Company No. 5631421
RT.
, 50 Victoria
www.littlebrown.co.uk

CLARENCE HOUSE

I have always thought that the National Gardens Scheme represents a unique celebration of the extraordinary range of plants that we can grow in the British Isles. From February, when Winter is still evident, until the end of October, when Autumn has begun to fade, thousands of gardens delight their visitors with seasonal displays. For the owners, sourcing and nurturing their plants, whether specialist rarities or widely-grown favourites, is one of the primary rewards derived from their gardens.

At a time when increasing numbers of these plants are threatened by various pests and diseases it is vitally important to appreciate how much is at stake. Our domestic gardens, of which those opening in aid of the National Gardens Scheme are a high-quality cross-section, provide the biggest single area of support for the plant trade. They also have the most to lose from the spread of plant pests and diseases. To take just one example, evergreen box has been for centuries a staple element in our gardens large and small, but in recent years it has been decimated by the imported disease 'box blight' and, as a result thousands of gardens have suffered – including, I am sad to say, my own.

The National Gardens Scheme showcases everything that is best in British gardens. In doing so, it provides enormous enjoyment both for visitors to gardens and for proud owners whose talent and hard work is on display. From Cornwall to Ceredigion and Cumbria, it uses the beauty of plants to reap spectacular charitable rewards; in 2017 alone nearly £4 million was raised at its gardens. At the same time it provides a constant reminder of how we all need to be as vigilant as possible in order to preserve the riches of our horticultural heritage.

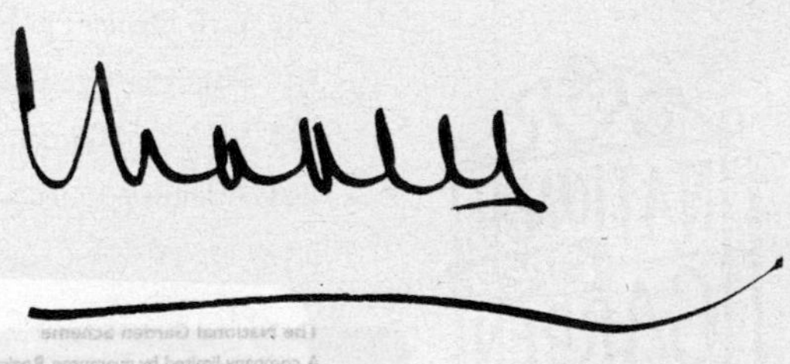

Right: Martin McMillan in front of the new NGS Macmillan Unit in Chesterfield

Who's Who

Chairman's Message

Our 90th anniversary in 2017 had some pretty momentous highlights, not least a record total of donations to our nursing beneficiaries of £3 million which we announced in March. In the summer we opened the brand new NGS Macmillan cancer unit at the Chesterfield Royal Hospital in Derbyshire. We were the major funder, contributing £1.5 million, and I think the unit is a wonderful embodiment of our support for nursing and caring in local communities.

We launched our new branding which has transformed our image and people's appreciation of what we do and we showcased the new look with our pioneering range of merchandise. We held our first-ever photographic competition, the winners of which we celebrated with an October party at the Garden Museum; a couple of weeks later our President, Mary Berry made a memorable contribution to the 90th at our annual lecture when she delighted the audience with stories about opening her garden for over 20 years.

For me the 90th anniversary showcased all that is best about the National Garden Scheme and confirmed its place as a unique, much-loved British institution. Built on the generosity and talents of our garden owners and our volunteers, it remains true to its roots in supporting nursing and inviting visitors into the best private gardens in the country. We are all raring to go for the new 2018 visiting season and look forward to seeing you at our gardens through the year.

Martin McMillan, OBE

Some tips on using your Handbook

This book lists all the gardens opening for the National Garden Scheme between January 2018 and early 2019. It is divided up into county sections, each including a calendar of opening dates and details of each garden, listed alphabetically.

Symbols explained

NEW Gardens opening for the first time this year or re-opening after a long break.

◆ Garden also opens on non-NGS days. (Gardens which carry this symbol contribute to the NGS either by opening on a specific day(s) and/or by giving a guaranteed contribution.)

Wheelchair access to at least the main features of the garden.

Dogs on short leads welcome.

Plants usually for sale.

NPC Plant Heritage National Plant Collection.

Gardens that offer accommodation.

Refreshments are available, normally at a charge.

D Garden designed by a Fellow, Member or Pre-registered Member of The Society of Garden Designers.

Garden accessible to coaches. Coach sizes vary so please contact garden owner or County Organiser in advance to check details.

Group Visits Group Organisers may contact the County Organiser or a garden owner direct to organise a group visit to a particular county or garden. See the front of each county section for County Organiser contact details, or visit www.ngs.org.uk

Children must be accompanied by an adult

Photography is at the discretion of the garden owner; please check first. Photographs must not be used for sale or reproduction without prior permission of the owner.

Donation To indicates that a proportion of the money collected will be given to the nominated charity.

Toilets are not usually available at private gardens.

If you cannot find the information you require from a garden or County Organiser, call the NGS office on 01483 211535

Where the money goes:
our nursing charities

We have donated over £50 million to our nursing and caring beneficiaries since our foundation in 1927, including £25 million during the last ten years. Our continuing support means that for most of our beneficiaries we are the largest cumulative donor in their histories.

"Through our annual donations over decades we have developed significant long-term partnerships with our beneficiaries to maximise our support for nursing charities and our contribution to local communities. The page opposite shows the full extent of our donations in 2017 and the new NGS Macmillan cancer unit mentioned in our Chairman's Message on page 3 is just one example of our impact in 2017; here are some more."

George Plumptre, Chief Executive

Below: George Plumptre with two Marie Curie volunteers at the Marie Curie Hospice in Solihull

Supporting Marie Curie's nurses
Since 1996 we have donated £8.4 million to fund Marie Curie's vital services and in 2017 we launched the National Garden Scheme Bursary Fund, to help Marie Curie clinical staff to achieve specialist qualifications in palliative and end of life care.

Supporting district nurses through our founders, the Queen's Nursing Institute
The Queen's Nursing Institute is the key support body for district and community nursing and we are their major funder. In 2017, in addition to our ongoing support for the national network of some 1,200 Queen's Nurses, we funded the launch of a new leadership programme for the QNI with the aim of getting community nurses into senior national nursing posts.

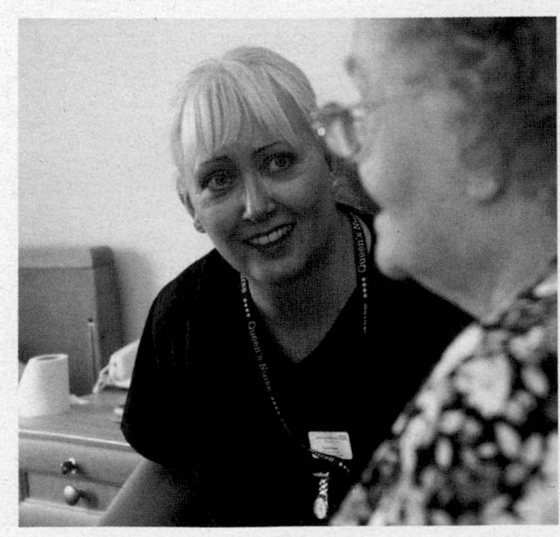

The Trials of a First-Time Opener by Chatu Madhvani

As a novice gardener, my first NGS visit in 2010 opened up a source of ideas and a network of encouraging gardeners. What I enjoyed about the gardens is that, as well as a special quality, they offer up something so personally 'home-made' and are 'real'.

Taking comfort in the odd dandelion spotted during my visits, I was inspired to work enthusiastically at my own shady garden. By 2016, previously barren areas were flourishing; it felt 'ready'. I admired its unintended successes and, with the assurance of unprompted compliments from tradesmen and a football-fanatical nephew, I wanted to share them. Soon I was proud to officially be a part of the NGS family.

Despite my determination to keep a relaxed approach to my first opening, I couldn't help a flurry of thoughts racing around the detail of the visitors' experience from entrance to plant sale to teas - not forgetting the garden!

Above: Chatu and her garden were featured in the 2017 Channel 4 series 'All Gardens Great and Small' presented by Dee Hart Dyke

Even with my frantic efforts and endless support from friends, I was conscious that my garden is inherently green and might lack interest. My concern quickly disappeared in the whirlwind of the opening. More than 200 visitors queued patiently outside the tiny plot and many went out of their way to make positive remarks. There was an immensely rewarding buzz.

For 2018, I know to enjoy the chaos.

Dates for your diary

Visiting a garden is one of the many ways you can support the National Garden Scheme in 2018, to help us raise more money for nursing charities. Through the coming months our gardens will have a number of spectacular highlights: tulips in April; peonies in May; roses in June; kitchen gardens in late-summer and autumn colour in October.

Here are some other events for your diary:

15th March – 28th August: Our annual photography competition, further information on page 14.

2 – 3 June: Annual Festival Weekend: our busiest weekend of the year with more than 300 gardens open through England and Wales.

August: Gardens and Health Week. During August we will be celebrating our second annual Gardens and Health Week. Look out for further information on our website and how you can get involved.

7 November: Annual Lecture at the Royal Geographical Society. Join us for a talk by Lord Heseltine. Tickets go on sale in August on our website.

For more information on the other ways you can support us visit www.ngs.org.uk

Visit one of our 1,200 gardens open by arrangement in 2018

Have you ever wanted a private tour of one of our gardens? Arrange a garden opening just for you and your friends, your group or society, giving you a personalised and exclusive experience.

You'll have direct contact with the garden owner, allowing you to liaise on everything from convenient times and dates to what you'll see and do once you're there.

There's something for everyone, and visitors can usually expect a talk from the garden owner and our famous tea and cakes – and maybe something extra depending on the time of year.

More than 1,000 of our gardens offer visits by arrangement. Full details are here in your book, otherwise simply check on the National Garden Scheme website where you'll find everything from minimum and maximum group sizes to the owner's contact details.

Photography competition

Calling all amateur photographers and garden enthusiasts! The National Garden Scheme is running its second annual photography competition in association with BBC Gardeners' World Magazine.

Shown here is the 2017 winning image by Corinna Potter, the 2018 competition runs from 15th March to 28th August 2018 and is free to enter. There are categories to inspire all budding photographers, including 'Town Gardens', 'Garden Wildlife' and the popular BBC *Gardeners' World* Magazine category: 'Fantastic Flowers'.

More information on the competition will be released on our website in February this year, so don't miss the opportunity to support the National Garden Scheme and celebrate the beauty of our gardens, whilst entering to win a host of amazing prizes!

To enter or to find out more information visit www.ngs.org.uk/photo

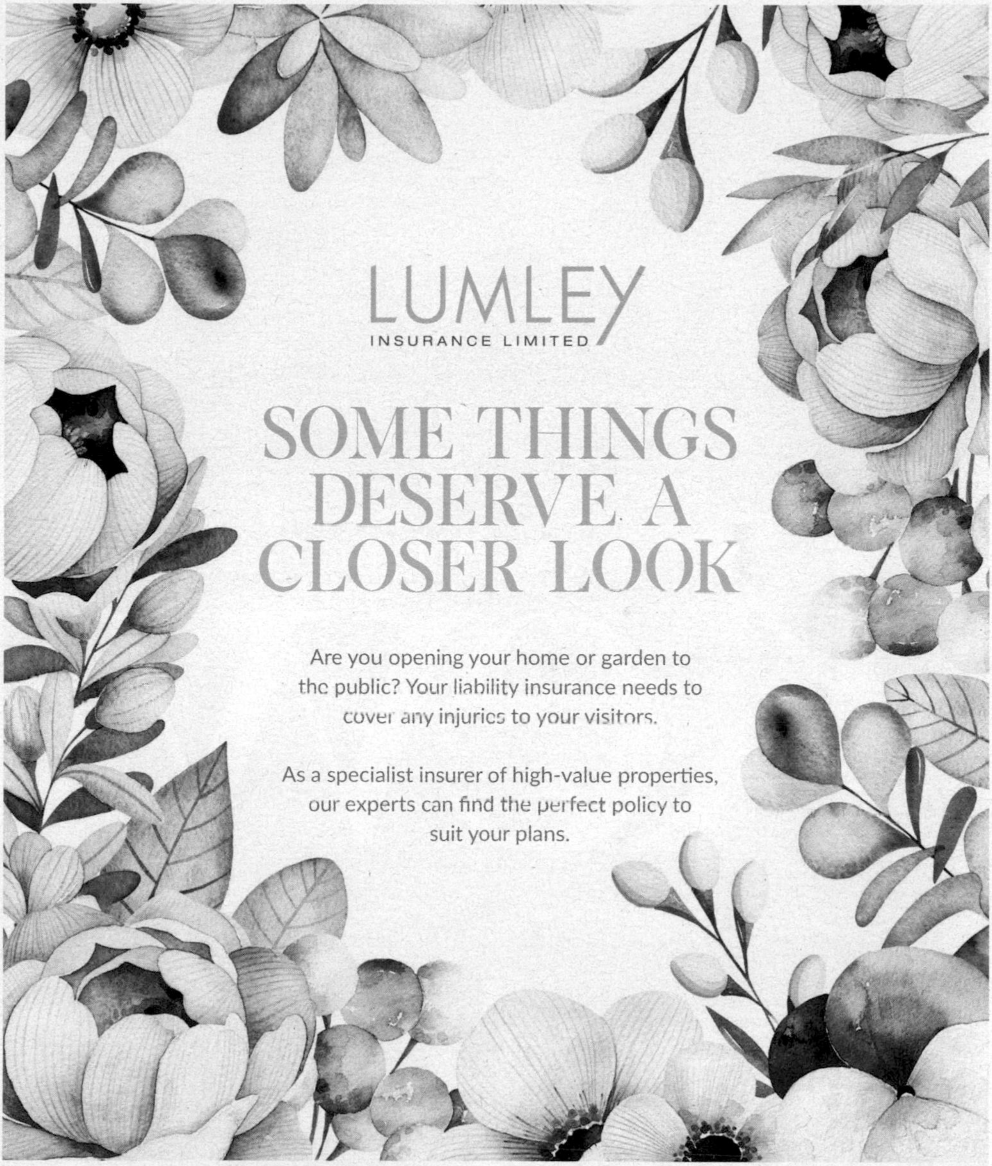

BEDFORDSHIRE

The Birthplace of John Bunyan, it is little wonder the county of Bedfordshire inspired the author of Pilgrim's Progress.

Running North to South through scenic countryside, a number of National Garden Scheme gardens lie along the John Bunyan Trail, from Stevington and Clapham, through Bedford, Ampthill, Steppingley to Westoning and Barton-le-Clay.

Bedfordshire also boasts a trio of 18th century gardens designed by Capability Brown, two of which open for the National Garden Scheme. First, Southill Park, an imposing country house with rolling lawns, flanked by belts, lakes and a Tuscan temple. It is also a founding garden which first opened its gates toNational Garden Scheme visitors in 1927. Second, Luton Hoo, where, wrote Samuel Johnson, "magnificence is not sacrificed to convenience, nor convenience to magnificence".

Once celebrated for its market gardens, many of the county's garden owners are as enthusiastic about their edibles as they are of their flowers. From the historic to the contemporary and from the village to the town, a warm welcome awaits you at a National Garden Scheme open garden in Bedfordshire. Join us for a truly British experience of garden, tea and well-being.

Volunteers

County Organiser
Indi Jackson
01525 713798
indi.jackson1@gmail.com

County Treasurer
Colin Davies
01525 712721
colin.davies@which.net

Publicity
Jolene Lynch
07779158593
jolene_akehurst@hotmail.com

Facebook
Jolene Lynch
(as above)

Newsletter
Kate Gardner
07725 307803
kgardner287@gmail.com

Booklet Co-ordinator
Indi Jackson
(as above)

Jolene Lynch
(as above)

Photography
Venetia Berrington
01525 280247
venetiajane.info@gmail.com

Talks
Victoria Diggle
01767 627247
victoria@diggledesign.com

Assistant County Organisers
Geoff & Davina Barrett
01908 585329
geoffanddean@gmail.com

Ann Davis
01525 712721
ann@no1colin.plus.com

Brenda Hands
brenda.iris@hotmail.co.uk

Left: 10 Alder Wynd

OPENING DATES

All entries subject to change. For latest information check **www.ngs.org.uk**

Map locator numbers are shown to the right of each garden name.

February

Snowdrop Festival

Sunday 11th
NEW The Folly 3
NEW The Knoll 8

Sunday 18th
The Swiss Garden 19

Saturday 24th
NEW The Folly 3
NEW The Knoll 8

Sunday 25th
◆ King's Arms Garden 7

March

Sunday 25th
NEW Gifla House 4
The Manor House, Barton-le-Clay 11
Wayside Cottage 22

April

Monday 2nd
The Old Rectory, Westoning 13

Sunday 22nd
Townsend Farmhouse 20
West Oak 23

May

Saturday 5th
Secret Garden 16

Monday 7th
The Old Rectory, Wrestlingworth 14

Saturday 19th
22 Elmsdale Road 2

Sunday 20th
22 Elmsdale Road 2
The Swiss Garden 19

Sunday 27th
The Old Rectory, Wrestlingworth 14

Monday 28th
NEW ◆ The Manor House, Stevington 12

June

Festival Weekend

Saturday 2nd
Steppingley Village Gardens 18

Sunday 3rd
Southill Park 17
Steppingley Village Gardens 18

Sunday 10th
The Hyde Walled Garden 5
The Old Rectory, Westoning 13

Saturday 16th
1-92 Kimbolton Road 6

Sunday 17th
NEW Gifla House 4
The Manor House, Barton-le-Clay 11
Wayside Cottage 22

July

Sunday 1st
10 Alder Wynd 1
The Hyde Walled Garden 5

Saturday 7th
22 Elmsdale Road 2
NEW Willow Lodge 24

Sunday 8th
22 Elmsdale Road 2
NEW Willow Lodge 24

Saturday 21st
Walnut Cottage 21

Sunday 22nd
Luton Hoo Hotel Golf & Spa 10
Walnut Cottage 21

August

Saturday 4th
1a St Augustine's Road 15

September

Sunday 16th
Lindy Lea 9
Townsend Farmhouse 20

October

Sunday 28th
◆ King's Arms Garden 7

November

Saturday 10th
Townsend Farmhouse 20

February 2019

Sunday 24th
◆ King's Arms Garden 7

By Arrangement

10 Alder Wynd 1
22 Elmsdale Road 2
NEW The Folly 3
NEW The Knoll 8
The Old Rectory, Wrestlingworth 14
1a St Augustine's Road 15
Secret Garden 16
Walnut Cottage 21

The Manor House, Stevington

THE GARDENS

1 10 ALDER WYND

Silsoe, Bedford, MK45 4GQ. David & Frances Hampson, 01525 861356, mail@davidhampson.com. *From Barton Rd, turn into the estate on Obelisk Way. At end of Obelisk Way turn R at school, then 1st L into Alder Wynd & bear R. 10 Alder Wynd is the 1st house on R.* **Sun 1 July (2-5). Adm £3, chd free. Home-made teas, cakes, and gluten free cake. Visits also by arrangement in July.**

Runners up in the 2017 Gardeners World Competition, 'Small Garden Category'. The garden demonstrates what can be achieved in a relatively small space, 10m x 11m. Created from scratch in the Autumn of 2014, the garden is roughly courtyard in style and formed from a series of raised beds and oak structures. Lush plantings of banana, tree ferns, hostas, bamboos and colourful herbaceous perennials. This small area has a wide selection of plants, tetrapanax, roses, wisteria, clematis, a variety of grasses and traditional perennials. A water feature provides a subtle background noise. The pathways are narrow and made of slate chippings, there are two shallow steps to the decked area.

2 22 ELMSDALE ROAD

Wootton, Bedford, MK43 9JN. Roy & Dianne Richards, 07733 222495, roy.richards60@ntlworld.com. *4m from J13 M1. Join old A421 towards Bedford, follow signs to Wootton. Turn R at The Cock PH follow Rd to Elmsdale Rd.* **Sat 19, Sun 20 May, Sat 7, Sun 8 July (12-5). Adm £4, chd free. Home-made teas, coffee and cakes. Visits also by arrangement Apr to Sept for groups 8+.**

Topiary garden greets visitors before they enter a genuine Japanese Feng Shui garden incl bonsai every plant is strictly Japanese, large Koi pond and lily pond and Japanese Tea House. The garden was created from scratch by the owners and has many interesting features. Japanese lanterns and a large collection of Japanese plants and bonsai. From China the Kneeling Archer terracotta soldier, Koi pond and lily pond. Partial wheelchair access. The Garden is on 2 levels and has gravel type paths but some of the garden can be viewed from the lower level.

3 NEW THE FOLLY

High Street, Pavenham, Bedford, MK43 7PE. Mr & Mrs J Kirby, 01234 825711, debby_horsman@hotmail.com. *Approx 6m N of Bedford off the A6 towards Kettering signed Oakley & Pavenham. Enter Pavenham. Garden is 3rd house on L past the 30 MPH sign.* **Sun 11, Sat 24 Feb (1-4.30). Combined adm with The Knoll £4, chd free. Visits also by arrangement in Feb please contact The Knoll.**

Medium sized cottage garden with an extensive collection of snowdrops, hellebores and other spring bulbs. Small parterre, pergola and pond. Gravel drive and narrow twisting paths so wheelchair access difficult.

4 NEW GIFLA HOUSE

Manor Road, Barton-Le-Clay, Bedford, MK45 4NR. Jim & Rosemary Bottoms. *The house is next door to the Manor House on the very sharp bend of Manor Rd on L. Entrance is via a white five bar gate down the long drive with parking at the rear of the Manor House.* **Sun 25 Mar, Sun 17 June (2-5). Combined adm with The Manor House, Barton-le-Clay £6, chd free**

When we first moved to the house (some 20+ years ago) the garden was essentially a field with a couple of trees in it. Over the years we have had the entire space carefully and sympathetically landscaped. Now there are beautiful decorative bridges over the natural river, many different shrubs in the flower beds, crazy paved pathways and patios which add to the character of this fantastic garden.

5 THE HYDE WALLED GARDEN

East Hyde, Luton, LU2 9PS. D J J Hambro Will Trust. *2m S of Luton. M1 exit/10a Exit to A1061 towards Harpenden take 2nd on L signed East Hyde. From A1 exit J4 follow A3057 N to r'about 1st L to B653 follow road to Wheathampstead/ Luton to East Hyde.* **Sun 10 June, Sun 1 July (2-5). Adm £4.50, chd free. Home-made teas.**

Walled garden adjoins the grounds of The Hyde (not open). Extends to approx 1 acre and features rose garden, seasonal beds and herbaceous borders, imaginatively interspersed with hidden areas of formal lawn. An interesting group of Victorian greenhouses, coldframes and cucumber house are serviced from the potting shed in the adjoining vegetable garden. Gravel paths.

6 192 KIMBOLTON ROAD

Bedford, MK41 8DP. Tricia Atkinson. *On B660 between Brickhill Drive & Avon Drive nr pedestrian crossing.* **Sat 16 June (1.30-4.30). Adm £3.50, chd free. Home-made teas.**

A third of acre cottage garden with grape vine, vegetable and soft fruit patch and an orchard. The garden includes over 90 roses. Wheelchair access with care. Some gravel.

Your support helps Carers Trust to provide more help to unpaid carers

7 ◆ KING'S ARMS GARDEN

1 Brinsmade Road, Ampthill, MK45 2PP. bryden.k@ntlworld.com. *8m S of Bedford. Free parking in town centre. Entrance opp Old Market Place, down King's Arms Yard.* **For NGS: Sun 25 Feb (2-4.30); Sun 28 Oct (2.30-5). Adm £3, chd free. 2019: Sun 24 Feb.** For other opening times and information, please phone or email.

Small woodland garden of about 1½ acres created by plantsman the late William Nourish. Trees, shrubs, bulbs and many interesting collections throughout the yr. Maintained since 1987 by 'The Friends of the Garden' on behalf of Ampthill Town Council. See us on Facebook Kings Arms Garden. Wheelchair access to most of the garden.

8 NEW THE KNOLL

High Street, Pavenham, Bedford, MK43 7PD. Mr & Mrs Terry & Debby Horsman, 01234 825711, debby_horsman@hotmail.com. *Approx 6m N of Bedford just off A6. From A6 north of Bedford take 2nd L signed Oakley & Pavenham. Follow directions for Pavenham. Garden is on the L, 300 metres inside the 30mph zone.* **Sun 11 Feb (1-4.30). Light refreshments at the Knoll. Sat 24 Feb (1-4.30). Combined adm with The Folly £4, chd free. Visits also by arrangement in Feb. Happy to accept bookings by phone, given due notice. Max 20.**

Cottage garden, ⅓ acre with a large collection of many varieties of snowdrops. Hellebores, spring bulbs and other colour. Pergolas, wildlife pond, kitchen garden and raised bed. Woodland area and island beds. There is a gravel drive but most parts of the garden can be accessed by wheelchair with care. This is difficult after heavy rain.

9 LINDY LEA

Ampthill Road, Steppingley, Bedford, MK45 1AB. Roy & Linda Collins. *On Steppingley Rd between Flitwick and Ampthill. From E L off A507 Ampthill towards Steppingley or from M1 J13 turn R at Millbrook r'about then L at 1st r'about, 1st entrance past Steppingley Hospital entrance.* **Sun 16 Sept (2-5). Adm £5, chd free. Home-made teas at Townsend Farmhouse. Combined opening with Townsend Farmhouse. Opening with Steppingley Village Gardens on Sat 2, Sun 3 June.**

Set within an acre, this garden is a haven for wildlife with two water features, cottage garden style perennial plantings, variety of shrubs and mature trees. There is also a vegetable garden and a sunny terrace furnished with pots and climbers. Some paths may be difficult to negotiate.

10 LUTON HOO HOTEL GOLF & SPA

The Mansion House, Luton Hoo, Luton, LU1 3TQ. Luton Hoo Hotel Golf & Spa, www.lutonhoo.co.uk. *Approx 1m from J10 M1, take London Rd A1081 signed Harpenden for approx ½m - entrance on L for Luton Hoo Hotel Golf & Spa.* **Sun 22 July (11-4). Adm £5, chd free. Light refreshments. Visitors wishing to have lunch/formal afternoon tea at the hotel must book in advance directly with the hotel.**

The gardens and parkland designed by Capability Brown are of national historic significance and lie in a conservation area. Main features - lakes, woodland and pleasure grounds, Victorian grass tennis court and late C19 sunken rockery. Italianate garden with herbaceous borders and topiary garden. Gravel paths.

11 THE MANOR HOUSE, BARTON-LE-CLAY

87 Manor Road, Barton-le-Clay, MK45 4NR. Mrs Veronica Pilcher. *Off A6 between Bedford & Luton. Take old A6 (Bedford Rd) through Barton-le-Clay Village (not the by-pass) & Manor Rd is off Bedford Rd. Parking in paddock.* **Sun 25 Mar, Sun 17 June (2-5). Combined adm with Gifla House £6, chd free. Home-made teas.**

The garden was beautifully landscaped during the 1930s and much interest is created by picturesque stream which incorporates a series of waterfalls and ponds. Colourful streamside planting incl an abundance of arum lilies. Sunken garden with lily pond and a magnificent wisteria thrives at the rear of the house. Children under supervision as there is a water hazard. Partial wheelchair access, 2ft wide bridges.

12 NEW ◆ THE MANOR HOUSE, STEVINGTON

Church Road, Stevington, Bedford, MK43 7QB. Kathy Brown, www.kathybrownsgarden.com. *5m NW of Bedford. Off A428 through Bromham.* **For NGS: Mon 28 May (1-5). Adm £5, chd free. Home-made teas.** For other opening times and information, please visit garden website.

The Manor House Garden is now 25 years old with many different rooms and views to enjoy. Clematis, wisteria and laburnum arches are under planted with alliums, poppies and foxgloves. White and yellow Banksian roses vye for space on the house walls. Bees feast on Allium christophii in the main herbaceous border, Allium siculum in the cottage garden and intersectional peonies near the drive. Kathy has surprising containers and plans an edible flower workshop for the afternoon. Partial wheelchair access. Disabled WC.

13 THE OLD RECTORY, WESTONING

Church Road, Westoning, MK45 5JW. Ann & Colin Davies. *2m S of Flitwick. Off A5120, 2m N of M1 J12. ¼m up Church Rd, next to church.* **Mon 2 Apr, Sun 10 June (2-5.30). Adm £4, chd free. Cream teas in C14 church next door.**

Ancient box and yew hedges surround the colour coordinated beds of this two acre garden. Spring is greeted by hellebores, primroses and daffodils with magnolias blooming in profusion. Roses, delphiniums and lupins complement the flowering trees and shrubs of summer with the romantic meadow full of poppies and cornflowers. Come and enjoy the the sight and and smell of a traditional English garden. Wheelchair access generally good.

♿ ✿ ☕

14 THE OLD RECTORY, WRESTLINGWORTH

Church Lane, Wrestlingworth, Sandy, SG19 2EU. Mrs Josephine Hoy, 01767 631204, hoyjosephine@hotmail.co.uk. *5m E of Sandy, 5m NE of Biggleswade. Wrestlingworth is situated on B1042. 5m from Sandy & 6m from Biggleswade. The Old Rectory is at the top of Church Lane, which is well signed, behind the church.* **Mon 7, Sun 27 May (2-5.30). Adm £5, chd free. Home-made teas. Visits also by arrangement Apr to July groups are welcome with prior appointment but only limited visits this year.**

4 acre garden full of colour and interest. The owner has a free style of gardening sensitive to wildlife. Beds overflowing with tulips, alliums, bearded iris, peonies, poppies, geraniums and much more. Beautiful mature trees and many more planted in the last 30 years. Incl a large selection of betulas. Gravel gardens, box hedging, woodland garden and wild flower meadows. Wheelchair access maybe limited on grass paths.

♿ ✿ 🚌 ☕

15 1A ST AUGUSTINE'S ROAD

Bedford, MK40 2NB. Chris Bamforth Damp, 01234 353730/01234 353465. *St Augustine's Rd is on L off Kimbolton Rd as you leave the centre of Bedford.* **Sat 4 Aug (12-4.30). Adm £3, chd free. Home-made teas. Visits also by arrangement June to Sept for groups of 6+.**

A colourful town garden with herbaceous borders, climbers, a green house and pond. Planted in cottage garden style with traditional flowers, the borders overflow with late summer annuals and perennials including salvias and rudbeckia. The pretty terrace next to the house is lined with ferns and hostas. The owners also make homemade chutneys and preserves which can be purchased on the day. The garden is wheelchair accessible.

♿ ✿ ☕

The Knoll

16 SECRET GARDEN

4 George Street, Clapham, Bedford, MK41 6AZ. Graham Bolton, 07746 864247, bolton_graham@hotmail.com. *3m N of Bedford (not the bypass). Clapham Village High St. R into Mount Pleasant Rd then L into George St. 1st white Bungalow on R.* **Sat 5 May (12.30-5.30). Adm £2.50, chd free. Light refreshments. Visits also by arrangement Apr & May.**

Alpine lovers can see a wide variety of alpines in two small scree gardens, front and back of bungalow plus pans, dwarf Salix, rhododendron, daphne's. Dwarf acers, conifers and pines, hellebores, epimediums. Two small mixed borders of herbaceous salvias, lavenders and potentillas. Alpine greenhouse plus one greenhouse and cold frames with plants for sale. Partial wheelchair access. No access at the rear of property due to narrow gravel paths but garden can be viewed from the patio.

♿ ✿ ☕

17 SOUTHILL PARK

Southill, Nr Biggleswade, SG18 9LL. Mr & Mrs Charles Whitbread. *3m W of Biggleswade. In the village of Southill. 3m from A1 junction at Biggleswade.* **Sun 3 June (2-5). Adm £5, chd free. Cream teas.**

Southill Park is one of the founder NGS gardens which first opened its gates to visitors in 1927. A large garden with mature trees and flowering shrubs, herbaceous borders, a formal rose garden, sunken garden, ponds and kitchen garden. It is on the south side of the 1795 Palladian house. The parkland was designed by Lancelot 'Capability' Brown. A large conservatory houses the tropical collection.

♿ ✿ ☕

GROUP OPENING

18 STEPPINGLEY VILLAGE GARDENS

Steppingley, Bedford, MK45 5AT. *Follow signs to Steppingley, pick up yellow signs at Fordfiled Rd r'about between Ampthill & Flitwick. Lindy Lea next to Hospital and village centre for West Oak & Townsend Farmhouse.* **Sat 2, Sun 3 June (2-6). Combined adm £6.50, chd free. Home-made teas at Townsend Farmhouse and Lower Barn.**

LINDY LEA
Roy & Linda Collins.
(See separate entry)

NEW **MIDDLE BARN**
Bruce & Pauline Henninger.

NEW **TOP BARN**
Tim & Nicky Kemp.

TOWNSEND FARMHOUSE
Hugh & Indi Jackson.
(See separate entry)

WEST OAK
John & Sally Eilbeck.
(See separate entry)

Steppingley is a picturesque Bedfordshire village on the Greensand ridge, close to Ampthill, Flitwick and Woburn. Although a few older buildings survive, most of Steppingley was built by 7th Duke of Bedford between 1840 and 1872. Five gardens in the village offer an interesting mix of planting styles and design to include pretty court yards, cottage garden style perennial borders, ponds, a well, glass houses, an orchard, vegetable gardens, a herb garden, wild life havens and country views. Live stock include chickens, ducks and fish. Some gravel paths and steps.

♿ ✿ ☕

19 THE SWISS GARDEN

Old Warden Aerodrome, Old Warden, Biggleswade, SG18 9ER. The Shuttleworth Trust, www.shuttleworth.org/the-swiss-garden/. *2m W of Biggleswade. Signed from A1 & A600.* **Sun 18 Feb, Sun 20 May (9.30-5). Adm £6, chd free. The Shuttleworth Restaurant - open all day.**

This enchanting garden was created in the 'Swiss Picturesque' style for the 3rd Lord Ongley in the early C19 and reopened in July 2014 after a major HLF-funded restoration. Serpentine paths lead to cleverly contrived vistas, many of which focus on the thatched Swiss Cottage. Beautiful wrought-iron bridges, ponds, sweeping lawns and the magnificent Pulhamite-lined Grotto Fernery have all been given a new lease of life by this landmark restoration. The pathways in the Swiss Garden are firm and even, with minimal gradients, and most are suitable for access by wheelchair users.

♿ ✿ 🚌 ☕

20 TOWNSEND FARMHOUSE

Rectory Road, Steppingley, Bedford, MK45 5AT. Hugh & Indi Jackson. *In Steppingley Village. Follow directions to Steppingley village and pick up yellow signs from village centre.* **Sun 22 Apr, Sun 16 Sept (2-5). Home-made teas. Evening opening Sat 10 Nov (4-7). Light refreshments. Adm £5, chd free. Combined with West Oak on April 22nd. Combined with Lindy Lea on 16 Sept. Opening with Steppingley Village Gardens on Sat 2, Sun 3 June.**

A tree lined driveway with young specimens and mature broad leaves rising above swathes of spring bulbs. Planted for year round interest, the cottage-garden style herbaceous borders are filled with early perennials in June. Hydrangeas, dahlias and asters flourish in September. A pretty cobbled courtyard with a glass house and a Victorian well 30 metres deep, viewed through a glass top. This garden is also open for Diwali on Saturday 10th November 4 pm - 7 pm. Join us for an evening of diya lamps, flower rangoli and sweetmeats. Wheelchair access - gravelled driveway and paths.

♿ ✿ ☕

21 WALNUT COTTAGE

8 Great North Road, Chawston, MK44 3BD. D G Parker, 07784 792975, dave.parkergnr@gmail.com. *2m S of St Neots. Between Wyboston & Blackcat r'about on S-bound lane of A1. Turn off at McDonalds, at end of filling station forecourt turn L. Off rd parking.* **Sat 21, Sun 22 July (2-6). Adm £4.50, chd free. Home-made teas. Visits also by arrangement Mar to Sept refreshments on request.**

Once a land settlement. 4 acre smallholding. 1 acre cottage garden. Over 2000 species give year round interest. Bulbs, herbaceous, water, bog plants, ferns, grasses, shrubs, trees, coppiced paulownias. Rare, exotic and unusual plants abound. Large pond, level grass paths. 1 acre young trees and shrubs. 2500sq metre glasshouse growing Chinese vegetable. 1½-acre picnic and party zone. Level grass paths.

♿ 🐕 ✿ 🚌 ☕

22 WAYSIDE COTTAGE

74 Manor Road, Barton-le-Clay, MK45 4NR. Nigel Barrett. *1m off A6. Take old A6 (Bedford Rd) through Barton-le-Clay Village (not the by-pass), Manor Rd is off Bedford Rd. Parking in paddock at the Manor House.* **Sun 25 Mar, Sun 17 June (2-5). Adm £6, chd free.**

The garden is sited on a ½-acre plot. Developed over 50 yrs it has mature trees, shrubs and flower borders. A well-stocked pond with fountain and waterfalls. A variety of attractive outbuildings nestle within the old walled garden for a tranquil scene with plenty of hidden corners.

♿ ☕

23 WEST OAK

50 Rectory Road, Steppingley, Bedford, MK45 5AT. John & Sally Eilbeck. *Steppingley Village. Follow signs to Steppingley from A507 r'about between Ampthill & Flitwick, pick up yellow signs from centre of village.* **Sun 22 Apr (2-5). Adm £5, chd free. Combined opening with Townsend Farmhouse. Opening with Steppingley Village Gardens on Sat 2, Sun 3 June.**

An informal garden of approx ¾ acre with open countryside on two sides. It consists of lawns and shrubs with perennial planting including some mature trees. There is a herb garden, greenhouse, vegetable gardens with soft fruit, and small orchard with chickens. The garden has been developed over nearly 30 years by the present owners from a completely bare plot. The garden is approached across a gravel drive and there are some steps

24 NEW WILLOW LODGE

20 Witts End, Eversholt, Milton Keynes, MK17 9DY. Catherine Doherty. *From the centre of Eversholt village with Green Man Pub on L, take next L & then Willow Lodge is approx 500 metres along, 1st house on R.* **Sat 7, Sun 8 July (9.30-5). Adm £4, chd free. Home-made teas, coffees, cakes and snacks. perhaps even a glass of Pimms.**

A Collaborative Vegetable garden in Catherine's garden. Tended by 4 local people each sharing in the toil and the spoils of the produce. Established 5 years ago we are all learning as we go. We have a no dig approach and love cut and come again produce. We are largely organic and we sell our fresh salad to fund the collective costs. There is parking on the same level as the garden, the access is grass, some paths are narrow.

Willow Lodge

BERKSHIRE

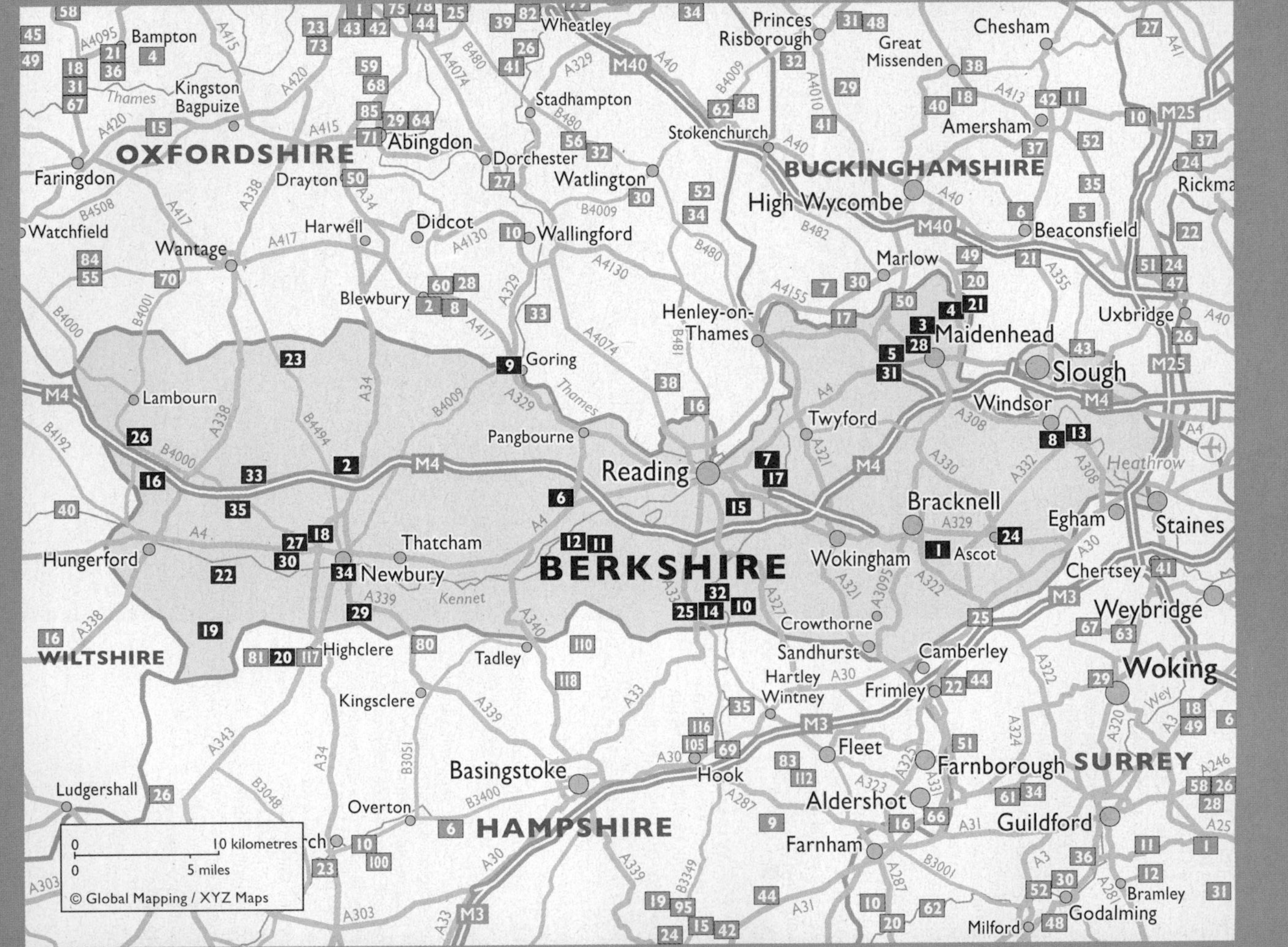

BERKSHIRE
BUCKINGHAMSHIRE
OXFORDSHIRE
SURREY
HAMPSHIRE
WILTSHIRE
Reading
Slough
Maidenhead
Windsor
Egham
Staines
Chertsey
Weybridge
Woking
Bracknell
Ascot
Wokingham
Crowthorne
Sandhurst
Camberley
Frimley
Farnborough
Guildford
Godalming
Bramley
Milford
Aldershot
Fleet
Farnham
Hartley Wintney
Hook
Basingstoke
Tadley
Kingsclere
Overton
Highclere
Newbury
Thatcham
Hungerford
Lambourn
Wantage
Faringdon
Watchfield
Bampton
Kingston Bagpuize
Abingdon
Drayton
Didcot
Harwell
Blewbury
Wallingford
Dorchester
Stadhampton
Wheatley
Watlington
Goring
Pangbourne
Henley-on-Thames
Twyford
Marlow
High Wycombe
Stokenchurch
Princes Risborough
Great Missenden
Amersham
Chesham
Beaconsfield
Uxbridge
Ludgershall
Heathrow
Thames
Kennet
Wey
10 kilometres
5 miles
© Global Mapping / XYZ Maps

The Royal County of Berkshire offers a wonderful mix of natural beauty and historic landmarks that are reflected in the portfolio of gardens opening for the National Garden Scheme.

The Thames flows right through the county, passing picturesque towns and villages, many of which have beautiful gardens opening in 2018. Private gardens at famous places such as Windsor Castle and Eton College offer rare opportunities for visitors to enjoy gardens not normally open to the public. All are generously opened to raise funds for the nursing and caring charities we support.

Our gardens come in every shape, size and style, and we are delighted to welcome back great examples of this at Estoril, Fairway and Handpost. We are also excited to introduce a new garden for 2018 – Compton Elms near Maidenhead – where you can book in advance to enjoy a Spring afternoon 'Talk & Walk'.

If you are organising a group visit, please see our gardens open 'by arrangement', or if you would like someone locally to give a talk about the National Garden Scheme, contact Angela at angela.oconnell@icloud.com. Some gardens may capture your interest due to their designers or their historic setting, while most have evolved thanks to the efforts of their enthusiastic owners. We think they all offer moments of inspiration and look forward to welcoming you at a garden soon.

Below: Wickham House

Volunteers

County Organiser
Heather Skinner
01189 737197
heatheraskinner@aol.com

County Treasurer
Hugh Priestley
01189 744349 Fri – Mon
hughpriestley@aol.com

Booklet Co-ordinator
Heather Skinner
(as above)

Talks & Group Visits
Angela O'Connell
01252 668645
angela.oconnell@icloud.com

Assistant County Organisers
Cathie Davies
07718 589317
cathieldavies@gmail.com

Claire Fletcher
07709 905908
cfletcher7@sky.com

Carolyn Foster
01628 624635
candrfoster@btinternet.com

Angela O'Connell
(as above)

Graham O'Connell
01252 668645
graham.oconnell22@gmail.com

Deborah Padwick
07824 999002
debspadwick@yahoo.co.uk

OPENING DATES

All entries subject to change. For latest information check **www.ngs.org.uk**

Map locator numbers are shown to the right of each garden name.

February

Snowdrop Festival

Wednesday 7th
◆ Welford Park 33

March

Saturday 17th
Stubbings House 31

Sunday 18th
Stubbings House 31

April

Wednesday 4th
Rookwood Farm House 27

Wednesday 18th
Inholmes 16
Rooksnest 26
St Timothee 28

Sunday 22nd
Odney Club 21
The Old Rectory, Farnborough 23
Sandleford Place 29

Thursday 26th
St Timothee 28

May

Saturday 5th
Stubbings House 31

Sunday 6th
Rookwood Farm House 27
Stubbings House 31

Monday 7th
Stubbings House 31

Sunday 13th
Sandleford Place 29

Sunday 20th
Handpost 14
The Old Rectory, Farnborough 23

June

Festival Weekend

Saturday 2nd
Cookham Gardens 4

Sunday 3rd
Swallowfield Village Gardens 32

Saturday 9th
Eton College Gardens 8

Sunday 10th
Chieveley Manor 2
Kirby House 19
The Old Rectory Inkpen 22

Wednesday 13th
Inholmes 16
Rooksnest 26

Saturday 16th
Estoril 7

Sunday 17th
Sandleford Place 29
Stockcross House 30

Wednesday 20th
Rookwood Farm House 27

July

Friday 6th
Deepwood Stud Farm 5

Sunday 8th
Deepwood Stud Farm 5
The Harris Garden 15
Jannaways 18
West Mills Allotments & Island Cottage 34

Tuesday 10th
Wickham House 35

Sunday 15th
Farley Hill Place Gardens 10
Ivydene 17

Wednesday 25th
The Old Rectory, Farnborough 23

August

Sunday 19th
Bracknell Gardens 1

Monday 27th
Rookwood Farm House 27
St Timothee 28
Stockcross House 30

September

Sunday 16th
Handpost 14

By Arrangement

NEW Compton Elms 3
Deepwood Stud Farm 5
Farley Hill Place Gardens 10
Field Farm Cottage 11
Handpost 14
Island Cottage, West Mills Allotments & Island Cottage 34
Ivydene 17
Old Waterfield 24
The Priory 25
Rooksnest 26
Rookwood Farm House 27
St Timothee 28
Sandleford Place 29
Stockcross House 30
Stubbings House 31

Compton Elms

The National Garden Scheme is Hospice UK's largest single funder

THE GARDENS

GROUP OPENING

1 BRACKNELL GARDENS

The Parks Community Centre, 8-10 Nicholson Park, Bracknell, RG12 9NF. *1m S of Bracknell. Follow NGS signs from all major routes into Bracknell. Parking available at Parks Community Centre (please note it is a reasonable walk between gardens). Limited street parking at Shaftesbury Close.* **Sun 19 Aug (1.30-5.30). Combined adm £5, chd free. Home-made teas at 10 Shaftesbury Close.**

DEVONIA
Andrew Radgick.

GLENWOOD ALLOTMENTS
Gill Cheetham.

10 SHAFTESBURY CLOSE
Gill Cheetham.

Two interesting town gardens, both completely different, and lovely local allotments. Devonia is a plantsman's garden designed for all seasons with areas showcasing different conditions. 10 Shaftesbury Close is a woodland garden, planted to reflect the challenges that pine trees offer. Glenwood Allotments have enthusiastic owners who plant a wide variety of vegetables for yr-round cropping. Plant sale at Devonia.

2 CHIEVELEY MANOR

Chieveley, Nr Newbury, RG20 8UT. Mr & Mrs CJ Spence. *5m N of Newbury. Take A34 N, pass under M4, then L to Chieveley. After ½m L up Manor Lane.* **Sun 10 June (2-5). Adm £5, chd free. Home-made teas.** Donation to St Mary's Church, Chieveley.

Large garden surrounding listed house (not open) in the heart of Chieveley village. Attractive setting with fine views over stud farm. Walled garden containing lovely borders, shrubs and rose garden, evolving every year. Box parterre filled with alliums, white geraniums and lavender. Many viticella clematis growing through shrubs.

3 NEW COMPTON ELMS

Marlow Road, Pinkneys Green, Maidenhead, SL6 6NR. Alison Kellett, 01628 634334, kellettaj@gmail.com. *Situated at the end of a gravel road located opp & in between the Arbour & Golden Ball Pubs on the A308.* **Visits by arrangement on 17 & 21 March at 2pm for Spring 'Talk & Walk'. Due to limited numbers, pre-booking essential. Adm £10, chd free. Talk & home-made teas included.**

You are invited to join us for an afternoon Spring 'Talk & Walk' on Sat 17 and Wed 21 Mar at 2pm at our pretty sunken woodland garden, lovingly recovered from clay pit workings. The atmospheric garden is filled with snowdrops, primroses, hellebores and fritillaria, interspersed with anemone and narcissi under a canopy of ash and beech. The talk will be indoors where you can enjoy tea and cake before exploring the garden. Space is limited so please phone or email to book.

GROUP OPENING

4 COOKHAM GARDENS

Cookham, SL6 9QD. *3½m N of Maidenhead. Two gardens in The Pound, Cookham, nr the train station. Please park your car at the NT car park at Cookham Moor, street parking or nr station. Tickets available at both gardens.* **Sat 2 June (2-5). Combined adm £5.50, chd free. Home-made teas at Hunters Lodge.**

2 BELLE VUE COTTAGES
Liz & William Wells.

HUNTERS LODGE
Daphne Wardell-Yerburgh.

Two contrasting gardens in the beautiful Thameside village of Cookham, within ½m of the Stanley Spencer Gallery. 2 Bellevue Cottages showcases innovative use of limited space. It is a small, stunning, modern garden, which has a curving walkway that weaves through arbours bordered by lush, exotic and evergreen planting, punctuated by dabs of intense colour. Sorry not suitable for children. Hunters Lodge is a country style garden with a series of rooms leading to a summerhouse and an established wildlife pool surrounded by aquatic plants. Filled with herbaceous and climbing plants, lawned areas and set behind an Edwardian house (not open) in heart of village, a lovely place to enjoy afternoon tea. During a recent BBC One 'Garden Rescue' episode, Belle Vue Cottages was used as the example of what can be done in a small space to produce a stunning garden.

5 DEEPWOOD STUD FARM

Henley Road, Stubbings, Nr Maidenhead, SL6 6QW. Mr & Mrs E Goodwin, 01628 822684, ed.goodwin@deepwoodproperties.com. *2m W of Maidenhead. M4 J8/9 take A404M N. 2nd exit for A4 to Maidenhead. L at 1st r'about on A4130 Henley, approx 1m on R.* **Evening opening Fri 6 July (6-8.30). Adm £10, chd free. Wine & cheese. Sun 8 July (2-5). Adm £4.50, chd free. Home-made teas on lawn or in conservatory. Visits also by arrangement Mar to Sept for groups of 10-40.**

4 acres of formal and informal gardens within a stud farm, so great roses! Small lake with Monet style bridge and 3 further water features. Several neo-classical follies and statues. Walled garden with windows cut in to admire the views and horses. Woodland walk and enough hanging baskets to decorate a pub! Partial wheelchair access.

6 ◆ ENGLEFIELD HOUSE GARDEN

Englefield, Theale, Reading, RG7 5EN. Mr & Mrs Richard Benyon, 01189 302221, peter.carson@englefield.co.uk, **www.englefieldestate.co.uk.** *6m W of Reading. M4 J12. Take A4 towards Theale. 2nd r'about take A340 to Pangbourne. After ⅙m entrance on the L.* **For opening times and information, please phone, email or visit garden website.**

The 12 acre garden descends dramatically from the hill above the historic house through woodland where mature native trees mix with Victorian conifers. Drifts of spring and summer planting are followed by striking autumn colour. Stone balustrades enclose the lower terrace, with wide lawns, roses, mixed borders and topiary. Open every Monday from Apr-Sept (10-6) and Oct-Mar (10-4). Please check Englefield website for any changes before travelling. Group bookings by arrangement from Apr-Sept with option of refreshments and tour with gardener. Wheelchair access to some parts of the gardens.

7 ESTORIL

9 Old Bath Road, Sonning, Reading, RG4 6SZ. Fiona & Jonathan Hill. *Just off A4 between Charvil & Woodley. Turn into Old Bath Rd close to pedestrian crossing, follow road around to the R, Estoril is 5th house on L.* **Sat 16 June (2-5). Adm £3.50, chd free. Home-made teas.**

An attractive ¼ acre family garden with a contemporary feel that has been lovingly developed by the owner over the last 12 yrs. The beautifully planted mixed borders are filled with a wide variety of shrubs, perennials, grasses and bulbs. There is a pretty summerhouse, wildlife pond, courtyard garden and a small vegetable garden and greenhouse.

8 ETON COLLEGE GARDENS

Eton, Nr Windsor, SL4 6DB. *½m N of Windsor. Parking signed off B3022, Slough Rd. Walk from car park across playing fields to entry. Cars with disabled badges will be directed closer. Follow signs for tickets & maps sold at gazebo near entrance.* **Sat 9 June (2-5). Adm £5, chd free. Home-made teas served in the Fellows garden.**

A rare chance to visit a group of central College gardens surrounded by historic school buildings, including Luxmoore's garden on a small island in the Thames reached across two attractive bridges. Also an opportunity to explore the fascinating Eton College Natural History Museum and a small group of other private gardens. Plant Sale. We are sorry but the gardens are not suitable for wheelchairs due to gravel, steps and uneven ground.

10 FARLEY HILL PLACE GARDENS

Church Road, Farley Hill, Reading, RG7 1TZ. Tony & Margaret Finch, 01189 762544, tony.finch7@btinternet.com. *From M4 J11, take A33 S to Basingstoke. At T-lights turn L for Spencers Wood, B3349. Go 2m turn L, through Swallowfield towards Farley Hill. Garden ½m on R.* **Sun 15 July (2-5). Adm £5, chd free. Home-made teas. Visits also by arrangement Mar to Aug for groups of 15+. Please mention NGS.**

A 4 acre, C18 cottage garden. 1½ acre walled garden with yr-round interest and colour. Well stocked herbaceous borders, large productive vegetable areas with herb garden, dahlia and cutting flower beds. Enjoy wandering around the garden, with spontaneous singing from a Barber's Shop Quartet. Victorian glasshouse recently renovated and small nursery. Plants, lovely cut flowers and produce for sale. Partial wheelchair access.

11 FIELD FARM COTTAGE

Sulhamstead Hill, Sulhamstead, RG7 4DA. Mrs Anne Froom, 01189 302735, anne.froom@knowall.it, **www.bandbwestberkshire.co.uk.** *From A4 take lane by The Spring Inn for 1m. Garden is on L, 150yds past 2 LH-turns.* **Visits by arrangement May to Sept for groups of 10+. Refreshments available on request. Adm £4, chd free.**

A pretty ¾ acre cottage garden planted with a wide variety of herbaceous perennials, set in a series of garden rooms. Lovely borders spill over the lawn and there is a large pond which is fed by a natural spring. Wild garden, small white garden and a variety of trees planted by the owner. Small vegetable garden and greenhouse. The terrain is rather uneven, but most of the garden can be viewed from a wheelchair.

12 FOLLY FARM

Sulhamstead Hill, Sulhamstead, RG7 4DG. *7m SW of Reading. From A4 between Reading & Newbury (2m W of M4 J12) take road marked Sulhamstead at The Spring Inn. Restricted car parking.* **Visits by arrangement on Wed 25 April & Wed 4 July for private small group tours. Very limited availability. Adm £25. Pre-booking essential, please phone 01483 211535. Tea & home-made pastries.**

Gardens laid out in 1912 by Sir Edwin Lutyens and Gertrude Jekyll. Garden designs evolved during culmination of their partnership and considered one of their most complex. Extensively restored and replanted by current owners assisted by Dan Pearson. Recently reopened for private group visits which include approximately 1½ hour guided tour and refreshments. Please note paths are uneven and there are many sets of steps between areas of the garden. Sorry no dogs.

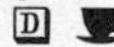

13 ◆ FROGMORE HOUSE GARDEN

Windsor, SL4 1LB. Her Majesty The Queen. *1m SE of Windsor. Entrance via Park St gate into Long Walk.* **For NGS: Date to be confirmed. For further information please visit www.ngs.org.uk or phone 01483 211535. Light refreshments & picnics welcome.**

The private royal garden at Frogmore House on the Crown Estate at Windsor. This landscaped garden set in 30 acres with notable trees, lawns, flowering shrubs and C18 lake, is rich in history. It is largely the creation of Queen Charlotte, who in the 1790s introduced over 4,000 trees and shrubs to create a model picturesque landscape. The historic plantings, incl tulip trees and redwoods, along with Queen Victoria's Tea House, remain key features of the garden today. Please note the Royal Mausoleum is closed due to long term restoration. To book optional garden history tours (approx 45 mins) with limited availability, go to 'Events' page at www.ngs.org.uk or phone 01483 211535. Tickets for garden and to visit the house are also available on the day by cash payment only. Last entry 4pm. Please note that Windsor traffic may be halted at 11am for Guard change.

14 HANDPOST

Basingstoke Road, Swallowfield, Reading, RG7 1PU. Faith Ramsay, faith@mycountrygarden.co.uk, www.mycountrygarden.co.uk. *From M4 J11, take A33 S. At 1st T-lights turn L on B3349 Basingstoke Rd. Follow road for 2¾m, garden on L.* **Sun 20 May, Sun 16 Sept (2.30-5). Adm £5, chd free. Home-made teas. Visits also by arrangement Apr to Oct for groups of 12+.**

4 acre designer's garden with many areas of interest. Features incl two lovely long borders attractively and densely planted in six colour sections, a formal rose garden, old orchard with a grass meadow, pretty pond and peaceful wooded area. Large variety of plants, trees and a productive fruit and vegetable patch.

15 THE HARRIS GARDEN

Whiteknights Campus, Pepper Lane entrance, Reading, RG6 6LA. The University of Reading, www.friendsoftheharrisgarden.org.uk. *1½m S of Reading. Off A327 Shinfield Rd. From Pepper Lane entrance to campus, turn R to car park.* **Sun 8 July (2-5). Adm £4, chd free. Home-made teas.**

Described as 'a real gem', the Harris Garden, in the Whiteknights campus of Reading University, is a 12 acre haven of peace and tranquillity. Planting provides yr-round interest, including notable trees, stream, pond, herbaceous borders and walled physic garden. With lots to enjoy it is an important amenity for University visitors, as well as for teaching and research.

16 INHOLMES

Woodlands St Mary, RG17 7SY. *3m SE Lambourn. M4 J14, take A338 N, take 1st L onto B4000. After 1½m Inholmes signed on L.* **Wed 18 Apr, Wed 13 June (11-3.30). Adm £5, chd free. Light refreshments. Last entry 3.30pm. Combined adm with Rooksnest £7.00, chd free.**

Set in 10 acres with wonderful views over parkland. A wide variety of different areas to enjoy such as a walled garden, many spring bulbs, inspirational herbaceous borders and rose beds. Walks to the lake and through the meadow. Most areas accessible by wheelchair over grass, gravel, and paving.

Inholmes

17 IVYDENE

283 Loddon Bridge Road, Woodley, Reading, RG5 4BE. Janet & Bill Bonney, 01189 697591, billabonney@aol.com. *3½m E of Reading. Loddon Bridge Rd is main road through Woodley. Garden approx 100yds S of Just Tiles r'about. Parking in adjacent roads.* **Sun 15 July (11-5). Adm £4, chd free. Home-made teas. Visits also by arrangement June & July for groups of 10-25. Please mention NGS.**

Small urban gardeners' garden with mature tree fern walkway and many unusual hostas. Overflowing herbaceous borders. The vertical garden is now mature. There is a new stumpery with many interesting ferns. A lavender bed surrounds a new pergola. The garden also features stained glass and ceramic art to complete the picture. Owner is a previous BBC Gardener of the Year finalist. Featured in Garden News and Garden of the Week.

18 JANNAWAYS

Bagnor, Newbury, RG20 8AH. Mr & Mrs Sharples. *3m W of Newbury. From M4 J13, S on A34. Take A4 exit towards Newbury. 1st L to Station Rd. Turn L to Lambourn Rd. 1st R to Bagnor, past Watermill Theatre, then follow NGS signs.* **Sun 8 July (2-5.30). Adm £5, chd free. Tea & biscuits included.**

This 5 acre garden encompasses a lake naturally fed by springs. A circular walk from formal beds near the house, leads along a woodland path, crossing a weir to wild flowers and specimen trees. A pitch perfect lawn, fish pond, pagodas and many hidden gems provide visitors with a rich panoply of vistas round every corner. Also a children's jungle gym and trampoline for young visitors.

19 KIRBY HOUSE

Upper Green, Inkpen, RG17 9ED. Mrs K Astor. *5m SE of Hungerford. A4 to Kintbury. At Xrds by Corner Stores take Inkpen Rd. Follow road into Inkpen. Pass common on L. Just past Crown & Garter Pub, turn L (to Combe & Faccombe), at T-junction turn L, house on R.* **Sun 10 June (2-5). Adm £4.50, chd free. Combined adm with The Old Rectory Inkpen £7, chd free.**

7 acres in beautiful setting with views of South Berkshire Downs and historical Combe Gibbet, across lawn with ha-ha and parkland. C18 Queen Anne House (not open). Formal borders, lily pond garden and terraces laid out by Harold Peto. Reflecting pond with fountain, lake, walled garden and contemporary sculptures. Some uneven paths. Refreshments available at The Old Rectory, Inkpen.

20 MALVERLEYS

Fullers Lane, East End, Newbury, RG20 0AA. *A34 S of Newbury, exit signed for Highclere. Follow A343 for ½m, turn R to Woolton Hill. Pass school & turn L to East End. After 1m R at village green, then after 100 metres, R onto Fullers Lane.* **Sun 29 Apr, Sun 29 July (2-5). Adm £12, chd free. Pre-booking essential, please go to 'Events' at www.ngs.org.uk or phone 01483 211535. Tea, cake and tour at 2pm or 3.30pm with Head Gardener included. Ticket availability is limited so please book early to avoid disappointment.**

10 acres of dynamic gardens which have been developed over the last 6 yrs to include magnificent mixed borders and a series of contrasting yew hedged rooms, hosting flame borders, a cool garden, a pond garden and new stumpery. A vegetable garden with striking fruit cages sit within a walled garden, also encompassing a white garden. Meadows open out to views over the parkland. Featured on BBC Gardener's World (July 2017).

21 ODNEY CLUB

Odney Lane, Cookham, SL6 9SR. John Lewis Partnership. *3m N of Maidenhead. Off A4094 S of Cookham Bridge. Signs to car park in grounds.* **Sun 22 Apr (2-6). Adm £5, chd free. Light refreshments served 2pm-5pm.**

This 120 acre site is beside the Thames with lovely riverside walks. A favourite with Stanley Spencer who featured our magnolia in his work. Lovely wisteria, specimen trees, side gardens, spring bedding and ornamental lake. The John Lewis Partnership Heritage Centre will be open, showcasing the textile archive and items illustrating the history of John Lewis and Waitrose. Some gravel paths. Dogs on leads please.

22 THE OLD RECTORY INKPEN

Lower Green, Inkpen, RG17 9DS. Mrs C McKeon. *4m SE of Hungerford. From centre of Kintbury at the Xrds, take Inkpen Rd. After ½m turn R, then go approx 3m (passing Crown & Garter Pub, then Inkpen Village Hall on L). Nr St Michaels Church, follow car park signs.* **Sun 10 June (2-5). Adm £4.50, chd free. Home-made teas. Combined adm with Kirby House £7, chd free.**

On a gentle hillside with lovely countryside views, the Old Rectory offers a peaceful setting for this pretty 2 acre garden. Enjoy strolling through the formal and walled gardens, herbaceous borders, pleached lime walk and wild flower meadow (some slopes).

23 THE OLD RECTORY, FARNBOROUGH

Nr Wantage, Oxon, OX12 8NX. Mr & Mrs Michael Todhunter, 01488 638298. *4m SE of Wantage. Take B4494 Wantage-Newbury road, after 4m turn E at sign for Farnborough. Approx 1m to village, Old Rectory on L.* **Sun 22 Apr, Sun 20 May (2-5); Wed 25 July (11-4). Adm £5, chd free. Home-made teas. Donation to Farnborough PCC.**

In a series of immaculately tended garden rooms, incl herbaceous borders, arboretum, secret garden, roses, vegetables and bog garden, there is an explosion of rare and interesting plants, beautifully combined for colour and texture. With stunning views across the countryside, it is the perfect setting for the 1749 rectory (not open), once home of John Betjeman, in memory of whom John Piper created a window in the local church. Plants and home-made preserves for sale. Awarded Finest Parsonage in England by Country Life and The Rectory Society. Featured in The Telegraph (Apr 2017). Some steep slopes and gravel paths.

24 OLD WATERFIELD

Winkfield Road, Ascot, SL5 7LJ. Hugh & Catherine Stevenson, catherine.stevenson@oldwaterfield.com. *6m SW of Windsor to E of Ascot Racecourse. On E side of A330 midway between A329 & A332.* **Visits by arrangement Apr to Oct for groups of 10-25. Light refreshments on request. Adm £4.50, chd free.**

Set in 4 acres between Ascot Heath and Windsor Great Park, the original cottage garden has been developed and extended over the past few years. Herbaceous borders, meadow with specimen trees, large productive vegetable garden, orchard and mixed hedging.

25 THE PRIORY

Beech Hill, RG7 2BJ. Mr & Mrs C Carter, 01189 883146, tita@getcarter.org.uk. *5m S of Reading. M4 J11, A33 S to Basingstoke. At T-lights, L to Spencers Wood. After 1½m turn R for Beech Hill. After approx 1½m, L into Wood Lane, R down Priory Drive.* **Visits by arrangement June to Aug for groups of 10+. Teas on request. Adm £4.50, chd free.**

Extensive gardens in grounds of former C12 French Priory (not open), rebuilt 1648. The mature gardens are in a very attractive setting beside the River Loddon. Large formal walled garden with espalier fruit trees, lawns, mixed and replanted herbaceous borders, vegetables and roses. Woodland, fine trees, lake and Italian style water garden. A lovely garden for group visits.

The National Garden Scheme is the largest single funder of Macmillan

26 ROOKSNEST

Ermin Street, Lambourn Woodlands, RG17 7SB. garden@rooksnest.net. *2m S of Lambourn on B4000. From M4 J14, take A338 Wantage Rd, turn 1st L onto B4000 (Ermin St). Rooksnest signed after 3m.* **Wed 18 Apr, Wed 13 June (11-3.30). Adm £5, chd free. Light refreshments. Last entry 3.30pm. Combined adm with Inholmes £7.00, chd free. Visits also by arrangement Mar to June for groups of 15+.**

Approx 10 acre exceptionally fine traditional English garden. Rose garden (redesigned 2017), herbaceous garden, pond garden, herb garden, fruit, vegetable and cutting garden, and glasshouses. Many specimen trees and fine shrubs, orchard and terraces. Garden mostly designed by Arabella Lennox-Boyd. All areas have step-free access, although surface consists of gravel and mowed grass. Plant Sale at June opening only.

27 ROOKWOOD FARM HOUSE

Stockcross, RG20 8JX. The Hon Rupert & Charlotte Digby, 01488 608676, charlotte@rookwoodfarmhouse.co.uk, www.rookwoodfarmhouse.co.uk. *3m W of Newbury. M4 J13, A34(S). After 3m exit for A4(W) to Hungerford. At 2nd r'about take B4000 towards Stockcross, after approx ¾m turn R into Rookwood.* **Wed 4 Apr, Sun 6 May, Wed 20 June (11-5). On Mon 27 Aug (11-5), also open Stockcross House. Adm £5, chd free. Home-made teas. Visits also by arrangement Apr to Sept for groups of 10+.**

This exciting valley garden, a work in progress, has elements all visitors can enjoy. A rose covered pergola, fabulous tulips, giant alliums, and a recently developed 'jungle garden' with banana plants and canas. A kitchen garden features a parterre of raised beds, which along with a bog garden and colour themed herbaceous planting, all make Rookwood well worth a visit. Gravel paths, some steep slopes.

28 ST TIMOTHEE

Darlings Lane, Maidenhead, SL6 6PA. Sarah & Sal Pajwani, 07976 892667, pajwanisarah@gmail.com. *1m N of Maidenhead. M4 J8/9 to A404M. 2nd exit onto A4 to Maidenhead. L at 1st r'about to A4130 Henley Rd. After ½m turn R onto Pinkneys Drive. At Pinkneys Arms Pub, turn L into Lee Lane, follow NGS signs.* **Wed 18, Thur 26 Apr (2-4.30); Mon 27 Aug (11-4.30). Adm £4, chd free. Home-made teas. Visits also by arrangement Apr to Sept for groups of 10+.**

Deep and gently flowing, colour themed borders planted for yr-round interest with a wide range of attractive grasses and perennials. Other features incl a box parterre, wildlife pond, rose terrace and wild areas in a 2 acre plot. Open this year in April and August to celebrate tulips and blossom, and the richness of the late summer garden. Special Event - Join us for a morning Winter Garden 'Talk & Walk' on 18 January 2018 at 10.30am. Limited numbers so pre-booking essential. Adm £10, including talk (indoors) and tea and cake. Please phone or email to book.

Kirby House

29 SANDLEFORD PLACE

Newtown, Newbury, RG20 9AY. Mel Gatward, 01635 40726, melgatward@btinternet.com. *House is on A339, 1½m S of Newbury on NW side of Swan r'about at Newtown. Parking through nearby field gate 50yds beyond entrance.* **Sun 22 Apr, Sun 13 May, Sun 17 June (2-6). Adm £5, chd free. Home-made teas. Visits also by arrangement Mar to Oct. For group bookings more than a month in advance pre-payment requested.**

A plantswoman's 4 acres, more exuberant than manicured with River Enborne flowing through. Various areas of shrub and mixed borders create a romantic, naturalistic effect. Wonderful old walled garden. Long herbaceous border flanks wild flower meadow. Yr-round interest from early carpets of snowdrops and daffodils, crocus covered lawn, to autumn berries and leaf colour. A garden for all seasons. Wheelchair access to most areas. Guide dogs only.

30 STOCKCROSS HOUSE

Church Road, Stockcross, Newbury, RG20 8LP. Susan & Edward Vandyk, 07765 674863, dragonflygardens@btinternet.com. *3m W of Newbury. M4 J13, A34(S). After 3m exit A4(W) to Hungerford. At 2nd r'about take B4000, 1m to Stockcross, 2nd L into Church Rd.* **Sun 17 June (11-4). On Mon 27 Aug (11-4), also open Rookwood Farm House. Adm £5, chd free. Home-made teas. Visits also by arrangement Apr to Sept for groups of 10+.**

A delightful two acre garden set around a Grade II listed former rectory (not open), with an emphasis on naturalistic planting. Romantic wisteria and clematis covered pergola, reflecting pond with folly, rich variety of roses, vegetable and cutting garden. Orangery with vines. Pond with cascade and duck house. Small stumpery with ferns. Sculptural elements by local artists. Partial wheelchair access with some gravelled areas.

31 STUBBINGS HOUSE

Henley Road, Maidenhead, SL6 6QL. Mr & Mrs D Good, 01628 825454, info@stubbingsgroup.com, www.stubbingsnursery.co.uk. *2m W of Maidenhead. From A4130 Henley Rd follow signed private access road opp Stubbings Church. See website for further directions.* **Sat 17 Mar (10-4); Sun 18 Mar (10.30-3); Sat 5 May (10-4); Sun 6, Mon 7 May (10.30-3). Adm £4, chd free. Visits also by arrangement Mar to Sept for groups of 10-20.**

Parkland garden accessed via adjacent retail nursery. Set around C18 house (not open), home to Queen Wilhelmina of Netherlands in WW2. Large lawn with ha-ha and woodland walks. Notable trees incl historic cedars and araucaria. March brings an abundance of daffodils and in May a 60 metre wall of wisteria. Attractions incl a C18 icehouse and access to adjacent NT woodland. A level site with firm gravel paths for wheelchair access.

GROUP OPENING

32 SWALLOWFIELD VILLAGE GARDENS

The Street, Swallowfield, RG7 1QY. *5m S of Reading. From M4 J11 take A33 S. At 1st T-lights turn L on B3349 signed Swallowfield. On entering the village follow signs for parking. Purchase of tickets & map, opp The Crown.* **Sun 3 June (2-6). Combined adm £6, chd free. Home-made teas at Loddon Lower Farm.**

BIRD IN HAND HOUSE
Margaret & John McDonald.

BRAMBLES
Sarah & Martyn Dadds.

BROOKSIDE NURSERY
David Maskell.

5 CURLYS WAY
Carolyn & Gary Clark.

GREENWINGS
Liz & Ray Jones.

LAMBS FARMHOUSE
Eva Koskuba.

LODDON LOWER FARM
Mr & Mrs J Bayliss.

NORKETT COTTAGE
Jenny Spencer.

RUSSETTS
Roberta Stewart.

This year Swallowfield is offering nine gardens to visit. A number are in the village itself, others are nearby, so there is a mix of walking to some, with those in different directions needing a car or bicycle to reach them comfortably. Whilst each provides its own character and interest, they all nestle in rural countryside by the Whitewater, Blackwater and Loddon rivers which create an abundance of wildlife and lovely views. The garden owners, many of whom are members of the local Horticultural Society, are always happy to chat and share their enthusiasm and experience. Plants for sale. Most of the gardens have wheelchair access, some have slight slopes but the area is generally flat.

33 ◆ WELFORD PARK

Welford, Newbury, RG20 8HU. Mrs J H Puxley, www.welfordpark.co.uk. *6m NW of Newbury. M4 J13, A34(S). After 3m exit for A4(W) to Hungerford. At 2nd r'about take B4000, after 4m turn R signed Welford. Entrance on Newbury-Lambourn road.* **For NGS: Wed 7 Feb (11-4). Adm £7. Light refreshments. For other opening times and information, please visit garden website.**

One of the finest natural snowdrop woodlands in the country, approx 4 acres, along with a wonderful display of hellebores throughout the garden and winter flowering shrubs. This is an NGS 1927 pioneer garden on the River Lambourn set around Queen Anne House (not open). Featured on BBC Gardener's World In October 2017. Also the stunning setting for Great British Bake Off 2014 - 2017. Dogs welcome on leads. Coach parties please book in advance.

GROUP OPENING

34 WEST MILLS ALLOTMENTS & ISLAND COTTAGE

West Mills, Newbury, RG14 5HT. *In centre of Newbury, nr the canal. Best to park in town centre car parks. Walk either side of St Nicholas Church or between Cote Restaurant & Holland & Barrett to canal. 100yds to Swing Bridge & follow signs. Limited side road parking.* **Sun 8 July (2-5). Combined adm £5, chd free. Home-made teas at Island Cottage (weather permitting).**

ISLAND COTTAGE
Karen Swaffield, karen@lockisland.com.
Visits also by arrangement May to Sept to Island Cottage only.

WEST MILLS ALLOTMENTS
Newbury Town Council (local contact Alison Martin).

Lovely allotments and small town garden in the centre of Newbury. You are welcome to visit the allotments on our 120 plot site with the opportunity to talk to some of the plot holders about their methods. A variety of fruit, vegetables and flowers to see, some in greenhouses and polytunnels. Island Cottage is a small town garden set between a backwater of the River Kennet and the Kennet and Avon Canal. You will find interesting combinations of colour and texture to look at rather than walk through, although you can do that too! A deck overlooks a sluiceway towards a lawn and border. Started from scratch in 2005, and mostly again after the floods of 2014. Plants for sale at the allotments. No dogs please.

35 WICKHAM HOUSE

Wickham, Newbury, RG20 8HD. Mr & Mrs James D'Arcy, www.wickhamhouse.com. *7m NW of Newbury or 6m NE of Hungerford. From M4 J14, take A338(N) signed Wantage. Approx ¾m turn R onto B4000 for Wickham & Shefford Woodlands. Through Wickham, entrance 100yds on R. From Newbury take B4000, house on L just before Wickham.* **Tue 10 July (11-4). Adm £5, chd free. Home-made teas & home cooked gammon rolls.**

In a beautiful country house setting, this exceptional ½ acre walled garden was created from scratch in 2008. Designed by Robin Templar-Williams, the different rooms have distinct themes and colour schemes. Delightful arched clematis and rose walkway. Wide variety of trees, planting, pots brimming with colour and places to sit and enjoy the views. Separate cutting and vegetable garden. Gravel paths.

D

BUCKINGHAMSHIRE

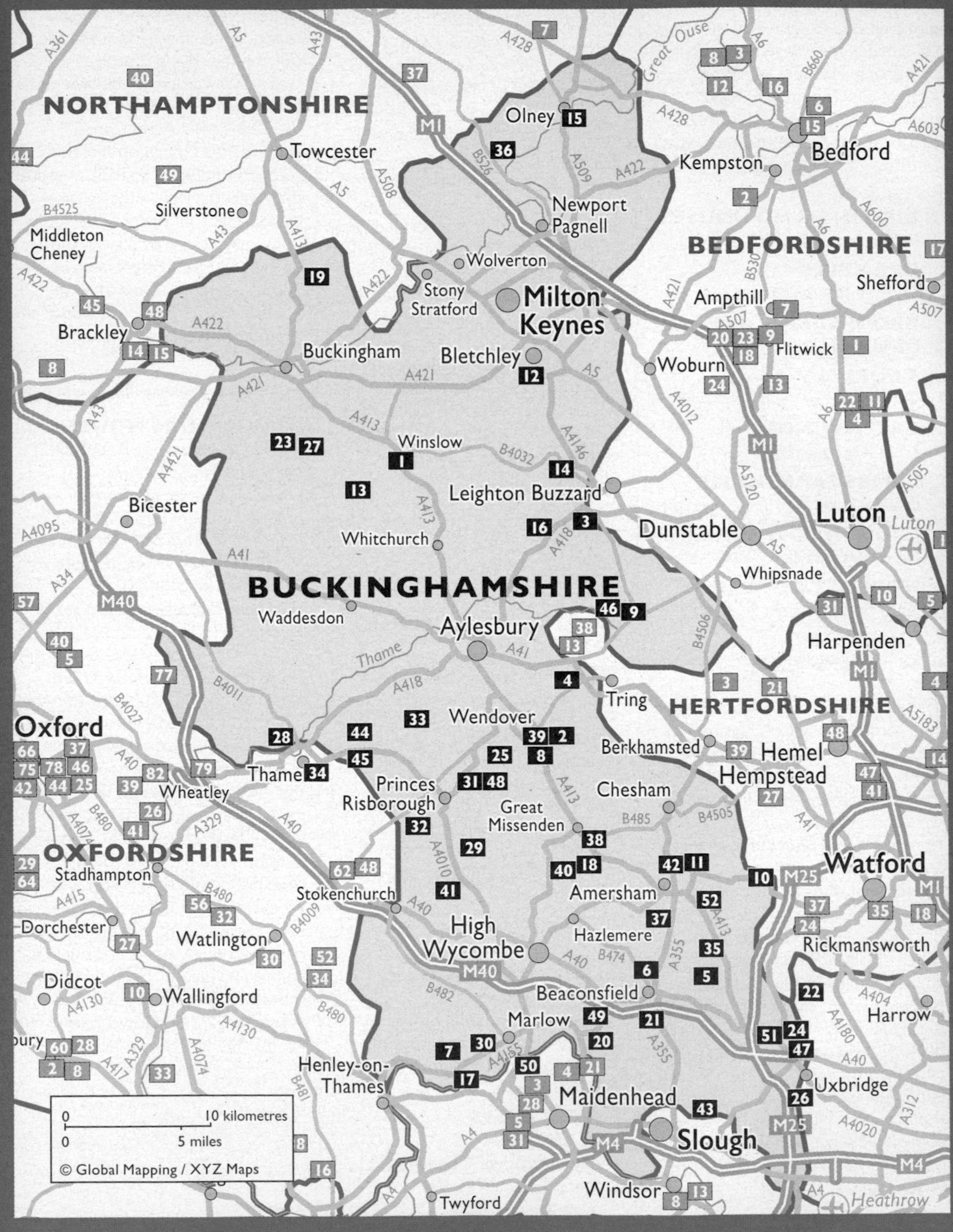

Buckinghamshire has a beautiful and varied landscape; edged by the River Thames to the south, crossed by the Chiltern Hills, and with the Vale of Aylesbury stretching to the north.

This year Buckinghamshire will hold six group openings, many of which can be found in villages of thatched or brick and flint cottages.

Many Buckinghamshire gardens have been used as locations for films and television, with the Pinewood Studios nearby and excellent proximity to London.

We also boast historical gardens including Ascott, Cowper and Newton Museum Gardens, Hall Barn, and Stoke Poges Memorial Gardens (Grade I listed).

Most of our gardens offer homemade tea and cakes to round off a lovely afternoon, visitors can leave knowing they have enjoyed a wonderful visit and helped raise money for nursing and caring charities at the same time.

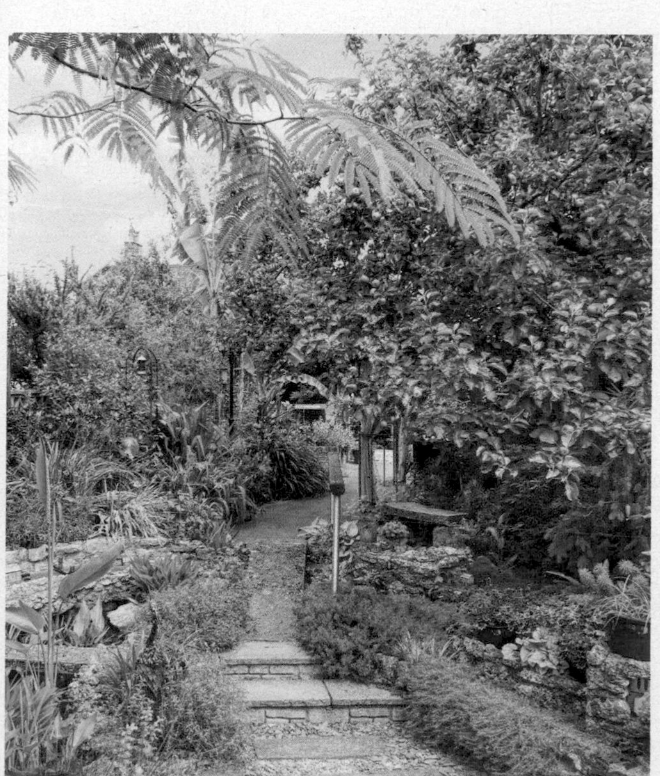

Volunteers

County Organiser
Maggie Bateson
01494 866265
maggiebateson@gmail.com

County Treasurer
Tim Hart
01494 837328
timgc.hart@btinternet.com

Publicity
Sandra Wetherall
01494 862264
sandracwetherall@gmail.com

Social Media
Lisa Wilhelmy
07493 442641
lisa.wilhelmy@yahoo.co.uk

Booklet Co-ordinator
Maggie Bateson
(as above)

Assistant County Organisers
Janice Cross
01494 728291
janicemaycross@gmail.com

Judy Hart
01494 837328
judy.elgood@gmail.com

Margaret Higgins
01844 347072
jhiggins816@btinternet.com

Mhairi Sharpley
01494 782870
mhairisharpley@btinternet.com

Left: 20 Whitepit Lane

OPENING DATES

All entries subject to change. For latest information check **www.ngs.org.uk**

Map locator numbers are shown to the right of each garden name.

March

Sunday 18th
Wind in the Willows 51

April

Sunday 1st
Overstroud Cottage 38

Monday 2nd
Westend House 46

Sunday 15th
NEW Iver Environmental Centre 26
Rivendell 42

Sunday 22nd
Hills House 24
Long Crendon Gardens 28
Orchard House 37
Overstroud Cottage 38

Sunday 29th
NEW Aston Clinton Gardens 4
NEW ◆ Chenies Manor Gardens 10

May

Sunday 6th
Close Cottage 14
◆ Nether Winchendon House 34

Monday 7th
◆ Ascott 3
Turn End 44

Sunday 13th
Overstroud Cottage 38
◆ Stoke Poges Memorial Gardens 43

Tuesday 15th
Red Kites 41

Sunday 20th
Higher Denham Gardens 22
The Manor House 32

Sunday 27th
Fressingwood 18
◆ Nether Winchendon House 34

Monday 28th
The Claydons 13
Glebe Farm 19

June

Sunday 3rd
Burrow Farm 7
Cublington Gardens 16
Loosley Dene 29
The White House 47

Saturday 9th
18 Brownswood Road 6
◆ Cowper & Newton Museum Gardens 15

Sunday 10th
18 Brownswood Road 6
◆ Cowper & Newton Museum Gardens 15
Long Crendon Gardens 28
Overstroud Cottage 38

Friday 15th
Lords Wood 30

Sunday 17th
NEW Aston Clinton Gardens 4
Cheddington Gardens 9
126 Church Green Road 12
Hillesden House 23
NEW Old Park Barn 36

Tuesday 19th
126 Church Green Road 12

Saturday 23rd
Acer Corner 2
11 The Paddocks 39

Sunday 24th
Acer Corner 2
11 The Paddocks 39
Tythrop Park 45

July

Sunday 1st
Burrow Farm 7
Lowthorpe House 31
NEW The White House, Askett 48

Saturday 7th
11 The Paddocks 39

Sunday 8th
11 The Paddocks 39

Tuesday 17th
Red Kites 41

Tuesday 24th
NEW Iver Environmental Centre 26

August

Wednesday 8th
Danesfield House 17

Friday 24th
NEW Iver Environmental Centre 26

Sunday 26th
Nether Winchendon House 34

Monday 27th
◆ Ascott 3

September

Tuesday 4th
NEW ◆ Chenies Manor Gardens 10

October

Saturday 20th
Acer Corner 2

Sunday 21st
Acer Corner 2

By Arrangement

Abbots House 1
Acer Corner 2
Beech House 5
Burrow Farm 7
Cedar House 8
Chesham Bois House 11
Close Cottage 14
Grange Drive Wooburn 20
Hall Barn 21
Hillesden House 23
Hills House 24
Homelands 25
Kingsbridge 27
Larkspur House, Cublington Gardens 16
Loosley Dene 29
Moat Farm 33
North Down 35
Overstroud Cottage 38
11 The Paddocks 39
Peterley Corner Cottage 40
Red Kites 41
NEW 20 Whitepit Lane 49
Whitewalls 50
Wind in the Willows 51
NEW Woodside 52

Danesfield House

THE GARDENS

1 ABBOTS HOUSE

10 Church Street, Winslow, MK18 3AN. Mrs Jane Rennie, 01296 712326, jane@renniemail.com. 9m N of Aylesbury. A413 into Winslow. From town centre take Horn St & R into Church St, L fork at top. Entrance 20 metres on L. Parking in town centre & adjacent streets. **Visits by arrangement Apr to Aug for groups of 20 max. Adm £4, chd free. Light refreshments.**

Garden on different levels divided into four; courtyard near house with arbour, pond with waterfall and pots; woodland garden with rose gazebo and swimming pool; garden with grasses; walled Victorian kitchen garden with glasshouses, potager, fruit pergola, wall trained fruit, many Mediterranean plants and recent meadow planting spring bulbs in April, a major feature in wild areas and woodland. Late spring bulbs, water feature and many pots. Experimental wild areas. Some sculptures. Partial wheelchair access, garden levels accessed by steps. Guide dogs and medical-aid dogs only.

2 ACER CORNER

10 Manor Road, Wendover, HP22 6HQ. Jo Naiman, 07958 319234, jo@acercorner.com, www.acercorner.com. 3m S of Aylesbury. Follow A413 into Wendover. L at clock tower r'about into Aylesbury Rd. R at next r'about into Wharf Rd, continue past schools on L, garden on R. **Sat 23, Sun 24 June, Sat 20, Sun 21 Oct (2-5). Adm £2.50, chd free. Home-made teas. Visits also by arrangement May to Oct for groups of 20 max.** Donation to South Bucks Jewish Community Charity.

Garden designer's garden with Japanese influence and large collection of Japanese maples. The enclosed front garden is Japanese in style. Back garden is divided into three areas; patio area recently redesigned in the Japanese style; densely planted area with many acers and roses; and the corner which includes a productive greenhouse and interesting planting. Featured in Woman's Weekly Gardening magazine (Sept 2017).

3 ◆ ASCOTT

Ascott, Wing, Leighton Buzzard, LU7 0PP. The National Trust, 01296 688242, amy@ascottestate.co.uk, www.ascottestate.co.uk. 2m SW of Leighton Buzzard, 8m NE of Aylesbury. Via A418. Buses: 150 Aylesbury - Milton Keynes, 100 Aylesbury & Milton Keynes. **For NGS: Mon 7 May, Mon 27 Aug (1-6). Adm £5, chd £2.50. (NT members are required to pay to enter the gardens on NGS days).** For other opening times and information, please phone, email or visit garden website.

Combining Victorian formality with early C20 natural style and recent plantings to lead it into the C21, with a recently completed garden designed by Jacques and Peter Wirtz who designed the gardens at Alnwick Castle, and also a Richard Long sculpture. Terraced lawns with specimen and ornamental trees, panoramic views to the Chilterns. Naturalised bulbs, mirror image herbaceous borders, and impressive topiary incl box and yew sundial. Ascott House is closed on NGS Days. Outdoor wheelchairs available from car park. Mobility buggy, prior booking advised.

The Lantern Cottage, Aston Clinton Gardens

GROUP OPENING

4 NEW ASTON CLINTON GARDENS

Green End Street, Aston Clinton, Aylesbury, HP22 5JE. 3m E of Aylesbury. From Aylesbury take A41 E. At large r'about, continue straight (signed Aston Clinton). Continue onto London Rd. L at The Bell Pub, parking on Green End St & side roads. **Sun 29 Apr, Sun 17 June (2-5). Combined adm £4, chd free. Home-made teas.**

NEW 101 GREEN END STREET
Sue Lipscomb.

NEW THE LANTERN COTTAGE
Jacki Connell.

These two cottage gardens, one well established and the other having recently undergone a radical redesign by its new owner, share a basis of seasonal interest underpinned by evergreens and perennial planting. At The Lantern Cottage, spring hellebores and an abundance of tulips give way to an early summer display of roses, peonies, bearded iris, alliums and climbers including various clematis, wisteria and akebia. A wide selection of salvias and herbaceous perennials, mostly raised from seed and cuttings. Pelargoniums provide yr-round colour in the conservatory, and the greenhouse is always full! At 101, the new owner took up residence in autumn 2015, quickly establishing raised beds for vegetable production, a number of fruit trees and a variety of soft fruits. There is also a wildlife pond, an arbour overlooking the Victorian greenhouse, plus herbaceous borders, ornamental grasses surrounding a red kite sculpture, and varied container planting. Wildlife is encouraged to visit.

5 BEECH HOUSE

Long Wood Drive, Jordans, Beaconsfield, HP9 2SS. Sue & Ray Edwards, raychessmad@hotmail.com. From A40, L to Seer Green & Jordans for approx 1m. Turn into Jordans Way on L. Long Wood Drive 1st L. From A413 turn into Chalfont St Giles. Straight ahead until L signed Jordans. 1st L Jordans Way. **Visits by arrangement Mar to Nov for groups of 2-30. Adm £3, chd free.**

2 acre plantsman's garden built up over the last 30 yrs, with a wide range of plants in a variety of habitats aimed at providing yr-round interest. Many perennials, shrubs, roses, ferns, trees planted for their foliage, ornamental bark and autumn colour. Popular features are two meadows with numerous bulbs and wild flowers in spring and early summer, followed by climbing roses later in the yr. Wheelchair access dependent upon weather conditions.

6 18 BROWNSWOOD ROAD

Beaconsfield, HP9 2NU. John & Bernadette Thompson. From New Town turn R into Ledborough Lane, L into Sandleswood Rd, 2nd R into Brownswood Rd. **Sat 9 June (11.30-5); Sun 10 June (1-5). Adm £3.50, chd free. Home-made teas & gluten free options.**

A plant filled garden designed by Barbara Hunt. A harmonious arrangement of arcs and circles introduces a rhythm that leads through the garden. Sweeping box curves, gravel beds, brick edging and lush planting. A restrained use of purples and reds dazzle against a grey and green background. There has been considerable replanning and replanting during the winter.

7 BURROW FARM

Hambleden, RG9 6LT. David Palmer, 01491 571256. 1m SE of Hambleden. On A4155 between Henley & Marlow, turn N at Mill End. After 300yds, R onto Rotten Row. After ½m, Burrow Farm entrance on R. **Sun 3 June, Sun 1 July (11-3.30). Adm £5, chd free. Home-made teas. Visits also by arrangement May to Aug for groups of 10-30.**

Burrow Farm and the adjacent cottages (not open) are part Tudor and part Elizabethan, set in the Chilterns above Hambleden Valley where it meets the Thames. Views of pasture and woodlands across the ha-ha greatly enhance the setting. Special features are the parterre, arboretum and C15 barn, where home-made teas will be served.

8 CEDAR HOUSE

Bacombe Lane, Wendover, HP22 6EQ. Sarah Nicholson, 01296 622131, sarahhnicholson@btinternet.com. 5m SE Aylesbury. From Gt Missenden take A413 into Wendover. Take 1st L before row of cottages, house at top of lane. Parking for no more than 10 cars. **Visits by arrangement May to Sept for groups of 10+. Adm £3.50, chd free. Light refreshments.**

A chalk garden in the Chiltern Hills with a steep sloping lawn leading to a natural swimming pond with aquatic plants. Wild flowers with native orchids. Shaped borders hold a great variety of trees, shrubs and perennials. A lodge greenhouse and a good collection of half-hardy plants in pots. Steep, sloping lawn.

GROUP OPENING

9 CHEDDINGTON GARDENS

Cheddington, Leighton Buzzard, LU7 0RQ. www.cheddington.org.uk. 7m E of Aylesbury, 5m S of Leighton Buzzard, 5m W of Dunstable. Turn off B489 at Pitstone. Turn off B488 at Cheddington Station. ¾m walk from train station to village, approx 15 mins. **Sun 17 June (1.30-5). Combined adm £6, chd free. Home-made teas in Methodist hall by the green.** Donation to St Giles Tower Restoration Fund.

CHEDDINGTON ALLOTMENTS
Cheddington Parish Council.

7 HIGH STREET
Irene & Tony Johnson.

THE OLD POST OFFICE
Alan & Wendy Tipple.

THE OLD READING ROOM
Mrs Kim Goldhagen.

SPRINGBRAE
Pier Thomas.

THE VICARAGE
Revd Gill Rowell.

WESTEND HOUSE
His Honour Judge & Mrs Richard Foster.
(See separate entry)

Mentioned in Domesday Book, Cheddington is a friendly, active, award-winning village, situated in the Vale of Aylesbury at the northern end of the Chilterns. 2018 we have 7 gardens to view, varying in size, aspect and content, each reflecting their owners' style and passions. Cheddington has St Giles Church which dates back to C12, the present buildings are C14/C15 (open) and located just a short walk from the allotments, through the old orchards or by car to Church Path. Cheddington is home to the world's first branch railway line (closed 1964), along with the infamous Great Train Robbery of 1963. Partial wheelchair access.

10 NEW ◆ CHENIES MANOR GARDENS

Chenies, Rickmansworth, WD3 6ER. Boo Macleod Mathews, 07798 558150, enquiries@cheniesmanorhouse.co.uk, www.cheniesmanorhouse.co.uk. Between Little Chalfont & Chorleywood on A404. Take J18 off M25 & follow road L onto the A404 towards Amersham. **For NGS: Sun 29 Apr, Tue 4 Sept (2-5). Adm £6, chd £3.50.**

Home-made teas in the garden. For other opening times and information, please phone, email or visit garden website.
C14/15 Manor House within award-winning gardens. Throughout the garden permanent herbaceous plantings are complemented by two distinct seasonal plantings for spring and summer. The gardens are divided into a series of compartments with various colour themes and structural forms combining imaginative planting and beautiful plant associations. Physic garden, kitchen garden and yew maze. Tulip Festival 7th May, Dahlia Festival 27th August, Plant Fair 15th July. Wheelchair access to the tea room. Limited access to the gardens and no access to the house. Disabled WC.

11 CHESHAM BOIS HOUSE

85 Bois Lane, Chesham Bois, HP6 6DF. Julia Plaistowe, 01494 726476, julia.plaistowe@yahoo.co.uk, cheshamboishouse.co.uk. 1m N of Amersham-on-the-Hill. Follow Sycamore Rd (main shopping centre road of Amersham) which becomes Bois Lane. Do not use SatNav once in lane as you will be led astray. **Visits by arrangement Mar to Sept. Adm £8, incl home-made teas.**
3 acre plantswoman's garden with primroses, daffodils and hellebores in early spring. Interesting for most of the year with lovely herbaceous borders, rill with small ornamental canal, walled garden, old orchard with wildlife pond, and handsome trees of which some are topiaried. It is a peaceful oasis. Close to the garden the 800 yr old church can also be visited. Featured in The Telegraph 'Gardens to Visit' (2017). Gravel in front of the house.

12 126 CHURCH GREEN ROAD

Bletchley, Milton Keynes, MK3 6DD. David & Janice Hale. 13m E of Buckingham, 11m N of Leighton Buzzard. Off B4034 into Church Green Rd, take L turn at mini-r'about. **Sun 17 June (2-6); Tue 19 June (2-5). Adm £3, chd free. Home-made teas.**
A gentle sloping mature garden of ½ acre is a plant lover's delight, which incl a small formal garden, shady areas and mixed borders of shrubs, perennials and roses. Features incl a thatched wendy house, pergola, formal pond, wildlife pond, productive fruit and vegetable garden, two greenhouses and patio.

GROUP OPENING

13 THE CLAYDONS

East Botolph and Middle Claydon, MK18 2ND. 1½m SW Winslow. In Winslow turn R off High St, by the Bell Pub & follow NT signs towards Claydon House & The Claydons. **Mon 28 May (2-6). Combined adm £5, chd free. Home-made teas in village hall.**

CLAYDON COTTAGE
Mr & Mrs Tony Evans.

THE OLD RECTORY
Mrs Jane Meisl.

THE OLD VICARAGE
Nigel & Esther Turnbull.

NEW **4 STATION COTTAGES**
Mr & Mrs Andrew & Alison Fenner.

Three small villages, originally part of the Claydon Estate with typical north Buckinghamshire cottages and two C13 churches. The Old Vicarage, a large garden on clay with mixed borders, scented garden, dell, shrub roses, vegetables and a natural clay pond. Small meadow area and planting to encourage wildlife, and beehives. A free children's quiz. Access via gravel drive. Claydon Cottage has many quirky features and surprises. The Old Rectory is a large garden with a wildflower meadow, herbaceous borders, a woodland walk and cloud hedging. 4 Station Cottages is a small, perfectly formed garden sculptured out of the railway embankment. Partial wheelchair access.

14 CLOSE COTTAGE

Church Lane, Soulbury, Leighton Buzzard, LU7 0BU. Rachel Belsham & Daniel Storey, belshamstorey@btinternet.com. Approx 3m NW of Leighton Buzzard. In centre of village, next to field below church, on narrow country lane leading uphill from The Boot Pub. Parking in field, clearly signed. **Sun 6 May (1.30-6). Adm £4.50, chd free. Home-made teas. Visits also by arrangement Mar to Aug for groups of 10+.**
The 3 acre garden at Close Cottage is 16 yrs old and encompasses a formal terraced garden, orchard and paddock. The garden is laid to lawn and planted with a wide variety of shrubs, bulbs and perennials. The orchard incl an avenue of cherry trees, various fruit trees, a wild flower meadow, woodland area, vegetable beds and a cutting garden.

15 ◆ COWPER & NEWTON MUSEUM GARDENS

Orchard Side, Market Place, Olney, MK46 4AJ. Anne Kempson, 01234 711833, www.cowperandnewtonmuseum.org.uk. 5m N of Newport Pagnell. 12m S of Wellingborough. On A509. Please park in public car park in East St. **For NGS: Sat 9, Sun 10 June (10.30-4.30). Adm £3, chd free. Home-made teas.** For other opening times and information, please phone or visit garden website.
The tranquil Flower Garden of C18 poet William Cowper, who said 'Gardening was of all employments, that in which I succeeded best', has plants introduced prior to his death in 1800, many mentioned in his writings. The Summer House Garden, with Cowper's 'verse manufactory', now a Victorian Kitchen Garden, has new and heritage vegetables organically grown, also a herb border and medicinal plant bed. Features incl Georgian dancing on Sunday, lacemaking demonstrations and local artists painting live art.

GROUP OPENING

16 CUBLINGTON GARDENS

Cublington, Leighton Buzzard, LU7 0LF. 5m SE Winslow, 5m NE Aylesbury. From Aylesbury take A413 Buckingham Rd. After 4m, at Whitchurch, turn R to Cublington. **Sun 3 June (2-6). Combined adm £5, chd free. Home-made teas in village hall.**

CHERRY COTTAGE, 3 THE WALLED GARDENS
Gwyneira Waters.

NEW **CUBLINGTON COTTAGE**
Mr & Mrs J Packer.

LARKSPUR HOUSE
Mr & Mrs S Jenkins, 01296 682615, gstmusketeers3@aol.com. **Visits also by arrangement June & July for groups of 20 max.**

NEW **1 MEADOW CLOSE**
Charlie & Andrea Toosey.

THE OLD STABLES
Mr & Mrs S George.

1 STEWKLEY ROAD
Tom & Helen Gadsby.

A group of diverse gardens in this attractive Buckinghamshire village listed as a conservation area. Cherry Cottage is adapted for wheelchair gardening with raised beds and artificial grass. Larkspur House is a beautifully maintained modern garden with hostas and alliums being firm favourites. It has a large, newly planted orchard and wild flower meadow. The Old Stables is a large garden divided into areas of different character, both formal and informal, featuring a revolving summerhouse and a circular hornbeam maze. 1 Stewkley Road has a strong focus on home grown food with an idyllic organic kitchen garden, small orchard and courtyard garden. New for 2018 is Cublington Cottage, a typical cottage garden and 1 Meadow Close, a garden with emphasis on recycling! Partial wheelchair access to some gardens.

♿ ☕

17 DANESFIELD HOUSE

Henley Road, Marlow, SL7 2EY. Danesfield House Hotel, 01628 891010, amoorin@danesfieldhouse.co.uk, www.danesfieldhouse.co.uk. 3m from Marlow. On the A4155 between Marlow & Henley-on-Thames. Signed on the LH-side Danesfield House Hotel and Spa. **Wed 8 Aug (10.30-4.30). Adm £4.50, chd free. Pre-booking essential for lunch and afternoon tea.**

The gardens at Danesfield were completed in 1901 by Robert Hudson, the Sunlight Soap magnate who built the house. Since the house opened as a hotel in 1991, the gardens have been admired by several thousand guests each yr. However, in 2009 it was discovered that the gardens contained outstanding examples of pulhamite in both the formal gardens and the waterfall areas. The 100 yr old topiary is also outstanding. Part of the grounds incl an Iron Age fort. Guided tours welcome on NGS open days. You may wander the grounds on your own or there will be two 1hr tours offered by our Head Gardener at 10.30am and 1.30pm for 30 max per tour. Pre-booking essential due to high demand. The gardeners will be available for questions after each tour. Restricted wheelchair access to the gardens due to gravel paths.

♿ 🛏 ☕

18 FRESSINGWOOD

Hare Lane, Little Kingshill, Great Missenden, HP16 0EF. John & Maggie Bateson. 1m S of Gt Missenden, 4m W of Amersham. From the A413 at Chiltern Hospital, turn L signed Gt & Lt Kingshill. Take 1st L into Nags Head Lane. Turn R under railway bridge, then L into New Rd & continue to Hare Lane. **Sun 27 May (2-5.30). Adm £4, chd free. Home-made teas.**

Thoughtfully designed garden with yr-round colour and many interesting features. Shrubbery with ferns, hostas, grasses and hellebores. Small formal garden, herb garden, pergolas with roses and clematis. Topiary and landscaped terrace. Newly developed area incorporating water with grasses. Herbaceous borders and bonsai collection. Children's quiz

✿ ☕

Larkspur House, Cublington Gardens

19 GLEBE FARM

Lillingstone Lovell, Buckingham, MK18 5BB. Mr David Hilliard, 01280 860384, thehilliards@talk21.com, www.glebefarmbarn.co.uk. Off A413, 5m N of Buckingham & 2m S of Whittlebury. From A5 at Potterspury, turn off A5 & follow signs to Lillingstone Lovell. **Mon 28 May (1.30-5.30). Adm £3, chd free. Home-made teas.**

A large cottage garden with an exuberance of colourful planting and winding gravel paths, amongst lawns and herbaceous borders on two levels. Ponds, a wishing well, vegetable beds, a knot garden, a small walled garden and an old tractor feature. Everything combines to make a beautiful garden full of surprises.

GROUP OPENING

20 GRANGE DRIVE WOOBURN

Wooburn Green, HP10 0QD. Elaine & Alan Ford, 01628 525818, lanforddesigns@gmail.com. On A4094, 2m SW of A40, between Bourne End & Wooburn. From Wooburn Church, direction Maidenhead, Grange Drive is on L before r'about. From Bourne End, L at 2 mini-r'abouts, then 1st R. **Visits by arrangement Feb to Sept. Combined adm £6, chd free. Light refreshments. Evening visits welcome in early summer.**

MAGNOLIA HOUSE
Elaine & Alan Ford.

THE SHADES
Pauline & Maurice Kirkpatrick.

Two diverse gardens in a private tree lined drive which formed the entrance to a country house now demolished. Magnolia House is a ½ acre garden with many mature trees incl magnificent copper beech and magnolia reaching the rooftop, a small cactus bed, fernery, stream leading to pond and greenhouses with small aviary. Front garden has natural pond. The Shades drive is approached through mature trees and beds of herbaceous plants and 60 various roses. A natural well is surrounded by shrubs and acers. The garden was developed in 2010 to incl a natural stone lawn terrace and changes made to the existing flower beds. A green slate water feature with alpine plants completes the garden. Child friendly. Partial wheelchair access.

21 HALL BARN

Windsor End, Beaconsfield, HP9 2SG. Mrs Farncombe, jenefer@farncombe01.demon.co.uk. ½m S of Beaconsfield. Lodge gate 300yds S of St Mary & All Saints' Church in Old Town centre. Please do not use SatNav. **Visits by arrangement Feb to Dec. Home-made teas & tours for groups, but individual visitors welcome. Adm £4.50, chd free.**

Historical landscaped garden laid out between 1680-1730 for the poet Edmund Waller and his descendants. Features 300 yr old cloud formation yew hedges, formal lake and vistas ending with classical buildings and statues. Wooded walks around the grove offer respite from the heat on sunny days. One of the original NGS garden openings of 1927. Chiltern Shakespeare Company open-air performances of Richard III in the garden 13-23 June. Information provided. Gravel paths, but certain areas can be accessed by car for those with limited mobility.

The National Garden Scheme is Marie Curie's largest single funder

GROUP OPENING

22 HIGHER DENHAM GARDENS

Higher Denham, UB9 5EA. 6m E of Beaconsfield. Turn off A412, approx ½m N of junction with A40 into Old Rectory Lane. After 1m enter Higher Denham straight ahead. Tickets for all gardens available at the community hall, 70yds into the village. **Sun 20 May (2-5). Combined adm £5, chd free. Home-made teas in the community hall.** Donation to Higher Denham Community CIO.

NEW **25 LOWER ROAD**
Mr & Mrs Malham.

30 LOWER ROAD
Mr & Mrs Mike Macgowan.

5 SIDE ROAD
Jane Blythe.

WIND IN THE WILLOWS
Ron James. (See separate entry)

Four gardens will open in 2018, incl one new, in the delightful chalk stream Misbourne Valley. Wind in the Willows has over 350 shrubs and trees, informal woodland and wild gardens incl riverside and bog plantings and a collection of 80 hostas and 12 striped roses in 3 acres. 'Really different' and 'stunning' are typical visitor comments. The garden at 5 Side Road is medium sized with lawns, borders and shrubs, and many features which children will love incl a competition to find hidden miniature characters! The new garden 25 Lower Road, where the front garden has been completely redesigned with raised beds, richly filled with plants and shrubs to create a vibrant instant garden, reminiscent of the way it is done in some TV programmes. 30 Lower Road is a well-stocked garden with charm and character, many new features since they last opened. In May the owner of Wind in the Willows will lead optional guided tours of the garden starting at 2pm and 4pm. Tours last approx 1 hour. Partial wheelchair access to some gardens.

23 HILLESDEN HOUSE

Church End, Hillesden, MK18 4DB. Mr & Mrs R M Faccenda, 01296 730451, suef@faccenda.co.uk. 3m S of Buckingham through Gawcott. Next to church in Hillesden. **Sun 17 June (2-5). Adm £5, chd free. Home-made teas. Visits also by arrangement June to Aug for groups of 20+.**

By superb church Cathedral in the Fields. Carp lakes, fountains and waterfalls with mature trees. Rose, alpine and herbaceous borders with 80 acres of deer park. Wild flower areas and extensive lakes developed by the owner. Lovely walks and plenty of wildlife. Also a woodland area and vegetable garden with raised beds. An orchard was created 3 yrs ago. Vines were planted this year. No wheelchair access to lakes.

24 HILLS HOUSE

Village Road, Denham Village, UB9 5BH. Mr & Mrs B Savory, 01895 833290, reminlondon@hotmail.com. Turn off M40 J1A towards London. Turn L at T-lights, stay in middle lane, turn L at r'about & stay in RH lane. Follow sign Village Only & follow road ¼ m. Turn L over bridge, next to St Mary's Church. **Sun 22 Apr (2-5). Adm £4, chd free. Cream teas. Visits also by arrangement in Apr.**

A C16, 3 acre garden, in Denham Village with an impressive collection of majestic specimen trees, walled garden and designated shrub borders. A large rose garden and perennial border frame a sunken buxus parterre, and annual display of baskets that flow to an orchard on long gravel paths. Walk through serene areas and woodland plantings, with a spring display of bulbs underneath mature trees. No wheelchair access to sunken parterre area. Gravel paths.

25 HOMELANDS

Springs Lane, Ellesborough, Aylesbury, HP17 0XD. Jean & Tony Young, 01296 622306, young.ellesborough@gmail.com. 6m SE of Aylesbury. On the B4010 between Wendover & Princes Risborough. Springs Lane is between village hall at Butlers Cross & the church. Narrow lane with an uneven surface. **Visits by arrangement May to Aug. Adm £4, chd free. Light refreshments.**

Secluded ¾ acre garden on difficult chalk, adjoining open countryside. Designed to be enjoyed from many seating positions. Progress from semi-formal to wild flower meadow and wildlife pond. Deep borders with all season interest, and gravel beds with exotic late summer and autumn planting.

26 NEW IVER ENVIRONMENTAL CENTRE

Slough Road, Iver, SL0 0EB. Ruth Shelton. Between Slough & Uxbridge. At Black Horse r'about take Slough Rd (A4007) to Uxbridge. **Sun 15 Apr, Tue 24 July, Fri 24 Aug (10-4). Adm £4, chd free. Home-made teas.**

The gardens at Iver Environment Centre are a hidden gem. A visual treat awaits you at every turn as you explore our 4½ acre site. Our winding pathways lead you through woodland, allotments, an orchard and a sensory garden. Embark on your own secret garden adventure past ponds, through willow tunnels and into our rainforest polytunnel. You can even try navigating your way through our hedge maze. If that's not for you then why not enjoy the view on our raised decking where tea is served.

27 KINGSBRIDGE

Steeple Claydon, MK18 2EJ. Mr & Mrs T Aldous, 01296 730224. 3m S of Buckingham. Halfway between Padbury & Steeple Claydon. Xrds with sign to Kingsbridge Only. **Visits by arrangement Apr to Aug for groups of 10+. Home-made teas.**

Stunning and exceptional 6 acre garden imaginatively created over last 26 yrs. Main lawn is enclosed by softly, curving, colour themed herbaceous borders, and many roses and shrubs interestingly planted with cleverly created landscaping features. Clipped topiary yews, pleached hornbeams lead out to the ha-ha and countryside beyond. A natural stream with bog plants, nesting kingfishers, meanders serenely through woodland gardens, with many walks. A garden to visit again and again.

GROUP OPENING

28 LONG CRENDON GARDENS

Long Crendon, HP18 9AN. Long Crendon village is situated on the B4011 Thame-Bicester road, 2m N of Thame. Maps showing the location of the gardens will be available at each garden & at Church House in the High St. **Sun 22 Apr, Sun 10 June (2-6). Combined adm £5, chd free. Home-made teas at Church House, High St.** Donation to Riding for the Disabled Shabbington Group.

BAKER'S CLOSE
Mr & Mrs Peter Vaines.
Open on Sun 22 Apr

BARRY'S CLOSE
Mr & Mrs Richard Salmon.
Open on Sun 22 Apr

NEW **13 BICESTER ROAD**
Rhona Hallaway & Paul Smith.
Open on Sun 10 June

48 CHILTON ROAD
Mr & Mrs M Charnock.
Open on Sun 10 June

COP CLOSE
Sandra & Tony Phipkin.
Open on Sun 10 June

25 ELM TREES
Carol & Mike Price.
Open on Sun 10 June

MANOR HOUSE
Mr & Mrs West.
Open on Sun 22 Apr

TOMPSONS FARM
Mr & Mrs T Moynihan.
Open on Sun 22 Apr

Four gardens open on Sun 22 Apr. Bakers Close, partly walled with terraced lawns, rockery, shrubs and wild area. A spring planting of 1000's of daffodils, narcissi and tulips. Barrys Close has a collection of spring flowering trees forming a backdrop to borders, pools and a water garden. The Manor House, a large garden with views towards the Chilterns, two ornamental lakes and a large variety of spring bulbs and shrubs. Along the High St, Tompsons Farm, a large woodland garden with mature trees and shrubs sweeping down to a lake. On Sun 10 June a different four gardens will open; two cottage style gardens, 25 Elm Trees with a terrace and small orchard area, wildlife pond, rockery and deep borders, also 48 Chilton Road, a garden with perennial borders and summerhouse. Cop Close a 1½ acre garden with vegetables, cutting garden and borders. New for this year, 13 Bicester Road, a secluded cottage garden designed to suit a busy lifestyle; colourful mixed borders surround a paved entertaining area with ornamental pond. No dogs please. Partial wheelchair access to some gardens.

♿ 🐕 ✿ ☕

29 LOOSLEY DENE

Lower Road, Loosley Row, Princes Risborough, HP27 0PE. Tim & Sarah Halliday, sarah@shgd.co.uk. 7m W of High Wycombe, 2m E of Princes Risborough off the A4010. From Princes Risborough, take L onto Woodway to Lacey Green. Up the hill after 1m take R fork into Lower Rd. After ⅓m turn R at small Xrds down into Loosley Hill, car parking in field on R (signed). **Sun 3 June (1-5). Adm £4, chd free. Home-made teas. Visits also by arrangement in July for groups of 10-20 during weekdays.**

Within 4½ acres, set into hillside, the garden has panoramic views of the Chiltern landscape. Well established trees and shrubs with yr-round interest has been redesigned in the last 6 yrs maintaining some original features dating to C19. Yorkstone terrace retained by Cotswold stone walls overlook lawns, steps and paths lead to small parterre, mixed borders with lavenders and roses. Chickens, ducks, pigs and Gruffalo!

✿ ☕

30 LORDS WOOD

Frieth Road, Marlow Common, SL7 2QS. Mr & Mrs Messum. 1½m NW Marlow. From Marlow turn off the A4155 at Platts Garage into Oxford Rd, towards Frieth for 1½m. Garden is 100yds past the Marlow Common turn, on the L, opp Valley View Stables. **Fri 15 June (11-4). Adm £4.50, chd free. Home-made teas.**

Lords Wood was built for the artist Mary Sargent Florence in 1899 and has been the Messum's family home since 1974. Lords Wood's artistic connections continue to this day. The 5 acre garden surrounding the house (not open) contains sculpture and water features, extensive mature borders in varying styles, vegetable, flower and herb gardens, large water gardens and rockery. There is an orchard with beehives, woodland walks and two wildflower meadows with fantastic views over the Chilterns. Partial wheelchair access; gravel paths and steep slopes.

♿ ☕

11 The Paddocks

31 LOWTHORPE HOUSE

Crowbrook Road, Askett, Princes Risborough, HP27 9LS. Margaret & John Higgins. 100 metre down Crowbrook Rd (north end) on LH-side. **Sun 1 July (2-5). Combined adm with The White House, Askett £4, chd free. Home-made teas.**

The narrow hornbeam-lined drive, opens out to reveal a sunny, secluded ⅔ acre garden, tucked away in the conservation area of Askett. Emphasis is on flowers in deep herbaceous borders; soft fruit cage, tree area, fern garden and grasses. Some interesting trees and conifers. Wheelchair access to all areas; gravel drive leads to a level garden with grass.

32 THE MANOR HOUSE

(Off Perry Lane), Bledlow, Nr Princes Risborough, HP27 9PB. The Lord Carrington. 9m NW of High Wycombe, 3m SW of Princes Risborough. ½m off B4009 in middle of Bledlow village. SatNav directions HP27 9PA. **Sun 20 May (2-5). Adm £5, chd free. Light refreshments.**

Paved garden, parterres, shrub borders, old roses and walled kitchen garden. Water garden with paths, bridges and walkways fed by 14 chalk springs, plus 2 acres of landscaped planting. Sculpture garden. Partial wheelchair access as there is stepped access or sloped grass to enter the gardens.

33 MOAT FARM

Water Lane, Ford, Aylesbury, HP17 8XD. Mr & Mrs P Bergqvist, 01296 748560, patricia@quintadelarosa.com. Turn up Water Lane by Dinton Hermit in the middle of Ford village, after approx 200yds, turn L over cattle grid between beech hedges into Moat Farm. **Visits by arrangement Apr to Sept for groups of 8+.**

A country garden with herbaceous borders, roses, hostas, trees and water. A moat that flows through the garden and a blind moat through the arboretum. Small walled garden and some vegetables.

34 ◆ NETHER WINCHENDON HOUSE

Nether Winchendon, Thame, Aylesbury, HP18 0DY. Mr Robert Spencer Bernard, 01844 290101, Contactus@netherwinchendonhouse.com, www.netherwinchendonhouse.com. 6m SW of Aylesbury, 6m from Thame. Approx 4m from Thame on A418, turn 1st L to Cuddington, turn L at Xrds, downhill turn R & R again to parking by house. **For NGS: Sun 6 May, Sun 27 May, Sun 26 Aug (2-5.30). Adm £4, chd free. Cream teas at the church (2.30-5).** For other opening times and information, please phone, email or visit garden website.

Nether Winchendon House has fine and rare trees, set in a stunning landscape surrounded by parkland, with 7 acres of lawned grounds running down to the River Thame. A Founder NGS Member (1927). Enchanting and romantic Mediaeval and Tudor House. Picturesque small village. Interesting Church. One of the most romantic of the historic houses of England and Grade I listed. Unfenced riverbank.

35 NORTH DOWN

Dodds Lane, Chalfont St Giles, HP8 4EL. Merida Saunders, 01494 872928. 4m SE of Amersham, 4m NE of Beaconsfield. Opp the green in centre of village, at Costa turn into UpCorner onto Silver Hill. At top of hill fork R into Dodds Lane. North Down is 7th on L. **Visits by arrangement May to Aug for groups of 2-40. Adm £4, chd free. Light refreshments.**

A passion for gardening is evident in this plantswomans lovely ¾ acre garden which has evolved over the yrs with scenic effect in mind. Colourful and interesting throughout the yr. Large grassed areas with island beds of mixed perennials, shrubs and some unusual plants. Variety of rhododendrons, azaleas, acers and clematis. Displays of sempervivum, alpines, grasses and ferns. Small patio and water feature, greenhouse and an Italianate front patio to owner's design.

36 NEW OLD PARK BARN

Dag Lane, Stoke Goldington, Newport Pagnell, MK16 8NY. Emily & James Chua. 4m N of Newport Pagnell on B526. Park on High St. A short walk up Dag Lane. Limited disabled parking near garden via Orchard Way. **Sun 17 June (2-5.30). Adm £4, chd free. Home-made teas.**

We made a garden from a rough field of just under 3 acres, 20 yrs ago. Near the house a series of terraces, cut into the sloping site, create the formal garden with long and cross vistas, lawns and deep borders. The aim is to provide interest throughout the yr with naturalistic planting and views borrowed from the surrounding countryside. Beyond is a wildlife pond, meadow and woodland garden. Partial wheelchair access.

37 ORCHARD HOUSE

Tower Road, Coleshill, Amersham, HP7 0LB. Mr & Mrs Douglas Livesey. From Amersham Old Town take the A355 to Beaconsfield. Appox ¾m along this road at top of hill, take the 1st R into Tower Rd. Parking in cricket club grounds. **Sun 22 Apr (2-5). Adm £5, chd free. Home-made teas in the barn.**

The 5 acre garden incl several wooded areas with eco bug hotels for wildlife. Two ponds with wild flower planting, large avenues of silver birches, a bog garden with board walk, and a wild flower meadow and orchard. There is a cut flower and vegetable garden with a dramatic collection of spring bulbs set amongst an acer glade. Meanwhile a collection of specimen trees compliment the native trees. Rear garden lawn slopes down.

38 OVERSTROUD COTTAGE

The Dell, Frith Hill, Gt Missenden, HP16 9QE. Mr & Mrs Jonathan Brooke, 01494 862701, susanmbrooke@outlook.com. ½m E Gt Missenden. Turn E off A413 at Gt Missenden onto B485 Frith Hill to Chesham Rd. White Gothic cottage set back in lay-by 100yds uphill on L. Parking on R at church. **Sun 1, Sun 22 Apr, Sun 13 May, Sun 10 June (2-5). Adm £3.50, chd free. Cream teas at parish church. Visits also by arrangement Apr to June for groups of 15-30. Home-made teas.**

Artistic chalk garden on two levels. Collection of C17/C18 plants incl auriculars, hellebores, bulbs, pulmonarias, peonies, geraniums, herbs and succulents. Many antique, species and rambling roses. Potager and lily pond. Cottage was once C17 fever house for Missenden Abbey. Features incl a garden studio with painting exhibition (share of flower painting proceeds to NGS).

39 11 THE PADDOCKS

Wendover, HP22 6HE. Mr & Mrs E Rye, 01296 623870, pam.rye@talktalk.net. 5m from Aylesbury on A413. From Aylesbury turn L at mini-r'about onto Wharf Rd. From Gt Missenden turn L at the Clock Tower, then R at mini-r'about onto Wharf Rd. **Sat 23, Sun 24 June, Sat 7, Sun 8 July (2-5). Adm £2.50, chd free. Visits also by arrangement June to Aug for groups of 30 max.** Donation to Bonnie People in South Africa.

Small peaceful garden with mixed borders of colourful herbaceous perennials, a special show of David Austin roses and a large variety of spectacular named Blackmore and Langdon delphiniums. A tremendous variety of colour in a small area. The White Garden with a peaceful arbour, The Magic of Moonlight created for the BBC. Most of the garden can be viewed from the lawn.

40 PETERLEY CORNER COTTAGE

Perks Lane, Prestwood, Great Missenden, HP16 0JH. Dawn Philipps, 01494 862198, dawn.philipps@googlemail.com. Turn into Perks Lane from Wycombe Rd (A4128), Peterley Corner Cottage is the 3rd house on the L. **Visits by arrangement May to Aug for groups of 10+. Adm £4.50, chd free. Light refreshments.**

A 3 acre mature garden, incl an acre of wild flowers and indigenous trees. Surrounded by tall hedges and a wood, the garden has evolved over the last 30 yrs. There are many specimen trees and mature roses incl a Paul's Himalaya Musk and a Kiftsgate. A large herbaceous border runs alongside the formal lawns with other borders like heathers and shrubs. The most recent addition is a potager.

41 RED KITES

46 Haw Lane, Bledlow Ridge, HP14 4JJ. Mag & Les Terry, 01494 481474, les.terry@lineone.net. 4m S of Princes Risborough. Off A4010 halfway between Princes Risborough & West Wycombe. At Hearing Dogs sign in Saunderton turn into Haw Lane, then ¾m on L up the hill. **Tue 15 May, Tue 17 July (2-5). Adm £4, chd free. Home-made teas. Visits also by arrangement May to Sept for groups of 15+.**

This much admired 1½ acre Chiltern hillside garden is planted for yr-round interest and is lovingly maintained with mixed and herbaceous borders, wild flower orchard, established pond, vegetable garden, managed woodland area and a lovely hidden garden. Many climbers used throughout the garden which changes significantly through the seasons. Sit and enjoy the superb views from the top terrace.

42 RIVENDELL

13 The Leys, Amersham, HP6 5NP. Janice & Mike Cross. Off A416. Take A416 N towards Chesham. The Leys is on L ½m after Boot & Slipper Pub. Park at Beacon School, 100yds N. **Sun 15 Apr (2-5). Adm £3.50, chd free. Home-made teas.**

S-facing garden comprising a series of different areas, incl a woodland area, gravel area with grasses and pond, fruit and vegetable garden, bug hotels, herbaceous beds containing a wide variety of shrubs, bulbs and perennials, all surrounding a circular lawn with a rose and clematis arbour.

43 ◆ STOKE POGES MEMORIAL GARDENS

Church Lane, Stoke Poges, Slough, SL2 4NZ. South Bucks District Council, 01753 523744, memorial.gardens@southbucks.gov.uk, www.southbucks.gov.uk/stokepogesmemorialgardens. 1m N of Slough, 4m S of Gerrards Cross. Follow signs to Stoke Poges & from there to the Memorial Gardens. Car park opp main entrance, disabled visitor parking in the gardens. Weekend disabled access through churchyard. **For NGS: Sun 13 May (1.30-4.30). Adm £4.50, chd free. Home-made teas.** For other opening times and information, please phone, email or visit garden website.

Unique 20 acre Grade I registered garden constructed 1934-9. Rock and water gardens, sunken colonnade, rose garden, 500 individual gated gardens. Spring garden with bulbs, wisteria and rhododendrons. Guided tours every half hour. Guide dogs only.

Your visit has already helped 600 more people gain access to a Parkinson's nurse

The Manor House

44 TURN END

Townside, Haddenham, Aylesbury, HP17 8BG. Peter & Maragret Aldington, 07591 018601, turnendtrustevents@gmail.com, www.turnend.org.uk. 3m NE of Thame, 5m SW of Aylesbury. Turn off A418 to Haddenham. Turn at Rising Sun to Townside. Please park at a distance with consideration for neighbours. **Mon 7 May (2-5.30). Adm £4.50, chd free. Home-made teas.**

Intriguing series of garden rooms each with a different planting style enveloping architect's own post-war 2* listed house (not open). Dry garden, small woodland, formal box garden, sunken gardens, mixed borders around curving lawn, framed by ancient walls and mature trees. Bulbs, irises, wisteria, roses, ferns and climbers. Courtyards with pools, pergolas, secluded seating, Victorian Coach House. Open studios with displays and demonstrations by creative artists. Steps, narrow archways, stone and gravel pathways.

45 TYTHROP PARK

Kingsey, HP17 8LT. Nick & Chrissie Wheeler. 2m E of Thame, 4m NW of Princes Risborough. Via A4129, at T-junction in Kingsey turn towards Haddenham, take L turn on bend. Parking in field on L. **Sun 24 June (2-5.30). Adm £6, chd free. Home-made teas.** Donation to St Nicholas Church, Kingsey.

10 acres of garden surrounds a C17 Grade I listed manor house (not open). This large and varied garden blends traditional and contemporary styles; a pool border rich with grasses and a green and white theme, walled kitchen/cutting garden with large greenhouse, and at its heart a box parterre. Deep mixed borders, water feature, rose garden, wild flower meadow, many old trees and shrubs.

46 WESTEND HOUSE

Cheddington, Leighton Buzzard, LU7 0RP. His Honour Judge & Mrs Richard Foster, 01296 661332, westend.house@hotmail.com, www.westendhousecheddington.co.uk. 5m N of Tring. From double mini-r'about in Cheddington take turn to Long Marston. Take 1st L & Westend House is on your R. **Mon 2 Apr (1.30-4.30). Adm £4, chd free. Home-made teas. Opening with Cheddington Gardens on Sun 17 June.**

A country garden of 2 acres restored and developed in recent yrs featuring herbaceous and shrub borders, a formal rose garden with swags, wild flower areas adjacent to the pond and in the orchard, a natural wildlife pond and stream with recently extended planting, potager with vegetables and picking flowers. Wood and metal sculptures. Rare breed hens, sheep and pigs in field next to garden. All cakes are home-made and tea is served in bone china with waitress service. Some bespoke sculptures and seasonal vegetables for sale. Wheelchair access to far side of pond restricted.

47 THE WHITE HOUSE

Village Road, Denham Village, UB9 5BE. Mr & Mrs P G Courtenay-Luck. 3m NW of Uxbridge, 7m E of Beaconsfield. Signed from A40 or A412. Parking in village road. The White House is in centre of village. **Sun 3 June (2-5). Adm £5, chd free. Home-made teas.**

Well established 6 acre formal garden in picturesque setting. Mature trees and hedges with River Misbourne meandering through lawns. Shrubberies, flower beds, rockery, rose garden and orchard. Large walled garden. Herb garden, vegetable plot and Victorian greenhouses. Gravel entrance and path to gardens.

48 NEW THE WHITE HOUSE, ASKETT

Askett, Princes Risborough, HP27 9LT. Terri Boyce. On the main road through Askett, at the junction of Letter Box Lane. Please park at Lowthorpe House, Crowbrook Rd & walk to White House (5 mins) **Sun 1 July (2-5.30). Combined adm with Lowthorpe House £4, chd free. Home-made teas at Lowthorpe House.**

A cottage garden surrounding a C17 thatched cottage (not open), with many flower borders, an ancient well in the small front garden, a secret garden, an evergreen border, pond, box edged herbaceous border and several peaceful seating areas.

49 NEW 20 WHITEPIT LANE

Flackwell Heath, High Wycombe, HP10 9HS. Trevor Jones, 01628 524876, trevorol4969@gmail.com. ¾ m E Flackwell Heath, 4m High Wycombe. From M40 J3 (west bound exit only) take 1st L, 300yds T-junction turn R, 300yds turn L uphill to centre of Flackwell Heath, turn L ¾ m, garden 75yds on R past mini-r'about. **Visits by arrangement May to Sept for groups up to 12 max. Adm incl refreshments. Adm £7, chd free.**

The front garden has a seaside type landscape with timber groynes and a rock pool. The rear garden is long and thin with colour from Apr to Oct, containing many unusual plants, with steps and bridges over two ponds. Amongst the plants are a large Banana, an Albizia, Grevillea, Callistemon Abutilon, Salvias and several Alstroemeria's. The beds are filled with mixed shrubs and herbaceous plants.

50 WHITEWALLS

Quarry Wood Road, Marlow, SL7 1RE. Mr W H Williams, 01628 482573. ½ m S Marlow. From Marlow crossover bridge. 1st L, 3rd house on L with white garden wall. **Visits by arrangement Mar to Oct. Adm £2.50, chd free.**

Thames side garden, approx ½ acre, with spectacular views of the weir. Large water lily pond, interesting planting of trees, shrubs, herbaceous perennials and bedding, and a large conservatory. Many chairs to sit by the river and view the weir.

51 WIND IN THE WILLOWS

Moorhouse Farm Lane, Off Lower Road, Higher Denham, UB9 5EN. Ron James, 07740 177038, r.james@company-doc.co.uk. Moorhouse Farm Lane, off Lower Rd, Higher Denham. Take lane next to the community centre & Wind in the Willows is the 1st house on L. **Sun 18 Mar (2-5). Adm £5, chd free. Home-made teas in the community hall. Opening with Higher Denham Gardens on Sun 20 May. Visits also by arrangement Mar to Aug for groups of 10+. Adm incl tea, coffee & biscuits.**

3 acre wildlife friendly, yr-round garden, comprising informal, woodland and wild gardens, separated by streams lined by iris and primulas. Over 350 shrubs and trees, many variegated or uncommon, marginal and bog plantings incl a collection of 80 hostas. 'Stunning' was the word most often used by visitors last year. 'Best private garden I have visited in 20 yrs of NGS visits' said another. Although unlikely to be seen on busy open days, 65 species of bird and 13 species of butterfly have been seen in and over the garden, which is also home to the now endangered water vole (Water Rat in the book Wind in the Willows), frogs and toads. Gravel paths and spongy lawns.

52 NEW WOODSIDE

23 Willow Lane, Amersham, HP7 9DW. Elin & Graham Stone, 01494 261236, glawderstone@hotmail.com. On A413, 1m SE from Old Amersham, between Barley Lane & Finch Lane. The garden is the last but one, on the RH-side. **Visits by arrangement on Fri 15, Sat 16 & Sun 17 June and Fri 10, Sat 11 & Sun 12 Aug (2-5). Adm £3, chd free. Home-made teas.**

A small cottage garden, recently created, on s-facing slope, cleverly integrating circular lawn, pond, gravel paths and steps to a curved rose pergola, colour-based rose beds and abundant humped borders. In contrast, a secret woodland path winds past a stumpery, a shade area and wildlife hedging leading to a kitchen garden. Patios and hidden seating areas abound. Artist's Studio.

Donations from the National Garden Scheme enable Perennial to care for horticulturalists

CAMBRIDGESHIRE

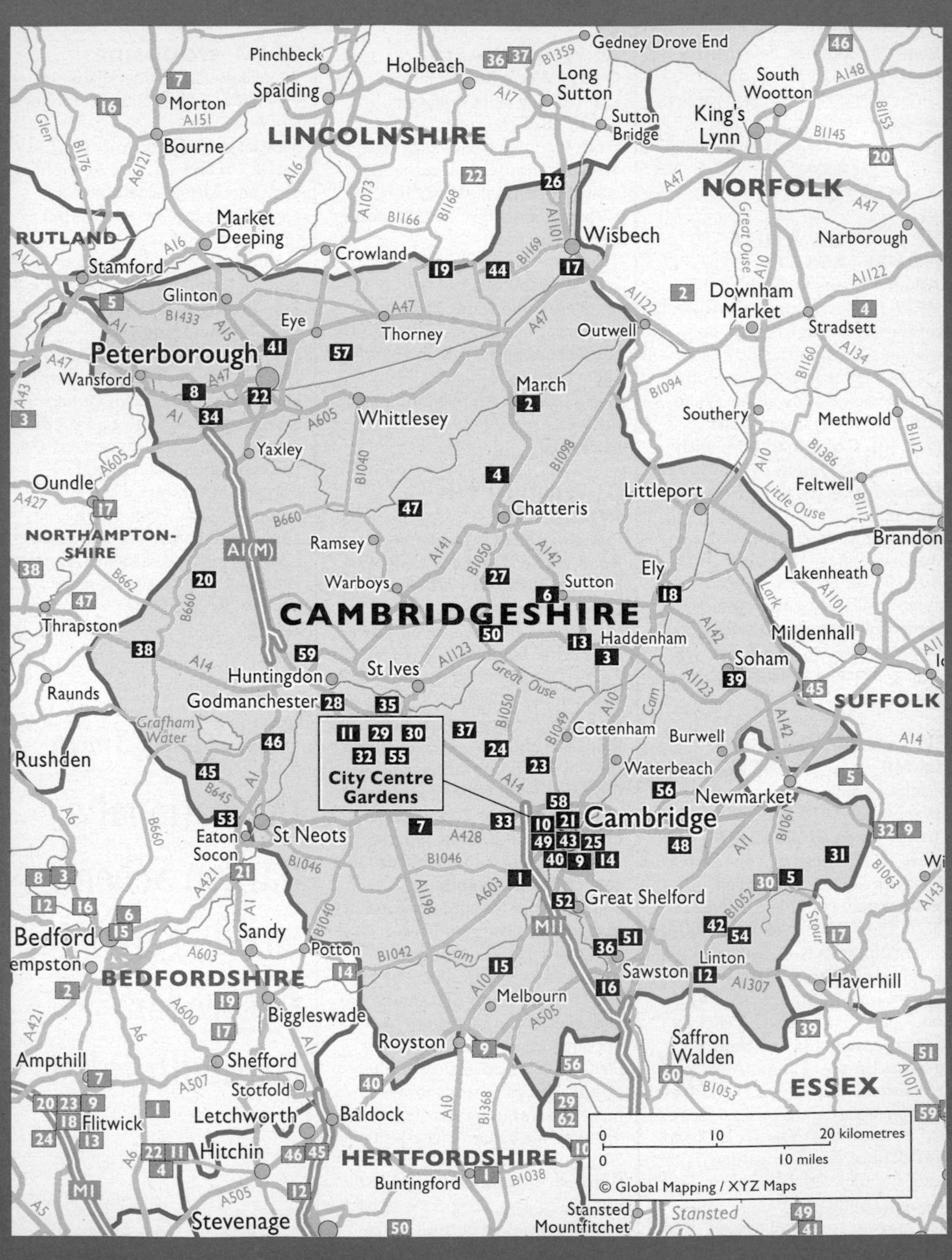

The low-lying flat lands of Cambridgeshire offer many diverse and interesting gardens.

The Cambridge University gardens are well worth a visit, and people interested in urban gardens can find plenty in the city of Cambridge - these smaller gardens are ideal for giving inspiration for back garden planting and design.

Peterborough has gardens showing an innovative approach to designing for smaller spaces. Ely has a delightful group of varied gardens in this historic Cathedral City.

The whole county embraces many delightful gardens, from former rectory gardens to very small urban gardens. There are many surprises waiting to be discovered in Cambridgeshire, and our generous garden owners invite you to come and take a closer look.

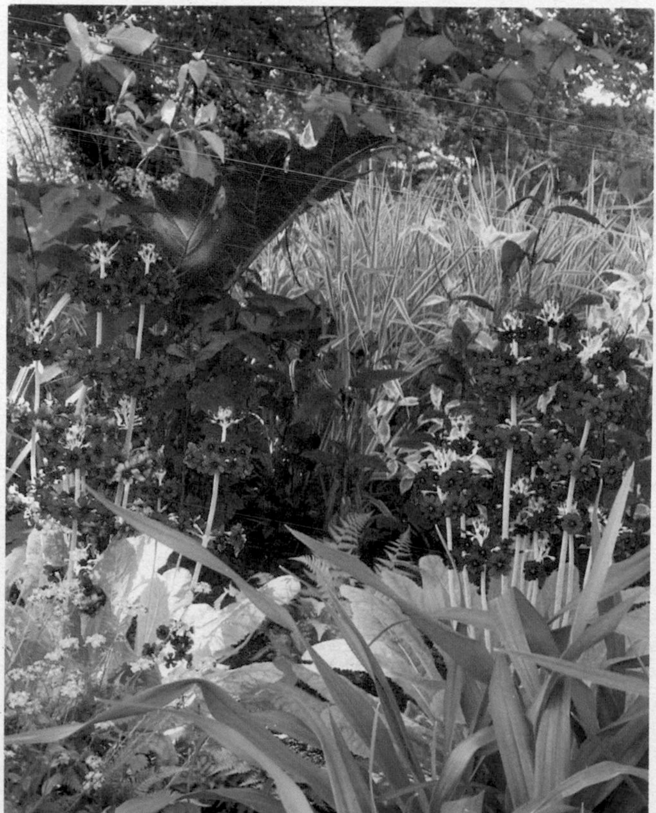

Volunteers

County Organiser
George Stevenson
01733 262698
chrisgeorge1a@aol.com

County Treasurer
Nicholas Kyberd
01954 200568
n.kyberd@ntlworld.com

Publicity
Amanda Wharrier
01223 882745
amanda.wharrier66@gmail.com

Booklet Coordinator
Robert Marshall
01733 555978
robfmarshall@btinternet.com

Assistant County Organisers
Pam Bullivant
01353 667355
pbu1@hotmail.co.uk

Patsy Glazebrook
01799 541180
glazebrc@doctors.org.uk

Angie Jones
01733 222367
janda.salix@gmail.com

Nicholas Kyberd
(as above)

Dulce Threlfall
01638 508470
dulce.quercus6065@btinternet.com

Annette White
01638 730876
annette323@btinternet.com

Left: The Windmill

OPENING DATES

All entries subject to change. For latest information check **www.ngs.org.uk**

Extended openings are shown at the beginning of the month.

Map locator numbers are shown to the right of each garden name.

January

Every Monday to Friday
Robinson College 49

Every Saturday and Sunday from Sunday 7th
Robinson College 49

February Snowdrop Festival

Every Sunday
Clover Cottage 12

Every Monday to Friday
Robinson College 49

Every Saturday and Sunday
Robinson College 49

March

Every Monday to Friday
Robinson College 49

Every Saturday and Sunday
Robinson College 49

Sunday 4th
Clover Cottage 12

Sunday 25th
Kirtling Tower 31
2a Nine Chimneys Lane 42

April

Every Monday to Friday to Friday 20th
Robinson College 49

Every Saturday and Sunday to Sunday 15th
Robinson College 49

Sunday 1st
Netherhall Manor 39

Sunday 8th
Barton Gardens 1
Trinity College, Fellows' Garden 55

Sunday 15th
Churchill College 10
Fitzwilliam College 21

Sunday 22nd
◆ Docwra's Manor 15

Sunday 29th
Lucy Cavendish College 32
NEW Newnham Croft Primary School 40

May

Sunday 6th
Chaucer Road Gardens 9
Netherhall Manor 39

Monday 7th
Chaucer Road Gardens 9

Saturday 12th
High Bank Cottage 26

Sunday 13th
◆ Ferrar House 20
High Bank Cottage 26

Saturday 19th
Bell Gables 3

Sunday 20th
Bell Gables 3
The Burystead, Sutton 6
NEW Foxelwood 23

Wednesday 23rd
Wild Rose Cottage 56

Saturday 26th
Staploe Gardens 53

Sunday 27th
The Burystead, Sutton 6
Cambourne Gardens 7
NEW Foxelwood 23
Island Hall 28
Staploe Gardens 53
Willow Holt 57

Monday 28th
Willow Holt 57

June

Every Monday to Friday from Monday 18th
Robinson College 49

Every Saturday and Sunday from Saturday 23rd
Robinson College 49

Festival Weekend

Sunday 3rd
Duxford Gardens 16
Streetly End & West Wickham Gardens 54

Saturday 9th
Sandpiper 50

Sunday 10th
Barton Gardens 1
NEW Benwick Road, Doddington 4
Ely Gardens 18
Madingley Hall 33
Mary Challis Garden 36
Molesworth & Brington Gardens 38
The Old Rectory 44
Ramsey Forty Foot 47
Sandpiper 50

Sunday 17th
Burrough Green Gardens 5
Manor House, Alwalton 34
Stapleford Gardens 52

Saturday 23rd
45 Beaver Lodge 2

Sunday 24th
45 Beaver Lodge 2
NEW Green End Farm 24
Kirtling Tower 31

Saturday 30th
NEW Cottage Garden 14

July

Every Monday to Friday
Robinson College 49

Every Saturday and Sunday
Robinson College 49

Sunday 1st
Clare College Fellows' Garden 11
NEW Cottage Garden 14
Fenleigh 19
Sawston Gardens 51
Wytchwood 59

Saturday 7th
10 Gwydir Street 25
Norfolk Terrace Garden 43

Sunday 8th
NEW Green End Farm 24
10 Gwydir Street 25
King's College Fellows' Garden and Provost's Garden 30
Norfolk Terrace Garden 43

Sunday 15th
Jesus College 29

August

Every Monday to Friday to Friday 10th
Robinson College 49

Every Saturday and Sunday to Sunday 5th
Robinson College 49

Every Monday to Friday from Monday 27th
Robinson College 49

Sunday 5th
◆ Elgood's Brewery Gardens 17
Netherhall Manor 39

Sunday 12th
Netherhall Manor 39

Saturday 18th
45 Beaver Lodge 2

Sunday 19th
45 Beaver Lodge 2
Castor House 8

September

Every Monday to Friday
Robinson College 49

Every Saturday and Sunday
Robinson College 49

Sunday 16th
◆ Ferrar House 20

October

Every Monday to Friday
Robinson College 49

Every Saturday and Sunday
Robinson College 49

November

Every Monday to Friday
Robinson College 49

Every Saturday and Sunday
Robinson College 49

December

Every Monday to Friday to Friday 28th
Robinson College 49

Every Saturday and Sunday
Robinson College 49

Friday 7th
Sandpiper 50

Saturday 8th
Sandpiper 50

Sunday 9th
Sandpiper 50

By Arrangement

45 Beaver Lodge 2
Clover Cottage 12
College Farm 13
NEW Cottage Garden 14
39 Foster Road 22
Horseshoe Farm 27
5 Moat Way 37
Netherhall Manor 39
NEW The Night Garden 41
2a Nine Chimneys Lane 42
The Old Rectory 44
The Old Vicarage 45
23a Perry Road 46
Quercus, Burrough Green Gardens 5
Reed Cottage 48
Wild Rose Cottage 56
The Windmill 58

THE GARDENS

GROUP OPENING

1 BARTON GARDENS

High Street, Barton, Cambridge, CB23 7BG. *3½m SW of Cambridge. Barton is on A603 Cambridge to Sandy Rd, ½m for J12 M11.* **Sun 8 Apr, Sun 10 June (2-5). Combined adm £5, chd free. Home-made teas in Barton Church (April) Village Hall (June). The White Horse Inn (118 High St) serves meals.**

BRYGHT BARN, 48 HIGH STREET
Jenny Robson Platt.
Open on Sun 10 June

FARM COTTAGE
Dr R M Belbin.
Open on all dates

GLEBE HOUSE
David & Sue Rapley.
Open on Sun 10 June

114 HIGH STREET
Meta & Hugh Greenfield.
Open on all dates

NEW **11 KINGS GROVE**
Mrs Judith Bowen.
Open on all dates

31 NEW ROAD
Drs D & M Macdonald.
Open on Sun 10 June

THE SIX HOUSES
Perennial.
Open on all dates

Varied group of large and small gardens reflecting different approaches to gardening. Farm Cottage: large landscaped cottage garden with herbaceous beds and themed woodland walk. Glebe House is a 1 acre mature, partly wooded and walled garden with large (unfenced) duck pond. Italiante style courtyard garden. Landscaped secret garden with gazebo. 114 High Street: small cottage garden with an unusual layout comprising several areas incl vegetables, fruit and a secret garden. 31 New Road: large, wildlife friendly cottage garden with a good show of spring flowers, mature shrubs, trees and a kitchen garden. The Six Houses: recently renovated gardens, incl winter and dry gardens, lovely spring bulbs and a small wood. Bryght Barn: a charming small garden being developed by new owner. 11 Kings Grove: a garden developed from a wilderness since 1992 with a lawn,flowers and shrub area and a fruit area. The White Horse Inn (118 High Street) serves meals. Some gardens have gravel paths.

2 45 BEAVER LODGE

Henson Road, March, PE15 8BA. Mr & Mrs Maria & Paul Nielsen Bom, 01354 656185, beaverbom@gmail.com. *A141 to Wisbech rd into March, turn L into Westwood Ave, follow rd leading to Henson Rd, turn R. Property opp school playground.* **Sat 23, Sun 24 June, Sat 18, Sun 19 Aug (10.30-4). Adm £3, chd free. Home-made teas. Visits also by arrangement June to Sept small groups welcome.**

An unusual town garden divided into different rooms in the oriental style with a large number of bonsai both large and small. In a different area surrounding a pond with koi carp, unusual trees , bonsai gardens and plants can be found. The overall effect is that of a peaceful and relaxing atmosphere with the sound of running water, with oriental statues, dragons and pagoda.

3 BELL GABLES

Church Lane, Wilburton, Ely, CB6 3RQ. Shona Mckay & William Bertram. *Church Lane is off A1123 between Stretham & Haddenham behind the parish church in Wilburton.* **Sat 19 May (11-5). Sun 20 May (11-5), also open The Burystead. Adm £3.50, chd free. Home-made teas in St Peter's Church, opp garden, coffee, tea with homemade cakes from 11- 5.**

Approx one acre of garden with a large natural pond with moorhens, grass snakes and other pond life, at its best in the spring. A small walled garden and formal fruit and flower parterre. Wheelchair access - level drive but with gravel finish. There is a concrete ramp down to the lawn.

Springfield, Benwick Road, Doddington

GROUP OPENING

4 NEW BENWICK ROAD, DODDINGTON

March, PE15 0TU. Jill Vaughan. *1m W of Doddington on Benwick Road (B1093). Use entrance for Delfland Nurseries and park in shop car park (limited parking at other three gardens - approx. 500m walk).* **Sun 10 June (1-5). Combined adm £5, chd free. Home-made teas at Fields End and Springfield.**

ALDERLEY
Jill Vaughan & John Overvoorde.

NEW **1 FIELDS END BUNGALOWS**
Mr Mark Latchford.

NEW **FIELDS END HOUSE**
Mr & Mrs Duncan & Viccy Boughton.

NEW **SPRINGFIELD**
Janice & Jonathan Holdich.

Four lovely rural gardens. Alderley, with professionally designed areas, interesting plants and a well-stocked kitchen garden. 1 Fields End Bungalows, a new renovation project in the hands of a landscape gardener. Fields End House, an established garden with sunken lawn, wild flower meadow, rockery and a productive vegetable plot. Springfield, 2½ acre informal garden with a large natural pond, orchard, wild flowers, woodland paths and established trees.

GROUP OPENING

5 BURROUGH GREEN GARDENS

Burrough Green, Newmarket, CB8 9NH. *5m S of Newmarket. Take B1061 out of Newmarket, & Burrough Green is signed to L 1m after Dullingham.* **Sun 17 June (2-5). Combined adm £5, chd free. Home-made teas at Village Hall.**

NEW **HOME FARM COTTAGE**
Mrs Alison Wilson.

QUERCUS
Dulce Threlfall, 01638 508470, thedulcethrelfall@gmail.com.
Visits also by arrangement Apr to Sept for groups of 10+.

New this year Home Farm Cottage has a large and secluded cottage style back garden incorporating a serpentine lawn with trees, bordered by delightful mixed borders with plenty of roses and herbaceous plants. A partially sunken terraced area by the house has many colourful pots. A small bridged watercourse divides the garden from the paddock, greenhouse and a small vegetable/ cutting garden, accessed through a rose covered pergola. Quercus is a newly modernised, replanted, redesigned contemporary and evolving 1½ acre garden on clay with 'English' planting. It features espaliered plums, roses, bearded iris, tulips and a variety of screening shrubs in the front. To the rear a large rose garden leads to 2 large mirrored mixed borders. Also find an arboretum, orchard, soft fruit, vegetable and cutting gardens and a large greenhouse. The two boundaries are planted with woodland plants and spring bulbs.

6 THE BURYSTEAD, SUTTON

Bury Lane, Sutton, Ely, CB6 2BB. Sarah Cleverdon & Stephen Tebboth. *6m W of Ely. Drive through Sutton towards Earith. Turn R, signed 'Sutton Gault' & 'Anchor Inn', Bury Lane. Our house is 1st on L, approx 300 metres.* **Sun 20 May (11-5), also open Bell Gables. Sun 27 May (11-5). Adm £3.50, chd free.**

½ acre walled courtyard garden of formal design, set against a backdrop of a restored C16 thatched barn. Orchard and sculpture at front of house. Also a cottage garden and a new vegetable plot.

GROUP OPENING

7 CAMBOURNE GARDENS

Great Cambourne, CB23 6AH. *8m W of Cambridge on A428. From A428: take Cambourne junction into Great Cambourne. From B1198, enter village at Lower Cambourne & drive through to Great Cambourne.*

Follow NGS signs via either route to start at any garden. **Sun 27 May (11-7). Combined adm £5.50, chd free.**

14 GRANARY WAY
Mrs Jackie Hutchinson.

NEW **88 GREENHAZE LANE**
Mr & Mrs Darren and Irette Murray.

5 MAYFIELD WAY
Debbie & Mike Perry.

14 MILLER WAY
Geoff Warmington.

43 MONKFIELD LANE
Tony & Penny Miles.

A unique and inspiring modern group, all created from new build in just a few years. This selection of seven demonstrates how imagination and gardening skill can be combined in a short time to create great effects from unpromising and awkward beginnings. The grouping includes a foliage garden, and many other beautiful borders showing their owners' creativity and love of growing fine plants well. Cambourne is one of Cambridgeshire's newest communities, and this grouping showcases the happy, vibrant place it has become. No garden is more than 17 years old, and most are much younger. New for 2018 include a large sloping garden skilfully converted into a sun-trap patio area, socialising space, children's play area and raised beds for produce, as well as a 'cool' garden focusing on alliums, lavender, agapanthus and an interesting collection of carnivorous pitcher plants.

8 CASTOR HOUSE

2, Peterborough Road, Castor, Peterborough, PE5 7AX.
Ian & Claire Winfrey, www.castorhousegardens.co.uk.
4m W of Peterborough. House on main Peterborough Rd in Castor. Parking in paddock off Water Lane. **Sun 19 Aug (2-5). Adm £6, chd free. Home-made teas.**

12 acres of gardens and woodland on a slope, terraced and redesigned 2010. Italianate spring fed ponds and stream gardens. Potager with greenhouse and exotic borders. Willow arbour and woodland garden. Peony and prunus walk. Rose and cottage gardens, 'Hot' double border, stumpery. Orchard in walled gardens. New loggia added in 2017. There is limited access for wheelchairs due to sloping nature of the garden.

GROUP OPENING

9 CHAUCER ROAD GARDENS

Cambridge, CB2 7EB. *1m S of Cambridge. Off Trumpington Rd (A1309), nr Brooklands Ave junction. Parking available at MRC Psychology Dept on Chaucer Rd.* **Sun 6, Mon 7 May (2-5). Combined adm £7, chd free. Home-made teas at Upwater Lodge.**

11 CHAUCER ROAD
Mark & Jigs Hill.
Open on all dates

12 CHAUCER ROAD
Mr & Mrs Bradley.
Open on Sun 6 May

16 CHAUCER ROAD
Mrs V Albutt.
Open on all dates

NEW **19 CHAUCER ROAD**
Tonia & Paul Forster.
Open on all dates

UPWATER LODGE
Mr & Mrs George Pearson.
Open on all dates

11 Chaucer Road is a ¾ acre Edwardian garden that has changed rapidly over the ensuing 110 yrs. A rock garden with pond and large weeping Japanese maple dates from about 1930. 16 Chaucer Road ½ acre garden, divided by arches and hedges into separate areas, each with its own character. Front rose garden. Unusual hawthorn and late summer borders. Blackberries and apple trees. Wildlife area with new sculpture. Waterproof footwear advised. Upwater Lodge is an Edwardian academic's house with 7acres of grounds. It has mature trees, fine lawns, old wisterias, and colourful borders. There is a small, pretty potager with vegetables and autumn fruits, and a well maintained grass tennis court. A network of paths through a wooded area lead down to a dyke, water meadows and a small flock of rare breed sheep. Enjoy a walk by the river and watch the punts go by. Buy home-made teas and sit in the garden or take them down to enjoy a lazy afternoon with ducks, geese, swans and heron on the riverbank. Cakes made with garden fruit where possible. Swings and climbing ropes. Stalls selling cards, prints and fabric crafts. Plant stall possible but please email to check. Some gravel areas and grassy paths with fairly gentle slopes.

10 CHURCHILL COLLEGE

Storey's Way, Cambridge, CB3 0DS. University of Cambridge, www.chu.cam.ac.uk. *1m from M11 J13. 1m NW of Cambridge city centre. Turn into Storeys Way from Madingley Rd (A1303), or from Huntingdon Rd (A1307). Parking on site.* **Sun 15 Apr (2-5). Combined adm with Fitzwilliam College £5, chd free. Light refreshments.**

42 acre site designed in 1960s for foliage and form, to provide year round interest in peaceful and relaxing surrounds with courtyards, large open spaces and specimen trees. 10m x 5m orchid house, herbaceous plantings. Beautiful grouping of Prunus Tai Haku (great white cherry) trees forming striking canopy and drifts of naturalised bulbs in grass around the site. The planting provides a setting for the impressive collection of modern sculpture. Orchid house, Sculptures. The greenhouse is restricted in size.

11 CLARE COLLEGE FELLOWS' GARDEN

Trinity Lane, Cambridge, CB2 1TL. The Master & Fellows, www.clare.cam.ac.uk. *Central to city. From Queens Rd or city centre via Senate House Passage, Old Court & Clare Bridge.* **Sun 1 July (2-5.30). Adm £4, chd free. Home-made teas. Tea, coffee, juice and cakes.**

2 acres. One of the most famous gardens on the Cambridge Backs. Herbaceous borders; sunken pond garden, fine specimen trees and tropical garden. Gravel paths.

12 CLOVER COTTAGE

50 Streetly End, West Wickham, CB21 4RP. Mr Paul & Mrs Shirley Shadford, 01223 893122, shirleyshadford@live.co.uk. *3m from Linton, 3m from Haverhill & 2m from Balsham. From Horseheath turn L, from Balsham turn R, thatched cottage opposite triangle of grass next to old windmill.* **Every Sun 4 Feb to 4 Mar (2-4). Adm £2.50, chd free. Light refreshments. Hot chocolate, tea and coffee during Snowdrop Festival. Opening with Streetly End & West Wickham Gardens on Sun 3 June. Visits also by arrangement in June adm incl tea or coffee & biscuits.**

In winter find a flowering cherry tree, borders of snowdrops, aconites, iris reticulata, hellebores and miniature narcissus throughout the packed small garden which has inspiring ideas on use of space. Pond and arbour, raised beds of fruit and vegetables. In summer arches of roses and clematis. Hardy geraniums, delightful borders of English roses and herbaceous plants. Pots of flowering bulbs for sale during Snowdrop Festival, plants for sale in the summer. Features in Country Homes and Interiors February 2018, and The English Garden March 2018. NO WHEELCHAIRS, PRAMS, PUSHCHAIRS, WHEELED WALKERS OR DOG ACCESS TO THE GARDEN AT ALL.

13 COLLEGE FARM

Station Road, Haddenham, Ely, CB6 3XD. Sheila & Jeremy Waller, 07779 302777, jeremyprimavera@aol.com, www.primaveragallery.co.uk. *From Stretham & Wilburton, at Xrds in Haddenham, turn R, past the church. Exactly at the bottom of the hill, turn L down narrow drive, with a mill wheel on R of the drive.* **Visits by arrangement May to Aug. Adm £5, chd free.**

40 acres around an intact Victorian farm. New walks, gallery and sculpture cattle yard. Further walks by ponds and through meadows. Roses, wild flowers, new water plants, foxgloves and new plantings of trees add colour and shape. Splendid fen views, lovely water features and ancient ridge and furrow pasture land with interesting wild flowers, original farm buildings and abundant wildlife. Amongst the farm buildings an outside gallery, and inside the house another gallery full of extraordinary paintings, art and craft. Wheelchair access is only possible around the garden near the house, but not through the gallery, farm, milking parlour and many of the walks.

The National Garden Scheme is the largest single funder of the Queen's Nursing Institute

14 NEW COTTAGE GARDEN

79 Sedgwick Street, Cambridge, CB1 3AL. Rosie Wilson, 01223 570890, p.wilson34@ntlworld.com. *From town centre or park & ride, go down Mill Rd over railway bridge. If driving take 2nd L Cavendish Rd, then 2nd R which leads into Sedgwick St.* **Sat 30 June, Sun 1 July (11-5). Adm £3, chd free. Tea. Visits also by arrangement June & July.**

Long narrow and planted in the cottage garden style with over 40 roses some on arches and growing through trees. Particularly planned to encourage wildlife with small pond, mature trees and shrubs. Perennials and some unusual plants interspersed with sculptures.

15 ◆ DOCWRA'S MANOR

2 Meldreth Road, Shepreth, Royston, SG8 6PS. Mrs Faith Raven, 01763 260677, www.docwrasmanorgarden.co.uk. *8m S of Cambridge. ½m W of A10. Garden is opp the War Memorial in Shepreth. King's Cross-Cambridge train stop 5 min walk.* **For NGS: Sun 22 Apr (2-4.30). Adm £5, chd free. Home-made teas. For other opening times and information, please phone or visit garden website.**

2½ acres of choice plants in a series of enclosed gardens. Tulips and Judas trees. Opened for the NGS for more than 40yrs. The garden is featured in great detail in a book published 2013 'The Gardens of England' edited by George Plumptre. Wheelchair access to most parts of the garden, gravel paths.

GROUP OPENING

16 DUXFORD GARDENS

Bustlers Cottage, 26 St Peters Street, Duxford, Cambridge, CB22 4RP. *All 6 gardens are close to the centre of the village of Duxford, just south of the A505 between the M11 J10 & Sawston.* **Sun 3 June (2-6). Combined adm £6, chd free. Home-made teas**

at United Reformed Church, Chapel Street a short walk from all the open gardens. WC.

BUSTLERS COTTAGE
John & Jenny Marks.

NEW **DUXFORD MILL**
Mrs Frankie Bridgwood.

NEW **2 GREEN STREET**
Mr Bruce Crockford.

31 ST PETER'S STREET
Mr David Baker.

6 THE BIGGEN
Mrs Bettye Reynolds.

NEW **9 THE BIGGEN**
Valerie Bennett.

Six gardens, 3 new to the NGS, of very different sizes and characters. The river Cam flows through three of them, including the Mill, which has historical associations and 11 acres of mature gardens. Two gardens in the Biggen with very different planting also lead down to the river. The garden at 2 Green Street is a charming small and colourful garden and 31 St Peters Street is packed with colour and slopes down to a rockery and secluded patio. Bustlers Cottage has an acre of traditional Cambridgeshire cottage garden including roses, herbaceous borders, vegetable garden and fruit trees.

17 ◆ ELGOOD'S BREWERY GARDENS

North Brink, Wisbech, PE13 1LW. Elgood & Sons Ltd, 01945 583160, info@elgoods-brewery.co.uk, www.elgoods-brewery.co.uk. *1m W of town centre. Leave A47 towards Wisbech Centre. Cross river to North Brink. Follow river & brown signs to brewery & car park beyond.* **For NGS: Sun 5 Aug (11.30-4.30). Adm £4, chd free. Light refreshments.** For other opening times and information, please phone, email or visit garden website.

Approx 4 acres of peaceful garden featuring 250 yr old specimen trees providing a framework to lawns, lake, rockery, herb garden and maze. Featured in 'The Fens' magazine July 2017. Wheelchair access to Visitor Centre and most areas of the garden.

GROUP OPENING

18 ELY GARDENS

Chapel Street, Ely, CB6 1AD. *14m N of Cambridge. Parking at Barton Rd car park, Tower Road or the Grange Council Offices. Map given at first garden visited.* **Sun 10 June (2-6). Combined adm £5, chd free.**

BISHOP OF HUNTINGDON'S GARDEN
David & Jean Thomson.

THE BISHOPS HOUSE
The Bishop of Ely.

42 CAMBRIDGE ROAD
Mr & Mrs J & C Switsur.

12 & 26 CHAPEL STREET
Ken & Linda Ellis, www.simplygardeningofely.co.uk.

A delightful and varied group of gardens in an historic Cathedral city: The Bishop's house is a monastic building adjoining Ely Cathedral and has mixed planting with a formal rose garden, wisteria and more. 12 & 26 Chapel Street: the former a small town garden reflecting the owners eclectic outlook, from alpine to herbaceous, all linked with a model railway! The latter is a green oasis of peace in the city. 42 Cambridge Road is a secluded town garden with interesting herbaceous borders, roses, shrubs and trees. The Bishop of Huntingdon's garden has a pond, well stocked borders, and a small orchard with mown paths. Lovely view of Ely Cathedral. Jane Frost, local environmental artist, will display and sell pieces in Bishops garden. 20% of sales to Littleport charity 'Branching Out'. Wheelchair access to areas of most gardens.

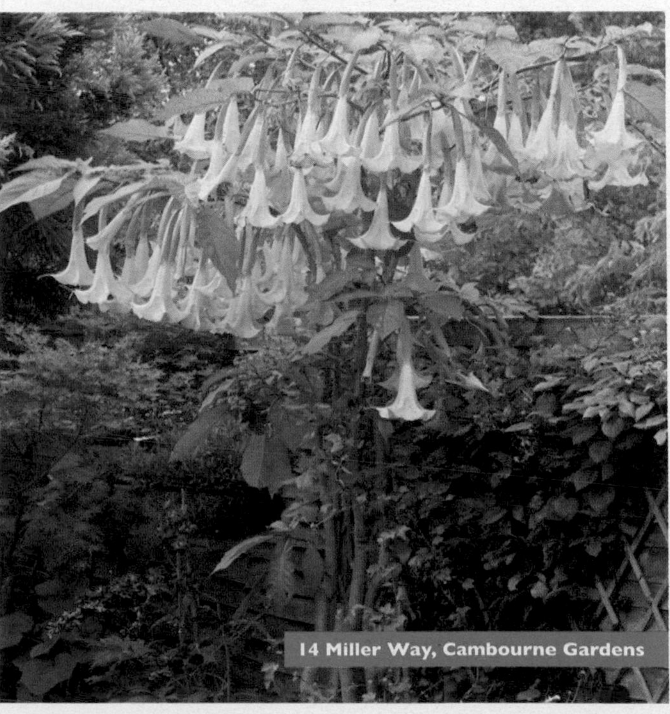

14 Miller Way, Cambourne Gardens

19 FENLEIGH

Inkerson Fen, Off Common Rd, Throckenholt, PE12 0QY. Jeff & Barbara Stalker. *2m from Gedney Hill. Turn R on to B1166 take next R into Common Rd following NGS signs approx 1m. From Parson Drove on B1166 turn L into Common Rd following NGS signs approx 3m.* **Sun 1 July (10-4). Adm £2.50, chd free. Light refreshments.**

Set in 4 acres incl 2 acre paddock. Quirky areas for easy maintenance. A fish pond dominates the garden surrounded with planting. Seating and two permanent gazebos if the weather is inclement. Patio with pots and raised beds, BBQ area containing ferns and acers. Small wooded area, poly tunnels and corners of the garden for wildlife. Large grass area for family fun and games.

20 ◆ FERRAR HOUSE

Little Gidding, Huntingdon, PE28 5RJ. Mrs Susan Capp, 01832 293383, info@ferrarhouse.co.uk, www.ferrarhouse.co.uk. *Take Mill Rd from Great Gidding (turn at Fox & Hounds) then after 1m turn R down single track lane. Car Park at Ferrar House.* **For NGS: Sun 13 May, Sun 16 Sept (10-5). Adm £4, chd free. Cream teas.** For other opening times and information, please phone, email or visit garden website.

A peaceful garden of a Retreat House with beautiful uninterrupted views across meadows and farm land. Adjacent to the historic Church of St John's it was here that a small religious community was formed in the C17. The poet T. S. Eliot visited in 1936 and it inspired the 4th of his Quartets named Little Gidding. Lawn and walled flower beds with a walled vegetable garden. WC accessible at Ferrar House.

21 FITZWILLIAM COLLEGE

University of Cambridge, Storey's Way, Cambridge, CB3 0DG. Master & Fellows, www.fitz.cam.ac.uk. *1m NW of Cambridge city centre. Turn into Storey's Way from Madingley Rd (A1303) or from Huntingdon Rd (A1307). Free parking on site.* **Sun 15 Apr (2-5). Combined adm with Churchill College £5, chd free. Cafe open for drinks and snacks.**

Traditional topiary, borders, woodland walk, lawns from the Edwardian period and specimen trees are complemented by modern planting and wild meadow. The avenue of limes, underplanted with spring bulbs, leads to The Grove, the 1813 house once belonging to the Darwin Family (not open). Some ramped pathways.

22 39 FOSTER ROAD

Campaign Ave, Sugar Way, Peterborough, PE2 9RS. Robert Marshall & Richard Handscombe, 01733 555978, robfmarshall@btinternet.com. *1m SW of Peterborough City Centre. A605 Oundle Rd, at T.L. turn N into Sugar Way. Cross 1st r'bout, L at 2nd r'bout to Campaign Ave. R at next r'bout on Campaign Ave. 2nd R to Foster Rd. Continue until very end. L into cul-de-sac.* **Visits by arrangement Feb to Sept weekends & weekdays possible, groups very welcome. Adm incl tea/coffee/biscuits (cake for groups). Adm £4, chd free. Light refreshments in garden pergola or indoor lounge, weather depending.**

Plantsman's garden in compact, new estate plot. Mixed borders; woodland/shade; 'vestibule' garden; exotics and ferns; espaliered fruit; pergola; patio; pond; parterre; many pots; octagonal greenhouse; seating and sculpture. Uncommon snowdrops, over 250 hostas, plus daphnes, acers and other choice/ unusual cultivars. Trees and hedges create enclosure and intimacy.
4 x British Shorthair cats. Compact 'town garden' conceals many design ideas to maximize planting and create intimacy - without grass to cut. See how trees (x12) and hedges can be used in a small garden. Large collection of Hostas (250+ cultivars). Rare snowdrops. Ensembles of unusual plants in pots extend interest and season. Featured in Garden News, Garden Answers, Modern Gardens, Mail on Saturday. All viewings accompanied by garden owner(s). Main garden and WC accessible by wheelchair.

23 NEW FOXELWOOD

Westwick, Oakington, Cambridge, CB24 3AR. Mr & Mrs David Mardle. *Opposite the Scallywags pre-school nursery at the Cottenham end of Westwick.* **Sun 20, Sun 27 May (2-5). Adm £5, chd free. Teas.**

Approximately 3 acres, partly woodland with more formal gardens, some designed by Sylvia Newman, featuring large herbaceous

Horseshoe Farm

borders, conifers, lawns, small pond garden and an enclosure for chickens. The garden includes several sculptures by local artists Wesley West and Carol Sinclair, and access to public footpaths for long walks across the surrounding fields.

24 NEW GREEN END FARM

Over Road, Longstanton, Cambridge, CB24 3DW. Sylvia Newman, www.sngardendesign.co.uk. *From A14 take the direction of Longstanton At the r'about, take the 2nd exit At the next r'about, turn L (this shows a dead end on the sign) We're a couple of hundred metres on L.* **Sun 24 June, Sun 8 July (12.30-4). Adm £3, chd free. Home-made teas**

A young garden that's beginning to blend well with the farm. An interesting combination of new and established spaces interlinked with a design eye. An established orchard with beehives; two wildlife ponds. A productive kitchen and cutting garden. Doves, chickens and sheep complete the picture!

25 10 GWYDIR STREET

Cambridge, CB1 2LL. Mrs Rosemary Catling. *A603 East Rd, R into St Matthews St, L into Norfolk Terrace then R at junction with Gwydir St.* **Sat 7, Sun 8 July (11-5). Combined adm with Norfolk Terrace Garden £4, chd free. Light refreshments at Norfolk Terrace.**

L shaped town garden, paved with some raised beds. The formal structure is informally planted with perennials, shrubs and small trees. Many in pots. There is a sitting area under a mature fig tree and small pond. An artist's garden with attention to form and colour combination.Some artwork also for sale. Some unusual plants and shrubs. Access for small wheelchair down narrow side passage.

26 HIGH BANK COTTAGE

Kirkgate, Tydd St. Giles, Wisbech, PE13 5NE. Mrs F Savill. *Heading from Wisbech, North Cambs. A1101 take turn signed Tydd St Giles. Parking at Tydd St Giles golf & country club, a few minutes walk from the garden. www.pure-leisure.co.uk/parks/tydd-st-giles/overview/.* **Sat 12, Sun 13 May (10.30-4). Adm £3.50, chd £1.50. Home-made teas. Meals are available at the golf course.**

The garden is a tranquil oasis from the hurry of life. A cottage garden, mainly, but it has many mature trees and shrubs. It is seperated into different areas with seating so that the views of the garden can be appreciated. There are two ponds, one of which has fish, and a river bank with areas for wildlife, and, also an allotment. Children must be supervised AT ALL TIMES. No dogs are allowed. There will be coffee/tea and homemade cakes and biscuits available to purchase. Also, plants and garden related craft items. There are gravelled areas, and some steps. The brick paths can be slippery when wet.

27 HORSESHOE FARM

Chatteris Road, Somersham, Huntingdon, PE28 3DR. Neil & Claire Callan, 01354 693546, nccallan@yahoo.co.uk. *9m NE of St Ives, Cambs. Easy access from the A14. Situated on E side of B1050, 4m N of Somersham Village. Parking for 8 cars in the drive.* **Visits by arrangement May to July groups max 20. Adm £4, chd free. Home-made teas.**

This ¾ acre plant-lovers' garden has a large pond with summer-house and decking, bog garden, alpine troughs, mixed rainbow island beds with over 25 varieties of bearded irises, water features, a small hazel woodland area, wildlife meadow, secret corners and a lookout tower for wide Fenland views and bird watching. Featured in WI Life, Amateur Gardening and Garden News.

28 ISLAND HALL

Godmanchester, PE29 2BA. Mr Christopher & Lady Linda Vane Percy, www.islandhall.com. *1m S of Huntingdon (A1). 15m NW of Cambridge (A14). In centre of Godmanchester next to free car park.* **Sun 27 May (11-4.30). Adm £4, chd free. Home-made teas.**

3-acre grounds. Tranquil riverside setting with mature trees. Chinese bridge over Saxon mill race to embowered island with wild flowers. Garden restored in 1983 to mid C18 formal design, with box hedging, clipped hornbeams, parterres, topiary, good vistas over borrowed landscape and C18 wrought iron and stone urns. The ornamental island has been replanted with Princeton elms (ulmus americana). Mid C18 mansion (not open).

29 NEW JESUS COLLEGE

Jesus Lane, Cambridge, CB5 8BL. Mr Paul Stearn. *Entrance via Victoria Ave, vehicle entrance. Free on site parking subject to numbers.* **Sun 15 July (11-4). Adm £4, chd free. Light refreshments.**

Historic College Gardens and Grounds dating from mid C12. Fine lawns and courtyards, colourful flowers in many courts. Shrubberies, arbour archways and sculptures. Fellows garden open on day.

30 KING'S COLLEGE FELLOWS' GARDEN AND PROVOST'S GARDEN

Queen's Road, Cambridge, CB2 1ST. Provost & Scholars of King's College. *In Cambridge, the Backs. Entry by gate at junction of Queen's Rd & West Rd. Parking at Lion Yard 10mins walk, or some pay & display places in West Rd & Queen's Rd.* **Sun 8 July (2-5). Adm £4, chd free.**

Fine example of a Victorian garden with rare specimen trees. With a small woodland walk and a kitchen/allotment garden created in 2011 and a rose pergola and herbaceous border created in 2013. Now with an exciting sub -tropical border together with a new Rond Pont entrance feature celebrating the mathematicians who studied and researched at King's over the centuries. Gravel paths.

31 KIRTLING TOWER

Newmarket Road, Kirtling, Newmarket, CB8 9PA. The Lord & Lady Fairhaven. *6m SE of Newmarket. From Newmarket head towards village of Saxon Street, through village to Kirtling, turn L at war memorial, signed to Upend, entrance is signed on the L.* **Sun 25 Mar, Sun 24 June (11-4). Adm £5, chd free. Light refreshments at the Church. Selection of hot & cold food, sandwiches & cakes, tea & coffee.**

Surrounded by a moat, formal gardens and parkland. In the spring there are swathes of daffodils, narcissi, crocus, muscari, chionodoxa and tulips. Closer to the house, vast lawn areas Secret and Cutting Gardens. In the summer the Walled Garden has superb herbaceous borders with anthemis, hemerocallis, geraniums and delphiniums. The Victorian Garden is filled with peonies. Views of surrounding countryside. A Classic car display will be in attendance. Mr Feinson and his Arcadia Recorder Group will be playing in the walled garden. Rougham Nurseries and Helens Herbaceous will bring a selection of plants for sale. There will be a variety of craft stalls on both dates as well as a display of Stonework from the Fairhaven Stoneyard. The Church will be providing delicious hot and cold refreshments throughout the day. Featured in the Newmarket News. Many of the paths and routes around the garden are grass - they are accessible by wheelchairs, but can be hard work if wet.

32 LUCY CAVENDISH COLLEGE

Lady Margaret Road, Cambridge, CB3 0BU. Lucy Cavendish College. *1m NW of Gt St Mary. College situated on the corner of Lady Margaret Rd & Madingley Rd (A1303). Entrance off Lady Margaret Rd.* **Sun 29 Apr (2-5). Adm £3.50, chd free.**

The gardens of 4 late Victorian houses have been combined and developed over past 25yrs into an informal 3 acre garden. Fine mature trees shade densely planted borders. An Anglo Saxon herb garden is situated in one corner. The garden provides a rich wildlife habitat.

33 MADINGLEY HALL

Cambridge, CB23 8AQ. University of Cambridge, 01223 746222, reservations@madingleyhall.co.uk, www.madingleyhall.co.uk. *4m W of Cambridge. 1m from M11 J13.* **Sun 10 June (2.30-5.30). Adm £5, chd free. Home-made teas at St Mary Magdalene Church adjacent to Madingley Hall Drive.**

C16 Hall (not open) set in 8 acres of attractive grounds landscaped by Capability Brown. Features incl landscaped walled garden with hazel walk, alpine bed, medicinal border and rose pergola. Historic meadow, topiary, mature trees and wide variety of hardy plants. Featured in BBC Look East.

34 MANOR HOUSE, ALWALTON

Church Street, Alwalton, Peterborough, PE7 3UU. Malcolm & Jane Holmes. *Alwalton Village. Turn into centre of old village, park on street or Village Hall carpark. Garden 100yds on the right after Village Hall.* **Sun 17 June (1.30-4.30). Adm £4, chd free. Home-made teas.**

Walled garden surrounding 17th century farmhouse, divided into rooms with tall hedges, topiary and mixed borders. Paths leading to wild garden overlooking Nene valley.

35 ◆ THE MANOR, HEMINGFORD GREY

Hemingford Grey, PE28 9BN. Mrs D S Boston, 01480 463134, diana_boston@hotmail.com, www.greenknowe.co.uk. *4m E of Huntingdon. Off A14. Entrance to garden by small gate off river towpath. Limited parking on verge halfway up drive, parking near house for disabled. Otherwise park in village.* For opening times and information, please phone, email or visit garden website.

Garden designed and planted by author Lucy Boston, surrounds C12 manor house on which Green Knowe books based (house open by appt). 3 acre 'cottage' garden with topiary; snowdrops, old roses, extensive collection of irises incl Dykes Medal winners and Cedric Morris varieties, herbaceous borders with mainly scented plants. Meadow with mown paths. Enclosed by river, moat and wilderness. Late May splendid show of Irises followed by the old roses. Care is taken with the planting to start the year with a large variety of snowdrops and to extend the flowering season right through to the first frosts. The garden is interesting even in winter with the topiary. Featured in 'The English Garden' magazine Irises, Old Roses and Topiary. Gravel paths but wheelchairs are encouraged to go on the lawns.

36 MARY CHALLIS GARDEN

68 High Street, Sawston, Cambridge, CB22 3BG. A M Challis Trust Ltd, www.challistrust.org.uk. *5m SE of Cambridge. Passageway between 60 High St & 66 High St (Billsons Opticians).* **Sun 10 June (2-6). Adm £3, chd free. Home-made teas. Opening with Sawston Gardens on Sun 1 July.**

Gifted to Sawston in 2006, a 2 acre garden maintained by volunteers to benefit wildlife and for the local community. Winter/spring long border, drifts of crocuses, snowdrops and aconites in spring; very colourful summer flowerbeds. Woodland, pond, raised vegetable beds, orchard, vine house, wild flower meadow and beehives. Regular opening hours all year round: 10-12 am Tues, Thurs & Sat; 2-4 pm summer and 1-3 pm winter on Sundays. Featured in Cambridgeshire Journal 'The Lost Garden'. Paths and lawns accessible by wheelchair from car-park.

The National Garden Scheme is committed to helping unpaid carers

37 5 MOAT WAY
Swavesey, CB24 4TR. Mr & Mrs N Kyberd, 01954 200568, n.kyberd@ntlworld.com. *Off A14, 2m beyond Bar Hill. Look for School Lane/Fen Drayton Rd, at mini r'about turn into Moat Way, no.5 is approx 100 metres on L.* **Visits by arrangement June & July. Adm £3, chd free.**
Colourful garden filled with collection of trees, shrubs and perennials. Large patio area displaying many specimen foliage plants in planters, incl pines, hostas and acers.

GROUP OPENING

38 MOLESWORTH & BRINGTON GARDENS
Molesworth, Huntingdon, PE28 0QD. *10m W of Huntingdon. A14 W for Molesworth & Brington exit at J16 onto B660.* **Sun 10 June (2-6). Combined adm £4, chd free. Home-made teas at Molesworth House and Yew Tree Cottage.**

MOLESWORTH HOUSE
John Prentis.

YEW TREE COTTAGE
Christine & Don Eggleston.
2 styles of planting showing how to make a garden complement the building it surrounds. Molesworth House is an old rectory garden with everything that you'd both expect and hope for, given its Victorian past. There are surprising corners to this traditional take on a happy and relaxed, yet also formal garden. Yew Tree Cottage, informal garden approx 1 acre, complements the C17 building (not open) and comprises flower beds, lawns, vegetable patch, boggy area, copses and orchard. Plants in pots and hanging baskets. Partial wheelchair access.

39 NETHERHALL MANOR
Tanners Lane, Soham, CB7 5AB. Timothy Clark, 01353 720269. *6m Ely, 6m Newmarket. Enter Soham from Newmarket, Tanners Lane 2nd R 100yds after cemetery. Enter Soham from Ely, Tanners Lane 2nd L after War Memorial.* **Sun 1 Apr, Sun 6 May, Sun 5, Sun 12 Aug (2-5). Adm £3, chd free. Home-made teas. Visits also by arrangement Mar to Aug (Best in March, early May, August.).**
An elegant garden 'touched with antiquity' Good Gardens Guide. An unusual garden appealing to those with historical interest in individual collections of plant groups: March-old primroses, daffodils & Victorian double flowered hyacinths. first garden hellebores hybrids. May-old English tulips. Crown Imperials. Aug-Victorian pelargonium,heliotrope,calceolaria, dahlias. Author-Margery Fish's Country Gardening & Mary McMurtrie's Country Garden Flowers. Historic Plants 1500-1900. The only bed of English tulips on display in the country. Author's books for sale. Featured in Country Life and The Garden. Flat garden with two optional steps. Lawns.

40 NEW NEWNHAM CROFT PRIMARY SCHOOL
Chedworth Street, Cambridge, CB3 9JF. Mrs Sharon Williams, www.newnhamcroft.cambs.sch.uk. *M11 J12. Follow Barton Rd to City Centre. There is no R turn into Grantchester St at T-lights. Follow rd L to Newnham garage r'about to return to Grantchester St. Chedworth St on L.* **Sun 29 Apr (1-5). Adm £3, chd free. Home-made teas.**
Children are encouraged to take part in gardening activities carried out by our volunteers. The gardens start with a courtyard with planters and woodland path. There are two herbaceous borders and a number of flower beds. The vegetable garden provides produce for the school kitchen. In spring bulbs and tree blossom from the many variety of trees dominate this beautiful learning environment.

41 NEW THE NIGHT GARDEN
37 Honeyhill, Paston, Peterborough, PE4 7DR. Andrea Connor, 07801987905, andrea.connors@ntlworld.com. *From A47 Soke Parkway at J19. Take exit N on Topmoor Way. R at next r'about (3rd exit) to Paston Ridings, over the speed humps. Take 4th L to Honeyhill. 1st R into car park. No37 at top L corner.* **Visits by arrangement June to Sept groups up to 15. Womens' health & well-being groups particularly welcome. Adm £4, chd free. Light refreshments in garden or house if weather inclement. Refreshments incl in adm.**
Small town garden with shrubs, roses, clematis, colourful bedding plants and Ash tree for shade, seclusion and privacy. Salvia collection for wellbeing. Arches and trellis give height, water adds tranquility. At dusk the solar powered lighting gradually transforms the space into an enchanting magical world. Sit and enjoy the gradual transformation from either seating area at the ends of the garden. Night time lighting brings an unusual dimension, transforming the experience.

42 2A NINE CHIMNEYS LANE

Balsham, CB21 4ES. Mr & Mrs Jim & Hilary Potter, 01223 891211, hppotter@btinternet.com. *In centre of Balsham just off High St. 3m E of A11, 12m S of Newmarket & 10m SE of Cambridge. Car parking in the High St or the Church car park. 2 disabled spaces in Nine Chimneys Lane.* **Sun 25 Mar (12-4). Adm £4, chd £1. Home-made teas. Visits also by arrangement Mar to Oct for groups of 10+ Max. 20.**

Two acres of garden with spring bulbs, herbaceous border, raised vegetable beds, gravel garden, large duck pond, wild flower meadow, an orchard and modern sculptures and human sundial. A Music Maze was planted in 1993 and has two types of trees in ½m of hedge; green yew (Taxus baccata) and golden yew (Taxus elegantissima) in the shape of a treble clef with viewing hill. Mature and new trees. Including the maze there are over 1500 trees in total. Also two paved areas form the shape of French horns which enclose an alpine garden and a mobile fountain. Refreshments provided by Macmillan Cancer Support, Cambridge Hard paths around formal garden area. Limited wheelchair access to grassland areas. Fine in dry weather with a good driver.

43 NORFOLK TERRACE GARDEN

38 Norfolk Terrace, Cambridge, CB1 2NG. John Tordoff & Maurice Reeve. *Central Cambridge. A603 East Rd turn R into St Matthews St to Norfolk St, L into Blossom St & Norfolk Terrace is at the end.* **Sat 7, Sun 8 July (11-6). Combined adm with 10 Gwydir Street £4, chd free. Light refreshments.**

A small, paved courtyard garden in Moroccan style. Masses of colour in raised beds and pots, backed by oriental arches. An ornamental pool done in patterned tiles offers the soothing splash of water. The garden has been included in the recently published book Secret Gardens of East Anglia.The owners' previous, London garden, was named by BBC Gardeners' World as 'Best Small Garden in Britain'. There will also be a displays of recent paintings by John Tordoff and handmade books by Maurice Reeve.

44 THE OLD RECTORY

312 Main Road, Parson Drove, Wisbech, PE13 4LF. Helen Roberts, 01945 700415, yogahelen@talk21.com. *SW of Wisbech. From Peterborough on A47 follow signs to Parson Drove L after Thorney Toll. From Wisbech follow the B1166 through Levrington Common.* **Sun 10 June (11-4). Adm £4, chd free. Home-made teas. Visits also by arrangement May to Aug gardening groups welcome.**

Walled Georgian cottage garden of 1 acre, opening into wild flower meadow and paddocks. Long herbaceous border, 2 ponds and unusual weeping ash tree. Terraced areas and outdoor kitchen! No hills but lovely open Fen views, bridge over wildlife dyke (Monet!) and par3 golf hole come and have a putt! Featured in Amateur Gardening magazine.

45 THE OLD VICARAGE

Causeway, Great Staughton, St Neots, PE19 5BF. Mr & Mrs Richard Edmunds, 01480 860397, elizabeth.edmunds4@btinternet.com. *5m off A1, 8m from St Neots. Take the B645 to Great Staughton.* **Visits by arrangement Apr to Oct groups of 10+. Adm £5, chd free. Light refreshments in the kitchen or the garden by summer houses. A nice place to have a picnic..**

A good Old Vicarage garden, redesigned in 2008/9 to enhance original plan. A Natural Swimming Pond which has pretty rockery planting with ferns and a man made waterway running into it over rocks. Also, a Wendy house on a platform with swings and slide off it. natural swimming pond, great garden for children and nice layout. Some gravel paths easily negotiable by wheelchair.

46 23A PERRY ROAD

Buckden, St. Neots, PE19 5XG. David & Valerie Bunnage, 01480 810553, d.bunnage@btinternet.com. *5m S of Huntingdon on A1. From A1 Buckden r'about take B661, Perry Rd approx 300yds on L.* **Visits by arrangement Apr to Oct. Adm £4, chd free.**

Approx 1 acre garden consisting of many garden designs incl Japanese interlinked by gravel paths. Large selection of acers, pines, rare and unusual shrubs. Also interesting features, a quirky garden. Plantsmans garden for all seasons, small bog garden. WC. Coaches welcome.

GROUP OPENING

47 RAMSEY FORTY FOOT

Ramsey, PE26 2YA. *3m N of Ramsey. From Ramsey (B1096) travel through Ramsey Forty Foot, just before bridge over river, turn into Hollow Rd at The George PH and carry on for 300m.* **Sun 10 June (2-6). Combined adm £3, chd free. Home-made teas.**

THE ELMS
Mr R Shotbolt.

FIRST COTTAGE
Kevin Brown.

LAKE VIEW HOUSE
Sir John & Lady O'reilly.

THE WILLOWS
Jane & Andrew Sills.

Four interesting and contrasting gardens in the village of Ramsey Forty Foot. The Elms is a 1½-acre informal garden with ancient water-filled clay pits teeming with wildlife and backed by massive elms. Large collection of shrubs, perennials, bog and aquatic plants. Woodland and arid plantings. The Willows is a cottage garden with riverside location filled with old roses, herbaceous beds; shrubs, ferns, pond and vegetable garden.
First Cottage is a rural cottage garden full of colour, with long herbaceous borders, shrub beds

and terraces with a natural pond. A rockery hosts a miniature steam railway. Lake View House is a garden of mixed beds and borders with some specimen trees, running down to a lake. A good place to finish your visit with tea/ coffee and cake, accompanied by gentle background music. Some wheelchair access.

48 REED COTTAGE

1 Rectory Farm Road, Little Wilbraham, Cambridge, CB21 5LB. Mr Robert Turner, rj-turner@hotmail.co.uk. *5m S of Newmarket, 5m E of Cambridge. In centre of village on corner opp grass triangle.* **Visits by arrangement Apr to Sept visit April to see 5000 tulips and spring bulbs. Visit July to see the garden in full flower. Adm £5, chd free. Light refreshments. Sandwiches, tea, coffee, wine.**

A delightful traditional cottage garden with stunning borders of many mature herbaceous perennials. 5000 bulbs in spring, and full colour in summer. A garden pond adds to the enjoyment and brings wildlife benefits. A well stocked vegetable garden makes us 60% self efficient. A shaded area hosts ferns and hostas.

49 ROBINSON COLLEGE

Grange Road, Cambridge, CB3 9AN. Warden and Fellows, www.robinson.cam.ac.uk/about-robinson/gardens/national-gardens-scheme. *Garden at main Robinson College site, report to Porters' Lodge. There is only on-street parking.* **Every Mon to Fri 1 Jan to 20 Apr (10-4). Every Sat and Sun 7 Jan to 15 Apr (2-4). Every Mon to Fri 18 June to 10 Aug (10-4). Every Sat and Sun 23 June to 5 Aug (2-4). Every Mon to Fri 27 Aug to 28 Dec (10-4). Every Sat and Sun 1 Sept to 30 Dec (2-4). Adm £4, chd free.**

10 original Edwardian gardens are linked to central wild woodland water garden focusing on Bin Brook with small lake at heart of site. This gives a feeling of park and informal woodland, while at the same time keeping the sense of older more formal gardens beyond. Central area has a wide lawn running down to the lake framed by many mature stately trees with much of the original planting intact. More recent planting incl herbaceous borders and commemorative trees. Please report to Porters' Lodge on arrival to pay for entry and guidebook. No picnics. Children must be accompanied at all times. NB from time to time some parts, or occasionally all, of Robinson College gardens may be closed for safety reasons involving work by contractors and our maintenance staff. Please report to Porters' Lodge on arrival for information. Ask at Porters' Lodge for wheelchair access.

50 NEW SANDPIPER

30 Colnefields, Somersham, PE28 3DL. Tim & Emma Procter, 01487 740896, emma.procter1@me.com. *4m NE of St Ives. Take B1040 from St Ives to Somersham. Drive through Somersham High St until you get to a sharp R corner (just after garage), take L turn signed Chatteris. Colnefields is 1st rd on R after 150m.* **Sat 9, Sun 10 June (12-5). Evening opening Fri 7, Sat 8, Sun 9 Dec (5-9). Adm £4, chd free. Light refreshments. Pre-booking essential, please phone or email. 01487 740896 emma.procter1@me.com.**

About an acre of herbaceous borders, lawn, rose arbour, secluded seating areas, kitchen, cottage and wildlife garden. A photo opportunity around every corner. Our Winter open evening provides an enchanted evening view of a garden full of nostalgia. The inspired creative lighting demonstrates the beauty and architecture of plants and trees in winter. A real winter tonic.

GROUP OPENING

51 SAWSTON GARDENS

Sawston, Cambridge, CB22 3HY. *5m SE of Cambridge. Midway between Saffron Walden & Cambridge on A1301.* **Sun 1 July (1-6). Combined adm £5, chd free. Enjoy a cream tea at the Sweet Tea café in the High Street.**

BROOK HOUSE
Mr & Mrs Ian & Mia Devereux.

MARY CHALLIS GARDEN
A M Challis Trust Ltd.
(See separate entry)

11 MILL LANE
Tim & Rosie Phillips.

22 ST MARY'S ROAD
Ann & Mike Redshaw.

VINE COTTAGE
Dr & Mrs Tim Wreghitt.

5 very varied gardens. Brook House has many lovely recently designed and planted features set in 1½ acres, including an impressive large walled kitchen garden and an expansive modern patio and pond. At 11 Mill Lane many big changes are taking place to both the hard and soft landscaping, with a re-designed orchard at the front, and a revamped sun dappled secluded back garden. The semi-circular lawn, roses and mixed borders remain. 22 St Mary's Road has views over Sawston Hall Meadows SSSI, wildlife friendly planting, a pond and colour-themed contemporary borders.
Vine Cottage's large mature garden of several 'rooms' incorporates a secret Japanese courtyard. Also open with the group this year is the Mary Challis Garden, a 2-acre varied garden gifted to the village in 2006 (see separate entry for more details). Many other features to be seen, something for everyone. Great value for £5. Most parts of the gardens are accessible by wheelchair.

GROUP OPENING

52 STAPLEFORD GARDENS

Stapleford, Cambridge, CB22 5DG. *4m S of Cambridge on A1301. In London Rd next to Church St. Parking available on site.* **Sun 17 June (2-5). Combined adm £5, chd free. Home-made teas at Johnson Hall, 1 Gog Magog Way CB22 5BQ.**

NEW 3A DUKES MEADOW
Jan & Lee Gruncell.

6 HAVERHILL ROAD
Mr & Mrs John & Joan King.

5 PRIAMS WAY
Tony Smith.

Contrasting gardens showing a range of size, planting and atmosphere in this village just S of Cambridge. 3a Dukes Meadow a beautiful tranquil south-facing established garden. Lawns, perennial plants, grasses, shrubs and trees. Pergola covered in roses. Large patio with water features. Sculptures and hanging baskets.
6 Haverhill Road is a well established and relaxing garden with grass, pergolas, flower beds, vegetable garden and soft fruit. Overlooking fields. Priam's Way has small mature borders with a wide variety of plants and shrubs.

GROUP OPENING

53 STAPLOE GARDENS

Staploe, St. Neots, PE19 5JA. *Great North Rd in western part of St Neots. At r'about just N of the Coop store, exit westwards on Duloe Rd. Follow this under the A1, through the village of Duloe & on to Staploe.* **Sat 26, Sun 27 May (1-5). Combined adm £4, chd free. Home-made teas.**

FALLING WATER HOUSE
Caroline Kent.

OLD FARM COTTAGE
Sir Graham & Lady Fry.

Old Farm Cottage: flower garden surrounding thatched house (not open), with 3 acres of orchard, grassland, young woodland and pond maintained for wildlife.
Falling Water House: a mature woodland garden, partly reclaimed from farmland 10yrs ago, it is constructed around several century old trees incl three Wellingtonia. Kitchen garden potager, courtyard and herbaceous borders, planted to attract bees and wildlife, through which meandering paths have created hidden vistas. Old Farm Cottage has rough ground and one steep slope.

GROUP OPENING

54 STREETLY END & WEST WICKHAM GARDENS

West Wickham, CB21 4RP. *3m from Haverhill & 3m from Linton. Clover Cottage, Streetly End is opp grass triangle next to old windmill. 25 High Street, West Wickham CB21 4RY is near T junction.* **Sun 3 June (12-5). Combined adm £4.50, chd free. Light refreshments at Clover Cottage.**

CLOVER COTTAGE
Mr Paul & Mrs Shirley Shadford. (See separate entry)

25 HIGH STREET
Mrs Jane Scheuer.

Find at Clover Cottage, Streetly End, arches of roses, clematis and many varieties of geraniums, and raised fruit and vegetable beds. Delightful pond and borders of English roses, climbers and herbaceous plants. Ferns and shade plants under an old tree, with views over open countryside from the summer house in the sunken white garden. This small garden has an inspiring use of space.
25 High Street, West Wickham is a charming informal cottage garden to ramble, wander and relax in, with many routes through borders and pathways. Plants are allowed to self-seed and hybridise freely. Several interesting and unusual shrubs and herbaceous perennials from many continents. Features about Clover Cottage in Country Homes and Interiors February 2018, and in The English Garden March 2018 issue. No access for wheelchairs, prams, pushchairs, wheeled walkers or dogs to gardens.

55 TRINITY COLLEGE, FELLOWS' GARDEN

Queens Road, Cambridge, CB3 9AQ. Master and Fellows' of Trinity College, www.trin.cam.ac.uk/about/gardens. *Short walk from city centre. At the Northampton St/Madingley Rd end of Queens Rd close to Garrett Hostel Lane.* **Sun 8 Apr (1-4). Adm £3.50, chd free. Home-made teas. Special dietary requirements are usually catered for.**
Interesting historic garden of about 8 acres with impressive specimen trees, mixed borders, drifts of spring bulbs and informal lawns with notable influences throughout from Fellows over the years. Across the gently flowing Bin Brook to Burrell's Field you will find some modern planting styles and plants nestled amongst the accommodation blocks in smaller intimate gardens. Members of the Gardening staff will be on hand to answer any queries. The teas and cakes are provided and served by a local Girl Guide unit. Wheelchair access - some gravel paths.

56 WILD ROSE COTTAGE

Church Walk, Lode, Cambridge, CB25 9EX. Mrs Joy Martin, 01223 811132, joymartin123@btinternet.com. *From A14 take the rd towards Burwell turn L in to Lode & park on L. Walk straight on between cottages to the archway of Wild Rose Cottage.* **Evening opening Wed 23 May (6-9). Adm £6, chd free. Wine. Visits also by arrangement Mar to Sept please email or phone in advance.**

Groups welcome.
A real cottage garden overflowing with plants. Gardens within gardens of abundant vegetation, roses climbing through trees, laburnum tunnel, a daffodil spiral which becomes a daisy spiral in the summer. Circular vegetable garden and wildlife pond. Described by one visitor as a garden to write poetry in! It is a truly wild and loved garden where flowers in the vegetable circle are not pulled up! Chickens ducks and dog, circular vegetable garden, wild life pond, and wild romantic garden! Lots of little path ways.

57 WILLOW HOLT

Willow Hall Lane, Thorney, PE6 0QN. Angie & Jonathan Jones. *4m E of Peterborough. From A47, between Eye & Thorney turn S into Willow Hall Lane. 1.6m on R. NOT in Thorney Village.* **Sun 27, Mon 28 May (11-5). Adm £4, chd free. Home-made teas.**
Two acres, part farmer's field part local tip, were combined as a building plot in 1960 and have been transformed over the past 25 years into a place of of peaceful relaxation. Trees and shrubs, wildflower meadow, wildlife ponds, scrap metal sculptures and an impressive and varied collection of plants and shrubs. 75% accessible by wheelchair users with a good pusher.

58 THE WINDMILL

10 Cambridge Road, Impington, CB24 9NU. Pippa & Steve Temple, 07775 446443, mill.impington@ntlworld.com, www.impingtonmill.org. *2½m N of Cambridge. Off A14 at J32, B1049 to Histon, L into Cambridge Rd at T-lights, follow Cambridge Rd round to R, the Windmill is approx 400yds on L.* **Visits by arrangement Apr to Oct by arrangement. Adm £5, chd free. Wine**
A previously romantic wilderness of 1½ acres surrounding windmill, now filled with bulbs, perennial beds, pergolas, bog gardens, grass bed and herb bank. Secret paths and wild areas with thuggish roses maintain the romance. Millstone seating area in smouldering borders contrasts with the pastel colours of the remainder of the garden. Also 'Pond Life' seat, 'Tree God' and amazing compost area! The Windmill - an C18 smock on C19 tower on C17 base on C16 foundations - is being restored. Featured in Daily Mail - local radio and press coverage. Guide dogs only.

59 WYTCHWOOD

7 Owl End, Great Stukeley, Huntingdon, PE28 4AQ. Mr David Cox. *2m N of Huntingdon on B1043. Parking available at Great Stukeley Village Hall in Owl End.* **Sun 1 July (1.30-5.30). Adm £3.50, chd free. Home-made teas. Cream teas and home made cakes.**
A 2 acre garden with borders of perennials, annuals and shrubs, lawns, fish pond and a larger wildlife pond. The garden includes 1 acre for wildlife with grasses set among rowan, birch, maple and field maple trees, foxgloves, ferns and bulbs. Roses are a special feature in June. Enjoy home made and cream teas, plenty of seats. Short gravel drive at the garden entrance.

Island Hall

CHESHIRE & WIRRAL

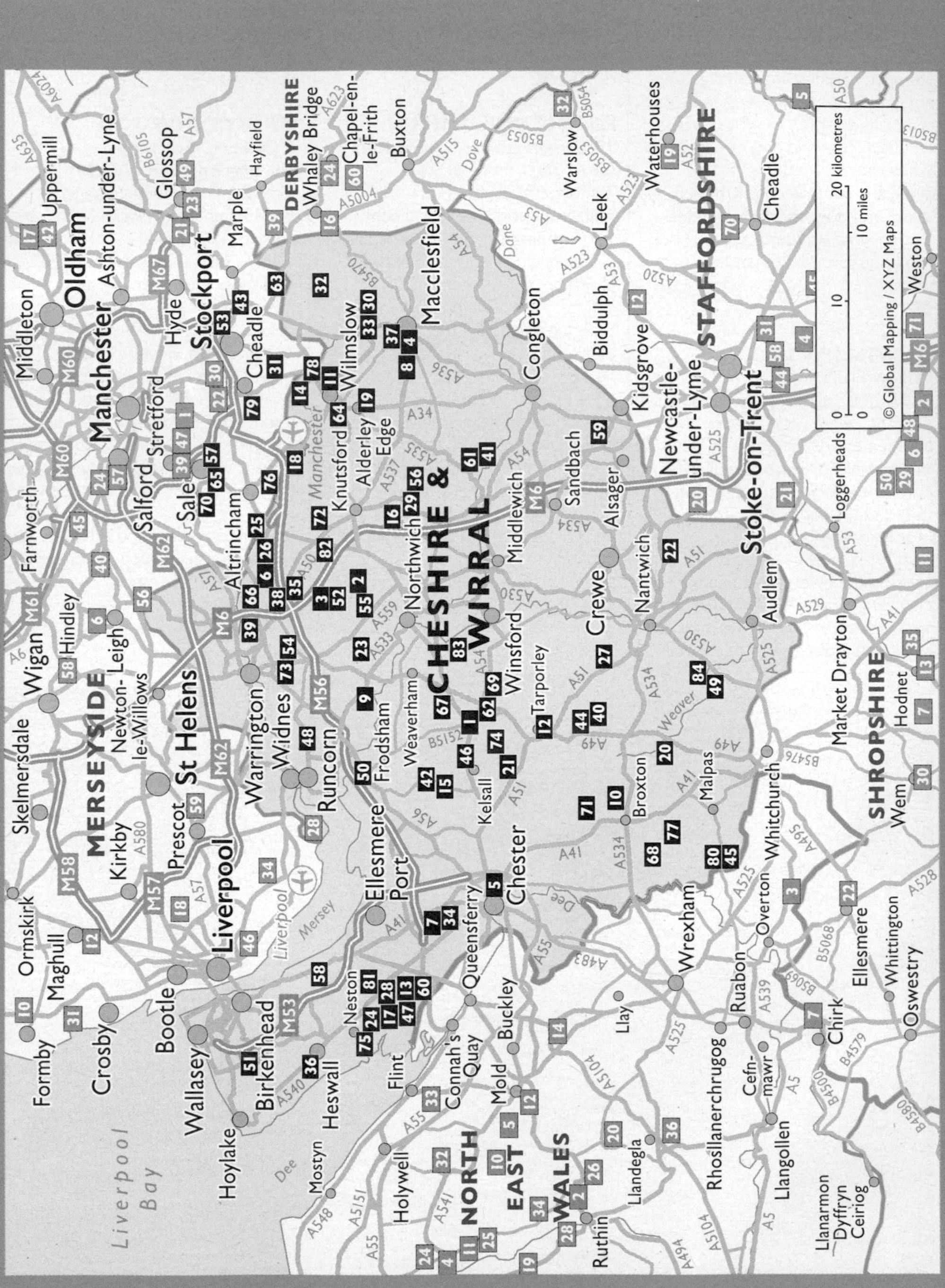

The area of Cheshire and Wirral comprises what are now the four administrative regions of West Cheshire and Chester, East Cheshire, Warrington and Wirral, together with gardens in the south of Greater Manchester, Trafford and Stockport.

The perception of the area is that of a fertile county dominated by the Cheshire Plain, but to the extreme west it enjoys a mild maritime climate, with gardens often sitting on sandstone and sandy soils and enjoying mildly acidic conditions.

A large sandstone ridge also rises out of the landscape, running some 30-odd miles from north to south. Many gardens grow ericaceous-loving plants, although in some areas, the slightly acidic soil is quite clayey. But the soil is rarely too extreme to prevent the growing of a wide range of plants, both woody and herbaceous.

As one travels east and the region rises up the foothills of the Pennine range, the seasons become somewhat harsher, with spring starting a few weeks later than in the coastal region.

As well as being home to one of the RHS's major shows, the region's gardens include two National Garden Scheme 'founder' gardens in Arley Hall and Peover Hall, as well as the University of Liverpool Botanic Garden at Ness.

Below: **18 Highfield Road**

Volunteers

County Organiser
Janet Bashforth
01925 349895
jan.bashforth@ngs.org.uk

County Treasurer
Andrew Collin
01513 393614
andrewcollin@btinternet.com

Social Media
Janet Bashforth
01925 349895
jan.bashforth@ngs.org.uk

Publicity
Linda Enderby
07949 496747
linda.enderby@ngs.org.uk

Booklet Co-ordinator
John Hinde
0151 353 0032
john.hinde@maylands.com

Assistant County Organisers
Graham Beech
01625 402946
gb.ngs@talktalk.net

Sue Bryant
0161 928 3819
suewestlakebryant@btinternet.com

Jean Davies
01606 892383
mrsjeandavies@gmail.com

Sandra Fairclough
0151 342 4645
sandra.fairclough@tiscali.co.uk

Juliet Hill
01829 732804
t.hill573@btinternet.com

Romy Holmes
01829 732053
romy@bowmerecottage.co.uk

Mike Porter
01925 753488
porters@mikeandgailporter.co.uk

OPENING DATES

All entries subject to change. For latest information check **www.ngs.org.uk**

Extended openings are shown at the beginning of the month.

Map locator numbers are shown to the right of each garden name.

February

Snowdrop Festival

Sunday 18th
West Drive Gardens 79

Saturday 24th
Briarfield 13

Sunday 25th
Briarfield 13
Bucklow Farm 16

April

Sunday 1st
All Fours Farm 2

Sunday 15th
Briarfield 13

Saturday 21st
Poulton Hall 58

Sunday 22nd
Long Acre 40
Poulton Hall 58

Sunday 29th
◆ Ness Botanic Gardens 47

May

Saturday 5th
◆ Mount Pleasant 46

Sunday 6th
◆ Mount Pleasant 46

Monday 7th
All Fours Farm 2
Framley 28

Thursday 10th
◆ Cholmondeley Castle Garden 20

Saturday 12th
NEW 64 Carr Wood 18
NEW Lane End Cottage Gardens 38

Sunday 13th
◆ Abbeywood Gardens 1
NEW Lane End Cottage Gardens 38
◆ Stonyford Cottage 67
Tirley Garth Gardens 74

Wednesday 16th
◆ Tatton Park 72

Saturday 19th
Inglewood 36

Sunday 20th
Inglewood 36
Sandymere 62
NEW Stretton Old Hall 68
Tattenhall Hall 71
Tirley Garth Gardens 74

Saturday 26th
NEW Cheriton 19

Sunday 27th
NEW Cheriton 19
73 Hill Top Avenue 31
Manley Knoll 42
Rowley House 61

Monday 28th
All Fours Farm 2
Delfan 24

Wednesday 30th
Oakfield Villa 49
Wren's Nest 84

June

Festival Weekend

Saturday 2nd
Brooklands 15
NEW Mayfield 44
The Old Cottage 50
The Old Parsonage 52
◆ Peover Hall Gardens 56
10 Statham Avenue 66
The White Cottage 80

Sunday 3rd
Brooklands 15
Free Green Farm 29
NEW Mayfield 44
NEW Mill House 45
The Old Cottage 50
The Old Parsonage 52
◆ Peover Hall Gardens 56
10 Statham Avenue 66
Sycamore Cottage 70
Tirley Garth Gardens 74
The White Cottage 80

Saturday 9th
Willaston Grange 81

Sunday 10th
◆ Norton Priory Museum & Gardens 48
24 Old Greasby Road 51
Twin Gates 75

Wednesday 13th
◆ Tatton Park 72

Saturday 16th
61 Birtles Road 8
60 Kennedy Avenue 37
NEW 15 Park Crescent 54
Thorncar 73

Sunday 17th
Bucklow Farm 16
60 Kennedy Avenue 37
Long Acre 40
NEW 34 Stanley Mount 65

Saturday 23rd
Ashmead 4
150 Barrel Well Hill Chester 5
Clemley House 21
18 Highfield Road 30
The Homestead 35
Winterbottom House 82

Sunday 24th
Ashmead 4
150 Barrel Well Hill Chester 5
Bowmere Cottage 12
Burton Village Gardens 17
Clemley House 21
18 Highfield Road 30

Saturday 30th
All Fours Farm 2
◆ Bluebell Cottage Gardens 9

July

Sunday 1st
◆ Bluebell Cottage Gardens 9
Bollin House 11
218 Marple Road 43
10 Statham Avenue 66
Well House 78

Saturday 7th
Brooke Cottage 14
NEW Mayfield 44
Rowley House 61

Sunday 8th
Brooke Cottage 14
Cogshall Grange 23
NEW Mayfield 44
NEW Mill House 45
Rowley House 61

Wednesday 11th
5 Cobbs Lane 22

Saturday 14th
5 Cobbs Lane 22
8a Warwick Drive 76

Sunday 15th
NEW Stretton Old Hall 68
8a Warwick Drive 76
West Drive Gardens 79

Saturday 21st
The Birches 7
17 Poplar Grove 57

Sunday 22nd
The Birches 7
17 Poplar Grove 57

Saturday 28th
The Firs 27

Sunday 29th
The Firs 27
NEW Hilltop 33
◆ Stonyford Cottage 67
Winterbottom House 82

August

Saturday 4th
NEW Field House 26
21 Scafell Close 63

Sunday 5th
◆ Arley Hall & Gardens 3
NEW Field House 26
73 Hill Top Avenue 31
21 Scafell Close 63

Saturday 11th
Laskey Farm 39

Sunday 12th
◆ Abbeywood Gardens 1
Laskey Farm 39

Sunday 19th
Beechwood Cottage 6

THE GARDENS

1 ◆ ABBEYWOOD GARDENS

Chester Road, Delamere, Northwich, CW8 2HS. The Rowlinson Family, 01606 889477, info@abbeywoodestate.co.uk, www.abbeywoodestate.co.uk. *11m E of Chester. On the A556 facing Delamere Church.* **For NGS: Sun 13 May, Sun 12 Aug (10-5). Adm £5, chd free. Light refreshments. Restaurant in garden.** For other opening times and information, please phone, email or visit garden website.

Superb setting near Delamere Forest. Total area 45 acres incl mature woodland, new woodland and new arboretum all with connecting pathways. Approx 4½ acres of gardens surrounding large Edwardian House. Vegetable garden, exotic garden, chapel garden, pool garden, woodland garden, lawned area with beds.

2 ALL FOURS FARM

Colliers Lane, Aston by Budworth, Northwich, CW9 6NF. Mr & Mrs Evans, 01565 733286. *M6 J19, take A556 towards Northwich. Turn immed R, past The Windmill Pub. Turn R after approx 1m, follow rd, garden on L after approx 2m. We're happy to allow direct access for drop off & collection for those with limited mobility.* **Sun 1 Apr, Mon 7, Mon 28 May, Sat 30 June (10-4). Adm £5, chd free. Light refreshments. Visits also by arrangement Apr to June parties of 16+ by arrangement. Please contact Hazel.**

A traditional and well established country garden with a wide range of roses, hardy shrubs, bulbs, perennials and annuals. You will also find a small vegetable garden, pond and greenhouse as well as vintage machinery and original features from its days as a working farm. The garden is adjacent to the families traditional rose nursery. Featured in Cheshire Life Magazine The majority of the garden is accessible by wheelchair.

3 ◆ ARLEY HALL & GARDENS

Northwich, CW9 6NA. Viscount Ashbrook, www.arleyhallandgardens.com. *10m from Warrington. Signed from J9 & 10 (M56) & J19 & 20 (M6) (20 min from Tatton Park, 40 min to Manchester). Please follow the brown tourist signs.* **For NGS: Sun 5 Aug (11-5). Adm £8.50, chd £3.50. All refreshments available.** For other opening times and information, please visit garden website.

One of Britain's finest gardens, Arley has been lovingly created by the same family over 550yrs and is famous for its double herbaceous border, thought to be the oldest in Europe, avenue of ilex columns, walled garden, pleached lime avenue and Victorian Rootree. A garden of great atmosphere, interest and vitality throughout the seasons.

4 ASHMEAD

2 Bramhall Way, off Gritstone Drive, Macclesfield, SK10 3SH. Peter & Penelope McDermott, 01625 434200, penelope.mcdermott@pmsurveying.plus.com. *1m W of Macclesfield. Turn onto Pavilion Way, off Victoria Rd , then immed L onto Gritstone Drive. Bramhall Way first on R.* **Sat 23, Sun 24 June (1-5). Adm £3.50, chd free. Visits also by arrangement May to Oct groups 30 or less. Teas £2.50, adm £3.50.**

⅛ acre suburban cottage garden, featuring plant packed mixed borders, rock gardens, kitchen garden, island beds, water feature, pond. The garden demonstrates how small spaces can be planted to maximum effect to create all round interest. Extensive range of plants favoured for colours, texture and scent. Pots used in a creative way to extend and enhance borders.

5 150 BARREL WELL HILL CHESTER

Boughton, Chester, CH3 5BR. Dr & Mrs John Browne, 01244 329988, john.browne@jwbcatalyst.co.uk. *On riverside ¾m E of Chester off A5115. No parking at garden. Preferred access via Chester Boats, on the hour from the Groves, central Chester. Cost £3.50 one way. Or bus to St Pauls Church. Parking 100m at Boughton Health Centre CH2 3DP.* **Sat 23, Sun 24 June (11-5). Adm £4, chd free. Home-made teas. Visits also by arrangement Apr to Sept groups of 10+.**

Spectacular terraced garden with views over the R Dee to the Meadows and Clwyd Hills. Uniquely, preferred method of arrival is by leisurely river cruiser from Chester. Informal cottage style garden on historic site by the Martyrs Memorial. Lawns running down to the river, prolific shrub and flower beds, productive vegetable patch and soft and hard fruit areas, springs, stream and lily pond. River cruisers leave the centre of Chester regularly and arrangements have been made that they will drop off and pick up garden visitors on their way up river. Not suitable for wheelchairs or children under eight due to steps and unprotected drop into river.

6 BEECHWOOD COTTAGE

64 Crouchley Lane, Lymm, WA13 0AT. Ian & Amber Webb. *8m S of Altrincham. 4m from J7 or 2m J21 M6 onto A56 turn into Crouchley Ln past Lymm Rugby Club on R, 300yds on R (opp Crouchley Mews).* **Sun 19 Aug (11-5). Adm £5, chd free. Home-made teas, tea room undercover.**

2 acre garden looking out to fields. Large lawn with herbaceous borders. Formal walkway with rose arches, topiary garden and orchard. Wild flower meadow - shaded area with tree ferns, hellebores and ferns. The grandest chicken shed outside Highgrove. Some gravel paths.

7 THE BIRCHES

Grove Road, Mollington, Chester, CH1 6LG. Martin Bentley & Colin Williams. *Lea by Backford, nr Chester. 3m N of Chester. From the A540 Parkgate Rd turn onto Coal Pit Lane & follow around until it becomes Grove Rd. Pass riding stables on R, gardens approx ¼m further on R.* **Sat 21, Sun 22 July (12-5). Adm £5, chd free. Home-made teas in Pemberley House front garden-next door adjoining. Tea/coffee/wine and locally baked cakes-traditional cakes and modern cupcakes.**

½ acre of gardens comprising of: Front night garden of pale/white herbaceous/mixed planting. Rear split into 4 areas 1, Koi and wildlife pond with herbaceous planting 2. Grasses/shrubs and fernery 3. Orchard and meadow with hens. 4, Vegetable and fruit trees and wildlife stream. Tea and locally baked cakes-traditional and modern cupcakes. Level garden with lawn or pathways to most areas.

8 61 BIRTLES ROAD

Macclesfield, SK10 3JG. Kate & Graham Tyson. *Close to Macclesfield Leisure Centre & Macclesfield Hospital. Follow NGS signs from Priory Road & A537 junction with Whirley Lane.* **Sat 16 June (1-5); Sun 16 Sept (12-3). Adm £3, chd free. Home-made teas.**

The rear garden of this south facing semi has been developed over the past few years to include a Rose garden and well stocked herbaceous borders and island beds. This planting has been created to give year round interest and a changing colour palette, whilst the wildlife pond creates a habitat for frogs and newts. There is a variety of seating around the garden to enjoy refreshments. Wheelchairs will be able to access onto the patio only and look down onto the garden.

9 ◆ BLUEBELL COTTAGE GARDENS

Lodge Lane, Dutton, WA4 4HP. Sue & Dave Beesley, 01928 713718, info@bluebellcottage.co.uk, www.bluebellcottage.co.uk. *5m NW of Northwich. From M56 (J10) take A49 to Whitchurch. After 3m turn R at T-lights towards Runcorn/ Dutton on A533. Then 1st L. Signed with brown tourism signs from A533.* **For NGS: Sat 30 June, Sun 1 July (10-5). Adm £4, chd free. Home-made teas.** For other opening times and information, please phone, email or visit garden website.

South facing country garden wrapped around a cottage on a quiet rural lane in the heart of Cheshire. Packed with thousands of rare and familiar hardy herbaceous perennials, shrubs and trees. Unusual plants available at adjacent nursery. The opening dates coincide with the peak of flowering in the herbaceous borders. Some gravel paths. Wheelchair access to 90% of garden. WC is not fully wheelchair accessible.

10 BOLESWORTH CASTLE

Tattenhall, CH3 9HQ. Mrs Anthony Barbour, 01829 782210, dcb@bolesworth.com. *8m S of Chester on A41. Enter by Lodge on A41.* **Visits by arrangement Apr & May groups of 10+. Light Refreshments by arrangement. Adm £5, chd free.**

Rock Walk above castle with one of the finest collections of rhododendrons, camellias and acers in any private garden in the NW. Set on a steep hillside accessed by a gently rising woodland walk and overlooking spectacular view of the Cheshire plain. Formal lawns beside and below castle with well stocked shrub borders. Regret no wheelchair access.

11 BOLLIN HOUSE

Hollies Lane, Wilmslow, SK9 2BW. Angela Ferguson & Gerry Lemon, 07828 207492, fergusonang@doctors.org.uk. *From Wilmslow past Station & proceed to T-junction. Turn L onto Adlington Rd. From Wilmslow past Station & proceed to T-junction. Turn L onto Adlington Rd. After ½m turn R into Hollies Lane. Go to turning circle at end & take 2nd exit to Bollin House. Ltd parking at house. Please park at The Unicorn. After ½m turn R into Hollies Lane. Go to turning circle at end & take 2nd exit to Bollin House. Ltd parking at house. Please park at The Unicorn. Parking is possible on Adlington Rd, Browns Lane, Hollies Lane or walk from The Unicorn car park 10 mins* **Sun 1 July (10.30-4.30). Combined adm with Well House £6.50, chd free. Visits also by arrangement June & July groups 8-25. Adm £4. Tea and cake or scones £3.50. If more than 10 cars anticipated please let us know.**

There are two components to this garden, the formal garden and the wild flower meadow. The garden contains richly planted, deep, herbaceous borders with a wide plant variety. Also an orchard, wild flower area and vegetable garden. The meadow contains both cornfield annuals and perennial wild flower areas which are easily accessible with meandering mown paths. We are opening with Well House on Sun 1 July to showcase our beautiful flower meadows. Bollin House sits on a location of dreams with the garden, orchard and meadow flowing into the Bollin Valley. Here the meadow is a combination of perennial and annual wild flowers areas. Ramps to gravel lined paths to most of the garden. Some narrow paths through borders. Mown pathways in the meadow.

♿ ✽ ☕

12 BOWMERE COTTAGE

5 Bowmere Road, Tarporley, CW6 0BS. Romy & Tom Holmes, 01829 732053, romy@bowmerecottage.co.uk. *10m E of Chester. From Tarporley High St (old A49) take Eaton Rd signed Eaton. After 100 metres take R fork into Bowmere Rd, Garden 100 metres on LH-side.* **Sun 24 June (1-5). Adm £4, chd free. Home-made teas. Visits also by arrangement from mid June to mid July.**

A mature 1 acre country style garden around a Grade II listed house with well stocked mixed shrub and herbaceous borders, pergolas, two plant filled courtyard gardens and a small kitchen garden. Shrub and rambling roses, clematis, hardy geraniums and a wide and colourful range of hardy plants make this a very traditional English garden. Cobbled drive and courtyard. Tea/coffee and home made cakes.

✽ ☕

13 BRIARFIELD

The Rake, Burton, Neston, CH64 5TL. Liz Carter, 0151 336 2304, carter.burton@btinternet.com. *9m NW of Chester. Turn off A540 at Willaston-Burton Xrds T-lights & follow rd for 1m to Burton village centre.* **Sat 24, Sun 25 Feb (1-4). Adm £3, chd free. Sun 15 Apr (2-5). Adm £4, chd free. Opening with Burton Village Gardens on Sun 24 June. Visits also by arrangement Apr to Sept.**

Tucked under the S-facing side of Burton Wood the garden is home to many specialist and unusual plants, some available in plant sale. This 2 acre garden is on two sites, a couple of minutes along an unmade lane. Shrubs, colourful herbaceous, bulbs, alpines and water features compete for attention as you wander through four distinctly different gardens. Always changing, Liz can't resist a new plant! Rare and unusual plants sold (70% to NGS) in Neston Market each Friday morning.

✽ 🚌 ☕

14 BROOKE COTTAGE

Church Road, Handforth, SK9 3LT. Barry & Melanie Davy. *1m N of Wilmslow. Centre of Handforth, behind Health Centre. Turn off Wilmslow Rd at St Chads, follow Church Rd round to R. Garden last on L. Parking in Health Centre car park.* **Sat 7, Sun 8 July (12-5). Adm £4, chd free. Home-made teas.**

Garden designer's plant-filled garden surrounded by trees and shrubs. 3 distinct areas and planting styles. Woodland garden: unusual water feature, many fern varieties incl tree ferns, astrantias, hydrangeas, foxgloves, shade-loving plants. Container garden: huge variety of hostas, daylilies, dahlias, bamboos, pond. Colourful naturalistic style herbaceous borders, island beds, grasses, late flowering perennials.

✽ ☕

15 BROOKLANDS

Smithy Lane, Mouldsworth, CH3 8AR. Barbara & Brian Russell-Moore, 01928 740413, ngsmouldsworth@aol.co.uk. *1½m N of Tarvin. 5½m S of Frodsham. Smithy Lane is off B5393 via A54 Tarvin/Kelsall rd or the A56 Frodsham/Helsby rd.* **Sat 2, Sun 3 June (2-5). Adm £4, chd free. Home-made teas and cakes using eggs from our own hens. Visits also by arrangement May to Aug for groups of 10+.**

A lovely country style, ¾ acre garden with backdrop of mature trees and shrubs. The planting is based around azaleas, rhododendrons, mixed shrub and herbaceous borders. There is a small vegetable garden, supported by a greenhouse and hens providing eggs for all the afternoon tea cakes!! Repeat visitors will notice significant changes following damage and tree loss caused by 'Storm Doris.'.

♿ ✽ 🚌 ☕

Visit a garden and support hospice care in your local community

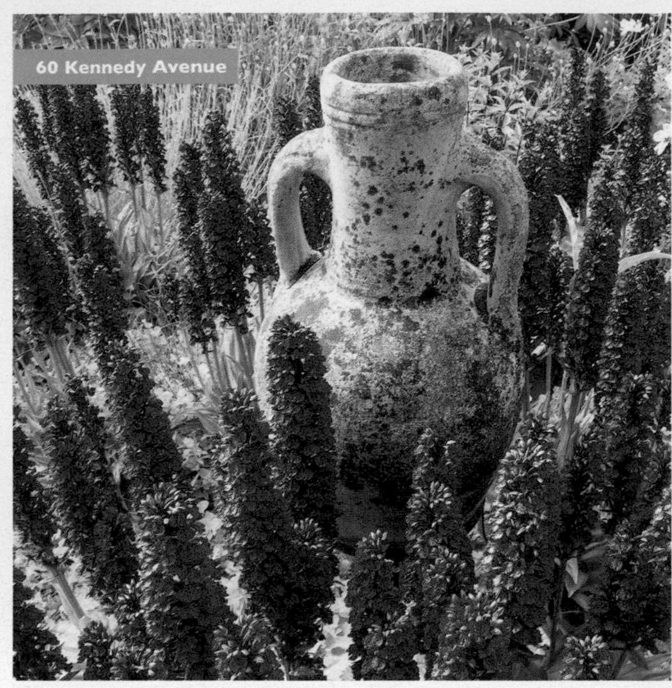
60 Kennedy Avenue

Burton is a medieval village built on sandstone overlooking the Dee estuary. Three gardens are open. Trustwood is a country wildlife garden with fruit, flowers and vegetables in raised beds at the front; at the back a more formal garden blends into the wood where the hens live. Briarfield's sheltered site, on the south side of Burton Wood (NT), is home to many specialist and unusual plants, some available in the plant sale at the house. The 1½ acre main garden invites exploration not only for its huge variety of plants but also for the imaginative use of ceramic sculptures. Period planting with a splendid vegetable garden surrounds the restored Edwardian glasshouse in Burton Manor's walled garden. Plants for sale at two gardens. Well signed free car parks. Maps available; all within easy walking distance. Briarfield is unsuitable for wheelchairs.

16 BUCKLOW FARM

Pinfold Lane, Plumley, Knutsford, WA16 9RP. Dawn & Peter Freeman. *2m S of Knutsford. M6 J19, A556 Chester. L at 2nd set of T-lights. In 1¼ m, L at concealed Xrds. 1st R. From Knutsford A5033, L at Sudlow Lane. becomes Pinfold Lane.* **Sun 25 Feb (1-3). Adm £3.50, chd free. Light refreshments. Sun 17 June (2-5). Adm £4.50, chd free. Cream teas in June, Mulled Wine in February. 2019: Sun 24 Feb.** Donation to Knutsford Methodist Church.

Country garden with shrubs, perennial borders, rambling roses, herb garden, vegetable patch, wildlife pond/water feature and alpines. Landscaped and planted over the last 30yrs with recorded changes. Free range hens. Carpet of snowdrops and spring bulbs. Leaf, stem and berries to show colour in autumn and winter. Featured in Cheshire Life. Cobbled yard from car park, but wheelchairs can be dropped off near gate.

GROUP OPENING

17 BURTON VILLAGE GARDENS

Burton, Neston, CH64 5SJ. *9m NW of Chester. Turn off A540 at Willaston-Burton Xrds T-lights & follow rd for 1m to Burton. Maps given to visitors. Buy your ticket at first garden.* **Sun 24 June (11-5). Combined adm £5, chd free. Home-made teas. In the Sports and Social Club behind the village hall.**

BRIARFIELD
Liz Carter.
(See separate entry)

◆ BURTON MANOR WALLED GARDEN
Burton Manor Gardens Ltd, 0151 3451107, www.burtonmanorgardens.org.uk.

TRUSTWOOD
Peter & Lin Friend, lin@trustwoodbnb.uk, , www.trustwoodbnb.uk.

18 NEW 64 CARR WOOD

Hale Barns, Altrincham, WA15 0EP. Mrs J.H. Booth. *10m S of Manchester city centre. 2m from J6 M56: Take A538 to Hale Barns. L at 'triangle' by church into Wicker Lane & L at mini r'about into Chapel Lane & 1st R into Carr Wood.* **Sat 12 May (2-6). Adm £4, chd free. Home-made teas.**

Two-thirds acre landscaped, S-facing garden overlooking Bollin Valley laid out in 1959 by Clibrans of Altrincham and recently restored. Gently sloping lawn, woodland walk, seating areas and terrace, extensive mixed shrub and plant borders. Partial wheelchair access and ample parking on Carr Wood. Wheelchair access to terrace overlooking main garden.

19 NEW CHERITON

34 Congleton Road, Alderley Edge, SK9 7AB. David & Jo Mottershead. *400yds S of Alderley Edge on R of A34. Park on rd.* **Sat 26, Sun 27 May (11-5). Adm £5, chd £3. Home-made teas.**

SW-facing, 1-acre garden with

views on a fine day to the Clwydian Range. Novice gardeners working in garden of mature rhododendron, magnolias and wisteria with early clematis, hellebores and a range of unusual herbaceous plants and young specimen trees' Previously open, but significant and exciting changes made. Large free-standing Wisteria. Interesting planted flowing water feature with ponds. Front garden now planted as a stunning winter garden, with white barked birches underplanted with heuchera and hellebore. Wheelchair access to rear garden only via a short flight (4) of low steps. No toilet facilities for wheelchair users.

20 ◆ CHOLMONDELEY CASTLE GARDEN

Cholmondeley, nr Malpas, SY14 8AH. Marquess of Cholmondeley, 01829 720383, dilys@cholmondeleycastle.co.uk, www.cholmondeleycastle.com. *4m NE of Malpas Sat Nav SY14 8ET. Signed from A41 Chester-Whitchurch rd & A49 Whitchurch-Tarporley rd SAT NAV SY14 8ET.* **For NGS: Thur 10 May (11-5). Adm £7, chd £4. Light lunches & home-made teas.** For other opening times and information, please phone, email or visit garden website.

Over 20 acres of romantically landscaped gardens with fine views and eye-catching water features, but still manages to retain its intimacy. Beautiful mature trees form a background to spring bulbs, exotic plants in season incl magnolias, rhododendrons, azaleas and camellias and many other, particularly *Davidia Involucrata* which will be in flower in late May. Magnificent magnolias. One of the finest features of the gardens are its trees, many of which are rare and unusual and Cholmondeley Gardens is home to over 35 county champion trees. Partial wheelchair access.

21 CLEMLEY HOUSE

Well Lane, Duddon Common, Tarporley, CW6 0HG. Sue & Tom Makin. *8m SE of Chester, 3m W of Tarporley. A51 from Chester towards Tarporley. 1m after Tarvin turn off, at bus shelter, turn L into Willington Rd. After community centre, 2nd L into Well Lane. Third house.* **Sat 23, Sun 24 June (1-5). Adm £5, chd free. Home-made teas. Home grown organic fruits used in jams & cakes. Gluten free & Vegan cakes usually available.**

2 acre organic, wildlife friendly, gold award winning cottage garden. Orchard, 3 wildlife ponds, wild flower meadow, fruit and vegetable areas, badger sett, rose pergola, gazebo, summer house, barn owl and many other nest and bat boxes. Drought tolerant gravel garden and shade garden, shepherd's hut and poly tunnel. Year round interest. 'Frogwatch' charity volunteers transport migrating amphibians to the safety of these ponds when they are found on the roads in early spring. Gravel paths may be difficult to use but most areas are flat and comprise grass paths or lawn.

22 5 COBBS LANE

Hough, Crewe, CW2 5JN. David & Linda Race. *4m S of Crewe. M6 J16 r'about take A500 towards Nantwich. At next r'about take 1st exit Keele/Nantwich (not the bypass) . Next r'about straight on Hough/ Nantwich. After 1m turn L into Cobbs Lane. From the W A51 Nantwich bypass to A500 r'about 3rd exit signed Shavington, continue 3m passing White Hart Pub, then R into Cobbs Lane. Pass No. 5, parking 300m at Village Hall, no parking on Lane* **Wed 11, Sat 14 July (11-5). Adm £5, chd free. Home-made teas at Village Hall 300m up Cobbs Lane.**

A plant person's ⅔ acre garden with island beds, wide cottage style herbaceous borders with bark paths. A large variety of hardy and some unusual perennials. Interesting features, shrubs, grasses and trees, with places to sit and enjoy the surroundings. A water feature runs to a small pond, wildlife friendly garden containing a woodland area. Finalists in Daily Mail Garden Competition. Featured in Amateur Gardening and Cheshire Life.

23 COGSHALL GRANGE

Hall Lane, Antrobus, Northwich, CW9 6BJ. Anthony & Margaret Preston. *3m NW of Northwich. Take A559 Northwich to Warrington. Turn into Wheatsheaf Lane or Well Lane. Head S on Sandiway Lane to grass triangle & then R into Hall Lane.* **Sun 8 July (11-5). Adm £6, chd free. Light refreshments.**

Set in the historic landscape of a late Georgian country house this is a contemporary garden, designed by the internationally renowned garden designer, Tom Stuart-Smith. The gardens contain a mixture of both informal and formal elements, modern herbaceous plantings, a walled garden, wild flower meadows, an orchard and woodland borders with views to parkland and the surrounding countryside.

D

24 DELFAN

Burton Road, Little Neston, Neston, CH64 4AF. Chris Sullivan. *10m NW of Chester situated between Neston & Ness Gardens. M53 J4, follow signs M56 & A5117 (signed N Wales). Turn onto A540 follow signs for Hoylake. Garden is 1m past Ness Gardens. Garden is near to Marshlands Rd. Parking at St Michael's Church.* **Mon 28 May (1-5). Adm £3.50, chd free. Light refreshments at St Michael's Church.**

The garden is surrounded by mature trees. Spring borders with camellias and rhododendrons, followed by herbaceous borders offering colour and variety of planting. The borders provide fragrance with roses climbing up obelisks. A tender plant area and fern bed sit amongst the cottage garden plants. Late summer colour is provided by echinaceas, heleniums and dahlias.

25 ◆ DUNHAM MASSEY

Altrincham, WA14 4SJ. National Trust, 0161 941 1025, dunhammassey@nationaltrust.org.uk, www.nationaltrust.org.uk/dunhammassey. *3m SW of Altrincham. Off A56; M6 exit J19; M56 exit J7. Foot: close to Trans-Pennine Trail & Bridgewater Canal. Bus: Nos 38 & 5.* For opening times and information, please phone, email or visit garden website.

Enjoy the elegance of this vibrant Edwardian garden. Richly planted borders packed with colour and texture, sweeping lawns, majestic trees and shady woodland all await your discovery. Explore the largest Winter Garden in Britain and marvel at the colourful, scent-filled Rose Garden. Water features. C18 Orangery, rare Victorian Bark House. Visitors to the garden, incl NT members, should collect ticket from Visitor Reception at Visitor Centre.

26 NEW FIELD HOUSE

Crouchley Lane, Lymm, WA13 0TQ. Emma Aspinall, emmalaspinall@gmail.com. *1m S/SE of Lymm Village. From Lymm Dam Head E along Church Rd (A56) past The Church Green pub. Take next R into Crouchley Lane for approx 1m garden on R. From M56 jct 7 follow A56 Lymm Turn L into Crouchley Lane.* **Sat 4, Sun 5 Aug (12.30-5). Adm £4, chd free. Home-made teas. Visits also by arrangement July to Sept for groups of ten+.**

An evolving garden designed and tended by local garden designer, Emma Aspinall. Set in peaceful countryside on an exposed plot extending to approx 0.4 acres together with a 1 acre paddock. Stable block with sedum roof. Well stocked herbaceous borders, vegetable/cut flower garden, fruit trees, orangery, water features and small rose/scented garden. Some gravel paths.

27 THE FIRS

Old Chester Road, Barbridge, Nantwich, CW5 6AY. Richard & Valerie Goodyear. *3m N of Nantwich on A51. After entering Barbridge turn R at Xrds after 100 metres. The Firs is 2nd house on L.* **Sat 28, Sun 29 July (1-5). Adm £4, chd free. Light refreshments.**

Canalside garden set idyllically by the Shropshire Union Canal. Approx 0.4 acre of varied trees, shrubs and herbaceous beds, with some wild areas. All leading down to an observatory at the bottom of the garden. There is wheelchair access to most of the garden.

28 FRAMLEY

Hadlow Road, Willaston, Neston, CH64 2US. Mrs Sally Reader, 07496 015259, sllyreader@yahoo.co.uk. *½m S of Willaston village centre. From Willaston Green, proceed along Hadlow Rd, crossing the Wirral Way. Framley is the next house on R.* **Mon 7 May (10.30-4). Adm £4, chd free. Light refreshments. Visits also by arrangement May to July please contact by email as early in year as possible.**

This 5 acre garden holds many hidden gems. Comprising extensive mature wooded areas, underplanted with a variety of interesting and unusual woodland plants - all at their very best in spring. A selection of deep seasonal borders surround a mystical sunken garden, planted to suit its challenging conditions. Wide lawns and sandstone paths invite you to discover what lies around every corner. Please phone ahead for parking instructions for wheelchair users - access around much of the garden although the woodland paths may be challenging.

29 FREE GREEN FARM

Free Green Lane, Lower Peover, WA16 9QX. Sir Philip Haworth. *3m S of Knutsford. Near A50 between Knutsford & Holmes Chapel. Off Free Green Lane.* **Sun 3 June (2-5.30). Adm £5, chd free. Home-made teas.**

2-acre garden with pleached limes, herbaceous borders, ponds, parterre, garden of the senses, British woodland with fernery, quasi-jungle area with Banana. Topiary. Wildlife friendly. Assortment of trees, and ten different forms of hedging. Ponds and underplanted woodland. Wheelchair access not easy in the wood.

30 18 HIGHFIELD ROAD

Bollington, Macclesfield, SK10 5LR. Mrs Melita Turner. *3m N of Macclesfield. A523 to Stockport. Turn R at B5090 r'about signed Bollington. Pass under viaduct. Take next R (by Library) up Hurst Lane. Turn R into Highfield Rd. Property on L. Park on wider road just past it.* **Sat 23, Sun 24 June (11-4). Adm £3.50, chd free. Home-made teas by East Cheshire Hospice.**

This small terraced garden packed with plants was designed by Melita and has evolved over the past 10 yrs. This plantswoman is a plantaholic and RHS Certificate holder. An attempt has been made to combine formality through structural planting with a more casual look influenced by the style of Christopher LLoyd. Steep step on to top tier at front. Steps up to higher tiers at rear.

31 73 HILL TOP AVENUE

Cheadle Hulme, Stockport, SK8 7HZ. Mrs Land, 0161 486 0055. *4m S of Stockport. Turn off A34 (new bypass) at r'about signed Cheadle Hulme (B5094). Take 2nd turn L into Gillbent Rd, signed Cheadle Hulme Sports Centre. Go to end, small r'about, turn R into Church Rd. 2nd rd on L is Hill Top Ave. From Stockport or Bramhall turn R or L into Church Rd by The Church Inn. Hill Top Ave is 1st rd on R.* **Sun 27 May, Sun 5 Aug (2-6). Adm £3.50, chd free. Tea. Visits also by arrangement May to Aug groups of 5+. Refreshments by prior arrangement.** Donation to Arthritis Research UK.

⅙ acre plantswoman's garden. Well stocked with a wide range of sun-loving herbaceous plants, shrub and climbing roses, many clematis varieties, pond and damp area, shade-loving woodland plants and some unusual trees and shrubs, in an originally designed, long narrow garden.

32 HILLSIDE COTTAGE

Shrigley Road, Pott Shrigley, SK10 5SG. Anne & Phil Geoghegan, 01625 572214, annegeoghegan@btinternet.com. *6m N of Macclesfield. From Macclesfield on A523 at Legh Arms T-lights turn R to Pott Shrigley. After approx 1½m take 3rd. L signed Higher Poynton. After 1m at Green Close Methodist Church turn R up hill to garden.* **Visits by arrangement July to Sept groups of 10+. Adm £6, chd free. Home-made teas, coffee & cakes or wine with nibbles for evening visits incl in adm**

A ¼-acre garden with panoramic views over the treetops. Packed with colourful perennials, roses, clematis, shrubs and small trees. Landscaped on several discreet levels with various places to sit and enjoy the garden incl a summerhouse, conservatory and rose covered arbour. Small walled patio with a water feature and container planting. Partial wheelchair access.

33 NEW HILLTOP

Flash Lane, Prestbury, SK10 4ED. Martin & Clare Gardner, 07768 337525, hughmartingardner@gmail.com, www.hilltopcountryhouse.co.uk. *2m N of Macclesfield. A523 to Stockport. Turn R at B5090 r'about signed Bollington, after ½m turn L at Cock & Pheasant pub into Flash Lane. At bottom of lane turn R into cul de sac. Hilltop Country House signed on R.* **Sun 29 July (1-5). Adm £5, chd free. Home-made teas. Visits also by arrangement May to Sept.**

Interesting country garden of approx 4 acres. Woodland walk, parterre, Herb garden, herbaceous borders, dry stone walled terracing, lily ponds with waterfall. Many paths, arches, gateways and steps to explore. Wisteria clad 1693 house (not open). Mature trees, orchard, magnificent views to Pennines and to West. Partial wheelchair access, disabled WC, easy parking.

34 HOME FARM HOUSE

Townfield Lane, Mollington, nr Chester, CH1 6NJ. Christine & Roger Jones, 01244 851842, chrisjones@hotmail.co.uk. *3m NW of Chester heading towards the Wirral on A540. From the A540 take turning into Mollington Village opp Crabwall Manor Hotel and follow ngs signs. Parking on road near the house is possible but car spaces are limited.* **Visits by arrangement May to July for groups of 10+. Adm £4, chd free. Light refreshments.**

C17 farm house and small walled garden provides the setting for your morning coffee or afternoon tea and cake. 2 mixed borders offer mid season colour while favourites such as established wisteria and climbing roses give a wow factor should you wish to view by arrangement earlier in the year. Gravel driveway, the garden is on two levels with steps in between. Wheelchairs have access to both levels through the use of two different entrances.

35 THE HOMESTEAD

2 Fanners Lane, High Legh, Knutsford, WA16 0RZ. Janet Bashforth. *J20 M6/J9 M56 at Lymm interchange take A50 for Knutsford, after 1m turn R into Heath Lane then 1st R into Fanners Lane. Follow parking signs.* **Sat 23 June (10-5). Adm £3.50, chd free. Home-made teas. Visits also by arrangement June to Aug groups of 10 - 20.**

Nestled in the Cheshire countryside this compact gem of a garden has been created over the last 2½ years by a keen gardener and plants woman. Enter past groups of Liquidamber and White Stemmed Birch, visit shaded nooks with their own distinctive planting. Past topiary nestled in grasses, enjoy the exuberant colours of the hot area. Greenhouse and a small pond. Further on there is a small pond with water lilies and Iris. Many types of roses and clematis adorn the fencing along the paths and into the trees.

36 INGLEWOOD

4 Birchmere, Heswall, CH60 6TN. Colin & Sandra Fairclough, www.inglewood-birchmere.blogspot.co.uk. *6m S of Birkenhead. From A540 Devon Doorway/Clegg Arms r'about go through Heswall. ¼m after Tesco, R into Quarry Rd East, 2nd L into Tower Rd North & L into Birchmere.* **Sat 19, Sun 20 May (1.30-4.30). Adm £4, chd free. Home-made teas.**

Beautiful ½ acre garden with stream, large koi pond, 'beach' with grasses, wildlife pond and bog area. Brimming with shrubs, bulbs, acers, conifers, rhododendrons, herbaceous plants and new hosta border. Interesting features including hand cart, antique mangle, wood carvings, bug hotel and Indian dog gates leading to a secret garden. Lots of seating to enjoy refreshments. Live music may be available.

37 60 KENNEDY AVENUE

Macclesfield, SK10 3DE. Bill North. *5min NW of Macclesfield Town Centre. Take A537 Cumberland St, 3rd r'bout (West Park) take B5087 Prestbury Rd. Take 5th turn on L into Kennedy Ave, last house on L before Brampton Ave opp Belong Care Home.* **Sat 16, Sun 17 June (12-5). Adm £3.50, chd free. Light refreshments, teas and cakes provided by The East Cheshire Hospice.**

Small suburban garden which featured in 2017 August edition of Amateur Gardening magazine, designed to provide Al Fresco dining and relaxed entertaining, also providing relaxing Cottage Garden tranquillity which includes display of 60 hanging baskets. A Bee Keeper's Garden. Unusually, front garden set out in Cottage Garden style. Seating. Not suitable for disabled access. Four-page feature in Amateur Gardening magazine.

38 NEW LANE END COTTAGE GARDENS

Old Cherry Lane, Lymm, WA13 0TA. Imogen & Richard Sawyer, www.laneendcottagegardens.co.uk. *1m SW of Lymm. J20 M6/J9 M56/A50 Lymm interchange. Take B5158 signed Lymm. Turn R 100 metres into Cherry Corner, turn immed R into Old Cherry Lane.* **Sat 12, Sun 13 May (10-5). Adm £4, chd free. Home-made teas.**

Formerly a nursery, this 1 acre cottage garden is densely planted for all year round colour and scent with many unusual plant varieties. Features include deep colour themed mixed borders, ponds, herb garden, walled orchard with trained fruit, shady woodland walk, sunny formal courtyard, vegetable garden and chickens. Teas served in large greenhouse. Wheelchair accessible WC.

39 LASKEY FARM

Laskey Lane, Thelwall, Warrington, WA4 2TF. Howard & Wendy Platt, 07740 804825, wendy.platt1@gmail.com, www.laskeyfarm.com. *2m From M6/M56. From M56/M6 follow directions to Lymm. At T-junction turn L onto the A56 in Warrington direction. Turn R onto Lymm Rd. Turn R onto Laskey Lane.* **Sat 11, Sun 12 Aug (11-5). Adm £5, chd free. Home-made teas. Visits also by arrangement June to Aug groups of 12+.**

1½ acre garden packed with late summer colour including herbaceous and rose borders, vegetable area, parterre and a maze showcasing grasses and prairie style planting. Interconnected pools for wildlife, fish and terrapins form an unusual water garden and there are also a greenhouse and treehouse to explore. Live music and an exhibition of the work of Lymm Artists will take place over the weekend. Exhibition of the work of Lymm Artists both days. Live music between 1pm and 4pm both days. Featured in Cheshire Life and Warrington Guardian Most areas of the garden may be accessed by wheelchair.

40 LONG ACRE

Wyche Lane, Bunbury, CW6 9PS. Margaret & Michael Bourne, 01829 260944, mjbourne249@tiscali.co.uk. *3½m SE of Tarporley. In Bunbury village, turn into Wyche Lane by Nags Head Pub car park, garden 400yds on L.* **Sun 22 Apr, Sun 17 June (2-5). Adm £5, chd free. Home-made teas. Visits also by arrangement Apr to June groups of 10+.**

61 Birtles Road

Donation to St Boniface Church Flower Fund and Bunbury Village Hall.
Plantswoman's garden of approx 1 acre with unusual and rare plants and trees including Kentucky Coffee Tree, Scadiopitys, Kalapanax Picta and others, pool garden, exotic conservatory with bananas, anthuriums and medinilla, herbaceous, greenhouses with Clivia in Spring and Disa Orchids in Summer.. Spring garden with camellias, magnolias, bulbs; roses and lilies in summer.

41 ◆ THE LOVELL QUINTA ARBORETUM

Swettenham, CW12 2LD. Tatton Garden Society, 01565 831981, admin@tattongardensociety.org.uk, www.lovellquintaarboretum.co.uk. *4m NW of Congleton. Turn off A54 N 2m W of Congleton or turn E off A535 at Twemlow Green, NE of Holmes Chapel. Follow signs to Swettenham. Park at Swettenham Arms. Do not follow Sat Nav.* **For NGS: Sun 30 Sept (1-4). Adm £5, chd free.** For other opening times and information, please phone, email or visit garden website.
The 28-acre arboretum has been established since 1960s and contains around 2,500 trees and shrubs, some very rare. Incl National Collections of Pinus and Fraxinus, large collection of oak, a collection of hebes and autumn flowering, fruiting and colouring trees and shrubs. A lake and way-marked walks. Autumn colour,winter walk and spring bulbs. Refreshments at the Swettenham Arms during licenced hours or by arrangement. Care required but wheelchairs can access much of the arboretum on the mown paths.
NPC

42 MANLEY KNOLL

Manley Road, Manley, WA6 9DX. Mr & Mrs James Timpson, 07961 202327, Jt.rowlinson@gmail.com, www.manleyknoll.com. *3m N of Tarvin. On B5393, via Ashton & Mouldsworth. 3m S of Frodsham, via Alvanley.* **Sun 27 May (12-5). Adm £5, chd free. Home-made teas. Visits also by arrangement Apr to June limited number of group visits taken each spring.**
Arts and Crafts garden created early 1900s. Covering 6 acres, divided into different rooms encompassing parterres, clipped yew hedging, ornamental ponds and herbaceous borders. Banks of rhododendron and azaleas frame a far-reaching view of the Cheshire Plain. Also a magical quarry/folly garden with waterfall and woodland walks.

43 218 MARPLE ROAD

Offerton, Stockport, SK2 5HE. Barry & Pat Hadfield. *3½m E of Stockport M60 J27 at the r'about, 5th exit A626 for Marple, follow the A626. parking on L at Offerton Sand & Gravel. Please note quarry closes at 3.45pm; Disabled drop-off only at the house.* **Sun 1 July (10-3.30). Adm £4, chd free. Home-made teas.**
This secret south-facing garden approx 1 acre, full of herbaceous plants, specimen trees, vegetable plot, plant growing area, plants for sale, topiary, unfenced ponds/water features, fun feature areas, developed from paddock to garden over 20yrs by current owners. We are trying to encourage children of all ages in this fun garden. Wheelchair access to most areas.

44 NEW MAYFIELD

Moss Lane, Bunbury Heath, Tarporley, CW6 9SY. Mrs Jeannie France Hayhurst, jeanniefh@me.com. *Moss Lane: just off Whitchurch/ Tarporley Rd (A49) and opp the main turn into the village of Bunbury (School Lane) & a yellow speed camera.* **Sat 2, Sun 3 June, Sat 7, Sun 8 July (10-4.30). Adm £5, chd free. Home-made teas. Visits also by arrangement May to Sept small groups.**
A thoroughly English mature garden with a wealth of colour and variety throughout the year. A background of fine trees, defined areas bordered by mixed hedging, masses of rhododendrons, azaleas, camellias,hydrangeas and colourful shrubs. Clematis and wisteria festoon the walls in early Summer. Easy access and random seating areas. Small lake with an island and broad lawns with glades of foxgloves. Garden statuary, little lake, swimming pool, near pretty villages and very good gastro-pubs and some beautiful gardens nearby. Cheshire Life featured a Garden Party here in 2015. Very wide wrought iron gates lead to the garden and it is entirely navigable.

45 NEW MILL HOUSE

Mill Lane, Threapwood, Malpas, SY14 7PD. Matthew Stevenson. *2m W of Malpas. From Malpas go past St Oswalds Church on B5069, follow rd to Threapwood post office/ garage turn 2nd L onto Sarn Rd. Yellow signs will be visible from this point.* **Sun 3 June, Sun 8 July (11-4). Adm £4, chd free. Home-made teas.**
A large garden set in the midst of a small holding, its split into three areas; a young meadow, an extensive vegetable garden and cottage garden. The majority of the plants have been grown from seeds and cuttings. The remains of an old orchard has provided a home for unusual and exotic plants. This is a true plantsman's garden. Teas and cakes will be available. Gravel paths and steps.

Macmillan and the National Garden Scheme, partners for more than 30 years

46 ◆ MOUNT PLEASANT
Yeld Lane, Kelsall, CW6 0TB. Dave Darlington & Louise Worthington, 01829 751592, louisedarlington@btinternet.com, www.mountpleasantgardens.co.uk. *8m E of Chester. Off A54 at T-lights into Kelsall. Turn into Yeld Lane opp Farmers Arms Pub, 200yds on L. Do not follow SatNav directions.* **For NGS: Sat 5, Sun 6 May, Sat 1, Sun 2 Sept (12-5). Adm £5, chd £2. Light refreshments.** For other opening times and information, please phone, email or visit garden website.
10 acres of landscaped garden and woodland started in 1994 with impressive views over the Cheshire countryside. Steeply terraced in places. Specimen trees, rhododendrons, azaleas, conifers, mixed and herbaceous borders; 4 ponds, formal and wildlife. Vegetable garden, stumpery with tree ferns, sculptures, wild flower meadow and Japanese garden. Bog garden, tropical garden. Sculpture trail. Sculpture Exhibition. Featured on North West Tonight. Please ring prior to visit for wheelchair access.

47 ◆ NESS BOTANIC GARDENS
Neston Road, Ness, Neston, CH64 4AY. The University of Liverpool, 0151 795 6300, nessgdns@liverpool.ac.uk, www.nessgardens.org.uk. *10m NW of Chester. Off A540. M53 J4, follow signs M56 & A5117 (signed N Wales). Turn onto A540 follow signs for Hoylake. Ness Gardens is signed locally.* **For NGS: Sun 29 Apr (10-5). Adm £7.50, chd £3.50. Light refreshments in our Café, based in our Visitor Centre.** For other opening times and information, please phone, email or visit garden website.
Looking out over the dramatic Dee Estuary from a lofty perch of the Wirral peninsula, Ness Botanic Gardens boasts 64 spectacular acres of landscaped and natural gardens overflowing with horticultural treasures. With a delightfully peaceful atmosphere, a wide array of events taking place, plus a cafe and gorgeous open spaces it's a great fun-filled day out for all. National Collection of Sorbus. Herbaceous borders, Rock Garden, Mediterranean Bank, Potager and conservation area. Mobility scooters and wheelchairs are available free to hire [donations gratefully accepted] but advance booking is highly recommended.
NPC

48 ◆ NORTON PRIORY MUSEUM & GARDENS
Tudor Road, Manor Park, Runcorn, WA7 1SX. Norton Priory Museum Trust, 01928 569895, info@nortonpriory.org, www.nortonpriory.org. *2m SE of Runcorn. If using Sat-Nav try WA7 1BD and follow the brown Norton Priory signs.* **For NGS: Sun 10 June (10-5). Adm £3.50, chd £3.50. Light refreshments at the museum.** For other opening times and information, please phone, email or visit garden website.
Beautiful 2½-acre Georgian Walled Garden, with fruit trees, herb garden, colour borders and rose walk. Home to the National Collection of Tree Quince (Cydonia Oblonga) and surrounded by historic pear orchard and wild flower meadow. Norton Priory is also home to medieval ruins and a brand new museum. Plant Hunters Fair will be held at the garden on Sunday 10 June. Garden paths are gravel but there is level access to the whole garden site.
NPC

49 OAKFIELD VILLA
Nantwich Road, Wrenbury, Nantwich, CW5 8EL. Carolyn & Jack Kennedy, 01270 781106. *6m S of Nantwich & 6m N of Whitchurch. Garden on main rd through village next to Dairy Farm. Parking in field between Oak Villas & School 1min walk to garden.* **Wed 30 May (10.30-5). Combined adm with Wren's Nest £6, chd free. Home-made teas. Visits also by arrangement June & July with refreshments £1.**
Romantic S-facing garden of densely planted borders and creative planting in containers, incl climbing roses, clematis and hydrangeas. Divided by screens into rooms, the garden incl a small fishpond and water feature. Pergola clothed in beautiful climbers provides relaxed sheltered seating area. Small front garden, mainly hydrangeas and clematis. Some gravelled areas.

50 THE OLD COTTAGE
44 High Street, Frodsham, WA6 7HE. John & Lesley Corfield, 07591 609311, corfield@rock44.plus.com. *DO NOT FOLLOW SATNAV - no parking at garden. On A56 close to Frodsham town centre. Follow signs from town centre to railway car park, garden signed from there (short walk). Or park in town centre and follow signs uphill N to cottage.* **Sat 2, Sun 3 June (1-6). Adm £5, chd free. Home-made teas. Visits also by arrangement June to Aug for groups of 6+.**
At the rear of the Grade II listed C16 cottage (not open) are ⅔ acre, organic and wildlife friendly garden featuring many aspects that support various forms of wildlife. Steps lead up to a large vegetable and herb garden, with further mixed planting in herbaceous borders. Wildlife pond and bog garden. Further areas of fruit trees and shady woodland borders. Extensive views over Mersey estuary. Numerous plants and trees found in the fossil records. Partial wheelchair access - please ring for details.

51 24 OLD GREASBY ROAD
Upton, Wirral, CH49 6LT. Lesley Whorton & Jon Price. *Approx 1m from J2A on M53 (Upton Bypass). M53 J2; follow Upton sign. At r'about (J2A) straight on to Upton Bypass. At 2nd r'about, turn L by Upton Cricket Club. 24 Old Greasby Rd on L.* **Sun 10 June (11-4). Adm £3.50, chd free. Home-made teas.**
A multi-interest and surprising suburban garden. Both front and rear gardens incorporate innovative features designed for climbing and rambling roses, clematis, under-planted with cottage garden plants

with a very productive kitchen garden. Unfortunately, due to narrow access and gravel paths, there is no wheelchair access.

52 THE OLD PARSONAGE

Arley Green, Northwich, CW9 6LZ. The Viscount & Viscountess Ashbrook, 01565 777277, ashbrook@arleyhallandgardens.com, www.arleyhallandgardens.com. *5m NNE of Northwich. 3m NNE of Great Budworth. M6 J19 & 20 & M56 J10. Follow signs to Arley Hall & Gardens. From Arley Hall notices to Old Parsonage which lies across park at Arley Green (approx 1m).* **Sat 2, Sun 3 June (2-5.30). Adm £5, chd free. Visits also by arrangement May & June for 10+. Refreshments available at Gardener's Kitchen, Arley Hall.** Donation to Save The Children Fund (2 & 3 June only).

2-acre garden in attractive and secretive rural setting in secluded part of Arley Estate, with ancient yew hedges, herbaceous and mixed borders, shrub roses, climbers, leading to woodland garden and unfenced pond with gunnera and water plants. Rhododendrons, azaleas, meconopsis, cardiocrinum, some interesting and unusual trees. Wheelchair access over mown grass, but some slopes and bumps and rougher grass further away from the house.

53 39 OSBORNE STREET

Bredbury, Stockport, SK6 2DA. Geoff & Heather Hoyle, www.youtube.com/user/Dahliaholic. *1½m E of Stockport, just off B6104. Follow signs for Lower Bredbury/Bredbury Hall. Leave M60 J27 (from S & W) or J25 (from N & E). Osborne St is adjacent to pelican crossing on B6104.* **Sat 8, Sun 9 Sept (1-5). Adm £4, chd free. Light refreshments, teas, coffees, and cakes.**

This dahliaholic's garden contains over 350 dahlias in 150+ varieties, many of exhibition standard. Shapely lawns are surrounded by deep flower beds that are crammed with dahlias of all shapes, sizes and colours, and complemented by climbers, soft perennials and bedding plants. An absolute riot of early autumn colour. The garden comprises two separate areas, both crammed with very colourful flowers. The dahlias range in height from 18 inches to 8 feet tall, and are in a wide variety of shapes and colours. They are interspersed with salvias, fuchsias, argyranthemums, and bedding plants. The garden is on YouTube: search for Dahliaholic.

54 NEW 15 PARK CRESCENT

Appleton, Warrington, WA4 5JJ. Linda & Mark Enderby, 07949 496 747, lmaenderby@outlook.com. *2½m S of Warrington. From M56 J10 take A49 towards Warrington for 1½m. At 2nd set of lights turn R into Lyons Lane , then 1st R into Park Crescent. No.15 is last house on R.* **Sat 16 June (12.30-4.30). Combined adm with Thorncar £6, chd free. Prosecco available by donation. Visits also by arrangement June to Aug for groups of 10+.**

An abundant garden containing many unusual plants, trees and a mini orchard. A waterfall, ponds and planting encourage wildlife. There are also vegetable and herb plots and many roses in various forms. The garden has been split into different areas, each with their own vista drawing one through the garden. A Chinese model railway will also be on show. Look out for the Seven Dwarves on your visit!

Your visit helps Marie Curie work night and day in people's homes

55 PARM PLACE

High Street, Great Budworth, CW9 6HF. Peter & Jane Fairclough, 01606 891131, janefair@btinternet.com. *3m N of Northwich. Great Budworth on E side of A559 between Northwich & Warrington, 4m from J10 M56, also 4m from J19 M6. Parm Place is W of village on S side of High St.* **Visits by arrangement Mar to Aug between 10 and 40. Tea/coffee and biscuits provided for donation. Adm £4, chd free.** Donation to Great Ormond Street Hospital.

Well-stocked ½ acre plantswoman's garden with stunning views towards S Cheshire. Curving lawns, parterre, shrubs, colour co-ordinated herbaceous borders, roses, water features, rockery, gravel bed with some grasses. Fruit and vegetable plots. In spring large collection of bulbs and flowers, camellias, hellebores and blossom.

56 ◆ PEOVER HALL GARDENS

Over Peover, Knutsford, WA16 9HW. Randle Brooks, 07443 429756, bookings@peoverhall.com, www.peoverhall.com. *4m S of Knutsford. Please do not rely on SATNAV after the A50. A50/Holmes Chapel Rd/Whipping Stocks PH turn onto Stocks Lane. Approx 0.9m turn onto Grotto Lane. ¼m turn onto Goostrey Lane. Main entrance on bend.* **For NGS: Sat 2, Sun 3 June (2-5). Adm £5, chd free. Hot drinks and cake available in the Park House tea room.** For other opening times and information, please phone, email or visit garden website.

The gardens to Peover Hall are set in 15 acres and feature five walled gardens or 'garden rooms' filled with clipped box, topiary, roses, lily pond, kitchen garden, Romanesque loggia, C19 dell and rockery, rhododendrons and pleached limes. There are Grade I listed Carolean Stables which are of significant architectural importance. Partial wheelchair access to garden.

57 17 POPLAR GROVE

Sale, M33 3AX. Mr Gordon Cooke, www.gordoncooke.co.uk. *3m N of Altrincham. From the A6144 at Brooklands Stn turn into Hope Rd. Poplar Grove 3rd on R.* **Sat 21, Sun 22 July (2-5). Adm £3.50, chd free. Home-made teas.**

This S-facing suburban garden is on many levels. Its strongly diagonal design features a pebble mosaic 'cave', topiary, sculpture garden, living roof and exotic planting. A mix of formality and dense planting in the contemporary 'English' style. Reopening this year after a break to make changes which include a viewing platform and bug hotel screen with ceramic lights. Exhibition of Garden Ceramics. The garden is not suitable for wheel chairs.

58 POULTON HALL

Poulton Lancelyn, Bebington, CH63 9LN. The Lancelyn Green Family, www.poultonhall.co.uk. *2m S of Bebington. From M53, J4 towards Bebington; at T-lights R along Poulton Rd; house 1m on R.* **Sat 21, Sun 22 Apr (1.30-4.30). Adm £5, chd free. Home-made teas.**

3 acres; lawns fronting house, wild flower meadow. Surprise approach to walled garden, with reminders of Roger Lancelyn Green's retellings, Excalibur, Robin Hood and Jabberwocky. Scented sundial garden for the visually impaired. Memorial sculpture for Richard Lancelyn Green by Sue Sharples. Rose, nursery rhyme, witch, herb and oriental gardens and new Memories Reading room. There are often choirs or orchestral music in the garden. Level gravel paths. Separate wheelchair access (not across parking field).

♿ ✲ ☕

59 ◆ RODE HALL

Church Lane, Scholar Green, ST7 3QP. Randle & Amanda Baker Wilbraham, 01270 873237, enquiries@rodehall.co.uk, www.rodehall.co.uk. *5m SW of Congleton. Between Scholar Green (A34) & Rode Heath (A50).* For opening times and information, please phone, email or visit garden website.

Nesfield's terrace and rose garden with view over Humphry Repton's landscape is a feature of Rode, as is the woodland garden with terraced rock garden and grotto. Other attractions incl the walk to the lake with a view of Birthday Island complete with heronry, restored ice house, working 2 acre walled kitchen garden and Italian garden. Fine display of snowdrops in Feb and Bluebells in May. Snowdrop Walks: 3 Feb - 4 March, 11-4 pm Tues - Sat (Closed Mons). Bluebell Walks: 28 Apr - 7 May. Summer: Weds and Bank Hol Mons, 11-5. Stables Tearooms offering wide variety of homemade cakes and light refreshments. Partial wheelchair access, some steep areas with gravel and woodchip paths, access to WC, kitchen garden and tearooms.

🐕 ✲ 🚌 ☕

60 ROSEWOOD

Old Hall Lane, Puddington, Neston, CH64 5SP. Mr & Mrs C E J Brabin, 0151 353 1193, angela.brabin@btinternet.com. *8m N of Chester. From A540 turn down Puddington Lane, 1½m. Park by village green. Walk 30yds to Old Hall Lane, turn L through archway into garden.* **Visits by arrangement individuals, medium or large groups. Adm £3, chd free. Tea.**

All yr garden; thousands of snowdrops in Feb, Camellias in autumn, winter and spring. Rhododendrons in April/May and unusual flowering trees from March to June. Autumn Cyclamen in quantity from Aug to Nov. Perhaps the greatest delight to owners is a large Cornus capitata, flowering in June. Bees kept in the garden. Honey sometimes available.

♿ ✲ 🚌 ☕

61 ROWLEY HOUSE

Forty Acre Lane, Kermincham, Holmes Chapel, CW4 8DX. Tim & Juliet Foden. *3m ENE from Holmes Chapel. J18 M6 to Holmes Chapel, from Holmes Chapel take A535 (Macclesfield). Take R turn at Twemlow (Swettenham) at Yellow Broom restaurant. Rowley House ½m on L.* **Sun 27 May, Sat 7, Sun 8 July (1.30-4.30). Adm £5, chd free. Home-made teas and cakes.**

Our aim is to give nature a home and create a place of beauty. There is a formal courtyard garden and informal gardens featuring rare trees, and herbaceous borders, a pond with swamp cypress and woodland walk with maples, rhododendrons, ferns and shade-loving plants. Beyond the garden there are wild flower meadows, natural ponds and a wood with ancient oaks. There are also wood sculptures.

🐕 ☕

62 SANDYMERE

Middlewich Road, Cotebrook, CW6 9EH. John Timpson. *5m N of Tarporley. On A54 approx 300yds W of T-lights at Xrds of A49/A54.* **Sun 20 May (12-5). Adm £6, chd free. Home-made teas.**

16 landscaped acres of beautiful Cheshire countryside with terraces, walled garden, extensive woodland walks and an amazing hosta garden. Turn each corner and you find another gem with lots of different water features including a new rill built in 2014, which links the main lawn to the hostas. Partial wheelchair access.

♿ ✲ 🚌 ☕

63 21 SCAFELL CLOSE

High Lane, Stockport, SK6 8JA. Lesley & Dean Stafford, 01663 763015, lesley.stafford@live.co.uk. *High Lane is on A6 SE of Stockport towards Buxton. From A6 take Russell Ave then Kirkfell Drive. Scafell Close on R.* **Sat 4, Sun 5 Aug (1-4.30). Adm £3, chd free. Light refreshments, tea/coffee and cakes. Visits also by arrangement July & Aug one group per day, wander round at your leisure.**

⅓ acre landscaped suburban garden. Colour themed annuals border the lawn featuring the

Kinder Ram statue in a heather garden, passing into vegetables, soft fruits and fruit trees. Returning perennial pathway leads to the fishpond and secret terraced garden with modern water feature and patio planting. Finally visit the blue front garden. Interview appeared on BBC Radio Manchester with a video on Facebook. Partial wheelchair access.

64 68 SOUTH OAK LANE

Wilmslow, SK9 6AT. Caroline Melliar-Smith, 01625 528147, caroline.ms@btinternet.com. *¾m SW of Wilmslow. From M56 (J6) take A538 (Wilmslow) R into Buckingham Rd. From centre of Wilmslow turn R onto B5086 , 1st R into Gravel Lane, 4th R into South Oak Lane.* **Visits by arrangement June & July max group 20. Adm £4, chd free.**

With year-round colour, scent and interest, this attractive, narrow, hedged cottage garden has evolved over the years into 5 natural 'rooms'. These Hardy Plant Society members passion for plants, is reflected in the variety of shrubs, trees, flower borders and pond, creating havens for wildlife. Share this garden with its' varied history from the 1890's. Some rare and unusual hardy, herbaceous and shade loving plants and shrubs.

65 NEW 34 STANLEY MOUNT

Sale, M33 4AE. Debbie &Steve Bedford. *1m from J7 M60 heading S on A56 (Washway Rd.) towards Altrincham. From A56 Altrincham N towards Sale (Washway Rd) Turning for Stanley Mount off Washway Rd, no.34 on R.* **Sun 17 June (1-5). Adm £4, chd free. Home-made teas.**

Informal small suburban garden designed and created from scratch. Mature trees, hedges, shrubs and climbers provide the framework. Colour and contrasting foliage are key. Planted areas feature herbaceous perennials, grasses bulbs, clematis, hostas, ferns and groundcover. Seated areas, creative pots, productive greenhouse, cacti, alpines and a shed hotel.

66 10 STATHAM AVENUE

Lymm, WA13 9NH. Mike & Gail Porter, 01925 753488, porters@mikeandgailporter.co.uk. *Approx 1m from J20 M6 /M56 interchange. Follow B5158 signed Lymm. Take A56 Booth's Hill Rd, towards Warrington, turn R on to Barsbank Lane, after passing under the Bridgewater canal turn R (50m) onto Statham Ave. No 10 is 100 metres on R.* **Sat 2, Sun 3 June, Sun 1 July (12-5). Adm £4.50, chd free. Home-made teas. Enjoy home made cakes or try Gail's famous meringues with fresh fruit and cream. Visits also by arrangement May to July for groups of 10+.**

Peaceful, pastel shades in early summer. Beautifully structured ¼ acre south facing garden carefully terraced and planted as it rises to the Bridgewater towpath. Hazel arch opens to clay paved courtyard with peach trees. Rose pillars lead to varied herbaceous beds and quiet shaded areas bordered by fuchsias, azaleas and rhododendrons. Wide variety of plants. Interesting garden buildings. A treasure hunt and quiz to keep the children occupied. Featured in Amateur Gardening. Short gravel driveway and some steps to access the rear garden. The rear garden is sloping.

67 ◆ STONYFORD COTTAGE

Stonyford Lane, Oakmere, CW8 2TF. Janet & Tony Overland, 01606 888970, info@stonyfordcottagegardens.co.uk, www.stonyfordcottagegardens.co.uk. *5m SW of Northwich. From Northwich take A556 towards Chester. ¾m past A49 junction turn R into Stonyford Lane. Entrance ½m on L.* **For NGS: Sun 13 May, Sun 29 July (11-4). Adm £4.50, chd free. Lunches and cream teas available.** For other opening times and information, please phone, email or visit garden website.

Set around a tranquil pool this Monet style landscape has a wealth of moisture loving plants, incl iris and candelabra primulas. Drier areas feature unusual perennials and rarer trees and shrubs. Woodland paths meander through shade and bog plantings, along boarded walks, across wild natural areas with views over the pool to the cottage gardens. Unusual plants available at the adjacent nursery. Open Tues - Sun & BH Mons Apr - Oct 10-5pm. Cottage Tea Room. Plant Nursery. Some gravel paths.

15 Park Crescent

24 Old Greasby Road

68 NEW STRETTON OLD HALL

Stretton, Tilston, Malpas, SY14 7JA. Stephen Gore Head Gardener, 07800 602225, stegore244@hotmail.com. *5m N of Malpas. From Chester follow A41, Broxton r'about follow signs for Stretton Water Mill, turn L at Cock o Barton. 2m on L.* **Sun 20 May, Sun 15 July (11-5). Adm £6, chd free. Home-made teas. Visits also by arrangement Apr to Oct.**

5 acre Cheshire countryside garden with a planting style best described as controlled exuberance with a definite emphasis upon perennials, colour, form and scale. Divided into several discrete and individual gardens incl stunning herbaceous borders, scree garden, walled kitchen garden and glass house. Wild flower meadows, wildlife walk around the lake with breathtaking vistas in every direction. Gravel paths.

♿ 🐕 ☕

69 SUNNYSIDE FARM

Shop Lane, Little Budworth, CW6 9HA. Mike & Joan Smeethe, 01829 760618, joan.ann.smeethe@btinternet.com. *4m NE of Tarporley. On A54 1m E of T-lights at A54/A49 junction. Turn off A54 into Shop Lane opp Shrewsbury Arms Pub. After 30yds take farm track on R & continue to end. Parking at house.* **Visits by arrangement June to Aug. Adm £5, chd free. Home made teas available by arrangement.**

A plant lover's and beekeeper's atmospheric country garden. Wildlife and child friendly the five acres encompass oak woodland, wildflower meadow, pool garden, potager and fruit garden, orchard with beehives, long border with naturalistic planting and cottage garden. With a wealth of unusual plants and interesting colour schemes this is a constantly evolving garden. Always something new. Wheelchair access to most parts of the garden.

♿ 🐕 ✿ ☕

70 SYCAMORE COTTAGE

Manchester Road, Carrington, Manchester, M31 4AY. Mrs C Newton. *From M60 J8 take Carrington turn (A6144) through 2 sets of T-lights. Garden approx 1m after 2nd set of T-lights on R. From M6 J20 signed for Partington/Carrington garden approx 1m on L.* **Sun 3 June (12-5). Adm £4, chd free. Light refreshments.**

Approx ⅕ acre cottage garden split into distinct areas, arches covered with rambling roses, colourful herbaceous borders, and a woodland area planted to encourage birds and wildlife. There is a natural spring, well, and ponds. There are plenty of seating areas to sit and enjoy this very pretty garden. Featured in an TV advert for Cuprinol paints used on the decking areas.

71 TATTENHALL HALL

High Street, Tattenhall, CH3 9PX. Jen & Nick Benefield, Chris Evered & Jannie Hollins, 01829 770654, janniehollins@gmail.com. *8m S of Chester on A41. Turn L to Tattenhall, through village, turn R at Letters Pub, past war memorial on L through Sandstone pillared gates. Park on rd or in village car park.* **Sun 20 May (2-5.30). Adm £5, chd free. Home-made teas. Visits also by arrangement Mar to Oct any size of group, limited parking facilities.**

Plant enthusiasts garden around Jacobean house (not open). 4½ acres, wild flower meadows, interesting trees, large pond, stream, walled garden, colour themed borders, succession planting, spinney walk with shade plants, yew terrace overlooking meadow, views to hills. Glasshouse and vegetable garden. Wildlife friendly sometimes untidy garden, interest throughout the year, continuing to develop. Articles in online magazine, Gardenista. Wheelchair access is difficult because of gravel paths, cobbles and some steps.

♿ 🐕 ✿ ☕

72 ◆ TATTON PARK

Knutsford, WA16 6QN. National Trust, leased to Cheshire East Council, 01625 374400, tatton@cheshireeast.gov.uk, www.tattonpark.org.uk. *2½m N of Knutsford. Well signed on M56 J7 & from M6 J19.* **For NGS: Wed 16 May, Wed 13 June (10-6). Adm £7, chd £5.** For other opening times and information, please phone, email or visit garden website.

Features incl orangery by Wyatt, fernery by Paxton, restored Japanese garden, Italian and rose gardens. Greek monument and African hut. Hybrid azaleas and rhododendrons; swamp cypresses, tree ferns, tall redwoods, bamboos and pines. Fully restored productive walled gardens. Wheelchair access apart from rose garden and Japanese garden.

73 THORNCAR

Windmill Lane, Appleton, Warrington, WA4 5JN. Mrs Kath Carey, 01925 267633, john.carey516@btinternet.com. *South Warrington. From M56 J10 take A49 towards Warrington for 1½m. At 2nd set of T-lights turn L into Quarry Lane, as the rd swings R it becomes Windmill Lane. Thorncar is 4th house on R.* **Sat 16 June (12.30-4.30). Combined adm with 15 Park Crescent £6, chd free. Light refreshments provided by WI. Visits also by arrangement Mar to Sept groups between 5 and 25.**

One third acre plantwoman's suburban garden planted since 2011 within the framework of part of an established garden. It is planted to give some colour 12 months of the year and to require no watering even in dry spells. Peonies are a passion of the owner and are at their best in June.

74 TIRLEY GARTH GARDENS

Mallows Way, Willington, Tarporley, CW6 0RQ. Tirley Garth. *2m N of Tarporley. 2m S of Kelsall. Entrance 500yds from village of Utkinton. At N of Tarporley take Utkinton rd.* **Sun 13, Sun 20 May, Sun 3 June (1-5). Adm £5, chd free. Home-made teas.**

40-acre garden, terraced and landscaped, designed by Thomas Mawson (considered the leading exponent of garden design in early C20), it is the only Grade II* Arts and Crafts garden in Cheshire that remains complete and in excellent condition. The gardens are an important example of an early C20 garden laid out in both formal and informal styles. By early May the garden is bursting into flower with almost 3000 Rhododendron and Azalea many 100 years old. Art Exhibition by local Artists. Wheelchair access to tea rooms, but limited in areas of gardens.

75 TWIN GATES

3 Earle Drive, Parkgate, Neston, CH64 6RY. John Hinde & Lilian Baker. *Approx ½m N of Neston town centre. From Neston (Tesco/ Brown Horse PH), N towards Methodist Church. At church (Brewers Arms on L), take L fork into Park St, becomes Leighton Rd. Continue for approx ½m, L into Earle Drive.* **Sun 10 June (1.30-5). Adm £4, chd free. Home-made teas.**

Garden developed over last 4 to 5 years and now looking mature. Mixed herbaceous and shrub borders, with some choice small trees all set in fully stocked sinuous borders. In June, peaonies and roses come to the fore, but there are plenty of other genus, too. Featured in Cheshire Life.

76 8A WARWICK DRIVE

Hale, Altrincham, WA15 9EA. Gill & Chris Turner, 01619 803258, gillandchris_turner@hotmail.com. *M56 J6, take A538 to Altrincham. Turn L at 2nd T-lights into Park Rd. Take 2nd R into Bower Rd & turn L immed into Warwick Drive. Garden is 200yds on L, on corner of Lindop Rd.* **Sat 14, Sun 15 July (2-5). Adm £4, chd free. Home-made teas. Visits also by arrangement June to Aug 10-30.**

We're here again but with a difference! Focusing on the rear garden in 2017, we had extensive tree work which changed the side and back borders, letting the sunlight in and increasing the potential for growth. Much new planting followed with pleasing results. The highlight in July is still the front herbaceous border, designed by a plantaholic flower arranger to provide glorious colour from Apr-Oct. Featured in Cheshire Life, Top 10 Secret Gardens of Cheshire.

77 THE WELL HOUSE

Wet Lane, Tilston, Malpas, SY14 7DP. Mrs S H French-Greenslade, 01829 250332. *3m NW of Malpas. On A41, 1st R after Broxton r'about, L on Malpas Rd through Tilston. House on L.* **Visits by arrangement Feb to Oct not open Aug. Open Feb for snowdrops. Adm £5, chd free. Pre-booked refreshments for small groups only..**

1-acre cottage garden, bridge over natural stream, spring bulbs, perennials, herbs and shrubs. Triple ponds. Adjoining ¾-acre field made into wild flower meadow; first seeding late 2003. Large bog area of kingcups and ragged robin. February for snowdrop walk. Not suitable for wheelchairs. Dogs on leads only.

78 WELL HOUSE

Dean Row Road, Wilmslow, SK9 2BU. Steven & Jill Kimber. *2m N of Wilmslow. On Dean Row Rd (B 5358), at junction with Adlington Rd (A5102). Park at the Unicorn Pub 300yds, from the house. Next to Shell garage. Less able visitors can drop off at house limited space.* **Sun 1 July (10.30-4.30). Combined adm with Bollin House £6.50, chd free. Home-made teas.**

This maturing 3 acre garden, tended with a gentle hand offers; shady woodland, formal borders, with lush herbaceous planting & wild flower areas. Both naturalised and planted the wild flowers are managed, cultivated and encouraged wherever possible. The meadow which now boasts many wild orchids is a particular joy, visit us alone or see group opening details. For those with special interest in Meadows we have teamed up with Bollin House a 10min walk away. Both gardens are passionate about their wild flower meadows and for those with a particular interest in sowing cultivation management of these precious spaces. Less then ½m apart the 2 gardens showcase very different styles. Wheelchair access through the main gate.

GROUP OPENING

79 WEST DRIVE GARDENS

6, 9 West Drive, Gatley, Cheadle, SK8 4JJ. Mr & Mrs D J Gane, Thelma Bishop & John Needham, 01614 280204, Davidjgane@btinternet.com. *4m N of Wilmslow on B5166. 4 m N of Wilmslow on B5166. From J5 (M56) drive past airpt. to B5166 (Styal Rd).L to Gatley. Go over T-lights at Heald Green. West Drive is last turn on R before Gatley(approx. 1½m from T-lights).* **Sun 18 Feb (1-3). Combined adm £3, chd free. Light refreshments. Sun 15 July (11-5). Combined adm £5, chd free. Home-made teas and WC at No 6. Visits also by arrangement Feb to Aug.**

Cul-de-sac, do not park beyond notice. Here are two gardens of very different character, reflecting their owner's gardening style. Although suburban , they are surrounded by mature trees and have a secluded feel. Rich variety of planting incl. ferns, hostas and herbaceous borders. with clematis,roses,phlox, astrantia at their best. Wild life pond at no.6 and other water features. Ceramics and containers with alpines complete the picture. Home-made teas, no.6. Opening in February for displays of hellebores and snowdrops. Access to top of gardens giving general overview, with shallow step leading onto gravel at no.6 and several steps and narrow paths at no.9.

The National Garden Scheme and Perennial, helping gardeners when they are in need

80 THE WHITE COTTAGE

Threapwood, Malpas, Cheshire, SY14 7AL. Chris & Carol Bennion, chrisbennion@btinternet.com. *3m W of Malpas. From Malpas take Wrexham Road B5069 W for 3m. From Bangor on Dee take B5069 E to Threapwood. Car Park signed off B5069.* **Sat 2, Sun 3 June (1-5). Adm £4, chd free. Light refreshments. Visits also by arrangement May & June for groups of 10-30.**

Behind a long beech hedge lies an interesting and relaxing country garden, featured in Cheshire Life, containing mature trees, shrubs, topiary, statuary and meandering herbaceous borders brimming with soft romantic planting. A formal area near the cottage is a delightful place to sit and relax. The orchard contains fruit trees, raised beds and borders. Lovely views across lush meadows. Many interesting features including a dovecote, pergola and horseshoe garden. Some steps around the cottage.

81 WILLASTON GRANGE

Hadlow Road, Willaston, Neston, CH64 2UN. Mr & Mrs M Mitchell. *Willaston. On the A540 (Chester High Rd) take the B5151 into Willaston. From the Village Green in the centre of Willaston turn onto Hadlow Rd, Willaston Grange is ½m on your L.* **Sat 9 June (11-4.30). Adm £5, chd free. Home-made teas.**

Willaston Grange returns after opening for the first time last year. The gardens extend to almost 6 acres with a small lake, wide range of mature and rare trees, herbaceous borders, woodland and vegetable gardens, orchard and magical tree house. The fully restored Arts and Crafts house provides the perfect backdrop, along with afternoon tea and live music. Most areas accessible by wheelchair.

82 WINTERBOTTOM HOUSE

Winterbottom Lane, Mere, Knutsford, WA16 0QQ. Neil & Verona Stott, thestotts@btinternet.com. *Half way between Mere T-lights & High Legh. Signed off A50. From A50 opp Kilton Inn turn into Hoo Green Lane, in ½m bear L down Winterbottom Lane (narrow lane - take care!). Winterbottom House at end . Follow signs for ample parking with wheelchair access.* **Evening opening Sat 23 June (5.30-9). Adm £10, chd free. Wine. Sun 29 July (1-5). Adm £5, chd free. Home-made teas, wine and light bites incl on 23 June. There will be a Jazz band in the garden. Delicious home made cakes on 29 July!. Visits also by arrangement May to Aug.**

We have gradually started to develop more of the areas of the garden over the last 40 years. A small duck pond is now a large pool filled with many interesting koi. The trees were all planted as saplings and are now fully mature. This contrasts with the much more formal areas round the house, which includes a sunken garden with box parterre, a water feature and many interesting statuary. The area includes a period summer house, ornamental rill and extensive lawns with plenty of seating areas. Home made cakes and teas. Some gravel paths but no steps.

83 WOOD END COTTAGE

Grange Lane, Whitegate, Northwich, CW8 2BQ. Mr & Mrs M R Everett, 01606 888236, woodendct@supanet.com. *4m SW of Northwich. Turn S off A556 (Northwich bypass) at Sandiway T-lights; after 1¾m, turn L to Whitegate village; opp school follow Grange Lane for 300yds.* **Visits by arrangement May to July. Adm £4.50, chd free. Home-made teas.**

Plantsman's ½ acre garden in attractive setting, sloping to a natural stream bordered by shade and moisture-loving plants. Background of mature trees. Well stocked herbaceous borders, trellis with roses and clematis, magnificent delphiniums, many phlox, meconopsis and choice perennials. Interesting shrubs and flowering trees. Vegetable garden.

84 WREN'S NEST

Wrenbury Heath Road, Wrenbury, Nantwich, CW5 8EQ. Sue & Dave Clarke, 07855 398803, wrenburysue@gmail.com. *12m from M6 J16. From Nantwich signs for A530 to Whitchurch, reaching Sound school turn 1st R Wrenbury Heath Rd, across the Xrds & bungalow is on L, telegraph pole right outside.* **Wed 30 May (10.30-5). Combined adm with Oakfield Villa £6, chd free. Visits also by arrangement May to Aug phone or email. Refreshments on request.**

Set in a semi-rural area, this bungalow has a Cottage Garden Style of lush planting and is 80ft x 45ft. The garden is packed with unusual and traditional perennials and shrubs incl over 100 hardy geraniums, campanulas, crocosmias, iris and alpine troughs. Plants for sale. Proceeds from this garden will be for the NGS. National collection of Hardy Geranium sylvaticum and renardii. Plant Heritage National Collection of Hardy Geraniums.

NPC

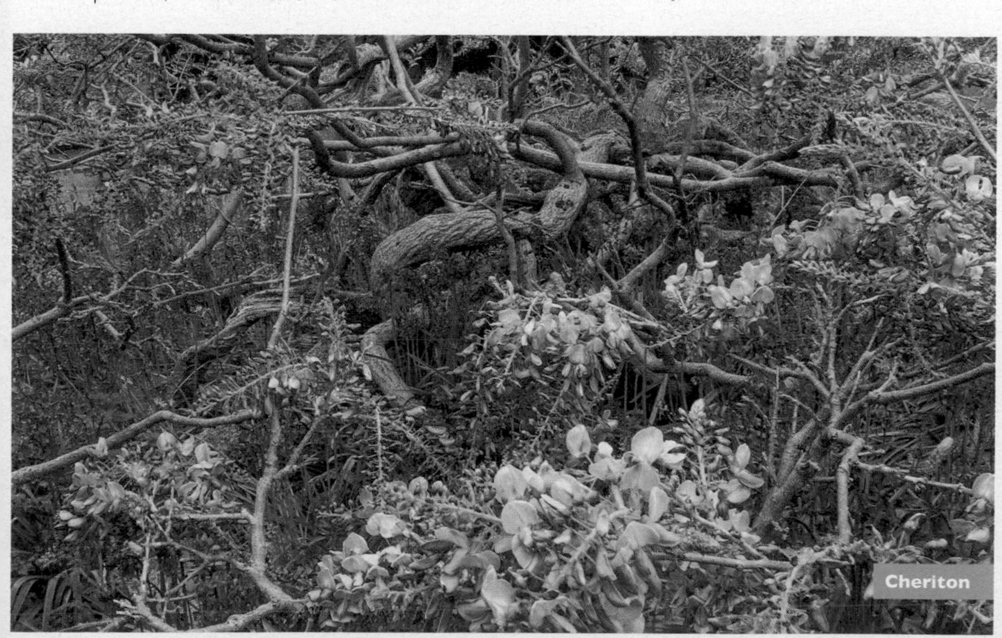
Cheriton

CORNWALL

ISLES OF SCILLY

Tresco
St Martin's
Bryher
Hugh Town
St Mary's
St Agnes

The Isles of Scilly lie about 28 miles or 45 kilometres south west of Land's End

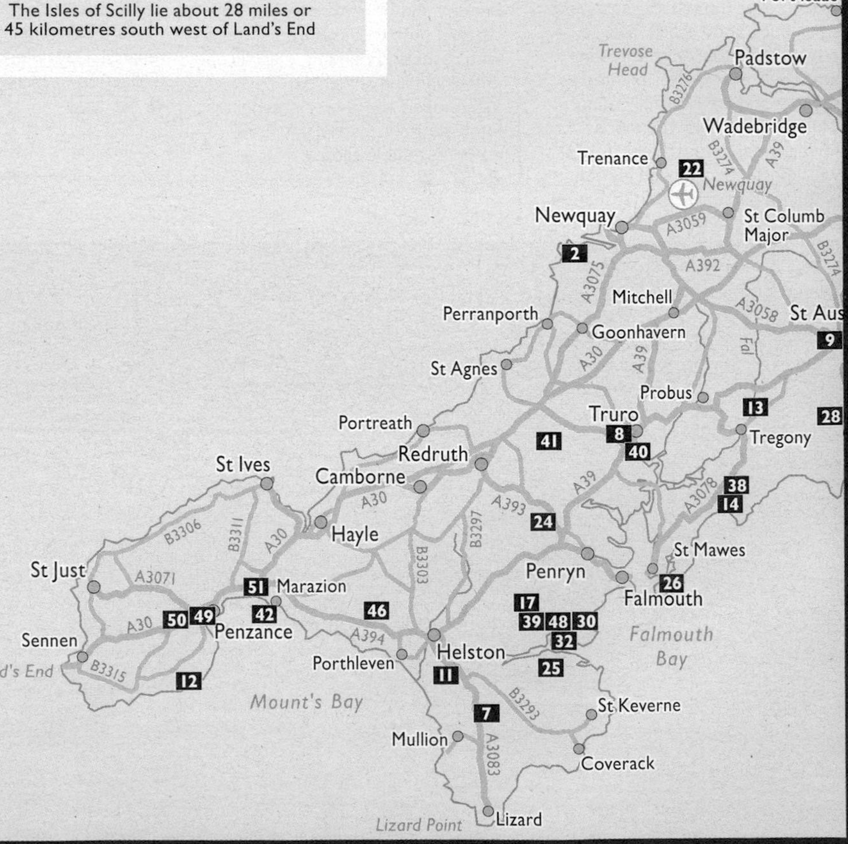

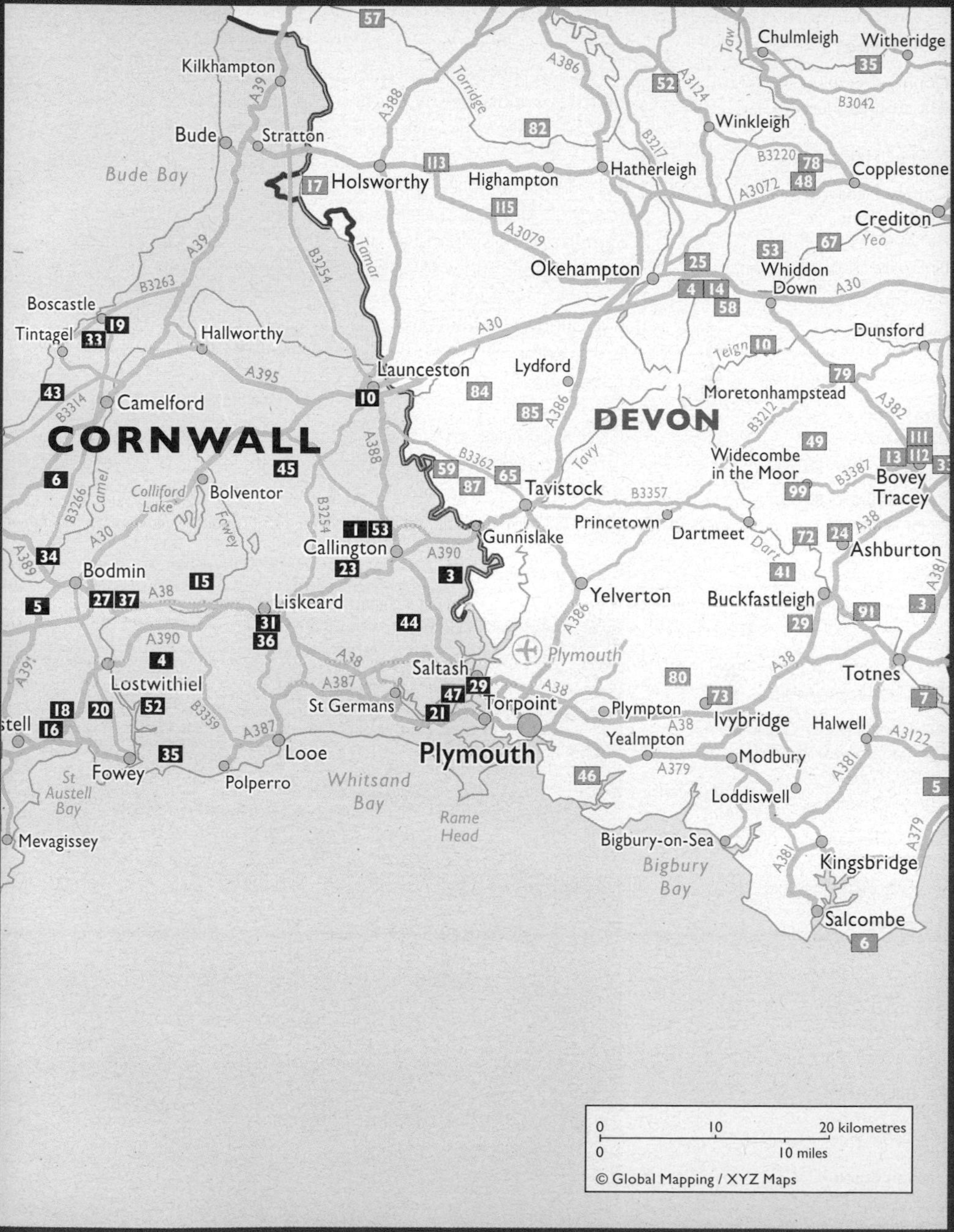

CORNWALL
DEVON
Kilkhampton
Bude
Stratton
Bude Bay
Holsworthy
Highampton
Hatherleigh
Chulmleigh
Witheridge
Winkleigh
Copplestone
Crediton
Yeo
Okehampton
Whiddon Down
Dunsford
Boscastle
Tintagel
Hallworthy
Launceston
Lydford
Moretonhampstead
Camelford
Widecombe in the Moor
Bovey Tracey
Tavistock
Princetown
Dartmeet
Ashburton
Colliford Lake
Bolventor
Callington
Gunnislake
Bodmin
Liskeard
Yelverton
Buckfastleigh
Lostwithiel
Saltash
Plymouth
Totnes
St Germans
Torpoint
Plympton
Ivybridge
Halwell
Yealmpton
Modbury
Fowey
Looe
Polperro
St Austell Bay
Whitsand Bay
Rame Head
Loddiswell
Mevagissey
Bigbury-on-Sea
Bigbury Bay
Kingsbridge
Salcombe
Tamar
Torridge
Taw
Teign
Tavy
Dart
Camel
Fowey
A39
A388
A386
A3124
B3217
B3042
B3220
A3072
A3079
B3254
B3263
A30
A395
B3314
B3362
B3212
A382
B3387
B3357
A38
A381
B3266
A389
A390
A391
B3359
A387
A379
A3122
0 10 20 kilometres
0 10 miles
© Global Mapping / XYZ Maps

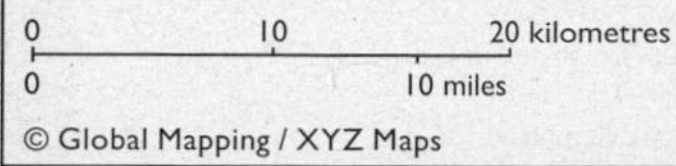

Volunteers

County Organiser
Christopher Harvey Clark
01872 530165
suffree2012@gmail.com

County Treasurer
Andrew Flint
01726 879336
flints@elizaholidays.co.uk

Publicity
Nutty Lim
01726 815247
christianne.gf.lim@gmail.com

Sara Gadd
07814 885141
sara@gartendesign.co.uk

Booklet Co-ordinator
Peter Stanley
01326 565868
stanley.m2@sky.com

Photographer

Lucie Averill
01736 711971
lucieaverill@ymail.com

Assistant County Organisers
Ginnie Clotworthy
01208 872612
ginnieclotworthy@hotmail.co.uk

Sarah Gordon
01579 362076
sar.gordon@talktalk.net

Katie Nichols
01872 275786
katherinemlambert@gmail.com

Alison O'Connor
01726 882460
tregoose@tregoose.co.uk

Rachel Ruttledge
07564 256916
rachel@ruttledgegardendesigns.com

Marion Stanley
01326 565868
stanley.m2@sky.com

Cornwall has some of the most beautiful natural landscapes to be found anywhere in the world.

Here, you will discover some of the country's most extraordinary gardens, a spectacular coastline, internationally famous surfing beaches, windswept moors and countless historic sites. Cornish gardens reflect this huge variety of environments particularly well.

A host of National Collections of magnolias, camellias, rhododendrons and azaleas, as well as exotic Mediterranean semitropical plants and an abundance of other plants flourish in our acid soils and mild climate.

Surrounded by the warm currents of the Gulf Stream, with our warm damp air in summer and mild moist winters, germination continues all year.

Cornwall boasts an impressive variety of beautiful gardens. These range from coastal-protected positions to exposed cliff-top sites, moorland water gardens, Japanese gardens and the world famous tropical biomes of the Eden Project.

Below: Kestle Barton

OPENING DATES

All entries subject to change. For latest information check **www.ngs.org.uk**

Extended openings are shown at the beginning of the month.

Map locator numbers are shown to the right of each garden name.

March

Every day from Sunday 25th
Ken Caro 23

Every Tuesday to Sunday from Saturday 24th
NEW Kestle Barton 25

Sunday 4th
Ince Castle 21

Sunday 18th
The Lodge 27

Sunday 25th
Ince Castle 21

April

Every day
Ken Caro 23

Every Tuesday to Sunday
NEW Kestle Barton 25

Every day
Waye Cottage 52

Saturday 7th
◆ Trewidden Garden 50

Sunday 8th
Meudon Hotel 30

Monday 9th
◆ Pencarrow 34

Saturday 14th
Bodwannick Manor Farm 5

Sunday 15th
The Lodge 27

Saturday 21st
NEW Ash Barn 3

Sunday 22nd
NEW Ash Barn 3
Riverside Cottage 40

Saturday 28th
◆ Chygurno 12

Sunday 29th
◆ Chygurno 12
Ethnevas Cottage 17
Ince Castle 21

May

Every day
Ken Caro 23

Every Tuesday to Sunday
NEW Kestle Barton 25

Sunday 6th
Carminowe Valley Garden 11
Navas Hill House 32
South Lea 44

Monday 7th
◆ Boconnoc 4
◆ Moyclare 31
NEW Penmilder 36

Sunday 13th
◆ The Japanese Garden 22
Trebartha 45

Monday 14th
◆ The Japanese Garden 22

Saturday 19th
◆ Pinsla Garden & Nursery 37

Wednesday 23rd
NEW Gardens Cottage 18

Sunday 20th
◆ Pinsla Garden & Nursery 37

Sunday 27th
NEW Bokelly 6

Monday 28th
Riverside Cottage 40

Wednesday 30th
NEW Gardens Cottage 18

June

Every Wednesday
NEW Gardens Cottage 18

Every day
Ken Caro 23

Every Tuesday to Sunday
NEW Kestle Barton 25

Every day from Monday 11th
Sea View 43

Every day
Waye Cottage 52

Festival Weekend

Sunday 3rd
Bodwannick Manor Farm 5

Friday 8th
◆ St Michael's Mount 42

Sunday 10th
Creed House & Creed Lodge 13
Mary Newman's Garden 29

Saturday 16th
Half Acre 19

Sunday 17th
Crugsillick Manor 14
Half Acre 19
The Lodge 27
◆ Poppy Cottage Garden 38
South Lea 44

Saturday 23rd
◆ Roseland House 41

Sunday 24th
Anvil Cottage 1
◆ Roseland House 41
Trenarth 48
Windmills 53

Friday 29th
Dye Cottage 15

Saturday 30th
Dye Cottage 15

July

Every Wednesday
NEW Gardens Cottage 18

Every day
Ken Caro 23

Every Tuesday to Sunday
NEW Kestle Barton 25

Every day to Sunday 15th
Sea View 43

Sunday 1st
Anvil Cottage 1
Dye Cottage 15
Windmills 53

Sunday 8th
◆ Bosvigo House 8
Byeways 10

Sunday 15th
Brookvale 9

Saturday 21st
◆ Chygurno 12

Sunday 22nd
◆ Chygurno 12
Mary Newman's Garden 29

Saturday 28th
NEW Kitpurva 26
Tregonning 46

Sunday 29th
NEW Kitpurva 26
Tregonning 46

August

Every Wednesday
NEW Gardens Cottage 18

Every day
Ken Caro 23

Every Tuesday to Sunday
NEW Kestle Barton 25

Saturday 4th
◆ Pinsla Garden & Nursery 37

Sunday 5th
◆ Pinsla Garden & Nursery 37

Wednesday 15th
◆ Bonython Manor 7

September

Every Wednesday to Wednesday 19th
NEW Gardens Cottage 18

Every day to Sunday 9th
Ken Caro 23

Every Tuesday to Sunday
NEW Kestle Barton 25

Sunday 2nd
Trebartha 45

October

Every Tuesday to Sunday

November

Every Tuesday to Sunday to Saturday 3rd

By Arrangement

The Queen's Nursing Institute founded the National Garden Scheme over 90 years ago

Ash Barn

THE GARDENS

1 ANVIL COTTAGE

South Hill, PL17 7LP. Geoff & Barbara Clemerson, 01579 362623, geoff@south-hill.co.uk. *3m NW of Callington. Head N on A388 from Callington centre. After ½m L onto South Hill Rd (signed South Hill), straight on for 3m. Gardens on R just before St Sampson's Church.* **Sun 24 June, Sun 1 July (1.30-5). Combined adm with Windmills £5, chd free. Home-made teas. Gluten free refreshements. Visits also by arrangement May & June.**

Essentially a plantsman's garden. Winding paths take you through a series of themed rooms housing both familiar and rare and unusual plants. Higher up, a wild flower garden leads through a formal rose garden to a raised viewpoint with spectacular views of Caradon Hill and Bodmin Moor. Very limited wheechair access due to steps.

2 ARUNDELL

West Pentire, Crantock, TR8 5SE. Brenda & David Eyles, 01637 831916, david@davideyles.com. *1m W of Crantock. From A3075 take signs to Crantock. At junction in village keep straight on to West Pentire (1m). Park in field (signed) or public car parks at W Pentire.* **Visits by arrangement May to Aug except Fridays, max group size 20. Adm £5, chd free. Cream teas & home-made biscuits.**

A garden where no garden should be! - on windswept NT headland between 2 fantastic beaches. 1 acre packed with design and plant interest round old farm cottage. Front: cottage garden. Side: Mediterranean courtyard. Rear: rockery and shrubbery leading to stumpery and fernery and on to stream and pond, Cornish Corner, herbaceous borders, Beth Chatto dry garden, small pinetum and jungle garden. As seen in Gardeners' World; Coast magazine;

Cornwall Today; Cornish Life. Wheelchair access from public car park with entrance via rear gate. 14 shallow steps in centre of garden useable with care.

3 NEW ASH BARN

Callington, PL17 8BP. Mary Martin. *3m E of Callington. Leaving Callington on A 390 (Tavistock direction) take 1st R signed Harrowbarrow. Turn R at T junction in village then 1m down hill to Glamorgan Mill parking on L.* **Sat 21, Sun 22 Apr (10-5). Adm £4.50, chd free. Home-made teas.**
Terraced 3 acre woodland garden, full of magnolias, camellias and fruit trees, under-planted with old roses, shrubs and Tamar Valley narcissi. Intensive herbaceous planting provides interest for most of the year, and contrasts with box and holly topiary. Narrow, uneven paths and steps reflect the wild wood atmosphere. There is also a quarry edge, so no dogs or unsupervised children. Regret no wheelchair access.

4 ◆ BOCONNOC

Lostwithiel, PL22 0RG. Elizabeth Fortescue, 01208 872507, office@boconnoc.com, www.boconnoc.com. *Off A390 between Liskeard & Lostwithiel. From East Taphouse follow signs to Boconnoc. (SatNav does not work well in this area).* **For NGS: Mon 7 May (2-5). Adm £5.50, chd free. Home-made teas in stable yard.** For other opening times and information, please phone, email or visit garden website.
20 acres surrounded by parkland and woods with magnificent trees, flowering shrubs and stunning views. The gardens are set amongst mature trees which provide the backcloth for exotic spring flowering shrubs, woodland plants, with newly-planted magnolias and a fine collection of hydrangeas. Bathhouse built in 1804, woodland gardens, obelisk built in 1771, house dating from Domesday, deer park, C15 church.

5 BODWANNICK MANOR FARM

Nanstallon, Bodmin, PL30 5LN. Gaia Trust, sarahmatta@btinternet.com, www.gaiatrust.org.uk/bodwannick. *From A30, take A389 signed to Lanivet and Bodmin. 1m after Lanivet turn L (signed to Nanstallon). From Bodmin, take A389 signed for A30. After 1½m turn R at Jim's hardware store.* **Sat 14 Apr, Sun 3 June (10.30-3.30). Adm by donation. Home-made teas in old farmhouse conservatory and on terrace. Visits also by arrangement Mar to Oct for groups of up to 20.**
1½-acre plantsman's garden with fern-rich rockery, water and kitchen gardens, daffodils, roses and shrubs. It is remarkable for its aura of peace and tranquillity, but its air of antiquity is deceptive as it was the lifetime creation of Martin Appleton and his family. Now in the care of the Gaia Trust, it has particular features of note and yr-round interest. Wheelchair access possible to much but not all of the garden.

6 NEW BOKELLY

St Kew, Bodmin, PL30 3DY. Toby & Henrietta Courtauld. *Follow road to Trelill from St Kew Highway, leaving Red Lion pub on L. Garden on L after approx 1m.* **Sun 27 May (1.30-5.30). Adm £5, chd free. Home-made teas.**
The 7-acre garden surrounds a beautiful C15 barn and lichened stone outbuildings. It has been expanded and rejuvenated with new plantings to suit the varied levels and soil types, including woodland and pond areas, herbaceous border, little orchard and vegetable plot, and raised beds massed with flowers for cutting (a particular passion of garden designer Henrietta).

7 ◆ BONYTHON MANOR

Cury Cross Lanes, Helston, TR12 7BA. Mr & Mrs Richard Nathan, 01326 240550, sbonython@gmail.com, www.bonythonmanor.co.uk. *5m S of Helston. On main A3083 Helston to Lizard Rd. Turn L at Cury Cross Lanes (Wheel Inn). Entrance 300yds on R.* **For NGS: Wed 15 Aug (2-4.30). Adm £8, chd £2. Home-made teas.** For other opening times and information, please phone, email or visit garden website.
Magnificent 20 acre colour garden incl sweeping hydrangea drive to Georgian manor (not open). Herbaceous walled garden, potager with vegetables and picking flowers; 3 lakes in valley planted with ornamental grasses, perennials and South African flowers. A 'must see' for all seasons colour.

8 ◆ BOSVIGO HOUSE

Bosvigo Lane, Truro, TR1 3NH. Wendy Perry, 01872 275774, www.bosvigo.com/. *Truro City Centre. At Highertown, nr Sainsbury r'about, turn down Dobbs Lane. After 500yds, entrance to house is on L, after sharp LH-bend.* **For NGS: Sun 8 July (2-6). Adm £5, chd free. Home-made teas. Teas served in the Servants Hall.** For other opening times and information, please phone or visit garden website.
Created by artist owner, the 2 acre garden surrounding the Georgian house has been designed to create dazzling displays of vivid colour and plant harmonies. Each garden room is designed with a different palette of colour. For the opening in July the Vean garden and walled garden will be looking their best. Very limited wheelchair access.

9 BROOKVALE

Gover Valley, St. Austell, PL25 5RA. Leslie & Myrna Baker. *1m from the town centre, close to Gover Viaduct.* **Sun 15 July (2-6). Adm £4, chd free. Cream teas.**
Brunel's GWR viaduct is a magnificent backdrop to this all yr-round garden created by the current owners over the past 30 years. Both sun and shade plantings with significant herbaceous borders and an extensive rockery.

10 BYEWAYS

Dunheved Road, Launceston, PL15 9JE. Tony Reddicliffe. *Launceston town centre. 100yds from multi-storey car park past offices of Cornish & Devon Post into Dunheved Rd, 3rd bungalow on R.* **Sun 8 July (1-5). Adm £5, chd free. Cream teas. Home-made teas.**

Small town garden developed over 5yrs by enthusiastic amateur gardeners. Herbaceous borders, rockery. Tropicals incl bananas, gingers and senecio. Stream and water features. Roof gardens. Butterfly house new this year. Many areas to sit and view.

11 CARMINOWE VALLEY GARDEN

Tangies, Gunwalloe, TR12 7PU. Mr & Mrs Peter Stanley, 01326 565868, stanley.m2@sky.com www.carminowevalleygarden.co.uk *3m SW of Helston. A3083 Helston-Lizard rd. R opp main gate to Culdrose. 1m downhill, garden on R.* **Sun 6 May (12-5). Adm £5, chd free. Home-made teas. Visits also by arrangement Apr to Aug.**

Overlooking the beautiful Carminowe Valley towards Loe Pool this abundant garden combines native oak woodland, babbling brook and large natural pond with more formal areas. Wild flower meadow, mown pathways, shrubberies, orchard, nectar beds, cutting garden, kitchen garden, summerhouse. Enclosed cottage garden, tulips in spring and roses early summer provide huge contrast. Gravel paths, slopes.

12 ◆ CHYGURNO

Lamorna, TR19 6XH. Dr & Mrs Robert Moule, 01736 732153, rmoule010@btinternet.com. *4m S of Penzance. Off B3315. Follow signs for The Lamorna Cove Hotel. Garden is at top of hill, past Hotel on L.* **For NGS: Sat 28, Sun 29 Apr, Sat 21, Sun 22 July (2-5). Adm £5, chd free.** For other opening times and information, please phone or email.

Beautiful, unique, 3 acre cliffside garden overlooking Lamorna Cove. Planting started in 1998, mainly S-hemisphere shrubs and exotics with hydrangeas, camellias and rhododendrons. Woodland area with tree ferns set against large granite outcrops. Garden terraced with steep steps and paths. Plenty of benches so you can take a rest and enjoy the wonderful views. Featured in Country Homes and Interiors magazine.

13 CREED HOUSE & CREED LODGE

Creed, Grampound, Truro, TR2 4SL. The Croggon family, 01872 530372, www.creedhouse.co.uk. *9m W of Truro. From the centre of Grampound on A390, take rd signed to Creed. After 1m turn L opp Creed Church, garden is on L.* **Sun 10 June (11-5). Adm £4.50, chd free. Home-made teas.**

5 acre landscaped Georgian rectory garden; tranquil rural setting; spacious lawns. Tree collection; rhododendrons; sunken cobbled yard and formal walled rose garden. Trickle stream to ponds and bog. Natural woodland walk together with recently planted small garden around new house. Herbaceous beds, shrubs and large terrace with rose bed below. Dogs welcome on leads.

14 CRUGSILLICK MANOR

Ruan High Lanes, Truro, TR2 5LJ. Dr Alison Agnew & Mr Brian Yule, 01872 501972, alisonagnew@icloud.com. *On Roseland Peninsula. Turn off A390 Truro-St Austell rd onto A3078 towards St Mawes. Approx 5m after Tregony turn 1st L after Ruan High Lanes towards Veryan, garden is 200yds on R.* **Sun 17 June (11-5). Adm £4, chd free. Light refreshments. Also open Poppy Cottage Garden. Visits also by arrangement May to Sept for groups of 15+ only.**

2 acre garden, substantially re-landscaped and planted - mostly over last 5 yrs. To the side of the C17/C18 house, a wooded bank drops down to walled kitchen garden and hot garden. In front, sweeping yew hedges and paths define oval lawns and broad mixed borders. On a lower terrace, the focus is a large pond and the planting is predominantly exotic flowering trees and shrubs. Partial wheelchair access. Garden is on several levels connected by fairly steep sloping gravel paths.

15 DYE COTTAGE

St Neot, PL14 6NG. Sue & Brian Williams. *Opp The London Inn in centre of St Neot village. Turn off A38 to St Neot. Street parking.* **Fri 29, Sat 30 June, Sun 1 July (2-5). Adm £4, chd free. Light refreshments.**

⅓ acre cottage garden, designed and completely maintained by the owners over the past 25 yrs. Many seating areas - down by the river, in courtyard garden, fire pit corner, and on rose terrace. Wisteria walk, potting shed, greenhouse, summerhouse, office (once the tree house!), fruit cage, mature borders, and roses everywhere. Regret no wheelchair access.

16 ◆ EDEN PROJECT

Bodelva, PL24 2SG. The Eden Trust, 01726 811911, www.edenproject.com. *4m E of St Austell. Brown signs from A30 & A390.* **For opening times and information, please phone or visit garden website.**

Described as 8th wonder of the world, the Eden Project is a global garden for the C21. Discover the story of plants that have changed the world and which could change your future. The Eden Project is an exciting attraction where you can explore your relationship with nature, learn new things and get inspiration about the world around you. Yr-round programme of talks, events and workshops. Wheelchairs available - booking of powered wheelchairs is essential; please call 01726 818895 in advance.

17 ETHNEVAS COTTAGE

Constantine, Falmouth, TR11 5PY. Lyn Watson & Ray Chun, 01326 340076. *6m SW of Falmouth. Nearest main rds A39, A394. Follow signs for Constantine. At lower village sign, at bottom of winding hill, turn off on private lane. Garden ¾m up hill.* **Sun 29 Apr (1-4). Adm £5, chd free. Home-made teas. Visits also by arrangement Apr to Sept for groups of 20 max.**

Isolated granite cottage in 2 acres. Intimate flower and vegetable garden. Bridge over stream to large pond and primrose path through semi-wild bog area. Hillside with grass paths among native and exotic trees. Many camellias and rhododendrons. Mixed shrubs and herbaceous beds, wild flower glade, spring bulbs. A garden of discovery of hidden delights.

18 NEW GARDENS COTTAGE

Prideaux, St Blazey, PL24 2SS. Sue & Roger Paine, 07786 367610, sue.newton@btinternet.com. *1m from railway Xing on A390 in St Blazey. Turn into Prideaux Rd opp Gulf petrol station on A390 in St Blazey (signed Luxulyan). Proceed ½m. Turn R (signed Luxulyan Valley and Prideaux) and follow signs.* **Every Wed 23 May to 19 Sept (2-5). Adm £4, chd free. Home-made teas. Visits also by arrangement May to Sept.**

Set in a stunning landscape and tranquil location on the edge of the Luxulyan Valley, Gardens Cottage is a newly created garden of about 1½ acres. Work commenced in 2015 on a comprehensive mix of herbaceous planting, dry terracing, rockeries, formal garden, enclosed courtyard, orchard/fruit garden, beehives, wildlife pond, productive kitchen garden and managed woodland. Check our Facebook page for special events - @gardenscottageprideaux.

19 HALF ACRE

Mount Pleasant, Boscastle, PL35 0BJ. Carole Vincent, 01840 250263, concretecarole@btinternet.com, www.carolevincent.org. *5m N of Camelford. Park at doctors' surgery at top of village (clearly signed). Limited parking for disabled at garden.* **Sat 16, Sun 17 June (1.30-5). Adm £4, chd free. Home-made teas provided by Boscastle Churches. Visits also by arrangement Mar to Sept, max group size 15.**

Old stone cottage with 2 studios overlooking cliffs and sea, set in 1½ acres of gardens - cottage, small wood and Blue Circle garden (RHS Chelsea 2001) constructed in colour concrete. Owner has a national reputation for her sculpture in concrete, and sculptures all around occupy small spaces or command a view. Mid-June should see the flowering of the roses and echiums. Studio open. Painting exhibition. Regret no dogs.

20 ◆ HIDDEN VALLEY GARDENS

Treesmill, Par, PL24 2TU. Tricia Howard, www.hiddenvalleygardens.co.uk. *2m SW of Lostwithiel. Directions: From A390 between Lostwithiel (2m) & St Austell (5m), turn onto B3269 towards Fowey, then R turn within 200 metres. From Fowey, take B3269 and turn L at garden sign just prior to A390.* **For opening times and information, please see below or visit garden website.**

Award-winning 3 acre colourful garden in hidden valley with nursery. Cottage-style planting with herbaceous beds and borders, grasses, ferns and fruit. Gazebo with country views. Iris fairy well and vegetable potager. Special displays of herbaceous plants including collections of crocosmia, agapanthus and dahlias and many other colourful flowers. Children's quiz. Dogs on lead. Open from 10 to 6, Thurs to Mon, 20 March to 15 Oct. Entry £5 incl complimentary tea/coffee. Children free. See website for special snowdrops opening in Feb. Tricia has a collection of some 80+ named snowdrops as well as hellebores and early flowering daffodils. Filmed for the BBC Garden Rescue programme as an exemplar garden for herbaceous plants. Special drop off parking for wheelchair access directly into garden area. Mainly wheelchair accessible, some gentle slopes.

21 INCE CASTLE

Saltash, PL12 4RA. Lord & Lady Boyd, 01752 842672, boydince@aol.com, www.incecastle.co.uk. *3m SW of Saltash. From A38 at Stoketon Cross take turn signed Trematon, then Elmgate. No large coaches.* **Sun 4, Sun 25 Mar, Sun 29 Apr (2-5). Adm £5, chd free. Home-made teas.**

Romantic garden at the end of winding lanes, surrounding C17 pink brick castle on a peninsula in R Lynher. Old apple trees with bulbs, woodland garden with fritillaries, camellias and rhododendrons. Extraordinary 1960s shell house on edge of formal garden. Partial wheelchair access.

22 ◆ THE JAPANESE GARDEN

St Mawgan, TR8 4ET. Natalie Hore & Stuart Ellison, 01637 860116, info@japanesegarden.co.uk, www.japanesegarden.co.uk. *6m E of Newquay. St Mawgan village is directly below Newquay Airport. Follow brown & white road signs on A3059 & B3276.* **For NGS: Sun 13, Mon 14 May (10-6). Adm £5, chd £2.50. Refreshments available in village 2-3 min walk from garden.** For other opening times and information, please phone, email or visit garden website.

Discover an oasis of tranquillity in a Japanese-style Cornish garden, set in approx one acre. Spectacular Japanese maples and azaleas, symbolic teahouse, koi pond, bamboo grove, stroll, woodland, zen and moss gardens. A place made for contemplation and meditation. Adm free to gift shop, bonsai and plant areas. Featured in BBC 2 Big Dreams Small Spaces. 90% accessible with gravel paths.

23 KEN CARO

Bicton, Liskeard, PL14 5RF. Mr & Mrs K R Willcock. *5m NE of Liskeard. From A390 to Callington turn off N at St Ive. Take Pensilva Rd, follow brown tourist signs, approx 1m off main rd. Plenty of parking. (SatNav is misleading).* **Daily Sun 25 Mar to Sun 9 Sept (10-5). Adm £5, chd £2.**

Connoisseurs' garden full of interest all yr round. Lily ponds, panoramic views, plenty of seating, picnic area, in all 10 acres. Garden started in 1970, recently rejuvenated. Woodland walk, which has one of the largest beech trees. Good collection of yellow magnolias and herbaceous plants. Large collection of hydrangeas. Over 200 camellias and collection of ilex. Partial wheelchair access.

24 KENNALL HOUSE

Ponsanooth, TR3 7HJ. Nick & Mary Wilson-Holt, 01872 870557, kennallvale@hotmail.com. *4m NW of Falmouth. Off A393 Falmouth-Redruth rd. Turn L at Ponsanooth PO for ⅓m. Garden at end of drive marked Kennall House.* **Visits by arrangement Apr to Nov. Adm £5.50, chd free.**

The 12-acre garden-cum-arboretum, beautifully situated in the Kennall Valley, is an intriguing combination of typical British species and exotics, sympathetically laid out in a variety of spacious settings, incl walled garden and fast-flowing stream with ponds. Wide variety of trees incl new plantings of rare specimens. An unusual Cornish garden with yr-round interest. Limited wheelchair access.

25 NEW KESTLE BARTON

Manaccan, Helston, TR12 6HU. Karen Townsend, info@kestlebarton.co.uk, http://www.kestlebarton.co.uk. *A3083 Helston - Lizard, 2m L B3293 for St Keverne. 2m L Helford, Newtown St Martin, R then L for Helford. 1m L at Xrds to Kestle Barton, R after several hundred yds, follow signs.* **Every Tue to Sun 24 Mar to 3 Nov (10.30-5). Adm by donation. Light refreshments. Visits also by arrangement Apr to Oct.**

A delightful garden near Frenchmans Creek, on the Lizard, which is the setting for Kestle Barton Gallery; wild flower meadow, Cornish orchard with named varieties and a formal garden with prairie planting in blocks by James Alexander Sinclair. It is a riot of colour in summer and continues to delight well into late summer. Parking, honesty box tea hut, good wheel chair access. Dogs on leads welcome. Large coaches cannot reach Kestle Barton.

26 NEW KITPURVA

St. Anthony, Portscatho, Truro, TR2 5EY. Jude Lynock. *Take the A3078 from Tregony to St Mawes but turn L at Trewithian to St Anthony. Kitpurva is 2.3m past Gerrans church. Also pass Trewince and Froe. Do not turn R to Bohortha.* **Sat 28, Sun 29 July (10.30-4.30). Adm £5, chd free. Home-made teas.**

Gardens Cottage

1920s coastal garden with some original features; extensively replanted by current owners over past 15 yrs. Agapanthus, hemerocallis, anemone, hydrangea, cordyline, trachycarpus thrive. Restoration ongoing incl paths which lead you around the garden to seating areas, borders and small pond from which to enjoy the panoramic sea and rural views. Newly planted escallonia maze with viewing areas to enjoy views from Nare Head to the Lizard. Visitors are welcome to walk the horses' track. Please note that some areas are work in progress. Most areas accessible by wheelchair.

27 THE LODGE

Fletchersbridge, Bodmin, PL30 4AN. Mr Tony Ryde. *2m E of Bodmin. From A38 at Glynn Crematorium r'about take rd towards Cardinham and continue through hamlet of Fletchersbridge. Garden first on R over river bridge.* **Sun 18 Mar, Sun 15 Apr, Sun 17 June (1-6). Adm £4, chd free. Cream teas.**

3-acre riverside garden some 20 yrs old specialising in trees and shrubs chosen for their flowers, foliage and form, embracing a Gothic lodge remodelled in 2016. Magnolias and camellias, prunus and pieris, azaleas and rhododendrons, paulownias and viburnums, with cornus, davidias and stewartia later. Recently extended water garden with sculptures. Informal setting complemented by ponds, waterfalls, spring bulbs and herbaceous flowers, surrounding a Gothic former lodge by the Glynn estate. Wheelchair access to gravelled areas around house and along two sides of garden.

28 ◆ THE LOST GARDENS OF HELIGAN

Pentewan, St Austell, PL26 6EN. Heligan Gardens Ltd, 01726 845100, info@heligan.com, www.heligan.com. *5m S of St Austell. From St Austell take B3273 signed Mevagissey, follow signs.* **For opening times and information, please phone, email or visit garden website.**

Lose yourself in the mysterious world of The Lost Gardens where an exotic sub-tropical jungle, atmospheric Victorian pleasure grounds, an interactive wildlife project and the finest productive gardens in Britain all await your discovery. Wheelchair access to Northern gardens. Armchair tour shows video of unreachable areas. Wheelchairs available at reception free of charge.

NPC

29 MARY NEWMAN'S GARDEN

48 Culver Road, Saltash, PL12 4DT. Tamar Protection Society, 01579 384381/01752 842132, brigettedixon32@gmail.com, www.tamarprotectionsociety. *200yds down from railway station. Lower end of Culver Rd near to Waterside of Saltash, ¼ m from Saltash Fore St. Plenty of parking in adj streets.* **Sun 10 June, Sun 22 July (11-4). Adm by donation. Cream teas. Light refreshments. Visits also by arrangement 15 Apr to 30 Sept on specific days agreed between the Trustees of the Tamar Protection Society and the NGS.**

Mary Newman's is a delightful Elizabethan cottage and garden - reputedly the home of Sir Francis Drake's first wife, Mary Newman. The garden is laid out in authentic Elizabethan style, showcasing the plants and herbs vital to a household of the period, and has the feeling of being a very secret garden which is a shelter from the humdrum of the busy world we live in. Plants for sale cultivated within garden. Also open 15 April to end Sept Wed, Thurs, Sat, Sun (12-4) by donation in aid of Tamar Protection Society. Ramp can be requested at reception for main access. Wheelchair access to ground floor of cottage.

30 MEUDON HOTEL

Maenporth Road, Mawnan Smith, Falmouth, TR11 5HT. Tessa Rabett, 01326 250541, wecare@meudon.co.uk, www.meudon.co.uk. *Follow signs for Mabe, then Mawnan Smith.* **Sun 8 Apr (1-5). Adm £7, chd free. Home-made teas. Bar drinks, snacks, cream teas.**

Meudon has 9 acres of sub-tropical valley garden created by the Fox family in 1800. Wealthy Quakers and shipping agents, their Packet ships provided transport for Meudon's wonderful collection of rare and exotic trees and shrubs from around the world. Terraces, pathways, meander down to Bream Cove (private beach). Formal garden, herbaceous borders, indigenous plants, and sunken pond area. Brazilian Gunnera manicata, Japanese banana trees Musa basjoo, Wollemia pine, Dicksonia antaractica, rhodendendrons, camellias, magnolia, Trachycarpus fortunei. Wheelchair access limited to upper terrace and ponds (although they take a little longer to get to).

31 ◆ MOYCLARE

Lodge Hill, Liskeard, PL14 4EH. Elizabeth & Philip Henslowe, 01579 343114, elizabethhenslowe@btinternet.com, www.moyclare.co.uk. *1m S of Liskeard centre. Approx 300yds S of Liskeard railway stn on St Keyne-Duloe rd (B3254).* **For NGS: Mon 7 May (11.30-5). Combined adm with Penmilder £6, chd free. Home-made teas. For other opening times and information, please phone, email or visit garden website.**

Gardened by one family for over 80yrs; mature trees, shrubs and plants (many unusual, many variegated). Once most televised Cornish garden. Now revived and rejuvenated and still a plantsman's delight, full of character. Camellia, brachyglottis and astrantia (all Moira Reid) and cytisus Moyclare Pink originated here. Meandering paths through fascinating shrubberies, herbacious borders and sunny corners. Wellstocked pond. Wildlife habitat area. Quite a lot of the garden can be enjoyed by wheelchair users.

32 NAVAS HILL HOUSE

Bosanath Valley, Mawnan Smith, Falmouth, TR11 5LL. Aline & Richard Turner, 01326 251233, alineturner@btinternet.com. *1½ m from Trebah & Glendurgan Gdns. Head for Mawnan Smith, pass Trebah and Glendurgan Gdns then follow yellow signs. Don't follow SatNav which suggests you turn right before Mawnan Smith - congestion alert!* **Sun 6 May (2-5). Adm £5, chd free. 'All you can eat' £3.50. Visits also by arrangement in May for groups of 10+.**

8½-acre elevated valley garden paddocks; woodland; kitchen garden and ornamental areas. The ornamental garden consists of 2 plantsman areas with specialist trees and shrubs; walled rose garden; ornamental garden with water features and rockery. Young and established wooded areas with bluebells, camellia walks and young large leafed rhododendrons. Seating areas with views across wooded valley. Partial, limited wheelchair access, some gravel and grass paths.

33 THE OLD RECTORY

Trevalga, Boscastle, PL35 0EA. Jacqueline M A Jarvis, 01840 250512, jacqueline@jacquelinejarvis.co.uk. *Coastal rd between Tintagel & Boscastle. At Trevalga Xrds turn inland away from hamlet. Garden ½ m up narrow, steep hill. Limited parking.* **Visits by arrangement Apr to June. Parking limited, larger groups would need to share cars and notify owner in advance. Adm £4, chd free. Light refreshments.**

On N Cornish coast ½ m inland with panoramic sea views, a challenging, exposed, NW-facing garden at an elevation of 500ft. 'From Field to Garden' a 32 yr project by artist owner. Informal incl woodland, perennial borders, sunken and walled areas. Lookout at front of garden (4-step spiral stair access) with stunning views across circa 50m of coastline - Hartland Point to Pentire Point. Previous articles in Cornish Guardian and Gardening Weekly. Gravel drive and partial wheelchair access to garden.

34 ◆ PENCARROW

Washaway, Bodmin, PL30 3AG. Molesworth-St Aubyn family, 01208 841369, info@pencarrow.co.uk, www.pencarrow.co.uk. *4m NW of Bodmin. Signed off A389 & B3266.* **For NGS: Mon 9 Apr (10-5). Adm £5.75, chd free. Light refreshments. For other opening times and information, please phone, email or visit garden website.**

50 acres of tranquil, family-owned Grade II* listed gardens. Superb specimen conifers, azaleas, magnolias and camellias galore. 700 varieties of rhododendron give a blaze of spring colour; blue hydrangeas line the mile-long carriage drive throughout the summer. Discover the Iron Age hill fort, lake, Italian gardens and granite rockery. Free parking, dogs welcome, café and children's play area. Gravel paths, some steep slopes.

35 NEW PENDOWER HOUSE

Lanteglos-by-Fowey, PL23 1NJ. Mr Roger Lamb, 01726 870884, rl@rogerlamb.com. *Near Polruan off the B3359 towards Bodinnick. 2m from Fowey using the Bodinnick ferry. Please ask for directions when arranging to visit the garden. Do not use SatNav.* **Visits by arrangement May & June for groups of 4+. Adm £4.50, chd free. Home-made teas. Other refreshments available by prior arrangement.**

Set in the heart of Daphne du Maurier country in its own valley this established garden surrounding a Georgian Rectory is now undergoing a revival having been wild and neglected for some years. It has formal herbaceous terraces, a cottage garden, orchard, ponds, streams and a C19 shrub garden with a fine collection of azaleas, camellias and rhododendrons plus rare mature specimen trees. House and garden available for filming and photography. Sadly difficult wheelchair access to much of this garden.

36 NEW PENMILDER

Lodge Hill, Liskeard, PL14 4EL. Chris & Mandy Deegan. *1m S of Liskeard town centre. On 3254 (Duloe road). Entrance on L directly opp 'Santa Trees'.* **Mon 7 May (11-5). Combined adm with Moyclare £6, chd free. Cream teas.**

Gently sloping, S-facing 2½ acre Cornish garden, with mature trees and shrubs. Bluebell woods, a haven for wildlife, and apple orchard which is particularly pretty with primroses, daffodils and bluebells in spring. Pond and vegetable garden. Sadly the garden is not suitable for wheelchair users due to gravel paths.

37 ◆ PINSLA GARDEN & NURSERY

Cardinham, PL30 4AY. Mark & Claire Woodbine, 01208 821339, cwoodbine@btinternet.com, www.pinslagarden.net. *3½ m E of Bodmin. From A30 or Bodmin take A38 towards Plymouth, 1st L to Cardinham & Fletchers Bridge, 2m on R.* **For NGS: Sat 19, Sun 20 May, Sat 4, Sun 5 Aug (9-5). Adm £3.50, chd free. Home-made teas. For other opening times and information, please phone, email or visit garden website.**

Romantic 1½-acre artist's garden set in tranquil woodland. Naturalistic cottage garden planting surrounds the C18 fairytale cottage. Imaginative design, intense colour and scent, bees and butterflies. Unusual shade plants, acers and ferns. Fantastic range of plants and statues on display and for sale. Friendly advice in nursery. Wheelchair access limited as some paths are narrow and bumpy.

38 ◆ POPPY COTTAGE GARDEN

Ruan High Lanes, Truro, TR2 5JR. Cazz Kenzie & Josh Hoole, 01872 501411, hello@poppycottage.garden,

www.poppycottage.garden. *Roseland Peninsula. From A390 between Truro and St Austell, take A3078 to St Mawes. Garden on R approx 3½ m after Tregony.* **For NGS: Sun 17 June (12.30-5). Adm £4, chd free. Home-made teas. Also open Crugsillick Manor.** For other opening times and information, please phone, email or visit garden website.
Situated on the beautiful Roseland Peninsula, this one acre garden is a plantsman's paradise. Planted for year round interest and divided into rooms, its dense planting of shrubs and herbaceous perennials, underplanted with bulbs, provides colourful and intriguing surprises around every corner. Small orchard with ornamental poultry, plant sales and seasonal flower bulb sales. Partial wheelchair access. Steps in one part of garden. Small step up to WC.

39 ◆ POTAGER GARDEN

High Cross, Constantine, Falmouth, TR11 5RF. Mr Mark Harris, 01326 341258, enquiries@potagergarden.org, www.potagergarden.org. *5m SW of Falmouth. From Falmouth, follow signs to Constantine. From Helston, drive through Constantine and continue towards Famouth.* **For opening times and information, please phone, email or visit garden website.**
Potager has emerged from the bramble choked wilderness of an abandoned plant nursery. With mature trees which were once nursery stock and lush herbaceous planting interspersed with fruit and vegetables Potager Garden aims to demonstrate the beauty of productive organic gardening. There are games to play, hammocks to laze in and boule and badminton to enjoy.

40 RIVERSIDE COTTAGE

St. Clement, Truro, TR1 1SZ. Billa & Nick Jeans, 01872 263830, billajeans@gmail.com. *1½m SE of Truro. From Trafalgar r'about on A39 in Truro, follow signs for St Clement, up St Clement Hill. R at top of hill, continue to car park by river; Riverside Cottage is first cottage on L.* **Sun 22 Apr, Mon 28 May (1.30-5). Adm £4, chd free. Cream teas. Home-made cakes. Visits also by arrangement Apr to June for groups, max 15; small coaches only please.**
Small garden on beautiful Tresillian River Estuary. Small Victorian orchard and nut walk with wild flower areas, wildlife pond, borders and vegetable patch. Steep paths and steps but plenty of seats, affording places of rest and views down the river. There's a swing and trampoline for the children. Walk through to C13 St Clement Church and 'Living Churchyard'. The best cream teas in the parish. Featured in Cornwall Life as Garden of the Month.

41 ◆ ROSELAND HOUSE

Chacewater, TR4 8QB. Mr & Mrs Pridham, 01872 560451, charlie@roselandhouse.co.uk, www.roselandhouse.co.uk. *4m W of Truro. At Truro end of main st. Park in village car park (100yds) or on surrounding rds.* **For NGS: Sat 23, Sun 24 June (1-5). Adm £4, chd free. Home-made teas. For other opening times and information, please phone, email or visit garden website.**
The 1-acre garden is a mass of rambling roses and clematis. Ponds and borders alike are filled with plants, many rarely seen in gardens. National Collection of clematis viticella cvs can be seen in garden and display tunnel, along with a huge range of other climbing plants. Some slopes.

NPC

42 ◆ ST MICHAEL'S MOUNT

Marazion, TR17 0HS. James & Mary St Levan, 01736 710507, mail@stmichaelsmount.co.uk, www.stmichaelsmount.co.uk. *2½m E of Penzance. ½m from shore at Marazion by Causeway; otherwise by motor boat.* **For NGS: Fri 8 June (10-5). Adm £7, chd £3.50. For other opening times and information, please phone, email or visit garden website.**
Infuse your senses with colour and scent in the unique sub-tropical gardens basking in the mild climate and salty breeze. Clinging to granite slopes the terraced beds tier steeply to the ocean's edge, boasting tender exotics from places such as Mexico, the Canary Islands and South Africa. Laundry lawn, mackerel bank, pill box, gun emplacement, tiered terraces, well, tortoise lawn. Walled gardens, seagull seat. The garden lawn can be accessed with wheelchairs although further exploration is limited due to steps and steepness.

43 SEA VIEW

Treligga, Delabole, PL33 9EE. Duncan Scott, 01840 211033, seaview.treligga@gmail.com. *Hamlet 1m W of Delabole, approached via no-through-rd signed to Treligga from B3314 at Westdowns. On entering the hamlet turn L at noticeboard - house is end-on to road at bottom of narrow lane.* **Daily Mon 11 June to Sun 15 July (2-5). Adm £4, chd free. Light refreshments.**
Imaginative garden in a remote coastal hamlet, designed as a series of varied, colourful and naturalistic enclosures - with flowers, vegetables, meadow and orchard. Although just a few fields away from the cliff edge with the sea 400 feet below, the feeling is more countryside than seaside and the garden sits sympathetically within the wider environment of its coastal setting. Sorry, not currently suitable for wheelchair users owing to steps.

Gardens are at the heart of hospice care

44 SOUTH LEA

Pillaton, Saltash, PL12 6QS. Viv & Tony Laurillard, 01579 350629, tony@laurillard.eclipse.co.uk. *4m S of Callington. Signed from r'bouts on A388 at St Mellion and Hatt, and on A38 at Landrake. In middle of village opp Weary Friar PH. Roadside parking. Please do not park in PH carpark.* **Sun 6 May, Sun 17 June (1-5). Adm £5, chd free. Home-made teas. Visits also by arrangement May to July for groups of 15+, eg gardening clubs or coach parties, please phone to discuss arrangements.**

Cottage style garden, about 0.3 acre, arranged with separate spaces. First an area of landscaped dry planting and a small pond. Outside the front door the theme is tropical with various palms, yuccas, agave and cannas. S-facing rear garden with views across the R Lynher valley, and sun terraces with plenty of seating. Sloping and level lawns and herbaceous borders, filled in spring with bulbs, flowering shrubs and clematis, a riot of colour in June. Fair sized pond and small shady woodland area. Due to steps there is only wheelchair access to the front dry garden and rear terrace, from which most of the rest of garden can be viewed.

45 TREBARTHA

Trebartha, nr Launceston, PL15 7PD. The Latham Family. *6m SW of Launceston. North Hill, SW of Launceston nr junction of B3254 & B3257. No coaches.* **Sun 13 May, Sun 2 Sept (2-5). Adm £5, chd free. Home-made teas.**

Historic landscape gardens featuring ponds, streams, cascades, rocks and woodlands, including fine American trees, bluebells in spring, ornamental walled garden and private garden at Lemarne (best seen in autumn). Allow at least 1 hour for a circular walk. Some steep and rough paths, which can be slippery when wet. Stout footwear advised. Interesting garden project in progress.

46 TREGONNING

Carleen, Breage, Helston, TR13 9QU. Andrew & Kathryn Eaton, tregonninggarden.co.uk. *1m S of Godolphin Cross. From Xrds in centre of Godolphin Cross head S towards Carleen. In ½m at fork signed Breage 1¼ turn R up narrow lane marked no through rd. After ½m parking on L opp Tregonning Farm.* **Sat 28, Sun 29 July (1-5). Adm £4, chd free. Home-made teas.**

Located 300ft up NE side of Tregonning Hill this small (less than 1 acre) maturing garden will hopefully inspire those thinking of making a garden from nothing more than a pond and copse of trees (in 2009). With the ever present challenge of storm force winds, garden offers yr-round interest and a self-sufficient vegetable and soft fruit paddock. Sculpted grass meadow, with panoramic views from Carn Brea to Helston. A section of the garden is designed in the form of a plant (incorporating a deck, leaf shaped beds, stream and large pond). Formal front garden, Spring garden, Mediterranean patio. Carp pond/small fernery. Packed vegetable garden. Parking in field, but access to garden is via short grass. Spring garden not accessible to wheelchairs. For front garden access see owners.

47 ◆ TREMATON CASTLE

Castle Hill, Trematon, Saltash, PL12 4QW. Bannerman, info@bannermandesign.com, www.bannermandesign.com/trematon. *2m SW of Saltash. Lanes surrounding the castle are very narrow, please approach from Trematon and Trehan.* **For opening times and information, please email or visit garden website.**

Property of Duchy of Cornwall since the Conquest, Trematon is a perfect miniature motte and bailey castle. On R Lynher estuary, '... one of the superb views of Cornwall .... all the more romantic for being still a private residence' (John Betjeman). Julian and Isabel Bannerman have begun to create a garden playing on its pre-Raphaelite glories, wild flowers, orchard, woodland, scented borders, seaside and exotic planting. Regrettably not suitable for wheelchair users, pea gravel throughout.

48 TRENARTH

High Cross, Constantine, Falmouth, TR11 5JN. Lucie Nottingham, 01326 340444, lmnottingham@btinternet.com, www.trenarthgardens.com. *6m SW of Falmouth. Main rd A39/A394 Truro to Helston, follow Constantine signs. High X garage turn L for Mawnan, 30yds on R down dead end lane, Trenarth is ½m at end of lane.* **Sun 24 June (2-5). Adm £5, chd free. Cream teas. Visits also by arrangement Mar to Oct garden clubs and groups especially welcome, tour and teas provided.**

4 acres round C17 farmhouse in peaceful pastoral setting. Yr-round interest. Emphasis on tender, unusual plants, structure and form. C16 courtyard, listed garden walls, yew rooms, vegetable garden, traditional potting shed, orchard, new woodland area with childrens' interest, palm and gravel garden. Circular walk down ancient green lane via animal pond to Trenarth Bridge, returning through woods. Abundant wildlife. Bees in tree bole, lesser horseshoe bat colony, swallows, wild flowers and butterflies. Family friendly, children's play area, the Wolery, and plenty of room to run, jump and climb. Featured in CGS magazine, article on growing dieramas.

49 TREREIFE PARK

Penzance, TR20 8TJ. Mr & Mrs T Le Grice, 01736 362750, trereifepark@btconnect.com, www.trereifepark.co.uk. *2m W of Penzance on A30 on Lands End rd. Garden and house signed R through estate gates.* **Visits by arrangement May to Sept, garden and house tours available. Adm £6, chd free. Cream teas.**

Mature gardens undergoing restoration in the historic setting of Trereife Park. Established specimen camellia, rhododendron, azalea walk under mature beech trees. Modern parterre, sculptural yew hedge, S-facing walled terrace with wisteria and magnolia. New hot border with unusual Mediterranean planting. Medlar collection around events lawn and old kitchen garden awaiting restoration.

50 ◆ TREWIDDEN GARDEN

Buryas Bridge, Penzance, TR20 8TT. Mr Alverne Bolitho - Richard Morton, Head Gardener, 01736 364275/363021, contact@trewiddengarden.co.uk, www.trewiddengarden.co.uk. *2m W of Penzance. Entry on A30 just before Buryas Bridge. SatNav TR19 6AU.* **For NGS: Sat 7 Apr (10.30-5.30). Adm £6.50, chd free. Light refreshments.** For other opening times and information, please phone, email or visit garden website.

Historic Victorian garden with magnolias, camellias and magnificent tree ferns planted within ancient tin workings. Tender, rare and unusual exotic plantings create a riot of colour thoughout the season. Water features, specimen trees and artefacts from Cornwall's tin industry provide a wide range of interest for all.

NPC

51 ◆ VARFELL FARM

Long Rock, Penzance, TR20 8AQ. Mr A Vickers, 01736 339276, avickers@greenyardfresh.co.uk, www.nationaldahliacollection.co.uk. *3m N of Penzance. Turn off A30 near Long Rock r'about, signed Varfell.* For opening times and information, please phone, email or visit garden website.

National Dahlia Collection growing in 2 acre field of riotous colour which delights the eye. All types of dahlias are exhibited from dainty pompoms to huge decoratives amounting to 1600 named varieties bred and grown here. Displayed in ordered rows, fully labelled for identification in mail order sales. Open to the public free of charge from Aug to mid Oct, donations to NGS welcomed. Come and see the extraordinary show. Coach parties welcome by prior arrangement. In dry conditions with some wheelchairs it is possible to move around the field or possible to view the field as a whole from road.

NPC

52 WAYE COTTAGE

Lerryn, nr Lostwithiel, PL22 0QQ. Malcolm & Jennifer Bell, 01208 872119. *4m S of Lostwithiel. Parking usually available at property or village parking, garden 10min, level stroll along riverbank/stepping stones. Open most days in April and June but do ring first - best after 6pm.* **Daily Sun 1 Apr to Mon 30 Apr (10-5). Daily Fri 1 June to Sat 30 June (10-5). Adm £4, chd free. Light refreshments. Visits also by arrangement Apr to June, garden and other groups welcomed at reduced rates.**

An enchanting cottage garden - good plants, enticing paths, secluded seats and stunning river views. 'Magical! The perfect place for a botanical recharge and horticultural inspiration.' Reproduced courtesy of Cornwall Life magazine. Featured in Cornwall Life and Cornwall Today. Steep paths and steps sadly make it impossible for the disabled.

53 WINDMILLS

South Hill, Callington, PL17 7LP. Mr & Mrs Peter Tunnicliffe, 01579 363981. *3m NW of Callington. Head N from Callington A388, after about ½m turn L onto South Hill Rd (signed South Hill). Straight on for 3m, gardens on R just before church.* **Sun 24 June, Sun 1 July (1.30-5). Combined adm with Anvil Cottage £5, chd free. Home-made teas. Gluten free cakes available. Visits also by arrangement May & June.**

Next to medieval church and on the site of an old rectory and there are still signs in places of that long gone building. A garden full of surprises, formal paths and steps lead up from the flower beds to extensive vegetable and soft fruit area. More paths lead to water feature with rustic stone bridge, past a pergola, and down into large lawns with trees and shrubs. Limited wheelchair access.

Trebartha

CUMBRIA

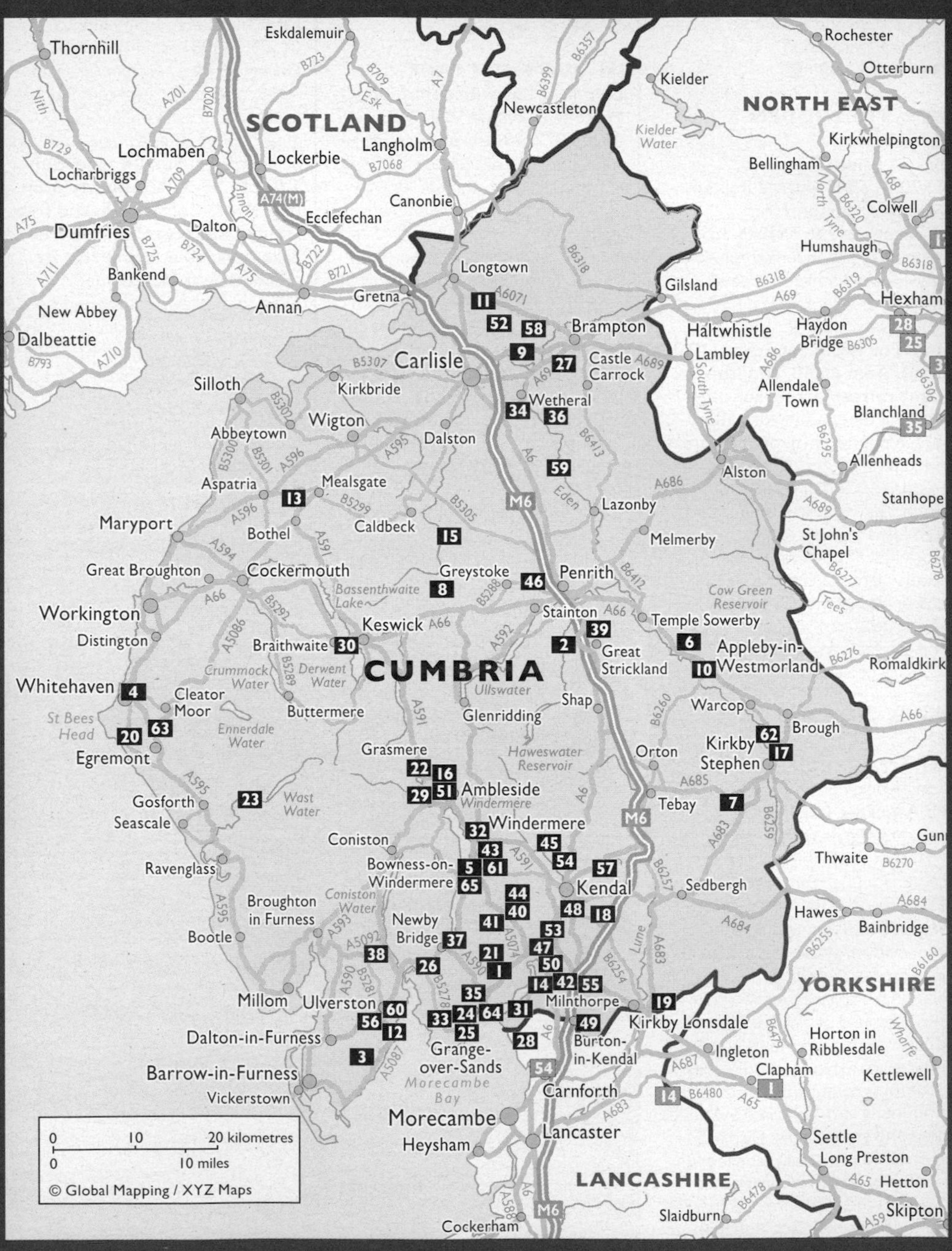
SCOTLAND
NORTH EAST
CUMBRIA
YORKSHIRE
LANCASHIRE
Thornhill
Eskdalemuir
Newcastleton
Kielder
Kielder Water
Rochester
Otterburn
Kirkwhelpington
Bellingham
Colwell
Humshaugh
Hexham
Haydon Bridge
Haltwhistle
Lambley
Allendale Town
Blanchland
Allenheads
Stanhope
St John's Chapel
Alston
Gilsland
Lochmaben
Lockerbie
Langholm
Locharbriggs
Canonbie
Ecclefechan
Dumfries
Dalton
Bankend
New Abbey
Dalbeattie
Annan
Gretna
Longtown
Brampton
Castle Carrock
Carlisle
Kirkbride
Silloth
Wigton
Dalston
Wetheral
Abbeytown
Aspatria
Mealsgate
Maryport
Bothel
Caldbeck
Lazonby
Melmerby
Great Broughton
Cockermouth
Workington
Distington
Greystoke
Penrith
Bassenthwaite Lake
Keswick
Braithwaite
Stainton
Temple Sowerby
Cow Green Reservoir
Appleby-in-Westmorland
Great Strickland
Romaldkirk
Whitehaven
Cleator Moor
Crummock Water
Derwent Water
Buttermere
Ullswater
Glenridding
Shap
Warcop
Brough
St Bees Head
Egremont
Ennerdale Water
Grasmere
Haweswater Reservoir
Orton
Kirkby Stephen
Ambleside
Windermere
Tebay
Gosforth
Seascale
Wast Water
Coniston
Ravenglass
Bowness-on-Windermere
Kendal
Sedbergh
Thwaite
Gunn
Hawes
Bainbridge
Broughton in Furness
Coniston Water
Newby Bridge
Bootle
Millom
Ulverston
Milnthorpe
Kirkby Lonsdale
Dalton-in-Furness
Grange-over-Sands
Burton-in-Kendal
Ingleton
Horton in Ribblesdale
Clapham
Kettlewell
Barrow-in-Furness
Vickerstown
Morecambe Bay
Carnforth
Morecambe
Lancaster
Heysham
Settle
Long Preston
Hetton
Skipton
Slaidburn
Cockerham
Nith
Esk
Annan
Eden
Lune
Tees
South Tyne
North Tyne
Wharfe
M6
A74(M)
A6071
A69
A6
A66
A591
A590
A595
A596
A686
A689
A683
A684
A685
A65
A687
A7
A75
A701
A709
A711
A710
B7020
B723
B709
B6357
B6399
B6318
B6320
B6319
B6305
B6306
B6295
B6278
B6277
B6276
B6270
B6260
B6259
B6257
B6255
B6254
B6160
B6413
B6412
B5305
B5307
B5302
B5300
B5301
B5299
B5292
B5289
B5288
A592
A5086
A5092
A593
A5074
B5278
B5281
A5087
A683
A588
B6479
B6480
B6478
A59
B7068
B729
B725
B724
B722
B721
B793
A594
A5092
0 10 20 kilometres
0 10 miles
© Global Mapping / XYZ Maps
1 2 3 4 5 6 7 8 9 10 11 12 13 14 15 16 17 18 19 20 21 22 23 24 25 26 27 28 29 30 31 32 33 34 35 36 37 38 39 40 41 42 43 44 45 46 47 48 49 50 51 52 53 54 55 56 57 58 59 60 61 62 63 64 65

Venture into Daniel Defoe's "... County eminent only for being the wildest, most barren and frightful of any that I have passed over in England, or even in Wales itself..." and be amazed by the gardens and horticultural excellence that Cumbria can offer.

From Rydal Halls 17th centaury Picturesque 'Viewing Room', through the C19 planting of Dora's Field (Wordsworth's remembrance of his dead daughter) and founding of the British Pteridological Society, to C21 gardens created by Chelsea Gold Medal winners – for more than 300 years Cumberland and Westmorland (now Cumbria) have provided England with gardens and scenery second to none. In 2017 much of the county gained UNESCO World Heritage Site status in recognition of its cultural heritage.

Considered by the knowledgeable worth the journey over 300 years ago it is still a county to visit for gardens that encompass all gardening traditions. From real cottage garden providing produce for the family to the set piece gardens of the great estates – all can be found in the far north west of England.

Below: Summerdale House

© Val Corbett

Volunteers

County Organiser
Diane Hewitt
01539 446238
dhewitt.kinsman@gmail.com

County Treasurer
Derek Farman
01539 444893
derek@derejam.myzen.co.uk

Publicity –
Publications & Special Interest
Carole Berryman
01539 443649
Carole.Berryman@student.sac.ac.uk

Publicity – Social Media
Gráinne Jakobson
01946 813017
gmjakobson22@gmail.com

Booklet Co-ordinator
Diane Hewitt (as above)

Assistant County Organisers

Central
Carole Berryman (as above)

East
Sue Sharkey
07811 710248
bsjsewebank@btinternet.com

North
Alannah Rylands
01697 320413
alannah.rylands@me.com

North East
Cate Bowman
01228 573903
catebowman@icloud.com

North East
Grace Kirby
01228 670076
gracekirby03@gmail.com

South East
Linda & Alec Greening
01524 781624
lindagreening48@gmail.com

West
Gráinne Jakobson (as above)

OPENING DATES

All entries subject to change. For latest information check **www.ngs.org.uk**

Extended openings are shown at the beginning of the month.

Map locator numbers are shown to the right of each garden name.

February

Snowdrop Festival

Every Friday and Saturday from Friday 23rd
Summerdale House 56

Every day from Monday 19th
◆ Swarthmoor Hall 57

Sunday 18th
Summerdale House 56

March

Every Friday and Saturday
Summerdale House 56

Every day to Sunday 11th
◆ Swarthmoor Hall 57

Sunday 25th
◆ Dora's Field 16
◆ High Close Estate and Arboretum 30
High Moss 31
◆ Holehird Gardens 33
◆ Rydal Hall 52

April

Every Friday and Saturday
Summerdale House 56

Saturday 7th
NEW Deer Rudding 15

Sunday 8th
Fern Bank 20

Saturday 21st
◆ Conishead Priory and Buddhist Temple 12

Sunday 22nd
◆ Conishead Priory and Buddhist Temple 12
Orchard Cottage 48

Thursday 26th
◆ Rydal Hall 52

Monday 30th
Newton Rigg College Gardens 47

May

Every Friday and Saturday
Summerdale House 56

Saturday 5th
NEW Deer Rudding 15

Sunday 6th
Brackenrigg Cottage 5
Low Fell West 42
Windy Hall 62

Monday 7th
Low Fell West 42

Saturday 12th
Highlands 32

Sunday 13th
Dallam Tower 14
Highlands 32
Woodend House 64

Friday 18th
Chapelside 8

Saturday 19th
Chapelside 8
Langholme Mill 39

Sunday 20th
Chapelside 8
Cherry Cottage 9
Church View 10
Langholme Mill 39
Matson Ground 44
Mirefoot 46
◆ Rydal Hall 52
Sprint Mill 55

Sunday 27th
Fell Yeat 19
Orchard Cottage 48
Tenter End Barn 58

June

Every Friday and Saturday
Summerdale House 56

Friday 1st
Chapelside 8

Festival Weekend

Saturday 2nd
Beckside Farm 3
Chapelside 8
NEW Deer Rudding 15
Galesyke 23
Trio of Armathwaite Gardens 60

Sunday 3rd
Brackenrigg Cottage 5
Chapelside 8
Galesyke 23
Low Blakebank 41
Middle Blakebank 45
Tithe Barn 59
Trio of Armathwaite Gardens 60
Windy Hall 62
Yewbarrow House 65

Wednesday 6th
Larch Cottage Nurseries 40

Saturday 9th
Beckside Farm 3

Sunday 10th
Hayton Village Gardens 27
Hazelwood Farm 29
8 Oxenholme Road 49
Yews 66

Friday 15th
Chapelside 8

Saturday 16th
Beckside Farm 3
Chapelside 8

Sunday 17th
Askham Hall 2
Chapelside 8
Summerdale House 56

Thursday 21st
Haverthwaite Lodge 26
Lakeside Hotel & Rocky Bank 38

Saturday 23rd
Beckside Farm 3

Sunday 24th
NEW Grange over Sands Hidden Gardens 25
Ivy House 37
Orchard Cottage 48
Sandhouse 53

Friday 29th
Chapelside 8

Saturday 30th
Beckside Farm 3
Chapelside 8

July

Every Friday and Saturday
Summerdale House 56

Sunday 1st
Chapelside 8
Ewebank Farm 18
Hazel Cottage 28
Ulverston Town & Country Gardens 61
Yewbarrow House 65

Saturday 7th
Beckside Farm 3

Sunday 8th
Abi and Tom's Garden Plants 1
NEW Cliffe Cottage, Kirklinton 11
Fernhill Coach House 21

Thursday 12th
◆ Holehird Gardens 33

Saturday 14th
Beckside Farm 3

Sunday 15th
Holme Meadow 35
Winton Park 63

Saturday 21st
Beckside Farm 3

Sunday 22nd
Eden Place 17

Saturday 28th
Beckside Farm 3

August

Every Friday and Saturday
Summerdale House 56

Saturday 4th
Beckside Farm 3

Sunday 5th
Fell Yeat 19
NEW HPB Merlewood 36
Yewbarrow House 65

Saturday 11th
Beckside Farm 3

Sunday 12th
Berriedale 4
NEW Rose Croft 51

Thursday 16th
Haverthwaite Lodge 26
Lakeside Hotel & Rocky Bank 38

Saturday 18th
Beckside Farm 3

Sunday 19th
Grange Fell Allotments 24

Thursday 23rd
◆ Holker Hall Gardens 34

Saturday 25th
Beckside Farm 3

September

Sunday 2nd
Yewbarrow House 65

Sunday 9th
Low Fell West 42

Monday 10th
◆ Sizergh Castle 54

Thursday 13th
◆ Rydal Hall 52

Sunday 30th
Church View 10

October

Monday 1st
Newton Rigg College Gardens 47

Wednesday 31st
Larch Cottage Nurseries 40

By Arrangement

Beckside Farm 3
Berriedale 4
Broom Cottage 6
The Chantry 7
Chapelside 8
Cherry Cottage 9
Church View 10
Crookdake Farm 13
NEW Deer Rudding 15
Ewebank Farm 18
Fell Yeat 19
Fernhill Coach House 21
Forest Side 22
Galesyke 23
Grange Fell Allotments 24
Haverthwaite Lodge 26
Hazelwood Farm 29
High Moss 31
Highlands 32
Holme Meadow 35
Ivy House 37
Kinrara, Hayton Village Gardens 27
Lakeside Hotel & Rocky Bank 38
Langholme Mill 39
Low Blakebank 41
Low Fell West 42
Lower Rowell Farm & Cottage 43
Matson Ground 44
Middle Blakebank 45
Newton Rigg College Gardens 47
Orchard Cottage 48
8 Oxenholme Road 49
Pear Tree Cottage 50
Sprint Mill 55
Tenter End Barn 58
West Garth Cottage, Hayton Village Gardens 27
Windy Hall 62
Woodend House 64
Yewbarrow House 65

THE GARDENS

1 ABI AND TOM'S GARDEN PLANTS

Halecat, Witherslack, Grange-Over-Sands, LA11 6RT. Abi & Tom Attwood, www.abiandtom.co.uk. *20 mins from Kendal. From A590 turn N to Witherslack. Follow brown tourist signs to Halecat. Rail Grange-over-sands 5m, Bus X6 2m, NCR 70.* **Sun 8 July (10-5). Combined adm with The Coach House £3.50, chd free. Home-made teas.**
The 1 acre nursery garden is a fusion of traditional horticultural values with modern approaches to the display, growing and use of plant material. Our full range of perennials can be seen growing alongside one another in themed borders be they shady damp corners or south facing hot spots. The propagating areas, stock beds and family garden, normally closed to visitors, will be open on the NGS day. More than 1,000 different herbaceous perennials are grown on the nursery, many that are excellent for wildlife. For other opening times and information please phone, e-mail or visit website. Sloping site that has no steps but steep inclines in places.

2 ASKHAM HALL

Askham, Penrith, CA10 2PF. Countess of Lonsdale, 01931 712350, enquiries@askhamhall.co.uk, www.askhamhall.co.uk. *5m S of Penrith. Turn off A6 for Lowther & Askham.* **Sun 17 June (11-5). Adm £2, chd free. Light refreshments. Cafe serving tea, coffee, light lunches, cake. Wood-fired pizza oven. BBQ and bar serving pimms and real ales in the courtyard. Donation to Askham and Lowther Churches.**
Askham Hall is a Pele Tower incorporating C14, C16 and early C18 elements in a courtyard plan. Opened in 2013 with luxury accommodation, a restaurant, spa, cafe and wedding barn. Splendid formal garden with terraces of herbaceous borders and topiary, dating back to C17. Meadow area with trees and pond, kitchen gardens and animal trails. Cafe serving tea, coffee, cake, lunch and ice-cream. Combined with Summer Fair.

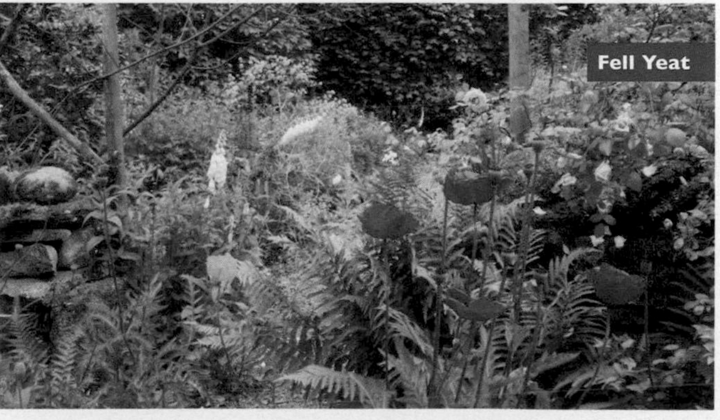
Fell Yeat
© Linda Greening

3 BECKSIDE FARM

Little Urswick, Cumbria, nr Ulverston, LA12 0PY. Anna Thomason, 01229 869151, anna@becksidefarm.eclipse.co.uk. *On outskirts of village - good off road parking. A590 towards Barrow. S off A590 to Urswick. Go through Great Urswick & Little Urswick. Park at T-junction. Rail Ulverston 4m, NCR 70 & 700 ½m.* **Sat 2, 9, 16, 23, 30 June, 7, 14, 21, 28 July, 4, 11, 18, 25 Aug (12-5). Adm £3.50, chd free. Light refreshments for day openings or groups need to be pre-ordered - phone 01229 869151. Visits also by arrangement June to Sept.**

Organic cottage garden with raised beds, herbaceous borders. Many unusual\new varieties of tender perennials and annuals, raised from seed and cuttings each year. Several interesting patio/seating areas. Productive greenhouse, again with unusual varieties. Ferns and summer flowering bulbs in pots. Ulverston is a pretty market town that has many tea shops and several pubs serving food.

4 BERRIEDALE

15 Loop Road South, Whitehaven, CA28 7TN. Enid & John Stanborough, 01946 695467. *From S, A595 through T-lights onto Loop Rd approx 150yds on R. From N, A595 onto Loop Rd at Pelican Garage, garden approx 1½m on L. Whitehaven rail stn 20 mins brisk walk, mainly up hill.* **Sun 12 Aug (2-5). Adm £3.50, chd free. Home-made teas.** Visits also by arrangement any numbers -refreshments by arrangement Parking for up to small mini bus or on estate or 1m away.

Suburban garden, surprisingly large with different areas and levels. Incl large vegetable plot (with award winning onions and leeks), pond, Japanese inspired border and many seating areas around the garden. Children love the fairy dell and mini trail. The owners raise over 1000 bedding plants which give riotous colour around the garden in mid to late summer. John wins prizes with his fuchsias at local shows and has many for sale. Partial wheelchair access to most of flower garden. Vegetable garden can be accessed by separate entrance with prior notice.

Chapelside

5 BRACKENRIGG COTTAGE

Windy Hall Road, Bowness-on-Windermere, LA23 3HY. Lynne Bush. *½m S of Bowness. Just off B5284 on Windy Hall Rd, opp Linthwaite Hotel entrance. Rail 2.6m; Bus 1m, 6, 599, 755, 800; NCR 6.* **Sun 6 May (10-5), also open Low Fell West. Sun 3 June (10-5). Combined adm with Windy Hall £7, chd free. Home-made teas at Windy Hall. Single garden adm £5.**

3 acres of wildlife garden run on organic lines with a combination of native and cultivated plants, shrubs and trees. Water features created from a diverted culvert giving streams, waterfall and pond. Woodland area, bog garden, wild flower meadows. The new deer fence works a treat. Stout footwear needed. The Cottage is a new build so please excuse where the builders have yet to finish. Thank you. Very limited access for wheelchairs but the garden can be viewed from a distance.

6 BROOM COTTAGE

Long Marton, Appleby-In-Westmorland, CA16 6JP. Mr & Mrs Peter & Janet Cox, 01768 362896, peter_janet_cox@hotmail.com. *From A66 1m E of Kirkby Thore, take turn signed Long Marton, then sharp R just before churchyard. From Appleby, follow signs to Long Marton (2m), L at church.* **Visits by arrangement June to Sept individuals and small groups max 20. Unsuitable for coaches, but minibus possible. Adm £4, chd free. Light refreshments.**

Peaceful 2 acre wildlife garden set around C18 former farmhouse. Wildlife pond with ducks and moorhens, stream, wild copse and wild flower hay meadow with mown paths. Beautiful views of the Pennines and surrounded by pastures. A haven for birds. Large productive organic fruit and vegetable garden. Bee friendly walled herb garden, shrub and cottage garden borders. Featured in Cumbria Life. Surfaces are tarmac, cobbles, slate chippings and mown grass which may be wheelchair accessible. An area of pebbles in the walled herb garden is not.

7 THE CHANTRY

Ravenstonedale, Kirkby Stephen, CA17 4NQ. Joan & John Houston, 01539 623468, joanbarnard@btinternet.com. *8mE J38 M6 (Tebay), 4m W Kirkby Stephen. From A685, follow signs for Ravenstonedale, into village.* **Visits by arrangement Apr to Sept for groups of 10 - 25. Refreshments and visits to other neighbouring gardens by arrangement. Teas, light lunches by arrangement.**
Formal areas around the fine Victorian house contrast with informal areas, which link the garden with panoramic views of the surrounding Howgill Fells. Herbaceous borders, large wildlife pond, vegetable beds. Various seating areas and features using reclaimed materials. In development since 2008, by trial and error rather than experience and still very much work in progress. What garden isn't?

8 CHAPELSIDE

Mungrisdale, Penrith, CA11 0XR. Tricia & Robin Acland, 017687 79672. *12m W of Penrith. On A66 take minor rd N signed Mungrisdale. After 2m, sharp bends, garden on L immed after tiny church on R. Park at foot of our short drive. On C2C Reivers 71, 10 cycle routes.* **Fri 18, Sat 19, Sun 20 May, Fri 1, Sat 2, Sun 3, Fri 15, Sat 16, Sun 17, Fri 29, Sat 30 June, Sun 1 July (1-5). Adm £3.50, chd free. Visits also by arrangement. Refreshments for groups by arrangement.**
1 acre organic windy garden below fell, around C18 farmhouse and outbuildings, latter mainly open. Fine views. Tiny stream, large pond. Alpine, herbaceous, raised, gravel, damp and shade beds, bulbs in grass. Extensive range of plants, many unusual. Relaxed planting regime. Art constructions in and out, local stone used creatively.

9 CHERRY COTTAGE

Crosby Moor, Crosby-On-Eden, Carlisle, CA6 4QX. Mr & Mrs John & Lesley Connolly, 01228 573614, jtlaconnolly@aol.com. *Off A689 midway between Carlisle & Brampton. Take turn signed 'Wallhead'. Cherry Cottage is on the corner of junction on R. Park in the lane.* **Sun 20 May (11-5). Adm £3.50, chd free. Light refreshments. £1.50 for 'tea & cake'. Visits also by arrangement Apr to Sept max 20.**
Relaxed country garden surrounding an C18 cottage on an approx. ⅓ acre site. It has a wide range of habitats incl herbaceous borders, wildlife pond, bog garden, shady woodland, productive fruit and vegetable area, 2 greenhouses and summer house. Various seating areas connected by grass and gravel paths. Not suitable for wheelchairs. Refreshment proceeds to Epilepsy Action. Featured in 'Cumberland News'.

10 CHURCH VIEW

Bongate, Appleby-in-Westmorland, CA16 6UN. Mrs H Holmes, 017683 51397, engcougars@btinternet.com, www.engcougars.co.uk/church-view. *0.4m SE of Appleby town centre. A66 W take B6542 for 2m St Michael's Church on L garden opp. A66 E take B6542 & continue to Royal Oak Inn, garden next door, opp church.* **Sun 20 May, Sun 30 Sept (12-4). Adm £4, chd free. Refreshments are available locally. Visits also by arrangement May to Oct.**
It's all about the plants! Less than ½ acre of garden but with layers of texture, colour and interest in abundance, this is a garden for plantaholics. Plant combinations are at the heart of the design. With self-contained vistas and maximum use of planting space, the garden photographs very well and has been a subject for many local and national publications and photographers over the last decade. Featured in the 90 gardens blog: thegardengateisopen.blog Partial wheelchair, main garden is on a sloping site with gravel paths.

11 NEW CLIFFE COTTAGE, KIRKLINTON

Carlisle, CA6 6DE. Mrs Michelle Marsh. *Turn off the A7 signed Scaleby & Cliff. From the A6701 from Longtown / Brampton turn on the bend signed Blackford 5m Carlisle 7m.* **Sun 8 July (10.30-4). Adm £4, chd free. Home-made teas. A selection of homemade baking available.**
Large garden with mature flower beds and trees. Productive vegetable patch and a small orchard. Wildlife pond with wild planting and bog garden. Homemade refreshments available. Parking available on driveway for wheelchair access.

12 ◆ CONISHEAD PRIORY AND BUDDHIST TEMPLE

A5087 Coast Road, Ulverston, LA12 9QQ. Manjushri Kadampa Meditation Centre, 01229 584029 Ext 234, visits@manjushri.com, www.manjushri.org. *2m S of Ulverston. 30 mins from M6 J36, follow A590 to Ulverston then S onto A5087 Coast Rd signed Croftlands, Bardsea & 'Coastal route to Barrow'. Rail 2 m, Bus 11, NCR 700.* **For NGS: Sat 21, Sun 22 Apr (11-5). Adm £3.60, chd free. Light refreshments. For other opening times and information, please phone, email or visit garden website.**
Conishead Priory was founded by Augustinian monks in 1160. 70 acres of gardens and woodland surround the Temple and Romantic Gothic mansion. Temple garden an oasis of peace, arboretum, wildlife and cottage gardens. Map of woodland walks to beach on Morecambe Bay. Free simple 15 min. Guided Meditations at 12.30, 2 and 3.30 and guided tours of Temple and part of the mansion at 1 and 2.30.

13 CROOKDAKE FARM

Aspatria, Wigton, CA7 3SH. Kirk & Alannah Rylands, 016973 20413, alannah.rylands@me.com. *3m NE of Aspatria. Between A595 & A596. From A595 take B5299 at Mealsgate signed Aspatria. After 2m turn sharp R in Watch Hill signed Crookdake. House 1m on L.* **Visits by arrangement June & July 10+ Refreshments by arrangement. Adm £4, chd free. Home-made teas.**

Windswept informal farmhouse (not open) garden with a careful colour combination of interesting planting sympathetic to the landscape incl various different areas with densely planted herbaceous borders, fenced vegetable patch, wild meadow and large pond area home to moisture-loving plants, hens, ducks and moorhens.

14 DALLAM TOWER

Milnthorpe, LA7 7AG. Mr & Mrs R T Villiers-Smith. *7m S of Kendal. 7m N of Carnforth. Nr J36 off M6. A6 & B5282. Stn: Arnside, 4m; Lancaster, 15m.* **Sun 13 May (2-5). Adm £4, chd free. Cream teas.**

Dallam Tower is set in 150 acres of parkland with a large herd of Fallow deer. The gardens have extensive sunken lawns, a natural stream feeding into a limestone rock garden, a gravel woodland path with mature trees and a Yew tree walk. Wander past shrubs, topiary, roses and enjoy afternoon tea by the stunningly beautiful C19 cast iron Orangery. Limited wheelchair access Deep gravel paths.

15 NEW DEER RUDDING

Hesket Newmarket, Wigton, CA7 8HU. Mrs Lynne Carruthers, deer.rudding@gmail.com, , http://deerrudding.garden. *Located off the road from Millhouse to Haltcliff Bridge, not in Hesket Newmarket. From Penrith J41 of M6 take B5305 6.8m, L to Hesket Newmarket 2.2m, at Millhouse L to Haltcliffe Bridge by village hall, continue 1m, R over cattle grid.* **Sat 7 Apr, Sat 5 May, Sat 2 June (11-4.30). Adm £5, chd free. Refreshments from local cafes at Caldbeck, Hesket Newmarket and Unthank. Visits also by arrangement Feb to Oct.**

Set in the lee of the Northern Fells and on the bank of the Caldew, enjoying views into the wider landscape, notably Carrock Fell. The garden surrounds a former Cumbrian farmhouse and outbuildings with a good range of planting: mixed shrub and perennial borders; woodland and meadow grass areas; extensive rockery. There are a number of gates and gravel pathways.

16 ◆ DORA'S FIELD

Rydal, Ambleside, LA22 9LX. National Trust, www.nationaltrust.org.uk. *1½m N of Ambleside. Follow A591 from Ambleside to Rydal. Dora's Field is next to St Mary's Church.* **For NGS: Sun 25 Mar (11-4). Adm by donation. Also open High Close Estate and Arboretum. For other opening times and information, please visit garden website.**

Named for Dora, the daughter of the poet William Wordsworth. Wordsworth planned to build a house on the land but, after her early death, he planted the area with daffodils in her memory. Now known as Dora's field the area is renowned for its spring display of daffodils and Bluebells. 25 March; Wordsworth's Daffodil Legacy.

17 EDEN PLACE

Kirkby Stephen, CA17 4AP. J S Parrot Trust. *½m N of Kirkby Stephen. A685 Kirkby Stephen to Brough.* **Sun 22 July (11-5). Adm £4, chd free. Home-made teas.**

3 acre garden with many large perennial borders and island beds enclosed by tall hedges. Part of the garden is made over to aviaries with exotic birds, some are free - flying. Also a lake and a woodland walk. Free-flying parrots and a display of Victorian costumes.

18 EWEBANK FARM

Old Hutton, Kendal, LA8 0NS. Sue & Barry Sharkey, 01539 722954. *3m NE of Kendal. Oxenholme Stn - B6254 - Old Hutton. 3rd turning on L. R turns at next 2 junctions. M6 take J37 A684 Sedbergh. 1st R & R again. After 3m turn L. Ewebank. From Oxenholme Station, bikes take (70)68.* **Sun 1 July (1-5). Adm £4, chd free. Light refreshments. Visits also by arrangement July to Sept for groups of 10 - 15.**

Relaxing, rural, wildlife friendly garden, 'green roof' and sink gardens. Welcoming hens and suggestions of music. Large lawn slopes down to a stream where curved decking follows the gentle contours of the land. Areas of shade for ferns, moisture-loving plants, over 70 varieties of hostas and new cobbled mosaics. Mixed borders, statues, topiary, raised vegetable beds, orchard and espaliered apples. Visitors from an Owl Sanctuary.

19 FELL YEAT

Casterton, Kirkby Lonsdale, LA6 2JW. Mrs A E Benson, 01524 271340. *1m E of Casterton Village. On the rd to Bull Pot. Leave A65 at Devils Bridge, follow A683 for 1m, take the R fork to High Casterton at golf course, straight across at two sets of Xrds, house on L, ¼m from no-through-rd sign.* **Sun 27 May, Sun 5 Aug (1-5). Adm £4, chd free. Home-made teas. Visits also by arrangement May to Sept groups of 10 to 25. No coaches. Refreshments by arrangement.**

1 acre country garden with mixed planting, incl unusual trees, shrubs and some topiary. Small woodland garden and woodland glades. 2 ponds which encourage dragonflies. Several arbours where you can sit and relax. New paved topiary garden. Many ferns in a designated area; old roses in mixed borders and a large collection of hydrangeas. A garden to explore. Metal sculptures in various areas. Adjoining nursery specialising in ferns, hostas, hydrangeas and many unusual plants. Featured in Cumbria Life. Mostly mown grass with one or two gravel paths.

Deer Rudding

20 FERN BANK

High House Road, St. Bees, CA27 0BZ. Chris & Charm Robson. *At the edge of the village going out towards A595. 2m from A595 down road signed St Bees unsuitable for long vehicles (or something like that), or B5345 from Whitehaven.* **Sun 8 Apr (12-5). Adm £3.50, chd free. Home-made teas.**

Located in St Bees village, this is a spring garden on different levels with natural planting. Nearest the house lawns and borders lead down to the 'secret' garden via a pergola clad with roses, wisteria and clematis. Hidden away are 5 ponds surrounded by trees and boardwalks, a haven for wildlife. In Spring this area is lit up by snowdrops, leucojum, marsh marigolds and daffodils. Poetry trail through the garden. The entrance level where teas are served is wheelchair accessible but because of the steep slopes the rest of the garden is not accessible.

21 FERNHILL COACH HOUSE

Bleacragg Road,, Witherslack, Grange-Over-Sands, LA11 6RX. Adele & Mike Walford, 015395 52102, mwandaj@btinternet.com. *From A950 turn North to Witherslack. Follow brown signs to Halecat, continue on lane for ½ m. Fern Hill on R. Rail Grange-over-sands 5m, Bus X6 2m, NCR 70.* **Sun 8 July (10-5). Combined adm with Abi and Tom's Garden Plants £3.50, chd free. Home-made teas and cakes, Coach House apple juice.** Visits also by arrangement June to Sept.

Approx one acre garden - a riot of chaotic exuberance. From a stable yard, old tip and remnants of an orchard, seven years of hard work have resulted in a garden. Mixed borders, lots of vegetables, greenhouse, polytunnel, ponds and lots of roses. We are members of the South Lakes Orchard Group, we have a young orchard and northern and heritage apple trees for sale. Witherslack orchard Group Apple juice, Damson and Apple juice. To be featured in Cumbria Life July 2018. Wheelchair access is limited to the flower garden only. Paths are uneven and on sloping ground.

Funds from National Garden Scheme gardens help Macmillan support thousands of people every year

22 FOREST SIDE

Grasmere, Ambleside, LA22 9RN. Mr Greg Stephenson, 015394 35250, info@theforestside.com, www.theforestside.com. *Located on R of A591, set back from the road appro ½m after the Wordsworth Trust approaching from Ambleside or 100 metres on L after Swan Lane approaching from Keswick.* **Visits by arrangement May to Sept garden tours are conducted for small groups of between 4 - 12 max visitors. Adm £40. Please advise regarding any dietary requirements at the time of booking..**

Pre-booked tickets only adm £40 includes tour, welcome drink, four course lunch, with tea and coffee. The informal gardens surrounding the main property have also been cleverly designed by Frances Truscott working with our gardeners to provide an array of provender for the table. Not only that the 43 acres of woodland surrounding the hotel also provides a rich bounty of forageable plants, shoots and stems, which Kevin and his team use to full effect in the food they create and for the bar team to use in the creation of their imaginative cocktails and mocktails. Planted with over 100 varieties of vegetable and 25 types of herb, the kitchen garden aims to supply 60-70% of the produce needed. All produce is picked fresh daily, with the aim of ensuring the freshest possible crops. By reducing the length of time from farm to fork this increases the nutrient content and flavour quality of the produce. The garden also supplies the kitchen with a broad selection of micro greens, used for garnishes, a growing technique that increases the nutrient content by up to ten times. These are grown in the garden's traditional greenhouse – a vital resource in Cumbria to supplement what is produced in the garden. http://www.aspect-county.co.uk/blog/post.php?s=what-does-it-take-to-earn-a-michelin-star http://www.lancashirelife.co.uk/food-drink/food-and-drink-features/kevin-tickle-the-award-winning-chef-at-the-forest-side-in-grasmere-1-5057067. Due to the nature of the site, which includes steep steps to access terraced areas and undulating hillside, wheelchair access is not possible.

23 GALESYKE

Wasdale, CA20 1ET. Christine & Mike McKinley, 01946 726267, mckinley2112@sky.com. *From Gosforth, follow signs to Nether Wasdale & then to Lake, approx 5m. From Santon Bridge follow signs to Wasdale then to Lake, approx 2¼m.* **Sat 2, Sun 3 June (10.30-5). Adm £4, chd free. Cream teas. Visits also by arrangement May to Sept.**

4 acre woodland garden with spectacular views of the Wasdale fells. The R Irt runs through the garden and both banks are landscaped, you can cross over the river via a picturesque, mini, suspension bridge. The garden has an impressive collection of rhododendrons and azaleas that light up the woodlands in springtime.

ALLOTMENTS

24 GRANGE FELL ALLOTMENTS

Fell Road, Grange-Over-Sands, LA11 6HB. Mr Bruno Gouillon, 01539 532317, brunog45@hotmail.com. *Opposite Grange Fell Golf Club. Rail 1.3 m, Bus 1m X6, NCR 70.* **Sun 19 Aug (11-5). Adm £3, chd free. Visits also by arrangement Apr to Oct groups of 30 max.**

The allotments are managed by Grange Town Council. Opened in 2010, 30 plots are now rented out and offer a wide selection of gardening styles and techniques. The majority of plots grow a mixture of vegetables, fruit trees and flowers. There are a few communal areas where local fruit tree varieties have been donated by plot holders with herbaceous borders and annuals.

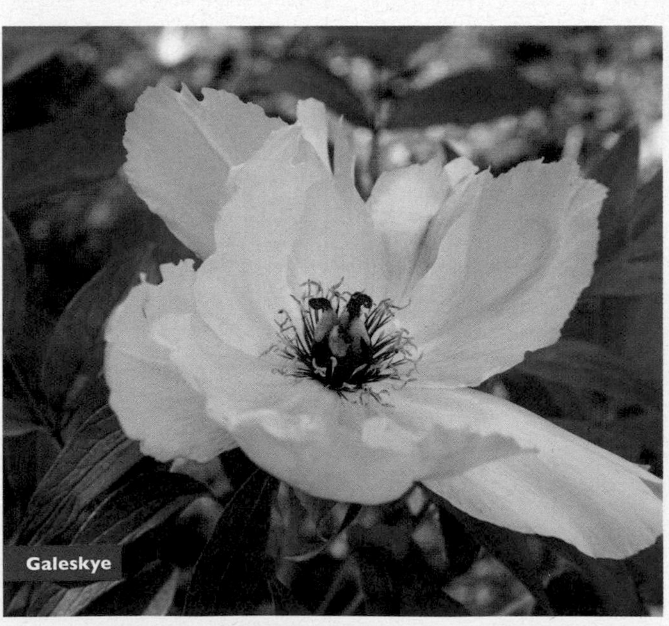

Galeskye

GROUP OPENING

25 NEW GRANGE OVER SANDS HIDDEN GARDENS

LA11 7AF. *Off Kents Bank Rd. 3 gardens are on Cart Lane and 2 Gardens on Kilmidyke Rd off Carter Rd. Rail 1.4m; Bus X6; NCR 70.*
Sun 24 June (11-5). Combined adm £4, chd free. Home-made teas.

NEW 21 CART LANE
Veronica Cameron.

NEW ELDER COTTAGE
Bruno Gouillon & Andrew Fairey.

NEW SUNBEAMS
Sue Lawton.

NEW SUNRISE COTTAGE
Mike & Mavis McKeown.

NEW WHISTLING GEM
Joan & Peter Lawton.

5 very different gardens hidden down narrow lanes off the road south out of Grange. Sunbeams and Sunrise are on a steep hillside with views across Morecambe Bay; neither have any flat areas. Sunbeams is managed without using pesticides and has a small pond to encourage wildlife. Lots of plants (and chickens) are packed into a small space. With no grass Sunrise is terraced with an emphasis on perennial planting providing colour throughout the year. There are challenging spaces, dry and damp and alpine areas. The 3 gardens on Cart Lane all back onto the railway embankment, providing shelter from the wind but also creating a frost pocket. 21 is a series of rooms designed to create an element of surprise with fruit and vegetables in raised beds. Elder cottage is an organised riot of fruit trees, vegetables, shrubby perennials and herbaceous plants. Productive and peaceful. Whistling Gem has been redesigned and replanted over the last 3 years to create a garden with colour and interest. Featured on and in Bay radio, Lakeland radio, Grange Now, Westmorland Gazette.

26 HAVERTHWAITE LODGE

Haverthwaite, LA12 8AJ. David Snowdon, 015395 39841, sheena.taylforth@lakesidehotel.co.uk.
100yds off A590 at Haverthwaite. Turn S off A590 opp Haverthwaite railway stn. Bus 6, NCR 70.
Thur 21 June, Thur 16 Aug (11-4). Combined adm with Lakeside Hotel & Rocky Bank £7.50, chd free. Single adm £3.50. Refreshments - 20% discount from Lakeside Hotel Conservatory Menu on the Open Day. Visits also by arrangement Mar to Sept.
Traditional Lake District garden that has been redesigned and replanted. A wonderful display of hellebores and spring flowers. Gardens on a series of terraces leading down to the R Leven and incl: rose garden, cutting garden, dell area, rock terrace, herbaceous borders and many interesting mature shrubs. In a stunning setting the garden is surrounded by oak woodland and was once a place of C18 and C19 industry.

GROUP OPENING

27 HAYTON VILLAGE GARDENS

Hayton, Brampton, CA8 9HR.
7m E of Carlisle. 5m E of M6 J43. ½m S of A69, 3m W of Brampton signed to Hayton. Map of gardens with tickets, narrow road, please park courteously on one side only. Facebook: Hayton Open Gardens.
Sun 10 June (12-5). Combined adm £4, chd free. Home-made teas at Hayton Village Primary School with live music. Other refreshments eg cava usually served in the conservatory at Millbrook depending on weather. Donation to Hayton Village Primary School.

CHESTNUT COTTAGE
Mr Barry Bryan.

CURLEW COTTAGE
Frances & David Scales.

HAYTON C OF E PRIMARY SCHOOL
Hayton C of E Primary School, www.hayton.cumbria.sch.uk.

KINRARA
Tim & Alison Brown, 01228 670067 (Ashton Design), tim@tjbgallery.com.
Visits also by arrangement Apr to Sept refreshments may be available depending on notice. No dogs please & back garden unsafe for children.

LITTLE GARTH
Dugald Campbell.

MILLBROOK
Emily & Angus Dawson.

THE PADDOCK
Phil & Louise Jones.

SOUTH VIEW COTTAGE
Mrs Anita Laird.

TOWNHEAD COTTAGE
Chris & Pam Haynes

WEST GARTH COTTAGE
Debbie Jenkins, 01228 670430, debbiejenkins.art@gmail.com, www.westgarth-cottage-gardens.co.uk.
Visits also by arrangement Apr to July tea/coffee and biscuits available for pre-arranged visits. Ideally 10 -20 (max 25).

A valley of gardens of varied size and styles all within ½m, mostly of old stone cottages. Smaller and larger cottage gardens, courtyards and containers, steep wooded slopes, lawns, exuberant borders, frogs, pools and poultry, colour and texture throughout. Home-made teas and live music at the school where the children annually create gardens within the main school garden. Often an informal treasure hunt for children young and old. Gardens additional to those listed also generally open and there are views into numerous others of very high standard. Facebook: Hayton Open Gardens. Two of the gardens; Westgarth Cottage and Kinrara are designed by artist/s and an architect with multiple garden design experience. Varying degrees of wheelchair access from full to minimal.

28 HAZEL COTTAGE

Armathwaite, CA4 9PG. Mr D Ryland & Mr J Thexton. *8m SE of Carlisle. Turn off A6 just S of High Hesket signed Armathwaite, after 2m house facing you at T-junction 1¼ m walk from Armathwaite railway station.* **Sun 1 July (12-5). Adm £3.50, chd free. Home-made teas. featuring home made cakes. Opening with Trio of Armathwaite Gardens on Sat 2, Sun 3 June.**

Flower arrangers and plantsman's garden. Extending to approx 5 acres. Includes mature herbaceous borders, pergola, ponds and planting of disused railway siding providing home to wildlife. Many variegated and unusual plants. Varied areas, planted for all seasons, S-facing, some gentle slopes. Has been featured in newspapers and magazines. BorderTV 'summer gardens'. Only partial access, small steps to toilet area . Main garden planted on gentle slope.

29 HAZELWOOD FARM

Hollins Lane, Silverdale, Carnforth, LA5 0UB. Glenn & Dan Shapiro, 01524 701276, glenn@hazelwoodfarm.co.uk, www.hazelwoodfarm.co.uk. *4m NW of M6 J35. From Carnforth follow signs to Silverdale, after 1m turn L signed Silverdale, after level Xing turn L then 1st L into Hollins Lane. Farm on R.* **Sun 10 June (11-5). Adm £4, chd free. Home-made teas.** Visits also by arrangement May & June groups of 20+.

A theatre of light curtained by backdrops of woodland. Steep paths winding up and through natural limestone cliff, intersected by a tumbling rill joining ponds, provide staging for alpine gems and drifts of herbaceous, prairie and woodland planting. Old and English roses, bulbs and the National Collection of Hepatica. Wildlife friendly garden surrounded by NT access land. New bird, bee and butterfly garden, rock garden, Hepatica collection, well-stocked plant sale. Chapter in 'Rock Gardening: Reimagining a Classic Style', Joseph Tychonievich, Timber Press, 'Hazelwood Hepaticas' in 'Gardening Japan'. Partial wheelchair access - lower level only.

NPC

30 ◆ HIGH CLOSE ESTATE AND ARBORETUM

Loughrigg, Ambleside, LA22 9HH. National Trust, 015394 37623, neil.winder@nationaltrust.org.uk, www.nationaltrust.org.uk/sticklebarn-and-the-langdales/features/high-close-estate. *10 min NW from Ambleside. Ambleside (A593) to Skelwith Bridge signed for High Close, turn R & head up hill until you see a white painted stone sign to 'Langdale', turn L, High Close on L.* **For NGS: Sun 25 Mar (11-4). Adm by donation. Light refreshments. Also open Dora's Field. Small cafe in house part of the YHA.** For other opening times and information, please phone, email or visit garden website.

Originally planted in 1866 by Edward Wheatley-Balme, High Close was designed in the fashion of the day using many of the recently discovered 'exotic' conifers and evergreen shrubs coming into Britain from America. Today the garden works in partnership with the Royal Botanic Gardens Edinburgh and International Conifer Conservation Programme, preserving endangered Conifers species. Tree trail. Guided walks throughout the day.

31 HIGH MOSS

Portinscale, Keswick, CA12 5TX. Christine & Peter Hughes, christine_hug25@hotmail.com. *1m W of Keswick. Enter village off A66, take 1st turning R through white gates, on R of rd after ⅓ m.* **Sun 25 Mar (2.30-5). Adm £6, chd free. Visits also by arrangement Mar to Oct on Thursday afternoons only. Donation to Hospice at Home.**

Lakeland Arts and Craft house (not open) and garden (mentioned in Pevsner). 4½ acres of formal and informal S-facing terraced gardens. Magnificent views of the fells. Many fine trees and shrubs, rhododendrons and azaleas. Spring meadow planted with daffodils and camassia. Old tennis court converted into vegetable/flower parterre for the Diamond Jubilee with rose garden and sun dial by Joe Smith. Open as part of Cumbria Daffodil Day. The garden is not suitable for wheelchair users.

32 HIGHLANDS

High Knott Road, Arnside, Carnforth, LA5 0AW. Judith & Stephen Slater, 01524 761535, judithslater@rocketmail.com. *12m J35 & J36 M6. From A6 MilnthorpeT-lights take B5282 to Arnside. Follow signs in village.* **Sat 12, Sun 13 May (10-5). Adm £4, chd free. Home-made teas and home made soups available.** Visits also by arrangement May to July for groups of 10+.

More new features added to this 1½ acre gently terraced garden. 3 types of rockery, well-stocked herbaceous borders leading to a tranquil woodland garden. Raised vegetable beds and orchard with mistletoe. Secluded and secret areas throughout. Courtyard garden with water feature and beech tunnel exit. Extensive hosta collection. Numerous unique sculptures with a twist. Wildlife friendly. Featured in Cumbria Life. Steps or steep incline to rear garden.

33 ◆ HOLEHIRD GARDENS

Patterdale Road, Windermere, LA23 1NP. Lakeland Horticultural Society, 015394 46008, enquiries@holehirdgardens.org.uk, www.holehirdgardens.org.uk. *1m N of Windermere. On A592, Windermere to Patterdale rd.* **For NGS: Sun 25 Mar, Thur 12 July (10-5). Adm by donation. Self-service hot drinks available.** For other opening times and information, please phone, email or visit garden website.

Run by volunteers with the aim of promoting knowledge of the cultivation of plants particularly suited to Lakeland conditions. One of the best labelled gardens in the

UK. National Collections of *astilbe*, daboecia, *polystichum* (ferns) and meconopsis. Set on the fellside with stunning views over Windermere. The walled garden gives protection to mixed borders whilst alpine houses display an always colourful array of tiny gems. Wheelchair access limited to walled garden and beds accessible from drive.

♿ ✿ NPC ☕

34 ◆ HOLKER HALL GARDENS

Cark-in-Cartmel, Grange-over-Sands, LA11 7PL. The Cavendish Family, 015395 58328, info@holker.co.uk, www.holker.co.uk. *4m W of Grange-over-Sands. 12m W of M6 (J36) Follow brown tourist signs. Rail 1m, NCR 700 ½m.* **For NGS: Thur 23 Aug (10.30-5). Adm by donation. NGS will receive the donations for guided tours on this day but not garden adm.** For other opening times and information, please phone, email or visit garden website.

25 acres of romantic gardens, with peaceful arboretum, inspirational formal gardens, flowering meadow and Labyrinth. Summer brings voluptuous mixed borders and bedding. Discover unusually large rhododendrons, magnolias and azaleas, and the National Collection of Styracaceae. Discover our latest garden feature - The Pagan Grove, designed by Kim Wilkie. Guided tour of the gardens with our experienced guide. Donation to NGS required.

♿ ✿ 🚌 NPC ☕

35 HOLME MEADOW

1 Holme Meadow, Cumwhinton, Carlisle, CA4 8DR. John & Anne Mallinson, 01228 560330, jwai.mallinson@btopenworld.com. *2m S of Carlisle. From M6 J42 take B6263 to Cumwhinton, in village take 1st L then bear R at Lowther Arms, Holme Meadow is immediately on R.* **Sun 15 July (11-4). Adm £3, chd free. Light refreshments.** Visits also by arrangement June to Aug for groups of 10+.

Village garden developed and landscaped from scratch by owners. Incl shrubbery, perennial beds supplemented by annuals;gazebo, pergola and trellis with climbers, slate beds and water feature, ornamental copse, pond, wild flower meadow and kitchen garden. Designed, planted and maintained to be wildlife friendly. Featured in Cumberland News.

✿ ☕

36 NEW HPB MERLEWOOD

Windermere Road, Grange-Over-Sands, LA11 6JT. Marion St Quinton Site Manager. *Merlewood is on the B5271 between Grange over Sands & Lindale. Rail 1m; Bus X6, NCR 70 (1m).* **Sun 5 Aug (10.30-4). Adm £4, chd free. Home-made teas.**

Extensive and varied gardens with a dramatic view to Morecambe Bay from the terrace. Newly planted formal and terraced gardens surround the house. A woodland including a nature trail for children. The wood on the limestone crags contain a variety of tree species many of which are from the original Victorian planting. The rockery is work in progress! Some areas are not accessible due to steps.

♿ ✿ ☕

37 IVY HOUSE

Cumwhitton, Brampton, CA8 9EX. Martin Johns & Ian Forrest, 01228 561851, martinjohns193@btinternet.com. *6m E of Carlisle. At the bridge at Warwick Bridge on A69 take turning to Great Corby & Cumwhitton. Through Great Corby & woodland until you reach a T-junction Turn R.* **Sun 24 June (1-5). Adm £4, chd free. Home-made teas in Cumwhitton village hall.** Visits also by arrangement May to Sept for groups up to 60.

Approx 2 acres of sloping fell-side garden with meandering paths leading to a series of 'rooms': pond, fern garden, gravel garden with assorted grasses, vegetable and herb garden. Copse with meadow leading down to beck. Trees, shrubs, ferns, bamboos and herbaceous perennials planted with emphasis on variety of texture and colour. Steep slopes.

🐕 ☕

38 LAKESIDE HOTEL & ROCKY BANK

Lake Windermere, Newby Bridge, Ulverston, LA12 8AT. Mr N Talbot, 015395 39841, sheena.taylforth@lakesidehotel.co.uk, www.lakesidehotel.co.uk. *1m N of Newby Bridge. Turn N off A590 across R Leven at Newby Bridge along W side of Windermere.* **Thur 21 June, Thur 16 Aug (11-4). Combined adm with Haverthwaite Lodge £7.50, chd free. Light refreshments. Single adm to Lakeside and Rocky Bank £5. Refreshments - 20% discount from Hotel Conservatory menu on the Open Day.** Visits also by arrangement Mar to Sept.

Two diverse gardens on the shores of Lake Windermere. Lakeside has been created for year round interest, packed with choice plants, incl some unusual varieties. Main garden area with herbaceous borders and foliage shrubs, scented and winter interest plants and seasonal bedding. Roof garden with lawn, espaliered local heritage apple varieties and culinary herbs. Lawn art on front lawn. Rocky Bank is a traditional garden with rock outcrops. Planted with unusual specimen alpines. Herbaceous borders, shrubs and ornamental trees. Woodland area with species rhododendrons. Working greenhouse and polytunnels. Wild flower garden and cut flower garden. Wheelchair access not available at Rocky Bank.

🚌 🛏 ☕

Donations from the National Garden Scheme help Parkinson's UK care for more people

39 LANGHOLME MILL

Woodgate, Lowick Green, LA12 8ES. Judith & Graham Sanderson, 01229 885215, judith@themill.biz. *7m NW of Ulverston. West on A590. At Greenodd, N on A5902 towards Broughton. Langholme Mill is approx 3m along this rd on L as rd divides on the hill.* **Sat 19, Sun 20 May (11-5). Adm £5, chd free. Home-made teas.** Visits also by arrangement Apr to Oct please phone Judith.

Approx 1 acre of mature woodland garden with meandering lakeland stone paths surrounding the mill race stream which can be crossed by a variety of bridges. The garden hosts well established bamboo, rhododendrons, hostas, acers and astilbes and a large variety of country flowers.

40 LARCH COTTAGE NURSERIES

Melkinthorpe, Penrith, CA10 2DR. Peter Stott, www.larchcottage.co.uk. *From N leave M6 J40 take A6 S. From S leave M6 J39 take A6 N signed off A6.* **Wed 6 June, Wed 31 Oct (1-4). Adm £4, chd free.**

For 2 days only Larch Cottage Nurseries are opening the new lower gardens and chapel for NGS visitors. The gardens include lawns, flowing perennial borders, rare and unusual shrubs, trees, small orchard and a kitchen garden. A natural stream runs into a small lake - a haven for wildlife and birds. At the head of the lake stands a chapel, designed and built by Peter for family use only. Larch Cottage has a Japanese Dry garden, ponds and Italianesque columned garden specifically for shade plants, the Italianesque tumbled down walls are draped in greenery acting as a backdrop for the borders filled with stock plants. Newly designed and constructed lower gardens and chapel. The gardens are accessible to wheelchair users although the paths are rocky in places.

41 LOW BLAKEBANK

Underbarrow, Kendal, LA8 8BN. Mrs Catherine Chamberlain, 07807 603108, catherinec99@btinternet.com. *Lyth Valley between Underbarrow & Crosthwaite. East off A5074 to Crossthwaite. Signed Red Scar & Broom Farm off the main rd between Crosthwaite & Underbarrow. 1st drive on R off Broom Lane.* **Sun 3 June (10.30-4.30). Combined adm with Middle Blakebank £6, chd free. Home-made teas at Middle Blakebank.** Visits also by arrangement in June for groups of 8+.

Charming and secluded 3 acre garden surrounding a C17 Lakeland farmhouse and bank barn. Plenty of seating to enjoy the beautiful views of the Lyth Valley and Scout Scar. Garden under development. Mixed borders, ponds, lawned areas, topiary, small bluebell wood and vegetable garden. Uneven ground, slopes and steps.

42 LOW FELL WEST

Crosthwaite, Kendal, LA8 8JG. Barbie & John Handley, 015395 68297, barbie@handleyfamily.co.uk. *4½m S of Bowness. Off A5074, turn W just S of Damson Dene Hotel. Follow lane for ½m.* **Sun 6 May (2-5); Mon 7 May (11-2); Sun 9 Sept (11-5). Adm £4, chd free. Home-made teas.** Visits also by arrangement nearest access for large coaches ½m away.

This 2 acre woodland garden in the tranquil Winster Valley has extensive views to the Pennines. The four season garden, restored since 2003, incl expanses of rock planted sympathetically with grasses, unusual trees and shrubs, climaxing for autumn colour. There are native hedges and areas of plant rich meadows. A woodland area houses a gypsy caravan and there is direct access to Cumbria Wildlife Trust's Barkbooth Reserve of Oak woodland, blue bells and open fellside. Wheelchair access to much of the garden, but some rough paths, steep slopes.

43 LOWER ROWELL FARM & COTTAGE

Milnthorpe, LA7 7LU. John & Mavis Robinson & Julie & Andy Welton, 015395 62270. *Approx 2m from Milnthorpe, 2m from Crooklands. Signed to Rowell off B6385, Milnthorpe to Crooklands Rd. Garden ½m up lane on L.* **Visits by arrangement Feb to July groups of 10-40, refreshments by arrangement.**

Approx 1¼ acre garden with views to Farleton Knott and Lakeland hills. Unusual trees and shrubs, plus perennial borders; architectural pruning; retro greenhouse; polytunnel with tropical plants; cottage gravel garden and vegetable plot. Fabulous display of snowdrops in spring followed by other spring flowers, with colour most of the year. Wildlife ponds and 2 friendly pet hens.

44 MATSON GROUND

Windermere, LA23 2NH. Matson Ground Estate Co Ltd, 015394 47892, info@matsonground.co.uk. *⅔m E of Bowness. Turn N off B5284 signed Heathwaite. From E 100yds after Windermere Golf Club, from W 400yds after Windy Hall Rd. Rail 2½m; Bus 1m, 6, 599, 755, 800; NCR 6 (1m).* **Sun 20 May (1-5). Adm £4, chd free. Home-made teas.** Visits also by arrangement for gardening groups of 4+.

2 acres of mature, south facing gardens. A good mix of formal and informal planting including topiary features, herbaceous and shrub borders, wild flower areas, stream leading to a large pond and developing arboretum. Rose garden, rockery, topiary terrace borders, ha-ha. Productive, walled kitchen garden c 1862, a wide assortment of fruit, vegetables, cut flowers, cobnuts and herbs. Greenhouse.

45 MIDDLE BLAKEBANK

Underbarrow, Kendal, LA8 8HP. Mrs Hilary Crowe, 015395 68959, hfcmbb@aol.com. *Lyth Valley between Underbarrow &*

Crosthwaite. East off A5074 to Crosthwaite. The garden is on Broom Lane, a turning between Crosthwaite & Underbarrow signed Red Scar & Broom Farm. **Sun 3 June (10.30-4.30). Combined adm with Low Blakebank £6, chd free. Home-made teas.** Visits also by arrangement May to Sept we are happy to open for small groups.
The garden extends to 4½ acres and overlooks the Lyth Valley with extensive views south to Morecambe Bay and east to the Howgills. We have orchards, wild flower meadow and more formal garden with a range of outbuildings. Over the last 6 years the garden has been developed with plantings that provide varying colour and texture all year. We enjoy providing home made cakes and sandwiches - under cover if necessary!

46 MIREFOOT

Potter Fell Road, Burneside, Kendal, LA8 9AB. Mark Baker & Kim Kremer, www.mirefoot.co.uk. *From A591 follow signs for Burneside. Head north on Burneside rd towards Bowston (0.5M). On entering Bowston turn 1st R and over bridge. Continue for ½m.* **Sun 20 May (10.30-5.30). Adm £3.50, chd free. Light refreshments, tea & cakes.**
'A mature and relaxed 4 acre country house garden, developed to be enjoyed by the family and neighbours, including young children, cats, dogs and (every gardener's nightmare), free-range pet rabbits. Extends to formal and informal areas, including rose terrace, herbaceous borders, sunken lavender garden, arboretum with many special trees, ponds with visiting heron.'. Arboretum with some unusual trees, large pond, combination of formal and informal garden areas. Wheelchair access over grass but not all areas (e.g. Sunken garden, gravel paths and part of the veranda).

47 NEWTON RIGG COLLEGE GARDENS

Newton Rigg, Penrith, CA11 0AH. Newton Rigg College, www.newtonrigg.ac.uk. *1m W of Penrith. 3m W from J40 & J41 off M6. ½m off the B5288 W of Penrith. We have The Coast to Coast cycle route (Route 7) & public pathway approx 500 metres from the garden entrance gates.* **Mon 30 Apr (1-4). Tea. Mon 1 Oct (1-4). Adm £4, chd free.** Visits also by arrangement 15+.
Our Educational Gardens have much of horticultural interest incl herbaceous borders, ten ponds, decorative and productive organic garden, woodland walk, seasonal borders, Pictorial Meadows, Pleached Hornbeam Walkway and extensive range of ornamental trees and shrubs. Our Horticultural and Forestry staff and students will give informative tours and a variety of demonstrations.

48 ORCHARD COTTAGE

Hutton Lane, Levens, Kendal, LA8 8PB. Shirley & Chris Band, 015395 61005, chrisband67@gmail.com. *6m S of Kendal. Turn N off A590 or A6 signed Levens. From Xrds by Methodist Church, 300 metres down Hutton Lane. Park near this Xrds. Garden access via 'The Orchard'.* **Sun 22 Apr, Sun 27 May, Sun 24 June (1-5). Adm £3.50, chd free.** Visits also by arrangement Mar to Oct any from 1 to 60.
¾ acre sloping garden in old orchard. Plantsperson's paradise. Winding paths, diverse habitats, secret vistas. All yr interest and colour. Collections of ferns (100+ varieties), hellebores (70+), grasses, cottage plants, geraniums, Acers (36) Hostas. Auricula theatres, 'imaginary' stream, bog garden. Trees support clematis, roses and honeysuckle. Wildlife friendly. Featured in Lancashire Magazine. Light refreshments at Sizergh Castle (not in aid of ngs).

49 8 OXENHOLME ROAD

Kendal, LA9 7NJ. Mr & Mrs John & Frances Davenport, 01539 720934, frandav8@btinternet.com. *SE Kendal. From A65 (Burton Rd, Kendal/Kirkby Lonsdale) take B6254 (Oxenholme Rd). No.8 is 1st house on L beyond red post box.* **Sun 10 June (10-5). Adm £3.50, chd free. Home-made teas.** Visits also by arrangement May to Sept for groups of 10+.
Artist and potters garden of approx ½ acre of mixed planting designed for year-round interest, incl two linked small ponds. Roses, grasses and colour themed borders surround the house, with a gravel garden at the front, as well as a number of woodland plant areas, vegetable and fruit areas and sitting spaces. John is a ceramic artist and Frances is a painter. Paintings and pots are a feature of the garden display. Garden essentially level, but access to WC is up steps.

Beckside Farm

Pear Tree Cottage

50 PEAR TREE COTTAGE
Dalton, Burton-in-Kendal, LA6 1NN. Linda & Alec Greening, 01524 781624, lindagreening48@gmail.com. *5m from J35 & J36 of M6. From northern end of Burton-in-Kendal (A6070) turn E into Vicarage Lane & continue approx 1m.* **Visits by arrangement May to July groups of 15+. Refreshments by arrangement.**
⅓ acre cottage garden in a delightful rural setting. A peaceful and relaxing garden, harmonising with its environment and incorporating many different planting areas, from packed herbaceous borders and rambling roses, to wildlife pond, bog garden, rock garden and gravel garden. A plantsperson's delight, incl over 200 different ferns, and many other rare and unusual plants.

51 NEW ROSE CROFT
Levens, Kendal, LA8 8PH. Enid Fraser. *M6 J36 take A590 toward Barrow. R turn Levens, L at pub, follow road to garden on L. From A6, into Levens, past shop, bear L, over Xrds, downhill. L turn signed 'PV Dobson'. Garden on R after Dobsons.* **Sun 12 Aug (1-5). Adm £4, chd free. Light refreshments.**
Gardening on a steep slope with wildlife in mind. Naturalistic plantings, perennials and grasses pouring away from the top terrace, shrubs, rose arches and silver birches for supporting structure. August sees the peak of this colourful drama: set against the views that dominate the westerly scene beyond the summer house, past the sown wild flowers and lawn which fold into the garden-bounding stream.

52 ◆ RYDAL HALL
Ambleside, LA22 9LX. Diocese of Carlisle, 01539 432050, gardens@rydalhall.org, www.rydalhall.org. *2m N of Ambleside. E from A591 at Rydal signed Rydal Hall. Bus 555, 599, X8, X55; NCR 6.* **For NGS: Sun 25 Mar, Thur 26 Apr, Sun 20 May, Thur 13 Sept (9-4). Adm by donation. Light refreshments in tea shop on site. For other opening times and information, please phone, email or visit garden website.**
Forty acres of Park, Woodland and Gardens to explore. The Formal Thomas Mawson Garden has fine examples of herbaceous planting, seasonal displays and magnificent views of the Lakeland Fells. Enjoy the peaceful atmosphere created in the Quiet Garden with informal planting around the pond and stunning views of the waterfalls from The Grot. Visit the Vegetable Garden and Orchard. The Grot, the UK's first viewing station. Limited Wheelchair access, top terrace only.

53 SANDHOUSE
Burnhill, Scaleby, Carlisle, CA6 4LU. John Dalton & Ken Dodd. *5m NE Carlisle. From A6071 turn at Smithfield, follow NGS signs. From M6 J44 follow A689 Hexham, follow NGS signs.* **Sun 24 June (1-5). Adm £3.50, chd free. Home-made teas.**
A cottage garden with island beds of herbaceous perennials, foliage plants suitable for the flower arranger. Hidden seating areas to surprise the visitor, and lots of nooks and crannies. John is a multiple award winner for his floral arrangements including Chelsea GOLD, his latest in 2017. Flower demonstration. Gravel paths.

54 ◆ SIZERGH CASTLE
Sizergh, Kendal, LA8 8DZ. National Trust, 015395 60951, sizergh@nationaltrust.org.uk, www.nationaltrust.org.uk. *3m S of Kendal. Approach rd leaves A590 close to & S of A590/A591 interchange.* **For NGS: Mon 10 Sept (10-4.30). Adm £7.50, chd £3.75. For other opening times and information, please phone, email or visit garden website.**
⅔ acre limestone rock garden, largest owned by National Trust; Wild flower areas, hot wall and herbaceous borders, Productive ornamental kitchen garden and fruit orchard with spring bulbs. Terrace garden and mirror lake. Holders of the National Collections of Asplenium scolopendrium, Cystopteris, Dryopteris and Osmunda. Stumpery garden built 2016. National Trust members are admitted free with an opportunity to donate to the good causes the NGS supports. Non National Trust members entrance fees are donated to the NGS. Featured in

The Times in their 20 best Great British gardens to visit in summer.

♿ ✻ 🚌 ☕

55 SPRINT MILL

Burneside, LA8 9AQ. Edward & Romola Acland, 01539 725168, mail@sprintmill.uk. *2m N of Kendal. From Burneside follow signs to Skelsmergh for ½m then L into drive of Sprint Mill. Or from A6 over 1m N of Kendal follow signs towards Burneside.* **Sun 20 May (10.30-5). Adm £3, chd free. Light lunches & home-made teas all day.** Visits also by arrangement Mar to Oct optional extended tour of traditional flower-rich hay meadows, orchard and coppice for groups of 6+.

Unorthodox organically run garden,the wild and natural alongside provision of owners' fruit, vegetables and firewood. Idyllic riverside setting, 5 acres to explore including wooded riverbank with hand-crafted seats. Large vegetable and soft fruit area, following no-dig and permaculture principles. Hand-tools prevail. Historic water mill with original turbine.The 3-storey building houses owner's art studio and personal museum, incl collection of old hand tools associated with rural crafts. Green woodworking demonstrations. Goats, hens, ducks, rope swing, family-friendly. Short walk to our flower-rich hay meadows. Mill and its collections featured in Lancashire Life. Access for wheelchairs to some parts of both garden and mill.

♿ 🐕 ✻ ☕

56 SUMMERDALE HOUSE

Nook, Lupton, LA6 1PE. David & Gail Sheals, www.summerdalegardenplants.co.uk. *7m S of Kendal, 5m W of Kirkby Lonsdale. From J36 M6 take A65 towards Kirkby Lonsdale, at Nook take R turn Farleton. Location not signed on highway. Detailed directions available on our website.* **Sun 18 Feb (11-4.30). Home-made soups & bread (Feb only). Every Fri and Sat 23 Feb to 31 Aug (11-4.30). Sun 17 June (11-4.30). Home-made teas (Sun only). Adm £4, chd free.**

1½ acre part-walled country garden set around C18 former vicarage. Several defined areas have been created by hedges, each with its own theme and linked by intricate cobbled pathways. Beautiful setting with fine views across to Farleton Fell. Traditional herbaceous borders, ponds, woodland and meadow planting provide year round interest. Large collections of auricula, primulas and snowdrops. Adjoining specialist nursery growing a wide range of interesting and unusual herbaceous perennials. Home made jams and chutneys for sale. RHS Gold Medal winning nursery featured on Gardener's World.

🐕 ✻ ☕

57 ♦ SWARTHMOOR HALL

Swarthmoor Hall Lane, Ulverston, LA12 0JQ. Jane Pearson, Manager, 01229 583204, info@swarthmoorhall.co.uk, www.swarthmoorhall.co.uk. *1½m SW of Ulverston. A590 to Ulverston. Turn off to Ulverston railway stn. Follow Brown tourist signs to Hall. Rail 0.9m. NCR70 & 700 (1m).* **For NGS: Daily Mon 19 Feb to Sun 11 Mar (10.30-4.30). Adm by donation. Light refreshments. For other opening times and information, please phone, email or visit garden website.**

Formal gardens and wild flower meadow. Wild purple crocus meadow in early spring: late February or early March depending on weather, earlier if mild winter later if cold and frosty. Also, good displays of snowdrops, daffodils and tulips in spring. Barn Cafe serves wonderful local food and recaptures the Hall's reputation for hospitality: delicious cakes and light lunches. Open 10.30-4.30 daily.

♿ ✻ 🛏 ☕

58 TENTER END BARN

Docker, Kendal, LA8 0DB. Mrs Hazel Terry, 01539 824447, hnterry@btinternet.com. *3m N Kendal. From Kendal take A685 Appleby rd. Then 2nd on R to Docker. At the junction bear L.* **Sun 27 May (11-4.30). Adm £3.50, chd free. Home-made teas.** Visits also by arrangement May to Sept for groups of 4+.

3 acres of cultivated and natural areas, in a secretive rural setting. A patio garden, large lawns, herbaceous borders and a small vegetable patch. Walks on the wild side around a mere and woodlands. Many birds can be seen at various feeding stations, also waterfowl on the mere. All managed by one OAP. Wheelchair access - rather uneven around the woodland paths. Could be difficult around mere in wet weather.

♿ 🐕 ✻ ☕

59 TITHE BARN

Laversdale, Irthington, Carlisle, CA6 4PJ. Mr & Mrs Gordon & Christine Davidson. *8m N E of Carlisle. Laversdale, N. Cumbria, ½m from Carlisle Airport. From 6071 turn for Laversdale, from M6 J44 follow A689 Hexham. Follow NGS signs.* **Sun 3 June (1-5). Adm £4, chd free.**

Set on a slight incline, the thatched property has stunning views of the Lake District, Pennines and Scottish Border hills. Planting follows the cottage garden style, the surrounding walls, arches, grottos and quirky features have all been designed and created by the owners. There is a peaceful sitting glade beside a rill and pond. Wheelchairs unable to view the small 'shaded woodland area' down steep steps.

♿ ✻ 🚌 ☕

GROUP OPENING

60 TRIO OF ARMATHWAITE GARDENS

Armathwaite, Carlisle, CA4 9PG. *Turn off A6 just S of High Hesket signed Armathwaite, after 2m Coombe House is on R & Hazel Cottage is at the junction. Turn R at junction to Armathwaite - 2 The Faulds is in the village.* **Sat 2, Sun 3 June (12-5). Combined adm £5, chd free. Home-made teas at Hazel Cottage, by Armathwaite village hall ladies group featuring home made cakes.**

COOMBE EDEN
Belinda & Mike.

HAZEL COTTAGE
Mr D Ryland & Mr J Thexton.
(See separate entry)

2 THE FAULDS
Mr & Mrs Phil & Jane Dutton, www.thebuzzshelter.wordpress.com.

Coombe Eden is approx 1 acre Victorian garden renovation project of traditional and contemporary beds. Steeply banked to a Japanese style bridge over the stream to a woodland area. Contemporary mixed beds, large rhododendrons give a breathtaking display in May. Hazel Cottage is a flower arranger's and plantsman's garden extending to 5 acres. Mature herbaceous borders with many unusual plants. Planted for a ll seasons. 2 The Faulds is a compact garden with rare and unusual trees, shrubs and herbaceous perennial. Collection of trees grown from seed. Art work and stained glass on display. Wheelchair: only partial access for Hazel Cottage and Coombe Eden as they are on gentle slopes. 2 The Faulds is not accessible by wheelchair.

GROUP OPENING

61 ULVERSTON TOWN & COUNTRY GARDENS

Ulverston, LA12 7LA. *A590 to Ulverston. 3 gardens near Booths Supermarket - a good start point. Rail Ulverston; Bus 6, 6X; NCR 70. Maps available at gardens.* **Sun 1 July (10.30-5). Combined adm £5, chd free. Light refreshments available at 11, Oubas Hill, The Glade, Hamilton Grove and 51, Daltongate.**

NEW **104 BIRCHWOOD DRIVE**
Jane Parker.

NEW **51 DALTONGATE**
Ian & Angela Hutt.

NEW **THE GLADE**
Paul & Alev Stoller.

1 GRASMERE ROAD
Wayne & Jude Evans.

HAMILTON GROVE
Helen & Martin Cooper.

11 OUBAS HILL
David & Janet Parratt.

14 OUBAS HILL
Pat & Barry Bentley.

7 gardens within a mile of historic market town, with its canal, lighthouse monument to Sir John Barrow and 18thC iron furnace - open to visitors at no extra charge. Hamilton Grove garden slopes down from a large terrace to the, now dry, canal feeder via beds of annuals and perennials. There is a collection of scented leaf pelargoniums. The two houses on Oubas Hill rise up towards the lighthouse and are busy and varied with unconventional features. Handmade pottery products at No 11 (income to NGS). 51 Daltongate is medium sized and wildlife friendly with a lovely wild flower area. 104 Birchwood makes the most of a small corner plot with roadside vegetables, formal front garden and delightful secret back garden. 1 Grasmere is a VERY small, low-maintenance, garden full of ideas and novelties with a Mediterranean feel. The Glade is a medium sized garden packed with ideas, which will surprise. Adjacent to The Glade is the Newland Blast Furnace (Listed Building Grade II*) which will be open on this day.

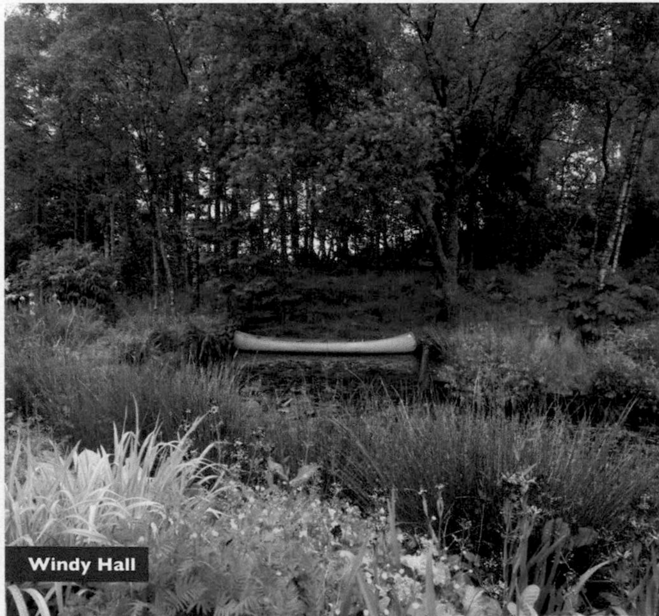

Windy Hall

62 WINDY HALL

Crook Road, Windermere, LA23 3JA. Diane Hewitt & David Kinsman, 015394 46238, dhewitt.kinsman@gmail.com, windy-hall.co.uk. *½m S of Bowness-on-Windermere. On western end of B5284, pink house up Linthwaite Hotel driveway. Rail 2.6m; Bus 1m, 6, 599, 755, 800; NCR 6 (1m).* **Sun 6 May (10.30-5), also open Low Fell West. Sun 3 June (10.30-5). Combined adm with Brackenrigg Cottage £7, chd free. Home-made teas. Single garden adm £5. We can provide Teas for any size group and Light Lunches for groups of 8+.** Visits also by arrangement Apr to Aug guided tours for groups of 8+.

"Paradise". "I was bowled over by the ecologically intelligent approach you and Diane take and the exquisitely planted back garden or hill with rare species and subspecies so elegantly placed where they will flourish. It was truly superb." "The garden left a lasting impression on all. It is beautiful, exciting and charming. It nestles so comfortably in its landscape and totally belongs there.". Plant Heritage Aruncus collection. Rare Hebridean sheep, exotic waterfowl and pheasants.

✿ 🚗 NPC 🛏 ☕

63 WINTON PARK

Appleby Road, Kirkby Stephen, CA17 4PG. Mr Anthony Kilvington. *2m N of Kirkby Stephen. On A685 turn L signed Gt Musgrave/Warcop (B6259). After approx 1m turn L as signed.* **Sun 15 July (11-5). Adm £6, chd free. Light refreshments.**

4- acre country garden bordered by the banks of the R Eden with stunning views. Many fine conifers, acers and rhododendrons, herbaceous borders, hostas, ferns, grasses, heathers and several hundred roses. Four formal ponds plus rock pool. Partial wheelchair access.

♿ ✿ ☕

64 WOODEND HOUSE

Woodend, Egremont, CA22 2TA. Grainne & Richard Jakobson, 019468 13017, gmjakobson22@gmail.com. *2m S of Whitehaven. Take the A595 from Whitehaven towards Egremont. On leaving Bigrigg take 1st turn L. Go down hill, garden at bottom on R opp Woodend Farm. Close to cycleways & Coast to Coast route.* **Sun 13 May (11-5). Adm £3.50, chd free. Home-made teas.** Visits also by arrangement Mar to Oct any number of people.

An interesting garden tucked away in a small hamlet. Meandering gravel paths lead around the garden with imaginative, colourful planting. Take a look around a productive, organic potager, wildlife pond, mini spring and summer meadows and a pretty summer house. Designed to be beautiful throughout the year and wildlife friendly. Plant sale, home-made teas, mini-quiz for children. Live Blues and Jazz in the garden. The gravel drive and paths are difficult for wheelchairs but more mobile visitors can access the main seating areas in the rear garden.

✿ 🚗 ☕

65 YEWBARROW HOUSE

Hampsfell Road, Grange-over-Sands, LA11 6BE. Jonathan & Margaret Denby, 015395 32469, jonathan@bestlakesbreaks.co.uk, www.yewbarrowhouse.co.uk. *¼m from town centre. Proceed along Hampsfell Rd passing a house called Yewbarrow to brow of hill then turn L onto a lane signed 'Charney Wood/ Yewbarrow Wood' & sharp L again. Rail 0.7m, Bus X6, NCR 70.* **Sun 3 June, Sun 1 July, Sun 5 Aug, Sun 2 Sept (11-4). Adm £5, chd free. Cream teas.** Visits also by arrangement Apr to Oct morning coffee, tea with biscuits for groups £2.50 a head. Cream teas £5 a head.

'More Cornwall than Cumbria' according to Country Life, a colourful 4 acre garden filled with exotic and rare plants, with dramatic views over the Morecambe Bay. Outstanding features include the Orangery; the Japanese garden with infinity pool, the Italian terraces and the restored Victorian kitchen garden. Dahlias, cannas and colourful exotica are a speciality. www.youtube.com/watch?v=v--VH2cLG18. There is limited wheelchair access owing to the number of steps.

🐕 ✿ 🚗 ☕

66 YEWS

Middle Entrance Drive, Storrs Park, Bowness-on-Windermere, LA23 3JR. Sir Christopher & Lady Scott. *1.4m S of Bowness-on-Windermere. On A5074, W on Middle Entrance Drive. About 0.3m N of Blackwell, The Arts & Crafts House. Rail Windermere 3m, Bus 1m, 6, 599, 755, 800; NCR 6 (1m).* **Sun 10 June (1-5.30). Adm £3.50, chd free. Teas and cakes all home-made.**

Medium-sized formal Edwardian garden; fine trees, ha-ha, herbaceous borders; glasshouse (by Messenger). Bog area with, bamboos, primuli, hostas. Young yew maze and vegetable garden. Designed by H. Avray Tipping in 1912. Rose garden under reconstruction. Wheelchair access is reasonable given the private nature of the garden.

♿ 🐕 ✿ ☕

DERBYSHIRE

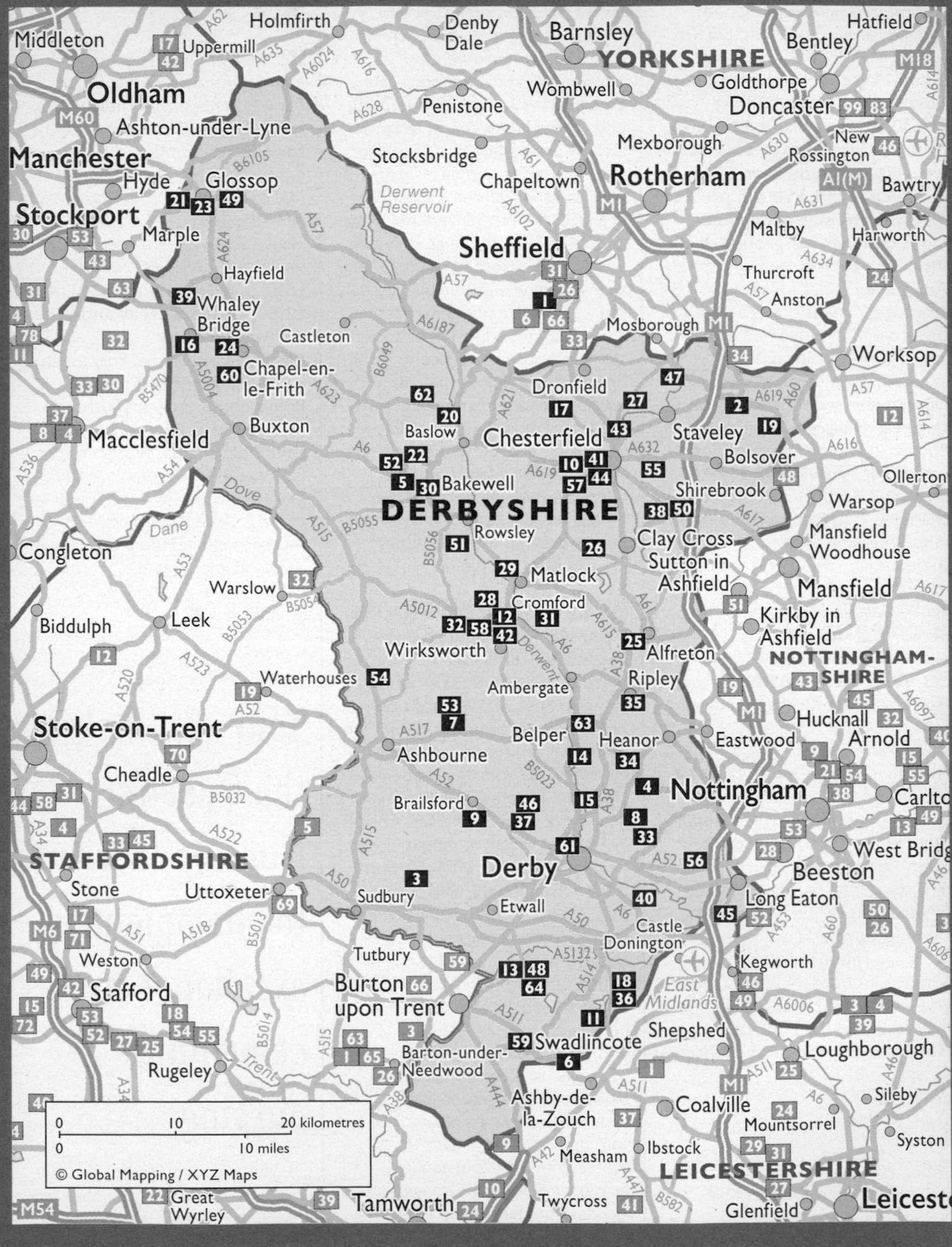

Holmfirth
Denby Dale
Barnsley
Hatfield
Middleton
Uppermill
YORKSHIRE
Bentley
Oldham
Wombwell
Goldthorpe
Penistone
Doncaster
Ashton-under-Lyne
Mexborough
New Rossington
Manchester
Stocksbridge
Hyde
Glossop
Chapeltown
Rotherham
Bawtry
Derwent Reservoir
Stockport
Maltby
Marple
Harworth
Sheffield
Thurcroft
Hayfield
Anston
Whaley Bridge
Castleton
Mosborough
Worksop
Chapel-en-le-Frith
Dronfield
Staveley
Buxton
Baslow
Chesterfield
Macclesfield
Bolsover
Ollerton
Bakewell
Shirebrook
Warsop
DERBYSHIRE
Rowsley
Clay Cross
Mansfield Woodhouse
Congleton
Sutton in Ashfield
Matlock
Mansfield
Warslow
Cromford
Biddulph
Leek
Kirkby in Ashfield
Wirksworth
Alfreton
NOTTINGHAM-SHIRE
Waterhouses
Ripley
Ambergate
Hucknall
Stoke-on-Trent
Belper
Heanor
Eastwood
Arnold
Ashbourne
Cheadle
Nottingham
Brailsford
Derby
West Bridg
STAFFORDSHIRE
Beeston
Stone
Uttoxeter
Sudbury
Long Eaton
Etwall
Castle Donington
Tutbury
Weston
Kegworth
Burton upon Trent
Stafford
East Midlands
Swadlincote
Shepshed
Loughborough
Barton-under-Needwood
Rugeley
Ashby-de-la-Zouch
Coalville
Sileby
Mountsorrel
Syston
Measham
Ibstock
LEICESTERSHIRE
Great Wyrley
Tamworth
Twycross
Glenfield
0 10 20 kilometres
0 10 miles
© Global Mapping / XYZ Maps

Derbyshire is the county where the Midlands meets the North, and visitors are attracted to the rugged hills of the High Peak, the high moorlands near Sheffield and the unspoilt countryside of the Dales.

There are many stately homes in the county with world famous gardens, delightful private country gardens, and interesting small cottage and town gardens.

Some of the northern gardens have spectacular views across the Peak District; their planting reflecting the rigours of the climate and long, cold winters. In the Derbyshire Dales, stone walls give way to hedges and the countryside is hilly with many trees, good agricultural land and very pretty villages.

South of Derby the land is much flatter, the architecture has a Midlands look with red brick replacing stone and softer planting in the gardens.

The east side of Derbyshire is different again, reflecting the recent past with small pit villages, and looking towards the rolling countryside of Nottinghamshire. There are fast road links with other parts of the country via the M1 and M6, making a day trip to a Derbyshire garden a very easy choice.

Below: Thornbridge Hall Gardens

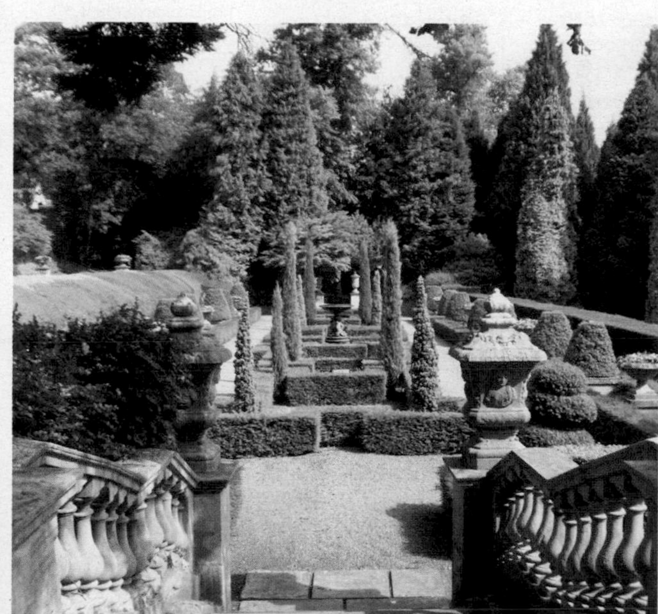

Volunteers

County Organiser
Peter Gardner
01335 372001
petergardner532@btinternet.com

County Treasurer
Robert Little
01283 702267
robert.little@ngs.org.uk

Publicity
Vanessa Charles
07950 186762
nesscharles1@gmail.com

Booklet Co-ordinator
Malcolm and Wendy Fisher
0115 9664 322
wendy.fisher111@btinternet.com

Valerie Booth
01283 221167
valerie.booth@sky.com

Assistant County Organisers
Gill & Colin Hancock
01159 301061
gillandcolin@tiscali.co.uk

Jane Lennox
01663 732381
jane@lennoxonline.net

Pauline Little
01283 702267
plittle@hotmail.co.uk

Christine and Vernon Sanderson
01246 570830
christine.r.sanderson@uwclub.net

Kate & Peter Spencer
01629 822499
pandkspencer@yahoo.co.uk

OPENING DATES

All entries subject to change. For latest information check **www.ngs.org.uk**

Map locator numbers are shown to the right of each garden name.

February

Snowdrop Festival

Saturday 17th
The Dower House 18

Sunday 18th
The Dower House 18

Saturday 24th
The Old Vicarage 42

Sunday 25th
10 Chestnut Way 13
The Old Vicarage 42

March

Sunday 4th
10 Chestnut Way 13

Sunday 18th
Chevin Brae 14

Saturday 24th
Treetops Hospice Care 56

Friday 30th
12 Ansell Road 1

Saturday 31st
12 Ansell Road 1

April

Sunday 1st
12 Ansell Road 1

Monday 2nd
12 Ansell Road 1

Sunday 8th
122 Sheffield Road 49

Sunday 15th
◆ Cascades Gardens 12
Coxbench Hall 15

Wednesday 18th
◆ Bluebell Arboretum and Nursery 6

Saturday 21st
◆ Old English Walled Garden, Elvaston Castle Country Park 40

Sunday 22nd
334 Belper Road 4

Sunday 29th
Moorfields 38
The Paddock 43

May

Sunday 6th
12 Ansell Road 1
122 Sheffield Road 49
12 Water Lane 58

Monday 7th
12 Ansell Road 1
Tilford House 53
12 Water Lane 58

Sunday 13th
◆ Cascades Gardens 12
Gamesley Fold Cottage 21
Locko Park 33

Tuesday 15th
◆ Renishaw Hall & Gardens 47

Wednesday 16th
◆ Bluebell Arboretum and Nursery 6

Saturday 19th
◆ Melbourne Hall Gardens 36

Sunday 20th
Broomfield Hall 8
Fir Croft 20
Higher Crossings 24
◆ Melbourne Hall Gardens 36

Sunday 27th
Barlborough Gardens 2
334 Belper Road 4

Monday 28th
◆ The Burrows Gardens 9
10 Chestnut Way 13
Rectory House 46
◆ Tissington Hall 54

June

Festival Weekend

Saturday 2nd
NEW Barton Hall 3
The Holly Tree 29

Sunday 3rd
NEW Barton Hall 3
Fir Croft 20
The Holly Tree 29
NEW Walton Cottage 57

Sunday 10th
Highfield House 25
Hollies Farm Plant Centre 28

Tuesday 12th
◆ Renishaw Hall & Gardens 47

Thursday 14th
◆ Bluebell Arboretum and Nursery 6

Saturday 16th
Holme Grange 30
The Dower House 18

Sunday 17th
◆ The Burrows Gardens 9
◆ Cascades Gardens 12
The Dower House 18
Fir Croft 20
13 Westfield Road 59

Friday 22nd
NEW 330 Old Road 41

Saturday 23rd
◆ Calke Abbey 11
NEW Hill Cottage 26
NEW 330 Old Road 41

Sunday 24th
High Roost 23
◆ Meynell Langley Trials Garden 37
Park Hall 44

Saturday 30th
Craigside 16
Elmton Gardens 19

July

Sunday 1st
Craigside 16
Elmton Gardens 19
The Lilies 32
NEW Walton Cottage 57

Saturday 7th
New Mills School and Sixth Form 39
The Old Vicarage 42
NEW Smithy House 50
26 Windmill Rise 63

Sunday 8th
◆ The Burrows Gardens 9
2 Manvers Street 35
Moorfields 38
New Mills School and Sixth Form 39
The Old Vicarage 42
26 Windmill Rise 63

Saturday 14th
Barlborough Gardens 2
NEW Hazeldene 22
NEW Stanton in Peak Gardens 51

Sunday 15th
Barlborough Gardens 2
◆ Cascades Gardens 12
NEW Hazeldene 22
◆ Meynell Langley Trials Garden 37
NEW Stanton in Peak Gardens 51

Wednesday 18th
◆ Bluebell Arboretum and Nursery 6

Sunday 22nd
Hollies Farm Plant Centre 28
The Paddock 43
Repton NGS Village Gardens 48

Tuesday 24th
Thornbridge Hall Gardens 52

Saturday 28th
12 Ansell Road 1
Byways 10

Sunday 29th
12 Ansell Road 1
Byways 10
NEW 18 Plant Lane 45
Wild in the Country 62

August

Saturday 4th
9 Main Street 34

Sunday 5th
9 Main Street 34

13 Westfield Road 59
Woodend Cottage 64

Saturday 11th
NEW Hazeldene 22

Sunday 12th
◆ Cascades Gardens 12
NEW Hazeldene 22
Hollies Farm Plant Centre 28

Wednesday 15th
◆ Bluebell Arboretum and Nursery 6

Saturday 18th
NEW 18 Plant Lane 45

Sunday 19th
◆ Meynell Langley Trials Garden 37

Sunday 26th
Coxbench Hall 15
Repton NGS Village Gardens 48
12 Water Lane 58

Monday 27th
◆ The Burrows Gardens 9
◆ Tissington Hall 54
12 Water Lane 58

September

Sunday 2nd
The Lilies 32
NEW 18 Plant Lane 45

Wednesday 12th
◆ Bluebell Arboretum and Nursery 6

Sunday 16th
◆ Meynell Langley Trials Garden 37

Saturday 22nd
◆ Calke Abbey 11

Sunday 23rd
Broomfield Hall 8

October

Sunday 7th
◆ Meynell Langley Trials Garden 37

Wednesday 17th
◆ Bluebell Arboretum and Nursery 6

By Arrangement

12 Ansell Road 1
334 Belper Road 4
Birchfield 5
Brick Kiln Farm 7
Byways 10
10 Chestnut Way 13
Chevin Brae 14
Craigside 16
Dam Stead 17
The Dower House 18
Gamesley Fold Cottage 21
NEW Hazeldene 22
High Roost 23
Higher Crossings 24
Highfield House 25
Hillside 27
Holme Grange 30
Holme Point, Repton NGS Village Gardens 48
9 Main Street 34
2 Manvers Street 35
New Mills School and Sixth Form 39
The Old Vicarage 42
The Paddock 43
Park Hall 44
NEW 18 Plant Lane 45
NEW Smithy House 50
Tilford House 53
NEW 206/208 Top Road 55
12 Water Lane 58
13 Westfield Road 59
Westgate 60
26 Wheeldon Avenue 61
Woodend Cottage 64

Hill Cottage

THE GARDENS

1 12 ANSELL ROAD

Ecclesall, Sheffield, S11 7PE. Dave Darwent, 01142 665881, dave.darwent@ngs.org.uk, www.poptasticdave.co.uk/_/Horticulture.html. *Approx 3m SW of City Centre. Travel to Ringinglow Rd (88 bus), then Edale Rd (opp Ecclesall C of E Primary School). 3rd R - Ansell Rd. No 12 on L ¾ way down, solar panel on roof.* **Fri 30, Sat 31 Mar, Sun 1, Mon 2 Apr, Sun 6, Mon 7 May, Sat 28, Sun 29 July (10.30-4). Adm £3, chd free. Light refreshments. Visits also by arrangement Apr to Sept groups 20 max. No parking for large coaches. Afternoon teas available on request when booking.**

Celebrating 90 years since the house was built and the garden first laid out by my grandparents. The weekend of July 28th and 29th marks 90 years to the day since my grandparents moved in. I have published a book about the garden to mark this milestone - all profits to the NGS. Afternoon Teas available during the 90th Anniversary Weekend openings: cucumber sandwiches, strawberries and cream, selection of dainties and unlimited tea or coffee. Then and now pictures of the garden in 1929 and 1950's Vs present. Map of landmarks up to 55m away which can be seen from garden.

✽ ☕

GROUP OPENING

2 BARLBOROUGH GARDENS

Barlborough, Chesterfield, S43 4ER. Christine Sanderson, 07956 203184, christine.r.sanderson@uwclub.net, http:/www.facebook.com/barlboroughgardens. *7m NE of Chesterfield. Off A619 midway between Chesterfield & Worksop. ½m E M1, J30. Follow signs for Barlborough then yellow NGS signs. Parking available in village. Coach parking available at Royal Oak PH.* **Sun 27 May (2-6). Combined adm £4, chd free. Sat 14, Sun 15 July (1-6). Combined adm £6, chd free. Home-made teas on 27th May at The Hollies. Refreshments available at both Stone Croft and The Hollies on 14th & 15th July.**

THE HOLLIES
Vernon & Christine Sanderson, christine.r.sanderson@uwclub.net.
Open on all dates

LINDWAY
Thomas & Margaret Pettinger.
Open on all dates

NEW **THE RED BRICK HOUSE**
Mr & Mrs Steven and Ashlyn Miller.
Open on Sun 27 May

NEW **2 SPEETLEY VIEW**
Tony Needham.
Open on Sat 14, Sun 15 July

STONE CROFT
Mrs June Widdowson.
Open on Sat 14, Sun 15 July

WOODSIDE HOUSE
Tricia & Adrian Murray-Leslie.
Open on Sat 14, Sun 15 July

Barlborough is an attractive historic village and a range of interesting buildings can be seen all around the village centre. The village is situated close to Renishaw Hall for possible combined visit. Map detailing location of all the gardens is issued with admission ticket, which can be purchased at any of the gardens listed. For more information visit our Facebook page - see details above. Local photographer, Lesley Carley will be displaying some of her work on 15th July. Digital prints will be available both as greeting cards and mounted/framed prints. Partial wheelchair access at The Hollies.

3 NEW BARTON HALL

Church Broughton, Derby, DE65 5AN. Francine Salisbury. *A50 take the turning for Hatton. Go through the T-lights, then take the 1st turning L for Church Broughton. Go straight on for approx 2 miles. Barton Blount is sign posted on the L.* **Sat 2, Sun 3 June (11-4). Adm £5, chd free. Home-made teas in the Engine Room.**

In the magnificent setting of Barton Blount a set of themed gardens containing wisteria archways, lavender lined pathways, rose gardens, glasshouses and a parterre garden. There is also 'Charlotte's Garden', a huge walled vegetable garden dedicated to charity. Toilets on site.

4 334 BELPER ROAD

Stanley Common, DE7 6FY. Gill & Colin Hancock, 01159 301061, gillandcolin@tiscali.co.uk, www.hamescovert.com. *7m N of Derby. 3m W of Ilkeston. On A609, ¾m from Rose & Crown Xrds (A608). Please park in field up farm drive or Working Men's Club rear car park if wet.* **Sun 22 Apr, Sun 27 May (12-4.30). Adm £3.50, chd free. Home-made teas. April highlight - home-made soup, bread & cakes. Visits also by arrangement Apr to June adm £7 incl tea/coffee/cake and our personal attention.**

Now in our 21st year of opening and still an evolving country garden. Plenty of seating to enjoy our highly recommended home-made cakes. Take a scenic walk to a 10 acre wood with glades and ½ acre lake. April: cowslips. May: laburnum tunnel and wisteria. June: wild flowers, hostas, ferns and roses. Streptocarpus in conservatory. Children welcome with plenty of activities to keep them entertained. Paths round wood and lake not suitable for wheelchairs.

5 BIRCHFIELD

The Dukes Drive, Ashford in the Water, Bakewell, DE45 1QQ. Brian Parker, 01629 813800. *2m NW of Bakewell. On A6 to Buxton between New Bridge & Sheepwash Bridge.* **Visits by arrangement adm £3 April - Sept, £2 Oct - March. Please leave message if no answer. Light refreshments.** Donation to Thornhill Memorial Trust.

Beautifully situated ¾ acre part terraced garden with pond and a 1¼ acre arboretum and wildflower meadow. An extremely varied collection of trees, shrubs, climbers, colourful perennials, bulbs and bamboos, all designed to give yr-round colour and interest. Many overgrown shrubs have been removed allowing for much new planting.

6 ◆ BLUEBELL ARBORETUM AND NURSERY

Annwell Lane, Smisby, Ashby de la Zouch, LE65 2TA. Robert & Suzette Vernon, 01530 413700, sales@bluebellnursery.com, www.bluebellnursery.com. *1m NW of Ashby-de-la-Zouch. Arboretum is clearly signed in Annwell Lane (follow brown signs), ¼m S, through village of Smisby off B5006, between Ticknall & Ashby-de-la-Zouch. Free parking.* **For NGS: Wed 18 Apr, Wed 16 May, Thur 14 June, Wed 18 July, Wed 15 Aug, Wed 12 Sept, Wed 17 Oct (9-4). Adm £5, chd free. Tea/coffee available on request at office. For other opening times and information, please phone, email or visit garden website.**

Beautiful 9 acre woodland garden with a large collection of rare trees and shrubs. Interest throughout the yr with spring flowers, cool leafy areas in summer and sensational autumn colour. Many information posters describing the more obscure plants. Bring wellingtons in wet weather. Adjacent specialist tree and shrub nursery. Please be aware this is not a wood full of bluebells, despite the name. The woodland garden is fully labelled and the staff can answer questions or talk at length about any of the trees or shrubs on display. Rare trees and shrubs. Educational signs. Woodland. Arboretum. Please wear sturdy, waterproof footwear during or after wet weather! Full wheelchair access in dry, warm weather however grass paths can become wet and inaccessible in snow or after rain.

7 BRICK KILN FARM

Hulland Ward, Ashbourne, DE6 3EJ. Mrs Jan Hutchinson, 01335 370440, robert.hutchinson123@btinternet.com. *4m E of Ashbourne (A517). 1m S of Carsington Water. From Hulland Ward take Dog Lane past church 2nd L. 100yds on R. From Ashbourne A517 Bradley Corner turn L follow sign for Carsington Water 1m on L.* **Visits by arrangement May to Aug (am, pm and evening visits), adm incl refreshments. Adm £5, chd free. Home-made teas.** Donation to Great Dane Adoption Society.

A small country garden which wraps around an old red brick farmhouse accessed through a courtyard with original well. Irregularly shaped lawn bounded by wide herbaceous borders leading to duck pond and pet's memorial garden. Small holding. Cattle and horses grazing. Search for us on YouTube. Level garden, some uneven flagstones, gravel drive, plenty of parking.

8 BROOMFIELD HALL

Morley, Ilkeston, Derbyshire, DE7 6DN. Derby College, www.facebook.com/BroomfieldPlantCentre. *4m N of Derby. 6m S of Heanor on A608.* **Sun 20 May, Sun 23 Sept (10-4). Adm £3, chd free. Light refreshments.**

25 acres of constantly developing educational Victorian gardens/woodlands maintained by students and volunteers. Trees, shrubs, herbaceous borders, walled garden, themed gardens, parterre, winter garden, plant centre, rose garden, rhododendrons, tropical garden, student plots, terrace views, lawns, garden tours and much more. Most of garden is accessible to wheelchair users.

9 ◆ THE BURROWS GARDENS

Burrows Lane, Brailsford, Ashbourne, DE6 3BU. Mrs N M Dalton, 01335 360745, enquiries@burrowsgardens.com, www.burrowsgardens.com. *5m SE of Ashbourne; 5m NW of Derby. A52 from Derby: turn L opp sign for Wild Park Leisure 1m before village of Brailsford. ¼m.* **For NGS: Mon 28 May, Sun 17 June, Sun 8 July, Mon 27 Aug (11-4). Adm £5, chd free. Home-made teas.** For other opening times and information, please phone, email or visit garden website.

5 acres of stunning garden set in beautiful countryside where immaculate lawns show off exotic rare plants and trees, mixing with old favourites in this outstanding garden. A huge variety of styles from temple to Cornish, Italian and English, gloriously designed and displayed. This is a must see garden. Non NGS: Open every Tues, Fri, and Sun from April - August incl. Look out for Special events such as Shakespeare productions and wine tasting. Refreshments can be provided for pre-booked groups. Most of garden accessible to wheelchairs.

10 BYWAYS

7A Brookfield Avenue, Brookside, Chesterfield, S40 3NX. Terry & Eileen Kelly, 01246 566376, telkel1@aol.com. *1½m W of Chesterfield. Follow A619 from Chesterfield towards Baslow. Brookfield Av is 2nd R after Brookfield Sch. Please park on Chatsworth Rd (A619).* **Sat 28, Sun 29 July (12.30-4.30). Adm £3, chd free. Home-made teas. Visits also by arrangement July & Aug adm £5.50 incl tea or coffee and cakes.** Donation to Ashgate Hospice.

Previous winners of the Best Back Garden over 80sq m, Best Front Garden, Best Container Garden and Best Hanging Basket in Chesterfield in Bloom. Well established perennial borders including helenium, monardas, phlox, penstenom, grasses, acers, giving a very colourful display. Rockery and many planters containing acers, hostas, fuchsias and roses. 5 seating areas.

11 ◆ CALKE ABBEY

Ticknall, DE73 7LE. National Trust, 01332 865587, www.nationaltrust.org.uk. *10m S of Derby. On A514 at Ticknall between Swadlincote & Melbourne.* **For NGS: Sat 23 June, Sat 22 Sept (10-5). Adm £10.20, chd £5.10.** For other opening times and information, please phone or visit garden website.

Late C18 walled gardens gradually repaired over the last 25yrs. Flower garden with summer bedding, herbaceous borders and the unique auricula theatre. Georgian orangery, impressive collection of glasshouses and garden buildings. Ice house, grotto and gardeners' tunnel. Vegetable garden growing unusual varieties of fruit and vegetables, often on sale to visitors. Restaurant at main visitor facilities for light refreshments and locally sourced food. Electric buggy available for those with mobility problems.

12 ◆ CASCADES GARDENS
Clatterway, Bonsall, Matlock, DE4 2AH. Alan & Alesia Clements, 01629 822813, cascadesgardens@gmail.com, www.cascadesgardens.com. *5m SW of Matlock. From Cromford A6 T-lights turn towards Wirksworth. Turn R along Via Gellia, signed Buxton & Bonsall. After 1m turn R up hill towards Bonsall. Garden entrance at top of hill before village car park.* **For NGS: Sun 15 Apr, Sun 13 May, Sun 17 June, Sun 15 July, Sun 12 Aug (1-4.30). Adm £5, chd free. Home-made teas. For other opening times and information, please phone, email or visit garden website.**
Fascinating 4 acre peaceful garden in spectacular natural surroundings, with woodland, cliffs, stream, pond, lead mine and ruined corn mill. Eastern philosophy inspired secluded garden rooms for relaxation and reflection and beautiful views of the wide collection of unusual perennials, conifers, shrubs and trees. Non NGS: open everyday March to October 10am to 5pm. Groups welcome. Bonsall open gardens weekend in June. Featured in Derby Telegraph and Nottinghamshire Magazine. Mostly accessible. Gravel paths, some steep slopes.

13 10 CHESTNUT WAY
Repton, DE65 6FQ. Robert & Pauline Little, 01283 702267, rlittleq@gmail.com, www.littlegarden.org.uk. *6m S of Derby. From A38/A50, S of Derby, follow signs to Willington, then Repton. In Repton turn R at r'about. Chestnut Way is ¼ m up hill, on L.* **Sun 25 Feb, Sun 4 Mar (11-3). Adm £3, chd free. Light refreshments. Mon 28 May (1.30-5.30). Adm £4, chd free. Home-made teas. Home-made soup (Feb/Mar). Home-made teas (all dates). Opening with Repton NGS Village Gardens on Sun 22 July, Sun 26 Aug. Visits also by arrangement for groups of 10+ (adm incl home-made tea and guided tour).**
Still changing even after 20 yrs. Wander through an acre of sweeping mixed borders, spring bulbs, mature trees to a stunning butterfly bed, maturing arboretum, established prairie. Meet a pair of passionate, practical, gardeners who gently manage this plantsman's garden. Designed and maintained by the owners. Expect a colourful display. Plenty of seats, conservatory if wet. Thousands of snowdrops. **Celebrate our 20 years of NGS openings on 28th May with activities for children young and old** Excellent plant stall in Spring. Special interest in viticella clematis, organic vegetables and composting. In Daily Telegraph Gardens to Visit. Level garden, good solid paths to main areas. Some grass/bark paths.

14 CHEVIN BRAE
Milford, Belper, DE56 0QH. Dr David Moreton, 01332 843553, david.moreton@lubrizol.com.

Park Hall

1½m S of Belper. Coming from S on A6 turn L at Strutt Arms & cont up Chevin Rd. Park on Chevin Road. After 300 yds follow arrow to L up Morrells Lane. After 300 yds Chevin Brae on L with silver garage. **Sun 18 Mar (1-5). Adm £2.50, chd free. Home-made teas. Visits also by arrangement Feb to Oct. For appointments please call and leave a message or email.**
A large garden, with swathes of daffodils in the orchard a spring feature. Extensive wild flower planting along edge of wood features aconites, snowdrops, wood anemones, fritillaries and dog tooth violets. Other parts of garden will have hellebores and early camelias. Tea and home-made pastries, many of which feature fruit and jam from the garden, served from the summer house in the middle of the orchard.

15 COXBENCH HALL

Alfreton Road, Coxbench, Derby, DE21 5BB. Mr Brian Ballin. *4m N of Derby close to A38. After passing thru Little Eaton, turn L onto Alfreton Rd for 1m, Coxbench Hall is on L next to Fox & Hounds PH between Little Eaton & Holbrook. From A38, take Kilburn turn & go towards Little Eaton.* **Sun 15 Apr, Sun 26 Aug (2.30-4.30). Adm £3, chd free. Home-made teas incl diabetic and gluten free cakes.**
Formerly the ancestral home of the Meynell family, the gardens reflect the Georgian house standing in 4½ acres of grounds most of which is accessible and wheelchair friendly. The garden has 2 fishponds connected by a stream, a sensory garden for the sight impaired, a short woodland walk through shrubbery, rockery, raised vegetable beds, an orchard and seasonal displays in the mainly lawned areas. As a Residential Home for the Elderly, our Gardens are developed to inspire our residents from a number of sensory perspectives - different colours, textures and fragrances of plants, growing vegetables next to the C18 potting shed. There is also a veteran (500 - 800 yr old) Yew tree. Most of garden is lawned or block paved including a block paved path around the edges of the main lawn. Regret no wheelchair access to woodland area.

16 CRAIGSIDE

Reservoir Road, Whaley Bridge, SK23 7BW. Jane & Gerard Lennox, 07939 012634, jane@lennoxonline.net, www.craigside.info. *11m SE of Stockport. 11m NNW of Buxton. Turn off A6 onto A5004 to Whaley Bridge. Turn R at train station 1st L under railway bridge onto Reservoir Rd. Park on roadside or in village. Garden ½m from village.* **Sat 30 June, Sun 1 July (12-5). Adm £3.50, chd free. Home-made teas incl gluten free and savoury options. Visits also by arrangement May to Aug please be aware that the garden is steep.**
1 acre garden rising steeply from the reservoir giving magnificent views across Todbrook reservoir into Peak District. Gravel paths, stone steps with stopping places. Many mature trees incl 500+yr old oak. Spring bulbs, summer fuchsias, herbaceous borders, alpine bed, steep mature rockery many heucheras and hydrangeas. Herbs, vegetables and fruit trees. Gluten free cakes available also savoury alternatives. Refreshments also available for 4 legged visitors with a selection of home-made dog biscuits! These are also edible for humans and were tested by some of the volunteers.

17 DAM STEAD

3 Crowhole, Barlow, Dronfield, S18 7TJ. Derek & Barbara Saveall, 01142 890802, barbarasaveall@hotmail.co.uk. *Chesterfield B6051 to Barlow. Tickled Trout Pub on L. Springfield Rd on L then R on unnamed rd. Last cottage on R.* **Visits by arrangement May to Sept. Adm £3, chd free. Light refreshments.**
Approx one acre with stream, weir, fragrant garden, rose tunnel, orchard garden and dam with an island. Long woodland path, alpine troughs, rockeries and mixed planting. A natural wildlife garden large summerhouse with seating inside and out. 3 village well dressings and carnival over one week mid August.

18 THE DOWER HOUSE

Church Square, Melbourne, DE73 8JH. William & Griselda Kerr, 01332 864756, griseldakerr@btinternet.com. *6m S of Derby. 5m W of exit 23A M1. 4m N of exit 13 M42. When in Church Square, turn R at board giving church service times just before church, gates then 50 yds ahead.* **Sat 17, Sun 18 Feb (10-4). Adm £3, chd free. Sat 2, Sun 3 June (10-5). Adm £4, chd free. Light refreshments. Visits also by arrangement Feb to Sept min group size 15, max group size 26 when tour, tea and cake are required.**
Beautiful view of Melbourne Pool from balustraded terrace running length of 1831 house. Garden drops steeply by paths and steps to lawn with herbaceous border and bank of flowering shrubs best in June/Sept. Interesting bog garden and other late summer beds. Rose tunnel, glade, orchard, hellebores and small woodland lovely in early spring. Herb garden, other small lawns and vegetable garden. Children can search for a bronze crocodile, a stone pig, a metal bug and a strange bird. They might also see an iron sunflower hanging in a tree, a bronze girl doing cartwheels, two sleeping dragons and a lion's face. There are seats around the garden for visitors to sit and take in the views. Derbyshire Life, The Melbourne Village Voice, Radio Derby. Wheelchair access top half of the garden only. Shoes with a good grip are highly recommended as some slopes are steep. No parking within 50 yards.

GROUP OPENING

19 ELMTON GARDENS

Elmton, Worksop, S80 4LS. *2m from Creswell, 3m from Clowne, 5m from J30, M1. From M1 take A616 to Newark. Follow approx 4m. Turn R at Elmton signpost. At junction turn R.* **Sat 30 June, Sun 1 July (1-5). Combined adm £5, chd free. Cream teas.**

ASH LEA
Jane & Graham Cooper.

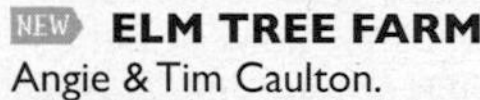

ELM TREE FARM
Angie & Tim Caulton.

PEAR TREE COTTAGE
Geoff & Janet Cutts.

PINFOLD
Nikki Kirsop Barry Davies.

Elmton is a lovely little village situated on a stretch of rare Magnesian limestone in the middle of attractive, rolling farm land. It has a pub, a church and a village green. Garden opening coincides with our annual Elmton Festival and Well Dressing celebrations. There are two exhibitions to view, one in the church showing local history devised by the History Group and a display of local farming history. Other attractions include a brass band performance in the courtyard of Elm Tree Farm and cream teas in the old School Room. The village green has an unimproved grassland area where quaking grass, bee orchids and harebells grow. The four very colourful but different open gardens are all surrounded by farm land and have wonderful views. They show a range of gardening styles, themed beds and all have a commitment to fruit and vegetable growing. Elmton received it's third silver gilt award from EMIB in 2017 and has been the East Midlands winner of the best small village 5 times. Food and drink is available throughout the day at the Elm Tree pub. Cream Teas are available from the old school house next to the church. Garden opening coincides with Elmton Festival and Well Dressing celebrations with exhibitions and a brass band.

20 FIR CROFT

Froggatt Road, Calver, S32 3ZD. Dr S B Furness, www.alpineplantcentre.co.uk. *4m N of Bakewell. At junction of B6001 with A625 (formerly B6054), adjacent to Power Garage.* **Sun 20 May, Sun 3, Sun 17 June (2-5). Adm by donation.**

Massive scree with many varieties. Plantsman's garden; rockeries; water garden and nursery; extensive collection (over 3000 varieties) of alpines; conifers; over 800 sempervivums, 500 saxifrages and 350 primulas. Many new varieties not seen anywhere else in the UK. Huge new tufa wall planted with many rare Alpines and sempervivums.

21 GAMESLEY FOLD COTTAGE

Gamesley Fold, Glossop, SK13 6JJ. Mrs G M Carr, 01457 867856, gcarr@gamesleyfold.co.uk, www.gamesleyfold.co.uk. *2m W of Glossop. Off A626 Glossop/ Marple Rd nr Charlesworth. Turn down lane directly opp St. Margaret's School, white cottage at the bottom Car parking in the adjacent field if weather is dry.* **Sun 13 May (1-4). Adm £3, chd free. Home-made teas. Visits also by arrangement May & June any number welcome.**

Old fashioned cottage garden with rhododendrons, herbaceous borders with candelabra primulas, cottage garden perennial flowers and herbs also a plant nursery selling a wide variety of these plus wild flowers. Small ornamental fish pond and an orchard. Lovely views of the surrounding countryside and plenty of seats available to relax and enjoy tea and cakes. A garden planted with wildlife in mind lots of native wild flower plants on sale to visitors. Featured in High Peak Review, Community paper and Glossop Chronicle.

22 NEW HAZELDENE

Glebe Avenue, Great Longstone, Bakewell, DE45 1TY. Colby Burke, nickell280@btinternet.com. *Glebe Avenue - Great Longstone. West - A623 - B6465 - NGS sign Monsal Head. South - Bakewell A6 - A6020 - NGS sign Great Longstone. East/ North - A619 or A623 Baslow - A619 - A6020 to Village NGS sign at War Memorial in Village.* **Sat 14, Sun 15 July, Sat 11, Sun 12 Aug (11-4). Adm £3, chd £3. Refreshments available at Hassop Bookshop. Visits also by arrangement July to Sept 10 - 20 people ideally.**

Hazeldene is a medium sized private garden offering colour themed perennials, a patio allotment and a 'silver-black ' border. The rear garden offers muted colours, sounds and textures, is hopefully relaxing and reflective and is designed to be appreciated in the rain and to maximise the space through the use of perspective and seasonal screening. Access slightly difficult to the back garden but can be done! Very accessible to the front.

23 HIGH ROOST

27 Storthmeadow Road, Simmondley, Glossop, SK13 6UZ. Peter & Christina Harris, 01457 863888, peter-harris9@sky.com. *3/4 m SW of Glossop. From Glossop A57 to M/CL at 2nd r'about, up Simmondley Ln nr top R turn. From Marple A626 to Glossop, in Chworth R up Town Ln past Hare & Hound PH 2nd L.* **Sun 24 June (12-5). Adm £3, chd free. Light refreshments. Visits also by arrangement May to July.** Donation to Manchester Dogs Home.

Garden on terraced slopes, views over fields and hills. Winding paths, archways and steps explore different garden rooms packed with plants, designed to attract wildlife. Alpine bed, gravel gardens; vegetable garden, water features, statuary, troughs and planters. A garden which needs exploring to discover its secrets tucked away in hidden corners. Craft stall, children's garden quiz and lucky dip. Photographed for Amateur Garden magazine.

24 HIGHER CROSSINGS

Crossings Road, Chapel-en-le-Frith, High Peak, SK23 9RX. Malcolm & Christine Hoskins, 01298 812970. *Turn off B5470 N from Chapel-en-le-Frith on Crossings Rd signed Whitehough/Chinley. Higher Crossings is 2nd house on R beyond 1st Xrds . Park best before crossroads on Crossings Rd or L on Eccles Rd.* **Sun 20 May (1.30-5). Adm £4, chd free. Light refreshments. Visits also by arrangement May to Aug.**

Nearly 2 acres of formal terraced country garden, sweeping lawns and magnificent Peak District views. Rhododendrons, acers, azaleas, hostas, herbaceous borders, Zen garden. Mature specimen trees and shrubs leading through a dell. Beautiful stone terrace and sitting areas. Garden gate leading into meadow. Featured in Pure Buxton magazine.

25 HIGHFIELD HOUSE

Wingfield Road, Oakerthorpe, Alfreton, DE55 7AP. Paul & Ruth Peat and Janet & Brian Costall, 01773 521342, highfieldhouseopengardens@hotmail.co.uk, www.highfieldhouse.weebly.com. *Rear of Alfreton Golf Club. A615 Alfreton-Matlock Rd.* **Sun 10 June (10.30-5). Adm £3, chd free. Home-made teas. Visits also by arrangement: 18-28 Feb, May & June. Adm £6 incl refreshments. Groups 15+.**

Lovely country garden of approx 1 acre, incorporating a shady garden, woodland, pond, laburnum tunnel, orchard, herbaceous borders and vegetable garden. Fabulous AGA baked cakes and lunches. Groups welcome by appointment - (including 18th -28th February for Snowdrops with afternoon tea or lunch inside by the fire). Lovely walk to Derbyshire Wildlife Trust nature reserve to see Orchids in June. Some steps, slopes and gravel areas.

26 NEW HILL COTTAGE

Ashover Road, Littlemoor, Ashover nr Chesterfield, S45 0BL. Jane Tomlinson and Tim Walls. *Littlemoor. 1.8 m from Ashover village, 6.3 m from Chesterfield and 6.1 m from Matlock. Hill Cottage is on Ashover Rd (also known as Stubben Edge Lane). Opp the end of Eastwood Lane.* **Sat 23 June (10.30-5). Adm £3.50, chd free. Light refreshments.**

Hill Cottage is a lovely example of an English country cottage garden. Whilst small, the garden has full, colourful and fragrant herbaceous borders with hostas and roses in pots along with a heart shaped lawn. A greenhouse full of chillies and scented geraniums and a small veg patch. Views to the horizon over a pastoral landscape. Teas, homemade cakes and plants are for sale. There are several steps.

27 HILLSIDE

286 Handley Road, New Whittington, Chesterfield, S43 2ET. Mr E J Lee, 01246 454960, eric.lee5@btinternet.com. *3m N of Chesterfield. Between B6056 & B0652 N of village. SatNav friendly.* **Visits by arrangement, groups and individual visitors. Adm £2.50, chd free. Light refreshments.**

⅓ acre sloping site. Herbaceous borders, rock garden, alpines, streams, pools, bog gardens, asiatic primula bed, and alpine house. Acers, bamboos, collection of approx 150 varieties of ferns, eucalypts, euphorbias, grasses, conifers, Himalayan bed. 1000+ plants permanently labelled. Yr round interest.

28 HOLLIES FARM PLANT CENTRE

Uppertown, Bonsall, Matlock, DE4 2AW. Robert & Linda Wells, www.holliesfarmplantcentre.co.uk. *From Cromford turn R off A5012 up The Clatterway. Keep R past Fountain Tearoom to village cross, take L up High St, then 2nd L onto Abel Lane. Garden straight ahead.* **Sun 10 June, Sun 22 July, Sun 12 Aug (11-3). Adm £3.50, chd free. Home-made teas.**

The best selection in Derbyshire with advice and personal attention from Robert and Linda Wells at their family run business. Enjoy a visit to remember in our beautiful display garden - set within glorious Peak District countryside. Huge variety of hardy perennials incl the rare and unusual. Vast selection of traditional garden favourites. Award winning hanging baskets. Ponds, herbaceous borders and glorious views. Plenty of parking available. Pure Buxton and Pure Bakewell magazines.

29 THE HOLLY TREE

21 Hackney Road, Hackney, Matlock, DE4 2PX. Carl Hodgkinson. *½m NW of Matlock, off A6. Take A6 NW past bus stn & 1st R up Dimple Rd. At T-junction, turn R & immed L, for Farley & Hackney. Take 1st L onto Hackney Rd. Continue ¾m.* **Sat 2, Sun 3 June (11-4.30). Adm £3, chd free. Home-made teas.**

The garden is in excess of 1½ acres and set on a steeply sloping S-facing site, sheltering behind a high retaining wall and incl a small arboretum, bog garden, herbaceous borders, pond, vegetables, fruits, apiary and chickens. Extensively terraced with many paths and steps and with spectacular views across the Derwent valley to Snitterton and Oker.

The National Garden Scheme is Hospice UK's largest single funder

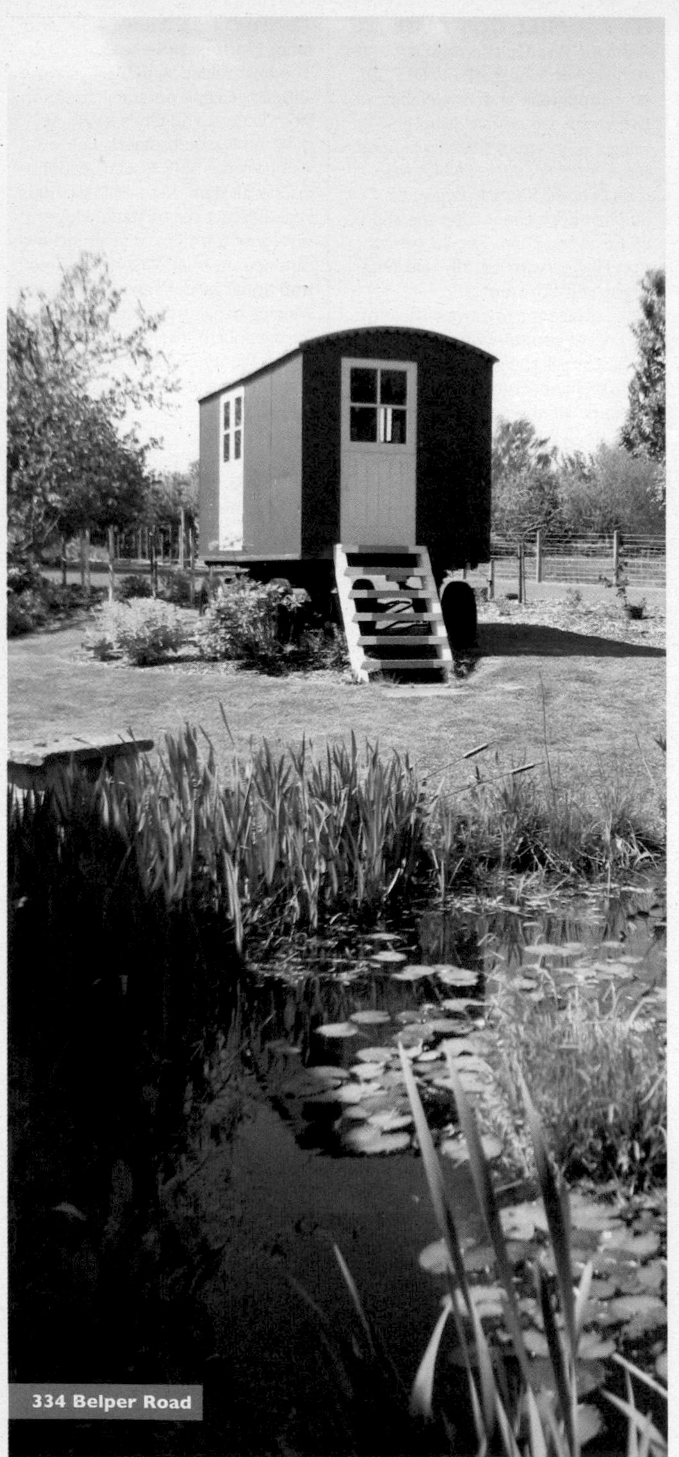
334 Belper Road

30 HOLME GRANGE

Holme Lane, Bakewell, DE45 1GF. Mrs Shirley Stubbs, 01629 814728, shirleystubbs@hotmail.co.uk. *Close to centre of Bakewell. From Bakewell town centre, follow the Baslow Rd and take the first L along Holme Lane, beside the river meadow. From Baslow turn R into Holme Lane.* **Sat 16 June (11-4). Adm £4, chd free. Home-made teas. Visits also by arrangement June & July min 10.**

Holme Grange has a garden of about an acre, and offers a range of mixed borders, large lawned area and woodland offering some unusual trees, shrubs and plants. Back gate access to level gravel paths and lawned area.

31 ◆ LEA GARDENS

Lea, Matlock, DE4 5GH. Mr & Mrs J Tye, 01629 534380, www.leagarden.co.uk. *5m SE of Matlock. Off A6 & A615.* **For opening times and information, please phone or visit garden website.**

Rare collection of rhododendrons, azaleas, kalmias, alpines and conifers in delightful woodland setting. Gardens are sited on remains of medieval quarry and cover about 4 acres. Specialised plant nursery of rhododendrons and azaleas on site. Open daily 1 March to 31 July (9-5). Plant sales by appointment out of season. Visitors welcome throughout the yr. Coffee shop noted for home baked cakes and light refreshments. Gravel paths, steep slopes. Free access for wheelchair users.

32 THE LILIES

Griffe Grange Valley, Grangemill, Matlock, DE4 4BW. Chris & Bridget Sheppard, www.thelilies.com. *4m N Cromford. On A5012 Via Gellia Rd 4m N Cromford. 1st house on R after junction with B5023 to Middleton. From Grangemill 1st house on L after Prospect Quarry (IKO Permatrack).* **Sun 1 July, Sun 2 Sept (11.30-4.30). Adm £3.50, chd free. Home-made teas. Light**

Lunches served 11.30 to 3.00, Homemade teas all day.
One acre garden gradually restored over the past 12yrs situated at the top of a wooded valley, surrounded by wildflower meadow and ash woodland. Area adjacent to house with seasonal planting and containers. Mixed shrubs and perennial borders many raised from seed. 3 ponds, vegetable plot, barn conversion with separate cottage style garden. Natural garden with stream developed from old mill pond. Walks in large wildflower meadow and ash woodland both SSSI's. Handspinning demonstration and natural dyeing display using materials from the garden and wool from sheep in the meadow. Locally made crafts for sale. Partial wheelchair access. Steep slope from car park, limestone chippings at entrance, some boggy areas if wet.

33 LOCKO PARK

Spondon, Derby, DE21 7BW. Mrs Lucy Palmer, www.lockopark.co.uk. *6m NE of Derby. From A52 Borrowash bypass, 2m N via B6001, turn to Spondon. More directions on www.lockopark.co.uk. NB. SatNav use DE21 7BW Via Locko Rd.* **Sun 13 May (2-4.30). Adm £3, chd free. Home-made teas.**
An original 1927 open garden for the NGS. Large garden; pleasure gardens; rose gardens designed by William Eames. House (not open) by Smith of Warwick with Victorian additions. Chapel (open) Charles II, with original ceiling. Tulip tree in the arboretum purported to be the largest in the Midlands. Large collection of rhododendron and azalea.

34 9 MAIN STREET

Horsley Woodhouse, DE7 6AU. Ms Alison Napier, 01332 881629, ibhillib@btinternet.com. *3m SW of Heanor. 6m N of Derby. Turn off A608 Derby to Heanor Rd at Smalley, towards Belper, (A609). Garden on A609, 1m from Smalley turning.* **Sat 4, Sun 5 Aug (1.30-4.30). Adm £3, chd free. Cream teas. Visits also by arrangement Apr to Sept.**
⅓ acre hilltop garden overlooking lovely farmland view. Terracing, borders, lawns and pergola create space for an informal layout with planting for colour effect. Features incl large wildlife pond with water lilies, bog garden and small formal pool. Emphasis on carefully selected herbaceous perennials mixed with shrubs and old fashioned roses. Gravel garden for sun loving plants and scree garden, both developed from former drive. Wide collection of home grown plants for sale. To be featured in Amateur Gardening. All parts of the garden accessible to wheelchairs. Wheelchair adapted WC.

35 2 MANVERS STREET

Ripley, DE5 3EQ. Mrs D Wood & Mr D Hawkins, 01773 743962, d.s.hawkins@btinternet.com. *Ripley Town centre to Derby Rd turn L opp Leisure Centre onto Heath Rd. 1st turn R onto Meadow Rd, 1st L onto Manvers St.* **Sun 8 July (1.30-5). Adm £3, chd free. Home-made teas. Visits also by arrangement July & Aug, refreshments on request when booking.**
Summer garden with backdrop of neighbouring trees, 10 borders bursting with colour surrounded by immaculate shaped lawn. Perennials incl 26 clematis, annuals, baskets, tubs and pots. Ornamental fish pond. Water features, arbour and summerhouse. Plenty of seating areas to take in this awe inspiring oasis.

36 ◆ MELBOURNE HALL GARDENS

Church Square, Melbourne, Derby, DE73 8EN. Melbourne Gardens Charity, 01332 862502, Melbhall@globalnet.co.uk, www.melbournehallgardens.com. *6m S of Derby. At Melbourne Market Place turn into Church St, go down to Church Sq. Garden entrance across visitor centre next to Melbourne Hall tea room.* **For NGS: Sat 19, Sun 20 May (1.30-5.30). Adm £5, chd free. For other opening times and information, please phone, email or visit garden website.**
A 17 acre historic garden with an abundance of rare trees and shrubs. Woodland and waterside planting with extensive herbaceous borders. Meconopsis, candelabra primulas, various Styrax and Cornus kousa. Other garden features incl Bakewells wrought iron arbour, a yew tunnel and fine C18 statuary and water features. 300yr old trees, waterside planting, feature hedges and herbaceous borders. Fine statuary and stonework. Gravel paths, uneven surface in places, some steep slopes.

37 ◆ MEYNELL LANGLEY TRIALS GARDEN

Lodge Lane (off Flagshaw Lane), Kirk Langley, Ashbourne, DE6 4NT. Robert & Karen Walker, 01332 824358, enquiries@meynell-langley-gardens.co.uk, www.meynell-langley-gardens.co.uk. *4m W of Derby, nr Kedleston Hall. Head W out of Derby on A52. At Kirk Langley turn R onto Flagshaw Lane (signed to Kedleston Hall) then R onto Lodge Lane. Follow Meynell Langley Gardens signs.* **For NGS: Sun 24 June, Sun 15 July, Sun 19 Aug, Sun 16 Sept, Sun 7 Oct (10-4). Adm £4, chd free. For other opening times and information, please phone, email or visit garden website.**
Formal ¾ acre Victorian style garden established over 20yrs, displaying and trialling new and existing varieties of bedding plants, herbaceous perennials and vegetable plants grown at the adjacent nursery. Over 180 hanging baskets and floral displays. 45 varieties of apple, pear and other fruit. Summer fruit pruning demonstrations on July NGS day and apple tasting on October NGS day. Adjacent tea rooms serving lunches and refreshments daily. Level ground and firm grass. Full disabled access to tea rooms.

38 MOORFIELDS

257/261 Chesterfield Road, Temple Normanton, Chesterfield, S42 5DE. Peter, Janet & Stephen Wright. *4m SE of Chesterfield. From Chesterfield take A617 for 2m, turn on to B6039 through Temple Normanton, taking R fork signed Tibshelf, B6039. Garden ¼m on R. Limited parking.* **Sun 29 Apr, Sun 8 July (1-5). Adm £3, chd free. Light refreshments.**

Two adjoining gardens each planted for seasonal colour. The larger one has mature, mixed island beds and borders, a gravel garden to the front, a small wild flower area, large wildlife pond, orchard and soft fruit, and vegetable garden. Show of late flowering tulips. The smaller gardens of No. 257 feature herbaceous borders and shrubs. Extensive views across to mid Derbyshire.

39 NEW MILLS SCHOOL AND SIXTH FORM

Church Lane, New Mills, High Peak, SK22 4NR. Mr Craig Pickering, 07833 373593, cpickering@newmillsschool.co.uk, www.newmillsschool.co.uk. *12m NNW of Buxton. From A6 take A6105 signed New Mills, Hayfield. At C of E Church turn L onto Church Lane. School on L. Parking on site.* **Sat 7 July (10-5); Sun 8 July (1-5). Adm £3, chd free. Home-made teas in School Library. Visits also by arrangement June to Aug for groups 10+.**

Mixed herbaceous perennials/shrub borders, with mature trees and lawns and gravel border situated in the semi rural setting of the High Peak incl a Grade II listed building with 4 themed quads. The school was awarded a distinction for their first garden at Tatton RHS Flower Show 2015 and highly commended for their entry in 2017. Hot and Cold Beverages and a selection of sandwiches, cream teas and home-made cakes are available. Featured in Pure Buxton; In and Around Glossop and High Peak and featuring in Derbyshire Life. Ramps allow wheelchair access to most of outside, flower beds and into Grade II listed building and library.

40 ◆ OLD ENGLISH WALLED GARDEN, ELVASTON CASTLE COUNTRY PARK

Borrowash Road, Elvaston, Derby, DE72 3EP. Derbyshire County Council, 01629 533870, www.derbyshire.gov.uk/elvaston. *4m E of Derby. Signed from A52 & A50. Car parking charge applies.* **For NGS: Sat 21 Apr (12-4). Adm £2.50, chd free. Light refreshments. For other opening times and information, please phone or visit garden website.**

Come and discover the beauty of the Old English walled garden at Elvaston Castle. Take in the peaceful atmosphere and enjoy the scents and colours of all the varieties of trees, shrubs and plants. Summer bedding and large herbaceous borders. After your visit to the walled garden take time to walk around the wider estate featuring romantic topiary gardens, lake, woodland and nature reserve. Estate gardeners on hand during the day. Delicious home-made cakes available.

41 NEW 330 OLD ROAD

Brampton, Chesterfield, S40 3QH. Christine Stubbs & Julia Stubbs. *1m from town centre. 50 yds from junc with Storrs Rd. 1st house next to grazing field; on-road parking available adjacent to tree-lined roadside stone wall.* **Fri 22, Sat 23 June (10.30-5). Adm £3, chd free. Home-made teas.**

Deceptive ⅓ acre plot of mature trees, landscaped lawns, orchard and cottage style planting. Unusual perennials, species groups such as astrantia, lychnis, thalictrum, heuchera and 40+ clematis. Acers, actea, hosta, ferns and acanthus lie within this interesting garden. Through a hidden gate, another smaller plot of similar planting, with delphinium, helenium, Echinacea, acers and hosta.

42 THE OLD VICARAGE

The Fields, Middleton by Wirksworth, Matlock, DE4 4NH. Jane Irwing, 01629 825010, irwingjane@gmail.com. *Garden located behind church on Main St & nr school. Travelling N on A6 from Derby turn L at Cromford, at top of hill turn R onto Porter Lane, at traffic lights, turn R onto Main St. Park in Village Hall. Walk through churchyard. No parking at house.* **Sat 24, Sun 25 Feb (12-4). Light refreshments. Sat 7, Sun 8 July (11-5). Home-made teas. Adm £3.50, chd free. Visits also by arrangement Mar to Sept.**

Traditional front garden with lawn and mixed summer borders in gentle valley overlooking Black Rocks. To the side a courtyard garden where acid loving plants are grown in pots and, in the fernery, tender ferns. Beyond is the orchard, fruit garden, vegetable patch and greenhouse, the home of honey bees, doves and hens. Spectacular Rambling Rector rose over front of house in late June early July. Cakes, tea and coffee and cold drinks served in the garden or in fernery if wet (limited space). Path through Churchyard ends in some steps leading onto the lane and into the garden gate. Once in the garden much can be seen from the terrace.

43 THE PADDOCK

12 Manknell Rd, Whittington Moor, Chesterfield, S41 8LZ. Mel & Wendy Taylor, 01246 451001, debijt9276@gmail.com. *2m N of Chesterfield. Whittington Moor just off A61 between Sheffield & Chesterfield. Parking available at Victoria Working Mens Club, garden signed from here.* **Sun 29 Apr, Sun 22 July (11-5). Adm £3.50, chd free. Cream teas. Visits also by arrangement Apr to Sept.**

½ acre garden incorporating small formal garden, stream and koi filled pond. Stone path over bridge, up some steps, past small copse, across the stream at the top and back down again. Past herbaceous border towards a pergola where cream teas can be enjoyed.

44 PARK HALL

Walton Back Lane, Walton, Chesterfield, S42 7LT. Kim & Margaret Staniforth, 01246 567412, kim.staniforth@btinternet.com. *2m SW of Chesterfield centre. From town on A 619 L into Somersall Lane. On A632 R into Acorn Ridge. Park on field side only of Walton Back Lane.* **Sun 24 June (2-5.30). Adm £5, chd free. Home-made teas. Visits also by arrangement Apr to July for groups 10+.** Donation to Bluebell Wood Childrens Hospice.

Romantic 2 acre plantsmans garden, in a stunningly beautiful setting surrounding C17 house (not open) 4 main rooms, terraced garden, parkland area with forest trees, croquet lawn, sunken garden with arbours, pergolas, pleached hedge, topiary, statuary, roses, rhododendrons, camellias, several water features. Featured in 'Historic Gardens and Parks of Derbyshire' Dianne Barre. Two steps down to gain access to garden.

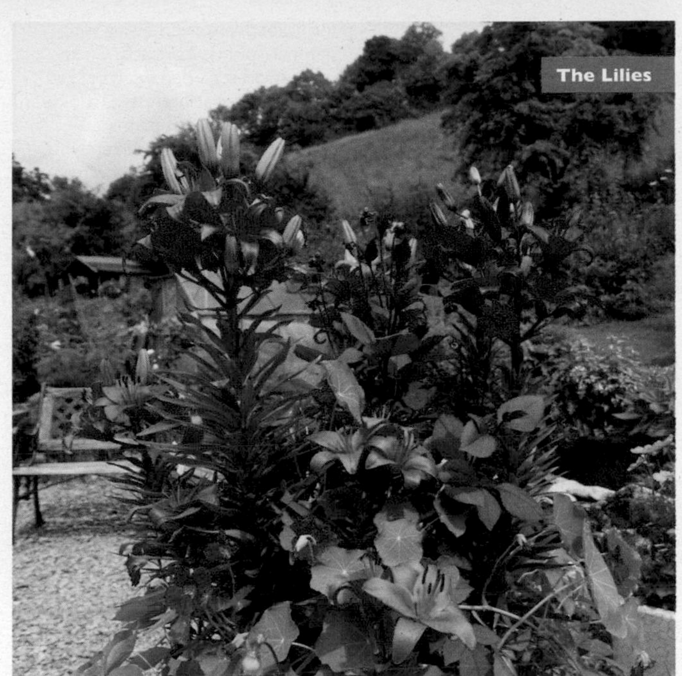
The Lilies

45 NEW 18 PLANT LANE

Long Eaton, Old Sawley, Nottingham, NG10 3BJ. Ernie & Averil Carver, 0115 8491960. *2m SW of Long Eaton from town centre take the B6540 to Old Sawley, R at Nags Head into Wilne Rd, 400yds take R turn into Plant Lane at the Railway Inn Garden on the L 200yds.* **Sun 29 July, Sat 18 Aug, Sun 2 Sept (2-6). Adm £3, chd free. Light refreshments. Visits also by arrangement July to Sept 10 to 20.**

Having opened the garden for the last ten years at 25 Plant Lane for the NGS, we have now moved across the road to 18 Plant Lane. A different kind of garden, larger than the last one. Major work has been done to bring it up to the standard we had at the last garden. Full of colour, nooks and crannies. A garden not to be missed. A slight slope to all of the garden.

46 RECTORY HOUSE

Kedleston, Derby, DE22 5JJ. Helene Viscountess Scarsdale. *5m NW Derby. A52 from Derby turn R Kedleston sign. Drive to village turn R. Brick house standing back from rd on sharp corner.* **Mon 28 May (2-5). Adm £5, chd free. Home-made teas.**

The garden is next to Kedleston Park and is of C18 origin. Many established rare trees and shrubs also rhododendrons, azaleas and unusual roses. Large natural pond with amusing frog fountain. Primulas, gunneras, darmeras and lots of moisture loving plants. The winding paths go through trees and past wild flowers and grasses. New fernery with rare plants. An atmospheric garden. Delicious teas and cakes available. Soft drinks. Featured in Derbyshire Countryside magazine. Wheelchair access possible with care. Uneven paths.

47 ◆ RENISHAW HALL & GARDENS

Renishaw, Sheffield, S21 3WB. Alexandra Hayward, 01246 432310, enquiries@renishaw-hall.co.uk, www.renishaw-hall.co.uk. *10m from Sheffield city centre. By car: Renishaw Hall only 3m from J30 on M1, well signed from junction r'about.* **For NGS: Tue 15 May, Tue 12 June (10.30-4.30). Adm £5.50, chd free. Light refreshments at The Cafe. For other opening times and information, please phone, email or visit garden website.**

Renishaw Hall and Gardens boasts 7 acres of stunning gardens created by Sir George Sitwell in 1885. The Italianate gardens feature various rooms with extravagant herbaceous borders. Rose gardens, rare trees and shrubs, National Collection of Yuccas, sculptures, woodland walks and lakes create a magical and engaging garden experience. The Cafe will be open for light meals, hot and cold drinks and cakes. Wheelchair route around garden.

NPC

GROUP OPENING

48 REPTON NGS VILLAGE GARDENS

Repton, Derby, DE65 6FQ. *6m S of Derby. From A38/A50, S of Derby, follow signs to Willington, then Repton.* **Sun 22 July, Sun 26 Aug (1.30-5.30). Combined adm £6, chd free. Home-made teas at 10 Chestnut Way.**

ASKEW COTTAGE
Louise Hardwick, www.hardwickgardendesign.co.uk.
Open on all dates

10 CHESTNUT WAY
Robert & Pauline Little.
Open on all dates
(See separate entry)

HOLME POINT
Mrs Janet Holmes, 01283 707445.
Open on Sun 22 July
Visits also by arrangement May to Sept.

22 PINFOLD CLOSE
Mr & Mrs O Jowett.
Open on all dates

REPTON ALLOTMENTS
Mr A Topping.
Open on Sun 22 July

WOODEND COTTAGE
Wendy & Stephen Longden.
Open on Sun 22 July
(See separate entry)

Repton is a thriving village dating back to Anglo Saxon times and was where Christianity was first preached in the Midlands. In the crypt of the church there are still well preserved remains of Saxon architecture. The village gardens are all quite different ranging from the very small to very large several of them have new features for 2018. Askew cottage is a professionally designed garden and has many structural features linked together by curving paths. 10 Chestnut Way is a plantoholic's garden often likened to a tardis - be prepared to be surprised. Holme Point is an exquisitely designed small garden, formal beds are overflowing with perennial plants, 22 Pinfold Close is the smallest garden but is packed full with a special interest in tropical plants. Repton allotments is a small set of allotments currently undergoing a revival with community area and attractive views across Derbyshire. Woodend Cottage is an organic garden with stunning views from the grass labyrinth. **Not all gardens are open at every opening** - check website for latest details. All gardens have plenty of seats. Featured in the Daily Telegraph and local press. Some gardens have grass or gravel paths but most areas accessible.

49 122 SHEFFIELD ROAD

Glossop, SK13 8QU. Simon Groarke. *1 mile from Glossop town centre. From Glossop town centre take A57 Snake Pass Sheffield. Cont on A57 3rd exit rdbt cont 3/4m. House on R. Park on Shirebrook Drive. From Sheffield take A57 Glossop. After long descent, house on L.* **Sun 8 Apr, Sun 6 May (12-5). Adm £3.50, chd free. Home-made teas.**

A woodland garden with an array of spring bulbs and a host of bluebells in May. Pathways meander through the garden and down to the brook. A summerhouse nestles in the trees taking a view of the woodland area. Nearer the house the garden opens up to perennial borders and lawns. There are plenty of seats to sit and enjoy the garden but please note there are several steps and uneven paths. Bluebell woodland garden with a babbling brook running through. Attractive perennial borders. Camellias, azaleas and rhododendrons are focal points.

50 NEW SMITHY HOUSE

Mansfield Road, Heath, Chesterfield, S44 5SB. Christine & Michael Hasty, 01246850361, c.hasty@sky.com. *5m SE of Chesterfield and 1m from J29 M1. From Chesterfield take A617 for 2m,then take B6039 through Temple Normanton and follow signs for Heath. From M1 take A6175 signed Clay Cross.After 400 metres turn R into Heath.* **Sat 7 July (11-5). Adm £4, chd free. Cream teas. Visits also by arrangement June to Sept for groups of 10+. Admission £5-50 includes tea and cakes.**

Set among mature trees is a one acre cottage garden. A broad gravel path takes you past a formal herb garden, patio, koi pond and pergola, before sweeping lawns lead you through colour themed herbaceous borders past a large wildlife pond overlooked by a deck and summerhouse to a vegetable parterre. Seating areas allow you to enjoy colourful containers, scented rose arbour and the sound of water.

GROUP OPENING

51 NEW STANTON IN PEAK GARDENS

Stanton-In-The-Peak, Matlock, DE4 2LR. *At the top of the hill in Stanton in Peak, on the road to Birchover. Stanton in Peak is 5m south of Bakewell. Turn off the A6 at Rowsley, or at the B5056 and follow signs up the hill. Postcode for Satnav is DE4 2LR.* **Sat 14, Sun 15 July (1-5). Combined adm £4, chd free. Home-made teas. Tea and cake at 2 Haddon View. Pop-up 'pub' serving draught local beer at Woodend.**

NEW 2 HADDON VIEW
Steve Tompkins.

NEW HARE HATCH COTTAGE
Bill Chandler.

NEW WOODEND COTTAGE
Will Chandler.

Stanton in Peak is a hillside, stone village with glorious views, and is a Conservation Area in the Peak District National Park. Three gardens are open. Steve's garden at 2 Haddon View is at the top of the village and is one tenth of an acre crammed with plants. Follow the winding path up the garden with a few steps. There are cacti flowering in the greenhouse, lots of patio pots, herbaceous borders, three wildlife ponds with red, pink and white water lilies, a koi pond, rhododendrons and a summerhouse. Tea and cakes served. Just down the hill is Woodend where Will has constructed charming roadside follies on a strip of raised land along the road. The hidden, rear garden has diverse planting, and an extended vegetable plot. All with breath-taking views. A pop-up 'pub' will have draught beer from a local brewery. Nearby is Hare Hatch where Bill's garden wraps around the cottage. This is carefully designed to get the best of every planting opportunity, with a little bit of everything!

52 THORNBRIDGE HALL GARDENS

Ashford in the Water, DE45 1NZ. Jim & Emma Harrison, www.thornbridgehall.co.uk. *2m NW of Bakewell. From Bakewell take A6, signed Buxton. After 2m, R onto A6020. ½m turn L, signed Thornbridge Hall.* **Tue 24 July (9-5). Adm £7, chd free. Light refreshments.**

A stunning C19, 12 acre garden, set in the heart of the Peak District overlooking rolling Derbyshire countryside. Designed to create a vision of 1000 shades of green, the garden has many distinct areas. These incl koi lake and water garden, Italian garden with statuary, grottos and temples, 100ft herbaceous border, kitchen garden, scented terrace, hot border and refurbished glasshouses. Contains statuary from Clumber Park, Sydnope Hall and Chatsworth. Tea, coffee, sandwiches and cakes available. Gravel paths, steep slopes, steps.

53 TILFORD HOUSE

Hognaston, Ashbourne, DE6 1PW. Mr & Mrs P R Gardner, 01335 372001, petergardner532@btinternet.com. *5m NE of Ashbourne. A517 Belper to Ashbourne. At Hulland Ward follow signs to Hognaston. Downhill (2m) to bridge. Roadside parking 100 metres.* **Mon 7 May (1-5). Adm £4, chd free. Visits also by arrangement May to Aug, groups of 10+.**

A 1½ acre streamside English country garden. Woodland, wildlife areas and ponds lie alongside colourful borders. Extensive collections of primulas, hostas, iris and clematis as well as many unusual plants and trees. Sit and relax in a magical setting to enjoy listening to the continuous sounds of the birds.

54 ◆ TISSINGTON HALL

Tissington, Ashbourne, DE6 1RA. Sir Richard & Lady FitzHerbert, 01335 352200, tisshall@dircon.co.uk, www.tissingtonhall.co.uk. *4m N of Ashbourne. E of A515 on Ashbourne to Buxton Rd in centre of the beautiful Estate Village of Tissington.* **For NGS: Mon 28 May, Mon 27 Aug (12-3). Adm £6, chd £5. Cream teas at Herbert's Fine English Tearooms. For other opening times and information, please phone, email or visit garden website.**

Large garden celebrating over 75yrs in the NGS, with stunning rose garden on west terrace, herbaceous borders and 5 acres of grounds. Refreshments available at the award winning Herberts Fine English Tearooms in village (Tel 01335 350501). Frequent Ashbourne News Telegraph & Derby Telegraph articles and Derbyshire Life Monthly Column. Wheelchair access advice from ticket seller.

55 NEW 206/208 TOP ROAD

Top Road, Calow, Chesterfield, S44 5TE. Janet Mort, 01246270103, janetmort0@gmail.com. *A632 Chesterfield to Bolsover Road. From Chesterfield, past Blacksmith Lane on L. Before The White Hart pub, 206 Top Rd is on the R.* **Visits by arrangement May to Aug for groups of 3-30. Adm £3.50, chd free. Light refreshments. £1.50 per person.**

Small suburban garden with over 200 clematis. Mixed planting. Pond. Trained fruit trees. Vegetable plot. Greenhouses. Large collection of clematis.

56 TREETOPS HOSPICE CARE

Derby Road, Risley, Derby, DE72 3SS. Treetops Hospice Care, www.treetopshospice.org.uk. *On main rd, B5010 in centre of Risley village. From J25 M1 take road signed to Risley. Turn L at T-lights, Treetops Hospice Care on L approx ½m through village. From Borrowash direction Treetops is on R just after church.* **Sat 24 Mar (11-3). Adm £3, chd free. Light refreshments.**

Beginning with a modest appeal for spring bulbs, the 12 acre site of woodland and grounds now has thousands of daffodils. It has been developed over the last 10yrs taking into consideration the needs and fundraising activities of the hospice. There is a raised wheelchair walkway to enable guests to access some woodland areas, and a 20 minute circular walk on bark chipped paths and raised walkways. Refreshments incl teas and coffees, soup and roll. Plants and homemade preserves stall. Wheelchair access along raised wooden walkways through part of the woods and along some tarmacked paths forms a circular walk.

The National Garden Scheme is the largest single funder of Macmillan

57 NEW **WALTON COTTAGE**
Matlock Road, Walton, Chesterfield, S42 7LG. Neil & Julie Brown. *3 miles from Chesterfield. 6.5 miles from Matlock. On A632 Matlock to Chesterfield main road. From Chesterfield 1 mile after junction near garage with T-lights. From Matlock 1 mile after B5057 junction.* **Sun 3 June, Sun 1 July (11-5). Adm £4, chd free. Home-made teas.**
A large garden that has both formal and informal areas, including woodland, orchard, kitchen garden and sweeping lawns with views over Chesterfield. Wheelchair/disabled access by car drop off in front of house which then gives easy access into garden. No easy access to woodland area.

58 12 WATER LANE
Middleton, Matlock, DE4 4LY. Hildegard Wiesehofer, 01629 825543, wiesehofer@btinternet.com. *Approx 2½m SW of Matlock. 1½m NW of Wirksworth. From Derby: at A6 & B5023 intersection take rd to Wirksworth. Right to Middleton. Follow NGS signs. From Ashbourne take Matlock road & follow signs. Park on main road. Limited parking in Water Lane.* **Sun 6, Mon 7 May, Sun 26, Mon 27 Aug (11-5.30). Adm £3.50, chd free. Home-made teas. Visits also by arrangement Apr to Aug for groups 10+.**
Small, eclectic hillside garden on different levels, created as a series of rooms over the last 15yrs. Each room has been designed to capture the stunning views over Derbyshire and Nottinghamshire and incl a woodland walk, ponds, eastern and infinity gardens. Glorious views and short distance from High Peak Trail, Middleton Top and Engine House. Very rare specimen of a limestone vaulted ceiling, so we are told. The garden has been featured on BBC East Midlands, Derbyshire Life, Amateur Gardener Weekly & Radio Derby. Light wheelchair access only to front terrace and conservatory, views over some of garden possible.

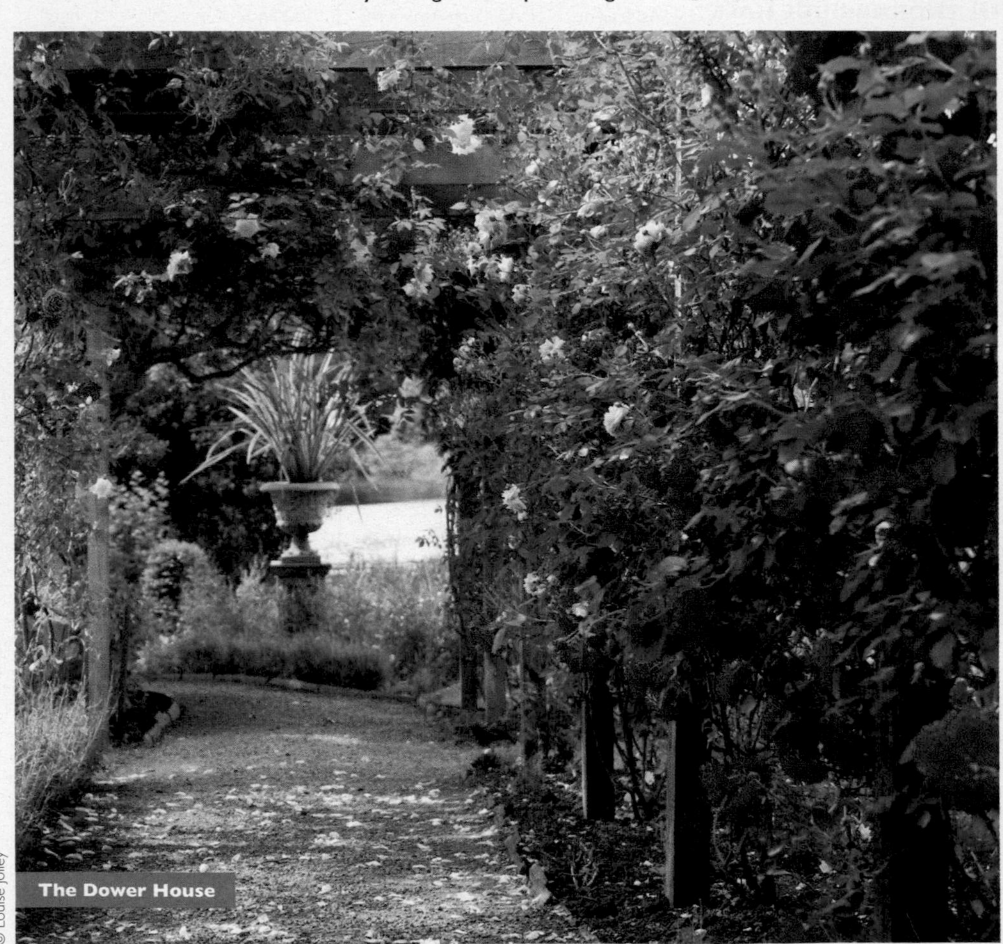
The Dower House

59 13 WESTFIELD ROAD

Swadlincote, DE11 0BG. Val & Dave Booth, 01283 221167 or 07891 436632, valerie.booth@sky.com. *5m E of Burton-on-Trent, off A511. Take A511 from Burton-on-Trent. Follow signs for Swadlincote. Turn R into Springfield Rd, take 3rd R into Westfield Rd.* **Sun 17 June, Sun 5 Aug (1-5). Adm £3, chd free. Home-made teas. Visits also by arrangement June to Aug adm £5 incl tea and cake.**

A garden on 2 levels of approx ½ acre. Packed herbaceous borders designed for colour. Roses and clematis scrambling over pergolas. A passion of ours are roses (over 60). Shrubs, baskets and tubs. Greenhouses, raised bed vegetable area, fruit trees and 2 ponds. Free range chicken area. Plenty of seating. (WC).

60 WESTGATE

Combs Road, Combs, Chapel-en-le-Frith, High Peak, SK23 9UP. Maurice & Chris Lomas, 07854 680170, ca-lomas@sky.com. *N of Chapel-en-le-Frith off B5470. Turn L immed before Hanging Gate PH, signed Combs Village. ¾m on L by railway bridge.* **Visits by arrangement Apr to July for groups 10+. Adm £3, chd free.**

Large sloping garden in quiet village with beautiful views. Features incl mixed borders and beds containing many perenials, hosta and heuchera. Large rockery. Vegetable and fruit beds. Wild flower area, grasses and fernery. Natural pond and stream with bog area. 3 formal ponds. Chicken area. Lots of places to sit and enjoy the views. Featured in Amateur Gardening.

61 26 WHEELDON AVENUE

Derby, DE22 1HN. Ian Griffiths, 01332 342204, idhgriffiths@gmail.com. *1m N of Derby. 1m from city centre & approached directly off Kedleston Rd or from A6 Duffield Rd via West Bank Ave. Limited on street parking.* **Visits by arrangement in June for groups 4+. Refreshments by prior arrangement and incl in adm price. Adm £3, chd free. Light refreshments.**

Tiny Victorian walled garden near to city centre. Lawn and herbaceous borders with newly expanded old rose collection, lupins, delphiniums and foxgloves. Small terrace with topiary, herb garden and lion fountain. Rose collection. Featured on BBC TV and now the subject of a new greetings card collection. Garden on one level, lawn may be soft if wet.

62 WILD IN THE COUNTRY

Hawkhill Road, Eyam, Hope Valley, S32 5QQ. Mrs Gill Bagshawe, www.wildinthecountryflowers.co.uk. *In Eyam, follow signs to public car park. Located next to Eyam Museum & opp public car park on Hawkhill Rd.* **Sun 29 July (11-4.30). Adm £2.50, chd free.**

A rectangular plot devoted totally to growing flowers and foliage for cutting. Sweet pea, rose, larkspur, cornflower, nigella, ammi. All the florist's favourites can be found here. There is a tea room, a village pub and several cafes in the village to enjoy refreshments.

63 26 WINDMILL RISE

Belper, DE56 1GQ. Kathy Fairweather. *From Belper Market Place take Chesterfield Rd towards Heage. Top of hill, 1st R Marsh Lane, 1st R Windmill Lane, 1st R Windmill Rise - limited parking on Windmill Rise - disabled mainly.* **Sat 7, Sun 8 July (11.30-4.30). Adm £3.50, chd free. Light refreshments.**

Behind a deceptively ordinary looking façade, lies a surprise. Meander along extensive pathways lined with a tapestry of texture and light and shade with a lush and restful atmosphere. A plant lovers' organic garden divided into sections: woodland, Japanese, secret garden, cottage, edible, ponds and small stream. A large collection of rare and unusual plants and fruit trees/shrubs. Live music and delicious home baking and light lunches available.

64 WOODEND COTTAGE

134 Main Street, Repton, DE65 6FB. Wendy & Stephen Longden, 01283 703259, wendylongden@btinternet.com. *6m S of Derby. From A38, S of Derby, follow signs to Willington, then Repton. In Repton straight on at r'about through village. Garden is 1m on R.* **Sun 5 Aug (1.30-5). Adm £3, chd free. Home-made teas. Opening with Repton NGS Village Gardens on Sun 22 July. Visits also by arrangement June to Aug for groups 10+.**

Plant lover's garden with glorious views on a sloping 2½ acre site developed organically for yr-round interest. On lower levels herbaceous borders are arranged informally and connected via lawns, thyme bed, pond and pergolas. Mixed woodland and grassed labyrinth lead naturally into fruit, vegetable and herb potager with meadows beyond. Especially colourful in July and August. Easy and unusual perennials and grasses for sale. Why not visit St Wystan's Church Repton with its Saxon crypt, as part of your visit? Wheelchair access on lower levels only.

The National Garden Scheme is Marie Curie's largest single funder

DEVON

Lundy
Ilfracombe
Combe Martin
Lynton
Morte Point
Woolacombe
Baggy Point
Croyde
Braunton
Muddiford
Barnstaple
Barnstaple or Bideford Bay
Appledore
Westward Ho!
Northam
Bishop's Tawton
Hartland Point
Clovelly
Hartland
Bideford
Great Torrington
South Molton
Chulmleigh
Kilkhampton
Winkleigh
DE
Bude
Stratton
Holsworthy
Highampton
Hatherleigh
Bude Bay
Okehampton
Boscastle
Tintagel
Hallworthy
Whiddon Down
Camelford
Launceston
Lydford
Moretonhampstead
Port Isaac
Trevose Head
Padstow
Bolventor
Colliford Lake
Widecombe in the Moor
Tavistock
Wadebridge
CORNWALL
Callington
Gunnislake
Princetown
Dartmeet
Ashburton
Trenance
Bodmin
Liskeard
Yelverton
Buckfastleigh
Newquay
St Columb Major
Saltash
Plymouth
Lostwithiel
St Germans
Plympton
Ivybridge
Goonhavern
St Austell
Looe
Modbury
Whitsand Bay
Yealmpton
Probus
Fowey
Polperro
St Austell Bay
Loddiswell
Truro
Mevagissey
Rame Head
Bigbury-on-Sea
Tregony
Bigbury Bay
Dodman Point
Salcombe
Penryn
St Mawes
Torridge
Tamar
Camel
Fowey
Tavy
Teign
Dart
Taw

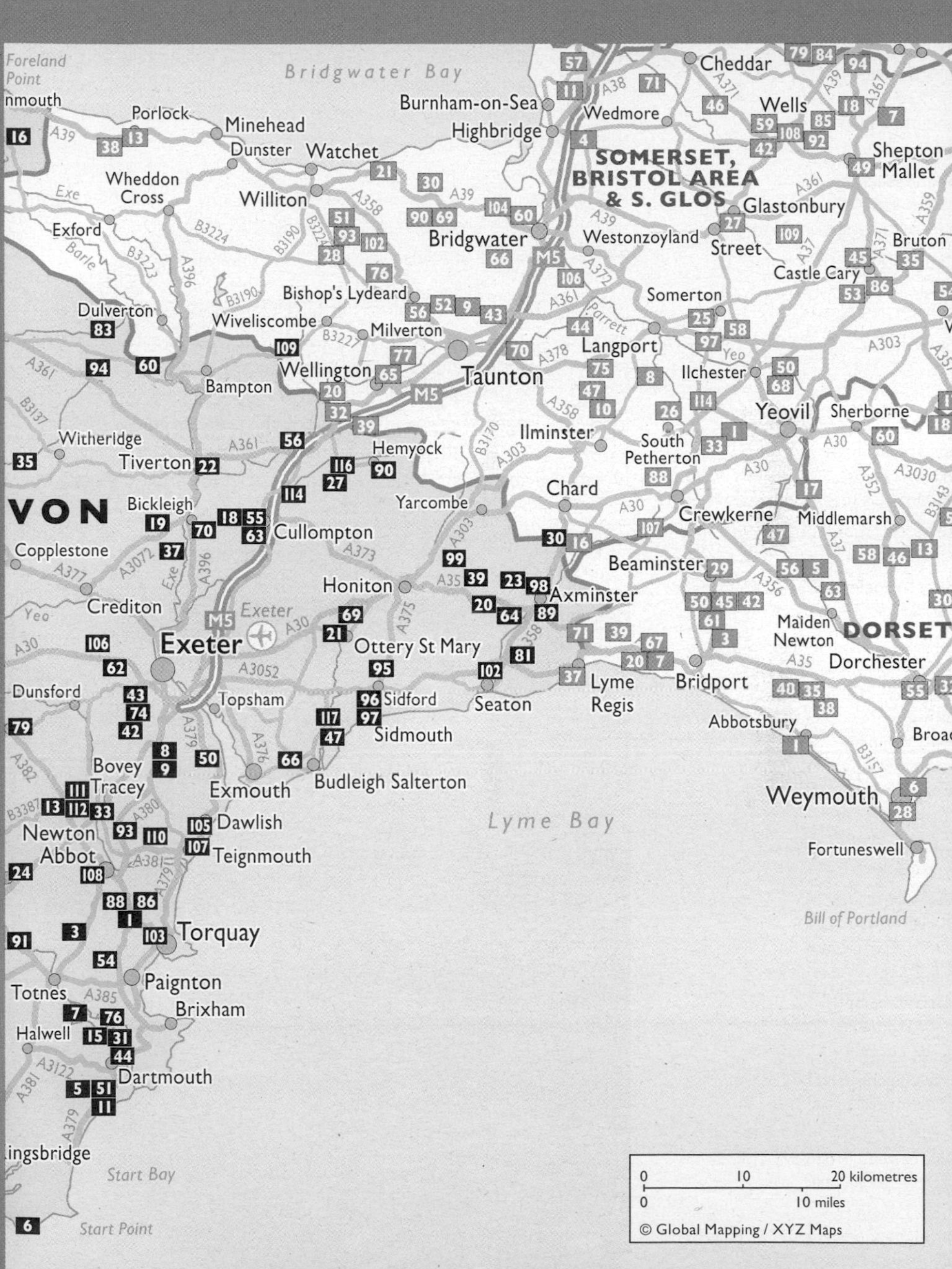
Foreland Point
Bridgwater Bay
nmouth
Porlock
Minehead
Dunster
Watchet
Burnham-on-Sea
Highbridge
Cheddar
Wedmore
Wells
Shepton Mallet
SOMERSET, BRISTOL AREA & S. GLOS
Glastonbury
Wheddon Cross
Williton
Exe
Exford
Barle
Bridgwater
Westonzoyland
Street
Bruton
Castle Cary
Bishop's Lydeard
Somerton
Dulverton
Wiveliscombe
Milverton
Parrett
Langport
Taunton
Wellington
Bampton
Ilchester
Yeo
Yeovil
Sherborne
Witheridge
Tiverton
Hemyock
Ilminster
South Petherton
Chard
Yarcombe
Crewkerne
Middlemarsh
VON
Bickleigh
Cullompton
Copplestone
Crediton
Honiton
Beaminster
Axminster
Exeter
Ottery St Mary
Maiden Newton
DORSET
Dorchester
Dunsford
Topsham
Sidford
Seaton
Lyme Regis
Bridport
Sidmouth
Abbotsbury
Broad
Bovey Tracey
Exmouth
Budleigh Salterton
Weymouth
Dawlish
Lyme Bay
Newton Abbot
Teignmouth
Fortuneswell
Bill of Portland
Torquay
Paignton
Totnes
Brixham
Halwell
Dartmouth
Kingsbridge
Start Bay
Start Point
0 10 20 kilometres
0 10 miles
© Global Mapping / XYZ Maps

Volunteers

County Organisers
& Central Devon
Edward & Miranda Allhusen
01647 440296
Miranda@allhusen.co.uk

County Treasurer
Julia Tremlett
01392 832671
jandjtremlett@hotmail.com

Publicity
Brian Mackness
01626 356004
brianmackness@clara.co.uk

Cath Pettyfer
01837 89024
cathpettyfer@gmail.com

Paul Vincent
01803 722227
paulvincent46@gmail.com

Booklet Co-ordinator
Edward Allhusen
01647 440296
edward@allhusen.co.uk

Assistant County Organisers

East Devon
Peter Wadeley 01297 631210
wadeley@btinternet.com

Exeter
Jenny Phillips 01392 254076
jennypips25@hotmail.co.uk

Exmoor
Anna Whinney
01598 760217
annawhinney@yahoo.co.uk

North Devon
Jo Hynes 01805 804265
hynesjo@gmail.com

North East Devon
Jill Hall 01884 38812
jill22hall@gmail.com

Plymouth
Maria Ashurst 01752 351396
maria.ashurst@sky.com

South Devon
Sally Vincent 01803 722227
salv@hotmail.co.uk

Torbay
Gill Treweek 01626 879313
gilltreweek@hotmail.co.uk

West Devon
Sara-Jane Cumming 01822 860281
sj@broadparkdesigns.co.uk

Devon is a county of great contrasts in geography and climate, and therefore also in gardening.

The rugged north coast has terraces clinging precariously to hillsides so steep that the faint-hearted would never contemplate making a garden there. But here, and on the rolling hills and deep valleys of Exmoor, despite a constant battle with the elements, NGS gardeners create remarkable results by choosing hardy plants that withstand the high winds and salty air.

In the south, in peaceful wooded estuaries and tucked into warm valleys, gardens grow bananas, palms and fruit usually associated with the Mediterranean.

Between these two terrains is a third: Dartmoor, 365 square miles of rugged moorland rising to 2000 feet, presents its own horticultural demands. Typically, here too are many NGS gardens.

In idyllic villages scattered throughout this very large county, in gardens large and small, in single manors and in village groups within thriving communities – gardeners pursue their passion.

Below: **AM Brook Meadow**

OPENING DATES

All entries subject to change. For latest information check **www.ngs.org.uk**

Extended openings are shown at the beginning of the month.

Map locator numbers are shown to the right of each garden name.

February

Snowdrop Festival

Every Tuesday to Friday from Tuesday 13th
High Garden 50

Friday 9th
Higher Cherubeer 52

Friday 16th
Higher Cherubeer 52

Saturday 17th
The Mount, Delamore 80

Sunday 18th
The Mount, Delamore 80

Saturday 24th
Bickham House 9

Sunday 25th
Higher Cherubeer 52

March

Every Tuesday to Friday
High Garden 50

Sunday 4th
East Worlington House 35

Sunday 11th
East Worlington House 35

Sunday 18th
Summers Place 106

Saturday 24th
Haldon Grange 42
The Haven 46

Sunday 25th
Bickham House 9
Gorwell House 40
Haldon Grange 42
The Haven 46
Heathercombe 49
NEW Linden Rise 68

Friday 30th
◆ Holbrook Garden 56

Saturday 31st
Haldon Grange 42
◆ Holbrook Garden 56
Monkscroft 78

April

Every Tuesday to Friday
High Garden 50

Sunday 1st
Haldon Grange 42
◆ Holbrook Garden 56
Kia-Ora Farm & Gardens 63
Monkscroft 78
Wood Barton 116
Yonder Hill 117

Monday 2nd
Haldon Grange 42
Kia-Ora Farm & Gardens 63
Wood Barton 116
Yonder Hill 117

Wednesday 4th
Shapcott Barton Knowstone Estate 94

Friday 6th
◆ Holbrook Garden 56

Saturday 7th
Haldon Grange 42
◆ Holbrook Garden 56

Sunday 8th
Haldon Grange 42
Shapcott Barton Knowstone Estate 94
Summers Place 106
Yonder Hill 117

Friday 13th
◆ Holbrook Garden 56
Sidbury Manor 95

Saturday 14th
Haldon Grange 42
◆ Holbrook Garden 56

Sunday 15th
Andrew's Corner 4
Haldon Grange 42
◆ Holbrook Garden 56
Kia-Ora Farm & Gardens 63
St Merryn 92
Shapcott Barton Knowstone Estate 94
Sidbury Manor 95
Yonder Hill 117

Wednesday 18th
Haldon Grange 42

Friday 20th
◆ Holbrook Garden 56

Saturday 21st
Bickham House 9
NEW Coombe Meadow 24
Haldon Grange 42
◆ Holbrook Garden 56

Sunday 22nd
Andrew's Corner 4
Bickham House 9
NEW Coombe Meadow 24
Haldon Grange 42
Yonder Hill 117

Wednesday 25th
◆ Hotel Endsleigh 59

Friday 27th
◆ Holbrook Garden 56

Saturday 28th
Haldon Grange 42
◆ Holbrook Garden 56
Sedgewell Coach House Gardens 93
Torview 108

Sunday 29th
Andrew's Corner 4
Gorwell House 40
Haldon Grange 42
Kia-Ora Farm & Gardens 63
Sedgewell Coach House Gardens 93
Torview 108
Whitstone Bluebells 111
Yonder Hill 117

May

Every day
The Gate House 38

Every Tuesday to Friday
High Garden 50

Saturday 5th
Dicot 30
Greatcombe 41
Haldon Grange 42
Sedgewell Coach House Gardens 93

Sunday 6th
Andrew's Corner 4
Chevithorne Barton 22
Dicot 30
Greatcombe 41
Haldon Grange 42
Kia-Ora Farm & Gardens 63
Sedgewell Coach House Gardens 93
Wood Barton 116
Yonder Hill 117

Monday 7th
Andrew's Corner 4
Dicot 30
Greatcombe 41
Haldon Grange 42
Kia-Ora Farm & Gardens 63
Wood Barton 116
Yonder Hill 117

Wednesday 9th
Haldon Grange 42

Saturday 12th
NEW East Woodlands Farmhouse 34
Haldon Grange 42
The Old Vicarage 83

Sunday 13th
Andrew's Corner 4
Bickham House 9
NEW East Woodlands Farmhouse 34
Gorwell House 40
Haldon Grange 42
Heathercombe 49
Higher Ash Farm 51
Higher Cherubeer 52
Kia-Ora Farm & Gardens 63
The Old Vicarage 83
Portington 87
Yonder Hill 117

Wednesday 16th
◆ Hotel Endsleigh 59

Friday 18th
Moretonhampstead Gardens 79

Saturday 19th

Bowdens 14
Brendon Gardens 16
Craddock House 27
Haldon Grange 42
NEW Kentlands 62
Kilmington (Shute Road) Gardens 64
Little Dorweeke 70
Lower Spitchwick Garden 72
Moretonhampstead Gardens 79

Sunday 20th

Brendon Gardens 16
Craddock House 27
Foamlea 36
Haldon Grange 42
Heathercombe 49
Higher Ash Farm 51
NEW Kentlands 62
Kilmington (Shute Road) Gardens 64
NEW Lamerton Gardens 65
Little Dorweeke 70
Lower Spitchwick Garden 72
Moretonhampstead Gardens 79
Portington 87
St Merryn 92
Wick Farm Gardens 113
Yonder Hill 117

Wednesday 23rd

Haldon Grange 42

Saturday 26th

NEW Blackaton 10
Bocombe Mill Cottage 12
Deancombe Farm 29
Greatcombe 41
Haldon Grange 42
Heathercombe 49
Lewis Cottage 67

Sunday 27th

NEW Blackaton 10
Bocombe Mill Cottage 12
◆ Cadhay 21
Deancombe Farm 29
Greatcombe 41
Haldon Grange 42
Heathercombe 49
Hillersdon 55
Kia-Ora Farm & Gardens 63
Lewis Cottage 67
The Mill House 77
Southcombe Gardens 100
Wick Farm Gardens 113
Yonder Hill 117

Monday 28th

Bocombe Mill Cottage 12
◆ Cadhay 21
Greatcombe 41
Haldon Grange 42
Hillersdon 55
Kia-Ora Farm & Gardens 63
Lewis Cottage 67
Southcombe Gardens 100
Wick Farm Gardens 113
Yonder Hill 117

Tuesday 29th

Heathercombe 49

Wednesday 30th

Heathercombe 49

Thursday 31st

Heathercombe 49

June

Every day

The Gate House 38

Every evening from Saturday 2nd

Goren Farm 39

Every Tuesday to Sunday from Saturday 16th

Heathercombe 49

Every Tuesday to Friday

High Garden 50

Friday 1st

Heathercombe 49

Festival Weekend

Saturday 2nd

Goren Farm 39
Haldon Grange 42
Heathercombe 49
Springfield House 102

Sunday 3rd

32 Allenstyle Drive 2
Andrew's Corner 4
The Bridge Mill 17
Burn Valley Butterleigh Gardens 18
Goren Farm 39
Haldon Grange 42
Hayne 48
Heathercombe 49
Southcombe Gardens 100
Yonder Hill 117

Friday 8th

Marshall Farm 74

Saturday 9th

Abbotskerswell Gardens 1
Bickham House 9
◆ Fursdon 37
Goren Farm 39
Haldon Grange 42
Little Ash Bungalow 69
Sidmouth June Gardens 97
Willand Old Village Gardens & Allotments 114

Sunday 10th

Abbotskerswell Gardens 1
◆ Docton Mill 32
◆ Fursdon 37
Goren Farm 39
Haldon Grange 42
Hole Farm 57
Kia-Ora Farm & Gardens 63
Marshall Farm 74
Sidmouth June Gardens 97
Southcombe Gardens 100
Willand Old Village Gardens & Allotments 114
Yonder Hill 117

Friday 15th

Bramble Torre 15
◆ Marwood Hill Garden 75

Saturday 16th

Bramble Torre 15
Goren Farm 39
NEW Halscombe Farm 43
Higher Orchard Cottage 54
NEW Lamerton Gardens 65
South Wood Farm 99
Venn Cross Engine House 109
◆ Winsford Walled Garden 115

Sunday 17th

Bramble Torre 15
The Croft 28
Goren Farm 39
Gorwell House 40
NEW Halscombe Farm 43
Higher Orchard Cottage 54
The Mill House 77
Regency House 90
Riverford Field Kitchen Garden 91
St Merryn 92
South Wood Farm 99
Southcombe Gardens 100
Venn Cross Engine House 109
◆ Winsford Walled Garden 115
Yonder Hill 117

Monday 18th

Regency House 90

Friday 22nd

NEW Hutswell Farm 60

Saturday 23rd

Ash Gardens 5
Bickham House 9
Bowdens 14
Greatcombe 41
Harbour Lights 45
NEW Hutswell Farm 60
Kentisbury Gardens 61
Lewis Cottage 67
Summers Place 106
Teignmouth Gardens 107

Sunday 24th

Ash Gardens 5
NEW Court Hall 26
Greatcombe 41
Harbour Lights 45
Kentisbury Gardens 61
Kia-Ora Farm & Gardens 63
Lewis Cottage 67
Southcombe Gardens 100
Teignmouth Gardens 107
Yonder Hill 117

Saturday 30th

Cleave Hill 23
NEW Musbury Barton 81
The Priory 88
Springfield House 102
Stone Farm 104

July

Every day

The Gate House 38

Every evening to Sunday 15th

Goren Farm 39

Every Tuesday to Sunday to Sunday 8th
Heathercombe 49

Every Tuesday to Friday
High Garden 50

Sunday 1st
Burn Valley Butterleigh Gardens 18
Cleave Hill 23
NEW Musbury Barton 81
The Priory 88
Southcombe Gardens 100
Stone Farm 104
Yonder Hill 117

Saturday 7th
NEW AM Brook Meadow 3
Dunley House 33
The Olde Cottage 84
Park House 85

Sunday 8th
NEW AM Brook Meadow 3
Bickham House 9
Dunley House 33
Kia-Ora Farm & Gardens 63
The Olde Cottage 84
Park House 85
Yonder Hill 117

Friday 13th
Socks Orchard 98

Saturday 14th
Bovey Tracey Gardens 13
Dittisham Gardens 31
Socks Orchard 98

Sunday 15th
Bovey Tracey Gardens 13
The Croft 28
Dittisham Gardens 31
Gorwell House 40
Hole Farm 57
NEW Linden Rise 68
Socks Orchard 98
Yonder Hill 117

Wednesday 18th
Shapcott Barton Knowstone Estate 94

Saturday 21st
Bowdens 14
Lewis Cottage 67
Venn Cross Engine House 109
NEW The Walled Garden, Lindridge 110

Sunday 22nd
Kia-Ora Farm & Gardens 63
Lewis Cottage 67
Shapcott Barton Knowstone Estate 94
Venn Cross Engine House 109
NEW The Walled Garden, Lindridge 110
Yonder Hill 117

Thursday 26th
Shapcott Barton Knowstone Estate 94

Saturday 28th
Lower Spitchwick Garden 72
Squirrels 103

Sunday 29th
Lower Spitchwick Garden 72
Shapcott Barton Knowstone Estate 94
Springfield House 102
Squirrels 103
Whitstone Farm 112
Yonder Hill 117

August

Every day
The Gate House 38

Every Tuesday to Friday
High Garden 50

Saturday 4th
Brendon Gardens 16
NEW Corscombe Gardens 25
Hole's Meadow 58

Sunday 5th
Brendon Gardens 16
NEW Corscombe Gardens 25
Hole's Meadow 58
Kia-Ora Farm & Gardens 63
Yonder Hill 117

Saturday 11th
Ash Gardens 5
NEW East Woodlands Farmhouse 34
The Old Vicarage 83
Torview 108

Sunday 12th
Ash Gardens 5
Bickham House 9
NEW Court Hall 26
NEW East Woodlands Farmhouse 34
The Old Vicarage 83
Torview 108
Yonder Hill 117

Saturday 18th
Bowdens 14
Moretonhampstead Gardens 79

Sunday 19th
The Croft 28
Kia-Ora Farm & Gardens 63
Little Ash Bungalow 69
Moretonhampstead Gardens 79
Yonder Hill 117

Saturday 25th
Burnbridge Cottage 19
Greatcombe 41
Lewis Cottage 67
Sedgewell Coach House Gardens 93
NEW Sidmouth August Gardens 96
Stone Farm 104
Venn Cross Engine House 109

Sunday 26th
32 Allenstyle Drive 2
Burnbridge Cottage 19
◆ Cadhay 21
Greatcombe 41
Kia-Ora Farm & Gardens 63
Lewis Cottage 67
Sedgewell Coach House Gardens 93
NEW Sidmouth August Gardens 96
Stone Farm 104
Venn Cross Engine House 109
Yonder Hill 117

Monday 27th
◆ Cadhay 21
Greatcombe 41
Kia-Ora Farm & Gardens 63
Lewis Cottage 67
NEW Sidmouth August Gardens 96
Yonder Hill 117

Friday 31st
Prospect House 89

September

Every day to Sunday 16th
The Gate House 38

Every Tuesday to Friday
High Garden 50

Saturday 1st
Prospect House 89
Sedgewell Coach House Gardens 93

Sunday 2nd
Chevithorne Barton 22
Prospect House 89
Riverford Field Kitchen Garden 91
Sedgewell Coach House Gardens 93
Yonder Hill 117

Saturday 8th
◆ Fursdon 37
Hawkern 47

Sunday 9th
32 Allenstyle Drive 2
Bickham House 9
◆ Fursdon 37
Hawkern 47
Kia-Ora Farm & Gardens 63

Saturday 15th
Ash Park 6

Sunday 16th
32 Allenstyle Drive 2
Ash Park 6
NEW Kentlands 62

Sunday 30th
Gorwell House 40

October

Every Tuesday to Friday
High Garden 50

Sunday 7th
Higher Ash Farm 51

Sunday 14th
Bickham Cottage 8
Regency House 90
Summers Place 106

Sunday 21st
Andrew's Corner 4

November

Every Tuesday to Friday
High Garden 50

February 2019

Friday 8th
Higher Cherubeer 52

Friday 15th
Higher Cherubeer 52

Saturday 23rd
Higher Cherubeer 52

By Arrangement

32 Allenstyle Drive 2
Andrew's Corner 4
Avenue Cottage 7
Bickham Cottage 8
Bickham House 9
Bocombe Mill Cottage 12
Brendon Gardens 16
The Bridge Mill 17
Burn Valley Butterleigh Gardens 18
Byes Reach, Sidmouth June Gardens 97
Cleave Hill 23
The Croft 28
The Gate House 38
Haldon Grange 42
Hamblyn's Coombe 44
Harbour Lights 45
The Haven 46
Hawkern 47
Heathercombe 49
Higher Cherubeer 52
Higher Cullaford 53
Hole's Meadow 58
NEW Hutswell Farm 60
NEW Kentlands 62
Kia-Ora Farm & Gardens 63
Lee Ford 66
Lewis Cottage 67
Little Ash Bungalow 69
Little Webbery 71
Lower Spitchwick Garden 72
NEW Middle Well 76
The Mill House 77
NEW Musbury Barton 81
Musselbrook Cottage Garden 82
The Old Vicarage 83
The Olde Cottage 84
Prospect House 89
Regency House 90
St Merryn 92
Shapcott Barton Knowstone Estate 94
Socks Orchard 98
South Wood Farm 99
Southcombe Barn, Southcombe Gardens 100
Springfield House 102
Squirrels 103
NEW Stonelands House 105
Summers Place 106
Sutton Mead, Moretonhampstead Gardens 79
Venn Cross Engine House 109
Whitstone Bluebells 111
Whitstone Farm 112
Wood Barton 116
Yonder Hill 117

THE GARDENS

GROUP OPENING

1 ABBOTSKERSWELL GARDENS

Abbotskerswell, TQ12 5PN. *2m SW of Newton Abbot town centre. A381 Newton Abbot/Totnes rd. Sharp L turn from NA, R from Totnes. Field parking at Fairfield. Maps available at all gardens and at Church House.* **Sat 9, Sun 10 June (1-5). Combined adm £6, chd free. Home-made teas at Church House. Teas available from 2pm. Maps and tickets from 1pm.**

ABBOTSFORD
Wendy & Phil Grierson.

ABBOTSKERSWELL ALLOTMENTS
Margaret Crompton.

1 ABBOTSWELL COTTAGES
Jane Taylor.

BRIAR COTTAGE
Peggy & David Munden.

FAIRFIELD
Brian Mackness.

NEW **4 LABURNUM TERRACE**
Ms Mary Down.

7 WILTON WAY
Mr & Mrs Cindy & Vernon Stunt.

10 WILTON WAY
Mrs Margaret Crompton.

16 WILTON WAY
Katy & Chris Yates.

For 2018, Abbotskerswell offers 8 gardens plus the village allotments. Ranging from very small to large they offer a wide range of planting styles and innovative landscaping. Cottage gardens, terracing, wild flower areas, a wild garden and specialist plants. Ideas for every type and size of garden. Visitors are welcome to picnic in the field or arboretum at Fairfield. See YouTube Abbotskerswell Gardens 2011. Sales of plants, garden produce, jams and chutneys and other creative crafts. Teas! Disabled access to 3 gardens.

2 32 ALLENSTYLE DRIVE

Yelland, Barnstaple, EX31 3DZ. Steve & Dawn Morgan, 01271 861433, fourhungrycats@aol.com, www.devonsubtropicalgarden.co.uk. *5m W of Barnstaple. From Barnstaple take B3233 towards Instow. Through Bickington & Fremington. L at Yelland sign into Allenstyle Rd. 1st R into Allenstyle Dr. Light blue bungalow. From Bideford go past Instow on B3233.* **Sun 3 June, Sun 26 Aug, Sun 9, Sun 16 Sept (11.30-5). Adm £4, chd free. Home-made teas. Visits also by arrangement Aug & Sept garden clubs welcome.**

Small (50x100ft) garden in mild estuary location, which combines sub-tropical, cottage and prairie planting. Bananas, hedychiums (gingers), palms, colocasia, aroids, brugmansias and an exotic collection of passionflowers and much more. Lots of seating so you can take your time and enjoy scent, colour and high impact planting. Featured in Garden Answers magazine.

3 NEW AM BROOK MEADOW

Torbryan, Ipplepen, Newton Abbot, TQ12 5UP. Jennie Marles. *5m from Newton Abbot on A381. Leaving A381 at 'Causeway Cross '* go through *Ipplepen village, heading towards Broadhempston. Stay on Orley Rd for ¾m. At Poole Cross Turn L signed Totnes, then 1st L into Am Brook Meadow.* **Sat 7, Sun 8 July (2-6). Adm £4, chd free. Home-made teas.**

Country garden developed over past 10 years to encourage wildlife. Beautiful perennial native wildflower meadows, large ponds with ducks and swans, streams and wild areas covering 10 acres are accessible by gravel and grass pathways. Formal courtyard garden and herbaceous borders with prairie-style planting together with poultry and bees close by. Wheelchair access to most gravel path areas is good, but grass pathways in larger wildflower meadow are weather dependent.

4 ANDREW'S CORNER

Skaigh Lane, Belstone, EX20 1RD. Robin & Edwina Hill, 01837 840332, **edwinarobinhill@outlook.com, www.andrewscorner.garden.** *3m E of Okehampton. Signed to Belstone from A30. In village turn L, signed Skaigh. Follow NGS signs. Garden approx ½m on R. Visitors may be dropped off at house, parking in nearby field.* **Every Sun 15 Apr to 13 May (2-5). Mon 7 May, Sun 3 June, Sun 21 Oct (2-5). Adm £4, chd free. Home-made teas. Visits also by arrangement Feb to Oct.**

Well established, wildlife friendly, well labelled plantsman's garden in stunning high moorland setting. Variety of garden habitats incl woodland areas and pond; wide range of unusual trees, shrubs, herbaceous plants for yr-round effect with blue poppies, rhododendrons, bulbs and maples; spectacular autumn colour. Family friendly, with quiz sheet, fairy doors, playhouse, fruit, vegetables and chickens. Featured on BBC Radio Devon and in The Moorlander publication. Wheelchair access difficult when wet.

GROUP OPENING

5 ASH GARDENS

Ash, Dartmouth, TQ6 0LR. *2m SW of Dartmouth. Leave A381 Totnes to Kingsbridge rd in Halwell taking A3122 for Dartmouth. Just before Sportsmans Arms turn R. At T junction turn R then 1st L. At Xrds turn R then parking 1st L.* **Sat 23, Sun 24 June, Sat 11, Sun 12 Aug (2-5). Combined adm £5, chd free. Home-made teas.**

BAY TREE COTTAGE
Jenny Goffe.

HIGHER ASH FARM
Mr Michael Gribbin & Mrs Jennifer Barwell.
(See separate entry)

2 delightful gardens in the tiny hamlet of Ash. The beautiful intimate little garden at Bay Tree Cottage sits in a quiet secluded valley with wonderful sunlit views across open farmland. The perfect curved lawn leads the eye to small rooms filled with surprise and clever planting. Ornamental trees punctuate the boundary and a tiny vegetable garden of raised beds overflows with produce. Higher Ash Farm has 2½ acres of established and developing garden situated around farmhouse and barn conversions. Large kitchen garden terraced into the hillside, orchard, pond, stream with bog planting and feature borders around the house offering seasonal and yr-round interest.

6 ASH PARK

East Prawle, Kingsbridge, TQ7 2BX. Chris & Cathryn Vanderspar. *Ash Park, East Prawle South Devon. Take A379 Kingsbridge to Dartmouth, at Frogmore after PH R to East Prawle, after 1.1m L, in 1.4m at Cousins Cross bear R (middle of 3 rds). In village head to Prawle Point.* **Sat 15, Sun 16 Sept (11-5). Adm £5, chd free. Home-made teas.**

In a stunning location, with 180° view of the sea, Ash Park nestles at the foot of the escarpment, with 3½ acres of sub-tropical gardens, paths to explore, woodland glades, ponds and hidden seating areas. In Sept, cannas, hydrangeas, ginger lilies, salvias and dahlias should be at their best. Limited access for wheelchairs.

7 AVENUE COTTAGE

Ashprington, Totnes, TQ9 7UT. Mr Richard Pitts & Mr David Sykes, 01803 732769, **richard.pitts@btinternet.com, www.avenuecottage.com.** *3m SW of Totnes. A381 Totnes to Kingsbridge for 1m; L for Ashprington, into village then L by PH. Garden ¼m on R after Sharpham Estate sign.* **Visits by arrangement Mar to Oct, groups and individuals welcome. Adm £4, chd free. Teas by arrangement.**

11 acres of mature and young trees and shrubs. Once part of an C18 landscape, the neglected garden has been cleared and replanted over the last 30 yrs. Good views of Sharpham House and R Dart. Azaleas and hydrangeas are a feature.

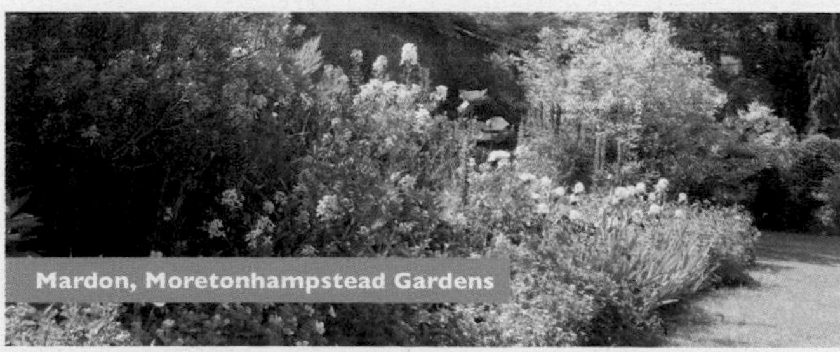
Mardon, Moretonhampstead Gardens

8 BICKHAM COTTAGE

Kenn, Exeter, EX6 7XL. Steve Eyre, 01392 833964, bickham@live.co.uk. *6m S of Exeter. 1m off A38. Leave A38 at Kennford Services, follow signs to Kenn. 1st R in village, follow lane for ¾m to end of no through rd.* **Sun 14 Oct (2-5). Adm £4, chd free. Light refreshments. Visits also by arrangement Sept to Nov.**

Small cottage garden divided into separate areas by old stone walls and hedge banks. Front garden with mainly South African bulbs and plants. Lawn surrounded by borders with agapanthus, eucomis, crocosmia, diorama etc. Stream garden with primulas. Pond with large Koi carp. Glasshouses with National Collection of Hardy Nerines, Nerine sarniensis and cultivars, 3500 pots with in excess of 450 varieties. Visitors are also welcome to wander around Bickham House gardens.

NPC

9 BICKHAM HOUSE

Kenn, Exeter, EX6 7XL. Julia Tremlett, 01392 832671, jandjtremlett@hotmail.com. *6m S of Exeter, 1m off A38. Leave A38 at Kennford Services, follow signs to Kenn, 1st R in village, follow lane for ¾m to end of no through rd.* **Sat 24 Feb, Sun 25 Mar, Sat 21, Sun 22 Apr, Sun 13 May, Sat 9, Sat 23 June, Sun 8 July, Sun 12 Aug, Sun 9 Sept (2-5). Adm £5, chd free. Home-made teas. Visits also by arrangement Apr to Sept coaches welcome.**

7 acres with borders, mature trees and shrubs. Banks of snowdrops and small named collection at Bickham Cottage. Formal parterre with lily pond. Walled garden with colourful profusion of vegetables and flowers. Palm tree avenue leading to millennium summerhouse. Late summer colour with dahlias, crocosmia, agapanthus etc. Cactus and succulent greenhouse. Pelargonium collection. New gravel beds. Lake. WC, disabled access

10 NEW BLACKATON

Chagford, Newton Abbot, TQ13 8HW. Anthony and Kit Newsome. *From Whiddon Down take A382 S; after 1½m R to Gidleigh, after ¾m R at white farmhouse, over staggered Xrd and straight on to bottom of hill. From Chagford follow signs to Thowleigh.* **Sat 26, Sun 27 May (12-5). Adm £5, chd free. Home-made teas.**

6 acre garden lying in a high wooded valley below Providence. Moorland trout and salmon stream flows over weir and beneath Monet bridge as it tumbles down beside sloping lawns. Borders at top of garden, mature rhododendrons and azaleas provide a swathe of colour. Mixed shrubs and perennials below 2 terraces. Through the orchard, a vegetable garden and small Japanese Zen garden. Partially surrounded by Woodland Trust land creating an extension to the existing garden. Very rural. Gravel drive and level paths for disabled access. Well behaved dogs on leads welcome.

11 ◆ BLACKPOOL GARDENS

Dartmouth, TQ6 0RG. Sir Geoffrey Newman, 01803 771801, beach@blackpoolsands.co.uk, www.blackpoolsands.co.uk. *3m SW of Dartmouth. From Dartmouth follow brown signs to Blackpool Sands on A379. Entry tickets, parking, toilets and refreshments available at Blackpool Sands. Sorry, no dogs permitted.* **For opening times and information, please phone, email or visit garden website.**

Carefully restored C19 subtropical plantsman's garden with collection of mature and newly planted tender and unusual trees, shrubs and carpet of spring flowers. Paths and steps lead gradually uphill and above the Captain's seat offering fine coastal views. Recent plantings follow the S hemisphere theme with callistemons, pittosporums, acacias and buddlejas. Open 1 Apr - 30 Sept (10-4) weather permitting.

12 BOCOMBE MILL COTTAGE

Bocombe, Parkham, Bideford, EX39 5PH. Mr Chris Butler & Mr David Burrows, 01237 451293, www.bocombe.co.uk. *6m E of Clovelly, 9m SW of Bideford. From A39 just outside Horns Cross village, turn to Foxdown. At Xrds follow signs for parking.* **Sat 26, Sun 27, Mon 28 May (12-5). Adm £4.50, chd £1. Ploughmans lunches & traditional home-made cakes & cream teas. Visits also by arrangement Apr to July for groups of 10+.**

12 themed flower gardens and many unique features that punctuate an undulating landscape of 5 acres in a wooded valley. Streams, 3 bog gardens - raised walkway, a dozen water features, 3 large pools. White pergola. Hillside orchard. Soft fruit and kitchen gardens. Wild meadow, a wildlife haven. Short flower garden walk or longer circular walk, boots suggested. Garden Plan incl 80+ specimen trees. Real hermit in the hermitage with adjoining shell grotto. Goats on hillside. Japanese pavilion with buddha cascade. Garden kaleidoscope. New gated stone archway to hermitage walk. All organic.

GROUP OPENING

13 BOVEY TRACEY GARDENS

Bovey Tracey, TQ13 9NA. *6m N of Newton Abbot. Gateway to Dartmoor. Take A382 to Bovey Tracey. Car parking at town car parks and on some rds.* **Sat 14, Sun 15 July (1.30-5.30). Combined adm £5, chd free. Teas at Gleam Tor. Wine at Ashwell.**

ASHWELL
TQ13 9EJ. Tony & Jeanette Pearce.

5 BRIDGE COTTAGES
TQ13 9DR. Cath Valentine.

NEW ELBURY
TQ13 9LZ. Peter & Hazel Murkin.

GLEAM TOR
TQ13 9DH. Gillian & Colin Liddy.

GREEN HEDGES
TQ13 9LZ. Alan & Linda Jackson.

PARKE VIEW
TQ13 9AD. Peter & Judy Hall.

2 REDWOODS
TQ13 9YG. Mrs Julia Mooney.

23 STORRS CLOSE
TQ13 9HR. Roger Clark & Chie Nakatani.

Bovey Tracey is a pretty cob and granite built town nestling in Dartmoor foothills. Ashwell: steeply sloping 1840s walled garden, vineyard, mixed borders, soft fruit, vegetables, orchard, wild flowers. Bridge Cottage: structured but quirky garden on historic pottery site; varied planting. Elbury: scented roses, mature shrubs, perennials and a spring fed pond. Gleam Tor: long colourful herbaceous border, white garden, wild flower meadow, prairie planting. Green Hedges: mature garden with well established colourful borders incl shrubs, bulbs, perennials, vegetables, soft fruit. Parke View: romantic 1 acre town centre garden. Meandering old stone walls lead to separate planted areas and colour themed herbaceous borders. Redwoods: mature trees, unusual fernery, moorland leat. Acid loving spring and summer shrubs. 23 Storrs Close: plantsman's small garden, main emphasis on plants, many very rare, from Japan and China. Most gardens have distant views, allow dogs and sell plants. Limited wheelchair access at some gardens.

14 BOWDENS

Cleave House, Sticklepath, EX20 2NL. Tim & Ruth Penrose, www.bowdenhostas.com. *3½ m E of Okehampton. Follow brown tourist signs for Bowden Hostas. From Okehampton, Cleave House is on L, covered with Virginia Creeper.* **Sat 19 May, Sat 23 June, Sat 21 July, Sat 18 Aug (10-4). Adm £4, chd free. Teas and Coffees. Further refreshments available within the village.** Donation to NCCPG.
Not just one, but two National Collections - Hostas (Halcyon and sports) and Agapanthus (Pine Cottage cultivars) - are housed in a beautifully mature garden of about ½ acre, alongside many interesting trees, shrubs and other plants. The newly completed stumpery provides a focal point for ferns. Hostas, ferns, tree ferns, bamboos and also agapanthus for sale with expert advice available. BBC1 coverage of Bowdens' Chelsea Flower Show display. Featured on BBC Radio Devon. Partial wheelchair access, some grassed areas.

15 BRAMBLE TORRE

Dittisham, nr Dartmouth, TQ6 0HZ. Paul & Sally Vincent, www.rainingsideways.com. *¾ m from Dittisham. Leave A3122 at Sportsman's Arms. Drop down into village, at Red Lion turn L to Cornworthy. Continue ¾ m Bramble Torre straight ahead.* **Fri 15, Sat 16, Sun 17 June (2-6). Adm £5, chd free. Cream teas.**
Set in 20 acres of farmland, the 3 acre garden follows a rambling stream through a steep valley: lily pond, herbaceous borders, camellias, shrubs and roses dominated by huge embothrium glowing scarlet in late spring against a sometimes blue sky! A formal herb and vegetable garden runs alongside the stream while chickens scratch in an orchard of Ditsum plums and cider apples. Well behaved dogs on leads welcome. Limited wheelchair access, parts of garden very steep and uneven. Tea area with wheelchair access and excellent garden view.

GROUP OPENING

16 BRENDON GARDENS

Brendon, Lynton, EX35 6PU. 01598 741343, lalindevon@yahoo.co.uk. *1m S of A39 North Devon coast rd between Porlock and Lynton.* **Sat 19, Sun 20 May, Sat 4 Aug (12-5). Light refreshments. Sun 5 Aug (12-5). Combined adm £5, chd free. Refreshments served at Brendon House & Higher Tippacott Farm. Light lunches, home-made cakes & cream teas. WCs available. Visits also by arrangement May to Sept.**

NEW **BRENDON HOUSE**
Pat Young & Martin Longhurst.

1 DEERCOMBE COTTAGES
Valerie & Stephen Exley.

DOONE COTTAGE
Carole & Jason Miller.

HALL FARM
Karen & Nick Wall.

HIGHER TIPPACOTT FARM
Angela & Malcolm Percival.

Stunning part of Exmoor National Park. All gardens have views. Excellent walking along river between Brendon & Rockford. Brendon Hse: C18 in idyllic village location. Established front garden, evolving kitchen garden, greenhouse. Emphasis on recycling and gardening in harmony with wildlife. 1 Deercombe Cottages: delightful small garden in steeply wooded valley, created using ditched stone to provide a variety of levels to display planting rich in contrasting foliage and variety of perennials. Doone Cottage (open subject to availability): C17 listed cottage at river's edge. Planted terraces with paths. River vistas. Designed for yr-round interest. Hall Farm: C16 Longhouse set in 2 acres of tranquil mature gardens, enclosed then opening out into lake area with wild area beyond. Rheas, chickens, rare-breed cattle and black bees feature. Higher Tippacott Farm: 950ft altitude on moor. Garden overlooking own idyllic valley with stream and pond. Sunny levels of planting and lawns. Organic. Plants, books and bric-a-brac for sale.

17 THE BRIDGE MILL

Mill Rd, Bridgerule, Holsworthy, EX22 7EL. Rosie & Alan Beat, 01288 381341, rosie@thebridgemill.org.uk, www.thebridgemill.org.uk. *In Bridgerule village on R Tamar between Bude and Holsworthy. Between the chapel by river bridge and the church at top of hill. The mill is at the bottom of the hill opp. Short and Abbott agricultural engineers. See website for detailed directions.* **Sun 3 June (11-5). Adm £4, chd free. Home-made teas. Refreshments in garden if fine or in stable if wet! Plenty of dry seating. Visits also by arrangement May & June for groups of 15+.**

One acre organic gardens set around mill house and restored working water mill. Small cottage garden; herb garden with medicinal and dye plants; productive fruit and vegetable garden, and a wild woodland and water garden by the mill. The 16 acre smallholding will be open for lake and riverside walks through wildflower meadows. Friendly sheep and hens. Exhibition of embroideries by Linda Chilton. The historic water mill was restored to working order in April 2012 and in 2017 was awarded a plaque by the Society for the Protection of Ancient Buildings. The mill and smallholding are open for free educational visits throughout the year to school groups. Details on website. Wheelchair access to some of the gardens. WC with access for wheelchairs.

GROUP OPENING

18 BURN VALLEY BUTTERLEIGH GARDENS

Butterleigh, Cullompton, EX15 1PG. 01884 38812, jill22hall@gmail.com. *Between Tiverton & Cullompton, Follow signs for Silverton from Butterleigh village. Take L fork 100yds after entrance to Pound Farm. Car park sign on L after 150yds.* **Sun 3 June, Sun 1 July (2-5.30). Combined adm £5, chd free. Home-made teas. Shutelake has indoor tea room if weather inclement. Visits also by arrangement May to Sept.**

HIGHER BURNHAIES
Richard & Virginia Holmes. 01884 855748
Visits also by arrangement May to Sept, no coaches, max group size 20.

SHUTELAKE
Jill & Nigel Hall. 01884 38812, jill22hall@gmail.com
Visits also by arrangement May to Sept, no coaches, min 10, max 20.

Two contrasting neighbouring gardens, Burnhaies is a 2½ acre site started in 1997. Situated in the beautiful Burn Valley, a plantsman's garden of herbaceous plantings with trees, shrubs, ponds and wildlife. Informal, country feel with Devon lane and wilderness walk. Vegetable garden. Uneven ground and steps. Live music. Cross a bridge over a stream to Shutelake, a garden terraced into a hillside. Several levels blend a Mediterranean feel with natural local landscape. Recently redesigned and planted herbaceous border in colours of a Turkish carpet. Large pond, sculptures, woodland walk. An oasis of calm with plenty of places to sit and relax. Uneven ground and steps in both gardens, not good for unsteady walkers.

19 BURNBRIDGE COTTAGE

Cadeleigh, Tiverton, EX16 8RY. Kate Leevers & Martin Callaghan. *From A3072 1½m from Bickleigh bridge, 6½m from Crediton, follow lane behind Blue Cross centre for ¾m. On R after stone bridge. From Cadeleigh village take lane opp PH. On L at bottom of hill.* **Sat 25, Sun 26 Aug (2-5). Adm £4, chd free. Home-made cakes and cream teas. Gluten free available.**

Mature trees and shrubs provide the backdrop for this informal, secluded 1¼ acre garden. Reclaimed from long neglect and developed for diversity of planting and wildlife. Late summer flowerbeds attract bees and butterflies. Other moods and habitats created by copse, hedges, pond, bog garden and stream. Mini arboretum and hillside wood can also be visited. Grassed sloping site - should be accessible by wheelchairs if dry.

20 ◆ BURROW FARM GARDENS

Dalwood, Axminster, EX13 7ET. Mary & John Benger, 01404 831285, enquiries@burrowfarmgardens.co.uk, www.burrowfarmgardens.co.uk. *3½m W of Axminster. From A35 turn N at Taunton Xrds then follow brown signs.* **For opening times and information, please phone, email or visit garden website.**

Beautiful 13 acre garden with unusual trees, shrubs and herbaceous plants. Traditional summerhouse looks towards lake and ancient oak woodland with rhododendrons and azaleas. Early spring interest and superb autumn colour. The more formal Millennium garden features a rill. Anniversary garden featuring late summer perennials and grasses. A photographer's dream. Open 30 March – 31 Oct (10am – 6pm). Adm £8. Café and gift shop. Various events incl spring and summer plant fair and open air theatre held at garden each year. Visit events page on Burrow Farm Gardens website for more details.

21 ◆ CADHAY

Ottery St Mary, EX11 1QT. Rupert Thistlethwayte, 01404 813511, jayne@cadhay.org.uk, www.cadhay.org.uk. *1m NW of Ottery St Mary. On B3176 between Ottery St Mary and Fairmile, follow signs for Cadhay. From E exit A30 at Iron Bridge. From W exit A30 at Patteson's Cross, follow brown signs for Cadhay.* **For NGS: Sun 27, Mon 28 May, Sun 26, Mon 27 Aug (2-5). Adm £4, chd £1. Cream teas. Our tea room serves a range of home-made**

cakes and cream teas. For other opening times and information, please phone, email or visit garden website.
Tranquil 2 acre setting for Elizabethan manor house. 2 medieval fish ponds surrounded by rhododendrons, gunnera, hostas and flag iris. Roses, clematis, lilies and hellebores surround walled water garden. 120ft herbaceous border walk informally planted with cottage garden perennials and annuals. Walled kitchen gardens have been turned into allotments and old apple store is now tea room. Gravel paths.

22 CHEVITHORNE BARTON

Tiverton, EX16 7QB. Chris McDonald (Head Gardener), oaksofchevithornebarton.com. *3m NE of Tiverton. Through Sampford Pev and Halberton to Tiverton, past Golf Club, turn R. R at next junction. Over bridge, L through Craze Lowman, carry on to T-junction, R then 1st L.* **Sun 6 May, Sun 2 Sept (12-5). Adm £5, chd free. Cream teas.**
Visit us during this exciting time of development. Newly planted areas complement walled garden, summer borders and woodland of rare trees and shrubs. In spring, garden features a large collection of magnolias, camellias, and rhododendrons. Home to a Plant Heritage National Collection of Quercus (Oaks) situated in 12 hectares of parkland and comprising over 400 different taxa. From time to time within the gardens are a flock of Jacob Sheep and rare breed woodland Pigs.

23 CLEAVE HILL

Membury, Axminster, EX13 7AJ. Andy & Penny Pritchard, 01404 881437, penny@tonybenger.com. *4m NW of Axminster. From Membury Village, follow rd down valley. 1st R after Lea Hill B&B, last house on drive, approx 1m.* **Sat 30 June, Sun 1 July (11-5). Adm £4, chd free. Light refreshments. Light lunches, cream teas and cakes. Visits also by arrangement coach parking 1m.**
Artistic garden in pretty village situated on edge of Blackdown Hills. Cottage style garden, planted to provide all season structure, texture and colour. Designed around pretty thatched house and old stone barns. Wonderful views, attractive vegetable garden and orchard, wild flower meadow. Featured in Country Homes and Interiors magazine.

24 NEW COOMBE MEADOW

Ashburton, Newton Abbot, TQ13 7HU. Angela Patterson & Mike Walker. *Coombe Meadow TQ13 7HU opp Waterleat. Enter Ashburton town centre, turn onto North St. After Victoria Inn, bear R at junction, do not cross bridge to Buckland in the Moor. Follow the signs.* **Sat 21, Sun 22 Apr (11-4). Adm £3.50, chd £1. Light refreshments. Tea, coffee, sandwiches and cake.**
This Lost Garden, by a beautiful Dartmoor stream was overgrown and neglected. Since 2016 its mature Magnolias, Camellias, Azaleas and other trees have been rescued. Paths and ponds cleared, archaeology preserved, borders created, bridges and terraces repaired and over 5000 bulbs planted. The meadows contain wild daffodils and bluebells, so in the spring the garden is a kaleidoscope of colour. Wheelchair access limited to front and rear patios.

GROUP OPENING

25 NEW CORSCOMBE GARDENS

Okehampton, EX20 1SD. *1m N of Dartmoor and the pretty village of Belstone. From A30 take slip rd to Okehampton. L towards Sticklepath. Past BP garage then next L to Sampford Courtenay. Over A30. At Crossways Jct take lane to Corscombe. Down hill ½m. EX20 1SD for SatNav.* **Sat 4, Sun 5 Aug (12-5). Combined adm £5, chd free. Home-made teas at Corscombe Barn.**

NEW CORSCOMBE BARN
Jackie & Phil Hammans.

NEW THE OLD COTTAGE
Mollie & Peter Fillingham.

2 very different gardens in delightful small hamlet. The Old Cottage sits, looking down on garden and slightly elevated, in one corner of ½ acre. 2 small ponds, fed by stream bordered with colourful herbaceous planting during spring, summer and autumn, and lavender walk below rose, clematis and honeysuckle arches. Behind the pretty, open-fronted stone built summerhouse, circled by various dogwoods, giving welcome winter colour, lies a well managed woodland area concentrating on the variation of colour texture and shape of the foliage. Corscombe Barn: a little bit of everything within ¾ acre. Pretty cottage garden with stone and sleeper patio and steps; orchard with a mix of trees and wildflower area; small spinney left partially wild with mix of planting; wildlife pond; bog garden and stream bordered with gunnera, skunk cabbage, astilbe; kitchen garden with raised beds and beautiful Victorian greenhouse; lawn with summerhouse. Dogs on leads only at Corscombe Barn. Some parking is available at both properties as well as Lower Corscombe Farm (close neighbour) by kind permission of the owners. Clearly signed. Wheelchair access only if dry. Some steps and gravel areas in both gardens.

Your visit has already helped 600 more people gain access to a Parkinson's nurse

26 NEW COURT HALL

North Molton, EX36 3HP. Mr & Mrs C Worthington. *2½m N from A361 Barnstaple-Tiverton rd. In N Molton drive up hill into square with church on your L take the only drive beside old school buildings and park outside the house.* **Sun 24 June, Sun 12 Aug (2-6). Adm £5, chd free. Cream teas.**

Parkland, and lawns with pleached hedge and avenue lead to a walled garden where rose, clematis and honeysuckle arbours surround a swimming pool garden with tender plants and rock wall with a large collection of agapanthus. A door leads to an old fashioned kitchen garden with flowers, vegetables and apple trees.

27 CRADDOCK HOUSE

Craddock, Cullompton, EX15 3LJ. Carina Persey. *Halfway between Uffculme and Culmstock.* **Sat 19, Sun 20 May (2.30-5.30). Adm £5, chd free. Home-made teas.**

Attractive extensive garden with small lake. House and grounds built early 1800's. Formal areas and herbaceous borders with large grasses border. Woodland area and extensive lawns and interesting water features. Large rose border with lavender and verbena. Not everywhere wheelchair accessible, but lots of nice areas that can be reached.

Prospect House

28 THE CROFT

Yarnscombe, Barnstaple, EX31 3LW. Sam & Margaret Jewell, 01769 560535. *8m S of Barnstaple, 10m SE of Bideford, 12m W of South Molton, 4m NE of Torrington. From A377, turn W opp Chapelton railway stn. Follow Yarnscombe signs for 3m. From B3232, ¼m N of Huntshaw Cross TV mast, turn E and follow Yarnscombe signs for 2m. Parking in village hall car park.* **Sun 17 June, Sun 15 July, Sun 19 Aug (2-6). Adm £4, chd free. Home-made teas. Visits also by arrangement June to Aug min 7 days notice required.** Donation to North Devon Animal Ambulance.

1 acre plantswoman's garden featuring exotic Japanese garden with tea house, koi carp pond and cascading stream, tropical garden with exotic shrubs and perennials, herbaceous borders with unusual plants and shrubs, bog garden with collection of irises, astilbes and moisture-loving plants, duck pond. Exotic borders, new beds around duck pond and bog area, large collection of rare and unusual plants. Featured in Amateur Gardening magazine.

29 DEANCOMBE FARM

Deancombe, Buckfastleigh, TQ11 0LZ. James & Deborah Hedger. *½m N of A38. Leave A38 at Dean Prior. From Exeter exit A38 at Lower Dean (after Buckfastleigh exit) then R under bridge, turn L and follow NGS signs. From Plymouth exit A38 at Dean Prior then turn L and follow NGS signs.* **Sat 26, Sun 27 May (2-5.30). Adm £4, chd free. Home-made teas.**

Nestling between old walls and a traditional Devon farm overlooked by meadows with sheep and cattle set in the southern foothills of Dartmoor. Small swimming lake, waterfalls and stream. Herbaceous beds, part walled and terraced vegetable garden, bog and woodland gardens, cider orchard and stream walks stretch over 4 acres in a naturalistic landscape. Home composting system. Grass paths and steep slopes adj to deep water. Dependent on size of wheelchair up to 50% accessible.

30 DICOT

Chardstock, EX13 7DF. Mr & Mrs F Clarkson, www.dicot.co.uk. *5m N of Axminster. Axminster to Chard A358 at Tytherleigh to Chardstock. R at George Inn, L fork to Hook, R to Burridge, 2nd house on L.* **Sat 5, Sun 6, Mon 7 May (2-5.30). Adm £4, chd free. Cream teas.**

Secret garden hidden in East Devon valley. 3 acres of unusual and exotic plants - some rare. Rhododendrons, azaleas and camellias in profusion. Meandering stream, fish pool, Japanese style garden and interesting vegetable garden with fruit cage, tunnel and greenhouses. Surprises round every corner. Partial wheelchair access.

GROUP OPENING

31 DITTISHAM GARDENS

Dittisham, Dartmouth, TQ6 0ES. www.dittisham.org.uk. *On R Dart at Dittisham between Totnes and Dartmouth. Leave A3122 Dartmouth rd at Hemborough Post by Sportsmans Arms PH. Continue 2½m then down steep hill with river views into village.* **Sat 14, Sun 15 July (2-5). Combined adm £6, chd free. Cream teas.**

Dittisham overlooks the widest stretch of the beautiful River Dart just three miles upstream from Dartmouth. The village, protected from the worst weather by rolling hills and the temperance of the Gulf Stream, is a gardener's paradise! A group of eight or more gardens will be opening their gates in July. Thatched cottages with gardens, filled with all the old fashioned favourites, look out across the river to Dartmoor in the distance. There are modern gardens too with contemporary planting and terraced gardens clinging to the hillside. Sheep graze quietly on surrounding farmland and the famous Ditsum Plum orchards flourish still. A cream tea and plant stall will complete the afternoon! Read more about the village on www.dittisham.org.uk. Beautiful village on steep slopes overlooking R Dart opp National Trust property Greenway (Agatha Christie). Very limited wheelchair access; the village is very steep.

32 ◆ DOCTON MILL

Lymebridge, Hartland, EX39 6EA. Lana & John Borrett, 01237 441369, docton.mill@btconnect.com, www.doctonmill.co.uk. *8m W of Clovelly. Follow brown tourist signs on A39 nr Clovelly.* **For NGS: Sun 10 June (10-5). Adm £4.50, chd free. Light refreshments. Cream teas and light lunches available all day. For other opening times and information, please phone, email or visit garden website.**

Situated in stunning valley location. Garden surrounds original mill pond and the microclimate created within the wooded valley enables tender species to flourish. Recent planting of herbaceous, stream and summer garden give variety through the season. Regret not suitable for wheelchairs.

33 DUNLEY HOUSE

Bovey Tracey, Newton Abbot, TQ13 9PW. Mr & Mrs F Gilbert. *2m E of Bovey Tracey on rd to Hennock. From A38 going W turn off slip rd R towards Chudleigh Knighton on B3344, in village follow yellow signs to Dunley House. From A38 eastwards turn off on Chudleigh K slip road L and follow signs.* **Sat 7, Sun 8 July (2-5). Adm £4, chd free. Home-made teas.**

9 acre garden set among mature oaks, sequoiadendrons and a huge liquidambar started from a wilderness in the mid eighties. Rhododendrons, camellias and over 40 different magnolias. Arboretum, walled garden with borders and fruit and vegetables, rose garden and new enclosed garden with lily pond. Large pond renovated 2016 with new plantings. Woodland walk around perimeter of property.

34 NEW EAST WOODLANDS FARMHOUSE

Alverdiscott, Newton Tracey, Barnstaple, EX31 3PP. Ed & Heather Holt. *5m NE of Great Torrington, 5m S of Barnstaple, off B3232. From Great Torrington turn R into single track rd before Alverdiscott; and from Barnstaple turn L after Alverdiscott. 1m down rd R fork at Y-junction.* **Sat 12, Sun 13 May, Sat 11, Sun 12 Aug (2-5). Adm £4, chd free. Home-made teas. Gluten free cakes available.**

Newly reopening in 2018, East Woodlands is a beautifully designed garden full of rooms packed with plants, shrubs and trees. Enjoy the spectacular bamboos, flowing grasses, colourful roses and giant phormiums all set in an acre looking out over the North Devon countryside. Sit in one of the seating areas and enjoy a cuppa. Unfenced pond and bog garden. Plants for sale. Partial wheelchair access.

35 EAST WORLINGTON HOUSE

East Worlington, Witheridge, Crediton, EX17 4TS. Barnabas & Campie Hurst-Bannister. *In centre of East Worlington, 2m W of Witheridge. From Witheridge Square R to East Worlington. After 1½m R at T-junction in Drayford, then L to Worlington. After ½m L at T-junction. 200 yds on L. Parking nearby, disabled parking at house.* **Sun 4, Sun 11 Mar (1.30-5). Adm £4, chd free. Cream teas in thatched parish hall next to house.**

Thousands of crocuses. In 2 acre garden, set in lovely position with views down valley to Little Dart river, these spectacular crocuses have spread over many years through the garden and into the neighbouring churchyard. Cream teas in the parish hall (in aid of its modernisation fund) next door. Dogs on leads please.

36 FOAMLEA

Chapel Hill, Mortehoe, EX34 7DZ. Beth Smith, foamlea.uk. *¼m S of Mortehoe village. A361 N from Barnstaple. L onto B3343 to Mortehoe car park. No parking at or near garden. On foot L past church, down hill, then 200yds.* **Sun 20 May (2-5). Adm £4, chd £1. Home-made teas.**

Coastal garden with uninterrupted view of Morte Point (NT), brim full of unusual and familiar plants originating around the world. Rockery, colour rooms, mixed beds and borders all linked by slate steps and shillet paths. Several changed plantings incl 2 new areas. Herbaceous and shrub varieties of Phlomis (Jerusalem Sage) occur throughout. Featured in RHS The Garden, Gardeners' World magazine, Devon Life and several national magazines, and on ITV Love Your Garden. Garden on gradient, narrow paths. Sorry, no dogs.

NPC

37 ◆ FURSDON

Cadbury, Thorverton, Exeter, EX5 5JS. David & Catriona Fursdon, 01392 860860, admin@fursdon.co.uk, www.fursdon.co.uk. *2m N of Thorverton. From Tiverton S on A396. Take A3072 at Bickleigh towards Crediton. L after 2½m. From Exeter N on A396. L to Thorverton and R in centre.* **For NGS: Sat 9, Sun 10 June, Sat 8, Sun 9 Sept (2-5). Adm £4.50, chd free. Home-made teas in Coach Hall from 2pm, also cream teas. Teas proceeds not for NGS. For other opening times and information, please phone, email or visit garden website.**

Garden surrounds Fursdon House, home of the same family for 7 centuries. Hillside setting with extensive views S over parkland and beyond. Sheltered by house, hedges and cob walls, there are terraces of roses, herbs and perennials in mixed traditional and contemporary planting. Woodland walk, seasonal wild flowers and pond in meadow garden. Fursdon House open for guided tours on NGS days (separate entrance fee not for NGS). Some steep slopes, grass and gravel paths.

38 THE GATE HOUSE

Lee, EX34 8LR. Mrs H Booker, 01271 862409. *3m W of Ilfracombe. Park in Lee village car park. Take lane alongside The Grampus PH. Garden approx 30 metres past inn buildings. Open most days but wise to check by phoning between 7pm & 9pm.* **Daily Tue 1 May to Sun 16 Sept (9.30-3). Adm by donation. Visits also by arrangement May to July, good refreshments available adjacent to garden, at The Grampus Inn.**

Described by many visitors as a peaceful paradise, this streamside garden incl National Collection of over 100 rodgersia (at their best end of June), interesting herbaceous areas, patio gardens with semi-hardy exotics, many unusual mature trees and shrubs and large organic vegetable garden. Level gravel paths.

NPC

39 GOREN FARM

Broadhayes, Stockland, Honiton, EX14 9EN. Julian Pady, www.goren.co.uk. *6m E of Honiton, 6m W of Axminster. Go to the Stockland television mast. Head 100 metres N signed from Ridge Cross.* **Every Sat and Sun 2 June to 17 June (10.30-5). Home-made teas. Evening openings Sat 2 June to Sun 15 July (5-9). Adm £3, chd free. Teas and home-made cakes with local produce from the farm available.**

Wander through 50 acres of natural species rich wild flower meadows. Dozens of varieties of wild flowers and grasses. Orchids early June, butterflies July. Stunning views of Blackdown Hills. Georgian house and walled gardens, guided walks 10.30 and 2.30 on open weekends. Species information signs and picnic tables around the fields. Partial wheelchair access to meadows.

40 GORWELL HOUSE

Goodleigh Rd, Barnstaple, EX32 7JP. Dr J A Marston, www.gorwellhousegarden.co.uk. *¾m E of Barnstaple centre on Bratton Fleming rd. Drive entrance between 2 lodges on L coming uphill (Bear Street) approx ¾m from Barnstaple centre.* **Sun 25 Mar, Sun 29 Apr, Sun 13 May, Sun 17 June, Sun 15 July, Sun 30 Sept (2-6). Adm £4.50, chd free. Cream teas by Goodleigh WI. Regret no teas in March.**

Created mostly since 1979, this 4 acre garden overlooking the Taw estuary has a benign microclimate which allows many rare and tender plants to grow and thrive, both in the open and in walled garden. Several strategically placed follies complement the enclosures and vistas within the garden. Opening in March especially for the magnolias. Featured in N Devon Journal, The English Garden and Devon Life magazines and on BBC Radio Devon and web-based SW1TV Summer Gardens. Mostly wheelchair access but some steep slopes.

41 GREATCOMBE

Holne, Newton Abbot, TQ13 7SP. Robbie & Sarah Richardson. *Michelcombe, Holne, TQ13 7SP. 4m NW Ashburton via Holne Bridge and Holne Village. 4m NE Buckfastleigh via Scorriton. Narrow lanes.* **Sat 5, Sun 6, Mon 7, Sat 26, Sun 27, Mon 28 May, Sat 23, Sun 24 June, Sat 25, Sun 26, Mon 27 Aug (1-5). Adm £4, chd free. Home-made teas.**

Charming, tranquil garden nestled in the southern slopes of Dartmoor, intersected by a babbling stream and featuring bright colours and textual foliage. Gentle undulating paths and lawns bordered by spring and summer flowering shrubs, herbaceous plants, ornamental grasses and spectacular rambling roses incl the famous Greatcombe White in June. Artist's Studio featuring brightly coloured acrylic paintings, prints and cards all available to purchase along with ornamental metal plant supports in all sizes and shapes. Sadly very limited wheelchair access.

42 HALDON GRANGE

Dunchideock, Exeter, EX6 7YE. Ted Phythian, 01392 832349. *5m SW of Exeter. From A30 through Ide Village to Dunchideock 5m. L to Lord Haldon, Haldon Grange is next L. From A38 (S) turn L on top of Haldon Hill follow Dunchideock signs, R at village centre to Lord Haldon.* **Sat 24, Sun 25, Sat 31 Mar, Sun 1, Mon 2, Sat 7, Sun 8, Sat 14, Sun 15, Wed 18, Sat 21, Sun 22, Sat 28, Sun 29 Apr, Sat 5, Sun 6, Mon 7, Wed 9, Sat 12, Sun 13, Sat 19, Sun 20, Wed 23, Sat 26, Sun 27, Mon 28 May, Sat 2, Sun 3, Sat 9, Sun 10 June (1-5). Adm £4.50, chd free. Home-made teas. Visits also by arrangement Mar to June, refreshments by arrangement in advance.**

12 acre well established garden with camellias, magnolias, azaleas, various shrubs and rhododendrons; rare and mature trees; small lake and ponds with river and water cascades. 5 acre arboretum planted 2011 with wide range of trees, shrubs and a large lilac circle. Wisteria pergola with views over Exeter and Woodbury. Daily Telegraph recommended. Wheelchair access to main parts of garden.

43 NEW HALSCOMBE FARM

Halscombe Lane, Ide, Exeter, EX2 9TQ. Prof J Rawlings. *From Exeter go through Ide to mini r'about take 2nd exit and continue to L turn into Halscombe Lane.* **Sat 16, Sun 17 June (2-5.30). Adm £3.50, chd free. Home-made teas.** Donation to The Friends of Exeter Cathedral.

Farmhouse garden created over last 5 years. Large collection of old roses and peonies, long and colourful herbaceous border, knot garden, productive fruit cage and vegetable garden all set within a wonderful borrowed landscape.

44 HAMBLYN'S COOMBE

Dittisham, Dartmouth, TQ6 0HE. Bridget McCrum, 01803 722228, mccrum.sculpt@waitrose.com, www.bridgetmccrum.com. *3m N of Dartmouth. From A3122 L to Dittisham. In village R at Red Lion, The Level, then Rectory Lane, past River Farm to Hamblyn's Coombe.* **Visits by arrangement, parking difficult for more than 20. Adm £5, chd free.**

7 acre garden with stunning views across the river to Greenway House and sloping steeply to R Dart at bottom of garden. Extensive planting of trees and shrubs with unusual design features accompanying Bridget McCrum's stone carvings and bronzes. Wild flower meadow and woods. Good rhododendrons and camellias, ferns and bamboos, acers and hydrangeas. Exceptional autumn colour. Featured in Country Life. No wheelchair access.

45 HARBOUR LIGHTS

Horns Cross, Bideford, EX39 5DW. Brian & Faith Butler, 01237451627, brian.nfu@gmail.com. *7m W of Bideford, 3m E of Clovelly. On main A39 between Bideford and Clovelly, halfway between Hoops Inn and Bucks Cross.* **Sat 23, Sun 24 June (11-6). Adm £4, chd free. Light lunches, home-made cakes and cream teas, or perhaps a glass of wine. Visits also by arrangement June to Aug for groups of 10+.**

½ acre colourful garden with Lundy views. A garden of wit, humour, unusual ideas, artwork, volcano and many surprises. Water features, shrubs, foliage area, grasses in an unusual setting, fernery, bonsai and polytunnel, time saving ideas. You will never have seen a garden like this! Superb conservatory for cream teas. Free leaflet. We like our visitors to leave with a smile! Child friendly. A 'must visit' garden. Intriguing artwork of various kinds. Featured in Amateur Gardening and Daily Mail.

46 THE HAVEN

Wembury Road, Hollacombe, Wembury, South Hams, PL9 0DQ. Mrs S Norton & Mr J Norton, 01752 862149, suenorton1@hotmail.co.uk. *20mins from Plymouth city centre. Use A379 Plymouth to Kingsbridge Rd. At Elburton r'about follow signs to Wembury. Parking on roadside. Bus stop nearby on Wembury Rd. Route 48 from Plymouth.* **Sat 24, Sun 25 Mar (12-4). Adm £4, chd free. Cream teas. Visits also by arrangement Mar to May for groups, max 20.**

½ acre sloping plantsman's garden in South Hams AONB. Tearoom and seating areas. 2 ponds. Substantial collection of large flowering Asiatic and hybrid tree magnolias. Large collection of camellias including camellia reticulata. Rare dwarf, weeping and slow growing conifers. Daphnes, early azaleas and rhododendrons, spring bulbs and hellebores. Magnolias, camellias. Wheelchair access to top part of garden.

Higher Cherubeer

47 HAWKERN

Ladram Road, Otterton, Budleigh Salterton, EX9 7HT. Tony Mills, 01395 567304, clairemills2@hotmail.co.uk. *Once in Otterton, follow signs to Ladram Bay by turning into Bell St. At top of hill, just past unrestricted speed signs Hawkern is on L opp last lamp post.* **Sat 8, Sun 9 Sept (2-5). Adm £5, chd free. Home-made teas. Wine for early evening visits if required. Visits also by arrangement May to Sept for groups 15+.**

The gardens, first planted in the 20s, are set in approx 3½ acres. Glorious panoramic views from Peak Hill round to Bicton and towards E Devon. 4 distinct planting areas with extensive mature trees, camellias, rhododendrons and a stump garden clothed in roses and underplanted with hostas and ferns together with a superb range of perennials in varied plantings.

48 HAYNE

Zeal Monachorum, Crediton, EX17 6DE. Tim & Milla Herniman, www.haynedevon.co.uk. *Located ½m S of Zeal Monachorum. From Zeal Monachorum, keeping church on L, drive through village. Continue on this road for ⅓m, garden drive is 1st entrance on R.* **Sun 3 June (2-6). Adm £4, chd free. Home-made teas.**

Hayne has a magical walled garden brimming with mature trees, shrubs, roses and borders. Highlights incl beautiful tree peonies, mature wisteria in both purple and white and rambling wild roses in combination with a more modern Piet Oudolf style perennial planting which surrounds the recently renovated grade II* farm buildings ... magic, mystery and soul by the spadeful! Live jazz band. Disabled WC. Wheelchair access to walled garden through orchard.

49 HEATHERCOMBE

Manaton, Nr Bovey Tracey, TQ13 9XE. Claude & Margaret Pike Woodlands Trust, 01626 354404, gardens@pike.me.uk, www.heathercombe.com. *7m NW of Bovey Tracey. From Bovey Tracey take scenic B3387 to Haytor/Widecombe. 1.7m past Haytor Rocks (before Widecombe hill) turn R to Hound Tor and Manaton. 1.4m past Hound Tor turn L at Heatree Cross to Heathercombe.* **Sun 25 Mar, Sun 13, Sun 20, Sat 26, Sun 27, Tue 29, Wed 30, Thur 31 May, Fri 1, Sat 2, Sun 3 June (1.30-5.30). Adm £5, chd free. Every Tue to Sun 16 June to 8 July (11-5.30). Adm £6, chd £2. Cream teas in pretty cottage garden or conservatory if wet. Visits also by arrangement Apr to Oct.** Donation to Rowcroft Hospice.

Secluded valley with streams tumbling through woods, ponds and lake; tranquil setting for 30 acres of spring/summer interest (many recent changes) - daffodils, extensive bluebells complementing large displays of rhododendrons, pretty cottage gardens, woodland walks, many specimen trees, bog/fern gardens, orchard and wild flower meadow, sculptures. Seats. 2m mainly level sandy paths. From 16 June to 8 July admission incl bi-annual Heathercombe 'EDGE' Sculpture Trail - approx 50 works in woodland/garden settings.

50 HIGH GARDEN

Chiverstone Lane, Kenton, EX6 8NJ. Chris & Sharon Britton, www.highgardennurserykenton.wordpress.com. *5m S of Exeter on A379 Dawlish Rd. Leaving Kenton towards Exeter, L into Chiverstone Lane, 50yds along lane. Entrance clearly marked at High Garden Nurseries. Phone for directions 01626 899106.* **Every Tue to Fri 13 Feb to 30 Nov (9-5). Adm £3.50, chd free. Light refreshments.** Donation to Hospiscare and FORCE cancer care charities.

Very interesting and wide ranging planting of trees, shrubs, climbers and perennials in relaxed but still controlled 12 yr old garden. 70 metre summer herbaceous border, colour-themed beds, grass walkways with surprises around each corner. Always something to enjoy. Lots of unusual and different species. Self-service tea room open March to November. Garden attached to plantsman's nursery, open at same time. Slightly sloping site but the few steps can be avoided.

51 HIGHER ASH FARM

Ash, Dartmouth, TQ6 0LR. Mr Michael Gribbin & Mrs Jennifer Barwell, 07595 507516, matthew.perkins18@yahoo.co.uk, www.higherashfarm.com. *Leave A381 at Halwell for Dartmouth A3122. Turn R before Sportsman's Arms to Bugford. At T-junction go R then next L. After 1½m at Xrds go R, Higher Ash Farm entrance is 1st L.* **Sun 13, Sun 20 May (2-5); Sun 7 Oct (1.30-4.30). Adm £5, chd free. Home-made teas. Opening with Ash Gardens on Sat 23, Sun 24 June, Sat 11, Sun 12 Aug.**

Evolving garden, high up in South Devon countryside. Sitting in 2½ acres there is a large kitchen garden terraced into the hillside with adjoining orchard. Vibrant array of azaleas and rhododendrons surround the barns and courtyard. Farmhouse is surrounded by a mix of herbaceous borders, shrubs and lawns. Pond, stream, autumn interest.

52 HIGHER CHERUBEER

Dolton, Winkleigh, EX19 8PP. Jo & Tom Hynes, 01805 804265, hynesjo@gmail.com, www.sites.google.com/site/cherubeergardens/the-gardens. *2m E of Dolton. From A3124 turn S towards Stafford Moor Fisheries, take 1st R, garden 500m on L.* **Fri 9, Fri 16, Sun 25 Feb (2-5); Sun 13 May (2.30-5.30). Adm £4, chd free. Home-made teas. 2019: Fri 8, Fri 15, Sat 23 Feb. Visits also by arrangement Feb to Oct for groups of 10+.**

1½ acre country garden with gravelled courtyard, raised beds and alpine house, lawns, large herbaceous border, shady woodland beds, potager style kitchen garden with large greenhouse. Winter openings for National Collection of Cyclamen species, hellebores and over 400 snowdrop varieties. Featured in The Telegraph.

53 HIGHER CULLAFORD
Spreyton, Crediton, EX17 5AX. Dr & Mrs Kennerley, 01837 840974, kenntoad@yahoo.com. *Approx ¾m from centre of Spreyton, 20m W of Exeter, 10 E of Okehampton. From A30 at Whiddon Down follow signs to Spreyton. Yellow signs from A3124, centre of village and Spreyton parish church.* **Visits by arrangement May to Oct, see www.ngs.org.uk for additional pop-up openings. Adm £3.50, chd free. Home-made teas.**
Traditional cottage style garden developed over past 12yrs from steep field and farmyard on northern edge of Dartmoor National Park. Mixed borders of herbaceous plants, roses and shrubs. 30ft pergola covered with seagull rose and many varieties of clematis. Wildlife pond. Newly planted pleached hornbeam hedge. Additional vegetable garden with polytunnel and fruit cage and fruit trees. Wheelchair access limited but can drive in to garden on request.

54 HIGHER ORCHARD COTTAGE
Aptor, Marldon, Paignton, TQ3 1SQ. Mrs Jenny Saunders. *1m SW of Marldon. A380 Torquay to Paignton. At Churscombe Cross r'about R for Marldon, L towards Berry Pomeroy, take 2nd R into Farthing Lane. Follow for exactly 1m. Turn R at NGS sign for parking at Aptor Farm.* **Sat 16, Sun 17 June (11-5). Adm £4, chd free. Home-made teas. Teas from 2pm to 4pm if weather permits.**
Set in a secluded rural area, this sloping 2 acre garden has abundant colour themed herbaceous borders. Large wildlife pond, productive raised vegetable beds, grass path walks through wild flower meadow areas and lovely countryside views. Examples of work by local artist and sculptor and crafts available if weather permits. Temporary installations by local Sculptor: Edward Netley www.netzfineart.com. Displays by textile artist: Jackie Wills www.jackiewills.com. Craft stalls if weather permits.

55 HILLERSDON
Cullompton, EX15 1LS. Mr Mike Lloyd, www.hillersdon.com/. *2m NW of Cullompton (M5 J28). From Fore St in Cullompton town centre (B3181) take Tiverton Rd (narrow entrance next to Costa). Continue along this road for approx 1½m then follow yellow signs to Hillersdon.* **Sun 27, Mon 28 May (10-5). Adm £5, chd free. Home-made teas on main terrace adjacent to house.**
After decades of neglect, the gardens at Hillersdon have been lovingly restored and developed, and this work is ongoing. The Gardens and Parkland now include several ornamental lakes, new collection of rhododendrons, restored walled garden, secret garden, stumpery, formal parterres, wild flower meadow, red deer and the ancient and enigmatic chestnut walk. Hillersdon has always been a very Private Garden. This is only the second time the Gardens have been open to the General Public in the last Century. Access to walled garden and formal garden areas but loose gravel on many paths. Limited wheelchair access to other areas (gradients and steps).

Donations from the National Garden Scheme enable Perennial to care for horticulturalists

56 ♦ HOLBROOK GARDEN
Sampford Shrubs, Sampford Peverell, EX16 7EN. Martin Hughes-Jones & Susan Proud, 01884 821164, www.holbrookgarden.com. *1m NW from M5 J27. From M5 J27 follow signs to Tiverton Parkway. At top of slip rd off A361 follow brown sign to Holbrook Garden, 1m from J27.* **For NGS: Fri 30, Sat 31 Mar, Sun 1, Fri 6, Sat 7, Fri 13, Sat 14, Sun 15, Fri 20, Sat 21, Fri 27, Sat 28 Apr (10-5). Adm £5, chd free. Light refreshments.** For other opening times and information, please phone or visit garden website.
2 acre s-facing garden on heavy clay, 35 yrs in the making. Diverse habitats and inspired by nature. Wet garden, stone garden, pink garden and woodland glades. Perfumes, songbirds and nests are everywhere in spring. Anemones, hellebores, tulips and snakeshead fritillaries with camellias, magnolias and rhododendrons in April. Productive vegetable garden and polytunnel. Coach parties by arrangement, please phone or see holbrookgarden.com. Donation to MSF UK (Medecin sans Frontieres). Narrow paths restrict access for wheelchairs and buggies.

57 HOLE FARM
Woolsery, Bideford, EX39 5RF. Heather Alford. *11m SW of Bideford. Follow directions for Woolfardisworthy, signed from A39 at Bucks Cross. From village follow NGS signs from school for approx 2m.* **Sun 10 June, Sun 15 July (2-6). Adm £4, chd free. Home-made teas in converted barn.**
3 acres of exciting gardens with established waterfall, ponds, vegetable and bog garden. Terraces and features incl round house have all been created using natural stone from original farm quarry. Peaceful walks through Culm grassland and water meadows border R Torridge and host a range of wildlife. Home to a herd of pedigree native Devon cattle. Riverside walk not wheelchair accessible.

58 HOLE'S MEADOW

Holes Meadow, South Zeal, Okehampton, EX20 2JS. Fi & Paul Reddaway, 07850 305040, fireddaway@gmail.com, https://holesmeadow.com. *4½m from Okehampton on B3260, 4m from Whiddon Down. Signed from main street when open. Half way between the King's Arms and Oxenham Arms and opp village hall. A minute's fairly level walk along private path.* **Sat 4, Sun 5 Aug (1.30-5.30). Adm £4, chd free. Home-made teas. Visits also by arrangement in July.**

Looking directly up to Dartmoor's Cawsand Beacon and set within a 2 acre burgage plot. The garden features Plant Heritage National Plant Collections of both Monarda and Nepeta. Also over 200 herbs plus a young prairie garden with monardas and complementary planting. Bottom half of garden incl orchard, ornamental trees and maturing native woodland area interspersed with pathways.

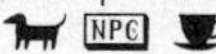

59 ◆ HOTEL ENDSLEIGH

Milton Abbot, Tavistock, PL19 0PQ. Olga Polizzi, 01822 870000, mail@hotelendsleigh.com, www.hotelendsleigh.com/garden. *7m NW of Tavistock, midway between Tavistock and Launceston. From Tavistock, take B3362 to Launceston. 7m to Milton Abbot then 1st L, opp school. From Launceston & A30, B3362 to Tavistock. At Milton Abbot turn R opp school.* **For NGS: Wed 25 Apr, Wed 16 May (11-4). Adm £5, chd free. For other opening times and information, please phone, email or visit garden website.**

200 year old Repton-designed garden in 3 parts; formal gardens around the house, picturesque dell with pleasure dairy and rockery and arboretum. Gardens were laid out in 1814 and have been carefully renovated over last 12yrs. Bordering the R Tamar, it is a hidden oasis of plants and views. Hotel was built in 1810 by Sir Jeffry Wyattville for the 6th Duchess of Bedford in the romantic cottage Orne style. Plant Nursery adjoins hotel's 108 acres. Partial wheelchair access.

60 NEW HUTSWELL FARM

Blackaller Lane, Oakford, Tiverton, EX16 9JE. Paul & Jean Marcus, 01398 351241, Barvanjack@aol.com. *1½m NNW of Oakford. Signed narrow lane off B3227. Turn L 12m E of S Molton. 2½m NW of Black Cat junction turn R. Signs to Hutswell.* **Fri 22, Sat 23 June (11-5). Adm £4.50, chd free. Light refreshments. Soup, ploughmans, afternoon teas. Visits also by arrangement Apr to Oct groups max 15.**

Delightful 8 acre S-facing country garden around old farmhouse. Ponds, bog garden, shrubaceous borders, prairie planting, maturing arboretum with Pyrus calleryana Chanticleer avenue, serpentine hornbeam walk, vegetable garden and orchard with local apple varieties. Walks through ancient wet woodland and recent plantation of over 11,000 native trees to viewpoints. Variety and interest all yr round.

The National Garden Scheme is the largest single funder of the Queen's Nursing Institute

GROUP OPENING

61 KENTISBURY GARDENS

Kentisbury, Barnstaple, EX31 4NT. *From Barnstaple follow A39 to Lynton. L at Kentisbury Ford, follow B3229 for about 2m, Little Ley on L. From S Molton follow A399, then L at Easter Close Cross onto B3229 then R.* **Sat 23 June (12-5). Cream teas at Beachborough Country House & Higher Patchole Farm, near Spring Cottage. Sun 24 June (12-5). Home-made teas at Beachborough Country House & Higher Patchole Farm. Combined adm £5, chd free.**

BEACHBOROUGH COUNTRY HOUSE
Viviane Clout, 01271 882487, viviane@beachboroughcountryhouse.co.uk, www.beachboroughcountryhouse.co.uk.

LITTLE LEY
Jerry & Jenny Burnett.

SPRING COTTAGE
Nerys Cadvan-Jones.

Kentisbury is situated high in the North Devon countryside a few miles inland from the dramatic coastline and bordering Exmoor National Park. These 3 gardens make good use of the landscape and views, providing a variety of planting and garden habitats. Beachborough Country House is a garden created from an artist's perspective and home to hundreds of roses. Interest incl herbaceous borders, lawns, stream, pond and large ornamental kitchen garden. Little Ley is a large country garden with pond, stream, mature trees and shrubs, perennial flower and shrub beds, plus wildlife areas. Productive fruit and vegetable area. Early spring interest and superb autumn colour. Spring Cottage is a pretty cottage garden with colourful flower borders, shrubs, climbers and small trees giving yr-round interest. Devon banks, a stream and stone walls afford varying views and conditions for planting and the growing collection of hardy geraniums.

---

62 NEW KENTLANDS

Whitestone, Exeter, EX4 2JR. David & Gill Oakey, 01392 811585, david.oakey3@hotmail.co.uk. *NW of Exeter mid way between Exwick and Tedburn St Mary. Follow NGS signs from centre of village.* **Sat 19, Sun 20 May (11-5); Sun 16 Sept (11-4). Adm £4, chd free. Light refreshments. Visits also by arrangement May to Sept maximum 20 people.**

Our 2 acre tucked away garden is s-facing with distant views across Exeter towards west Devon and Sidmouth. The Garden was started in 2010 and is still developing. The planting is mainly perennials with some shrubs, large salvia collection, orchids and alpines, productive vegetable garden with poly tunnel, fruit cage and fruit trees. Sloping garden.

63 KIA-ORA FARM & GARDENS

Knowle Lane, Cullompton, EX15 1PZ. Mrs M B Disney, 01884 32347, rosie@kia-orafarm.co.uk, www.kia-orafarm.co.uk. *On W side of Cullompton and 6m SE of Tiverton. M5 J28, through town centre to r'about, 3rd exit R, top of Swallow Way turn L into Knowle Lane, garden beside Cullompton Rugby Club.* **Sun 1, Mon 2, Sun 15, Sun 29 Apr, Sun 6, Mon 7, Sun 13, Sun 27, Mon 28 May, Sun 10, Sun 24 June, Sun 8, Sun 22 July, Sun 5, Sun 19, Sun 26, Mon 27 Aug, Sun 9 Sept (2-5.30). Adm £3.50, chd free. Home-made teas at Kia-ora, available inside or outside depending on personal preference and the weather! Teas and sales not for NGS charities. Visits also by arrangement Apr to Sept.**

Charming, peaceful 10 acre garden with lawns, lakes and ponds. Water features with swans, ducks and other wildlife. Mature trees, shrubs, rhododendrons, azaleas, heathers, roses, herbaceous borders and rockeries. Nursery avenue, novelty crazy golf. Stroll leisurely around and finish by sitting back, enjoying a traditional homemade Devonshire cream tea or choose from the wide selection of cakes!

GROUP OPENING

64 KILMINGTON (SHUTE ROAD) GARDENS

Kilmington, Axminster, EX13 7ST. www.Kilmingtonvillage.com. *1½ m W of Axminster. Signed off A35.* **Sat 19, Sun 20 May (1.30-5). Combined adm £6, chd free. Home-made teas at Breach.**

NEW BETTY'S GROUND
Michael & Mary-Anne Driscoll.

BREACH
J A Chapman & B J Lewis.

SPINNEY TWO
Paul & Celia Dunsford.

Set in rural E Devon in AONB yet easily accessed from A35. 3 gardens just under 1 mile apart. Spinney Two: ½ acre garden planted for yr-round colour, foliage and texture. Mature oaks and beech. Views. On gentle southerly slope. Spring bulbs, hellebores and shrubs incl azaleas, camellias, cornus, pieris, skimmias, viburnums. Roses, acers, flowering trees, clematis and other climbers. Mixed borders and vegetable patch. Breach: set in over 3 acres with majestic woodland partially underplanted with rhododendrons and hydrangeas; shrubberies, areas of grass, colourful mixed border, vegetable garden, small orchard and ponds. Established bog garden using natural springs. Betty's Ground, Haddon Corner: 1½ acres mixed garden. ⅓ at front of house has been designed/replanted 3 yrs ago. Remaining ⅔ has been restored/replanted and continues to evolve. Good selection of mature trees and large shrubs including beautiful wisteria walk. Beds with yr-round colour united by repeat planting.

GROUP OPENING

65 NEW LAMERTON GARDENS

Orchard Court, Lamerton, Tavistock, PL19 8SF. *At Blacksmith's Arms PH in Lamerton on Tavistock-Launceston Road, turn into village; follow road for ¼ m crossing bridge, following NGS signs.* **Sun 20 May, Sat 16 June (1-5). Combined adm £5, chd free. Teas, coffee, soft drinks and home made cakes 50% to St. Luke's Hospice.**

NEW OAKWOOD
Karen & Rod Dreher.

NEW PENDENE
Ellie Hill.

2 adjacent s-facing sloping gardens on edge of W Devon village Oakwood: created in 2008 garden provides all yr-round interest with winding paths through well stocked borders and sloping beds, water features, laburnum and wisteria tunnel, mature specimen trees, intimate garden rooms taking advantage of the landscape. Soft fruit and vegetable areas and small potting shed. Pendene: created in 1999 then extended in 2007 this evolving garden has sweeping lawn, borders of mixed shrubs and herbaceous with spring bulbs, water features and plenty of early season colour; polytunnel and raised vegetable beds. Grassland with stands of mostly native trees at Orchard Court providing parking for both gardens provided ground dry otherwise parking on Green Hill with 50 yd walk up moderate incline. Well behaved dogs on leads welcome in grassland area but not in gardens. Regret neither garden suitable for wheelchairs or those with impaired mobility.

---

66 LEE FORD

Knowle Village, Budleigh Salterton, EX9 7AJ. Mr & Mrs N Lindsay-Fynn, 01395 445894, crescent@leeford.co.uk, www.leeford.co.uk/. *3½m E of Exmouth. For SatNav use postcode EX9 6AL.* **Visits by arrangement Mar to Oct, groups of 20+ discount, adm £5. Refreshments for groups of 10+, coffee/tea & cake, cream teas. Home-made teas. Numbers and special dietary requests must be pre-booked.** Donation to Lindsay-Fynn Trust.

Extensive, formal and woodland garden, largely developed in 1950s, but recently much extended with mass displays of camellias, rhododendrons and azaleas, incl many rare varieties. Traditional walled garden filled with fruit and vegetables, herb garden, bog garden, rose garden, hydrangea collection, greenhouses. Ornamental conservatory with collection of pot plants. Lee Ford has direct access to the Pedestrian route and National Cycle Network route 2 which follows the old railway line that linked Exmouth to Budleigh Salterton. Garden is ideal destination for cycle clubs or rambling groups. Formal gardens are lawn with gravel paths. Moderately steep slope to woodland garden on tarmac with gravel paths in woodland.

67 LEWIS COTTAGE

Spreyton, nr Crediton, EX17 5AA. Mr & Mrs M Pell and Mr R Orton, 07773 785939, rworton@mac.com, www.lewiscottageplants.co.uk. *5m NE of Spreyton, 8m W of Crediton. From Hillerton Cross, keep Stone Cross to your R. Drive approx 1½m, Lewis Cottage on L, proceed across cattle grid down farm track. From Crediton follow A377 to Barnstaple for 1m turn L at NGS sign.* **Sat 26, Sun 27, Mon 28 May, Sat 23, Sun 24 June, Sat 21, Sun 22 July, Sat 25, Sun 26, Mon 27 Aug (11-5). Adm £4.50, chd free. Light refreshments. Home made cakes and savoury tarts, tea and coffee available. Visits also by arrangement May to Sept, groups welcome (max 20), garden talks given or Q&A sessions if required.**

Located on SW-facing slope in rural Mid Devon, the 4 acre garden at Lewis Cottage has evolved primarily over the last 25 yrs, harnessing and working with the natural landscape. Using informal planting and natural formal structures to create a garden that reflects the souls of those who garden in it, it is an incredibly personal space that is a joy to share. Spring camassia cricket pitch, Rose garden, large natural dew pond, woodland walks, bog garden, hornbeam rondel planted with late flowering narcissi, newly planted winter garden, hot and cool herbaceous borders, picking garden, outdoor poetry reading room and small plant nursery. Featured on BBC Gardeners World and in Devon Life. Wheelchairs/ motorised buggies not advised due to garden being on a slope (though many have successfully tried!).

68 NEW LINDEN RISE

Chapel Lane, Combe Martin, Ilfracombe, EX34 0HJ. Professor Chris & Jenny Sheppard. *In Combe Martin high street turn R at old PO on to Chapel lane and LInden RIse is on R opp Hollands park where parking is available.* **Sun 25 Mar, Sun 15 July (2-5). Adm £4, chd free. Home-made teas.**

In an area of outstanding natural beauty with countryside and sea views, 1½ acre garden of lawns, mature trees and shrubs. Children's play area, pergola, decorative ponds, small orchard and seasonal flower borders. Plenty of early spring colour and a great variety of daffodils. Tarmacadam drive with wheelchair access to most areas.

69 LITTLE ASH BUNGALOW

Fenny Bridges, Honiton, EX14 3BL. Helen & Brian Brown, 01404 850941, helenlittleash@hotmail.com, www.facebook.com/littleashgarden. *3m W of Honiton. Leave A30 at Iron Bridge from Honiton 1m, Patteson's Cross from Exeter ½m and follow NGS signs.* **Sat 9 June, Sun 19 Aug (1-5). Adm £4, chd free. Light refreshments. Visits also by arrangement June to Oct for groups of 10+.**

Country garden of 1½ acres, packed with different and unusual herbaceous perennials, trees, shrubs and bamboos. Designed for yr-round interest, wildlife and owners' pleasure. Naturalistic planting in colour coordinated mixed borders, highlighted by metal sculptures, provides a backdrop to the view. Natural stream, pond and damp woodland area, mini wildlife meadows and raised gravel/alpine garden. Grass paths.

70 LITTLE DORWEEKE

Silverton, Exeter, EX5 4BZ. Helen & Paul Cooper. *From Exeter take the A396 towards Tiverton. Take R turn signed Butterleigh. Property approx 1½m up rd on R.* **Sat 19, Sun 20 May (11-5). Adm £4, chd free. Home-made teas.**

2 acre garden nestling in valley beside stream and surrounding thatched Devon longhouse. Developed over 45 years from original smallholding. Many areas, incl koi, lily and natural ponds, bog area and vegetable garden. The natural planting includes mature trees and shrubs with many rhododendrons and azaleas to provide all yr round colour. A wildlife haven.

The National Garden Scheme is committed to helping unpaid carers

71 LITTLE WEBBERY

Webbery, Bideford, EX39 4PS. Mr & Mrs J A Yewdall, 01271 858206, jyewdall1@gmail.com. *2m E of Bideford. From Bideford (East the Water) along Alverdiscott Rd, or from Barnstaple to Torrington on B3232. Take rd to Bideford at Alverdiscott, pass through Stoney Cross.* **Visits by arrangement May to Sept. Adm £4, chd free. Home-made teas.**

Approx 3 acres in valley setting with pond, lake, mature trees, 2 ha-has and large mature raised border. Large walled kitchen garden with yew and box hedging incl rose garden, lawns with shrubs and rose and clematis trellises. Vegetables and greenhouse and adj traditional cottage garden. Partial wheelchair access.

72 LOWER SPITCHWICK GARDEN

Poundsgate, TQ13 7NU. Pauline Lee, 01364 631593, paulineleeceramics@hotmail.com. *4m NW of Ashburton. By Spitchwick Common, nr New Bridge, Dartmoor.* **Sat 19, Sun 20 May, Sat 28, Sun 29 July (11-5). Adm £4, chd free. Home-made teas. Visits also by arrangement May to Sept.**

Beautiful valley alongside R Dart. East Lower Lodge: atmospheric woodland garden with imaginative planting in natural setting. Contains jungle area with bamboo teahouse, meandering grass pathways, lawns, borders with stream, potager and vegetable garden. Artist/ designer's gallery garden showing plant inspired sculpture placed in and amongst plantings to create a symphony of forms, colour and texture. Visitors can buy or commission directly from the artist. Partial wheelchair access.

73 ◆ LUKESLAND

Harford, Ivybridge, PL21 0JF. Mrs R Howell and Mr & Mrs J Howell, 01752 691749, lorna.lukesland@gmail.com, www.lukesland.co.uk. *10m E of Plymouth. Turn off A38 at Ivybridge. 1½m N on Harford rd, E side of Erme valley.* For opening times and information, please phone, email or visit garden website.

24 acres of flowering shrubs, wild flowers and rare trees with pinetum in Dartmoor National Park. Beautiful setting of small valley around Addicombe Brook with lakes, numerous waterfalls and pools. Extensive and impressive collections of camellias, rhododendrons, azaleas and acers; also spectacular Magnolia campbellii and huge Davidia involucrata. Superb spring and autumn colour. Children's trail. Open Suns, Weds and BH (11-5) 25 March - 10 June and 7 Oct - 11 November. Adm £5, chd free. Partial wheelchair access incl tearoom and WC.

74 MARSHALL FARM

Ide, nr Exeter, EX2 9TN. Jenny Tuckett. *Between Ide and Dunchideock. Drive through Ide to top of village r'about, straight on for 1½m. Turn R onto concrete drive, parking in farmyard at rear of property.* **Fri 8, Sun 10 June (1-5). Adm £3, chd free. Home-made teas.** Donation to Spinal Injuries Association.

Garden approached along lane lined with home grown lime, oak and chestnut trees. A country garden created approx 1967. One acre featuring wild flower gardens, gravel beds, pond, parterre garden and a vegetable and cutting garden. Stunning views of Woodbury, Sidmouth gap and Haldon. Limited wheelchair access.

Green Hedges, Bovey Tracey Gardens

75 ◆ MARWOOD HILL GARDEN

Marwood, EX31 4EB. Dr J A Snowdon, 01271 342528, info@marwoodhillgarden.co.uk, www.marwoodhillgarden.co.uk. *4m N of Barnstaple. Signed from A361 & B3230. Look out for brown signs. See website for map and directions. Coach & Car park.* **For NGS: Fri 15 June (10-4.30). Adm £7, chd £3. Light refreshments. Garden Tea Room offers selection of light refreshments throughout the day, all home-made or locally sourced delicious food to suit most tastes.** For other opening times and information, please phone, email or visit garden website.

Marwood Hill is a very special private garden covering an area of 20 acres with lakes and set in a valley tucked away in N Devon. From early spring snowdrops through to late autumn there is always a colourful surprise around every turn. National Collections of astilbe, iris ensata and tulbaghia, large collections of camellia, rhododendron and magnolia. Winner of MacLaren Cup at rhododendron and camellia show RHS Rosemoor. Articles in The English Garden. Partial wheelchair access.

NPC

76 NEW MIDDLE WELL

Waddeton Road, Stoke Gabriel, Totnes, TQ9 6RL. Neil & Pamela Millward, 01803 782981, neilandpamela@talktalk.net. *A385 from Totnes towards Paignton, R at Riviera Motors signed Stoke Gabriel. Straight on for 1m to Four Cross. Straight across. From A380, R at A385 toward Totnes, L in 400m, L at Four Cross.* **Visits by arrangement Mar to Oct, groups/individuals welcome. Soup lunches, tea/coffee/cakes by arrangement. Coach parking 400yds. Adm £4, chd free. Home-made teas.**

2 acre garden plus woodland and streams contain a wealth of interesting plants chosen for colour, form and long season of interest. Many seating places from which to enjoy the vistas. Interesting structural features (rill, summerhouse, pergola, cobbling, slate bridge). Heady mix of exciting perennials, shrubs, bulbs, climbers and specimen trees. Vegetable garden. Child friendly. Featured in Totnes Times and on The Breeze radio. Mostly accessible by wheelchair.

77 THE MILL HOUSE

Fremington, Barnstaple, EX31 3DQ. Martin & Judy Ash, 01271 344719, martin_s_ash@yahoo.co.uk. *3m W of Barnstaple. Off A39, take A3125 N. At 3rd r'about (Cedars) L on B3233. In Fremington L at top of Church Hill onto Higher Rd. All parking signed 100m away.* **Sun 27 May, Sun 17 June (12-5). Adm £4, chd free. Home-made teas. Visits also by arrangement May to Sept, 25 max.**

¾ acre garden, surrounding thatched mill house and bordered by Fremington water; the topography is the first wow factor here. Stepped ups and downs, ins and outs, surprises around every corner. There is so much on a small scale; bridges, borders, ponds, walkways, rockery, terracing, lawns, bog garden, quarry garden, wild garden, a small gallery, oh and a henge. Wandering minstrels!

78 MONKSCROFT

Zeal Monachorum, Crediton, EX17 6DG. Mr & Mrs Ken and Jane Hogg. *Lane opp Church.* **Sat 31 Mar, Sun 1 Apr (11-5). Adm £3.50, chd free. Cream teas.**

Pretty, medium sized garden of oldest cottage in village. Packed with spring colours, primroses, primulas, daffodils, tulips, magnolias and camellias. Views to far hills. Also tranquil fishing lake with daffodils and wild flowers in beautiful setting, home to resident kingfisher. Steep walk to lake approx 20mins, or 5mins by car. Dogs on leads welcome. Parking and WC at lake.

GROUP OPENING

79 MORETONHAMPSTEAD GARDENS

Moretonhampstead, TQ13 8PW. *12m W of Exeter, 12m N of Newton Abbot. Signs from the Xrd of A382 and B3212. On E slopes of Dartmoor National Park. Parking at both gardens.* **Fri 18, Sat 19, Sun 20 May, Sat 18, Sun 19 Aug (2-6). Combined adm £6, chd free. Home-made teas at both gardens.**

MARDON
Graham & Mary Wilson.

SUTTON MEAD
Edward & Miranda Allhusen, 01647 440296, miranda@allhusen.co.uk.
Visits also by arrangement, coach possible, short walk from main rd.

2 large gardens close to moorland town. One in a wooded valley, the other higher up with magnificent views of Dartmoor. Dogs on leads welcome. Plant sale, teas are a must. Both have mature orchards and yr round vegetable gardens. Substantial rhododendron, azalea and tree planting, croquet lawns, summer colour and woodland walks through hydrangeas and acers. Something for all the family. Mardon: 4 acres based on its original Edwardian design. Long herbaceous border, rose garden and formal granite terraces supporting 2 borders of agapanthus. Fernery beside stream-fed pond with its thatched boathouse. Arboretum with 60 specimen trees. Sutton Mead: Paths wander through tranquil woodland, unusual planting. Lawns surrounding granite-lined pond with seat at water's edge. Elsewhere dahlias, grasses, bog garden, rill-fed round pond, secluded seating and an unusual concrete greenhouse. Sedum roofed summerhouse. A garden of variety. Featured in Daily Telegraph, Radio Devon. Limited wheelchair access.

80 THE MOUNT, DELAMORE

Cornwood, Ivybridge, PL21 9QP. Mr & Mrs Gavin Dollard. *Delamore Park PL21 9QP. Please park in car park for Delamore Park Offices not in village. From Ivybridge turn L at Xrds keep PH on L, follow wall on R to sharp R bend, turn R.* **Sat 17, Sun 18 Feb (11-3). Adm £4.50, chd free.**

Welcome one of the first signs of spring by wandering through swathes of thousands of unusual varieties of snowdrops in this lovely wood. Closer to the village than to Delamore gardens (open only in May for the Sculpture and Art Exhibition), paths meander through a sea of these lovely plants, some of which are unique to Delamore and which were sold as posies to Covent Garden as late as 2002. Main house and garden open for sculpture exhibition every day in May. mainly rough paths/woodland tracks so difficult wheelchair access.

81 NEW MUSBURY BARTON

Musbury, Axminster, EX13 8BB. Lt Col Anthony Drake, 01297 552255, Ajmdrake@btinternet.com. *3m S of Axminster off A358. Turn E into village, follow yellow arrows. Garden next to church, parking for 12 cars, otherwise park on road in village.* **Sat 30 June, Sun 1 July (1.30-5). Adm £5, chd free. Home-made teas. Tea proceeds to Musbury Church. Visits also by arrangement Mar to Oct.**

5 acres. Formal rose garden. Extensive areas of trees and shrubs, many rare or unusual. Stream. Pond. Lots of steps and bridges. Never perfect, always interesting.

82 MUSSELBROOK COTTAGE GARDEN

Sheepwash, Beaworthy, EX21 5PE. Richard Coward, 01409 231677, coward.richard@sky.com. *1.4m N of Sheepwash. Leave Okehampton joining A386 going N. L onto A3072 in Hatherleigh. R in Highampton to Sheepwash. 1.6m after Sheepwash sign, turn L onto farm track signed Lake Farm. Take L fork. Cottage on R.* **Visits by arrangement Apr to Oct late afternoon, evening visits possible. Adm £4, chd free. Tea.**

1 acre naturalistic/wildlife/plantsman's garden of all season interest. Many rare/unusual plants on sloping site. 9 ponds (koi, orfe, lilies). Stream, Japanese gdn, oriental features, Mediterranean gdn, wildflower meadow, clock golf, 1000s of bulbs. Many ericaceous plants incl acers, rhododendron, magnolias. Euphorbia, diorama, crocosmia, grasses . Aquatic nursery incl lilies. Planting extremely labour intensive - ground is full of rocks. A mattock soon became my indispensable tool, even for planting bulbs.

83 THE OLD VICARAGE

West Anstey, South Molton, EX36 3PE. Tuck & Juliet Moss, 01398 341604, julietm@onetel.com. *9m E of South Molton. From S Molton go E on B3227 to Jubilee Inn. From Tiverton r'about take A396 7m to B3227 then L to Jubilee Inn. Follow NGS signs to garden.* **Sat 12, Sun 13 May, Sat 11, Sun 12 Aug (12-5). Adm £4.50, chd free. Cream teas. Visits also by arrangement May to Aug, coach turning and parking is available.**

Croquet lawn leads to multi-level garden overlooking 3 large ponds with winding paths, climbing roses and overviews. Brook with waterfall flows through garden past fascinating summerhouse built by owner. Benched deck overhangs first pond. Features rhododendrons, azaleas and primulas in spring and large collection of Japanese iris in July and wonderful hydrangeas in August. New wall fountain mounted on handsome, traditional dry wall above house. Access by path through kitchen garden. A number of smaller standing stones echoing local Devon tradition.

84 THE OLDE COTTAGE

Dippertown, Lewdown, Okehampton, EX20 4PT. Emma Bending & Joe Baker, bendinge@yahoo.com. *8m E of Launceston signed off West Devon Drive. From Exeter follow A30 dual carriageway W, passing Okehampton. Turn off at Sourton, signed Tavistock. Bottom of slip road turn R and then immediately L, signed Lewdown. From Lewdown follow signs.* **Sat 7, Sun 8 July (11-4). Adm £5, chd free. Home-made teas. All home made cakes, scones and biscuits. Visits by arrangement in July (6th July only). Adm £5, chd free. Home-made teas.**

Attractive cottage garden set in the tiny hamlet of Dippertown. A range of mixed borders full of traditional cottage plants and fruit wind their way up steeply to the top of the garden where a wildlife pond sits, encouraging you stop and view the sweep of interesting trees and shrubs that lead to a more formal lawned area. Productive kitchen garden of stepped raised beds and soft fruit. Not good access for wheelchairs.

85 PARK HOUSE

Liddaton, Coryton, Okehampton, EX20 4AB. Mr Roger Jennings. *9m outside Tavistock and near Brentor. From A386, turn R at Dartmoor Inn, follow signs for Brentor and Tavistock and look for yellow signs. From A30 dual carriageway get to Lewdown, follow signs from there.* **Sat 7, Sun 8 July (11-5). Adm £5, chd free. Home-made teas.**

Situated in the beautiful Lyd Valley this is an attractive 3 acre garden in two parts. Walk through banks of unusual and interesting planting combinations to a meadow with stunning views of Dartmoor and meandering mown paths leading to vibrant, traditional herbaceous borders, running water, a productive greenhouse and orchard. Not good wheelchair access.

Springfield House

86 ◆ **PLANT WORLD**
St Marychurch Road, Newton Abbot, TQ12 4SE. Ray Brown, 01803 872939, raybrown@plant-world-seeds.com, www.plant-world-gardens.co.uk. *2m SE of Newton Abbot. 1½m from Penn Inn turn-off on A380. Follow brown tourist signs at end of A380 dual carriageway from Exeter.* **For opening times and information, please phone, email or visit garden website.**
The 4 acres of landscape gardens with fabulous views have been called Devon's 'Little Outdoor Eden'. Representing each of the five continents, they offer an extensive collection of rare and exotic plants from around the world. Superb mature cottage garden and Mediterranean garden will delight the visitor. Attractive new viewpoint café and shop. Open April 1st to the end of Sept (9.30-5.00). Wheelchair access to café and nursery only.

87 PORTINGTON
Lamerton, PL19 8QY. Mr & Mrs I A Dingle. *3m NW of Tavistock. From Tavistock take rd past hospital to Lamerton. Beyond Lamerton L at Carrs garage. 1st R (signed Horsebridge), next L then L again. From Launceston turn R at Carrs garage then as above.* **Sun 13, Sun 20 May (3-5). Adm £3, chd free. Home-made teas.** Donation to The Lions Club of Plymouth.
Garden in peaceful rural setting with fine views over surrounding countryside. Mixed planting with shrubs and borders. Walk to a small lake through woodland and fields at bluebell time. Limited wheelchair access.

88 THE PRIORY
Priory Road, Abbotskerswell, Newton Abbot, TQ12 5PP. Priory Residents. *2m SW of Newton Abbot town centre. A381 Newton Abbot/ Totnes Rd. Sharp L turn from NA. R from Totnes. At mini r'about in village centre turn L into Priory Rd.* **Sat 30 June, Sun 1 July (1-5). Adm £5, chd free. Home-made teas.**
The Priory is a Grade II* listed building, originally a manor house extended in Victorian times as a home for an Augustinian order of nuns, now a retirement complex of 43 apartments and cottages. The grounds extend to approx 5 acres and incl numerous flower borders, a wild flower meadow, an area of woodland with some interesting specimen trees, cottage gardens and lovely views. Small Mediterranean garden and area of individually owned raised beds and greenhouses. Wheelchair access difficult when wet.

89 PROSPECT HOUSE
Lyme Road, Axminster, EX13 5BH. Peter Wadeley, 01297 631210, wadeley@btinternet.com. *½m uphill from centre of Axminster. Just before service station.* **Fri 31 Aug, Sat 1, Sun 2 Sept (1-5). Adm £4, chd free. Home-made teas. Visits also by arrangement May to Oct for groups of 10+.**
1 acre plantsman's garden hidden behind high stone walls with Axe Valley views. Well stocked borders with rare shrubs, many reckoned to be borderline tender. 200 varieties of salvia, and other late summer perennials incl rudbeckia, helenium, echinacea, helianthus, crocosmia and grasses creating a riot of colour. A gem, not to be missed. Artist Zee Jones will be showing and selling her work. Zee uses mixed media to produce contemporary colourful semi abstract paintings. In her own words, Zee tries to portray her intuitive understanding of the way colours work together and how they can affect emotion. Featured in Garden Answers magazine and Gardeners' World.

90 REGENCY HOUSE
Hemyock, EX15 3RQ. Mrs Jenny Parsons, 01823 680238, jenny.parsons@btinternet.com, www.regencyhousehemyock.co.uk. *8m N of Honiton. M5 J26. From Catherine Wheel pub and church in Hemyock take Dunkeswell-Honiton Rd. Entrance ½m on R. Disabled parking (only) at house.* **Sun 17, Mon 18 June, Sun 14**

Oct (2-5.30). Adm £5, chd free. Home-made teas. Visits also by arrangement June to Oct, no coaches.
5 acre plantsman's garden approached across private ford. Many interesting and unusual trees and shrubs. Visitors can try their hand at identifying plants with the plant list or have a game of croquet. Plenty of space to eat your own picnic. Walled vegetable and fruit garden, lake, ponds, bog plantings and sweeping lawns. Horses, Dexter cattle and Jacob sheep. Gently sloping gravel paths give wheelchair access to the walled garden, lawns, borders and terrace, where teas are served.

91 RIVERFORD FIELD KITCHEN GARDEN

Wash Farm, Buckfastleigh, TQ11 0JU. Riverford Farm. *Take A384 between Totnes and Buckfastleigh. Take turning for Riverford Organic (not the Farm Shop) and follow yellow NGS signs.* **Sun 17 June, Sun 2 Sept (11-5). Adm £4, chd free. Home-made teas. Tasty refreshments, hot and cold drinks available all day. Booking essential for the Field Kitchen Restaurant 01803 762000.**
Impressive 4yr old large allotment style kitchen garden with enormous 60m x 9m polytunnel. Planted up with an interesting range of organic vegetables, herbs and flowers used to feed and beautify our two fantastic restaurants, the Field Kitchen here and the Duke of Cambridge, Islington, London. Come and be inspired to grow your own! Practical demos throughout the day. The head gardener will be here to welcome visitors and answer any questions.

92 ST MERRYN

Higher Park Road, Braunton, EX33 2LG. Dr W & Mrs Ros Bradford, 01271 813805, ros@st-merryn.co.uk. *5m W of Barnstaple. On A361, R at 30mph sign, then at mini r'about, R into Lower Park Rd, then L into Seven Acre Lane, at top of lane R into Higher Park Rd. Pink house 200 yds on R.* **Sun 15 Apr, Sun 20 May, Sun 17 June (2-5.30). Adm £4, chd free. Cream teas. Visits also by arrangement Apr to July for small groups, max 20.**
Very sheltered, peaceful, gently sloping, S-facing, artist's garden, emphasis on shape, colour, scent and yr-round interest. A garden for pleasure with swimming pool. Thatched summerhouse leading down to herbaceous borders. Winding crazy paving paths, many seating areas. Shrubs, mature trees, fish ponds, grassy knoll, gravel areas, hens. Many environmental features. Open gallery (arts & crafts).

93 SEDGEWELL COACH HOUSE GARDENS

Olchard, TQ12 3GU. Heather Jansch, www.heatherjansch.com. *4m N of Newton Abbot. 12m S of Exeter on A380, L for Olchard, straight ahead on private drive.* **Sat 28, Sun 29 Apr, Sat 5, Sun 6 May, Sat 25, Sun 26 Aug, Sat 1, Sun 2 Sept (11-5). Adm £4.50, chd free. Cream teas.**
Heather Jansch, world-famous sculptor, brings innovative use of recycled materials to gardening. 14 acres incl stunning driftwood sculpture, fabulous views from thrilling woodland bluebell trail down to timeless stream-bordered water meadow walk, pools, herbaceous border, medicinal herb garden. Plentiful seating, come and picnic. Most sculpture is on level areas near the house. Limited disabled parking but there is a drop off point. Sorry no wheelchair accessible WC.

94 SHAPCOTT BARTON KNOWSTONE ESTATE

(East Knowstone Manor), East Knowstone, South Molton, EX36 4EE. Anita Allen, 01398 341664. *13m NW of Tiverton. J25 M5 take Tiverton exit. 6½m to r'about take exit South Molton 10m on A361. Turn R signed Knowstone. Leave A361 travel ¼m to Roachhill through hamlet turn L at Wiston Cross, entrance on L ¼m.* **Wed 4, Sun 8, Sun 15 Apr, Wed 18, Sun 22, Thur 26, Sun 29 July (10.30-4.30). Adm £4, chd free. Home-made teas on Suns when fine. Visits also by arrangement Apr to Aug.** For other opening times and information, please phone. Donation to Cats Protection.
Large, ever developing garden of 200 acre estate around ancient historic manor house. Wildlife garden. Restored old fish ponds, stream and woodland rich in bird life. Unusual fruit orchard. Scented historic narcissi bulbs in Apr. Flowering burst July/Aug of National Plant Collections Leucanthemum superbum (shasta daisies) and buddleja davidii. Many butterfly plants incl over 40 varieties of phlox, fernery. Ghost talks. Dowsing lessons. Very limited wheelchair access, steep slopes.

NPC

95 SIDBURY MANOR

Sidmouth, EX10 0QE. Sir John & Lady Cave, www.sidburymanor.co.uk. *1m NW of Sidbury. Sidbury village is on A375, S of Honiton, N of Sidmouth.* **Fri 13, Sun 15 Apr (2-5). Adm £5, chd free. Home-made teas.**
Built in 1870s this Victorian manor house built by owner's family and set within E Devon AONB comes complete with 20 acres of garden incl substantial walled gardens, extensive arboretum containing many fine trees and shrubs, a number of champion trees, and areas devoted to magnolias, rhododendrons and camellias. Partial wheelchair access.

GROUP OPENING

96 NEW SIDMOUTH AUGUST GARDENS

Sidmouth, EX10 9DX. *From Exeter on A3052 10m. R at Woolbrook Rd. In ½m R at St Francis Ch.. Fr. Exeter on A3052 11m R at Sidford T-Lights. ¾m turn L at Coulsdon Rd. Fr Exeter 10m L. B3174 1½m R. Broadway, 1st L.* **Sat 25, Sun 26, Mon 27 Aug (1.30-5.30). Combined adm £5, chd free. Home-made teas at Byes Reach and 21 Coulsdon Rd EX10 9JJ (No refreshments at Fairpark & Rowan Bank). Gluten free, lactose free cakes available.**

BYES REACH
26 Coulsdon Road, EX10 9JP. Lynette Talbot & Peter Endersby.

NEW **21 COULSDON ROAD**
EX10 9JJ. Denise Rendell.

NEW **FAIRPARK**
Knowle Drive, EX10 8HP. Helen & Ian Crackston.

ROWAN BANK
44 Woolbrook Park, EX10 9DX. Barbara Mence.

Situated on Jurassic Coast World Heritage Site, Sidmouth has fine beaches, beautiful gardens and magnificent coastal views. 4 contrasting ¼ acre gardens 1m apart. Byes Reach: edible garden, potager beds, espalier fruit archway, colour-themed flower beds, herbs ferns, hosts, pond, rill rockery, greenhouses, studio. Backs onto nature reserve with walks. Rowan Bank is NW facing, sloping, generously planted with trees, shrubs, perennials, bulbs. Steps lead to wide zigzag path leading to woodland and Mexican pine. Seats and summerhouse. Fairpark lies behind a 12ft red brick wall, terraces, rockery, impressionist palette of colour, texture, many acres, small woodland and greenhouse. 21 Coulsdon is evolving, a cottage garden meeting minimalist design. Grasses punctuate blocks of colour, raised beds, willow creatures, seating areas. No wheelchair access at Rowan Bank and Fairpark.

GROUP OPENING

97 SIDMOUTH JUNE GARDENS

Sidmouth, EX10 9DX. *Sidmouth. For Rowan Bank from Exeter on A3052 10m. R at Woolbrook Rd. In ½m R at St Francis church. For Byes Reach from Exeter on A3052 11m. R at Sidford T-lights. In ¾m turn L into Coulsdon Rd.* **Sat 9, Sun 10 June (1.30-5.30). Combined adm £4, chd free. Home-made teas at Byes Reach only. Gluten free available.**

BYES REACH
26 Coulsdon Rd, EX10 9JP. Lynette Talbot & Peter Endersby, 01395 578081, latalbot01@gmail.com. **Visits also by arrangement 5 May to 2 Sept for groups of 6-20.**

ROWAN BANK
44 Woolbrook Park, EX10 9DX. Barbara Mence.

Situated on Jurassic Coast World Heritage Site, Sidmouth has fine beaches, beautiful gardens and magnificent coastal views. 2 contrasting gardens about 1m apart. Byes Reach: edible garden of ⅕ acre. Potager style, raised beds, espalier fruit trees on arched walkway, designed for those with mobility problems. Herbaceous borders, colour themed flower beds combining perennials, herbs, ferns and hostas. Pond, rockery, greenhouse and studio. Backing onto The Byes nature reserve and R Sid, offering an opportunity for a short walk from the garden gate. Rowan Bank is approx ¼ acre on a NW facing slope, generously planted with trees, shrubs, perennials and bulbs for yr-round interest. Steps lead to an easy, wide zigzag path rising gently to woodland edge of birch and rowan, with shady bench under Mexican pine. Seats at every corner and summerhouse looking towards wooded hills. Wheelchair access at Byes Reach, regret none at Rowan Bank.

98 SOCKS ORCHARD

Smallridge, Axminster, EX13 7JN. Michael & Hilary Pritchard, 01297 33693, michael.j.pritchard@btinternet.com. *2m from Axminster. From Axminster on A358 L at Weycroft Mill T-lights. Pass Ridgeway Hotel on L. Continue on lane for ½m. Park in field opp.* **Fri 13, Sat 14, Sun 15 July (1-5). Adm £4, chd free. Home-made teas. Visits also by arrangement Mar to Sept for small groups up to 30 with car sharing.**

1 acre plus plantaholic's garden designed for yr-round structure and colour. Many specimen trees, large collection of herbaceous plants, over 200 roses, woodland shrubs, dahlias, gravel and grass borders, small orchard, vegetable patch, small pond. Steep bank inset with shrubs underplanted with wild flowers (ongoing project). Chickens. Limited wheelchair access.

99 SOUTH WOOD FARM

Cotleigh, Honiton, EX14 9HU. Professor Clive Potter, williamjamessmithson@gmail.com. *3m NE of Honiton. From Honiton head N on A30, take 1st R past Otter Dairy layby. Follow for 1m. Go straight over Xrds and take first L. Entrance after 1m on R.* **Sat 16, Sun 17 June (2-5). Adm £5, chd free. Home-made teas. Visits also by arrangement May to Sept for groups of 15+, guided tours of garden.**

Designed by the renowned Arne Maynard around C17 thatched farmhouse, this country garden in the Blackdown Hills exemplifies how contemporary design can be integrated into a traditional setting. Herbaceous borders, roses, yew topiary, knot garden, wildflower meadows, orchards, lean-to greenhouses and a mouthwatering kitchen garden combine to create an unforgettable sense of place.

Featured in Country Life. Gravel pathways, cobbles and steps.

GROUP OPENING

100 SOUTHCOMBE GARDENS

Dartmoor, Widecombe-in-the-Moor, TQ13 7TU. 01364 621332, amandasabin1@hotmail.com. *6m W of Bovey Tracey. B3387 from Bovey Tracey after village church take rd SW for 400yds then sharp R signed Southcombe, after 200yds pass C17 farmhouse and park on L.* **Sun 27, Mon 28 May, Sun 3, Sun 10, Sun 17, Sun 24 June, Sun 1 July (2-5). Combined adm £5, chd free. Home-made teas at Southcombe Barn. Southcombe cakes are lavish, adventurous and lovely.**

SOUTHCOMBE BARN
Amanda Sabin & Stephen Hobson, 01364 621332, amandasabin1@hotmail.com. **Visits also by arrangement May & June.**

SOUTHCOMBE HOUSE
Dr & Mrs J R Seale.

Village famous for its fair, Uncle Tom Cobley and its C14 church - the Cathedral of the Moor. Featured in RHS The Garden. Southcombe Barn: 4 acres, trees and drifts of flowers, abundantly wild and intensely colourful. Beautiful all yr-round and busy with wildlife but this is its zenith 6 weeks of breathtaking glory. You can spend hours in it. People do. Southcombe House: 5 acres, SE-facing garden, arboretum and orchid rich restored wild flower meadow with bulbs in spring and four orchid species (early purple, southern marsh, common spotted and greater butterfly). On steep slope at 900ft above sea level with fine views to nearby tors. The teas are legendary. People starting their own wild flower meadows have used Southcombe House seed-rich fresh-cut hay to seed their newly cleared ground. Yellow rattle is then usually abundant in 1st year and orchids begin to appear in the 4th year. With a bit of a bumpy 100yds along the flat and then 1 step wheelchair users can access the tea lawn and look down on some of the garden.

102 SPRINGFIELD HOUSE

Seaton Road, Colyford, EX24 6QW. Wendy Pountney, 01297 552481, pountneys@talktalk.net. *Colyford. Starting on A3052 coast rd, at Colyford PO take Seaton Rd. House 500m on R. Ample parking in field.* **Sat 2, Sat 30 June, Sun 29 July (10.30-5). Adm £4, chd free. Tea and cake/coffee/cream teas. Visits also by arrangement for groups, max 35.**

1 acre garden of mainly fairly new planting. Numerous beds, majority of plants from cuttings and seed keeping cost to minimum, full of colour spring to autumn. Vegetable garden, fruit cage and orchard with ducks and chicken. New large formal pond. Wonderful views over R Axe and bird sanctuary, which is well worth a visit, path leads from the garden. Featured in Amateur Gardening magazine.

103 SQUIRRELS

98 Barton Road, Torquay, TQ2 7NS. Graham & Carol Starkie, 01803 329241, calgra@talktalk.net. *5m S of Newton Abbot. From Newton Abbot take A380 to Torquay. After ASDA store on L, turn L at T-lights up Old Woods Hill. 1st L into Barton Rd. Bungalow 200yds on L. Also could turn by B&Q. Parking nearby.* **Sat 28, Sun 29 July (2-5). Adm £4, chd free. Home-made teas. Visits also by arrangement in July (14 July to 27 July).**

Plantsman's small town environmental garden, landscaped with small ponds and 7ft waterfall. Interlinked through abutilons to Japanese, Italianate, tropical areas. Specialising in fruit incl peaches, figs, kiwi. Tender plants incl bananas, tree fern, brugmansia, lantanas, oleanders. Mandevilla. Collections of fuchsia, abutilons, bougainvilleas, topiary and more. Enviromental and Superclass Winners. 27 cleverly hidden rain water storage containers. Advice on free electric from solar panels and solar hot water heating and fruit pruning. 3 sculptures. Many topiary birds, animals and balls. Huge 20ft Torbay palm. 9ft geranium. 15ft abutilons. Featured on Gardeners' World. Regret no wheelchair access. Conservatory for shelter and seating.

Abbotsford, Abbotskerswell Gardens

104 STONE FARM

Alverdiscott Rd, Bideford, EX39 4PN. Mr & Mrs Ray Auvray. *1½m from Bideford towards Alverdiscott. From Bideford cross river using Old Bridge and turn L onto Barnstaple Rd. 2nd R onto Manteo Way and 1st L at mini r'about.* **Sat 30 June, Sun 1 July, Sat 25, Sun 26 Aug (2-5). Adm £4, chd free. Home-made teas.**

1 acre country garden with striking herbaceous borders, dry stone wall terracing, white garden, dahlia bed, wild meadow area and woodland area. Extensive fully organic vegetable garden with raised beds, soft fruit cage and polytunnels, together with an orchard with traditional varieties of apples, pears and nuts. Some gravel paths but wheelchair access to whole garden with some help.

105 NEW STONELANDS HOUSE

Dawlish, EX7 9BQ. Mr Kerim Derhalli (Owner) Mr Saul Walker (Head Gardener), 07815 807832, saulwalkerstonelands@outlook.com. *Outskirts of NW Dawlish. From A380 take junction for B3192 and follow signs for Teignmouth, after 2m R at Xrds onto Luscombe Hill, further 2m main gate is on L.* **Visits by arrangement May to Sept, Weds only, for groups of 10-30. Please ring/email to book. Adm £5, chd free.**

Beautiful 12 acre pleasure garden surrounding late C18 property designed by John Nash. Mature specimen trees, shrubs and rhododendrons, large formal lawn, recently landscaped herbaceous beds, vegetable garden, woodland garden, orchard with wild-flower meadow and river walk. An atmospheric and delightful horticultural secret! Wheelchair access limited to lower area of gardens, paths through woodland, meadow and riverside walk may be unsuitable for wheelchairs.

106 SUMMERS PLACE

Little Bowlish, Whitestone, EX4 2HS. Mr & Mrs Stafford Charles, 01647 61786. *6m NW of Exeter. From M5, A30 Okehampton. After 7m R to Tedburn St Mary R at r'about past golf course 1st L after ½m signed Whitestone straight ahead at Xrds follow signs. From Exeter on Whitestone rd 1m beyond Whitestone, follow sign from Heath Cross. From Crediton follow Whitestone rd through Fordton.* **Sun 18 Mar, Sun 8 Apr (12-5); Sat 23 June (5-9); Sun 14 Oct (12-5). Adm £4.50, chd free. Lunches 12-1.45, soup and sandwiches. Home-made teas 2.15-4.30. Teas and barbecued sausages on 23 June. Visits also by arrangement Mar to Oct, 24 hrs notice required. Refreshments by arrangement.** Donation to Stroke Unit Royal Devon and Exeter Hospital.

Rambling rustic paths and steps (some steep) lead down a shaded woodland garden; unusual trees and shrubs (profusion of spring bulbs) to ornamental orchard (berries, fruit, hip, autumn colour) with follies, sculpture, stream and ponds. Conservation as important as horticulture (wild flowers). Intimate gardens round house. Nurseries attend. Willow sculptress with demos and sales table usually attends. Further new amusing features.

The Village Allotments, Willand Old Village Gardens & Allotments

GROUP OPENING

107 TEIGNMOUTH GARDENS

Ferndale Road, Teignmouth, TQ14 8NH. *½m from Teignmouth town centre. From Teignmouth town centre take A379 towards Dawlish for 9 The Rowdens (½m on R) and 65 Teignmouth Rd (1m on R). For Grosvenor Green Gdns and 26 Hazeldown Rd park in New Rd.* **Sat 23, Sun 24 June (1-5). Combined adm £5, chd free. Home-made teas. Teas at Grosvenor Green Gardens, 9 The Rowdens and 26 Hazeldown Rd.**

GROSVENOR GREEN GARDENS
Michelle & Neal Fairley, www.grosvenorgreengardens.co.uk.

26 HAZELDOWN ROAD
Mrs Ann Sadler.

65 TEIGNMOUTH ROAD
Mr Terry Rogers.

NEW **9 THE ROWDENS**
Mr Michael Brown.

A new garden joins the popular Teignmouth Gardens group in 2018. 9 The Rowdens uses its hillside setting to provide shelter for its mature fruit trees, pond, generous flower borders and a productive greenhouse. 26 Hazeldown Rd has an immaculate garden featuring clipped topiary and a large raised pond stocked with koi carp. At 65 Teignmouth Rd the lovely sea views are framed by plentiful flower beds planted with colourful and pollinator friendly plants. At Grosvenor Green the stunning ⅓ acre plantsman's garden has a cottage garden feel and incl naturalistic pond, large productive greenhouse, fruit trees and vegetable beds. Limited wheelchair access at 65 Teignmouth Rd and 26 Hazeldown Rd.

108 TORVIEW

44 Highweek Village, Newton Abbot, TQ12 1QQ. Ms Penny Hammond. *On N of Newton Abbot accessed via A38. From Plymouth: A38 to Goodstone, A383 past Hele Park, L onto Mile End Rd. From Exeter: A38 to Drumbridges then A382 past Forches X, R signed Highweek. R at top of hill. Locally take Highweek signs.* **Sat 28, Sun 29 Apr, Sat 11, Sun 12 Aug (12-5). Adm £4.50, chd free. Home-made teas.**

Run by 2 semi-retired horticulturists: formal Mediterranean front garden, with wisteria-clad Georgian house, small alpine house. Rear courtyard with tree ferns, pots/troughs, lean-to 7m conservatory with tender plants and climbers. Steps to 30x20m walled garden - flowers, vegetables and trained fruit. Shade tunnel of woodlanders. Many rare/unusual plants. Rear garden up 7 steps, pebble areas in front garden.

109 VENN CROSS ENGINE HOUSE

Venn Cross, Waterrow, Taunton, TA4 2BE. Kevin & Samantha Anning, 01398 361392, venncross@btinternet.com. *Devon/Somerset border. Use main B3227 between Bampton and Wiveliscombe.* **Sat 16, Sun 17 June, Sat 21, Sun 22 July, Sat 25, Sun 26 Aug (2-5.30). Adm £5, chd free. Home-made teas. Selection of gluten-free cakes also available. Visits also by arrangement May to Sept.**

Former GWR goods yard. 4 acres of formal and less formal gardens of interest to gardeners and railway buffs alike. An acre of orchid rich wild flower meadow. Areas of mass-planted candelabra primulas start the summer with many large sweeping herbaceous borders bursting into colour as the season progresses. Sculptures, streams, ponds, vegetable beds and woodland walk, railway relics and historic pictures. Featured on BBC Radio Devon. Wheelchair access to main areas.

110 NEW THE WALLED GARDEN, LINDRIDGE

Humber, Teignmouth, TQ14 9TE. Mr & Mrs Will Patterson. *12m S of Exeter. From B3192 turn alongside Teignmouth golf course to Gipsy Corner then follow signs for Bishopsteignton. After 1m, at Rowden Cross, turn R to Lindridge. Garden 0.7m further on L.* **Sat 21, Sun 22 July (2-5). Adm £5, chd free. Light refreshments. Home-made cakes.**

1 acre historical walled former kitchen garden of the Lindridge Park Estate, fallow for over 50 years. Now in 3rd yr of renovation, the garden has a geometric layout, lawns, mixed borders, juvenile hedges, trained fruit trees, wild flower meadow, ponds, woodland area, set in attractive countryside with far reaching views. Managed on an organic basis to provide a haven for wildlife. Sloping site with gravel and woodchip paths. Some steps. Limited accessible parking.

111 WHITSTONE BLUEBELLS

Bovey Tracey, Newton Abbot, TQ13 9NA. 01626 832258, katie@whitstonefarm.co.uk. *Whitstone Lane. From A382 turn towards hospital (sign opp golf range), after ⅓m L at swinging sign 'Private road leading to Whitstone'. Follow NGS signs.* **Sun 29 Apr (2-5). Combined adm £5, chd free. Home-made teas at Whitstone Farm. Tea/coffee/home-made cakes incl gluten free option. Visits also by arrangement Apr & May Whitstone Farm only.**

Stunning spring garden with far reaching views over Dartmoor. Bluebells throughout the garden along with camellias, rhododendrons and magnolias. Display of architectural metal sculptures and ornaments.

112 WHITSTONE FARM

Whitstone Lane, Bovey Tracey, TQ13 9NA. Katie & Alan Bunn, 01626 832258, katie@whitstonefarm.co.uk. *½m N of Bovey Tracey. From A382 turn towards hospital (sign opp golf range), after ⅓m L at swinging sign 'Private road leading to Whitstone'. Follow NGS signs.* **Sun 29 July (2-5). Adm £5, chd free. Tea and home-made cakes, gluten free option. Visits also by arrangement May to Sept for group and society tours.**

Nearly 4 acres of steep hillside garden with stunning views of Haytor and Dartmoor. Arboretum planted 40 yrs ago, over 200 trees from all over the world incl magnolias, camellias, acers, alders, betula, davidias and sorbus. Major plantings of rhododendron and cornus. Late summer opening for flowering eucryphias and hydrangeas. National Collection of Eucryphias. Beautiful yr-round garden.

113 WICK FARM GARDENS

Cookbury, Holsworthy, EX22 6NU. Martin & Jenny Sexton. *3m E of Holsworthy. From Holsworthy take Hatherleigh Rd for 2m, L at Anvil Corner, ¼m then R to Cookbury, garden 1½m on L.* **Sun 20, Sun 27, Mon 28 May (11.30-6). Adm £5, chd free. Light lunches, home-made cakes, cream teas.**

8 acre pleasure garden around Victorian farmhouse arranged in rooms with many attractive features. Fernery, ornamental pond, borders, sculptures, oriental garden with stone bell, lake with carp. Plants in long border to attract butterflies and bees. Crocosmia, croquet lawn, tropical oasis, stone henge with sacrificial stone, arboretum with over 300 trees, flowering cherries, rhododendrons and azaleas. Woodland bluebell walk 1m. Some gravel paths, motor wheelchair friendly. Woodland not suitable for wheelchairs.

GROUP OPENING

114 WILLAND OLD VILLAGE GARDENS & ALLOTMENTS

Willand Old Village, Cullompton, EX15 2RH. *From J27 or J28 of M5 follow signs B3181 to Willand. Turn at PO sign, gardens approx 200 yds, follow yellow signs. Parking in village & at Allotments (EX15 2RG) yellow signs off B3181.* **Sat 9, Sun 10 June (2-5.30). Combined adm £5, chd free. Home-made teas.**

4 BUTTERCUP ROAD
John & Sally Holmes.

8 BUTTERCUP ROAD
Julie De-Ath-Lancaster.

CHURCH LEA
Mrs D Anderson.

NEW **COOMBE COURT**
Mrs Bernice Philbrick.

NEW **THE OLD RECTORY**
Chris Borne.

THE VILLAGE ALLOTMENTS
c/o Mrs S. Statham.

The gardens and allotments and award-winning composting scheme which make up the group offer a mix from small gardens to larger ones in different parts of the village. All show what can be achieved in a more limited space, whilst meeting various owners' needs e.g. wheelchair user, and providing yr-round interest and colour. Each garden reflects differing interests and tastes. The allotment plots demonstrate a wide range of skills and production methods. St. Mary's Church and churchyard is open and interesting to explore. We can promise visitors a welcoming, full, and varied afternoon whether you plan to walk the trail or park and re-park. You can take refreshments on the way round. Start points will be indicated. Gardens, village and church have good accessibility for wheelchair users with modest slopes and few changes of level. Allotments have partial access.

115 ◆ WINSFORD WALLED GARDEN

Halwill Junction, EX21 5XT. Dugald & Adel Stark, 01409 221477, dugald@dugaldstark.co.uk, www.winsfordwalledgarden.org.uk. *10m NW of Okehampton. On A3079 follow brown tourism signs from centre of Halwill Junction (1m). Straight on through Anglers Paradise and then follow yellow NGS signs.* **For NGS: Sat 16, Sun 17 June (10-5). Adm £5, chd free. Cream teas.** For other opening times and information, please phone, email or visit garden website.

Historic walled gardens, redesigned and brimming with colourful, tall and lush planting. Large restored Victorian glasshouses and romantic ruins. Extensive mature bamboo grove. Giant pergola, fruit, vegetable and herb areas. Home of the painter, Dugald Stark. Studio open. Visits also by prior arrangement, groups welcome. Access is very good.

116 WOOD BARTON

Kentisbeare, EX15 2AT. Mrs Rosemary Horton, 01884 266285. *8m SE of Tiverton, 3m E of Cullompton. 3m from M5 J28. A373 Cullompton to Honiton. 2m L to Bradfield/Willand, Horn Rd. After 1m at Xrds turn R. Farm drive ½m on L. Bull on sign.* **Sun 1, Mon 2 Apr, Sun 6, Mon 7 May (2.30-5.30). Adm £5, chd free. Home-made teas. Visits also by arrangement Mar to Oct entry incl tea/biscuits. Small buses only (max 30). Also Evening visits with wine & nibbles £10/head.**

Established 2 acre arboretum with species trees on S-facing slope. Magnolias, 2 davidia, azaleas, camellias, rhododendrons, acers; several ponds and water feature. Autumn colour. New planting of woodland trees and bluebells opp house (this part not suitable for wheelchairs but dogs are welcome here). Sculptures and profiles in bronze resin plus new sculptures this year. Small Japanese garden.

117 YONDER HILL

Shepherds Lane, Colaton Raleigh, Sidmouth, EX10 0LP. Judy McKay, Eddie Stevenson, Sharon Attrell, Bob Chambers, 07864 055532, judy@yonderhill.me.uk, www.yonderhill.org.uk. *4m N of Budleigh Salterton B3178 between Newton Poppleford and Colaton Raleigh. Take turning signed to Dotton and immed R into Shepherds Lane, ¼m 1st R at top of hill opp public footpath.* **Sun 1, Mon 2, Sun 8, Sun 15, Sun 22, Sun 29 Apr, Sun 6, Mon 7, Sun 13, Sun 20, Sun 27, Mon 28 May, Sun 3, Sun 10, Sun 17, Sun 24 June, Sun 1, Sun 8, Sun 15, Sun 22, Sun 29 July, Sun 5, Sun 12, Sun 19, Sun 26, Mon 27 Aug, Sun 2 Sept (1.30-4.30). Adm £3.50, chd £1. Light refreshments. Good selection of teas and coffee (make it yourself as you like it) and biscuits. Picnics welcome. Visits also by arrangement Apr to Aug for groups up to 30. No minimum number.**

Enjoy a warm welcome to 3½ acres planted with love. Blazing herbaceous borders buzzing with insects, cool woods and sunny glades alive with birdsong, rustling bamboos, Eucalyptus, grasses, conifer and fern collections. Rare plants, unusual planting, wildlife ponds, wild flower meadow, lots of benches. New features. and planting for 2018. This garden will awaken your senses and soothe your soul. Garden attracts great variety of birds, insects and other wildlife. Limited wheelchair access, some slopes.

Visit a garden and support hospice care in your local community

Greatcombe

DORSET

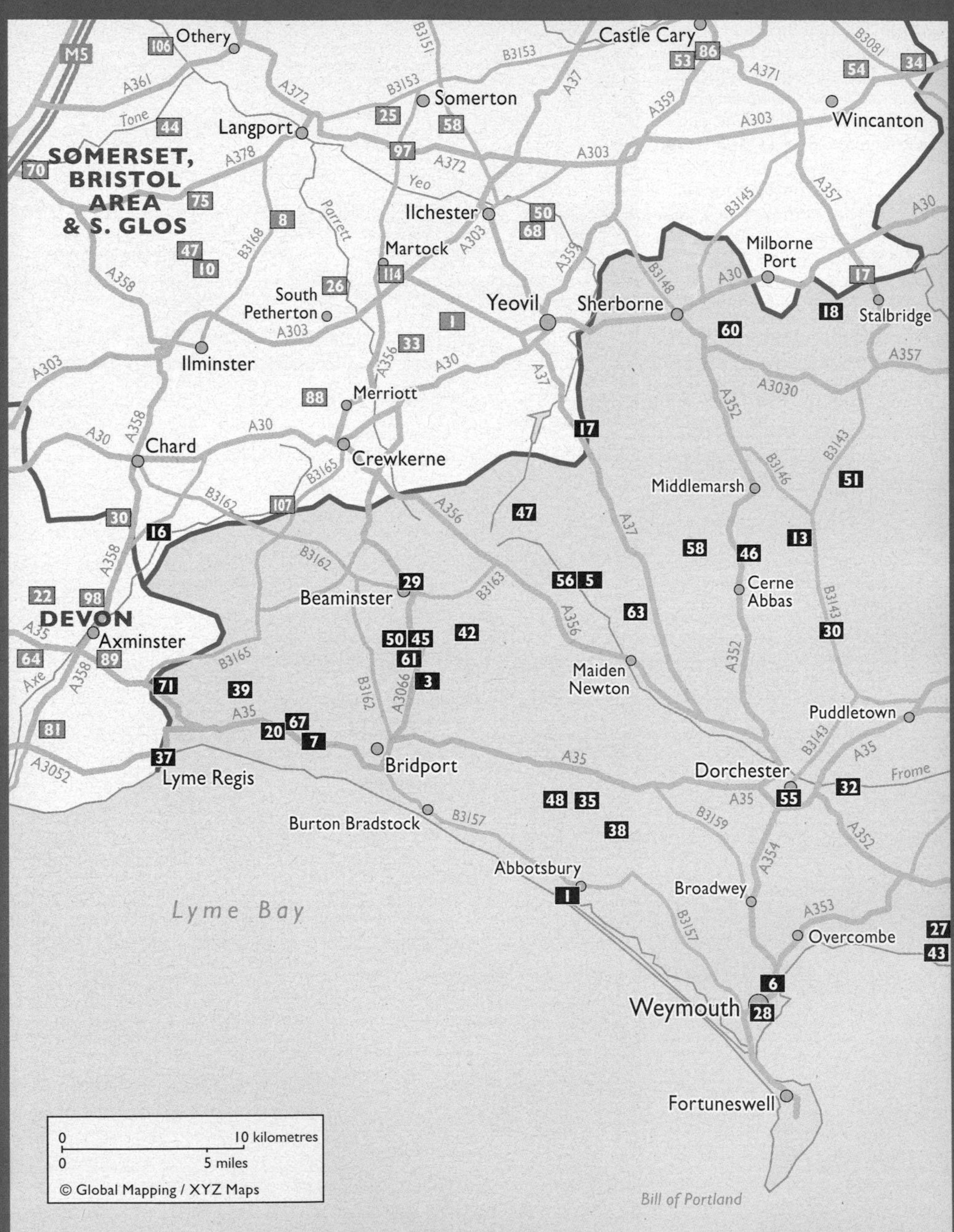

Othery
Castle Cary
Somerton
Wincanton
Langport
SOMERSET, BRISTOL AREA & S. GLOS
Ilchester
Martock
Milborne Port
Yeovil
Sherborne
Stalbridge
South Petherton
Ilminster
Merriott
Chard
Crewkerne
Middlemarsh
Beaminster
Cerne Abbas
DEVON
Axminster
Maiden Newton
Puddletown
Lyme Regis
Bridport
Dorchester
Burton Bradstock
Abbotsbury
Broadwey
Overcombe
Lyme Bay
Weymouth
Fortuneswell
Bill of Portland
0 10 kilometres
0 5 miles
© Global Mapping / XYZ Maps

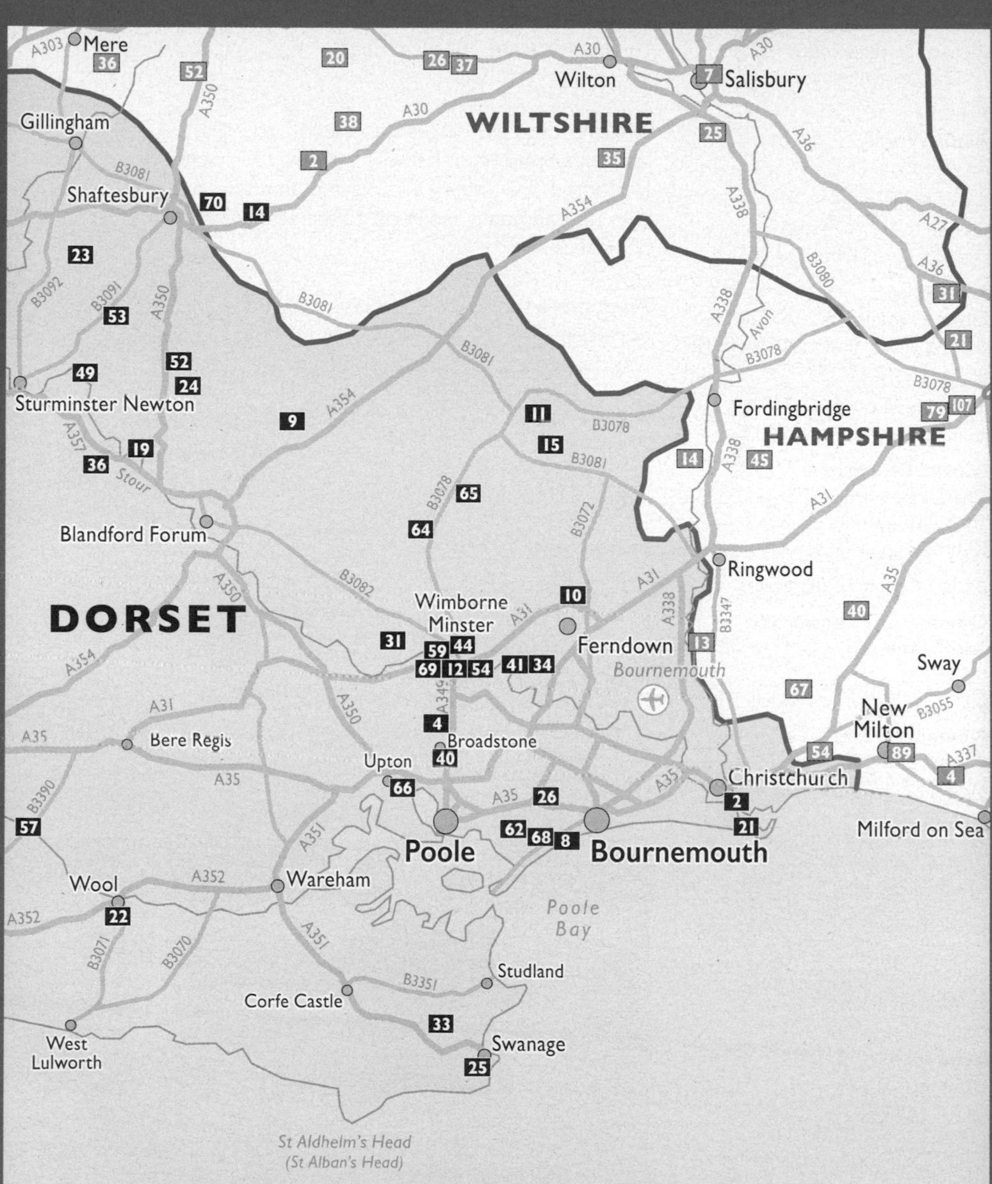
Mere
Gillingham
Shaftesbury
Sturminster Newton
Blandford Forum
DORSET
WILTSHIRE
HAMPSHIRE
Wilton
Salisbury
Fordingbridge
Ringwood
Wimborne Minster
Ferndown
Bournemouth
Sway
New Milton
Christchurch
Milford on Sea
Bere Regis
Broadstone
Upton
Poole
Poole Bay
Wool
Wareham
Studland
Corfe Castle
Swanage
West Lulworth
St Aldhelm's Head
(St Alban's Head)
Stour
Avon

Volunteers

County Organiser
Alison Wright 01935 83652
wright.alison68@yahoo.com

County Treasurer
Richard Smedley 01202 528286
richard@carter-coley.co.uk

Publicity
Alison Wright
(as above)

Social Media
Di Reeds 07973 241028
digardengate@hotmail.co.uk

Photographer
Edward Griffiths 01202 572288
eandj-griffiths@bhdorset.fsnet.co.uk

Booklet Editor
Judith Hussey 01258 474673
judithhussey@hotmail.com

Booklet Distributors
Charles Le Hardy 01258 860352
Trish Neale 01425 403565
trishneale1@yahoo.co.uk

Assistant County Organisers

Central East/Bournemouth
Trish Neale
(as above)

North Central
Alexandra Davies 01747 860351
alex@theparishhouse.co.uk

North East/Ferndown/
Christchurch
Mary Angus 01202 872789
mary@gladestock.co.uk

North West & Central
Annie Dove 01300 345450
anniedove1@btinternet.com

South Central/East
Helen Hardy 01929 471379
helliehardy@hotmail.co.uk

South Central/West
Di Reeds (as above)

South West
Christine Corson 01308 863923
christinekcorson@gmail.com

West Central
Alison Wright (as above)

Dorset is not on the way to anywhere. We have no cathedral and no motorways. The county has been inhabited forever and the constantly varying landscape is dotted with prehistoric earthworks and ancient monuments, bordered to the south by the magnificent Jurassic Coast.

Discover our cosy villages with their thatched cottages, churches and pubs. Small historic towns including Dorchester, Blandford, Sherborne, Shaftesbury and Weymouth are scattered throughout, with Bournemouth and Poole to the east being the main centres of population.

Amongst all this, we offer the visitor a wonderfully diverse collection of gardens, found in both towns and deep countryside. They are well planted and vary in size, topography and content. In between the larger ones are the tiniest, all beautifully presented by the generous garden owners who open for the National Garden Scheme. Most of the county's loveliest gardens in their romantic settings also support us.

Each garden rewards the visitor with originality and brings joy, even on the rainiest day! They are never very far away from an excellent meal and comfortable bed.

So do come, discover and explore what the gardens of Dorset have to offer with the added bonus of that welcome cup of tea and that irresistible slice of cake, or a scone laden with clotted cream and strawberry jam!

Below: Frankham Farm

OPENING DATES

All entries subject to change. For latest information check **www.ngs.org.uk**

Extended openings are shown at the beginning of the month.

Map locator numbers are shown to the right of each garden name.

February

Snowdrop Festival

Sunday 4th
◆ Mapperton Gardens 42

Sunday 11th
◆ Mapperton Gardens 42
The Old Rectory, Netherbury 50

Saturday 24th
Manor Farm, Hampreston 41

Sunday 25th
Lawsbrook 36
Manor Farm, Hampreston 41

March

Sunday 11th
Frankham Farm 17
Q 55

Sunday 18th
Herons Mead 22
22 Holt Road 26
The Old Vicarage 53
Q 55

Sunday 25th
Q 55

April

Sunday 1st
Chideock Manor 7
Herons Mead 22
Ivy House Garden 30
The Old Rectory, Netherbury 50

Monday 2nd
Chideock Manor 7
◆ Edmondsham House 15
Ivy House Garden 30

Tuesday 3rd
The Old Rectory, Netherbury 50

Wednesday 4th
◆ Edmondsham House 15

Friday 6th
The Old Vicarage 53

Sunday 8th
Q 55

Wednesday 11th
◆ Edmondsham House 15

Friday 13th
The Old Vicarage 53

Sunday 15th
22 Holt Road 26
Ivy House Garden 30
Q 55

Wednesday 18th
◆ Cranborne Manor Garden 11
◆ Edmondsham House 15
The Old Vicarage 53

Sunday 22nd
Broomhill 5
Frankham Farm 17
Ivy House Garden 30
Q 55

Wednesday 25th
◆ Edmondsham House 15
Horn Park 29

Friday 27th
The Old Vicarage 53

Saturday 28th
Marren 43

Sunday 29th
Manor Farm, Hampreston 41
Marren 43
The Old Rectory, Litton Cheney 48

May

Thursday 3rd
Little Cliff 37

Saturday 5th
The Secret Garden 58

Sunday 6th
Herons Mead 22
Holworth Farmhouse 27
Ivy House Garden 30
Little Cliff 37
The Secret Garden 58

Monday 7th
Holworth Farmhouse 27
Ivy House Garden 30

Tuesday 8th
Braddocks 3

Saturday 12th
Harcombe House 20

Sunday 13th
Harcombe House 20
Mayfield 44
The Old Rectory, Pulham 51
The Old Vicarage 53
Q 55
Wincombe Park 70
Wolverhollow 71

Monday 14th
Wolverhollow 71

Tuesday 15th
Stanbridge Mill 65

Wednesday 16th
Mayfield 44
Wincombe Park 70

Thursday 17th
NEW Chine View 8
The Old Rectory, Pulham 51

Sunday 20th
NEW Chine View 8
22 Holt Road 26
The Old Rectory, Netherbury 50
Well Cottage 67

Monday 21st
Deans Court 12
Well Cottage 67

Tuesday 22nd
The Old Rectory, Netherbury 50

Friday 25th
Knitson Old Farmhouse 33

Saturday 26th
Knitson Old Farmhouse 33

Sunday 27th
Annalal's Gallery 2
Holworth Farmhouse 27
Knitson Old Farmhouse 33
Lawsbrook 36
Mayfield 44
Slape Manor 61
Staddlestones 64

Monday 28th
Holworth Farmhouse 27
Knitson Old Farmhouse 33
Lawsbrook 36
Staddlestones 64

Wednesday 30th
Manor Farm, Hampreston 41

June

Friday 1st
24 Carlton Road North 6

Festival Weekend

Saturday 2nd
24 Carlton Road North 6

Sunday 3rd
Annalal's Gallery 2
24 Carlton Road North 6
Frankham Farm 17

Monday 4th
24 Carlton Road North 6

Wednesday 6th
Mayfield 44
NEW Stable Court 63

Thursday 7th
Little Cliff 37

Saturday 9th
Marren 43

Sunday 10th
Hanford School 19
Little Cliff 37
Marren 43
The Old Vicarage 53
NEW Rampisham Gardens 56
NEW Stable Court 63

Tuesday 12th
Braddocks 3

Wednesday 13th
Donhead Hall 14
Mayfield 44

Sunday 17th
Donhead Hall 14
22 Holt Road 26
NEW Norwood House 47
The Old Rectory, Manston 49
NEW The Old School House 52
Western Gardens 68

Tuesday 19th
Deans Court 12
◆ Littlebredy Walled Gardens 38

Wednesday 20th
Horn Park 29
The Old Rectory, Manston 49
NEW The Old School House 52

Thursday 21st
NEW Norwood House 47
Staddlestones 64

Saturday 23rd
Chideock Manor 7
The Hollow, Blandford Forum 24

Sunday 24th
Annalal's Gallery 2
Chideock Manor 7
The Hollow, Blandford Forum 24

Tuesday 26th
◆ Littlebredy Walled Gardens 38

Wednesday 27th
The Hollow, Blandford Forum 24

Saturday 30th
Lower Abbotts Wootton Farm 39

July

Every Wednesday
The Hollow, Swanage 25

Sunday 1st
NEW Chine View 8
Holworth Farmhouse 27
Lower Abbotts Wootton Farm 39
The Old Rectory, Litton Cheney 48

Wednesday 4th
The Old Rectory, Litton Cheney 48
◆ Sculpture by the Lakes 57

Thursday 5th
Little Cliff 37

Saturday 7th
◆ Cranborne Manor Garden 11

Sunday 8th
Little Cliff 37

Tuesday 10th
Braddocks 3

Sunday 15th
Broomhill 5
Hilltop 23

Thursday 19th
The Secret Garden and Serles House 59

Saturday 21st
Holy Trinity Primary School Garden 28

Sunday 22nd
Annalal's Gallery 2
Cottesmore Farm 10
Hilltop 23
22 Holt Road 26
Holy Trinity Primary School Garden 28
The Secret Garden and Serles House 59
Well Cottage 67

Monday 23rd
Well Cottage 67

Friday 27th
◆ Knoll Gardens 34

Saturday 28th
44 Lower Blandford Road 40

Sunday 29th
Cottesmore Farm 10
Hilltop 23
44 Lower Blandford Road 40
Manor Farm, Hampreston 41
The Secret Garden and Serles House 59
Western Gardens 68

August

Every Wednesday
The Hollow, Swanage 25

Wednesday 1st
Manor Farm, Hampreston 41

Thursday 2nd
The Secret Garden and Serles House 59

Sunday 5th
Annalal's Gallery 2
10 Brookdale Close 4
Cottesmore Farm 10
Hilltop 23
Holworth Farmhouse 27
The Old Rectory, Pulham 51
The Secret Garden and Serles House 59

Thursday 9th
The Old Rectory, Pulham 51

Saturday 11th
Harcombe House 20

Sunday 12th
10 Brookdale Close 4
Broomhill 5
Harcombe House 20
Hilltop 23
Manor Farm, Hampreston 41

Tuesday 14th
Harcombe House 20

Saturday 18th
44 Lower Blandford Road 40

Sunday 19th
Hilltop 23
22 Holt Road 26
44 Lower Blandford Road 40
The Secret Garden and Serles House 59

Sunday 26th
The Secret Garden and Serles House 59

Monday 27th
The Secret Garden and Serles House 59

Thursday 30th
The Secret Garden and Serles House 59

September

Saturday 1st
The Secret Garden and Serles House 59

Sunday 2nd
The Secret Garden and Serles House 59

Friday 7th
◆ Knoll Gardens 34

Sunday 9th
The Secret Garden and Serles House 59

Sunday 16th
Herons Mead 22

October

Wednesday 3rd
◆ Edmondsham House 15

Wednesday 10th
◆ Edmondsham House 15

Sunday 14th
Frankham Farm 17

Wednesday 17th
◆ Edmondsham House 15

Wednesday 24th
◆ Edmondsham House 15

November

Sunday 4th
Lawsbrook 36

By Arrangement

Annalal's Gallery 2
Braddocks 3
10 Brookdale Close 4
Broomhill 5
Chideock Manor 7
Cottage Row 9
Cottesmore Farm 10
Deans Court 12
Domineys Yard 13
Frith House 18
Harcombe House 20
Herons Mead 22
The Hollow, Swanage 25
22 Holt Road 26
Holworth Farmhouse 27

THE GARDENS

1 ◆ ABBOTSBURY GARDENS

Abbotsbury, Weymouth, DT3 4LA. Ilchester Estates, 01305 871387, www.abbotsburygardens.co.uk. *8m W of Weymouth. From B3157 Weymouth-Bridport, 200yds W of Abbotsbury village.* **For opening times and information, please phone or visit garden website.**

30 acres, started in 1760 and considerably extended in C19. Much recent replanting. The maritime micro-climate enables Mediterranean and southern hemisphere garden to grow rare and tender plants. National collection of Hoherias (flowering Aug in NZ garden). Woodland valley with ponds, stream and hillside walk to view the Jurassic Coast. Open all yr except Christmas week. Featured on Countrywise and Gardeners' World and in Country Life. Limited wheelchair access, some very steep paths and rolled gravel.

2 ANNALAL'S GALLERY

25 Millhams Street, Christchurch, BH23 1DN. Anna & Lal Sims, 01202 567585, anna.sims@ntlworld.com, www.annasims.co.uk. *Town centre. Park in Saxon Square PCP - exit to Millhams St via alley at side of church.* **Suns 27 May, 3, 24 June, 22 July, 5 Aug (2-4). Adm £3, chd free. Visits also by arrangement May to Aug, max 10.**

Enchanting 150 yr-old cottage, home of two Royal Academy artists. 32ft x 12½ft garden on 3 patio levels. Pencil gate leads to colourful scented Victorian walled garden. Sculptures and paintings hide among the flowers and shrubs. Unusual studio and garden room. Not suitable for wheelchairs; not suitable for dogs.

3 BRADDOCKS

Oxbridge, Bridport, DT6 3TZ. Dr & Mrs Roger Newton, 01308 488441, rogernewton329@btinternet.com, www.braddocksgarden.co.uk. *3m N of Bridport. From Bridport, A3066 to Beaminster 3m, just before Melplash, L into Camesworth Lane signed Oxbridge. Single track rd, down steep hill. Garden signed.* **Tue 8 May, Tue 12 June, Tue 10 July (2-5). Adm £4.50, chd free. Home-made teas. Adults tea and cake £3, children drink and cake £1.50. Visits also by arrangement Mar to Sept, groups of 10+ will be offered refreshments by arrangement.**

3 acres of plant-packed sloping gardens, conceived, planted and looked after by owner. 'A feast of a garden at all times of the year'. Wild flower meadows and water. Herbaceous, underplanted shrubs and roses of all types and hues. Shady woodland garden and fine mature specimen trees. Steep slopes and gravel paths make the garden unsuitable for wheelchairs.

4 10 BROOKDALE CLOSE

Broadstone, BH18 9AA. Michael & Sylvia Cooper, 01202 693280. *Located just 100yds from centre of Broadstone, Brookdale Close is on Higher Blandford Rd, with additional parking in the next road, Fairview Crescent.* **Sun 5, Sun 12 Aug (2-5). Adm £3, chd free. Home-made teas. Visits also by arrangement in Aug, afternoon visits only.**

Described as a 'little piece of paradise', our 70 foot by 50 foot garden is centred around a wildlife pond and tumbling waterfall. A rich kaleidoscope of colour combining both tropical and cottage garden with tree ferns, bananas, lilies, grasses, and beautiful perennials with a different view at every turn. Featured in Amateur Gardening and on Radio Solent. Limited wheelchair access.

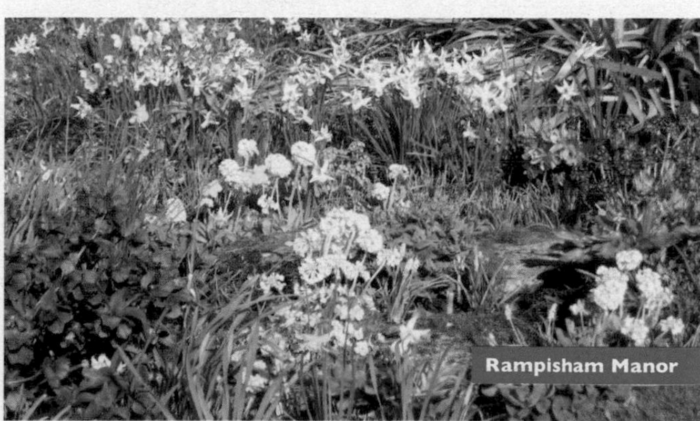

Rampisham Manor

5 BROOMHILL

Rampisham, Dorchester, DT2 0PU. Mr & Mrs D Parry, 01935 83266, carol.parry2@btopenworld.com. *11m NW of Dorchester. From Dorchester A37 Yeovil, 4m L A356 to Crewkerne, 6m R to Rampisham. From Yeovil A37 Dorchester, 7m R Evershot. From Crewkerne A356, 1½m after Rampisham Garage L Rampisham. Follow signs.* **Sun 22 Apr, Sun 15 July, Sun 12 Aug (2-5). Adm £4.50, chd free. Home-made teas. Opening with Rampisham Gardens on Sun 10 June. Visits also by arrangement May to Aug for groups of 8+.**

Once a farmyard now a delightful, tranquil garden set in 1½ acres. Island beds and borders are planted with shrubs, roses, masses of unusual perennials and choice annuals to give vibrancy and colour into the autumn. Lawns and paths lead to a less formal area with a large wildlife pond, meadow, shaded areas, bog garden and late summer border. Gravel entrance, the rest is grass, some gentle slopes.

6 24 CARLTON ROAD NORTH

Weymouth, DT4 7PY. Anne & Rob Tracey. *8m S of Dorchester. A354 from Dorchester, R into Carlton Rd North. From Town Centre follow esplanade towards A354 Dorchester and L into C Rd N.* **Fri 1, Sat 2, Sun 3, Mon 4 June (2-5). Adm £3, chd free. Home-made teas.**

Long garden on several levels. Steps and narrow sloping paths lead to beds and borders filled with trees, shrubs and herbaceous plants incl many unusual varieties. A garden which continues to evolve and reflect an interest in texture, shape and colour. Wildlife is encouraged by the provision of homes. A small pond is the latest addition. Raised beds create a space for vegetable growing.

7 CHIDEOCK MANOR

Chideock, Bridport, DT6 6LF. Mr & Mrs Howard Coates, 07885 551795, deirdrecoates9@gmail.com. *2m W of Bridport on A35. In centre of village turn N at church. The Manor is ¼m along this rd on R.* **Sun 1, Mon 2 Apr, Sat 23, Sun 24 June (2-5). Adm £6, chd free. Home-made teas. Visits also by arrangement Apr to June.**

6/7 acres of formal and informal gardens. Bog garden beside stream and series of ponds. Yew hedges and mature trees. Lime and crab apple walks, herbaceous borders, colourful rose and clematis arches, fernery and nuttery. Walled vegetable garden and orchard. Woodland and lakeside walks. Fine views. Partial wheelchair access.

8 NEW CHINE VIEW

15a Cassel Avenue, Poole, BH13 6JD. Andy & Mel Leach. *2m W of Bournemouth. From centre of Westbourne turn S into Alumhurst Rd, take 8th turning on R into Mountbatten Rd then 1st L into Cassel Ave.* **Thur 17, Sun 20 May, Sun 1 July (1-5). Adm £4, chd free. Home-made teas.**

Unique Chine garden adjacent to public footpath leading to beach. Features incl extensive terraced rockery incorporating 330 tons of Purbeck stone, palladian rotunda, subtropical plants and profusion of azaleas and rhododendrons. Wavelength A Cappella ladies choir will be singing at 3pm on Sun 1 July. Steep steps and uneven paths make it unsuitable for the less mobile.

9 COTTAGE ROW

School Lane, Tarrant Gunville, nr Blandford Forum, DT11 8JJ. Carolyn & Michael Pawson, 01258 830212, michaelpawson637@btinternet.com. *6m NE of Blandford Forum. From Blandford take A354 towards Salisbury, L at Tarrant Hinton. After 1½m R in Tarrant Gunville into School Lane.* **Visits by arrangement Apr to Sept for groups of 6+. Roses/clematis at best June/July, cyclamen Sept. Adm £4.50, chd free. Home-made teas. Refreshments for groups discussed in advance.**

Maturing ½ acre partly walled garden. Formal and informal areas separated by yew hedges. Pergola, arbours, brick paths, tree house, kitchen garden and the sound of water; bees and butterflies abound in this tranquil spot. This sophisticated cottage garden reflects the owners' love of unusual plants, structure and an artist's eye for sympathetic colour. Featured in Dorset Life.

10 COTTESMORE FARM

Newmans Lane, West Moors, Ferndown, BH22 0LW. Paul & Valerie Guppy, 07413 925372, paulguppy@googlemail.com. *1m N of West Moors. Off B3072 Bournemouth to Verwood rd. Car parking in owner's field.* **Every Sun 22 July to 5 Aug (2-5). Adm £4, chd free. Home-made teas. Visits also by arrangement in Aug for groups of 10+, afternoons only.**

Gardens of over an acre, created from scratch over 19yrs. Wander through a plantsman's tropical paradise of giant gunneras, bananas, towering bamboos and over 100 palm trees, into a floral extravaganza. Large borders and sweeping island beds overflowing with phlox, heliopsis, helenium and much more combine to drown you in scent and colour. Wheelchair access to garden to avoid 2 lots of steps, please ask on arrival to make use of level route through main drive gate.

11 ◆ CRANBORNE MANOR GARDEN

Cranborne, BH21 5PP. Viscount Cranborne, 01725 517289, info@cranborne.co.uk, www.cranborne.co.uk. *10m N of Wimborne on B3078. Enter garden via Cranborne Garden Centre, on L as you enter top of village of Cranborne.* **For NGS: Wed 18 Apr, Sat 7 July (9-4). Adm £6, chd £1. Light refreshments in Café, Cranborne Garden Centre www.cranbornegardencentre.co.uk. Breakfast, hot & cold lunches,**

afternoon tea. For other opening times and information, please phone, email or visit garden website.
Beautiful and historic garden laid out in C17 by John Tradescant and enlarged in C20, featuring several gardens surrounded by walls and yew hedges: blue and white garden, cottage style and mount gardens, water and wild garden. Many interesting plants, with fine trees and avenues. Mostly wheelchair access.

12 DEANS COURT

Deans Court Lane, Wimborne Minster, BH21 1EE. Sir William Hanham, 01202 849314, info@deanscourt.org, www.deanscourt.org. *¼m SE of Minster. Pedestrians: From Deans Court Lane, continuation of High St, over Xrds at Holmans shop (BH21 1EE). Cars: Follow yellow NGS signs to entrance on A349, Poole Rd, Wimborne (BH21 1QF).* **Mon 21 May, Tue 19 June (11-5). Adm £4, chd free. Light lunches and teas. Visits also by arrangement usually require a minimum of 15. Visit involves tour of house and garden.** Donation to Friends of Victoria Hospital.
13 acres of peaceful, partly wild gardens in ancient setting with mature specimen trees, Saxon fish pond, herb garden and apiary beside R Allen close to town centre. Apple orchard with wild flowers. 1st Soil Association accredited kitchen garden within C18 serpentine walls. Lunches and teas served in café, using estate produce (also for sale). Tours of house £5 at 12 and 2pm, book upon arrival. For disabled access, follow signs within grounds for parking closer to the gardens. Some paths have deeper gravel.

13 DOMINEYS YARD

Buckland Newton, Dorchester, DT2 7BS. Mr & Mrs W Gueterbock, 01300 345295, cottages@domineys.com, www.domineys.com. *11m N of Dorchester, 11m S of Sherborne. 2m E A352 or take B3143. No through road between church & Gaggle of Geese pub. Car Park 90yds on R, enter 100yds on L.* **Visits by arrangement all year, individuals and groups up to 30. Adm £5, chd free. Light refreshments by request on booking.**
Welcome to our 32nd year of opening for the NGS and 57th year here. Varied layout, which we continue to change, in attractive setting around thatched house and cottages. Separate naturalised arboretum. Superb soil, good micro climate. Plant diversity to enjoy throughout the year. Rare and well known trees, shrubs, herbaceous, bulbs, annuals, pots, fruit and vegetables. A garden to revisit all year. Children under 15 very welcome and enter free of charge. Featured in Blackmore Vale Magazine, Dorset Echo and on Radio Solent. Wheelchair access excludes arboretum.

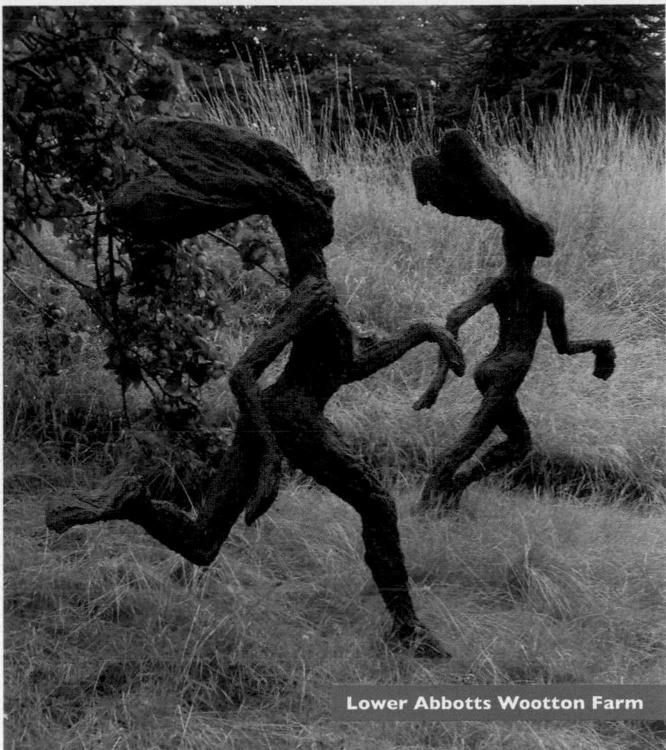

Lower Abbotts Wootton Farm

14 DONHEAD HALL

Donhead St Mary, Shaftesbury, SP7 9DS. Paul & Penny Brewer. *4m E of Shaftesbury. A30 towards Shaftesbury. In Ludwell turn R opp brown sign to Tollard Royal. Follow rd for ¾m and bear R at T-junction. Donhead Hall 50 yds on L on corner of Watery Lane, cream gates.* **Evening opening Wed 13 June (6-8.30). Wine. Sun 17 June (3-6). Home-made teas. Adm £5, chd free.**
Walled garden overlooking deer park. The house and garden are built into the side of a hill with uninterrupted views to Cranborne Chase. Martin Lane Fox designed the terracing and advised on the landscaping of the gardens which are on 4 different levels. Large mixed borders and specimen trees, kitchen garden with glasshouses. Regret no wheelchair access.

15 ◆ EDMONDSHAM HOUSE

Edmondsham, Wimborne, BH21 5RE. Mrs Julia Smith, 01725 517207, julia.edmondsham@homeuser.net. *9m NE of Wimborne. 9m W of Ringwood. Between Cranborne & Verwood. Edmondsham off B3081. Wheelchair access and disabled parking at West front door.* **For NGS: Mon 2, Weds 4, 11, 18, 25 Apr, Weds 3, 10, 17, 24 Oct (2-5). Adm £2.50, chd £0.50. Tea, coffee, cake and soft drinks 3.30-4pm in Edmondsham House Weds only. For other opening times and information, please phone or email.**

6 acres of mature gardens, grounds, views, trees and shaped hedges surrounding C16/C18 house, giving much to explore incl C12 church adjacent to garden. Large Victorian walled garden is productive and managed organically (since 1984) using 'no dig' vegetable beds. Wide herbaceous borders planted for seasonal colour. Traditional potting shed and working areas. House also open on NGS days. Coaches welcome by appointment only. Some grass and gravel paths.

♿ ✿ 🚌 ☕

16 ◆ FORDE ABBEY GARDENS

Forde Abbey, Chard, TA20 4LU. Mr & Mrs Julian Kennard, 01460 221290, info@fordeabbey.co.uk, www.fordeabbey.co.uk. *4m SE of Chard. Signed off A30 Chard-Crewkerne and A358 Chard-Axminster. Also from Broadwindsor B3164.* **For opening times and information, please phone, email or visit garden website.**

30 acres of fine shrubs, magnificent specimen trees, ponds, herbaceous borders, rockery, bog garden containing superb collection of Asiatic primulas, Ionic temple, working walled kitchen garden supplying the tearoom. Centenary fountain, England's highest powered fountain. Gardens open daily (10am-5.30pm, last adm 4.30pm). Please ask at reception for best wheelchair route. Wheelchairs available to borrow/hire, advance booking advised.

♿ 🐕 ✿ 🚌 ☕

17 FRANKHAM FARM

Ryme Intrinseca, Sherborne, DT9 6JT. Susan Ross, www.Facebook.com/frankhamfarmgarden. *3m S of Yeovil. A37 Yeovil-Dorchester; turn E; ¼m; drive is on L.* **Suns 11 Mar, 22 Apr, 3 June, 14 Oct (11.30-5). Adm £5, chd free. Home produced lunch 12-2.30 pulled pork or sausage in a roll, vegetarian soup. Home made teas 3-5.**

3½ acre garden, created since 1960 by the late Jo Earle for yr-round interest. This large and lovely garden is filled with a wide variety of well grown plants, roses, unusual labelled shrubs and trees from around the world. Productive vegetable garden. Climbers cover the walls. Spring bulbs through to autumn colour, particularly oaks. Sorry, no dogs.

✿ 🚌 ☕

18 FRITH HOUSE

Stalbridge, DT10 2SD. Mr & Mrs Patrick Sclater, 01963 250809, rosalynsclater@btinternet.com. *5m E of Sherborne. Between Milborne Port and Stalbridge. From A30 1m, follow sign to Stalbridge. From Stalbridge 2m and turn W by PO.* **Visits by arrangement Apr to July for groups of 10+ Mon-Fri only. Adm £5, chd free. Home-made teas.**

Approached down long drive with fine views. 4 acres of garden around Edwardian house and self-contained hamlet. Range of mature trees, lakes and flower borders. House terrace edged by rose border and featuring Lutyensesque wall fountain and game larder. Well stocked kitchen gardens.

♿ ☕

19 HANFORD SCHOOL

Child Okeford, Blandford Forum, DT11 8HN. Rory & Georgina Johnston. *From Blandford take A350 to Shaftesbury. Approx 2m after Stourpaine take L turn for Hanford. From Shaftesbury take A350 to Poole. After Iwerne Courtney take next R to Hanford.* **Sun 10 June (2-4.30). Adm £4.50, chd free. Home-made teas.**

Perhaps the only school in England with a working kitchen garden growing quantities of seasonal vegetables, fruit and flowers for the table. The rolling lawns host sports matches, gymnastics, dance and plays while ancient cedars look on. The stable clock chimes the hour and the chapel presides over it all. Teas in Great Hall (think Hogwarts). What a place to go to school or visit. Several steps/ramp to main house. No wheelchair access to WC.

♿ 🐕 ☕

20 HARCOMBE HOUSE

Pitmans Lane, Morcombelake, Bridport, DT6 6EB. Jan & Martin Dixon, 01297 489229, harcombe@hotmail.co.uk, jdmc49.wixsite.com/harcombe-house. *4m W of Bridport - ignore SatNav. A35 from Bridport: R to Whitchurch just past The Artwave Gallery. Immed R, bear L into Pitmans Lane. Approx 800m, park in paddock on L.* **Sat 12, Sun 13 May, Sat 11, Sun 12, Tue 14 Aug (11-5). Adm £5, chd free. Home-made teas. All cakes are home-made by Jan Dixon. Visits also by arrangement May to Aug, groups are welcome but lane is too narrow for coaches.**

Landscaped into the hillside 500ft above the Char Valley with spectacular views across Charmouth and Lyme Bay, the ¾ acre garden, maintained by the owners, is laid out as a series of gravel paths and terraces connected by steps. Featuring an abundance of shrubs and perennials, many of which are unusual and visually stunning, the garden offers something for every season. Majestic rhododendrons and azaleas complement spring bulbs in a blaze of colour in May/June and in August the beautiful eucryphia is the star of the garden. Whilst the garden is easily navigable, it will present a challenge to the less mobile visitor and is definitely unsuitable for wheelchairs and buggies.

21 ◆ HENGISTBURY HEAD VISITOR CENTRE

Broadway, Southbourne, Bournemouth, BH6 4EN. Bournemouth Borough Council, 01202 451618, hengistbury.head@bournemouth.gov.uk, www.visithengistburyhead.co.uk. *Near Christchurch on southern side of Christchurch Harbour. From B'mouth, take Southbourne Overcliff Drive, then Southbourne Coast Rd. Eventually, turn R onto Broadway. From Christchurch, cross R Stour on B3059. After r'about turn L onto Broadway.* **For opening times and information, please phone, email or visit garden website.**

The Visitor Centre garden was designed to inspire visitors to try things in their own seaside gardens. Features incl raised pond, wildflower meadow, woodland section, borders, raised bed, bug hotels and vegetable plot. Bird boxes with cameras, log pile and gateway for hedgehogs. Plants incl wild flowers (to reflect the nature reserve) and a variety of garden plants. Visitors can also explore the Hengistbury Head Visitor Centre and its gift shop. Interactive exhibitions about the history, geology and wildlife of Hengistbury Head and regular art exhibitions. One free hot drink for visitors who bring along their NGS Dorset Handbook - just show your handbook at reception to receive your drink. The Visitor Centre and garden (apart from the woodland section) are accessible to wheelchairs and mobility scooters.

22 HERONS MEAD

East Burton Road, East Burton, Wool, BH20 6HF. Ron & Angela Millington, 01929 463872, ronamillington@btinternet.com. *6m W of Wareham on A352. Approaching Wool from Wareham, turn R just before level crossing into East Burton Rd. Herons Mead ¾m on L.* **Suns 18 Mar, 1 Apr, 6 May, 16 Sept (2-5). Adm £3.50, chd free. Home-made teas. Visits also by arrangement Mar to Sept for groups of 10+.**

½ acre plantlover's garden full of interest from spring (bulbs, many hellebores, pulmonaria, fritillaries) through abundant summer perennials, old roses scrambling through trees and late seasonal exuberant plants amongst swathes of tall grasses. Wildlife pond and plants to attract bees, butterflies, etc. Tiny woodland. Cacti. Small wheelchairs can gain partial access - as far as the tea house!

23 HILLTOP

Woodville, Stour Provost, Gillingham, SP8 5LY. Josse & Brian Emerson, www.hilltopgarden.co.uk. *7m N of Sturminster Newton, 5m W of Shaftesbury. On B3092 turn E at Stour Provost Xrds, signed Woodville. After 1¼m thatched cottage on R. On A30, 4m W of Shaftesbury, turn S opp Kings Arms. 2nd turning on R signed Woodville, 100 yds on L.* **Every Sun 15 July to 19 Aug (2-6). Adm £3, chd free. Home-made teas.**

Summer at Hilltop is a gorgeous riot of colour and scent, the old thatched cottage barely visible amongst the flowers. Unusual annuals and perennials grow alongside the traditional and familiar, boldly combining to make a spectacular display, which attracts an abundance of wildlife. Always something new, the unique, gothic garden loo a great success.

24 THE HOLLOW, BLANDFORD FORUM

Tower Hill, Iwerne Minster, Blandford Forum, DT11 8NJ. Sue Le Prevost. *Between Blandford and Shaftesbury. Follow signs on A350 to Iwerne Minster. Turn off at Talbot Inn, continue straight to The Chalk, bear R along Watery Lane for parking in Parish Field on R. 5 min uphill walk to house.* **Sat 23, Sun 24, Wed 27 June (2-5). Adm £3, chd free. Cream teas. Home-made cakes and gluten-free available.**

Hillside cottage garden built on chalk, about ⅓ acre with an interesting variety of plants in borders that line the numerous sloping pathways. Water features for wildlife and well placed seating areas to sit back and enjoy the views. Productive fruit and vegetable garden in converted paddock with raised beds and greenhouses. A high maintenance garden which is constantly evolving. Slopes, narrow gravel paths and steep steps so sadly not suitable for wheelchairs or limited mobility.

Macmillan and the National Garden Scheme, partners for more than 30 years

25 THE HOLLOW, SWANAGE

25 Newton Road, Swanage, BH19 2EA. Stuart & Suzanne Nutbeem, 01929 423662, gdnsuzanne@gmail.com. *½m S of Swanage town centre. From town follow signs to Durlston Country Park. At top of hill turn R at red postbox into Bon Accord Rd. 4th turn R into Newton Rd.* **Every Wed 4 July to 29 Aug (2-5.30). Adm £3, chd free. Visits also by arrangement July & Aug.**

Come and wander around a dramatic sunken garden on the site of an old stone quarry, a surprising find at the top of a hill above the seaside town of Swanage. Drystone terraces hold original plants and grasses with vast richness of colour & texture attracting butterflies and bees, changing from year to year showing the owners' passion for plants. Pieces of mediaeval London Bridge lurk in the walls. Exceptionally wide range of plants including succulents and airplants. Featured in Amateur Gardening, The English Garden and BBC Radio Solent.

26 22 HOLT ROAD

Branksome, Poole, BH12 1JQ. Alan & Sylvia Lloyd, 01202 387509, alan.lloyd22@ntlworld.com. *2½m W of Bournemouth Square, 3m E of Poole Civic Centre. From Alder Rd turn into Winston Ave, 3rd R into Guest Ave, 2nd R into Holt Rd, at end of cul de sac. Park in Holt Rd or in Guest Ave.* **Suns 18 Mar, 15 Apr, 20 May, 17 June, 22 July, 19 Aug (2-5). Adm £3.50, chd free. Home-made teas. Visits also by arrangement Mar to Sept for groups of 10+.**

¾ acre walled garden for all seasons. Garden seating throughout the diverse planting areas, incl Mediterranean courtyard garden and wisteria pergola. Walk up slope beside rill and bog garden to raised bed vegetable garden. Return through shrubbery and rockery back to waterfall cascading into a pebble beach. Partial wheelchair access.

27 HOLWORTH FARMHOUSE

Holworth, Dorchester, DT2 8NH. Anthony & Philippa Bush, 01305 852242, bushinarcadia@yahoo.co.uk. *7m E of Dorchester. 1m S of A352. Follow signs to Holworth. Through farmyard with duckpond on R. 1st L after 200yds of rough track. Ignore No Access signs.* **Sun 6, Mon 7, Sun 27, Mon 28 May, Sun 1 July, Sun 5 Aug (2-5). Adm £4, chd free. Home-made teas. Visits also by arrangement Feb to Oct for individuals or groups, refreshments by arrangement.**

This unusual garden is tucked away without being isolated and has an atmosphere of extraordinary peace and tranquility. At no point do visitors perceive any idea of the whole, but have to discover, by degrees and at every turn, its element of surprise, its variety of features and its appreciation of space. At all times you are invited to look back, to look round and to look up. Beautiful unspoilt views. Large vegetable garden. Ponds, fish, and water features. Many unusual trees and shrubs. Featured on radio Solent. Limited wheelchair access.

28 HOLY TRINITY PRIMARY SCHOOL GARDEN

Cross Rd, Weymouth, DT4 9QX. Holy Trinity C E Primary School & Nursery, www.holytrinityenvironmentalgarden.blogspot.co.uk. *1m W of Weymouth centre. Take A354 from Weymouth Harbour junction by Asda. R at top of hill into Wyke Rd. 3rd L into Cross Rd. 200m on R school car park.* **Sat 21, Sun 22 July (1-5). Adm £4, chd free. Light refreshments in Gracewell (Weymouth) Residential Home adjoining the garden.**

An award winning wildlife garden, started in 2008 with the donation of a winning RHS Show Garden. Children's raised beds, large wildlife pond, WWII garden with Anderson shelter, tranquil Memory Corner, Dorset's largest living willow classroom, small orchard and bird garden. Lush Jurassic garden with many ferns and plants from the time of the dinosaurs completes the garden! Butterfly hunt and Mud Kitchen for children. Wheelchair access to most of garden and composting WC.

29 HORN PARK

Tunnel Rd, Beaminster, DT8 3HB. Mr & Mrs David Ashcroft, 01308 862212, angieashcroft@btinternet.com. *1½m N of Beaminster. On A3066 from Beaminster, L before tunnel (see signs).* **Wed 25 Apr, Wed 20 June (2.30-4.30). Adm £4.50, chd free. Home-made teas. Visits also by arrangement Apr to Sept, Tues to Thurs only.**

Large, plantsman's garden with magnificent view to sea. Many rare and mature plants and shrubs in terraced, herbaceous, rock and water gardens. Woodland garden and walks in bluebell woods. Good autumn colouring. Wild flower meadow with 164 varieties incl orchids. Very limited access for wheelchair users, gravel paths and some steep slopes.

30 IVY HOUSE GARDEN

Piddletrenthide, DT2 7QF. Bridget Bowen, 07586 377675, beepeebee66@icloud.com. *9m N of Dorchester. On B3143. In middle of Piddletrenthide village, opp Village Stores near Piddle Inn.* **Sun 1, Mon 2, Sun 15, Sun 22 Apr, Sun 6, Mon 7 May (2-5). Adm £4, chd free. Home-made teas. Visits also by arrangement Mar to May for groups of 10+.**

Unusual and challenging ½ acre garden set on steep hillside with fine views. Wildlife friendly garden with mixed borders, ponds, propagating area, vegetable garden, fruit cage, greenhouses and polytunnel, chickens and bees,

Langebride House

nearby allotment. Daffodils, tulips and hellebores in quantity for spring openings. Come prepared for steep terrain and a warm welcome! Run on organic lines with plants to attract birds, bees and other insects. Insect-friendly plants usually for sale. Honey and hive products usually available and, weather permitting, observation hive of honey bees in courtyard. Beekeeper present to answer queries.

31 ◆ KINGSTON LACY

Wimborne Minster, BH21 4EA. National Trust, 01202 883402, kingstonlacy@nationaltrust.org.uk, www.nationaltrust.org.uk/kingston-lacy. *2½m W of Wimborne Minster. On Wimborne-Blandford rd B3082.* **For opening times and information, please phone, email or visit garden website.**

35 acres of formal garden, incorporating parterre and sunk garden planted with Edwardian schemes during spring and summer. 5 acre kitchen garden and allotments, Victorian fernery containing over 35 varieties. Rose garden, mixed herbaceous borders, vast formal lawns and Japanese garden restored to Henrietta Bankes' creation of 1910. 2 National Collections: Convallaria and Anemone nemorosa. Snowdrops, blossom, bluebells, autumn colour and Christmas light display. Deep gravel on some paths but lawns suitable for wheelchairs. Slope to visitor reception and South Lawn.

32 ◆ KINGSTON MAURWARD GARDENS AND ANIMAL PARK

Kingston Maurward, Dorchester, DT2 8PY. Kingston Maurward College, 01305 215003, events@kmc.ac.uk, www.morekmc.com. *1m E of Dorchester. Off A35. Follow brown Tourist Information signs.* **For opening times and information, please phone, email or visit garden website.**

Stepping into the grounds you will be greeted with 35 impressive acres of formal gardens. During the late spring and summer months, our National Collection of penstemons and salvias display a lustrous rainbow of purples, pinks, blues and whites, leading you on through the ample hedges and stonework balustrades. An added treat is the Elizabethan walled garden, offering a new vision of enchantment. Open early Jan to mid Dec. Hours will vary in winter depending on conditions - check garden website or call before visiting. Partial wheelchair access only, gravel paths, steps and steep slopes. Map provided at entry, highlighting the most suitable routes.

33 KNITSON OLD FARMHOUSE

Corfe Castle, Wareham, BH20 5JB. Rachel Helfer, 01929 421681, rjehelfer@gmail.com. *2m NW of Swanage. 3m E of Corfe Castle. Signed L off A351 to Knitson. Very narrow rds for 1m. Ample parking in yard or in adjacent field.* **Fri 25 May (2-6). Cream teas. Sat 26, Sun 27 May (2-8). Light refreshments. Mon 28 May (2-6). Cream teas. Adm £4, chd free. Cream teas and delicious home-made cakes from 2-6pm. On Sun, after 6pm, tea available or BYO bottle of wine/drinks, savoury picnic snacks for sale. Visits also by arrangement Apr to Nov, max 30.**

Mature cottage garden nestled at base of chalk downland. Herbaceous borders, rockeries, climbers and shrubs, evolved and designed over 50yrs for yr-round colour and interest. Large wildlife friendly kitchen garden for self sufficiency. Rachel is delighted to welcome visitors, discuss all aspects of sustainable gardening and the benefits of gardening for mental and physical wellbeing. We have used a lot of local stone in the design and have interesting old stones and stone baths around the garden. Uneven, sloping paths.

34 ◆ KNOLL GARDENS

Hampreston, Wimborne, BH21 7ND. Mr Neil Lucas, 01202 873931, enquiries@knollgardens.co.uk, www.knollgardens.co.uk. *2½m W of Ferndown. ETB brown signs from A31. Large car park.* **For NGS: Fri 27 July, Fri 7 Sept (10-4). Adm £6.50, chd £4.50. Self catering drinks and pre-wrapped cakes and biscuits. For other opening times and information, please phone, email or visit garden website.**

Taking its inspiration from the natural world, Knoll's naturalistic planting style mimics nature, building on the way plants co-exist to create a glorious garden packed with year-round interest. Practical planting ideas abound. A mini-arboretum of rare and unusual trees and shrubs provides the perfect backdrop for more recent informal plantings of glorious grasses and flowering perennials. The garden is also home to a registered charity, the Knoll Gardens Foundation. The Foundation researches and promotes wildlife friendly gardening and regularly hosts events in the garden frequently with other wildlife charities. More information at www.knollgardensfoundation.org. Some slopes. Various surfaces incl gravel, paving, grass and bark.

NPC

35 LANGEBRIDE HOUSE

Long Bredy, DT2 9HU. Mrs J Greener, 01308 482257. *8m W of Dorchester. S off A35, midway between Dorchester and Bridport. Well signed. 1st gateway on L in village.* **Visits by arrangement Feb to July. Adm £4.50, chd free.**

This old rectory garden has carpets of spring bulbs spreading out under huge copper beech tree on lawn. A lovely place to visit in spring and early summer, with a large variety of daffodils and early spring bulbs amongst flowering shrubs, trees and herbaceous borders with kitchen garden. Limited wheelchair access if wet.

36 LAWSBROOK

Brodham Way, Shillingstone, DT11 0TE. Clive Nelson, 01258 860148, cne70bl@aol.com, www.facebook.com/Lawsbrook. *5m NW of Blandford. To Shillingstone on A357. Turn up Gunn Lane (PO box) - up lane (past Wessex Avenue on L & Everetts Lane on R) then turn R as rd bends to L. Lawsbrook 250m on R.* **Sun 25 Feb (10-4); Sun 27, Mon 28 May (10-6). Home-made teas. Sun 4 Nov (10-4). Adm £3, chd free. Tea, coffee, cold drinks, cakes. Visits also by arrangement Feb to Nov, garden can accommodate large numbers.**

10th Year of opening for NGS! More than 130 different tree species spread over 6 acres in a garden founded in 1959. Significant numbers of native species and many unusual specimens incl Dawn Redwood, Damyio Oak and Wollemi Pine. Formal borders and raised bed vegetable and flower garden. You can be assured of a relaxed and friendly day out, lovely opportunity for family walks in all areas incl wildlife, stream and meadow. Children's activities, all day teas/cakes and dogs are very welcome. Large scale snowdrop day in Feb, double May opening and intense autumn hues in Nov. It is open and accessible with enough space and interest for everyone. Gravel path at entrance, grass paths over whole garden.

♿ 🐕 ✿ 🚌 ☕

37 LITTLE CLIFF

Sidmouth Road, Lyme Regis, DT7 3EQ. Mrs Debbie Bell, 01297 444833, debbie@debbiebell.co.uk. *Edge of Lyme Regis. Turn off A35 onto B3165 to Lyme Regis. Through Uplyme to mini r'about by Travis Perkins. 3rd exit on R, up to fork and L down Sidmouth Rd following NGS arrows from mini r'about. Garden on R.* **Thur 3, Sun 6 May, Thur 7, Sun 10 June, Thur 5, Sun 8 July (2-5). Adm £4, chd free. Visits also by arrangement May to July, please arrange in advance.**

S-facing seaward, Little Cliff looks out over spectacular views of Lyme Bay. Spacious garden sloping down hillside through series of garden rooms where visual treats unfold. Vibrant herbaceous borders incl hot garden and bog garden intermingled with mature specimen trees, shrubs and wall climbers. Jungle walkway at bottom of garden, Indian influenced pavilion leading to white borders and vegetable garden. New hidden garden amongst the palms and rich colours of the hot garden. Steep slopes.

✿

38 ◆ LITTLEBREDY WALLED GARDENS

Littlebredy, DT2 9HL. The Walled Garden Workshop, 01305 898055, secretary@wgw.org.uk, www.littlebredy.com. *8m W of Dorchester. 10m E of Bridport. 1½m S of A35. NGS days: park on village green then walk 300yds. For the less mobile (and on normal open days) use gardens car park.* **For NGS: Tue 19, Tue 26 June (2-6). Adm £5, chd free. Home-made teas. For other opening times and information, please phone, email or visit garden website.**

1 acre walled garden on S-facing slopes of Bride River Valley. Herbaceous borders, riverside rose walk, lavender beds and potager vegetable and cut flower gardens. Original Victorian glasshouses, one under renovation. Gardens also open 2-5pm on Wed & Sun (see website for other days) from Mid-April to mid-Sept, weather permitting. Featured in Country Living, Dorset Gardens Trust, Dorset Magazine, Western Daily Press. Partial wheelchair access, some steep grass slopes. For disabled parking please follow signs to main entrance.

♿ 🐕 ✿ ☕

39 LOWER ABBOTTS WOOTTON FARM

Whitchurch Canonicorum, Bridport, DT6 6NL. Johnny & Clare Trenchard. *6m W of Bridport. Well signed from A35 at Morecombe Lake (2m) and Bottle Inn at Marshwood on B3165 (1.5m). Some disabled off-road parking.* **Sat 30 June, Sun 1 July (2-5). Adm £4, chd free. Home-made teas.**

Sculptor owner reflects her creative flair in garden form, shape and colour. New open gravel garden contrasts with main garden consisting of lawns, borders and garden rooms, making a perfect setting for sculptures. The naturally edged pond provides a tranquil moment of calm, but beware of being led down the garden path by the running hares! Partial wheelchair access.

🐕 ✿ ☕

40 44 LOWER BLANDFORD ROAD

Broadstone Poole, BH18 8NY. Mike and Tina Clifford, 01202 904203, addicted2tropical44@icloud.com. *Take Lower Blandford Rd leading up to Broadstone centre approaching from Derbys Corner r'about. Take 1st turning on R. (Fontmell Rd) then sharp L. Extra parking in Fontmell Rd.* **Sat 28, Sun 29 July, Sat 18, Sun 19 Aug (1-5). Adm £3.50, chd free. Home-made teas. Visits also by arrangement July to Sept for groups of 10+.**

Exotic garden full of bananas, palms and lush tropical planting, the garden is filled to the brim with unusual and rare plants, many seldom seen in British gardens. Paths lead you through to the greenhouses and an Abbotsbury inspired colonial summerhouse and water feature surrounded by tree ferns and shade loving plants. A true plantaholic's paradise!

✿ ☕

41 MANOR FARM, HAMPRESTON

Wimborne, BH21 7LX. Guy & Anne Trehane, 01202 574223, anne.trehane@live.co.uk. *2½m E of Wimborne, 2½m W of Ferndown. From Canford Bottom r'about on A31, take exit B3073 Ham Lane. ½m turn R at Hampreston Xrds. House at bottom of village.* **Sat 24 Feb (10-1); Sun 25 Feb (1-4). Light refreshments. Sun 29 Apr, Wed 30 May, Sun 29 July, Wed 1, Sun 12 Aug (1-5). Home-made teas. Adm £4, chd free. Soup also**

available at Feb openings. Visits also by arrangement Feb to Aug for groups of 15+.
Traditional farmhouse garden designed and cared for by 3 generations of the Trehane family through over 100yrs of farming and gardening at Hampreston. Garden is noted for its herbaceous borders and rose beds within box and yew hedges. Mature shrubbery, water and bog garden. Open for hellebores and snowdrops in Feb. Dorset Hardy Plant Society sales at openings. Hellebores for sale in Feb.

42 ◆ MAPPERTON GARDENS

Mapperton, Beaminster, DT8 3NR. The Earl & Countess of Sandwich, 01308 862645, office@mapperton.com, www.mapperton.com. *6m N of Bridport. Off A356/A3066. 2m SE of Beaminster off B3163.* **For NGS: Sun 4, Sun 11 Feb (11-3.30). Adm £4.50, chd free. Tea, coffee and cake in Church on 4 & 11 Feb.** For other opening times and information, please phone, email or visit garden website.
Terraced valley gardens surrounding Tudor/Jacobean manor house. On upper levels, walled croquet lawn, orangery and Italianate formal garden with fountains, topiary and grottoes. Below, C17 summerhouse and fishponds. Lower garden with shrubs and rare trees, leading to woodland and spring gardens. Garden open 1 Mar to 31 Oct (except Sat) (11-5); Café open 2 Apr to 31 Oct (except Sat); House open 2 Apr to 31 Oct (except Fri and Sat). Snowdrop Sundays 4 & 11 February 2018. Partial wheelchair access (lawn and upper levels).

43 MARREN

Holworth, Dorchester, DT2 8NJ. Mr & Mrs Peter Cartwright, 01305 851503, wcartwright@tiscali.co.uk, www.wendycartwright.net. *SE of Dorchester. Don't use SatNav. Off A353 At Poxwell turn towards Ringstead. Straight ahead in NT Car Park at top of hill. Park before gate marked No Cars. Walk through gate, signed path, on R or walk down track.* **Sat 28, Sun 29 Apr, Sat 9, Sun 10 June (2-5). Adm £5, chd free. Visits also by arrangement Apr to Sept, refreshments by arrangement for groups of 10+.**
4 acres. From NT car park down steep public footpath and 64 grass steps to woodland garden with chainsaw tree sculptures. More formal Italianate garden around house with wonderful arbours. Mediterranean feel. Strong structural planting. Wildlife and seaside garden. Children's summerhouse, hornbeam house. Willow arbour to discover at the bottom. Fabulous sea views. Featured on Gardeners' World and in Country Homes and Interiors. Stout footwear and strong knees recommended. Not suitable for wheelchairs but disabled access to house for tea by prior arrangement.

44 MAYFIELD

4 Walford Close, Wimborne Minster, BH21 1PH. Mr & Mrs Terry Wheeler, 01202 849838, terry.wheeler@tesco.net. *½m N of Wimborne Town Centre. B3078 out of Wimborne, R into Burts Hill, 1st L into Walford Close.* **Sun 13, Wed 16, Sun 27 May, Wed 6, Wed 13 June (2-5). Adm £3.50, chd free. Home-made teas. Visits also by arrangement May & June for groups of 6+.** Donation to The Friends of Victoria Hospital, Wimborne.
Town garden of approx ¼ acre. Front: formal hard landscaping planted with drought-resistant shrubs and perennials. Shaded area has wide variety of hostas. Back garden contrasts with a seductive series of garden rooms containing herbaceous perennial beds separated by winding grass paths and rustic arches. Pond, vegetable beds and greenhouses containing succulents and vines. Garden access is across a pea-shingle drive. If this is manageable, wheelchairs can access the back garden provided they are no wider than 65cms.

45 THE MILL HOUSE

Crook Hill, Netherbury, DT6 5LX. Michael & Giustina Ryan, 01308 488267, themillhouse@dsl.pipex.com. *1m S of Beaminster. Turn R off A3066 Beaminster to Bridport rd signed Netherbury. Car park at Xrds at bottom of hill.* **Visits by arrangement min 6, max 30.**
6½ acres of garden around R Brit, incl mill stream and mill pond. Extensive garden consisting of formal walled, terraced and vegetable gardens and bog garden. Emphasis on spring bulbs, scented flowers, hardy geraniums, lilies, clematis and water irises. Wander through the wild garden planted with many rare and interesting trees incl conifers, magnolias, oak and fruit trees. Collection of Magnolias flowering March to Sept. Walled garden with water feature. Collection of crab apples flowering April to May and fruiting Aug to Nov. Partial wheelchair access.

46 ◆ MINTERNE HOUSE

Minterne Magna, Dorchester, DT2 7AU. The Hon Henry & Mrs Digby, 01300 341370, enquiries@minterne.co.uk, www.minterne.co.uk. *2m N of Cerne Abbas. On A352 Dorchester-Sherborne rd.* **For opening times and information, please phone, email or visit garden website.**
As seen on BBC Gardeners' World and voted one of the 10 prettiest gardens in England by The Times. Famed for their display of rhododendrons, azaleas, Japanese cherries and magnolias in April/May. Small lakes, streams and cascades offer new vistas at each turn around the 1m horseshoe shaped gardens covering 23 acres. The season ends with spectacular autumn colour. Snowdrops in Feb. Spring bulbs, blossom and bluebells in April. Garden at its peak in April/May with historic rhododendron collection, magnolias and azaleas. Over 200 acers provide spectacular autumn colour in Sept/Oct. Regret unsuitable for wheelchairs.

47 NEW NORWOOD HOUSE

Corscombe, Dorchester, DT2 0PD. Mr & Mrs Jonathan Lewis, 07836 600185, jonathan.lewis@livegroup.co.uk. *1m on R from The Fox Inn in Corscombe, going towards Halstock.* **Sun 17, Thur 21 June (2-5). Adm £5, chd £2. Home-made teas and cream teas. Visits also by arrangement May to Aug for groups of 8+.**

Our garden is hidden away in a stunning West Dorset Valley surrounded by our small family estate. We started our landscaping adventure from scratch in 2011. Today the glorious purple, pink and white borders surround the house and lawn. Many varieties of geranium and other perennials, grasses, shrubs and a rockery. Lake walks recommended, weather permitting.

48 THE OLD RECTORY, LITTON CHENEY

Dorchester, DT2 9AH. Richard & Emily Cave. *9m W of Dorchester. 1m S of A35, 6m E of Bridport. Small village in the beautiful Bride Valley. Park in village and follow signs.* **Sun 29 Apr, Sun 1, Wed 4 July (2-5). Adm £6, chd free. Home-made teas.**

Steep paths lead to beguiling 4 acres of natural woodland with many springs, streams, 2 pools one a natural swimming pool planted with native plants. Front garden with pleached crabtree border, topiary and soft planting incl tulips, peonies, roses and verbascums. Walled garden with informal planting, kitchen garden, orchard and 350 rose bushes for a cut flower business. Formal front garden designed by Arne Maynard. Not suitable for wheelchairs.

49 THE OLD RECTORY, MANSTON

Manston, Sturminster Newton, DT10 1EX. Andrew & Judith Hussey, 01258 474673, judithhussey@hotmail.com. *6m S of Shaftesbury, 2½m N of Sturminster Newton. From Shaftesbury, take B3091. On reaching Manston, past Plough Inn, L for Child Okeford on R-hand bend. Old Rectory last house on L.* **Sun 17, Wed 20 June (2-5). Adm £5, chd free. Home-made teas. Visits also by arrangement May to July for groups of 4+.**

Beautifully restored 5 acre garden. S-facing wall with 120ft herbaceous border edged by old brick path. Enclosed yew hedge flower garden. Wildflower meadow marked with mown paths and young plantation of mixed hardwoods. Well maintained walled Victorian kitchen garden with new picking flower section. Large new greenhouse also installed. Knot garden now well established. Featured in Country Life and Dorset Life.

50 THE OLD RECTORY, NETHERBURY

Beaminster, DT6 5NB. Simon & Amanda Mehigan, www.oldrectorynetherbury.tumblr.com. *2m SW of Beaminster. Please park considerately in the village as directed. Parking for the less mobile available at house.* **Sun 11 Feb (11-3.30). Light refreshments. Sun 1, Tue 3 Apr, Sun 20, Tue 22 May (11-5). Home-made teas. Adm £6, chd free. Refreshments from 12 noon.**

5 acre garden developed by present owners over last 20 yrs. Formal areas with topiary near house, naturalistic planting elsewhere. Many bulbs including fritillaries, erythroniums, tulips and wood anemones. Extensive bog garden with pond and stream planted with candelabra primroses and other moisture lovers. Hornbeam walk. Decorative kitchen garden.

51 THE OLD RECTORY, PULHAM

Dorchester, DT2 7EA. Mr & Mrs N Elliott, 01258 817595, gilly.elliott@hotmail.com. *13m N of Dorchester. 8m SE of Sherborne. On B3143 turn E at Xrds in Pulham. Signed Cannings Court.* **Sun 13, Thur 17 May, Sun 5, Thur 9 Aug (2-5). Adm £6, chd free. Home-made teas. Visits also by arrangement May to Aug for groups, weekdays only.**

4 acres formal and informal gardens surround C18 rectory, splendid views. Yew pyramid allées and hedges, circular herbaceous borders with late summer colour. Exuberantly planted terrace, purple and white beds. Box parterres, mature trees, pond, fernery, ha-ha, pleached hornbeam circle. 10 acres woodland walks. Flourishing extended bog garden with islands; awash with primulas and irises in May. Interesting plants for sale. Featured on ITV and in Country Life, Dorset Life, Homes and Gardens, Country Homes and Interiors. Mostly wheelchair access.

52 NEW THE OLD SCHOOL HOUSE

The Street, Sutton Waldron, Blandford Forum, DT11 8NZ. David Milanes. *Turn into Sutton Waldron from A351, continue for 300 yds, 1st house on the L in The Street. Entrance past house through gates in wall.* **Sun 17, Wed 20 June (2-5). Adm £3.50, chd free. Home-made teas. Gluten free cakes available.**

Small village garden laid out in last 4 yrs with planting of hedges into rooms incl orchard, secret garden and pergola walkway. Strong framework of existing large trees, beds are mostly planted with roses and herbacious plants. Pleached hornbeam screen. A designer's garden with interesting semi-tender plants close to house. Level lawns.

53 THE OLD VICARAGE

East Orchard, Shaftesbury, SP7 0BA. Miss Tina Wright, 01747 811744, tina_lon@msn.com. *4½m S of Shaftesbury, 3½m N of Sturminster Newton. Between 90 degree bend and lay-bye with old red phone box. Parking is on opp corner towards Hartgrove.* **Sun 18 Mar, Fri 6, Fri 13, Wed 18, Fri 27 Apr, Sun 13 May, Sun 10 June (2-5). Adm £4, chd free. Home-made teas.**

Cottesmore Farm

Teas will be inside if raining, with wood stove if cold. Visits also by arrangement for any size group.
1.7 acre, award-winning wildlife friendly garden. Swathes of crocus, primula and unusual snowdrops in spring. Many different daffodils and a tulip extravaganza with over 1000 tulip bulbs, then herbaceous borders and wild flowers. Sit by the bubbling stream or gaze at beautiful reflections in the swimming pond. Dogs welcome and children can pond dip. Swing and tree platform overlooking Duncliffe woods. Various shelters around garden if wet. Featured in Homes & Gardens, the Saturday Telegraph, the Mail on Sunday, the Independent, the Dorset magazine. Not suitable for wheelchairs if very wet.

54 ◆ PRIEST'S HOUSE MUSEUM & GARDEN

23-27 High Street, Wimborne, BH21 1HR. Priest's House Museum Trust, 01202 882533, museum@priest-house.co.uk, www.priest-house.co.uk.
Wimborne town centre. Wimborne is just off A31. From W take B3078, from E take B3073 towards town centre. From Poole and Bournemouth enter town from S on A341. **For opening times and information, please phone, email or visit garden website.**
Discover a real gem tucked away in the centre of Wimborne. The walled garden, with its path leading from the back door to the mill stream, is 100 metres long. Colourful herbaceous borders and old varieties of apple and pear trees line the path further down. The garden is sheltered by brick walls, which mark ancient property boundaries and a medieval burgage plot. Groups are asked to pre-book. Wheelchair access throughout the ground floor, garden and tearoom.

55 Q

113 Bridport Road, Dorchester, DT1 2NH. Heather & Chris Robinson, 01305 263088, hmrobinson45@gmail.com.
Approx 300m W of Dorset County Hospital. From Top o' Town r'about head W towards Dorset County Hospital, Q 300 metres further on from Hospital on R. **Suns 11, 18, 25 Mar, 8, 15, 22 Apr, 13 May (2-5). Adm £3, chd free. Tea and home-made cakes. Visits also by arrangement Feb to Sept min number 8, 40 max, 1week notice preferred.**
Q is essentially all things to all men, a modern cottage town garden with many facets, jam packed with bulbs, shrubs, trees, climbers and herbaceous plants. Gazebo, statutes, water, bonsai and topiary. Planting reflects the owners many and varied interest including over 100 clematis, different types and varieties of spring bulbs purchased yearly. In spring the garden flourishes with bulbs from early snowdrops, herbaceous plants incl hellebores, clematis, daphne The garden is divided into rooms providing differing areas of interest. Vegetable garden and fruit trees dotted around the garden. We celebrate Mothering Sunday by providing a small gift for each Mum Featured in Gardeners' World, TV West Country and German tourist guide. Small number of paths available for wheelchair users.

GROUP OPENING

56 NEW RAMPISHAM GARDENS

Rampisham, DT2 0PR. *11m NW of Dorchester. From Dorchester A37 Yeovil, 4m L A356 to Crewkerne, 6m R to Rampisham. From Yeovil A37 Dorchester, 7m R Evershot. From Crewkerne A356, 1½m after Rampisham Garage L Rampisham. Follow signs.* **Sun 10 June (11-5). Combined adm £6, chd free. Home-made teas in the village hall.**

BROOMHILL
Mr & Mrs D Parry.
(See separate entry)

NEW **BROOMHILL COTTAGE**
Mr & Mrs Oz Osborne.

NEW **THE CURATAGE**
Mr & Mrs Tim Hill.

NEW **THE OLD RECTORY**
Mr & Mrs Peter Thomas.

NEW **PUGIN HALL**
Mr & Mrs Tim Wright.

NEW **RAMPISHAM MANOR**
Robert Boileau.

NEW **ROSEMARY COTTAGE**
Lady Gillian Ford.

NEW **THATCHERS REST**
David & Carole Angel.

Parking signed at village hall and in field opp church. This beautiful historic village hosts a wide variety of gardens with 8 hidden gems and several open for the first time, incl some large well established gardens and smaller cottage gardens. Extensive borders planted with shrubs, roses, unusual perennials and annuals, enabling them all to display a vibrancy of colour. Walled vegetable garden, lawns, meadows and meandering pathways leading to bog gardens, wildlife ponds, garden sculptures and streams. C15 church with modifications in the 1840s by Pugin, it will be decorated for the occasion with flowers. The Old Rectory Cottage will also open its wood turner workshop for visitors, as part of Dorset Arts Week. Wheelchair access to most gardens.

57 ◆ SCULPTURE BY THE LAKES

Pallington Lakes, Pallington, Dorchester, DT2 8QU. Mrs Monique Gudgeon, 07720 637808, sbtl@me.com, www.sculpturebythelakes.co.uk. *6m E of Dorchester. ½m E of Tincleton, see beech hedge and security gates. From other direction ¾m from Xrds. No children under 14. No dogs allowed.* **For NGS: Wed 4 July (10-5). Adm £7.50. Light refreshments in our onsite Gallery Cafe serving hot & cold drinks, light lunches & snacks, cream teas & cakes, using ingredients grown onsite or from local area.** For other opening times and information, please phone, email or visit garden website.

Recently created modern garden with inspiration taken from all over the world. Described as a modern arcadia it follows traditions of the landscape movement, but for C21. Where sculpture has been placed, the planting palette has been kept simple, but dramatic, so that the work remains the star. Home to Monique and her husband, renowned British sculptor Simon Gudgeon, the sculpture park features over 30 of his most iconic pieces including Isis, which is also in London's Hyde Park and a dedicated gallery where some of his smaller pieces can be seen and purchased. Disabled access limited though possible to go round paths on mobility scooter or electric wheelchair if care taken.

58 THE SECRET GARDEN

The Friary, Hilfield, Dorchester, DT2 7BE. The Society of St Francis, 01300 341345, hilfieldssf@franciscans.org.uk, www.hilfieldfriary.org.uk. *10m N of Dorchester, on A352 between Sherborne & Dorchester. 1st L after Minterne Magna, 1st turning on R signed The Friary. From Yeovil turn off A37 signed Batcombe, 3rd turning on L.* **Sat 5, Sun 6 May (2-5). Adm £5, chd free. Light refreshments. Range of home-made cakes. Visits also by arrangement Apr to Sept, please phone.**

Ongoing reclamation of neglected woodland garden. Mature trees, bamboo, rhododendrons, azaleas, magnolias, camellias, other choice shrubs with stream on all sides crossed by bridges, and in spring a growing collection of loderi hybrids. New plantings of viburnums. Stout shoes recommended for woodland garden. Friary grounds open where meadows, woods and livestock can be viewed. Friary Shop selling a variety of gifts. Wheelchair access along our private road and main areas.

59 THE SECRET GARDEN AND SERLES HOUSE

47 Victoria Road, Wimborne, BH21 1EN. Ian Willis, 01202 880430. *Centre of Wimborne. On B3082 W of town, very near hospital, Westfield car park 300yds. Off-road parking close by.* **Thur 19, Sun 22, Sun 29 July, Thur 2, Sun 5, Sun 19, Sun 26, Mon 27, Thur 30 Aug, Sat 1, Sun 2, Sun 9 Sept (2-5). Adm £3.50, chd free. Home-made teas. Visits also by arrangement July to Sept, home-made teas can be**

arranged. Donation to Wimborne Civic Society and NADFAS.
Alan Titchmarsh described this amusingly creative garden as 'one of the best 10 private gardens in Britain'. The ingenious use of unusual plants complements the imaginative treasure trove of garden objects d'art. The enchanting house is also open. A feeling of a bygone age accompanies your tour as you step into a world of whimsical fantasy that is theatrical and unique. 'Deliciously bonkers'. Antiques and bric-a-brac on sale. Dorset Heritage Week Booklet. Wheelchair access to garden only. Narrow steps may prohibit wide wheelchairs.

60 ◆ SHERBORNE CASTLE

New Rd, Sherborne, DT9 5NR. Mr E Wingfield Digby, www.sherbornecastle.com. *½m E of Sherborne. On New Rd B3145. Follow brown signs from A30 & A352.* **For opening times and information, please visit garden website.**
40+ acres. Grade I Capability Brown garden with magnificent vistas across surrounding landscape, incl lake and views to ruined castle. Herbaceous planting, notable trees, mixed ornamental planting and managed wilderness are linked together with lawn and pathways. Dry grounds walk. Partial wheelchair access, gravel paths, steep slopes, steps.

61 SLAPE MANOR

Netherbury, DT6 5LH. Mr & Mrs Antony Hichens, 01308 488232, sczhichens@btinternet.com. *1m S of Beaminster. Turn W off A3066 to Netherbury. House ½m S of Netherbury on back rd to Bridport signed Waytown.* **Sun 27 May (2-5). Adm £4.50, chd free. Home-made teas. Visits also by arrangement for groups of 10+.**
River valley garden with spacious lawns and primula fringed streams down to lake. Walk over the stream with magnificent hostas, gunneras and horizontal cryptomeria Japonica Elegans, and around the lake. Admire the mature wellingtonias, ancient wisterias, rhododendrons and planting around the house. Mostly flat with some sloping paths and steps.

62 2 SPUR GATE

24 Spur Hill Avenue, Parkstone, Poole, BH14 9PH. Mr & Mrs R J P Butler, 01202 732342, annebbutler@icloud.com. *3m W of Bournemouth. At end of Wessex Way (A 338) take 3rd exit (Lindsay Rd). Continue to end. R at T-Lights. After next T-Lights, 2nd L into Kings Ave. Top of hill turn R into Spurhill Ave. Please park on rd.* **Visits by arrangement Apr to Oct, 20 max. Home-made teas.**
Town garden designed around modern house on steep slope. Over 9 years this challenging site has been converted into a series of banks and terraces which progress from the formality of pool terraces to a gravel garden, Japanese area and woodland. The Teahouse offers a peaceful and sheltered destination from which to view the house set above its bank of Stipa grasses. New living roof. Featured on Radio Solent. Regret no wheelchair access.

63 NEW STABLE COURT

Chalmington, Dorchester, DT2 0HB. Jenny & James Shanahan. *From A37 travel down towards Cattistock & Chalmington for 1½m turn R at triangle to Chalmington. ½m house on R with red letter box on gate.* **Wed 6, Sun 10 June (2-5.30). Adm £4.50, chd free. Home-made teas.**
This exuberant garden was begun in 2010. Extending to about 1½ acres, it is naturalistic in style with a shrubbery, gravel garden, wild garden and pond where many trees have been planted. Overflowing with roses scrambling up trees, over hedges and walls. More formal garden closer to house with lawns and herbaceous borders. Lovely views over Dorset countryside. Exhibition of paintings in studio. Gravel path partway around garden, otherwise the paths are grass, not suitable for wheelchairs in wet weather.

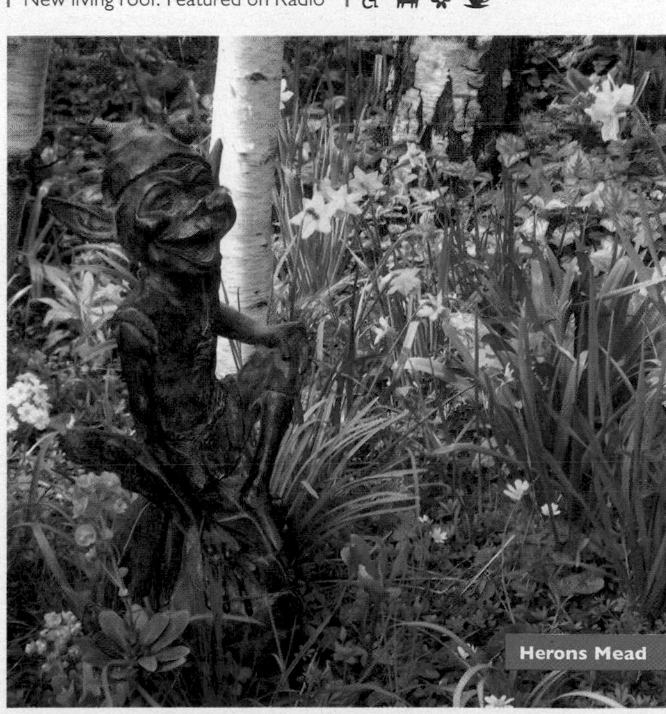

Herons Mead

64 STADDLESTONES
14 Witchampton Mill, Witchampton, Wimborne, BH21 5DE. Annette & Richard Lockwood, 01258 841405. *5m N of Wimborne off B3078. Follow signs through village and park in sports field, 7 min walk to garden, limited disabled parking near garden.* **Sun 27, Mon 28 May, Thur 21 June (2-5). Adm £4, chd free. Home-made teas. Visits also by arrangement Apr to Sept, tea and cake available if required.**
A beautiful setting for a cottage garden with colour themed borders, pleached limes and hidden gems, leading over chalk stream to shady area which has some unusual plants incl hardy orchids and arisaemas. Plenty of areas just to sit and enjoy the wildlife. Wire bird sculptures by local artist. Featured in Dorset Life & Amateur Gardening. Wheelchair access to 1st half of garden.

65 STANBRIDGE MILL
Gussage All Saints, BH21 5EP. Lord and Lady Phillimore. *7m N of Wimborne. On B3078 to Cranborne 150yds from Horton Inn on Shaftesbury road.* **Tue 15 May (10-4.30). Adm £5, chd free. Tea.**
Hidden garden created in 1990s around C18 water mill (not open) on R Allen. Series of linked formal gardens featuring herbaceous and iris borders, pleached limes, white walk and wisteria-clad pergola. 20-acre nature reserve with reed beds and established shelter belts. Grazing meadows with wild flowers and flock of rare breed Dorset Horn sheep. Some areas around river not suitable for wheelchairs.

66 ♦ UPTON COUNTRY PARK
Upton, Poole, BH17 7BJ. Borough of Poole, 01202 262753, uptoncountrypark@poole.gov.uk, www.uptoncountrypark.com. *3m W of Poole town centre. On S side of A35/A3049. Follow brown signs.* **For opening times and information, please phone, email or visit garden website.**
Over 130 acres of award winning parkland incl formal gardens, walled garden, woodland and shoreline. Maritime micro-climate offers a wonderful collection of unusual trees, vintage camellias and stunning roses. Home to Upton House, Grade II* listed Georgian mansion. Regular special events. Plant centre, art gallery and tea rooms. Car parking pay + display (cash or card), free entry to the park. Open 8am - 6pm (winter) and 8am - 9pm (summer). www.facebook.com/uptoncountrypark.

67 WELL COTTAGE
Ryall, Bridport, DT6 6EJ. John & Heather Coley. *Less than 1m N of A35 from Morcombelake. From E: R by farm shop in Morcombelake. Garden 0.9m on R. From W: L entering Morcombelake, immed R by village hall and L on Pitmans Lane to T junc. Turn R, Well Cott on L. Parking on site and nearby.* **Sun 20, Mon 21 May, Sun 22, Mon 23 July (11-5). Adm £4, chd free. Home-made teas.**
1 acre garden brought back to life over last 5½ yrs. There is now much more light after some trees were taken down and new areas have been cultivated. The planting is intended to be natural and the emphasis is very much on colour. A number of distinct areas, some quite surprising but most still enjoy wonderful views over Marshwood Vale. Heather's textile art studio will be open to view. Wheelchair access possible but there are a few hard surface paths, slopes and steps.

Your visit to a garden will help more people be cared for by a Parkinson's nurse

68 WESTERN GARDENS
24A Western Ave, Branksome Park, Poole, BH13 7AN. Mr Peter Jackson, 01202 708388, pjbranpark@gmail.com. *3m W of Bournemouth. From S end Wessex Way (A338) at gyratory take The Avenue, 2nd exit. At T-lights turn R into Western Rd then at bottom of hill L. At church turn R into Western Ave.* **Sun 17 June, Sun 29 July (2-5). Adm £4, chd free. Tea and delicious home-made cakes. Visits also by arrangement June to Aug, refreshments by arrangement, min 12.**
'This secluded and magical 1-acre garden captures the spirit of warmer climes and begs for repeated visits' (Gardening Which?). Created over 40 yrs it offers enormous variety with rose, Mediterranean courtyard and woodland gardens, herbaceous borders and cherry tree and camellia walk. Lush foliage and vibrant flowers give yr-round colour and interest enhanced by sculpture and topiary. Home-made jams and chutneys for sale. Wheelchair access to ¾ garden.

69 NEW ♦ WIMBORNE MODEL TOWN & GARDENS
King Street, Wimborne, BH21 1DY. Wimborne Minster Model Town Ltd Registered Charity No 298116, 01202 881924, info@wimborne-modeltown.com, www.wimborne-modeltown.com. *2 mins walk from Wimborne Town Centre & the Minster Church. Follow Wimborne signs from A31; From Poole/Bournemouth follow Wimborne signs on A341; from N follow Wimborne signs B3082/B3078. Public parking opp in King Street Car Park.* **For opening times and information, please phone, email or visit garden website.**
Attractive garden surrounding the intriguing model town buildings, with herbaceous borders, rockery, perennials, shrubs and rare trees. Miniature river system incl bog garden and other water features. Sensory area incorporates the vegetable garden, grasses, a

seasonally fragrant and colourful border, wind and water elements. Plentiful seating. Open 24 Mar to 28 Oct (10 - 5). Seniors discount; groups welcome. For admission charges see website. The original 1950s miniature buildings of Wimborne nestle within the garden area. Tea room, shop, miniature dolls' house collection and digital model railway. Gardens, model buildings and facilities are wheelchair accessible. Two wheelchairs available for use by visitors.

The National Garden Scheme and Perennial, helping gardeners when they are in need

70 WINCOMBE PARK

Shaftesbury, SP7 9AB. John & Phoebe Fortescue, phoebe.fortescue@btinternet.com. *2m N of Shaftesbury. A350 Shaftesbury to Warminster, past Wincombe Business Park, 1st R signed Wincombe & Donhead St Mary. ¾m on R.* **Sun 13, Wed 16 May (2-5). Adm £5, chd free. Cream teas. Home-made cakes and biscuits, tea, coffee, squash. Dairy and gluten free available. Visits also by arrangement May & June, groups are welcome, parking for a coach.**

Extensive mature garden with sweeping panoramic views from lawn over parkland to lake and enchanting woods through which you can wander amongst bluebells. Garden is a riot of colour in spring with azaleas, rhododendrons and camellias in flower amongst shrubs and unusual trees. Beautiful walled kitchen garden. Partial wheelchair access only, slopes and gravel paths.

71 WOLVERHOLLOW

Elsdons Lane, Monkton Wyld, DT6 6DA. Mr & Mrs D Wiscombe, 01297 560610. *4m N of Lyme Regis. 4m NW of Charmouth. Monkton Wyld is signed from A35 approx 4m NW of Charmouth off dual carriageway. Wolverhollow next to church.* **Sun 13, Mon 14 May (11.30-4). Adm £4, chd free. Home-made teas. Visits also by arrangement.**

Over 1 acre of informal mature garden on different levels. Lawns lead past borders and rockeries down to a shady lower garden. Numerous paths take you past a variety of uncommon shrubs and plants. A managed meadow has an abundance of primulas growing close to stream. A garden not to be missed! Cabin in meadow area from which vintage, retro and other lovely things can be purchased.

44 Lower Blandford Road

ESSEX

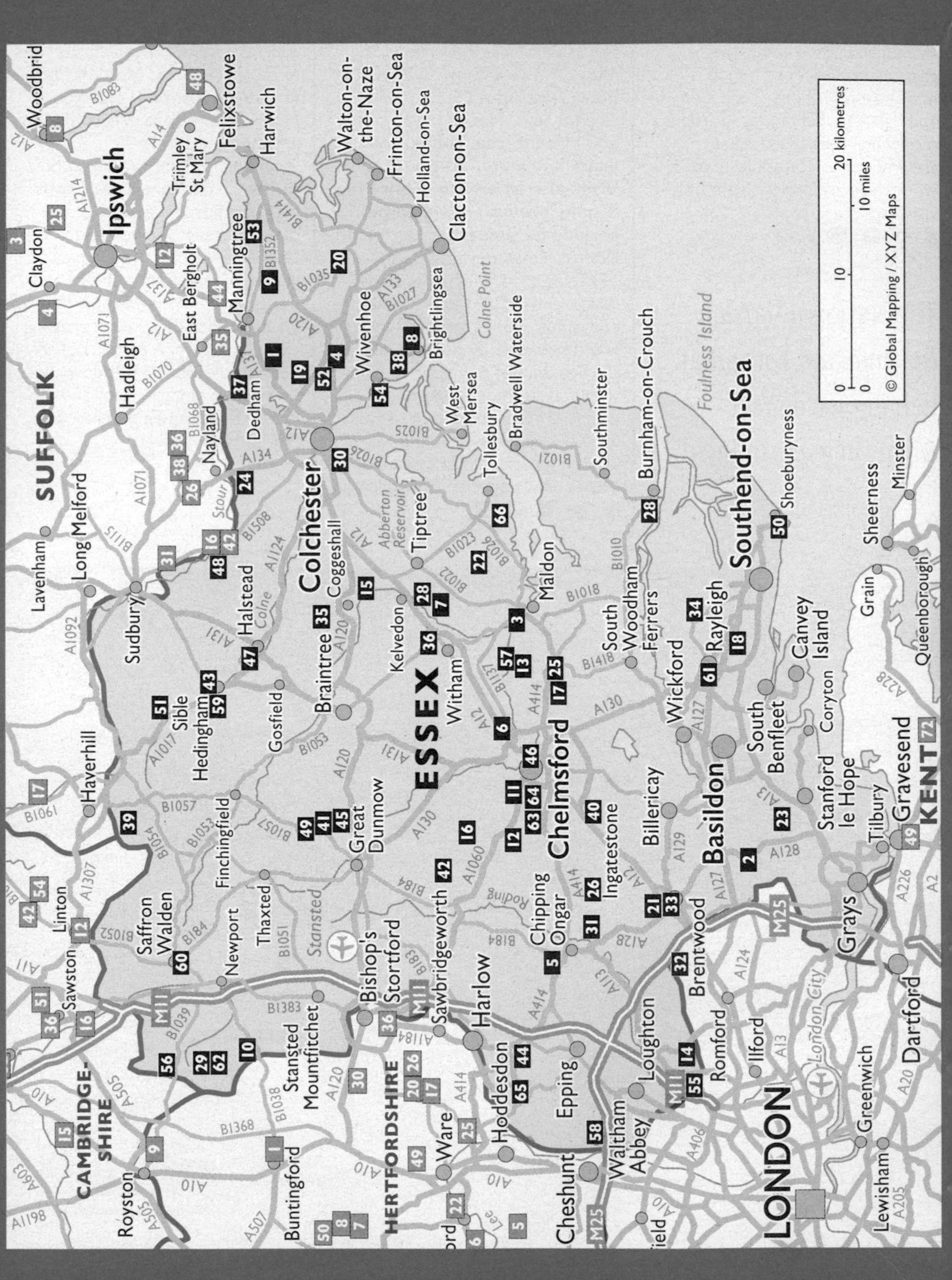
ESSEX
SUFFOLK
CAMBRIDGE-SHIRE
HERTFORDSHIRE
KENT
LONDON
Ipswich
Colchester
Chelmsford
Southend-on-Sea
Basildon
Harlow
Woodbridge
Felixstowe
Trimley St Mary
Harwich
Walton-on-the-Naze
Frinton-on-Sea
Holland-on-Sea
Clacton-on-Sea
Claydon
East Bergholt
Manningtree
Brightlingsea
Colne Point
Wivenhoe
Hadleigh
Dedham
Nayland
Stour
West Mersea
Bradwell Waterside
Tollesbury
Southminster
Burnham-on-Crouch
Foulness Island
Shoeburyness
Minster
Sheerness
Long Melford
Lavenham
Sudbury
Halstead
Colne
Coggeshall
Abberton Reservoir
Tiptree
Kelvedon
Maldon
South Woodham Ferrers
Rayleigh
Canvey Island
Grain
Queenborough
Braintree
Witham
Wickford
South Benfleet
Coryton
Gosfield
Sible Hedingham
Haverhill
Great Dunmow
Finchingfield
Billericay
Ingatestone
Stanford le Hope
Tilbury
Gravesend
Linton
Saffron Walden
Thaxted
Newport
Stansted
Bishop's Stortford
Sawbridgeworth
Chipping Ongar
Rodina
Brentwood
Grays
Sawston
Stansted Mountfitchet
Epping
Loughton
Romford
Ilford
London City
Dartford
Royston
Buntingford
Ware
Hoddesdon
Waltham Abbey
Greenwich
Lewisham
Cheshunt
Lee
M11
M25
A12
A14
A120
A127
A130
A13
A10
0
10
20 kilometres
10 miles
© Global Mapping / XYZ Maps

Close to London but with its own unique character, Essex is perhaps England's best kept secret - with a beautiful coastline, rolling countryside and exquisite villages. It is a little known fact that over seventy per cent of Essex is rural. There are wide horizons, ancient woodlands and hamlets pierced by flint church spires.

Please come and visit our Essex gardens and gain inspiration for your own keenly cultivated patch. It is full of surprises with glorious gardens spread across one amazing county. Essex is the home of 'Constable Country', and we have a range of attractive gardens in and around that delightful picturesque area. Indeed, from the four corners of Essex we offer lots to explore, from a garden featuring the smallest thatched cottage in England within its grounds, to grand country estates.

Essex is proud to have a collection of exciting and beautiful gardens for you to discover including our renowned tulip gardens, fragrant rose gardens and newly designed modern gardens. You will find gardens to suit all tastes. So why not take a few hours out of the hurly burly of life, unwind and wander around our county's picturesque gardens? Or plan a whole day out by making arrangements to visit a garden with a group. Remember, some of our gardens aren't just for plant enthusiasts but are perfect for the whole family to enjoy.

Visitors can be assured of a warm welcome at every open garden gate, whether hidden away down narrow country lanes, in attractive towns or along the estuaries of the east coast. Forget the clichés - rediscover Essex!

Below: **3 Church Path, Wendons Ambo Gardens**

Volunteers

County Organiser
Susan Copeland
01799 550553
susan.copeland@ngs.org.uk

County Treasurer
Richard Steers
07392 426490
steers123@aol.com

Publicity & Booklet Co-ordinator
Doug Copeland
01799 550553
dougcopeland@btinternet.com

Maria Miola
01279 731352
maria.miola@btinternet.com

Social Media Coordinator
Debbie Thomson
01279 600241
dmthomson43@gmail.com

Assistant County Organisers
Tricia Brett
01255 870415
brett.milestones@hotmail.co.uk

Avril & Roger Cole-Jones
01245 225726
randacj@gmail.com

David Cox
01245 222165
elwylodge@gmail.com

Linda & Frank Jewson
01992 714047
frank.jewson@btconnect.com

Groups and Talks
Linda Holdaway
01621 782137
lindaholdaway@btinternet.com

Talks
Neil Holdaway
01621 782137
mail@neilholdaway.com

OPENING DATES

All entries subject to change. For latest information check **www.ngs.org.uk**

Extended openings are shown at the beginning of the month.

Map locator numbers are shown to the right of each garden name.

February

Snowdrop Festival

Friday 16th
Dragons 12

Sunday 25th
Horkesley Hall 24

March

Saturday 17th
◆ Beth Chatto Gardens 4

Sunday 25th
Peacocks 40
Wickets 62

April

Every Thursday from Thursday 19th
Barnards Farm 2

Every Thursday and Friday
Feeringbury Manor 15

Sunday 8th
30 Glenwood Avenue 18

Monday 9th
NEW Jericho Cottage (Megarry's Antiques & Teashop) 26

Sunday 15th
Peacocks 40
NEW 30 Sandford Road 46

Sunday 22nd
Ulting Wick 57

Wednesday 25th
Furzelea 17

Friday 27th
◆ Beeleigh Abbey Gardens 3
Ulting Wick 57

Saturday 28th
NEW Loxley House 33
Tudor Roost 54

Sunday 29th
Furzelea 17
South Shoebury Hall 50
Tudor Roost 54

May

Every Thursday
Barnards Farm 2

Every Thursday and Friday
Feeringbury Manor 15

Sunday 6th
◆ Green Island 19

Monday 7th
Fairwinds 14

Saturday 12th
NEW Ardleigh Gardens 1

Sunday 13th
NEW Ardleigh Gardens 1
Elwy Lodge 13

Thursday 17th
8 Dene Court 11

Friday 18th
Wycke Farm 66

Sunday 20th
Peacocks 40
NEW Sandy Lodge 47
The White Garden 61
Wycke Farm 66

Monday 21st
Miraflores 36

Tuesday 22nd
NEW Jericho Cottage (Megarry's Antiques & Teashop) 26

Thursday 24th
Writtle University College 64

Sunday 27th
Langley Village Gardens 29
Tudor Roost 54

Monday 28th
Rookwoods 43
Tudor Roost 54
Washlands 59

Tuesday 29th
8 Dene Court 11
Dragons 12

June

Every Thursday
Barnards Farm 2

Every Thursday and Friday
Feeringbury Manor 15

Festival Weekend

Saturday 2nd
Boreham Gardens 6

Sunday 3rd
Boreham Gardens 6
Clavering Gardens 10
Furzelea 17
◆ Spencers 51
NEW Two Cottages 56
Waltham Abbey Group 58

Tuesday 5th
Braxted Park Estate 7

Thursday 7th
8 Dene Court 11

Friday 8th
Elwy Lodge 13

Saturday 9th
Spring Cottage 52
NEW Two Cottages 56

Sunday 10th
Blake Hall 5
Havendell 22
Horkesley Hall 24
NEW 30 Sandford Road 46
Spring Cottage 52
Washlands 59
The White Garden 61
NEW Writtle Gardens 63
NEW Wychwood 65

Wednesday 13th
Long House Plants 32

Friday 15th
Miraflores 36

Sunday 17th
Elwy Lodge 13
Parsonage House 39
Peacocks 40
Snares Hill Cottage 49
37 Turpins Lane 55
NEW Two Cottages 56

Tuesday 19th
8 Dene Court 11

Saturday 23rd
3 Pound Gate 41
St Helens 45

Sunday 24th
Barnards Farm 2
Chippins 9
Fudlers Hall 16
NEW 73 Layer Road 30
Miraflores 36

Thursday 28th
8 Dene Court 11

Friday 29th
Keeway 27

July

Every Thursday
Barnards Farm 2

Every Thursday and Friday
Feeringbury Manor 15

Sunday 1st
NEW Hilldrop 23
Little Myles 31
37 Turpins Lane 55
Wendens Ambo Gardens 60

Wednesday 4th
Keeway 27
NEW The Punchbowl Restaurant 42

Thursday 5th
NEW Jericho Cottage (Megarry's Antiques & Teashop) 26

Saturday 7th
NEW The Punchbowl Restaurant 42
Tudor Roost 54

Sunday 8th
Fudlers Hall 16
262 Hatch Road 21
Tudor Roost 54
Washlands 59

Tuesday 10th
8 Dene Court 11
Dragons 12

Wednesday 11th
Long House Plants 32

Friday 13th
Elwy Lodge 13

Saturday 14th
NEW Loxley House 33
69 Rundells 44

Sunday 15th
Elwy Lodge 13
NEW 24 Hyde Lane 25
262 Main Road 34

Thursday 19th
8 Dene Court 11
NEW Jericho Cottage (Megarry's Antiques & Teashop) 26

Sunday 22nd
NEW Brightlingsea Gardens 8
262 Hatch Road 21

Sunday 29th
South Shoebury Hall 50
37 Turpins Lane 55

Tuesday 31st
8 Dene Court 11

August

Every Thursday
Barnards Farm 2

Sunday 5th
30 Glenwood Avenue 18

Tuesday 7th
8 Dene Court 11
Dragons 12

Saturday 11th
Tudor Roost 54

Sunday 12th
Tudor Roost 54

Wednesday 15th
Long House Plants 32

Sunday 19th
262 Main Road 34

Monday 27th
Ulting Wick 57

September

Every Thursday and Friday
Feeringbury Manor 15

Sunday 2nd
Barnards Farm 2
◆ Spencers 51
Writtle University College 64

Sunday 9th
Furzelea 17
Parsonage House 39
Snares Hill Cottage 49
Waltham Abbey Group 58

Wednesday 12th
Furzelea 17
Long House Plants 32

Sunday 16th
NEW Sandy Lodge 47

Wednesday 19th
Dragons 12

Sunday 23rd
NEW Wychwood 65

Sunday 30th
◆ Beth Chatto Gardens 4

October

Every Thursday and Friday to Friday 12th
Feeringbury Manor 15

Sunday 14th
◆ Green Island 19

By Arrangement

Barnards Farm 2
Caynton Cottage, Boreham Gardens 6
Chippins 9
NEW 44 Church Road, Brightlingsea Gardens 8
8 Dene Court 11
Dragons 12
62 Eastbrook Road, Waltham Abbey Group 58
Elwy Lodge 13
Fairwinds 14
Feeringbury Manor 15
Fudlers Hall 16
Furzelea 17
30 Glenwood Avenue 18
Hannams Hall 20
NEW Hilldrop 23
Horkesley Hall 24
NEW Jericho Cottage (Megarry's Antiques & Teashop) 26
Kelvedon Hall 28
Long House Plants 32
Miraflores 36
Monks Cottage 37
Moverons 38
Peacocks 40
3 Pound Gate 41
Rookwoods 43
69 Rundells 44
St Helens 45
NEW Sandy Hook, Brightlingsea Gardens 8
Shrubs Farm 48
Snares Hill Cottage 49
South Shoebury Hall 50
Strandlands 53
Tudor Roost 54
37 Turpins Lane 55
NEW Two Cottages 56
Ulting Wick 57
Waltham Abbey Group 58
Washlands 59
Wickets 62
Writtle University College 64

Barnards Farm

THE GARDENS

GROUP OPENING

1 NEW ARDLEIGH GARDENS

CO7 7LZ. *3½m NE of Colchester. From Ardleigh village centre continue on A137 to Manningtree. 3rd R Tile Barn Lane. R again Hungerdown Lane. 500yds gardens on R. As narrow lane please follow this clockwise route to the gardens.* **Sat 12, Sun 13 May (11-4). Combined adm £5, chd free. Home-made teas at Mayfield Farm.**

NEW CHARITY FARM
Jacqueline & Arthur Cork.

NEW MAYFIELD FARM
Ed Fairey & Jennifer Hughes.

Two lovely, large country gardens set in the beautiful setting of nearby Constable country of north east Essex. Refreshments, and parking in paddock at Mayfield Farm.
Mayfield Farm a 3 acre garden which 3 years ago was largely a field with a huge glass house on 46 tonnes of concrete footings. Now planted with long borders, a secret garden and yew hedging for topiary. In autumn '16, 31,000 bulbs were planted and an additional 41,000 last year. Charity Farm is a 4½ acre garden created from an open and empty site since 2001. Woodland walks and 2 avenues of trees create vistas. A large lake surrounded with natural planting and contains lots of pool frogs which sing loudly in early summer. Parts of the garden are delineated with beech and yew hedging, and the latest planting is a birch grove containing 12 different kinds of birch trees.

2 BARNARDS FARM

Brentwood Road, West Horndon, Brentwood, CM13 3LX. Bernard & Sylvia Holmes & The Christabella Charitable Trust, 01268 454075, vanessa@barnardsfarm.eu, www.barnardsfarm.eu. *5m S of Brentwood. On A128 1½m S of A127 Halfway House flyover. From Junction continue on A128 under the railway bridge. Garden on R just past bridge.* **Every Thur 19 Apr to 30 Aug (11-4.30). Adm £7.50, chd £2.50. Light refreshments, tea, coffee, cakes and light lunches (Thurs), Sun 24 June, Sun 2 Sept (1-5.30). Adm £10, chd £2.50. Home-made teas and cakes, tea, coffee (Suns). Visits also by arrangement Jan to Nov for groups of min 30. Special needs groups min 10.** Donation to St Francis Church.

So much to explore! Climb the Belvedere for the wider view and take the train for a woodland adventure. Spring bulbs and blossom, summer beds and borders, ponds, lakes and streams, walled vegetable plot. 'Japanese garden', sculptures grand and quirky enhance and delight. Barnards Miniature Railway rides (BMR) :Separate charges apply. Sunday extras: Bernard's Sculpture tour 2.30pm Car collection. 1920s Cycle shop. Archery. Model T Ford Rides. Collect loyalty points on Thur visits and earn a free Sun or Thur entry. Aviators welcome (PPO), see website for details. One of the featured gardens in ' Secret Gardens of East Anglia' by Barbara Segall, photographs by Marcus Harper published September 7th 2017. Wheelchair accessible WC Golf buggy tours available.

NPC

3 ◆ BEELEIGH ABBEY GARDENS

Abbey Turning, Beeleigh, Maldon, CM9 6LL. Christopher & Catherine Foyle, 07506 867122, www.visitmaldon.co.uk/beeleigh-abbey. *1m NW of Maldon. Leaving Maldon via London Road take 1st R after Cemetery into Abbey Turning.* **For NGS: Fri 27 Apr (10.30-4.30). Adm £6, chd £2.50. Light refreshments. For other opening times and information, please phone or visit garden website.**

3 acres of secluded gardens in rural historic setting C12 abbey incorporated into private house (not open). Mature trees surround variety of planting and water features, woodland walks underplanted with bulbs leading to tidal river, cottage garden, kitchen garden, orchard, wild flower meadow, rose garden, wisteria walk, magnolia trees, lawn with 85yd long herbaceous border. Scenic backdrop of remains of C12 abbey incorporated into private house (not open). Refreshments including Hot and Cold Drinks, Cakes and Rolls. Gravel paths, some gentle slopes and some steps. Large WC with ramp and handlebars.

4 ◆ BETH CHATTO GARDENS

Elmstead Market, Colchester, CO7 7DB. Mrs Beth Chatto, 01206 822007, info@bethchatto.co.uk, www.bethchatto.co.uk. *¼m E of Elmstead Market. On A133 Colchester to Clacton Rd in village of Elmstead Market.* **For NGS: Sat 17 Mar (9-5). Adm £4.50, chd free. Sun 30 Sept (9-5). Adm £7.95, chd free. Light refreshments. For other opening times and information, please phone, email or visit garden website.**

Internationally famous gardens, including dry, damp, shade, reservoir and woodland areas. The result of over 50 years of hard work and application of the huge body of plant knowledge possessed by Beth Chatto and her late husband Andrew. Visitors cannot fail to be affected by the peace and beauty of the garden. The new Reservoir Garden was opened by Beth in 2017: a wonderful area, and a must-visit for those who haven't seen it yet. Large plant nursery. Audio trail. Tree Trail. Gift Shop. Free parking. Garden courses and events held all year. Open all year round. We have a large Tearoom overlooking the Gravel Garden and Nursery, offering homemade breakfasts, lunches and teas. It is also fully licensed. Featured on and in BBC Gardeners' World interview with Carol Klein, various newspaper and magazine articles and book mentions. Disabled WC &

parking. Wheelchair access around all of the gardens - on gravel or grass (concrete in Nursery, Giftshop and Tearoom areas).

5 BLAKE HALL

Bobbingworth, CM5 0DG. Mr & Mrs H Capel Cure, www.blakehall.co.uk. *10m W of Chelmsford. Just off A414 between Four Wantz r'about in Ongar & Talbot r'about in North Weald. Signed on A414.* **Sun 10 June (11-4). Adm £4, chd free. Home-made teas in C17 barn.**

25 acres of mature gardens within the historic setting of Blake Hall (not open). Arboretum with broad variety of specimen trees. Spectacular rambling roses clamber up ancient trees. Traditional formal rose garden and herbaceous border. Sweeping lawns. Some gravel paths.

GROUP OPENING

6 BOREHAM GARDENS

Boreham, Chelmsford, CM3 3EF. *4m NE Chelmsford. Take B1137 Boreham Village, turn into Church Rd at Lion Inn. Caynton Cottage is 50mtrs on L. the other gardens are all within walking distance. a map will be available.* **Sat 2, Sun 3 June (1-5). Combined adm £6.50, chd free. Delicious home made cakes and cream teas at Brookfield.**

BROOKFIELD
Bob & Linda Taylor.

CAYNTON COTTAGE
Les & Lynn Mann, 01245 463490, mannlynn15@gmail.com.
Visits also by arrangement in June for groups up to 20. Tea/ Coffee and home-made cake included in the admission fee.

NEW **17 FITZWALTER ROAD**
Lee & Nina Marston.

MONALEE
Andrew & Debora Overington.

Four stunning, inspirational and different gardens in the lovely village of Boreham. At Brookfield a rose covered wall and perennial border greets you, a raised bed vegetable garden, perennial island beds and pond with shrub bank. A buttercup meadow, bordered by a camellia and rhododendron woodland walk. The new garden at Caynton Cottage has been designed and planted from a neglected plot with a C15 thatched cottage. It is planted with a selection of shrubs and perennials for maximum all year interest, with a small wildlife pond and dry stream. Monalee is an ever evolving garden that has many features to attract you including an oriental garden, cut flower bed, enclosed and patio and summer house, with a wide variety of shrubs, trees and perennials. 17 Fitzwalter Road. is a small family garden, modern design softened with natural cottage style planting. Raised beds and decking made from scaffold boards, overcomes flooding issues due to underground springs, and is south west facing. Brookfield, accessible, partial access to meadow. Caynton Cottage, gravel paths, Monalee not wheelchair friendly, 17 Fitzwalter Road partial access.

The Queen's Nursing Institute founded the National Garden Scheme over 90 years ago

7 BRAXTED PARK ESTATE

Braxted Park Road, Great Braxted, Witham, CM8 3EN. Mr Duncan & Mrs Nicky Clark, www.braxtedpark.com. *A12 north, by-pass Witham,. Turn L to Rivenhall & Silver End. Turn L by closed Fox pub. Turn L to Rivenhall & Great Braxted. At T junction turn R to Gt Braxted & Witham. Follow brown sign to Braxted Pk (NOT Braxted Golf Course).* **Tue 5 June (10-4). Adm £5.50, chd free. Light refreshments in the Walled Garden Pavilion. Light lunches and afternoon tea available.**

At 12 noon, the celebrated garden designer, Tom Stuart-Smith will be giving an exclusive talk. Tickets for the talk must be purchased in advance and will support Horatio's Garden charity. To book please visit www.horatiosgarden.org.uk/Braxted or ring 01722 326 834. Braxted Park, Grade II* park of "exceptional significance" is again opening its gardens for the NGS which last year resulted in a record breaking weekday attendance. Meander around the parkland's ponds, lakes and walled gardens. Experience the execution of the 10-year Parkland Restoration Management Plan. Enter walled garden 'rooms' through long Wisteria broad walk and admire Mulberry parasol trees, unique to Braxted. Head Gardener will be on hand to show round and answer questions. There will also be information about Horatio's Garden charity. Perennials on sale in aid of Horatio's Garden.. Guide dogs only.

Braxted Park Estate

GROUP OPENING

8 NEW BRIGHTLINGSEA GARDENS

Colchester, CO7 0JF. *Approx 10m SE of Colchester. Go to Thorrington on B1027 & then head S for approx 3m towards Brightlingsea on B1029. Group gardens are either side of Church Rd. 100yds beyond Autosmith Garage.* **Sun 22 July (10-5). Combined adm £5, chd free. Light refreshments. at 44 Church Road.**

NEW 44 CHURCH ROAD

Mandy Livingstone & Steven Nicholson, 01206 303455, peter.sedwell@gmail.com. **Visits also by arrangement July & Aug 44 Church Rd is opening jointly with Sandy Hook. Contact Sandy Hook. Contact details above.**

NEW 51 CHURCH ROAD

Mr & Mrs John & Maureen McAuley.

NEW SANDY HOOK

Mr & Mrs Peter & Elaine Sedwell, 01206 303455, peter.sedwell@gmail.com. **Visits also by arrangement July & Aug Sandy Hook is opening jointly with 44 Church Rd. Contact Sandy Hook to book a visit.**

Three very interesting and contrasting gardens to enjoy in the unique and ancient maritime town of Brightlingsea. Sandy Hook boasts a raised rose bed, dahlias, penstemons and salvias, with a small woodland stream and a sheltered "White Garden". For old car enthusiasts there are also some pre-war Austins and a model engineering workshop on view.
44 Church Road has a traditional country garden, lovingly transformed over the years, with gentle colours, mature trees, evergreen shrubs, a water feature and a wisteria covered pergola.The garden offers various places to relax and contemplate the different features of this quintessentially English garden.
The garden at 51 Church Road is guaranteed to make you smile – and gasp! A garden that could truly be said to have some depth, with clever landscaping and use of pottery and natural stones. At Brightlingsea the spectacular award winning floral displays adorning the centre are not to be missed.There is much to see along the harbour, the marina with bracing walks along the promenade. Brightlingsea is blessed with plenty of watering holes and places to eat. Wheelchair access restricted to main border garden at Sandy Hook and to the patio at 51 Church Road.

Sandy Hook, Brightlingsea Gardens

9 CHIPPINS

Heath Road, Bradfield, CO11 2UZ. Kit & Ceri Leese, 01255 870730, ceriandkit1@btinternet.com. *3m E of Manningtree. Take A137 from Manningtree Station, turn L opp garage. Take 1st R towards Clacton. At Radio Mast turn L into Bradfield continue through village. Bungalow is opp primary school.* **Sun 24 June (11-4.30). Adm £3.50, chd free. Home-made teas. Delicious home made cakes also available!. Visits also by arrangement May to July groups very welcome - Kit is also an artist, and will happily show people around the studio!.**

Artist's garden and plantaholics' paradise packed with interest. Springtime heralds irises, hostas and alliums. Stream, with wildlife pond and Horace the Huge! Summer hosts an explosion of colour with daylilies and rambling roses. Later dahlias, salvias and exotics. Front features hanging baskets and a 'dry' bed with aeonium schwarzkopf, unusual agaves and cacti Studio open with etching press. Kit is a landscape artist and printmaker, pictures always on display. Afternoon tea with delicious homemade cakes is also available for small parties on specific days if booked in advance.

GROUP OPENING

10 CLAVERING GARDENS

Middle Street, Clavering, CB11 4QL. *7m N of Bishop's Stortford. On B1038. Turn W off B1383 at Newport. Parking at Fox & Hounds Pub & in Middle St.* **Sun 3 June (11-5). Combined adm £5, chd free. Home-made teas at Chestnut Cottage.**

NEW BLACKSMITHS COTTAGE

Michael Sonenscher & Elizabeth Allen.

CHESTNUT COTTAGE

Carol & Mike Wilkinson.

Popular village with many C16/17 timber-framed dwellings. Beautiful C14 church, village green with thatched cricket pavilion and pitch. Chestnut Cottage is 1 acre cottage garden with sweeping lawns and wide flower borders, opposite Clavering Ford. Lots of pathways and seats to sit and contemplate, and stunning views over the medieval heart of the village. Come and see 'The Little House', (open), built in 1760 and reputedly the smallest thatched cottage in England. Blacksmiths Cottage boasts an attractive cottage garden with some unusual plants bordering the historic cottage and old smithy barn. Jamie Oliver was brought up in Clavering where his parents still run 'The Cricketers Pub.' Middle Street is the medieval heart of the village with the ford crossing the River Stort. Local honey for sale.

---

11 8 DENE COURT

Chignall Road, Chelmsford, CM1 2JQ. Mrs Sheila Chapman, 01245 266156. *W of Chelmsford (Parkway). Take A1060 Roxwell Rd for 1m. Turn R at T-lights into Chignall Rd. Dene Court 3rd exit on R. Parking in Chignall Rd.* **Thur 17 May (2-5). Tue 29 May (2-5), also open Dragons. Thur 7, Tue 19, Thur 28 June (2-5). Tue 10 July (2-5), also open Dragons. Thur 19, Tue 31 July (2-5). Tue 7 Aug (2-5), also open Dragons. Adm £3, chd free. Visits also by arrangement May to Aug.**

Beautifully maintained and designed compact garden (250sq yds). Owner is well-known RHS gold medal-winning exhibitor (now retired). Circular lawn, long pergola and walls festooned with roses and climbers. Large selection of unusual clematis. Densely-planted colour coordinated perennials add interest from May to Sept in this immaculate garden.

12 DRAGONS

Boyton Cross, Chelmsford, CM1 4LS. Mrs Margot Grice, 01245 248651, mandmdragons@tiscali.co.uk. *3m W of Chelmsford. On A1060. ½m W of The Hare Pub.* **Fri 16 Feb (12-3). Light refreshments. Tue 29 May, Tue 10 July, Tue 7 Aug (2-5). Also open 8 Dene Court. Home-made teas. Wed 19 Sept (2-5). Home-made teas. Adm £4, chd free. Visits also by arrangement Feb to Sept for groups of 10+.**

A plantswoman's ¾ acre garden, planted to encourage wildlife. Sumptuous colour-themed borders with striking plant combinations, featuring specimen plants, fernery, clematis,and grasses. Meandering paths lead to ponds, patio, scree garden and small vegetable garden. Two summerhouses, one overlooking stream and farmland.

13 ELWY LODGE

West Bowers Rd, Woodham Walter, CM9 6RZ. David & Laura Cox, 01245 222165, elwylodge@gmail.com. *Just outside Woodham Walter village. From Chelmsford, A414 to Danbury. L at 2nd mini r'about into Little Baddow Rd. From Colchester, A12 to Hatfield Peverel, L onto B1019. Follow NGS signs.* **Sun 13 May (11-5); Fri 8 June (12-5); Sun 17 June (11-5); Fri 13 July (12-5); Sun 15 July (11-5). Adm £5, chd free. Home-made teas. Seasonal and Special home made cakes on Sunday openings, not to be missed. Visits also by arrangement May to July.**

Tucked away in the gentle Essex countryside, the glorious garden at Elwy Lodge offers a welcome that is hard to beat. Join the growing numbers of visitors who regularly return each season to sit and savour the different sights this exceptional garden has to offer in late spring, midsummer and then again in late summer. Plenty of seating throughout the garden. Flowing lawns, herbaceous borders, scented roses, clematis, trees, wildlife pond and a small meadow area. A secluded chamomile-scented lower garden with raised vegetable. beds and fruit trees leads to a delightful summer house, where visitors relax and enjoy the peaceful surroundings and amazing views. Featured in the Saturday Telegraph as an Essex garden that must be seen. Sloping uneven lawn in parts. Please check wheelchair access with garden owner before visiting.

14 FAIRWINDS

Chapel Lane, Chigwell Row, IG7 6JJ. Sue & David Coates, 07731 796467, scoates@forest.org.uk. *2m SE of Chigwell. Grange Hill Tube, turn R at exit, 10 mins walk uphill. Car: Nr M25 J26 & N Circular Waterworks r'about. Follow signs for Chigwell. Fork R for Manor/Lambourne Rd. Park in Lodge Close Car Park.* **Mon 7 May (2-5). Adm £3.50, chd free. Home-made teas. Free refills of tea/coffee. Visits also by arrangement Apr to Sept refreshments by arrangement. Groups of 10 to 20 only. Tours if requested.**

Gravelled front garden and three differently styled back garden spaces with planting changes every year. Places for you to sit, relax and enjoy. Start with themed flower borders - planting influenced by Beth Chatto, Penelope Hobhouse and Christopher Lloyd. Move on to a woodland garden - shade planting and home to our hens. Beyond the rustic fence, lies the wildlife pond and vegetable plot. Happy hens. Happy insects in bee house, bug house, log piles and sampling the spring pollen. Newts in pond. There be dragons a plenty!! Space for 2 disabled cars to park by the house. Wood chip paths in woodland area may require assistance.

With your support we can help raise awareness of Carers Trust and unpaid carers

15 FEERINGBURY MANOR

Coggeshall Road, Feering, Colchester, CO5 9RB. Mr & Mrs Giles Coode-Adams, 01376 561946, seca@btinternet.com, www.ngs.org.uk. *12m SW of Colchester. Between Feering & Coggeshall on Coggeshall Rd, 1m from Feering village.* **Every Thur and Fri 5 Apr to 27 July, 6 Sept to 12 Oct (9-4). Adm £5, chd free. Visits also by arrangement. Conducted tours on request There is a charge for this.** Donation to Feering Church.

There is always plenty to see in this 10 acre garden with two ponds and river Blackwater. Jewelled lawn in early April then spectacular tulips and blossom lead on to a huge number of different and colourful plants, many unusual, culminating in a purple explosion of michaelmas daisies in Sept. Wonderful sculpture by Ben Coode-Adams. No wheelchair access to arboretum, steep slope.

16 FUDLERS HALL

Fox Road, Mashbury, Chelmsford, CM1 4TJ. Mr & Mrs A J Meacock, 01245 231335. *7m NW of Chelmsford. Chelmsford take A1060, R into Chignal Rd. ½m L to Chignal St James approx 5m, 2nd R into Fox Rd signed Gt Waltham. Fudlers FROM GT WALTHAM. Take Barrack Lane for 3m.* **Sun 24 June, Sun 8 July (2-5). Adm £5, chd free. Home-made teas. Visits also by arrangement in July.**

An award winning, romantic 2 acre garden surrounding C17 farmhouse with lovely pastoral views, across the Chelmer Valley. Old walls divide garden into many rooms, each having a different character, featuring long herbaceous borders, ropes and pergolas festooned with rambling old fashioned roses. Enjoy the vibrant hot border in late summer. Yew hedged kitchen garden. Ample seating.

17 FURZELEA

Bicknacre Road, Danbury, CM3 4JR. Avril & Roger Cole-Jones, 01245 225726, randacj@gmail.com. *4m E of Chelmsford, 4m W of Maldon A414 to Danbury. At village centre turn S into Mayes Lane Take 1st R. Go past Cricketers Pub, L on to Bicknacre Rd park in NT carpark immed on L Garden 50m further on R. Extra parking 200 metres past on L.* **Wed 25 Apr (2-5); Sun 29 Apr, Sun 3 June, Sun 9 Sept (11-5); Wed 12 Sept (2-5). Adm £4, chd free. Home-made teas. Visits also by arrangement Apr to Sept groups 15+ mid April to Sept (not Aug) refreshments available.**

A Victorian house surrounded by a garden designed, created and maintained by the owners to provide all year round interest. The colour coordinated borders and beds are enhanced with topiary, grasses,and climbers. April starts with thousands of tulips followed by Alliums. By June the roses are blooming with many perennials, July is hemerocallis show time, Sept includes Dahlias Asters, late exotics. The garden has many unusual plants and shrubs. Opp Danbury Common (NT), short walk to Danbury Country Park and Lakes and short drive to RHS Hyde Hall. Featured in Womans Weekly Garden supplement, English Garden, Garden News and numerous magazines and newspapers. Very limited wheelchair access, with some steps and gravel paths and drive.

18 30 GLENWOOD AVENUE

Leigh-On-Sea, SS9 5EB. Joan Squibb, 07543 031772, squibb44@gmail.com. *Follow A127 towards Southend. Past Rayleigh Weir. At Progress Rd T-lights turn L. At next T-lights turn L down Rayleigh Rd A1015. Past shops turn 2nd L into Glenwood Ave . Garden halfway down on R.* **Sun 8 Apr, Sun 5 Aug (11-4). Adm £3.50, chd free. Tea, coffee and home made cakes. Visits also by arrangement Apr to Aug groups of 10-20.**

Nestled next to the busy A127 lies a beautifully transformed town garden. Homemade raised beds with tulips in spring, dahlias and roses in the summer. From a corridor of Cyprus trees and grass emerges an open garden giving a vista of colour, inspiration and peaceful harmony, with many different scents to savour. Hanging baskets bloom in the fruit trees and along the fences. A paved area allows one to enjoy the view of the garden as does a deck at the back where herbs and some vegetables live alongside the flowers. A peaceful vista , to sit in and restore the batteries . Vegetables are also grown in raised beds.

19 ◆ GREEN ISLAND

Park Road, Ardleigh, CO7 7SP. Fiona Edmond, 01206 230455, fionaedmond7@aol.com, www.greenislandgardens.co.uk. *3m NE of Colchester. From Ardleigh village centre, take B1029 towards Great Bromley. Park Rd is 2nd on R after level Xing. Garden is last on L.* **For NGS: Sun 6 May, Sun 14 Oct (10-5). Adm £7.50, chd £2.50. Light refreshments. For other opening times and information, please phone, email or visit garden website.**

'A garden for all seasons' A plantsman's paradise with 20 acres packed with rare and unusual plants. Carved within mature woodland are huge island beds, Japanese garden, terrace, gravel garden, seaside garden, water gardens and extensive woodland plantings. Also tearoom with home-made cakes and snacks and nursery offering plants all seen growing in the gardens. Bluebells and Azalea weekend on the 5 & 6 May. Sunday 6 May is in aid of the NGS. It is a chance to see the the stunning azaleas amongst the carpets of bluebells over 20 acres. Bluebells and azaleas, acers and rhododendrons in May. Water gardens, island beds all summer. Stunning Autumn colour. Light lunches, home-made teas and cream teas served. Flat and easy walking /pushing wheelchairs. Ramps at entrance and tearoom. Disabled parking and WC.

20 HANNAMS HALL

Thorpe Road, Tendring, CO16 9AR. Mr & Mrs W Gibbon, 01255 830292, w.gibbon331@btinternet.com. *10m E of Colchester. From A120 take B1035 at Horsley Cross, through Tendring Village (approx 3m) pass Bicycle Pub on R, after ⅓m over small bridge 1st house L.* **Visits by arrangement Mar to Nov max 30. Adm £6.50, chd free. Tea. Wine and light refreshments also available for evening appointments.**

C17 house (not open) set in 6 acres of formal and informal gardens and grounds with extensive views over open countryside. Herbaceous borders and shrubberies, many interesting trees incl flowering paulownias. Lawns and mown walks through wild grass and flower meadows, woodland walks, ponds and stream. Walled vegetable potager and orchard. Lovely autumn colour. Some gravel paths.

8 Dene Court

21 262 HATCH ROAD

Pilgrims Hatch, Brentwood, CM15 9QR. Mike & Liz Thomas. *2m N of Brentwood town centre. On A128 N toward Ongar turn R onto Doddinghurst Rd at mini-r'about (to Brentwood Centre) After the Centre turn next L into Hatch Rd. Garden 4th on R.* **Sun 8, Sun 22 July (11.30-4.30). Adm £4.50, chd free. Home-made teas.**

A formal frontage with lavender. An eclectic rear garden of around an acre divided into 'rooms' with themed borders, several ponds, three green houses, fruit and vegetable plots and oriental garden. There is also a secret white garden, spring and summer wild flower meadows, Yin and Yang borders, a folly and an exotic area. There is plenty of seating to enjoy the views and a cup of tea and cake.

22 HAVENDELL

Beckingham Street, Tolleshunt Major, Maldon, CM9 8LJ. Malcolm & Val. *5m E of Maldon 3m W of Tiptree. From B1022 take Loamy Hill rd. At the Xrds L into Witham rd. Follow NGS signs.* **Sun 10 June (11-4.30). Adm £4, chd free. Home-made teas.**

Set in ⅓ acre, this garden lends itself to a cottage style. A garden of many surprises from the glory of roses - including the rambling rector (a must to see) to a vast collection of Hostas and a sub-tropical section. Don't miss the mini stumpery in this ever evolving garden. Sit for a while in one of the many places and allow nature to relax you with a ' cuppa ' WC available.

23 NEW HILLDROP

Laindon Road (B1007), Horndon-On-The-Hill, Stanford-le-Hope, SS17 8QB. John Little & Fiona Crummay, 07967 733720, grassroofcompany@gmail.com, www.grassroofcompany.co.uk. *Just N of Horndon on the Hill. 80m E of junction B1007 & Lower Dunton Rd.* **Sun 1 July (2-7). Adm £5, chd free. Wine. Vegetarian savoury snacks. Visits also by arrangement May to Sept educational groups welcomed.**

This garden is not all about roses! It is a wild flower and wildlife paradise. Since building our turf roof house in 1995 we have trialled waste materials to grow plants and mimic brownfield habitats as well as getting plants and soils onto buildings and urban infrastructure. These parts of the garden are now our most important and diverse habitats. The garden features 6 green roofs, 3 ponds, brownfield habitat which gives ideas for difficult areas, green roof shipping container garden room, wildlife friendly hedges incl laid hedges. 2 wild flower meadows and ephemeral wetland. Featured on 'BBC Gardeners' World' Sept. Some wheelchair friendly paths and grass paths that may be accessible depending on rabbit damage. Garden is on a slight slope.

24 HORKESLEY HALL

Little Horkesley, Colchester, CO6 4DB. Mr & Mrs Johnny Eddis, 078085 99290, pollyeddis@hotmail.com, www.airbnb.co.uk/rooms/10354093. *6m N of Colchester City Centre. 2m W of A134. Drive right into Little Horkesley Church car park to the very far end - access is via low double black gates at the far end. 10 mins from A12, 20 from Sudbury & 1hr from Newmarket.* **Sun 25 Feb (1.30-4). Adm £5, chd free. Light refreshments. Sun 10 June (11-5). Adm £6, chd free. Home-made teas, cream teas and soups. Visits also by arrangement Feb to Oct very flexible and warm welcome assured! Coffee, teas, wine or light lunch available by arrangement.**

8 acres of romantic garden surrounding classical house in mature parkland setting. 2 lakes, one with jungle walk. Unusual, ancient and enormous trees. Largest ginkgo tree outside Kew. Walled garden, snowdrops, wild flower garden, blossom, spring bulbs, roses, hydrangeas. Formal terrace overlooking sweeping lawns to woodland. A timeless, family garden with recent and ongoing improvements. Wonderful natural setting, vast plane trees, Snowdrop Walk, Jungle walk. Walled garden, wild flower garden, snowdrops, established climbers including many roses, clematis, wisteria, hydrangea. A charming enclosed swimming pool garden and long-established bay and yew. A well-stocked Plant Stall. Limited wheelchair access to some areas, gravel paths and slopes quite easy access to tea area with lovely views over lake and garden.

25 NEW 24 HYDE LANE

Danbury, Chelmsford, CM3 4QS. Mr Ray Collings. *4m E of Chelmsford. 4m W of Maldon. From Chelmsford A414 to Danbury, edge of village past Tesco express take 2nd turning R. At small Xrd turn R (Hyde Lane) Park in The Hawthorns or Dilston.* **Sun 15 July (11-4.30). Adm £4, chd free. Light refreshments.**

Nestled in a leafy lane you will find a little piece of Asia, which has been developed over last 3 years. We wanted the same feel that we had experienced on our holidays to Bali, as we had fallen in love with Architectural forms of the type of plants that we saw there. So we decided to create the same type of look in our own garden. No wheelchair access, small easy steps up.

26 NEW JERICHO COTTAGE (MEGARRY'S ANTIQUES & TEASHOP)

The Green, Blackmore, Ingatestone, CM4 0RR. Judi Wood, 01277 821031, megarrys@yahoo.co.uk, www..antique-teashop.co.uk. *4m E of Chipping Ongar 4m N of Brentwood. At centre of Blackmore village head for village green. Turn by the war memorial into Blacksmith Alley. Jericho Cottage straight ahead.* **Mon 9 Apr, Tue 22 May, Thur 5, Thur 19 July (2-5). Adm £3, chd free. Home-made teas. Visits also by arrangement Apr to July.**

Small walled wildlife, woodland garden with mature trees, shrubs, bamboos, palms and ponds. Historic Romany Vardo and Victorian Glasshouse. Primroses, bluebells, camellias, rhododendrons and later hydrangeas, euphorbias and geraniums clothe the ground, while a canopy of wisteria, rambling roses, honeysuckle and kiwi vine shade the patio and pergola. The garden is an untamed hidden oasis. Antique shop, Teashop. A gentle paved path leads to the pergola and patio where there is access to the garden through a wrought iron gate onto the lawn.

Gardens are at the heart of hospice care

27 KEEWAY

Ferry Road, Creeksea, nr Burnham-on-Crouch, CM0 8PL. John & Sue Ketteley. *2m W of Burnham-on-Crouch. B1010 to Burnham on Crouch. At town sign take 1st R into Ferry Rd signed Creeksea & Burnham Golf Club & follow NGS signs.* **Fri 29 June, Wed 4 July (2-5). Adm £4, chd free. Home-made teas.**

Large, mature country garden with stunning views over the R Crouch. Formal terraces surround the house with steps leading to sweeping lawns, mixed borders packed full of bulbs and perennials, formal rose and herb garden with interesting water feature. Further afield there are wilder areas, paddocks and lake. A productive greenhouse, vegetable and cutting gardens complete the picture.

28 KELVEDON HALL

Kelvedon, Colchester, CO5 9BN. Mr & Mrs Jack Inglis, 07973 795955, victoria.inglis@me.com. *Take Maldon Rd from Kelvedon High St. Go over bridge over Blackwater & A12 at T-junction turn R onto Kelvedon Rd. Take 1st L, single gravel road, oak tree on corner.* **Visits by arrangement May & June min group of 20. Adm £4.50, chd free. Home-made teas in the Pool House Walled Garden, weather permitting. Teas, Coffees and Cakes.**

Varied 6 acre garden surrounding a pretty C18 Farmhouse. A blend of formal and informal spaces interspersed with modern sculpture. Pleached hornbeam and yew and box topiary provide structure. Courtyard walled garden juxtaposes a modern walled pool garden, both providing season long displays. Herbaceous borders offset an abundance of roses around the house. Lily covered ponds with a wet garden. Topiary, sculpture, tulips and roses. Homes and Gardens. Wheelchair access not ideal as there is a lot of gravel.

GROUP OPENING

29 LANGLEY VILLAGE GARDENS

Langley Upper Green, Saffron Walden, CB11 4RY. *7m W of Saffron Walden 10m N of Bishops Stortford. At Newport take B1038. After 3m turn R at Clavering, signed Langley. Upper Green is 3m further on. Sheepcote Green will also be signed on day.* **Sun 27 May (11-5). Combined adm £7.50, chd free. Light refreshments at Village Hall on Langley Village Green. Light lunches & home-made teas.**

APRIL COTTAGE
Anne & Neil Harris.

THE CHESTNUTS
Jane & David Knight.

CHURCH COTTAGE
Jago Russell & Maeve Polkinhorn, 01799 551085, maevepolkinhorn@hotmail.co.uk.

DUDDENHOE GRANGE
Peter & Bridget Murphy.

WICKETS
Susan & Doug Copeland.
(See separate entry)

April Cottage, Sheepcote Green 2m from Langley. Charming thatched cottage, with well established, colourful garden with unusual plants; old fashioned roses, clematis, wildlife and ornamental ponds, damp garden, hosta collection. Church Cottage, a pretty cottage garden surrounding a C17 thatched house with lovely countryside views. Seating to relax and enjoy the garden. Duddenhoe Grange nestles at end of 150yd drive. Farm pond, lawns, woodland. Mature trees incl. silver birch and oak. Mown paths via meadows with long pastoral views. Roses and clematis border house. Sit and relax in 'Rose and Soft Fruit Garden'. The Chestnuts boasts mature trees.. Planting beds designed and installed by Tristen Knight, RHS Young Designer 2012. Water feature with reclaimed sleeper jetty. Productive garden with oak walkways, sandstone paving and water feature. Meadow. Tranquil place to linger and enjoy. Wickets has wide, mixed borders, roses, two landscaped meadows, lily pond, parterre and gravel garden. Langley is highest Essex village set in rolling countryside. St John the Evangelist Church, Langley, also open for a Flower Festival. Featured in Essex Life magazine. Gravel drives at Wickets and Duddenhoe Grange.

30 NEW 73 LAYER ROAD

Colchester, CO2 7JP. Margaret & Jim Stewart. *1¼m from Colchester town centre. From J26 A12 take A1124 to Colchester. At lights go R into Straight Rd. Continue to Shrub End Rd & turn L. Go R at Boudiccea Way. At end turn L into Layer Rd.* **Sun 24 June (2-5). Adm £3, chd free. Tea, coffee, cakes.**

A town garden approx 27 ft x 125 ft with a winding gravel path dissecting the area into smaller spaces. Mature trees and shrubs provide areas of deep shade, opening into brightness. Colour themed borders contain a wide selection of perennials including phlox, day lilies, clematis,salvias and veronicas.There is a small patio area and seating dotted throughout the garden.

31 LITTLE MYLES

Ongar Road, Stondon Massey, Brentwood, CM15 0LD. Judy & Adrian Cowan. *1½m SE of Chipping Ongar. Off A128 at Stag Pub, Marden Ash, towards Stondon Massey. Over bridge, 1st house on R after 'S' bend. 400yds Ongar side of Stondon Church.* **Sun 1 July (11-4). Adm £5, chd free. Home-made teas. Seating in Tea Room, also under trees and on main lawn.**

A romantic, naturalistic garden full of hidden features, set in 3 acres. Full borders, meandering paths to Beach Garden, Perennial Prairie border, Exotic Jungle around elephant, monkeys and giraffe. Fountains, sculptures and tranquil benches. Hidden Asian garden, Slate garden, hornbeam pergola, ornamental vegetable patch and natural pond. Herb garden that inspired Little Myles herbal cosmetics. Hand painted jungle mural. Crafts and handmade herbal cosmetics for sale. Explorers sheet and map for children. Gravel paths. No disabled WC available.

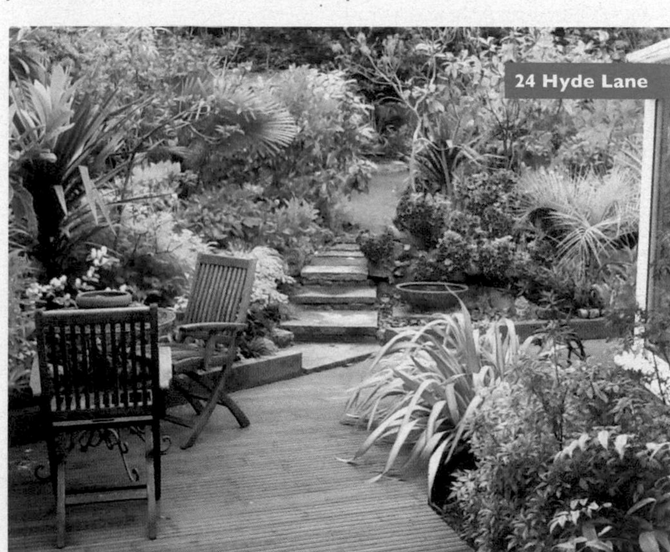
24 Hyde Lane

32 LONG HOUSE PLANTS

Church Road, Noak Hill, Romford, RM4 1LD. Tim Carter, 01708 371719, tim@longhouse-plants.co.uk, www.longhouse-plants.co.uk. *3½m NW of J28 M25. J28 M25 take A1023 Brentwood. At 1st T-lights, turn L to South Weald after 0.8m turn L at T junction. After 1.6m turn L, over M25 after ½m turn R into Church Rd, nursery opp church.* **Wed 13 June, 11 July, 15 Aug, 12 Sept (11-4). Adm £5, chd £3. Home-made teas. Visits also by arrangement June to Sept Mon - Thur inclusive (not Bank Hol). Groups of 25+. Additional fee for conducted tours.**

A beautiful garden - yes, but one with a purpose. Long House Plants has been producing home grown plants for more than 10 years - here is a chance to see where it all begins! With wide paths and plenty of seats carefully placed to enjoy the plants and views. It has been thoughtfully designed so that the collections of plants look great together through all seasons.

33 NEW LOXLEY HOUSE

49 Robin Hood Road, Brentwood, CM15 9EL. Robert & Helen Smith. *1m N of Brentwood town centre. On A128 N towards Ongar turn R onto Doddinghurst Rd at mini r'about. Take the 1st rd on L into Robin Hood Rd. 2 houses before the bend on L.* **Sat 28 Apr, Sat 14 July (11.30-3.30). Adm £3, chd free. Home-made teas.**

On entering the rear garden you will be surprised and delighted by this town garden. A colourful patio with pots and containers. Steps up onto a circular lawn surrounded by hedges, herbaceous borders, trees and climbers. 2 water features, one a Japanese theme and another with ferns in a quiet seating area. The garden is planted to offer colour from spring to autumn with bulbs and perennials.

34 262 MAIN ROAD

Hawkwell, Hockley, SS5 4NW. Karen Mann. *3m NE of Rayleigh. From A127 at Rayleigh Weir take B1013 towards Hockley. Garden on L after White Hart Pub & village green.* **Sun 15 July, Sun 19 Aug (12.30-5). Adm £4, chd free. Home-made teas.**

The garden comprises of 185 metres of island beds and borders sited on ⅓ acre. Some of the borders are elevated from the house resulting in steep banks which provide a different and interesting aspect. Salvia, dahlia, hedychium, brugmansia peak in the summer months.

35 ◆ MARKS HALL GARDENS & ARBORETUM

Coggeshall, CO6 1TG. Marks Hall Estate, 01376 563796, enquiries@markshall.org.uk, www.markshall.org.uk. *1½m N of Coggeshall. Follow brown & white tourism signs from A120 Coggeshall bypass.* **For opening times and information, please phone, email or visit garden website.**

Marks Hall Gardens and Arboretum features a tree collection from all the temperate areas of the world set in more than 200 acres of historic landscape providing interest and enjoyment throughout the year. Highlights include: the Millennium Walk designed for structure, colour and scent on the shortest days of the year; the largest planting in Europe of Wollemi pine and the inspired combination of traditional and contemporary planting in the C18 Walled Garden. Spring snowdrop and autumn colour displays are annual highlights. Tea room serving homemade cakes, hot and cold beverages, light lunches including homemade soup and daily specials. See website for opening times. Hard paths lead to all key areas of interest. Wheelchairs or staff-driven buggy available for visitors with mobility issues (booking essential).

Wycke Farm

36 MIRAFLORES

5 Rowan Way, Witham, CM8 2LJ. Yvonne & Danny Owen, 07976 603863, danny@dannyowen.co.uk. *Access is ONLY by rear gate off of FOREST RD... Postcode CM8 2TP .... Please follow yellow signs.* **Mon 21 May, Fri 15, Sun 24 June (2-5). Adm £3.50, chd free. Teas, coffee, soft drinks, herbal teas, Plus fab homemade cakes...some even Gluten free !. Visits also by arrangement in June min 10. max 30, £7 inc cream tea.**

An award-winning, medium-sized garden described by one visitor as a "Little Bit of Heaven'. A blaze of colour with roses, clematis, pergola, rose arch, triple fountain with box hedging and deep herbaceous borders. See our 'Folly', exuberant and cascading hanging baskets... find our Secret Door. Featured in Garden Answers, Amateur Gardening and Essex Life Home made cakes are on sale, some Gluten free. We have tranquil seating areas and homemade cakes to die for, and some being Gluten free. No access for wheelchair users as step up to garden.

37 MONKS COTTAGE

Monks Lane, Dedham nr Colchester, CO7 6DP. Nicola Baker, 01206 322210, nicola_baker@tiscali.co.uk. *6m NE of Colchester. Leave Dedham village with the church on L. Take 2nd main rd on R (Coles Oak Lane) Monks Lane is 1st rd on L.* **Visits by arrangement May to July small groups, daytime or evening visits welcome. Adm £3.50, chd free.**

½ acre cottage garden on a sloping site in the heart of Constable country. A constantly evolving garden which features mature trees, pond, box-edged parterre beds, boggy area with strong foliage shapes, rill garden with cascade and small woodland garden. A gin-and-tonic balcony gives a high level vantage point over the garden and a raised terrace looks out over the surrounding countryside.

38 MOVERONS

Brightlingsea, CO7 0SB. Lesley & Payne Gunfield, 01206 305498, lesleyorrock@me.com, www.moverons.co.uk. *7m SE of Colchester. At old church turn R signed Moverons Farm. Follow lane & garden signs for approx 1m. Beware some SatNavs take you the wrong side of the river.* **Visits by arrangement May to Sept for groups of 10+ only. Adm £5, chd free. Home-made teas.**

Beautiful tranquil 4 acre garden in touch with its surroundings and enjoying stunning estuary views. A wide variety of planting in mixed borders to suit different growing conditions and provide all year colour. Courtyard, reflection pool, large natural ponds, sculptures and barn for rainy day teas! Magnificent trees some over 300yrs old give this garden real presence. Featured in the East Anglian Daily Times and on BBC Radio Essex. Most of the garden is accessible by wheelchair via grass and gravel paths, There are some steps and bark paths.

39 PARSONAGE HOUSE

Wiggens Green, Helions Bumpstead, Haverhill, CB9 7AD. The Hon & Mrs Nigel Turner. *3m S of Haverhill. From Xrds in the village centre go up past the Church for approx 1m. Parking on R through a five bar gate into the orchard. Garden on L of the lane.* **Sun 17 June, Sun 9 Sept (2-5). Adm £4, chd free. Home-made teas. Apple juice from the orchard available on the day for sale.**

C15 house (not open) surrounded by 3 acres of formal gardens with mixed borders, topiary, pond, potager and greenhouse. Further 3-acre wild flower meadow with orchids and rare trees and further 3 acre orchard of old East Anglian apple varieties in two small fields across the lane. Featured in the recently published book 'Secret Gardens of East Anglia' with photographs by Marcus Harpur. Gravel drive and small step into WC.

40 PEACOCKS

Main Road, Margaretting, CM4 9HY. Phil Torr, 07802 472382, phil.torr@btinternet.com. *Margaretting Village Centre. From village Xrds go 75yds in the direction of Ingatestone, entrance gates will be found on L set back 50 feet from the road frontage.* **Sun 25 Mar, Sun 15 Apr, Sun 20 May (1-4); Sun 17 June (1-5). Adm £5, chd free. Home-made teas. Visits also by arrangement Mar to June min 15. For smaller groups please ask for available dates before consulting members.** Donation to St Francis Hospice.

5-acre garden with mature native and specimen trees. Restored horticultural buildings. Series of garden rooms including Paradise Garden, Garden of Reconciliation, Alhambra fusion. Long herbaceous/ mixed border. Temple of Antheia on the banks of a lily lake. Large areas for wildlife incl woodland walk, a nuttery and orchard. Traditionally managed wild flower meadow. Sunken dell with waterfall. Display of old Margaretting postcards. Small art exhibition. Garden sculpture. Wild flower meadow in traditional orchard. Most of garden wheelchair accessible.

NPC

41 3 POUND GATE

Stebbing, near Great Dunmow, CM6 3RH. Wal & Jenny Hudgell, 01371 856406, jenny_hudgell@yahoo.co.uk. *3m E of Great Dunmow. Leave Gt Dunmow on B1256. Take first L to Stebbing. At the War Memorial junction turn L, down hill to High Street. Take 2nd R past the School, signed to Garden Fields.* **Sat 23 June (1-5). Combined adm with St Helens £7, chd free. Light refreshments. Visits also by arrangement June to Aug groups 10-20. Refreshments incl in adm fee.**

Third of an acre plant lovers garden reinvented in 2010 and an ongoing project. Borders packed with an eclectic mix of perennials and shrubs for all year round interest including Iris, hemerocallis and hostas in abundance. All punctuated by numerous shrub roses. Approximately 40 new trees planted around the garden to provide height to a very flat site. There is a medium size vegetable garden. The garden is fully accessible to wheelchairs.

Your visit helps fund 389 Marie Curie Nurses

42 NEW THE PUNCHBOWL RESTAURANT

The Street, High Easter, Chelmsford, CM1 4QW. Penny Kelsey. *Centre of High Easter. Next to the church.* **Wed 4, Sat 7 July (2-5). Adm £5, chd free. Home-made teas.**

Found in the village centre next to the church, this garden offers a mixture of mature shrubs and trees and coloured themed herbaceous borders. Lawns and paths lead through entertainment spaces littered with animal sculptures. With a small pond and plenty of seating the garden is accessible to wheelchairs.

43 ROOKWOODS

Yeldham Road, Sible Hedingham, CO9 3QG. Peter & Sandra Robinson, 07770 957111, sandy1989@btinternet.com. *8m NW of Halstead. Entering Sible Hedingham from the direction of Haverhill on A1017 take 1st R just after 30mph sign.* **Mon 28 May (10.30-4.30). Combined adm with Washlands £7.50, chd free. Home-made teas. Single adm £5. Visits also by arrangement May to Sept groups of 8+ welcome.**

Rookwoods is a tranquil garden. The herbaceous borders feature columns of tumbling roses, Pleached hornbeam rooms lead to a wild flower bed, buttercup meadow and ancient oak wood. There is no need to walk far, you can come and linger over tea, under a dreamy wisteria canopy, while enjoying the garden view. Gravel drive.

Funds from National Garden Scheme gardens help Macmillan support thousands of people every year

44 69 RUNDELLS

Harlow, CM18 7HD. Mr & Mrs K Naunton, 01279 303471, k_naunton@hotmail.com. *From M11 J7 A414 exit T-lights take L exit Southern Way, mini r'about 1st exit Trotters Rd leading into Commonside Rd, take 2nd L into Rundells.* **Sat 14 July (2-5). Adm £2.50, chd free. Home-made teas and cakes, tea, coffee and soft drinks. Visits also by arrangement June to Oct please give plenty of notice, groups of 10+ can be accommodated (within reason).**

As featured on Alan Tichmarsh's first 'Love Your Garden' series ('The Secret Garden') 69, Rundells is a very colourful, small town garden packed with a wide variety of shrubs, perennials, herbaceous and bedding plants in over 200 assorted containers. Hard landscaping on different levels incl's summer house, various seating areas and water features. Steep steps. Access to adjacent allotment open to view. Various small secluded seating areas. A small fairy garden has been added to give interest for younger visitors. The garden is next to a large allotment and this is open to view with lots of interesting features including a bee apiary. Honey and other produce for sale (conditions permitting).

45 ST HELENS

High Street, Stebbing, CM6 3SE. Stephen & Joan Bazlinton, 01371 856495, revbaz@phonecoop.coop. *3m E of Great Dunmow. Leave Gt Dunmow on B1256. Take 1st L to Stebbing, at T-junction turn L into High St, garden 2nd on R.* **Sat 23 June (1-5). Combined adm with 3 Pound Gate £7, chd free. Home-made teas. Visits also by arrangement June & July.** Donation to Dentaid.

A garden of contrasts due to moist and dry conditions, laid out on a gentle Essex slope from a former willow plantation. These contours give rise to changing vistas and unanticipated areas of seclusion framed with hedging and generous planting. Walkways and paths alongside natural springs and still waters. Partial wheelchair access.

46 NEW 30 SANDFORD ROAD

Chelmsford, CM2 6DQ. John & Mary Hawkes. *Limited parking for disabled only (gravel drive). Visitors are advised to park at nearby Chelmer Village Retail Park CM2 6XE. Take footpath opp Next, cross T-lights (A138) 5mins walk.* **Sun 15 Apr, Sun 10 June (10-5). Adm £4, chd free. Home-made teas and cakes. Tea, coffee, cold drinks.**

A surprising ⅓ acre town garden which is divided into 3 areas. A formal garden with lawn, monkey puzzle tree, flowering borders, fishpond, pergola with wisteria and a large patio. Enter through the rose arbour into a shaded area with a variety of specimen fruit and ornamental trees. Then finally, through a gate to a secret landscaped kitchen garden. We opened the garden for the first time 2017 for Springfield Open Gardens (Farleigh Hospice). Limited wheelchair access due to gravel drive and some uneven areas.

47 NEW SANDY LODGE

Howe Drive, Hedingham Road, Halstead, CO9 2QL. Emma & Rick Rengasamy. *8m NE of Braintree. Turn off Hedingham Rd into Ashlong Grove. Howe Drive is on L. Please park in Ashlong Grove & walk up Howe Drive.* **Sun 20 May, Sun 16 Sept (11-5). Adm £4.50, chd free. Home-made teas.**

A garden for all seasons. ¾ acre created over the last 5 years. Minutes from Halstead Town centre yet a very peaceful garden with stunning views over the countryside. Enter to a two-tier gravel Bee Border; wander to our Winter Wedding border then the Woodlands Walk. Across the lawn you find the Prairie decking borders. Lots of seating/viewing spots. Garden on a slight slope; gravel at front. Wheelchair access restricted due to large amount of gravel.

48 SHRUBS FARM

Lamarsh, Bures, CO8 5EA. Mr & Mrs Robert Erith, 01787 227520, bob@shrubsfarm.co.uk, www.shrubsfarm.co.uk. *1¼m from Bures. On rd to Lamarsh, the drive is signed to Shrubs Farm.* **Visits by arrangement May to Sept groups min 6, no max. Tours £7 led by owner. Refreshments served in barn £5. Adm £7, chd free. Home-made teas. Wine & canapes..**

2 acres with shrub borders, lawns, roses and trees. 50 acres parkland with wild flower paths and woodland trails. Over 60 species of oak. Superb 10m views over Stour valley. Ancient coppice and pollards incl largest goat (pussy) willow (*Salix caprea*) in England. Wollemi and Norfolk pines, and banana trees. Full size black rhinoceros. Display of Bronze Age burial urns. Large grass maze. Guided Tour to incl park and ancient woodland. Restored C18 Essex barn is available for refreshment by prior arrangement. Featured in East Anglian Daily Times. Some ground may be boggy in wet weather.

49 SNARES HILL COTTAGE

Duck End, Stebbing, CM6 3RY. Pete & Liz Stabler, 01371 856565, petestabler@gmail.com. *Between Dunmow & Bardfield. On B1057 from Great Dunmow to Great Bardfield, ½m after Bran End on L.* **Sun 17 June, Sun 9 Sept (10.30-4). Adm £4, chd free. Home-made teas. Visits also by arrangement.**

A 'quintessential English Garden' - Gardeners World. Our quirky 1½ acre garden has surprises round every corner and many interesting sculptures. A natural swimming pool is bordered by romantic flower beds, herb garden and Victorian folly. A bog garden borders woods and leads to silver birch copse, beach garden and 'Roman' temple. Natural Swimming Pond. Classic cars. Sculptures. Not wheelchair friendly as it is a hilly garden with some steep slopes.

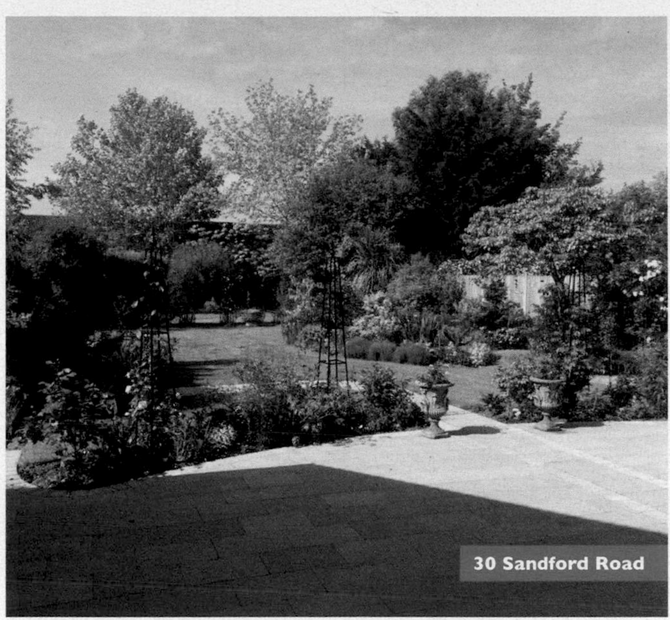

30 Sandford Road

50 SOUTH SHOEBURY HALL

Church Road, Shoeburyness, SS3 9DN. Mr & Mrs M Dedman, 01702 299022, michael@shoeburyhall.co.uk. *4m E of Southend-on-Sea. Enter Southend on A127 to Eastern Ave A1159 signed Shoebury. R at r'about to join A13. Proceed S to Ness Rd. R into Church Rd. Garden on L 50 metres.* **Sun 29 Apr, Sun 29 July (2-5). Adm £4, chd free. Home-made teas. Visits also by arrangement May to Aug for groups of 10 + to a coach party.**

Delightful, 1-acre established walled garden surrounding Grade II listed house (not open) and bee house. Charming agapanthus and hydrangea beds. April is ablaze with 3000 tulips and fritillaria. July shows 200+ varieties of agapanthus incl 'Queen Mum' and 'Black Magic'. Unusual trees, shrubs, rose borders, with 50yr old plus geraniums, Mediterranean and Southern Hemisphere planting in dry garden. C11 St Andrews Church open to visitors (by arrangement). Garden close to sea. Bumper agapanthus sale at both open days.

51 ◆ SPENCERS

Tilbury Road, Great Yeldham, CO9 4JG. Mr & Mrs Colin Bogie, 01787 238175, lynne@spencersgarden.net, www.spencersgarden.net. *Just N of Gt Yeldham on Tilbury Rd. In village centre, turn off A1017 at the 'Blasted Oak' (huge oak stump). Keep L, following stream (signed 'The Belchamps/Tilbury Juxta Clare'). Spencers is clearly signed on L after approx ½m.* **For NGS: Sun 3 June, Sun 2 Sept (2-5). Adm £5, chd free. Home-made teas. For other opening times and information, please phone, email or visit garden website.**

Romantic C18 walled garden laid out by Lady Anne Spencer, overflowing with blooms following Tom Stuart-Smith's renovation. Huge wisteria, armies of Lord Butler delphiniums ('Rab' lived at Spencers). Spectacular rose and herbaceous borders. Parkland with many specimen trees including Armada Oaks. Victorian woodland walk along River Colne.

52 SPRING COTTAGE

Chapel Lane, Elmstead Market, Colchester, CO7 7AG. Mr & Mrs Roger & Sharon Sciachettano. *3m from Colchester. Overlooking village green N of A133 through Elmstead Market. Parking limited adjacent to cottage, village car park nearby on S side of A133.* **Sat 9, Sun 10 June (2-5). Adm £3.50, chd free. Home-made teas. Refreshments provided by the Elmstead in Bloom group served on the village green in front of Spring Cottage.**

From Acteas to Zauschenerias and Aressima to Zebra grass we hope our large variety of plants will please. Our award winning garden features a range of styles and habitats e.g. woodland dell, stumpery, Mediterranean area, perennial borders and pond. Our C17 thatched cottage and garden show case a number of plants found at the world famous Beth Chatto gardens ½m down the road.

53 STRANDLANDS

off Rectory Road, Wrabness, Manningtree, CO11 2TX. Jenny & David Edmunds, 01255 886260, strandlands@outlook.com. *1km along farm track from the corner of Rectory Rd. If using a SatNav, the post code will leave you at the corner of Rectory Rd. Turn onto a farm track, signed to Woodcutters Cottage & Strandlands, & continue for 1km.* **Visits by arrangement May to July for groups of 10 to 20. Adm £5, chd free. Light refreshments. Tea, coffee & a slice of home made cake.**

Cottage surrounded by 4 acres of land bordering beautiful and unspoilt Stour Estuary. One acre of decorative garden: formal courtyard with yew, box and perovskia hedges, lily pond, summerhouse and greenhouse; 2 large island beds, secret 'moon garden', madly and vividly planted 'Madison' garden, 3 acres of wildlife meadows with groups of native trees, large wildlife pond, also riverside bird hide. View the Stour Estuary from our own bird hide. Grayson Perry's 'A House for Essex' can be seen just one field away from Strandlands. Mostly accessible and flat although parking area is gravelled.

54 TUDOR ROOST

18 Frere Way, Fingringhoe, Colchester, CO5 7BP. Chris & Linda Pegden, 01206 729831, pegdenc@gmail.com. *5m S of Colchester. In Fingringhoe by Whalebone PH follow sign to Ballast Quay, after ½m turn R into Brook Hall Rd, then 1st L into Frere Way.* **Sat 28, Sun 29 Apr, Sun 27, Mon 28 May, Sat 7, Sun 8 July, Sat 11, Sun 12 Aug (2-5). Adm £4, chd free. Home-made teas. Large conservatory to sit in if inclement weather. Visits also by arrangement Apr to Aug adm incl tea & cake £7. Min payment £70 (i.e. 10 people).**

An unexpected hidden colourful ¼-acre garden. Well manicured grassy paths wind round island beds and ponds. Densely planted subtropical area with architectural and exotic plants - cannas, bananas, palms, agapanthus, agaves and tree ferns surround a colourful gazebo. Garden planted to provide yr-round colour and encourage wildlife. Many peaceful seating areas. Within 1m of Fingringhoe Wick Nature Reserve. PLEASE CONFIRM OPENING DATES ON NGS WEBSITE OR TELEPHONE. Featured in Look magazine.

55 37 TURPINS LANE

Chigwell, IG8 8AZ. Fabrice Aru & Martin Thurston, 0208 5050 739, martin.thurston@talktalk.net. *Between Woodford & Epping. Tube: Chigwell, 2m from North Circular Rd at Woodford, follow the signs for Chigwell (A113) through Woodford Bridge into Manor Rd & turn L, Bus 275 & W14.* **Sun 17 June, Sun 1, Sun 29 July (11-6). Adm £3, chd free. Visits also by arrangement May to Oct max 8.**

An unexpected hidden, magical, part-walled garden showing how much can be achieved in a small space. An oasis of calm with densely planted rich, lush foliage, tree ferns, hostas, topiary and an abundance of well maintained shrubs complemented by a small pond and 3 water features designed for yr round interest. Featured on BBC TV Gardeners World. Runner up Daily Mail National Garden Competition Awarded 2nd place by Gardeners News for Best Small Garden.

56 NEW TWO COTTAGES

Church Road, Chrishall, Saffron Walden, SG8 8QT. Michelle Thomas, 01763 838682, mrsdthomas@btinternet.com. *7m W of Saffron Walden. Continue on B1039, take R turn to Chrishall. Bury Lane leading into Church Rd. You will find Two Cottages on your 1st L with an old planted boat on the bank.* **Sun 3 June (11-5). Adm £4, chd free. Home-made teas. Evening opening Sat 9 June (5-9). Adm £5, chd free. Light refreshments. Sun 17 June (11-5). Adm £4, chd free. Home-made teas. Visits also by arrangement Apr to Oct.**

Magic lurks within this charming 1½ acre garden, which has evolved over 30 yrs. Many treasures hidden amongst a variety of planting. Over 215 roses showcased in island borders. Meandering lawn paths lead through the wisteria walkway to find two miniature Shetland ponies at the bottom of the garden keen to show off to guests. Tranquil seating areas, teas, local crafts and plants sometimes for sale. Large smoking dragon, once on display at Hampton Court garden show. Superb views over undulating countryside to the village church. Fragrance and colour that only Mother Nature can create.

57 ULTING WICK

Crouchmans Farm Road, Maldon, CM9 6QX. Mr & Mrs B Burrough, 01245 380216, philippa.burrough@btinternet.com, www.ultingwickgarden.co.uk. *3m NW of Maldon. Take R turning to Ulting off B1019 as you exit Hatfield Peverel by a green. Garden on R after 2m.* **Sun 22 Apr (11-5). Light refreshments, homemade soup using ingredients from the garden, filled rolls &**

home-made teas on 22 April. Fri 27 Apr, Mon 27 Aug (2-5). Home-made teas. Adm £5, chd free. Visits also by arrangement Mar to Oct groups of 15+. Other catering by arrangement. Donation to All Saints Ulting Church.

Listed black barns provide backdrop for vibrant and exuberant planting in 8 acres. Thousands of colourful tulips, flowing innovative spring planting, herbaceous borders, pond, mature weeping willows, kitchen garden, dramatic late summer beds with zingy, tender, exotic plant combinations. Drought tolerant perennial and mini annual wild flower meadows. Woodland. Many plants propagated in-house. Lots of unusual plants for sale. All Saints Church Ulting will be open in conjunction with the garden for talks on its history. Beautiful dog walks along the R Chelmer from the garden. Featured in Period Homes, Rustica (France), Waitrose magazine, Daily Mail, Essex Life and one of only 22 gardens included in new book 'Secret Gardens of East Anglia,. Some gravel around the house but main areas of interest are accessible for wheelchairs.

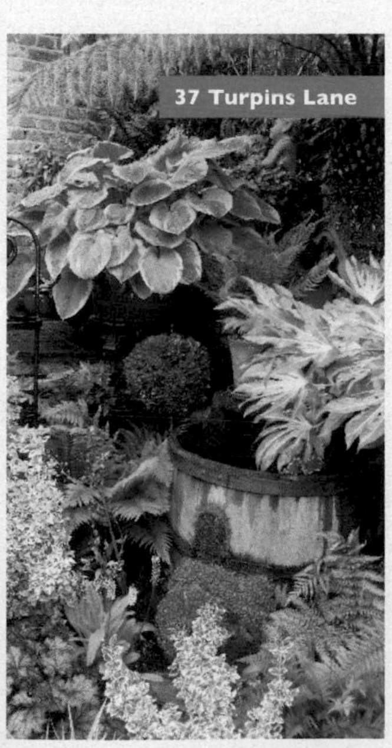

37 Turpins Lane

GROUP OPENING

58 WALTHAM ABBEY GROUP

Waltham Abbey, EN9 1LG. 01992 714047, frank.jewson@btconnect.com. *M25, J26 to Waltham Abbey. At T-lights by McD turn R to r'about. Take 2nd exit to next r'about. Take 3rd exit (A112) to T-lights. L to Monkswood Av.* **Sun 3 June, Sun 9 Sept (12-5.30). Combined adm £5, chd free. Home-made teas at Silver Birches, Quendon Drive. Visits also by arrangement May to Sept groups of 10 - 20.**

62 EASTBROOK ROAD
Caroline Cassell, 07973 551196, cvcassell@gmail.com.
Open on Sun 3 June
Visits also by arrangement May to Sept, and open for vintage Afternoon Tea for 3-4 guests, please call for individual dates. 2017 Winner of Small Garden category in the Gardeners World magazine.

39 HALFHIDES
Chris Hamer.
Open on all dates

76 MONKSWOOD AVENUE
Cathy & Dan Gallagher.
Open on all dates

SILVER BIRCHES
Linda & Frank Jewson.
Open on all dates

Historic Waltham Abbey is near Epping Forest. The Abbey is purported to be last resting place of King Harold. Lee Valley Regional Park is nearby. Silver Birches boasts 3 lawns on 2 levels. This surprisingly secluded garden has many mixed borders packed with all year interest. Mature shrubs and trees create a short woodland walk. At 39 Halfhides the garden has evolved over 45yrs. It features mixed shrubs and perennial borders on 2 levels. Waterfall linking two ponds leads to shade garden. Alpines thrive on scree and in troughs. Beautiful autumn colour. 76 Monkswood Ave is a plantswoman's garden . Mixed borders filled with specimen trees, shrubs and perennials incl asters, dahlias and late-flowering anemones. Wildlife pond. 62 Eastbrook Rd. off Honey Lane (Limited Parking). Walking distance from Halfhides and The Glade Way approx. 7 mins. This is a small cottage garden, traditional perennial planting, topiary and circular themed hard landscaping. Monkswood Avenue - Reclaimed chimney pots for sale as planters. 62 Eastbrook Rd not suitable for wheelchairs.

59 WASHLANDS

Prayors Hill, Sible Hedingham, CO9 3LE. Tony & Sarah Frost, 01787 460732, tony@washlands.co.uk. *¼ m NW of Sible Hedingham Church. At former Sugar Loaves Pub on A1017 turn SW into Rectory Rd, R at former White Horse Pub, pass St Peters Church on R, ¼ m NW on Prayors Hill.* **Mon 28 May (2-5). Combined adm with Rookwoods £7.50, chd free. Single adm £4. Sun 10 June, Sun 8 July (2-5). Adm £4, chd free. Home-made teas. Visits also by arrangement May to Aug groups of 10+.**

Charming one-acre country garden surrounding a former farmhouse,with good views over rolling countryside. A former horse pond features a beach with landing stage. Rose garden, wide herbaceous, shrub and woodland borders, hidden walks and opportunities to sit and relax. Alpines, grasses and alliums. Featured in Essex Life. Come and see! Woodland walk unsuitable for wheelchairs.

GROUP OPENING

60 WENDENS AMBO GARDENS

Saffron Walden, CB11 4JX. *Parking at village hall nr Church & at village pubs, all signed on day. Gardens and woodland are within walking distance. Map available on day.* **Sun 1 July (12-4). Combined adm £5, chd free. Light refreshments at Loxley.**

3 CHURCH PATH
Ms Liz Hartley.

KATIE'S MILLENNIUM WOOD
Dr Katie Petty-Saphon.

LOXLEY
Robert Chappell & Tomi Ciglenecki.

3 Church Path, quintessential cottage garden adjacent to historic church set behind a chocolate box thatched cottage. Terraced garden with mixed shrubs, perennials, beautiful clematis and roses. Hidden vegetable garden and fruit trees. Katie's Millennium Wood, 10,000 trees planted as whips in 2000 – 2001. Remarkable height and girth achieved in 17yrs. Good recovery from Ash die-back disease which affected 2000 trees. Loxley is a young garden; both, front and rear, have been recently landscaped and planted and completed in late spring 2016. The garden itself features a good size Koi pond, surrounded by a lawn and flower beds which includes various ericaceous plants, bamboos, grasses, some rare plants as well as some traditional shrubs and flowers all of which offers interest all year around. Wendens Ambo is a meandering historic village with a busy B road through village. Please use car parks. Beware. There is a lack of pavements in places so take great care if walking on the road. Village very close to Audley End House.

61 THE WHITE GARDEN

35 Langdon Road, Rayleigh, Essex, SS6 9HY. Mrs Louise Reed. *From A129 turn R into Langdon Rd.* **Sun 20 May, Sun 10 June (12-5). Adm £3.50, chd free. Light refreshments.**

A delightful white garden with 100 David Austin roses, unusual perennials and shrubs nestled into a tiny plot. Shady fernery walk with white hydrangeas, waterfalls, pond and blooms surrounding a lush lawn provide interest all summer long. Front garden has fragrant flowers and shrub borders, with roses, enclosed by box hedging and topiary for an evergreen curb appeal. Small back garden is a profusion of delicate cottage style planting in a scented, white, cream and pastel colour scheme. Inspiration from Beatrix Potter Tales and the White Garden at Sissinghurst. New Victorian greenhouse. Woodland style path and plants beneath Pergola with Clematis and Rambling roses leading to Arbour. Bird nesting boxes, unusual glass and rusted iron sculptures. Louise has written for The Rayleigh Review Magazine. Featured in The Amateur Gardening magazine.

62 WICKETS

Langley Upper Green, CB11 4RY. Susan & Doug Copeland, 01799 550553, susan.copeland@ngs.org.uk. *7m W of Saffron Walden, 10m N of Bishops Stortford. At Newport take B1038 After 3m turn R at Clavering, signed Langley. Upper Green is 3m further on. At cricket green turn R. House 200m on R.* **Sun 25 Mar (1-4). Adm £4.50, chd free. Home-made teas. Opening with Langley Village Gardens on Sun 27 May. Visits also by arrangement Mar to July groups of 10+.**

Peaceful country garden 'Far from the Madding Crowd'. Wide, informal mixed borders include narcissi, camassia, shrub roses and perennials. Two landscaped meadows and shepherd's hut with fine pastoral views. Large lily pond sheltered by silver birch. Griffin Glasshouse nearby. Curvilinear design links themed planting areas. Espalier apples enclose parterre with standard weeping roses and lavender. Secluded gravel garden and views over rolling Essex countryside. Stout shoes or wellies recommended in March. Featured in House Beautiful, Garden Answers, Essex Life Magazine. Gravel drive. www.thegardengateisopen.blog

GROUP OPENING

63 NEW WRITTLE GARDENS

Chelmsford, CM1 3NA. *Writtle can be approached from 3 directions. From the A1060, A1016 and A414 follow the yellow signs to Writtle Village.* **Sun 10 June (12-5). Combined adm £6, chd free.**

NEW **8 THE GREEN**
CM1 3DU. Andrea Johnson.

NEW **53 LONG BRANDOCKS**
CM1 3JL. Roger & Margaret Barker.

NEW **65 ONGAR ROAD**
CM1 3NA. Doug & Jean Pinkney.

NEW **40 ST JOHNS ROAD**
CM1 3EB. Catherine Eubanks.

Four contrasting, colourful and interesting gardens to enjoy in the delightful village of Writtle. 8 The Green offers creatively planted borders and a tapestry of colour, texture and form, with perennials, shrubs, ornamental trees, annuals and alpines, and a south-facing summerhouse. The front of the new garden at 40 St John's Road is being designed to encourage wildlife, with the rear garden offering a surprising contrast, with a more modern, landscaped Italian feel. The garden at 65 Ongar Road will transport visitors to tropical destinations, with its colour and "summer living" features. And 53 Long Brandocks is a true plantsman's garden with a wealth of unusual shrubs, plants and trees in its small but cleverly designed space. The ancient and traditional village of Writtle, with its delightful Norman church, village green and pond, dates back to pre-Roman times, and was featured in the Doomsday Book. No refreshments are offered at these gardens. But Writtle offers a number of pubs and cafes, incl the renowned Tiptree Tea Room in Lordship Rd.

64 WRITTLE UNIVERSITY COLLEGE

Writtle, CM1 3RR. Writtle University College, 01245 424200 x 25758, Charlotte.Power@writtle.ac.uk, www.writtle.ac.uk. *4m W of Chelmsford. On A414, nr Writtle village.* **Thur 24 May (10-3.30); Sun 2 Sept (10-4). Adm £4, chd free. Light refreshments in The Garden Room (main campus) & The Lordship tea room (Lordship campus). Visits also by arrangement May to Oct.**
15 acres; informal lawns with naturalised bulbs and wild flowers. Large tree collection, mixed shrubs, herbaceous borders. Landscaped gardens designed and built by students. Landscaped glasshouses and wide range of seasonal bedding displays. New Dry/Mediterranean garden designed and built by staff and students on our RHS courses. Herbaceous perennial borders. Extended naturalised bulb areas on front campus lawns. Renovated Rockery Open Day is coordinated by Level 3 Horticultural Students who are on hand to assist visitors. Some gravel, however majority of areas accessible to all.

65 NEW WYCHWOOD

Epping Road, Roydon, Harlow, CM19 5DW. Mrs Madeleine Paine. *At Tylers Cross r'about head in the direction of Roydon. You will find the garden on R approx 400 metres from the r'about. Parking is available in Redrick's nursery next to garden.* **Sun 10 June, Sun 23 Sept (11-4). Adm £4, chd free. Home-made teas.**
A garden of around ¾ of an acre with a large pond, attracting much wildlife, as well as the owners resident ducks. Free ranging chickens roam in the shrubbery and budgerigar aviary. There are numerous features incl, vegetable and fruit plot, mixed shrub and herbaceous borders, 1920's summer house and Scandinavian cabin. English roses are a particular feature of the garden.

66 WYCKE FARM

Pages Lane, Tolleshunt D'Arcy, Maldon, CM9 8AB. Nancy & Anthony Seabrook. *5m E of Maldon, 10m SW of Colchester. B1023 from Tolleshunt D'Arcy 1m towards Tollesbury. Turn R into Pages Lane. Follow for 1m to Wycke Farm.* **Fri 18, Sun 20 May (11-5). Adm £4, chd free. Home-made teas.**
Large cottage style farmhouse garden situated in the peaceful Essex countryside with mature trees, mixed borders, vegetables, greenhouses and a small flock of sheep. Developed from a neglected state over 12 years ago with a fine view of the Blackwater Estuary. Some gravel and grass paths.

Jericho Cottage (Megarry's Antiques & Teashop)

GLOUCESTERSHIRE

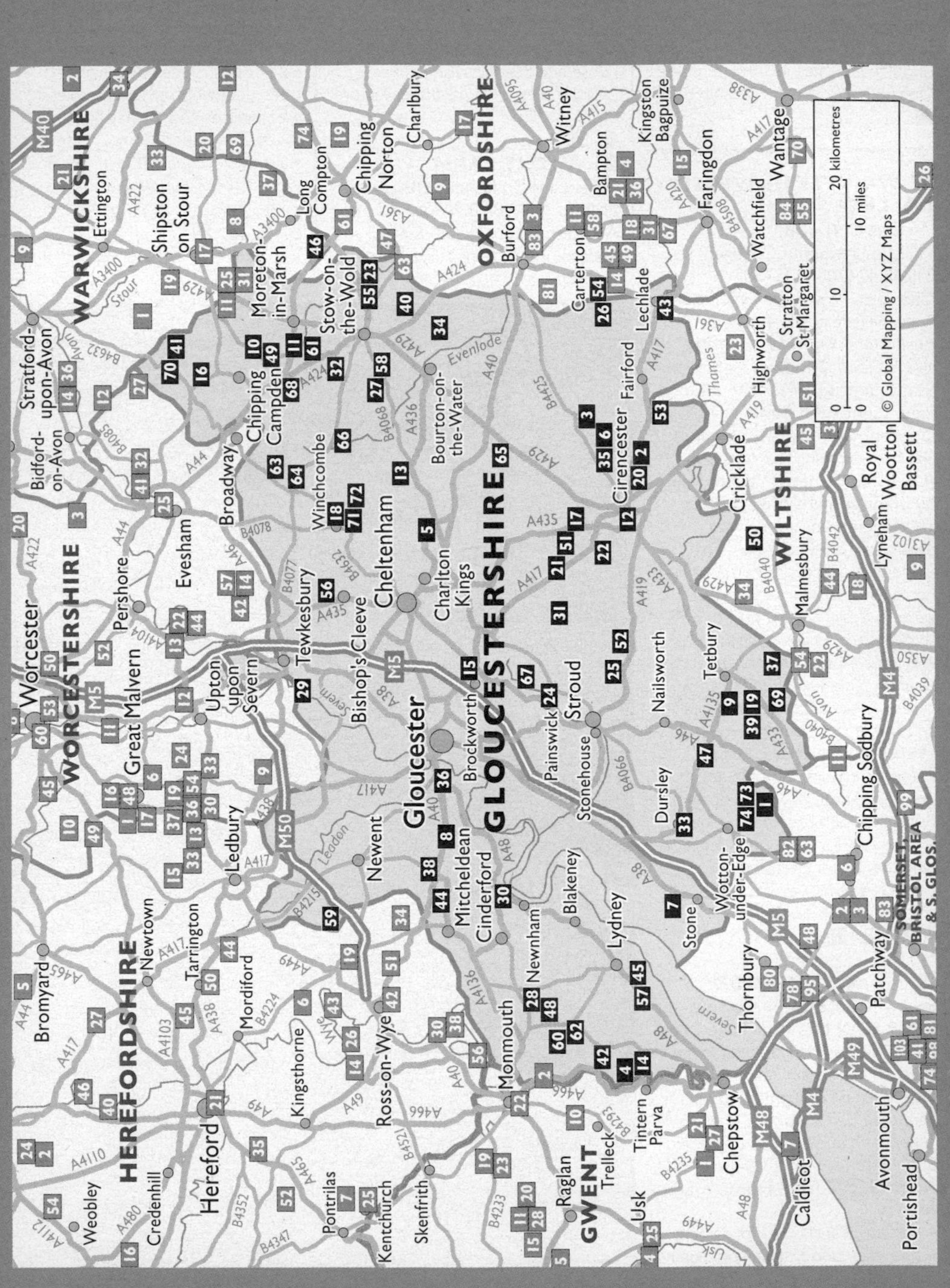

Gloucestershire is one of the most beautiful counties in England, spanning as it does a large part of the area known as the Cotswolds as well as the Forest of Dean and Wye and Severn Valleys.

The Cotswolds is an expanse of gently sloping green hills, wooded valleys and ancient, picturesque towns and villages; it is designated as an area of Outstanding Natural Beauty, and its quintessentially English charm attracts many visitors.

Like the county itself many of the gardens that open for the National Garden Scheme are simply quite outstanding. There are significant gardens which open for the public as well, such as Kiftsgate and Bourton House. There are also some large private gardens which only open for us, such as Highnam Court and Stowell Park.

There are however many more modest private gardens whose doors only open on the National Garden Scheme open day, such as Bowling Green Road in Cirencester with over 300 varieties of Hemerocallis. This tiny garden has now opened for over 35 years. The National collection of Rambling Roses is held at Moor Wood and that of Juglans and Pterocarya at Upton Wold.

Several very attractive Cotswold villages also open their gardens and a wonderful day can be had strolling from cottage to house marvelling at both the standard of the gardens and the beauty of the wonderful buildings, only to pause for the obligatory tea and cake!

Volunteers

County Organiser
Norman Jeffery
01793 762805
norman.jeffery@ngs.org.uk

County Treasurer
Pam Sissons
01242 573942
pamsissons1@gmail.com

Publicity
Vanessa Berridge
01242 609535
vanessa.berridge@sky.com

Booklet Coordinator
Nick Kane
07768 478668
nick@kanes.org

Assistant County Organisers
Sue Hunt
01453 521263
suehunt2@btinternet.com

Trish Jeffery
01793 762805
trishjeffery@aol.com

Valerie Kent
01993 823294

Colin & Verena Olle
01452 863750
colin.olle@ngs.org.uk

Pat Willey
01285 762946
patwilley1@gmail.com

Gareth & Sarah Williams
01531 821654
dgwilliams84@hotmail.com

Left: **Stowell Park**

OPENING DATES

All entries subject to change. For latest information check **www.ngs.org.uk**

Map locator numbers are shown to the right of each garden name.

January

Sunday 28th
Home Farm 38

February

Snowdrop Festival

Sunday 11th
Home Farm 38
Trench Hill 67

Saturday 17th
Lindors Country House 42

Sunday 18th
Beverston Castle 9
NEW The Garden House 32
Lindors Country House 42
Trench Hill 67

March

Saturday 10th
Lindors Country House 42

Sunday 11th
Home Farm 38
Lindors Country House 42

Sunday 18th
NEW The Garden House 32

Saturday 31st
Lindors Country House 42

April

Sunday 1st
Lindors Country House 42
Trench Hill 67

Monday 2nd
Lindors Country House 42
Trench Hill 67

Sunday 8th
Highnam Court 36
Home Farm 38
South Lodge 62

Monday 9th
◆ Kiftsgate Court 41

Tuesday 10th
Barnsley House 6

Sunday 15th
20 Forsdene Walk 28
Meadow Cottage 48
Pear Tree Cottage 56
Upton Wold 68

Sunday 22nd
Blockley Gardens 10
NEW Charlton Down House 19
◆ The Coach House Garden 20
◆ The Garden at Miserden 31
Trench Hill 67

Sunday 29th
Home Farm 38

May

Saturday 5th
Lindors Country House 42
South Lodge 62

Sunday 6th
Eastcombe, Bussage and Brownshill Gardens 25
Highnam Court 36
Lindors Country House 42
Ramblers 57
◆ Stanway Fountain & Water Garden 64

Monday 7th
Eastcombe, Bussage and Brownshill Gardens 25
Lindors Country House 42

Wednesday 9th
◆ Lydney Park Spring Garden 45

Wednesday 16th
Downton House 24
20 Forsdene Walk 28

Saturday 19th
Charingworth Court 18

Sunday 20th
Charingworth Court 18
◆ Matara Gardens 47
◆ Mill Dene Garden 49
South Lodge 62
Stowell Park 65

Monday 21st
NEW ◆ Oxleaze Farm 54

Tuesday 22nd
NEW ◆ Oxleaze Farm 54

Saturday 26th
Hookshouse Pottery 39
Lindors Country House 42
Longhope Gardens 44

Sunday 27th
Greenfields, Little Rissington 34
Hookshouse Pottery 39
Lindors Country House 42
Longhope Gardens 44
Pasture Farm 55

Monday 28th
Hookshouse Pottery 39
Lindors Country House 42
Pasture Farm 55

Tuesday 29th
Hookshouse Pottery 39

Wednesday 30th
Hookshouse Pottery 39

Thursday 31st
Hookshouse Pottery 39

June

Friday 1st
Hookshouse Pottery 39

Festival Weekend

Saturday 2nd
Hookshouse Pottery 39
Pasture Farm 55
Wortley Farm House 73

Sunday 3rd
Highnam Court 36
Hodges Barn 37
Hookshouse Pottery 39
The Manor 46
Pasture Farm 55
Wortley Farm House 73

Monday 4th
Hodges Barn 37

Wednesday 6th
Daylesford House 23
Eyford House 27
20 Forsdene Walk 28
Rockcliffe House 58
Trench Hill 67

Thursday 7th
Campden House 16

Saturday 9th
Cotswold Farm 21
Longhope Gardens 44
White House 70

Sunday 10th
Barn House, Sandywell Park 5
Blockley Gardens 10
NEW Charlton Down House 19
Cotswold Farm 21
The Gables 30
Longhope Gardens 44
South Lodge 62
White House 70

Monday 11th
Berkeley Castle 7

Wednesday 13th
Trench Hill 67

Thursday 14th
Campden House 16

Sunday 17th
20 Forsdene Walk 28
Meadow Cottage 48
Oakridge Lynch Open Gardens 52
◆ Sezincote 61
Stanton Village Gardens 63

Tuesday 19th
Wortley House 74

Wednesday 20th
Trench Hill 67

Saturday 23rd
Berrys Place Farm 8

Sunday 24th
Berrys Place Farm 8

Brocklehurst 13
Minety and Upper Minety Open Gardens and Plant Fair 50
Stowell Park 65

Wednesday 27th
Berrys Place Farm 8
Eyford House 27
◆ Herbs for Healing 35
Rockcliffe House 58

Thursday 28th
Berrys Place Farm 8

Saturday 30th
South Lodge 62

July

Sunday 1st
Ampney Brook House 2
Awkward Hill Cottage 3
25 Bowling Green Road 12
◆ Cerney House Gardens 17
Forthampton Court 29
Highnam Court 36
Icomb Gardens 40
Moor Wood 51
NEW Winchcombe Gardens 71

Monday 2nd
25 Bowling Green Road 12

Sunday 8th
Barn House, Sandywell Park 5
25 Bowling Green Road 12
◆ Herbs for Healing 35

Monday 9th
25 Bowling Green Road 12
Brockworth Court 15

Wednesday 11th
20 Forsdene Walk 28

Sunday 15th
25 Bowling Green Road 12
NEW The Garden House 32
◆ Westonbirt School Gardens 69

Monday 16th
25 Bowling Green Road 12

Sunday 22nd
Trench Hill 67

August

Wednesday 1st
Woodlands Farm 72

Sunday 5th
Highnam Court 36
Woodlands Farm 72

Wednesday 8th
20 Forsdene Walk 28
Woodlands Farm 72

Sunday 12th
◆ Bourton House Garden 11
The Old Rectory, Quenington 53
Woodlands Farm 72

Monday 13th
◆ Kiftsgate Court 41

Sunday 19th
The Gables 30
The Manor 46

Saturday 25th
Lindors Country House 42

Sunday 26th
Barn House, Sandywell Park 5
Lindors Country House 42
Trench Hill 67

Monday 27th
Barn House, Sandywell Park 5
Lindors Country House 42

September

Saturday 1st
Loders Gate 43
Rose Cottage 59

Sunday 2nd
Highnam Court 36
Rose Cottage 59

Sunday 9th
NEW Brockweir Gardens 14
Trench Hill 67

Sunday 16th
◆ Mill Dene Garden 49

Sunday 23rd
◆ Stanway Fountain & Water Garden 64

January 2019

Sunday 27th
Home Farm 38

February 2019

Sunday 10th
Home Farm 38

By Arrangement

Alderley Grange 1
Ampney Brook House 2
Awkward Hill Cottage 3
Barn House, Chepstow 4
25 Bowling Green Road 12
Brockworth Court 15
Charingworth Court 18
Cotswold Farm 21
Daglingworth House 22
Eastleach House 26
20 Forsdene Walk 28
The Gables 30
NEW Green Bowers 33
Home Farm 38
Longhope Gardens 44
Meadow Cottage 48
Moor Wood 51
Pear Tree Cottage 56
Scatterford 60
South Lodge 62
Trench Hill 67
White House 70
Woodlands Farm 72
Wortley House 74

Awkward Hill Cottage

THE GARDENS

1 ALDERLEY GRANGE

Alderley, GL12 7QT. The Hon Mrs Acloque, 01453 842161, milly@acloque-alderley.co.uk. *2m S of Wotton-under-Edge. Turn NW off A46 Bath to Stroud rd at Dunkirk. L signed Hawkesbury Upton & Hillesley. In Hillesley follow sign to Alderley.* **Visits by arrangement May to July small or large groups, max 40. Adm £6, chd free.**

Originally designed by Alvilde Lees-Milne in the early 1960's, this quintessentially English garden boasts an abundance of old-fashioned roses and many aromatic and medicinal plants and herbs. Features include a pleached lime walk, fine trees and a Regency summerhouse. Some gravel paths.

2 AMPNEY BROOK HOUSE

School Lane, Ampney Crucis, Cirencester, GL7 5RT. Allan Hirst, 01285 851098, allan.hirst@clmail.co.uk. *From Cirencester go E on A417 toward Fairford. After passing the Crown of Crucis take 1st L and also immed L again onto School Lane and L again into the gated (open automatically) drive.* **Sun 1 July (11-4). Adm £5, chd free. Light refreshments. Visits also by arrangement Apr to Oct for groups of all sizes - we've had 1-55 so far. Discuss refreshments when booking.**

Striking Grade II Cotswold country house on 4.3 acres fronting Ampney Brook. The gardens are at the end of a 5yr project to create a haven for wildlife with fun and stimulating spaces yr-round. Incl woodland, kitchen garden, herbaceous borders, meadows, newly planted arbor. Ample areas and lawns for picnicking (encouraged). No wheelchair access to kitchen garden/greenhouse.

3 AWKWARD HILL COTTAGE

Awkward Hill, Bibury, GL7 5NH. Mrs Victoria Summerley, v.summerley@hotmail.com, www.awkwardhill.co.uk. *Bibury, Gloucestershire. No parking at the property, so best to park in village and walk past Arlington Row up Awkward Hill, or up Hawkers Hill from Catherine Wheel PH.* **Sun 1 July (2-6). Adm £3.50, chd free. Home-made teas. Visits also by arrangement June to Sept for groups between 10 and 20, preferably weekdays (parking is easier).**

This country Cotswold garden is a work in progress. Since 2012, when the current owner bought the property, it has been redesigned to reflect the local landscape and encourage wildlife. Planting is both formal and informal contributing yr-round interest. Pond and waterfall. The owner, a journalist, is author of Secret Gardens of the Cotswolds and Great Gardens of London. Wonderful view over neighbouring meadow and woodland, small pond jetty, 2 sunny terraces and plenty of places to sit and relax.

4 BARN HOUSE, CHEPSTOW

Brockweir Common, Chepstow, NP16 7PH. Mrs Kate Patel, 01291 680041, barnhousegarden@gmail.com, www.thegardenbarnhouse.com. *10m S of Monmouth & N of Chepstow, under 1 hr from Hereford, Cheltenham & Cardiff. From Chepstow A466 to Monmouth. 2m past Tintern Abbey R Brockweir Bridge then up Mill Hill ½m, 1st L at The Rock (cottage) continue uphill 1½m. BH on R. No large coaches.* **Visits by arrangement June to Aug. Adm £4.50, chd free. Refreshments available by arrangement at additional £2.50 per person.**

Boldly and generously planted garden of an acre. Wealth of ornamental grasses plus long, late flowering perennials. Stunning mass plantings incl 70m miscanthus hedge. Imaginatively designed contrasting areas incl tranquil sunken terrace with lush Asian grasses, hot border of potted tender perennials and dramatic bamboo screening. Featured in BBC Gardeners World, Country Homes and Interiors, The English Garden, Saturday Telegraph.

5 BARN HOUSE, SANDYWELL PARK

Whittington, Cheltenham, GL54 4HF. Shirley & Gordon Sills. *4m E of Cheltenham on A40. Between Andoversford and Whittington villages on A40.* **Sun 10 June, Sun 8 July, Sun 26, Mon 27 Aug (11-5). Adm £5, chd free. Home-made teas.**

Final Year of Opening. 2½ acre plantaholic's walled garden. Designed, created and maintained solely by the owners as a series of enclosures both formal and informal, sometimes quirky. Profusely and exuberantly planted for form, scent and colour and to attract wildlife. Herbaceous, climbers, shrubs, trees, lawns, hedges, structures, vistas, water features.

6 BARNSLEY HOUSE

Barnsley, Cirencester, GL7 5EE. Calcot Health & Leisure Ltd, 01285 740000, reception@barnsleyhouse.com, www.barnsleyhouse.com. *4m NE of Cirencester. From Cirencester, take B4425 to Barnsley. House entrance on R as you enter village.* **Tue 10 Apr (10-4). Adm £5, chd free. Tea.**

The beautiful garden at Barnsley House, created by Rosemary Verey, is one of England's finest and most famous gardens incl knot garden, potager garden and mixed borders in Rosemary Verey's successional planting style. The house also has an extensive kitchen garden which will be open with plants and vegetables available for purchase. Narrow paths mean restricted wheelchair access but happy to provide assistance.

7 BERKELEY CASTLE

Berkeley, GL13 9PJ. Mr & Mrs RJG Berkeley, www.berkeley-castle.com. *Half-way between Bristol & Gloucester, 10mins from J13 & 14 of M5. Follow signs to Berkeley from A38 & B4066. Visitors' entrance is on L of Canonbury St, just before town centre.* **Mon 11 June (11-5). Adm £6, chd free. Light refreshments in yurt restaurant, next to ticket office/gift shop. Delicious home-made cakes, savouries and locally sourced items available.**

Unique historic garden of a keen plantsman, with far-reaching views across R Severn. Gardens contain many rare plants which thrive in the warm micro-climate against stone walls of mediaeval castle. Woodland, historic trees and stunning terraced borders. Butterfly house with free-flying tropical butterflies. Difficult for wheelchairs due to terraced nature of gardens.

8 BERRYS PLACE FARM

Bulley Lane, Churcham, Gloucester, GL2 8AS. Anne Thomas, 07950 808022, gary.j.thomas1953@gmail.com. *6m W of Gloucester. A40 towards Ross. Turning R into Bulley Lane at Birdwood.* **Sat 23, Sun 24, Wed 27, Thur 28 June (11-5). Adm £3.50, chd free. Home-made teas. Ploughmans lunches, cream teas.**

Country garden, approx 2 acres, surrounded by farmland and old orchards. Lawns and large sweeping mixed herbaceous borders with over 100 roses. Formal kitchen garden and beautiful rose arbour leading to lake and summerhouse with a variety of water lilies and carp. All shared with peacocks and ducks.

9 BEVERSTON CASTLE

Beverston, nr Tetbury, GL8 8TU. Mrs A L Rook. *2m W of Tetbury. On A4135 to Dursley between Tetbury & Calcot Xrds.* **Sun 18 Feb (12.30-3.30). Adm £5, chd free. Home-made teas in the Norman church.**

New opening time in the spring to appreciate drifts of snowdrops overlooked by romantic C12-C17 castle ruin (not open). Terrace with steps lead from C18 house (private and not open) across bridge and moat to sloping lawn with spring bulbs in abundance. Snowdrops in castle grounds and Norman churchyard. Partial wheelchair access.

GROUP OPENING

10 BLOCKLEY GARDENS

Blockley, GL56 9DB. *3m NW of Moreton-in-Marsh. Just off the Morton-in-Marsh to Evesham Rd A44.* **Sun 22 Apr, Sun 10 June (2-6). Combined adm £6, chd free. Home-made teas at Mill Dene & St George's Hall on April 22, at St George's Hall & The Manor House on June 10.**

NEW **BLOCKLEY ALLOTMENTS**
Open on Sun 10 June

CHURCH GATES
Mrs Brenda Salmon.
Open on all dates

LANDGATE
Mrs Hilary Sutton.
Open on all dates

THE MANOR HOUSE
George & Zoe Thompson.
Open on all dates

◆ **MILL DENE GARDEN**
Mrs B S Dare.
Open on all dates
(See separate entry)

MILL GARDEN HOUSE
Andrew & Celia Goodrick-Clarke.
Open on Sun 22 Apr

THE OLD CHEQUER
Mr & Mrs H Linley.
Open on all dates

PORCH HOUSE
Mr & Mrs Johnson.
Open on Sun 22 Apr

◆ **'RODNEYS'**
Mr Duncan & Mrs Amelia Stewart.
Open on Sun 10 June

SNUGBOROUGH MILL
Rupert & Mandy Williams-Ellis, 01386 701310, rupert.williams-ellis@talk21.com.
Open on Sun 10 June

WOODRUFF
Paul & Maggie Adams.
Open on all dates

This popular historic hillside village has a great variety of high quality, well-stocked gardens - large and small, old and new. Blockley Brook, an attractive stream which flows right through the village, graces some of the gardens; these incl gardens of former water mills, with millponds attached. From some gardens there are wonderful rural views. Shuttle coach service provided. Children welcome but close supervision is essential. Access to some gardens quite steep and allowances should be made.

Donations from the National Garden Scheme help Parkinson's UK care for more people

11 ◆ BOURTON HOUSE GARDEN

Bourton-on-the-Hill, GL56 9AE. Mr & Mrs R Quintus, 01386 700754, info@bourtonhouse.com, www.bourtonhouse.com. *2m W of Moreton-in-Marsh. On A44.* **For NGS: Sun 12 Aug (10-5). Adm £7, chd free. Home-made teas in Grade I listed C16 Tithe Barn. Light refreshments & home-made cakes.** For other opening times and information, please phone, email or visit garden website.

Award winning 3 acre garden featuring imaginative topiary, wide herbaceous borders with many rare, unusual and exotic plants, water features, unique shade house and many creatively planted pots. Fabulous at any time of year but magnificent in summer months. Walk in 7 acre pasture with free printed guide to specimen trees available to garden visitors. Featured in The English Garden. 70% access for wheelchairs.

12 25 BOWLING GREEN ROAD

Cirencester, GL7 2HD. Mrs Sue Beck, 01285 653778, sjb@beck-hems.org.uk. *On NW edge of Cirencester. Take A435 to Spitalgate/Whiteway T-lights, turn into The Whiteway (Chedworth turn), then 1st L into Bowling Green Rd, garden in bend in rd between Nos 23 & 27.* **Sun 1 July (2-5); Mon 2 July (11-4); Sun 8 July (2-5); Mon 9 July (11-4); Sun 15 July (2-5); Mon 16 July (11-4). Adm £3.50, chd free. Visits also by arrangement June & July, also open by appt in Sept for grasses, max 30. Tea/coffee/ biscuits can be provided for small groups by arrangement.**

Expect the unexpected as you wander at will along winding walkways and billowing borders in a naturalistic mini-jungle of heavenly hemerocallis, gorgeous grasses, curvaceous clematis, romantic roses and plentiful perennials to glimpse friendly frogs and a graceful giraffe, rated by visitors as an amazing hidden gem. See http://thechattygardener.com/?p=2585. Featured in local publications. Sadly not suitable for wheelchair access.

13 BROCKLEHURST

Hawling, Cheltenham, GL54 5TA. Mrs Anne Wood. *from A40 Cheltenham to Oxford at Andoversford turn onto A436 towards Stow-on-theWold and follow signed rd to Hawling.* **Sun 24 June (11-5). Adm £4, chd free. Home-made teas.**

¼ acre romantic Cotswold garden surrounded by beautiful countryside with far reaching views. Traditional herbaceous borders with lawn leading down to raised lily pond surrounded by scented planting incl roses, peonies and summerhouse. Hidden woodland wildlife garden with pond and productive cottage vegetable patch. New for 2018, courtyard garden with Zen influence. Limited wheelchair access, some gravel paths.

GROUP OPENING

14 NEW BROCKWEIR GARDENS

Brockweir, Chepstow, NP16 7PJ. *Small village in Wye Valley, 6.7m N of Chepstow and 10.6m S of Monmouth, off A466, across Brockweir Bridge.* **Sun 9 Sept (12-5). Combined adm £7.50, chd free. Home-made teas at Cloud's Rest. Tea, coffee, cakes.**

NEW CLOUDS REST
Mrs Jan Brassford.

NEW THE PATCH
Mrs Immy Lee.

NEW SPRING FARM
Mrs Sue Burrows.

Brockweir is a medieval village, nestled between the River Wye and the Offas Dyke Path. The gardens are of contrasting styles and sited in elevated positions offering extensive views over the Wye Valley and beyond. All gardens have parking close by. Cloud's Rest's transformation from a stony paddock into the current garden started in 2012. Set within meandering gravel pathways, the garden contains a mixture of roses and perennials, with a wide selection of michaelmas daisies providing a riot of colour. The garden at The Patch, restructured over the last few yrs, is now a well designed garden with fine borders containing an abundance of roses, shrubs and perennials, providing variety and colour throughout the yr. Spring Farm is the more mature garden, set in a stunning landscape, with a variety of unusual trees and shrubs culminating in an attractive small lake. Plants featured in the gardens will be for sale. Partial wheelchair access at the Patch. Wheelchair access is limited at Cloud's rest and Spring Form, but some areas are accessible.

15 BROCKWORTH COURT

Court Road, Brockworth, GL3 4QU. Tim & Bridget Wiltshire, 01452 862938, timwiltshire@hotmail.co.uk. *6m E of Gloucester. 6m W of Cheltenham. Adj St Georges Church on Court Rd. From A46 turn into Mill Lane, turn R, L, R at T junctions. From Ermin St, turn into Ermin Park, then R at r'about then L at next r'about.* **Mon 9 July (2-5.30). Adm £5, chd free. Home-made teas in tithe barn. Visits also by arrangement Apr to Sept, light refreshments by arrangement, groups of 10+.**

This intense yet informal tapestry style garden beautifully complements the period manor house which it surrounds. Organic, naturalistic, with informal cottage-style planting areas that seamlessly blend together. Natural fish pond, with Monet bridge leading to small island with thatched Fiji house. Kitchen garden once cultivated by monks. Historic tithe barn. Views to Crickley and Coopers Hill. Adj Norman Church (open). Small vintage tractor collection. Featured in Cotswold Life, The Citizen, Garden News, Gloucester radio. Partial wheelchair access.

16 CAMPDEN HOUSE

Dyers Lane, Chipping Campden, GL55 6UP. The Hon Philip & Mrs Smith. *Entrance on Chipping Campden to Weston Subedge Rd (Dyers Lane), approx ¼m SW of Campden, 1¼m drive. Do not use SatNav.* **Thur 7, Thur 14 June (2-6). Adm £6, chd free. Home-made teas.**

2 acres featuring mixed borders of plant and colour interest around house and C17 tithe barn (neither open). Set in fine parkland in hidden valley with lakes and ponds. Woodland garden and walks, vegetable garden. Gravel paths, steep slopes.

17 ◆ CERNEY HOUSE GARDENS

North Cerney, Cirencester, GL7 7BX. Mr N W Angus & Dr J Angus, 01285 831300, janet@cerneygardens.com, www.cerneygardens.com. *4m NW of Cirencester. On A435 Cheltenham rd turn L opp Bathurst Arms, follow rd past church up hill, then go straight towards pillared gates on R (signed Cerney House).* **For NGS: Sun 1 July (10-5). Adm £5, chd £1. Tea, coffee, home-made cakes and cream teas in The Bothy.** For other opening times and information, please phone, email or visit garden website.

Romantic walled garden filled with old-fashioned roses and long herbaceous borders. Knot garden filled with spring tulip display and dahlias later in the year. Working kitchen garden with heritage vegetables, scented garden and lavender walk. Drifts of naturalised snowdrops end Jan/ Feb. Large collection of hellebores and woodland bluebell walk. Herb garden (in development), koi carp pond, woodland walks. Limited wheelchair access.

18 CHARINGWORTH COURT

Broadway Road, Winchcombe, GL54 5JN. Susan & Richard Wakeford, 01242 603033, susanwakeford@gmail.com, www.charingworthcourtcotswoldsgarden.com. *8m NE of Cheltenham. 400 metres N of Winchcombe town centre car park in Bull Lane; walk down Chandos St, L onto Broadway Rd. Garden is on L or limited parking along Broadway Rd.* **Sat 19, Sun 20 May (11-5.30). Adm £5, chd free. Home-made teas from 12noon. Visits also by arrangement May to July for groups of 10+, day or eve.**

Artistically and lovingly created 1½ acre garden surrounding restored Georgian/Tudor house (not open). Relaxed country style with Japanese influences, large pond and walled vegetable/flower garden, created over 20 years from a blank canvas. Mature copper beech trees, Cedar of Lebanon and Wellingtonia; and younger trees replacing an earlier excess of Cupressus leylandii. Garden will be the backdrop for 7th annual Charingworth Court Garden sculpture selling exhibition once again curated by Jane Smoczynski of Winds of Change Gallery. Most paths gravelled, several areas accessible without steps. Disabled parking next to house.

Charlton Down House

19 NEW CHARLTON DOWN HOUSE

Charlton Down, Tetbury, GL8 8TZ. Neil & Julie Record. *2m SW of Tetbury, Gloucs. From Tetbury, take A433 towards Bath for 1½m; turn R (north) just before the Hare and Hounds, then R again after 200yds into Hookshouse Lane. Charlton Down House is 600yds on R.* **Sun 22 Apr, Sun 10 June (12-6). Adm £5, chd free. Home-made teas.**

Extensive country house gardens in 180 acre equestrian estate. Formal terraces, perennial borders, walled topiary garden, enclosed cut flower garden and large glasshouse. Newly planted copse. Rescue animals. Ample parking. Largely flat terrain; most garden areas accessible.

20 ◆ THE COACH HOUSE GARDEN

Ampney Crucis, Cirencester, GL7 5RY. Mr & Mrs Nicholas Tanner, 01285 850256, mel@thegenerousgardener.co.uk, www.thegenerousgardener.co.uk. *3m E of Cirencester. Turn into village from A417, immed before Crown of Crucis Inn. Over hump-back bridge, parking immed to R on cricket field (weather permitting) or signed nearby field.* **For NGS: Sun 22 Apr (2-5). Adm £5, chd free. Home-made teas. For other opening times and information, please phone, email or visit garden website.**

Approx 1½ acres, full of structure and design. Garden is divided into rooms incl rill garden, gravel garden, rose garden, herbaceous borders, green garden with pleached lime allee and potager. Created over last 28yrs by present owners and constantly evolving. Visitors welcome during April - July (groups of 15+), please see above website. Rare plant sales (in aid of James Hopkins Trust) and garden lecture days. Featured in Gardens Illustrated Magazine & Telegraph. Limited wheelchair access. Ramp available to enable access to main body of garden, steps to other areas.

21 COTSWOLD FARM

Duntisbourne Abbots, Cirencester, GL7 7JS. Mrs Mark Birchall, 01285 821857, iona@cotswoldfarmgardens.org.uk, www.cotswoldfarmgardens.org.uk. *5m NW of Cirencester off old A417. From Cirencester L signed Duntisbourne Abbots Services, R and R underpass. Drive ahead. From Gloucester L signed Duntisbourne Abbots Services. Pass Services. Drive L.* **Sat 9, Sun 10 June (2-5). Adm £5, chd free. Home Made Teas by WI. Visits also by arrangement all yr, individuals and groups welcome.** Donation to A Rocha.

Arts and Crafts garden in lovely position overlooking quiet valley on descending levels with terrace designed by Norman Jewson in 1930s. Snowdrops named and naturalised, aconites in Feb. Winter garden. Bog garden best in May, White border overflowing with texture and scent. Shrubs, trees, shrub roses. Allotments in old walled garden, 8 native orchids, hundreds of wild flowers and Roman snails. Family day out. Rare orchid walks. Picnics welcome. Partial wheelchair access.

22 DAGLINGWORTH HOUSE

Daglingworth, nr Cirencester, GL7 7AG. David & Henrietta Howard, 01285 885626, ettajhoward@gmail.com. *3m N of Cirencester off A417/419. House with blue gate beside church in Daglingworth.* **Visits by arrangement Apr to Sept for groups between 4 & 25. Adm £6.**

Walled garden, water features, temple and grotto. Classical garden of 2 acres, views and vistas with humorous contemporary twist. Attractive planting, hedges, topiary shapes, herbaceous borders. Pergolas, woodland, pool, cascade and mirror canal. Lovely Cotswold village setting beside church - see www.ngs.org.uk for further details on garden. Featured in Cotswold Life, Wilts & Glos Standard and other publications. Due to many changes of level and steps this garden is regretfully not suitable for wheelchairs.

23 DAYLESFORD HOUSE

Daylesford, GL56 0YG. Lord Bamford & Lady Bamford. *5m W of Chipping Norton. Off A436. Between Stow-on-the-Wold & Chipping Norton.* **Wed 6 June (1-5). Adm £6, chd free. Home-made teas.**

Magnificent C18 landscape grounds created 1790 for Warren Hastings, greatly restored and enhanced by present owners. Lakeside and woodland walks within natural wild flower meadows. Large walled garden planted formally, centred around orchid, peach and working glasshouses. Trellised rose garden. Collection of citrus within period orangery. Secret garden with pavilion and formal pools. Very large garden with substantial distances to be walked. Partial wheelchair access.

24 DOWNTON HOUSE

Gloucester St, Painswick, GL6 6QN. Ms Jane Kilpatrick. *Entry to garden via Hollyhock Lane only. Please note: no cars in Lane. Parking in Stamages Lane village car park below church or in Churchill Way (1st R off Gloucester Street – B4073).* **Wed 16 May (1.30-5). Adm £5, chd free. Home-made teas.**

Enthusiast's walled ¼ acre garden in heart of historic Painswick. Planted for yr-round foliage colour and interest and packed with rare and unusual plants. Collection of tender plants in heated glasshouse. Looks good even in the rain!

GROUP OPENING

25 EASTCOMBE, BUSSAGE AND BROWNSHILL GARDENS

Eastcombe, GL6 7DS. *3m E of Stroud. 2m N of A419 Stroud to Cirencester rd on turning signed to Bisley & Eastcombe. Please park considerately in villages. Not all gardens listed may be open on the day so please check before arrival.* **Sun 6, Mon 7 May (2-6). Combined adm £7, chd free. Home-made teas at Eastcombe Village Hall. Cream teas/home-made cakes.** Donation to Hope for Tomorrow; Myeloma UK; Sarcoma UK.

NEW **BREWERS COTTAGE**
Jackie & Nick Topman.

21 FARMCOTE CLOSE
Mr & Mrs Robert Bryant.

HAWKLEY COTTAGE
Helen Westendorp.

1 HIDCOTE CLOSE
Mr & Mrs J Southall.

12 HIDCOTE CLOSE
Mr & Mrs K Walker.

HIGHLANDS
Helen & Bob Watkinson.

1 THE LAURELS
Andrew & Ruth Fraser.

MARYFIELD AND MARYFIELD COTTAGE
Mrs M Brown.

NEW **PARK VIEW**
Anne & Paul Hutt.

REDWOOD
Rita Collins.

NEW **50 STONECOTE RIDGE**
Julie & Robin Marsland.

YEW TREE COTTAGE
Andy & Sue Green.

Medium and small gardens, set in picturesque hilltop location. Some approachable only by foot. (Exhibitions may be on view in Eastcombe village hall). Plants for sale in Eastcombe village hall and possibly in some gardens. New event – children's trail around the gardens. Wheelchair access to some gardens. Please check at village hall.

26 EASTLEACH HOUSE

Eastleach Martin, Cirencester, GL7 3NW. Mrs David Richards, garden@eastleachhouse.com, www.eastleachhouse.com. *5m NE of Fairford, 6m S of Burford. Entrance opp church gates in Eastleach Martin. Lodge at gate, gravel driveway is quite steep and curves up to house.* **Visits by arrangement Feb to Oct any size group. Adm £10.**
Large traditional all-yr-round garden. Wooded hilltop position with long views S and W. New parkland, lime avenue and arboretum. Wild flower walk, wildlife pond, lawns, walled and rill gardens, with modern herbaceous borders, yew and box hedges, iris and paeony borders, lily ponds, formal herb garden and topiary. Rambling roses into trees. Limited wheelchair access.

27 EYFORD HOUSE

Upper Slaughter, Cheltenham, GL54 2JN. Mrs C Heber-Percy. *2½m from Stow on the Wold on B4068 Stow to Andoversford Rd.* **Wed 6, Wed 27 June (11-5). Adm £4, chd free. Home-made teas. Also open Rockcliffe House.**
1½ acre sloping N facing garden, ornamental shrubs and trees. Laid out originally by Graham Stuart Thomas, 1976. West garden and terrace, red border, walled kitchen garden, two lakes with pleasant walks and views, boots recommended! Holy well. Walled garden now open after reconstruction.

28 20 FORSDENE WALK

Coalway, Coleford, GL16 7JZ. Pamela Buckland, 01594 837179. *From Coleford take Lydney/Chepstow Rd at T-lights. L after police station ½m up hill turn L at Xrds then 2nd R (Old Road) straight on at minor Xrds then L into Forsdene Walk.* **Sun 15 Apr (1-5). Combined adm with Meadow Cottage £5, chd free. Wed 16 May, Wed 6 June (2-6). Adm £3, chd free. Sun 17 June (2-6). Combined adm with Meadow Cottage £5, chd free. Wed 11 July, Wed 8 Aug (2-6). Adm £3, chd free. Home-made teas. Visits also by arrangement May to Sept for individuals and small groups.**
Corner garden filled with interest and design ideas to maximise smaller spaces. A series of interlinking colour themed rooms, some on different levels. Packed with perennials, grasses, ferns and bamboos. A pergola, small man made stream, fruit and vegetables and pots in abundance on gravelled areas.

29 FORTHAMPTON COURT

Forthampton, Tewkesbury, GL19 4RD. John Yorke. *W of Tewkesbury. From Tewkesbury A438 to Ledbury. After 2m turn L to Forthampton. At Xrds go L towards Chaceley. Go 1m turn L at Xrds.* **Sun 1 July (12-4). Adm £5, chd free. Home-made teas.**
Charming and varied garden surrounding North Gloucestershire medieval manor house (not open) within sight of Tewkesbury Abbey. Incl borders, lawns, roses and magnificent Victorian vegetable garden.

30 THE GABLES

Riverside Lane, Broadoak, Newnham on Severn, GL14 1JE. Bryan & Christine Bamber, 01594 516323, bryanbamber@sky.com. *1m NE of Newnham on Severn. Park in White Hart PH overspill car park, to R of PH when facing river. Please follow signs to car park. Walk, turning R along rd towards Gloucester for approx 250yds. Access through marked gate.* **Sun 10 June, Sun 19 Aug (11-5). Adm £3.50, chd free. Home-made teas. Visits also by arrangement June to Aug for groups of 10+.**
Garden established 12 yrs ago from blank canvas. Large flat garden with formal lawns, colourful herbaceous borders, shrubberies and long border with mini stumpery. Incl wild flower meadow incorporating soft fruits and fruit trees, allotment-size productive vegetable plot, greenhouse and composting area. Disabled parking information available at entrance. All areas of garden visible for wheelchair users but with limited access.

Your visit helps the Queen's Nursing Institute to champion excellence in community nursing

31 ◆ THE GARDEN AT MISERDEN

Miserden, Stroud, GL6 7JA. Mr Nicholas Wills, 01285 821303, estate.office@miserdenestate.org, www.miserden.org. *6m NW of Cirencester. Follow signs off A417 or B4070 from Stroud.* **For NGS: Sun 22 Apr (10-5). Adm £7.50, chd free. Cream teas in plant nursery alongside.** For other opening times and information, please phone, email or visit garden website.

This lovely unspoilt garden, positioned high on the Wolds and commanding spectacular views, was created in C17 and still retains a wonderful sense of timeless peace and tranquillity. Perhaps finest features in garden are double 92metre mixed border incl roses and clematis, in different colour sections. Much of original garden is found within ancient Cotswold stone walls. Stunning gardens. Featured in Cotswold Life and Gardens to Visit book. Partial wheelchair access.

32 NEW THE GARDEN HOUSE

Manor Farm, Condicote, Cheltenham, GL54 1ES. Mr Nick Mahony. *Take B4077 or A424 2m W of Stow on the Wold signed Condicote. Park at village hall.* **Sun 18 Feb, Sun 18 Mar, Sun 15 July (2-5). Adm £3, chd free. Home-made teas in Condicote Village Hall.**

This is the retirement home of Pamela Schwerdt and Sibylle Kreutzberger. ⅓ acre packed with rare and interesting plants. Large plantings of named snowdrops In Feb. In March there is a carpet of woodland plants and unusual bulbs, notably fritillaries. Summer is a riot of colour with mainly herbaceous perennials.

33 NEW GREEN BOWERS

The Broadway, Dursley, GL11 6AG. Amanda Songer, 07791 659932, amandacant@yahoo.co.uk. *Up steps by white garage. If using SatNav, go to The Old Spot pub. Green Bowers is 200m up a steep hill from car park opp pub. For a first visit, it's easier to come via the town, rather than the country lanes.* **Visits by arrangement for individuals/groups, max 6, on Tue 24, Wed 25, Sat 28, Sun 29, Mon 30 Apr, Tue 1 May (8-3). Adm £4. Home-made teas. Proceeds from refreshments will support both NGS charities and Dursley Walking Festival, a local charity. Please arrange a time via email.**

Delightful East facing steep woodland garden with extensive views, next to The Cotswold Way. This planted hillside takes its character from the proximity of the woods, wildlife activity and the gradient of the site. You'll find a mixture of both garden plants and wild flowers. There is also a wild flower roof garden as well as acers, and a recently planted pieris bed. Due to the character of the site, we would prefer no children or pets. Terrain is uneven, lots of steps and not all areas have handrails. Please wear suitable footwear. Regrettably, this site is not suitable for individuals with any access or mobility requirements.

34 GREENFIELDS, LITTLE RISSINGTON

Cheltenham, GL54 2NA. Mrs Diana MacKenzie-Charrington. *Greenfields is on the Rissington Road between Bourton-on-the-Water and Little Rissington, opp the turn to Great Rissington (Leasow Lane). SatNav using postcode does not take you to house.* **Sun 27 May (2-5). Adm £5, chd free. Home-made teas.**

The honey coloured Georgian Cotswold stone house sits in 2 acres of garden, created by current owners over last 17 yrs. Lawns are edged with borders full of flowers and later flowering bulbs. A small pond and stream overlook fields. Bantams roam freely. Mature apple trees in wild garden, greenhouse in working vegetable garden. Sorry no dogs. Partial wheelchair access.

35 ◆ HERBS FOR HEALING

Claptons Lane (behind Barnsley House Hotel), Barnsley, GL7 5EE. Davina Wynne-Jones, 07773 687493, davina@herbsforhealing.net, www.herbsforhealing.net. *4m NE of Cirencester. Coming into Barnsley from Cirencester - turn R after Barnsley House Hotel and R again at dairy barn. Follow signs.* **For NGS: Wed 27 June (10.30-5); Sun 8 July (11-4). Adm £3, chd free. Teas, herb teas and home-made**

Berrys Place Farm

cakes. For other opening times and information, please phone, email or visit garden website.
Not a typical NGS garden, rural and naturalistic. Davina, the daughter of Rosemary Verey, has created a unique nursery, specialising in medicinal herbs and a tranquil organic garden in secluded field where visitors can enjoy the beauty of plants and learn more about properties and uses of medicinal herbs. Informative tours of the garden with Davina at 11.30 and 2.30. Products made from the herbs are available. Access to WC is difficult for wheelchair users however the garden itself is all level.

36 HIGHNAM COURT

Highnam, Gloucester, GL2 8DP. Mr & Mrs R J Head, www.HighnamCourt.co.uk. *2m W of Gloucester. On A40/A48 from Gloucester.* **Sun 8 Apr, Sun 6 May, Sun 3 June, Sun 1 July, Sun 5 Aug, Sun 2 Sept (11-5). Adm £5, chd free. Light refreshments in Orangery. Tea, coffee from 11.00am. Sandwiches available until 1.30pm. Cream teas served from 1.30 to 5pm.**
40 acres of Victorian landscaped gardens surrounding magnificent Grade I house (not open), set out by artist Thomas Gambier Parry. Lakes, shrubberies and listed Pulhamite water gardens with grottos and fernery. Exciting ornamental lakes, and woodland areas. Extensive 1 acre rose garden and many features, incl numerous wood carvings. Some gravel paths and steps into refreshment area. Disabled WC outside.

37 HODGES BARN

Shipton Moyne, Tetbury, GL8 8PR. Mr & Mrs N Hornby, www.hodgesbarn.com. *3m S of Tetbury. On Malmesbury side of village.* **Sun 3, Mon 4 June (2-6). Adm £5, chd free. Home-made teas.**
Very unusual C15 dovecote converted into family home. Cotswold stone walls host climbing and rambling roses, clematis, vines, hydrangeas and together with yew, rose and tapestry hedges create formality around house. Mixed shrub and herbaceous borders, shrub roses, water garden, woodland garden planted with cherries, magnolia and spring bulbs.

38 HOME FARM

Newent Lane, Huntley, GL19 3HQ. Mrs T Freeman, 01452 830210, torill@ukgateway.net. *4m S of Newent. On B4216 ½m off A40 in Huntley travelling towards Newent.* **Sun 28 Jan, Sun 11 Feb (11-3); Sun 11 Mar, Sun 8, Sun 29 Apr (11-4). Adm £3, chd free. 2019: Sun 27 Jan, Sun 10 Feb. Visits also by arrangement Jan to May.**
Set in elevated position with exceptional views. 1m walk through woods and fields to show carpets of spring flowers. Enclosed garden with fern border, sundial and heather bed. White and mixed shrub borders. Stout footwear advisable in winter.

39 HOOKSHOUSE POTTERY

Hookshouse Lane, Tetbury, GL8 8TZ. Lise & Christopher White, www.hookshousepottery.co.uk. *2½m SW of Tetbury. Follow signs from A433 at Hare and Hounds Hotel, Westonbirt. Alternatively take A4135 out of Tetbury towards Dursley and follow signs after ½m on L.* **Daily Sat 26 May to Sun 3 June (11-5.30). Adm £4, chd free. Home-made teas.**
Garden offers a combination of dramatic open perspectives and intimate corners. Planting incl wide variety of perennials, with emphasis on colour interest throughout the seasons. Borders, shrubs, woodland glade, water garden containing treatment ponds (unfenced) and flowform cascades. Kitchen garden with raised beds, orchard. Sculptural features. Run on organic principles. Pottery showroom with hand thrown wood-fired pots incl frostproof garden pots. Art & Craft exhibition incl garden furniture and sculptures. Garden games and tree house. Mostly wheelchair accessible.

GROUP OPENING

40 ICOMB GARDENS

Icomb, Stow-on-the-Wold, GL54 1JL. *3m S of Stow-on-the-Wold. Take Icomb Rd off A424 Burford-Stow Rd. After 1m turn R signed Icomb. Parking near gardens as directed by stewards. No parking on street.* **Sun 1 July (1.30-5). Combined adm £5, chd free. Home-made teas in village hall.**

GUYS FARM
Vanda Palmer.

HOME FARM
Miss Ellen Fisher.

LITTLE DORMERS
Vanessa & Jonathan Curry.

MANOR FARM
Eleanor & Hugh Paget.

1 ORCHARD ROW
John & Janet Bauser.

2 PARK VIEW COTTAGES
David Cowdery.

PARK VIEW HOUSE
Mr & Mrs Ros & Steve Watson.

Small pretty village with glorious views and early C13 church. Manor Farm: Well laid out large garden with unusual plants, orchard and ornamental vegetable plot and exceptional views. 2 Park View Cottages: Pretty well-stocked small front garden with courtyard at back acting as outdoor room. Guys Farm: Peaceful cottage garden with terrace and herbaceous border. Home Farm: Extensive well-stocked cottage garden with fruit and vegetables and lovely views. Little Dormers: Terraced cottage garden with dry stone walls. 1 Orchard Row: Well stocked small cottage garden. Park View House: Charming cottage garden with different rooms taking advantage of varying aspects and levels. 2 ParkView Cottages & Little Dormers have no wheelchair access. Dogs on leads welcome in all gardens.

41 ◆ KIFTSGATE COURT

Chipping Campden, GL55 6LN. Mr & Mrs J G Chambers, 01386 438777, info@kiftsgate.co.uk, www.kiftsgate.co.uk. *4m NE of Chipping Campden. Adj to Hidcote NT Garden. 3m NE of Chipping Campden.* **For NGS: Mon 9 Apr, Mon 13 Aug (2-6). Adm £8.50, chd £2.50. Home-made teas.**

For other opening times and information, please phone, email or visit garden website.

Magnificent situation and views, many unusual plants and shrubs, tree peonies, hydrangeas, abutilons, species and old-fashioned roses incl largest rose in England, Rosa filipes Kiftsgate. Steep slopes and uneven surfaces.

42 LINDORS COUNTRY HOUSE

The Fence, St. Briavels, Lydney, GL15 6RB. Christian Guild, 01594 530283, lindors@christianguild.co.uk, www.lindors.co.uk. *Lower Wye Valley. Monmouth 7m, Chepstow 9m, Coleford 4m. From Monmouth/ Chepstow use Wye Valley rd (A466). Turn at Bigswier Bridge towards St Briavels for ½m. From St Briavels Castle head downhill towards River Wye. On L ½m before bottom of hill.* **Sat 17, Sun 18 Feb, Sat 10, Sun 11, Sat 31 Mar, Sun 1, Mon 2 Apr, Sat 5, Sun 6, Mon 7, Sat 26, Sun 27, Mon 28 May, Sat 25, Sun 26, Mon 27 Aug (10-4.30). Adm £3.50, chd free. Light refreshments. Refreshments available all day. Light meals 12–4pm, Hot meals 12–2pm.**

9 acres of mature woodland gardens with streams, ponds, formal gardens with over 80 varieties of trees. Wild flower meadows host a variety of wild Orchids species. Traditional games on the lawns and lunches served on the terraces. Garden tours available. Putting green, bowls, tennis, croquet. Some gravel paths.

43 LODERS GATE

Fairford Road, Downington, Lechlade, GL7 3DL. Mr Jim Pymer. *½m from centre of Lechlade off A417 to Fairford. Turn R into gravel drive 100yds past West Alcott sign. No Parking.* **Sat 1 Sept (1-4.30). Adm £5, chd free. Tea.**

A plant lover's haven of 1½ acres. Front garden with long deep borders of herbaceous plants, ornamental grasses and yew hedging, is repeated in walled garden to rear of house. Beyond is large garden with 2 wildlife ponds, small wooded area, greenhouse, lawns, mature trees, rose garden and long herbaceous and shrub borders.

GROUP OPENING

44 LONGHOPE GARDENS

Longhope, GL17 0NA. 01452 830406, sally.j.gibson@btinternet.com. *10m W of Gloucester. 7m E of Ross on Wye. A40 take Longhope turn off to Church Rd. From A4136 follow Longhope signs and turn onto Church Rd. Parking available on Church Rd.* **Sat 26 May (12-5); Sun 27 May (2-6); Sat 9 June (12-5); Sun 10 June (2-6). Combined adm £5, chd free. Home-made teas.**
Visits also by arrangement May & June for groups of 10+.

3 CHURCH ROAD
Rev Clive & Mrs Linda Edmonds.

SPRINGFIELD HOUSE
Sally & Martin Gibson.

WOODBINE COTTAGE
Mrs Lucille Roughley.

3 beautiful gardens set in the valley of Longhope. Each garden has its own style and delights for you to discover with sweeping views across the valley to May Hill and the Forest of Dean. 3 Church Road is a long garden divided into rooms with a large collection of hardy geraniums. Springfield House: a large enclosed garden with terraced lawns, a wide variety of shrubs and trees mingling with sweeping herbaceous borders. Woodbine Cottage: a tranquil garden with a natural pond and unusual plants. Home-made cakes, refreshments and plant sales. Keep up to date with Longhope Gardens on our Facebook page. 3 Church Road and Springfield House featured in Amateur Gardening magazine. Springfield House also appeared in an Austrian TV special 'Classic English Gardens'.

45 ◆ LYDNEY PARK SPRING GARDEN

Lydney, GL15 6BU. The Viscount Bledisloe, 01594 842844/842922, www.lydneyparkestate.co.uk. *½m SW of Lydney. On A48 Gloucester to Chepstow rd between Lydney & Aylburton. Drive is directly off A48.* **For NGS: Wed 9 May (10-5). Adm £5, chd £0.50. Home-made teas. light lunches.**

For other opening times and information, please phone or visit garden website.

Spring garden in 8 acre woodland valley with lakes, profusion of rhododendrons, azaleas and other flowering shrubs. Formal garden; magnolias and daffodils (April). Picnics in deer park which has fine trees. Important Roman Temple site and museum. Not suitable for wheelchairs due to rough pathway through garden and steps to WC.

46 THE MANOR

Little Compton, Moreton-In-Marsh, Gloucestershire, GL56 0RZ. Reed Foundation (Charity). *Next to church in Little Compton. ½m from A44 or 2m from A3400. Follow signs to Little Compton and then pick up yellow NGS signs.* **Sun 3 June, Sun 19 Aug (2-5). Adm £5.50, chd free. Home-made teas.**

4 acres of stunning gardens surrounding historic manor house (not open), and set in a beautiful location within the village of Little Compton. Enjoy the many garden rooms, long herbaceous palette, deer walk, Japanese garden, flower garden, extended gardens including arboretum walks, and specimen

trees. Home to the country's smallest deer park and a flock of rare-breed sheep. Garden staff on site, croquet and tennis courts available to play. Featured in Cotswold Life.

47 ◆ MATARA GARDENS

Kingscote, Tetbury, GL8 8YA. Matara, 01453 861050, info@matara.co.uk, www.matara.co.uk. *5½m NW of Tetbury. Approx 20 mins from either J18 of M4 (12m) or J13 of M5 (8.5m). On A4135 between Tetbury and Dursley in Kingscote village. Entrance opp Hunter's Hall PH.* **For NGS: Sun 20 May (1-5). Adm £5, chd free. Home-made teas. You are welcome to bring your own picnics if you would like to picnic in the gardens. For other opening times and information, please phone, email or visit garden website.**

Trees of life - enjoy the tranquil beauty of Matara's Gardens and its dedication to the symbolic, spiritual and cultural role of trees. What makes us special are our Chinese Scholar's garden, Japanese tea garden, Shinto woodlands, Celtic wishing tree, labyrinth, healing spiral, field of dreams and ornamental herb and flower gardens. Woodland walk, Chinese cloistered courtyard, barefoot trail, ponds, strolling walk, walled herb garden and vegetable garden. Limited wheelchair access. Some steps and grass paths.

48 MEADOW COTTAGE

59 Coalway Road, Coalway, Coleford, GL16 7HL. Matt & Ella Beard, 01594 834672, ellabeard_1@hotmail.com. *1m SE of Coleford. From Coleford take Lydney & Chepstow Rd at T-lights in town. Turn L after police stn, signed Coalway & Parkend. Garden on L ½m up hill opp layby.* **Sun 15 Apr (1-5); Sun 17 June (2-6). Combined adm with 20 Forsdene Walk £5, chd free. Home-made teas. Visits also by arrangement Apr to June, max 20. Full afternoon tea can be provided for small groups, please contact for details.**

⅓-acre cottage garden with modern touches, from early spring. Gravelled entry, borders with shrubs, large-leaf plants, and lavenders. Newly planted white border. Corner area with Japanese elements leading to paths which wind around colourful shrubs, climbers and perennial-filled borders. Small pond with waterfall. Vegetable/fruit garden in raised beds. Shade plants in pots. Many containers. Joint opening with Meadow Cottage's previous owner in her new garden at 20 Forsdene Walk.

49 ◆ MILL DENE GARDEN

School Lane, Blockley, Moreton-in-Marsh, GL56 9HU. Mrs B S Dare, 01386 700457, info@milldenegarden.co.uk, www.milldenegarden.co.uk. *3m NW of Moreton-in-Marsh. From A44 follow brown signs from Bourton-on-the-Hill to Blockley. Approx 1¼m down hill turn L behind village gates. Limited parking. Coaches by appt.* **For NGS: Sun 20 May, Sun 16 Sept (10.30-5). Adm £10, chd free. Light refreshments. Opening with Blockley Gardens on Sun 22 Apr, Sun 10 June. For other opening times and information, please phone, email or visit garden website.**

50 shades of green (!) at least in this 2½ acre garden hidden in the Cotswolds. Centrepiece is water mill dating from C10 (probably), with mill pond and stream. The owners have had fun creating a varied garden, from informal woodland full of bulbs, to rose walk, cricket lawn, then herb garden looking out over hills with church as backdrop. Talk on the garden given by owner for groups of 10+ (£25) Garden trail for children. Free booklet re development of garden. Half of garden wheelchair accessible. Please ring for reserved parking/ramps. Garden in a valley but sides have slope or step alternatives.

GROUP OPENING

50 MINETY AND UPPER MINETY OPEN GARDENS AND PLANT FAIR

Upper Minety, Malmesbury, SN16 9PY. Mr & Mrs C Gallop, 01666 860286, katiegallop@btinternet.com. *7m SE of Cirencester. Follow signs from A429 (Cotswold Water Park) or alternatively from B4040 to Minety Church. Ample parking.* **Sun 24 June (11-5). Combined adm £5, chd free. Home-made teas.**

Minety and Upper Minety which takes its name from the wild mint plant found growing in and around the villages will be offering 7 inspirational gardens from sweeping herbaceous borders, productive fruit/veg plots, country estate grounds, tranquil nature reserve and arboretum, open meadows with St Leonard's Church floral arrangements. Specialist plant nurseries and imaginative stalls offering accessories for your home and garden will be hosted at Oakwood Farm with teas on the farm lawn and where garden maps can be obtained. Some gravel, mostly grass. Disabled parking available. Coaches by prior arrangement only.

51 MOOR WOOD

Woodmancote, GL7 7EB. Mr & Mrs Henry Robinson, 01285 831397, henry@moorwoodhouse.co.uk, www.moorwoodroses.co.uk. *3½m NW of Cirencester. Turn L off A435 to Cheltenham at North Cerney, signed Woodmancote 1¼m; entrance in village on L beside lodge with white gates.* **Sun 1 July (2-6). Adm £5, chd free. Home-made teas. Visits also by arrangement 2-30 June only. No coach parking. Walk down drive, approx 150m. Conducted tours incl.**

2 acres of shrub, orchard and wild flower gardens in beautiful isolated valley setting. Holder of National Collection of Rambler Roses. Not recommended for wheelchairs.

NPC

GROUP OPENING

52 OAKRIDGE LYNCH OPEN GARDENS

Oakridge Lynch, Stroud, GL6 7NS. *2m S of Bisley, off Bisley to Eastcombe rd. From Bisley, turn L on leaving village. From Stroud, on A419, turn L to Chalford Hill, follow signs to Bisley. Turn R before entering Bisley. Please park considerately in the village.* **Sun 17 June (1.30-5.30). Combined adm £5 per person, chd free. Home-made teas at Edgehill, The Broadway, Oakridge Lynch. Also at Edgehill, a plant stall in aid of mental health charities for the young.**

THE COTTAGE
Mr Mark Wright.

NEW **EDGEHILL**
Pat Willey.

HOPE COTTAGE
Gillian Wimperis.

OLD COTTAGE
Richard & Judy Mackie.

OLD POST OFFICE COTTAGE
Eileen Herbert.

SWEETBRIAR COTTAGE
David & Caroline Cook.

Beautiful hillside village of pretty cottages and stunning views. Selection of small to medium sized lovely gardens packed with interesting plants: herbaceous borders, roses, herbs, climbers, fruit and vegetables. Featured in Amateur Gardening. Limited wheelchair access at most gardens.

53 THE OLD RECTORY, QUENINGTON

Church Rd, Quenington, Cirencester, GL7 5BN. Mr & Mrs David Abel Smith, www.freshairsculpture.com. *Opp St Swithins Church at bottom of village. 8m NE of Cirencester. Garden well signed once in village.* **Sun 12 Aug (2-5.30). Adm £5, chd free. Home-made teas.**

On the banks of the mill race and the River Coln, this is an organic garden of great variety. Mature trees, large vegetable garden, herbaceous borders, shade garden, pool and bog gardens. The majority of the garden is accessible by wheelchair.

54 NEW ◆ OXLEAZE FARM

Between Eastleach & Filkins, Lechlade, GL7 3RB. Mr & Mrs Charles Mann, 01367 850216, chipps@oxleaze.co.uk, www.oxleazebarn.co.uk. *5m S of Burford, 3m N of Lechlade off A361 to W (signed Barringtons). Take 2nd L then follow signs.* **For NGS: Mon 21, Tue 22 May (2-6). Adm £6, chd free. Home-made teas. For other opening times and information, please phone, email or visit garden website.**

Set amongst beautiful traditional farm buildings, plantsperson's good size garden combining formality and informality. Yr round interest; mixed borders, vegetable potager, decorative fruit cage, pond and bog garden, bees, potting shed, wild meadow, and topiary for structure when the flowers fade. Garden rooms off central lawn with reflective corners in which to enjoy this Cotswold garden. Featured in The English Garden magazine. Mostly wheelchair access.

55 PASTURE FARM

Upper Oddington, Moreton-In-Marsh, GL56 0XG. Mr & Mrs John LLoyd. *Mid-way between Upper and Lower Oddington. Oddington lies about 3m from Stow-on-the-Wold just off A436.* **Sun 27, Mon 28 May (11-6); Sat 2, Sun 3 June (11-5). Adm £5, chd free. Home-made teas.**

Informal country garden developed over 30 yrs by current owners. Mixed borders, topiary, orchard and many species of trees. Gravel garden in 'the ruins', new concrete garden and wild flower area leads to vegetable patch. Big spring-fed pond with ducks. Also bantams, chickens and 2 kunekune pigs. Large plant sale 27/28 May with proceeds to Kate's home nursing. Public footpath across 2 small fields arrives at C11 church, St Nicholas, with doom paintings, set in ancient woodlands. Truly worth a visit. See Simon Jenkins' Book of Churches.

56 PEAR TREE COTTAGE

58 Malleson Road, Gotherington, GL52 9EX. Mr & Mrs E Manders-Trett, 01242 674592, edandmary@talktalk.net. *4m N of Cheltenham. From A435, travelling N, turn R into Gotherington 1m after end of Bishop's Cleeve bypass at garage. Garden on L approx 100yds past Shutter Inn.* **Sun 15 Apr (2-5). Adm £4, chd free. Light refreshments. Visits also by arrangement Mar to June, max 30.**

Mainly informal country garden of approx ½ acre with pond and gravel garden, grasses and herbaceous borders, trees and shrubs surrounding lawns. Wild garden and orchard lead to greenhouses and vegetable garden. Spring bulbs, early summer perennials and shrubs particularly colourful.

57 RAMBLERS

Lower Common, Aylburton, Lydney, GL15 6DS. Jane & Leslie Hale. *1½m W of Lydney. Off A48 Gloucester to Chepstow Rd. From Lydney through Aylburton, out of de-limit turn R signed Aylburton Common, ¾m along lane.* **Sun 6 May (1.30-5.30). Adm £4, chd free. Home-made teas.**

Peaceful medium sized country garden with informal cottage planting, herbaceous borders and small pond looking through hedge windows onto wild flower meadow and mature apple orchard. Some shade loving plants and topiary. Large productive vegetable garden. Past winner of The English Garden magazine's Britain's Best Gardener's Garden competition.

58 ROCKCLIFFE HOUSE

Upper Slaughter, Cheltenham, GL54 2JW. Mr & Mrs Simon Keswick. *2m from Stow-on-the-Wold. 1½m from Lower Swell on B4068 towards Cheltenham. Leave Stow on*

the Wold on B4068 through Lower Swell. Continue on B4068 for 1½m. Rockcliffe is well signed on R. **Wed 6 June (11-5). Wed 27 June (11-5), also open Eyford House. Adm £7, chd free. Home-made teas. Donation to Kates Home Nursing.**
Large traditional English garden of 8 acres incl pink garden, white and blue garden, herbaceous borders, rose terrace, large walled kitchen garden and orchard. Greenhouses and pathway of topiary birds leading up through orchard to stone dovecot. Featured in several books and magazines, incl Gardens Illustrated. Sorry no dogs. 2 wide stone steps through gate, otherwise good wheelchair access.

59 ROSE COTTAGE

Kempley, Nr Dymock, GL18 2BN. Naomi Cryer. *3m from Newent towards Dymock. From Newent on B4221 take turning just after PH, on R from Gloucester direction, signed Kempley. Follow rd for approx 3m.* **Sat 1, Sun 2 Sept (11-5). Adm £4, chd free. Home-made teas.**
Approx 1 acre of flat garden, mostly herbaceous borders. Dahlias and salvias in profusion. Long borders leading to borrowed view, small parterre in orchard area, grass bed and wildlife pond. Small wild flower pasture, at its best in June. Rose garden, iris bed, hydrangea bed, vegetable and nursery beds and cutting garden. Home-made cakes, cards and plants for sale. Featured in Cotswold Life. Although quite flat, wheelchair access mostly via lawn and grass which may make wheelchair use a little difficult especially in damp weather.

60 SCATTERFORD

Newland, Coleford, GL16 8NG. 01291 675483, kelly@kellyweare.plus.com, www.scatterfordgarden.com. *1m S of Newland and just N of Clearwell, opp junction to Coleford. From Monmouth take A466/Redbrook Rd to Redbrook. From Chepstow take B4228 turn off to Clearwell. From Coleford take Newland Street.* **Visits by arrangement June to Oct for horticultural, garden and design groups of 10+. Adm by donation.**
Well-crafted and maintained 2-acre garden between Wye valley and Forest of Dean. Formal pond, walled garden, sculpted terraces, courtyards, haha, hedges, orchards, hedgrows, natural pond and extensive borders. A contemporary design with serene atmosphere. Head Gardener: Kelly Weare. Designed by Sean Swallow and Askew Nelson Landscape Architects.

61 ◆ SEZINCOTE

Moreton-in-Marsh, GL56 9AW. Mrs D Peake, 01386 700444, enquiries@sezincote.com, www.sezincote.co.uk. *3m SW of Moreton-in-Marsh. From Moreton-in-Marsh turn W along A44 towards Evesham; after 1½m (just before Bourton-on-the-Hill) turn L, by stone lodge with white gate.* **For NGS: Sun 17 June (2-6). Adm £5, chd free. Home-made teas. Teas provided by Longborough School, profits to Longborough School. For other opening times and information, please phone, email or visit garden website.**
Exotic oriental water garden by Repton and Daniell with lake, pools and meandering stream, banked with massed perennials. Large semi-circular orangery, formal Indian garden, fountain, temple and unusual trees of vast size in lawn and wooded park setting. House in Indian manner designed by Samuel Pepys Cockerell. Garden on slope with gravel paths, so not all areas wheelchair accessible.

62 SOUTH LODGE

Church Road, Clearwell, Coleford, GL16 8LG. Andrew & Jane MacBean, 01594 837769, southlodgegarden@btinternet.com, www.southlodgegarden.co.uk. *2m S of Coleford. Off B4228. Follow signs to Clearwell. Garden on L of castle driveway. Please park on rd in front of church or in village. No parking on castle drive.* **Sun 8 Apr, Sat 5, Sun 20 May, Sun 10, Sat 30 June (1-5). Adm £4, chd free. Home-made teas. Visits also by arrangement Apr to June for groups of 15+. For coach visits only, home made teas served in the village hall.**
Peaceful country garden in 2 acres with stunning views of surrounding countryside. High walls provide a backdrop for rambling roses, clematis, and honeysuckles. Organic garden with large variety of perennials, annuals, shrubs and specimen trees with yr-round colour. Vegetable garden, wildlife and formal ponds. Rustic pergola planted with English climbing roses and willow arbour in gravel garden. Rosy Hardy (from Hardys Cottage Garden Plants), award winning plantswoman and designer, winner of countless RHS medals incl 22 Chelsea Golds, will be in the garden to talk about all aspects of perennials on Sunday 10 June (1-5). Featured in The English Garden. Gravel paths and steep grassy slopes.

GROUP OPENING

63 STANTON VILLAGE GARDENS

Stanton, nr Broadway, WR12 7NE. *3m S of Broadway. Off B4632, between Broadway (3m) & Winchcombe (6m).* **Sun 17 June (2-6). Combined adm £7.50, chd free. Home-made teas in The Burland Hall in centre of the village & several open gardens. Ice cream trike in the village. Donation to village charities.**
Approx 15 gardens open in this picturesque, unspoilt Cotswold village. Many houses border the street with long gardens hidden behind. Gardens vary, from houses with colourful herbaceous borders, established trees, shrubs and vegetable gardens to tiny cottage gardens. Some also have attractive, natural water features fed by the stream which runs through the village. Plants for sale & book stall. Legendary home-made teas. Free parking. An NGS visit not to be missed. Regret not all gardens suitable for wheelchair users.

64 ◆ STANWAY FOUNTAIN & WATER GARDEN

Stanway, Cheltenham, GL54 5PQ. The Earl of Wemyss & March, 01386 584528, stanwayhse@btconnect.com, www.stanwayfountain.co.uk. *9m NE of Cheltenham. 1m E of B4632 Cheltenham to Broadway rd on B4077 Toddington to Stow-on-the-Wold rd.* **For NGS: Sun 6 May, Sun 23 Sept (2-5). Adm £6, chd £2. Home-made teas in Stanway Tea Room.** For other opening times and information, please phone, email or visit garden website.

20 acres of planted landscape in early C18 formal setting. The restored canal, upper pond and 165ft high fountain have re-created one of the most interesting Baroque water gardens in Britain. Striking C16 manor with gatehouse, tithe barn and church. Britain's highest fountain at 300ft, the world's highest gravity fountain which runs at 2.45 & 4.00pm for 30 mins each time. Limited wheelchair access in garden, some flat areas, able to view fountain and some of garden. House is not wheelchair suitable.

65 STOWELL PARK

Yanworth, Northleach, Cheltenham, GL54 3LE. The Lord & Lady Vestey, www.stowellpark.co.uk. *8m NE of Cirencester. Off Fosseway A429 2m SW of Northleach.* **Sun 20 May, Sun 24 June (2-5). Adm £6, chd free. Home-made teas.**

Magnificent lawned terraces with stunning views over Coln Valley. Fine collection of old-fashioned roses and herbaceous plants, with pleached lime approach to C14 house (not open). 2 large walled gardens containing vegetables, fruit, cut flowers and range of greenhouses. Long rose pergola and wide, plant filled borders divided into colour sections. New water features and hazel arch at bottom of garden. Open continuously for 50yrs. Plants for sale at May opening only.

67 TRENCH HILL

Sheepscombe, GL6 6TZ. Celia & Dave Hargrave, 01452 814306, celia.hargrave@btconnect.com. *1½m E of Painswick. From Cheltenham A46 take 1st turn signed Sheepscombe and follow lane (about 1¼m) to bottom of hill then continue up hill towards Sheepscombe. Garden on L opp lane.* **Sun 11, Sun 18 Feb (11-5); Sun 1, Mon 2, Sun 22 Apr (11-6). Every Wed 6 June to 20 June (2-6). Sun 22 July, Sun 26 Aug, Sun 9 Sept (11-6). Adm £4, chd free. Home-made teas. Visits also by arrangement Feb to Oct, not suitable for large coaches, small coaches only, advise garden owner in advance.**

Approx 3 acres set in small woodland with panoramic views. Variety of herbaceous and mixed borders, rose garden, extensive vegetable plots, wild flower areas, plantings of spring bulbs with thousands of snowdrops and hellebores, woodland walk, 2 small ponds, waterfall and larger conservation pond. Interesting wooden sculptures, many within the garden. Run on organic principles. Wide variety of wooden sculptures in garden. Children's play area. Variety of local and national magazines. Mostly wheelchair access but some steps and slopes.

68 UPTON WOLD

Moreton-in-Marsh, GL56 9TR. Mr & Mrs I R S Bond, www.uptonwoldcotswoldgarden.co.uk. *4½m W of Moreton-in-Marsh. On A44, ¾ mile past A424 junction at Troopers Lodge Garage, on R, opp deer warning sign. Follow road between fields, turn L at Xrds, and park in Estate Yard. Follow signs to garden.* **Sun 15 Apr (11-5). Adm £12, chd free. Home-made teas.**

Ever developing and changing garden, architecturally and imaginatively laid out around C17 house (not open) with commanding views. Yew hedges, herbaceous walk, some unusual plants and trees, vegetables, pond and woodland gardens, labyrinth. National Collections of Juglans and Pterocarya. 2 Star award from GGG.

NPC

69 ◆ WESTONBIRT SCHOOL GARDENS

Tetbury, GL8 8QG. Holfords of Westonbirt Trust, 01666 881373, jbaker@holfordtrust.com, www.holfordtrust.com. *3m SW of Tetbury. Opp Westonbirt Arboretum, on A433. Enter via Holford wrought iron gates to Westonbirt House.* **For NGS: Sun 15 July (11-5). Adm £5, chd free. Tea, coffee & cake available to purchase in Holford Dining Room.** For other opening times and information, please phone, email or visit garden website.

28 acres. Former private garden of Robert Holford, founder of Westonbirt Arboretum. Formal Victorian gardens incl walled Italian garden now restored with early herbaceous borders and exotic border. Rustic walks, lake, statuary and grotto. Rare, exotic trees and shrubs. Beautiful views of Westonbirt House open with guided tours to see fascinating Victorian interior on designated days of the year. Afternoon tea with sandwiches and scones available for pre-booked private tours, groups of 10-60. Only some parts of garden accessible to wheelchairs. Ramps and lift allow access to house.

70 WHITE HOUSE

Chapel Lane, Mickleton, Chipping Campden, GL55 6SD. Mr & Mrs James Bend, 07831 106518, clare.bend@agrii.co.uk. *2m NW of Chipping Campden. Approaching Mickleton heading N on B4632, turn L into Chapel Lane by Three Ways House Hotel. After 100yds garden on L opp Butchers Arms PH.* **Sat 9, Sun 10 June (11-5). Adm £3.50, chd free. Visits also by arrangement June & July.**

An Arts & Crafts inspired cottage garden encircling the house and arranged in a series of informal rooms. Incl rose garden, holly-pop walk, sunken terrace and collection of topiary faces originally established by artist Richard Sorrell.

Garden has been designed to offer peaceful sitting areas from which to enjoy the plants or simply relax in contemplation. Featured in Daily Telegraph, Gloucestershire Echo, Amateur Gardening and Daily Mail Weekend magazines.

GROUP OPENING

71 NEW WINCHCOMBE GARDENS

North Street, Winchcombe, Cheltenham, GL54 5PS. *80 North Street, and St Mary's, Cowl Lane. Winchcombe lies on B4632 mid-way between Cheltenham and Broadway. Parking behind Winchcombe Library in Back Lane car park which has steps to Cowl Lane.* **Sun 1 July (2-6). Combined adm £6, chd free. Home-made teas at St Mary's, Cowl Lane.**

NEW **THE GATE**
Vanessa Berridge & Chris Evans.

NEW **ST MARY'S**
Lynne & David Banks.

Two contrasting country gardens, both peaceful retreats, in the centre of an historic Cotswold town. The Gate is a cottage-style garden planted with perennials, annuals, climbers and herbs in the walled courtyard of a former C17 Coaching Inn. Separate, productive kitchen garden with espaliers and other fruit trees. St. Mary's garden is approx ½ acre on the site of what was once part of Winchcombe Abbey. Mixed borders with repeat planting in drifts of hardy perennials providing colour all-year-round. Grasses and beds edged with box give structure and definition. Entry to The Gate is on North Street and exit via Cowl Lane to visit kitchen garden and then St Mary's, also in Cowl Lane, on the corner of Abbey Terrace. Plants for sale at The Gate; home-made teas at St Mary's. The Gate appeared in the March 2017 issue of The English Garden. Limited wheelchair access to both gardens.

72 WOODLANDS FARM

Rushley Lane, Winchcombe, GL54 5JE. Mrs Morag Dobbin, 01242 604261, mdobbin@btinternet.com. *On N side of Winchcombe, just off B4632. Rushley Lane comes off B4632 through Winchcombe, at Footbridge. Proceed up Rushley Lane for 50yds, gate is behind Stancombe Lane sign. Parking available in field next to garden.* **Wed 1, Sun 5, Wed 8, Sun 12 Aug (10-4). Adm £4, chd free. Home-made teas. Visits also by arrangement June to Sept min 10, max 20.**

1½ acre garden with generously sized garden rooms. The planting and landscaping are both thoughtful and tranquil. Generous borders throughout with colourful and harmonious planting schemes. Tall hornbeam hedge creates dramatic vista to stone monolith. Long contemporary pond. New prairie style border, cottage borders. Featured in Country Life. Wheelchair assistance needed with one steepish slope to access garden.

73 WORTLEY FARM HOUSE

Wortley, Wotton-Under-Edge, GL12 7QP. Sean & Annabel Mills. *1m out of Wotton Under Edge, 15 mins from M5 J14 and from M4 J18. From A46: Take L turn to Hawkesbury Upton, continue through Hillesley & Alderley towards Wotton into Wortley. From Wotton head to Wortley & Alderley.* **Sat 2 June (11-5); Sun 3 June (2-6). Adm £4, chd free. Home-made teas.**

1½ acres on different levels with wild area, pond, herbaceous borders, textural planting, vegetable garden and disabled garden. Sean is a garden designer. Plant sales. There will be help for wheelchair users on gravel drive. Thereafter the entire garden is accessible via ramps.

74 WORTLEY HOUSE

Wortley, Wotton-Under-Edge, GL12 7QP. Simon and Jessica Dickinson, 01453 843174, jessica@wortleyhouse.co.uk. *1m from Wotton-under-Edge. Full directions will be provided with ticket.* **Tue 19 June (3-6). Adm £12, chd free. Pre-booking essential, please visit www.ngs.org.uk or phone 01483 211535 for information & booking. Home-made teas. Visits also by arrangement.**

This diverse garden of over 20 acres has been created through the last 30 yrs by current owners and incl walled garden, pleached lime avenues, nut walk, potager, ponds, Italian garden, shrubberies and wild flower meadows. Follies urns and statues have been strategically placed throughout to enhance extraordinary vistas, and the garden has been filled with plants, arbours, roses through trees and up walls and herbaceous borders. The stunning surrounding countryside is incorporated into the garden with views up the steep valley that are such a feature in this part of Gloucestershire. Wheelchair access to most areas of the garden, golf buggy available as well.

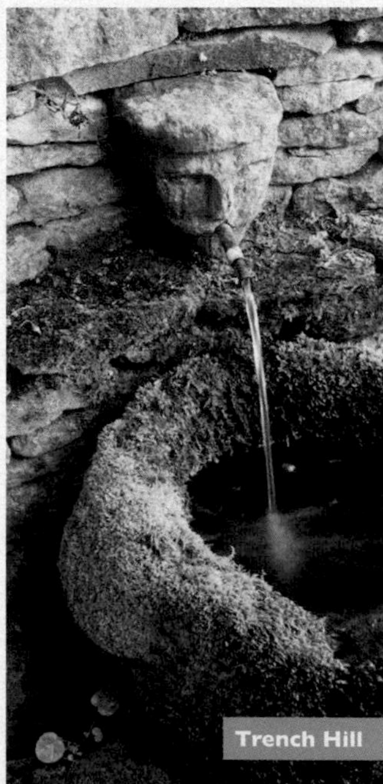

Trench Hill

HAMPSHIRE

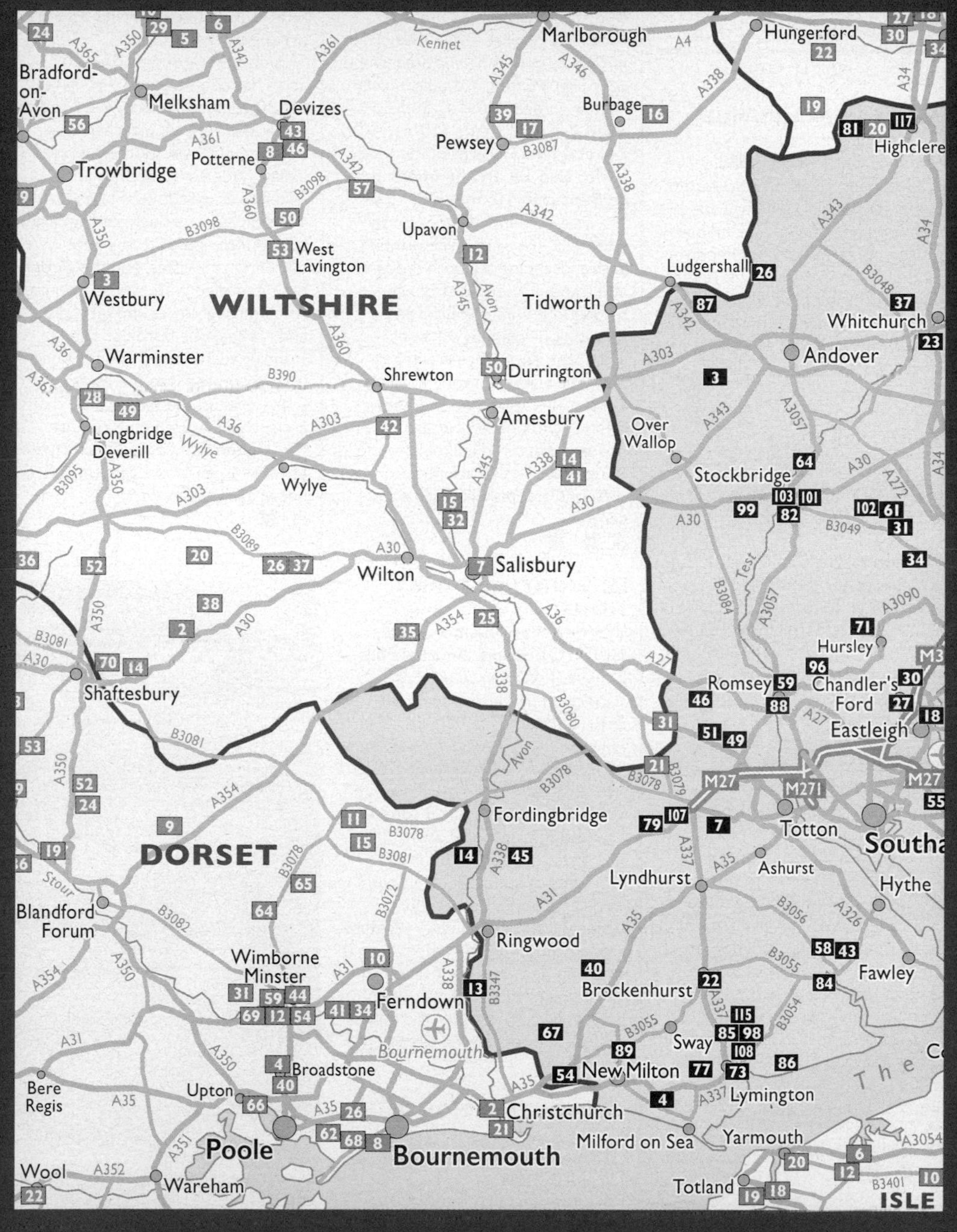

Marlborough
Hungerford
Bradford-on-Avon
Melksham
Devizes
Burbage
Pewsey
Highclere
Potterne
Trowbridge
Upavon
West Lavington
Ludgershall
Westbury
WILTSHIRE
Tidworth
Whitchurch
Andover
Warminster
Shrewton
Durrington
Amesbury
Over Wallop
Longbridge Deverill
Wylye
Stockbridge
Salisbury
Wilton
Hursley
Shaftesbury
Romsey
Chandler's Ford
Eastleigh
Fordingbridge
Totton
DORSET
Lyndhurst
Ashurst
Southa
Hythe
Blandford Forum
Ringwood
Wimborne Minster
Brockenhurst
Fawley
Ferndown
Sway
Bournemouth
Broadstone
New Milton
Lymington
Bere Regis
Upton
Christchurch
Milford on Sea
Yarmouth
Poole
Bournemouth
Wool
Wareham
Totland
ISLE
Kennet
Avon
Wylye
Test
Stour

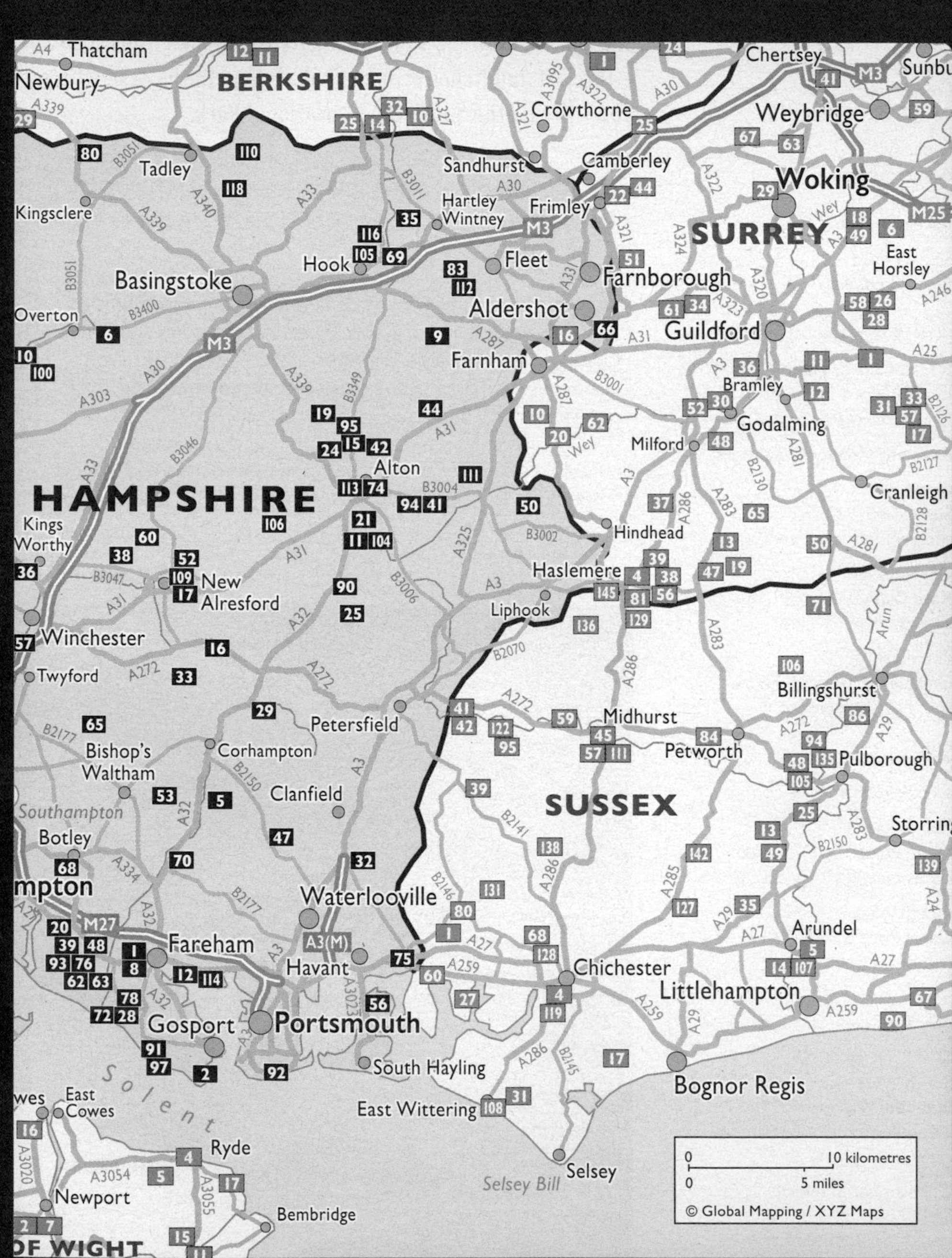
BERKSHIRE
HAMPSHIRE
SURREY
SUSSEX
Thatcham
Newbury
Tadley
Kingsclere
Basingstoke
Overton
Crowthorne
Sandhurst
Camberley
Hartley Wintney
Frimley
Hook
Fleet
Farnborough
Aldershot
Farnham
Chertsey
Sunbu
Weybridge
Woking
East Horsley
Guildford
Bramley
Godalming
Milford
Cranleigh
Hindhead
Haslemere
Liphook
Alton
Kings Worthy
New Alresford
Winchester
Twyford
Petersfield
Bishop's Waltham
Corhampton
Clanfield
Southampton
Botley
mpton
Waterlooville
Fareham
Havant
Gosport
Portsmouth
South Hayling
East Wittering
Solent
wes
East Cowes
Ryde
Newport
Bembridge
OF WIGHT
Selsey
Selsey Bill
Chichester
Midhurst
Petworth
Billingshurst
Pulborough
Storrin
Arundel
Littlehampton
Bognor Regis
0
10 kilometres
0
5 miles
© Global Mapping / XYZ Maps

Volunteers

County Organiser
Mark Porter 01962 791054
markstephenporter@gmail.com

County Treasurer
Fred Fratter 01962 776243
fred@fratter.co.uk

Publicity
Ann Freeborn
07917 280169
traveleventstyle@gmail.com

Social Media
Richard Loader
01425 655698
richardloader@aol.com

Booklet Co-ordinator
John Huxford 01256 893518
john.huxford@btinternet.com

Assistant County Organisers

Central
Sue Cox 01962 732043
suealex13@gmail.com

Central West
Kate Cann 01794 389105
kategcann@gmail.com

East
Linda Smith 01329 833253
linda.ngs@btinternet.com

North
Cynthia Oldale 01420 520438
c.k.oldale@btinternet.com

North East
Lizzie Powell 01420 23185
lizzie.powell@btconnect.com

North West
Carol Pratt 01264 710305
carolacap@yahoo.co.uk

South
Barbara Sykes 02380 254521
barandhugh@aol.com

South West
Elizabeth Walker 01590 677415
elizabethwalker13@gmail.com

West
Christopher Stanford
01425 652133
stanfordsnr@gmail.com

Hampshire is a large, diverse county. The landscape ranges from clay/gravel heath and woodland in the New Forest National Park in the south west, across famous trout rivers – the Test and Itchen – to chalk downland in the east, where you will find the South Downs National Park.

Our open gardens are spread right across the county and offer a very diverse range of interest for both the keen gardener and the casual visitor.

We have a large number of gardens with rivers running through them such as those in Longstock, Bere Mill, Dipley Mill and Weir House; gardens with large vegetable kitchen gardens such as Dean House and Bramdean House; and fifteen new gardens will open for the very first time.

You will be assured of a warm welcome by all our garden owners and we hope you enjoy your visits.

Below: 27 Russell Road

OPENING DATES

All entries subject to change. For latest information check **www.ngs.org.uk**

Extended openings are shown at the beginning of the month.

Map locator numbers are shown to the right of each garden name.

February

Snowdrop Festival

Sunday 18th
Bramdean House 16
Brandy Mount House 17
The Down House 38
Little Court 61

Monday 19th
Little Court 61

Sunday 25th
◆ Chawton House Library 21
Little Court 61

Monday 26th
Little Court 61

March

Sunday 11th
Bere Mill 10

Saturday 17th
Pilley Hill Cottage 85

Sunday 18th
Pilley Hill Cottage 85

Sunday 25th
2 Church Cottages 23
The Deane House 34

Wednesday 28th
Beechenwood Farm 9

Friday 30th
Crawley Gardens 31

April

Every Wednesday
Beechenwood Farm 9

Sunday 1st
Pylewell Park 86

Monday 2nd
Crawley Gardens 31

Saturday 7th
The Island 59

Sunday 8th
Bramdean House 16
Durmast House 40
The Island 59
Old Thatch & The Millennium Barn 83

Saturday 14th
Pilley Hill Cottage 85

Sunday 15th
Little Court 61
Pilley Hill Cottage 85

Monday 16th
Little Court 61

Sunday 22nd
2 Church Cottages 23
Terstan 103

Saturday 28th
Bluebell Wood 15

Sunday 29th
Bluebell Wood 15
The Dower House 36
Oaklands 79
28 St Ronan's Avenue 92
◆ Spinners Garden 98
Tylney Hall Hotel 105
Walhampton 108

May

Every Wednesday
Beechenwood Farm 9

Wednesday 2nd
Down Farm House 37

Sunday 6th
The Cottage 27
Little Court 61
Rotherfield Park 90

Monday 7th
Ashe Park 6
The Cottage 27
Little Court 61

Saturday 12th
NEW 146 Bridge Road 20
2 Church Cottages 23
2 Sampan Close 93

Sunday 13th
Berry Cottage 11
NEW 146 Bridge Road 20
The Cottage 27
Crookley Pool 32
The House in the Wood 58
2 Sampan Close 93
The Thatched Cottage 104

Monday 14th
The Cottage 27

Tuesday 15th
NEW ◆ Apple Court 4

Saturday 19th
21 Chestnut Road 22
Hollybrook 55
99 Locks Heath Park Road 62
101 Locks Heath Park Road 63
Selborne 94
NEW Spitfire House 99

Sunday 20th
Aviemore 7
Beechenwood Farm 9
21 Chestnut Road 22
Hinton Admiral 54
Hollybrook 55
Little Court 61
99 Locks Heath Park Road 62
101 Locks Heath Park Road 63
Selborne 94
Spring Pond 100

Wednesday 23rd
Bisterne Manor 13
Dean House 33

Saturday 26th
Hollybrook 55

Sunday 27th
Amport & Monxton Gardens 3
Hollybrook 55
1 Maple Cottage 69
Meon Orchard 70
Pylewell Park 86
Romsey Gardens 88
West Silchester Hall 110

Monday 28th
Amport & Monxton Gardens 3
Bere Mill 10
1 Maple Cottage 69
Romsey Gardens 88
West Silchester Hall 110

Wednesday 30th
Bisterne Manor 13

June

Festival Weekend

Saturday 2nd
Froyle Gardens 44
1 Maple Cottage 69

Sunday 3rd
Dipley Mill 35
Froyle Gardens 44
1 Maple Cottage 69
Oaklands 79
28 St Ronan's Avenue 92
Waldrons 107

Wednesday 6th
Beechenwood Farm 9

Thursday 7th
Lake House 60

Saturday 9th
◆ Alverstoke Crescent Garden 2
21 Chestnut Road 22

Sunday 10th
Bramdean House 16
21 Chestnut Road 22
2 Church Cottages 23
Cranbury Park 30
The Deane House 34
Furzehill Farm 45
Lake House 60
Spindles 97
Tylney Hall Hotel 105
Weir House 109

Monday 11th
Spindles 97

Thursday 14th
Stockbridge Gardens 101

Friday 15th
Walden 106

Saturday 16th
2 Church Cottages 23
NEW 27 Russell Road 91

Sunday 17th
Conholt Park 26
Dipley Mill 35
Furzehill Farm 45
Longstock Park 64
NEW Oakcroft 78
NEW 27 Russell Road 91
Shalden Park House 95
Stockbridge Gardens 101
Walden 106

Monday 18th
NEW Oakcroft 78

Tuesday 19th
Tanglefoot 102

Wednesday 20th
Dean House 33

Thursday 21st
Tanglefoot 102

Saturday 23rd
7 Downland Close 39
East Worldham Manor 41
NEW Lower Baybridge House 65
Selborne 94

Sunday 24th
Colemore House Gardens 25
61 Cottes Way 28
7 Downland Close 39
Durmast House 40
East Worldham Manor 41
Hambrooks Show Gardens 48
NEW Lower Baybridge House 65
23 New Brighton Road 75
Selborne 94
Spring Pond 100
Terstan 103
Wicor Primary School Community Garden 114

Monday 25th
Colemore House Gardens 25
61 Cottes Way 28

Friday 29th
26 Lower Newport Road 66

Saturday 30th
26 Lower Newport Road 66

July

Every Tuesday to Tuesday 24th
Old Swan House 82

Sunday 1st
19 Barnwood Road 8
Berry Cottage 11
Bleak Hill Nursery & Garden 14
The Old Rectory 81
Old Thatch & The Millennium Barn 83
The Thatched Cottage 104

Monday 2nd
The Old Rectory 81

Wednesday 4th
Dean House 33

Thursday 5th
Crawley Gardens 31

Saturday 7th
The Island 59
Oak Tree Cottage 77

Sunday 8th
Bramdean House 16
2 Church Cottages 23
Crawley Gardens 31
The Island 59
Merdon Manor 71
Michaelmas 72
Oak Tree Cottage 77
NEW Oakcroft 78
West Silchester Hall 110
1 Wogsbarne Cottages 116
NEW Woolton House 117

Monday 9th
Michaelmas 72
NEW Oakcroft 78
1 Wogsbarne Cottages 116
NEW Woolton House 117

Wednesday 11th
Wychwood 118

Saturday 14th
NEW Manor Lodge 68
NEW 27 Russell Road 91
Selborne 94

Sunday 15th
Bleak Hill Nursery & Garden 14
Dipley Mill 35
NEW Manor Lodge 68
NEW 27 Russell Road 91
Selborne 94

Tuesday 17th
Tanglefoot 102

Wednesday 18th
Wychwood 118

Thursday 19th
Tanglefoot 102

Saturday 21st
8 Birdwood Grove 12
21 Chestnut Road 22

Sunday 22nd
21 Chestnut Road 22
Conholt Park 26
Dean House 33
◆ The Hospital of St Cross 57

Saturday 28th
Fairweather's Nursery 43
NEW Hamdown Corner 49
Hideaway 51
4 Nightingale Mews 76
Willows 115

Sunday 29th
Berry Cottage 11
Bleak Hill Nursery & Garden 14
Fairweather's Nursery 43
NEW Hamdown Corner 49
Hideaway 51
Meon Orchard 70
4 Nightingale Mews 76
Terstan 103
The Thatched Cottage 104
Willows 115

August

Saturday 4th
Old Camps 80
NEW Rotherfield Greys 89
Selborne 94

Sunday 5th
Dean House 33
Dipley Mill 35
The Homestead 56
Old Camps 80
NEW Rotherfield Greys 89
Selborne 94
West Silchester Hall 110

Monday 6th
Selborne 94

Tuesday 7th
NEW ◆ Apple Court 4

Thursday 9th
Hill House 52

Saturday 11th
22 Mount Pleasant Road 74
NEW Rotherfield Greys 89
42 Whitedown 113

Sunday 12th
Hill House 52
22 Mount Pleasant Road 74
NEW Rotherfield Greys 89
42 Whitedown 113

Tuesday 14th
Hill House 52

Wednesday 15th
Dean House 33

Saturday 18th
Moore Blatch 73
Wheatley House 111

Sunday 19th
Berry Cottage 11
21 Chestnut Road 22
Moore Blatch 73
The Thatched Cottage 104
Wheatley House 111

Saturday 25th
Willows 115

Sunday 26th
Gilberts Dahlia Field 46
Willows 115

Monday 27th
Hambledon House 47
Willows 115

September

Sunday 2nd
Berry Cottage 11
Dipley Mill 35
Meon Orchard 70
Old Thatch & The Millennium Barn 83
Terstan 103
The Thatched Cottage 104

Sunday 9th
Bramdean House 16
2 Church Cottages 23
NEW Court House 29
Weir House 109

Sunday 16th
Bere Mill 10
2 Church Cottages 23
Hill Top 53

Tuesday 18th
NEW Redenham Park House 87

Wednesday 19th
NEW Redenham Park

THE GARDENS

1 80 ABBEY ROAD

Fareham, PO15 5HW. Brian & Vivienne Garford, 01329 843939, vgarford@aol.com. *1m W of Fareham. From M27 J9 take A27 E to Fareham for approx 2m. At top of hill, turn L at lights into Highlands Rd. Turn 4th R into Blackbrook Rd. Abbey Rd is 4th L.* **Visits by arrangement Apr to Aug for groups of 25 max. Light refreshments.**

Unusual small garden with large collection of herbs and plants of botanical and historical interest, many for sale. Box hedging provides structure for relaxed planting. Interesting use of containers and ideas for small gardens. Two ponds and tiny meadow for wildlife. Living willow seat, summerhouse, and trained grapevine. Remodelled herb garden for 2018. A garden trail for children.

2 ◆ ALVERSTOKE CRESCENT GARDEN

Crescent Road, Gosport, PO12 2DH. Gosport Borough Council, www.alverstokecrescentgarden.co.uk. *1m S of Gosport. From A32 & Gosport follow signs for Stokes Bay. Continue alongside bay to small r'about, turn L into Anglesey Rd. Crescent Garden signed 50yds on R.* **For NGS: Sat 9 June (10-4). Adm by donation. Home-made teas. For other opening times and information, please visit garden website.**

Restored Regency ornamental garden, designed to enhance fine crescent (Thomas Ellis Owen 1828). Trees, walks and flowers lovingly maintained by community and council partnership. Garden's of considerable local historic interest highlighted by impressive restoration and creative planting. Adjacent to St Mark's churchyard, worth seeing together. Heritage, history and horticulture, a fascinating package. Plant sale and teas. Green Flag Award.

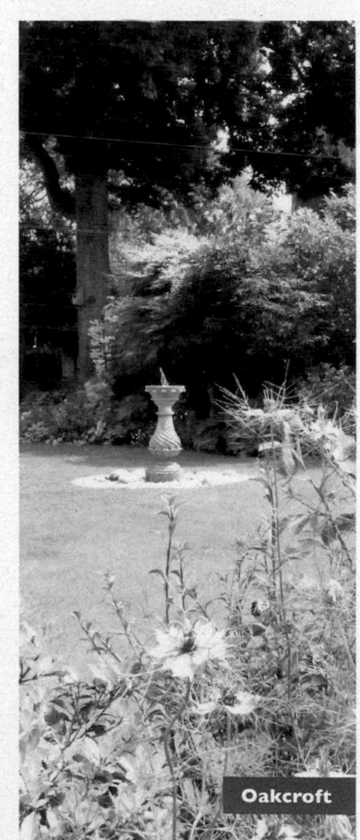
Oakcroft

GROUP OPENING

3 AMPORT & MONXTON GARDENS

Amport and Monxton, SP11 8AY. *3m SW of Andover. Turn off the A303 signed East Cholderton from the E or Thruxton village from the W. Follow signs to Amport. Car parking in a field next to Amport village green. Please drive between the two villages.* **Sun 27, Mon 28 May (2-5.30). Combined adm £6, chd free. Cream teas at village hall, Monxton.**

AMPORT PARK MEWS
Amport Park Mews Ltd.

BRIDGE COTTAGE
John & Jenny Van de Pette.

FLEUR DE LYS
Ian & Jane Morrison.

NEW **THE WHITE COTTAGE**
Mrs Angela Reckitt.

WHITE GABLES
Mr & Mrs D Eaglesham.

Monxton and Amport are two pretty villages linked by Pill Hill Brook. Visitors have five gardens to enjoy. Bridge Cottage a 2 acre haven for wildlife, with the banks of the trout stream and lake planted informally with drifts of colour, a large vegetable garden, fruit cage, small mixed orchard and arboretum with specimen trees. Amport Park Mews has eleven borders arranged around a communal space surrounded by converted stable and carriage blocks in historic mews. Fleur de Lys garden is a series of rooms with glorious herbaceous borders, leading to a large orchard. White Gables a cottage style garden with a collection of trees, incl a young giant redwood, along with old roses and herbaceous plants. Amport has a lovely village green, come early and bring a picnic to enjoy the views of the thatched cottages, before the gardens open. No wheelchair access to White Gables.

4 NEW ◆ APPLE COURT

Hordle Lane, Hordle, Lymington, SO41 0HU. Mrs Emma Taylor, 07388 562749, applecourtgarden@icloud.com, www.applecourtgarden.co.uk. *4m W of Lymington. From A337 between Lymington & New Milton, turn into Hordle Lane opp the Royal Oak at Downton Xrds.* **For NGS: Tue 15 May, Tue 7 Aug (10-4). Adm £5, chd free. Home-made teas.** For other opening times and information, please phone, email or visit garden website.

I acre formally designed and exuberantly planted sheltered walled garden. Theatrical white garden, extensive ornamental grass plantings and subtropical borders. 70 metre hosta walk. International display gardens of daylilies and Japanese style garden with koi pond. Well stocked nursery with interesting variety. Featured in Lymington Times (2017). The garden is mostly flat. WC is not accessible to wheelchair users.

5 APPLETREE HOUSE

Station Road, Soberton, SO32 3QU. Mrs J Dover, 01489 877333, jennie.dover@yahoo.co.uk. *10m N of Fareham. A32 to Droxford, at Xrds turn onto B2150. Turn R under bridge into Station Rd, follow road for 1m to garden. Roadside parking or in lay-by 300yds away.* **Visits by arrangement July & Aug. Adm £3.50, chd free. Tea.**

Designed to look larger than its 40ft x 90ft, this garden has both a shady woodland style area and also sunny areas allowing a variety of planting. Winding paths lead to different views across the garden and of the meadows beyond. Lots of ideas for the smaller garden. Large collection of over 90 clematis, mainly viticella hybrids.

6 ASHE PARK

nr Ashe, Overton, RG25 3AF. Graham & Laura Hazell. *2m E of Overton. Entrance on B3400, approx 500yds W of Deane.* **Mon 7 May (2-5). Adm £5, chd free. Home-made teas.**

An extensive developing garden within the grounds of a Georgian country house and estate, now becoming more established with further initiatives in progress. Parkland and specimen trees, mature lime avenue, woodland and bluebell walks, wild flower areas, a large contemporary potager, and a series of land sculpted features.

7 AVIEMORE

Chinham Road, Bartley, Southampton, SO40 2LF. Sandy & Alex Robinson, 02380 813651, hears2u@gmail.com. *3m N of Lyndhurst, 7m W of Southampton. From M27 J1 go towards Lyndhurst on A337. After ¾ m turn L to Bartley & follow NGS signs.* **Sun 20 May (2-5). Adm £3.50, chd free. Home-made teas. Visits also by arrangement May to July for groups of 15-50. Refreshments on request.**

A richly planted, small garden in north New Forest with lawns, gravel areas and a vegetable plot. Oak bridges criss-cross a small stream. Old alpine troughs and quirky artifacts add to its structure, texture and colour. We aim to please plant connoisseurs and show enthusiasts new plants and ideas for smaller gardens. No wheelchair access to some gravel and stream areas.

8 19 BARNWOOD ROAD

Fareham, PO15 5LA. Jill & Michael Hill, 01329 842156, Jillhillflowers@icloud.com. *1m W of Fareham. M27 J9, A27 towards Fareham. At top of Titchfield Hill, L at T-lights, 4th R Blackbrook Rd, 4th R Meadow Bank. Barnwood Rd is off Meadow Bank. Please consider neighbours when parking.* **Sun 1 July (11-4). Adm £3.50, chd free. Home-made teas. Visits also by arrangement May to July for groups of 10-30.**

Step through the gate to an enchanting garden designed for peace with an abundance of floral colour and delightful features. Greek style courtyard leads to natural pond with bridge and bog garden, complemented by a thatched summerhouse and jetty, designed and built by owners. Secret pathways, hexagonal greenhouse and new mosaic seating area.

9 BEECHENWOOD FARM

Hillside, Odiham, Hook, RG29 1JA. Mr & Mrs M Heber-Percy, 01256 702300, beechenwood@totalise.co.uk. *5m SE of Hook. Turn S into King St from Odiham High St. Turn L after cricket ground for Hillside. Take 2nd R after 1½m, modern house ½m.* **Wed 28 Mar (2-5). Every Wed 4 Apr to 30 May (2-5). Sun 20 May, Wed 6 June (2-5). Adm £4, chd free. Home-made teas. Visits also by arrangement Mar to June. Regret no coaches due to narrow lane.**

2 acre garden in many parts. Lawn meandering through woodland with drifts of spring bulbs. Rose pergola with steps, pots with spring bulbs and later aeoniums. Fritillary and cowslip meadow. Walled herb garden with pool and exuberant planting. Orchard incl white garden and hot border. Greenhouse and vegetable garden. Rock garden extending to grasses, ferns and bamboos. Shady walk to belvedere. 8 acre copse of native species with grassed rides. Assistance available with gravel drive, and some avoidable shallow steps.

10 BERE MILL

London Road, Whitchurch, RG28 7NH. Rupert & Elizabeth Nabarro, 01256 892210, rupertnab@gmail.com. *9m E of Andover, 12m N of Winchester. In centre of Whitchurch, take London Rd at r'about. Uphill 1m, turn R 50yds beyond The Gables on R. Drop-off point for disabled at garden.* **Sun 11 Mar, Mon 28 May, Sun 16 Sept (1.30-5). Adm £5, chd free. Home-made teas. Visits also by arrangement Feb to Oct for groups of 15+.** Donation to Smile Train.

On the Upper Test with water meadows and wooded valleys, this garden offers herbaceous borders, bog and Mediterranean plants as well as a replanted orchard and two small arboretums. Features incl early bulbs, species tulips, Japanese prunus, peonies, wisteria, irises, roses, and semi-tropical planting. At heart it aims to complement the natural beauty of the site, and to incorporate elements of oriental garden design and practice. The working mill was where Portals first made paper for the Bank of England in 1716. Unfenced and unguarded rivers and streams. Wheelchair access unless very wet.

11 BERRY COTTAGE

Church Road, Upper Farringdon, Alton, GU34 3EG. Mrs P Watts, 01420 588318. *3m S of Alton off A32. Turn L at Xrds, 1st L into Church Rd. Follow road past Massey's Folly, 2nd house on R, opp church.* **Sun 13 May, Sun 1, Sun 29 July, Sun 19 Aug, Sun 2 Sept (2-5.30). Combined adm with The Thatched Cottage £6, chd free. Home-made teas. Visits also by arrangement Apr to Sept for groups of 10+.**

Small organic cottage garden with yr-round interest, designed and maintained by owner, surrounding C16 house (not open). Spring bulbs, roses, clematis and herbaceous borders. The borders are colour themed and contain many unusual plants. Pond, bog garden and shrubbery. Close to Massey's Folly built by the Victorian rector incl 80ft tower with unique handmade floral bricks, C11 church and some of the oldest yew trees in the county. Featured in Hampshire Life magazine (May 2017). Partial wheelchair access.

12 8 BIRDWOOD GROVE

Downend, Fareham, PO16 8AF. Jayne & Eddie McBride, 01329 280838, jayne.mcbride@ntlworld.com. *½m E of Fareham. M27 J11, L lane slip to Delme r'about, L on A27 to Portchester over 2 T-lights, completely around small r'about, Birdwood Grove 1st L.* **Sat 21 July (1-5). Adm £3, chd free. Home-made teas. Visits also by arrangement July & Aug for groups of 2-25 max.**

The subtropics in Fareham! This small garden is influenced by the flora of Australia and New Zealand and incl many indigenous species and plants that are widely grown 'down under'. The 4 climate zones; arid, temperate, lush fertile and a shady fernery, are all densely planted to make the most of dramatic foliage, from huge bananas to towering cordylines. Fareham in Bloom gold award Small Plantsman's Back Garden and Best In Category for the 5th year running! Short gravel path not suitable for mobility scooters.

13 BISTERNE MANOR

Bisterne, Ringwood, BH24 3BN. Mr & Mrs Hallam Mills. *2½m S of Ringwood on B3347 Christchurch Rd, 500yds past church on L. Entrance signed Stable Family Home Trust on L (blue sign), just past lodge. Disabled parking signed near the house.* **Wed 23, Wed 30 May (2-5). Adm £5, chd free. Home-made teas.**

Glorious rhododendrons and azaleas form a backdrop for our C19 garden first opened in the 1930s for the fledgling NGS, now under restoration. The C16 manor house (not open) overlooks a grand parterre with box hedges and lavender. Rare tree specimens grace fine lawns and wild flower planting, leading to a boundary woodland walk with glimpses of surrounding pastures. There is a small kitchen garden. Wheelchair access to a level garden with wide gravel paths.

14 BLEAK HILL NURSERY & GARDEN

Braemoor, Bleak Hill, Harbridge, Ringwood, BH24 3PX. Tracy & John Netherway & Judy Spratt, 01425 652983, jnetherway@btinternet.com. *2½ m S of Fordingbridge. Turn off A338 at Ibsley. Go through Harbridge village to T-junction at top of hill, turn R for ¼ m.* **Sun 1, Sun 15, Sun 29 July (2-5.30). Adm £4, chd free. Home-made teas. Visits also by arrangement in July.**

Through the moongate and concealed from view are billowing borders contrasting against a seaside scene, with painted beach huts and a boat on the gravel. Herbaceous borders fill the garden with colour wrapping around a pond and small stream. Greenhouses with cacti and sarracenias. Vegetable patch and bantam chickens. Small adjacent nursery.

15 BLUEBELL WOOD

Stancombe Lane, Bavins, New Odiham Road, Alton, GU34 5SX. Mrs Jennifer Ospici, 01420 82171, www.bavins.co.uk. *On the corner of Stancombe Lane & the B3349 2½ m N of Alton.* **Sat 28, Sun 29 Apr (11-4). Adm £5, chd free. Light refreshments. Visits also by arrangement Apr & May.**

Unique 100 acre ancient bluebell woodland. If you are a keen walker you will have much to explore on the long meandering paths and rides dotted with secluded seats. Those who enjoy a more leisurely pace will experience the perfume of the carpet of blue, listen to the birdsong and watch the contrasting light through the trees nearer to the entrance of the woods. Refreshments will be served in an original rustic wooden building and incl soups using natural woodland ingredients. Featured in Sunday Times. No wheelchair access.

16 BRAMDEAN HOUSE

Bramdean, Alresford, SO24 0JU. Mr & Mrs H Wakefield, 01962 771214, victoria@bramdeanhouse.com. *4m S of Alresford. In centre of village on A272. Entrance opp sign to the church.* **Sun 18 Feb, Sun 8 Apr, Sun 10 June, Sun 8 July, Sun 9 Sept (2-4). Adm £5, chd free. Home-made teas. Visits also by arrangement Feb to Sept for groups of 10+.**

Beautiful 5 acre garden famous for its mirror image herbaceous borders. Carpets of spring bulbs especially snowdrops. A large and unusual collection of plants and shrubs giving yr-round interest. 1 acre walled garden featuring prize-winning vegetables, fruit and flowers. Small arboretum. Trial of hardy Nerine cultivars in association with RHS. Features incl a wild flower meadow, boxwood castle, a large collection of old fashioned sweet peas. Home of the nation's tallest sunflower 'Giraffe'. Flowering cherries recently imported from Japan.

17 BRANDY MOUNT HOUSE

Alresford, SO24 9EG. Michael Baron. *Nr Alresford centre. From centre, 1st R in East St before Sun Lane. Please leave cars in Broad St, station car park, at Perins School or Longbarn Lavender Farm.* **Sun 18 Feb (12-4). Adm £5, chd free. Home-made teas. Also open The Down House.**

1 acre, informal plantsman's garden. Spring bulbs, hellebores, species geraniums, a wonderful snowdrop collection and daphnes. European primulas, collection of dwarf narcissi, herbaceous and woodland plants. Raised beds to display early spring bulbs and alpines. Limited access for wheelchairs and mobility vehicles. Please keep to the main paths and grass.

18 6 BREAMORE CLOSE

Boyatt Wood, Eastleigh, SO50 4QB. Mr & Mrs R Trenchard, 02380 611230, dawndavina6@yahoo.co.uk. *1m N of Eastleigh. M3 J12, follow signs to Eastleigh. Turn R at r'about into Woodside Ave, then 1st L into Broadlands Ave (park here). Breamore Close 3rd on L.* **Visits by arrangement May to July for groups of 10+. Adm £3.50, chd free. Home-made teas.**

Delightful plant lover's garden with coloured foliage and unusual plants, giving a tapestry effect of texture and colour. Many hostas displayed in pots and in May a wonderful wisteria scrambles over a pergola. The garden is laid out in distinctive planting themes with seating areas to sit and contemplate. In July many clematis scramble through roses and there are many varieties of phlox. Small gravel areas.

19 BRICK KILN COTTAGE

The Avenue, Herriard, Nr Alton, RG25 2PR. Barbara Jeremiah, 01256 381301, barbara@klca.co.uk. *4m NE of Alton. A339 Basingstoke to Alton, 7m out of Basingstoke turn L along The Avenue, past Lasham Gliding Club on R, then past Back Lane on L & take next track on L, one field later.* **Visits by arrangement Apr to July. Adm £4, chd free. Home-made teas.**

Bluebell woodland garden with 2 acres incl treehouse, pebble garden, billabong, stumpery, ferny hollow, shepherd's hut and a traditional cottage garden filled with herbs. The garden is maintained using eco-friendly methods as a haven for wild animals, butterflies, birds and bees and English bluebells. Families, schools and groups welcome to this wild garden in a former brick works, with excellent cream teas, home-made cakes, sandwiches and pots of tea. Received a Hampshire & Isle of Wight Wildlife Trust Award for a wildlife friendly garden and featured in Hampshire Life and Period Living. Wheelchair access to some parts of the garden.

20 NEW 146 BRIDGE ROAD

Sarisbury Green, Southampton, SO31 7EJ. Audrey & Jonathan Crutchfield. *4m W of Fareham. On A27 (Bridge Rd) at Sarisbury Green between Glen Rd & Chapel Rd. Drop off at house available for disabled.*

Please park at the Bold Forester Pub, 200yds E. **Sat 12, Sun 13 May (2-5.30). Adm £3.50, chd free. Home-made teas.**
A rambling, deceptively large and tranquil cottage garden that is accessed from a side gate and unexpectedly removed from the sometimes bustling A27. Creatively divided with rooms, richly filled borders, patios and lawns giving intense variety. These are interspersed with nooks, arbours, mirrors, statues and unexpected resting spots that offer promise, privacy and the chance to unwind and reflect.

21 ◆ CHAWTON HOUSE LIBRARY
Chawton, Alton, GU34 1SJ. Andrew Bentley, 01420 595903, andrew.bentley@chawtonhouselibrary.org, www.chawtonhouse.org. *2m S of Alton. Take the road opp Jane Austen's House museum towards St. Nicholas church. Property is at the end of this road on the L.* **For NGS: Sun 25 Feb (11-4). Adm £5, chd free.** For other opening times and information, please phone, email or visit garden website.
Snowdrops are scattered through this 14 acre listed English landscape garden which is gradually being restored. Sweeping lawns, ha-ha, wilderness, terraces, fernery and shrubbery walk surround the Elizabethan manor house. The walled garden designed by Edward Knight now includes rose garden, vegetable beds, orchard, and 'Elizabeth Blackwell' garden based on her book 'A Curious Herbal' of 1737-39. Due to slopes and gravel paths, we regret this garden is not suitable for wheelchairs.

22 21 CHESTNUT ROAD
Brockenhurst, SO42 7RF. Iain & Mary Hayter, 01590 622009, maryiain.hayter@gmail.com, www.21-chestnut-rdgardens.co.uk. *New Forest, 4m S of Lyndhurst. At Brockenhurst turn R, B3055 Grigg Lane. Limited parking, village car park nearby. Leave M27 J2, follow Heavy Lorry Route. Mainline station less than 10 mins walk.* **Sat 19 May (11-5). Sun 20 May (1-5), also open Aviemore. Sat 9 June (11-5); Sun 10 June (1-5); Sat 21 July (11-5); Sun 22 July (1-5). Sun 19 Aug (11-5), also open Moore Blatch. Adm £3.50, chd free. Home-made teas & gluten free option. Visits also by arrangement Apr to Sept for groups of 10+.**
Be amazed at how much you will see in this third of an acre mature garden. Inspirational ideas where features and plants combine with artistic flare. Seasonal planting, being wildlife friendly, productive and relaxing, all aimed to inspire. Home-made refreshments can be enjoyed in various locations incl summerhouse and raised deck over pond, and children can see the fairies in the secret garden. Some areas are not suitable for wheelchair users in wet weather.

23 2 CHURCH COTTAGES
Tufton, Whitchurch, RG28 7RF. Jane & John Huxford, 01256 893518, jane.huxford@icloud.com. *N on A34 at Whitchurch exit, turn L off slip road, R at Xrds, house 2nd on R. From Whitchurch centre take Winchester Rd S. Before slip road bear R, turn R, turn R at Xrds, house 2nd on R.* **Sun 25 Mar, Sun 22 Apr, Sat 12 May, Sun 10, Sat 16 June, Sun 8 July, Sun 9, Sun 16 Sept (2-5). Adm £4, chd free. Home-made teas. Visits also by arrangement Mar to Sept for groups of 10+.**
2 ½ acres. A stone's throw from the River Test, formerly an estate cowman's dwelling, the front and back is a traditional cottage garden, but there's much more! Through a gate in the hedge you'll find a nursery, greenhouses, raised beds, cutting garden and orchard. A stroll in the field leads to a new wildlife pond and a woodland walk, both in development. Tea in the barn completes your visit. Photographed for Hampshire Life.

24 CLOVER FARM
Shalden Lane, Shalden, Alton, GU34 4DU. Tom & Sarah Floyd, 01420 862294. *Approx 3m N of Alton in the village of Shalden. Take A339 out of Alton. After approx 2m turn R up lane. At top, turn sharp R next to church sign.* **Visits by arrangement Apr to Oct for groups of 10+. Adm £5, chd free. Light refreshments.**
3 acre garden with views to die for! Herbaceous borders and sloping lawns down to reflection pond, wild flower meadow, lime avenue, rose and kitchen garden.

25 COLEMORE HOUSE GARDENS
Colemore, Alton, GU34 3RX. Mr & Mrs Simon de Zoete, 01420 588202, simondezoete@gmail.com. *4m S of Alton (off A32). Approach from N on A32, turn L (Shell Lane), ¼m S of East Tisted. Go under bridge, keep L until you see Colemore Church. Park on verge of church.* **Sun 24, Mon 25 June (2-6). Adm £5, chd free. Home-made teas. Visits also by arrangement May to Sept.**
4 acres in lovely unspoilt countryside, featuring rooms containing many unusual plants and different aspects. A spectacular arched rose walk, water rill, mirror pond, herbaceous and shrub borders and a new woodland walk. Many admire the lawns, new grass gardens and thatched pavilion (built by students from the Prince's Trust). A small arboretum is being planted. Change and development is ongoing, and increasing the diversity of interesting plants is a prime motivation. We propagate and sell plants, many of which can be found in the garden. Some are unusual and not readily available elsewhere.

26 CONHOLT PARK

Hungerford Lane, Andover, SP11 9HA. Conholt Park Estate, 07917 796826, conholtgarden17@outlook.com. *7m N of Andover. Turn N off A342 at Weyhill Church, 5m N through Clanville. L at T-junction, Conholt ½m on R, opp Chute Causeway. A343 to Hurstbourne Tarrant, turn R, go through Vernham Dean, L signed Conholt.* **Sun 17 June, Sun 22 July (11-5). Adm £6, chd free. Home-made teas. Visits also by arrangement May to July on weekdays only.**

10 acres of varied garden styles and lawns with mature cedars. Large walled garden recently replanted and established beds. Orchard with wisteria walk. Formal rose garden, rhyl, secret gardens with hostas, geranium and macleaya. Other features include large laurel maze (good for children) and croquet lawn (play if you like). Visitors welcome to picnic. Free-range chickens and guineafowl. Deep gravel and steps, not suitable for wheelchairs.

27 THE COTTAGE

16 Lakewood Road, Chandler's Ford, SO53 1ES. Hugh & Barbara Sykes, 02380 254521, barandhugh@aol.com. *2m NW of Eastleigh. Leave M3 J12, follow signs to Chandler's Ford. At King Rufus on Winchester Rd, turn R into Merdon Ave, then 3rd road on L.* **Sun 6, Mon 7, Sun 13, Mon 14 May (2-6). Adm £4, chd free. Home-made teas. Visits also by arrangement Apr & May.**

¾ acre. Azaleas, rhododendrons and over 30 camellias with trilliums and erythroniums under old oaks and pines. Since 1982 we've planted 30 new trees incl P.montezuma. Herbaceous cottage style borders with unusual plants for yr-round interest. Bog garden, ponds, kitchen garden. Bantams, bees and birdsong, with over 30 bird species recorded. Wildlife areas. NGS sundial for opening for 30yrs. Childrens' quiz. 'A lovely tranquil garden', Anne Swithinbank. Hampshire Wildlife Trust Wildlife Garden Award. Honey from our garden hives for sale.

28 61 COTTES WAY

Hill Head, Fareham, PO14 3NL. Norma Matthews & Alan Stamps. *4½m S of Fareham. From Fareham follow signs to Stubbington, then Hill Head. Turn R into Bells Lane, L bend to Crofton Lane, R opp shops into Carisbrooke Ave, L into Cottes Way.* **Sun 24, Mon 25 June (11-4). Adm £3, chd free. Home-made teas.**

33ft x 33ft garden, designed by owner in 2015, a fine example of a low maintenance, spacious and relaxing outdoor living room. Colourful with a wide variety of shrubs, perennials and climbers. Interesting art and metal work, water features and patterned natural stone patio. Many pots and containers incl chimney pots and champagne bottles create a blaze of colour. Small vegetable patch. Winner of 3 Gold Awards in the Fareham in Bloom 2017.

29 NEW COURT HOUSE

West Meon, Petersfield, GU32 1JG. Mr & Mrs Paul & Tina Over. *150yds W of the A32 in the centre of the village; follow signs.* **Sun 9 Sept (2-5). Adm £5, chd free. Home-made teas.**

Redesigned some 20 yrs ago, 26 acres with a 3 acre garden. Plenty of interest which incl orchard, wild area, courtyard and the River Meon. A combination of short and long grass with trees and shrubs has been used to create shape and interest, to reflect the natural countryside within a listed building setting. Herbaceous borders enhance the C14 house (not open). Partial wheelchair access.

30 CRANBURY PARK

Otterbourne, nr Winchester, SO21 2HL. Mrs Chamberlayne-Macdonald. *3m NW of Eastleigh. Main entrance on old A33 at top of Otterbourne Hill. Entrances also in Hocombe Rd, Chandlers Ford & next to Otterbourne Church.* **Sun 10 June (2-6). Adm £5, chd free. Home-made teas.** Donation to St Mark's Church, Ampfield.

Extensive pleasure grounds laid out in late C18 and early C19 by Papworth; fountains, rose garden, specimen trees and pinetum, lakeside walk and fern walk. Family carriages and collection of prams will be on view, also photos of King George VI, Eisenhower and Montgomery reviewing Canadian troops at Cranbury before D-Day. Disabled WC. All dogs on leads please.

GROUP OPENING

31 CRAWLEY GARDENS

Crawley, Winchester, SO21 2PR. F J Fratter, 01962 776243, fred@fratter.co.uk. *5m NW of Winchester. Between B3049 (Winchester - Stockbridge) & A272 (Winchester - Andover). Parking throughout village.* **Fri 30 Mar, Mon 2 Apr, Thur 5, Sun 8 July (2-5.30). Combined adm £7.50, chd free. Home-made teas in the village hall.**

BAY TREE HOUSE
Julia & Charles Whiteaway.
Open on all dates

LITTLE COURT
Mrs A R Elkington.
Open on Fri 30 Mar, Mon 2 Apr
(See separate entry)

PAIGE COTTAGE
Mr & Mrs T W Parker.
Open on all dates

TANGLEFOOT
Mr & Mrs F J Fratter.
Open on Thur 5, Sun 8 July
(See separate entry)

Crawley is an exceptionally pretty period village nestling in chalk downland with thatched houses, C14 church and village pond with ducks. The spring gardens are Bay Tree House, Little Court and Paige Cottage; the summer gardens are Bay Tree House, Paige Cottage and Tanglefoot; providing seasonal interest of varied character, and with traditional and contemporary approaches to landscape and planting. Most of the gardens have beautiful country views and there are other good gardens to be seen from the road. Bay Tree House has bulbs, wild flowers, a Mediterranean garden, pleached limes, a rill and contemporary borders of perennials and grasses. Little Court is a 3 acre traditional English country garden with carpets of spring bulbs and a large meadow. Paige Cottage is a 1 acre traditional English country garden surrounding a period thatched cottage (not open) with bulbs and wildflowers in spring, and old climbing roses in summer. Tanglefoot has colour themed borders, herb wheel, exceptional kitchen garden, traditional Victorian boundary wall supporting trained fruit incl apricots; and a large wildflower meadow. Plants from the garden for sale at Little Court and Tanglefoot.

32 CROOKLEY POOL

Blendworth Lane, Horndean, PO8 0AB. Mr & Mrs Simon Privett. *5m S of Petersfield. 2m E of Waterlooville, off A3. From Horndean up Blendworth Lane between bakery & hairdresser. Entrance 200yds before church on L with white railings. Parking in field.* **Sun 13 May (2-5). Adm £4.50, chd free. Home-made teas.**

Here the plants decide where to grow. Californian tree poppies elbow valerian aside to crowd round the pool. Evening primroses obstruct the way to the door and the steps to wisteria shaded terraces. Hellebores bloom under the trees. Salvias, Pandorea jasminoides, Justicia, Pachystachys lutea and passion flowers riot quietly with tomatoes in the greenhouse. Not a garden for the neat or tidy minded, although this is a plantsman's garden full of unusual plants and a lot of tender perennials. Bantams stroll throughout. Watercolour paintings of flowers found in the garden will be on display and for sale in the studio.

33 DEAN HOUSE

Kilmeston Road, Kilmeston, Alresford, SO24 0NL. Mr P H R Gwyn, www.deanhousegardens.co.uk. *5m S of Alresford. Via village of Cheriton or off A272 signed at Cheriton Xrds. Follow signs for Kilmeston, through village & turn L at Dean House sign after the bus shelter.* **Wed 23 May, Wed 20 June, Wed 4 July (10-4); Sun 22 July, Sun 5 Aug (12-4.30); Wed 15 Aug (10-4). Adm £6, chd free. Home-made cream teas & a wide selection of cakes in the Orangery.**

The 7 acres have been described as 'a well-kept secret hidden behind the elegant facade of its Georgian centrepiece'. Sweeping lawns, York stone paths, gravel pathways, many young and mature trees and hedges, mixed and herbaceous borders. Rose garden, pond garden, working walled garden with glasshouses growing 125 different varieties of vegetables, which help to create a diverse and compact sliver of Eden. Over 1700 individually documented plant species and cultivars in our collection. 60 metre laburnum and wisteria tunnel. Gravel paths.

34 THE DEANE HOUSE

Sparsholt, Winchester, SO21 2LR. Mr & Mrs Richard Morse, 01962 776425, chrissie@morse.eclipse.co.uk. *3½m NW of Winchester. Off A3049 Stockbridge Rd, onto Woodman Lane, signed Sparsholt. Turn L at 1st cottage on L, white with blue gables, at top of drive.* **Sun 25 Mar (1.30-4.30); Sun 10 June (1.30-5). Adm £6, chd free. Home-made teas. Visits also by arrangement for groups of 10+.**

Flowering cherry trees, statuesque copper beech and tulip trees grace the sweeping lawns at The Deane House (not open), leading the eye to the landscape beyond. Come and pick daffodils in March, and the walled garden is best in June when the heady perfume of roses fills the air. Stained glass and modern water features abound. Sorry No Dogs.

The National Garden Scheme is Hospice UK's largest single funder

Rotherfield Greys

35 DIPLEY MILL

Dipley Road, Hartley Wintney, Hook, RG27 8JP. Miss Rose McMonigall, www.dipley-mill.co.uk. *2m NE of Hook. Turn E off B3349 at Mattingley (1½m N of Hook) signed Hartley Wintney, West Green & Dipley. Dipley Mill ½m on L just over bridge.* **Sun 3, Sun 17 June, Sun 15 July, Sun 5 Aug, Sun 2, Sun 30 Sept (2-5.30). Adm £6, chd free. Cream teas.** Donation to St Michael's Hospice.

A romantic adventure awaits as you wander by the meandering streams surrounding this Domesday Book listed mill! Explore many magical areas, such as the rust garden, the pill box grotto and the ornamental courtyard, or just escape into wild meadows. Alpacas. 'One of the most beautiful gardens in Hampshire' according to Alan Titchmarsh in his TV programme Love Your Garden. Featured on BBC TV and other press coverage as a result of a show garden at Hampton Court for Turismo De Galicia and the Spanish Tourist Office. Featured in Weranda magazine, Mediterranean Gardening, and Basingstoke Gazette. Regret no dogs.

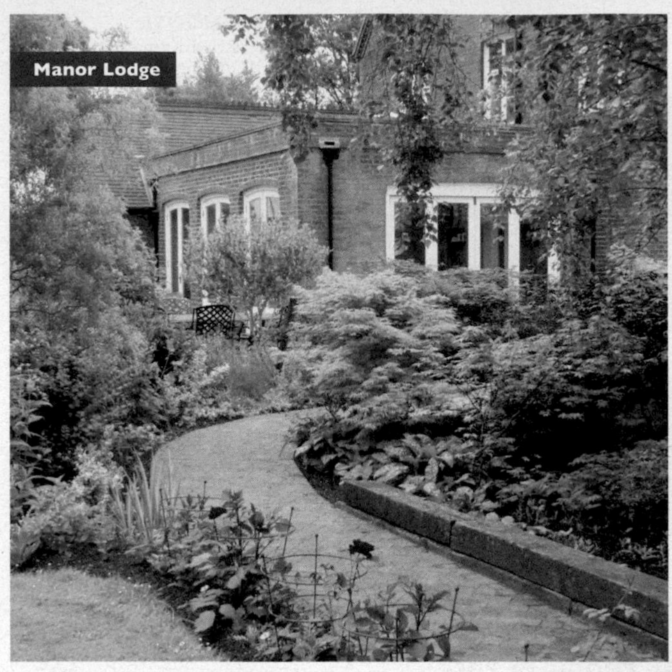
Manor Lodge

36 THE DOWER HOUSE

Springvale Road, Headbourne Worthy, Winchester, SO23 7LD. Mrs Judith Lywood, 01962 882848, hannahlomax@thedowerhousewinchester.co.uk, www.thedowerhousewinchester.co.uk. *2m N of Winchester. Entrance is directly opp watercress beds in Springvale Rd & near The Good Life Farm Shop. Parking at main entrance to house, following path to garden.* **Sun 29 Apr (2.30-5.30). Adm £4.50, chd free. Home-made teas. Visits also by arrangement Mar to Sept for groups of 20-30.**

The Dower House is set within 5½ acres of gardens with meandering paths allowing easy access around the grounds. There are plenty of places to sit, relax and enjoy the surroundings. Areas of interest incl a scented border, iris bed, geranium bed, shrubbery, a pond populated with fish and water lilies, bog garden, bluebell wood and secret courtyard garden.

37 DOWN FARM HOUSE

Whitchurch, RG28 7FB. Pat & Steve Jones, 01256 892490, patthehound@gmail.com. *1½m from the centre of Whitchurch. Please do not use SatNav. From the centre of Whitchurch take the Newbury road up the hill, over railway bridge & after approx 1m turn L.* **Wed 2 May (1.30-5). Adm £4, chd free. Home-made teas. Visits also by arrangement May & June for groups of 10+.**

Step back in time in this 2 acre garden, created from an old walled farmyard and the surrounding land. Many of the original features are used as hard landscaping, incl organic vegetables, succulents, alpine bed created from the old concrete capped well, informal and naturalistic planting, wooded area and orchard. The garden has been created slowly over the last 30 yrs. Wildlife pond built in 2017. Wheelchair access by gravel drive onto lawn.

38 THE DOWN HOUSE

Itchen Abbas, SO21 1AX. Jackie & Mark Porter, 01962 791054, markstephenporter@gmail.com, www.thedownhouse.co.uk. *5m E of Winchester on B3047. 5th house on R after the Itchen Abbas village sign if coming on B3047 from Kings Worthy. 400yds on L after Plough Pub if coming on B3047 from Alresford.* **Sun 18 Feb (12-4). Adm £5, chd free. Home-made teas. Visits also by arrangement in late February for groups of 20+.**

A 3 acre garden laid out in rooms overlooking the Itchen Valley, adjoining the Pilgrim's Way, with walks to the river. In February come and see the snowdrops, aconites and crocus, plus borders of coloured dogwoods, willow stems and white birches. A garden of structure with pleached hornbeams, a rope-lined fountain garden and yew lined avenues - plus a pruned and trained vineyard!

39 7 DOWNLAND CLOSE

Locks Heath, nr Fareham, SO31 6WB. Roy & Carolyn Dorland, 07768 107779, roydorland@hotmail.co.uk. *3m W of Fareham. M27 J9 follow A27 on Southampton Rd to Park Gate. Past Kams Palace Restaurant, L into Locks Rd, 3rd R into Meadow Ave. 2nd L into Downland Close. Please park in Locks Rd (only 2 mins from garden).* **Sat 23, Sun 24 June (1-5). Adm £3, chd free. Home-made teas. Visits also by arrangement May to Aug for groups of 15-25.**

Visit this prize-winning, beautiful, restful and inspirational 50ft x 45ft plantsman's garden, packed with ideas for the modest sized plot. Many varieties of hardy geraniums, hostas, heucheras, shrubs, ferns and other unusual perennials, weaving a tapestry of harmonious colour. Attractive water feature, plenty of seating areas and charming summerhouse. A garden to fall in love with!

40 DURMAST HOUSE

Bennetts Lane, Burley, BH24 4AT. Mr & Mrs P E G Daubeney, 01425 402132, philip@daubeney.co.uk, www.durmasthouse.co.uk. *5m SE of Ringwood. Off Burley to Lyndhurst Rd, nr White Buck Hotel.* **Sun 8 Apr, Sun 24 June (2-5). Adm £5, chd free. Cream teas. Visits also by arrangement Apr to Oct, incl talk on the history and planting of the garden for groups only.** Donation to Delhi Commonwealth Women's Assn Medical Clinic.

Designed by Gertrude Jekyll, Durmast has contrasting hot and cool colour borders, formal rose garden edged with lavender and a long herbaceous border. Many old trees, Victorian rockery and orchard with beautiful spring bulbs. Rare azaleas; Fama, Princeps and Gloria Mundi from Ghent. Features incl new rose bowers with rare French roses; Eleanor Berkeley, Psyche and Reine Olga Wurtemberg. New Jekyll border with a blue, yellow and white scheme. Many old trees incl Monterey Pine, about 140 yrs old. Many stone paths and some gravel paths.

41 EAST WORLDHAM MANOR

Worldham Hill, East Worldham, Alton, GU34 3AX. Hermione Wood, www.worldham.org. *2m SE of Alton on B3004. Coming from Alton, turn R by village hall, signed car park.* **Sat 23, Sun 24 June (2-5.30). Combined adm with Selborne £5, chd free. Home-made teas.**

A rambling double-walled garden laid out in the 1870s with far-reaching views to the South Downs. Illustrates a substantial Victorian garden with fruit, vegetables and flower borders, rose garden, many shrubs, herbaceous plants, apple and pear orchard and large productive greenhouses. Gravel paths, some naturalised with white foxgloves and campanulas, wind through many parts of the garden. WC at village hall.

42 FAIRBANK

Old Odiham Road, Alton, GU34 4BU. Jane & Robin Lees, 01420 86665, j.lees558@btinternet.com. *1½m N of Alton. From S, past Sixth Form College, then 1½m beyond road junction on R. From N, turn L at Golden Pot & then 50yds turn R. Garden 1m on L before road junction.* **Visits by arrangement June to Sept for individuals or groups of 30 max. Adm £4, chd free. Home-made teas.**

The planting in this large garden reflects our interest in trees, shrubs, fruit and vegetables. A wide variety of herbaceous plants provide colour and are placed in sweeping mixed borders that carry the eye down the long garden to the orchard and beyond. Near the house, there are rose beds and herbaceous borders, as well as a small formal pond. There is a range of acers, ferns and unusual shrubs, with 60 different varieties of fruit, along with a large vegetable garden. Please be aware of uneven ground in some areas.

43 FAIRWEATHER'S NURSERY

Hilltop, Beaulieu, SO42 7YR. 01590 612113, info@fairweathers.co.uk, www.fairweathers.co.uk. *1½m NE of Beaulieu village. Signed Hilltop Nursery on B3054 between Heath r'about (A326) & Beaulieu village.* **Sat 28, Sun 29 July (11-4). Adm £3, chd free. Cream teas at Aline Fairweather's garden.**

Fairweather's hold a specialist collection of over 400 agapanthus grown in pots and display beds, incl plants being trialled for the RHS AGM. Features incl guided tours of the nursery at 11.30am and 2.30pm, demonstrations of how to get the best from agapanthus and companion planting. Agapanthus and a range of other traditional and new perennials for sale. Aline Fairweather's garden (adjacent to the nursery) will also be open, with mixed shrub and perennial borders containing many unusual plants. Also open Patrick's Patch at Fairweather's Garden Centre.

NPC

The National Garden Scheme is the largest single funder of Macmillan

GROUP OPENING

44 FROYLE GARDENS

Lower Froyle, Froyle, GU34 4LG. www.froyle.com/ngs. *5m NE of Alton. Access to Lower Froyle from A31 between Alton & Farnham at Bentley, or via Upper Froyle at Hen & Chicken Pub, or via B3349 & Golden Pot Pub. Park at recreation ground. Maps given to all visitors.* **Sat 2, Sun 3 June (2-6). Combined adm £7.50, chd free. Home-made teas at Froyle Village Hall.**

NEW **ALDERSEY HOUSE**
Nigel & Julie Southern.

BRAMLINS
Anne Blunt.

6 COLDREY COTTAGES
Roy & Sue Cranford.

DAY COTTAGE
Nick & Corinna Whines, www.daycottage.co.uk.

GLEBE COTTAGE
Barbara & Michael Starbuck.

NEW **MANOR COTTAGE**
Russell & Victoria Pearn.

OLD BREWERY HOUSE
Vivienne & John Sexton.

WARREN COTTAGE
Gillian & Jonathan Pickering.

NEW **WELL LANE CORNER**
Mark & Sue Lelliott.

You will certainly receive a warm welcome as nine Froyle Gardens open their gates again this year, enabling visitors to enjoy a wide variety of gardens. We have three new gardens (one in Upper Froyle) which has recently undergone a great deal of development and will be looking splendid. All the Froyle gardens harmonise well with the surrounding landscape and most have spectacular views. The gardens themselves are diverse with rich planting often incorporating unusual plants. You will also see greenhouses, water features, vegetables, roses, clematis and wild flower meadows as well as a gem of a courtyard garden. Lots of ideas to take away with you along with plants for sale. The delicious teas served in the village hall are famous and close by there is a new children's playground with a zip wire and climbing frame where younger visitors can let off steam. The main parking area is at the recreation ground, close to the village hall, additional signed parking available. In conjunction with Froyle Open Gardens there is an exhibition of richly decorated vestments to be held in St Mary's Church, Upper Froyle GU34 4LB (separate donation). Parking by the church. No wheelchair access to Glebe Cottage and Manor Cottage. Gravel drive at Bramlins. Gravel area at Warren Cottage with disabled access on request.

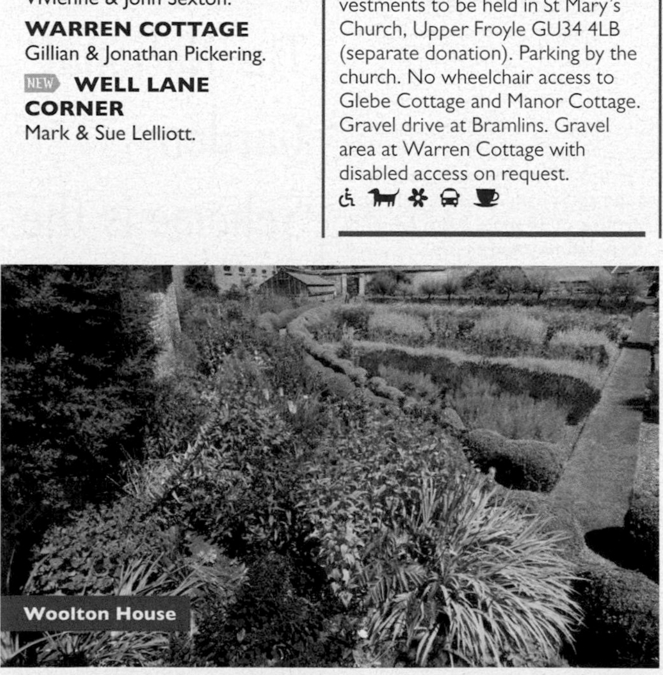

Woolton House

45 FURZEHILL FARM

FurzeHill, South Gorley, Fordingbridge, SP6 2PT. Richard & Sue Loader, www.furzehillfarm.garden. *In the New Forest between Ringwood & Fordingbridge. At Ibsley Church on A338 between Fordingbridge & Ringwood, follow yellow NGS signs for 2½ m.* **Sun 10, Sun 17 June (2-5). Adm £4.50, chd free. Home-made teas.** Donation to Cancer Research UK.

A 3 acre wildlife friendly garden in a New Forest smallholding setting. It has evolved over the last 20 yrs with a pretty cottage garden, vegetable plots, wildlife zones and a tiny oak wood coppice, all combining delightfully into a rambling mix that has a broad appeal whatever your gardening interests. Don't expect tidiness throughout, some areas are informal with nature allowed free rein. Walk through our wildflower meadow plots, see new plant varieties in patio containers, learn about innovative ways to grow garden produce and see interesting garden structures made from New Forest greenwood. Not suitable for wheelchairs due to inclines and loose surfaces.

46 GILBERTS DAHLIA FIELD

Gilberts Nursery, Dandysford Lane, Sherfield English, nr Romsey, SO51 6DT. Nick & Helen Gilbert, www.gilbertsdahlias.co.uk. *Midway between Romsey & Whiteparish on A27, in Sherfield English Village. From Romsey 4th turn on L, just before small petrol station on R, visible from main road.* **Sun 26 Aug (10-4). Adm £3, chd free. Light refreshments.**

This may not be a garden but do come and be amazed by the sight of over 300 varieties of dahlias in our dedicated 1½ acre field. Prize winning blooms are in all colours, shapes and sizes and can be closely inspected from wheelchair friendly hard grass paths. An inspiration for all gardeners.

47 HAMBLEDON HOUSE

East Street, Hambledon, PO7 4RX. Capt & Mrs David Hart Dyke, 02392 632380, dianahartdyke@talktalk.net. *8m SW of Petersfield, 5m NW of Waterlooville. In village centre, driveway leading to house in East St. Do not go up Speltham Hill even if advised by SatNav.* **Mon 27 Aug (2-5). Adm £5, chd free. Home-made teas. Visits also by arrangement Apr to Oct. Teas by prior request.**

3 acre partly walled plantsman's garden for all seasons. Large borders filled with a wide variety of unusual shrubs and perennials with imaginative plant combinations culminating in a profusion of colour in late summer. Hidden, secluded areas reveal surprise views of garden and village rooftops. Planting a large central area, started in 2011, has given the garden an exciting new dimension. Partial wheelchair access as garden is on several levels.

48 HAMBROOKS SHOW GARDENS

135 Southampton Road, Titchfield, Fareham, PO14 4PR. Mr Mike Hodges. *On the old A27 opp B&Q.* **Sun 24 June (12-4); Sat 27 Oct (1-5); Sat 24 Nov (12-5). Adm by donation.**

16 individually designed showcase gardens ranging from the traditional to the contemporary, featuring outdoor kitchens, fireplaces, garden sofas, chandeliers, obelisks, ponds and streams. Our 3 special NGS events will be dressed for the season and lit after dark. We will also have live music, refreshments and entertainment. There is a covered walkway to protect you from the elements. Sun 24 June Midsummer Fete, Sat 27 Oct Spooky Afternoon and Sat 24 Nov Winter Walk Into Christmas.

49 NEW HAMDOWN CORNER

Whinwhistle Road, East Wellow, Romsey, SO51 6BH. Jacky Petretic. *Turn SE into Whinwhistle Rd from A36 (Salisbury 13m/Southampton 9m). Follow NGS signs.* **Sat 28, Sun 29 July (2-5.30). Combined adm with Hideaway £5, chd free. Home-made teas at Hideaway only.**

This ¼ acre plot is surrounded by mixed hedging. There is a generous use of box and gravel to offset the curvaceous lawns. Although abundantly planted with a wide variety of trees, shrubs, grasses and flowers, a relaxed look is intended through coordinating colours and textures. There are several seating areas and an imposing garden and potting shed.

50 HANGING HOSTA GARDEN

Narra, Frensham Lane, Lindford, Bordon, GU35 0QJ. June Colley & John Baker, 01420 489186, hanginghostas@btinternet.com. *Approx 1m E of Bordon. From the A325 at Bordon take the B3002, then B3004 to Lindford. Turn L into Frensham Lane, 3rd house on L.* **Visits by arrangement in July (Mon 2 to Fri 6 only). Adm £3.50, chd free.**

This garden is packed with almost 2000 plants. The collection of over 1500 hosta cultivars is one of the largest in England. Hostas are displayed at eye level to give a wonderful tapestry of foliage and colour. Islamic garden, waterfall and stream garden, cottage garden. Talks given to garden clubs.

51 HIDEAWAY

Hamdown Crescent, East Wellow, Romsey, SO51 6BJ. Caroline & Colin Hart, 01794 322445, hart.caroline@yahoo.com. *3m W of Romsey. From M27 J2 take A36 NW towards Salisbury. After 2m, turn R by speed camera into Whinwhistle Rd. Hamdown Crescent is 3rd L.* **Sat 28, Sun 29 July (2-5.30). Combined adm with Hamdown Corner £5, chd free. Home-made teas. Visits also by arrangement June & July for groups of 30+.**

Winding paths lead through our peaceful ½ acre garden, where diverse and unusual plants grow in different habitats; shade, woodland, sunny borders, grass gardens, wildlife pond and bog gardens. Fountains play amidst the yr-round colour and somehow fruit and vegetables also find a place to grow. Plants propagated by the owner are for sale, as is a variety of art work.

52 HILL HOUSE

Old Alresford, SO24 9DY. Mrs S Richardson, 01962 732720, hillhouseolda@yahoo.co.uk. *N of Alresford. From Alresford, 1m along B3046 towards Basingstoke, then R by church.* **Thur 9, Sun 12, Tue 14 Aug (1.30-5). Adm £4, chd free. Home-made teas. Visits also by arrangement from mid July to mid Aug only.**

Traditional English 2 acre garden with a relaxed feel, established 1938, divided by yew hedge. Large croquet lawn framing the star of the garden, the huge multicoloured herbaceous border. Dahlia bed and butterfly attracting sunken garden in lavender shades. Prolific old fashioned kitchen garden with hens and bantams both fluffy and large. Small Dexter cows. Dried flowers.

53 HILL TOP

Damson Hill, Upper Swanmore, SO32 2QR. David Green, 01489 892653, tricia1960@btinternet.com. *1m NE of Swanmore. Junction of Swanmore Rd & Church Rd, up Hampton Hill, sharp L bend. After 300yds junction with Damson Hill, house on L. Disabled parking by house.* **Sun 16 Sept (1.30-5). Adm £4, chd free. Home-made teas. Visits also by arrangement May to Aug for groups of 20+.**

2 acres with extensive colourful borders and wide lawns, this garden has stunning views to the Isle of Wight. The glasshouses produce unusual fruit and vegetables from around the world. The outdoor vegetable plots bulge with well grown produce, much for sale in season. Potted specimen plants and interesting annuals.

54 HINTON ADMIRAL

Lyndhurst Road, Hinton, Christchurch, BH23 7DY. Sir George & Lady Meyrick. *4m NE of Christchurch. On N side of A35, ¾m E of Cat & Fiddle Pub.* **Sun 20 May (1-4.30). Adm £7, chd free.** Donation to Julia's House Childrens Hospice.

Magnificent 20 acre garden within a much larger estate, now being restored and developed. Mature plantings of deciduous azaleas and rhododendrons amidst a sea of bluebells. Wandering paths lead through rockeries and beside ponds, and a stream with many cascades. Orchids appear in the large lawns. The two walled gardens are devoted to herbs and wild flowers, and a very large greenhouse. The terrace and rock garden were designed by Harold Peto. Gravel paths and some steps.

55 HOLLYBROOK

20a Chalk Hill, West End, Southampton, SO18 3BZ. Michael Hook & Janet Galpin. *3m E of Southampton. Exit M27 J7, take A27 to West End, at T-lights turn L into Chalk Hill. Two disabled spaces on drive. Other parking on hill, side roads & at Master Builder Pub on A27, 2 mins from Chalk Hill.* **Sat 19, Sun 20, Sat 26, Sun 27 May (1-5). Adm £3, chd free. Home-made teas.**

Small 82ft x 39ft town garden started in 2008. Raised beds built using railway sleepers and imaginative use of other recycled and new materials to make interesting artistic garden pieces, to complement small herbaceous border, pergola and two ponds, one with a variety of fish. Structural planting incl bamboos, grasses and hostas. Small vegetable patch. New summerhouse made from recycled materials.

56 THE HOMESTEAD

Northney Road, Hayling Island, PO11 0NF. Stan & Mary Pike, 02392 464888, jhomestead@aol.com, www.homesteadhayling.co.uk. *3m S of Havant. From A27 Havant & Hayling Island r'about, travel S over Langstone Bridge & turn immed L into Northney Rd. Car park entrance on R after Langstone Hotel.* **Sun 5 Aug (2-5.30). Adm £4, chd free. Home-made teas. Visits also by arrangement June to Sept for groups of 10+.**

1¼ acre garden surrounded by working farmland with views to Butser Hill and boats in Chichester Harbour. Trees, shrubs, colourful herbaceous borders and small walled garden with herbs, vegetables and trained fruit trees. Large pond and woodland walk with shade-loving plants. A quiet and peaceful atmosphere with plenty of seats to enjoy the vistas within the garden and beyond. Some gravel paths.

57 ◆ THE HOSPITAL OF ST CROSS

St Cross Road, Winchester, SO23 9SD. The Hospital of St Cross & Almshouse of Noble Poverty, 01962 851375, porter@hospitalofstcross.co.uk, www.hospitalofstcross.co.uk. *½m S of Winchester. From city centre take B3335 (Southgate St & St Cross Rd) S. Turn L immed before The Bell Pub. If on foot follow riverside path S from Cathedral & College, approx 20 mins.* **For NGS: Sun 22 July (2-5). Adm £4, chd free. Home-made teas in the Hundred Men's Hall in the Outer Quadrangle. For other opening times and information, please phone, email or visit garden website.**

The Medieval Hospital of St Cross nestles in water meadows beside the River Itchen and is one of England's oldest almshouses. The tranquil, walled Master's Garden, created in the late C17 by Bishop Compton, now contains colourful herbaceous borders, old fashioned roses, interesting trees and a large fish pond. The Compton Garden has unusual plants of the type he imported when Bishop of London. There is wheelchair access, but please be aware surfaces are uneven in places.

58 THE HOUSE IN THE WOOD

Beaulieu, SO42 7YN. Victoria Roberts. *New Forest. 8m NE of Lymington. Leaving the entrance to Beaulieu Motor Museum on R (B3056), take next R signed Ipley Cross. Take 2nd gravel drive on RH-bend, approx ½m.* **Sun 13 May (2-5). Adm £5, chd free. Cream teas.**

Peaceful 12 acre woodland garden with continuing progress and improvement. New areas and streams have been developed and good acers planted among mature azaleas and rhododendrons. Used in the war to train the Special Operations Executive. A magical garden to get lost in and popular with birdwatchers.

59 THE ISLAND

Greatbridge, Romsey, SO51 0HP. Mr & Mrs Christopher Saunders-Davies, 01794 512100, ssd@littleroundtop.co.uk. *1m N of Romsey on A3057. Entrance alongside Greatbridge (1st bridge Xing the River Test), flanked by row of cottages on roadside.* **Sat 7, Sun 8 Apr, Sat 7, Sun 8 July (2-5). Adm £5, chd under 12 yrs free. Home-made teas.**

6 acres either side of the River Test. Fine display of paeonies, wisteria and spring flowering trees. Main garden has herbaceous and annual borders, fruit trees, rose pergola, lavender walk and extensive lawns. An arboretum planted in the 1930s by Sir Harold Hillier contains trees and shrubs providing interest throughout the yr. Please Note: No Dogs Allowed.

60 LAKE HOUSE

Northington, SO24 9TG. Lord Ashburton, 07795 364539, lukeroeder@hotmail.com. *4m N of Alresford. Off B3046. Follow English Heritage signs to The Grange, and then to Lake House.* **Thur 7, Sun 10 June (12-5). Adm £5, chd free. Home-made teas. Visits also by arrangement June to Oct for groups of 10+.**

Two large lakes in Candover Valley

set off by mature woodland with waterfalls, abundant birdlife, long landscaped vistas and folly. 1½ acre walled garden with rose parterre, mixed borders, long herbaceous border, rose pergola leading to moon gate. Flowering pots, conservatory and greenhouses. Picnicking by lakes. Grass paths and slopes to some areas of the garden.

61 LITTLE COURT

Crawley, Winchester, SO21 2PU. Mrs A R Elkington, 01962 776365, elkslc@btinternet.com. *5m NW of Winchester. Between B3049 (Winchester - Stockbridge) & A272 (Winchester - Andover) 400yds from either pond or church.* **Sun 18, Mon 19, Sun 25, Mon 26 Feb (2-4.30). Adm £4, chd free. Sun 15, Mon 16 Apr, Sun 6, Mon 7, Sun 20 May (2-5.30). Adm £5, chd free. Home-made teas in the village hall. 2019: Sun 17, Mon 18, Sun 24, Mon 25 Feb. Opening with Crawley Gardens on Fri 30 Mar, Mon 2 Apr. Visits also by arrangement Feb to July with home-made teas in the garden.**

A 3 acre walled and sheltered traditional country garden, well known for its naturalised bulbs, special snowdrops, a sea of wild crocus, hellebores, perennials in harmonious colours, punctuated by box balls. Loved by old and young, there are swings and a treehouse. Many seats, with views for miles to the south, increasing wildlife and butterflies. In 2017 a visitor said 'a heavenly garden'. Good butterflies in early July. A great place to relax.

62 99 LOCKS HEATH PARK ROAD

Locks Heath, Southampton, SO31 6LY. Linda & David Goringe. *2m W of Fareham. From M27 J9 take A27 to Park Gate. At 2nd r'about sharp L into Hunts Pond Rd. R at 1st of 2 mini-r'abouts into Church Rd. Then L into Locks Heath Park Rd.* **Sat 19, Sun 20 May (11-5). Combined adm with 101 Locks Heath Park Road £4, chd free. Home-made teas.**

Delightful plant lover's 150ft x 50ft garden designed for yr-round interest, replanted over the last 7 yrs with emphasis on coloured foliage. Island bed, varied ground cover perennials, sun and shade loving plants, with hellebores and bulbs in spring. Fish pond with water lilies, 5 raised vegetable beds, and 2 greenhouses. Wheelchair access: one small step (12cm) from patio to main garden area and gentle slope around raised vegetable beds.

63 101 LOCKS HEATH PARK ROAD

Locks Heath, SO31 6LY. Barbara & Graham Peckham. *2m W of Fareham. From M27 J9 take A27 to Park Gate. At 2nd r'about sharp L into Hunts Pond Rd. R at 1st of 2 mini-r'abouts into Church Rd. Then L into Locks Heath Park Rd.* **Sat 19, Sun 20 May (11-5). Combined adm with 99 Locks Heath Park Road £4, chd free. Home-made teas.**

A garden 120ft x 40ft that has been created over the yrs by Barbara & Graham, who just enjoy gardening. Busy borders with yr-round interest, incl many plants that attract butterflies and bees. Herb and pot garden. Unusual and varied selection of fruit trees and bushes incl Asian pear, honey berry and blueberry. Vegetable plot with greenhouse.

64 LONGSTOCK PARK

Leckford, Stockbridge, SO20 6EH. Leckford Estate Ltd, part of John Lewis Partnership, www.longstockpark.co.uk. *4m S of Andover. From Leckford village on A3057 towards Andover, cross the river bridge & take 1st turning to the L signed Longstock.* **Sun 17 June (1-4). Adm £6, chd £2. Light refreshments.**

Famous water garden with extensive collection of aquatic and bog plants set in 7 acres of woodland with rhododendrons and azaleas. A walk through the park leads to National Collections of *Buddleja* and *Clematis viticella*; arboretum and herbaceous border. Light refreshments at Leckford Farm Shop, at Longstock Nurseries (last orders at 3.45pm). Assistance dogs only.

NPC

The National Garden Scheme is Marie Curie's largest single funder

Lower Baybridge House

65 NEW LOWER BAYBRIDGE HOUSE

Lower Baybridge Lane, Owslebury, Winchester, SO21 1JN. Sophie & Jon Adams. *5m S of Winchester. Take the Morestead Rd out of Winchester, turn R at Xrds towards Owslebury, 1st L after the cricket pitch into Baybridge Lane & take next R. Parking in field opp. Disabled drop off at house.* **Sat 23, Sun 24 June (1-5). Adm £3.50, chd free. Home-made teas.**

A garden on chalk designed and planted by the owner. Features incl a sunken lawn bordered by classical flower border, a hummocky shaded evergreen border and a hillock meadow. A lavender walk leads to a kitchen garden enclosed by espalier fruit trees. Also open grassland with mown pathways and a wilderness area for bees. Warm sheltered walls for climbers, a choice of areas to sit and enjoy.

66 26 LOWER NEWPORT ROAD

Aldershot, GU12 4QD. Mr & Mrs P Myles. *From the A331 coming off at the Aldershot junction, head towards Aldershot. Take the 1st R turn, opp the Fiat Showroom into North Lane & then 1st L into Lower Newport Rd.* **Fri 29, Sat 30 June (11-4). Adm £3, chd free. Light refreshments.**

A 'T' shaped small town garden full of ideas, split into four distinct sections; a semi-enclosed patio area with pots and water feature; a free-form lawn with a tree fern, perennials, bulbs and shrubs; secret garden with a 20ft x 6ft raised pond, exotic planting backdrop and African carvings; and a potager garden with a selection of vegetable, roses and plant storage. We also have over 50 named varieties of hosta.

67 ◆ MACPENNYS WOODLAND GARDEN & NURSERIES

Burley Road, Bransgore, Christchurch, BH23 8DB. Mr & Mrs T M Lowndes, 01425 672348, office@macpennys.co.uk, www.macpennys.co.uk. *6m S of Ringwood, 5m NE of Christchurch. From Crown Pub Xrds in Bransgore take Burley Rd, following sign for Thorney Hill & Burley. Entrance ¼m on R.* **For opening times and information, please phone, email or visit garden website.**

4 acre woodland garden originating from worked out gravel pits in the 1950s, offering interest yr-round, but particularly in spring and autumn. Attached to a large nursery that offers for sale a wide selection of home-grown trees, shrubs, conifers, perennials, hedging plants, fruit trees and bushes. Tearoom offering home-made cakes, afternoon tea (pre-booking required), and light lunches using locally sourced produce wherever possible. Nursery closed Christmas through to the New Year. Partial wheelchair access.

68 NEW MANOR LODGE

Brook Lane, Botley, Southampton, SO30 2ER. Gary & Janine Stone. *6m E of Southampton. From A334 to the W of Botley village centre, turn into Brook Lane. Manor Lodge is ½m on the R. Limited disabled parking. Continue past Manor Lodge to parking (signed).* **Sat 14, Sun 15 July (2-5). Adm £3.50, chd free. Home-made teas.**

Close to Manor Farm Country Park, this mid-Victorian house (not open), set in over 1½ acres is the garden of an enthusiastic plants woman. A garden in evolution with established areas and new projects, a mixture of informal and formal planting, woodland and grass meadow areas. There are large established and new specimen trees, common and exotic perennials, planting combinations for extended seasonal interest. Largely flat with hard paving but some gravel and grass to access all areas.

69 1 MAPLE COTTAGE

Searles Lane, off London Road (A30), Hook, RG27 9EQ. John & Pat Beagley. *A30: Hartley Wintney side of Hook opp Hampshire Prestige Cars. Up Searles Lane (approx ¼m) parking close to rear of property. Follow yellow ribbons.* **Sun 27, Mon 28 May, Sat 2, Sun 3 June (2-5). Adm £3.50, chd free. Home-made cakes, gluten free cakes & biscuits.**

½ acre garden evolved over 25 yrs, many ideas for smaller gardens. Shady, herbaceous and hot borders, wildlife pond with many hosta varieties, vegetable plots plus a wild area, and views towards River Whitewater. Features incl a tree cave for children, and we feel we offer the most varied and quality plants for sale, from three experienced producers, incl a renowned local, retired nursery owner from Whispers. Some paved paths, mainly grassed areas.

70 MEON ORCHARD

Kingsmead, North of Wickham, PO17 5AU. Doug & Linda Smith, 01329 833253, meonorchard@btinternet.com. *5m N of Fareham. From Wickham take A32 N for 1½m. Turn L at Roebuck Inn. Garden in ½m. Park on verge or in field N of property.* **Sun 27 May, Sun 29 July, Sun 2 Sept (2-6). Adm £5, chd free. Home-made teas.**

1½ acre garden designed and constructed by current owners. An exceptional range of rare, unusual and architectural plants incl National Collection of Eucalyptus. Dramatic foliage plants from around the world, see plants you have never seen before! Flowering shrubs in May/June; perennials in July; bananas, tree ferns, cannas, gingers, palms dominate in Sept; and streams and ponds, plus an extensive range of planters complete the display. Visitors are welcome to explore the 20 acre meadow and ½m of Meon River frontage attached to the garden. Extra big plant sale of the exotic and rare on Sun 3 Sept. Garden fully accessible by wheelchair, reserved parking.

NPC

71 MERDON MANOR

Merdon Castle Lane, Hursley, Winchester, SO21 2JJ. Mr & Mrs J C Smith, 01962 775215, vronk@fastmail.com. *5m SW of Winchester. From A3090 Winchester to Romsey road, turn R at Standon, onto Merdon Castle Lane. Proceed for 1¼ m. Entrance on R between 2 curving brick walls.* **Sun 8 July (2-6). Adm £4, chd free. Home-made teas. Visits also by arrangement May to Sept for groups of up to 35 max.**

5 acre country garden surrounded by panoramic views; pond with ducks, damsel flies, dragonflies and water lilies; large wisteria, roses, fruit-bearing lemon trees, extensive lawns, impressive yew hedges and small secret walled garden with fountains. Black Hebridean sheep (St. Kildas). Very tranquil and quiet. All areas are accessible but wheelchairs have to go down the drive to reach the sunken garden where azaleas rhododendrons and camelias grow.

72 MICHAELMAS

2 Old Street, Hill Head, Fareham, PO14 3HU. Ros & Jack Wilson, 01329 662593, jazzjack00@gmail.com. *4½m S of Fareham. From Fareham follow signs to Stubbington, then Hill Head. Turn R into Bells Lane. After 1m pass Osborne View Pub on L, next R is Old St.* **Sun 8, Mon 9 July (2-5). Adm £3.50, chd free. Home-made teas. Visits also by arrangement June & July for groups of 10-20.**

Very cheerful, colourful small garden with the wow factor. A variety of tall plants for a tall lady! Many are grown from seed or cuttings. Small vegetable garden, greenhouse, garden room, pot grown vegetables and flowers. Styled in the fashion of a country garden with a wide range of plants attracting many bees and butterflies. As pictured in preface of The Gardens of England book. 1 min walk from beach, 5 mins walk from Titchfield Haven Nature Reserve.

73 MOORE BLATCH

48 High Street, Lymington, SO41 9ZQ. Moore Blatch Solicitors. *Top end of Lymington High St, opp Poundland. Follow signs for Lymington town centre & use High St car parks.* **Sat 18 Aug (9.30-1); Sun 19 Aug (2-5). Adm £3.50, chd free. Tea, coffee & cakes.**

Situated behind this elegant Georgian town house lies a surprising s-facing walled garden of 1 acre. From the raised terrace, enjoy the long vista across the croquet lawn to mature gardens beyond with glimpses of the Isle of Wight. Amusing and varied topiary underplanted with mixed herbaceous. Dahlia bed(s) should be at their peak with rose's repeat flowering and vegetable beds in full production. Attractions close by incl the Lymington Saturday Market and the lively waterfront at the bottom of the High St.

74 22 MOUNT PLEASANT ROAD

Alton, GU34 1NN. Phyllida McCormick. *From A31 take A339 Alton. Follow signs for town centre, past Butts Green on L & garage on R. Next R is Mount Pleasant Rd. Car park on L. No 22 on R. Spaces on road for residents only please.* **Sat 11, Sun 12 Aug (2-5). Combined adm with 42 Whitedown £5, chd free.**

A small garden, a few minutes' walk away from the town centre, yet quiet and peaceful. Three garden rooms are divided by arches and espalier fruit trees. There are perennials, roses and clematis, against a backdrop of mature shrubs and trees, with a covered path of clematis Viticella 'Mary Rose' in August which greets you at the gate.

75 23 NEW BRIGHTON ROAD

Emsworth, PO10 7PR. Lucy Watson & Mike Rogers. *7m W of Chichester, 2m E of Havant. From Emsworth main r'about head N, under the railway bridge, under the flyover & the garden is immed on the LH-side up a slope. Parking at Horndean Recreation Ground (approx 5 min walk).* **Sun 24 June (2-5). Adm £3.50, chd free. Home-made teas. Gluten-free available.**

Variously described as exuberant, chaotic, romantic and restful, this is a garden of surprises. The further you travel down the 250ft gently sloped plot, the more you will discover from ponds to garden rooms, art studio to library. A plantaholic's garden with a heavy emphasis on full shade plantings together with full sun. From Horndean Recreation Ground visitors will have the opportunity to walk through the small but delightfully planted Memorial Garden situated in the corner. No access for wheelchairs. Narrow, gravelled entrance may prove difficult for those with mobility issues.

76 4 NIGHTINGALE MEWS

Locks Heath, Southampton, SO31 6GA. Mrs Kath Stratton. *3m W of Fareham. M27 J9 follow A27 Southampton. Turn L into Hunts Pond Rd, R into Church Rd, 2nd L into St Johns Rd, R into Woodpecker Copse & Nightingale Mews on the L. Please park in Woodpecker Copse.* **Sat 28, Sun 29 July (1-5). Adm £3.50, chd free. Home-made teas.**

Very colourful, steeply sloping terraced garden 65ft x 75ft, established over 7yrs and divided into varied sections incl a shady garden and crystal granite hide. A shelled gazebo at the top has stunning views of the striking planting, sculptures and planted roof garden. A lower patio, with hanging baskets and pots, has seats to see different perspectives of trees and shrubs in the tiered garden. Finalist in the Daily Mail Competition 2017 'Best Garden in England'. Fareham in Bloom gold award for Large Plantsman's Back Garden and cup for overall winner in Large Plantsman's category. Wheelchair access to lower patio only.

77 OAK TREE COTTAGE

Upper Common Road, Pennington, Lymington, SO41 8LD. Sue Kent. *2m NW of Lymington. From N off A337, turn into Sway Rd, 1½m to Wheel Inn. Turn L into Ramley Rd & follow signs. Leave M27 J2 & follow Heavy Lorry Route to avoid traffic in Lyndhurst.* **Sat 7, Sun 8 July (2-5). Adm £4, chd free. Home-made teas.**

This 1½ acre garden has a wealth of surprises, but with continuity. Using a limited palette of plants, with repetition of blue and silver, it flows from one secluded space to another. Designed with a gentle variation of levels and using many trees, contrasting foliage and flowers, one can become delightfully lost.

78 NEW OAKCROFT

98 Titchfield Road, Stubbington, Fareham, PO14 3EL. Ginny & Nick Foy. *2m SW of Fareham. From A27 at Titchfield take the Stubbington road B3334, cross T-lights at Cuckoo Lane, Oakcroft is on the L after 300yds. Parking in side roads. Drop-off point for disabled at garden.* **Sun 17, Mon 18 June, Sun 8, Mon 9 July (2-6). Adm £3, chd free. Home-made teas.**

Nick & Ginny welcome you to their new 150ft x 50ft garden created in just 3 yrs. The restful top garden is primarily hardy perennials in and around a lawn. Shade-loving plants nestle under a large oak tree. A wisteria covered pergola leads to the next area with trees, shrubs and a rockery. Espalier red apple and pear trees lead to a newly evolving fruit and vegetable area. Seafaring themed folly. Wheelchair access to most of the garden.

79 OAKLANDS

Brook, Bramshaw, Nr Lyndhurst, SO43 7HD. Chris & Caroline Biggin, christopherbiggin@yahoo.com. *Via M27 J1 signed Bramshaw & Brook, follow the B3078 for 1m to Brook. Then follow NGS signs.* **Sun 29 Apr (2-5). Adm £3.50, chd free. Sun 3 June (2-5). Combined adm with Waldrons £5, chd free. Home-made teas. Visits also by arrangement Apr to June.**

Oaklands is in an elevated position overlooking paddocks and the New Forest, surrounded by a cottage style garden with mixed borders. Climbers, roses, wisteria and clematis abound, potted grasses and hostas jostle for space with planters on the patios. The vegetable garden, fruit cage and orchard provide produce yr-round. Walk around the orchard, paddock and large pond or sit and admire the view. Some paths have a step, but adjacent lawns allow access to all areas.

80 OLD CAMPS

Newbury Road, Headley, Thatcham, RG19 8LG. Mr & Mrs Adam & Heidi Vetere, 07720 449702, adamvetere465@msn.com. *Please do not use SatNav! Turn off the A339 into Galley Lane & after 100yds turn R into Plumtrees Farm. Follow the concrete road to the car park (signed). Walk 400yds to garden.* **Sat 4, Sun 5 Aug (10-5). Adm £5, chd free. Home-made teas. Visits also by arrangement May to Sept for groups of up to 25 max.**

A breathtaking garden set over an acre, which benefits from panoramic views of Watership Down. Surprises await, ranging from traditional herbaceous borders through desert and prairie planting, an enchanted knot garden, formal potager to exuberant and exotic subtropical schemes; featuring bananas, cannas, hedychiums and much more. Enjoy teas surrounded by Brugmansia and lemons in toning colours. The garden is built on the site of a Roman Camp and Bath House. Partial wheelchair access. Non-disabled WC.

81 THE OLD RECTORY

East Woodhay, Newbury, RG20 0AL. David & Victoria Wormsley. *6m SW of Newbury. Turn off A343 between Newbury & Highclere to Woolton Hill. Turn L to East End, continue ¾m beyond East End. Crossover at T-junction to parking in field. Garden opp St Martin's Church.* **Sun 1, Mon 2 July (2-5). Adm £5, chd free. Home-made teas.**

Classic English country garden of about 2 acres surrounding Regency Gothic former rectory (not open). Tranquil views over parkland, croquet lawn, large walled garden incl formal topiary, roses and unusual perennials, Mediterranean pool garden, wildflower meadow and fruit garden. Gravel drive and some steps.

82 OLD SWAN HOUSE

High Street, Stockbridge, SO20 6EU. Mr Herry Lawford. *9m W of Winchester. The garden is accessed from Recreation Ground Lane which is off the eastern end of the High St, next to the Framing Shop.* **Every Tue 3 July to 24 July (2-5). Adm £4, chd free. Lemonade & biscuits included. Opening with Stockbridge Gardens on Thur 14, Sun 17 June.**

Replanted in 2013/4 this town garden is designed around seven areas defined by the sun at different times of the day. Planting is modern perennial with euphorbias, rosemary and lavender used extensively. Surprise is provided by a grass and gravel garden and a small wildflower meadow. There is an ancient hazel against a brick and flint wall, a loggia hung with creeper, an orchard and a pond.

GROUP OPENING

83 OLD THATCH & THE MILLENNIUM BARN

Sprats Hatch Lane, Winchfield, Hook, RG27 8DD. *3m W of Fleet. 1½m E of Winchfield Station, follow NGS signs. Parking in Sprats Hatch Lane in adjacent field to Old Thatch if dry, or car park at Barley Mow Slipway (opp Barley Mow Pub). Garden is ½m walk via lane or canal towpath, cross at Baseleys Bridge.* **Sun 8 Apr, Sun 1 July, Sun 2 Sept (2-6). Combined adm £4, chd free. Home-made teas. Pimms if hot & mulled wine if cool.**

THE MILLENNIUM BARN

OLD THATCH

Jill Ede, www.old-thatch.co.uk.

Who could resist visiting Old Thatch, a chocolate box thatched cottage, featured on film and TV, a smallholding with a 5 acre garden and woodland alongside the Basingstoke Canal (unfenced). A succession of spring bulbs, a profusion of wild flowers, perennials and home-grown annuals pollinated by our own bees and fertilised by the donkeys, who await your visit. Over 30 named clematis and rose cultivars. Sometimes lambs in April and donkey foals in summer. Children enjoy our garden quiz, adults enjoy tea and home-made cakes. New for 2018, fernery walk. Arrive by narrow boat! Trips on 'John Pinkerton' may stop at Old Thatch on NGS days www.basingstoke-canal.org.uk. Also Accessible Boating shuttle available from Barley Mow wharf approx every 30 mins. Featured in Hampshire Life (2017). Blue badge holders go beyond main car park to second entrance by red telephone box. Paved paths and grass slopes give access to the whole garden.

Meon Orchard

84 ◆ PATRICK'S PATCH

Fairweather's Garden Centre, High Street, Beaulieu, SO42 7YB. 01590 612307, info@ fairweathers.co.uk www.fairweathers.co.uk. *SE of New Forest at head of Beaulieu River. Leave M27 at J2 & follow signs for Beaulieu Motor Museum. Go up High St & park in Fairweather's on LH-side.* **For opening times and information, please phone or visit garden website.**

Model kitchen garden with a full range of vegetables, trained top and soft fruit and herbs. Salads in succession used as an educational project for all ages. Maintained by volunteers, primary school children and a part-time head gardener. Open daily by donation from dawn to dusk.

85 PILLEY HILL COTTAGE

Pilley Hill, Pilley, Lymington, SO41 5QF. Steph & Sandy Glen, 01590 677844, stephglen@hotmail.co.uk. *New Forest. 2m N of Lymington off A337. To avoid traffic delays in Lyndhurst leave M27 at J2 & follow Heavy Lorry Route.* **Sat 17, Sun 18 Mar, Sat 14, Sun 15 Apr (2-5). Adm £3, chd free. Cream teas. Visits also by arrangement Mar & Apr for groups of 20+.**

Pilley Hill Cottage garden changes constantly through the seasons. Entering through the creeper covered lych gate, the garden reveals itself, via winding pathways with surprises around every corner. Dogwood, cornus and ghost bramble supply spring structure. Gnarled fruit trees provide shelter for bulbs, and wildflowers are making a welcome debut. Enjoy a cream tea to complete your visit. Steph will be giving a demonstration of spring bulb propagation at 3pm on each open day, of particular interest to those who may wish to increase their stock of snowdrops. Some slippery slopes. Visitors with wheelchairs have managed our garden, so please phone to discuss.

86 PYLEWELL PARK

South Baddesley, Lymington, SO41 5SJ. Lord Teynham. *Coast road 2m E of Lymington. From Lymington follow signs for Car Ferry to Isle of Wight, continue for 2m to South Baddesley.* **Sun 1 Apr, Sun 27 May (2-5). Adm £4, chd free.**

A large parkland garden laid out in 1890. Enjoy a walk along the extensive informal grass and moss paths, bordered by fine rhododendrons, magnolias, embothriums and cornus. Wild daffodils in bloom at Easter and bluebells in May. Large lakes are bordered by giant gunnera. Distant views of the Isle of Wight across the Solent. Lovely for families and dogs. Bring your own tea or picnic. Old glasshouses and other out buildings are not open to visitors. Wear suitable footwear for muddy areas.

87 NEW REDENHAM PARK HOUSE

Redenham Park, Andover, SP11 9AQ. Lady Olivia Clark, 01264 772511, oliviaclark@redenhampark.co.uk. *Approx 1½m from Weyhill on the A342 Andover to Ludgershall road.* **Tue 18, Wed 19 Sept (2.30-4.30). Adm £5.50, chd free. Home-made teas. Visits also by arrangement in Sept for groups only.**

Redenham Park built in 1784. The garden sits behind the house (not open). The formal rose garden is planted with white flowered roses. Steps lead up to the main herbaceous borders which peak in late summer. A calm green interlude, a gate opens into gardens with espaliered pears, apples, mass of scented roses, shrubs and perennial planting surrounds the swimming pool. A door opens onto a kitchen garden. Featured in Homes & Gardens and House & Gardens magazines.

GROUP OPENING

88 ROMSEY GARDENS

Town Centre, Romsey, SO51 8LD. *All gardens are within walking distance of each other & are clearly signed. Use Lortemore Place public car park (SO51 8LD), free on Sundays & BH.* **Sun 27, Mon 28 May (11-4.30). Combined adm £6, chd free.**

KING JOHN'S GARDEN
Friends of King John's Garden & Test Valley Borough, www.facebook.com/KingJohnsGarden/.

4 MILL LANE
Miss J Flindall, 01794 513926. **Visits also by arrangement May to Sept for groups of 10+. Combined opening with The Old Thatched Cottage.**

THE OLD THATCHED COTTAGE
Genevieve & Derek Langford.

Romsey is a small, unspoilt, historic market town with the majestic C12 Norman Abbey as a backdrop to 4 Mill Lane, a garden described by Joe Swift as 'the best solution for a long thin garden with a view'. King John's Garden, with its fascinating listed C13 house (not open), has all period plants that were available before 1700; it also has an award-winning Victorian garden with a courtyard where tea is served (no dogs, please). The Old Thatched Cottage (C15) has a small garden undergoing further development by new owners; it features a variety of shrubs, lawn, vegetable patch, fruit cordons, rockery and water feature. No wheelchair access at 4 Mill Lane.

89 NEW ROTHERFIELD GREYS

Fernhill Lane, New Milton, BH25 5ST. Dr Peter Clode & Dr David Smith, 07899 895215 / 01425 627679, pclode@gmail.com. *1m N of New Milton Station. Leave New Milton on B3058, on L just N of Ballard School, before junction of B3055.* **Sat 4, Sun 5, Sat 11, Sun 12 Aug (1.30-5). Adm £3.50, chd free. Home-made teas. Visits also by arrangement May to Sept for groups of 12+.**

Sumptuous delights. This 1 acre garden features vibrant borders of salvia, lobelia, dahlia, canna, helenium and rose. A stunning avenue of ancient olives. 3 metre oak pergola, bog gardens oozing with interest, romantic white garden, hosta and begonia gazebo, gushing water features, wildflower meadow and a woodland walk and spotting trail. Come relax, soak up the beauty and enjoy teas in many seating areas. Wheelchair access to most areas. Some gravel paths, summerhouse and gazebo accessed by steps only.

90 ROTHERFIELD PARK

East Tisted, Alton, GU34 3QE. Sir James & Lady Scott. *4m S of Alton on A32. Please turn off your SatNav. Entry from A32 only.* **Sun 6 May (2-5). Adm £5, chd free. Home-made teas. Visitors may picnic in the park from noon.**

Take some ancient ingredients: ice house, lime avenue and walled garden. Add fruit, vegetables, trees and topical topiary (will the rabbit eat the carrot?). Set this 12 acre plot in an early C19 park. Mix in a bluebell wood, a willow chapel and Kim Wilkie's take on an amphitheatre. A good day out for all the family. Retail therapy from top local growers including Charleshurst Farm Nursery, Marcus Dancer and Seale Nursery. Wheelchair access to walled garden.

91 NEW 27 RUSSELL ROAD

Lee-on-the-Solent, PO13 9HR. Kerry & Neil Littleales. *4½m S of Fareham. From Fareham on B3385 follow signs for Lee-on-the-Solent. Continue S past The Bun Penny Pub on L. Turn L after pub into Grove Rd & L again into Russell Rd.* **Sat 16, Sun 17 June, Sat 14, Sun 15 July (2-5.30). Adm £3, chd free. Home-made teas.**

A suburban 40ft x 40ft plot championing the small garden. A variety of shrubs and perennials for shade and sun in a colourful and exuberant style, attracting bees and butterflies, a pond full of newts with hovering damsel flies, a sedum green roof with solitary bee house and a bonsai collection. There are quirky recycled pieces created by the owners and a small craft studio open for viewing and sales. Winner of Best Back Garden & Best Newcomers in Gosport in Bloom 2017.

92 28 ST RONAN'S AVENUE

Southsea, Portsmouth, PO4 0QE. Ian & Liz Craig. *St Ronan's Rd can be found off Albert Rd, Southsea. Follow signs from Albert Rd or Canoe Lake on seafront. Parking in Craneswater School.* **Sun 29 Apr, Sun 3 June (2-6). Adm £3.50, chd free. Home-made teas.**

Town garden 145ft x 25ft, 700 metres from the sea. A mixture of tender, exotic and dry loving plants, along with more traditional incl king protea, bananas, ferns, agaves, echeverias, echium and puya. Wild flower area and wildlife pond. Two different dry gardens showing what can be grown in sandy soil. Recycled items have been used to create sculptures.

93 2 SAMPAN CLOSE

Warsash, Southampton, SO31 9BU. Amanda & Robert Bailey. *4½m W of Fareham. M27 J9 take A27 W, L at Park Gate into Brook Lane by Esso garage. Straight over 3 r'abouts, L at 4th r'about into Schooner Way. Sampan Close, 4th on R. Please park in Schooner Way.* **Sat 12, Sun 13 May (12-4). Adm £3, chd free. Home-made teas.**
Sited on former strawberry fields this compact garden 50ft x 27ft was designed by the owner, an enthusiastic horticulturalist, to give yr-round interest. Inspirational design ideas for tiny plots with perennials, grasses, old roses, trough planting and raised vegetable beds. A small brick rill edges a circle of lawn. A blue, lean-to glasshouse, against a brick garden wall is an attractive feature.

94 SELBORNE

Caker Lane, East Worldham, Alton, GU34 3AE. Brian & Mary Jones, www.worldham.org. *2m SE of Alton. On B3004 at Alton end of the village of East Worldham near The Three Horseshoes Pub. Please note: 'Selborne' is the name of the house, it is not in the village of Selborne. Parking signed.* **Sat 19, Sun 20 May (2-5). Adm £3.50, chd free. Sat 23, Sun 24 June (2-5.30). Combined adm with East Worldham Manor £5, chd free. Sat 14, Sun 15 July, Sat 4, Sun 5, Mon 6 Aug (2-5). Adm £3.50, chd free. Home-made teas in the orchard, with plenty of seating.** Donation to East Worldham Church & Tafara Mission Zimbabwe (Aug).
This much-loved ½ acre mature garden with wide views across farmland provides visitors with surprises around every corner. It features a productive 60 yr old orchard of named varieties, mixed, densely-planted borders, shrubs and climbers, especially clematis. Metal and stone sculptures enhance the borders. Enjoy tea in the dappled shade of the orchard. Summerhouses and conservatory provide shelter. Book stall, garden quizzes for children and a sandpit for small children. Wheelchair access, please note some gravel paths.

95 SHALDEN PARK HOUSE

The Avenue, Shalden, Alton, GU34 4DS. Mr & Mrs Michael Campbell. *4½m NW of Alton. B3349 from Alton or M3 J5 onto B3349. Turn W at Golden Pot Pub marked Herriard, Lasham, Shalden. Entrance ¼m on L. Disabled parking on entry.* **Sun 17 June (2-5). Adm £4.50, chd free. Home-made teas.**
Large 4 acre garden to stroll around with beautiful views. Herbaceous borders incl kitchen walk and rose garden, all with large-scale planting and foliage interest. Pond, arboretum, perfect kitchen garden and garden statuary.

96 ◆ SIR HAROLD HILLIER GARDENS

Jermyns Lane, Ampfield, Romsey, SO51 0QA. Hampshire County Council, 01794 369317, info@hants.gov.uk, www.hilliergardens.org.uk. *2m NE of Romsey. Follow brown tourist signs off M3 J11, or off M27 J2, or A3057 Romsey to Andover. Disabled parking available.* **For opening times and information, please phone, email or visit garden website.**
Established by the plantsman Sir Harold Hillier, this 180 acre garden holds a unique collection of 12,000 different hardy plants from across the world. It incl the famous Winter Garden, Magnolia Avenue, Centenary Border, Himalayan Valley, Gurkha Memorial Garden, Magnolia Avenue, spring woodlands, Hydrangea Walk, fabulous autumn colour, 14 National Collections and over 400 champion trees. The Centenary Border is believed to be the longest double mixed border in the country, a feast from early summer to autumn. Celebrated Winter Garden is one of the largest in Europe. Electric scooters are available for hire (please pre-book). Disabled WC. Guide and hearing dogs only.

NPC

97 SPINDLES

24 Wootton Road, Lee-on-the-Solent, Portsmouth, PO13 9HB. Peter & Angela Arnold, 02393 115181, angelliana62@gmail.com. *6m S of Fareham. Exit A27, turn L onto Gosport Rd A32. At r'about take 2nd exit Newgate Lane B3385. Through 3 r'abouts, turn L into Marine Parade B3333 onto Wootton Rd.* **Sun 10, Mon 11 June (2-5.30). Adm £3, chd free. Home-made teas. Visits also by arrangement June to Aug for groups of 6-30 (day & eve). Art groups welcome.**
Plantaholics' small but exciting garden, only 3 mins from the beach. This creative garden enjoys traditional cottage style planting with a nod to Christopher Lloyd. Topiary plays an important part with cloud pruned box and a cherished plaited bay tree. Many unusual shrubs and trees add to the mix. As seen in Amateur Gardening magazine (Oct 2017).

Donations from the National Garden Scheme enable Perennial to care for horticulturalists

98 ◆ SPINNERS GARDEN

School Lane, Pilley, Lymington, SO41 5QE. Andrew & Vicky Roberts, 07545 432090, info@spinnersgarden.co.uk, www.spinnersgarden.co.uk. *1½m N of Lymington. Follow the brown signs off the A337 between Lymington & Brockenhurst. Also signed off the B3054 Beaulieu to Lymington road. Map available on website.* **For NGS: Sun 29 Apr (2-5). Adm £5, chd free. Cream teas.** For other opening times and information, please phone, email or visit garden website.

Peaceful woodland garden with azaleas, rhododendrons, magnolias, acers and other rare shrubs underplanted with a wide variety of choice woodland and ground cover plants. The garden has been extended over the last 5 yrs and the views opened up over the Lymington valley. More recently, building work has been completed on a new house in the grounds designed to complement the garden. Partial wheelchair access.

99 NEW SPITFIRE HOUSE

Chattis Hill, Stockbridge, SO20 6JS. Tessa & Clive Redshaw. *2m from Stockbridge. Follow the A30 W from Stockbridge for 2m. Go past the Broughton/Chattis Hill Xrds & take the next R towards the Wallops, then next R up private drive to Spitfire House.* **Sat 19 May (2-5). Adm £3.50, chd free. Home-made teas.**

A country garden situated high on chalk downland. On the site of a WW11 Spitfire assembly factory with Spitfire tethering rings still visible. Established garden including vegetables and an orchard, but with several recently developed areas including large wildflower meadow. Wander through woodland to the wild flowers and on across the downs to be rewarded with extensive views. Some areas of gravel and a slope up to wildflower meadow.

100 SPRING POND

Laverstoke, Whitchurch, RG28 7PD. Julian & Carolyn Sheffield, info@springpondgarden.co.uk, www.springpondgarden.co.uk. *1m S of the B3400 in Laverstoke. 8m W of Basingstoke, 3m W of Overton. In Laverstoke turn L opp Bombay Sapphire brick building on B3400 to Micheldever Station. Spring Pond is 1m along road on the L.* **Sun 20 May, Sun 24 June (2-5). Adm £6, chd free. Home-made teas.**

Spring Pond is full of colour coordinated borders, with an abundance of roses and clematis, while hornbeam, yew and box hedges add structure to the garden. There is a pond with a wide variety of marginal plants, an arboretum full of ornamental trees, and a conservatory with Mediterranean and tropical plants. Hardy Garden Plants Nursery is 1m from Spring Pond.

GROUP OPENING

101 STOCKBRIDGE GARDENS

Stockbridge, SO20 6EX. *9m W of Winchester. On A30, at junction of A3057 & B3049. Parking on High St. All gardens on High St & Winton Hill.* **Thur 14, Sun 17 June (2-5.30). Combined adm £7, chd free. Home-made teas on the lawn at St Peter's Church.** Donation to St Peter's Church.

LITTLE WYKE
Mrs Mary Matthews.

THE OLD RECTORY
Robin Colenso & Chrissie Quayle.

OLD SWAN HOUSE
Mr Herry Lawford.
(See separate entry)

SHEPHERDS HOUSE
Kim & Frances Candler.

Stockbridge with its many listed houses, excellent shops and hostelries is on the famous River Test. Four gardens are open this yr offering a variety of styles and character. Little Wyke, next to the Town Hall, has a long mature town garden with mixed borders and fruit trees. The Old Rectory has a partially walled garden with formal pond, fountain and planting near the house, with a stream-side walk through woodland trees, shrubs and bog area. Old Swan House, at the east end of the High St, is a newly designed garden offering mature fish pond with waterlilies, long lawn facing mirror herbaceous borders, sheltering mixed planting and shrub roses, a gravel grass garden and orchard. Shepherds House is a s-facing, ¾ acre garden on rising ground with informal shrubberies, colourful borders, terraces, lawns, ponds, woodland glade and small orchard.

102 TANGLEFOOT

Crawley, Winchester, SO21 2QB. Mr & Mrs F J Fratter, 01962 776243, fred@fratter.co.uk. *5m NW of Winchester. Between B3049 (Winchester - Stockbridge) & A272 (Winchester - Andover). Lane beside Crawley Court (Arqiva). Parking in adjacent mown field.* **Tue 19, Thur 21 June, Tue 17, Thur 19 July (2-5.30). Adm £4, chd free. Soft drinks & biscuits included. Opening with Crawley Gardens on Thur 5, Sun 8 July. Visits also by arrangement June & July.**

Designed and developed by owners since 1976, Tanglefoot's ½ acre garden is a blend of influences, from Monet-inspired rose arch and small wildlife pond to Victorian boundary wall with trained fruit trees. Highlights include a raised lily pond, herbaceous bed (a riot of colour later in the summer), herb wheel, large productive kitchen garden and unusual flowering plants. In contrast to the garden, a 2 acre field with views over the Hampshire countryside has recently been converted into spring and summer wildflower meadows, with mostly native trees and shrubs; it has delighted visitors in recent summers. Watercolour flower paintings. Plants from the garden for sale.

103 TERSTAN

Longstock, Stockbridge, SO20 6DW. Alexander & Penny Burnfield, paburnfield@gmail.com,www. pennyburnfield.wordpress.com. *½m N of Stockbridge. From Stockbridge (A30) turn N to Longstock at bridge. Garden ½m on R.* **Sun 22 Apr, Sun 24 June, Sun 29 July, Sun 2 Sept (2-6). Adm £4, chd free. Home-made teas. Visits also by arrangement Apr to Sept. Coach parking available.**

A garden for all seasons. An acre of rough ground has been developed over 40 yrs into a profusely planted, contemporary cottage garden in peaceful surroundings. There is a constantly changing display in pots, starting with tulips and continuing with many unusual plants. Gravel garden, raised walkway, water features, cutting garden and Showman's Caravan. Art Groups welcome. Live music for NGS openings. Featured on Radio Solent. Wheelchair access, but some gravel paths and steps.

104 THE THATCHED COTTAGE

Church Road, Upper Farringdon, Alton, GU34 3EG. Mr David & Mrs Cally Horton, 01420 587922, dwhorton@btinternet.com. *3m S of Alton off A32. From the A32, take the road to Upper Farringdon. At the top of the hill turn L into Church Rd, follow round corner, past Masseys Folly & we are the 1st house on the R.* **Sun 13 May, Sun 1, Sun 29 July, Sun 19 Aug, Sun 2 Sept (2-5.30). Combined adm with Berry Cottage £6, chd free. Home-made teas at Berry Cottage. Visits also by arrangement May to Sept for groups of 10+.**

The Thatched Cottage (not open) is a Grade II listed C16 cottage in the conservation area, opp the church. Having been somewhat neglected in the past, the 1½ acre garden has been rescued and developed over the past 7 yrs. Featured in Hampshire Life (2017). Fully accessible by wheelchair after a short gravel drive.

105 TYLNEY HALL HOTEL

Ridge Lane, Rotherwick, RG27 9AZ. Elite Hotels, 01256 764881, sales@tylneyhall.com, www.tylneyhall.co.uk. *3m NW of Hook. From M3 J5 via A287 & Newnham, M4 J11 via B3349 & Rotherwick.* **Sun 29 Apr, Sun 10 June, Sun 7 Oct (10-4). Adm £5, chd free. Light refreshments in the Chestnut Suite from 12pm.**

Large garden of 66 acres with extensive woodlands and fine vista being restored with new planting. Fine avenues of wellingtonias; rhododendrons and azaleas, Italian garden, lakes, large water and rock garden, dry stone walls originally designed with assistance of Gertrude Jekyll. Partial wheelchair access.

106 WALDEN

Common Hill, Medstead, Alton, GU34 5LZ. Terri & Neil Burman. *5m S of Alton. From N on A31 turn R into Boyneswood Rd signed Medstead. At small Xrds go R into Roedowns Rd. At T-junction at village green turn L. After church Common Hill is 1st turning on L.* **Fri 15, Sun 17 June (1-5). Adm £3.50, chd free. Home-made teas.**

2 acre sloping garden on chalk, designed by the owners, with panoramic views towards Winchester. Restored 60ft rockery with many alpine species. Early summer colour with hardy perennials, peonies, roses, mature shrubs and fruit trees. Interesting sculptures enhance the garden whilst recycled objects add interest and humour.

The National Garden Scheme is the largest single funder of the Queen's Nursing Institute

107 WALDRONS

Brook, Lyndhurst, SO43 7HE. Mrs J Robinson. *4m N of Lyndhurst. On B3079 1m W from M27 J1. 1st house L past Green Dragon Pub & directly opp Bell Pub.* **Sun 3 June (2-5). Combined adm with Oaklands £5, chd free. Home-made teas.**

A thick high hedge and a selection of trees and shrubs surround our 1 acre garden and C18 New Forest cottage (not open). Raised beds and island beds have been developed for shade and sun loving plants, incl hostas, ferns, alpines, unusual perennials, cottage garden plants, flowering shrubs and wild flowers. A small area of the garden has raised vegetable beds, three compost bins and greenhouse.

108 WALHAMPTON

Beaulieu Road, Walhampton, Lymington, SO41 5ZG. Walhampton School Trust Ltd, 07928 385694, d.hill@walhampton.com. *1m E of Lymington. From Lymington follow signs to Beaulieu (B3054) for 1m & turn R into main entrance at 1st school sign 200yds after top of hill.* **Sun 29 Apr (2-6). Adm £5, chd free. Home-made teas in school dining room. Visits also by arrangement Apr & May for groups of up to 20 max.** Donation to St John's Church, Boldre.

Glorious walks through large C18 landscape garden surrounding magnificent mansion (not open). Visitors will discover three lakes, serpentine canal, climbable prospect mount, period former banana house and orangery, fascinating shell grotto, plantsman's glade and Italian terrace by Peto (c1907), drives and colonnade by Mawson (c1914). Excedrae and sunken garden, rockery, Roman arch, and fountain. Seating. Guided Tours with garden history available on the day. Gravel paths, some slopes.

109 WEIR HOUSE

Abbotstone Road, Old Alresford, SO24 9DG. Mr & Mrs G Hollingbery, 01962 735549, jhollingbery@me.com. *½m N of Alresford. From New Alresford down Broad St (B3046), past Globe Pub, take 1st L signed Abbotstone. Weir House is 1st drive on L. Park in signed field.* **Sun 10 June, Sun 9 Sept (2-5). Adm £5, chd free. Home-made teas. Visits also by arrangement for groups of 10+, but no refreshments available.**

Spectacular riverside garden with sweeping lawn backed by old walls, yew buttresses and mixed perennial beds. Contemporary vegetable garden at its height in Sept. Also incl contemporary garden around pool area, bog garden (at its best in May/June) and wilder walkways through wooded areas. Children welcome. Wheelchair access to most of the garden.

♿ 🐕 ✽ ☕

110 WEST SILCHESTER HALL

Bramley Road, Silchester, RG7 2LX. Mrs Jenny Jowett, 01189 700278, www.jennyjowett.com. *8m N of Basingstoke. 9m S of Reading, off A340 (signed from centre of village).* **Sun 27, Mon 28 May, Sun 8 July, Sun 5 Aug (2-5.30). Adm £4, chd free. Home-made teas. Visits also by arrangement May to Sept for groups of 10+.**

This much loved 2 acre garden is full of fascinating colour combinations inspired by the artist owner, with many spectacular herbaceous borders filled with rare and unusual plants. Pots with half hardies, a wild garden with orchids surrounding a pond, banks of rhododendrons and a kitchen garden. Always a large plant sale with a tempting selection of plants propagated from the garden. Large studio with exhibition of the owner's botanical, landscape and portrait paintings, cards and prints. Near Roman site. Wheelchair access to large part of the garden, gravel drive.

♿ 🐕 ✽ 🚌 ☕

111 WHEATLEY HOUSE

Wheatley Lane, between Binsted & Kingsley, Bordon, GU35 9PA. Mr & Mrs Michael Adlington, 01420 23113, adlingtons36@gmail.com. *4m E of Alton, 5m SW of Farnham. Take A31 to Bentley, follow sign to Bordon. After 2m, R at Jolly Farmer Pub towards Binsted, 1m L & follow signs to Wheatley.* **Sat 18, Sun 19 Aug (1.30-5.30). Adm £5, chd free. Home-made teas. Visits also by arrangement Apr to Oct for groups of 10+. Refreshments on request.**

Situated on a rural hilltop with panoramic views over Alice Holt Forest and the South Downs. The owner admits to being much more of an artist than a plantswoman, but has had great fun creating this 1½ acre garden full of interesting and unusual planting combinations. The sweeping, mixed borders and shrubs are spectacular with colour throughout the season, particularly in late summer. The black and white border, now with bright red accents, is very popular with visitors. Local variety of craft and produce and home-made teas in Old Barn. Wheelchair access with care on lawns, good views of garden and beyond from terrace.

♿ ✽ 🚌 ☕

112 WHISPERS

Chatter Alley, Dogmersfield, RG27 8SS. Mr & Mrs John Selfe, 01252 613568, Sally.selfe@googlemail.com. *3m W of Fleet. Turn N to Dogmersfield off A287 Odiham to Farnham Rd. Turn L by Queen's Head Pub.* **Visits by arrangement June to Aug for groups of 15+. Adm £6, chd free.**

Come and discover new plants in this 2 acre garden of manicured lawns surrounded by large borders of colourful shrubs, trees and long flowering perennials. Wild flower area, water storage system, greenhouse, kitchen garden and living sculptures. Spectacular waterfall cascades over large rock slabs and magically disappears below the terrace. A garden not to be missed. Gravel entrance.

♿ ✽ 🚌

113 42 WHITEDOWN

Alton, GU34 1LU. Jo Carter & Richard Farrington, www.richardfarrington.com. *In Alton, leave The Butts Green on your L, go past stone fountain & L into Borovere Gardens. Go down to T-junction then L into Whitedown, follow road round. 42 is on R. Park on road or at Butts Green.* **Sat 11, Sun 12 Aug (2-5). Combined adm with 22 Mount Pleasant Road £5, chd free. Home-made teas.**

Garden Designer Jo and professional Sculptor Richard have created their small town garden from scratch since 1997. An abundant haven of late flowering planting with creativity around every corner. A pollinator friendly, naturalistic style blends with tropical and traditional planting. Intimate places to sit, numerous stunning sculptures and a hand built wooden studio. Come and see our green roof garden and polytunnel, and have home-made teas in our conservatory tea room. There is inspiration for all! Featured in Hampshire Life and Amateur Gardening magazines.

✽ ☕

114 WICOR PRIMARY SCHOOL COMMUNITY GARDEN

Portchester, Fareham, PO16 9DL. Louise Moreton. *Halfway between Portsmouth & Fareham on A27. Turn S at Seagull Pub r'about into Cornaway Lane, 1st R into Hatherley Drive. Entrance to school is almost opp. Parking on-site, pay at main gate.* **Sun 24 June (12-4). Adm £3.50, chd free. Home-made teas.**

As shown on Gardeners' World in 2017. Beautiful school gardens tended by pupils, staff and community gardeners. Wander along Darwin's path to see the new coastal garden, Jurassic garden, orchard, tropical bed, wildlife areas, allotment and apiary, plus one of the few camera obscuras in the south of England. Wheelchair access to all areas, flat ground.

♿ 🐕 ✽ ☕

115 WILLOWS

Pilley Hill, Boldre, Lymington, SO41 5QF. Elizabeth & Martin Walker, 01590 677415, elizabethwalker13@gmail.com, www.willowsgarden.co.uk. *New Forest. 2m N Lymington off A337. To avoid traffic in Lyndhust, leave M27 at J2 & follow Heavy Lorry Route. Disabled parking at gate.* **Sat 28, Sun 29 July (2-5), also open Fairweather's Nursery. Sat 25, Sun 26, Mon 27 Aug (2-5). Adm £3.50, chd free. Cream teas. Visits also by arrangement July & Aug for groups of 20+. Talk, demonstration, garden tour & cream teas included.**

Golden bamboo greets you as you enter our vibrant front garden. Borders overflow with colourful dahlias, cannas, crocosmias, swathes of heleniums and rudbeckias. It's our Golden Year! Exciting exotics contrast with a jungly mix of gunneras, ferns and giant hostas around the tranquil pond and bog garden. Sunny upper borders have dark leaved dahlias with billowing grasses and interesting topiary. Willows is holding Dahlia Demo Days on Sat 25, Sun 26 and Mon 27 Aug. At 3pm Elizabeth will demonstrate how to plant seeds, take cuttings and plant and separate mature tubers. Also how to over winter plant dahlia tubers in the ground, protect them, dig them up and store if ground is unsuitable. Featured in Amateur Gardener and Country Garden magazines. Wheelchairs usually manage to access all of Willows garden.

116 1 WOGSBARNE COTTAGES

Rotherwick, RG27 9BL. Miss S & Mr R Whistler. *2½m N of Hook. M3 J5, M4 J11, A30 or A33 via B3349.* **Sun 8, Mon 9 July (2-5). Adm £3, chd free. Home-made teas.**

Small traditional cottage garden with a roses around the door look, much photographed for calendars, jigsaws and magazines. Mixed flower beds and borders. Vegetables grown in abundance. Ornamental pond and alpine garden. Views over open countryside to be enjoyed whilst you take afternoon tea on the lawn. The garden has been open for the NGS for more than 30 yrs. Small vintage motorcycle display (weather permitting). Some gravel paths.

117 NEW WOOLTON HOUSE

Woolton Hill, Newbury, RG20 9TZ. Rosamond Brown. *8m S of Newbury. From A343 take road to Woolton Hill, keep L at Xrds. Continue through village, turn L on 1st lane after short downhill & sign to Woolton Hill Sports Ground (Fullers Lane) & immed R on 1st driveway.* **Sun 8, Mon 9 July (2-5.30). Adm £5, chd free. Home-made teas.**

Spectacular, contemporary walled garden set in 4 acres, designed by Pascal Cribier with influence of Mondrian and planted in blues and yellows, interspersed with vegetables. Unique red and green 'tramline' garden. Red courtyard picking garden and new walled sedum and cactus garden. Rose garden with majestic pond. Stunning use of colour and texture.

118 WYCHWOOD

Silchester Road, Little London, Tadley, RG26 5EP. Jenny Inwood. *Please do not park in The Plough car park. Access to Wychwood garden is by rear access. Follow the signs opp Beach's Crescent.* **Wed 11, Wed 18 July (2-5). Adm £3.50, chd free. Light refreshments.**

A joyful garden comprising a stunning water feature with statuary and countless containers brimming with annuals. A tranquil and peaceful atmosphere invites you to sit and enjoy the many seating areas, amidst shrubs, roses and trees. The garden offers gentle access to different levels and habitats, and extends into a natural wooded area with views over the fields beyond. Wheelchair access may be difficult on gravel path and through the woods.

Spitfire House

HEREFORDSHIRE

Herefordshire is essentially an agricultural county, characterised by small market towns, black and white villages, fruit and hop orchards, meandering rivers, wonderful wildlife and spectacular, and often remote, countryside (a must for keen walkers).

As a major region in the Welsh Marches, Herefordshire has a long and diverse history, as indicated by the numerous prehistoric hill forts, medieval castles and ancient battle sites. Exploring the quiet country lanes can lead to many delightful surprises.

For garden enthusiasts the National Garden Scheme offers a range of charming and interesting gardens ranging from informal cottage plots to those of grand houses with parterres, terraces and parkland. Widely contrasting in design and plantings they offer inspiration and innovative ideas.

National collections of Asters and Siberian Iris can be found at The Picton Garden and Aulden Farm, respectively; and, for Galanthophiles, Ivycroft will not disappoint. The numerous specialist nurseries offer tempting collections of rare and unusual plants.

You can always be sure of a warm welcome at a National Garden Scheme open garden.

© Val Corbett

Volunteers

County Organiser
Rowena Gale
01568 615855
rowena.jimgale@btinternet.com

County Treasurer
Angela Mainwaring
01981 251331
angela@millfield.net

Publicity
Sue Evans
01568 614501
s.evans.gp@btinternet.com

Booklet Coordinator
Chris Meakins
01544 370215
christine.meakins@btinternet.com

Booklet Distribution
Andrew Hallett
01981 570401
ar.hallett@gmail.com

Assistant County Organisers
David Hodgson
01531 640622
dhodgson363@btinternet.com

Sue Londesborough
01981 510148
slondesborough138@btinternet.com

Gill Mullin
01989 750593
gill@longorchard.plus.com

Penny Usher
01568 611688
pennyusher@btinternet.com

Left: Kentchurch Court

OPENING DATES

All entries subject to change. For latest information check **www.ngs.org.uk**

Extended openings are shown at the beginning of the month.

Map locator numbers are shown to the right of each garden name.

February

Snowdrop Festival

Thursday 1st
Ivy Croft 24

Thursday 8th
Ivy Croft 24

Tuesday 13th
Coddington Vineyard 15

Thursday 15th
Ivy Croft 24

Friday 16th
Coddington Vineyard 15

Sunday 18th
The Old Corn Mill 34

Thursday 22nd
Ivy Croft 24

March

Sunday 11th
The Old Corn Mill 34

Saturday 17th
◆ Ralph Court Gardens 39

Sunday 18th
◆ The Picton Garden 37
◆ Ralph Court Gardens 39

Monday 26th
◆ Moors Meadow Gardens 29

April

Sunday 1st
The Old Corn Mill 34
◆ Stockton Bury Gardens 48

Monday 2nd
The Old Corn Mill 34

Sunday 8th
Bury Court Farmhouse 11
Lower Hope 27
◆ The Picton Garden 37
NEW Seabournes 43
Whitfield 52

Sunday 15th
The Old Corn Mill 34
NEW Revilo 40

Saturday 21st
Aulden Farm 2
Ivy Croft 24
◆ Ralph Court Gardens 39

Sunday 22nd
Aulden Farm 2
Ivy Croft 24
◆ The Picton Garden 37
◆ Ralph Court Gardens 39
Woodview 56

Monday 23rd
◆ Moors Meadow Gardens 29

Sunday 29th
Hill House Farm 22
The Old Corn Mill 34

May

Every Tuesday and Wednesday from Tuesday 29th
Church Cottage 14

Every Tuesday and Thursday from Tuesday 22nd
Windsor Cottage 54

Sunday 6th
◆ The Picton Garden 37
Southbourne & Pine Lodge 46

Monday 7th
◆ Bryan's Ground 9
Coddington Vineyard 15
Southbourne & Pine Lodge 46

Sunday 13th
NEW Broxwood Court 8
The Old Corn Mill 34

Sunday 20th
Hill House Farm 22
Lower Hope 27

Monday 21st
◆ Moors Meadow Gardens 29

Thursday 24th
◆ The Picton Garden 37

Saturday 26th
NEW Ardendale 1
Stapleton Castle Court Garden 47

Sunday 27th
NEW Ardendale 1
Aulden Farm 2
Ivy Croft 24
The Old Corn Mill 34
Perrycroft 36
Sheepcote 44
Stapleton Castle Court Garden 47

Monday 28th
Aulden Farm 2
Ivy Croft 24
The Old Corn Mill 34
Stapleton Castle Court Garden 47

June

Every Tuesday and Wednesday
Church Cottage 14

Every day from Monday 11th to Friday 15th
Newport House 31

Every Tuesday and Thursday to Thursday 14th
Windsor Cottage 54

Every Tuesday and Thursday from Tuesday 26th
Windsor Cottage 54

Friday 1st
Rhodds Farm 41

Festival Weekend

Saturday 2nd
Bredenbury, Mistletoe Lodge 4
Bredenbury, The Coppice 5
Rhodds Farm 41
NEW Seabournes 43

Sunday 3rd
Bredenbury, Mistletoe Lodge 4
Bredenbury, The Coppice 5
Kentchurch Court 25

Friday 8th
Lower House Farm 28

Saturday 9th
Bredenbury, Mistletoe Lodge 4
Bredenbury, The Coppice 5
Lower House Farm 28

Sunday 10th
Bredenbury, Mistletoe Lodge 4
Bredenbury, The Coppice 5
The Brooks 7
◆ Caves Folly Nurseries 13
Mulberry House 30
Old Colwall House 33
The Vine 50
Whitfield 52

Friday 15th
◆ Hereford Cathedral Gardens 21

Saturday 16th
Wolferlow House 55

Sunday 17th
Darkley 16
Hill House Farm 22
◆ The Picton Garden 37
NEW Revilo 40

Tuesday 19th
NEW Hillcroft 23

Wednesday 20th
NEW Hillcroft 23

Thursday 21st
NEW Hillcroft 23

Saturday 23rd
◆ The Garden of the Wind at Middle Hunt House 17
NEW Newton St Margarets Gardens 32
◆ Ralph Court Gardens 39

Sunday 24th
◆ The Garden of the Wind at Middle Hunt House 17
NEW Newton St Margarets Gardens 32
◆ Ralph Court Gardens 39

Monday 25th
◆ Moors Meadow Gardens 29

Saturday 30th
Byecroft 12

July

Every Tuesday and Wednesday
Church Cottage 14

Every Tuesday and Thursday to Thursday 19th
Windsor Cottage 54

Sunday 1st
Byecroft 12

Friday 6th
Rhodds Farm 41

Saturday 7th
Hill House Farm 22
Rhodds Farm 41
Ross-on-Wye Community Garden 42

Sunday 8th
Hill House Farm 22
Lower Hope 27
Woodview 56

Saturday 14th
NEW Herbfarmacy 20
◆ Ralph Court Gardens 39

Sunday 15th
Burnt House Farm 10
Kentchurch Court 25
◆ Ralph Court Gardens 39

Thursday 19th
NEW Herbfarmacy 20

Sunday 22nd
Burnt House Farm 10
Woodview 56

Sunday 29th
◆ The Picton Garden 37

Monday 30th
◆ Moors Meadow Gardens 29

Tuesday 31st
Windsor Cottage 54

August

Every Tuesday and Wednesday to Wednesday 15th
Church Cottage 14

Every Tuesday and Thursday to Thursday 23rd
Windsor Cottage 54

Sunday 5th
Aulden Farm 2
Ivy Croft 24

Wednesday 8th
◆ The Picton Garden 37

Sunday 12th
Hill House Farm 22

Sunday 19th
◆ The Picton Garden 37

Saturday 25th
◆ The Garden of the Wind at Middle Hunt House 17

Sunday 26th
◆ The Garden of the Wind at Middle Hunt House 17

Monday 27th
◆ The Picton Garden 37

September

Sunday 2nd
Brockhampton Cottage 6
NEW Broxwood Court 8
Grendon Court 19

Sunday 9th
The Brooks 7

Sunday 16th
Hill House Farm 22
Lower Hope 27
Wigmore Gardens 53

Monday 17th
◆ The Picton Garden 37

October

Saturday 6th
Southbourne & Pine Lodge 46

Sunday 7th
Southbourne & Pine Lodge 46

Monday 8th
◆ The Picton Garden 37

Saturday 13th
◆ Ralph Court Gardens 39

Sunday 14th
Hill House Farm 22
◆ Ralph Court Gardens 39

Saturday 20th
◆ The Picton Garden 37

Sunday 28th
NEW Seabournes 43

February 2019

Thursday 7th
Ivy Croft 24

Thursday 14th
Ivy Croft 24

Thursday 21st
Ivy Croft 24

Friday 22nd
◆ The Picton Garden 37

Thursday 28th
Ivy Croft 24

By Arrangement

Aulden Farm 2
Bachefield House 3
Bredenbury, Mistletoe Lodge 4
NEW Brighton House, Newton St Margarets Gardens 32
Bury Court Farmhouse 11
Byecroft 12
Church Cottage 14
Coddington Vineyard 15
Grantsfield 18
Grendon Court 19
Hill House Farm 22
Ivy Croft 24
Lawless Hill 26
Lower Hope 27
Newport House 31
Old Colwall House 33
The Old Corn Mill 34
The Old Rectory 35
Perrycroft 36
Poole Cottage 38
Shucknall Court 45
Stapleton Castle Court Garden 47
Upper Tan House 49
Weston Hall 51
Whitfield 52
Windsor Cottage 54
Woodview 56

Ivy Croft

THE GARDENS

1 NEW ARDENDALE

Old Hollow, West Malvern, Great Malvern, WR14 4DY. Mrs Julia Millidge. *½m W of Great Malvern. A449 N from Malvern turn L onto B4232 to W Malvern. Follow signs: turning R, then L, then R at T junction. Car park at W Malvern Playing Field. Garden 50m down lane on L, opp Malvern Outdoor Elements.* **Sat 26, Sun 27 May (1-5). Adm £4, chd free. Home-made teas.**

1½ acre informal country gdn and woodland created over 10 yrs on higher slopes of the Malvern Hills. The steep gradient is terraced with grass paths, banks of mixed shrubs and herbaceous plantings. Fine views to the Malvern Hills. Vegetables, soft fruit and fruit trees as well as beehives! Not suitable for wheelchairs or people with limited mobility. Sensible shoes essential.

2 AULDEN FARM

Aulden, Leominster, HR6 0JT. Alun & Jill Whitehead, 01568 720129, web@auldenfarm.co.uk, www.auldenfarm.co.uk. *4m SW of Leominster. From Leominster take Ivington/Upper Hill rd, ¾m after Ivington church turn R signed Aulden. From A4110 signed Ivington, take 2nd R signed Aulden.* **Sat 21, Sun 22 Apr, Sun 27, Mon 28 May, Sun 5 Aug (2-5.30). Combined adm with Ivy Croft £7. Home-made teas & ice cream. Single garden adm £4. Visits also by arrangement Apr to Sept groups or individuals.**

Informal country garden surrounding old farmhouse, 3 acres planted with wildlife in mind. Emphasis on structure and form, with a hint of quirkiness, a garden to explore with eclectic planting. Irises thrive around a natural pond, shady beds and open borders, seats abound, feels mature but ever evolving. Our own ice cream and home-burnt cakes, Lemon Chisel a speciality! National Collection of Siberian Iris and plant nursery. BBC Gardeners World television with Monty Don.

3 BACHEFIELD HOUSE

Kimbolton, HR6 0EP. Jim & Rowena Gale, 01568 615855, rowena.jimgale@btinternet.com. *3m E of Leominster. Take A4112 off A49 (signed Leysters), after 10yds 1st R (signed Stretford/Hamnish). 1st L to Grantsfield, over Xrds (signed Bache), continue for approx 1m, garden on R 200yds past rd to Gorsty Hill.* **Visits by arrangement individuals and groups (max 25) from mid May - 30 June. Adm £4, chd free. Home-made teas.**

Charming traditional cottage-style garden of 1 acre on gentle hill slope. Beds and borders bulge with beautiful blooms and foliage. Part-walled kitchen and cutting garden, gravel and herbaceous beds, rockery and pond. Good collections of roses, peonies, heritage pinks and irises. Summerhouse with fine views.

4 BREDENBURY, MISTLETOE LODGE

Wacton Lane, Bromyard, HR7 4TF. Jewels Williams Peplow & Mark Peplow, 01885 488029, jewelswilliams@hotmail.co.uk, www.jewelsporcelain.com. *A44 between Bromyard & Leominster. At Bredenbury turn onto Wacton Lane between Three Pines Garage & Barneby Inn. Garden 50yds on L. Drop off for disabled, other parking at Three Pines Garage.* **Sat 2, Sun 3, Sat 9, Sun 10 June (11-5). Combined adm with Bredenbury, The Coppice £5, chd free. Home-made teas, gluten free options available. Single garden adm £3., Visits also by arrangement 4 - 8 June.**

Small but charming, secluded garden, centred around a natural pond with lush planting. 'A tranquil hidden gem.' Complimented by a mixed media art exhibition, 'Coast and Garden'. Home-made cakes, teas and coffee to enjoy in the garden. Suitable for wheelchairs with large wheels for graveled paths.

5 BREDENBURY, THE COPPICE

Wacton Lane, Bromyard, HR7 4TF. Peter & Wendy Kirk. *A44 between Bromyard & Leominster. At Bredenbury turn onto Wacton Lane between Three Pines Garage & Barneby Inn. Garden is 50 yards on L. Disabled drop off at garden. Parking at the Barneby Inn.* **Sat 2, Sun 3, Sat 9, Sun 10 June (11-5). Combined adm with Bredenbury, Mistletoe Lodge £5, chd free. Single garden adm £3. Homemade teas at Mistletoe Lodge.**

In collaboration with and in contrast to Mistletoe Lodge, next door, The Coppice garden is a mature garden with some recent changes by the present owners. The garden is a mixture of perennial borders with mature Japanese acers, a fern garden, koi pond and a natural pond. In the front, a small coppice of white birch trees with woodland plants, and new rhododendron border. Suitable for wheelchairs with large wheels for some gravelled paths and grass.

6 BROCKHAMPTON COTTAGE

Brockhampton, HR1 4TQ. Peter Clay. *8m SW of Hereford. 5m N of Ross-on-Wye on B4224. In Brockhampton take rd signed to church, cont up hill for ½m, after set of farm buildings, driveway on L, over cattle grid. Car park 500yds from garden.* **Sun 2 Sept (1-4). Combined adm with Grendon Court £10, chd free. Single garden adm £6. Teas at Grendon Court.**

Created from scratch in 1999 by the owner and Tom Stuart-Smith, this beautiful hilltop garden looks S and W over miles of unspoilt countryside. On one side a woodland garden and 5 acre wild flower meadow, on the other side a Perry pear orchard and in valley below: lake, stream and arboretum. The extensive borders are planted with drifts of perennials in the modern romantic style. Allow 1hr 30 mins. Picnic parties welcome by the lake . Visit Grendon Court (2 - 5.30) after your visit to us.

7 THE BROOKS

Pontrilas, HR2 0BL.
Marion & Clive Stainton,
www.marionet.co.uk/the_brooks. *12m SW of Hereford. From the A465 Hereford to Abergavenny rd, turn L at Pontrilas onto B4347, take next R, then immediate L signed Orcop & Garway Hill. Garden 1¾m on L.* **Sun 10 June, Sun 9 Sept (2-5). Adm £4, chd free. Home-made teas.**
This 2½ acre Golden Valley garden incl part-walled enclosed vegetable garden and greenhouse (wind/solar-powered), orchard, ornamental, perennial, shade and shrub borders, wildlife pond, evolving arboretum cum coppice, and meadows with stunning views. Surrounding a stone 1684 farmhouse (not open), the garden has mature elements, but much has been created since 2006, with future development plans.

8 NEW BROXWOOD COURT

Broxwood, nr Pembridge, Leominster, HR6 9JJ. Richard Snead-Cox & Mike & Anne Allen. *From Leominster follow signs to Brecon A44/A4112. After approx 8m, just past Weobley turn off, go R to Broxwood/Pembridge. After 2m straight over Xrds to Lyonshall. 500yds on L over cattle grid.* **Sun 13 May, Sun 2 Sept (2-6). Adm £5, chd free. Home-made teas.**
Stunning 29 acre garden and arboretum, designed in 1859 by W. Nesfield for great-grandfather of present owner. Magnificent yew hedges and km long avenue of cedars and Scots pines. Spectacular view of Black Mountains, sweeping lawns, rhododendrons, gentle walks to summer house, chapel and ponds. Rose garden, mixed borders, rill, gazebo and fountain. Peacocks and white doves. Featured in The English Garden. Some gravel, but mostly lawn. Gentle slopes. Disabled WC.

9 ◆ BRYAN'S GROUND

Letchmoor Lane, Stapleton, Presteigne, LD8 2LP. David Wheeler & Simon Dorrell, 01544 260001, simonjdorrell@gmail.com, www.bryansground.co.uk. *12m NW of Leominster. Between Kinsham & Stapleton. At Mortimer's Cross take B4362 signed Presteigne. At Combe, follow signs. SATNAV is misleading. Coaches: please pre-book.* **For NGS: Mon 7 May (2-5). Adm £6, chd £2. Home-made teas.** For other opening times and information, please phone, email or visit garden website.
8 acre internationally renowned contemporary reinterpretation of an Arts and Crafts garden dating from 1912, conceived as series of rooms with yew and box topiary, parterres, colour-themed flower and shrub borders, reflecting pools, potager, Edwardian greenhouse, heritage apple orchard, follies. Arboretum of 400 specimen trees and shrubs with wildlife pool beside R Lugg. Home of Hortus, garden journal. Gardenista (on-line). The majority of the garden is accessible by wheelchair, though there are some steps adjoining the terrace.

10 BURNT HOUSE FARM

Ashford Carbonel, Ludlow, SY8 4LD. Julie Alviti. *3m SE Ludlow. Turn L off A49 (Ludlow - Leominster) at Xrds 0.25m past B4361 signed Ashford Carbonel, over 2 bridges, over 1st Xrds, R at 2nd Xrds signed Little Hereford, Tenbury. Large white FM house on L in 0.75m.* **Sun 15, Sun 22 July (2-6). Adm £4, chd free. Home-made teas.**
¾ acre farmhouse garden developed over 35 years by current owners. Lawn with mixed borders, patio, pond and gazebo. Garden rooms including vegetable garden with raised beds, cut flower garden, parterre and gravel garden. Extensively planted stream and pond, orchard, cottage garden with traditional potting shed and vintage tools. Unusual plants, 60+ clematis. Many seating areas. Some deep water. Indoor tearoom. House Beautiful Magazine Glorious Gardens winner - large garden category. Some steps.

Brockhampton Cottage

11 BURY COURT FARMHOUSE

Ford Street, Wigmore, Leominster, HR6 9UP. Margaret & Les Barclay, 01568 770618, l.barclay@zoho.com. *10m from Leominster, 10m from Knighton, 8m from Ludlow. On A4110 from Leominster, at Wigmore turn R just after shop & garage. Follow signs to parking and garden.* **Sun 8 Apr (2-5). Adm £4, chd free. Home-made teas. Opening with Wigmore Gardens on Sun 16 Sept. Visits also by arrangement Feb to Oct individual visitors and groups up to 50.**

¾ acre garden, 'rescued' since 1997, surrounds the 1840's stone farmhouse (not open). The courtyard contains a pond, mixed borders, fruit trees and shrubs, with steps up to a terrace which leads to lawn and vegetable plot. The main garden (semi-walled) is on two levels with mixed borders, greenhouse, pond, mini-orchard with daffodils in spring, and wildlife areas. Year-round colour. Massive new plantings of spring bulbs for 2018. Mostly accessible for wheelchairs by arrangement.

12 BYECROFT

Welshman's Lane, Bircher, Leominster, HR6 0BP. Sue & Peter Russell, 01568 780559, peterandsuerussell@btinternet.com, www.byecroft.weebly.com. *6m N of Leominster. From Leominster take B4361. Turn L at T-junction with B4362. ¼m beyond Bircher village turn R at war memorial into Welshman's Lane, signed Bircher Common.* **Sat 30 June, Sun 1 July (1.30-5.30). Adm £4, chd free. Home-made teas. Visits also by arrangement May & June for groups of 10+.**

Developed almost from scratch over 10 yrs, Byecroft is a compact garden stuffed full of interesting plants, many grown from seed. Herbaceous borders, pergola with old roses, formal pond, lots of pots, vegetable garden, wild flower orchard, soft fruit area. Sue and Peter are retired nursery owners and hope to offer a good sales table. Most areas accessible with assistance. Some small steps.

13 ◆ CAVES FOLLY NURSERIES

Evendine Lane, Colwall, WR13 6DX. Wil Leaper & Bridget Evans, 01684 540631, bridget@cavesfolly.com, www.cavesfolly.com. *1¼m NE of Ledbury. B4218. Between Malvern & Ledbury. Evendine Lane, off Colwall Green.* **For NGS: Sun 10 June (2-5). Adm £3, chd free. Home-made teas.** For other opening times and information, please phone, email or visit garden website.

Organic nursery and display gardens. Specialist growers of cottage garden plants herbs and alpines. All plants are grown in peat free organic compost. This is not a manicured garden! It is full of drifts of colour and wild flowers and a haven for wildlife.

14 CHURCH COTTAGE

Hentland, Ross-on-Wye, HR9 6LP. Sue Emms & Pete Weller, 01989 730222, sue.emms@mac.com, www.wyegardensbydesign.com. *6m from Ross-on-Wye. A49 from Ross. R turn Hentland/Kynaston. Sharp R to St Dubricius at bottom of hill. Narrow lane with few passing places - please take care. Unsuitable for motor homes. We are just before church.* **Every Tue and Wed 29 May to 15 Aug (2-5). Adm £3, chd free. Home-made teas. Visits also by arrangement June to Aug groups welcome.**

Garden designer and plantswoman's ½ acre evolving garden packed with plants, many unusual varieties mixed with old favourites, providing interest over a long period. Wildlife pond, rose garden, potager, mixed borders, white terrace, gravel garden. Interesting plant combinations and design ideas to inspire.

15 CODDINGTON VINEYARD

Coddington, HR8 1JJ. Sharon & Peter Maiden, 01531 641817, sgmaiden@yahoo.co.uk, www.coddingtonvineyard.co.uk. *4m NE of Ledbury. From Ledbury to Malvern A449, follow brown signs to Coddington Vineyard.* **Tue 13, Fri 16 Feb (11-3); Mon 7 May (2-4.30). Adm £4.50, chd free. Home-made teas. Visits also by arrangement Feb to Sept open for groups of 10+.**

5 acres incl 2 acre vineyard, listed farmhouse, threshing barn and cider mill. Garden with terraces, wild flower meadow, woodland with massed spring bulbs, large pond with wildlife, stream garden with masses of primula and hosta. Hellebores and snowdrops, hamamelis and parottia. Azaleas followed by roses and perennials. Lots to see all year.

16 DARKLEY

Norton Canon, Hereford, HR4 7BT. Mrs Samantha Maskery. *10m NW of Hereford. On A480 towards Kington. Take 1st L after Norton Canon sign. Towards Norton Wood. Gdn 1¼ m from the turning on L.* **Sun 17 June (12-5). Adm £4, chd free. Light refreshments all day.**

Beautiful 3½ acre garden with stunning views over countryside. Collection of clematis and roses. Herbaceous borders incl specimen trees and shrubs. Decorative walled, gravel, herb and kitchen gardens. Wildlife pond and flower meadows. Some gravel paths.

17 ◆ THE GARDEN OF THE WIND AT MIDDLE HUNT HOUSE

Middle Hunt House, Walterstone, Hereford, HR2 0DY. Rupert & Antoinetta Otten, 01873 860359, rupertotten@gmail.com, www.gardenofthewind.co.uk. *4m W of Pandy, 17m S of Hereford, 10m N of Abergavenny. A465 to Pandy, West towards Longtown, turn R at Clodock Church, 1m on R. Disabled parking available.* **For NGS: Sat 23, Sun 24 June, Sat**

25, Sun 26 Aug (2-5.30). Adm £5, chd free. Home-made teas.
For other opening times and information, please phone, email or visit garden website.
A modern garden using swathes of herbaceous plants and grasses, surrounding stone built farmhouse and barns with stunning views of the Black Mountains. Special features: rose border, hornbeam alley, formal parterre and bespoke water rill and fountains, William Pye water feature, architecturally designed greenhouse complex, vegetable gardens. Carved lettering and sculpture throughout, garden covering about 4 acres. Garden seating throughout the site on stone, wood and metal benches including some with carved lettering. The garden is also the home of part of the National Collection of Contemporary Memorial Art on loan from the Lettering and Commemorative Arts Trust. Partial wheelchair access.

18 GRANTSFIELD

nr Kimbolton, Leominster, HR6 0ET. Mrs R Polley, 01568 613338. *3m NE of Leominster. A49 N from Leominster, at A4112 turn R, then immed R (signed Hamnish), 1st L, then R at Xrds. Garden on R after ½m.* **Visits by arrangement Apr to Sept individuals and groups (max 30). Adm £4, chd free. Home-made teas.**
Large, informal country garden in contrasting styles surrounding old stone farmhouse. Wide variety of unusual plants, mature specimen trees and shrubs, old roses, climbers, herbaceous borders, superb views. 1½ acre orchard and kitchen garden. Spring bulbs. Flat from field gate entrance.

19 GRENDON COURT

Upton Bishop, Ross on Wye, Herefordshire, HR9 7QP. Mark & Kate Edwards, 07971 339126, kate@grendoncourt.co.uk. *3m NE of Ross-on-Wye. M50, J3 . Hereford B4224 Moody Cow PH, 1m open gate on R. From Ross. A40, B449, Xrds R Upton Bishop. 100yds on L by cream cottage.* **Sun 2 Sept (2-5.30). Combined adm with Brockhampton Cottage £10, chd free. Single garden adm £5. Home made teas in the barn. Visits also by arrangement June to Oct, lunch provided for groups up to 65. Private functions.**
A contemporary garden designed by Tom Stuart-Smith. Planted on 2 levels, a clever collection of mass-planted perennials and grasses of different heights, textures and colour give all-yr interest. The upper walled garden with a sea of flowering grasses makes a highlight. Views of the new pond and valley walk. Visit Brockhampton Cottage (1-4) before you visit us (picnic in parking field). Please note that Grendon Court garden does not open until 2pm. Wheelchair access possible.

20 NEW HERBFARMACY

The Field, Eardisley, Hereford, HR3 6NB. Paul Richards, www.herbfarmacy.com. *11m NW of Hereford. Take A338 from Hereford, turn onto A4112 to Leominster, then A4111 to Eardisley. In Eardisley turn L off A4111 by Tram Inn & turn R 3 times. Farm is at end of No Through Road on L.* **Sat 14, Thur 19 July (10-4). Adm £5, chd free. Home-made teas.**
A 4 acre organic herb farm overlooking the Wye valley with views to the Black Mountains. Featured on BBC Countryfile, crops are grown for use in herbal skincare and medicinal products. Colourful plots of Echinacea, Marshmallow, Mullein (Verbascum) and Calendula will be on show as well as displays on making products. Refreshments will be available along with a shop selling Herbfarmacy products. Wheelchair Access possible when dry with assistance but some ground rough and some slopes.

21 ◆ HEREFORD CATHEDRAL GARDENS

Hereford, HR1 2NG. Dean of Hereford Cathedral, 01432 374202, visits@herefordcathedral.org, www.herefordcathedral.org. *Centre of Hereford. Approach rds to the Cathedral are signed. Tours leave from information desk in the cathedral building or as directed.* **For NGS: Fri 15 June (10-4). Adm £5, chd free. Light refreshments in Cathedral's Cloister Café.**
For other opening times and information, please phone, email or visit garden website.
Guided tours of historic award winning gardens which won 2 top awards in 'It's Your Neighbourhood 2012 &13'. The tour incl: courtyard garden; an atmospheric cloisters garden enclosed by C15 buildings; the Vicar's Choral garden; the Dean's garden; and 2 acre Bishop's garden with fine trees, vegetable and cutting garden, outdoor chapel for meditation in floral settiing, leading to the R Wye. Collection of plants with ecclesiastical connections in College Garden. For Open Day please see website:. Featured in Country Life magazine and BBC 'Escape to the Country' programme. Partial wheelchair access.

The National Garden Scheme is committed to helping unpaid carers

22 HILL HOUSE FARM

Knighton, LD7 1NA. Simon & Caroline Gourlay, 01547 528542, simongourlay@btinternet.com, www.hillhousefarmgarden.com. *4m SE of Knighton. S of A4113 via Knighton (Llanshay Lane, 4m) or Bucknell (Reeves Lane, 3m).* **Sun 29 Apr, Sun 20 May, Sun 17 June (2-5). Light refreshments. Sat 7, Sun 8 July (2-5). Home-made teas. Sun 12 Aug, Sun 16 Sept, Sun 14 Oct (2-5). Light refreshments. Adm £5, chd free. Visits also by arrangement Apr to Oct home made teas only on July 7/8. Self service on other days.**

5 acre south facing hillside garden developed over past 40 years with magnificent views over unspoilt countryside. Some herbaceous around the house with extensive lawns and mown paths surrounded by roses, shrubs and specimen trees leading to the half acre Oak Pool 200ft below house. Transport available from bottom of garden if required. A very peaceful garden. Only one other dwelling is visible at a distance of half a mile - from part of the garden. Otherwise it is surrounded by pastureland with distant views of the Black Mountains. : limited to the top of the garden. Please park at the side of the house.

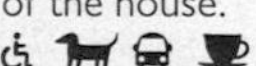

23 NEW HILLCROFT

Coombes Moor, Presteigne, LD8 2HY. Liz O'Rourke & Michael Clarke. *North Herefordshire. 10m from Leominster. Coombes Moor is under Wapley Hill on the B4362, between Shobdon & Presteigne. The house is on R just beyond Byton Cross when heading east.* **Tue 19, Wed 20, Thur 21 June (11-5.30). Adm £4, chd free. Tea, coffee and cold drinks along with delicious home-made cakes are available and can be enjoyed in the garden or the conservatory.**

The garden is part of a 5 acre site on the lower slopes of Wapley Hill in the beautiful Lugg Valley. The highlight in mid summer is the romantic Rose Walk, combining sixty roses with mixed herbaceous planting set in an old cider apple orchard. In addition to the garden area around the house, there is a secret garden, wild flower meadow and a vegetable and fruit area.

24 IVY CROFT

Ivington Green, Leominster, HR6 0JN. Sue & Roger Norman, 01568 720344, ivycroft@homecall.co.uk, www.ivycroftgarden.co.uk. *3m SW of Leominster. From Leominster take Ryelands Rd to Ivington. Turn R at church, garden ¾m on R. From A4110 signed Ivington, garden 1¾m on L.* **Every Thur 1 Feb to 22 Feb (9-4). Adm £4, chd free. Sat 21, Sun 22 Apr, Sun 27, Mon 28 May, Sun 5 Aug (2-5.30). Combined adm with Aulden Farm £7, chd free. Home-made teas. Single garden adm £4. 2019: Every Thur 7 to 28 Feb. Visits also by arrangement all year.**

A maturing rural garden with areas of meadow, wood and orchard, blending with countryside and providing habitat for wildlife. The cottage is surrounded by borders, raised beds, trained pears and containers giving all year interest. Paths lead to the wider garden including herbaceous borders, vegetable garden framed with espalier apples and seasonal pond with willows, ferns and grasses. Snowdrops. Featured in Sunday Telegraph and Country Homes and Interiors. Partial wheelchair access.

25 KENTCHURCH COURT

Pontrilas, HR2 0DB. Mrs Jan Lucas-Scudamore, 01981 240228, jan@kentchurchcourt.co.uk, www.kentchurchcourt.co.uk. *12m SW of Hereford. From Hereford A465 towards Abergavanny, at Pontrilas turn L signed Kentchurch. After 2m fork L, after Bridge Inn. Garden opp church.* **Sun 3 June, Sun 15 July (11-5). Adm £5, chd free. Home-made teas.**

Kentchurch Court is sited close to the Welsh border. The large stately home dates to C11 and has been in the Scudamore family for over 1000yrs The deer-park surrounding the house dates back to the Knights Hospitallers of Dinmore and lies at the heart of an estate of over 5000 acres. Historical characters associated with the house incl Welsh hero Owain Glendower, whose daughter married Sir John Scudamore. The house was modernised by John Nash in 1795. First opened for NGS in 1927. Formal rose garden, traditional vegetable garden redesigned with colour, scent and easy access. Walled garden and herbaceous borders, rhododendrons and wild

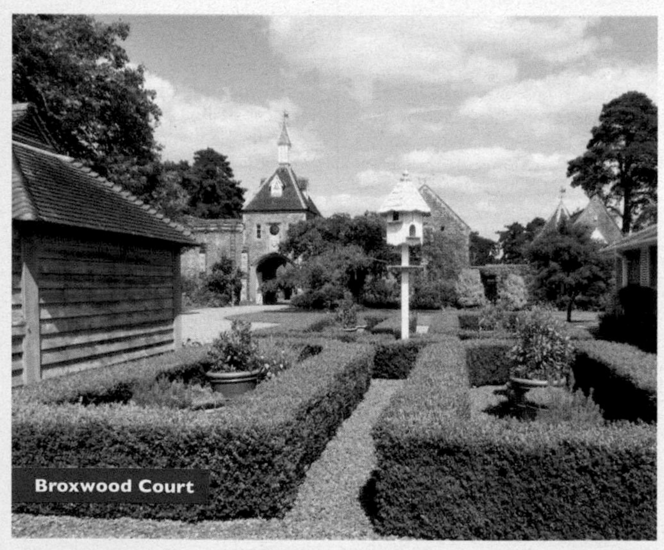

Broxwood Court

flower walk. Deer-park and ancient woodland. Extensive collection of mature trees and shrubs. Stream with habitat for spawning trout. Gravel (shallow), some slopes.

26 LAWLESS HILL

Sellack, Ross-on-Wye, HR9 6QP. Katalin & Keith Meehan, 07595 678837, Lawlesshill@gmail.com, www.facebook.com/Lawless-Hill-315093135189525. *4m NW of Ross-on-Wye. Western end of M50. On A49 to Hereford, take 2nd R, signed Sellack. After 2m, turn R by white house, to Sellack church. At next church sign, turn L. Garden halfway down lane, before church.* **Visits by arrangement Mar to Oct individuals and small groups welcome. Adm £5, chd free. Teas, coffees and cakes available upon request..**

Modernist Japanese-influenced garden with dramatic views over R Wye. Collection of 'rooms' sculpted from the steep hillside using network of natural stone walls and huge rocks. Among exotic and unusual plantings, natural ponds are held within the terracing, forming waterfalls between them. Due to steep steps and stepping stones by open water, the garden is unsuitable for the less mobile and young children. - magical views overlooking waterfall and the river Wye - infinity pond offers great photographic opportunities - cloud shaped pines and taxus trees from Japan - new zen meditation / gravel garden. - Garden featured in Historic Gardens of Herefordshire by Timothy Mowl and Jane Bradney - Amateur gardening.

27 LOWER HOPE

Lower Hope Estate, Ullingswick, Hereford, HR1 3JF. Mr & Mrs Clive Richards, 01432 820557, cliverichards@crco.co.uk, www.lowerhopegardens.co.uk. *5m S of Bromyard. A465 N from Hereford, after 6m turn L at Burley Gate onto A417 towards Leominster. After approx 2m turn R to Lower Hope. After ½m garden on L. Disabled parking available.* **Sun 8 Apr, Sun 20 May, Sun 8 July, Sun 16 Sept (2-5). Adm £6, chd £1. Tea and cakes. Visits also by arrangement Apr to Sept for private parties of 20+, only in week following each NGS open day.**

Outstanding 5 acre garden with wonderful seasonal variations. Impeccable lawns with herbaceous borders, rose gardens, white garden, Mediterranean, Italian and Japanese gardens. Natural streams, man-made waterfalls, bog gardens. Woodland with azaleas and rhododendrons with lime avenue to lake with wild flowers and bulbs. Glasshouses with exotic plants and breeding butterflies. Prizewinning Hereford cattle and Suffolk sheep. to most areas.

Ardendale

28 LOWER HOUSE FARM

Vine Lane, Sutton, Tenbury Wells, WR15 8RL. Mrs Anne Durstan Smith, 01885 410233, www.kyre-equestrian.co.uk. *3m SE of Tenbury Wells; 8m NW of Bromyard. From Tenbury take A4214 to Bromyard. After approx 3m turn R into Vine Lane, then R fork to Lower House Farm.* **Fri 8, Sat 9 June (2-6). Adm £3.50, chd free. Home-made teas.**

Award-winning country garden surrounding C16 farm-house (not open) on working farm. Herbaceous borders, roses, box-parterre, productive kitchen and cutting garden, spring garden, ha-ha allowing wonderful views. Wildlife pond and children's activities in adjoining field. Walkers can enjoy numerous footpaths across the farm land. Home to Kyre Equestrian Centre with access to safe rides and riding events.

29 ◆ MOORS MEADOW GARDENS

Collington, Bromyard, HR7 4LZ. Ros Bissell, 01885 410318/07812 041179, moorsmeadow@hotmail.co.uk, www.moorsmeadow.co.uk. *4m N of Bromyard, on B4214. ½m up lane follow yellow arrows.* **For NGS: Mon 26 Mar, 23 Apr, 21 May, 25 June, 30 July (11-5). Adm £6.50, chd £1.50.** For other opening times and information, please phone, email or visit garden website.

Gaining international recognition for its phenomenal range of wildlife and rarely seen plant species, this inspirational 7-acre organic hillside garden is a 'must see'. Full of peace, secret corners and intriguing features and sculptures with fernery, grass garden, extensive shrubberies, herbaceous beds, meadow, dingle, pools and kitchen garden. Resident Blacksmith. Huge range of unusual and rarely seen plants from around the world. Unique home-crafted sculptures.

30 MULBERRY HOUSE

Knapp Close, Goodrich, HR9 6JW. Tina & Adrian Barber. *Centre of Goodrich. 5m from Ross on Wye 7m from Monmouth. Close to Goodrich Castle in Wye Valley AONB. Goodrich signed from A40 or take B4234 from Ross on Wye. Park in village & follow signs to the garden.* **Sun 10 June (11-5). Adm £4, chd free. Home-made teas.**

Mulberry House: a delightful rear garden with views out to beautiful listed village buildings. Imaginatively planted and nurtured by a plant lover with an artistic eye. Themed herbaceous borders and areas of shrub planting provide a long season of colour and interest. Roses, peonies and alliums enhance the predominately cottage garden feel. New vegetable garden added in 2017.

31 NEWPORT HOUSE

Almeley, HR3 6LL. David & Jenny Watt, 07754 234903, david.gray510@btinternet.com. *5m S of Kington. 1m from Almeley Church, on rd to Kington. From Kington take A4111 to Hereford. After 4m turn L to Almeley, continue 2m, garden on L.* **Daily Mon 11 June to Fri 15 June (11-5.30). Adm £5, chd free. Home-made teas. Visits also by arrangement May to Sept.**

20 acres of garden, woods and lake (with walks). Formal garden set on 3 terraces with large mixed borders framed by formal hedges, in front of Georgian House (not open). 2½-acre walled organic garden in restoration since 2009.

GROUP OPENING

32 NEW NEWTON ST MARGARETS GARDENS

Newton St. Margarets, Hereford, HR2 0JU. Sue Londesborough. *17m SW of Hereford, 9m SE of Hay-on-Wye. A465 S from Hereford, R onto B4348, then L to Vowchurch & Michaelchurch Escley. After approx. 3m take either 1st or 3rd L turns. Follow yellow signs. From Hay B4348, R to Vowchurch, then as above.* **Sat 23, Sun 24 June (2-6). Combined adm £6, chd free. Home-made teas at Court Y Pella.**

NEW BRIGHTON HOUSE
Sue Londesborough, 01981 510148, slondesborough138@btinternet.com.
Visits also by arrangement Apr to Oct individuals or groups, adm £4.

NEW COURT Y PELLA
Linda Martin and G Lamb, 01981 510152, lindamartin250@gmail.com.

NEW ROCK COTTAGE
Mrs Sue Robinson, 01981 510360, robinsrockcottage@gmail.com, www.rockcottagebandb.co.uk.

Three country gardens with very different styles in the picturesque Herefordshire Golden valley. Brighton House: a plantswoman's garden of just over an acre, divided into several distinct areas crammed with many unusual and interesting plants. Herbaceous borders, ornamental and fruit trees, kitchen garden, two small ponds. The garden is planted to encourage wildlife. Views to the Black Mountains. Children's garden trail and play area. Plants for sale propagated from the garden. Court Y Pella: a south facing 4-acre garden started from scratch in 2013 and still in development. Mixed roses and perennials below the house merging into 2 acres of wildflower meadow with meandering paths. Wildlife pond, stream and over 100 young trees. A large grass sculpture and viewing mound. Dogs welcome.

Rock Cottage: a cottage garden including rose beds, rockery, herbaceous borders, shrubs, small wildlife pond, shady area with ferns and foxgloves and orchard. Plants for sale at Brighton House.

33 OLD COLWALL HOUSE

Old Colwall, Malvern, WR13 6HF. Mr & Mrs Roland Trafford-Roberts, 01684 540618, garden1889@aol.com. *3m NE of Ledbury. From Ledbury, turn L off A449 to Malvern towards Coddington. Signed from 2½m along lane. Signed from Colwall & Bosbury.* **Sun 10 June (2-5). Adm £5, chd free. Home-made teas. Visits also by arrangement, groups of 10+ from mid April - mid October. Children very welcome.**

Early C18 garden on a site owned by the Church till Henry VIII. Walled lawns and terraces on various levels. The heart is the yew walk, a rare survival from the 1700s: 100 yds long, 30ft high, cloud clipped, and with a church aisle-like quality inside. Later centuries have brought a summer house, water garden, and rock gardens. Fine trees, incl enormous veteran yew; fine views. Steep in places.

34 THE OLD CORN MILL

Aston Crews, Ross-on-Wye, HR9 7LW. Mrs Jill Hunter, 01989 750059, www.theoldcornmillgarden.com. *5m E of Ross-on-Wye. A40 Ross to Gloucester. Turn L at T-lights at Lea Xrds onto B4222 signed Newent, Garden ½m on L. Parking for disabled down drive. DO NOT USE THE ABOVE POSTCODE IN YOUR SATNAV - try HR9 7LA.* **Sun 18 Feb, Sun 11 Mar, Sun 1, Mon 2, Sun 15, Sun 29 Apr, Sun 13, Sun 27, Mon 28 May (1-5). Adm £5, chd free. Adm incl tea or coffee and cake. Visits also by arrangement Feb to Oct max 50. Refreshments incl in £5 adm.**
4 acres of woodland, meadows, ponds and streams. A tranquil and relaxed country garden of scents, sights and sounds. Interest all year with drifts of tulips, wild daffodils and common spotted orchids in spring. Good Autumn colour. Pop-up Art Exhibition in house. Featured in Daily Telegraph.

35 THE OLD RECTORY

Thruxton, HR2 9AX. Mr & Mrs Andrew Hallett, 01981 570401, ar.hallett@gmail.com, www.thruxtonrectory.co.uk. *6m SW of Hereford. A465 to Allensmore. At Locks (Shell) garage take B4348 towards Hay-on-Wye. After 1½m turn L towards Abbey Dore & Cockyard. Car park 150yds on L.* **Visits by arrangement May to Sept, min adm £60 if less than 15 people. Adm £4, chd free. Home-made teas.**
With breathtaking views over Herefordshire countryside this four acre garden - two acres formal and two acres paddock with ornamental trees and shrubs, and heritage apples - has been created since 2007. Constantly changing plantsman's garden stocked with unusual perennials and roses, together with woodland borders, gazebo, vegetable parterre, glasshouse and natural pond. Many places to sit and relax. Most plants labelled. Chickens, Mr Reynard permitting. Mainly level with some gravel paths.

36 PERRYCROFT

Jubilee Drive, Upper Colwall, Malvern, WR13 6DN. Gillian & Mark Archer, 07858 393767, gillianarcher@live.co.uk, www.perrycroft.co.uk. *Between Malvern & Ledbury. On B4232 between British Camp & Wyche cutting. Park in Gardiners Quarry pay & display car park on Jubilee Drive, short walk to the garden. No parking at house except for disabled by prior arrangement.* **Sun 27 May (2-5). Adm £5, chd free. Home-made teas. Visits also by arrangement Mar to Dec, closed July and August. For other opening times, please phone, email or visit garden website.**
10-acre garden and woodland on the upper slopes of the Malvern Hills with magnificent views, around an Arts and Crafts house designed by CFA Voysey. Walled formal garden, mixed and herbaceous borders, yew and box hedges and topiary. Natural wild flower meadows, ponds, bog garden, wild and woodland walks. Some steep and uneven paths. Featured in RHS The Garden. This garden is not suitable for wheelchairs, due to steep and uneven grass and gravel paths, and steps.

37 ♦ THE PICTON GARDEN

Old Court Nurseries, Walwyn Road, Colwall, WR13 6QE. Mr & Mrs Paul Picton, 01684 540416, oldcourtnurseries@btinternet.com, www.autumnasters.co.uk. *3m W of Malvern. On B4218 (Walwyn Rd) N of Colwall Stone. Turn off A449 from Ledbury or Malvern onto the B4218 for Colwall.* **For NGS: Sun 18 Mar, Sun 8, Sun 22 Apr, Sun 6, Thur 24 May, Sun 17 June, Sun 29 July, Wed 8, Sun 19, Mon 27 Aug, Mon 17 Sept, Mon 8, Sat 20 Oct (11-5). Adm £3.50, chd free. 2019: Fri 22 Feb.** For other opening times and information, please phone, email or visit garden website.
1½ acres W of Malvern Hills. Bulbs and a multitude of woodland plants in spring. Interesting perennials and shrubs in Aug. In late Sept and early Oct colourful borders display the National Plant Collection of Michaelmas daisies, backed by autumn colouring trees and shrubs. Many unusual plants to be seen, incl bamboos, more than 100 different ferns and acers. Features raised beds and silver garden. National Plant Collection of autumn-flowering asters and an extensive nursery that has been growing them since 1906. Featured on and in Gardeners World, Garden News. Wheelchair access gravel paths but all fairly level, no steps.

NPC

38 POOLE COTTAGE

Coppett Hill, Goodrich, Ross on Wye, HR9 6JH. Jo Ward-Ellison & Roy Smith, 01600 890148, jo@ward-ellison.com, www.herefordshiregarden.wordpress.com. *5m from Ross on Wye, 7m from Monmouth. Above Goodrich Castle in Wye Valley AONB. Goodrich signed from A40 or take B4234 from Ross. From centre of Goodrich follow rd uphill signed Welsh Bicknor & youth hostel. Turn R up narrow steep lane after red phone box.* **Visits by arrangement June to Sept for individuals and groups of up to 20. Parking limited to 5 cars close to garden. Adm £4, chd free. Home-made teas.**
Poole Cottage garden was created from scratch 7 years ago. Home to designer Jo Ward-Ellison, the 2 acre hillside garden has a naturalistic style and a long season of interest which, with many grasses and later flowering perennials, extends into Autumn. Some steep slopes, steps and uneven paths. Features include a pond loved by wildlife, small orchard and a kitchen garden with fabulous views.

Visit a garden and support hospice care in your local community

39 ◆ RALPH COURT GARDENS

Edwyn Ralph, Bromyard, HR7 4LU. Mr & Mrs Morgan, 01885 483225, ralphcourtgardens@aol.com, www.ralphcourtgardens.co.uk. *From Bromyard follow the Tenbury rd for approx 1m. On entering the village of Edwyn Ralph take 1st turning on R towards the church.* **For NGS: Sat 17, Sun 18 Mar, Sat 21, Sun 22 Apr, Sat 23, Sun 24 June, Sat 14, Sun 15 July, Sat 13, Sun 14 Oct (10-5). Adm £9, chd £6. Light refreshments.** For other opening times and information, please phone, email or visit garden website.

12 amazing gardens set in the grounds of a gothic rectory. A family orientated garden with a twist, incorporating an Italian Piazza, an African Jungle, Dragon Pool, Alice in Wonderland and the elves in their conifer forest and new for 2017 'The Monet Garden'. These are just a few of the themes within this stunning garden. Licenced Restaurant overlooks the Malvern Hills. 120 seater Licenced Restaurant offering a good selection of daily specials, delicious Sunday roasts, Afternoon tea and our scrumptious homemade cakes. All areas ramped for wheelchair and pushchair access. Some grass areas, without help can be challenging during wet periods.

♿ ✿ 🚌 ☕

40 NEW REVILO

Wellington, Hereford, HR4 8AZ. Mrs Shirley Edgar. *6m N of Hereford. On A49 from Hereford turn L into Wellington village, pass church on R. Then just after barn on L, turn L up driveway in front of The Harbour, to furthest bungalow.* **Sun 15 Apr, Sun 17 June (2-5). Adm £3.50, chd free. Home-made teas.**

Third of an acre garden surrounding bungalow includes mixed borders, meadow and woodland areas, scented garden, late summer bed, gravelled herb garden and vegetable/fruit garden. Flower arranger's garden. Wheelchair access to all central areas of the garden from the garage side.

♿ 🐕 ✿ ☕

41 RHODDS FARM

Lyonshall, HR5 3LW. Richard & Cary Goode, 01544 340120, cary.goode@russianaeros.com, www.rhoddsfarm.co.uk. *1m E of Kington. From A44 take small turning S just E of Penrhos Farm, 1m E of Kington. Continue 1m, garden straight ahead.* **Fri 1, Sat 2 June, Fri 6, Sat 7 July (11-5). Adm £5, chd free. tea and cake will be available for guests to help themselves in return for a donation.**

The garden began in 2005. The site is challenging with steep banks rising to overhanging woodland but has wonderful views. Formal garden leads to dovecote and through to mixed borders with interest throughout the year. Double herbaceous borders of hot colours, several ponds, new arboretum, woodland planting. See garden website for detailed description. Featured in English Garden House and Garden Country Life.

✿ 🛏 ☕

42 ROSS-ON-WYE COMMUNITY GARDEN

Old Gloucester Rd, Ross-On-Wye, HR9 5PB. Haygrove Ltd. *The garden is situated halfway along Old Gloucester Rd & opp the former Walter Scott School.* **Sat 7 July (10-4). Adm £2.50, chd free.**

The Community Garden is a three and a half acre site in the centre of Ross. The project works mainly with adults with learning disabilities, mental health illnesses, dementia and those who are long term unemployed. Plants are for sale. Half of the site is accessible for those using wheelchairs.

♿ 🐕 ✿

43 NEW SEABOURNES

Fawley, Hereford, HR1 4SP. Karen Birch, 01432 840 217, karen@riverseaholdings.com. *10m from Hereford. 7m from Ross-on-Wye. From Hereford B4224, via Fownhope, on 3.4m, turn R in How Caple. 2.2m, then L to Seabournes. From Ross/M50 take B4224, turn L at How Caple. After 2.2m turn L to Seabournes.* **Sun 8 Apr, Sat 2 June, Sun 28 Oct (11-6). Adm £5, chd £2. Home-made teas.**

10 acre garden on gentle slope on banks of R. Wye. Magnificent mature Magnolia, Acers, Ginko, Katsura and other fine trees and shrubs. Arts and Crafts summerhouse, original A&C garden layout under reconstruction. Ornamental pond with pagoda from Kerala. Woodland walk with views to the river. C12 chapel open. The beauty of the garden is in its setting overlooking the Wye. Romantic but not perfect !

🛏 ☕

44 SHEEPCOTE

Putley, Ledbury, HR8 2RD. Tim & Julie Beaumont. *5m W of Ledbury off the A438 Hereford to Ledbury rd. Passenger drop off; parking 4min walk.* **Sun 27 May (1-5.30). Adm £5, chd free. Home-made teas.**

⅓ acre garden taken in hand from 2011 retaining many quality plants, shrubs and trees from earlier gardeners. Topiary holly, box, hawthorn, privet and yew formalise the varied plantings around the croquet lawn and gravel garden; beds with heathers, azaleas, lavender surrounded by herbaceous perennials and bulbs; pond in shade of ancient apple tree; kitchen garden with raised beds.

✿ ☕

45 SHUCKNALL COURT

Hereford, HR1 4BH. Mrs Cessa Moore, 01432 850230. *5m E of Hereford. On A4103, signed (southerly) Weston Beggard, 5m E of Hereford towards Worcester.* **Visits by arrangement 10 April - 30 June. Adm £5, chd free.**

Tree paeonies in May. Large collection of species, old-fashioned and shrub roses. Mixed borders in old walled farmhouse garden. Wild garden, vegetables and fruit. Himalayan type roses growing into trees, from mid June. Partial wheelchair access.

♿ ✿ 🚌

46 SOUTHBOURNE & PINE LODGE

Dinmore, Hereford, HR1 3JR. Lavinia Sole & Frank Ryding. *8m N of Hereford; 8m S of Leominster. From*

Hereford on A49, turn R at bottom of Dinmore Hill towards Bodenham, gardens 1m on L. From Leominster on A49, L onto A417, 2miles turn right and through Bodenham, following NGS signs to garden. **Sun 6, Mon 7 May, Sat 6, Sun 7 Oct (11-4.30). Adm £5, chd free. Tea/coffee and home-made cakes.**

2 south facing adjacent gardens totalling 4½ acres, opened as one, with panoramic views over Bodenham Lakes to the Black Mountains and Malvern Hills. Southbourne: Steep access to 2 acres of terraced lawns, herbaceous beds, shrubs and developing woodland. Pine Lodge: Goblin Wood is 2½ acres of woodland featuring most of Britain's native trees plus some unusual oaks. Paths wind throughout the site. Steep but surfaced drive to Tea area can be accessed by wheelchair but the majority of the garden is not accessible.

47 STAPLETON CASTLE COURT GARDEN

Stapleton, Presteigne, LD8 2LS. Margaret & Trefor Griffiths, 01544 267327. *2m N of Presteigne. From Presteigne cross Lugg Bridge at bottom of Broad St & continue to Stapleton. Do not turn towards Stapleton but follow signs to garden on R.* **Sat 26, Sun 27, Mon 28 May (2-5.30). Adm £5, chd free. Home-made teas. Visits also by arrangement May to July min group charge £25.**

Situated on a gentle slope overlooked by the remains of Stapleton Castle. The garden, developed over the past 10 yrs by an enthusiastic plants-woman, benefits from considered and colour-themed borders. Guided tour of the castle 2.30 and 3.30 daily. Display of site history incl house ruins, mill pond, mill pit and disused turbine, etc. Wheelchairs not suitable for castle tour.

48 ◆ STOCKTON BURY GARDENS

Kimbolton, HR6 0HA. Raymond G Treasure, 07880 712649, twstocktonbury@outlook.com, www.stocktonbury.co.uk. *2m NE of Leominster. From Leominster to Ludlow on A49 turn R onto A4112. Gardens 300yds on right.* **For NGS: Sun 1 Apr (12-5). Adm £7, chd £3. Home-made teas in Tithe Barn café.** For other opening times and information, please phone, email or visit garden website.

Superb, sheltered 4-acre garden with colour and interest from April until October. Extensive collection of plants, many rare and unusual set amongst medieval buildings. Features pigeon house, tithe barn, grotto, cider press, auricula theatre, pools, ruined chapel and rill, all surrounded by unspoilt countryside. We pride ourselves in offering great plant and gardening advice to our visitors. Café serves coffee, tea, homemade cakes and lunches made from local and seasonal produce open 11am - 4.30pm. Last lunches served at 2.45pm.. Children under 5 free. All plants sold are grown on site. Stockton Bury has a small garden school - all classes to be found at. www.stocktonbury.co.uk.. Featured every fortnight in Amateur Gardening. Listed in top 20 great gardens to visit in summer The Times. The café was listed in top 30 garden cafes in The Telegraph. Partial wheelchair access.

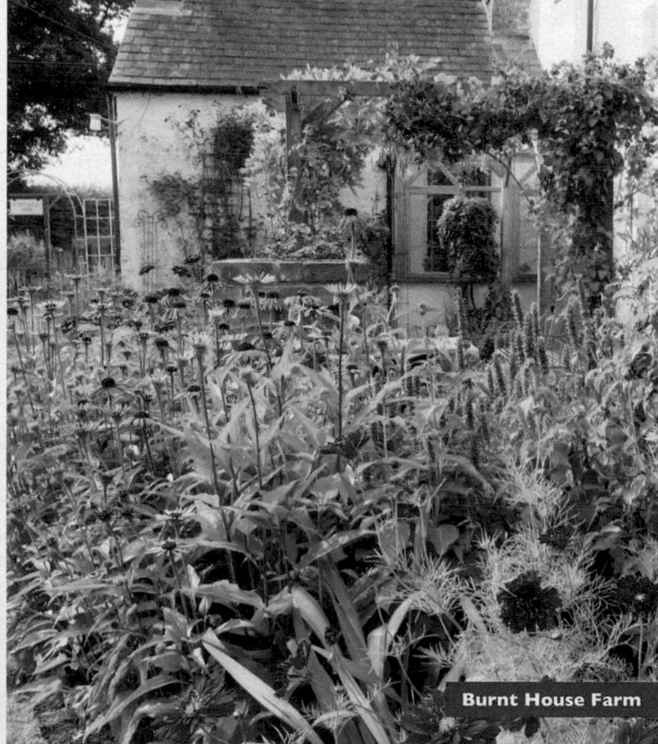

Burnt House Farm

Macmillan and the National Garden Scheme, partners for more than 30 years

49 UPPER TAN HOUSE

Stansbatch, Leominster, HR6 9LJ. James & Caroline Weymouth, 01544 260574, caroline.weymouth@btopenworld.com, www.uppertanhouse.com. *4m W of Pembridge. From A44 in Pembridge take turn signed Shobdon & Presteigne. After exactly 4m & at Stansbatch Nursery turn L down hill. Garden on L 100yds after chapel.* **Visits by arrangement June & July individuals and groups (16 max). Adm £5, chd free. Tea.**
S-facing garden sloping down to Stansbatch brook in idyllic spot. Deep herbaceous borders with informal and unusual planting, pond and bog garden, formal vegetable garden framed by yew hedges and espaliered pears. Reed beds, wild flower meadow with orchids. Diverse wildlife. Featured in Country Life, Country Living and Garden News.

50 THE VINE

Tarrington, HR1 4EX. Richard Price. *Between Hereford & Ledbury on A438. Follow signs from Tarrington Arms on A438. Park as directed. Disabled parking only at house.* **Sun 10 June (2-6). Adm £4.50, chd free. Cream teas.**
Mature, traditional garden in peaceful setting with stunning views of the surrounding countryside. Consisting of various rooms with mixed and herbaceous borders. Secret garden in blue/yellow/white, croquet lawn with C18 summer house, temple garden with ponds, herb and nosegay garden, vegetable/cutting/soft fruit garden around greenhouse on the paddock. Cornus avenues with obelisk and willow bower.

51 WESTON HALL

Weston-under-Penyard, Ross-on-Wye, HR9 7NS. Mr P & Miss L Aldrich-Blake, 01989 562597, aldrichblake@btinternet.com. *1m E of Ross-on-Wye. on A40 towards Gloucester.* **Visits by arrangement Apr to Sept groups only. Light refreshments by request at modest extra cost. Adm £5, chd free.**
6 acres surrounding Elizabethan house (not open). Large walled garden with herbaceous borders, vegetables and fruit, overlooked by Millennium folly. Lawns with both mature and recently planted trees, shrubs with many unusual varieties. Ornamental ponds and lake. 4 generations in the family, but still evolving year on year.

52 WHITFIELD

Wormbridge, HR2 9BA. Mr & Mrs Edward Clive, 01981 570202, tclive@whitfield-hereford.com, www.whitfield-hereford.com. *8m SW of Hereford. The entrance gates are off the A465 Hereford to Abergavenny rd, ½m N of Wormbridge.* **Sun 8 Apr, Sun 10 June (2-5). Adm £5, chd free. Visits also by arrangement Apr to Oct tour & refreshments available for 15+ groups at an extra charge.**
Parkland, wild flowers, ponds, walled garden, many flowering magnolias (species and hybrids), 1780 ginkgo tree, 1½m woodland walk with 1851 grove of coastal redwood trees. Picnic parties welcome. Dogs on leads welcome. Delicious teas. Partial access to wheelchair users, some gravel paths and steep slopes.

GROUP OPENING

53 WIGMORE GARDENS

Wigmore, Leominster, HR6 9UP. *10m from Leominster, 10m from Knighton. On A4110 from Leominster, at Wigmore turn R just after shop & garage into Ford St. Follow signs to parking & gardens.* **Sun 16 Sept (2-5). Combined adm £7, chd free. Home made teas at Bury Court Farmhouse.**

BURY COURT FARMHOUSE
Margaret & Les Barclay.
(See separate entry)

2 BURY COURT PARK
Ivan & Cathy Jones.

The ancient village of Wigmore is known for its C12 castle, home to the Mortimer family and now a 'romantic ruin', and its medieval church. The two gardens are both within 100yds of the parking area. Bury Court Farmhouse: ¾ acre garden, 'rescued' since 1997, surrounds the 1840's stone farmhouse (not open). The courtyard contains a pond, mixed borders, fruit trees and shrubs, with steps up to a terrace which leads to lawn and vegetable plot. The main garden (semi-walled) is on two levels with mixed borders, greenhouse, pond, mini-orchard with daffodils in spring, and wildlife areas. Massive new plantings of spring bulbs for 2018.
2 Bury Court: Small garden with beautiful views. Herbaceous and evergreen shrub borders, pond, bog garden, gravelled areas, patio, pergola with climbers, raised beds with companion planting, greenhouse, arbour, paved seating and sun areas, lawns. Specimen trees, fruit area and watering system. Exhibition of paintings in pastel by Ivan Jones at 2 Bury Court Park.

54 WINDSOR COTTAGE

Dilwyn, Hereford, HR4 8HJ. Jim & Brenda Collins, 01544 319011, jandb.windsor@gmail.com. *6m W of Leominster off A4112. Turn L off A4112 into Dilwyn. From centre of village, with Pub on L, continue for 100yds & turn R. Cottage 400yds on L. Limited parking.* **Every Tue and Thur 22 May to 14 June, 26 June to 19 July, 31 July to 23 Aug (2-5.30). Adm £3.50, chd free. Home-made cakes, ground coffee and choice of teas, Gluten free available. Visits also by arrangement May to Aug groups 10 to 20. Adm £6 incls home-made teas.**
½-acre wildlife friendly garden redesigned over the last 7yrs by present owners. Herbaceous borders, shrub bed, wildlife ponds, fruit and vegetables in raised beds. Extensive use of gravel beds. Wide selection of plants for all year

interest including peonies, irises, hostas and clematis. Exhibition of watercolour and oil paintings. Wildlife friendly garden. Plants chosen to encourage bees, birds, and butterflies. Featured in Amateur Gardening, Garden News, and Herefordshire Society. Gravelled drive giving access to level, lawned garden.

55 WOLFERLOW HOUSE

Wolferlow, nr Upper Sapey, HR7 4QA. Stuart & Jill Smith, 01886 853311, hillheadfm@aol.com, www.holidaylettings.co.uk/rentals/worcester/210892. *5m N of Bromyard. Off B4203 or B4214 between Upper Sapey & Stoke Bliss. Disabled parking at the house.* **Sat 16 June (10.30-5). Adm £4.50, chd free. Home-made teas.**

Surrounded by farmland this former Victorian rectory is set within formal and informal gardens with planting to attract wildlife. Walks through the old orchard and ponds to sit by, space to relax and reflect taking in the views of borrowed landscape. Fruit, vegetable and cutting garden and wild flower meadow. Gravel paths.

56 WOODVIEW

Great Doward, Whitchurch, Ross-on-Wye, HR9 6DZ. Janet & Clive Townsend, 01600 890477, clive.townsend5@homecall.co.uk. *6m SW of Ross-on-Wye, 4m NE of Monmouth. A40 Ross/Mon At Whitchurch follow signs to Symonds Yat west, then to Doward Park campsite. Take forestry rd 1st L garden 2nd L - follow NGS signs.* **Sun 22 Apr, Sun 8, Sun 22 July (1-6). Adm £5, chd free. Home-made teas. Visits also by arrangement Apr to Sept please phone for details.**

Formal and informal gardens approx 4 acres in woodland setting. Herbaceous borders, hosta collection, mature trees, shrubs and seasonal bedding. Gently sloping lawns. Statuary and found sculpture, local limestone, rockwork and pools. Woodland garden, wild flower meadow and indigenous orchids. Collection of vintage tools and memorabilia. Croquet, clock golf and garden games.

Court Y Pella, Newton St Margarets Gardens

HERTFORDSHIRE

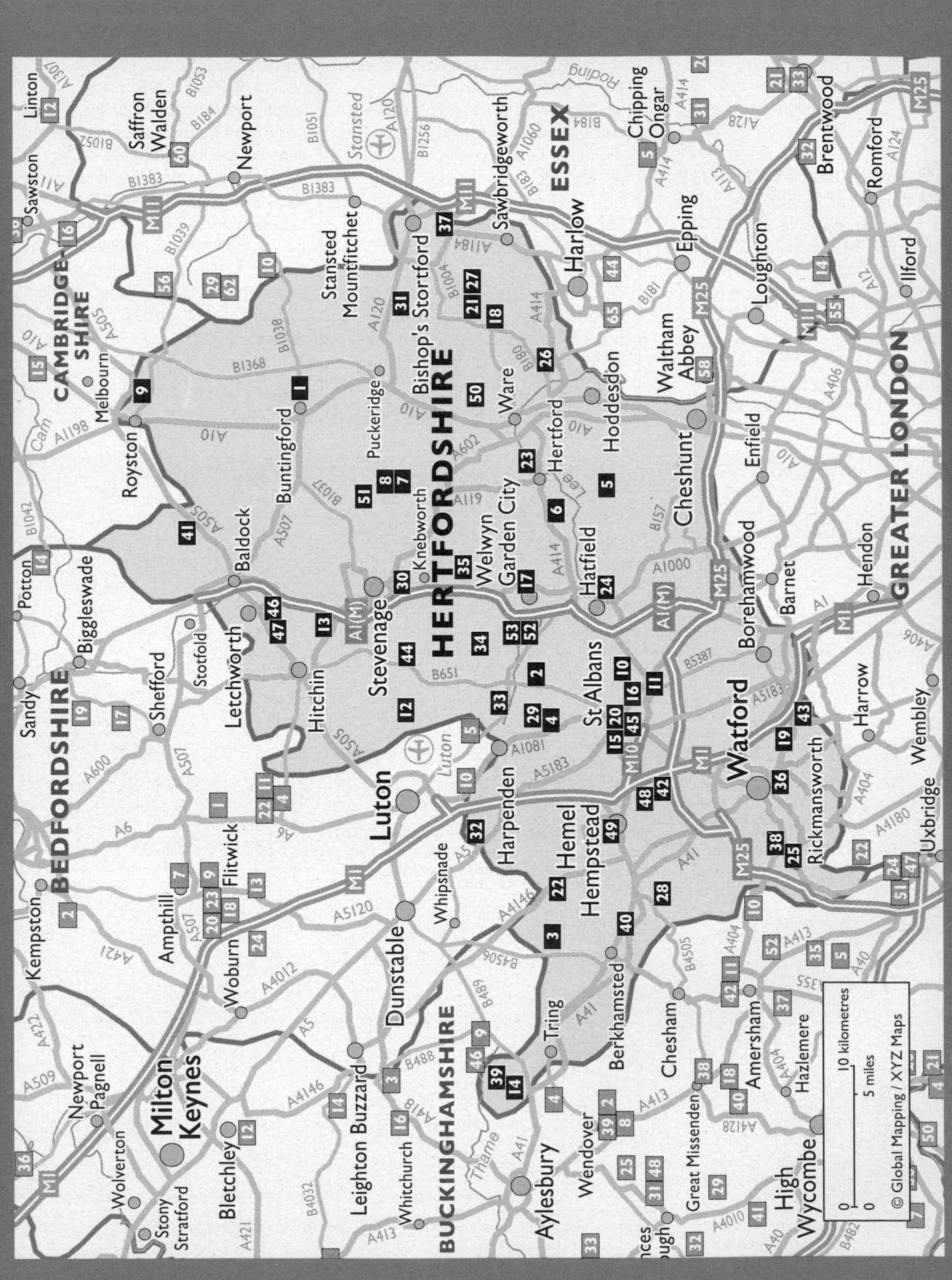

With its proximity to London, Hertfordshire became a breath of country air and a retreat for wealthy families wishing to escape the grime of the city – hence the county is peppered with large and small country estates, some of which open their garden gates for the NGS.

Hertfordshire was home for a long time to a flourishing fruit, vegetable and cut-flower trade, with produce sent up from nurseries and gardens to the London markets. There is a profusion of inviting rural areas with flower-filled country lanes and some of the best ancient woodlands carpeted with bluebells in late spring. Pretty villages sit in these rural pockets, with farmhouse and cottage gardens to visit.

Our diverse urban areas, such as St Albans with its abbey, the 'new town' of Hemel Hempstead, and Welwyn and Letchworth, the original garden cities, provide an array of interesting town gardens, both modern and traditional in their approach.

We have many gardens open 'by arrangement', and we are happy to arrange tours for large groups.

So next time you are heading through our county, don't just drive on – stop and visit one of our gardens to enjoy the warm welcome Hertfordshire has to offer.

Below: 120 Parkway

Volunteers

County Organiser
Julie Knight
01727 752375
julie.knight@ngs.org.uk

County Treasurer
Peter Barrett
01442 393508
peter.barrett@ngs.org.uk

Publicity
Kerrie Lloyd-Dawson
07736 442883
ker ield@yahoo.co.uk

Social Media
Helene Iley
07805 454310
iley.helene@gmail.com

Booklet Coordinator
Julie Loughlin
01438 871488
jloughlin11@gmail.com

New Gardens
Julie Wise
01438 821509
juliewise@f2s.com

Group Tours
Sarah Marsh
07813 083126
sarahkmarsh@hotmail.co.uk

Assistant County Organisers
Kate de Boinville
07973 558838
katedeboinville@btconnect.com

Christopher Melluish
01920 462500
c.melluish@btopenworld.com

Jacky O'Leary
07889 939325
jacky@jackyodesign.co.uk

Karen Smith
07850 406403
hertsgardeningangel@gmail.com

OPENING DATES

All entries subject to change. For latest information check **www.ngs.org.uk**

Map locator numbers are shown to the right of each garden name.

February

Snowdrop Festival

Saturday 10th
Walkern Hall 51

Sunday 11th
Walkern Hall 51

Friday 16th
1 Elia Cottage 18

Sunday 18th
1 Elia Cottage 18

Saturday 24th
Old Church Cottage 39
NEW Waterend House 52

Sunday 25th
Old Church Cottage 39

March

Saturday 17th
NEW Waterend House 52

Saturday 24th
◆ Hatfield House West Garden 24
Walkern Hall 51

Sunday 25th
Walkern Hall 51

April

Sunday 15th
Alswick Hall 1
◆ St Paul's Walden Bury 44

Friday 20th
Serendi 47

Sunday 22nd
Amwell Cottage 2
Serendi 47

Sunday 29th
NEW Hill House 26
◆ Pembroke Farm 41

May

Sunday 6th
Patchwork 40

Sunday 13th
NEW Pie Corner 42
◆ St Paul's Walden Bury 44

Sunday 20th
The Manor House, Ayot St Lawrence 34

Friday 25th
The White Cottage 53

Sunday 27th
◆ Benington Lordship 7
The Cherry Tree 13
15 Gade Valley Cottages 22

Monday 28th
43 Mardley Hill 35
The White Cottage 53

June

Friday 1st
Mackerye End House 33

Festival Weekend

Saturday 2nd
124 Highfield Way 25

Sunday 3rd
124 Highfield Way 25

Sunday 10th
◆ Ashridge House 3
NEW 14 Corinium Gate 15
Mackerye End House 33
◆ St Paul's Walden Bury 44
St Stephens Avenue Gardens 45
Serge Hill Gardens 48
Thundridge Hill House 50

Friday 15th
The Millers Cottage 37

Saturday 16th
The Lodge 32

Sunday 17th
Bayford Musical Gardens Day 5
Burloes Hall 9
The Lodge 32

Saturday 23rd
NEW Cunningham Hill Road Gardens 16

Sunday 24th
NEW Cunningham Hill Road Gardens 16

Friday 29th
The Cherry Tree 13
NEW 28 Fishpool Street 20

July

Sunday 1st
NEW 28 Fishpool Street 20

Friday 6th
NEW Foxglove Cottage 21
NEW ◆ Hoglands Garden 27

Sunday 8th
NEW Foxglove Cottage 21
9 Tannsfield Drive 49

Friday 13th
NEW 102 Cambridge Road 10

Sunday 15th
NEW 102 Cambridge Road 10
Scudamore 46

Sunday 22nd
2 Barlings Road 4
NEW Benington Park 8
15 Gade Valley Cottages 22

Saturday 28th
42 Falconer Road 19

Sunday 29th
35 Digswell Road 17
42 Falconer Road 19
NEW 9 Lloyd Taylor Close 31

August

Saturday 4th
42 Falconer Road 19

Sunday 5th
42 Falconer Road 19
9 Tannsfield Drive 49

Sunday 12th
NEW Church Barn 14

Friday 17th
8 Gosselin Road 23

Sunday 19th
8 Chapel Road 12
8 Gosselin Road 23
Patchwork 40

Saturday 25th
Beechleigh 6

Sunday 26th
Reveley Lodge 43

Monday 27th
Beechleigh 6
8 Kingcroft Road 29

Friday 31st
8 Kingcroft Road 29

September

Sunday 2nd
Huntsmoor 28
St Stephens Avenue Gardens 45

November

Saturday 10th
42 Falconer Road 19

By Arrangement

NEW 102 Cambridge Road 10
NEW Church Barn 14
NEW Cunningham Hill Road Gardens 16
35 Digswell Road 17
1 Elia Cottage 18
42 Falconer Road 19
Huntsmoor 28
8 Kingcroft Road 29
NEW 9 Lloyd Taylor Close 31
NEW 89 Mildred Avenue 36
Morning Light 38
Patchwork 40
Serendi 47
9 Tannsfield Drive 49
Thundridge Hill House 50
The White Cottage 53

THE GARDENS

1 ALSWICK HALL

Hare Street Road, Buntingford, SG9 0AA. Mike & Annie Johnson, www.alswickhall.co.uk. *1m from Buntingford on B1038. From the S take A10 to Buntingford, drive into town & take B1038 E towards Hare Street Village. Alswick Hall is 1m on R.* **Sun 15 Apr (12-4). Adm £5, chd free. Home-made teas. Bar and Hog Roast.**
Listed Tudor House with 5 acres of landscaped gardens set in unspoiled farmland. Two well established natural ponds with rockeries. Herbaceous borders, shrubs, woodland walk and wild flower meadow with a fantastic selection of daffodils, tulips, camassias and crown imperial. Spring blossom, formal beds, orchard and glasshouses. Licensed Bar, Hog Roast, Teas, delicious home-made cakes, plant stall and various other trade stands, children's entertainment. Good access for disabled with lawns and wood chip paths. Slight undulations.

Your visit helps Marie Curie work night and day in people's homes

2 AMWELL COTTAGE

Amwell Lane, Wheathampstead, AL4 8EA. Colin & Kate Birss. *½m S of Wheathampstead. From St Helen's Church, Wheathampstead turn up Brewhouse Hill. At top L fork (Amwell Lane), 300yds down lane, park in field opp.* **Sun 22 Apr (2-5). Adm £4, chd free. Home-made teas.**
Informal garden of approx 2½ acres around C17 cottage. Large orchard of mature apples, plums and pear laid out with paths. Extensive lawns with borders, framed by tall yew hedges and old brick walls. A large variety of roses, stone seats with views, woodland pond, greenhouse, vegetable garden with raised beds and fire-pit area. Gravel drive.

3 ◆ ASHRIDGE HOUSE

Berkhamsted, HP4 1NS. Ashridge (Bonar Law Memorial) Trust, 01442 843491, events@ashridge.hult.edu, www.ashridgehouse.org.uk. *3m N of Berkhamsted. A4251, 1m S of Little Gaddesden.* **For NGS: Sun 10 June (2-6). Adm £4.50, chd £2.50. Light refreshments.** For other opening times and information, please phone, email or visit garden website.
The gardens cover 190 acres forming part of the Grade II Registered Landscape of Ashridge Park. Based on designs by Humphry Repton in 1813 modified by Jeffry Wyatville. Small secluded gardens, as well as a large lawn area leading to avenues of trees. 2013 marked the 200th anniversary of Repton presenting Ashridge with the Red Book, detailing his designs for the estate.

4 2 BARLINGS ROAD

Harpenden, AL5 2AN. Liz & Jim Machin. *1m S of Harpenden. Take A1081 S from Harpenden, after 1m turn R into Beesonend Lane, bear R into Burywick to T-junction. Turn R and follow signs.* **Sun 22 July (2-5.30). Adm £3, chd free. Home-made teas.**
A compact garden for all seasons. Borders and island beds packed with perennials, climbers, shrubs and small trees. Small plant-filled formal pond. Colourful courtyard with unusual water feature. Shady gold and silver corner. Some areas re-planted every year for extra interest.

GROUP OPENING

5 BAYFORD MUSICAL GARDENS DAY

Bayford, SG13 8PX. www.bayfordgardensday.org. *3m S of Hertford. Off B158 between Hatfield & Hertford. Car parking.* **Sun 17 June (11.30-5). Combined adm £10, chd free. Light Refreshments available in gardens, village school, village hall. Incl BBQ, home made teas, bars, ice cream.**
A popular biennial event held for over 20yrs. More than a dozen gardens from large, long established formal layouts to pretty cottage gardens. 5 live bands incl jazz, steel and brass add a festive backdrop, while visitors can enjoy a variety of ploughman's lunches, cream teas and licensed bars. Stalls sell plants, local produce, cakes and ice-cream. For the more active there are a number of signed walks, complementary transport around the village is also provided and there is ample car parking. Bayford itself remains an oasis of countryside even though it is just 3m S of Hertford, and 10mins from Potters Bar. The village has a station which is on the Stevenage to Moorgate line. Mentioned in the Doomsday book of 1086 as Begesford, the village today is fortunate to retain much of its old world charm, incl a fine church with C15 font. Please see website for more details. All proceeds are for charitable causes; so far the Bayford open days have raised more than £250,000. People return year after year and many regard it as a great day out in the countryside. Coverage in local and national publications as well as online. Wheelchairs are of course welcome but we would ask people to remember that garden surfaces can be difficult.

Hill House

6 BEECHLEIGH

Birch Green, Hertford, SG14 2LP. Jacky & Gary O'Leary, www.jackyodesign.co.uk. *From A1M follow signs to Hertford along A414. From Hertford on A414, take 1st L after Hertingfordbury r'about & immed R along Old Coach Rd. House is mid way along Old Coach Rd.* **Evening opening Sat 25 Aug (5-8). Wine. Mon 27 Aug (12-5). Adm £5, chd free. Home made tea and cakes.**

Set in 2½ acres, the garden combines bold confident lines of contemporary planting with more traditional herbaceous borders. The house and outbuildings formed part of the historic Panshanger Estate with the new design incorporating reclaimed stone and red brick from the original buildings. Long beds of perennial grasses surround the 13m reflective pool, forming a focal point to the main house. Contemporary perennial grass borders. Wild flower meadow. Integrated fire pit and surrounding area. Artisan stalls, children's quiz. Featured in Hertfordshire Life, Telegraph and Garden and Homes. Some gravelled/stone areas.

7 ◆ BENINGTON LORDSHIP

Stevenage, SG2 7BS. Mr & Mrs R Bott, 01438 869668, garden@beningtonlordship.co.uk, www.beningtonlordship.co.uk. *4m E of Stevenage. In Benington Village, next to church. Signs off A602.* **For NGS: Sun 27 May (12-4). Adm £5, chd free. Light refreshments in Benington parish hall.**

For other opening times and information, please phone, email or visit garden website.

7 acre garden incl historic buildings, kitchen garden, lakes. Spectacular herbaceous borders, unspoilt panoramic views. Wheelchair access is limited as garden is on a steep slope. Accessible WC available in parish hall only.

8 NEW BENINGTON PARK

Benington, SG2 7BU. Marcus & Debbie Taverner. *5m E of Stevenage. Off A602 between Stevenage and Hertford through Aston Village into Benington R at village green follow signs.* **Sun 22 July (12-5). Adm £4.50, chd free. Home-made teas.**

The remains of earthwork terraces from early C17 make this one of the best archaeological gardens of its date. A Georgian House alongside a formal garden with lovely views of surrounding countryside. Garden laid out with an avenue of pleached Hornbeam trees , mature yew hedges and herbaceous borders. Refreshments in aid of the Hertfordshire Breast Unit. Wheelchair access to part of garden but all gravel paths. No disabled WC.

9 BURLOES HALL

Newmarket Road, Royston, SG8 9NE. Lady Newman, www.burloeshallweddings.co.uk. *From M11/A505 turn L on Newmarket rd. 200yds 1st turning on L Burloes Hall.* **Sun 17 June (12-5). Adm £5, chd free. Home-made teas in marquee.**

Formal gardens with deep colourful mixed herbaceous borders. Bountiful Nepeta and white rose pergolas. Handsome beech trees and mature yew hedges with extensive lawns.

10 NEW 102 CAMBRIDGE ROAD

St. Albans, AL1 5LG. Anastasia Rezanova & Keith Robertson, arezanova@gmail.com. *Nr Ashley Road end of Cambridge Road in The Camp neighbourhood on east side of city. S of the A1057 (Hatfield Rd). Take the A1057 from the A1(M) J3. Take the A1081 from M25 J22.* **Evening opening Fri 13 July (6-9). Wine. Sun 15 July (2-6). Light refreshments. Adm £4, chd free. Selection of teas, barista/coffee-shop coffee, homemade cakes. Visits also by arrangement May to Sept.**

Newly-planted contemporary space sympathetically redesigned to keep as much of the existing plants, trees and shrubs in a 1930s semi's garden. Modern take on the classic garden in two halves: ornamental and vegetable. All-year interest gabion borders packed with perennials and annuals, central bed featuring a pond and a mature Japanese maple. All vegetable, annuals and some perennials grown from seed. Count the Frog activity for children and young-at-heart.

11 NEW ◆ THE CELEBRATION GARDEN

North Orbital Road, St Albans, AL2 1DH. Aylett Nurseries Ltd, 01727 822255, info@aylettnurseries.co.uk, www.aylettnurseries.co.uk. *Aylett Nurseries is situated & A414 North Orbital Rd dual carriageway S of St Albans between J8 of M1 & A1M junction at Hatfield. The car park can be entered from the eastbound carriageway between Park St r'about & London Colney r'about. On entering the car park bear L taking the rd closest to the nursery buildings. Drive through the car park to the green gates & park on the grass next to garden.* For opening times and information, please phone, email or visit garden website.

The Celebration Garden is sited next to our famous Dahlia Field. Dahlias are planted amongst other herbaceous plants and shrubs. We also have a wild flower border complete with insect hotel. The garden is open all year to visit, during the garden centre opening hours, but it is especially spectacular from July to early autumn when the dahlias are in flower. Annual Autumn Festival between 8 and 16 Sptember. Grass paths.

12 8 CHAPEL ROAD

Breachwood Green, Hitchin, SG4 8NU. Mr & Mrs Melvin Gore. *Midway between Hitchin, Harpenden & Luton, Breachwood Green is well signed. We are just 2 doors from Red Lion Pub.* **Sun 19 Aug (12-5). Adm £3, chd free. Home-made teas.**

Standing in the heart of the village surrounding a C17 cottage is an informal garden having no lawns or straight level pathways with a good selection of perennials, shrubs and alpines. The paths meander past ponds and waterfalls. With one of the largest collections of vintage garden tools and machinery on display as featured in Garden Answers. Featured in Hertfordshire Life, Garden News, Garden Answers and Amateur Gardening.

13 THE CHERRY TREE

Stevenage Road, Little Wymondley, Hitchin, SG4 7HY. Patrick Woollard & Jane Woollard. *½m W of J8 off A1M. Follow sign to Little Wymondley; under railway bridge & house is R at central island flower bed opp Bucks Head Pub. Parking in adjacent rds.* **Sun 27 May (1-5). Light refreshments. Evening opening Fri 29 June (6-8.30). Wine. Adm £3.50, chd free.**

The Cherry Tree is a small, secluded garden on several levels containing shrubs, trees and climbers, many of them perfumed. Much of the planting, including exotics, is in containers that are cycled in various positions throughout the seasons. A heated greenhouse and summerhouse maintain tender plants in winter. The garden has been designed to be a journey of discovery as you ascend.

14 NEW CHURCH BARN

Church Road, Puttenham, Tring, HP23 4PR. Rebecca Barker, bec.barker@btinternet.com. *Set in the heart of Puttenham, this is one of the 51 Thankful Villages of England and Wales. From A41 take B4009 Tring/ Wendover exit. Take 1st exit on to Tring Hill towards Aston Clinton. At r'about exit to Lower Icknield Way. After 0.9m turn L. Follow signs from here.* **Sun 12 Aug (2-5.30). Adm £4, chd free. Home-made teas. Visits also by arrangement June to Sept for groups of 10 to 30. Times to be agreed.**

Started from scratch in 2014, rural crafts and bee-friendly plants have been chosen to blend the garden within its environs. Willow stock fencing, woven in situ, a shelter crafted in locally grown sweet chestnut, hedges of Hornbeam give structure to tall, wild, colourful borders. Later flowering perennials and grasses self-seed amongst roses, annuals and dahlias. Various seats welcome any visitor. Mainly flat with lawn and stone path.

Church Barn

15 NEW 14 CORINIUM GATE

St. Albans, AL3 4HX. Amanda Shipman, www.amandashipman.com/projects/2671945/small-town-garden-no-lawn. *1m SW of central St Albans, nr Waitrose. From King Harry Lane, take r'about into Mayne Avenue (signed 'supermarket'), then 1st L into Corinium Gate. Follow rd as it turns R, no.14 is on L. Parking in rd or nearby.* **Sun 10 June (2-5). Adm £3.50, chd free. Light refreshments.**

Designed for relaxation, this low maintenance garden makes the most of a 10m x 10m urban plot. Features include a spacious south-facing terrace, wisteria-clad gazebo, an ornamental water feature surrounded by wild flower turf, shed with sedum roof, borders in dappled shade, and zonal lighting. Soft fruit bushes and small fruit trees are integrated with herbaceous planting in the front garden. Practical, space-saving and sustainably-aware elements for every-day living are built into the design. E.g. compact, wall-hung washing line, water butts with small footprints, retractable hose, and contemporary shed with well-ordered internal space.

GROUP OPENING

16 NEW CUNNINGHAM HILL ROAD GARDENS

St Albans, AL1 5BX. annemyles@ymail.com. *1m S of St Albans City Centre. At A414 London Colney r'about turn onto London Road (City Centre). Turn R at sign 30mph.* **Sat 23, Sun 24 June (2-5.30). Combined adm £6, chd free. Home-made teas in garden of no 25. Gluten free cakes and scones. Visits also by arrangement May to Sept for group of 10 - 20.**

25 CUNNINGHAM HILL ROAD
David & Anne Myles.

NEW 28 CUNNINGHAM HILL ROAD
Rosemarie & Steve Frost.

Set on opposite sides of a tree lined road, these two ½ acre gardens have a similar mature backdrop, but differ in their aspects and design. No. 25 has been developed by the owner for more than 20 years to include ponds and a rock/ bog garden, large lawns, double herbaceous borders, a wild meadow area, and a rose trellis concealing a sizeable fruit, vegetable and nursery garden with seating. No. 28 while retaining many of the mature planting from its origins in the thirties, has mainly been planted in the last 4 years, by an established garden designer, to provide a peaceful haven of lawns, flanked by mixed borders, leading to a mature wooded area. Not all of no 28 is wheelchair accessible.

17 35 DIGSWELL ROAD

Welwyn Garden City, AL8 7PB. Adrian & Clare de Baat, 01707 324074, adrian.debaat@ntlworld.com, www.adriansgarden.org. *½m N of Welwyn Garden City centre. From the Campus r'about in city centre take N exit just past the Public Library into Digswell Rd. Over the White Bridge, 200yds on L.* **Sun 29 July (2-5.30). Adm £4, chd free. Home-made and cream teas Visits also by arrangement July to Oct groups of up to 20 - adm £7, incl tea & cake.**

Town garden of around a third of an acre with naturalistic planting inspired by the Dutch garden designer, Piet Oudolf. The garden has perennial borders plus a small meadow packed with herbaceous plants and grasses. The contemporary planting gives way to the exotic, incl a succulent bed and under mature trees, a lush jungle garden incl bamboos, bananas, palms and tree ferns. Daisy Roots Nursery will be selling plants. Video shoot for BBC Gardeners' World Magazine website. Grass paths and gentle slopes to all areas of the garden.

18 1 ELIA COTTAGE

Nether Street, Widford, Ware, SG12 8TH. Margaret & Hugh O'Reilly, 01279 843324, hughoreilly56@yahoo.co.uk. *B1004 from Ware, Wareside to Widford past Green Man Pub into dip at Xrd take R Nether St. 8m W of Bishop's Stortford on B1004 through Much Hadham at Widford sign turn L. B180 from Stanstead Abbots.* **Fri 16, Sun 18 Feb (12-4). Adm £3.50, chd free. Home-made teas. Visits also by arrangement Feb to Sept for groups up to 10. For snowdrops or spring opening please telephone.**

A garden forever changing to reflect the seasons, this year starting with one of our earliest flowers, the snowdrop. Approximately a third acre informal cottage garden with steep meandering paths on different levels, leading to stream with mini Monet-style bridge and pond beyond. Plenty of seats to rest upon, if it's not too chilly, but crumpets and teacakes available to warm up with. Due to the steep nature of the garden we are very sorry but there is no wheelchair access.

19 42 FALCONER ROAD

Bushey, Watford, WD23 3AD. Mrs Suzette Fuller, 077142 94170, suzettesdesign@btconnect.com. *M1 J5 follow signs for Bushey. From London A40 via Stanmore towards Watford. From Watford via Bushey Arches, through to Bushey High St, turn L into Falconer Rd, opp St James church.* **Sat 28, Sun 29 July, Sat 4, Sun 5 Aug (12-6). Evening opening Sat 10 Nov (5-8). Adm £3, chd free. Light refreshments. Visits also by arrangement in July.**

Enchanting magical unusual Victorian style space. Children so very welcome. Winter viewing for fairyland lighting, for all ages, bring a torch. Bird cages and chimneys a feature, plus a walk through conservatory with orchids.

20 NEW **28 FISHPOOL STREET**

St. Albans, AL3 4RT. Jenny & Antony Jay. *A5183 to St Albans city centre. Turn into George St. onto Romeland then Fishpool St. Free parking on Sunday signed opp Lower Red Lion Pub. Otherwise use town parking.* **Evening opening Fri 29 June (6-8). Wine. Sun 1 July (2-5). Home-made teas. Adm £5, chd free.**

Sculpted box and yew hedging and a C17 Tripe House feature strongly in this tranquil oasis set in the vicinity of St Albans Cathedral. Gravel paths lead to a lawn surrounded by late flowering sustainable herbaceous perennial borders and a relaxed woodland retreat. Imaginative planting in these areas offer unique perspectives. Not suitable for wheelchairs due to differing levels.

21 NEW **FOXGLOVE COTTAGE**

Perry Green, Much Hadham, SG10 6EF. Jennifer & John Flexton. *6m SW of Bishops Stortford. Follow brown signs to Henry Moore Foundation garden is 2 mins walk from Hoops Inn & HMF. Satnav postcode SG10 6EE. Parking Fri eve HMF & Hoops Inn Sun afternoon Hoops Inn only.* **Evening opening Fri 6 July (6-8.30). Combined adm with Hoglands Garden £6, chd free. Wine. Sun 8 July (2-5.30). Adm £4, chd free. Home-made teas.** Donation to Amy May Trust.

A beautiful thatched cottage in an idyllic setting on ⅔ of an acre, the epitome of English country charm. Colourful abundant successional planting and classic cottage garden plants fill the overflowing herbaceous borders. A hardworking greenhouse is bordered by organic vegetables, herbs and rose garden. Vibrant blooms attract bees, butterflies and bird boxes abound. Foxgloves pop up everywhere!

22 **15 GADE VALLEY COTTAGES**

Dagnall Road, Great Gaddesden, Hemel Hempstead, HP1 3BW. Bryan Trueman. *3m N of Hemel Hempstead. Follow B440 N from Hemel Hempstead. Past Water End. Go past turning for Great Gaddesden. Gade Valley Cottages on R. Park in village hall car park.* **Sun 27 May, Sun 22 July (1.30-5). Adm £3.50, chd free. Home-made teas.**

165ft x 30ft sloping rural garden. Patio, lawn, borders and pond. Paths lead through a woodland area emerging by wildlife pond and sunny border. A choice of seating offers views across the beautiful Gade valley or quiet shady contemplation with sounds of rustling bamboos and bubbling water. Featured in Garden News and local publications.

23 **8 GOSSELIN ROAD**

Bengeo, Hertford, SG14 3LG. Annie Godfrey & Steve Machin, www.daisyroots.com. *Take B158 from Hertford signed to Bengeo. Gosselin Rd 2nd R after White Lion PH.* **Evening opening Fri 17 Aug (6-8.30). Sun 19 Aug (1-5). Adm £4, chd free.**

Owners of Daisy Roots nursery, garden acts as trial ground and show case for perennials and ornamental grasses grown there. Lawn replaced in 2010 by a wide gravel path, flanked by deep borders packed with perennials and grasses. Sunken area surrounded by plants chosen for scent. Small front garden with lots of foliage interest. Regret no dogs.

24 **◆ HATFIELD HOUSE WEST GARDEN**

Hatfield, AL9 5HX. The Marquess of Salisbury, 01707 287010, visitors@hatfield-house.co.uk, www.hatfield-house.co.uk. *Pedestrian Entrance to Hatfield House is opp Hatfield Railway Stn, from here you can obtain directions to the gardens. Free parking is available, please use AL9 5HX with a sat nav.* **For NGS: Sat 24 Mar (11-5). Adm £6, chd free.** For other opening times and information, please phone, email or visit garden website.

Visitors can enjoy the spring bulbs in the lime walk, sundial garden and view the famous Old Palace garden, childhood home of Queen Elizabeth I. The adjoining woodland garden is at its best in spring with masses of naturalised daffodils and bluebells. Beautifully designed gifts, jewellery, toys and much more can be found in the Stable Yard shops. Visitors can also enjoy relaxing at the Coach House Restaurant which serves a variety of delicious foods throughout the day. There is a good route for wheelchairs around the West garden and a plan can be picked up at the garden kiosk.

25 124 HIGHFIELD WAY

Rickmansworth, WD3 7PH. Mrs Barbara Grant. *1m E of J18 M25, 1m NW of Rickmansworth. Easily accessible from J17 or J18 M25.* **Sat 2, Sun 3 June (2-5.30). Adm £4.50, chd free. Home-made teas.**

Gently sloping from terrace at the top down to deck at the bottom the plethora of plants and trees provide an ever-changing burst of colour and interest throughout the year. Clipped yew and bamboo hedging, together with mixed shrub and perennial borders seamlessly surround cutting garden, woodland area, bog garden, fruit patch, greenhouse and an enormous pond packed with many fish including koi. May include sale of artworks on Open Days. Wide paths - although a little bumpy in places.

26 NEW HILL HOUSE

Stanstead Abbotts, Ware, SG12 8BX. Mr & Mrs J M Pilkington, johnniepilk@hotmail.com. *nr Stanstead Abbotts from A10 turn E on to A414; then B181 for Stanstead Abbotts; L at end of High St, garden 1st R past Church.* **Sun 29 Apr (10-5). Adm £5, chd free. Home-made teas.**

9 acres incl wood; species roses, herbaceous border, water garden, conservatory, woodland walks. Lovely view over Lea Valley. Gravel paths and steep contours do not make it easy.

27 NEW ◆ HOGLANDS GARDEN

Perry Green, Much Hadham, SG10 6EE. Henry Moore Studios & Gardens, 01279 843333, visitorservices@henry-moore.org, www.henry-moore.org/visit/henry-moore-studios-gardens. *20 mins drive from M11 J8 or A10. Most Sat Nav will find correctly with SG10 6EE. Follow brown signs from Much Hadham / Bishop's Stortford. Full directions on website. Henry Moore's former home, near Much Hadham.* **For NGS: Evening opening Fri 6 July (6-8.30). Combined adm with Foxglove Cottage £6, chd free.** For other opening times and information, please phone, email or visit garden website.

A vibrant cottage garden created by Irina Moore, wife of modernist sculptor Henry Moore. Hoglands House was home to the Moore's from 1940 until their deaths. Irina was a keen gardener and transformed the garden into a perfect backdrop to her husband's work. The garden is now part of Henry Moore Studios and Gardens, owned and maintained by the Henry Moore Foundation. Regret no dogs. Wheelchair access is possible. Alternative routes avoid steps.

28 HUNTSMOOR

Stoney Lane, Bovingdon, Hemel Hempstead, HP3 0DP. Mr & Mrs Brian & Jane Bradnock, 01442 832014, b.bradnock@btinternet.com. *Between Bovingdon & Hemel Hempstead. Do not follow SatNav directions along Stoney Lane. Huge pot holes and ruts in lane. Approach from Bushfield Rd. Huntsmoor is facing you at the end of Bushfield Road.* **Sun 2 Sept (2-5). Adm £6, chd free. Home-made teas. Gluten free provided. Visits also by arrangement May to Sept for groups of 10+.**

Rose garden, rhododendron border, arboretum, Koi pond, nature pond, shrub and herbaceous borders. Also has a 'cave', and lots of places to sit. Full access to garden including easy access to WC.

29 8 KINGCROFT ROAD

Southdown, Harpenden, AL5 1EJ. Zia Allaway, 07770 780 231, zia.allaway@ntlworld.com, www.ziaallaway.com. *1½m S of Harpenden town centre. From Harpenden take the St Albans Rd A1081 S. At 1st r'about turn L onto Southdown Rd. Continue straight over 3 r'abouts to Grove Rd. Take the 3rd turning on R to Coleswood Rd. Take 1st turning on L.* **Mon 27 Aug (2-6). Home-made teas. Evening opening Fri 31 Aug (5-8). Wine. Adm £3.50, chd free. Visits also by arrangement July to Sept for small groups.**

Beautiful mature town garden designed by garden writer and designer in a contemporary informal style, with small pond and pebbled beach area, gravel garden, a wide range of summer bulbs, herbaceous perennials and shrubs, mature trees, shady borders, greenhouse, and inspirational container displays. A small courtyard features flower-filled window boxes and vegetables in raised beds.

30 ◆ KNEBWORTH HOUSE GARDENS

Knebworth, SG1 2AX. The Hon Henry Lytton Cobbold, 01438 812661, info@knebworthhouse.com, www.knebworthhouse.com. *Nr Stevenage. Direct access from A1(M) J7 at Stevenage.* For opening times and information, please phone, email or visit garden website.

Knebworth's magnificent 28 acre gardens were laid out by Lutyens in 1910. Lutyens' garden rooms and pollarded lime walks, Gertrude Jekyll's herb garden, the restored maze, yew hedges, roses and herbaceous borders are key features of the formal gardens with peaceful woodland walks beyond. Gold garden, green garden, brick garden and walled kitchen garden. Delicious afternoon teas are served in the Garden Terrace Tea Room. Plants for sale in Gift shop. Ideal for gardening group visits, garden tours can be arranged. Maze and Dinosaur trail for children, plus large Adventure Playground in the Park. For more details please see website.

31 NEW 9 LLOYD TAYLOR CLOSE

Little Hadham, Ware, SG11 2NB. Anne & David Willett, 01279 771564, annemread@msn.com. *3m W of Bishop Stortford, 4m E of Standon. From A10 follow A120 to Bishop Stortford through Standon to Little Hadham lights. Turn R towards Much Hadham. Within 100yds*

turn R - The Smithy - then R, then L and through white gate. **Sun 29 July (2-5). Adm £4, chd free. Home-made teas. Visits also by arrangement June to Aug groups of 10+.**
A colourful contemporary garden completely redesigned by the owners in 2013 with a small woodland garden to the side. The garden is planted to provide year round interest and colour through careful planting of bulbs, perennials, shrubs, trees and unusual plants. Also a water feature, pergola, wind spinner, garden ornaments and insect hotel with various seating areas. Step into woodland.

32 THE LODGE

Luton Road, Markyate, St Albans, AL3 8QA. Jan & John Paul. *2m N of M1 J9. Turn off A5 to Luton on B4540. The garden is between the villages of Markyate & Slip End.* **Sat 16 June (11-5); Sun 17 June (11-4.30). Adm £4.50, chd free. Light refreshments, tea, coffee or squash and homemade cakes.**
The garden, of nearly 3 acres, has evolved over 47yrs, partly through our own efforts and partly through nature growing plants wherever it chooses. The garden, mainly informal with a series of rooms, with small wooded area, a wild flower meadow and remains of an orchard full of common spotted orchids and other lovely wild flowers all of which arrived by themselves. Come and see for yourself. Main entrance gravel. Garden mostly flat.

33 MACKERYE END HOUSE

Mackerye End, Harpenden, AL5 5DR. Mr & Mrs G Penn. *3m E of Harpenden. A1 J4 follow signs Wheathampstead, then turn R Marshalls Heath Lane. M1 J10 follow Lower Luton Road B653. Turn L Marshalls Heath Lane. Follow signs.* **Evening opening Fri 1 June (6-9). Wine. Sun 10 June (12-5). Home-made teas. Adm £6, chd free. Friday evening wine with canapés.**
C16 (Grade I listed) Manor House (not open) set in 15 acres of formal gardens, parkland and woodland, front garden set in framework of formal yew hedges. Victorian walled garden with extensive box hedging and box maze, cutting garden, kitchen garden and lily pond. Courtyard garden with extensive yew and box borders. West garden enclosed by pergola walk of old English roses. All proceeds from the refreshments will be donated to the Isabel Hospice. Walled garden access by gravel paths.

34 THE MANOR HOUSE, AYOT ST LAWRENCE

Welwyn, AL6 9BP. Rob & Sara Lucas. *4m W of Welwyn. 20 mins J4 A1M. Take B653 Wheathampstead. Turn into Codicote Rd follow signs to Shaws Corner. Parking in field, short walk to garden. A disabled drop-off point is available at the end of the drive.* **Sun 20 May (11-5). Adm £5, chd free. Home-made cakes and tea for sale.**
A 6-acre garden set in mature landscape around Elizabethan Manor House (not open). 1-acre walled garden incl glasshouses, fruit and vegetables, double herbaceous borders, rose and herb beds. Herbaceous perennial island beds, topiary specimens. Parterre and temple pond garden surround the house. Gates and water features by Arc Angel. Garden designed by Julie Toll. Home-made cakes and tea/ coffee and produce for sale.

35 43 MARDLEY HILL

Welwyn, AL6 0TT. Kerrie & Pete, www.agardenlessordinary.blogspot.co.uk. *5m N of Welwyn Garden City. On B197 between Welwyn & Woolmer Green, on crest of Mardley Hill by bus stop for Arriva 300/301.* **Mon 28 May (1-5). Adm £4, chd free. Home-made teas.**
An unexpected garden created by plantaholics and packed with unusual plants and inspiring combinations. Foliage in a wide range of colours and textures forms the backdrop to ever-changing flowers. Several seating areas offer different perspectives on the design and planting composition. From a small bridge see the man-made stream cascade to the pond. For sale: cakes, teas and home-grown plants. Featured in the Garden Answers Chelsea Special.

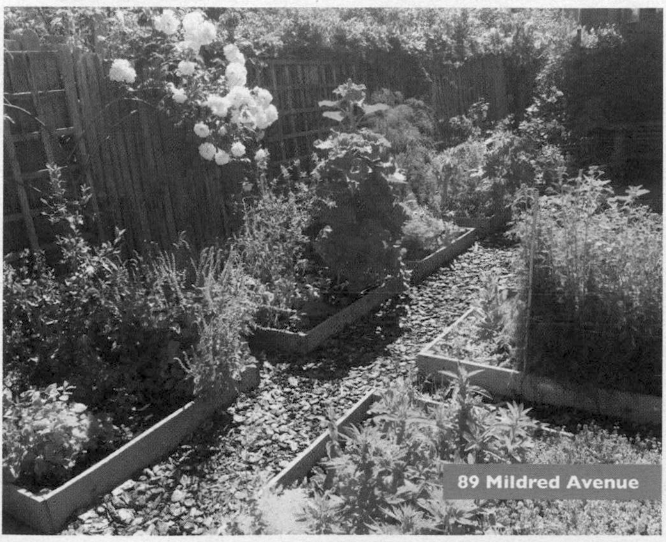
89 Mildred Avenue

Your visit to a garden will help more people be cared for by a Parkinson's nurse

36 NEW 89 MILDRED AVENUE (KEARNS & MEIRING PHYSIC GARDEN)

Watford, WD18 7DU. Victoria Kearns & Pieter Meiring, 07864 945 086, info@kmherbalists.co.uk, www.kmherbalists.co.uk. *Please note that there are daytime parking restrictions on Mildred Avenue. Limited free parking is available on Shepherds Road (Opp Watford Grammar School for Boys) or at Cassiobury Park.* **Visits by arrangement May to Aug please contact Victoria or Pieter to arrange your visit. Adm by donation. Home-made teas. Selection of herbal teas..**

The Kearns & Meiring Physic Garden – an impressive display of medicinal herbs from Europe and beyond by practising herbalists Victoria Kearns & Pieter Meiring, based in Watford, Hertfordshire. The garden is divided by medicinal plants from various families incl the Lamiaceae, Asteraceae, Solanaceae, Papaveraceae and others. The garden evolves according to the medicines they make and currently features 50+ different herbs with medicinal qualities. Featured in Optima Magazine. Wheelchair access is available through the side passage.

37 THE MILLERS COTTAGE

Pig Lane, Bishop's Stortford, CM22 7PA. Mandy & Marcus Scarlett. *1m S of Bishop's Stortford. Leave Bishop's Stortford on A1060 towards Hallingbury, after approx 1m turn R into Pig Lane. The Miller's Cottage is the first track on L - after about 300yds. Car parking available.* **Evening opening Fri 15 June (6-9). Adm £5, chd free. Wine.**

Essentially a romantic cottage garden with hundreds of roses that - like Topsy - just growed. Now over three acres the garden embraces many different themes from the woodland brook side walk and a formal wedding pavilion, through formal parterre and kitchen gardens, an architectural pool garden to the wide vistas of the open fields. Most of all it is a garden in development with much still to do. Some steps but largely accessible by wheelchair.

38 MORNING LIGHT

7 Armitage Close, Loudwater, Rickmansworth, WD3 4HL. Roger & Patt Trigg, 01923 774293, roger@triggmail.org.uk. *From M25 J18 take A404 towards Rickmansworth, after ¾m turn L into Loudwater Lane, follow bends, then turn R at T-junction and R again into Armitage Close.* **Visits by arrangement Apr to Sept or evenings May to Aug, restricted parking (minibus OK). Adm £4, chd free. Light refreshments.**

Compact, south-facing plantsman's garden, densely planted with mainly hardy and tender perennials and shrubs in shady environment. Features include island beds, pond, chipped cedar paths and raised deck. Tall perennials can be viewed advantageously from the deck. Large conservatory (450 sq ft) stocked with sub-tropicals.

39 OLD CHURCH COTTAGE

Chapel Lane, Long Marston, Tring, HP23 4QT. Dr John & Margaret Noakes. *A41 to Aylesbury take Tring exit. On outskirts of Tring take B488 towards Ivinghoe. At 1st r'about go on to Long Marston. Park at village hall, disabled parking & drop off only at house.* **Sat 24, Sun 25 Feb (11.30-3). Adm £5, chd free. Wine. At venue mulled wine and shortbreads served, incl in adm**

Small garden around a 400yr old thatched cottage adjoining a disused churchyard with ancient yews and Norman tower being the remnant of a Chapel of Ease. Many species and varieties of snowdrops together with cyclamen, crocuses, irises and other early spring bulbs. Garden is at the end of a very narrow country lane hence request to park at Village Hall. Ancient listed buildings in a conservation zone. Garden laid out with raised beds with many unusual snowdrops. Difficult for wheelchairs but we can help.

40 PATCHWORK

22 Hall Park Gate, Berkhamsted, HP4 2NJ. Jean & Peter Block, 01442 864731. *3m W of Hemel Hempstead. Entering E side of Berkhamsted on A4251, turn L 200yds after 40mph sign.* **Sun 6 May, Sun 19 Aug (2-5). Adm £4, chd free. Light refreshments. Visits also by arrangement Mar to Oct groups of 10 to 30.**

¼-acre garden with lots of year-round colour, interest and perfume, particularly on opening days. Sloping site containing rockeries, 2

14 Corinium Gate

small ponds, herbaceous border, island beds with bulbs in Spring and dahlias in Summer, roses, fuchsias, patio pots and tubs galore - all set against a background of trees and shrubs of varying colours. Seating and cover from the elements. Not suitable for wheelchairs, as side entrance is narrow, and there are many steps and levels.

41 ◆ PEMBROKE FARM

Slip End, Ashwell, Baldock, SG7 6SQ. Krysia Selwyn-Gotha, 01462 743100, Pembrokefarmgarden@gmail.com, www.pembrokefarmgarden.co.uk. *½m S of Ashwell. Turn off A505 (The Ashwell turn opp the Wallington & Rushden junction.) Go under railway bridge & past a cottage on R, after 200 yards enter the white farm gates on R. Car park close to garden entry.* **For NGS: Sun 29 Apr (12-5). Adm £4.50, chd free. Light refreshments in the courtyard. Also open Hill House.** For other opening times and information, please phone, email or visit garden website.

A country house garden with a wildlife walk and formal surprises. You are invited to meander through changing spaces creating a palimpsest of nature and structure.

42 NEW PIE CORNER

Millhouse Lane, Bedmond, Abbots Langley, WD5 0SG. Bella & Jeremy Stuart-Smith. *Between Watford & Hemel Hempstead. 1½m from J21 M25. 3m from Junction 8 of M1. Go to the centre of Bedmond. Millhouse Lane is opp the shops. Entrance is 50m down Millhouse Lane.* **Sun 13 May (2-5). Adm £4.50, chd free. Home-made teas.**

A garden designed to complement the modern classical house. Formal areas near the house, with views down the valley, include lawns and a formal pool. The garden becomes more informal towards the woodland edge. A dry garden leads through new meadow planting to the vegetable garden. Enjoy blossom, bulbs, wild garlic and bluebells in late spring. Access to all areas on grass or gravel paths except the formal pond where there are steps.

43 REVELEY LODGE

88 Elstree Road, Bushey Heath, WD23 4GL. Bushey Museum Property Trust, www.reveleylodge.org. *3½m E of Watford & 1½m E of Bushey Village. From A41 take A411 signed Bushey & Harrow. At mini-r'about 2nd exit into Elstree Rd. Garden ½m on L. Disabled parking only onsite.* **Sun 26 Aug (2-6). Adm £4, chd free. Home-made teas.**

2½-acre garden surrounding a Victorian house bequeathed to Bushey Museum in 2003 and in process of re-planting and renovation. Featuring colourful annual, tender perennial and medicinal planting in beds surrounding a mulberry tree. Conservatory, lean-to greenhouse, vegetable garden and beehive. Analemmatic (human) sundial constructed in stone believed unique to Hertfordshire. Partial wheelchair access.

44 ◆ ST PAUL'S WALDEN BURY

Whitwell, Hitchin, SG4 8BP. Simon & Caroline Bowes Lyon, stpaulswalden@gmail.com, , www.stpaulswaldenbury.co.uk. *5m S of Hitchin. On B651; ½m N of Whitwell village. From London leave A1(M) J6 for Welwyn (not Welwyn Garden City). Pick up signs to Codicote, then Whitwell.* **For NGS: Sun 15 Apr, Sun 13 May, Sun 10 June (2-7). Adm £5, chd £1. Home-made teas.** For other opening times and information, please email or visit garden website.

Spectacular formal woodland garden, Grade I listed, laid out 1720. Long rides lined with clipped beech hedges lead to temples, statues, lake and a terraced theatre. Seasonal displays of snowdrops, daffodils, cowslips, irises, magnolias, rhododendrons, lilies. Wild flowers are encouraged. This was the childhood home of the late Queen Mother. Children welcome. 10 June, Open Garden combined with Open Farm Sunday with free tours of the farm. Wheelchair access to part of the garden. Steep grass slopes in places.

GROUP OPENING

45 ST STEPHENS AVENUE GARDENS

St Albans, AL3 4AD. *1m S of St Albans City Centre. From A414 take A5183 Watling St. At double mini-r'about by St Stephens Church/ King Harry Pub take B4630 Watford Rd. St Stephens Ave is 1st R.* **Sun 10 June (2-5.30); Sun 2 Sept (2.30-5.30). Combined adm £5, chd free. Home-made teas at No 20. WC.**

20 ST STEPHENS AVENUE
Heather & Peter Osborne.

30 ST STEPHENS AVENUE
Carol & Roger Harlow.

Two gardens of similar size and the same aspect, developed in totally different ways. The plantswoman's garden at Number 20 is 'a master class in making the most of a long and narrow plot' (Amateur Gardening magazine). Varied habitats include cool and moist, dry gravel, and lush pondside displays. Paths meander through and behind the carefully maintained borders, giving access to all areas; specimen trees and fences clothed with climbers contribute to the peaceful seclusion. Seating in both sun and shade is positioned to appreciate different views, a large conservatory provides shelter. Number 30 has a southwest facing gravelled front garden that has a Mediterranean feel. Herbaceous plants, such as sea hollies and achilleas, thrive in the poor, dry soil. Clipped box, beech and hornbeam in the back garden provide a cool backdrop for the strong colours of the herbaceous planting. A gate beneath a beech arch frames the view to the park beyond. Plants for sale at June opening only. Compost making demonstrations. Number 20 featured in 'Amateur Gardening' magazine.

46 SCUDAMORE

1 Baldock Road, Letchworth Garden City, SG6 3LB. Michael & Sheryl Hann. *Opp Spring Rd, between Muddy Lane & Letchworth Lane. J9 A1M. Follow directions to Letchworth. Turn L to Hitchin A505. After 1m House on L opp corner shop. Parking in Muddy Lane & Spring Rd.* **Sun 15 July (11-5). Adm £5, chd free. Light refreshments.** Donation to Garden House Hospice.

½ acre garden surrounding early C17 cottages that were converted and extended in 1920s to form current house (not open). Garden of mature trees, mixed herbaceous borders with shrubs, pond and stream, wet bed, wilder garden and orchard/vegetable area. Many sculptures add interest to the garden.

47 SERENDI

22 Hitchin Road, Letchworth Garden City, SG6 3LT. Valerie & Ian Aitken, 01462 635386, valerie.aitken@ntlworld.com. *1m from city centre. A1(M) J9 signed Letchworth on A505. At 2nd r'about take first exit Hitchin A505. Straight over T-lights. Garden 1m on R.* **Evening opening Fri 20 Apr (5.30-8.30). Wine. Sun 22 Apr (11-5). Home-made teas. Adm £5, chd free. Visits also by arrangement June to Sept for groups of 10+.**

Tulips and Spring exuberance balanced by strong design throughout the garden. Meander through to the large mirror reflecting bulbs, acers, pots and topiary. Roses climbing 5 pillars, magnolias, wallflowers, clematis with a montana assailing an old pear tree. This is quietly contrasted by the knot garden and gravel area. Stop for tea and to view the photo book showing the garden in June last year. Gravel entrance driveway and paths, plenty of lawns.

GROUP OPENING

48 SERGE HILL GARDENS

Serge Hill Lane, Bedmond, Watford, WD5 0RT. *½m E of Bedmond. Go to Bedmond & take Serge Hill Lane, where you will be directed past the lodge & down the drive.* **Sun 10 June (2-5). Combined adm £8, chd free. Home-made teas at Serge Hill.**

THE BARN
Sue & Tom Stuart-Smith.
D

SERGE HILL
Kate Stuart-Smith.

Two very diverse gardens. At its entrance the Barn has an enclosed courtyard, with tanks of water, herbaceous perennials and shrubs tolerant of generally dry conditions. To the N there are views over the 5-acre wild flower meadow, and the West Garden is a series of different gardens overflowing with bulbs, herbaceous perennials and shrubs. The house at Serge Hill results principally from the work of Charles Augustin Busby (1786-1817), an architect and engineer perhaps most renowned for a development west of Brighton christened Brunswick Town and for his 1808 publication: A series of designs for villas and country houses. In 1811 Busby exhibited his designs for Serge Hill House at the Royal Academy. It has wonderful views over the ha-ha to the park; a walled vegetable garden with a large greenhouse, roses, shrubs and perennials leading to a long mixed border. At the front of the house there is an outside stage used for family plays, and a ship.

The National Garden Scheme and Perennial, helping gardener's when they are in need

49 9 TANNSFIELD DRIVE

Hemel Hempstead, HP2 5LG. Peter & Gaynor Barrett, 01442 393508, tterrabjp@ntlworld.com, www.peteslittlepatch.co.uk. *Approx 1m NE of Hemel Hempstead town centre & 2m W of J8 on M1. From M1, J8 cross r'about, A414 to Hemel Hempstead. Under ftbridge, cross r'about then 1st R across dual c'way to Leverstock Green Rd then on to High St Green. L into Ellingham Rd then follow signs.* **Sun 8 July, Sun 5 Aug (1.30-5). Adm £3.50, chd free. Home-made teas. Visits also by arrangement June to Sept groups (min 4 adults max 10) are very welcome. Tea/coffee available by prior arrangement.**

This small, town garden is decorated with over 450 plants which, together with the ever-present sound of water, create a welcoming oasis of calm for visitors to savour. Narrow paths divide, leading visitors on a voyage of discovery of the garden's many features. The owners regularly experiment with the garden planting scheme which ensures the look of the garden alters from year to year. Water features, metal sculptures, wall art and mirrors run throughout the garden. As a time and cost saving experiment all hanging baskets are planted with hardy perennials most of which are normally used for ground cover.

50 THUNDRIDGE HILL HOUSE

Cold Christmas Lane, Ware, SG12 0UE. Christopher & Susie Melluish, 01920 462500, c.melluish@btopenworld.com. *2m NE of Ware. ¾m from The Sow & Pigs Pub off the A10 down Cold Christmas Lane, crossing bypass.* **Sun 10 June (2-5.30). Adm £4.50, chd free. Cream teas. Visits also by arrangement Apr to Sept for groups of 10+.**

Well-established garden of approx 2½ acres; good variety of plants, shrubs and roses, attractive hedges. Visitors often ask for the unusual yellow-only bed. Several delightful places to sit. Wonderful views in and out of the garden

9 Lloyd Taylor Close

especially down to the Rib Valley to Youngsbury, visited briefly by Lancelot 'Capability' Brown. 'A most popular garden to visit'. Featured in the Hertfordshire Gardens Trust newsletter.

51 WALKERN HALL

Walkern, Stevenage, SG2 7JA. Mrs Kate de Boinville. *4m E of Stevenage. Turn L at War Memorial as you leave Walkern, heading for Benington (immed after small bridge). Garden 1m up hill on R.* **Sat 10, Sun 11 Feb (12-4); Sat 24, Sun 25 Mar (12-5). Adm £5, chd free. Light refreshments. Warming homemade soup.**
Walkern Hall is essentially a winter woodland garden. Set in 8 acres, the carpet of snowdrops and aconites is a constant source of wonder in Jan/Feb. This medieval hunting park is known more for its established trees such as the tulip trees and a magnificent London plane tree which dominates the garden. Following on in March and April is a stunning display of daffodils and other spring bulbs. There is wheelchair access but quite a lot of gravel. No disabled WC.

52 NEW WATEREND HOUSE

Waterend Lane, St. Albans, AL4 8EP. Mr & Mrs J Nall-Cain. *2m E of Wheathampstead. Approx 10 mins from J4 of A1M. Take B653 to Wheathampstead, past Crooked Chimney Pub, after ½m turn R into Waterend Lane. Cross river, house is immed on R.* **Sat 24 Feb, Sat 17 Mar (12-4). Adm £5, chd free. Home-made teas. Hot soup & bread.**
A hidden garden of 4 acres sets off an elegant Jacobean Manor House (not open). Stunning display of spring bulbs, orchard carpeted in snowdrops. Steep grass slopes and fine views of glorious countryside. Formal flint-walled garden, informal gardens leading into woodland. Mature specimen trees, newly created vegetable garden, bantams and Indian runner ducks. Over 40 varieties of daffodils. Hilly garden. Wheelchair access to lower gardens only. No disabled WC.

53 THE WHITE COTTAGE

Waterend Lane, Wheathampstead, St. Albans, AL4 8EP. Sally Trendell, 07775 897713 01582 834617, sallytrendell@me.com. *2m E of Wheathampstead. Approx 10 mins from J5 A1M Take B653 to Wheathampstead. Soon after Crooked Chimney Pub turn R into Waterend Lane, garden 300yds on L. Parking in field opp.* **Evening opening Fri 25 May (5-9). Wine. Mon 28 May (2-6). Home-made teas. Adm £5, chd free. Picnickers are welcome. Visits also by arrangement.**
An idyllic and atmospheric setting. A riverside retreat of over an acre in rural position adjacent to a ford. The River Lea widens and forms the boundary to this wildlife haven which could be a setting for 'Wind in the Willows'. Sally's cottage garden reflects her unique eclectic style. Picnickers welcome.

ISLE OF WIGHT

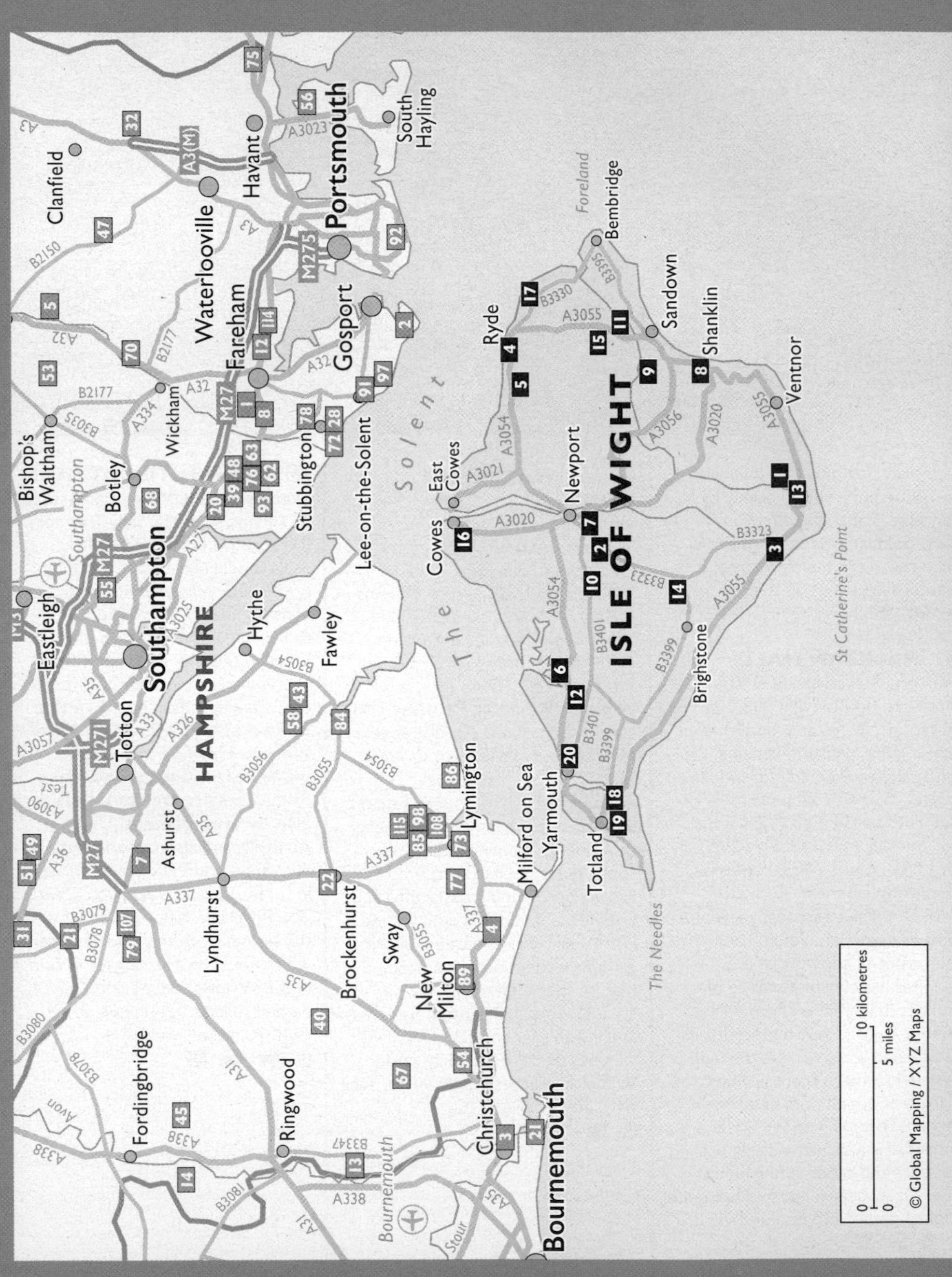

The island is a very special place to those who live and work here and to those who visit and keep returning. We have a range of natural features, from a dramatic coastline of cliffs and tiny coves to long sandy beaches.

Inland, the grasslands and rolling chalk downlands contrast with the shady forests and woodlands. Amongst all of this beauty nestle the picturesque villages and hamlets, many with gardens open for the National Garden Scheme. Most of our towns are on the coast and many of the gardens have wonderful sea views.

The one thing that makes our gardens so special is our climate. The moderating influence of the sea keeps hard frosts at bay, and the range of plants that can be grown is therefore greatly extended.

Conservatory plants are planted outdoors and flourish. Pictures taken of many island gardens fool people into thinking that they are holiday snaps of the Mediterranean and the Canaries.

Our gardens are very varied and our small enthusiastic group of garden owners are proud of their gardens, whether they are small town gardens or large manor gardens, and they love to share them for the National Garden Scheme.

Below: **324 Park Road**

Volunteers

County Organiser
Jennie Fradgley
01983 730805
jenniemf805@yahoo.co.uk

County Treasurer
Jennie Fradgley
(as above)

Publicity
Jennie Fradgley
(as above)

Booklet Co-ordinator
Jennie Fradgley
(as above)

Assistant County Organisers
Mike Eastwood
01983 721060
mike@aristia.co.uk

Sally Parker
01983 612495
sallyparkeriow@btinternet.com

OPENING DATES

All entries subject to change. For latest information check **www.ngs.org.uk**

Map locator numbers are shown to the right of each garden name.

April

Sunday 8th
NEW The Dairy 7

May

Sunday 6th
Morton Manor 11

Sunday 13th
Northcourt Manor Gardens 14

Sunday 20th
Badminton 2

Saturday 26th
Sunny Patch 18

Sunday 27th
Sunny Patch 18

June

Festival Weekend

Sunday 3rd
Meadowsweet 10
Thorley Manor 20

Saturday 9th
NEW 324 Park Road 16

Sunday 10th
◆ Nunwell House 15
NEW 324 Park Road 16

Saturday 16th
Niton Gardens 13

Sunday 17th
Niton Gardens 13

Saturday 23rd
Ashknowle House 1

Sunday 24th
Ashknowle House 1
Lansdown 9

Saturday 30th
Carpe Diem 5

July

Sunday 1st
Carpe Diem 5

Sunday 8th
Seaview Gardens 17
The Thatch 19

Saturday 14th
The Beeches 3

Saturday 28th
NEW Haven Hall 8

August

Saturday 11th
Blenheim House 4

Sunday 12th
Blenheim House 4

Sunday 19th
Crab Cottage 6
Morton Manor 11

Saturday 25th
NEW 324 Park Road 16

Sunday 26th
NEW 324 Park Road 16

By Arrangement

The Beeches 3
Crab Cottage 6
Morton Manor 11
Ningwood Manor 12
Northcourt Manor Gardens 14
NEW 324 Park Road 16
Sunny Patch 18

THE GARDENS

1 ASHKNOWLE HOUSE

Ashknowle Lane, Whitwell, Ventnor, PO38 2PP. Mr & Mrs K Fradgley. *4m W of Ventnor. Take the Whitwell Rd from Ventnor or Godshill. Turn into unmade lane next to Old Rectory. Field parking. Disabled parking at house.* **Sat 23, Sun 24 June (12.30-4.30). Adm £4, chd free. Home-made teas.**
A variety of features to explore in the grounds of this Victorian house (not open). Woodland walks, wildlife and fish ponds. Many colourful beds and borders. The large, well maintained, kitchen garden is highly productive and boasts a wide range of fruit and vegetables grown in cages, tunnels, glasshouses and raised beds. Young productive orchard incl protected cropping of strawberries, peaches and apricots. Display and DVD of red squirrel antics.

2 BADMINTON

Clatterford Shute, Carisbrooke, Newport, PO30 1PD. Mr & Mrs G S Montrose. *1½m SW of Newport. Parking in Carisbrooke Castle car park. Garden signed approx 200yds. Parking for disabled can be arranged, please phone 01983 526143, prior to opening.* **Sun 20 May (2-5). Adm £3.50, chd free. Home-made teas.**
1 acre garden on sheltered south and west facing site with good vistas. Planted for yr-round interest with many different shrubs, trees and perennials to give variety, structure and colour. Natural stream with bridges and waterfall. Pond being developed alongside kitchen garden.

3 THE BEECHES

Chale Street, Chale, Ventnor, PO38 2HE. Mr & Mrs Andrew & Anne Davidson, 01983 551876, andrewdavidson06@btinternet .com. *Turn off A3055 at Chale onto B3399. Entrance between Old Rectory & bus stop, in gap in stone wall.* **Sat 14 July (10-5). Adm £3, chd free. Light refreshments. Visits also by arrangement Mar to Sept for individuals, families or small groups.**
The garden is laid out mainly to shrubs and border plants designed for colour and texture. A haven of peace with extensive 270 degree views of the countryside incl the south west coast of the island down to The Needles and Dorset beyond. Features incl a wildflower meadow and a deep pond home to fish and wildlife (children to be supervised because of deep water). Come and see how the new wildflower meadow is settling in. The garden is not easy for wheelchairs due to gravel driveway and some steps, however can be accommodated with prior arrangement.

4 BLENHEIM HOUSE

9 Spencer Road (use Market St entrance), Ryde, PO33 2NY. David Rosewarne & Magie Gray. *Market St entrance behind Ryde Town Hall/ Theatre off Lind St.* **Sat 11, Sun 12 Aug (11-4). Adm £3, chd free. Home-made teas.**
A garden developed over 12 yrs, exploring the decorative qualities and long term effects of pattern making, colour and texture. This terraced

116ft x 30ft sloping site is centred on a twisting red brick path that both reveals and hides interesting and contrasting areas of planting, creating intimate and secluded spaces that belie its town centre location.

5 CARPE DIEM

75 Newnham Road, Binstead, Ryde, PO33 3TE. Tim & Tracy Welstead. *From the A3045 Newport to Ryde road, at Binstead Hill r'about, turn into Newnham Rd.* **Sat 30 June, Sun 1 July (10.30-4). Adm £3.50, chd free. Home-made teas.**

This ¼ acre garden has evolved over 14 yrs. It is a garden that is run on organic principles, for the benefit of both the gardeners and nature. It is divided into separate areas incl a vegetable plot, woodland areas, ponds, herb plantings, grass border and herbaceous borders. Insects and birds visit the garden in large numbers taking advantage of the plants chosen for their benefit.

6 CRAB COTTAGE

Mill Road, Shalfleet, PO30 4NE. Mr & Mrs Peter Scott, 07768 065756, mencia@btinternet.com. *4½m E of Yarmouth. At New Inn, Shalfleet, turn into Mill Rd. Continue 400yds. Please park in NT car park on L. Garden is further 200yds through NT gates on L, less than 5 mins walk.* **Sun 19 Aug (11-5). Adm £4, chd free. Home-made teas, soft drinks & cakes. Visits also by arrangement Apr to Sept.**

1¼ acres on gravelly soil. Part glorious views across croquet lawn over Newtown Creek and Solent leading to wild flower meadow, woodland walk and hidden waterlily pond. Part walled garden protected from westerlies, with mixed borders, leading to terraced sunken garden with ornamental pool and pavilion; planted with exotics, tender shrubs and herbaceous perennials. Featured in The Daily Telegraph, Gardening Section (12 Aug 2017) and The Isle of Wight County Press. Gravel and uneven grass paths.

7 NEW THE DAIRY

196 Carisbrooke Road, Newport, PO30 1DL. David & Louisa Killpack. *Situated near the junction of Carisbrooke Rd & Cedar Hill. Parking is at Carisbrooke Health Centre, 2 mins walk.* **Sun 8 Apr (2-5). Adm £3.50, chd free. Home-made teas.**

The first spring opening for this unexpected ½ acre garden, tucked behind busy Carisbrooke Rd. It features spring bulbs, herbaceous beds, a pergola of roses and fruit trees, and a kitchen garden. A natural stream feeds a watercress bed. A further ¾ acre woodland is home to much wildlife and provides an oasis of calm. A boardwalk and several benches have been made from trees felled in the wood. The garden is flat and mostly accessible to wheelchairs, although grassy paths may be soft.

8 NEW HAVEN HALL

5 Howard Road, Shanklin, PO37 6HD. David Barratt, 07914 796494, David@HavenHall.uk, www.HavenHall.uk. *Located between Shanklin & Lake on the cliff path. Howard Rd is opp Wiltons Garage. Extra car parking at Winchester House YMCA which is 5 mins walk along cliff path.* **Sat 28 July (11-4). Adm £4. Sorry no children. Teas.**

2 acres of gardens on the cliff top with stunning views overlooking the sea. This garden was completely created in the last 2 yrs with all new planting of established plants. The garden was awarded the 'Best Commercial Garden' in Wight in Bloom 2017.

9 LANSDOWN

Burnt House Lane, Alverstone, Sandown, PO36 0HB. Lynda & Larry Darby. *From the A3056, Arreton to Lake road. At Apse Heath r'about turn up Alverstone Rd. Follow road for about 1½m, Lansdown is on the R opp Youngwoods Way, by the bus stop. Parking in adjacent field.* **Sun 24 June (11.30-4.30). Adm £4, chd £1. Home-made teas.**

A garden within a 3 acre plot. A s-facing, sloping, exposed site with sandy soil. Different areas of interest; a terrace, formal garden with pond, some vines, a fernery, large organic vegetable plot, a souvenir garden set within the remains of an old glasshouse, mown paths though natural meadow and a pond for wildlife, beds and borders. Two pet alpacas and a truly 180 degree view. Sloping site with access to most of the garden without using steps.

Kings Manor Farm, Niton Gardens

10 MEADOWSWEET

5 Great Park Cottages, off Betty-Haunt Lane, Carisbrooke, PO30 4HR. Gunda Cross. *4m SW of Newport. From A3054 Newport/ Yarmouth road, turn L at Xrd Porchfield/Calbourne, over bridge into 1st lane on R. Parking along one side, on grass verge & past house.* **Sun 3 June (11.30-4.30). Adm £3.50, chd free. Home-made teas.**

From windswept barren 2 acre cattle field to developing tranquil country garden. Natural, mainly native planting and wild flowers. Cottagey front garden, herb garden, orchard, fruit cage and large pond. The good life and a haven for wildlife! Flat level garden with grass paths.

11 MORTON MANOR

Morton Manor Road, Brading, Sandown, PO36 0EP. Mr & Mrs G Godliman, 07768 605900, patricia.godliman@yahoo.co.uk. *Off A3055 5m S of Ryde, just out of Brading. At Yar Bridge T-lights turn into lower Adgestone Rd. Take next L into Morton Manor Rd.* **Sun 6 May, Sun 19 Aug (11-4). Adm £4, chd free. Light refreshments. Visits also by arrangement Apr to Sept.**

A colourful garden of great plant variety. Mature trees incl many acers with a wide variety of leaf colour. Early in the season a display of rhododendrons, azaleas and camellias. Ponds, sweeping lawns, roses set on a sunny terrace and much more to see in this extensive garden surrounding a picturesque C16 manor house (not open). Gravel driveway.

12 NINGWOOD MANOR

Station Road, Ningwood, Nr Newport, PO30 4NJ. Nicholas & Claire Oulton, 01983 761352, claireoulton@gmail.com. *Nr Shalfleet. From Newport, turn L opp the Horse & Groom Pub. Ningwood Manor is 300-400yds on the L. Please use 2nd set of gates.* **Visits by arrangement May to Aug for individuals or large groups of 30 max. Light refreshments.**

A 3 acre, landscape designed country garden divided into several rooms; a walled courtyard, croquet lawn, white garden and kitchen garden. They flow into each other, each with their own gentle colour schemes, the exception to this is the croquet lawn garden which is a riot of colour, mixing oranges, reds, yellows and pinks. Much new planting has taken place over the last few yrs. The owners have several new projects underway, so the garden is a work in progress. Features incl a vegetable garden with raised beds and a small summerhouse, part of which is alleged to be Georgian.

GROUP OPENING

13 NITON GARDENS

Niton, PO38 2AZ. *5m W of Ventnor. Parking at football ground (Blackgang Rd), in village & Allotment Rd car park. Tickets & maps from the library in the heart of the village on Niton Gardens open days only.* **Sat 16, Sun 17 June (11.30-4.30). Combined adm £5, chd free. Home-made teas at selected gardens on route.**

NEW **8 GLEN APPROACH**
Mrs K Harris.

KINGS MANOR FARM
Ian & Catherine Hoare.

SOUTHCLIFF
Mr & Mrs Martin & Eleanor Bowen.

SPRING COTTAGE
Mr & Mrs Neil White.

TALSA
Frances Pritchard.

TILLINGTON VILLA
Paul & Catherine Miller.

WINFRITH
Mrs Janet Tedman.

NEW **YAFFLES**
Mr & Mrs R Russell.

Niton is a delightful village with a busy community spirit, blessed with lovely churches, two pubs (one of which was renowned for smuggling), PO and shops, lovely walks and bridleways, school, football and cricket pitches and recreation ground. The gardens of this walk are very varied in both style and size and are full of colour, fragrance and interest; from cottage and country gardens to vegetable plot and havens for wildlife. The gardens are situated both in the heart of the village and the undercliff. We do hope you will enjoy them all.

14 NORTHCOURT MANOR GARDENS

Main Road, Shorwell, PO30 3JG. Mr & Mrs J Harrison, 01983 740415, john@northcourt.info, www.northcourt.info. *4m SW of Newport. On entering Shorwell from Newport, entrance at bottom of hill on R. If entering from other directions head through village in direction of Newport. Garden on the L, on bend after passing the PO.* **Sun 13 May (12-5). Adm £5, chd free. Home-made teas. Visits also by arrangement Mar to Oct. Teas or light lunch for groups.**

15 acre garden surrounding large C17 manor house (not open), incl walled kitchen garden, chalk stream, terraces, magnolias and camellias. Boardwalk along jungle garden. A large variety of plants enjoying the different microclimates. There are roses, primulas by the stream and hardy geraniums in profusion. Picturesque wooded valley around the stone manor house. Bathhouse and snail mount leading to terraces. 1 acre walled garden being restored. Last yr the house celebrated its 402nd yr anniversary. Wheelchair access on main paths only, some paths are uneven and the terraces are hilly.

15 ◆ NUNWELL HOUSE

West Lane, Brading, PO36 0JQ. Mr & Mrs S Bonsey, 01983 407240, info@nunwellhouse.co.uk, www.nunwellhouse.co.uk. *3m S of Ryde. Signed off A3055 into Coach Lane.* **For NGS: Sun 10 June (1-4). Adm £5, chd free.**

Home-made teas. For other opening times and information, please phone, email or visit garden website.
5 acres of beautifully set formal and shrub gardens, and old fashioned shrub roses prominent. Exceptional Solent views from the terraces. Small arboretum and walled garden with herbaceous borders. House developed over 5 centuries and full of architectural interest.

16 NEW 324 PARK ROAD

Cowes, PO31 7NN. Andrea Richter, 07970 433905, andrea@richters.co.uk. *Park Rd is the route to the Red Jet passenger ferry terminal. The property is towards the top of the road on the R as you travel from The Roundhouse r'about.* **Sat 9, Sun 10 June, Sat 25, Sun 26 Aug (10-4.30). Adm £3, chd free. Light refreshments. Visits also by arrangement May to Sept.**
This garden is an escape to the Mediterranean. The hard landscaping takes inspiration from Moorish design. The plants are a mixture of origin, from all over the world, with particular attention to the Antipodes. The garden changes dynamic throughout the year and there is always something unusual in flower. A microclimate using planting means less hardy species thrive. For visitors looking for more than tea and cake, try Watersedge at Gurnard Beach. Wheelchair access throughout the main parts of the garden, although some smaller pathways may prove difficult.

GROUP OPENING

17 SEAVIEW GARDENS

Duver Road, Seaview, PO34 5AJ. *Along E coast of Ryde. Follow signs for Seaview from Ryde or Brading along A3055. Parking in village or Duver Rd. Tickets & map available at each garden.* **Sun 8 July (11-5). Combined adm £5, chd free. Home-made teas at Northbank Hotel, Circular Road.**

NEW **ARMADALE**
Mrs Mary Johnston-Taylor.

RED CROSS COTTAGE
Mr & Mrs Stephen Jones.

SALTERNS COTTAGE
Susan & Noël Dobbs.

NEW **SEAFIELD HOUSE**
Mrs Sue Wakefield.

10 SPITHEAD CLOSE
Mr Peter Muspratt.

Enjoy a variety of garden styles set in the popular village resort of Seaview. Colourful borders of herbaceous perennials and annual bedding, trees, shrubs and climbers, grasses and water features. Raised vegetable beds, glasshouses and potager, plus colourful sunny patios with a touch of the exotic.

18 SUNNY PATCH

Victoria Road, Freshwater, PO40 9PP. Mrs Eileen Pryer, 01983 752974, Freshair33@hotmail.com. *Halfway between Freshwater Village & Freshwater Bay. Down Afton Rd, L at garage up Stroud Rd. Keep L, just up from Parish Hall on same side. Parking in road outside house.* **Sat 26, Sun 27 May (9.30-4.30). Adm £4, chd free. Light refreshments. Visits also by arrangement Mar to Sept, mainly at weekends and advanced notice only.**
A garden of an eccentric plantaholic and sculpture collector. This large and constantly evolving area has been created over 30 yrs to accommodate and reflect the owner's passion. Seasonal interest is sustained and nurtured through an extensive and interesting collection of trees, shrubs, perennials and bulbs incl some rare specimens. Features incl a fairy wood, two ponds and a variety of seated areas from which to view the landscape. This garden is a celebration of fun, fantasy and life, so look closely to appreciate its diversity. There are no paved paths and yrs of mole activity has made the ground uneven.

19 THE THATCH

Bedbury Lane, Moon's Hill, Freshwater, PO40 9RN. Mrs Val Hudson. *Approx 1m from Freshwater Bay. From Freshwater Bay, drive up Bedbury Lane past Farringford. Take next L, Farringford Farm Rd, for parking at Farringford Farm. 5 mins walk to The Thatch at the bottom of Moon's Hill.* **Sun 8 July (11.30-4.30). Adm £3.50, chd free. Home-made teas & light lunches.**
1 acre organic wildlife garden surrounds an C18 cottage (not open) in an AONB. Nectar rich borders with wild flowers, ornamental grasses, cottage garden plants, herbs, shrubs and roses, plus mature trees, young crabs and limes. Mown paths and informal lawns. Dragonfly and wildlife ponds, small orchard, hay meadow and wild hedgerows draw birds, insects and mammals. Gardening for both wildlife and people. Elements of coastal garden design integrating with a country garden setting. The site is in a rural landscape but within a mile of the sea and can often be dry and windy. Gardening for wildlife tours (HIWWT). Featured twice in the Isle of Wight County Press. Gravel drive, uneven grass and steps.

20 THORLEY MANOR

Thorley, Yarmouth, PO41 0SJ. Mr & Mrs Anthony Blest. *1m E of Yarmouth. From Bouldnor take Wilmingham Lane. House ½m on L.* **Sun 3 June (2-5). Adm £3.50, chd free. Home-made teas.**
Delightful informal gardens of over 3 acres surrounding manor house (not open). Garden set out in a number of walled rooms incl herb garden, colourful perennial and self-seeding borders, shrub borders and lawns, plus unusual island croquet lawn seamlessly blending in to the surrounding farmland.
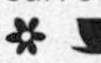

KENT

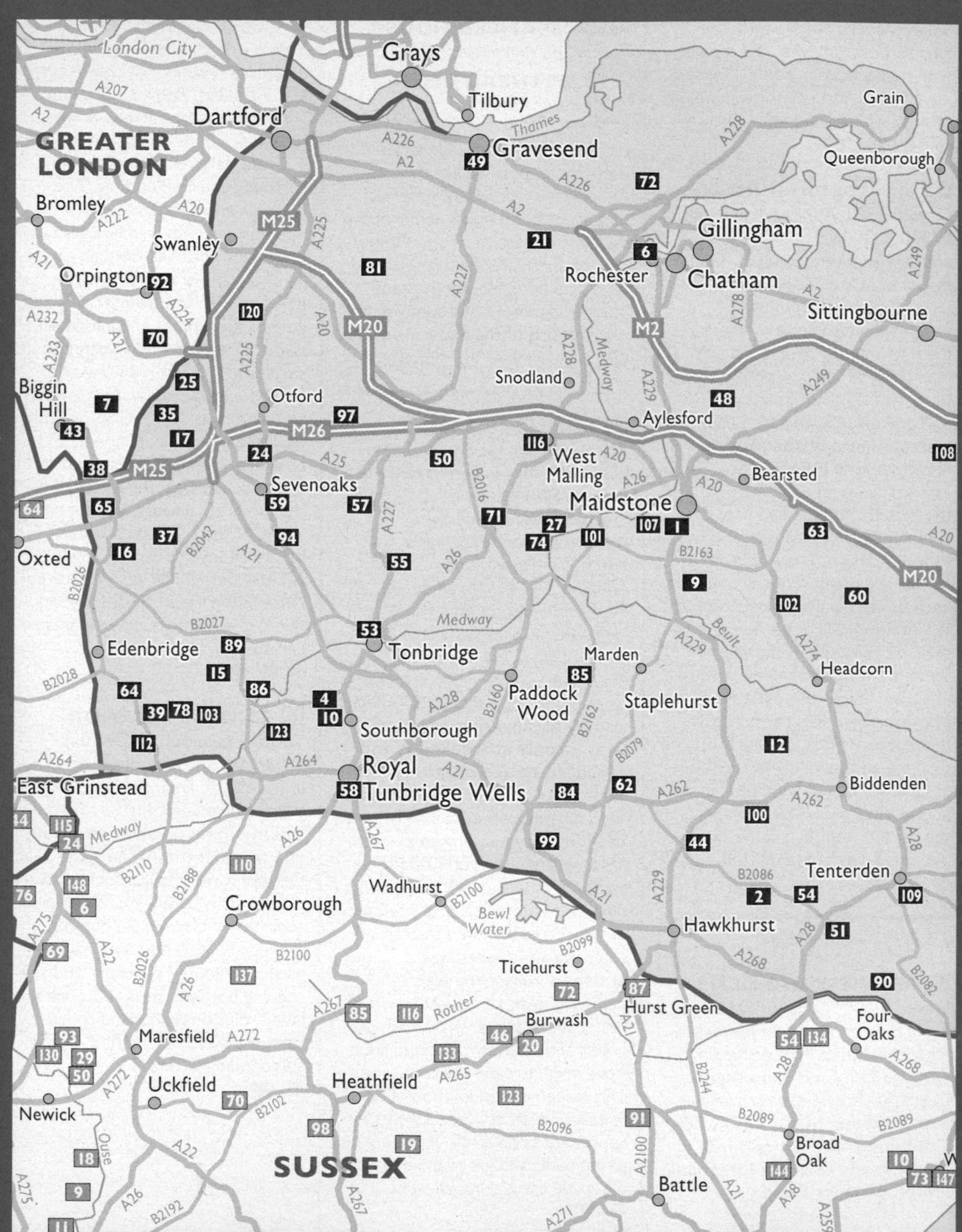
London City
Grays
Tilbury
Grain
Dartford
Thames
GREATER LONDON
Gravesend
Queenborough
Bromley
Swanley
Gillingham
Rochester
Chatham
Orpington
Sittingbourne
Snodland
Medway
Biggin Hill
Otford
Aylesford
West Malling
Bearsted
Sevenoaks
Maidstone
Oxted
Tonbridge
Edenbridge
Marden
Beult
Headcorn
Paddock Wood
Staplehurst
Southborough
Royal Tunbridge Wells
East Grinstead
Biddenden
Tenterden
Wadhurst
Crowborough
Bewl Water
Hawkhurst
Ticehurst
Hurst Green
Burwash
Rother
Four Oaks
Maresfield
Uckfield
Heathfield
Newick
Ouse
Broad Oak
SUSSEX
Battle

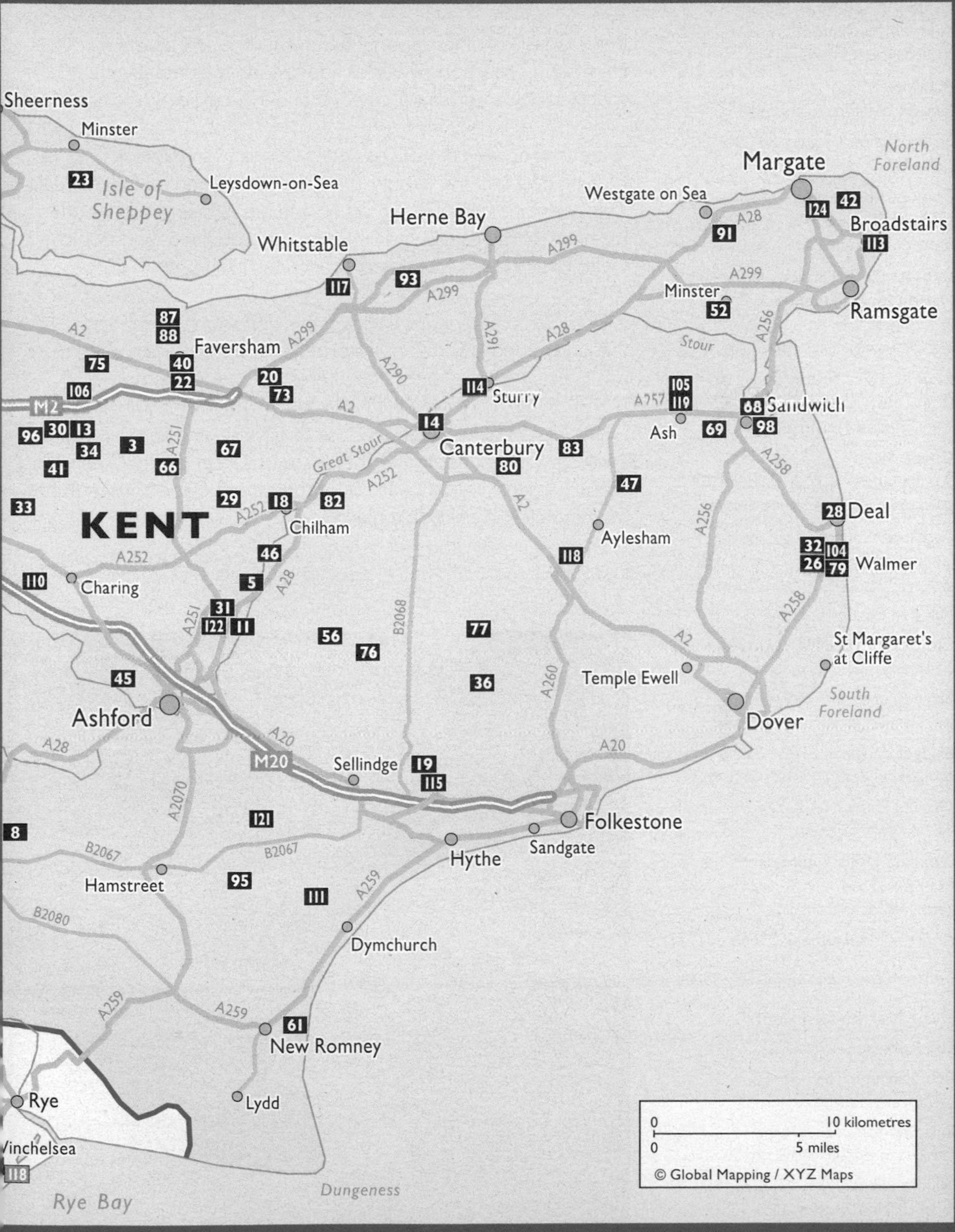
Sheerness
Minster
Isle of Sheppey
Leysdown-on-Sea
Whitstable
Herne Bay
Westgate on Sea
Margate
North Foreland
Broadstairs
Ramsgate
Minster
Stour
Faversham
Sturry
Sandwich
Ash
Canterbury
Great Stour
Chilham
KENT
Charing
Aylesham
Deal
Walmer
St Margaret's at Cliffe
South Foreland
Temple Ewell
Dover
Ashford
Sellindge
Folkestone
Sandgate
Hythe
Hamstreet
Dymchurch
New Romney
Lydd
Rye
Winchelsea
Rye Bay
Dungeness
A2
M2
A299
A291
A290
A28
A257
A256
A258
A251
A252
A20
M20
A2070
B2067
B2080
A259
B2068
A260
0 10 kilometres
0 5 miles
© Global Mapping / XYZ Maps

Volunteers

County Organiser
Jane Streatfeild 01342 850362
janestreatfeild@btinternet.com

County Treasurer
Andrew McClintock 01732 838605
mcclintockandrew@gmail.com

Publicity
Jane Streatfeild (as above)

Seann Carter 07565 239 270, seann.carter@outlook.com

Booklet Advertising
Marylyn Bacon 01797 270300
ngsbacon@ramsdenfarm.co.uk

Booklet Co-ordinator
Ingrid Morgan Hitchcock
01892 528341
ingrid@morganhitchcock.co.uk

Booklet Distribution
Diana Morrish 01892 723905
diana.morrish@hotmail.co.uk

Group Tours
Sue Robinson 01622 729568
suerobinson.timbers@gmail.com

Assistant County Organisers
Jacqueline Anthony 01892 518879
jacquelineanthony7@gmail.com

Marylyn Bacon (as above)

Clare Barham 01580 241386
clarebarham@holepark.com

Mary Bruce 01795 531124
mary.bruce@churchmans.co.uk

Bridget Langstaff 01634 842721
bridget.langstaff@btinternet.com

Virginia Latham 01303 862881
lathamvj@gmail.com

Caroline Loder-Symonds
01227 831203
caroline@dennehill.co.uk

Andrew Montgomery 01843 822971, andrew.montgomery2012@btinternet.com

Diana Morrish (as above)

Sue Robinson (as above)

Ros Scarlett 01689 851835
ros@scarlettonline.org.uk

Julia Stanton 01227 700421
familystanton@hotmail.com

Nicola Talbot 01342 850526
nicola@falconhurst.co.uk

Famously known as 'The Garden of England', Kent is a county full of natural beauty, special landscapes and historical interest.

Being England's oldest county, Kent unsurprisingly boasts an impressive collection of castles and historic sites, notably the spectacular Canterbury Cathedral, and the medieval Ightham Mote.

Twenty eight per cent of the county forms two Areas of Outstanding Natural Beauty: the Kent Downs and the High Weald. The landscapes of Kent are varied and breathtaking, and include haunting marshes, rolling downs, ancient woodlands and iconic white cliffs.

The gardens of Kent are well worth a visit too, ranging from the landscaped grounds of historic stately homes and castles, to romantic cottage gardens and interesting back gardens.

Never has a county been so close to London and yet feels so far away, so why not escape to the peace of a Kent garden? The variety of the gardens and the warmth of the garden owners will ensure a memorable and enjoyable day out.

Below: **Calico House**

OPENING DATES

All entries subject to change. For latest information check www.ngs.org.uk

Map locator numbers are shown to the right of each garden name.

January

Wednesday 31st
Spring Platt 102

February

Snowdrop Festival

Saturday 3rd
Knowle Hill Farm 60
Spring Platt 102

Sunday 4th
Knowle Hill Farm 60
Spring Platt 102

Wednesday 7th
Spring Platt 102
Yew Tree Cottage 123

Sunday 18th
Copton Ash 22
◆ Doddington Place 30
◆ Goodnestone Park Gardens 47
Mere House 71
Yew Tree Cottage 123

Sunday 25th
Mere House 71

Wednesday 28th
Yew Tree Cottage 123

March

Sunday 11th
NEW The Courtyard 23
Yew Tree Cottage 123

Sunday 18th
Copton Ash 22
◆ Mount Ephraim 73

Wednesday 21st
Yew Tree Cottage 123

Sunday 25th
◆ Godinton House & Gardens 45
Godmersham Park 46
◆ Great Comp Garden 50
Mere House 71
Potmans Heath House 90

Thursday 29th
Potmans Heath House 90
◆ The Salutation Garden 98

Friday 30th
Haven 52

April

Every Monday
NEW The Courtyard 23

Sunday 1st
NEW The Courtyard 23
Haven 52
Yew Tree Cottage 123

Monday 2nd
◆ Cobham Hall 21
Haven 52
Mere House 71

Sunday 8th
Copton Ash 22
◆ Goodnestone Park Gardens 47
◆ Hole Park 54

Wednesday 11th
Yew Tree Cottage 123

Sunday 15th
Copton Ash 22
Frith Old Farmhouse 41

Thursday 19th
◆ Ightham Mote 57

Friday 20th
Oak Cottage 76

Saturday 21st
Oak Cottage 76
Old Buckhurst 78

Sunday 22nd
Bilting House 5
Boldshaves 8
34 Cross Road 26
Old Buckhurst 78
Yew Tree Cottage 123

Tuesday 24th
◆ Riverhill Himalayan Gardens 94

Wednesday 25th
Great Maytham Hall 51

Saturday 28th
Watergate House 114

Sunday 29th
Balmoral Cottage 2
Copton Ash 22
Eagleswood 33
Frith Old Farmhouse 41
Ladham House 62
43 The Ridings 93

May

Every Monday
NEW The Courtyard 23

Tuesday 1st
NEW 14 Anglesey Avenue 1

Wednesday 2nd
NEW 14 Anglesey Avenue 1
1 Brickwall Cottages 12
◆ Hole Park 54
Yew Tree Cottage 123

Thursday 3rd
NEW 14 Anglesey Avenue 1

Saturday 5th
Little Gables 65
Old Buckhurst 78

Sunday 6th
Balmoral Cottage 2
1 Brickwall Cottages 12
NEW The Courtyard 23
Haven 52
Little Gables 65
Old Buckhurst 78
Stonewall Park 103

Monday 7th
Haven 52

Wednesday 9th
◆ Doddington Place 30

Sunday 13th
◆ Boughton Monchelsea Place 9
Copton Ash 22
Elgin House 35
Torry Hill 108
Yew Tree Cottage 123

Tuesday 15th
◆ Scotney Castle 99

Wednesday 16th
◆ Riverhill Himalayan Gardens 94

Sunday 20th
Bilting House 5
Frith Old Farmhouse 41
◆ Godinton House & Gardens 45
The Orangery 82
◆ Orchard House, Spenny Lane 85
St Clere 97

Wednesday 23rd
Great Maytham Hall 51
Yew Tree Cottage 123

Friday 25th
Oak Cottage 76

Saturday 26th
Canterbury Cathedral Gardens 14
NEW Denne Manor Farm 29
NEW Manwood House 68
Oak Cottage 76
Orchard End 84
3 Post Office Cottages 89

Sunday 27th
1 Brickwall Cottages 12
Canterbury Cathedral Gardens 14
The Coach House 20
Copton Ash 22
NEW Denne Manor Farm 29
Eagleswood 33
NEW Grange Oast 48
Haven 52
Old Bladbean Stud 77
Orchard End 84
3 Post Office Cottages 89

Monday 28th
The Coach House 20
Falconhurst 39
Haven 52

Wednesday 30th
1 Brickwall Cottages 12

June

Every Monday
NEW The Courtyard 23

Festival Weekend

Saturday 2nd
NEW The Courtyard 23
Faversham Gardens 40
Wyckhurst 121

Sunday 3rd
Chevening 17
NEW The Courtyard 23
Godmersham Park 46
Haven 52

NEW Ivy Chimneys 58
12 The Meadows 70
West Malling Early Summer Gardens 116
Wyckhurst 121
Yew Tree Cottage 123

Tuesday 5th
NEW 14 Anglesey Avenue 1

Wednesday 6th
NEW 14 Anglesey Avenue 1
◆ Chartwell 16

Thursday 7th
NEW 14 Anglesey Avenue 1

Friday 8th
NEW La Mouette 61
NEW Trieston House 111

Saturday 9th
Bishopscourt 6
Little Gables 65
The Old Palace 80
Tram Hatch 110
NEW Trieston House 111
Wyckhurst 121

Sunday 10th
Bishopscourt 6
◆ Boughton Monchelsea Place 9
NEW Chantlers 15
NEW La Mouette 61
Little Gables 65
Nettlestead Place 74
Old Bladbean Stud 77
The Old Palace 80
Rock Cottage 95
Torry Hill 108
Townland 109
NEW Trieston House 111
Whitstable Gardens 117
Wyckhurst 121

Monday 11th
Norton Court 75
NEW Tawnyhill Kennels 106

Tuesday 12th
Norton Court 75
NEW Tawnyhill Kennels 106

Wednesday 13th
◆ Hole Park 54
Yew Tree Cottage 123

Thursday 14th
◆ Mount Ephraim 73

Friday 15th
Falconhurst 39

Saturday 16th
Elham Gardens 36
Watergate House 114

Sunday 17th
34 Cross Road 26
Elham Gardens 36
NEW Saddlers 96
◆ The World Garden at Lullingstone Castle 120
Wye Gardens 122

Wednesday 20th
◆ Doddington Place 30
◆ Emmetts Garden 37
Upper Pryors 112

Friday 22nd
◆ Godinton House & Gardens 45

Saturday 23rd
Womenswold Gardens 118

Sunday 24th
37 The Haydens 53
Old Bladbean Stud 77
Womenswold Gardens 118

Wednesday 27th
Great Maytham Hall 51

Friday 29th
Falconhurst 39

Saturday 30th
◆ Belmont 3

July

Every day
The Blacksmiths Arms 7

Every Monday
NEW The Courtyard 23

Sunday 1st
◆ Belmont 3
NEW The Courtyard 23
Deal Gardens 28
NEW 196 Downs Road 32
Haven 52
Old Church House 79
Smiths Hall 101
NEW Sunnybank 104

Saturday 7th
142 Cramptons Road 24
Eureka 38

Sunday 8th
Bidborough Gardens 4
Calico House 13
142 Cramptons Road 24
Eureka 38
Goddards Green 44
Lords 66
Old Bladbean Stud 77
NEW 86 Ramsden Road 92
Townland 109
Tram Hatch 110

Tuesday 10th
◆ Knole 59

Friday 13th
Falconhurst 39

Saturday 14th
NEW The Garden Gate 42
NEW Yoakley House 124

Sunday 15th
3 Bramble Close 11
◆ Cobham Hall 21
Knowle Hill Farm 60
◆ Quex Gardens 91
Rock Cottage 95
Torry Hill 108

Saturday 21st
NEW Eastling Manor 34
Eureka 38
Gravesend Gardens Group 49
NEW Hurst House 56
Orchard End 84

Sunday 22nd
Eureka 38
Gravesend Gardens Group 49
Haven 52
NEW Hurst House 56
Old Bladbean Stud 77
Orchard End 84
NEW Yoakley House 124

Wednesday 25th
Great Maytham Hall 51

Thursday 26th
◆ Leeds Castle 63

Saturday 28th
The Orangery 82

Sunday 29th
The Orangery 82
Sweetbriar 105
NEW 12 Woods Ley 119

August

Every day
The Blacksmiths Arms 7

Every Monday
NEW The Courtyard 23

Saturday 4th
NEW Denne Manor Farm 29
Eureka 38
Falconhurst 39
The Watch House 113

Sunday 5th
NEW The Courtyard 23
NEW Denne Manor Farm 29
Eureka 38
Leydens 64
Old Bladbean Stud 77
◆ Orchard House, Spenny Lane 85
The Watch House 113

Tuesday 7th
◆ Knole 59

Sunday 12th
NEW 86 Ramsden Road 92
Tram Hatch 110

Saturday 18th
◆ Chilham Castle 18

Sunday 19th
NEW Gardenview 43
Old Bladbean Stud 77
Sweetbriar 105
NEW 12 Woods Ley 119

Wednesday 22nd
Great Maytham Hall 51

Sunday 26th
Haven 52

Monday 27th
Haven 52

September

Every Monday to Monday 17th
NEW The Courtyard 23

Sunday 2nd
NEW The Courtyard 23
◆ Goodnestone Park Gardens 47

Sunday 9th
Boldshaves 8
Rock Cottage 95

Wednesday 12th
◆ Penshurst Place & Gardens 86

Sunday 16th
◆ Doddington Place 30

Wednesday 19th
◆ The Salutation Garden 98

Thursday 20th
◆ Ightham Mote 57

Sunday 23rd
Haven 52

Sunday 30th
◆ Mount Ephraim 73
Nettlestead Place 74
Sweetbriar 105
NEW 12 Woods Ley 119

October

Monday 1st
◆ Sissinghurst Castle Garden 100

Sunday 7th
◆ Hole Park 54

Sunday 21st
Haven 52
Mere House 71

Sunday 28th
◆ Great Comp Garden 50

February 2019

Sunday 10th
Copton Ash 22

Saturday 16th
Knowle Hill Farm 60

Sunday 17th
Copton Ash 22
Knowle Hill Farm 60
Mere House 71

Monday 18th
Knowle Hill Farm 60

Sunday 24th
Mere House 71

By Arrangement
The Old Rectory 81

By Arrangement

NEW 14 Anglesey Avenue 1
Bilting House 5
The Blacksmiths Arms 7
Boundes End 10
1 Brickwall Cottages 12
Churchfield 19
The Coach House 20
Copton Ash 22
NEW The Courtyard 23
142 Cramptons Road 24
Cromlix 25
Crowmarsh House 27
Downs Court 31
Eagleswood 33
Eureka 38
Falconhurst 39
Frith Old Farmhouse 41
NEW The Garden Gate 42
NEW Gardenview 43
Goddards Green 44
Haven 52
Hookwood House 55
Knowle Hill Farm 60
NEW La Mouette 61
Lords 66
Luton House 67
Marshborough Farmhouse 69
The Mount 72
Norton Court 75
The Old Palace 80
The Old Rectory 81
The Orangery 82
The Orchard 83
Orchard End 84
Pheasant Barn 87
Pheasant Farm 88
43 The Ridings 93
Rock Cottage 95
Spring Platt 102
Spring Platt 102
Sweetbriar 105
Timbers 107
Torry Hill 108
Townland 109
Watergate House 114
West Court Lodge 115
Womenswold Gardens 118
Wyckhurst 121

The National Garden Scheme and Perennial, helping gardeners when they are in need

Doddington Place

THE GARDENS

1 NEW 14 ANGLESEY AVENUE

Maidstone, ME15 9SH. Mr & Mrs Mike Brett, 01622 299932, mandh.brett@tiscali.co.uk. *2m S of Maidstone. From Maidstone take A229 (bus routes 5 & 89) and after Swan pub take 1st R into Anglesey Avenue. Limited street parking.* **Tue 1, Wed 2, Thur 3 May, Tue 5, Wed 6, Thur 7 June (11-5). Adm £3. Light refreshments. Visits also by arrangement Apr to June for groups of up to 15.**

Plantsman's 120ft x 30ft garden created over 4 years with many unusual plants. Raised beds, rockeries and troughs accommodating alpine/rock garden plants. Herbaceous and shrub borders plus a shady woodland area at the end of the garden with Hellebores, Erythroniums, Trilliums, Anemones etc.

2 BALMORAL COTTAGE

The Green, Benenden, Cranbrook, TN17 4DL. Charlotte Molesworth, thepottingshedholidaylet@gmail.com. *Few 100 yards down unmade track to W of St George's Church, Benenden.* **Sun 29 Apr, Sun 6 May (12-6). Adm £6, chd £2.50. Refreshments available at Hole Park (separate adm price).**

An owner created and maintained garden now 33yrs mature. Varied, romantic and extensive topiary form the backbone for mixed borders. Vegetable garden, organically managed. Particular attention to the needs of nesting birds and small mammals lend this artistic plantswoman's garden a rare and unusual quality. Featured on All Gardens Great and Small, More 4.

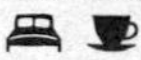

3 ◆ BELMONT

Belmont Park, Throwley, Faversham, ME13 0HH. Harris (Belmont) Charity, 01795 890202, administrator@belmont-house.org, www.belmont-house.org. *4½m SW of Faversham. A251 Faversham-Ashford. At Badlesmere, brown tourist signs to Belmont.* **For NGS: Sat 30 June, Sun 1 July (12-5). Adm £5, chd free. Home-made teas. For other opening times and information, please phone, email or visit garden website.**

Belmont House is surrounded by large formal lawns that are landscaped with fine specimen trees, a pinetum and a walled garden containing long borders, wisteria and large rose border. There is a second walled kitchen garden, restored in 2000 (to a design by Arabella Lennox Boyd), featuring lawns, hop arbours, pleached fruit, vegetables and flowers. During the season (April- Sept) the tea room is open on Wednesdays from 12pm for light lunches and afternoon teas. At the weekend tea and home-made cake available between 1-5pm. Out of season the tea room is open on a self service basis and welcomes visitors.

GROUP OPENING

4 BIDBOROUGH GARDENS

Bidborough, Tunbridge Wells, TN4 0XB. *3m N of Tunbridge Wells, between Tonbridge & Tunbridge Wells W off A26. Take B2176 Bidborough Ridge signed to Penshurst. Take 1st L into Darnley Drive, then 1st R into St Lawrence Ave.* **Sun 8 July (1-5). Combined adm £5, chd free. Home-made teas. Gluten and dairy free cake available.** Donation to Hospice in the Weald.

The Bidborough gardens (collect garden list from Boundes End) are in a small village at the heart of which are The Kentish Hare pub (book in advance), the church, village store and primary school. It is a thriving community with many clubs incl a very active Garden Association! In the surrounding countryside there are several local walks. The gardens are owner designed. Enjoy a variety of formal and informal features in front and main gardens, raised beds, a pebble bed, terraces and pergolas. There are specimen trees, interesting plants and plenty of places to sit and enjoy the peaceful surroundings. Partial wheelchair access, some gardens have steps.

5 BILTING HOUSE

nr Ashford, TN25 4HA. Mr John Erle-Drax, 07764 580011, jdrax@marlboroughfineart.com. *5m NE of Ashford. A28, 9m S from Canterbury. Wye 1½m.* **Sun 22 Apr, Sun 20 May (2-6). Adm £5, chd free. Home-made teas. Visits also by arrangement Apr to June for groups 10+.**

6 acre garden with ha-ha set in beautiful part of Stour Valley. Wide variety of rhododendrons, azaleas and ornamental shrubs. Woodland walk with spring bulbs. Mature arboretum with recent planting of specimen trees. Rose garden and herbaceous borders. Conservatory.

6 BISHOPSCOURT

24 St Margaret's Street, Rochester, ME1 1TS. Mrs Bridget Langstaff, 07816 828439. *Central Rochester, nr castle & cathedral. On St Margaret's St at junction with Vines Lane. Rochester train stn 7 mins walk. Disabled parking only at garden but many car parks within 5-7 mins walk.* **Sat 9, Sun 10 June (1-5). Adm £4, chd free. Home-made teas. Home-made cakes for sale. Tea and coffee is free.**

The residence of the Bishop of Rochester, this 1 acre historic walled garden is a peaceful oasis in the heart of Rochester with views of the castle from a raised lookout. Mature trees, lawns, yew hedges, rose garden, sculptures, fountain, wild flowers and mixed borders with perennials. Greenhouse and small vegetable garden. WC incl disabled.

7 THE BLACKSMITHS ARMS

Cudham Lane South, Cudham, Sevenoaks, TN14 7QB. Joyce Cole, 01959 572678,

mail@theblacksmithsarms.co.uk. *Leave M25 at J4. At Hewitts r'about take 3rd exit onto A21. At Pratts Bottom r'about take 2nd exit onto A21. At r'about take 1st exit onto Cudham Lane North & follow for 4m.* **Daily Sun 1 July to Fri 31 Aug (1-7). Adm by donation. Light refreshments. Lunches are available 12pm-3pm & Dinner 7pm-9pm If any group would like Cream Teas please arrange by phoning the Pub. Visits also by arrangement July & Aug. Please phone the Pub to let us know how many people.**
Exceptionally pretty and colourful summer garden set in the grounds of a C17 inn. Unusual varieties of summer bedding plants and annuals, mostly grown and cared for by the landlady. Decking and seating areas surrounded by spectacular hanging baskets and patio displays. Open lawn area with deep colour coordinated beds. We also are proud of our small natural area to attract and sustain wildlife. Partial wheelchair access inside PH.

8 BOLDSHAVES

Woodchurch, nr Ashford Kent, TN26 3RA. Mr & Mrs Peregrine Massey, 01233 860302, masseypd@hotmail.co.uk, www.boldshaves.co.uk. *Between Woodchurch & High Halden off Redbrook St. From A28 towards Ashford turn R in High Halden at village green; 2nd R on to Redbrook St, then R down unmarked lane after ½m to brick entrance to Boldshaves at bottom of hill.* **Sun 22 Apr, Sun 9 Sept (2-6). Adm £6, chd free. Home-made teas in C17 Barn.** Donation to Kent Minds.
7 acre garden, partly terraced, S-facing, with wide range of ornamental trees and shrubs, walled garden, Italian garden, Diamond Jubilee garden, camellia dell, herbaceous borders (incl flame bed, red borders and rainbow border), bluebell walks in April, woodland and ponds. **For details of other opening times see garden website www.boldshaves.co.uk**. Grass paths.

9 ◆ BOUGHTON MONCHELSEA PLACE

Church Hill, Boughton Monchelsea, Maidstone, ME17 4BU. Mr & Mrs Dominic Kendrick, 01622 743120, mk@boughtonplace.co.uk, www.boughtonplace.co.uk. *4m SE of Maidstone. From Maidstone follow A229 (Hastings Rd) S for 3½m to major T-lights at Linton Xrds, turn L onto B2163, house 1m on R; or take J8 off M20 & follow Leeds Castle signs to B2163, house 5½m on L.* **For NGS: Sun 13 May, Sun 10 June (2-5.30). Adm £5, chd £1. Home-made teas. Fantastic selection of cakes supplied and served by ladies from St. Peter's Church. For other opening times and information, please phone, email or visit garden website.**
150 acre estate mainly park and woodland, spectacular views over own deer park and the Weald. Grade I manor house (not open). Courtyard herb garden, intimate walled gardens, box hedges, herbaceous borders, orchard. Planting is romantic rather than manicured. Terrace with panoramic views over deer park, bluebell woods, wisteria tunnel, David Austin roses, traditional greenhouse and kitchen garden. Do not miss St. Peter's Church next door. Regret, no dogs.

10 BOUNDES END

2 St Lawrence Avenue, Bidborough, Tunbridge Wells, TN4 0XB. Carole & Mike Marks, 01892 542233, carole.marks@btinternet.com, www.boundesendgarden.co.uk. *Between Tonbridge & Tunbridge Wells off A26. Take B2176 Bidborough Ridge signed to Penshurst. Take 1st L into Darnley Drive, then 1st R into St Lawrence Ave.* **Visits by arrangement June to Aug groups 20 max. Adm £3, chd free. Home-made teas. Home-made teas incl gluten and dairy free..** Donation to Hospice in the Weald.
Garden, designed by owners, on an unusually shaped ⅓ acre plot formed from 2 triangles of land. Front garden features raised beds, and the main garden divided into a formal area with terrace, pebble bed and 2 pergolas, an informal area in woodland setting with interesting features and specimen trees. Plenty of places to sit and enjoy the garden. Some uneven ground in lower garden.

Townland

© Leigh Clapp

11 3 BRAMBLE CLOSE

Wye, TN25 5QA. Dr M Copland. *Bramble Close is off Bramble Lane, nearly opp Wye Motors and close to Wye Stn where parking is available.* **Sun 15 July (2-6). Adm £3.50, chd free. Opening with Wye Gardens on Sun 17 June.**

A very wild, experimental garden sown from seed 1987-89. Wild flower meadow, pond and ditches, mown paths, native copse and hedges buzzing with wildlife - a unique experience. Demonstrating how plants manipulate diseases, insects and other animals to establish and maintain their natural population density. Featured on BBC Gardeners World in July 2017. Some soft ground with some uneven pathways due to mole and rabbit activity but with attempts to stabilise these patches on the day.

12 1 BRICKWALL COTTAGES

Frittenden, Cranbrook, TN17 2DH. Mrs Sue Martin, 01580 852425, sue.martin@talktalk.net, www.geumcollection.co.uk. *6m NW of Tenterden. E of A229 between Cranbrook & Staplehurst & W of A274 between Biddenden & Headcorn. Park in village & walk along footpath opp school.* **Wed 2, Sun 6, Sun 27, Wed 30 May (2-5). Adm £4.50, chd free. Home-made teas. Visits also by arrangement Apr & May groups 30 max.**

Although less than ¼ acre, the garden gives the impression of being much larger as it is made up of several rooms all intensively planted with a wide range of hardy perennials, bulbs and shrubs, with over 100 geums which comprise the National Collection planted throughout the garden. Pergolas provide supports for climbing plants and there is a small formal pond. Featured in Landscape magazine, in article entitled 'Brimming over with beauty'. Some paths are narrow and wheelchairs may not be able to reach far end of garden.

NPC

13 CALICO HOUSE

The Street, Newnham, Sittingbourne, ME9 0LN. Graham Lloyd-Brunt, lloydbrunt.com. *Garden located in middle of village on road that runs through Newnham from A2 to A20. Parking in field off Sharsted Hill.* **Sun 8 July (1-6). Adm £5, chd free. Cream teas. Also open Lords.**

The garden at Calico House was made over the past decade utilising yew hedges and topiary dating from the 1920s. Terraced lawns and themed flower borders are set within a traditional English garden framework of hedges and walks. All borders have contemporary plantings of tall herbaceous flowers in distinct cool, exotic and white palettes.

GROUP OPENING

14 CANTERBURY CATHEDRAL GARDENS

Canterbury, CT1 2EP. 01227 762862, events@canterbury-cathedral.org, www.canterbury-cathedral.org. *Canterbury Cathedral Precincts.* **Enter precincts via main Christchurch gate.** *No access for cars, use park & ride or public car parks.* **Sat 26 May (11-5), Sun 27 May (2-5). Combined adm £5, chd free. Home-made teas on Green Court. Please note - on Sat, in addition to £5 adm, precinct charges apply. On Sun there are no precinct charges.**

ARCHDEACONRY
Archdeacon Jo Kelly-Moore.

THE DEANERY
The Dean.

15 THE PRECINCTS
Canon Papadapulos.

19 THE PRECINCTS
Canon Librarian.

22 THE PRECINCTS
Canon Clare Edwards.

A wonderful opportunity to visit and enjoy 5 Canonical gardens within the historic precincts of Canterbury Cathedral. The Deanery Garden with wonderful roses, wildflower planting and orchard, unusual medlar tree, vegetable garden and wild fowl enclosure; the Archdeaconry includes the ancient mulberry tree, contrasting traditional and modern planting and now both a Japanese and New World influence. Three further gardens, reflecting each Canon's style, offer sweeping herbaceous banks, delightful enclosed spaces, and areas planted to attract and support wildlife. Step back in time and see the herb garden, which show the use of herbs for medicinal purposes in the Middle Ages. The walled Memorial Garden has wonderful wisteria, formal roses, mixed borders and the stone war memorial at its centre, and hidden Bastion Chapel in the city wall. A new garden planted in the Friends' name surrounds the Buff's statue. Gardeners' plant stall and home-made refreshments. Dover Beekeepers Association, up close and personal opportunity with Birds of Prey and unique access to Bastion Chapel. Classic cars on Green Court. Archdeaconry has separate entrance for people who require a flat entrance.

15 NEW CHANTLERS

Wellers Town Road, Chiddingstone, Edenbridge, TN8 7BD. Fiona & J Leathers. *½ mile from Chiddingstone village going south. From Chiddingstone Causeway going west take 1st L turn to Chiddingstone. At top of hill turn L by Oast house. 300m on L.* **Sun 10 June (1.30-5.30). Adm £5, chd free. Home-made teas.**

One acre informal garden around C16 Wealden farmhouse, developed over 15 years. Divided into different areas, with views and seating. Mixed borders, prairie garden, small ha-ha, pond and vegetable potager. Main areas on the flat, with no steps.

16 ◆ CHARTWELL

Mapleton Road, Westerham, TN16 1PS. National Trust, 01732 868381, chartwell@nationaltrust.org.uk, www.nationaltrust.org.uk/chartwell. *4m N of Edenbridge, 2m S of Westerham. Fork L off B2026 after 1½m.* **For NGS: Wed 6 June (10-5). Adm £7.20, chd £3.60. For other opening times and information, please phone, email or visit garden website.**

Informal gardens on hillside with glorious views over Weald of Kent. Water features and lakes together with red brick wall built by Sir Winston Churchill, former owner of Chartwell. Lady Churchill's rose garden. Avenue of golden roses runs down the centre of a must-see productive kitchen garden. Hard paths to Lady Churchill's rose garden and the terrace. Some steep slopes and steps.

17 CHEVENING

Nr Sevenoaks, TN14 6HG. The Board of Trustees of the Chevening Estate, www.cheveninghouse.com. *4m NW of Sevenoaks. Turn N off A25 at Sundridge T-lights on to B2211; at Chevening Xrds 1½m turn L.* **Sun 3 June (2-5). Adm £7, chd £1. Home-made teas.**

The pleasure grounds of the Earls Stanhope at Chevening House are today characterised by lawns and wooded walks around an ornamental lake. First laid out between 1690 and 1720 in the French formal style, in the 1770s a more informal English design was introduced. In early C19 lawns, parterres and a maze were established and many specimen trees planted to shade woodland walks. The garden is being gradually restored following a plan by Elizabeth Banks, developed by George Carter, which reflects all the main periods of its development. Group guided tours of parks and gardens can sometimes be arranged with the Estate Office when house is unoccupied. Gentle slopes, gravel paths throughout.

18 ◆ CHILHAM CASTLE

Canterbury, CT4 8DB. Mr Stuart Wheeler, 01227 733100, chilhamcastleinfo@gmail.com, www.chilham-castle.co.uk. *6m SW of Canterbury, 7m NE of Ashford, centre of Chilham Village. Follow NGS signs from A28 or A252 up to Chilham village square & through main gates of Chilham Castle.* **For NGS: Sat 18 Aug (10-4). Adm £5, chd free. Light refreshments. For other opening times and information, please phone, email or visit garden website.**

The garden surrounds Jacobean house 1616 (not open). C17 terraces with herbaceous borders. Topiary frames the magnificent views with lake walk below. Extensive kitchen and cutting garden beyond spring bulb filled quiet garden. Established trees and ha-ha lead onto park. Check website for other events and attractions. Partial wheelchair access.

19 CHURCHFIELD

Pilgrims Way, Postling, Hythe, CT21 4EY. Chris and Nikki Clark, 01303 863558, coulclark@hotmail.com. *2m NW of Hythe. From M20 J11 turn S onto A20. 1st L after ½m on bend take rd signed Lyminge. 1st L into Postling.* **Visits by arrangement May to Sept with West Court Lodge. Groups 35 max. Home-made teas.**

At the base of the Downs, springs rising in this garden form the source of the East Stour. Two large ponds are home to wildfowl and fish and the banks have been planted with drifts of primula, large leaved herbaceous bamboo and ferns. The rest of the 5 acre garden is a Kent cobnut platt and vegetable garden, large grass areas and naturally planted borders and woodland. Postling Church open for visitors. Areas around water may be slippery. Children must be carefully supervised.

20 THE COACH HOUSE

Kemsdale Road, Hernhill, Faversham, ME13 9JP. Alison & Philip West, 07801 824867, alison.west@kemsdale.plus.com. *3m E of Faversham. At J7 of M2 take A299, signed Margate. After 600 metres take 1st exit signed Hernhill, take 1st L over dual carriageway to T-junction, turn R & follow yellow NGS signs.* **Sun 27, Mon 28 May (11-6). Adm £4, chd free. Cream teas. Visits also by arrangement May to Sept. Cream teas or coffee/tea and biscuits by prior arrangement.**

The ¾ acre garden has views over surrounding fruit producing farmland. Sloping terraced site, and island beds with yr-round interest, a pond room, herbaceous borders containing bulbs, shrubs, perennials, and a tropical bed. The different areas are connected by flowing curved paths. Unusual planting on light sandy soil where wildlife is encouraged. Kent Wild for Wildlife gold award winner. Gold Award from Kent Wildlife Trust - Wild about Wildlife. Most of garden accessible to wheelchairs. Seating available in all areas.

21 ◆ COBHAM HALL

Cobham, DA12 3BL. Mr D Standen (Bursar), 01474 823371, www.cobhamhall.com. *3m W of Rochester, 8m E of M25 J2. Ignore SatNav directions to Lodge Lane. Entrance drive is off Brewers Rd, 50 metres E from Cobham/Shorne A2 junction.* **For NGS: Mon 2 Apr, Sun 15 July (2-5). Adm £3, chd free. Home-made teas in the Gilt Hall. For other opening times and information, please phone or visit garden website.**

1584 brick mansion (open for tours) and parkland of historical importance, now a boarding and day school for girls. Some herbaceous borders, formal parterres, drifts of daffodils, C17 garden walls, yew hedges and lime avenue. Humphry Repton designed 50 hectares of park, most garden follies restored in 2009. Combined with tours to the Darnley Mausoleum. Film location for BBC's

Bleak House series and films by MGM and Universal. ITV serial The Great Fire. CBBC filmed serial 1 & 2 of Hetty Feather. Gravel and slab paths through gardens. Land uneven, many slopes. Stairs and steps in Main Hall. Please call in advance to ensure assistance.

22 COPTON ASH

105 Ashford Road, Faversham, ME13 8XW. Drs Tim & Gillian Ingram, 01795 535919, coptonash@yahoo.co.uk, www.coptonash.plus.com. *½m S of A2, Faversham. On A251 Faversham to Ashford rd. Opp E bound J6 with M2. Park in nearby laybys.* **Sun 18 Feb (12-4). Sun 18 Mar (12-5), also open Mount Ephraim. Sun 8, Sun 15 Apr (12-5). Sun 29 Apr (12-5), also open Eagleswood. Sun 13 May (12-5). Sun 27 May (12-5), also open The Coach House. Adm £4, chd free. Home-made teas. Home-made soup (Feb only). 2019: Sun 10, Sun 17 Feb. Visits also by arrangement Feb to June groups of 10+.**

Garden grown out of a love and fascination with plants. Contains very wide collection incl many rarities and newly introduced species raised from wild seed. Special interest in woodland flowers, snowdrops and hellebores with flowering trees and shrubs of spring. Refreshed Mediterranean plantings to adapt to a warming climate. Raised beds with choice alpines and bulbs. Small alpine nursery. Gravel drive, shallow step by house and some narrow grass paths.

23 NEW THE COURTYARD

Elmley Road, Minster On Sea, Sheerness, ME12 3SS. Kyle Ratcliffe, 07875 507937, ratcliffekyle@yahoo.co.uk. *Located on The Isle of Sheppey, 11 miles from the M2. From the A2500, travel past the rugby club, over several small roundabouts and turn immediately R after the 2nd hand car lot. Our garden is situated to the rear of the 5th bungalow on the L.* **Sun 11 Mar, Sun 1 Apr (10.30-2). Every Mon 2 Apr to 17 Sept (10.30-2). Sun 6 May, Sat 2, Sun 3 June, Sun 1 July, Sun 5 Aug, Sun 2 Sept (10.30-2). Adm £5, chd free. Home-made teas. Visits also by arrangement Mar to Sept. To buy tickets email for Paypal/Internet Banking info. Families & larger groups (up to 20) welcome.**

A young garden and home created in October 2016 by the BBC DIY SOS team. This is our family garden and smallholding which is enjoyed by our four young children daily. Our family garden has planted borders and raised beds. Having raised flower beds aids our two young sons who are full-time wheelchair users, to enjoy their garden too. Sensory based, family focused garden. We are smallholding with a few hens, pigs, sheep, honey bees and hives, a small raised fish pond and a little pony. We welcome all families - especially those with children with special needs. Tarmac and hard stone pathways and drive.

24 142 CRAMPTONS ROAD

Sevenoaks, TN14 5DZ. Mr Bennet Smith, bennet.smith@hotmail.co.uk. *4m from M25 J5. 1½m N of Sevenoaks, off Otford Road (A225) between Bat & Ball T-lights & Otford. Access to garden via side/rear passage. Limited parking in Cramptons Rd.* **Sat 7, Sun 8 July (11-5.30). Adm £3, chd free. Light refreshments. Visits also by arrangement June to Sept group size c.10-15.**

A very small, lush and leafy plantsman's oasis. A tapestry of carefully chosen plants from around the world selected for their texture, elegance, leaf size and shape or long season interest, or perhaps for their unusual habit or rarity: schefflera, wildlife-friendly umbellifers, trochodendron, tetrapanax, pseudopanax & Aesculus wangii. Discover what can be created and combined in a tiny space! Gardeners' World Small Garden of the Year Finalist & The English Garden Magazine.

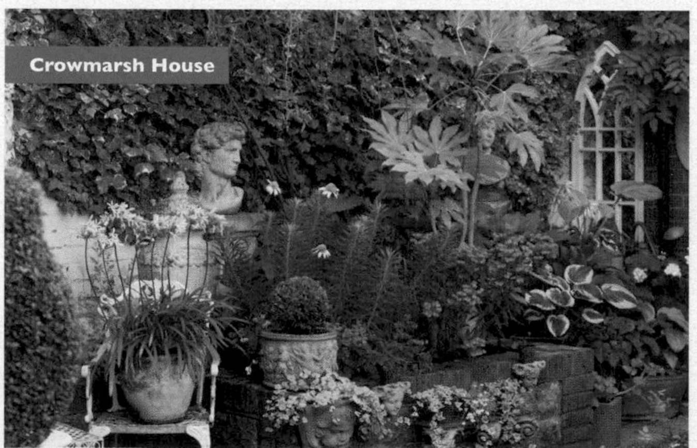

Crowmarsh House

© Leigh Clapp

25 CROMLIX

Otford Lane, Halstead, Sevenoaks, TN14 7EB. The Kitchener family, 01959 532282, geoffreykitchener@yahoo.com. *5m NW of Sevenoaks, 3m from M25 J4. Exit M25 at J4 for A21/A224. After ½m, 1st exit at r'bout for Badgers Mount A224. At next r'bout 3rd exit to Shoreham Ln, past PH, turn L at Xrds to Otford Ln. Field access to garden 400yds on L.* **Visits by arrangement June & July groups 10+. Adm £5, chd free. Light refreshments.** Donation to West Kent Cruse Bereavement Care.

13 acre grounds, of which 7 acres are a botanist's garden with some unusual plants. Colourful herbaceous

borders, scented garden, croquet and tennis lawns contrast with informal wooded walks opening up varied vistas. Laid out in the 1960s with specimen trees incl Giant Redwood and further enhanced since 2010; many bamboos. Wisteria covers tree tops and shaded areas accommodate c.400 ferns.

26 34 CROSS ROAD

Walmer, CT14 9LB. Mr Peter Jacob & Mrs Margaret Wilson. *A258 Dover to Deal. In Upper Walmer turn L into Station Rd. Under railway bridge, Cross Rd is 2nd R. Do not approach from Ringwould as SatNav suggests.* **Sun 22 Apr, Sun 17 June (11-5). Adm £3.50, chd free.**

An exciting and lovely garden combining great artistic sensibility with an extensive and fascinating variety of plants. ⅓ acre plantsman's garden. Collection of daphnes, hardy geraniums, herbaceous beds, unusual trees, shrubs and alpines.

27 CROWMARSH HOUSE

Boormans Mews, Wateringbury, Maidstone, ME18 5DU. Mrs Yvonne Marks, 01622 434897, dandymarks@hotmail.co.uk. *5m WSW of Maidstone. Located in private rd in centre of village nr A26 Xrds & opp free public village hall car park on B2015. Visitors should park here & follow yellow NGS signs.* **Visits by arrangement in June max 8 people. Adm £3.50, chd free. Home-made teas. Teas £3.**

Inspirational small courtyard Mediterranean style white garden created since 2004 and nestled in the heart of Wateringbury. Parterre with box topiary, lonicera nitida hedging and mind your own business paths. Fig and olive trees. Wisteria, roses, hibiscus and lavender. Raised beds with perennials. Water features, antique statuary and chimney pots. Seating to enjoy the garden. Featured in Kent Life Magazine and winner of Kent Life Garden competition. Please contact owner on arrival to enable access for wheelchairs.

GROUP OPENING

28 DEAL GARDENS

Deal, CT14 6EB. *A258 to Deal. Signs from all town car parks, maps & tickets at all gardens.* **Sun 1 July (11-5). Combined adm £5, chd free. Home-made teas at 53 Sandown Rd.**

4 GEORGE ALLEY
Lyn Freeman & Barry Popple, 07889572676, lynandbarry10@yahoo.co.uk, www.gleaners.co.uk.

THE LANDMARK GARDEN
Imogen Jenkins on behalf of the DWCA, www.facebook.com/thelandmarkgarden.

NEW **4 ROBERT STREET**
Christine Hayes-Watkins.

NEW **10 ST GEORGES ROAD**
Peter Tullo, 01304694144, bearswell@gmail.com.

53 SANDOWN ROAD
Robin Green & Ralph Cade.

88 WEST STREET
Lyn & Peter Buller.

Start tour from any town car park (signs from here). 88 West Street: Small cottage garden, full of perennials, shrubs, clematis and roses. Finalist Kent Life Amateur Gardener Award. 53 Sandown Road: Three rooms incl decked terrace with pots, courtyard with water feature and olive trees. Studio and greenhouse. Landmark Community Garden: Useful native plants, self seeding, edible annuals, fruiting perennials and useful foliage. 130 labelled plants. Gleaners: Down a pretty alleyway a secret garden. Colourful courtyard leading to a vibrant cottage garden with summer house. Robert Street: A small walled garden divided into four separate areas each holding little surprises; bedding plants, perennials, shrubs, trees, a small water feature and mature bamboos. 10 St Georges Rd: North facing walled garden attached to 18 Century house. Lawn, borders and pond overlooked by majestic willow tree. Partial wheelchair access at 53 Sandown Rd, 4 Robert Street and 88 West Street. No access at Gleaners.

29 NEW DENNE MANOR FARM

Denne Manor Lane, Shottenden, Canterbury, CT4 8JJ. Louisa Mills. *Into the centre of the hamlet of Shottenden at the only 4 way Xrds sign posted to Denne Manor Lane - No Through Rd continue R to very end of Denne Manor Lane.* **Sat 26, Sun 27 May, Sat 4, Sun 5 Aug (12-4). Adm £5, chd free. Light refreshments.**

Denne Manor House & Barn is a 15th & 17th Century farm house & restored barn. It is set in approx 10 acres of parkland with 2 Rare Breed Sheep paddocks. The Manor Gardens are intricate and at the front have a Kentish apple tree designed Buxus topary miniature maze. There is detail and interest plus open lawns for picnicking. Toilet with wheel chair access is available but not specifically a disabled toilet.

30 ◆ DODDINGTON PLACE

Church Lane, Doddington, Sittingbourne, ME9 0BB. Mr & Mrs Richard Oldfield, 01795 886101, enquiries@doddingtonplacegdns.co.uk, www.doddingtonplacegardens.co.uk. *6m SE of Sittingbourne. From A20 turn N opp Lenham or from A2 turn S at Teynham or Ospringe (Faversham), all 4m.* **For NGS: Sun 18 Feb (11-4); Wed 9 May, Wed 20 June, Sun 16 Sept (11-5). Adm £7, chd £2. Cream teas. For other opening times and information, please phone, email or visit garden website.**

10 acre garden, landscaped with wide views; trees and cloud clipped yew hedges; woodland garden with azaleas and rhododendrons; Edwardian rock garden recently renovated (not wheelchair accessible); formal garden with mixed borders. New gothic folly. Snowdrops in February. Wheelchair access possible to majority of gardens except rock garden.

31 DOWNS COURT

Church Lane, Boughton Aluph, Ashford, TN25 4EU. Mr & Mrs Bay Green, 07984 558945, bay@baygee.com. *4m NE of Ashford. From A28 Ashford or Canterbury, after Wye Xrds take next turn NW to Boughton Aluph Church. Fork R at pillar box, garden only drive on R.* **Visits by arrangement June & July. Adm £5, chd free. Refreshments by prior arrangement and charged separately.**

3 acre downland garden on alkaline soil with fine trees, mature yew and box hedges, mixed borders with many unusual plants. Shrub roses and rose arch pathway, small parterre. Sweeping lawns and lovely views over surrounding countryside.

32 NEW 196 DOWNS ROAD

Walmer, Deal, CT14 7TN. Sue Turner. *A258 Deal towards Dover. At Walmer turn R into Palmerston rd. At second Xrds turn L into Downs rd. From Dover A258 to Walmer. After Esso garage turn L into Palmerston rd then as above.* **Sun 1 July (10-4). Adm £3.50, chd free. Also open Sunnybank.**

New to the National Garden scheme, this typical town house garden has a long plot divided into spaces with different planting schemes. Enter via a side gate and walk through an arch of Wisteria into an array of shrubs and perennials in mixed borders with fruit trees, clematis and roses. A variety of plants homegrown from seed and cuttings includes shrubs, delphiniums, penstemon and agapanthus. Narrow side entrance with steps. From patio area more steps to main garden.

33 EAGLESWOOD

Slade Road, Warren Street, Lenham, ME17 2EG. Mike & Edith Darvill, 01622 858702, mike.darvill@btinternet.com. *Going E on A20 nr Lenham, L into Hubbards Hill for approx 1m then 2nd L into Slade Rd. Garden 150yds on R. Coaches permitted.* **Sun 29 Apr (11-5), also open Frith Old Farmhouse. Sun 27 May (11-5); Sun Oct 14 (11-5). Adm £4, chd free. Light refreshments. Visits also by arrangement Apr to Oct.** Donation to Demelza House Hospice.

2 acre plantsman's garden situated high on N-Downs, developed over the past 30yrs. Wide range of trees and shrubs (many unusual), herbaceous material and woodland plants grown to give yr-round interest, particularly in spring and for autumn colour. Some gravel areas. Grass paths may be uneven and slippery when wet.

34 NEW EASTLING MANOR

Eastling, Faversham, ME13 0AX. John & Bay Lees. *In the centre of Easting. opp the Carpenters Arms Pub in the centre of Eastling.* **Sat 21 July (2-5.30). Adm £5, chd free. Home-made teas.**

The garden surrounds a historically important, medieval village house and incl a knot garden, herbaceous borders, ponds, walled gardens and an orchard. The owners inherited a well established structure of topiary and hard landscaping but have softened the garden with the addition of new beds filled with drifts of lavender, airy grasses, roses and a mixture of perennial and annual plants. Opp the village pub where food is served. Good B&Bs in the village. Attractive and interesting village with church. Partial wheelchair access.

35 ELGIN HOUSE

Main Road, Knockholt, Sevenoaks, TN14 7LH. Mrs Avril Bromley. *Off A21 between Sevenoaks/Orpington at Pratts Bottom r'about road signed Knockholt (Rushmore Hill) 3m on R, follow yellow NGS signs. Main Road is continuation of Rushmore Hill.* **Sun 13 May (12-5). Adm £5, chd free. Home-made teas.**

Victorian family house surrounded by a garden which has evolved over the last 49yrs - rhododendrons, azaleas, wisteria, camellias, magnolias, mature trees, incl a magnificent cedar tree, and spacious lawns. This garden is on the top of the North Downs.

GROUP OPENING

36 ELHAM GARDENS

Elham, CT4 6TU. *10m S of Canterbury, 6m N of Hythe. Enter Elham from Lyminge (off A20) or Barham (off A2). Car parking in village school grounds, weather permitting. Tickets & maps from gazebo on main road opp Browns estate agents.* **Sat 16 June (11-4.30); Sun 17 June (2-5.30). Combined adm £5, chd free. Light refreshments in St Mary's Church for Ploughman's lunches, and home made teas in the Old Vicarage gardens available on both days.**

Elham has a thriving community of amateur gardeners, many of whom will open their gardens in this idyllic setting. The wide range of styles of garden are all within easy walking distance of each other and owners will be on hand to ensure you make the most of your visit. This picturesque village with its beautiful Grade I listed St Mary's church at its centre, is situated in glorious countryside within the Elham Valley Area of Outstanding Natural Beauty. The Elham Summer Farmers Market will be open in The Square between 11.00am and 2.00pm on Sunday 17th June.

37 ◆ EMMETTS GARDEN

Ide Hill, Sevenoaks, TN14 6BA. National Trust, 01732 751507, emmetts@nationaltrust.org.uk, www.nationaltrust.org.uk/emmetts-garden. *5m SW of Sevenoaks. 1½m S of A25 on Sundridge-Ide Hill Rd. 1½m N of Ide Hill off B2042.* **For NGS: Wed 20 June (10-4). Adm £8.50, chd £4.25. For other opening times and information, please phone, email or visit garden website.**

5 acre hillside garden, with the highest tree top in Kent, noted for its fine collection of rare trees and flowering shrubs. The garden

is particularly fine in spring, while a rose garden, rock garden and extensive planting of acers for autumn colour extend the interest throughout the season. Hard paths to the Old Stables for light refreshments and WC. Some steep slopes. Volunteer driven buggy available for lifts up steepest hill.

38 EUREKA

Buckhurst Road, Westerham Hill, TN16 2HR. Gordon & Suzanne Wright, 01959 570848, sb.wright@btinternet.com. *Off A233, 1½m N of Westerham, 1m S from centre of Biggin Hill. 5m from J5 & J6 of M25 Parking at Westerham Heights Garden Centre at top of Westerham Hill on A233, 200yds from garden. SATNAV use TN16 2HW. Disabled parking at house.* **Sat 7, Sun 8, Sat 21, Sun 22 July, Sat 4, Sun 5 Aug (12-4). Adm £5, chd free. Home-made teas. Visits also by arrangement July & Aug for groups 30+.**
Approx 1 acre garden with a blaze of colourful displays in perennial borders and the 8 cartwheel centre beds. Hundreds of annuals in 50 tubs and troughs and 50 hanging baskets. Sculptures, garden art, chickens, lots of seating, and stairs to a viewing platform. Many quirky surprises at every turn. Great fun for children incl a Treasure Trail. Garden art incl 12ft dragon, a horse's head carved out of a 200yr old yew tree stump and a 10ft dragonfly on a reed. Wheelchair access to most of the garden.

39 FALCONHURST

Cowden Pound Road, Markbeech, Edenbridge, TN8 5NR. Mr & Mrs Charles Talbot, 01342 850526, nicola@falconhurst.co.uk, www.falconhurst.co.uk. *3m SE of Edenbridge. B2026 at Queens Arms PH turn E to Markbeech. 2nd drive on R before Markbeech village.* **Mon 28 May, Fri 15, Fri 29 June, Fri 13 July, Sat 4 Aug (1.30-5). Adm £5, chd free. Home-made teas. Visits also by arrangement May to Oct. Groups 10 - 50 max. Refreshments available.**
4 acre garden with fabulous views devised and cared for by the same family for 160yrs. Deep mixed borders with old roses, peonies, shrubs and a wide variety of herbaceous and annual plants; ruin garden; walled garden; interesting mature trees and shrubs; kitchen garden; wildflower meadows with woodland and pond walks. Woodland pigs; orchard chickens; lambs in the paddocks.

GROUP OPENING

40 FAVERSHAM GARDENS

Faversham, ME13 8QN. *On edge of town, short distance from A2 & train stn. From M2 J6 take A251, L into A2, R into The Mall, cont along Forbes Road, then L before zebra crossing/into Athelstan Road. Combined tickets & maps from No 54.* **Sat 2 June (10-5). Combined adm £5, chd free.**

54 ATHELSTAN ROAD
Sarah Langton-Lockton OBE.

19 NEWTON ROAD
Posy Gentles, www.posygentles.co.uk.

17 NORMAN ROAD
Mary & John Cousins.

3 distinctive walled gardens in historic Faversham. Start at 54 Athelstan Road. Newly planted on a neglected site, the garden mirrors the angular 1922 house. Ornamental vegetable beds take centre stage. Climbing roses, clematis, thalictrums, Regale lilies, sibirica irises and unusual shrubs thrive, sheltered by old walls. On to 17 Norman Road, an established town garden offering privacy and delight. A large apple tree gives dappled shade, wisteria and clematis clothe the walls. Small ponds teem with wildlife. Vegetables and herbs are near the kitchen door; perennials interwoven with mature shrubs throughout. 19 Newton Road, a long, thin town garden, where the plant loving owner has used billowing roses, shrubs, climbers and perennials to blur boundaries. The judicious planting of trees, and curving paths, veil rather than conceal the garden as you move through it. Predominately soft colour scheme of creams, peaches and faded lilacs. Teas widely available in Faversham. Level access to 54 Athelstan Road.

41 FRITH OLD FARMHOUSE

Frith Road, Otterden, Faversham, ME13 0DD. Drs Gillian & Peter Regan, 01795 890556, peter.regan@cantab.net. *½m off Lenham to Faversham rd. From A20 E of Lenham turn N up Hubbards Hill, follow signs Eastling; after 4m turn L into Frith Road. From A2 in Faversham turn S (Brogdale Rd); continue 7m (thro' Eastling), turn R into Frith Road.* **Sun 15 Apr (11-5), also open Copton Ash. Sun 29 Apr (11-5), also open Eagleswood. Sun 20 May (11-5). Adm £4, chd free. Home-made teas. Visits also by arrangement Apr to Sept groups 2 to 50 max; please contact owners in advance.**
A riot of plants growing together as if in the wild, developed over 40 yrs. No neat edges or formal beds, but several hundred interesting (& some very unusual) plants. Trees and shrubs chosen for year-round appeal. Special interest in bulbs and woodland plants. 'Wild about Gardening' Gold award. Visitor comments - 'a plethora of plants', 'inspirational', 'a hidden gem'. Altered habitat areas to increase the range of plants grown. Fetaured in RHS 'The Garden', Kent Life, 'The English Garden'.

The Queen's Nursing Institute founded the National Garden Scheme over 90 years ago

42 NEW THE GARDEN GATE

Northdown Park, Northdown Park Road, Margate, Kent, CT9 3TP. The Garden Gate Project Ltd, 07714742456, gardengateproject@yahoo.co.uk, www.thegardengateproject.co.uk. *We're based in an old plant nursery/ vegetable garden within Northdown Park. Located within Northdown Park opposite Friends Corner on Northdown Park Road B2052 between Margate and Broadstairs near to Northdown House.* **Sat 14 July (2-5). Adm £3, chd free. Light refreshments. Also open Yoakley House. Visits also by arrangement Feb to Oct. We have a wood fired pizza oven so can provide pizzas topped with produce from the garden.**

The Garden Gate is a community garden based in Northdown Park, growing a mixture of plants, flowers and vegetables using organic methods. We also have a wildlife pond, two polytunnels, a shade house, some coppiced woodland and a green roof on one of our buildings. The garden is flat and on one level with grass or wood chip paths.

43 NEW GARDENVIEW

6 Edward Road, Biggin Hill, Westerham, TN16 3HL. Freda Davis, 07958534074, fredagdavis@aol.com, www.fredasgarden.co.uk. *Off A233, 7½m S of Bromley, 3½m N of Westerham. Edward Road is located at the southern end of Main Road, Biggin Hill by the pedestrian crossing. Parking available on road. Buses 246 (Village Green Way stop) and 320 (Lebanon Gardens stop).* **Sun 19 Aug (12-4). Adm £4, chd free. Light refreshments. Visits also by arrangement July & Aug for groups of 10+.**

Full of interest with a wide variety of shrubs, small orchard, veg beds and tranquil seating areas with beautifully placed statuary, this garden has been transformed into a beautiful, peaceful and welcoming oasis. Various musicians will entertain visitors during the garden's main opening. There is also a small art exhibition available to view.

44 GODDARDS GREEN

Angley Road, Cranbrook, TN17 3LR. John & Linde Wotton, 01580 715507, jpwotton@gmail.com, www.goddardsgreen.btck.co.uk. *½m SW of Cranbrook. On W of Angley Rd. (A229) at junction with High St, opp War Memorial.* **Sun 8 July (12.30-4.30). Adm £5, chd free. Home-made teas. Visits also by arrangement May to Sept groups preferably 10+ coaches welcome. NB: no coach parking on site.**

Gardens of about 5 acres, surrounding beautiful 500+yr old clothier's hall (not open), laid out in 1920s and redesigned over past 25yrs to combine traditional and modern planting schemes. Fountain and rill, water garden, fern garden, mixed borders, flowering shrubs, trees and exotics, birch grove, grass border, pond, kitchen garden, meadows, arboretum and mature orchard.

45 ◆ GODINTON HOUSE & GARDENS

Godinton Lane, Ashford, TN23 3BP. The Godinton House Preservation Trust, 01233 643854, info@godintonhouse.co.uk, www.godintonhouse.co.uk. *1½m W of Ashford. M20 J9 to Ashford. Take A20 towards Charing & Lenham, then follow brown tourist signs.* **For NGS: Sun 25 Mar, Sun 20 May, Fri 22 June (1-6). Adm £5, chd free. Home-made teas. For other opening times and information, please phone, email or visit garden website.**

12 acres complement the magnificent Jacobean house. Terraced lawns lead through herbaceous borders, rose garden and formal lily pond to intimate Italian garden and large walled garden with delphiniums, potager, cut flowers and iris border. March/ April the wild garden is a mass of daffodils, fritillaries, other spring flowers. Large collection of Bearded Iris flowering late May. Delphinium Festival (15 June - 24 June). Garden sculpture show (21 July-12 Aug). Macmillan Coffee Morning (Sept). Garden workshops and courses throughout the yr. Unveiling of Emily Young sculpture in the gardens on BBC news. Partial wheelchair access to ground floor of house and most of gardens.

46 GODMERSHAM PARK

Godmersham, CT4 7DT. Mrs Fiona Sunley. *5m NE of Ashford. Off A28, midway between Canterbury & Ashford.* **Sun 25 Mar, Sun 3 June (1-5). Adm £5, chd free. Home-made teas in The Mansion Orangery. Donation to Godmersham Church.**

24 acres of restored wilderness and formal gardens set around C18 mansion (not open). Topiary, rose garden, herbaceous borders, walled kitchen garden and recently restored Italian garden. Superb daffodils in spring and roses in June. Historical association with Jane Austen. Also visit the Heritage Centre. Deep gravel paths.

47 ◆ GOODNESTONE PARK GARDENS

Wingham, Canterbury, CT3 1PL. Francis Plumptre, 01304 840107, www.goodnestoneparkgardens.co.uk. *6m SE of Canterbury. Village lies S of B2046 from A2 to Wingham. Brown tourist signs off B2046.* **For NGS: Sun 18 Feb (12-4.30); Sun 8 Apr, Sun 2 Sept (12-5). Adm £7, chd £2. Home-made teas. For other opening times and information, please phone or visit garden website.**

One of Kent's outstanding gardens and the favourite of many visitors. 14 acres around C18 house (not open) and with views over cricket ground and parkland. Something special yr-round from snowdrops and spring bulbs to the famous walled garden with old fashioned roses and kitchen garden. Outstanding trees and woodland garden with cornus collection and hydrangeas later. 2 arboretums, contemporary gravel garden. Picnics welcome. Featured in The Lady magazine and Country Life.

48 NEW GRANGE OAST

Lidsing Road, Boxley, Maidstone, ME14 3EL. Robert Attwood & Seann Carter. *Between Boxley and Bredhurst on top of the North Downs. Turn off Lidsing Road in front of a cottage and continue along the long farm drive. Upon reaching the farm, bear R and follow the road to the last house.* **Sun 27 May (11-5). Adm £3.50, chd free. Light refreshments. Sweet and savoury refreshments offered and a range of hot or cold drinks.**

A front garden approx 15x40m built in 2014 for a recently restored property. A formal layout with mixed informal planting incorporating many unusual plants. Located on an exposed site where plants have to cope with hot summers and wet winters. Also a small vegetable patch, a patio with a collection of tender potted plants and a conservatory housing a collection of exotic plants and orchids.

GROUP OPENING

49 GRAVESEND GARDENS GROUP

Gravesend, DA12 1JZ. *Approx ½m from Gravesend town centre. From A2 take A227 towards Gravesend. At T-lights with Cross Lane turn R then L at next T-lights following yellow NGS signs. Park in Sandy Bank Rd or Leith Park Rd.* **Sat 21, Sun 22 July (12-5). Combined adm £4, chd free. Cream teas.**

58A PARROCK ROAD
Mr Barry Bowen.

68 SOUTH HILL ROAD
Judith Hathrill.

Enjoy two lovely gardens, very different in character, close to Windmill Hill which has extensive views over the Thames estuary. 58A Parrock Road is a beautiful, well established town garden, approx 120ft x 40ft, nurtured by owner for 55yrs. There is a stream running down to a pond, luscious planting along the rocky banks, fascinating water features, mature trees and shrubs, magnificent display of hostas and succulents. 68 South Hill Road is an award winning wildlife garden, showing that wildlife friendly gardens need not be wild. Flowers, herbs and vegetables in the raised beds. Ferns, grasses, perennials and shrubs in the borders and fruit and vegetables grown in containers on the terrace. Tender vegetables thrive in the greenhouse, two ponds planted with native species and wild flowers. Jazz Trio at 58A Parrock Road.

50 ♦ GREAT COMP GARDEN

Comp Lane, Platt, nr Borough Green, Sevenoaks, TN15 8QS. Great Comp Charitable Trust, 01732 885094, office@greatcompgarden.co.uk, www.greatcompgarden.co.uk. *7m E of Sevenoaks. 2m from Borough Green Station. Accessible from M20 & M26 motorways. A20 at Wrotham Heath, take Seven Mile Lane, B2016; at 1st Xrds turn R; garden on L ½m.* **For NGS: Sun 25 Mar, Sun 28 Oct (11-5). Adm £8, chd £3. Light refreshments at The Old Dairy Tearooms. For other opening times and information, please phone, email or visit garden website.**

Skilfully designed 7 acre garden of exceptional beauty. Spacious setting of well maintained lawns and paths lead visitors through plantsman's collection of trees, shrubs, heathers and herbaceous plants. Early C17 house (not open). Magnolias, hellebores and snowflakes (leucojum), hamamellis and winter flowering heathers are a great feature in the spring. A great variety of perennials in summer incl salvias, dahlias and crocosmias. Tearoom open daily for morning coffee, home-made lunches and afternoon teas. Most of garden accessible to wheelchair users. Disabled WC.

51 GREAT MAYTHAM HALL

Maytham Road, Rolvenden, Tenterden, TN17 4NE. The Sunley Group. *3m from Tenterden. Maytham Rd off A28 at Rolvenden Church, ½m from village on R. Designated parking for visitors.* **Wed 25 Apr, Wed 23 May, Wed 27 June, Wed 25 July, Wed 22 Aug (1-4). Adm £6, chd free.**

Lutyens designed gardens famous for having inspired Frances Hodgson Burnett to write The Secret Garden (pre Lutyens). Parkland, woodland with bluebells. Walled garden with herbaceous beds and rose pergola. Pond garden with mixed shrubbery and herbaceous borders. Interesting specimen trees. Large lawned area, rose terrace with far reaching views.

52 HAVEN

22 Station Road, Minster, Ramsgate, CT12 4BZ. Robin Roose-Beresford, 01843 822594, robin.roose@hotmail.co.uk. *Off A299 Ramsgate Rd, take Minster exit from Manston r'bout, straight rd, R fork at church is Station Rd.* **Fri 30 Mar, Sun 1, Mon 2 Apr, Sun 6, Mon 7, Sun 27, Mon 28 May, Sun 3 June, Sun 1, Sun 22 July, Sun 26, Mon 27 Aug, Sun 23 Sept, Sun 21 Oct (10-4). Adm £4, chd free. There are several local venues where refreshments are available. Visits also by arrangement Mar to Nov any day or time. 24hrs notice required.**

Award winning 300ft garden, designed in the Glade style, similar to Forest gardening but more open and with use of exotic and unusual trees, shrubs and perennials, with wildlife in mind, devised and maintained by the owner, densely planted in a natural style with stepping stone paths. Two ponds (one for wildlife, one for fish with water lilies), gravel garden, rock garden, fernery, Japanese garden, cactus garden, hostas and many exotic, rare and unusual trees, shrubs and plants incl tree ferns and bamboos and yr-round colour. Greenhouse cactus garden.

53 37 THE HAYDENS

Tonbridge, TN9 1NS. Angie Boakes. *N Tonbridge, off Yardley Park Rd (between Shipbourne Rd & Hadlow Rd). Please park on Yardley Park Rd by green & follow signs. Limited disabled parking on rd.* **Sun 24 June (11.30-5). Adm £4, chd free. Home-made teas.**

A small modern garden redesigned by the current owner in 2014 after trying to grow a peony on a N facing wall! Split into sections which mirror the house, the borders (separated by a slate path) feature roses, cornus, birches, salvia, perennials and grasses plus a small area of planting from a Chelsea Show Garden. Hopefully it will give visitors ideas for typical modern house sized gardens. Slate paths.

54 ◆ HOLE PARK

Benenden Road, Rolvenden, Cranbrook, TN17 4JB. Mr & Mrs Edward Barham, 01580 241344, info@holepark.com, www.holepark.com. *4m SW of Tenterden. Midway between Rolvenden & Benenden on B2086. Follow brown tourist signs from Rolvenden.* **For NGS: Sun 8 Apr, Wed 2 May, Wed 13 June, Sun 7 Oct (11-6). Adm £7.50, chd £1. Light refreshments. Cream teas, home-made teas and light lunches served in The Coach House. For other opening times and information, please phone, email or visit garden website.**

Hole Park is proud to stand amongst the group of gardens which first opened in 1927 soon after it was laid out by my great grandfather. Our 15 acre garden is surrounded by parkland with beautiful views and contains fine yew hedges, large lawns with specimen trees, walled gardens, pools and mixed borders combined with bulbs, rhododendrons and azaleas. Massed bluebells in woodland walk, standard wisterias, orchids in flower meadow and glorious autumn colours make this a garden for all seasons. Light lunches available on all openings. Wheelchairs are available for free hire and may be reserved.

55 HOOKWOOD HOUSE

Puttenden Road, Shipbourne, Tonbridge, TN11 9RJ. Mr & Mrs Nicholas Ward, 01732 810525, hookwood1@yahoo.co.uk. *2m N of Tonbridge. From A227 1m N of Tonbridge, turn on to Puttenden Rd. After 1m Hookwood House is on R.* **Visits by arrangement Apr to June. Home-made teas.**

Charming country garden of 2 acres of formal features; old brick paths lead through small garden rooms enclosed by clipped native and yew hedges; Tulips, mixed and herbaceous border, topiary, herb and vegetable garden, nut plat, chickens, fruit orchard, cobbled Kentish ragstone yard and planted containers.

56 NEW HURST HOUSE

Waltham Road, Hastingleigh, Ashford, TN25 5JD. Mrs Lynn Smith. *On the top of the downs above Wye Village, between Ashford and Canterbury, 10 mins from A28. From A28 go through Wye towards Hastingleigh. Follow road over Downs to x-roads, L towards Waltham. Ignore first R. Second house on R set back off road.* **Sat 21, Sun 22 July (10.30-5.30). Adm £4, chd free. Home-made teas.**

3 acre idyllic secluded garden surrounded by bluebell woods. Mature Borders, winding beds, ponds/ornamental trees perennials/shrubs/annuals designed for year round colours. Damp shady borders/dry sunny borders, unusual plants, huge pieris, acers and rhododendrons. Newly formed stumpery planted with ferns/shade loving plants – woodland walk/Painted Forest, intriguing features and sculptures. Whilst it is possible to use a wheelchair - the drive is gravel and there can be muddy paths around and through the woods.

57 ◆ IGHTHAM MOTE

Mote Road, Ivy Hatch, Sevenoaks, TN15 0NT. National Trust, 01732 810378, ighthammote@nationaltrust.org.uk, www.nationaltrust.org.uk/ightham-mote. *6m E of Sevenoaks. Off A25, 2½m S of Ightham. Buses from train stations Sevenoaks or Borough Green to Ivy Hatch & Ightham Mote on weekdays.* **For NGS: Thur 19 Apr, Thur 20 Sept (10-5). Adm £13, chd £6.50. Light refreshments in The Mote Café. A range of hot and cold food and drinks are available. For other opening times and information, please phone, email or visit garden website.**

14 acre garden and moated medieval manor c1320, open for NGS since 1927. Herbaceous borders, lawns, C18 cascade, pools, courtyard and cutting gardens provide formal interest, while the informal north lake, pleasure gardens, fernery, stumpery and orchard all contribute to the sense of charm and tranquillity. Wheelchairs available from visitor reception and shop. Please ask for wheeled access guide at visitor reception. Last admission 4.30.

58 NEW IVY CHIMNEYS

Mount Sion, Tunbridge Wells, TN1 1TW. Laurence and Christine Smith. *At the end of Tunbridge Wells High St, with Pizza Express on the corner, turn L up Mount Sion. Ivy Chimneys is a red brick Queen Anne house at the top of the hill on the R.* **Sun 3 June (11-5). Adm £3, chd free. Light refreshments. Pimms.**

Town centre garden with herbaceous borders and masses of roses set on three layers of lawns enclosed in an old walled garden. This property also boasts a large vegetable garden with flowers for cutting and chickens for eggs! The property dates back to the late 1600's. Parking in public carparks near the Pantiles. Winner of best back garden in Tunbridge Wells in Bloom competition.

59 ◆ KNOLE

Knole, Sevenoaks, TN15 0RP. Lord Sackville, 01732 462100, knole@nationaltrust.org.uk, www.nationaltrust.org.uk/knole. *1½m SE of Sevenoaks. Leave M25 at J5 (A21). Park entrance S of Sevenoaks town centre off A225 Tonbridge Rd (opp St Nicholas Church). For SatNav use TN13 1HU.* **For NGS: Tue 10 July, Tue 7 Aug (11-4). Adm £9, chd £4.75. For other opening times and information, please phone, email or visit garden website.**

Lord Sackville's private garden at Knole is a magical space, featuring sprawling lawns, a walled garden, an untamed wilderness area and a medieval orchard. Access is through the beautiful Orangery, off Green Court, where doors open to reveal the secluded lawns of the 26 acre garden and stunning views of the house. Last entry at 3.30pm. Refreshments are available in the Brewhouse Café. Bookshop in Green Court. Gift shop and plant sales in the Brewhouse Café. Wheelchair access via the bookshop into the Orangery. Some paths may be difficult in poor weather. Assistance dogs are allowed in the garden.

♿ 🚌 ☕

60 KNOWLE HILL FARM

Ulcombe, Maidstone, ME17 1ES. The Hon Andrew & Mrs Cairns, 01622 850240, elizabeth@knowlehillfarm.co.uk, www.knowlehillfarmgarden.co.uk. *7m SE of Maidstone. From M20 J8 follow A20 towards Lenham for 2m. Turn R to Ulcombe. After 1½m, L at Xrds, after ½m 2nd R into Windmill Hill. Past Pepper Box PH, ½m 1st L to Knowle Hill.* **Sat 3, Sun 4 Feb (11-3). Light refreshments. Sun 15 July (2-5.30). Home-made teas. Adm £5, chd free. Hot food in February. 2019: Sat 16, Sun 17, Mon 18 Feb. Visits also by arrangement Feb to Sept access only for 25-30 seater coaches.**

2 acre garden created over 30yrs on S-facing slope of N Downs. Spectacular views. Snowdrops and hellebores, many tender plants, china roses, agapanthus, verbenas, salvias and grasses flourish on light soil. Topiary continues to evolve with birds at last emerging. Lavender ribbons hum with bees. Pool and rill enclosed in small walled white garden. New green garden is nearly complete. Some steep slopes.

♿ 🐕 ✿ 🚌 ☕

61 NEW LA MOUETTE

Blenheim Road, Littlestone, New Romney, TN28 8PR. Sheila Georgiades, 01797 369189. *From A259 at New Romney take B2071 for approx. 1m, then follow NGS signs.* **Fri 8, Sun 10 June (2-5). Adm £3.50, chd free. Visits also by arrangement Apr to Sept up to 10.**

Interestingly designed densely planted small south facing garden making the most of the available space to create different areas and microclimates. Mixed planting within the constraints of the dry, windy coastal location to provide all year interest. Many grasses and Med. plants. The low maintenance front garden was landscaped 6 years ago and planted with a scheme of white and lime green. Partial access.

♿ ✿

62 LADHAM HOUSE

Ladham Road, Goudhurst, TN17 1DB. Guy & Nicola Johnson. *8m E of Tunbridge Wells. On NE of village, off A262. Through village towards Cranbrook, turn L at The Goudhurst Inn. 2nd R into Ladham Rd, main gates approx 500yds on L.* **Sun 29 Apr (2-5). Adm £5, chd free. Home-made teas. Tea, coffee, delicious home-made cakes and biscuits.**

Ten acres of garden with many interesting plants, trees and shrubs, incl rhododendrons, camellias, azaleas and magnolias. A beautiful rose garden, arboretum, an Edwardian sunken rockery, a woodland walk leading to bluebell woods, ponds & a vegetable garden. The garden also has spectacular 60 meter twin borders and a white pool garden designed by Chelsea Flower Show Gold Medal winner, Jo Thompson. Small Classic Car Display.

☕

Mount Ephraim

63 ◆ LEEDS CASTLE

Maidstone, ME17 1PL. Leeds Castle Trustees, 01622 765400, accommodation@leeds-castle.co.uk. *Off J8 of M20.* **For NGS: Evening opening Thur 26 July (6-8). Adm £15, chd free. Booking information available at www.ngs.org.uk from early 2018. See www.leeds-castle.com to pre-order food. For other opening times and information, please phone or email.**

Visitors to the 'loveliest castle in the world' are often surprised and enchanted by the glorious gardens which surround this magnificent moated building. Natural woodland walks, the Culpeper Garden - a quintessential English cottage garden - and the Lady Baillie Garden - a Mediterranean style terraced garden overlooking the Great Water - are complemented by the beautiful surrounding parkland. Fully wheelchair accessible with smooth paths through gardens, disabled WC and mobility bus.

64 LEYDENS

Hartfield Road, Edenbridge, TN8 5NH. Roger Platts, www.rogerplatts.com. *1m S of Edenbridge. On B2026 towards Hartfield (use Nursery entrance & car park).* **Sun 5 Aug (12-5). Adm £5, chd free. Home-made teas.**

Small private garden of garden designer, nursery owner and author who created NGS Garden at Chelsea in 2002, winning Gold and Best in Show, and in 2010 Gold and People's Choice for the M&G Garden and Gold in 2013. A wide range of shrubs and perennials incl late summer flowering perennial border adjoining wild flower hay meadow. Kitchen garden. Plants clearly labelled and fact sheet available.

65 LITTLE GABLES

Holcombe Close, Westerham, TN16 1HA. Mrs Elizabeth James. *Centre of Westerham. Off E side of London Rd A233, 200yds from The Green. Please park in public car park. No parking available at house.* **Sat 5, Sun 6 May, Sat 9, Sun 10 June (2-5). Adm £3, chd free. Home-made teas.**

¾ acre plant lover's garden extensively planted with a wide range of trees, shrubs, perennials etc, incl many rare ones. Collection of climbing and bush roses. Large pond with fish, water lilies and bog garden. Fruit and vegetable garden. Large greenhouse.

66 LORDS

Sheldwich, Faversham, ME13 0NJ. John Sell CBE & Barbara Rutter, 01795 536900, john@sellwade.co.uk. *On A251 4m S of Faversham & 3½m N of Challock Xrds. From A2 or M2 take A251 towards Ashford. ½m S of Sheldwich church find entrance lane on R adjacent to wood. (51.2654N 0.8803E).* **Sun 8 July (2-5). Adm £5, chd free. Home-made teas. Also open Calico House. Visits also by arrangement Apr to June refreshments and adm by arrangement.**

C18 walled garden and greenhouse. A herb terrace overlooks a citrus standing. Flowery mead beneath medlar and quince trees. Across a grass tennis court a cherry orchard grazed by Jacob sheep. A shady fernery, lawns, ponds and wild area. Old specimen trees incl sweet chestnut, planes, copper beech, yew hedges and 120ft tulip tree. Daffodils, fritillaries, tulips in spring. Some gravel paths.

67 LUTON HOUSE

Selling, ME13 9RQ. Lady Swire, 07866 601230, wendyestokes@gmail.com. *4m SE of Faversham. From A2 (M2) or A251 make for White Lion in Selling, entrance 30yds E on same side of rd.* **Visits by arrangement Apr to Oct. Adm £5, chd free.**

6 acres. C19 landscaped garden with ornamental ponds, trees underplanted with azaleas, camellias, woodland plants, hellebores, spring bulbs, magnolias, cherries, daphnes, halesias, maples, Judas trees and cyclamen. Depending on the weather, those interested in camellias, early trees and bulbs may like to visit in late Mar/early April. Some parts not wheelchair accessible.

♿

68 NEW MANWOOD HOUSE

Strand Street, Sandwich, CT13 9HX. Mr & Mrs Philip & Rebecca Croall. *Access to the garden is through white gates in Paradise Row, which is a small lane off Strand Street.* **Sat 26 May (2-5). Adm £5, chd free. Light refreshments.**

The gardens of Manwood House (not open) built in 1564 as the first home of the free founded by Sir Roger Manwood, a favourite of Elizabeth I are abundantly planted.The main gardens, designed by Fiona Cadwallader and bounded by flint walls, feature a remarkable and ancient robinia tree, an ornamental pond and luxuriantly planted borders. Sandstone paths into and through large parts of the garden, though narrow in places. A small number of shallow steps to access certain areas.

♿ D ☕

69 MARSHBOROUGH FARMHOUSE

Farm Lane, Marshborough, Sandwich, CT13 0PJ. David & Sarah Ash, 01304 813679. *1½m W of Sandwich, ½m S of Ash. From Ash take R fork to Woodnesborough. After 1m Marshborough sign. L into Farm Lane at white thatched cottage, garden 100yds on L. Coaches must phone for access information.* **Visits by arrangement (18 June - 29 June & 20 Aug - 31 Aug only). Groups 10+. Adm £5, chd free.**

Interesting 2½ acre plantsman's garden, developed enthusiastically over 20yrs by the owners. Paths and lawns lead to many unusual shrubs, trees and perennials in island beds, borders, rockery and raised dry garden creating yr-round colour and interest. Tender pot plants, succulents in glass house, pond and water features. Over 70 varieties of Salvia both hardy and tender.

70 12 THE MEADOWS

Chelsfield, Orpington, BR6 6HS. Mr Roger & Mrs Jean Pemberton. *3m from J4 on M25. Exit M25 at J4. At r'about 1st exit for A224, next r'about 3rd exit - A224, ½m, take 2nd L, Warren Rd. Bear L into Windsor Drive. 1st L The Meadway, follow signs to garden.* **Sun 3 June (11-5.30). Adm £4, chd free. Home-made teas.**

Front garden Mediterranean style gravel with sun loving plants. Rear ¾ acre garden in 2 parts. Semi-formal Japanese style area with two ponds, one Koi and one natural (lots of spring interest). Mature bamboos, acers, grasses etc and semi wooded area, children's path with 13ft high giraffe, Sumatran tigers and lots of points of interest. Designated children's area. Only children allowed access! Wheelchair access to all parts except small stepped area at very bottom of garden.

71 MERE HOUSE

Mereworth, ME18 5NB. Mr & Mrs Andrew Wells, www.mere-house.co.uk. *7m E of Tonbridge. From A26 turn N on to B2016 & then R into Mereworth village. 3½m S of M20/M26 junction, take A20, then B2016 to Mereworth.* **Sun 18, Sun 25 Feb, Sun 25 Mar, Mon 2 Apr, Sun 21 Oct (2-5). Adm £5, chd free. Home-made teas. 2019: Sun 17, Sun 24 Feb.**

C18 landscape surrounding 6 acre garden, completely replanted since 1958, bounded to the south by lake created 1780. Increasing areas of snowdrops and daffodils in spring. Extensive lawns set off herbaceous borders, ornamental shrubs and trees with yr-round foliage contrast and striking autumn colour. Major tree planting since 1987 storm; woodland, park and lake walks can be enjoyed beyond the garden. Country Life feature article.

72 THE MOUNT

Haven Street, Wainscott, Rochester, ME3 8BL. Susie Challen & Marc Beney, 01634 727434, challensusie@gmail.com. *3½m N of Rochester. 7 mins from M2 J1: take A289 twds Grain. At roundabout, R into Wainscott. Co-op ahead, turn R into Higham Rd. R into Islingham Farm Rd which turns sharply L. House is on L through white metal gate.* **Visits by arrangement May to July for groups 10 - 25 max. Adm £4, chd free. Home-made teas.**

Ongoing renovation of 1.75-acre plot. Walled kitchen garden with espaliered fruit trees, climbing roses, vegetable beds and a 25m colourful herbaceous border. Croquet lawn area with yellow and white colour scheme, including a 25m herbaceous border. Old grass tennis court with assorted nut trees at one end. Mature specimen trees include a rare surviving elm. Lovely views of surrounding farmland. Gravel drive, uneven paths and steps.

73 ◆ MOUNT EPHRAIM

Hernhill, Faversham, ME13 9TX. Mr & Mrs E S Dawes & Mr W Dawes, 01227 751496 / 07927137627, info@mountephraim.co.uk, www.mountephraimgardens.co.uk. *3m E of Faversham. From end of M2, then A299 take slip rd 1st L to Hernhill, signed to gardens.* **For NGS: Sun 18 Mar, Thur 14 June, Sun 30 Sept (11-5). Adm £7, chd £2.50. Cream teas. Light refreshments, lunches, wine. For other opening times and information, please phone, email or visit garden website.**

Herbaceous border, topiary, daffodils and rhododendrons, rose terraces leading to small lake. Rock garden with pools, water garden, young arboretum. Rose garden with arches and pergola planted to celebrate the Millennium. Magnificent trees. Grass maze. Superb views over fruit farms to Swale estuary. Village craft centre. Partial wheelchair access; top part manageable, but steep slope. Disabled WC. Full access to tea room.

74 NETTLESTEAD PLACE

Nettlestead, ME18 5HA. Mr & Mrs Roy Tucker, www.nettlesteadplace.co.uk. *6m W/SW of Maidstone. Turn S off A26 onto B2015 then 1m on L, next to Nettlestead Church.* **Sun 10 June, Sun 30 Sept (2-5). Adm £6, chd free. Home-made teas.**

C13 manor house in 10 acre plantsman's garden. Large formal rose garden. Large herbaceous garden of island beds with rose and clematis walkway leading to garden of China roses. Fine collection of trees and shrubs; sunken pond garden, terraces, bamboos, glen garden, acer lawn. Young pinetum adjacent to garden. Sculptures. Wonderful open country views. Gravel paths, partial access: sunken pond garden. New large steep bank and lower area in development.

75 NORTON COURT

Teynham, Sittingbourne, ME9 9JU. Tim & Sophia Steel, 07798 804544, sophia@nortoncourt.net. *Off A2 between Teynham & Faversham. L off A2 at Texaco garage into Norton Lane; next L into Provender Lane; L signed Church for car park.* **Mon 11, Tue 12 June (2-5). Adm £5, chd free. Home-made teas. Visits also by arrangement groups min 10, max 30. Also open Tawnyhill Kennels.**

10 acre garden within parkland setting. Mature trees, topiary, wide lawns and clipped yew hedges. Orchard with mown paths through wild flowers. Walled garden with mixed borders and climbing roses. Pine tree walk. Formal box and lavender parterre. Tree house in the Sequoia. Church open, adjacent to garden. Flat ground except for 2 steps where ramp is provided.

76 OAK COTTAGE

Elmsted, Ashford, TN25 5JT. Martin & Rachael Castle. *6m NW of Hythe. From Stone St (B2068) turn W opp the Stelling Minnis turning. Follow signs to Elmsted. Turn L at Elmsted village sign. Limited parking at house, further parking at Church (7mins walk).* **Fri 20, Sat 21 Apr, Fri 25, Sat 26 May (11-4). Adm £4, chd free. Cream teas.**

Get off the beaten track and discover this beautiful ½ acre cottage garden in the heart of the Kent countryside. This plantsman's garden is filled with unusual and interesting perennials, incl a wide range of salvias. There is a small specialist nursery packed with herbaceous perennials. For our April opening a large auricula collection will be showcased in a range of traditional theatres. Partial wheelchair access.

77 OLD BLADBEAN STUD

Bladbean, Canterbury, CT4 6NA. Carol Bruce, www.oldbladbeanstud.co.uk. *6m S of Canterbury. From B2068, follow signs into Stelling Minnis, turn R onto Bossingham Rd, then follow yellow NGS signs through single track lanes.* **Sun 27 May, Sun 10, Sun 24 June, Sun 8, Sun 22 July, Sun 5, Sun 19 Aug (2-6). Adm £6, chd free. Home-made teas.**

5 interlinked gardens all designed and created from scratch by the garden owner on 3 acres of rough grassland between 2003 and 2011. Romantic walled rose garden with over 90 labelled old fashioned rose varieties, tranquil yellow and white garden, square garden with blended pastels borders and Victorian style greenhouse, 300ft long colour schemed symmetrical double borders. An experimental self sufficiency project comprises a wind turbine, rain water collection, solar panels and a ground source heat pump, an organic fruit and vegetable garden. The gardens are maintained entirely by the owner and were designed to be managed as an ornamental ecosystem with a large number of perennial species encouraged to set seed, and with staking, irrigation, mulching and chemical use kept an absolute minimum. Each garden has a different season of interest – please see the garden website for more information.

78 OLD BUCKHURST

Markbeech, Edenbridge, TN8 5PH. Mr & Mrs J Gladstone. *4m SE of Edenbridge. B2026, at Queens Arms PH turn E to Markbeech. In approx 1½m, 1st house on R after leaving Markbeech. Parking in paddock if dry. Last entry 4.30pm.* **Sat 21, Sun 22 Apr, Sat 5 May (11-5). Sun 6 May (11-5), also open Stonewall Park. Adm £4, chd free.**

1 acre partly walled cottage garden around C15 Grade II listed farmhouse with catslip roof (not open). Comments from Visitors' Book: 'perfect harmony of vistas, contrasts and proportions. Everything that makes an English garden the envy of the world'. 'The design and planting is sublime, a garden I doubt anyone could forget'. Stefan Buczacki in Garden News said - 'My favourite cottage garden is Old Buckhurst in Kent'. Mixed borders with roses, clematis, wisteria, poppies, iris, peonies, lavender.

Old Rectory

© Leigh Clapp

79 OLD CHURCH HOUSE

26a Church Street, Walmer, Deal, CT14 7RT. Christine & Mark Symons. *A258 Dover to Deal. In Upper Walmer turn on to Church St.* **Sun 1 July (1-5). Adm £4, chd free. Home-made teas. Also open 196 Downs Road.**

Delightful small garden packed with a wide variety of interesting plants. Gravelled front garden and several areas on different levels divided by pergola, paths and steps, each with their own character. Perennials, shrubs and trees, bamboos and palms, with pond area. Salvias, hydrangeas and waving grasses combine to make a tranquil garden.

80 THE OLD PALACE

Old Palace Road, Bekesbourne, Canterbury, CT4 5ES. Mrs Nicky Fry, 01227 830319, nicolafry@cscope.co.uk. *2m S of Canterbury. A2 towards Dover take Bridge/Bekesbourne exit. Turn R into School Lane, in 500 yds turn R into Old Palace Rd. Parking for small coaches only.* **Sat 9, Sun 10 June (1-5). Adm £5, chd free. Home-made teas. Visits also by arrangement May to Aug for groups of 10+.**

The site of Thomas Cranmer's Old Palace and home of Ian Fleming. 4 acre garden created by present owner with many interesting features. A natural pond, planted to encourage wildlife. 100yr old Scots pines, other specimen trees incl large flowering tulip tree. Walled potager with rose pergola and espaliered fruit trees. New laburnum and allium walkway and herbaceous border planted in 2013.

81 THE OLD RECTORY

Valley Road, Fawkham, Longfield, DA3 8LX. Karin & Christopher Proudfoot, 01474 707513, keproudfoot@gmail.com. *1m S of Longfield. Midway between A2 & A20, on Valley Rd 1½m N of Fawkham Green, 0.3m S of Fawkham church, opp sign for Gay Dawn Farm/Corinthian Sports Club. Parking on drive only. Not suitable for coaches.* **Visits by arrangement in Feb for individuals and groups, 20 max. Also open by arrangement Feb 2019. Adm £4, chd free. Home-made teas.**

1½ acres with impressive display of long established naturalised snowdrops and winter aconites; 100 named snowdrops added more recently. Garden developed around the snowdrops over 30yrs, incl hellebores, pulmonarias and other early bulbs and flowers, with foliage perennials, shrubs and trees, also natural woodland. Garden illustrated in article on snowdrops by Val Bourne, Daily Telegraph Gardening; also featured in French garden magazine Rustica. Gentle slope, gravel drive, some narrow paths.

82 THE ORANGERY

Mystole, Chartham, Canterbury, CT4 7DB. Rex Stickland & Anne Prasse, 01227 738348, rex.mystole@btinternet.com. *5m SW of Canterbury. Turn off A28 through Shalmsford Street. In 1½m at Xrds turn R downhill. Cont, ignoring rds on L & R. Ignore drive on L (Mystole House only). At sharp RH bend in 600yds turn L into private drive.* **Sun 20 May (1-6); Sat 28, Sun 29 July (1-5). Adm £5, chd free. Home-made teas. Visits also by arrangement Mar to Oct for groups of 5-60 with or without conducted tour.**

1½ acre gardens around C18 orangery, now a house (not open). Magnificent extensive herbaceous border & impressive ancient wisteria. Large walled garden with a wide variety of shrubs, mixed borders & unusual specimen trees. Water features & intriguing collection of modern sculptures in natural surroundings. Refreshments on terrace with splendid views over ha-ha to the lovely Chartham Downs. Ramps to garden.

83 THE ORCHARD

Bramling, Canterbury, CT3 1NB. Mark Lane, 01227 207013, www.marklanedesigns.com. *5m E of Canterbury. Please call for further directions. Limited parking available.* **Visits by arrangement July & Aug for small groups of 4 max (slightly larger groups may be considered). Adm £4, chd free. Light refreshments.**

The Orchard is the home to Mark Lane, the UK's first wheelchair-bound garden designer, published gardening writer and BBC TV presenter, and his civil partner Jasen. The acre garden incl: herb garden, blue and yellow border, white garden, grass borders with stepped granite water feature, roses and peonies, as well as a small orchard, lawn and the large colourful herbaceous borders. Featured on BBC Gardeners' World, Guardian Newspaper, Which? Gardening, RHS The Garden. Limited wheelchair access - gravel paths. A complete circle of the garden can be done using an alternative route.

84 ORCHARD END

Cock Lane, Spelmonden Road, Horsmonden, TN12 8EQ. Mr Hugh Nye, 01892 723118, hughnye@aol.com. *8m E of Tunbridge Wells. From A21 going S turn L at r'bout onto B2162 to Horsmonden. After 2m turn R onto Spelmonden Rd. After ½m turn R into Cock Lane. Garden on R.* **Sat 26, Sun 27 May, Sat 21, Sun 22 July (11-5). Adm £5, chd free. Home-made teas. Visits also by arrangement May to July, groups 40 max.** Donation to The Amyloidosis Foundation.

Contemporary classical garden within a 4 acre site. Made over 15yrs by resident landscape designer. Divided into rooms with linking vistas. Incl hot borders, white garden, exotics, oak and glass summerhouse amongst magnolias. Dramatic changes in level. Formal pool with damp garden, ornamental vegetable potager. Wildlife orchards and woodland walks.

85 ◆ ORCHARD HOUSE, SPENNY LANE

Claygate, Marden, Tonbridge, TN12 9PJ. Mr & Mrs Lerwill, 01892 730662, jeanette@lerwill.com. *Just off B2162 between Collier St & Horsmonden. Spenny Lane is adjacent to White Hart PH. Orchard House is 1st house on R about 400m from PH.* **For NGS: Sun 20 May, Sun 5 Aug (11-4). Adm £5, chd free. Home-made teas. For other opening times and information, please phone or email.**

A relatively new garden created within the last 12yrs. Gravel garden with potted tender perennials, cottage garden and herbaceous borders. Potager with vegetables, fruit and flowers for cutting. Bee friendly borders. Hornbeam avenue underplanted with camassia. Small nursery on site specialising in herbaceous perennials and ornamental grasses. Productive beehives and honey for sale. Featured in The English Garden and Kent Life. Access for wheelchairs, some pathways are gravel, grassed areas uneven in places.

Gardens are at the heart of hospice care

86 ◆ PENSHURST PLACE & GARDENS

Penshurst, TN11 8DG. Lord & Lady De L'Isle, 01892 870307, contactus@penshurstplace.com, www.penshurstplace.com. *6m NW of Tunbridge Wells. SW of Tonbridge on B2176, signed from A26 N of Tunbridge Wells.* **For NGS: Wed 12 Sept (10.30-6). Adm £9, chd £6. Cream teas. For other opening times and information, please phone, email or visit garden website.**

11 acres of garden dating back to C14. The garden is divided into a series of rooms by over a mile of yew hedge. Profusion of spring bulbs, formal rose garden and famous peony border. Woodland trail and arboretum. Yr-round interest. Toy museum. Some paths not paved and uneven in places; own assistance will be required. 2 wheelchairs available for hire.

87 PHEASANT BARN

Church Road, Oare, ME13 0QB. Paul & Su Vaight, 07843 739301, paul.vaight@btinternet.com. *2m NW of Faversham. Entering Oare from Faversham, turn R at Three Mariners PH towards Harty Ferry. Garden 400yds on R, before church. Parking on roadside.* **Visits by arrangement June & July refreshments by arrangement. Adm £5, chd free.**

Series of smallish gardens around award winning converted farm buildings in beautiful situation overlooking Oare Creek. Main area is nectar rich planting in formal design with a contemporary twist inspired by local landscape. Also vegetable garden, new dry garden, water features, wild flower meadow and labyrinth. July optimum for wild flowers. Kent Wildlife Trust Oare Marshes Bird Reserve within 1m. Two village inns serving lunches/ dinners.

88 PHEASANT FARM

Church Road, Oare, Faversham, ME13 0QB. Jonathan & Lucie Neame, 01795 535366, neamelucie@gmail.com. *2m NW of Faversham. Enter Oare from Western Link Road. L at T-junction. R at Three Mariners PH into Church Road. Garden 450yds on R, beyond Pheasant Barn, before church. Parking on roadside & as directed.* **Visits by arrangement Apr to June groups 10 - 30 max welcome. Adm £4, chd free. Home-made teas.**

Redesigned in 2008, a walled garden surrounding C17 farmhouse with outstanding views over Oare marshes and creek. Main garden with shrubs and herbaceous plants. Infinity lawn overlooking Oare marshes and creek. Circular walk through orchard and adjoining churchyard. Two local public houses serving lunches. Period Living July 2017. Kent Life June 2017. Wheelchair access in main garden only.

89 3 POST OFFICE COTTAGES

Chiddingstone Causeway, Tonbridge, TN11 8JP. Julie & Graham Jones-Ellis. *Approx 6m W of Tonbridge & approx 6m E of Edenbridge. On B2027 Clinton Lane into Chiddingstone Causeway same side as PO, garden is end of terrace cottage with hedge & small gravel driveway.* **Sat 26, Sun 27 May (11-5.30). Adm £3.50, chd free. Home-made teas incl gluten free cake.**

Small, but charming cottage garden, showing good use of space. With large selection of clematis and over 30 varieties of roses. Herbaceous borders filled with colour in May. Several seating areas and small water features.

90 POTMANS HEATH HOUSE

Wittersham, TN30 7PU. Dr Alan & Dr Wilma Lloyd Smith. *1½m W of Wittersham. Between Wittersham & Rolvenden, 1m from junction with B2082. 200yds E of bridge over Potmans Heath Channel.* **Sun 25, Thur 29 Mar (1-5). Adm £5, chd free. Home-made teas.**

NEW EARLY SPRING OPENINGS 2018. Large compartmentalised country garden. Widespread naturalised daffodils. Early tulips and other bulbs. Ornamental flowering cherries. Part walled vegetable garden, greenhouses. Specimen trees, some unusual. Orchards. Adjoining parkland with duck ponds. Rich variety of garden birds. Recent new plantings of variety of acers, flowering cherry, mountain ash, candy floss tree and others. Some awkward slopes but generally accessible.

91 ◆ QUEX GARDENS

Quex Park, Birchington, CT7 0BH. Powell-Cotton Museum, 01843 842168, enquiries@quexmuseum.org, www.quexpark.co.uk/museum/quex-gardens/. *3m W of Margate. Follow signs for Quex Park on approach from A299 then A28 towards Margate, turn R into B2048 Park Lane. Quex Park is on L.* **For NGS: Sun 15 July (10-5). Adm £4.95, chd £3.50. Light refreshments. For other opening times and information, please phone, email or visit garden website.**

10 acres of woodland and gardens with fine specimen trees unusual on Thanet, spring bulbs, wisteria, shrub borders, old figs and mulberries, herbaceous borders. Victorian walled garden with cucumber house, long glasshouses, cactus house, fruiting trees. Peacocks, dovecote, woodland walk, wildlife pond, children's maze, croquet lawn, picnic grove, lawns and fountains. Head Gardener will be available on NGS open days to give tours and answer questions. Mama Feelgood's Boutique Café serving morning coffee, lunch or afternoon tea. Quex Barn farmers market selling local produce and serving breakfasts to evening meals. Picnic sites available. Garden almost entirely flat with tarmac paths. Sunken garden has sloping lawns to the central pond.

92 NEW 86 RAMSDEN ROAD

Orpington, BR5 4LT. Patricia Dow. *from M25 take J4 follow A21 for Bromley then at r'about take 4th exit (A224) for about 1½m and at second set of T-lights turn R into Ramsden Rd.* **Sun 8 July, Sun 12**

Aug (1-5). Adm £3, chd free. Tea.
Driving down Ramsden Road offers no clue that there is a really pretty plant lover's garden to the rear of the house. Packed full of colour and interest many plants grown from seed and cuttings from our greenhouse. Very personal small garden designed over many years by owners with ingenious economical solutions to garden needs.

93 43 THE RIDINGS

Chestfield, Whitstable, CT5 3QE. David & Sylvie Sayers, 01227 500775, sylviebuat-menard@hotmail.com. *Nr Whitstable. From M2 heading E cont onto A299. In 3m take A2990. From r'about on A2990 at Chestfield, turn onto Chestfield Rd, 5th turning on L onto Polo Way which leads into The Ridings.* **Sun 29 Apr (11-4). Adm £3.50, chd free. Home-made teas. Visits also by arrangement Apr to Sept for groups 8+. Coach 25 seater max.**

Delightful small garden brimming with interesting plants both in the front and behind the house. Many different areas. Dry gravel garden in front, raised beds with alpines and bulbs and borders with many unusual perennials and shrubs. The garden ornaments are always a source of interest for the visitors. The water feature will be of interest for those with a tiny garden as well as the smoky cauldron. There are many alpine troughs and raised beds as well as dry shade borders and mixed borders all in a fairly small space.

94 ◆ RIVERHILL HIMALAYAN GARDENS

Riverhill, Sevenoaks, TN15 0RR. The Rogers Family, 01732 459777, info@riverhillgardens.co.uk, www.riverhillgardens.co.uk. *2m S of Sevenoaks on A225. Leave A21 at A225 & follow signs for Riverhill Himalayan Gardens.* **For NGS: Tue 24 Apr, Wed 16 May (10.30-5). Adm £8.50, chd £6.25. For other opening times and information, please phone, email or visit garden website.**

Sweetbriar

© Leigh Clapp

Beautiful hillside garden, privately owned by the Rogers family since 1840. Extensive views across the Weald of Kent. Spectacular rhododendrons, azaleas and fine specimen trees. Bluebell and natural woodland walks. Rose garden. Walled garden has extensive new planting, terracing and water feature. Children's adventure playground, den building trail, hedge maze and Yeti spotting. Café serving freshly-ground coffee, speciality teas, light lunches, home-made cream teas, cakes, gluten free cakes and soya milk. Wheelchair access to Walled Garden only. Good access to café, shop and tea terrace (no disabled WC).

95 ROCK COTTAGE

New Church Road, Bilsington, Ashford, TN25 7LA. Bill & Penny Sisley, 01233 720416, hello@kentcottageholiday.co.uk, https://kentcottageholiday.co.uk/ngs. *6½m SE of Ashford. From M20, J10 take A2070 to Hastings. Join B2067 to Hamstreet, turn L on B2067 towards Bilsington, at White Horse PH turn R, onto New Church Rd. After 1m Rock Cottage is on L.* **Sun 10 June, Sun 15 July, Sun 9 Sept (10.30-4.30). Adm £5, chd free. Home-made teas. Visits also by arrangement May to Sept minimum group size of 10.**

Runners up in Kent Life Garden of the Year. Tranquil 2 acre garden with a surprise around every corner, a series of garden rooms and a mixture of styles. Collections of clematis, rambling roses, wisteria walk, topiary garden, lime avenue, arboretum, meadow, living willow & native hedges, restored pond, fruit orchard, dahlia bed, Specimen trees & shrubs, Mediterranean garden, Agaves. Kent Life Magazine September Garden Feature Dahlias Shortlisted by the Daily Mail in the top 12 Amateur Garden of the Year. Partial wheelchair access.

96 NEW SADDLERS

The Street, Doddington, Sittingbourne, ME9 0BH. Alan & Liz Wright. *Saddlers is in the centre of Doddington village opp. Chequers pub on Faversham road between A20 & A2.* **Sun 17 June (1-5). Adm £4, chd free. Home-made teas.**

½ acre garden hidden behind mature yew and beech hedges. Features incl a box knot garden & topiary, wisteria clad ragstone pergola under planted with hostas & ferns. A variety of trees & shrubs, lawned areas, central gravel path edged with lavenders & pleached limes. Rose arbours, herbaceous borders & seating in most areas.

97 ST CLERE

Kemsing, Sevenoaks, TN15 6NL. Mr & Mrs Simon & Eliza Ecclestone, www.stclere.com. *6m NE of Sevenoaks. 1m E of Seal on A25, turn L signed Heaverham. In Heaverham turn R signed Wrotham. In 75yds straight ahead marked Private Rd; 1st L to house.* **Sun 20 May (2-5). Adm £5, chd £1. Home-made teas in Garden Room.**

4 acre garden, full of interest. Formal terraces surrounding C17 mansion (not open), with beautiful views of the Kent countryside. Herbaceous and shrub borders, productive kitchen and herb gardens, lawns and rare trees. Garden tours with Head Gardener at 2.30pm and 3.45pm (£1 per person). Some gravel paths and small steps.

98 ◆ THE SALUTATION GARDEN

Knightrider Street, Sandwich, CT13 9EW. Mr J Fothergill, 01304 619919, enquiries@the-salutation.com, www.the-salutation.com. *In the heart of Sandwich. Turn L at Bell Hotel & into Quayside car park. Entrance in far R corner of car park.* **For NGS: Thur 29 Mar, Wed 19 Sept (10-5). Adm £8, chd free. Home-made teas. For other opening times and information, please phone, email or visit garden website.**

3½ acres of ornamental and formal gardens designed by Sir Edwin Lutyens in 1911 surrounding Grade I listed house. Designated historic park and garden. White, yellow, spring, woodland, gardens, vegetable garden, herbaceous borders and exotic garden, Designed to provide yr-round changing colour. Unusual plants for sale.

99 ◆ SCOTNEY CASTLE

Lamberhurst, TN3 8JN. National Trust, 01892 893820, scotneycastle@nationaltrust.org.uk, www.nationaltrust.org.uk/scotneycastle. *6m SE of Tunbridge Wells. On A21 London - Hastings, brown tourist signs. Bus: (Mon to Sat) Tunbridge Wells - Wadhurst, alight Lamberhurst Green.* **For NGS: Tue 15 May (10-4.30). Adm £14.30, chd £7.20. Light refreshments. For other opening times and information, please phone, email or visit garden website.**

The medieval moated Old Scotney Castle lies in a peaceful wooded valley. In C19 its owner Edward Hussey III set about building a new house, partially demolishing the Old Castle to create a romantic folly, the centrepiece of his picturesque landscape. From the terraces of the new house, sweeps of rhododendron and azaleas cascade down the slope in summer, mirrored in the moat. In the house three generations have made their mark, adding possessions and character to the homely Victorian mansion which enjoys far reaching views out across the estate. Wheelchairs available for loan.

100 ◆ SISSINGHURST CASTLE GARDEN

Sissinghurst, TN17 2AB. National Trust, 01580 710700, sissinghurst@nationaltrust.org.uk, www.nationaltrust.org.uk. *On A262 1m E of Sissinghurst. Bus: Arriva Maidstone-Hastings, alight Sissinghurst 1¼m. Approx 30 mins walk from village.* **For NGS: Mon 1 Oct (11-5). Adm £14.50, chd £7.50. For other opening times and information, please phone, email or visit garden website.**

Garden created by Vita Sackville-West and Sir Harold Nicolson. Spring garden, herb garden, cottage garden, white garden, rose garden. Tudor building and tower, partly open to public. Moat. Vegetable garden and estate walks. Free welcome talks and estate walks leaflets. Café, restaurant and shop open from 10am-5.30pm. Some areas unsuitable for wheelchair access due to narrow paths and steps.

101 SMITHS HALL

Lower Road, West Farleigh, ME15 0PE. Mr S Norman, www.smithshall.com. *3m W of Maidstone. A26 towards Tonbridge, turn L into Teston Lane B2163. At T-junction turn R onto Lower Rd B2010. Opp Tickled Trout PH.* **Sun 1 July (11-5). Adm £5, chd free. Home-made teas.** Donation to Heart of Kent Hospice.

Delightful 3 acre gardens surrounding a beautiful 1719 Queen Anne House (not open). Lose yourself in numerous themed rooms: sunken garden, iris beds, scented old fashioned rose walk, formal rose garden, intense wild flowers, peonies, deep herbaceous borders and specimen trees. Walk 9 acres of park and woodland with great variety of young native and American trees and fine views of the Medway valley. Cakes and quiche available. Gravel paths.

102 SPRING PLATT

Boyton Court Road, Sutton Valence, Maidstone, ME17 3BY. Mr & Mrs John Millen, 01622 843383, carolyn.millen1@gmail.com, www.kentsnowdrops.com. *5m SE of Maidstone. From A274 nr Sutton Valence follow yellow NGS signs. Limited parking.* **Wed 31 Jan, Sat 3, Sun 4, Wed 7 Feb (10.30-3.30). Adm £4, chd free. Light refreshments. Visits also by arrangement in Feb 2018 and Feb 2019 for groups 6+ only.**

One acre garden under continual development with panoramic views of the Weald. Over 600 varieties of snowdrop grown in tiered display beds with spring flowers in borders. An extensive collection of alpine plants in a large greenhouse. Vegetable garden and natural spring fed water feature. Home-made soup, home-made bread, tea/coffee and cake. Garden on a steep slope and many steps.

103 STONEWALL PARK

Chiddingstone Hoath, nr Edenbridge, TN8 7DG. Mr & Mrs Fleming. *4m SE of Edenbridge. Via B2026. ½way between Markbeech & Penshurst.* **Sun 6 May (2-5). Adm £8, chd free. Home-made teas in the conservatory. Also open Old Buckhurst.** Donation to Sarah Matheson Trust & St Mary's Church, Chiddingstone.

Romantic woodland garden in historic setting featuring species rhododendrons, magnolias, azaleas, bluebells, a range of interesting trees and shrubs, sandstone outcrops, wandering paths and lakes. Historic parkland with cricket ground.

104 NEW SUNNYBANK

12 Herschell Road East, Walmer, Deal, CT14 7SQ. Mr & Mrs James & Flora Cockburn. *Turn W off Dover Rd, Walmer at Corner Café. Last house on R before Herschell Sq.* **Sun 1 July (10-4). Adm £3.50, chd free. Home-made teas in the garden. Also open Old Church House.**

Gem of a little back garden rejuvenated in 2016 whilst retaining lovely old trees, shrubs and hedges. Gravel paths in straight lines with a lawn worthy of Wimbledon, surround 2 beds planted with hardy perennials and bright annuals. The colours ramp up as the season progresses. Side gates open onto terrace with full view of beds.

105 SWEETBRIAR

69 Chequer Lane, Ash, nr Sandwich, CT3 2AX. Miss Louise Dowle & Mr Steven Edney, 01304 448476, lou.dowle@hotmail.co.uk. *8m from Canterbury, 3m from Sandwich. Turn off A257 into Chequer Lane, 100 meters from junction opp field.* **Sun 29 July, Sun 19 Aug, Sun 30 Sept (11-5). Adm £3.50, chd free. Home-made teas. Also open 12 Wood Ley. Visits also by arrangement July to Oct for groups min 10, max 20.**

An average sized back garden transformed into an exotic jungle paradise full of fabulous foliage. A real plantsman's collection of many rare hardy and tender exotics to transport you into a lawn free tropical oasis. The front garden is a traditional cottage kitchen garden combining flowers and vegetables with fruit and herbs. Wildlife friendly, chemical free with 3 small ponds and eco grass drive.

106 NEW TAWNYHILL KENNELS

Homestall Road, Doddington, Sittingbourne, ME9 0HF. Jean Price. *Junction 6 off M2 - A2 towards Sittingbourne. L into Faversham Rd. Under motorway bridge, first R into Straight Hill. Junction 8 off M20 - A20 to Lenham. L into Faversham Rd. Drive for nearly 7m.* **Mon 11, Tue 12 June (1-6). Adm £5, chd free. Home-made teas. Also open Norton Court.**

The garden started off as an overgrown orchard in 2002. ⅓ of an acre and is all on one level. The soil is Faversham brick earth. The garden consists of two man made ponds linked by a stream. A lawn area with flower borders, a herb border, 6 raised vegetable beds, a rose garden at the front of the bungalow, 2 greenhouses. Cutting garden. Plant lover's wildlife garden. Short Listed for the Gardeners World Wildlife garden. Access to most of the garden by wheelchair. Disabled parking near to house.

107 TIMBERS

Dean Street, East Farleigh, nr Maidstone, ME15 0HS. Mrs Sue Robinson, 07905281764, suerobinson.timbers@gmail.com, www.timbersgardenkent.co.uk. *2m S of Maidstone. From Maidstone take B2010 to East Farleigh. After Tesco's on R follow Dean St for ½m. Timbers on L behind 8ft beech hedge. Parking through gates. Access for 54 seater coaches.* **Visits by arrangement Apr to July for groups of 10+. Adm £5, chd free. Home-made teas. Light lunches by arrangement.**

Beautiful 5 acre garden surrounding house designed with flower arranger's eye and with colour a priority. Unusual perennials, annuals and shrubs. Tulips in spring. New partly walled garden, parterre, arbour, pergola, island beds, lawns and mature specimen trees plus 100yr old Kentish cobnut plat, wildflower meadows and woodland. Rock pool with waterfalls. Valley views. Plant List. Tea room. Featured in The English Garden Magazine. Most of garden is flat, some steep slopes to rear.

108 TORRY HILL

Frinsted/Milstead, Sittingbourne, ME9 0SP. Lady Kingsdown, 01795 830258, lady.kingsdown@btinternet.com. *From M20 J8 take A20 (Lenham). At r'about by Hotel turn L Hollingbourne (B2163). Turn R at Xrds at top of hill (Ringlestone Rd). Then Frinsted-Doddington (not suitable for coaches), then Torry Hill/NGS signs. From M2 J5 take A249 towards Maidstone, then 1st L (Bredgar), Lagain (follow Bredgar signs), R at War Memorial, 1st L (Milstead), Torry Hill/NGS signs from Milstead. Please use entrance marked D (on red background) for disabled parking.* **Sun 13 May, Sun 10 June, Sun 15 July (2-5). Adm £5, chd free. Home-made teas. Visits also by arrangement Apr to July (Mon - Fri only). Groups min.10, max 30. Adm £8.00 incl tea/coffee and biscuits.** Donation to St Dunstan's Church, Frinsted and L'Arche (May & June only).

8 acres; large lawns, specimen trees, flowering cherries, rhododendrons, azaleas and naturalised daffodils; walled gardens with lawns, shrubs, herbaceous borders, rose garden incl shrub roses, wild flower areas and vegetables. Extensive views to Medway and Thames estuaries. Some shallow steps. No wheelchair access to rose garden due to very uneven surface but can be viewed from pathway.

109 TOWNLAND

Sixfields, Tenterden, TN30 6EX. Alan & Lindy Bates, 01580 764505, alanandlindybates@yahoo.co.uk. *Just off Tenterden High St. Park in Bridewell Lane car park (Sunday free). From centre of Tenterden High St, walk down Jackson's Lane next to Webbs Ironmongers. Follow lane to end (400m). Phone for disabled parking.* **Sun 10 June, Sun 8 July (2-5.30). Adm £5, chd free. Home-made teas. Visits also by arrangement June & July for groups 10+.** Donation to Pilgrims Hospice.

A 1 acre family garden in a unique position. Mixed borders, with a wide range of shrubs and flowers providing a riot of colour throughout the year, flow into the more naturalistic planting which is adjacent to meadow areas and fruit trees. A gravel garden, rose arbour and intensive fruit and vegetable areas complete the experience. Wide range of plants.

110 TRAM HATCH

Charing Heath, Ashford, TN27 0BN. Mrs P Scrivens, www.tramhatchgardens.co.uk. *10m NW of Ashford. A20 turn towards Charing Railway Stn on Pluckley Rd, over motorway then 1st R signed Barnfield to end, turn L carry on past Barnfield, Tram Hatch ahead.* **Sat 9 June, Sun 8 July, Sun 12 Aug (12-5). Adm £5, chd free. Home-made teas.**

Meander your way off the beaten track to a mature, extensive garden changing through the seasons. You will enjoy a garden laid out in rooms - what surprises are round the corner? Large selection of trees, vegetable, rose and gravel gardens, colourful containers. The River Stour and the Angel of the South enhance your visit. Please come and enjoy, then relax in our new garden room for tea. Featured in Kent Life Magazine The garden is totally flat, apart from a very small area which can be viewed from the lane.

111 NEW TRIESTON HOUSE

Church Road, Burmarsh, Romney Marsh, TN29 0JF. Mr and Mrs Andrew Winter. *10 miles South East of M20 J10. From M20/J10: 2nd exit (A20). 2m to Xrds - R to Aldington. 2m to T junction: R & immed L by Walnut Tree. Bottom of hill turn L - Boat Lane. Continue 3m & turn L to Burmarsh: Trieston House 1m on R.* **Fri 8, Sat 9, Sun 10 June (10.30-5). Adm £5, chd free. Home-made teas. Home-made cakes and refreshments on the back lawn.**

C14th Trieston House (not open) is a charming new ½ acre garden nestled in Romney Marsh. An extensive rose garden (over 200) sits alongside formal lawns and herbaceous beds where peonies, salvias, heucheras, hostas and friends jostle for attention. Go on to a rambunctious cottage garden filled with an abundance of life and laughter. Rest awhile and absorb the tranquillity of true timelessness. Georgian fronted medieval house settled for over 600 years. Wrap around garden featuring extensive views over the Romney Marsh and escarpment towards Lympne Castle. Owner of garden is disabled so garden has been designed to accommodate everyone.

112 UPPER PRYORS

Butterwell Hill, Cowden, TN8 7HB. Mr & Mrs S G Smith. *4½m SE of Edenbridge. From B2026 Edenbridge-Hartfield, turn R at Cowden Xrds & take 1st drive on R.* **Wed 20 June (12-5). Adm £5, chd free. Home-made teas.**

10 acres of English country garden surrounding C16 house - a garden of many parts; colourful profusion, interesting planting arrangements, immaculate lawns, mature woodland, water and a terrace on which to appreciate the view, and tea!

113 THE WATCH HOUSE

7 Thanet Road, Broadstairs, CT10 1LF. Dan Cooper, www.frustratedgardener.com. *Off Broadstairs High St on narrow side rd. At Broadstairs station, cont along High St (A255) towards sea front. Turn L at Terence Painter Estate Agent then immed turn R.* **Sat 4, Sun 5 Aug (12-4). Adm £3.50, chd free. Home-made teas.**

Adjoining an historic fishermen's cottage, two small courtyard gardens shelter an astonishing array of unusual plants. Thanks to a unique microclimate, the east-facing garden is home to an array of exotic plants and trees, chosen principally for exuberant, jungly foliage. In the west-facing courtyard a garden room leads onto a terrace where flowering plants jostle for space around a greenhouse. Within a few mins walk of Viking Bay, The Dickens Museum and Bleak House.

114 WATERGATE HOUSE

King Street, Fordwich, Canterbury, CT2 0DB. Fiona Cadwallader, 01227 710470, fiona@cadwallader.co.uk, www.cadwallader.co.uk. *2m E of Canterbury. From Canterbury A257 direction, Sandwich, 1m L to Fordwich. 1m L on Moat Lane, direct to Watergate House bottom of High St. Follow parking instructions.* **Sat 28 Apr, Sat 16 June (2-6). Adm £4.50, chd free. Home-made teas. Visits also by arrangement Apr to Aug for groups 10+.**

Magical walled garden by the River Stour: Defined areas of formal, spring, woodland, vegetable and secret garden reveal themselves in a naturally harmonious flow, each with its own colour combinations. Ancient walls provide the garden's basic structure, while a green oak pergola echoes a monastic cloister. See website for film of Fiona's Chelsea Garden The garden is mainly on one level with one raised walkway under pergola.

D

115 WEST COURT LODGE

Postling Court, The Street, Postling, nr Hythe, CT21 4EX. Mr & Mrs John Pattrick, 01303 863285, malliet@hotmail.co.uk. *2m NW of Hythe. From M20 J11 turn S onto A20. Immed 1st L. After ½m on bend take rd signed Lyminge. 1st L into Postling.* **Visits by arrangement May to Sept combined with Churchfield. Groups 35 max. Adm £6, chd free. Home-made teas in Village Hall or garden.**

S-facing one acre walled garden at the foot of the N Downs, designed in 2 parts: main lawn with large sunny borders and a romantic woodland glade planted with shadow loving plants and spring bulbs, small wildlife pond. Lovely C11 church will be open next to the gardens.

GROUP OPENING

116 WEST MALLING EARLY SUMMER GARDENS

West Malling, ME19 6LW. *On A20, nr J4 of M20. Park in West Malling for Brome House, Lucknow ,Town Hill Cottage ; and for Went House and 77 Swan Street, where maps and directions to 1 & 2 New Barns Cottages & New Barns Oasts are available.* **Sun 3 June (12-5). Combined adm £6.50, chd free. Home-made teas at New Barns Cottages.** Donation to St Mary's Church, West Malling.

NEW **ABBEY BREWERY COTTAGE**
Dr & Mrs David and Lynda Nunn.

BROME HOUSE
John Pfeil & Shirley Briggs.

NEW **LUCKNOW, 117 HIGH STREET**
Ms Jocelyn Granville.

NEW BARNS COTTAGES
Mr & Mrs Anthony Drake.

2 NEW BARNS OAST
Nick Robinson & Becky Robinson Hugill.

TOWN HILL COTTAGE
Mr & Mrs P Cosier.

WENT HOUSE
Alan & Mary Gibbins.

West Malling is an attractive small market town with some fine buildings. Enjoy seven lovely gardens that are entirely different from each other and cannot be seen from the road. Brome House and Went House have large gardens with specimen trees, old roses, mixed borders, attractive kitchen gardens and garden features incl a coach house, Roman temple, fountain and parterre. Lucknow and Town Hill Cottage are walled town gardens with mature and interesting planting. Abbey Brewery Cottages is a recent example of garden restoration and development. New Barns Cottages has serpentine paths leading through woodland to roomed gardens: tea and cakes in the courtyard garden of the cottages. New Barns Oasts has bespoke landscape features and is a child friendly adults' garden. Town Hill Cottage garden, Abbey Brewery Cottages and New Barns Cottages are difficult to access but the other gardens have wheelchair access.

GROUP OPENING

117 WHITSTABLE GARDENS

Whitstable, CT5 4LT. *Off A299, or A290. Down Borstal Hill, L by garage into Joy Lane to collect map of participating gardens (also available at other gardens). Parking at Joy Lane School (free) and Gorrell Tank.* **Sun 10 June (10-5). Combined adm £6, chd free. Home-made teas at Stream Walk Community Gardens and Umbrella Centre Cafe.**

87 ALBERT STREET
Paul Carey & Phil Gomm.

56 ARGYLE ROAD
Emma Burnham & Mel Green.

5 CLARE ROAD
Janet Maxwell & Philip Adam.

THE GUINEA
Sheila Wyver.

19 JOY LANE
Francine Raymond, www.kitchen-garden-hens.co.uk.

NEW **96 JOY LANE**
Vernon & Teresa Brown.

KENT ENTERPRISE TRUST
Stream Walk Community Gardens.

OCEAN COTTAGE
Katherine Pickering.

34 VICTORIA STREET
Caroline Burgess.

NEW **30A WESTGATE TERRACE**
Graeme Jenkins and Jane Davidson.

Enjoy a day of eclectic gardens by the sea. 10 people are showing off their gardens, but others, marked with yellow balloons, are there to admire from the street. From fishermen's yards to formal gardens, residents of Whitstable are making the most of quirky plots, enjoying the mild climate and the range of plants we can grow. Drop in and admire wildlife (96 & 19 Joy Lane), gravel gardens (The Guinea & Clare Rd), vertical gardening (Westgate Terrace), and those starting from scratch (56 Argyle Rd & 34 Victoria St). We're maximising our space, be it tiny (87 Albert St & Ocean Cottage), on a busy road or in deep shade. We garden on heavy Kent clay and are prone to northerly winds. Stream Walk is the heart of our gardening community, where residents can learn new skills & buy surplus produce - the ideal spot for those without outside space of their own. By opening, we're hoping to encourage those new to gardening with our ingenuity and style, rather than rolling acres. Combined adm £6 per adult or £10 for 2. Plant stalls at 19 Joy Lane and the Umbrella Centre.

Watergate House

© Leigh Clapp

118 WOMENSWOLD GARDENS

Womenswold, Canterbury, CT4 6HE. Mrs Maggie McKenzie, 01227 831414, Maggiemckenzie@vfast.co.uk. *6m S of Canterbury, midway between Canterbury & Dover. Take B2046 for Wingham at Barham Xover. Turn 1st R, following signs.* **Sat 23, Sun 24 June (1.30-6). Adm £5, chd free. Home-made teas. Visits also by arrangement May to Aug groups of 10+.**

A diverse variety of cottage gardens in an idylic situation in an unspoilt hamlet, mostly surrounding C13 Church. Cottage garden with variety of old, climbing and shrub roses, and clematis, vegetable bed & beehives; a traditional thatched cottage garden; colourful garden with ponds and other interesting features; a garden with a large display of perennials, incl kniphofias & hemerocallis; a 2 acre plantsman's garden-with vegetables, orchard & alpines. A picturesque terraced cottage garden, with unusual plants, feature pond. Easy walking distance between gardens. North Downs Way runs through village. Many unusual plants for sale. Teas in lovely restful garden with home-made cakes. Produce stall; Church open. Most gardens have good wheelchair access although some areas may be inaccessible.

119 NEW 12 WOODS LEY

Woods Ley, Ash, Canterbury, CT3 2HF. Philip Oostenbrink. *20 minutes from Canterbury. From A257 turn right at Chequer Lane. Go down Chequer Lane and turn left into Chilton Field. Keep going down the road and turn the second left into Woods Ley.* **Sun 29 July, Sun 19 Aug, Sun 30 Sept (11-5). Adm £2.50, chd free. Wine. Also open Sweetbriar. Prosecco served in the garage.**

A tropical style showing what can be achieved in the smaller modern garden, filled with colourful flowers and unusual foliage. The front and side garden have an array of ferns and unusual shrubs. The back garden is full of plants like tree ferns, bamboos, Canna, Hedychium and a selection of the National Collection of Hakonechloa macra. Indoors you will find a collection of Aspidistra. Private garden of the Head Gardener of Canterbury Cathedral.

NPC

120 ◆ THE WORLD GARDEN AT LULLINGSTONE CASTLE

Eynsford, DA4 0JA. Guy Hart Dyke, 01322 862114, info@lullingstonecastle.co.uk, www.lullingstonecastle.co.uk. *1m from Eynsford. Over Ford Bridge in Eynsford Village. Follow signs to Roman Villa. Keep Roman Villa immed on R then follow Private Rd to Gatehouse.* **For NGS: Sun 17 June**

Ivy Chimneys

(12-5). Adm £9, chd £4.50. Light refreshments. For other opening times and information, please phone, email or visit garden website.
Interactive world map of plants laid out as a map of the world within a walled garden. The oceans are your pathways as you navigate the world in one acre. You can see Ayers Rock and walk alongside the Andes whilst reading tales of intrepid plant hunters. Discover the origins of some 6,000 different plants - you'll be amazed where they come from! Plant Hunters Nursery and Lullingstone World Garden seeds for sale. Wheelchairs available upon request.

NPC

121 WYCKHURST

Mill Road, Aldington, Ashford, TN25 7AJ. Mr & Mrs Chris Older, 01233 720395, cdo@rmfarms.co.uk. *4m SE of Ashford. From M20 J10 take A20 2m E to Aldington turning; turn R at Xrds & proceed 1½m to Aldington Village Hall. Turn R & immed L by Walnut Tree Inn down Forge Hill. After ¼m turn R into Mill Rd.* **Sat 2, Sun 3, Sat 9, Sun 10 June (12-6). Adm £5, chd free. Home-made teas on the Sun Terrace. Visits also by arrangement in June, groups 20 max.**
Delightful C16 Kent Cottage (not open) nestles in romantic seclusion at the end of a drive. This enchanting 1 acre garden is a mixture of small mixed herbaceous borders, roses and much unusual topiary incl a wildflower meadow. There is plenty of seating round the lawns to enjoy the garden and teas with extensive views of the Kent Countryside across to the Romney Marsh on towards the sea. There is a dell with a small water feature and in the wildflower meadow is a shepherd's hut to enjoy after a stroll. The garden is under continuous redesign and development with fresh plantings each year to provide changing interest for every visitor. Some gentle slopes which limit wheelchair access to some small areas.

GROUP OPENING

122 WYE GARDENS

Harville Road, Wye, TN25 5EY. *3m NE of Ashford. From A28 take turning signed Wye. Bus: Ashford to Canterbury via Wye. Train: Wye. Next door to Spring Grove School.* **Sun 17 June (2-6). Combined adm £5, chd free. Home-made teas at Wye Church.**

3 BRAMBLE CLOSE
Dr M Copland.
(See separate entry)

NEW **MIDDLEFIELD HOUSE**
TN25 5EP. Kathy and Steve Bloom.

NEW **3 ORCHARD DRIVE**
TN25 5AU. Liz Coulson.

SPRING GROVE FARM HOUSE
TN25 5EY. Heather Van den Bergh.

There are four very different gardens open in the village this year including two new and interesting locations. At Orchard Drive, the owner has been busy planting out her new garden, an exciting project. In her own words "A new garden based upon the good bones established by the previous owner.' Our second new garden this year is Middlefield House, Olantigh Road, and a well-established venue including every aspect of a country garden that you could wish for with outstanding views of the surrounding countryside. Bramble Close is a wild experimental garden/meadow which demonstrates how plants maintain their natural population density. The garden was recently featured on BBC Gardeners World. Spring Grove Farmhouse is a large country garden full of colour and many interesting features incl a lake, pond and a gravel garden. Wye Gardens opening coincides with Stour Music Festival. Wheelchair access to Spring Grove Farm House only.

123 YEW TREE COTTAGE

Penshurst, TN11 8AD. Mrs Pam Tuppen, 01892 870689. *4m SW of Tonbridge. From A26 Tonbridge to Tunbridge Wells, join B2176 Bidborough to Penshurst Rd. 2m W of Bidborough, 1m before Penshurst. Unsuitable for coaches.* **Wed 7, Sun 18, Wed 28 Feb, Sun 11, Wed 21 Mar, Sun 1, Wed 11, Sun 22 Apr, Wed 2, Sun 13, Wed 23 May, Sun 3, Wed 13 June (12-5). Adm £3, chd free. Light refreshments.**
Small, romantic cottage garden with steep hillside entrance. Lots of seats and secret corners, many unusual plants - hellebores, spring bulbs, old roses, many special perennials. Small pond; something to see in all seasons. Created and maintained by owner, a natural garden full of plants. Featured in Garden Answers

124 NEW YOAKLEY HOUSE

Drapers Close, Margate, CT9 4AH. Michael Yoakley's Charity, www.yoakleycare.co.uk. *Drapers Close, Margate. Near Margate QEQM Hospital, Drapers Close is a cul de sac turning off St Peters Road. At the end of Drapers Close is access to the Yoakley car park, through the hedge.* **Sat 14 July (2.30-4.30), also open The Garden Gate. Sun 22 July (2.30-4.30). Adm £5, chd £2.50. Light refreshments in Yoakley House Care Home on site. Served in the garden if weather permits.**
Set in 2½ acres of grounds, cultivated the old fashioned way to complement the ancient almshouses it serves. Well-manicured lawns with extensive borders and densely planted display beds: summer bedding, carpet bedding, specimen trees, shrubs and rockery plants, herbaceous planting, shrub rose beds with standard roses. Magnificent hanging baskets. Accessible pathways from the main carpark throughout the grounds.

LANCASHIRE

Merseyside, Greater Manchester

The gardens of the Red Rose County of Lancashire offer a wide range of horticultural excellence and inspiration.

Hidden behind walls, hedges and fences lie some of the most exquisite private gardens in the country; a range of expertly tended plots full of colour, innovation and seasonal interest. There is something here to inspire all the family, whether it be allotments, wildlife sanctuaries, rows of back to back terrace gardens, inner city sanctuaries with water features or rolling acres with lakes.

So, whatever size your own patch, why not visit some of our stunning gardens and maybe take away a few brilliant ideas to copy at home- all with the added pleasure of home- made cakes and tea, and often plants for sale too.

Our gardeners look forward to welcoming you!

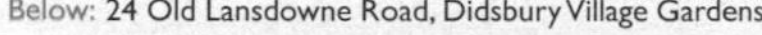

Below: **24 Old Lansdowne Road, Didsbury Village Gardens**

Volunteers

County Organiser
Margaret Fletcher
01704 567742
margaret.fletcher@ngs.org.uk

County Treasurer
Geoff Fletcher
01704 567742
geoffwfletcher@hotmail.co.uk

Publicity
Lynn Kelly
01704 563740
lynn-kelly@hotmail.co.uk

Christine Ruth
01517 274877
caruthchris@aol.com

Booklet Co-ordinator
Brenda Doldon
01704 834253
doldon@btinternet.com

Assistant County Organisers
Anne & Jim Britt
01614 458100
annebritt@btinternet.com

Peter & Sandra Curl
01704 893713
peter.curl@btinternet.com

Deborah Jackson
debs136@icloud.com

Carole Ann & Stephen Powers
01254 824903
chows3@icloud.com

Eric & Sharon Rawcliffe
01253 883275
ericrawk@talktalk.net

OPENING DATES

All entries subject to change. For latest information check **www.ngs.org.uk**

Extended openings are shown at the beginning of the month.

Map locator numbers are shown to the right of each garden name.

February

Snowdrop Festival

Sunday 11th
Weeping Ash Garden 56

Sunday 18th
Weeping Ash Garden 56

Sunday 25th
Weeping Ash Garden 56

March

Sunday 4th
Weeping Ash Garden 56

April

Saturday 14th
Dale House Gardens 20

Sunday 15th
Dale House Gardens 20

May

Tuesday 1st
NEW 6 Birch Road 6

Thursday 3rd
Warton Hall 55

Friday 4th
Warton Hall 55

Saturday 5th
Warton Hall 55

Sunday 6th
Didsbury Village Gardens 22
Warton Hall 55

Monday 7th
◆ The Ridges 44
Warton Hall 55

Sunday 20th
79 Crabtree Lane 16
NEW Hightown Gardens 31
Warton Gardens 54

Sunday 27th
Bretherton Gardens 8
◆ Clearbeck House 14
NEW Hillside Gardens 32
12 The Croft 50
Waddow Lodge Garden 53

Monday 28th
Bretherton Gardens 8
◆ Clearbeck House 14

June

Friday 1st
NEW 6 Birch Road 6

Festival Weekend

Saturday 2nd
Dent Hall 21
Mill Barn 38

Sunday 3rd
Birkdale Gardens 7
Dent Hall 21
NEW Meresands Kennels & Cattery 37
Mill Barn 38
The Secret Valley 45

Saturday 9th
136 Buckingham Road 12
NEW Giles Farm 25
Mill Barn 38

Sunday 10th
8 Andertons Mill 2
90 Brick Kiln Lane 9
136 Buckingham Road 12
NEW 31 Cousins Lane 15
Didsbury Village Gardens 22
NEW Giles Farm 25
Mill Barn 38
Woodstock Barn 61

Saturday 16th
35 Ellesmere Road 24
NEW The Old Vicarage 40
11 Westminster Road 57

Sunday 17th
79 Crabtree Lane 16
◆ Hazelwood 29
NEW The Old Vicarage 40
NEW Parkers Lodge 41

Saturday 23rd
Dale House Gardens 20
Hale Village Gardens 28

Sunday 24th
Bridge Inn Community Farm 10
◆ Clearbeck House 14
Dale House Gardens 20
Dutton Hall 23
Green Farm Cottage 26
Hale Village Gardens 28
NEW Tottington Gardens 51

Wednesday 27th
Dutton Hall 23

Saturday 30th
Alderbank 1
Becconsall 5
5 Crib Lane 17
NEW 19 Cumberland Avenue 19
NEW 11 Platt Lane 42
Warton Gardens 54

July

Sunday 1st
8 Andertons Mill 2
8 Balfour Road 3
Becconsall 5
◆ Clearbeck House 14
5 Crib Lane 17
Heaton Gardens 30
NEW 28 Lockwood Avenue 35
NEW 11 Platt Lane 42
91 Station Road 48
Warton Gardens 54
81 Windsor Road 60
Woodstock Barn 61

Sunday 8th
Birkdale Gardens 7
Bretherton Gardens 8
NEW Hightown Gardens 31
The Stones & Roses Garden 49

Saturday 14th
The Stones & Roses Garden 49

Sunday 15th
NEW 6 Birch Road 6
79 Crabtree Lane 16
Pool Foot Barn 43
Sefton Park Gardens 46
Waddow Lodge Garden 53
Wigan & Leigh Hospice 58

Saturday 21st
8 Bankfield Lane 4
Liverpool Marie Curie Hospice 34

Sunday 22nd
8 Bankfield Lane 4
NEW Hillside Gardens 32
Southlands 47

Sunday 29th
NEW 19 Cumberland Avenue 19
NEW Moss Park Allotments 39

August

Wednesday 1st
NEW 6 Birch Road 6

Saturday 4th
Lower Dutton Farm 36

Sunday 5th
Lower Dutton Farm 36

Saturday 11th
The Growth Project 27

Saturday 18th
Willowbrook Hospice Gardens 59

Sunday 19th
Willowbrook Hospice Gardens 59

Sunday 26th
Bretherton Gardens 8
NEW Croxteth Park Walled Garden 18

Monday 27th
◆ The Ridges 44

September

Sunday 9th
NEW 6 Birch Road 6
Weeping Ash Garden 56

By Arrangement

8 Andertons Mill 2
NEW 6 Birch Road 6
Bridge Inn Community Farm 10
4 Brocklebank Road 11
Casa Lago 13
79 Crabtree Lane 16

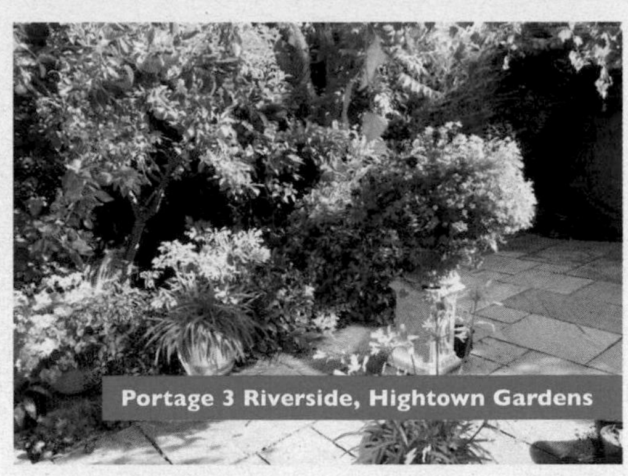
Portage 3 Riverside, Hightown Gardens

THE GARDENS

1 ALDERBANK

40c Edge Lane, Chorlton, Manchester, M21 9JW. Carolyn Shearman & Paul Harnett. *4m SE Manchester. On the R of Edge Lane heading towards Stretford from Chorlton.On the corner of Alderfield Rd just before Longford Park.* **Sat 30 June (12-5). Adm £3, chd free. Home-made teas.**

A quirky Chorlton garden! Recycled materials. Wildlife friendly areas. Great variety of lush naturalistic cottage style planting. Wildlife friendly pond with bridge. Potager style front garden with organic fruit, vegetables, flowers and herbs. Hundreds of container plantings. Roses, clematis, grasses, and some unusual plants. Secluded pergola with mosaics. Featured in Amateur Gardening magazine. Narrow paths and several steps so sorry not suitable for wheelchairs.

2 8 ANDERTONS MILL

Mawdesley, Ormskirk, L40 3TW. Mr & Mrs R Mercer, 01257 450636, margaret.mercer6@btinternet.com. *9m E of Ormskirk. M6 J27 A5209 over Parbold Hill, R Lancaster Lane/Chorley Rd, L after Farmers Arms to Bentley Lane/Andertons Mill. Garden 500yds on R. From Burscough A59,A5209 towards Parbold, L Lancaster Lane.* **Sun 10 June, Sun 1 July (12-5). Combined adm with Woodstock Barn £4.50, chd free. Home-made teas. Visits also by arrangement June & July for groups of 10+.**

This ½ acre cottage garden started in 2010, has many colourful borders of perennials, shrubs, and roses. A patio with raised beds, secluded potted plant area, large vegetable garden. Rose and clematis covered arches and many wrought iron features. An extensive bed of scented roses and a wonderful view of Harrock Hill. Wheelchair access to most areas across lawns.

3 8 BALFOUR ROAD

Southport, PR8 6LE. Mr & Mrs Stephenson, www.leadingahorticulture.wordpress.com. *1.4m SE of Southport. Off A570 Southport to Ormskirk rd. Turn L 1st rd up from football ground.* **Sun 1 July (12-5). Combined adm with 81 Windsor Road £3.50, chd free.**

Walled garden given mainly to a plantswoman's collection of perennials and shrubs. Large Edwardian conservatory stocked with tropicals and an extensive cactus collection.

4 8 BANKFIELD LANE

Churchtown, Southport, PR9 7NJ. Alan & Gill Swift. *2½ m N of Southport. Turn R at T-lights on A565 in Churchtown, 1st L at r'about past Hesketh Arms Pub & Botanic Gardens main entrance on L. Garden is 200yds on R.* **Sat 21, Sun 22 July (11-5). Adm £4, chd free. Home-made teas.** Donation to NW Spinal Injuries Unit, Southport Hospital.

Open aspect to rear of garden, double herbaceous borders, small vegetable garden, greenhouse, chickens coup, two raised patio areas. Front garden has trees, shrubs and roses. Restricted parking on Bankfield Lane. Parking available at rear of Botanic Gardens on Veralum Rd. A short walk through Botanic Gardens to Bankfield Lane via main or side gate. Wheelchair access to most areas.

5 BECCONSALL

Hunters Lane, Tarleton Moss, Tarleton, Preston, PR4 6JL. John & Elizabeth Caunce. *11m S of Preston, 6m N of Southport. Situated off A565. Preston/ Ormskirk A59 to Tarleton. A565 signed Southport. After 2m, turn R into Moss Hey Lane. Southport A565 left into Moss Hey Lane Parking in nearby field. Disabled parking, on driveway.* **Sat 30 June, Sun 1 July (11-5). Adm £4, chd free. Home-made teas. Wine.**

An interesting 1 acre garden, combining different areas of lawn, rill, arboretum, herbaceous border, and raised beds. Brass Band will be playing each afternoon, weather permitting. Featured in Lancashire Life. Wheelchair access to most of the garden.

33 Beryl Avenue, Tottington Gardens

6 NEW 6 BIRCH ROAD

Leigh, WN7 5SU. Ryan Forshaw, 01942 672307, info@growyourideas.co.uk. *8m E of M6 J23. Take A580 East Lancs Rd towards Manchester L on A579. At r'about 1st L onto Atherleigh Way. L at Kirkhall Ln, R at Heather Grove, L at Maple Cres signed from here.* **Tue 1 May, Fri 1 June (11-3). Adm £3, chd free. Sun 15 July (10-4). Combined adm with Wigan & Leigh Hospice £3, chd free. Wed 1 Aug, Sun 9 Sept (11-3). Adm £3, chd free. Also open Weeping Ash Garden. Tea. Visits also by arrangement May to Aug.** Donation to Horatio's Garden & SUAG.

A small wild life friendly garden brimming with colour making the most of its potential. Large collection of alpines and succulents and used in interesting and creative ways. Extensive and inspirational use of recycled materials giving them a new lease of life. Winner of several Borough in Bloom Awards. I have a spinal cord injury myself so the garden is completely wheelchair accessible.

GROUP OPENING

7 BIRKDALE GARDENS

Birkdale, Southport, PR8 2AX. *1m S of Southport. Gardens signed from A565 Southport to Liverpool rd & A5267 S through Birkdale Village. Maps available at each location.* **Sun 3 June, Sun 8 July (11-5). Combined adm £5, chd free. Home-made teas at 14 Saxon Rd. Bacon sandwiches at 22 Hartley Cres.**

22 HARTLEY CRESCENT

Sandra & Keith Birks, 01704 567182, sandie.b@talktalk.net. **Visits also by arrangement May to Aug groups of 10+.**

10 MEADOW AVENUE

John & Jenny Smith.

14 SAXON ROAD

Margaret & Geoff Fletcher, 01704 567742, margaret.fletcher@ngs.org.uk. **Visits also by arrangement May to Aug for groups of 10+.**

An established group of gardens surrounding the bustling Victorian village of Birkdale, reached by a short car journey. Gardens feature a delightful plants woman's L shaped garden with a very special secret garden, a walled garden with an array of tender plants amongst informal island beds and a family garden full of surprises with imaginative use of reclaimed materials. Wheelchair access to some gardens.

GROUP OPENING

8 BRETHERTON GARDENS

South Road, Bretherton, Leyland, PR26 9AD. *8m SW of Preston. Between Southport & Preston, from A59, take B5247 towards Chorley for 1m. Gardens signed from South Rd (B5247).* **Sun 27, Mon 28 May, Sun 8 July, Sun 26 Aug (12-5). Combined adm £5, chd free. Home-made teas at Bretherton Congregational Church. Light lunches (8 July only).**

GLYNWOOD HOUSE

Terry & Sue Riding.

HAZEL COTTAGE

John & Kris Jolley, 01772 600896, jolley@johnjolley.plus.com. **Visits also by arrangement.**

OWL BARN

Richard & Barbara Farbon, 01772 600750, farbons@btinternet.com. **Visits also by arrangement May to Aug small groups up to 20.**

PEAR TREE COTTAGE

John & Gwenifer Jackson.

Four contrasting gardens spaced across attractive village with conservation area. Glynwood House has ¾ acre mixed borders, pond with drystone-wall water feature, woodland walk, patio garden with pergola and raised beds, all in a peaceful location with spectacular open aspects. Pear Tree Cottage garden blends seamlessly into its rural setting with informal displays of ornamental and edible crops, water and mature trees, against a backdrop of open views to the West Pennine Moors. Owl Barn has herbaceous borders with cottage garden and hardy plants, a productive kitchen garden providing fruit, vegetables and cut flowers, and two ponds with fountains which complement the C18 converted barn (not open). Hazel Cottage garden has evolved from a Victorian subsistence plot to encompass a series of themed spaces packed with plants to engage the senses and the mind. Live music at Glynwood. Home-made preserves for sale at Pear Tree Cottage. Narrow or uneven paths in some parts of all the gardens.

9 90 BRICK KILN LANE

Rufford, Ormskirk, L40 1SZ. Mrs Jacky Soper. *From M6 J27, follow signs for Parbold then Rufford. Turn L onto the A59. Turn R at Hesketh Arms Pub. Turn 3rd L.* **Sun 10 June (11-4.30). Combined adm with 31 Cousins Lane £3.50, chd free. Light refreshments.**

A small, continually evolving, cottage garden, with a variety of different garden rooms containing shrubs, perennials, alpines, climbers, cobbled courtyard and a small pond. Wheelchair access limited: due to narrow paths and large step down to cobbled courtyard.

10 BRIDGE INN COMMUNITY FARM

Moss Side, Formby, Liverpool, L37 0AF. Bridge Inn Community Farm, 01704 830303, bridgeinnfarm@talktalk.net, www.bridgeinncommunityfarm.co.uk. *7m S of Southport. Formby by-pass A565, L onto Moss Side.* **Sun 24 June (10-4). Adm £3.50, chd free. Light refreshments in canteen. Visits also by arrangement.**

Bridge Inn Community Farm was established in 2010 in response to a community need. Our farm sits on a beautiful 4 acre small holding with views looking out over the countryside. We provide a quality service of training in a real life work environment and experience in horticulture, conservation and animal welfare.

11 4 BROCKLEBANK ROAD

Southport, PR9 9LP. Alan & Heather Sidebotham, 01704 543389, alansidebotham@yahoo.co.uk. *1¼ m N of Southport. Off A565 Southport to Preston Rd, opp North entrance to Hesketh Park.* **Visits by arrangement, groups of 8+. Adm £3.50, chd free.**

A walled garden incorporating a church folly. Landscaped with reclaimed materials from historic sites in the Southport area. There are several water features, an extensive herbaceous border and various areas of differing planting, thus creating a garden with much interest.

12 136 BUCKINGHAM ROAD

Maghull, L31 7DR. Debbie & Mark Jackson. *7m N of Liverpool. End M57/M58, A59 to Ormskirk after ½m, 1st L after car superstore onto Liverpool Rd South, cont' on past Meadows pub, 3rd R into Sandringham Rd, L into Buckingham Rd.* **Sat 9, Sun 10 June (12-5). Adm £2.50, chd free. Home-made teas.** Donation to Breast Unit Fazakerley Hospital.

A profusion of plants within a small suburban garden, cottage style planting, shrubs, climbers, perennials and containers brimming with hostas, acers and much more. Rose bed, wisteria covered pergola and fishpond. The garden is planted to attract butterflies and bees. Plenty of seating available, exceedingly good cakes and a large selection of plants for sale.

13 CASA LAGO

1 Woodlands Park, Whalley, BB7 9UG. Carole Ann & Stephen Powers, 01254 824903, chows3@icloud.com. *2½m S of Clitheroe. From M6 J31, take A59 to Clitheroe. 9m take 2nd exit at r'about for Whalley. After 2m reach village & follow yellow signs. Parking in village car parks or nearby.* **Visits by arrangement May to Sept. Adm £4, chd free. Light refreshments.**

Travel the globe through horticultural specimens with the rare and unusual, bonsai trees, koi ponds, succulent garden, oak pergolas, alpine displays, black limestone wall, hostas, decked elevated glass areas, Consistent visitor comments, paradise, breath taking, inspiring, absolutely fab u lous!

14 ◆ CLEARBECK HOUSE

Mewith Lane, Higher Tatham via Lancaster, LA2 8PJ. Peter & Bronwen Osborne, 01524 261029, www.clearbeckgarden.org.uk. *13m NE of Lancaster. Signed from Wray (M6 J34, A683, B6480) & Low Bentham.* **For NGS: Sun 27, Mon 28 May, Sun 24 June, Sun 1 July (11-5). Adm £4, chd free. Light refreshments.** For other opening times and information, please phone or visit garden website.

'A surprise round every corner' is the most common response as visitors encounter fountains, streams, ponds, sculptures, boathouses and follies: Rapunzel's tower, temple, turf maze, giant fish made of CDs, walk-through pyramid. 2 acre wildlife lake attracts many species of insects and birds. Planting incl herbaceous borders, grasses, bog plants and many roses. Vegetable and fruit garden. Painting studio open. Children- friendly incl quiz. Artists and photographers welcome by arrangement. Wheelchair access -many grass paths, some sloped.

15 NEW 31 COUSINS LANE

Rufford, Ormskirk, L40 1TN. Brenda & Roy Caslake. *From M6 J27, follow signs for Parbold then Rufford. Turn L onto the A59. Turn R at Hesketh Arms Pub. 4th turn.* **Sun 10 June (11-4.30). Combined adm with 90 Brick Kiln Lane £3.50, chd free. Home-made teas.**

As the sound of 'cork on willow' competes with the laughter of grandchildren, this family garden provides views for the sedentary, bug hunts for the active and a riot of colour for the artisitic. Adjacent to the village cricket ground this corner plot, with 2 small ponds, is planned with discrete areas offering the visitor colour, calm and contentment.

16 79 CRABTREE LANE

Burscough, L40 0RW. Sandra & Peter Curl, 01704 893713, peter.curl@btinternet.com, www.youtube.com/watch?v=TqpxW7_8HT4. *3m NE of Ormskirk. A59 Preston - Liverpool Rd. From N before bridge R into Redcat Lane signed for Martin Mere. From S over 2nd bridge L into Redcat Lane after ¾m L into Crabtree Lane.* **Sun 20 May, Sun 17 June, Sun 15 July (11-4). Adm £3.50, chd free. Home-made teas. Visits also by arrangement May to July short talk on how the garden developed.**

¾ acre all year round plants person's garden with many rare and unusual plants. Herbaceous borders and colour themed island beds leading to a pond and rockery, rose garden, spring area and autumn hot bed. Many stone features built with reclaimed materials. Shrubs and rhododendrons, Koi pond with waterfall, hosta and fern walk. Gravel garden with Mediterranean plants. Patio, surrounded by shrubs and raised alpine bed. Trees giving areas for shade loving plants. Featured on Ormskirk Champion Radio Lancashire. Flat grass paths.

17 5 CRIB LANE

Dobcross, Oldham, OL3 5AF. Helen Campbell. *5m E of Oldham. From Dobcross village-head towards Delph on Platt Lane, Crib Lane opp Dobcross Band Club - go straight up the lane, limited parking for disabled visitors only opp double green garage door.* **Sat 30 June, Sun 1 July (1-4). Combined adm with 11 Platt Lane £3, chd free. Home-made teas.**

A well loved and used family garden which is challenging as on a high stony hillside and encompasses hens, some small wildlife ponds, vegetable garden, a poly tunnel and areas that are always being re thought and dug up and changed depending on time and aged bodies aches and pains! An art gallery in the garden is of additional interest with visiting artists. Art gallery in the garden and 2017 saw Zimbabwean stone sculptors showing visitors how to sculpt. Featured in local Dobcross Diary and Saddleworth monthly magazines. Plants for sale by the National Trust.

18 NEW CROXTETH PARK WALLED GARDEN

Liverpool, L11 1EH. Liverpool City Council (Jim Cable is Head Gardener), www.liverpoolcityhalls.co.uk/croxteth-hall/about/victorian-walled-garden. *6m NE of Liverpool. From M57 Exit J4 take A580 towards Liverpool. Look for brown tourist signs directing L. Hall is off r'about at junction of Dwerryhouse Lane & Muirhead Av.* **Sun 26 Aug (11.30-5). Adm £3.50, chd free. Home-made teas.**

The two acre Victorian Walled Garden at Croxteth Hall was built around 1850. It produced a year round supply of fresh fruit, vegetable and cut flowers for the Hall until the last Earl died in 1972. Bedding display, herbaceous and mixed borders, trained fruit trees, herb garden, roses, soft fruits and a fuchsia collection. The garden houses part of Liverpool's historic botanical collection under glass. The estate offers ample opportunities for walking. The walled garden was used for filming the BBC series 'The Victorian Kitchen Garden'. More recently it featured in the November issue of Lancashire Life. There is disabled permit parking available near to the Hall and Garden – use the service entrance from Croxteth Hall Lane (Satnav postcode L12 0HB).

NPC

19 NEW 19 CUMBERLAND AVENUE

Leyland, PR25 1BE. Maureen Duggan, 01772 423068, mduggan22@gmail.com, www.maureenduggan.wordpress.com/. *M6(J28) to town centre on Turpin Green Lane (B5256) then Towngate (B5254). R on Church Rd (B5248) follow to Fox Lane. After Tennis club L Royal Ave, 2nd L Cumberland Ave.* **Sat 30 June, Sun 29 July (1-5). Adm £3, chd free. Light refreshments. Visits also by arrangement May to Aug.**

Well planted garden with island flower beds. Trees and shrubs with some unusual perennials. Also a pond and a view of Worden Park and woods. Visited by a lot of wildlife. Partial wheelchair access but some paths are too narrow.

20 DALE HOUSE GARDENS

off Church Lane, Goosnargh, Preston, PR3 2BE. Caroline & Tom Luke, 01772 862464, tomlukebudgerigars@hotmail.com. *2½ m E of Broughton. M6 J32 signed Garstang Broughton, T-lights R at Whittingham Lane, 2½ m to Whittingham at PO turn L into Church Lane garden between nos 17 & 19.* **Sat 14, Sun 15 Apr, Sat 23, Sun 24 June (10-4). Adm £3.50, chd free. Home-made teas. Visits also by arrangement Apr to June.** Donation to St Francis School, Goosnargh.

½ acre tastefully landscaped gardens comprising of limestone rockeries, well stocked herbaceous borders, raised alpine beds, well stocked koi pond, lawn areas, greenhouse and polytunnel, patio areas, specialising in alpines rare shrubs and trees, large collection unusual bulbs. All year round interest. New features for 2017. Large indoor budgerigar aviary. 300+ budgies to view. Gravel path, lawn areas.

21 DENT HALL

Colne Road, Trawden, Colne, BB8 8NX. Mr Chris Whitaker-Webb & Miss Joanne Smith, 01282 861892, denthall@tiscali.co.uk. *Turn L at end of M65. Follow A6068 for 2m; just after 3rd r'about turn R down B6250. After 1½ m, in front of church, turn R, signed Carry Bridge. Keep R, follow road up hill, garden on R after 300yds.* **Sat 2, Sun 3 June (12-5). Adm £5, chd free. Home-made teas. Visits also by arrangement June to Sept for groups of 10+.** Donation to Widowed & Young and MIND.

Nestled in the oldest part of Trawden villlage and rolling Lancashire countryside, this mature and evolving country garden surrounds a 400 year old grade II listed hall (not open); featuring a parterre, lawns, herbaceous borders, shrubbery, wildlife pond with bridge to seating area and a hidden summerhouse in a woodland area. Plentiful seating throughout. Some uneven paths and gradients.

GROUP OPENING

22 DIDSBURY VILLAGE GARDENS

Tickets: Any Village Garden, or Moor Cottage, Grange Lane, Didsbury, Manchester, M20 6RW. *5m S of Manchester. From M60 J5 follow signs to Northenden. Turn R at T-lights onto Barlow Moor Rd to Didsbury. From M56 follow A34 to Didsbury.* **Sun 6 May (12-5). Combined adm £5, chd free. Sun 10 June (12-5). Combined adm £6, chd free. Home-made teas at Moor Cottage & 68 Brooklawn Drive.**

68 BROOKLAWN DRIVE
Anne & Jim Britt, www.thefruitygardener.com.
Open on Sun 10 June

3 THE DRIVE
Peter Clare & Sarah Keedy, www.theshadegarden.com.
Open on all dates

ESTHWAITE, 52 BARLOW MOOR ROAD
Margaret & Derek Crowther.
Open on all dates

MOOR COTTAGE
William Godfrey.
Open on all dates

NEW **24 OLD LANSDOWNE ROAD**
Sarah and Stuart Chilvers.
Open on Sun 10 June

2 PARKFIELD ROAD SOUTH
Conrad & Kate Jacobson, Mary Butterworth.
Open on Sun 10 June

38 WILLOUGHBY AVENUE
Simon Hickey.
Open on Sun 10 June

Didsbury is an attractive South Manchester suburb which retains its village atmosphere. There are interesting shops, cafes and restaurants, well worth a visit in themselves! This year we have 7 gardens, including a new and very stylish low-maintenance contemporary garden.The gardens demonstrate a variety of beautiful spaces- one is a large family garden surrounding a Georgian cottage, divided into several enchanting areas, another is an expertly planted shade garden with many rarities, whilst another reflects the charm of the cottage garden ethos with rose covered pergola, old fashioned perennials and tranquil raised pool. Our smaller gardens show beautifully how suburban plots, with limited space, can be packed full of interesting features and a range of planting styles. Dogs allowed at some gardens. 68 Brooklawn Drive has appeared in Alan Titchmarsh's 'Love Your Garden'. Moor Cottage, 68 Brooklawn Drive & The Drive have all featured in Cheshire Life and Lancashire Life. Wheelchair access to some gardens.

23 DUTTON HALL

Gallows Lane, Ribchester, PR3 3XX. Mr & Mrs A H Penny, www.duttonhall.co.uk. *2m NE of Ribchester. Signed from B6243 & B6245 also directions on website.* **Sun 24 June (1-5). Home-made teas. Evening opening Wed 27 June (6-8.30). Light refreshments. Adm £5, chd free.**

An increasing range of interesting trees and shrubs have been added to the existing collection of old fashioned roses, including rare and unusual varieties and Plant Heritage National Collection of Pemberton Hybrid Musk roses. Formal garden at front with backdrop of C17 house (not open). A range of other features and extensive views over the Ribble Valley. Analemmatic Sundial, pond, meadow areas all with extensive views over Ribble Valley. Teas provided by St John's Church. Plant Heritage Plant Stall with unusual varieties for sale. Disabled access difficult due to different levels and steps.

NPC

24 35 ELLESMERE ROAD

Eccles, Salford, Manchester, M30 9FE. Enid Noronha. *3m W of Salford, 4m W of Manchester. From M60 exit at M602 for Salford.Take A576 for Trafford Park & Eccles, stay on A576. Turn L onto Half Edge Lane, keep L to Monton on Half Edge Lane. Turn R onto Stafford Rd & L onto Ellesmere Rd.* **Sat 16 June (12-5). Combined adm with 11 Westminster Road £4.50, chd free. Home-made teas.**

Amidst the busy urban environment of Eccles in Salford, lies a hidden pocket of grand houses with wide roads,and these two havens of tranquillity. 35 Ellesmere Road is a peaceful country garden with deep herbaceous borders filled with shrubs, scented roses, and perennials. A climber covered pergola leads to a productive vegetable garden where raised beds and fruit trees add to the feeling of abundance.

25 NEW GILES FARM

Four Acre Lane, Thornley, Preston, PR3 2TD. Kirsten & Phil Brown. *3m NE of Longridge. From J31A or J32 of M6 follow signs for Longridge. Pass through Longridge & follow signs for Chipping. Pass The Derby Arms on the L & then turn R at the old school. Parking at the farm.* **Sat 9, Sun 10 June (1-5). Adm £4, chd free. Home-made teas.**

Nestled high on the side of Longridge fell, with beautiful long-reaching views across the Ribble Valley, the gardens surround the old farmhouse and buildings. The gardens are ever evolving and include an acre of perennial wildflower meadows, wildlife pond, woodland areas and cottage gardens. There are plentiful areas to sit and take in the views. There are steps and uneven surfaces in the gardens. Disabled access difficult due to different levels, surface areas and steps.

26 GREEN FARM COTTAGE

42 Lower Green, Poulton-le-Fylde, FY6 7EJ. Eric & Sharon Rawcliffe, ericrawk@talktalk.net. *500yds from Poulton-le-Fylde Village. M55 J3 follow A585 Fleetwood. T- lights turn L. Next lights bear L A586. Poulton 2nd set of lights turn R Lower Green. Cottage on L.* **Sun 24 June (10-5). Adm £3.50, chd free. Home-made teas. Visits also by arrangement June & July, groups of 15+.**

½ acre well established formal cottage gardens. Feature koi pond, paths leading to different areas. Lots of climbers and rose beds. Packed with plants of all kinds. Many shrubs and trees. Well laid out lawns. Collections of unusual plants. A surprise round every corner. Said by visitors to be 'a real hidden jewel'. Featured in Lancashire Life.

27 THE GROWTH PROJECT

Kellett Street Allotments, Rochdale, OL16 2JU. Karen Hayday, k.hayday@hourglass.org.uk, , www.rochdalemind.org.uk/growth-project. *From A627M. R A58 L Entwistle Rd R Kellett St.* **Sat 11 Aug (11.30-3.30). Adm £3.50, chd free. Home-made teas. Visits also by arrangement June to Nov wednesdays & Thursdays only.** Donation to The Growth Project.

With excellent home made lunches, cut flowers and vegetables to buy plus guides to give horticultural advice and over an acre of organic unusual vegetable varieties the Project incl wildlife pond, insect hotels, formal flower and wild flower borders, and potager. Visit the Elizabethan straw bale house, stroll down the pergola walk and under the handcrafted arches to the wild flower meadow and orchard. Afternoon tea is served in the Victorian style ornate 'Woodland Green' woodworking station. Cut flowers and fresh organic vegetables, Jams and cakes to buy. The Growth Project is a partnership between Hourglass and Rochdale and District mind. No disabled WC, ground can be uneven.

GROUP OPENING

28 HALE VILLAGE GARDENS

Liverpool, L24 4BA. *6m S of M62 J6. Take A5300, A562 towards Liverpool, then A561, L for Hale opp the RSPCA. From S L'pool head for the airport then L sign for Hale. The 82A bus runs through the village from Widnes/Runcorn to L'pool.* **Sat 23, Sun 24 June (2-5). Combined adm £4, chd free. Home-made teas at 2 Pheasant Field & 66 Church Rd.**

NEW **54 CHURCH ROAD**
Norma & Ray Roe.

66 CHURCH ROAD
Liz Kelly-Hines & David Hines.

NEW **2 PHEASANT FIELD**
Roger & Tania Craine.

The delightful village of Hale, is set in rural S Merseyside between Widnes and Liverpool Airport. It is home to the cottage, sculpture and grave of the famous giant known as the Childe of Hale. Gardens at different ends of the village have arranged a combined opening and each has been fully developed by the present owners. No 2 Pheasant Field at the west of the village has a lovely waterfall in a well-planted area and lots of summer colour everywhere. Nos 54 and 66 Church Road at the south of the village are on the way to the old lighthouse at Hale Point and have wonderful views over the river Mersey and the distant Welsh Hills. A wildlife pond and mixed planting for structure, colour and fragrance, along with a substantial allotment, all feature.

29 ◆ HAZELWOOD

North Road, Bretherton, Leyland, PR26 9AY. Jacqueline Iddon & Thompson Dagnall, 01772 601433, jacquelineiddon@gmail.com, www.jacquelineiddon.co.uk. *8m SW of Preston. Between Southport & Preston, from A59, take B5247 for 1m then L onto (B5248) Garden signed from North Rd.* **For NGS: Sun 17 June (1-5). Adm £3.50, chd free. Cream teas. For other opening times and information, please phone, email or visit garden website.**

1½ acre garden and hardy plant nursery, originally orchard, now has gravel garden with pots and seating area bottle wall and folly, shrubs, herbaceous borders, large stream-fed pond with woodland walk. Sculpture, Victorian fern house. Oak-framed, summerhouse, log cabin as sculpture gallery fronted by cottage garden beds. Sculpture demonstration at 2 pm, live music. Beach area,Teas in Coach house. Extensive sculpture collection, the work of Thompson Dagnall. The majority of the garden is accessible to wheel chairs.

GROUP OPENING

30 HEATON GARDENS

Tickets: Any Garden or 6 Cannock Drive, Heaton Moor, Stockport, SK4 3JB. *5m S of Manchester. 1½m NW of J1 (Stockport) off M60, then A5154 (Didsbury Rd).The rd takes a slight ascent & you need to turn into Lodge Court, & next L into Cannock Drive.* **Sun 1 July (12-5). Combined adm £5, chd free. Home-made teas. Sparkling wine and nibbles at Clifton Road. Wine, coffee/tea and cakes at Cannock Drive.**

6 CANNOCK DRIVE
Andrea & Stefan Schumacher.

33 CLIFTON ROAD
Dr Guy Makin.

NEW **RICHMOND ROAD GARDENS**
Richmond Road Gardens.

Heaton Moor is a leafy, attractive suburb in south Manchester. These gardens are all hidden gems, and together, demonstrate the huge variety of gardens to be found in one small area: the first, Cannock Drive, has a lawn that sweeps down to a beautiful small lake with central fountain, offering views over the surrounding area. This is a substantial garden with well- stocked, developing borders. In contrast, Clifton Road is a smaller corner plot which has recently been completely redesigned to provide a garden of two halves, one a pretty family garden , the other a decorative and productive potager with raised beds and espaliered fruit trees. And finally, new to the group, Richmond Road is a row of eight tiny terrace gardens, each with its own unique design. These little plots demonstrate just how different even the smallest plot can look with a bit of imagination.

GROUP OPENING

31 NEW HIGHTOWN GARDENS

Liverpool, L38 0BU. *11m N of Liverpool & 11m S of Southport. M 57/58 Join A5758 keep L, at r'about take 2nd exit A565 Turn 2nd L onto B5193/Orrell Hill Lane Turn R Moss Lane Turn L onto Alt Rd Turn R to Kerslake Way At r'about take 5th exit to Church Hall.* **Sun 20 May, Sun 8 July (1-5). Combined adm £5, chd free. Home-made teas at St Stephen's Church Hall.**

NEW **5 BLUNDELL AVENUE**
Denise & Dave Ball.

NEW **11 BLUNDELL AVENUE**
Karen Rimmer.

NEW **PORTAGE 3 RIVERSIDE**
Val & Geoff Bailey.

NEW **20 RIVERSIDE**
Pamela Howard.

NEW **34 RIVERSIDE**
Hilary & Stuart Munro.

A group of gardens in the village of Hightown. Visit a courtyard with a 'quaint sweet shop', and nearby a quirky garden full of surprises then three gardens in the same Riverside location. A cottage garden with a spectacular view across to the Welsh Hills, an amazing collection of tropical plants and azaleas and an eco friendly garden with blossoms and tubs of bedding plants. Licensed bar, art work on sale. Partial access to the Riverside gardens.

GROUP OPENING

32 NEW HILLSIDE GARDENS

Liverpool Road, Southport, PR8 3DE. *3m S of Southport. Gardens signed from A565 Waterloo Rd & A5267 Liverpool Rd.* **Sun 27 May, Sun 22 July (11-5). Combined adm £5, chd free. Home-made teas at 339 Liverpool Rd.**

23 ASHTON ROAD
John & Jennifer Mawdsley.

33 CLOVELLY DRIVE
Bob & Eunice Drummond.

LINKS VIEW, 18 CLOVELLY DRIVE
Christine & Dave McGarry.

NEW **339 LIVERPOOL ROAD**
Ian & Sue Dexter.

A group of four gardens ranging from the smaller to medium sized - each with many features including pergolas, water features and special plants, shrubs and trees. Limited wheelchair access to 3 Gardens.

33 NEW KIBBOTH CREW

Ramsbottom, BL0 9DR. Gill Wild, 01706 822639, wildgill@aol.com. *4m N of Bury. From Ramsbottom centre - take Carr St up hill, 2nd R Springwood St, L to Old MIll Hotel, private rd through car parks, Kibboth Crew house up hairpin bend, 1st L.* **Visits by arrangement May to July. Adm £4.50, chd free. Light refreshments.** Donation to Bury Hospice.

An exciting and challenging 4½ acre garden developed during the last 15yrs. A sloping site with streams, ponds, natural waterfall and bog garden, archaeological dig. Herbaceous borders, trees, large lawns and extensive kitchen garden. Planting incl grasses, penstemons, astrantias and many perennials linked by paths , metal sculptures and patios. Rose expert available for advice at times.. Archaeological dig on site several years ago. A varied garden and peaceful. The owner is hoping to make it into a Healing Garden.

34 LIVERPOOL MARIE CURIE HOSPICE

Speke Road, Woolton, Liverpool, L25 8QA. Hayley Hawkins. *From the city centre, Woolton Rd or Menlove Ave, follow the signs for Woolton, at T-lights go onto Kings Drive for Hospice entrance. There is a small car park on Hospice grounds.* **Sat 21 July (12-4). Adm £3, chd free. Home-made teas.**

A wrap around garden, with well planted ornamental flower beds, shrubs and mature trees, including various seating areas, in which to relax and unwind. In addition, there are two internal courtyards. All areas of the grounds are wheelchair accessible.

35 NEW 28 LOCKWOOD AVENUE

Poulton-Le-Fylde, FY6 7AB. Tracy Mollart. *Located at the end of a cul de sac opp Poulton train stn. 3hrs parking at Booths which is only a 2 mins walk away. The property has a shared drive.* **Sun 1 July (1-4.30). Adm £4, chd free. Light refreshments.**

Two gardens in one quietly hidden behind a family home. The rear classic formal garden has four square lawns and central water feature which is softened by herbaceous borders and paved walkways. The lower cottage garden connects down stone stairs which shelters a gardeners hideaway, raised beds of fruit, vegetables and companion planting. Only the classic formal garden can be accessed as the cottage garden has 15 steps to access it.

36 LOWER DUTTON FARM

Gallows Lane, Ribchester, PR3 3XX. Mr R Robinson, 01254 878405, aforrest_50@outlook.com. *1½m NE of Ribchester. Leave M6 J31. Take A59 towards Clitheroe, turn L at T-lights towards Ribchester. Signed from B6243 & B6245. Ample car parking in adjacent field.* **Sat 4, Sun 5 Aug (1-5). Adm £4, chd free. Home-made teas. Visits also by arrangement May to Aug groups of 10+.**

Traditional long Lancashire farmhouse and barn, with 2 acre gardens. Formal gardens nr house with mixed herbaceous beds and shrubs. Sweeping lawns lead down past island beds to wildlife area and established large pond with small woodland. Orchard at rear of house with mix of fruit-trees and roses. Several seating areas. Lawns may be difficult in very wet weather.

37 NEW MERESANDS KENNELS & CATTERY

Holmeswood Rd, Rufford, Ormskirk, L40 1TG. Mrs Bridget Street. *6m N of Ormskirk. From the A59 Rufford, turn L on to Holmeswood Rd, past the Hesketh Arms on R. 1m on L Signed to Meresands Kennels & Cattery.* **Sun 3 June (10.30-4.30). Adm £3.50, chd free. Home-made teas.**

A relatively new garden of approx 3 acres which has been developed alongside a mature woodland. With koi pond and formal gardens. A laburnum arch leads you to the woodland area with paths, seating and stumpery. A natural pond with summer house/ pavilion, duck house and a jetty, is home to an abundance of wildlife, including the occasional kingfisher.

38 MILL BARN

Goosefoot Close, Samlesbury, Preston, PR5 0SS. Chris Mortimer, 01254 853300, chris@millbarn.net, www.millbarn.net. *6m E of Preston. From M6 J31 2½m on A59/A677 B/burn. Turn S. Nabs Head Lane, then Goosefoot Lane.* **Sat 2, Sun 3, Sat 9, Sun 10 June (12-5). Adm £4, chd free. Cream teas. Visits also by arrangement May to July min group donation £40 or £4 per head.**

The unique and quirky garden at Mill Barn is a delight: or rather a series of delights. Along the R Darwin, through the tiny secret grotto, past the suspension bridge and view of the fairytale tower, visitors can a stroll past folly, sculptures, lily pond, and lawns, enjoy the naturally planted flowerbeds, then enter the secret garden and through it the pathways of the wooded hillside beyond. A garden developed on the site of old mills gives a fascinating layout which evolves at many levels. Partial wheelchair access, visitors have not been disappointed in the past.

ALLOTMENTS

39 NEW MOSS PARK ALLOTMENTS

Lesley Road, Stretford, Manchester, M32 9EE. Allison Sterlini. *Lesley Road. J7 of M60 (Manchester), A56 (Manchester), A5181 Barton Road, L onto B5213 Urmston Lane, ½m L onto Lesley Rd signed Stretford Cricket Club. Parking at second gate.* **Sun 29 July (11-4). Adm £4, chd free. Home-made teas.**

Moss Park is a stunning, award winning allotment site in Stretford, Manchester. Wide grass paths flanked by pretty flower borders give way to a large variety of well-tended plots bursting with ideas to try at home, from insect hotels to unusual fruits and vegetables. Take tea and cake on the lawn outside the quirky society clubhouse that looks like a beamed country pub. A great day out. Limited wheelchair access.

40 NEW THE OLD VICARAGE

Church Road, Astley, Manchester, M29 7FS. Susan & Neil Kinsella. *½ way between Leigh & Worsley off A580 East Lancs Rd. Opp the site of the old St Stephens Astley CE Church & next to Dam House, 250 yds from the mini r'about junction at Church Rd (A5082) & Manchester Rd(A572). Close to the Bull's Head.* **Sat 16, Sun 17 June (9.30-5.30). Adm £4, chd free. Cream teas.**

Recently restored medium sized gardens of Grade 2* vernacular Georgian vicarage comprising both formal and informal planting and statuary as the garden narrows to follow the woodland stream which runs through it. There are six separate areas/rooms which gradually merge into the surrounding trees ending several hundred yards from the frontage to the property. Most of the garden is flat although paths and some areas are gravel.

41 NEW PARKERS LODGE

28 Lodge Side, Bury, BL8 2SW. Keith Talbot, wcp1964@gmail.com. *2m W of M66 J2. From A58 then B6196 Ainsworth Rd turn R onto Elton Vale Rd, drive past the sports club onto a small estate, and follow the road round to car park.* **Sun 17 June (11-4). Adm £4, chd free. Light refreshments. Visits also by arrangement.**

Parkers Lodge is set on the site of a demolished Victorian Mill that was used for bleaching. Since the houses were completed in 2014 a small group of volunteers have been working to transform what was a jungle into a manicured wild space that still allows the local wildlife to flourish. Set in 12 acres with 2 lakes with 50 percent of them open for a leisurely stroll round.

42 NEW 11 PLATT LANE

Dobcross, Oldham, OL3 5AD. Marilyn McNeill. *5m E of Oldham. From Dobcross village square the exit to Platt Lane, the garden is last house on L. From Delph take the turning opposite the Bell Inn and continue the garden is on the R.* **Sat 30 June, Sun 1 July (1-4). Combined adm with 5 Crib Lane £3, chd free. Cream teas.**

A cottage garden with a front garden planted with shrubs. The main garden has herbaceous borders with shrubs, roses and perennials. There is a wildlife pond and a summerhouse with an exhibition of textiles. The rear garden has a mixture of flowers, vegetables and fruit. There is also a small wildlife pond and a greenhouse.

43 POOL FOOT BARN

Poolfoot Lane, Little Singleton, Poulton-Le-Fylde, FY6 8LY. Mrs Amanda Ackroyd. *Blackpool 6m. 2m from Jct3 M55 off A585 to Fleetwood. Poolfoot Lane is opp the Shell Garage at the 5 lanes end T-lights. Park on lane, one side only.* **Sun 15 July (10.30-5.30). Adm £4, chd free. Home-made teas.** Donation to World Horse Welfare, Penny Farm, Blackpool.

Our 2 acre garden has several distinct areas including a cottage garden, kitchen garden, greenhouse, small pond, butterfly bed, shrub borders, hot summer beds and an area for moisture loving plants. In addition the terrace by the duck pond has alpine beds and is surrounded by perennial borders. Behind the breeze house is a copse leading to a wild flower area and field with Shetlands.

44 ◆ THE RIDGES

Weavers Brow (cont. of Cowling Rd), Limbrick, Chorley, PR6 9EB. Mr & Mrs J M Barlow, 01257 279981, barbara@barlowridges.co.uk, www.bedbreakfast-gardenvisits.com. *2m SE of Chorley town centre. From M6 J27. From M61 J8. Follow signs for Chorley A6 then signs for Cowling & Rivington. Passing Morrison's up Brook St, mini r'about 2nd exit, Cowling Brow. Pass Spinners Arms on L. Garden on R.* **For NGS: Mon 7 May, Mon 27 Aug (11-5). Adm £4.50, chd free. Home-made teas. For other opening times and information, please phone, email or visit garden website.**

3 acres, incl old walled orchard garden, cottage-style herbaceous borders, with perfumed rambling roses and clematis thru fruit the trees. Arch leads to formal lawn, surrounded by natural woodland, shrub borders and specimen trees with contrasting foliage. Woodland walks and dell. Natural looking stream, wildlife ponds. Walled water feature with Italian influence, and walled herb garden. Classical music played. Home made cakes, baked and served by ladies of St James Church, Chorley. Wheelchair access some gravel paths and woodland walks not accessible.

45 THE SECRET VALLEY

Christ the King Primary School Carpark, Worsley, Manchester, M28 3DW. Sally Berry, 0161 7300128, info@thesecretvalley.com, www.thesecretvalley.com. *7½ m from central Manchester. 1½ m from J13 M60. Straight over r'about onto Walkden Rd, at 1st T-lights turn R onto A580 Take 2nd L onto Holly Ave, park in Christ the King Primary School. No parking on 'Hopefold Dr' or 'The Reach'.* **Sun 3 June (10-5). Adm £5, chd free. Light refreshments. A selection of cakes, teas, coffee. Visits also by arrangement June to Aug groups max 30. £5 a head. Min £50. Toilets, water, cabin, power, wifi.**

Large 2 acre water garden with ponds, streams, waterfalls, islands and lake. High variety of trees, plants and climbers. It is a haven for waterfowl and local wildlife (incl swans, ducks, geese, coots, moorhens, grebes, herons and kingfishers). Adjoining gardens and allotment are also open. Waterfall, 1 acre lake, smaller ponds, streams, fountain, statues, wild swans and ducks, lots of seating and areas to relax. Featured in and on Gardeners World, BBC News, ITV News, Daily Mail, Manchester Evening News, Evening Standard, Mirror, The Sun. The entrance, central area are wheelchair friendly. However many paths are not and if its very wet then the wheelchair may struggle on grassy areas.

Willowbrook Hospice Gardens

GROUP OPENING

46 SEFTON PARK GARDENS

Liverpool, L8 3SD. *1m S of Liverpool city centre. From end of M62 take A5058 Queens Drive ring rd S through Allerton to Sefton Park. Parking roadside in Sefton Park.* **Sun 15 July (12-5). Combined adm £5, chd free. Home-made teas at Fern Grove Community Garden, Parkmount and Sefton Park Allotments.**

THE COMMUNITY ORCHARD AND WILDLIFE GARDEN
The Society of Friends, www.tann.org.uk.

6 CROXTETH GROVE
Stuart Speeden.

FERN GROVE COMMUNITY GARDEN
Liverpool City Council.

PARKMOUNT
L17 3BP. Jeremy Nicholls.

SEFTON PARK ALLOTMENTS
L17 1AS. Sefton Park Allotments Society.

THAT BLOOMIN' GREEN TRIANGLE
Mrs Helen Hebden.

This is a fascinatingly varied group of Liverpool gardens. In That Bloomin' Green Triangle, Architecture group Assemble won the Turner Prize 2015 for their work with the four streets. It was the guerrilla gardening of local residents which led to the area's regeneration. See long colour themed borders and rare plants in the garden and for sale at Parkmount, plus the delightful small garden in Croxteth Grove. Vegetables and flowers abound in the ninety allotments, which include a children's and disabled plots. Two local gardening projects to see: Fern Grove Community garden has children's activities and a beekeeping demonstration, and a Community Orchard is under development in the former Quaker Burial Ground in Arundel Avenue. Wheelchair access WC at Sefton Park Allotments. Featured on and in BBC Gardeners' World, Amateur Garden Magazine and The Guardian Magazine gardening section.

47 SOUTHLANDS

12 Sandy Lane, Stretford, M32 9DA. Maureen Sawyer & Duncan Watmough, www.southlands12.com. *3m S of Manchester. Sandy Lane (B5213) is situated off A5181 (A56) ¼m from M60 J7.* **Sun 22 July (12-6). Adm £4, chd free. Home-made teas. Cake-away service (take a slice of your favourite cake home).**

Described by visitors as 'totally inspirational', this artists' multi-award winning garden unfolds into a series of beautiful spaces including Mediterranean, Ornamental and Woodland gardens. Organic kitchen garden with large glasshouse. Extensive herbaceous borders,hanging baskets and stunning container plantings throughout the garden, 2 ponds and a water feature. Featured on and in BBC North West tonight and Garden News magazine.

48 91 STATION ROAD

Banks, Southport, PR9 8AY. Mr & Mrs P Edwards. *4m N of Southport. Take the A365 Southport to Preston rd. From Southport take 1st L by the car wash plant. From Preston take 3rd exit at Banks r'about then 1st L.* **Sun 1 July (11-5). Adm £4, chd free. Light refreshments.**

In a semi rural setting a charming garden of surprises featuring a courtyard with water feature and raised beds. Steps to the next level with secluded seating, winding paths with lush borders of cottage garden favourites and many roses. Another area features a pond with waterfall, a fruit bed and summer house. The garden is wildlife and bird friendly. Wheelchair access to courtyard only. Different levels with some steps and narrow winding paths.

49 THE STONES & ROSES GARDEN

White Coppice Farm, White Coppice, Chorley, PR6 9DF. Raymond & Linda Smith, 01257 277633, stonesandroses@btinternet.com, www.stonesandroses.org. *3m NE of Chorley. J8 M61 (next to the Mormon Temple & Botany Bay) take A674 to Blackburn, 3rd R to Heapey & White Coppice. Parking up hill next to the garden.* **Sun 8, Sat 14 July (11-4). Adm £4, chd free. Cream teas. Visits also by arrangement in July individuals may be added to groups 3 - 18 July.**

The garden where the cows used to live set in the beautiful hamlet of White Coppice with wonderful views. Sunken rose garden, fountains, waterfalls, herbaceous borders, all with colour themed planting and formal kitchen garden. Fruit tree walk down to the small lake with wild flower planting. Wonderful walking area with beautiful cricket field. Gravel paths, ⅔ of main garden accessible by wheelchair and entrance into the house.

50 12 THE CROFT

Euxton, Chorley, PR7 6LH. Mr & Mrs David & Jean Robinson. *3m NW of Chorley. A49 from Standish to Preston L at Bay Horse in Euxton. A49 Preston to Standish R into Runshaw Lane 4th Rd on L into Glencroft follow the Rd.* **Sun 27 May (12-5). Adm £3.50, chd free. Light refreshments.**

A small quirky garden with many interesting features. Amongst our collection of plants are acers, ferns, auriculas. Interesting use of gravel leading to the hot tub.The summer house provides one of the many seating areas. Come along and meet Henry!

GROUP OPENING

51 NEW TOTTINGTON GARDENS

Bury, BL8 3NF. Anne Ernill.
4m N of Bury. From M66 J2 follow A58 onto B6213 towards Tottington, follow Tottington rd yellow arrows pointing down Kirklees St. **Sun 24 June (11-4.30). Combined adm £4, chd free. Cream teas at both gardens. WC facilities at 33 Beryl Ave.**

NEW **33 BERYL AVE**
Anne Ernill.

NEW **17 RHINE CLOSE**
Paul Kelly.

2 gardens open for the first time. A suburban garden created over the past 9 yrs from a blank canvas into a creative oasis. Organically managed to attract birds,bees and butterflies. Stunning views across fields to Knowl Hill.Quirky poly tunnel disguise,rustic potting shack, 2 ponds, 2 water features, gravel paths, vegetable plot, natural wooden sculptures, mosaic floor panels and many reclaimed vintage items. A garden created with a touch of humour and a focus on using reclaimed and recycled materials to create interesting features.

6 Cannock Drive, Heaton Gardens

52 VARLEY FARM

Anna Lane, Forest Becks, Bolton-by-Bowland, Clitheroe, BB7 4NZ. Mr & Mrs B Farmer, 07887 638436, varleyforestbecks@btinternet.com. *7m N of Clitheroe. A59 off at Sawley follow Settle 2nd L after Copy Nook onto Settle Rd turn L at rd sign on L. Follow lane 1m to a sharp R hand bend garden on L.* **Visits by arrangement June & July for groups of 10+. Adm incl tea, cake and biscuits. Adm £5, chd free. Home-made teas.**
1½-acre garden that's been developing from 2004. Varley Farm is 700ft above sea level with views across the Forest of Bowland and Pendle. Herbaceous lawned cottage garden, flagged herb garden and walled gravel garden, steps to orchard. Stream and pond area planted in 2009 still maturing with a grassed walk through natural meadow and wild flower meadow.

53 WADDOW LODGE GARDEN

Clitheroe Road, Waddington, Clitheroe, BB7 3HQ. Liz & Peter Foley, www.gardentalks.co.uk. *1½m N of Clitheroe. From M6 J31 take A59 (Preston-Skipton). A671 to Clitheroe then B6478. 1st house on L in village. Parking available on rd before entering village; blue badges in drive parking area on gravel.* **Sun 27 May, Sun 15 July (1-5). Adm £4, chd free. Home-made teas.**

Inspirational 2-acre organic garden for all seasons surrounding Georgian house (not open) with views to Pendle and Bowland. An enthusiast's collection of many unusual plants with herbaceous borders, large island beds, shrubs, heathers, rhododendrons, small mature wooded area, old fashioned and hybrid roses. Extensive kitchen garden of vegetables and soft fruit, interesting heritage apple orchard, herbs, alpines and greenhouse, wildlife meadow and bog garden. Colourful containers. Circa 500 year old Yew Tree. Featured in Lancashire Life and on BBC Radio Lancashire. Some gravel/bark paths, otherwise level surfaces.

GROUP OPENING

54 WARTON GARDENS

Warton, LA5 9PJ. *1½m N of Carnforth. From M6 J35 take A601M NW for 1m, then N on A6 for 0.7m turn L signed Warton Old Rectory. Warton Village 1m down Borwick Lane. From Carnforth pass train stn & follow signs Warton & Silverdale.* **Sun 20 May, Sat 30 June, Sun 1 July (11-4.30). Combined adm £5, chd free. Home-made teas at 109/111 Main Street.**

2 CHURCH HILL AVENUE
Mr & Mrs J Street.
Open on all dates

111 MAIN STREET
Mr & Mrs J Spendlove,
01524 727 770,
claire@lavenderandlime.co.uk.
Open on all dates
Visits also by arrangement May to July gardening groups up to 20.

TUDOR HOUSE
Mr & Mrs T Singleton.
Open on Sat 30 June, Sun 1 July

The Old Vicarage

The 3 gardens are spread across the village and offer a wide variety of planting and design ideas incl. cottage charm on limestone pavement, unusual herbaceous and more formal approaches. Parking at the bottom of village (LA5 9NU) or the public car park, next to Old School Brewery (LA5 9PL). Warton has 2 Pubs and WCs. It is the birthplace of the medieval ancestors of George Washington, of which the family coat of arms can be seen in St Oswald's Church. The ruins of the Old Rectory (English Heritage) is the oldest surviving building in the village. Ascent of Warton Crag (AONB), provides panoramic views across Morecambe Bay to the Lakeland hills beyond. 111 Main Street, Warton featured on ITV 'Love Your Garden' Aug '17. All gardens have steps and uneven surfaces unsuitable for wheelchair access.

55 WARTON HALL

Lodge Lane, Lytham, Lytham St. Annes, FY8 5RP. Nicola & David Thompson, nicci_thompson@hotmail.co.uk, , www.total-art.co.uk. *J3 exit M55. L for Kirkham, follow signs for Wrea Green, L towards Warton to the BAE T-lights, R, Lodge Lane on R after The Golf Academy & 2m before Lytham town centre.* **Thur 3, Fri 4, Sat 5, Sun 6, Mon 7 May (10-5). Adm £4, chd free. Light refreshments. Visits also by arrangement in May groups of 8+.**

Georgian Manor House (not open) set in 4 acre garden with Bluebell woodland walk, Bog Garden and Sculpture Trail. Japanese Water Garden and Dry Garden, and Gallery Courtyard. Creativity Classes in the Garden and Studio and Yoga under the 400 year old Weeping Hornbeam tree (book online) Art, plants and garden gifts for sale in the Conservatory. The Tearoom will be serving light refreshment including homemade cakes. Woodland walk and Sculpture Trail. Craft and Art classes in the Garden and Art Studio can be booked online at www.total-art.co.uk' Gardens of Warton Hall' on Facebook for updates and booking classes. Featured in Daily Telegraph Gardens section, Gazette St Annes Express, Radio Lancashire. Wheelchair access to most of the garden.

56 WEEPING ASH GARDEN

Bents Garden & Home, Warrington Road, Glazebury, WA3 5NS. John Bent, www.bents.co.uk. *15m W of Manchester. Located next to Bents*

Garden & Home, just off the East Lancs Rd A580 at Greyhound r'about near Leigh. Follow brown 'Garden Centre' signs. **Sun 11, Sun 18, Sun 25 Feb, Sun 4 Mar, Sun 9 Sept (10-4). Adm by donation.**
Created by retired nurseryman and photographer John Bent, Weeping Ash is a garden of all-year interest with a beautiful display of early snowdrops. Broad sweeps of colour lend elegance to this stunning garden which is much larger than it initially seems with hidden paths and wooded areas creating a sense of natural growth. Weeping Ash Garden is located immed adjacent to Bents Garden & Home with its award winning Fresh Approach Restaurant and outdoor adventure play area. Partial wheelchair access and weather dependent.

57 11 WESTMINSTER ROAD

Eccles, Manchester, M30 9HF. Lynne Meakin. *3m W of Salford, 4m W of Manchester. 1st exit M602 Manchester direction 1st exit (r'about) 2nd T-lights turn L. After Xing turn R, Victoria Rd 2nd R (Westminster Rd) no.11 on L.* **Sat 16 June (12.30-5). Combined adm with 35 Ellesmere Road £4.50, chd free. Wine. Home-made teas at Ellesmere Road.**
The garden at 11 Westminster Road has a pretty front garden with topiary chickens and is well stocked with perennials. mature trees, and box hedge. The garden is divided by a trellis and rose arch which separates the flower beds and lawn from the fruit growing area, and there are a large number of fuchsias grown in pots. A coach house to the rear of the garden where wine/nibbles will be served. The garden is on the flat except for a small area in the front garden, care will need to be taken in case the path is slippy.

58 WIGAN & LEIGH HOSPICE

Kildare Street, Hindley, Wigan, WN2 3HZ. Wigan & Leigh Hospice, 01942525566, j.nicholson@wlh.org.uk, thehospicegardener.com. *1½m SW of Wigan. From Wigan on A577 Leigh/Manchester Rd. In Hindley turn R at St Peter's Church onto Liverpool Rd A58. After 200 metres turn R into Kildare St.* **Sun 15 July (10-4). Combined adm with 6 Birch Road £3, chd free. Home-made teas. Visits also by arrangement Mar to Sept.**
Large attractive gardens surround the Hospice creating a place of tranquillity. At the front are beautiful raised beds, at the rear 3 large ponds and a Chinese bridge. Outside patients' rooms are colourful tubs and flower beds. A memorial daisy garden and 2 courtyards also feature. A new wild flower garden is being developed - 'The Amberswood Garden'. The gardens are a haven for wildlife. Fully accessible, including WC.

59 WILLOWBROOK HOSPICE GARDENS

Portico Lane, Eccleston Park, Prescot, L34 2QT. Willowbrook Hospice. *Portico Lane, Eccleston Park, Prescot L34 2QT. Leave M6 at exit 21A to M62. At J7 take A57 to Prescot/Liverpool. Continue on A57, turn R onto B5201 Willowbrook is on the R.* **Sat 18, Sun 19 Aug (11-4). Adm £3, chd free. Light refreshments.**
An oasis containing three distinctive National Japanese Garden Society built gardens; a "willowbrook" flower bed designed by RHS Wisley students and a community vegetable garden.

60 81 WINDSOR ROAD

Southport, PR9 9BX. Jeanette Grimley, 07739 789431, jghygienist@gmail.com. *From Southport on A570 turn L at Ash St T-lights after sharp bend turn L into Windsor Rd.* **Sun 1 July (12-5.30). Combined adm with 8 Balfour Road £3.50, chd free. Cream teas. Prosecco. Visits also by arrangement June to Aug cheese, wine and garden chatter.**
This developing garden flows well with the house interior, making clever use of reclaimed materials to create an oasis of calm in a chaotic world! The borders are ever changing with the seasons and include a pretty mix of cottage plants, perennials and shrubs. The owners love of cooking is evident keeping hens, a varied range of herbs and edible planting, including a spectacular Fig tree.

61 WOODSTOCK BARN

Andertons Mill, Mawdesley, Ormskirk, L40 3TW. Mr & Mrs J Bean, 01772 641033, johnpatbean@sky.com. *9m E of Ormskirk. M6 J27 A5209 over Parbold hill, R Lancaster Lane/ Chorley Rd, L after Farmers Arms to Bentley Lane/Andertons Mill. Garden 500 yds on L. From Burscough A59, A5209 towards Parbold, L Lancaster Lane.* **Sun 10 June, Sun 1 July (12-5). Combined adm with 8 Andertons Mill £4.50, chd free. Home-made teas. Some seating under cover available for upto 30 people. Visits also by arrangement June to Sept groups 10+ garden visit with or without textile demonstrations (workshops available).**
An established country garden of over ¾ acre with form, texture and a green tapestry all year round. Developed from a barren wilderness to one with wildlife, amidst tall trees, shrubs, mixed borders, pond, vegetable patch, woodland area and stream. There are several seating areas to enjoy the tranquil atmosphere of this relaxing garden. Limited wheelchair access - main pathway only if lawns are wet.

Funds from National Garden Scheme gardens help Macmillan support thousands of people every year

LEICESTERSHIRE & RUTLAND

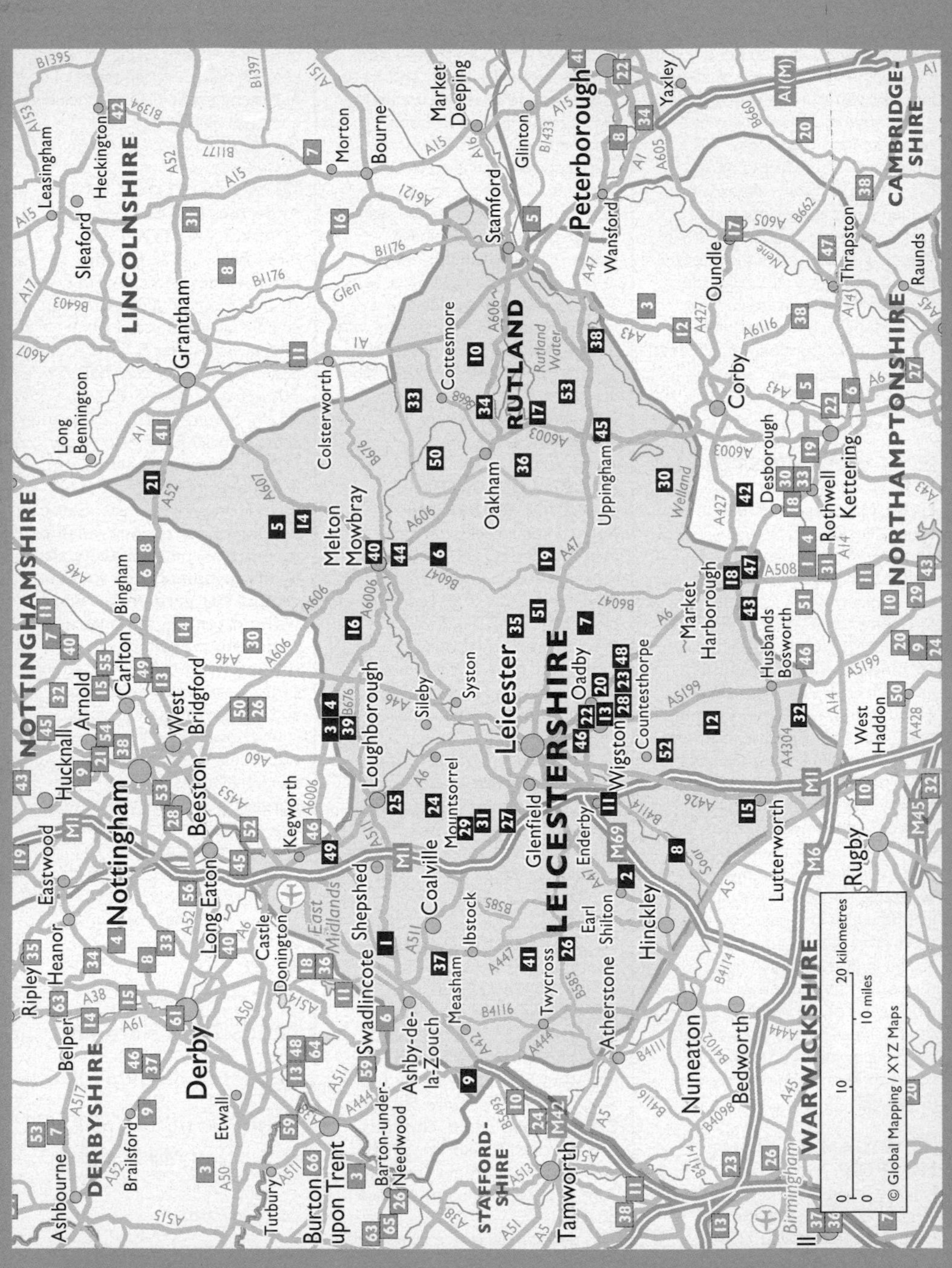

Leicestershire is very much in the centre of England, and has a diverse landscape and wide range of settlements.

Our open gardens are of corresponding variety. From compact Victorian terraces with inspirational planting, large country houses with broad vistas, an arboretum with four national champion trees, to an allotment with over 100 plots. Most gardens welcome groups, sell plants and offer tea and cake.

Confident in the knowledge that your donation goes to wonderful causes, you can look for inspiration for your own garden or plot, or simply take pleasure looking at beautiful gardens.

'Much in Little' is Rutland's motto. They say small is beautiful and never were truer words said.

Rutland is rural England at its best. Honey-coloured stone cottages make up pretty villages nestling amongst rolling hills; the passion for horticulture is everywhere you look, from stunning gardens to the hanging baskets and patio boxes showing off seasonal blooms in our two attractive market towns of Oakham and Uppingham.

There's so much to see in and around Rutland whatever the time of year, including many wonderful NGS gardens.

Below: Prebendal House, Empingham Gardens

Volunteers

Leicestershire

County Organiser
Pamela Shave 01858 575481
pamelashave@btconnect.com

County Treasurer
Martin Shave 01455 556633
martinshave@kilworthaccountancy.co.uk

Publicity
Janet Currie 01509 212191
janet.currie@ngs.org.uk

Talks
Pat Beeson 07940771185
pat.beeson@ngs.org.uk

Assistant County Organisers
Mary Hayward 07545 817664
mary.hayward@ngs.org.uk

David and Beryl Wyrko
01664 840385

Howard Grant 07968 131711
thefirsgarden@gmail.com

Roger Whitmore and Shirley Jackson 01162 787179
whitmorerog@hotmail.co.uk

Rutland

County Organiser
Rose Dejardin
01572 737788
rosedejardin@btopenworld.com

County Treasurer
David Wood
01572 737465
rdavidwood1@gmail.com

Publicity
Jane Alexander-Orr
01572 737368
janealexanderorr@hotmail.com

Assistant County Organiser
Sally Killick 01572 737816
sally.killick@aol.co.uk

Jennifer Wood
01572 737465
rdavidwood1@gmail.com

Leicestershire & Rutland
Booklet Co-ordinator
Mary Hayward
07545 817664
mary.hayward@ngs.org.uk

OPENING DATES

All entries subject to change. For latest information check **www.ngs.org.uk**

Extended openings are shown at the beginning of the month.

Map locator numbers are shown to the right of each garden name.

February

Snowdrop Festival

Saturday 24th
Hedgehog Hall 19

Sunday 25th
Hedgehog Hall 19
Westview 48

March

Saturday 3rd
Westview 48

Sunday 4th
Westview 48

Sunday 25th
Gunthorpe Hall 17

April

Every Wednesday to Sunday from Wednesday 4th
Long Close 24

Sunday 29th
The Old Hall 33

May

Every Wednesday to Sunday
Long Close 24

Sunday 6th
Burrough Hall 5
Hedgehog Hall 19
Tresillian House 44
Westbrooke House 47

Monday 7th
Hedgehog Hall 19
Long Close 24
Newtown Linford Gardens 31

Sunday 13th
Quaintree Hall 36
Willoughby Gardens 52

Saturday 19th
NEW 1 The Dairy, Hurst Court 9
NEW Grimston Gardens 16

Sunday 20th
NEW Grimston Gardens 16
Mill House 28
The Old Vicarage, Burley 34
Ravenstone Hall 37
◆ Whatton Gardens 49

Wednesday 23rd
Thorpe Lubenham Hall 43

Sunday 27th
Whissendine Gardens 50

Monday 28th
Long Close 24
Westview 48

June

Every Wednesday to Sunday
Long Close 24

Every Wednesday
Stoke Albany House 42

Festival Weekend

Sunday 3rd
Dairy Cottage 8
NEW Enderby Gardens 11
Nevill Holt Hall 30
Uppingham Gardens 45

Saturday 9th
28 Gladstone Street 13
Goadby Marwood Hall 14
13 Highcroft Avenue 20

Sunday 10th
Crossfell House 6
28 Gladstone Street 13
13 Highcroft Avenue 20
Honeytrees Tropical Garden 21
Ridgewold Farm 39

Saturday 16th
Loughborough Gardens 25

Sunday 17th
Loughborough Gardens 25
Wing Gardens 53

Saturday 23rd
The Paddocks 35

Sunday 24th
Empingham Gardens 10
Market Bosworth Gardens 26
The Paddocks 35

Saturday 30th
Shipmeadow 41

July

Every Wednesday
Stoke Albany House 42

Sunday 1st
Long Close 24
Mill House 28
Redhill Lodge 38
Shipmeadow 41
Tresillian House 44
Westbrooke House 47

Saturday 7th
28 Gladstone Street 13
NEW 7 Little Dale 23

Sunday 8th
28 Gladstone Street 13
Green Wicket Farm 15
Honeytrees Tropical Garden 21
NEW 7 Little Dale 23
Mountain Ash 29

Wednesday 11th
Green Wicket Farm 15

Sunday 15th
Mountain Ash 29

Saturday 21st
Cupplesfield 7

Sunday 22nd
Cupplesfield 7
Willoughby Gardens 52

Sunday 29th
119 Scalford Road 40

August

Every day from Saturday 4th to Friday 10th
NEW 221 Markfield Road 27

Sunday 5th
Honeytrees Tropical Garden 21
Knighton Sensory 22
NEW The White House Farm 51

Sunday 12th
The Firs 12

Saturday 18th
NEW 1 The Dairy, Hurst Court 9
13 Highcroft Avenue 20

Sunday 19th
13 Highcroft Avenue 20

Sunday 26th
Tresillian House 44

September

Saturday 1st
Westview 48

Sunday 2nd
Honeytrees Tropical Garden 21
Washbrook Allotments 46
Westview 48

October

Sunday 7th
Hammond Arboretum 18

Sunday 21st
Tresillian House 44

By Arrangement

NEW Aqueduct Cottage 1
Barracca 2
88 Brook Street 3
109 Brook Street 4
Crossfell House 6
Dairy Cottage 8
Farmway, Willoughby Gardens 52
Goadby Marwood Hall 14
Green Wicket Farm 15
Hedgehog Hall 19

THE GARDENS

1 NEW AQUEDUCT COTTAGE

Gelsmoor Road, Coleorton, Coalville, LE67 8JF. Jayne Wright, 07713 624595, jaynewright38@yahoo.co.uk. *Nr Ashby de la Zouch. Corner of Gelsmoor Rd and Aqueduct Rd. Access is via gate on Aqueduct Rd.* **Visits by arrangement in June. Adm £6, chd free. Light refreshments.**

Mature, classic English garden, in excess of 3 acres. It is flanked by a disused (1836) railway line which is wooded and boasts a large variety of specimen trees. There are formal perennial beds and specimen rose beds with a lot of roses! A small classic fish pond in the formal part of the garden and a 30m open pond in a wildlife friendly setting.

2 BARRACCA

Ivydene Close, Earl Shilton, LE9 7NR. Mr & Mrs John & Sue Osborn, 01455 842609, susan.osborn1@btinternet.com, www.barraccagardens.co.uk. *10m W of Leicester. From A47 after entering Earl Shilton, Ivydene Close is 4th on L from Leicester side of A47.* **Visits by arrangement Feb to July for groups of any size. Short notice bookings possible. Adm £7, chd free. Home-made teas. incl in adm price.**

1 acre garden with lots of different areas, silver birch walk, wildlife pond with seating, apple tree garden, Mediterranean planted area and lawns surrounded with herbaceous plants and shrubs. Patio area with climbing roses and wisteria. There is also a utility garden with greenhouse, vegetables in beds, herbs and perennial flower beds, lawn and fruit cage. Part of the old gardens owned by the Cotton family who used to open approx 9 acres to the public in the 1920's. Adm incl tea/coffee and home-made cakes. Additional catering (such as High Tea or full lunches) considered on request. Partial wheelchair access.

3 88 BROOK STREET

Wymeswold, LE12 6TU. Adrian & Ita Cooke, 01509 880155, itacooke@btinternet.com. *4m NE of Loughborough. From A6006 Wymeswold turn S by church onto Stockwell, then E along Brook St. Roadside parking on Brook St.* **Visits by arrangement May to July combined visits to include 109 Brook Street are possible.**

The ½ acre garden is set on a hillside, which provides lovely views across the village, and comprises 3 distinct areas: firstly, a cottage style garden; then a water garden with a stream and champagne pond; and finally at the top there is a vegetable plot, small orchard and wildflower meadow. The ponds are a breeding ground for great crested and common newts, frogs and toads.

4 109 BROOK STREET

Wymeswold, LE12 6TT. Maggie & Steve Johnson, 01509 880866, steve@brookend.org, www.brookend.org. *4m NE of Loughborough. From A6006 Wymeswold turn S onto Stockwell, then E along Brook St. Roadside parking along Brook St. Steep drive with limited disabled parking at house.* **Visits by arrangement May & June for groups 10+. Min 2 weeks notice please. (Combined visits to incl 88 Brook Street possible). Home-made teas.**

S-facing ¾ acre gently sloping garden with views to open country. Mature garden much improved. Patio with roses and clematis, wildlife and fish ponds, mixed borders, vegetable garden, orchard, hot garden and woodland garden. Something for everyone! Demonstration of rain water harvesting on limited budget. Superb home-made cakes served with beverages. Some gravel paths.

5 BURROUGH HALL

Burrough on the Hill, LE14 2QZ. Richard & Alice Cunningham. *Somerby Rd, Burrough on the Hill. Close to B6047. 10 mins from A606. 20 mins from Melton Mowbray.* **Sun 6 May (2-5). Adm £4, chd free. Home-made teas.**

Burrough Hall was built in 1867 as a classic Leicestershire hunting lodge. The garden, framed by mature trees and shrubs, was extensively redesigned by garden designer George Carter in 2007. The garden continues to develop. This family garden designed for all generations to enjoy and is surrounded by magnificent views across High Leicestershire. Gravel paths and lawn. In addition to the garden there will be a small collection of vintage and classic cars on display. Gravel paths & lawn.

Your visit helps fund 389 Marie Curie Nurses

Fourwinds, Grimston Gardens

6 CROSSFELL HOUSE

4d Nether End, Great Dalby, Melton Mowbray, LE14 2EY. Jane & Ian West, 01664 500585, 07912 066976, janeawest@gmail.com. *3m S of Melton Mowbray on B6047. On entering Great Dalby from Melton Mowbray remain on B6047. Crossfell House is on L approx 300 yards from village 30mph sign.* **Sun 10 June (11-5). Adm £3, chd free. Home-made teas. Visits also by arrangement June & July for groups 10-30 (smaller groups considered).**

A formal garden consisting of a terraced herbaceous border and rockery, flanked by a border of shrubs, two small areas of lawn and a sweeping path leading to a two acre meadow with wild grasses, flowers and a recently created wildlife pond. Paths crisscross the meadows, culminating in spectacular countryside views from our Shepherd's Hut and picnic area. We welcome you to bring your own picnic as well as the refreshments we provide. Featured in The Rutland Pride lifestyle magazine. Access to patio and garden area, only partial access to meadow.

7 CUPPLESFIELD

2 Stoughton Road, Gaulby, LE7 9BB. Roger & Ruth Harris. *6m E of Leicester. Follow NGS yellow arrows.* **Sat 21, Sun 22 July (2-5.30). Adm £4, chd free. Home-made teas.**

One acre garden packed full of surprises! Themes range from a contemporary Japanese style area to a long informal herbaceous border and Piet Oudolf inspired prairie beds. Interesting borders incl a hidden jungle, a small wild life pond and low walled potager. The garden is alive with sculptures and hedge art which add that extra interest. Such a lot in so little. Most parts accessible by wheelchair in dry conditions but reduced when wet.

8 DAIRY COTTAGE

15 Sharnford Road, Sapcote, LE9 4JN. Mrs Norah Robinson-Smith, 01455 272398, nrobinsons@yahoo.co.uk. *9m SW of Leicester. Sharnford Rd joins Leicester Rd in Sapcote to B4114 Coventry Rd. Follow NGS signs at both ends.* **Sun 3 June (1-5). Adm £3, chd free. Home-made teas. Visits also by arrangement May & June for groups 10+.**

From a walled garden with colourful mixed borders to a potager approached along a woodland path, this mature cottage garden combines extensive perennial planting with many unusual shrubs and specimen trees. More than 90 clematis and climbing roses are trained up pergolas, arches and into trees 50ft high – so don't forget to look up.

9 NEW 1 THE DAIRY, HURST COURT

Netherseal Road, Chilcote, Swadlincote, DE12 8DU. Alison Dockray. *3m from J11 of the M42. 10m from Tamworth and Ashby de la Zouch. Hurst Court is situated on Netherseal Rd but sat navs show it as Church Rd. Due to limited parking it is advisable to park on Netherseal Rd.* **Sat 19 May, Sat 18 Aug (11-2.30). Adm £3, chd free. Light refreshments.**

Developed over the last 10 years from a muddy ¼ acre patch attached to a barn conversion, the garden now contains a large Japanese Koi Carp pond and goldfish pond with planting having a Japanese connection viewed from winding paths. With many rhododendrons, camellias and azaleas combined with cloud pruning and a variety of other plants, an air of peace pervades the garden.

Donations from the National Garden Scheme help Parkinson's UK care for more people

GROUP OPENING

10 EMPINGHAM GARDENS

Empingham, LE15 8PS. *Empingham Village. 5m E of Oakham, 5m W of Stamford on A606.* **Sun 24 June (2-5.30). Combined adm £5, chd free. Home-made teas at Prebendal House.**

HOME FARM HOUSE
Mr & Mrs David & Susan Painter.

NEW **HONEYLEA**
Mr & Mrs Barry & Janet Chalmers-Stevens.

LAVANDER COTTAGE
Virginia Todd.

PREBENDAL HOUSE
Matthew & Rebecca Eatough.

4 very different gardens in a lovely village. Park and start your visit at Prebendal House, next door to the Church. 4 acres surround the house (not open), built in 1688 as a summer palace for the Bishop of Lincoln. Incl are extensive herbaceous borders, topiary and a sunken water garden. The garden of Home Farm House is entered via a rose arch, the path leads around the house via a sunken paved area with circular pool, a terrace enclosed by shrub roses and scented plants, a shady border and informal lawn with mature trees to the formal road frontage. The tiny garden of Lavander Cottage in Nook Lane has been developed over 10yrs into a series of rooms linked by rose and honeysuckle arches and packed with climbing, shrub and standard roses, richly underplanted with lavender, alliums and clematis and full of colour & scent. Honeylea, opposite, is an 'Enabled Garden'. The owner is registered disabled and has designed it for maximum accessibility & relaxation with yr round interest. Wheelchair access at Prebendal House and Honeylea.

GROUP OPENING

11 NEW ENDERBY GARDENS

Enderby, Leicester, LE19 4NA. Mrs Pat Beeson. *4m south of Leicester. From M1 J21 take A5460 to Fosse Park, turn R on B4114. Turn R to Enderby at next r'about, straight on to church then follow yellow NGS signs.* **Sun 3 June (11-5). Combined adm £4, chd free. Home-made teas at 12 Alexander Ave.**

12 ALEXANDER AVENUE
Mr & Mrs J Beeson.

NEW **13 BANTLAM LANE**
Clive and Helen Biggs.

A large Parish with a long history incl the Roman Fosse Way, the church of St. John the Baptiste and modern retail outlets. The two small town gardens are quite different with interesting features and many creative ideas.

12 THE FIRS

Main Street, Bruntingthorpe, LE17 5QF. Howard & Carmel Grant. *5m NE of Lutterworth. Exit J20 M1 to Lutterworth A426. Turn R to Gilmorton & Bruntingthorpe opp petrol station. From Leicester A5199 to Arnesby. Turn R & follow rd 2m to T-junction. Turn L to Bruntingthorpe.* **Sun 12 Aug (11-5). Adm £4, chd free. Home-made teas.**
A tranquil garden of 1½ acres with views over open countryside. The front garden features terraced borders and paving. The main rear garden has large areas of sweeping lawn and grass walkways around many flowing borders. There is a large variety of themed coloured planting, shrubs and trees. In amongst the borders can be found many unusual design features, artefacts and seating areas. Large sequoia tree at the front of the property was damaged by a bomber returning from a night training flight during the WW II. Short gravel drive, some paving, rest grass.

13 Bantlam Lane, Enderby Gardens

13 28 GLADSTONE STREET

Wigston Magna, LE18 1AE. Chris & Janet Huscroft. *4m S of Leicester. Off Wigston by-pass (A5199) follow signs off Mcdonalds r'about.* **Sat 9, Sun 10 June (11-5). Combined adm with 13 Highcroft Avenue £4.50, chd free. Sat 7, Sun 8 July (11-5). Combined adm with 7 Little Dale £4.50, chd free. Home-made teas.**

Our mature small town garden is divided into rooms and bisected by a pond with a bridge. It is brimming with unusual hardy perennials, including collections of ferns and hostas. David Austin roses chosen for their scent feature throughout, incl a 30' rose arch. A shade house with unusual hardy plants. Regular changes to planting and for 2018 we are moving the lawn! Come and see the difference! Frameworks Knitters Museum nearby - open Suns.

14 GOADBY MARWOOD HALL

Goadby Marwood, LE14 4LN. Mr & Mrs Westropp, 01664 464202. *4m NW of Melton Mowbray. Between Waltham-on-the-Wolds & Eastwell, 8m S of Grantham. Plenty of parking space available.* **Sat 9 June (10.30-5). Adm £5, chd free. Light refreshments in Village Hall. Visits also by arrangement with refreshments on request.**

Redesigned in 2000 by the owner based on C18 plans. A chain of 5 lakes (covering 10 acres) and several ironstone walled gardens all interconnected. Lakeside woodland walk. Planting for yr-round interest. Landscaper trained under plantswoman Rosemary Verey at Barnsley House. Beautiful C13 church open. Gravel paths and lawns.

15 GREEN WICKET FARM

Ullesthorpe Road, Bitteswell, Lutterworth, LE17 4LR. Mrs Anna Smith, 01455 552646, greenfarmbitt@hotmail.com. *2m NW of Lutterworth J20 M1. From Lutterworth follow signs through Bitteswell towards Ullesthorpe. Garden situated behind Bitteswell Cricket Club. Field parking available subject to weather conditions.* **Sun 8, Wed 11 July (2-5). Adm £3.50, chd free. Home-made teas. Visits also by arrangement June to Sept for groups min 10, max 30.**

Created in 2008 on a working farm. Clay soil and very exposed but beginning to look established. Many unusual hardy plants along with a lot of old favourites have been used to provide a long season of colour and interest. Anemone nemorosa, Pacific coast iris, sedums and salvias are of particular interest. Formal ponds and water features. Featured in Garden News - Garden of the Week. Some gravel paths.

GROUP OPENING

16 NEW GRIMSTON GARDENS

Main Street, Grimston, Melton Mowbray, LE14 3BZ. *5m NW Melton Mowbray. Follow Yellow NGS signs. The gardens are situated either side of the Church.* **Sat 19, Sun 20 May (11-5). Combined adm £5, chd free. Tea.**

NEW **FOURWINDS**
Monica and Brian Ravenscroft.

NEW **RED HOUSE FARM**
Claire Watson.

Grimston is a small village with a c13 church restored in 1856. The village green has a large stone and stocks set under a mature Chestnut. Fourwinds is approx. 1 acre, with mature trees and shrubs, extensive flower beds, vegetable garden and long stretches of lawns. The multi level ½ an acre of Red Brick Farm House has lawns, specimen shrubs, mature trees and mixed borders. Fourwinds Drive rather uneven in places, with a rather sharp slope. Assistance with wheelchairs available if necessary.

17 GUNTHORPE HALL

Gunthorpe, Oakham, LE15 8BE. Tim Haywood. *A6003 between Oakham & Uppingham; 1m from Oakham, up drive between lodges. Proceed over railway bridge to gardens, 600 yards ahead. Please follow the signs for parking.* **Sun 25 Mar (2-5). Adm £4, chd free. Home-made teas.**

Large garden in a country setting with extensive views across the Rutland landscape with the carpets of daffodils being the outstanding feature. A great deal of recent re-design has transformed this garden with more recent works being undertaken on the kitchen garden and around the (former) stable yard.

18 HAMMOND ARBORETUM

Burnmill Road, Market Harborough, LE16 7JG. The Robert Smyth Academy, www.hammondarboretum.org.uk. *15m S of Leicester on A6. From High St, follow signs to The Robert Smyth Academy via Bowden Lane to Burnmill Rd. Park in 1st entrance on L.* **Sun 7 Oct (2-4.30). Adm £4, chd free. Home-made teas.**

A site of just under 2½ acres containing an unusual collection of trees and shrubs, many from Francis Hammond's original planting dating from 1913 to 1936 whilst headmaster of the school. Species from America, China and Japan with malus and philadelphus walks and a moat. Proud owners of 4 champion trees identified by national specialist. Guided walks and walk plans available. Some steep slopes.

19 HEDGEHOG HALL

Loddington Road, Tilton on the Hill, LE7 9DE. Janet & Andrew Rowe, 01162597339. *8m W of Oakham. 2m N of A47 on B6047 between Melton & Market Harborough. Follow yellow NGS signs in Tilton towards Loddington.* **Sat 24, Sun 25 Feb (11-4). Light refreshments. Sun 6, Mon 7 May (11-4). Home-made teas. Adm £3.50, chd free. Visits also by arrangement in June for groups 10+.**

½ acre organically managed plant lover's garden. Steps leading to three stone walled terraced borders filled with shrubs, perennials, bulbs and a patio over looking the valley. Lavender walk, herb border, beautiful spring garden, colour themed herbaceous borders. Courtyard with collection of hostas and acers and terrace planted for yr-round interest with topiary and perennials. Snowdrop collection. Cakes for sale May opening. Regret, no wheelchair access to terraced borders.

20 13 HIGHCROFT AVENUE

Oadby, Leicester, LE2 5UH. Sharon Maher & Mike Costall. *Just off A6, 5m S Leicester & 9m N Market Harborough. Follow NGS yellow arrows.* **Sat 9, Sun 10 June (10-5). Combined adm with 28 Gladstone Street £4.50, chd free. Sat 18, Sun 19 Aug (10-5). Adm £2.50, chd free. Home-made teas.**

Our garden continues to be a work in progress. It is approx 22 metres x 14 metres. We have a rose bed with lots of David Austin roses, a bed full of hot colours, a herbaceous border, a wildlife area, alpine bed, patio planters and a small wildlife pond. There's plenty of room on the patio to sit and enjoy the tea and cake too!

21 HONEYTREES TROPICAL GARDEN

85 Grantham Road, Bottesford, NG13 0EG. Julia Madgwick & Mike Ford, 01949 842120, julia_madgwick@hotmail.com. *7m E of Bingham on A52. Turn into village. Garden is on L on slip road behind hedge going out of village towards Grantham. Parking on grass opp property.* **Sun 10 June, Sun 8 July, Sun 5 Aug, Sun 2 Sept (10-5). Adm £3, chd free. Home-made teas. Visits also by arrangement June to Sept small groups very welcome 10 - 30.**

The garden is on a S-facing slope which has evolved over 15 years into a tropical escape. Exotic planting as you enter the garden gives way on a gentle incline to more surprises to incl glass houses dedicated to various climatic zones interspersed with more exotic planting. There are steps and some gravel but plenty to view and enjoy from a wheelchair.

22 KNIGHTON SENSORY

Knighton Park, Leicester, LE2 3YQ. Mike Chalk, 0116 2104217, kpgc@hotmail.co.uk, www.knightonparkgardeningclub.com. *Off A563 (Outer Ring Rd) S of Leicester. From Palmerston Blvd, turn into South Kingsmead Rd then 1st L into Woodbank Rd. Park entrance at end of rd. Enter park, follow path to R, garden on R.* **Sun 5 Aug (1-5). Adm by donation. Home-made teas. Visits also by arrangement for groups 10 - 30.**

This ¼ acre community garden stands in a secluded corner of Knighton Park away from the bustle of the city. It is a feast for all the senses incl shrubs, some traditional bedding, herbaceous borders, bog garden with bridge, dry riverbed with wild flowers and wildlife area, Separate area contains raised beds for edibles. Awarded outstanding by the It's Your Neighbourhood Scheme.

23 NEW 7 LITTLE DALE

Wigston Harcourt, Leicester, LE18 3LF. Zoe Lewin & Neil Garner. *1m S of Wigston, follow signs from the cemetery r'about on the A5199.* **Sat 7, Sun 8 July (11-5). Combined adm with 28 Gladstone Street £4.50, chd free. Home-made teas.**

Come and see our 144m² maturing wildlife friendly garden. Although not massive we've managed to pack plenty in. Featuring mixed planting including wild flowers, potted trees and produce with a greenhouse for chillies, tomatoes and aubergines. Lawn laid to meadow with mown paths. The garden incorporates crafts and upcycled pieces throughout with a wooden gazebo for you to enjoy your tea and cake.

Westbrooke House

24 LONG CLOSE

60 Main St, Woodhouse Eaves, LE12 8RZ. John Oakland, 01509 890376, www.longclose.org.uk. *4m S of Loughborough. Nr M1 J23. From A6, W in Quorn.* **Every Wed to Sun 4 Apr to 1 July (10.30-4.30). Mon 7, Mon 28 May (10.30-4.30). Adm £4, chd £0.50** **Visits also by arrangement Apr to June, groups 15+.**

5 acres spring bulbs, rhododendrons, azaleas, camellias, magnolias, many rare shrubs, mature trees, lily ponds; terraced lawns, herbaceous borders, potager in walled kitchen garden, wildflower meadow walk. Winter, spring, summer and autumn colour, a garden for all seasons. 100yr old wild flower meadows open 2nd May to 1st July.

GROUP OPENING

25 LOUGHBOROUGH GARDENS

Herrick Road, Loughborough, LE11 2BU. www.thesecateur.com. *1m SW Loughborough. From M1 J23 take A512 Ashby Rd to Loughborough. At r'about R onto A6004 Epinal Way. At Beacon Rd r'about L, Herrick Rd 1st on R.* **Sat 16th and Sun 17th June (11-5). Combined adm £3, chd free. Light refreshments.**

94 HERRICK ROAD
Marion Smith.

134 HERRICK ROAD
Janet Currie, 01509 212191, janet.currie@me.com, www.thesecateur.com. **Visits also by arrangement June to Aug, groups 10+ daytime or early evening.**

Herrick Road, Loughborough is a quiet leafy area with a mix of Victorian and mid century homes. The gardens in this group contain plenty of horticultural and creative interest. 134 Herrick Road is a small long garden, cleverly designed to make use of the space, full of attractive features and planting and brimming with creative flair. The excellent Secret Craft Fair held during the open gardens weekend provides additional delight and surprises for visitors. 94 Herrick Road is a traditional old-fashioned English garden at rear of Victorian house. Mainly perennial planting with interest in hardy geraniums and heucheras, small pond and three active beehives. This peaceful walled garden also has a Coach House. Herrick Road Honey will be on sale. Loughborough NGS Open Gardens & Secret Craft Fair is part of a weekend trail of gardens, growing, creativity and wellbeing across Loughborough in 2018, check the website for more details as they become available. 134 Herrick Road is featured in the book 'Sunshine Over Clover - Gardens of Wellbeing' by Sarah Wint.

GROUP OPENING

26 MARKET BOSWORTH GARDENS

Market Bosworth, CV13 0LE. *13m W of Leicester; 8m N of Hinckley. 1m off A447 Coalville to Hinckley Rd, 3m off A444. Burton to Nuneaton Rd.* **Sun 24 June (1-6). Combined adm £5, chd free. Light refreshments at 13 Spinney Hill.** Donation to Bosworth in Bloom.

GLEBE FARM HOUSE
Mr Peter Ellis & Ms Ginny Broad.

HOME FARM COTTAGE
Anne Kitching.

4 LANCASTER AVENUE
Mr Peter Bailiss.

26 NORTHUMBERLAND AVENUE
Mrs Kathy Boot.

4 PRIORY ROAD
Mrs Margaret Barrett, 01455 290112, info@margaretbarrett.co.uk. **Visits also by arrangement Apr to July.**

5 PRIORY ROAD
David & Linda Chevell.

RAINBOW COTTAGE
Mr David Harrison.

13 SPINNEY HILL
Mrs J Buckell.

17 STATION ROAD
Carol Thomas.

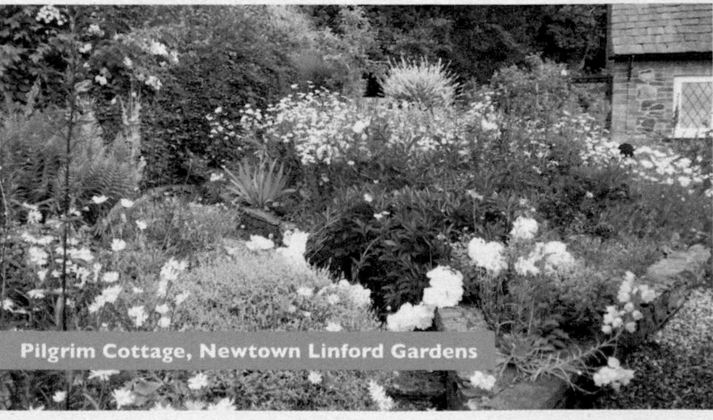

Pilgrim Cottage, Newtown Linford Gardens

Market Bosworth is an attractive market town, with an enviable record for the quality of its regular entry in the annual East Midlands in Bloom competition. There are a number of gardens open, some for the first time, and all within walking distance of the Market Square. The gardens show various planting styles and different approaches to small and intimate spaces in the historic town centre, as well as larger plots in more recent developments. Tickets and descriptive maps obtainable in the Market Place, with refreshments available there and at one of the gardens. Plants will be on sale at a number of gardens. A proportion of the proceeds from the Gardens Open Day will be used to support Bosworth in Bloom, the voluntary group responsible for the town's floral displays; see www.bosworthinbloom.co.uk. Farmers' Market in town centre (9-2) local produce, hot and cold food.

27 NEW 221 MARKFIELD ROAD

Groby, Leicester, LE6 0FT. Jackie Manship, 01530 249363, jmanship@btinternet.com. *From M1 J22 take A50 towards Leicester. In approx 3 miles at the T-lights junction with Lena Drive turn L. Parking available along this road, no parking on A50.* **Daily Sat 4 Aug to Fri 10 Aug (10-4). Adm £4, chd free. Light refreshments. Visits also by arrangement, groups of 25-30 are invited to book for evening visits from 6pm on 4th to 10th Aug.**

A S facing plot of land nestled between the village of Groby and Markfield approx 1 acre in size. The hidden treasures are deceptive from the front of the property which sits on one of the main trunk roads out of Leicester. Packed with interest and created over the last 20 years from a dishevelled overgrown plot you will be presented with a garden full of delight.

Home Farm House, Empingham Gardens

28 MILL HOUSE

118 Welford Road, Wigston, LE18 3SN. Mr & Mrs P Measures, 01162 885409. *4m S of Leicester. From Leicester to Wigston Magna follow A5199 Welford Rd S towards Kilby, up hill past Mercers Newsagents, 100yds on L.* **Sun 20 May, Sun 1 July (12-5). Adm £2.50, chd free. Home-made teas. Visits also by arrangement May to July flexible times for groups 3 - 25; refreshments at an additional cost.**

Walled town garden with an extensive plant variety, many rare and unusual. A plant lovers garden, with interesting designs incorporated in the borders, rockery and scree. It is full of surprises with memorabilia and bygones a reminder of our past. Good variety of reasonably priced plants on sale both open days. Bargain plant sale 14th July 11am till 4pm.

29 MOUNTAIN ASH

140 Ulverscroft Lane, Newtown Linford, LE6 0AJ. Mike & Liz Newcombe. *7m SW of Loughborough, 7m NW of Leicester, 1m NW of Newtown Linford. Head ½m N along Main St towards Sharpley Hill, fork L into Ulverscroft Lane and Mountain Ash (No 140) is about ½m along on the L. Parking is along the opp verge.* **Sun 8, Sun 15 July (11-5). Adm £4, chd free. Home-made teas.**

2 acre garden with stunning views across Charnwood countryside. Nr the house are patios, lawns, water feature, flower & shrub beds, fruit trees, soft fruit cage, greenhouses & vegetable plots. Lawns slope down to a gravel garden, large wildlife pond and small areas of woodland with walks through many species of trees. Many statues and ornaments. Several places to sit and relax around the garden. Only the top part of the garden around the house is reasonably accessible by wheelchair.

30 NEVILL HOLT HALL

Drayton Road, Nevill Holt, Market Harborough, LE16 8EG. Mr David Ross. *5m NE of Market Haborough. Signed off B664 at Medbourne.* **Sun 3 June (12-4). Adm £5, chd free. Tea.**

The gardens are at their peak in June and July. Whilst the walled kitchen garden shows signs of a harvest to come, our two other walled gardens and adjoining cedar lawn garden are full of colour and texture, all working together to create a summer scene that feels warm and summery, even on the dullest days. Please do join us for tea and cake – we would love to share our garden with you.

GROUP OPENING

31 NEWTOWN LINFORD GARDENS

On Main Street & Groby Lane, Newtown Linford, Leicester, LE6 0AD. *6m NW Leicester. 2½m from M1 J22. The gardens are along Main St (starting at Bradgate Park) heading slightly up hill past the Primary School and Bradgate Arms beyond Markfield Lane, and also on Groby Lane.* **Mon 7 May (11-4.30). Combined adm £5, chd free. Home-made teas at The Old Vicarage and 32 Main Street.**

APPLETREE COTTAGE
Katherine Duffy Anthony.

BANK COTTAGE
Jan Croft.

DINGLE HOUSE
Mr & Mrs R Howard.

NEW **32 GROBY LANE**
Mr & Mrs David Couling.

NEW **52 GROBY LANE**
Mr & Mrs Steve Palethorpe.

NEW **32 MAIN STREET**
Mrs Carol Ann Sugden.

PILGRIM COTTAGE
Mr & Mrs S Salter.

WOODLANDS
Mary Husseini.

Newtown Linford is a historic village bordering Bradgate Park with the River Lin flowing through it and is part of the Charnwood Forest. Two of the gardens opening have river banks from where you can see brown trout and the occasional kingfisher. The gardens opening are each quite different. Appletree Cottage has a charming enclosed garden surrounding a C17 thatched cottage with interesting paths leading to lawns, borders, sun terrace and small lily pond. Bank Cottage, Pilgrim Cottage, and Dingle House have cottage gardens set on different levels that provide yr-round colour but are prettiest in spring. The River Lin runs through Woodlands, a 1 acre garden where many varied shrubs and spring flowers grow around mature trees. There will also be plant sales and other stalls. Come and enjoy your day with us! Plant sales, and old garden tool sales together with other stalls at both refreshment venues, The Old Vicarage and 32 Main Street.

32 OAK TREE HOUSE

North Road, South Kilworth, LE17 6DU. Pam & Martin Shave, 01858 575481, pamelashave@btconnect.com. *15m S of Leicester. From M1 J20, take A4304 towards Market Harborough. At North Kilworth turn R, signed South Kilworth. Garden on L after approx 1m.* **Visits by arrangement June to Sept, no min. number for groups, price includes refreshments. Adm £6, chd free. Home-made teas.**

⅔ acre beautiful country garden full of colour, formal design, softened by cottage style planting. Stone circle and sculpture. Large herbaceous borders, vegetable plots, pond, greenhouse, shady area, colour-themed borders. Extensive collections in pots, incl perennial violas. Trees chosen for attractive bark. Nearly 40 types of clematis and many more roses. Dramatic arched pergola. Featured as Garden of the Week in Garden News magazine.

33 THE OLD HALL

Main Street, Market Overton, LE15 7PL. Mr & Mrs Timothy Hart, 01572 767145, stefa@hambleton.co.uk. *6m N of Oakham. Beyond Cottesmore, 6m N of Oakham; 5m from A1 via Thistleton. 10m E from Melton Mowbray via Wymondham.* **Sun 29 Apr (2-6). Adm £4.50, chd free. Home-made teas. incl Hambleton Bakery cakes, in aid of local charity 'For Rutland'.**

Set on a southerly ridge overlooking Catmose Vale. Stone walls and yew hedges divide the garden into enclosed areas with herbaceous borders, shrubs, and young and mature trees. In 2006 the lower part of garden was planted with new shrubs to create a walk with mown paths.There are interesting plants flowering most of the time. Neil Hewertson has been involved in the gardens design since 1990s. Partial wheelchair access. Gravel and mown paths. Return to house is steep.

34 THE OLD VICARAGE, BURLEY

Church Road, Burley, Nr Oakham, LE15 7SU. Jonathan & Sandra Blaza, 01572 770588, sandra.blaza@btinternet.com, www.theoldvicarageburley.com. *1m NE of Oakham. In Burley just off B668 between Oakham & Cottesmore. Church Rd is opp village green.* **Sun 20 May (11-5). Adm £4.50, chd free. Home-made teas. Visits also by arrangement May & June for groups 10+.**

Country garden, planted for yr round interest, incl a walled garden (with vine house) producing fruit, herbs, vegetables and cut flowers. Formal lawns and borders, lime walk, rose gardens and a rill with an avenue of standard wisteria. Wildlife garden with pond, 2 orchards and mixed woodland. Some gravel and steps between terraces.

Shipmeadow

35 THE PADDOCKS

Main Street, Hungarton, LE7 9JY. Helen Martin, 01162 595230, Michael.c.martin@talk21.com. *8m E of Leicester. Follow NGS signs in village.* **Sat 23, Sun 24 June (11-5). Adm £4, chd free. Home-made teas in the garden. Visits also by arrangement May to July for groups 20+.**

2 acre garden with mature and specimen trees, rhododendrons, azaleas, magnolia grandiflora, wisterias. Two lily ponds and stream. Three lawn areas surrounded by herbaceous and shrub borders. Woodland walk. Pergola with clematis and roses, hosta collection and two rockeries, fern bed. Large well established semi permanent plant stall in aid of local charities. Partial wheelchair access due to steep slopes at rear of garden. Flat terrace by main lawn provides good viewing area.

36 QUAINTREE HALL

Braunston, LE15 8QS. Mrs Caroline Lomas. *Braunston, nr Oakham. 2m W of Oakham, in the centre of the village of Braunston in Rutland on High St.* **Sun 13 May (2-6). Adm £4, chd free. Home-made teas.**

An established garden surrounding the medieval hall house (not open) incl a formal box parterre to the front of the house, a woodland walk, formal walled garden with yew hedges, a small picking garden and terraced courtyard garden with conservatory. A wide selection of interesting plants can be enjoyed, each carefully selected for its specific site by the knowledgeable garden owner.

37 RAVENSTONE HALL

Ashby Road, Ravenstone, Coalville, LE67 2AA. Jemima Wade, 07976 302260, jemimawade@hotmail.com. *Ravenstone village is situated off the A511 between Ashby de la Zouch and Coalville. The house is 1st on the L if approached from Ashby.* **Sun 20 May (11-5). Adm £5, chd free. Home-made teas. Visits also by arrangement Apr to Sept for groups 20 max.**

The garden was transformed in 2009 when the new owners moved to the house and planting and development has been on-going since that time. Azaleas and rhododendrons are planted on the bank of the drive. Beech trees and a beech hedge line the main front lawn. There is a woodland walk planted with bluebells. The main garden comprises a sunken garden, a rose garden, gravel path with herbaceous planting one side and iris and tulip on the other, a vegetable garden, an orchard, and a koi pond situated in a courtyard with white flowering plants and mixed foliage. Bluebell walk for groups from mid April, please call for details.

38 REDHILL LODGE

Seaton Road, Barrowden, Oakham, LE15 8EN. Richard & Susan Moffitt, 01572 748 653, s.moffitt@yahoo.co.uk, www.m360design.co.uk. *Redhill Lodge is 1m from village of Barrowden along Seaton Rd.* **Sun 1 July (12-5.30). Adm £5, chd free. Home-made teas. Visits also by arrangement May to July.**

Still evolving bold contemporary design with formal lawns, grass amphitheatre and turf viewing mound, herbaceous borders and cutting garden. Praire style planting showing vibrant colour in late summer. Also natural swimming pond surrounded by Japanese style planting, stream with marginal planting, bog garden and meadow area.

39 RIDGEWOLD FARM

Burton Lane, Wymeswold, LE12 6UN. Robert & Ann Waterfall. *5m SE of Loughborough. Off Burton Lane between A6006 & B676. Ample car parking.* **Sun 10 June (12-4). Adm £4, chd free. Home-made teas.**

2½ acre rural garden in the Leicestershire Wolds. A working farm. Impressive sweeping drive of specimen trees. beech, laurel and saxon hedges divide different areas. Lawn, rill, water feature, summer house, shrubs, rose fence, clematis arch, wisteria, ivy tunnel, rose garden, herbaceous planting, orchard, vegetable patch and pickery. Natural pond with seated viewing platform. Birch avenue with view of the village. Woodland walk. Natural Wildlife pond.

40 119 SCALFORD ROAD

Melton Mowbray, LE13 1JZ. Richard & Hilary Lawrence, 01664 562821, randh1954@me.com. *½m N of Melton Mowbray. Take Scalford Rd from town centre past Cattle Market. Garden 100yds after 1st turning on L (The Crescent). Some parking available on the drive but The Crescent is an easy walk.* **Sun 29 July (11-5). Adm £3, chd free. Home-made teas incl gluten free and cream teas. Visits also by arrangement June to Aug for groups 10 - 25 max.**

Larger than average town garden which has evolved over the last 28yrs. Mixed borders with traditional and exotic plants, enhanced by container planting particularly begonias. Vegetable parterre and greenhouse. Various seating areas for viewing different aspects of the garden. Water features incl ponds. New additions to the garden are a Red Border and a Succulents bed. Melton Times. Partial wheelchair access. Gravelled drive, ramp provided up to lawn but paths not accessible.

41 SHIPMEADOW

55 Main St, Barton in the Beans, Nr Nuneaton, CV13 0DJ. Viv McKee & Ian Woolley, 01455 291684, vivmckee@aol.com. *12m W of Leicester. From Barton towards Congerstone, follow NGS yellow arrows.* **Sat 30 June, Sun 1 July (10.30-6.30). Adm £4, chd free. Light refreshments. Visits also by arrangement June to Aug by prior agreement.**

The garden covers an acre plus with a variety of structures and planting. It has been developed over a period of five yrs. Areas of interest incl: a large natural pond; a coppice; a gravel garden; two large herbaceous beds; a herb garden and a formal garden with box hedging. Most of the vistas have a seating area from which to enjoy the view. Teas, cake and prosecco available in the studio. Beach, sculptures, artists studio, bridge and water lilies, varied planting.

42 STOKE ALBANY HOUSE

Desborough Road, Stoke Albany, Market Harborough, LE16 8PT. Mr & Mrs A M Vinton, 01858 535227, del.jones7@googlemail.com, www.stokealbanyhouse.co.uk. *4m E of Market Harborough. Via A427 to Corby, turn to Stoke Albany, R at the White Horse (B669) garden ½m on the L.* **Every Wed 6 June to 25 July (2-4.30). Adm £4.50, chd free. Visits also by arrangement June & July for groups 10+ (Weds preferably).** Donation to Marie Curie Cancer Care.

4 acre country house garden; fine trees and shrubs with wide herbaceous borders and sweeping striped lawn. Good display of bulbs in spring, roses June and July. Walled grey garden; nepeta walk arched with roses, parterre with box and roses. Mediterranean garden. Heated greenhouse, potager with topiary, water feature garden and sculptures.

43 THORPE LUBENHAM HALL

Farndon Road, Lubenham, LE16 9TR. Sir Bruce & Lady MacPhail. *2m W of Market Harborough. From Market Harborough take 3rd L off main rd, down Rushes Lane, past church on L, under old railway bridge & straight on up private drive.* **Wed 23 May (10-4). Adm £5, chd free. Cream teas.**

15 acres of formal and informal garden surrounded by parkland and arable. Many mature trees. Traditional herbaceous borders and various water features. Walled pool garden with raised beds. Ancient moat area along driveway. Gravel paths, some steep slopes and steps.

♿ ✿ ☕

44 TRESILLIAN HOUSE

67 Dalby Road, Melton Mowbray, LE13 0BQ. Mrs Alison Blythe, 01664 481997, tresillianhouse@aol.com, www.tresillianhouse.com. *Situated on B6047 Dalby Rd (Melton to Gt Dalby) going S. Parking on site. NB: We are not actually in Great Dalby but on the south side of Melton Mowbray.* **Sun 6 May, Sun 1 July, Sun 26 Aug, Sun 21 Oct (11-4). Adm £3, chd free. Cream teas. Visits also by arrangement Apr to Oct groups no min, 30 max. Parking on site.**

¾ acre garden re-established by current owner since 2009. Beautiful blue cedar trees, excellent specimen tulip tree. Parts of garden original, others reinstated with variety of plants and bushes. Original bog garden and natural pond. Koi pond added in 2015. Vegetable plot. Cowslips and bulbs abound in Springtime. Quiet and tranquil oasis. Two new beds of cut flowers and plants for shady/dry. Ploughmans lunches, cream teas, home-made cakes. October opening offers stew & dumplings or soup and cream teas. Appeared in Melton Times, Radio Leicester, Local Radio 103 The Eye, Garden News. Slate paths, steep in places but manageable.

♿ 🐕 ✿ 🛏 ☕

GROUP OPENING

45 UPPINGHAM GARDENS

7 Stockerston Road, Uppingham, LE15 9UD. Lawrence & Jennifer Fenelon. *6m S of Oakham. 7m N of Corby. 5m SW of Rutland Water. On A47 halfway between Leicester & Peterborough. Car parking in market town centre, along Stockerston Rd and in Uppingham School sports centre car park. WC in Market Square.* **Sun 3 June (2-5.30). Combined adm £5. Home-made teas in Church Hall, Market Place. Home Made Teas in aid of Church.**

GOWER LODGE
Dr C R & Mrs E L Jones.

HILLSIDE
Mr & Mrs Lawrence Fenelon.

THE ORCHARD
Doug & Margaret Stacey.

From the Sports Centre Car Park or from Stockerston Rd pass through the School West Quad with its dramatic paving, planting and sculptures. On exiting onto Stockerston Rd, diagonally to the R is Hillside, a 1 acre S facing garden with spring fed pond, terraces and patio, orchard, vegetable garden & woodland walk. Continue towards town centre along Stockerston Rd and turn R along Spring Back Way, passing new planting at Uppingham School. Gower Lodge, on the R, has a 1-acre S-facing sloping garden. a stream and wild flower areas incl meconopsis and primulas, also herbaceous borders, some interesting trees & kitchen garden. Continue along Spring Back Way, across London Rd into South View to its junction with Station Rd .The Orchard is on the R. It's S facing garden also takes advantage of the stream which runs through the lower reaches of the town. With its view out over the stream to sheep pastures beyond, the garden is full of interesting trees, shrubs, bulbs and perennials. Picturesque town centre and Uppingham School historic buildings with new Science Centre nationally recognised in the 2015 Royal Institute of British Architects Awards (RIBA) as making a significant contribution to the country's architecture. Partial wheelchair access is available at Hillside.

♿ ✿ ☕

46 WASHBROOK ALLOTMENTS

Welford Road, Leicester, LE2 6FP. Sharon Maher. *Approx 2½m S of Leicester, 1½ m N of Wigston. Regret no onsite parking. Welford Rd difficult to park on. Please use nearby side rds & Pendlebury Drive (LE2 6GY).* **Sun 2 Sept (11-3). Adm £3, chd free. Home-made teas.**

Our allotment gardens have been described as a hidden oasis off the main Welford Road. There are over 100 whole, half and quarter plots growing a wide variety of fruit and vegetables. We have a fledgling wildflower meadow, other wildlife friendly areas and a composting toilet! Keep a look out for the remains of Anderson Shelters, and other 'Heath Robinson' constructions. Circular route around the site is uneven in places but is suitable for wheelchairs.

♿ ✿ ☕

47 WESTBROOKE HOUSE

52 Scotland Road, Little Bowden, Market Harborough, LE16 8AX. Bryan & Joanne Drew, 07872 316153, Jwsd1980@hotmail.co.uk. *½m S Market Harborough. From Northampton Rd follow NGS arrows.* **Sun 6 May, Sun 1 July (11-5). Adm £5, chd free. Cream teas. Refreshments will be served in the 'Courtyard Cafe'. Visits also by arrangement May to July.**

Westbrooke House is a late Victorian property built in 1887. The gardens comprise 6 acres in total and are approached through a tree lined driveway of mature limes and wellingtonias. Key features are walled flower garden, walled kitchen garden, pond area, spring garden, lawns, woodland paths and a meadow with a wild flower area, ha-ha and hornbeam avenue.The new lower garden was added in May 2017.

48 WESTVIEW

1 St Thomas's Road, Great Glen, LE8 9EH. Gill & John Hadland, 01162592170, gillhadland1@gmail.com. *7m S of Leicester. Take either r'about from A6 into village centre then follow NGS signs. Please park in Oaks Rd.* **Sun 25 Feb, Sat 3, Sun 4 Mar (12-4); Mon 28 May, Sat 1, Sun 2 Sept (12-5). Adm £2.50, chd free. Home-made teas. Visits also by arrangement Feb to Sept for groups 20 max.**

Organically managed small walled cottage garden with year-round interest. Rare and unusual plants, many grown from seed. Formal box parterre herb garden, courtyard garden, herbaceous borders, woodland garden, small wildlife pond, greenhouse, vegetable and fruit garden. Display of auriculas and alpines. Collection of Galanthus (snowdrops). Recycled materials used to make quirky garden ornaments. Restored Victorian outhouse functions as a garden office and houses a collection of old garden tools and ephemera.

49 ◆ WHATTON GARDENS

Long Whatton, Loughborough, LE12 5BG. Lord & Lady Crawshaw, 01509 842225, whattonhouse@gmail.com, www.whattonhouseandgardens.co.uk. *4m NE of Loughborough. On A6 between Hathern & Kegworth; 2½m SE of M1J24.* **For NGS: Sun 20 May (10-6). Adm £4, chd free. Home-made teas. Refreshments 2pm - 5pm. For other opening times and information, please phone, email or visit garden website.**

Often described by visitors as a hidden gem, this 15 acre C19 Country House garden is a relaxing experience for all the family. Listen to the birds, and enjoy walking through the many fine trees, spring bulbs and shrubs, large herbaceous border, traditional rose garden, ornamental ponds and lawns. Open daily (excl Sat) March to Oct. Available for group bookings. Gravel paths.

GROUP OPENING

50 WHISSENDINE GARDENS

Whissendine, Nr Oakham, LE15 7HG. *5m N of Oakham. Whissendine is signed from A606 between Melton Mowbray & Oakham.* **Sun 27 May (2-5). Combined adm £5, chd free. Home-made teas at St Andrew's Church.**

NEW HAYES HOUSE
Judy & Tony Tullett.

THE OLD VICARAGE, WHISSENDINE
Prof Peter & Dr Sarah Furness, www.pathology.plus.com/Garden.

2 beautiful, very different, gardens in this Rutland village. The Old Vicarage, next door to the church, up the hill: ⅔ acre packed with variety. Terrace with topiary, a formal fountain courtyard and raised beds backed by small gothic orangery burgeoning with tender plants. Herbaceous borders surround main lawn. Wisteria tunnel leads to orchard filled with naturalised bulbs, home to four beehives, Gothic hen house plus six rare breed hens. Hidden 'white walk', unusual plants and much, much more! Just around the corner, Hayes House is a complete contrast and an excellent example of maximising a small space with very formal planting. A small garden created in three parts, designed and planted by the garden owners. To the front box squares and window boxes, to the rear of the house a small courtyard for outside dining and, beyond this, an enclosed garden with raised terrace and pergola. Clipped box creates a structured look, softened with predominantly blue and white planting. Partial wheelchair access due to gravel paths, slopes and steps.

51 NEW THE WHITE HOUSE FARM

Billesdon Road, Ingarsby, nr Houghton-on-the-Hill, LE7 9JD. Pam & Richard Smith, Pamsmithtwhf@aol.com. *7m E of Leicester. 12m W of Uppingham. Take A47 from Leicester through Houghton-on-the-Hill towards Uppingham. 1m after Houghton, turn L (signed Tilton). After 1m turn L (signed Ingarsby), garden is 1m further on.* **Sun 5 Aug (11-5). Adm £5, chd free. Light refreshments. Visits also by arrangement May to Oct.**

Former Georgian farm in 2 acres of country garden. Beautiful views. Box, yew & beech hedges divide a cottage garden of gaily coloured perennials and roses; a formal herb garden; a pergola draped with climbing plants; an old courtyard with roses, shrubs & trees. Herbaceous borders lead to pools with water lilies & informal cascade. Then orchard, wild garden and lake. Home for lots of wildlife.

GROUP OPENING

52 WILLOUGHBY GARDENS

Willoughby Waterleys, LE8 6UD. *9m S of Leicester. From A426 heading N turn R at Dunton Bassett lights. Follow signs to Willoughby. From Blaby follow signs to Countesthorpe. 2m S to Willoughby.* **Sun 13 May (11-5). Combined adm £3.50, chd free. Sun 22 July (11-5). Combined adm £5, chd free. Home-made teas. At Farmway in May, Village Hall in July.**

2 CHURCH FARM LANE
Valerie & Peter Connelly.
Open on Sun 22 July

FARMWAY
Eileen Spencer, 01162 478321, eileenfarmway9@msn.com.
Open on all dates
Visits also by arrangement July & Aug no min, 25 max.

HIGH MEADOW
Phil & Eva Day.
Open on all dates

JOHN'S WOOD
John & Jill Harris.
Open on all dates

3 ORCHARD ROAD
Diane Brearley.
Open on Sun 22 July

WILLOUGHBY LODGE FARM
Liz & David Winterton.
Open on Sun 22 July

Willoughby Waterleys lies in the South Leicestershire countryside. The Norman Church will be open, hosting a film of the local bird population filmed by a local resident. 6 gardens will be open. John's Wood is a 1½ acre nature reserve planted to encourage wildlife. 2 Church Farm Lane has been professionally designed with many interesting features. Farmway is a plant lovers garden with many unusual plants in colour themed borders. High Meadow has been evolving over 9yrs. Incl mixed planting and ornamental vegetable garden. 3 Orchard Road is a small garden packed with interest. Willoughby Lodge Farm is a country garden incl a walled garden, pond area, summer house, mown grass paths and wildflower area and numerous native trees. Lawncare advice clinic 2-4pm. Willoughby embroidery on display in village hall.

GROUP OPENING

53 WING GARDENS

Wing, Oakham, LE15 8SA. *2m S of Rutland Water. Off A6003 between Oakham & Uppingham.* **Sun 17 June (11-5). Combined adm £5, chd free. Home-made teas in Wing Village Hall. In aid of Wing Church.**

AUTUMN HOUSE
Jane & Jeremy Wood.

16 CHURCH STREET
Mr & Mrs Mick & Mary Rodgers.

DOVE COTTAGE
Mr & Mrs David & Alison Seviour.

GREYSTONES
Mr & Mrs Alisdair & Jane Alexander-Orr.

33 MORCOTT ROAD
Angela Harding.

NEW **STONECROP HOUSE**
Mr & Mrs Matthew & Nicky Lyttelton.

TOWNSEND HOUSE
David & Jeffy Wood.

7 very different gardens in pretty stone village of Wing with medieval church and turf maze. For map and directions start visit at Townsend House opp Village Hall. Each planted in traditional cottage garden style but with the distinctive touch of their individual owners, the larger with mature trees and lawns, and all with mixed borders of shrubs, perennials and grasses, roses, fruit trees and vegetable and herb gardens. Sizes range from the 2 largest, ½ acre gardens, Stonecrop House (with stunning wildflower meadow) and Autumn House, through medium sized cottage gdns at Dove Cottage, Greystones and Townsend House, to the very small at 16 Church St and 33 Morcott Rd. The 2 latter, both with panoramic views over the Rutland countryside from sitting areas, along with Dove Cottage both have Open Studios displaying work by the garden owners. Partial wheelchair access to some gardens.

The National Garden Scheme is Hospice UK's largest single funder

Red House Farm, Grimston Gardens

LINCOLNSHIRE

Lincolnshire is a county shaped by a rich tapestry of fascinating heritage, passionate people and intriguing traditions; a mix of city, coast and countryside.

The city of Lincoln is dominated by the iconic towers of Lincoln Cathedral. The eastern seaboard contains windswept golden sands and lonely nature reserves. The Lincolnshire Wolds is a nationally important landscape of rolling chalk hills and areas of sandstone and clay, which underlie this attractive landscape.

To the south is the historic, religious and architectural heritage of The Vales, with river walks, the fine Georgian buildings of Stamford and historic Burghley House. In the east the unqiue Fens landscape thrives on an endless network of waterways inhabited by an abundance of wildlife.

Beautiful gardens of all types, sizes and designs are cared for and shared by their welcoming owners. Often located in delightful villages, a visit to them will entail driving through quiet roads often bordered by verges of wild flowers.

Lincolnshire is rural England at its very best. Local heritage, beautiful countryside walks, aviation history and it is the home of the Red Arrows.

Volunteers

County Organisers
Helen Boothman
01652 628424
boothmanhelen@gmail.com

Sally Grant
01205 750486
sallygrant50@btinternet.com

County Treasurer
Helen Boothman
(as above)

Publicity
Margaret Mann
01476 585905
marg_mann2000@yahoo.com

Erica McGarrigle
01476 585909
ericamcg@hotmail.co.uk

Assistant County Organisers
Lynne Barnes
01529 497462
lynnebarnes14@googlemail.com

Tricia Elliot
01427 788517
t.elliott575@gmail.com

Colin Johnson
01775 822808
colinj04@hotmail.com

Stephanie Lee
01507 442151
marigoldlee@btinternet.

Rita Morgan
01472 597529
rita.morgan1@sky.com

Sylvia Ravenhall
01507 526014
sylvan@btinternet.com

Jo Rouston
01673 858656
jo@rouston-gardens.co.uk

Left: Willow Cottage

OPENING DATES

All entries subject to change. For latest information check **www.ngs.org.uk**

Map locator numbers are shown to the right of each garden name.

February

Snowdrop Festival

Saturday 24th
21 Chapel Street 7

Sunday 25th
Ashfield House 1
21 Chapel Street 7

March

Saturday 24th
The Manor House 27

Friday 30th
◆ Easton Walled Gardens 11

April

Sunday 1st
Woodlands 50

Saturday 7th
◆ Burghley House Private South Gardens 5

Sunday 8th
Ashfield House 1
◆ Burghley House Private South Gardens 5
Firsby Manor 12
◆ Grimsthorpe Castle 16

Sunday 22nd
◆ Goltho House 14
The Old Rectory 35

Saturday 28th
Marigold Cottage 28

Sunday 29th
Marigold Cottage 28

May

Sunday 6th
Fotherby Gardens 13

Sunday 13th
Dunholme Lodge 10
The Old Vicarage 36
Old White House 37

Sunday 20th
Holly House 21
The Old Rectory 35
66 Spilsby Road 43

Saturday 26th
Marigold Cottage 28

Sunday 27th
Manor House 26
Marigold Cottage 28
Pottertons Nursery 39

Monday 28th
Firsby Manor 12
Willow Cottage 49

June

Festival Weekend

Saturday 2nd
Oasis Garden - Your Place 33

Sunday 3rd
◆ Mill Farm 30
Oasis Garden - Your Place 33
The Old Vicarage 36
Woodlands 50

Wednesday 6th
◆ Grimsthorpe Castle 16

Sunday 10th
Hackthorn Hall 18
Sedgebrook Manor 41
48 Westgate 47

Thursday 14th
NEW Corner House Farm 8

Friday 15th
NEW Corner House Farm 8

Sunday 17th
Aubourn Hall 2
Inner Lodge 23
Manor Farm 25
Shangrila 42
NEW Springfield 44

Saturday 23rd
Marigold Cottage 28
NEW The Old Rectory 34

Sunday 24th
The Hawthorns 20
Marigold Cottage 28
Pine Fields 38

July

Sunday 1st
Dunholme Lodge 10
Gosberton Gardens 15
◆ Hall Farm 19
Woodlands 50

Sunday 15th
Inner Lodge 23
68 Watts Lane 46

Saturday 21st
Marigold Cottage 28

Sunday 22nd
Ballygarth 3
Marigold Cottage 28
The Stables 45

Sunday 29th
68 Watts Lane 46
Yew Tree Farm 51

August

Every Sunday
68 Watts Lane 46

Saturday 4th
School House 40

Sunday 5th
◆ Gunby Hall & Gardens 17
Woodlands 50

Thursday 16th
◆ Brightwater Gardens 4

Sunday 19th
Inner Lodge 23
Willoughby Road Allotments 48

Saturday 25th
Marigold Cottage 28

Sunday 26th
Manor House 26
Marigold Cottage 28

September

Sunday 2nd
Fotherby Gardens 13
◆ Hall Farm 19
48 Westgate 47

Saturday 15th
Inley Drove Farm 22

Sunday 16th
Inley Drove Farm 22

Wednesday 19th
◆ Doddington Hall Gardens 9

Sunday 23rd
◆ Goltho House 14

October

Sunday 7th
Woodlands 50

February 2019

Saturday 23rd
21 Chapel Street 7

Sunday 24th
21 Chapel Street 7

By Arrangement

Ashfield House 1
Aubourn Hall 2
Ballygarth 3
45 Chapel Lane 6
21 Chapel Street 7
Firsby Manor 12
Hackthorn Hall 18
Holly House 21
Ludney House Farm 24
Manor Farm 25
Manor House 26
Marigold Cottage 28
Mere House 29
◆ Mill Farm 30
The Moat 31
Nova Lodge 32
The Old Rectory 35
NEW The Old Rectory 34
The Old Vicarage 36
68 Watts Lane 46
Willow Cottage 49

THE GARDENS

1 ASHFIELD HOUSE

Lincoln Road, Branston, Lincoln, LN4 1NS. John & Judi Tinsley, 07977 505682, john@tinsleyfarms.co.uk. *3m S of Lincoln on B1188. From Branston off B1188 Lincoln Rd on L. ½m from Branston Hall Hotel signed Ashfield Farms.* **Sun 25 Feb (10.30-3); Sun 8 Apr (10.30-4). Adm £3.50, chd free. Home-made teas. Visits also by arrangement Feb to Oct groups of 15+.**

10 acre garden with sweeping lawns constructed around a planting of trees and shrubs. The main feature in the spring is the collection of some 110 flowering cherries of 40 different varieties along with massed plantings of spring flowering bulbs. We recently planted a magnolia collection in a newly constructed woodland garden. In the autumn the colours can be amazing. Fairly level garden. Grass paths.

2 AUBOURN HALL

Harmston Road, Aubourn, Lincoln, LN5 9DZ. Mr & Mrs Christopher Nevile, 01522 788224, paula@aubournhall.co.uk, www.aubournhall.co.uk. *7m SW of Lincoln. Signed off A607 at Harmston & off A46 at Thorpe on the Hill.* **Sun 17 June (2-5). Adm £5.50, chd free. Home-made teas. Visits also by arrangement May to Sept private Tours for 12+.**

Approx 9 acres. Lawns, mature trees, shrubs, roses, mixed borders, rose garden, large prairie and topiary garden, spring bulbs, woodland walk and ponds. C11 church adjoining. Access to garden is fairly flat and smooth. Depending on weather some areas may be inaccessible to wheelchairs. Parking in field not on tarmac.

3 BALLYGARTH

Post Office Lane, Whitton, Scunthorpe, DN15 9LF. Joanne & Adrian Davey, 07871 882339, joanne.davey1971@gmail.com. *From Scunthorpe on A1077 follow signs to West Halton. Through West Halton approx 3m to Whitton. Follow signs for parking at Village Hall.* **Sun 22 July (11-4). Adm £3, chd free. Home-made teas in Whitton Village Hall. Visits also by arrangement June to Aug max group of 15 people evenings only.**

Set in the rural village of Whitton our end terraced house has approx ⅓ acre garden with large herbaceous and grass borders and two water features. Seating areas overlooking the garden, countryside. Many home-made garden artifacts using recycled materials incl a small folly. Everything in wood, brick and metal has been made by us. Drop off for those with limited mobility but parking is at village hall.

4 ◆ BRIGHTWATER GARDENS

The Garden House, Saxby, Market Rasen, LN8 2DQ. Chris Neave & Jonathan Cartwright, 01673 878820, info@brightwatergardens.co.uk, www.brightwatergardens.co.uk. *8m N of Lincoln; 2¼m E of A15. Turn off A15 signed Saxby.* **For NGS: Thur 16 Aug (11-4). Adm £5, chd free. Light refreshments.** For other opening times and information, please phone, email or visit garden website.

8 acre landscaped garden. Yew hedging and walls enclose magical garden rooms full of roses and herbaceous plants. Solar garden, long terrace, Dutch, pergola and obelisk gardens, lavender walk. Large natural damp garden. Dry garden, specimen trees overlooking a large reflective pond. Native woodland areas, prairie and wild lower meadow planted with massed bulbs. Adjacent St. Helen's Church attributed to Lancelot Capability Brown. Featured in Garden News. Gravel paths, steep slopes.

5 ◆ BURGHLEY HOUSE PRIVATE SOUTH GARDENS

Stamford, PE9 3JY. Burghley House Preservation Trust, 01780 752451, burghley@burghley.co.uk, www.burghley.co.uk. *1m E of Stamford. From Stamford follow signs to Burghley via B1443.* **For NGS: Sat 7, Sun 8 Apr (11-4). Adm £4, chd free.** For other opening times and information, please phone, email or visit garden website.

On 7 and 8 April the Private South Gardens at Burghley House will open for the NGS with spectacular spring bulbs in park like setting with magnificent trees and the opportunity to enjoy Capability Brown's famous lake and summerhouse. Entry to the Private South Gardens via Orangery. The Garden of Surprises, Sculpture Garden and House are open as normal. (Regular adm prices apply). Food Fair. Gravel paths.

Corner House Farm

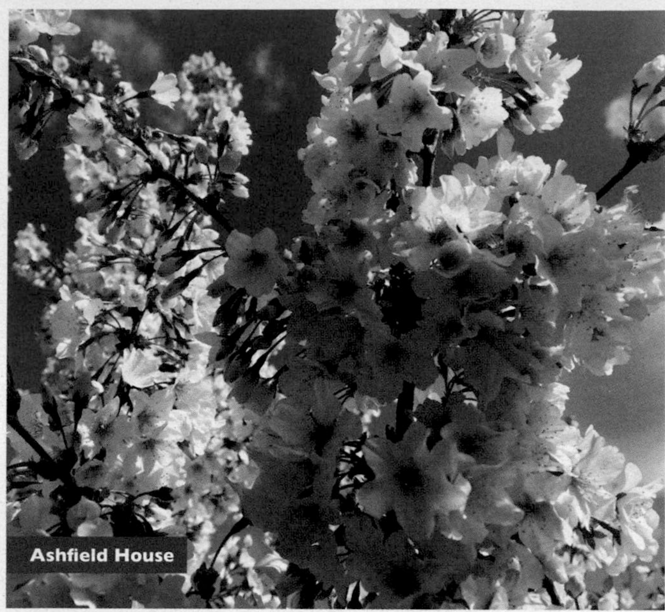
Ashfield House

This diverse garden continues to be a work in progress. A cottage garden with David Austin roses backs the Grade 2 listed farmhouse (C17), and lawns with informal mixed borders rise gently to the front. There is an intriguing bog garden, a small orchard and raised veg plot. The generous paddock beyond the attractive farmyard is responding to a programme of tree planting. Partial wheelchair access. Parking in field.

6 45 CHAPEL LANE

North Scarle, Lincoln, LN6 9EX. Michael & Anna Peacock, 01522 778461, jpeacock123@btinternet.com. *12m SW of Lincoln; 9m NW Newark. From A46 follow signs to Whisby & Eagle. On entering Eagle take 1st R, cont for approx 1m take 1st L. Cont to Xrds in centre of N Scarle. Turn R into Chapel Lane. Garden last on L.* **Visits by arrangement Mar to Sept morning, afternoon or evening visits to suit for groups of 10+. Adm £3, chd free. Home-made teas.**

A garden designed by the owners to give an all season, cottage style feel to a relatively modern edge of the village property. The ⅓ acre garden was started from a blank canvas in 2011. Three offset circular lawns, connected by archways, are edged with bee friendly hardy perennials and annuals, lavenders, roses, shrubs and fruit trees. Gravel area with low rockery. Pretty gazebo. Some features made from recycled materials. Single cobble path may prove difficult to wheelchair users.

7 21 CHAPEL STREET

Hacconby, Bourne, PE10 0UL. Cliff & Joan Curtis and Sharon White, 01778 570314, cliffordcurtis@btinternet.com. *3m N of Bourne. A15, turn E at Xrds into Hacconby, L at village green.* **Sat 24, Sun 25 Feb (11-4). Adm £3, chd free. Home-made teas. Hot soup (Feb). 2019: Sat 23, Sun 24 Feb. Visits also by arrangement Jan to Oct.**

A cottage garden behind a 300yr old cottage. Snowdrops, primroses, hellebores and many different spring flowering bulbs. Colour with bulbs and herbaceous plants through the yr, autumn with asters, dahlias, salvias and many of the autumn flowering yellow daises. Part gravel and part grass paths.

8 NEW CORNER HOUSE FARM

Little Humby, Grantham, NG33 4HW. Colin & Erica McGarrigle. *6m SE of Grantham. Turn off A52 signed Ropsley. ½m E of Ropsley, turn R to Humby.* **Evening opening Thur 14, Fri 15 June (6-8.30). Adm £5, chd free. Wine. Adm incl glass of wine.**

9 ◆ DODDINGTON HALL GARDENS

Doddington, Lincoln, LN6 4RU. Claire & James Birch, 01522 812503, info@doddingtonhall.com, www.doddingtonhall.com. *5m W of Lincoln on B1190. Signed from the A46 Newark to Lincoln rd. Also from the A57 between the A1 & Lincoln. If you are using 'sat nav', the post- code to enter is LN6 4RU.* **For NGS: Wed 19 Sept (11-4.30). Adm £7, chd £3.50. For other opening times and information, please phone, email or visit garden website.**

5 acres of romantic walled and wild gardens. Naturalised autumn crocus and colchicums, cyclamen, shrubs, grasses, roses and late flowering perennials. Turf maze and ancient chestnut trees. Fully productive working walled kitchen garden with pleached, espaliered and fan-trained fruit trees, dahlias, herbs and plants for butterflies and bees. Wheelchair access possible via gravel paths. Ramps also in use. Access map available from Gatehouse Shop.

10 DUNHOLME LODGE

Dunholme, Lincoln, LN2 3QA. Hugh & Lesley Wykes. *4m NE of Lincoln. Turn off A46 towards Welton at hand car wash garage. After ½m turn L up long private road. Garden at top.* **Sun 13 May (11-5). Home-made teas. Sun 1 July (11-5). Cream teas. Adm £3.50, chd free.**

3 acre garden. Spring bulb area, shrub borders, fern garden, topiary, large natural pond, wild flower area,

orchard and vegetable garden. RAF Dunholme Lodge Museum and War Memorial in the grounds. Most areas wheelchair accessible but some loose stone and gravel.

11 ◆ EASTON WALLED GARDENS

Easton, NG33 5AP. Sir Fred & Lady Cholmeley, 01476 530063, info@eastonwalledgardens.co.uk, www.visiteaston.co.uk. *7m S of Grantham. 1m from the A1, off the B6403.* **For NGS: Fri 30 Mar (11-4). Adm £7.50, chd £3.50. Light refreshments & lunches.** For other opening times and information, please phone, email or visit garden website.

A 400-year-old, restored, 12 acre garden set in the heart of Lincolnshire. Home to snowdrops, sweet peas, roses and meadows. The tearoom serves delicious light lunches and cream teas and there is a well-stocked gift shop and plants for sale. Other highlights include a turf maze, swing, yew tunnel and bird hide. Featured in the 20th anniversary souvenir edition of The English Garden as an iconic garden of the last 2 decades. Regret no wheelchair access to lower gardens but tearoom, shop and upper gardens all accessible.

12 FIRSBY MANOR

Firsby, Spilsby, PE23 5QJ. David & Gill Boldy, 01754 830386, gillboldy@gmail.com. *5m E of Spilsby. From Spilsby take B1195 to Wainfleet all Saints. In Firsby, turn R into Fendyke Rd. Firsby Manor is 0.8m along lane on L.* **Sun 8 Apr, Mon 28 May (1-4.30). Adm £3, chd free. Home-made teas. Visits also by arrangement Feb to May garden/photographic societies welcome.**

Firsby Manor, a garden of 3 acres, has been developed to provide interest throughout the year, A visit in April offers a chance to see many different daffodil cultivars as the owners exhibit at the annual Lincolnshire Daffodil Society show. May is also beautiful with borders of hardy geraniums, allium and other early summer perennials. Partial wheelchair access due to large areas of shingle and uneven ground and no toilet access.

GROUP OPENING

13 FOTHERBY GARDENS

Peppin Lane, Fotherby, Louth, LN11 0UW. *2m N of Louth on A16 signed Fotherby. Please park on R verge opp allotments & walk to gardens. Free taxi service between Woodlands & Nut Tree Farm. No parking at gardens. Please do not park beyond designated area.* **Sun 6 May, Sun 2 Sept (11-5). Combined adm £5, chd free. Home-made teas at Woodlands.**

NUT TREE FARM
Tim & Judith Hunter.

SHEPHERDS HEY
Barbara Chester.

WOODLANDS
Ann & Bob Armstrong.
(See separate entry)

Start your visit at Shepherds Hey, a small garden packed with unusual and interesting perennials. Its open frontage gives a warm welcome, with a small pond, terraced border and steep bank side to a small stream. The rear garden, with colour themed borders, takes advantage of the panoramic views over open countryside. Recently featured in Lincolnshire Life. 350yds along Peppin Lane is Woodlands, a lovely mature woodland garden with many unusual plants set against a backdrop of an ever changing tapestry of greenery. A peaceful garden where wildlife can thrive and the front garden is a crevice area for alpine plants. There is a Plant Heritage collection of Codonopsis and the nursery, featured in RHS Plantfinder, gives visitors the opportunity to purchase plants seen in the garden. An award winning professional artist's studio/ gallery is also open. The garden was featured in Lincolnshire Pride magazine. Complete your visit at Nut Tree Farm. The garden, est in 2007, is over an acre and enjoys stunning views of Lincolnshire Wolds. A sweeping herbaceous border frames the lawn and a double wall, planted with seasonal annuals, surrounds the house. From the raised terrace a rill runs to the large pond. As well as a raised brick edged vegetable garden, there is a prize winning flock of Hampshire Down sheep in fields surrounding part of garden. Locally made honey for sale.

14 ◆ GOLTHO HOUSE

Lincoln Road, Goltho, Wragby, Market Rasen, LN8 5NF. Mr & Mrs S Hollingworth, 01673 857768, bookings@golthogardens.com, www.golthogardens.com. *10m E of Lincoln. On A158, 1m before Wragby. Garden on L (not in Goltho Village).* **For NGS: Sun 22 Apr, Sun 23 Sept (10-4). Adm £5, chd free. Light refreshments.** For other opening times and information, please phone, email or visit garden website.

4½ acre garden started in 1998 but looking established with long grass walk flanked by abundantly planted herbaceous borders forming a focal point. Paths and walkway span out to other features incl nut walk, prairie border, wild flower meadow, rose garden and large pond area. Snowdrops, hellebores and shrubs for winter interest.

The National Garden Scheme is the largest single funder of Macmillan

GROUP OPENING

15 GOSBERTON GARDENS

Gosberton, Spalding, PE11 4NQ. *Entering Gosberton on A152, from Spalding , Salem St on L & Mill Lane on R opp the War Memorial. Continue through the village 21 Quadring Rd on R.* **Sun 1 July (11-4). Combined adm £5, chd free. Light refreshments at 21 Quadring Road.**

MILLSTONE HOUSE
Mrs J Chatterton.

NEW **21 QUADRING ROAD**
Julie Crunkhorn.

4 SALEM STREET
Patricia Hogben.

The village of Gosberton welcomes visitors to 3 private houses to view their gardens. We hope that everyone will find interesting features during their tour and enjoy the 3 locations.Millstone House. Colourful herbaceous borders are hidden by a privet hedge. Dappled shade creates a feeling of relaxation at the rear of the house. 21 Quadring Road. Redeveloped over recent years, the front garden includes bee friendly herbaceous beds divided by slate paths.
4 Salem Street. Delightful secluded garden. Mixed borders including a small water feature lead to a productive vegetable plot. Partial wheelchair access.

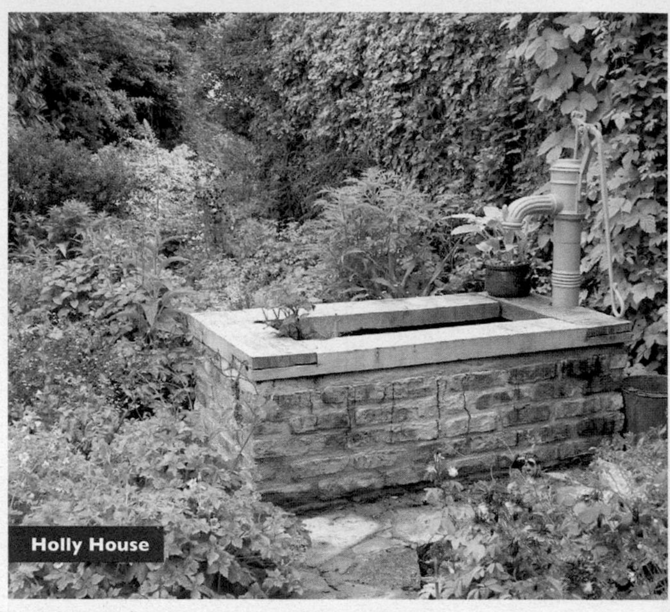
Holly House

16 ◆ GRIMSTHORPE CASTLE

Grimsthorpe, Bourne, PE10 0LZ. Grimsthorpe & Drummond Castle Trust, 01778 591205, ray@grimsthorpe.co.uk, www.grimsthorpe.co.uk. *3m NW of Bourne. 8m E of A1 on A151 from Colsterworth junction. Main entrance indicated by brown tourist sign.* **For NGS: Sun 8 Apr, Wed 6 June (10.30-6). Adm £7, chd £3. Light refreshments.** For other opening times and information, please phone, email or visit garden website.

The Grade I listed gardens encompass nearly 65 acres and incl large formal lawns, fine topiary and formal hedges, ornamental and productive kitchen garden, large herbaceous borders, rose parterre and woodland walks with spring bulb displays. Visitors can explore the surrounding 3000 acre estate that encompasses a Capability Brown landscape, in addition to the tranquil and relaxing gardens. Home-made lunches, afternoon tea and cakes. Gift shop, cycle hire and adventure playground, historic house, park trails. Gravel paths.

17 ◆ GUNBY HALL & GARDENS

Spilsby, PE23 5SS. National Trust, 01754 890102, gunbyhall@nationaltrust.org.uk, www.nationaltrust.org.uk. *2½m NW of Burgh-le-Marsh. 7m W of Skegness. On A158. Signed off Gunby r'about.* **For NGS: Sun 5 Aug (11-5). Adm £6.50, chd £4.50. Light refreshments in Gunby tea-room.** For other opening times and information, please phone, email or visit garden website.

Eight acres of formal and walled gardens. Old roses, herbaceous borders, herb garden and kitchen garden with fruit trees and vegetables. Greenhouses, carp pond and sweeping lawns. Tennyson's Haunt of Ancient Peace. House built by Sir William Massingberd in 1700. Wheelchair access in gardens and with Gunby's dedicated wheelchair on ground floor of house.

The National Garden Scheme is Marie Curie's largest single funder

18 HACKTHORN HALL

Hackthorn, Lincoln, LN2 3PQ. Mr & Mrs William Cracroft-Eley, 01673 860423, office@hackthorn.com, www.hackthorn.com. *6m N of Lincoln. Follow signs to Hackthorn. Approx 1m off A15 N of Lincoln.* **Sun 10 June (1-5). Adm £3.50, chd free. Home-made teas at Hackthorn Village Hall. Visits also by arrangement June to Sept for groups of 20+.**

Formal and woodland garden, productive and ornamental walled gardens surrounding Hackthorn Hall and church extending to approx 15 acres. Parts of the formal gardens designed by Bunny Guinness. The walled garden boasts a magnificent Black Hamburg vine, believed to be second in size to the vine at Hampton Court. Partial wheelchair access, gravel paths, grass drives.

19 ◆ HALL FARM

Harpswell, Gainsborough, DN21 5UU. Pam & Mark Tatam, 01427 668412, pam.tatam@gmail.com, www.hall-farm.co.uk. *7m E of Gainsborough. On A631, 1½ m W of Caenby Corner.* **For NGS: Sun 1 July, Sun 2 Sept (1-5). Adm £4, chd free. Light refreshments. For other opening times and information, please phone, email or visit garden website.**

The 3 acre garden encompasses formal and informal areas, incl a parterre, a sunken garden, a courtyard with rill, a walled Mediterranean garden, double herbaceous borders for late summer, lawns, pond, giant chess set, and a flower and grass meadow. It is a short walk to the medieval moat, which surrounds over an acre of wild semi-woodland garden with picnic table, benches and 'beach'. Free seed collecting on Sun 2 Sept. Most of garden suitable for wheelchairs.

20 THE HAWTHORNS

Bicker Road, Donington, PE11 4XP. Colin & Janet Johnson. *½m NW of Donington. Bicker Rd is directly off A52 opp Church Street. Parking available in Church Street or village centre car park.* **Sun 24 June (11-4). Adm £3.50, chd free. Home-made teas.**

Traditional garden with extensive herbaceous borders, pond, large old English rose garden, vegetable and fruit areas with feature greenhouse. Cider orchard and area housing rare breed animals incl goats, pigs, sheep, cattle and chickens. Home produce available incl honey and goat's milk dairy products. Featured in Lincolnshire Pride. Some gravel paths.

21 HOLLY HOUSE

Fishtoft Drove, Frithville, Boston, PE22 7ES. Sally & David Grant, 01205 750486, sallygrant50@btinternet.com. *3m N of Boston. 1m S of Frithville. Unclassified rd. On W side of West Fen Drain. Marked on good maps.* **Sun 20 May (12-5). Adm £3.50, chd free. Home-made teas. Visits also by arrangement May & June for groups 10+. Adm £5 incl refreshments.**

Approx 1 acre informal mixed borders, steps leading down to pond with cascade and stream. Small woodland area. Quiet garden with water feature. Extra 2½ acres devoted to wildlife, especially bumble bees and butterflies. Partial wheelchair access with some steep slopes and steps.

22 INLEY DROVE FARM

Inley Drove, Sutton St James, Spalding, PE12 0LX. Francis & Maisie Pryor, www.pryorfrancis.wordpress.com/. *Just off rd from Sutton St James to Sutton St Edmund. 2m S of Sutton St James. Look for yellow NGS signs on double bend.* **Sat 15, Sun 16 Sept (11-5). Adm £4, chd free. Home-made teas.**

Over 3 acres of Fenland garden and meadow plus 6½ acre wood developed over 20yrs. Garden planted for colour, scent and wildlife. Double mixed borders and less formal flower gardens all framed by hornbeam hedges. Unusual shrubs and trees, incl fine stand of Black Poplars, vegetable garden, woodland walks and orchard. Some gravel and a few steps but mostly flat grass.

23 INNER LODGE

Somerby, Gainsborough, DN21 3HG. Paul & Karen Graves. *On A631 Gainsborough to Grimsby rd. From Gainsborough, track on R at Very end of the dual carriageway, follow ½m track to find marked parking areas in small woodland glades.* **Sun 17 June, Sun 15 July, Sun 19 Aug (11-4). Adm £3, chd free. Home-made cakes, hot & cold drinks.**

Set in woodland our colourful cottage garden of approx 1 acre was started in 2013 and is still developing. We have mixed borders, shrubs, fernery, several quirky features, vegetable garden, and small secret garden. Plenty of seating around the garden but regret it is not suitable for wheelchairs. There will also be Craft sales (open on all the days) with a percentage of takings donated to the NGS.

24 LUDNEY HOUSE FARM

Ludney, Louth, LN11 7JU. Jayne Bullas, 07733 018710, jayne@theoldgatehouse.com. *Between Grainthorpe & Conisholme.* **Visits by arrangement Apr to Sept for groups of 10 (smaller groups considered). Adm £6, chd free. Home-made teas and cakes incl.**

A beautiful landscaped garden of several defined spaces containing formal and informal areas. There is an excellent mix of trees, shrubs, perennials and roses, also a long wild grass area which is home to the bee hives. In spring there is a nice selection of bulbs and spring flowers. There are plenty of seats positioned around to sit and enjoy a cuppa and piece of cake! Wheelchair access to most parts.

Your visit has already helped 600 more people gain access to a Parkinson's nurse

25 MANOR FARM

Horkstow Road, South Ferriby, Barton-upon-Humber, DN18 6HS. Geoff & Angela Wells, 01652 635214, wells.farming@btinternet.com. *3m from Barton-upon-Humber on A1077, turn L onto B1204, opp Village Hall.* **Sun 17 June (11-5). Combined adm with Springfield £5, chd free. Home-made teas. Visits also by arrangement May to Aug.**

A garden which is much praised by visitors. Set within approx 1 acre with mature shrubberies, herbaceous borders, gravel garden and pergola walk. There is also a rosebed, white garden and fernery. Many old trees with preservation orders. Wildlife pond set within a paddock.

26 MANOR HOUSE

Manor Road, Hagworthingham, Spilsby, PE23 4LN. Gill Maxim & David O'Connor, 01507 588530, vcagillmaxim@aol.com. *5m E of Horncastle. S of A158 in Hagworthingham, turn into Bond Hayes Lane downhill, becomes Manor Rd. Please follow signs down gravel track to parking area.* **Sun 27 May, Sun 26 Aug (2-5). Adm £3.50, chd free. Home-made teas. Visits also by arrangement May to Sept.**

2 acre garden on S-facing slope, partly terraced and well protected by established trees and shrubs. Redeveloped over 18yrs with natural and formal ponds. Shrub roses, laburnum walk, hosta border, gravel bed and other areas mainly planted with hardy perennials, trees and shrubs.

27 THE MANOR HOUSE

Manor House Street, Horncastle, LN9 5HF. Mr Michael & Dr Marilyn Hieatt. *Manor House St runs off Market Square in middle of Horncastle, beside St Mary's Church. The Manor House is approx 100 metres from Market Square (on R).* **Sat 24 Mar (12-4). Adm £3, chd free.**

An informal spring garden and orchard bordered by the R Bain, hidden in the middle of Horncastle. The garden includes a short section of the 3rd/4th Century wall that formed part of a Roman fort (Scheduled Ancient Monument) with the remnants of an adjacent medieval well. Restricted wheel chair access (some parts not accessible).

28 MARIGOLD COTTAGE

Hotchin Road, Sutton-on-Sea, LN12 2NP. Stephanie Lee & John Raby, 01507 442151, marigoldlee@btinternet.com, www.rabylee.uk/marigold/. *16m N of Skegness on A52. 7m E of Alford on A1111. 3m S of Mablethorpe on A52. Turn off A52 on High St at Cornerhouse Cafe. Follow rd past playing field on R. Rd turns away from the dunes. House 2nd on L.* **Sat & Sun 28, 29 Apr, 26, 27 May, 23, 24 June, 21, 22 July, 25, 26 Aug (2-5). Adm £3, chd free. Home-made teas. Visits also by arrangement Apr to Sept for groups 10+.**

Slide open the Japanese gate to find secret paths, lanterns, a circular window in a curved wall, water lilies in pots and a gravel garden, vegetable garden and propagation area. Take the long drive to see the sea. Back in the garden, find a seat, enjoy the birds and bees. We face the challenges of heavy clay and salt ladened winds but look for unusual plants not the humdrum for these conditions. Most of garden accessible to wheelchairs along flat, paved paths.

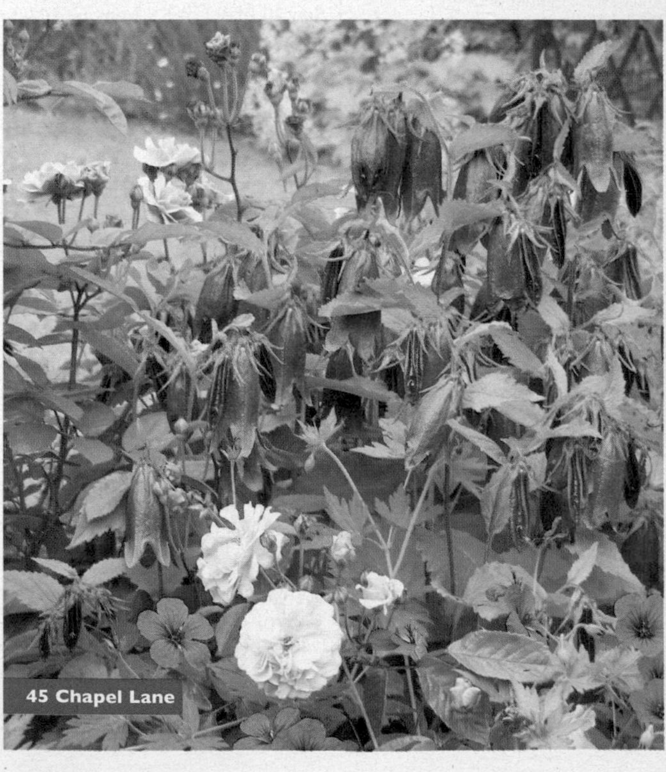

45 Chapel Lane

29 MERE HOUSE

Stow Road, Sturton by Stow, Lincoln, LN1 2BZ. Nigel & Alice Gray, 07932 442349, alice@merehouse.com. *10m NW of Lincoln between Sturton & Stow. 1m from centre of Sturton village heading to Stow, house on L. NB: Postcode will not bring you far enough out of Sturton village.* **Visits by arrangement Mar to Sept we have ample parking for groups, mini-bus or even coaches. Adm by donation. Home-made teas.**

Approx 1½ acres of established garden planted for the first time in 1975, redesigned in 1996. Renovated over the last 4yrs to incl new beds with drift planting but still incl the formal parterre. Spring bulbs and late summer colour are highlights. There is also a cutting garden, pleached hedge, vegetable garden and orchard. Work in progress incl a new garden project and long herbaceous border. There is the highly acclaimed Cross Keys Pub in Stow Village that does a very good lunch. The garden is wheelchair accessible on grass.

30 ◆ MILL FARM

Caistor Road, Grasby, Caistor, DN38 6AQ. Mike & Helen Boothman, 01652 628424, boothmanhelen@gmail.com, www.millfarmgarden.co.uk. *3m NW of Caistor on A1084. Between Brigg & Caistor. From Cross Keys PH towards Caistor for approx 200yds. Do not go into Grasby village.* **For NGS : Sun 3 June (11-4). Adm £4, chd free. Home-made teas.**
For other opening times and information, please phone, email or visit garden website.

This is a garden which continues to be developed. Over 3 acres of garden with many diverse areas. Formal frontage with shrubs and trees. The rear is a plantsman haven with a peony and rose garden, specimen trees, vegetable area, old windmill adapted into a fernery, alpine house and shade house with a variety of shade loving plants. Herbaceous beds with different grasses and hardy perennials. Small nursery on site with home grown plants available. Mainly grass, but with some gravelled areas.

31 THE MOAT

Newton, NG34 0ED. Mr & Mrs Mike Barnes, 01529 497462, lynnebarnes14@gmail.com. *Off A52 10m E of Grantham. In Newton village, opp church. Please park sensibly in village.* **Visits by arrangement May to Sept for groups 15+, evening visits welcome,with wine and canapes. Home-made teas.**

Delightful 3 acre garden designed to blend into its country location. Beautiful herbaceous island beds planted with imagination to give yr-round colour. Small vegetable garden, orchard, pretty courtyard garden and formal box parterre, also a lovely natural pond which is a magnet for wildlife. This garden contains many unusual plants and trees. Featured in Lincolnshire Life. Garden on slope but accessible to wheelchair users.

32 NOVA LODGE

150 Horncastle Road, Roughton Moor, Woodhall Spa, LN10 6UX. Leo Boshier, 01526 354940, moxons555@btinternet.com. *On B1191. Approx 2m E of centre of Woodhall Spa on Horncastle Rd. Roadside parking.* **Visits by arrangement 21 May to July for groups 10+. Adm £3, chd free. Home-made teas.**

⅔ acre traditional garden set within mature trees started 2009. Herbaceous borders and beds, rare and unusual perennials. Shrub beds with grasses and ferns, large collection of hostas and heucheras, area for vegetables, fruit and herbs. Summerhouse, greenhouses, lawns and ponds. Central arbour with climbing roses and clematis. Lightweight wheelchairs only; not suitable for motorised chairs.

33 OASIS GARDEN - YOUR PLACE

Wellington Street, Grimsby, DN32 7JP. Grimsby Neighbourhood Church, www.yourplacegrimsby.com. *Enter Grimsby (M180) over flyover, along Cleethorpe Rd. Turn R into Victor Street, Turn L into Wellington Street. Your Place is on the R on junction of Wellington Street & Weelsby Street.* **Sat 2, Sun 3 June (10-2). Adm £3, chd free. Light refreshments.**

The multi award winning Oasis Garden, Your Place, recently described by the RHS as the 'Most inspirational garden in the six counties of the East Midlands', is approximately 1½ acres and nestles in the heart of Great Grimsby's East Marsh Community. A working garden producing 15k plants per year, grown by local volunteers of all ages and abilities. Lawns, fruit, vegetable, perennial and annual beds.

34 NEW THE OLD RECTORY

Main Road, Benniworth, Market Rasen, LN8 6JW. Ian & Sally Waterhouse, ianandsallywaterhouse@hotmail.com. *The Old Rectory is on Main Rd in Benniworth, but car parking and entrance for the Open Day is in the Church grounds at the end of Church Lane which is signed LN8 6JP.* **Sat 23 June (12-5). Adm £3.50, chd free. Home-made teas. Visits also by arrangement May to Oct small groups are welcome by arrangement for visits of up to 2 hours.**

The garden is set in the 2½ acre grounds of a C19 rectory adjacent to the picturesque village church which has C12 origins. Surrounded by mature trees the garden has wide lawns with extensive herbaceous borders. There is a large polytunnel and fruit cage, vegetable plot and pond, a woodland garden, cutting garden, flower borders and a charming courtyard. Teas and cakes will be provided courtesy of Riding for the Disabled and there is a substantial plant sale. Wheelchairs can access the majority of the garden, but it might be a bit difficult on the gravel drive and the woodchip paths.

35 THE OLD RECTORY

Church Lane, East Keal, Spilsby, PE23 4AT. Mrs Ruth Ward, 01790 752477, rfjward@btinternet.com. *2m SW of Spilsby. Off A16. Turn into Church Lane by PO.* **Sun 22 Apr, Sun 20 May (2-4.30). Adm £3.50, chd free. Home-made teas. Visits also by arrangement Mar to Oct refreshments on request.**

Beautifully situated, with fine views, rambling cottage garden on different levels falling naturally into separate areas, with changing effects and atmosphere. Steps, paths and vistas to lead you on, seats well placed for appreciating special views or relaxing and enjoying the peace. Dry border, vegetable garden, orchard, woodland walk, wild flower meadow. Yr-round interest. Welcoming to wildlife. limited.

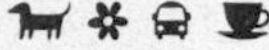

36 THE OLD VICARAGE

Low Road, Holbeach Hurn, PE12 8JN. Mrs Liz Dixon-Spain, 01406 424148, lizdixonspain@gmail.com. *2m NE of Holbeach. Turn off A17 N to Holbeach Hurn, past post box in middle of village, 1st R into Low Rd. Old Vicarage on R approx 400yds.* **Sun 13 May (1-5). Combined adm with Old White House £5, chd free. Light refreshments at Old White House. Sun 3 June (1-5). Adm £3, chd free. Visits also by arrangement Mar to Sept.**

2 acres of garden with 150yr old tulip, plane and beech trees: borders of shrubs, roses, herbaceous plants. Shrub roses and herb garden in old paddock area, surrounded by informal areas with pond and bog garden, wild flowers, grasses and bulbs. Small fruit and vegetable gardens. Kids love exploring winding paths through the wilder areas. Garden is managed environmentally. fun for kids ! Gravel drive, some paths, mostly grass access.

The Old Vicarage

37 OLD WHITE HOUSE

Holbeach Hurn, PE12 8JP. Mr & Mrs A Worth. *2m N of Holbeach. Turn off A17 N to Holbeach Hurn, follow signs to village, cont through, turn R after Rose & Crown Pub at Baileys Lane.* **Sun 13 May (1-5). Combined adm with The Old Vicarage £5, chd free. Home-made teas.**

1½ acres of mature garden, featuring herbaceous borders, roses, patterned garden, herb garden and walled kitchen garden. Large catalpa, tulip tree that flowers, ginko and other specimen trees. Flat surfaces, some steps, wheelchair access to all areas without using steps.

38 PINE FIELDS

Wells Road, Healing, Grimsby, DN41 7QQ. Rita & Geoff Morgan. *3m W of Grimsby. From B1210 Stallingborough Rd turn into Wells Rd, Lane entrance ½m on L. From A18 take A1173, turn R into Wells Rd Lane entrance on R immed after white Healing sign.* **Sun 24 June (11-5). Adm £3.50, chd free. Light refreshments.**

Large garden with herbaceous borders and beds interspersed with a mixture of trees and shrubs. Wildlife pond with water lilies and aquatic plants. Two pergolas in formal beds with box and yew hedging lead onto a winter garden and fruit orchard. A new formal parterre garden established 2016 is an ongoing project, the whole backed by a small woodland area.

39 POTTERTONS NURSERY

Moortown Road, Nettleton, Caistor, LN7 6HX. Rob & Jackie Potterton, www.pottertons.co.uk. *1m W of Nettleton. From A46 at Nettleton turn onto B1205 (Moortown). Nursery 1¼m, turn by edge of wood.* **Sun 27 May (9-5). Adm £3, chd free. Home-made teas.**

5 acre garden of alpine rockeries, stream and waterfall, raised beds, troughs, tufa bed, crevice garden, woodland beds, extensively planted with alpines, bulbs and woodland plants, which will be at their flowering peak. On the day we have invited Plant Hunters Fairs to the garden, with 9 specialist nurseries offering a range incl acers, shrubs, alpines, rare perennials and cottage garden plants. Access mostly on mixed grass surfaces.

40 SCHOOL HOUSE

Market Rasen Road, Holton-le-Moor, Market Rasen, LN7 6AE. Chris & Rosemary Brown. *15m N of Lincoln. A46 towards Caistor, take B1434 to Holton le Moor. School House on R next to village (Moot) hall.* **Sat 4 Aug (12.30-5). Adm £5, chd free. Light refreshments. Adm incl tea/ coffee and biscuits.**

An all around the house garden, ranging from shaded early area to summer and autumn flowering areas. Central gravel garden with alliums followed by agapanthus and supplemented with grasses. Designed and built by Chris Brown a now retired garden designer.

41 SEDGEBROOK MANOR

Church Lane, Sedgebrook, Grantham, NG32 2EU. Hon James & Lady Caroline Ogilvy. *2m W of Grantham on A52. In Sedgebrook village by church.* **Sun 10 June (1-5). Adm £4, chd free. Home-made teas.**

Yew and box topiary surround this charming Manor House (not open). Croquet lawn, herbaceous border and summer house. Bridge over small pond and two larger ponds. Ancient mulberry tree. Tennis court, vegetable patch, woodland area with chickens. Swimming pool in enclosed garden. Wheelchair access to most areas.

42 SHANGRILA

Little Hale Road, Great Hale, Sleaford, NG34 9LH. Marilyn Cooke & John Knight. *On B1394 between Heckington & Helpringham.* **Sun 17 June (11-5). Adm £4.50, chd free. Home-made teas.**

Approx 3 acre garden with sweeping lawns long herbaceous borders, colour themed island beds, hosta collection, lavender bed with seating area, topiary, acers, small raised vegetable area, 3 ponds and new exotic borders. Wheelchair access to all areas.

43 66 SPILSBY ROAD

Boston, PE21 9NS. Rosemary & Adrian Isaac. *From Boston town take A16 towards Spilsby. On L after Trinity Church. Parking on Spilsby Rd.* **Sun 20 May (11-4). Adm £4, chd free. Home-made teas.**

1⅓ acre with mature trees, moat, Venetian Folly, summer house and orangery, lawns and herbaceous borders. Children's Tudor garden house, gatehouse and courtyard. Wide paths.

44 NEW SPRINGFIELD

Main Street, Horkstow, Barton-Upon-Humber, DN18 6BL. Mr & Mrs G Allison. *4m from Barton on Humber. Take the A1077 towards Scunthorpe & in South Ferriby bear L onto the B1204, after 2m Springfield is on the hillside on L.* **Sun 17 June (11-5). Combined adm with Manor Farm £5, chd free.**

This beautiful hillside garden on the edge of the Wolds was renovated and redesigned in 2011 from an overgrown state. It features many shrubs and perennials with a rose pergola and stunning views over the Ancholme Valley.

Donations from the National Garden Scheme enable Perennial to care for horticulturalists

45 THE STABLES

Ranby, Market Rasen, LN8 5LN. Russ & Chris Hibbins. *SW corner of Lincolnshire Wolds - between Horncastle & Market Rasen. On A158, halfway between Wragby & Horncastle, is Baumber. Here, turn N on B1225 (direction Caistor & Belmont tv mast) for 3m. Garden well signed. From N follow B1225 - Ranby is 3m N of Baumber.* **Sun 22 July (12.30-5). Adm £3.50, chd free. Home-made teas.**

The garden approaches ½ acre and has been developed over last 15yrs as a place to sit, relax and look at a variety of trees, shrubs and plants (some not so common), together with statuary and sculptures. S-facing and extremely fertile, well drained soil helps most plants to quickly become established. The many seats around the garden are intended for use! Some covered seating and tables if needed. Wonderfully rural setting, in a quiet hamlet, the garden is not really visible from the road and often surprises people who see it for the first time. Features a much admired pair of ornamental gates. For wheelchair users there is a slightly different entry to the garden, along a flat gravel drive, with no steps.

46 68 WATTS LANE

Louth, LN11 9DG. Jenny & Rodger Grasham, 07977 318145, sallysing@hotmail.co.uk, www.facebook.com/thesecretgardenoflouth. *½m S of Louth town centre. Watts Lane off Newmarket (on B1200). Turn by pedestrian lights & Co-op into gated lane. Please open and close the gate. Some SatNavs unreliable. Try LN119DJ for Mount Pleasant Av, this leads on to Watts Lane.* **Sun 15, Sun 29 July (11-4). Every Sun 5 Aug to 26 Aug (11-4). Adm £2.50, chd free. Home-made teas. Visits also by arrangement Aug & Sept refreshments available. No minimum number.**

Blank canvas of ⅕ acre in early 90s. Developed into lush, colourful, exotic plant packed haven. A whole new world on entering from street. Exotic borders, raised exotic island, long hot border, ponds, stumpery, developing prairie style border. Conservatory, grapevine. Intimate seating areas along garden's journey. Facebook page - The Secret Garden of Louth. Children, find where the frogs are hiding! Many butterflies and bees but how many different types? Feed the fish, find Cedric the spider and Simon the snake. Grass pathways, main garden area accessible. Wheelchairs not permitted on bridge over pond, both sides can be reached via pathways.

The National Garden Scheme is the largest single funder of the Queen's Nursing Institute

47 48 WESTGATE

Louth, LN11 9YD. Kenneth Harvey. *Approx 100 yrds before The Wheatsheaf Pub, nr to Church.* **Sun 10 June, Sun 2 Sept (11-4). Adm £3.50, chd free. Home-made teas.**

Large town garden of about 1½ acres that crosses the R Ludd. Hidden away behind the high Georgian facades of Louth is a good example of a town garden of trees, herbaceous borders, two small ponds, a fern and white garden and formal vegetable parterre. Wonderful views of Louth church spire. The garden was originally planted in the late 1950s, but has been remodelled over the last 7yrs.

ALLOTMENTS

48 WILLOUGHBY ROAD ALLOTMENTS

Willoughby Road, Boston, PE21 9HN. Willoughby Road Allotments Association, **willoughbyroadallotments.org.uk.** *Entrance is adjacent to 109 Willoughby Road, Boston, PE21 9HN. Street Parking only.* **Sun 19 Aug (10-4). Adm £3, chd free. Light refreshments.**

Set in 5 acres the allotments comprise 60 plots growing fine vegetables, fruit, flowers and herbs. There is a small orchard and wild flower area and a community space adjacent. Grass paths run along the site. Several plots will be open to walk round. There will be a seed and plant stall. Light refreshments are available. Small orchard and wild flower beds.

49 WILLOW COTTAGE

Gravel Pit Lane, Burgh-le-Marsh, PE24 5DW. Bob & Karen Ward, 01754 811450, robertward055@aol.com, www.Birdsongtouringpark.com. *6m W of Skegness. S of Gunby r'about on A158, take 1st R signed Bratoft & Burgh-le-Marsh. 1st R again onto Bratoft Lane. L at T-junction, parking on R 25yds.* **Mon 28 May (2-5). Adm £4, chd free. Home-made teas on the terrace. Sumptuous homemade cakes, tea in china pots. Visits also by arrangement Apr to Sept friends love to gather take tea and cakes on the terrace, 15 or more makes for a happy gathering.**

Peering through the cottage window nestled sweetly amidst a garden of splendour! A kaleidoscope of colourful borders, a feast for the eyes. Fragrances linger in the air lifting the spirit. Intriguing walkways through shady cool woodland soothing to the soul. Late afternoon sunshine illuminates the new prairie border down at the end of the meadow. There's so much more to discover so please come! Woodland walk and Victorian glasshouse, new prairie border and caravan site pond walk now open. Featured in Lincolnshire Today Magazine. Partial wheelchair access. For assistance please phone ahead of visit.

50 WOODLANDS

Peppin Lane, Fotherby, Louth, LN11 0UW. Ann & Bob Armstrong, www.woodlandsplants.co.uk. *2m N of Louth off A16 signed Fotherby. Please park on R verge opp allotments & walk approx 350 yds to garden. No parking at garden. Please do not drive beyond designated area.* **Sun 1 Apr, Sun 3 June, Sun 1 July, Sun 5 Aug (11-5); Sun 7 Oct (11-4). Adm £3, chd free. Home-made teas. Opening with Fotherby Gardens on Sun 6 May, Sun 2 Sept.**

A lovely mature woodland garden where a multitude of unusual plants are the stars, many of which are available from the well stocked RHS listed nursery. The two new areas completed last year have developed well and this year there will be a new border for late interest to coincide with an October opening. Award winning professional artist's studio/gallery open to visitors. Specialist collection of Codonopsis for which Plant Heritage status has been granted.

NPC

51 YEW TREE FARM

Westhorpe Road, Gosberton, Spalding, PE11 4EP. Robert & Claire Bailey-Scott. *Nr Spalding. Enter the village of Gosberton. Turn into Westhorpe Rd, opp The Bell Inn, cont for approx. 1½m. Property is 3rd on R after bridge.* **Sun 29 July (11-5). Adm £4, chd free. Home-made teas.**

A lovely country garden, 1½ acres. Large herbaceous and mixed borders surround the well kept lawns. Wildlife pond with two bog gardens, woodland garden and shaded borders containing many unusual plants. A mulberry tree forms the centre piece of one lawn. Picturesque annual flower meadow, wild flower meadow and large vegetable plot. Stunning annual flower meadow. Two magnificent yew trees, organic vegetable plot and orchard, under planted with a wild flower meadow. Featured in Lincolnshire Free Press, Spalding Guardian and Garden News magazine. Gravel driveway, some gravel paths.

Yew Tree Farm

LONDON

HERTFORDSHIRE
BUCKINGHAMSHIRE
BERKSHIRE
SURREY
River Thames
London Heathrow
EN5
Barnet
EN4
Southgate
N20
N14
NW7
HA7
HA8
Edgware
HA6
HA5
HA3
UB9
Ruislip
HA4
HA2
Harrow
HA1
NW9
NW4
Hendon
NW11
N3
Finchley
N12
N11
N10
N22
N2
N8
N6
N19
Hampstead
NW2
NW3
NW5
N7
Islington
HA9
HA0
Wembley
NW10
NW6
NW8
NW1
UB10
Uxbridge
Northolt
UB5
UB6
UB8
Hillingdon
UB4
West Drayton
UB1
Southall
UB3
UB7
UB2
W7
W13
Ealing
W5
W3
W12
W11
W10
W9
Bayswater
W2
W1
WC1
WC2
W8
Westminster
SW1
W14
Hammersmith
W6
W4
Brentford
TW8
TW5
Hounslow
TW7
TW6
TW4
TW3
TW9
Richmond
TW1
TW14
Feltham
TW13
TW2
TW10
Twickenham
Teddington
TW11
TW12
Hampton
KT8
KT1
Kingston
KT2
KT7
KT6
KT5
KT3
KT9
SW13
SW14
SW6
SW5
SW7
SW3
SW10
SW8
Battersea
SW11
SW9
SW4
Wandsworth
SW15
SW18
SW12
SW2
SW17
Wimbledon
SW19
SW20
SW16
SM4
CR4
Mitcham
KT4
SM3
SM1
Sutton
SM2
SM5
SM6
Purley
Coulsdon
CR5

ESSEX
KENT
EN1
EN3
N9
Edmonton
Chingford
E4
N18
Woodford Green
IG8
Tottenham
N17
E17
E18
Walthamstow
N15
IG5
IG6
IG7
IG4
IG2
IG
E11
E10
N16
E5
E
Ilford
IG1
IG3
E12
E7
E8
E9
Stratford
E15
Barking
IG11
E2
E3
E13
E6
E1
EC1
EC2
EC3
EC4
E14
E16
London City
D O N
SE1
SE16
SE28
Thamesmead
SE10
SE7
SE18
SE2
SE8
Greenwich
SE3
SE15
SE14
SE17
SE5
Peckham
Lewisham
SE4
SE13
SE22
Eltham
SE9
SE12
SE23
SE6
SE21
SE26
SE19
SE20
SE25
SE
RM4
RM5
RM1
RM3
RM6
Romford
RM2
RM7
RM11
RM
RM8
RM10
RM12
Upminster
RM14
RM9
Rainham
RM13
DA18
DA17
DA8
DA16
DA7
Bexleyheath
DA6
DA1
DA
DA15
DA5
Bexley
Sidcup
DA14
Chislehurst
BR1
BR7
BR3
Bromley
BR5
BR2
BR
BR4
Orpington
BR6
CR0
Addington
CR
CR2
TN14
TN16
TN
Biggin Hill
River Thames
0
5
10 kilometres
0
5 miles
© Global Mapping / XYZ Maps

Volunteers

County Organiser
Penny Snell
01932 864532
pennysnellflowers@btinternet.com

County Treasurer
John McNicholas
07785 701770
john@jandjmcnicholas.com

Publicity
Penny Snell (as above)

Booklet Co-ordinator
Sue Phipps
07771 767196
sue@suephipps.com

Booklet Distributor
Joey Clover
020 8870 8740
joeyclover@hotmail.com

Assistant County Organisers

Central London
Eveline Carn
07831 136069
evelinecbcarn@icloud.com

Clapham & surrounding area
Sue Phipps
(as above)

Croydon & outer South London
Ben & Peckham Carroll
0208 777 9012
b.j.carroll@btinternet.com

Dulwich & surrounding area
Clive Pankhurst
07941 536934
alternative.ramblings@gmail.com

E London
Teresa Farnham
07761 476651
farnhamz@yahoo.co.uk

Hackney
Philip Lightowlers
020 8533 0052
plighto@gmail.com

Hampstead
Joan Arnold
020 8444 8752
joan.arnold40@gmail.com

Hampstead Garden Suburb, Finchley & Barnet
Caroline Broome
020 8444 2329
carosgarden@virginmedia.com

Islington
Penelope Darby Brown
020 7226 6880
pendarbybrown@blueyonder.co.uk

Gill Evansky
020 7359 2484
gevansky@gmail.com

Northwood, Pinner, Ruislip & Harefield
Hasruty Patel
07815 110050
hasruty@gmail.com

NW London
Susan Bennett & Earl Hyde
020 8883 8540
suebearlh@yahoo.co.uk

Outer NW London
James Duncan Mattoon
020 8830 7410
jamesmattoon@msn.com

Outer W London
Julia Hickman
020 8339 0931
julia.hickman@virgin.net

SE London
Janine Wookey
07711 279636
j.wookey@btinternet.com

SW London
Joey Clover
(as above)

W London, Barnes & Chiswick
Siobhan McCammon
07952 889866
siobhan.mccammon@gmail.com

From the tiniest to the largest, London gardens offer exceptional diversity. Hidden behind historic houses in Spitalfields are exquisite tiny gardens, while on Kingston Hill there are 9 acres of landscaped Japanese gardens.

The oldest private garden in London boasts 5 acres, while the many other historic gardens within these pages are smaller – some so tiny there is only room for a few visitors at a time – but nonetheless full of innovation, colour and horticultural excellence.

London allotments have attracted television cameras to film their productive acres, where exotic Cape gooseberries, figs, prizewinning roses and even bees all thrive thanks to the skill and enthusiasm of city gardeners.

The traditional sit comfortably with the contemporary in London – offering a feast of elegant borders, pleached hedges, topiary, gravel gardens and the cooling sound of water – while to excite the adventurous there are gardens on barges and green roofs to explore.

The season stretches from April to October, so there is nearly always a garden to visit somewhere in London. Our gardens opening this year are the beating heart of the capital just waiting to be visited and enjoyed.

LONDON GARDENS LISTED BY POSTCODE

Inner London postcodes

E and EC London

Spitalfields Gardens E1
17 Greenstone Mews E11
37 Harold Road E11
51 Tweedmouth Road E13
12 Western Road E13
Richard House Children's Hospice E16
87 St Johns Road E17
46 Cheyne Avenue E18
Victoria Lodge E18
5 Brodie Road E4
16 Maida Way E4
79 Royston Avenue E4
Lower Clapton Gardens E5
42 Latimer Road E7
84 Lavender Grove E8
Mapledene Gardens E8
12 Bushberry Road E9
The Charterhouse EC1
The Inner and Middle Temple Gardens EC4

N & NW London

37 Alwyne Road N1
Arlington Square Gardens N1
Barnsbury Group N1
Canonbury House N1
4 Canonbury Place N1
13 College Cross N1
De Beauvoir Gardens N1
Diespeker Wharf N1
41 Ecclesbourne Road N1
58 Halliford Street N1
King Henry's Walk Garden N1
2 Lonsdale Square N1
Malvern Terrace Gardens N1
5 Northampton Park N1
19 St Peter's Street N1
55 Dukes Avenue N10
Princes Avenue Gardens N10
5 St Regis Close N10
33 Wood Vale N10
21 Woodland Rise N10
Golf Course Allotments N11
46 Ollerton Road N11
53 Manor Road N16
15 Norcott Road N16
21 Gospatrick Road N17
77 Handsworth Road N17
159 Higham Road N17
36 Ashley Road N19
79 Church Lane N2
26 Ringwood Avenue N2
24 Twyford Avenue N2
1 Wades Grove N21
10 York Road N21
23 Imperial Road N22
Railway Cottages N22
Gordon Road Allotments N3
31 Hendon Avenue N3
18 Park Crescent N3
7 The Grove N6
3 The Park N6
Southwood Lodge N6
10 Woodside Avenue N6
5 Blackthorn Av, Apartment 5 N7
9 Furlong Road N7
33 Huddleston Road N7
1a Hungerford Road N7
60 & 62 Hungerford Road N7
19 Coolhurst Road N8
12 Fairfield Road N8
11 Park Avenue North N8
69 Gloucester Crescent NW1
70 Gloucester Crescent NW1
The Holme NW1
4 Park Village East (Tower Lodge Gardens) NW1
Royal College of Physicians' Medicinal Garden NW1
18 Dorchester Gardens NW11
48 Erskine Hill NW11
121 Erskine Hill NW11
74 Willifield Way NW11
86 Willifield Way NW11
27 Menelik Road NW2
72 Tanfield Avenue NW2
93 Tanfield Avenue NW2
208 Walm Lane, The Garden Flat NW2
Fenton House NW3
Marie Curie Hospice, Hampstead NW3
27 Nassington Road NW3
Tudor Herbalist Garden NW3
Highwood Ash NW7

S, SE and SW London

Garden Barge Square at Downings Roads Moorings SE1
The Garden Museum SE1
Lambeth Palace SE1
41 Southbrook Road SE12
Blackheath Gardens SE13
Choumert Square SE15
Lyndhurst Square Group SE15
85 Calton Avenue SE21
122 Court Lane SE21
125 Court Lane SE21
Dulwich Village Two Gardens SE21
4 Cornflower Terrace SE22
16 Landells Road SE22
174 Peckham Rye SE22
4 Piermont Green SE22
Forest Hill Gardens Group SE23
5 Burbage Road SE24
South London Botanical Institute SE24
Stoney Hill House SE26
33 Weyman Road SE3
35 Camberwell Grove SE5
Camberwell Grove Gardens SE5
24 Grove Park SE5
Cadogan Place South Garden SW1
Eaton Square Garden SW1
Eccleston Square SW1
61 Arthur Road SW19
97 Arthur Road SW19
Brixton Water Lane Gardens SW2
31 Trelawn Road SW2
11 Ernle Road SW20
Paddock Allotments & Leisure Gardens SW20
Chelsea Physic Garden SW3
51 The Chase SW4
2 Littlebury Road SW4
Royal Trinity Hospice SW4
The Hurlingham Club SW6

W London

Rooftopvegplot W1
57 St Quintin Avenue W10
Arundel & Elgin Gardens W11
Arundel & Ladbroke Gardens W11
12 Lansdowne Road W11
49 Loftus Road W12
Acacia House W3
Capel Manor College, Gunnersbury Park Campus W3
41 Mill Hill Road W3
65 Mill Hill Road W3
Zen Garden at Japanese Temple W3
Chiswick Mall Gardens W4
Park Road Gardens W4
All Seasons W5
38 York Road W5
57 Prebend Gardens W6
27 St Peters Square W6
1 York Close W7
Edwardes Square W8
7 Upper Phillimore Gardens W8

Outer London postcodes

153 Portland Road BR1
81 Baston Road BR2
40 Greenways BR3
12 Overbrae BR3
White Cottage BR5
40 Croham Manor Road CR2
Whitgift School CR2
45 Cotswold Way EN2
Oak Farm/Homestead EN2
West Lodge Park EN4
190 Barnet Road EN5
57 King Edward Road EN5
26 Normandy Avenue EN5
31 Arlington Drive HA4
4 Manningtree Road HA4
12 Haywood Close HA5
470 Pinner Road HA5
4 Ormonde Road HA6
254 Ashurst Drive IG6
74 Glengall Road IG8
20 Goldhaze Close IG8
Hurst House IG8
7 Woodbines Avenue KT1
9 Imber Park Road KT10
The Watergardens KT2
The Circle Garden KT3
Hampton Court Palace KT8
61 Wolsey Road KT8
18 Pettits Boulevard RM1
22 Shirley Avenue SM1
40 The Crescent SM2
7 St George's Road TW1
Ormeley Lodge TW10
Petersham House TW10
Stokes House TW10
Hampton Hill Gardens TW12
20 Beechwood Avenue TW9
Kew Green Gardens TW9
Trumpeters House & Sarah's Garden TW9
29 West Park Road TW9
31 West Park Road TW9
Dragon's Dream, Grove Lane UB8
Church Gardens UB9

OPENING DATES

All entries subject to change. For latest information check **www.ngs.org.uk**

February

Snowdrop Festival

Sunday 18th
7 The Grove, N6

March

Sunday 18th
5 Burbage Road, SE24

April

Saturday 7th
Cadogan Place South Garden, SW1

Sunday 8th
7 The Grove, N6
Royal Trinity Hospice, SW4

Sunday 15th
4 Canonbury Place, N1

Thursday 19th
◆ Hampton Court Palace, KT8

Friday 20th
◆ Chelsea Physic Garden, SW3

Sunday 22nd
51 The Chase, SW4
Edwardes Square, W8
Petersham House, TW10
South London Botanical Institute, SE24
7 Upper Phillimore Gardens, W8

Thursday 26th
51 The Chase, SW4

Saturday 28th
11 Ernle Road, SW20

Sunday 29th
11 Ernle Road, SW20
5 St Regis Close, N10

May

Sunday 6th
Eaton Square Garden, SW1W
Eccleston Square, SW1
27 St Peters Square, W6

Monday 7th
Hurst House, IG8
King Henry's Walk Garden, N1

Thursday 10th
12 Lansdowne Road, W11

Saturday 12th
The Circle Garden, KT3

Sunday 13th
NEW 13 College Cross, N1
NEW 40 Croham Manor Road, CR2
9 Furlong Road, N7
NEW 74 Glengall Road, IG8
Highwood Ash, NW7
NEW 2 Lonsdale Square, N1
Malvern Terrace Gardens, N1
Oak Farm/Homestead, EN2
4 Ormonde Road, HA6
Princes Avenue Gardens, N10
Southwood Lodge, N6
The Watergardens, KT2
West Lodge Park, EN4

Saturday 19th
The Circle Garden, KT3
The Hurlingham Club, SW6

Sunday 20th
Arundel & Elgin Gardens, W11
Arundel & Ladbroke Gardens, W11
5 Burbage Road, SE24
Canonbury House, N1
NEW 19 Coolhurst Road, N8
Diespeker Wharf, N1
55 Dukes Avenue, N10
NEW 12 Fairfield Road, N8
Forest Hill Gardens Group, SE23
Garden Barge Square at Downings Roads Moorings, SE1
Lower Clapton Gardens, E5
3 The Park N6, N6
Richard House Children's Hospice, E16
26 Ringwood Avenue, N2
Royal Trinity Hospice, SW4
19 St Peter's Street, N1
Stoney Hill House, SE26
Whitgift School, CR2
33 Wood Vale, N10

Monday 21st
Lambeth Palace, SE1

Friday 25th
Chiswick Mall Gardens, W4

Saturday 26th
Hampton Hill Gardens, TW12
4 Park Village East (Tower Lodge Gardens), NW1

Sunday 27th
36 Ashley Road, N19
190 Barnet Road, EN5
Chiswick Mall Gardens, W4
NEW Dragon's Dream, Grove Lane, UB8
Hampton Hill Gardens, TW12
Kew Green Gardens, TW9
NEW 16 Landells Road, SE22
12 Western Road, E13

Monday 28th
36 Ashley Road, N19
NEW 79 Royston Avenue, E4

June

Festival Weekend

Saturday 2nd
Acacia House, W3
7 St George's Road, TW1
Zen Garden at Japanese Temple, W3

Sunday 3rd
Acacia House, W3
37 Alwyne Road, N1
31 Arlington Drive, HA4
Barnsbury Group, N1
85 Calton Avenue, SE21
35 Camberwell Grove, SE5
Choumert Square, SE15
NEW 45 Cotswold Way, EN2
48 Erskine Hill, NW11
70 Gloucester Crescent, NW1
77 Handsworth Road, N17
31 Hendon Avenue, N3
159 Higham Road, N17
Kew Green Gardens, TW9
Mapledene Gardens, E8
4 Park Village East (Tower Lodge Gardens), NW1
Royal College of Physicians' Medicinal Garden, NW1
Stokes House, TW10
1 Wades Grove, N21
208 Walm Lane, The Garden Flat, NW2
29 West Park Road, TW9
31 West Park Road, TW9
Zen Garden at Japanese Temple, W3

Tuesday 5th
The Charterhouse, EC1

Saturday 9th
Capel Manor College, Gunnersbury Park Campus, W3
41 Southbrook Road, SE12

Sunday 10th
NEW Brixton Water Lane Gardens, SW2
5 Brodie Road, E4
4 Cornflower Terrace, SE22
Dulwich Village Two Gardens, SE21
7 The Grove, N6
12 Haywood Close, HA5
53 Manor Road, N16
27 Nassington Road, NW3
174 Peckham Rye, SE22
4 Piermont Green, SE22
41 Southbrook Road, SE12
NEW 31 Trelawn Road, SW2
Trumpeters House & Sarah's Garden, TW9

White Cottage, BR5
61 Wolsey Road, KT8

Tuesday 12th
◆ Fenton House, NW3

Thursday 14th
49 Loftus Road, W12

Saturday 16th
Paddock Allotments & Leisure Gardens, SW20
Spitalfields Gardens, E1

Sunday 17th
Arlington Square Gardens, N1
61 Arthur Road, SW19
97 Arthur Road, SW19
122 Court Lane, SE21
125 Court Lane, SE21
De Beauvoir Gardens, N1
11 Ernle Road, SW20
1a Hungerford Road, N7
60 & 62 Hungerford Road, N7
Lyndhurst Square Group, SE15
Ormeley Lodge, TW10
18 Park Crescent, N3
5 St Regis Close, N10
72 Tanfield Avenue, NW2
21 Woodland Rise, N10
NEW 10 York Road

Monday 18th
Lambeth Palace, SE1

Tuesday 19th
The Inner and Middle Temple Gardens, EC4

Saturday 23rd
18 Pettits Boulevard, RM1
Zen Garden at Japanese Temple, W3

Sunday 24th
Blackheath Gardens, SE13
NEW 5 Blackthorn Av, Apartment 5, N7
NEW 40 The Crescent, SM2
41 Ecclesbourne Road, N1
NEW 58 Halliford Street, N!
33 Huddleston Road, N7
9 Imber Park Road, KT10
84 Lavender Grove, E8
Marie Curie Hospice, Hampstead, NW3
11 Park Avenue North, N8
NEW Park Road Gardens, W4
18 Pettits Boulevard, RM1
NEW 22 Shirley Avenue, SM1
NEW 33 Weyman Road, SE3
74 Willifield Way, NW11
Zen Garden at Japanese Temple, W3

Friday 29th
5 Northampton Park, N1

Saturday 30th
The Holme, NW1
5 Northampton Park, N1
NEW Victoria Lodge, E18
1 York Close, W7

July

Sunday 1st
NEW 18 Dorchester Gardens, NW11
NEW 121 Erskine Hill, NW11
NEW 40 Greenways, BR3
The Holme, NW1
16 Maida Way, E4
27 Menelik Road, NW2
26 Normandy Avenue, EN5
12 Overbrae, BR3
Railway Cottages, N22
1 York Close, W7

Friday 6th
41 Mill Hill Road, W3
65 Mill Hill Road, W3

Saturday 7th
21 Gospatrick Road, N17

Sunday 8th
20 Beechwood Avenue, TW9
Camberwell Grove Gardens, SE5
46 Cheyne Avenue, E18
57 St Quintin Avenue, W10
NEW Tudor Herbalist Garden, NW3

Thursday 12th
◆ Hampton Court Palace, KT8

Saturday 14th
NEW Rooftopvegplot, W1

Sunday 15th
190 Barnet Road, EN5
12 Bushberry Road, E9
NEW 57 King Edward Road, EN5
NEW 46 Ollerton Road, N11
NEW Rooftopvegplot, W1
NEW 24 Twyford Avenue, N2
7 Woodbines Avenue, KT1

Sunday 22nd
NEW 81 Baston Road, BR2
42 Latimer Road, E7
NEW 46 Ollerton Road, N11
57 St Quintin Avenue, W10
5 St Regis Close, N10
86 Willifield Way, NW11
38 York Road, W5

Saturday 28th
All Seasons, W5

Sunday 29th
All Seasons, W5
254 Ashurst Drive, IG6
79 Church Lane, N2
20 Goldhaze Close, IG8
37 Harold Road, E11
4 Manningtree Road, HA4
93 Tanfield Avenue, NW2

August

Wednesday 1st
57 Prebend Gardens, W6

Saturday 4th
The Holme, NW1
57 Prebend Gardens, W6

Sunday 5th
70 Gloucester Crescent, NW1
20 Goldhaze Close, IG8
The Holme, NW1
41 Mill Hill Road, W3
65 Mill Hill Road, W3
153 Portland Road, BR1
87 St Johns Road, E17
10 Woodside Avenue, N6

Friday 17th
NEW 45 Cotswold Way, EN2

Sunday 19th
5 Brodie Road, E4
NEW 51 Tweedmouth Road, E13

Monday 27th
NEW Church Gardens, UB9
Gordon Road Allotments, N3

September

Sunday 2nd
190 Barnet Road, EN5
Golf Course Allotments, N11
24 Grove Park, SE5
Royal Trinity Hospice, SW4

Saturday 8th
◆ The Garden Museum, SE1

Sunday 9th
2 Littlebury Road, SW4
53 Manor Road, N16

Sunday 16th
15 Norcott Road, N16
470 Pinner Road, HA5

Sunday 30th
23 Imperial Road, N22

October

Sunday 14th
The Watergardens, KT2

Sunday 21st
West Lodge Park, EN4

By Arrangement

31 Arlington Drive, HA4
Arundel & Elgin Gardens, W11
Arundel & Ladbroke Gardens, W11
36 Ashley Road, N19
254 Ashurst Drive, IG6
190 Barnet Road, EN5
1 Battlebridge Court, Barnsbury Group, N1
20 Beechwood Avenue, TW9
5 Burbage Road, SE24
Cadogan Place South Garden, SW1
35 Camberwell Grove, SE5
2 Dorset Road, Railway Cottages, N22
48 Erskine Hill, NW11
70 Gloucester Crescent, NW1
69 Gloucester Crescent,

NW1
21 Gospatrick Road, N17
17 Greenstone Mews, E11
7 The Grove, N6
12 Haywood Close, HA5
27 Horniman Drive, Forest Hill Gardens Group, SE23
1a Hungerford Road, N7
9 Imber Park Road, KT10
84 Lavender Grove, E8
49 Loftus Road, W12
53 Mapledene Road, Mapledene Gardens, E8
27 Menelik Road, NW2
41 Mill Hill Road, W3
65 Mill Hill Road, W3
18 Park Crescent, N3
3 The Park N6, N6
4 Park Village East (Tower Lodge Gardens), NW1
Petersham House, TW10
Royal College of Physicians' Medicinal Garden, NW1
NEW 79 Royston Avenue, E4
7 St George's Road, TW1
27 St Peters Square, W6
57 St Quintin Avenue, W10
5 St Regis Close, N10
41 Southbrook Road, SE12
Southwood Lodge, N6
Stokes House, TW10
72 Tanfield Avenue, NW2
93 Tanfield Avenue, NW2
West Lodge Park, EN4
12 Western Road, E13
White Cottage, BR5
74 Willifield Way, NW11
86 Willifield Way, NW11
61 Wolsey Road, KT8
33 Wood Vale, N10

THE GARDENS

1 ACACIA HOUSE, W3

Centre Avenue, Acton, London, W3 7JY. Lucy Maxwell. *Adjoining Acton Park. Centre Ave is off Uxbridge Rd directly opp Total Garage, KwikFit & Access SelfStorage. Far end of Centre Ave on R by park gate. Acton Central 4mins walk across park. 207, 266 & 70 bus at end of rd.* **Evening opening Sat 2 June (6-8.30). Adm £6, chd free. Wine. Sun 3 June (2-5). Adm £5, chd free. Home-made teas.**

Hidden oasis in Acton. Once the home of Sean Connery, this densely planted walled cottage garden redesigned in 2015 now combines clipped box hedges, a wisteria covered pergola and a series of brick pathways leading you around the garden. Bordered by Acton Park on two sides.

2 ALL SEASONS, W5

97 Grange Road, Ealing, W5 3PH. Dr Benjamin & Mrs Maria Royappa. *Tube: Ealing Broadway/ South Ealing/Ealing Common: 10-15 mins walk.* **Sat 28 July (1-6); Sun 29 July (12.30-6). Adm £3.50, chd free. Home-made teas.**

Garden designed, built and planted by owners, with new interesting planting, features incl ponds, pergolas, Japanese gardens, tropical house for orchids, exotics and aviaries. Several recycled features, composting and rain water harvesting, orchard, kiwi, grape vines, architectural and unusual plants incl ferns, bamboos, conifers and cacti. Partial wheelchair access.

3 37 ALWYNE ROAD, N1

London, N1 2HW. Mr & Mrs J Lambert. *Buses: 38, 56, 73, 341 on Essex Rd; 4, 19, 30, 43 on Upper St, alight at Town Hall; 271 on Canonbury Rd, A1. Tube: Highbury & Islington.* **Sun 3 June (2-5). Adm £4, chd free. Home-made teas.** Donation to The Friends of the Rose Bowl.

The New River curves around the garden, freeing it from the constraints of the usual London rectangle and allowing differing degrees of formality - roses along the river, topiary, a secluded spot where the life of the river is part of the charm. Visitors return to see what's new and to enjoy the spectacular array of very good home-made cakes. Shelter if it rains. Wheelchair access only with own assistant for 3 shallow entrance steps.

4 31 ARLINGTON DRIVE, HA4

Ruislip, HA4 7RJ. John & Yasuko O'Gorman, johnogorman@outlook.com. *Tube: Ruislip. Then bus H13 to Arlington Drive, or 15 mins walk up Bury St. Arlington Drive is opp Millar & Carter Steakhouse on Bury St.* **Sun 3 June (2-5). Adm £3.50, chd free. Home-made teas. Visits also by arrangement June to Aug groups of up to 20.**

Cottage garden at heart with a wonderful oriental influence. Traditional cottage garden favourites have been combined with Japanese plants - a reflection of Yasuko's passion for plants and trees of her native Japan. Acers, paeonies, rhododendrons and flowering cherries underplanted with hostas, ferns and hellebores, create a lush exotic scheme. Emphasis on structure and texture. Featured in House Beautiful & Garden Answers.

GROUP OPENING

5 ARLINGTON SQUARE GARDENS, N1

London, N1 7DP. www.arlingtonassociation.org.uk. *South Islington. Off New North Rd via Arlington Ave or Linton St. Buses: 21, 76, 141, 271.* **Sun 17 June (2-5.30). Combined adm £5, chd free. Home-made teas at St James' Vicarage, 1A Arlington Square.**

26 ARLINGTON AVENUE
Thomas Blaikie.

25 ARLINGTON SQUARE
Michael Foley.

30 ARLINGTON SQUARE
James & Maria Hewson.

ST JAMES' VICARAGE, 1A ARLINGTON SQUARE
John & Maria Burniston.

Behind the early Victorian facades of Arlington Square and Arlington Avenue are 4 contrasting town gardens; 3 plantsmen's gardens and a delightful spacious garden with impressive herbaceous border created over the last few years. The group reflects the diverse tastes and interests of each garden owner who have got to know each other through the community gardening of Arlington Square. It is hard to believe you are minutes from the bustle of the City of London. Live music in the vicarage garden.

6 61 ARTHUR ROAD, SW19

Wimbledon, SW19 7DN. Daniela McBride. *Tube: Wimbledon Park, then 8 mins walk. Mainline: Wimbledon, 18 mins walk.* **Sun 17 June (2-6). Adm £4, chd free. Home-made teas. Also open 97 Arthur Road.**

This steeply sloping garden comprises woodland walks, filled with flowering shrubs and ferns. In early summer the focus is the many roses grown around the garden, then later the autumn colour is provided by trees and shrubs. Partial wheelchair access to top lawn and terrace only, steep slopes elsewhere.

7 97 ARTHUR ROAD, SW19

Wimbledon, SW19 7DP. Tony & Bella Covill. *Wimbledon Park tube, then 200yds up hill on R.* **Sun 17 June (2-6). Adm £5, chd free. Light refreshments. Also open 61 Arthur Road.**

⅓ acre garden of an Edwardian house. Garden established for more than 20yrs and constantly evolving with a large variety of plants and shrubs. It has grown up around several lawns with pond and fountains. Abundance of wildlife and a bird haven. A beautiful place with much colour, foliage and texture.

8 ARUNDEL & ELGIN GARDENS, W11

Kensington Park Road, Notting Hill, W11 2JD. Residents of Arundel Gardens & Elgin Crescent, 07850135766, fbassociates@btopenworld.com, www.arundelandelgingardens.org. *Entrance opposite 174 Kensington Park Road. Nearest tube within walking distance: Ladbroke Grove (3mins) or Notting Hill (8mins). Buses: 52, 452, 23, 228 all stop opposite garden entrance.* **Sun 20 May (2-5.30). Adm £5, chd free. Home-made teas. Also open Arundel & Ladbroke Gardens W11. Visits also by arrangement in June for groups up to 20 max.**

A friendly and informal garden square with mature and rare trees, plants and shrubs laid out according to the original Victorian design of 1862, one of the best preserved gardens of the Ladbroke estate. The central hedged garden area is an oasis of tranquillity with extensive and colourful herbaceous borders. The garden incl several topiary hedges, a rare Mulberry tree, a pergola and benches from which the vistas can be enjoyed. Gardeners Chris Jelston & Anna Park. Play areas for young children.

♿ ☕

9 ARUNDEL & LADBROKE GARDENS, W11

Kensington Park Road, Notting Hill, W11 2EP. Arundel & Ladbroke Gardens Committee, 07941 296375 (texts preferred), susan.lynn1@ntlworld.com, www.arundelladbrokegardens.co.uk. *Entrance on Kensington Park Rd, between Ladbroke & Arundel Gardens. Tube: Notting Hill Gate or Ladbroke Grove. Buses: 23, 52, 228, 452. Alight at stop for Portobello Market/Arundel Gardens.* **Sun 20 May (1.30-6). Adm £5, chd free. Home-made teas. Also open Arundel & Elgin Gardens W11. Visits also by arrangement Mar to Oct, groups welcome.**

This private communal garden is one of the few that retains its mid Victorian design. It has evolved into a woodland garden, with year-round colour and interest, particularly in spring with rhododendrons, camellias, foreign exotics and glades of spring bulbs. Live music on the lawn during tea. Playground for small children. A few steps and gravel paths to negotiate.

♿ 🐕 ☕

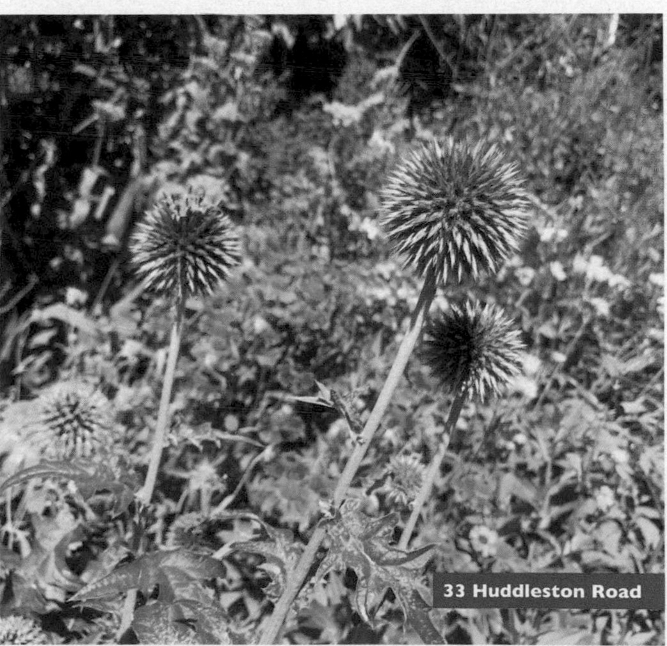

33 Huddleston Road

10 36 ASHLEY ROAD, N19

London, N19 3AF. Alan Swann & Ahmed Farooqui, 07506 128638, swann.alan@googlemail.com. *Between Stroud Green & Crouch End. Underground: Archway or Finsbury Park. Overground: Crouch Hill. Buses: 210 or 41 from Archway to Hornsey Rise. W7 from Finsbury Park to Heathville Road. Car: Free parking in Ashley Road at weekends.* **Sun 27, Mon 28 May (2-6). Adm £3.50, chd free. Cream teas. Visits also by arrangement May to Aug.**

A lush town garden rich in textures, colour and forms. At its best in late spring as Japanese maple cultivars display great variety of shape and colour whilst ferns unfurl fresh, vibrant fronds over a tumbling stream and alpines and clematis burst into flower on the rockeries and pergola. The garden has a number of micro habitats incl. ferneries, a bog garden, stream and pond plantings, rockeries, alpines and shade plantings. Young ferns and plants propagated from specimens in the garden for sale. Cream teas for sale. Indoor pop-up cafe with views over the garden when wet. The garden is regularly featured in the Ham and High. Cited as one of Penny Snell's, former chair of NGS, most favourite gardens in the Daily Telegraph. It was also featured in a photo essay in Naturaleza, the number 1 garden magazine in Brazil.

The National Garden Scheme is committed to helping unpaid carers

11 254 ASHURST DRIVE, IG6

Barkingside, IG6 1EW. Maureen Keating, 0208 550 0934. *2m S of Chigwell. Nearest tube: Barkingside on Central Line approx 8 mins walk. Bus: 150 stops outside Tesco's on Cranbrook Rd. go round right side of Tescos car park. keep right. alleyway leads to Ashurst Drive.* **Sun 29 July (1-5). Adm £3.50, chd free. Home-made teas. Visits also by arrangement June to Aug.**

Bird friendly colour filled town garden with interesting nooks and crannies each telling a story. Contains 7 water features, 6 seating areas, waterfall, pond and stream, miniature railway, model village and vibrant planting all in 40 ft square area! Regret, garden unsuitable for children.

12 190 BARNET ROAD, EN5

Arkley, Barnet, EN5 3LF. Hilde & Lionel Wainstein, 020 8441 4041, hildewainstein@hotmail.co.uk. *1m S of A1, 2m N of High Barnet tube. Garden is located on corner of A411 Barnet Rd & Meadowbanks cul-de-sac. Nearest tube: High Barnet, then 107 bus, Glebe Lane stop. Plenty of unrestricted roadside parking.* **Sun 27 May, Sun 15 July, Sun 2 Sept (2-6). Adm £4, chd free. Home-made teas. Visits also by arrangement Apr to Sept.**

Garden designer's walled garden, approx 90ft x 36ft. Modern, asymmetric design thickly planted in flowing, natural drifts around trees, shrubs and central pond; changing array of interesting containers, recycled objects and sculptures. Copper trellis divides the space into contrasting areas. The garden continues to evolve as planted areas are expanded. We now have a tin can sculpture garden. Selection of home-made cakes worthy of Mary Berry! Favourite at last opening was raspberry and white chocolate layer cake. Gluten free cakes also available. Wide range of interesting plants for sale, all propagated from the garden. Single steps within garden.

NPC

GROUP OPENING

13 BARNSBURY GROUP, N1

Islington, N1 1DB. *Barnsbury, London N1. Tube: King's Cross, Caledonian Rd or Angel. Overground: Caledonian Rd & Barnsbury. Buses: 17, 91, 259 to Caledonian Rd.* **Sun 3 June (2-6). Combined adm £7, chd free. Home-made teas at 57 Huntingdon Street N1 1BX.**

◆ BARNSBURY WOOD
London Borough of Islington, ecologycentre@islington.gov.uk.

1 BATTLEBRIDGE COURT
Mike Jackson, michaeljackson215@me.com. **Visits also by arrangement Mar to Sept for groups of 10 max.**

44 HEMINGFORD ROAD
Peter Willis & Haremi Kudo.

57 HUNTINGDON STREET
Julian Williams.

Walk through Islington's historic Georgian squares and terraces to these four contrasting spaces, all within walking distance of the vibrant development at King's Cross. Barnsbury Wood is London's smallest nature reserve and Islington's hidden secret, a tranquil oasis of wild flowers and massive trees just minutes from Caledonian Road. The three gardens have extensive collections of unusual plants; 57 Huntingdon St is a secluded garden room - an understorey of silver birch and hazel shades ferns, native perennials and grasses and a container pond. 44 Hemingford Road is a small, dense composition of trees (some unusual), shrubs, perennials and lawns – and a small pond. Battlebridge Court is a plantsman's small garden making optimum use of sun and shade beside the canal basin, together with four contrasting beds in front of the block of flats. All the gardens have evolved over many years, to incl plants to suit their particular growing conditions, and show what can be achieved while surmounting the difficulties of dry walls and shade.

14 NEW 81 BASTON ROAD, BR2

Baston Road, Hayes, Bromley, BR2 7BS. Mrs Jill Wimble. *On B265, 2m S of Bromley. 10 mins walk from Hayes, Kent Rail station, 146 & 353 bus-stop outside property. Opp Hayes Secondary School. Free on-site parking.* **Sun 22 July (2-5.30). Adm £3.50, chd free. Home-made teas.**

A generous ½ acre plot converted by the owners into a colourful, plant-filled garden, with many features of interest. A gravel garden influenced in style by Beth Chatto greets visitors. Detailed paving and brick work give a structure to the garden and divide areas of interest incl exotics, vegetable garden, water features and fabulous pebble mosaic. Mainly level with grass and paved paths. A few steps and slopes.

15 20 BEECHWOOD AVENUE, TW9

Kew, Richmond, TW9 4DE. Dr Laura de Beden, 02083921969, lauradebeden@hotmail.com, www.lauradebeden.co.uk. *Within walking distance of Kew Gardens Tube Station on North side.* **Evening opening Sun 8 July (5-7). Adm £5.50, chd free. Wine. Visits also by arrangement in July for groups of 10 max.**

Delightful town garden minutes away from Royal Botanic Gardens and Kew Retail Park. Joseph Campbell's words 'Follow your Bliss' guided the creation of this place by the designer owner. A decidedly minimalist layout offsets exquisite favourite plant combinations. Writing shed holds pride of place as main idea production centre. Topiary, pots, sculpture, surprises and good humour are all on offer.

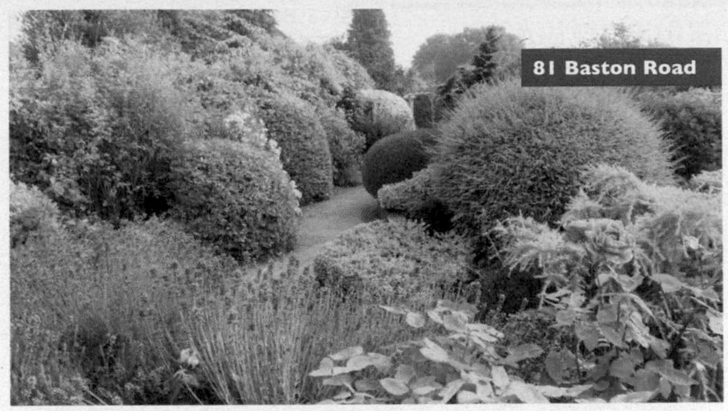

81 Baston Road

GROUP OPENING

16 BLACKHEATH GARDENS, SE13

Lewisham, London, SE13 7EA. *Gardens sit between Lewisham & Blackheath stns. DLR: Buses 54, 89, 108, 122, 178, 261, 321, 621 Free parking on Sundays but space limited.* **Sun 24 June (2-5.30). Combined adm £6, chd free. Home-made teas at Lee Rd and Michael's Close. Also open 33 Weyman Road.**

28 GRANVILLE PARK
Joanna Herald, www.joannaherald.com.
D

49 LEE ROAD
Jane Glynn & Colin Kingsnorth.

1 MICHAEL'S CLOSE
Jeffrey Warren.

Set among the airy hills of Blackheath are 3 gardens ranging from small to amazingly large, each with its own idiosyncratic style. All designed to be lived in and enjoyed. In Michael's Close, a magnificent rambling rector rose blankets the tall hawthorn hedge backing on a small enclosed garden wrapped round three sides of a modern flat on with densely planted borders defined by paths, steps and low retaining walls. A garden designer's 100ft x 35ft relaxing and softly contoured elegant family garden in Granville Park offers a wildlife friendly pool garden; herbaceous and shrubs and a gravel garden. A sunken terrace with pots by the house provides a suntrap seating area. The third garden in Lee Road is an substantial spacious oasis of calm in the city. Benches are set beneath rambling roses overlooking generous formal lawns with flowerbeds. Winding paths through silver birches and grasses reveal a treehouse clad with roses and clematis. Serious vegetable growing goes on here too. Plants at Granville Park. Lee Road and Michael's Close.

17 NEW 5 BLACKTHORN AV, APARTMENT 5, N7

London, N7 8AQ. Juan Carlos Cure Hazzi. *Barnsbury. 5 min walk from Highbury & Islington Stn. Building is on south side of Arundel Sq.* **Sun 24 June (11-5). Adm £5, chd free. Light refreshments. Pre-booking essential, please phone 01483 211535 to book.**

Small patio garden with lush tropical, sub-tropical and temperate plants. Garden was featured on the cover of the BBC Gardeners' World magazine and was a nationwide finalist in the Small Space category competition. This garden has a beautiful connection with the house and hasn't wasted an inch of space. It has plenty of colour, texture and year-round interest. Featured in BBC Gardeners' World magazine and on YouTube.

GROUP OPENING

18 NEW BRIXTON WATER LANE GARDENS, SW2

Brixton, London, SW2 1QB. *Tube: Brixton. Mainline: Herne Hill, both 10 mins. Buses: 3, 37, 196 or 2, 415, 432 along Tulse Hill.* **Sun 10 June (2-5.30). Combined adm £5, chd free. Home-made teas. Also open 31 Trelawn Road.**

NEW 60 BRIXTON WATER LANE

Caddy & Chris Sitwell.

NEW 62 BRIXTON WATER LANE

Daisy Garnett & Nicholas Pearson.

Two 90ft gardens backing onto Brockwell Park with original apple trees from the old orchard. No 60 has a large garden with floral borders and a mature wisteria covering the house. Strong colour comes from laburnum and lilac under which teas will be served. Number 62 is a country garden with exuberant borders of soft colours, a productive greenhouse and a mass of pots on the terrace. Plenty of colour from old fashioned roses, peonies and other perennials.

19 5 BRODIE ROAD, E4

Chingford, London, E4 7HF. Mr & Mrs N Booth. *N E London. From Chingford train station take any bus to Chingford Green (Co-op), turn L at Prezzo restaurant, 2nd R (Scholars Rd), then 1st L to Brodie Road.* **Sun 10 June, Sun 19 Aug (2-5). Adm £3.50, chd free. Light refreshments.**

An unconventional suburban garden. Herbaceous borders, trellises, arches and secret arbour overflow with flowers loved by bees and butterflies. Masses of colour throughout spring and summer. New and unusual plantings every year to add interest and create new vistas. A visual feast for garden enthusiasts. Featured in 'Amateur Gardening'.

20 5 BURBAGE ROAD, SE24

Herne Hill, SE24 9HJ. Crawford & Rosemary Lindsay, 020 7274 5610, rl@rosemarylindsay.com, www.rosemarylindsay.com. *Nr junction with Half Moon Lane. Herne Hill & N Dulwich mainline stns, 5 mins walk. Buses: 3, 37, 40, 68, 196, 468.* **Sun 18 Mar (2-5). Adm £3.50, chd free. Sun 20 May (2-5). Adm £4, chd free. Home-made teas. (May date only). Visits also by arrangement Mar to July.**

The much photographed garden of a member of The Society of Botanical Artists. 150ft x 40ft with large and varied range of plants. Herb garden, herbaceous borders for sun and shade, climbing plants, pots, terraces, lawns. Gravel areas to reduce watering. Immaculate topiary. A garden for all seasons. See our website for what the papers say. Incl in The London Garden Book A-Z.

21 12 BUSHBERRY ROAD, E9

Hackney, E9 5SX. Molly St Hilaire. *Overground stn: Homerton, then 5 mins walk. Buses: 26, 30, 488, alight last stop in Cassland Rd.* **Sun 15 July (2-6). Adm £3, chd free. Home-made teas.**

Petite courtyard garden with water feature. Rambling roses, jasmine, vine and clematis cover the overarching pergola. Small but beautifully formed. A pure joy to see.

22 CADOGAN PLACE SOUTH GARDEN, SW1

Sloane Street, Chelsea, SW1X 9PE. The Cadogan Estate, 07890 452992, Ric.Glenn@cadogan.co.uk. *Entrance to garden opp 97 Sloane St.* **Sat 7 Apr (10-4). Adm £4, chd free. Visits also by arrangement. Tours with head gardener by request weekdays only between 8am-4pm.**

Many surprises and unusual trees and shrubs are hidden behind the railings of this large London square. The first square to be developed by architect Henry Holland for Lord Cadogan at the end of C18, it was then called the London Botanic Garden. Mulberry trees planted for silk production at end of C17. Cherry trees, magnolias and bulbs are outstanding in spring, when the fern garden is unfurling. Award winning Hans Sloane Garden exhibited at the Chelsea Flower Show. Pond. Spring walk on East side of garden. Feel free to bring a picnic to enjoy in the garden.

23 85 CALTON AVENUE, SE21

Dulwich, London, SE21 7DF. Ian & Frances Twinn. *From Dulwich Village turn into Calton Av past St Barnabas Church opp Alleyn's School playing fields. From East Dulwich (37 bus): East Dulwich Grove, turn into Townley Rd. Calton Av next R.* **Sun 3 June (2-5.30). Adm £3.50, chd free. Home-made teas.**

A labour of love! Lovers of roses and peonies will be entranced by this immaculate garden that balances a spacious serpentine lawn with a choice of rooms – offering a quiet spot for contemplation against elegant found masonry walls and corners perfect for tea. Bold blocks of planting fill the borders, persicarias are a favourite.

24 35 CAMBERWELL GROVE, SE5

London, SE5 8JA. Lynette Hemmant & Juri Gabriel, 020 7703 6186, juri@jurigabriel.com. *Backing onto St Giles Church, Camberwell Church St. From Camberwell Green go down Camberwell Church St. Turn R into Camberwell Grove.* **Sun 3 June (12-6.30). Adm £3.50, chd free. Light refreshments. Also open Choumert Square. Visits also by arrangement June to Sept min charge £70. Groups 30 max.** Donation to St Giles Church.

Plant packed 120ft x 20ft garden with charming backdrop of St Giles Church. Evolved over 30yrs into a romantic country style garden brimming with colour and overflowing with pots. In June, spectacular roses stretch the full length of the garden, both on the artist's studio and festooning an old iron staircase. Artist's studio open. Lynette has painted the garden obsessively for the past 20yrs; see her (lynettehemmant.com) and NGS websites.

GROUP OPENING

25 CAMBERWELL GROVE GARDENS, SE5

Camberwell, SE5 8JE. *10 mins from Denmark Hill mainline & overgound stn. Buses: 12, 36, 68, 148, 171, 176, 185, 436. Entrance through garden rooms at rear.* **Sun 8 July (2-6). Combined adm £5, chd free. Home-made teas.**

81 CAMBERWELL GROVE
Jane & Alex Maitland Hudson.

83 CAMBERWELL GROVE
Robert Hirschhorn & John Hall.

This year these neighbouring walled gardens behind C18 houses in this beautiful tree lined street will be opening in July. At No.81 a tall Trachycarpus Palm and a magnolia grandiflora shade York stone paving and borders filled with herbaceous perennials and shade loving ground cover. There is a pond and bog garden. Pots of all sizes line the steps to the kitchen door and the terrace outside the garden room and greenhouse. No. 83 is a mature beautifully designed plant lovers' garden. Abundant unusual planting within a structure of box hedging provides varied and interesting areas of peace and privacy. As trees mature the nature of the garden is changing, and more shade tolerant perennials are being introduced. Contemporary garden room, gravel and York stone paths and seating areas, calming pool and lovely views of parish church. Delicious home-made cakes and tea at 81 and sparkling wine at 83.

26 CANONBURY HOUSE, N1

Canonbury Place, London, N1 2NQ. Mr & Mrs Gavin Ralston. *Junction of Canonbury Place & Alwyne Villas, next to Canonbury Tower. Tube & Overground: Highbury & Islington. Buses to Canonbury Sq. Entrance by side gate opp 1 Canonbury Place.* **Sun 20 May (2-5.30). Adm £4, chd free. Home-made teas.**

Large secluded garden next to historic Canonbury Tower and 500yr old mulberry. Magnificent mature trees, woodland planting, clipped box lining lawn. Sheltered herbaceous border. Fountain and well stocked pond; hidden children's play area. Wheelchair entry via shallow ramp to patio area from which garden can be viewed.

27 4 CANONBURY PLACE, N1

London, N1 2NQ. Mr & Mrs Jeffrey Tobias. *Highbury & Islington Tube & Overground. Buses: 271 to Canonbury Square. Located in old part of Canonbury Place, off Alwyne Villas, in a cul de sac.* **Sun 15 Apr (2-5.30). Adm £3.50, chd free. Home-made teas.**

A paved, 100ft garden behind a 1780 house. Spectacular mature trees enclosed in a walled garden. Mostly pots and also interesting shrubs and climbers. Daffodlils, tulips and bluebells abound for this springtime opening. Artisan pastries and sourdough bread as supplied to Fortnum & Mason.

28 CAPEL MANOR COLLEGE, GUNNERSBURY PARK CAMPUS, W3

The Walled Garden, Gunnersbury Park, Popes Lane, Ealing, London, W3 8LQ. Sarah Neophytou, www.capel.ac.uk/gunnersbury-park-centre.html. *Entering Popes Lane from the A406, park is on the L. Entrance to free car park is approx 200 metres on L, just past a pedestrian crossing.* **Sat 9 June (1-4). Adm £4, chd free. Light refreshments in Gunnersbury Park itself is a restaurant/café offering more substantial meals.**

Sited within the Walled Garden in Gunnersbury Park, formerly owned by the Rothschild family, is one of the Capel Manor College campuses, specialising in teaching landbased industries such as Horticulture, Arboriculture, Animal Care and Floristry. Usually closed to the public, this garden is maintained entirely by horticulture students, one member of staff and a handful of student volunteers. There are a range of loosely themed borders, tropical, Mediterranean, herbaceous, and kitchen garden beds. At the top of the student practice area is a stumpery garden, recently built by students. Tree ferns, a range of deciduous trees, woodland planting, give a magical feel while an imaginative use of dead wood and stumps contrast eerily with the planting. Paths through stumpery not suitable for wheelchair users but area can be viewed. Borders, and new garden have good access.

12 Fairfield Road

29 THE CHARTERHOUSE, EC1

Charterhouse Square, London, EC1M 6AN. The Governors of Sutton's Hospital, www.thecharterhouse.org. *Buses: 4, 55. Tube: Barbican. Turn L out of stn, L into Carthusian St & into square. Entrance around or through Charterhouse Square.* **Evening opening Tue 5 June (6-9). Adm £5, chd free. Wine. Evening to incl BBQ (additional charge).**

Enclosed courtyard gardens within the grounds of historic Charterhouse, which dates back to 1347. English country garden style featuring roses, herbaceous borders, ancient mulberry trees and small pond. Various garden herbs found here are still used in the kitchen today. In addition, two other areas are being opened for the NGS. Pensioners Court, which is partly maintained by the private tenants and Master's Garden, the old burial ground which now consists of lawns, borders and wildlife garden planted to camouflage a war time air raid shelter. A private garden for the Brothers of Charterhouse, not usually open to the public. (Buildings not open).

30 51 THE CHASE, SW4

London, SW4 0NP. Mr Charles Rutherfoord & Mr Rupert Tyler, www.charlesrutherfoord.net. *Off Clapham Common Northside. Tube: Clapham Common. Buses: 137, 452.* **Sun 22 Apr (12-5). Evening opening Thur 26 Apr (6-8). Light refreshments. Adm £4, chd free.**

Member of the Society of Garden Designers, Charles has created the garden over 30yrs. In 2015 the main garden was remodelled, to much acclaim. Spectacular in spring, when 2000 tulips bloom among irises and tree peonies. Scented front garden. Rupert's geodetic dome shelters seedlings, succulents and subtropicals.

D

31 ◆ CHELSEA PHYSIC GARDEN, SW3

66 Royal Hospital Road, London, SW3 4HS. Chelsea Physic Garden Company, 020 7352 5646, www.chelseaphysicgarden.co.uk. *Tube: Sloane Square (10 mins). Bus: 170. Parking: Battersea Park (charged). Entrance in Swan Walk.* **For NGS: Fri 20 Apr (11-6). Adm £10.50, chd £6.95. Lunches and afternoon tea at Tangerine Dream Café. For other opening times and information, please phone or visit garden website.**

Come and explore London's oldest botanic garden situated in the heart of Chelsea. With a unique living collection of around 5000 plants, this walled garden is a celebration of the importance of plants and their beauty. Highlights incl Europe's oldest pond rockery, the Garden of Edible and Useful Plants, the Garden of Medicinal Plants and the World Woodland Garden. Tours available. Wheelchair access is via 66 Royal Hospital Rd.

32 46 CHEYNE AVENUE, E18

South Woodford, Essex, E18 2DR. Helen Auty. *Nearest tube S Woodford. Short walk. From station take Clarendon Rd. Cross High Rd into Broadwalk, 3rd on L Bushey Ave. 1st R Cheyne Ave.* **Sun 8 July (12-5). Adm £4, chd free. Home-made teas.**

On site of Lord Cheyne's original market garden, typical suburban garden with lawn and borders of shrubs, climbers and perennials - greenhouse and productive fruit and vegetable garden.

GROUP OPENING

33 CHISWICK MALL GARDENS, W4

Chiswick, W4 2PR. *Car: Towards Hogarth r'about, A4 (W) turn Eyot Grds S. Tube: Stamford Brook or Turnham Green. Buses: 27, 190, 267 & 391 to Young's Corner. From Chiswick High Rd or Kings St S under A4 to river.* **Evening opening Fri 25 May (6-8). Combined adm £12, chd free. Sun 27 May (2-5). Combined adm £8, chd free. Tea at 16 Eyot Gardens. On Friday, wine at Swan House & Field House.**

16 EYOT GARDENS
Dianne Farris.
Open on all dates

FIELD HOUSE
Rupert King, www.fieldhousegarden.co.uk.
Open on all dates

LONGMEADOW
Charlotte Fraser.
Open on all dates

ST PETERS WHARF
Barbara Brown.
Open on Sun 27 May

SWAN HOUSE
Mr & Mrs George Nissen.
Open on all dates

This peaceful riverside setting offers five unique gardens. Two walled gardens - one large and one small, artists' studio garden, exotic water garden and town house garden with extensive vegetable garden.

34 CHOUMERT SQUARE, SE15

Peckham, SE15 4RE. The Residents. *Off Choumert Grove. Trains from London Victoria, London Bridge, London Blackfriars, Clapham Junction to Peckham Rye; buses (12, 36, 37, 63, 78, 171, 312, 345). Free Car park (1 min) in Choumert Grove.* **Sun 3 June (1-6). Adm £4, chd free. Light refreshments. Also open 35 Camberwell Grove. We will be serving afternoon teas, Pimms and a variety of homemade cakes.** Donation to St Christopher's Hospice.

About 46 mini gardens with maxi planting in Shangri-la situation that the media has described as a Floral Canyon, which leads to small communal secret garden. The day is primarily about gardens and sharing with others our residents' love of this little corner of the inner city; but it is also renowned for its demonstrable community spirit. Lots of stalls and live music. The popular open gardens will combine this year with our own take on a village fete with home produce stalls, arts, crafts and music. No steps within the Square just a tiny step to a raised paved space in the communal garden area.

35 NEW CHURCH GARDENS, UB9

Church Hill, Harefield, Uxbridge, UB9 6DU. Patrick McHugh. *If coming from Harefield Village, continue for ¼ mile down Church Hill to 1st Yellow sign. If coming from from A40 Uxbridge junction, follow signs to Harefield.* **Mon 27 Aug (2-5). Adm £5, chd £2. Light refreshments. Tea and cakes.**

Harefield's own 'secret garden'. 17th Century Renaissance walled gardens on the outskirts of Harefield, incl a traditional organic kitchen garden, consisting of 56 geometrically arranged raised beds, 60m long herbaceous borders, trained fruit trees, herb garden and an orchard with rare arcaded wall, dating back to the early 1600's. Unique opportunity to view ongoing restoration project. Good wheelchair friendly paths in kitchen garden, short access to kitchen garden possible for wheelchairs but not ideal surfaces.

36 79 CHURCH LANE, N2

London, N2 0TH. Caro & David Broome. *Tube: E Finchley, then East End Rd for ¾ m, R into Church Lane. Buses: 143 to Five Bells PH, 3 min walk; 263 to E Finchley Library, 5 min walk.* **Sun 29 July (2-6). Adm £4, chd free. Home-made teas and cakes incl gluten free.**

Award winning garden full of vibrant planting, humour and innovation. Contemporary front garden leads through to exotic plant filled catatorium, opening out into the garden beyond. Borders bursting with shrubs, roses and unusual perennials, central curved rill with quirky water features. Rustic archway leads to secluded fernery, secret hideaway with beach hut summer house and prairie roof terrace. Locally propagated perennials ideal for London clay soils. Ever popular raffle, children's treasure hunt. Home-made teas incl new recipes and old favourites. London Gardens Society: Best Small Back Garden. Columnist for Garden News Over The Fence. As seen on BBC1 The One Show and ITV Love Your Garden. Blogger for Thompson & Morgan.

37 THE CIRCLE GARDEN, KT3

33 Cambridge Avenue, New Malden, KT3 4LD. Vincent & Heidi Johnson-Paul-McDonnell, www.thecirclegarden.com. *1¼ m N of A3 Malden junction. Bus: 213. 10 mins walk from New Malden railway station; A3 signposted for Kingston; 213 bus stop located a short distance from end of rd; our house is pink!* **Sat 12, Sat 19 May (2-6). Adm £3.50, chd free. Home-made teas.**

A welcoming front garden with cottage style planting leading to an unexpected rear garden with intriguing vistas where you will find herbaceous and annuals in mixed borders. Relax in the Japanese area, stroll through the potager and chat to our suburban hens. An ever evolving garden with plans for further developments.

38 NEW 13 COLLEGE CROSS, N1

London, N1 1YY. Diana & Stephen Yakeley. *Barnsbury, Islington. Tube: Highbury & Islington. Buses: 19, 73, 277.* **Sun 13 May (1.30-6). Adm £3.50, chd free. Also open Malvern Terrace Gardens.**

An award winning walled garden 5m x 17m, behind a Georgian terraced house, enclosed by evergreen climbers with mature Bay, Box, Olive and Fig trees. Architectural plants chosen for form and texture in shades of green, enlivened by pots of white flowers. Black slate bench and a glass balustrade provide contemporary design interest.

39 NEW 19 COOLHURST ROAD, N8

Hornsey, London, N8 8EP. Jane Muirhead. *Exit tube at Highgate onto Priory gardens, L on Shepherd's Hill, R on Stanhope Road, L on Hurst Ave, R on Coolhurst Road (15mins) W7 from Finsbury Park to Crouch End & 5min walk 41 & 91 busses nearby.* **Sun 20 May (2-6). Adm £4, chd free. Home-made teas. Also open 12 Fairfield Road.**

Evolving, organic and wildlife garden with dappled sunlight, bees, birds and butterflies. Informal woodland planting under magnificent deciduous trees with interesting shrubs, box shapes and perennials. Small vegetable patch & wild flower garden where knapweed, campion, honesty, wild carrot & sweet rocket have naturalised. Large lawn with seating. (Some steps and uneven surfaces).

40 4 CORNFLOWER TERRACE, SE22

East Dulwich, London, SE22 0HH. Clare Dryhurst. *5 mins walk from 63 bus stop at bottom of Forest Hill Rd. Turn into Dunstans Rd, then 2nd on L. Stn: Peckham Rye or Honor Oak Park.* **Sun 10 June (2-5.30). Combined adm with 4 Piermont Green £5, chd free. Home-made teas. Also open 174 Peckham Rye.**

This little East Dulwich terraced cottage is among the smallest gardens featured. Both front and back have had a gentle makeover in 2017 to simplify and introduce more perfume. A calm and charming front has camellia, roses, lavender and heuchera. The sanctuary of the tiny courtyard back garden offers climbing roses, star jasmine, daphne, ferns & annuals around a sunken patio, bench & fountain.

41 NEW 45 COTSWOLD WAY, EN2

Oakwood, Enfield, EN2 7HD. Ian Brownhill & Michael Hirschl. *Short bus ride from either Oakwood underground station or Enfield Chase train stn. Use buses 121 or 307 and alight at Cotswold Way.* **Sun 3 June (2-6). Adm £4, chd free. Home-made teas. Evening opening Fri 17 Aug (5.30-8.30). Adm £5, chd free. Wine. June: Selection of homemade cakes and biscuits served with tea or coffee August: A glass of wine or soft drink offered with each entry.**
Designed and created in 2016 this contemporary, sunny, medium sized garden looks out over London's Green Belt. The garden contains a number of features incl an imposing outdoor fireplace with dining area, raised Koi pond and large deck. These provide a backdrop to the overflowing, densely planted borders featuring a wide range of trees, grasses, perennials and annuals.

42 122 COURT LANE, SE21

Dulwich, SE21 7EA. Jean & Charles Cary-Elwes. *Buses P4, 12, 40, 176, 185 (to Dulwich Library) 37. Mainline; North Dulwich then 12 mins walk. Ample free parking.* **Sun 17 June (2-5.30). Combined adm with 125 Court Lane £7, chd free.**
Generously proportioned, mature garden with deep herbaceous borders and unusual plants. Roses, agapanthus, a signature plant followed by oleander and a splendid clerodendron. Backing onto Dulwich Park, it has a countryside feel - a family garden with sandpit, swings and hammock mingling with a hardworking greenhouse. Live jazz band on the terrace, children's trail, plant sales, wormery demonstration. Featured in Dulwich Society Magazine and Dulwich Society Garden Brochure. Wheelchair access to terrace only but good view of garden.

43 125 COURT LANE, SE21

Dulwich, SE21 7EE. Stephen Henden & Neil Ellis. *15 mins walk from North Dulwich Station/ 5 mins walk from Dulwich Library for buses. Buses P4, 12, 40, 176, 185 (to Dulwich Library) 37. Mainline; North Dulwich then 12 mins walk. Ample free parking.* **Sun 17 June (2-5.30). Combined adm with 122 Court Lane £7, chd free. Home-made teas.**
Unique garden created over 14 yrs. Winding paths weave between eclectic herbaceous borders of myriad colours and plants. The eye is constantly drawn to beds filled with riotous colour and the planting seems to embrace and entice you to explore further. Hidden at the bottom of the garden is a secretive Druid Chair from which to contemplate the passing of time. Renowned for their teas and cakes. Reasonable access through house but with two low steps.

44 NEW 40 THE CRESCENT, SM2

Belmont, Sutton, SM2 6BJ. Mrs Barbara Welch. *Train: 5 min walk from Belmont Stn. or from Sutton Stn. take Bus 280 to Belmont. Then over bridge into Station Rd, 1st L into The Crescent. No 40 half way up on R. Street parking.* **Sun 24 June (1-5). Adm £4, chd free. Home-made teas.**
Semi-formal - some say Italianate - evergreen layout, containing informal planting of roses, cottage garden plants, many different shrubs, this NW facing 80' x 50' rectangular garden sits on chalk, with a central lawn bordered by clipped box and topiary-lined beds and pathways leading to unexpected shady areas, with a circular tree seat, small water features, an arbor with swing.

45 NEW 40 CROHAM MANOR ROAD, CR2

South Croydon, CR2 7BE. Mr Terry Eccles. *Rail East Croydon, then bus 433 or 64 to St Pauls Church. Road has ample free parking but caution should be used, as traffic can travel fast on the road. House has a dark blue double garage door.* **Sun 13 May (1-5). Adm £4, chd free. Home-made teas.**
Compact, Italian style terraces, sculptures & water features, deal with a challenging plot encompassing difficult slopes, shade & soil types. This garden shows what can be achieved using tonal planting, pots, lighting & architectural structures, with pleasing, peaceful dining & seating areas to take advantage of sun & shade at different times of day and night.

GROUP OPENING

46 DE BEAUVOIR GARDENS, N1

London, N1. *Highbury & Islington tube then 30 or 277 bus; Angel tube then 38, 56 or 73 bus; Bank tube then 21, 76 or 141 bus. 10 mins walk from Dalston Overground stations. Street parking available.* **Sun 17 June (11-3). Combined adm £6, chd free. Home-made teas at 158 Culford Road.**

132 CULFORD ROAD
Joan Ward.

158 CULFORD ROAD
Gillian Blachford.

21 NORTHCHURCH TERRACE
Nancy Korman.

Three gardens to explore in De Beauvoir, a leafy enclave of Victorian villas near to Islington and Dalston. The area boasts some of Hackney's keenest gardeners and a thriving garden club. The walled garden at 21 Northchurch Terrace has a formal feel, with deep herbaceous borders, pond, fruit trees, pergola, patio pots and herb beds. 132 Culford Road is a town garden of 110ft x 30ft featuring a large pergola, shingle, chippings and boulder landscaping, with a sunken garden and many shrubs, trees and a fern stumpery. 158 Culford Road is a long narrow garden with a romantic feel and a path winding through full borders with shrubs, small trees, perennials and many unusual plants.

47 DIESPEKER WHARF, N1

38 Graham Street, London, N1 8JX. Pollard Thomas Edwards. *Beside Regents Canal, Angel, Islington. Underground & Buses: 5 mins from Angel.* **Sun 20 May (2-5.30). Adm £4, chd free. Also open 19 St Peter's Street.**
An intriguing and unexpected garden in an historic industrial setting alongside the Regents Canal owned and converted by a firm of architects. The garden has become an enticing and unique space enjoyed both socially and for business. Interesting climbers clothe the high wall. Canalside beds incl aster monarch, verbena bonariensis, acanthus spinosis, astrantia major and euphorbia silver edge. The garden has won numerous awards from Islington in Bloom and London in Bloom.

48 NEW 18 DORCHESTER GARDENS, NW11

London, NW11 6BN. Sarah Oxby, www.hampsteadgardendesign.com. *Golders Green tube, then 102 bus for 18 min to Beaufort Drive, then 3 min walk to garden.* **Sun 1 July (2-6). Adm £4, chd free. Home-made teas. Also open 121 Erskine Hill.**
Contemporary town garden, created by the garden designer owner. The strong geometry of the garden layout is complemented by soft planting. Beds and borders brim with hydrangea, lavender and an abundance of perennials in shades of blue, purple and white. Olive and bay trees give structure to the sunny borders while tree ferns and shady plantings give interest in the darker corners of the garden.

49 NEW DRAGON'S DREAM, GROVE LANE, UB8

Grove Lane, Uxbridge, UB8 3RG. Chris and Meng Pocock. *Garden is in a small lane that is very close to Hillingdon Hospital. Parking is available in the nearby Royal Lane. Buses from Uxbridge Tube Station: U1,U3,U4,U5,U7. Buses from West Drayton: U1, U3.* **Sun 27 May (2-5). Adm £3.50, chd free. Home-made teas.**
Opening for the first time, is an established private and mature garden. This is a quiet oasis that is planted with cordon fruit trees and herbaceous shrubs. The main feature is an unusually large wisteria which forms a canopy of scented blooms. Other features include a huge and well established gunnera manicata, a romneya poppy, ferns, rose and herb beds, tree peony and a pond.

50 55 DUKES AVENUE, N10

Muswell Hill, N10 2PY Jo de Banzie & Duncan Lampard. *W3 Bus (Alexandra Palace Garden Centre stop) or W7 Bus (Muswell Hill stop). Free on-street parking available on Dukes Av.* **Sun 20 May (2-6). Adm £3.50, chd free.**
A photographer's small town garden uses curves and spheres to add shape and interest to a pretty, shady space. Gravel, paving, decking and a planting platform in an old apple tree create structure, whilst black bamboo, ferns and box provide the backdrop for a gentle palette of white and purple planting. Unfortunately not suitable for wheelchair access due to steps.

GROUP OPENING

51 DULWICH VILLAGE TWO GARDENS, SE21

London, SE21 7BJ. Mr & Mrs A Rutherford, Mr and Mrs N Annesley. *Rail: N Dulwich or W Dulwich then 10 -15 mins walk. Tube: Brixton then P4 bus, alight Dulwich Picture Gallery stop. Street parking.* **Sun 10 June (2-5). Combined adm £7, chd free. Home-made teas at 103 Dulwich Village.** Donation to Macmillan Cancer Care.

103 DULWICH VILLAGE
Mr & Mrs N Annesley.

105 DULWICH VILLAGE
Mr & Mrs A Rutherford.

2 Georgian houses with large gardens, 3 mins walk from Dulwich Picture Gallery and Dulwich Park. 103 Dulwich Village is a country garden in London with a long herbaceous border, lawn, pond, roses and fruit and vegetable gardens. 105 Dulwich Village is a very pretty garden with many unusual plants, lots of old fashioned roses, fish pond and water garden. Amazing collection of plants for sale from both gardens.

52 EATON SQUARE GARDEN, SW1W

Eaton Square, London, SW1W 9BD. The Grosvenor Estate, www.grosvenorlondon.com. *Entry to garden via gate opp no. 42 Eaton Sq. Easy walk from Victoria Station or Sloane Sq. Many bus routes passing close to square incl C1, C2, 16, 38, 52 & 73.* **Sun 6 May (11-3). Adm £3, chd free. Also open Eccleston Square. Tea, coffee and cakes.**
Thomas Cubitt laid out the 6 formal gardens flanking either side of the Kings Rd in 1826 in what was the main approach to Buckingham Palace. Eaton Square Gardens today combines well-manicured lawns, shady pathways and mixed borders with quiet seating and contemporary sculptures. The fabulously preserved regency buildings form a fine backdrop, complemented by the square's mature London planes. This is a level access site with paths suitable for wheelchairs running the perimeter of the garden and a hard landscaped central area.

53 41 ECCLESBOURNE ROAD, N1

London, N1 3AF. Steve Bell & Sandie Macrae. *Canonbury. Tube: Highbury & Islington 12 mins walk or 271 bus to Ecclesbourne Rd. Angel tube 15 mins walk or bus 73, 38, 56, 341, 476 to Northchurch Rd. Cross Essex Rd, down Halliford St, R on Ecclesbourne Rd.* **Sun 24 June (2-6). Combined adm with 58 Halliford Street £5.50, chd free. Home-made teas.**

A delightful, interesting and surprising artists' minimalistic Mediterranean garden complemented by new contemporary architecture. This garden has a hoggin surface with trees and pots on two levels. There is a birch, a handkerchief tree, herbs, trailing clematis, roses and, unbelievably a bay tree hand-gilded in gold leaf.

54 ECCLESTON SQUARE, SW1

London, SW1V 1NP. Roger Phillips & the Residents, www.rogerstreesandshrubs.com. *Off Belgrave Rd nr Victoria Stn, parking allowed on Suns.* **Sun 6 May (2-5). Adm £4, chd free. Home-made teas. Also open Eaton Square Garden SW1.**

Planned by Cubitt in 1828, the 3 acre square is subdivided into mini gardens with camellias, iris, ferns and containers. Dramatic collection of tender climbing roses and 20 different forms of tree peonies. National Collection of ceanothus incl more than 70 species and cultivars. Notable important additions of tender plants being grown and tested. World collection of ceanothus, tea roses and tree peonies.

NPC

55 EDWARDES SQUARE, W8

South Edwardes Square, Kensington, London, W8 6HL. Edwardes Square Garden Committee. *Tube: Kensington High St & Earls Court. Buses: 9, 10, 27, 28, 31, 49 & 74 to Odeon Cinema. Entrance in South Edwardes Square.* **Sun 22 Apr (11-5). Adm £4, chd free. Home-made teas. Also open 7 Upper Phillimore Gardens W8.**

One of London's prettiest secluded garden squares. 3½ acres laid out differently from other squares, with serpentine paths by Agostino Agliothe, Italian artist and decorator who lived at no.15 from 1814-1820, and a beautiful Grecian temple which is traditionally the home of the head gardener. Romantic rose tunnel winds through the middle of the garden. Good displays of bulbs and blossom. Tea, coffee and home-made cakes, Pimms if sunny. Children's play area. WC.

56 11 ERNLE ROAD, SW20

Wimbledon, London, SW20 0HH. Theresa-Mary Morton. *¼ m from Wimbledon Village, 200yds from Crooked Billet PH. Exit A3 at A238 to Wimbledon, turning L at Copse Hill. Mainline: Wimbledon or Raynes Park. Tube: Wimbledon; Bus: 200 to High Cedar Drive; 200 yds walk.* **Sat 28, Sun 29 Apr (2.30-6). Adm £4, chd free. Home-made teas. Evening opening Sun 17 June (6-8). Adm £5, chd free. Wine.**

Established suburban garden of ¼ acre on sandy acid soil, spatially organised into separate sections: oak pergola framing the main vista, hidden parterre, woodland, pool, yew circle, flower garden and summerhouse. Country Life, Garden News and Garden Answers. Beaten gravel paths, one step up to main garden.

Church Gardens

58 48 ERSKINE HILL, NW11

Hampstead Garden Suburb, London, NW11 6HG. Marjorie & David Harris, 020 8455 6507, marjorieharris@btinternet.com. *1m N of Golders Green. Nr A406 & A1. Tube: Golders Green. H2 Hail & Ride bus from Golders Green to garden, or 13, 460, 102 buses to Temple Fortune (10 mins walk).* **Sun 3 June (2-6). Adm £4, chd free. Home-made teas. Visits also by arrangement May to Sept no min, max 20. Tea/cake incl in adm price.**

Organic garden, wrapped around Arts and Crafts artisan's cottage. Bird and bee friendly, with wide borders containing colourful perennials, shrubs, masses of roses and clematis, trees and containerised vegetable plot with greenhouse. Lots of pots. Secret brick paved area with raised beds. Nest boxes, organic and pesticide free. Quirky water feature. Some single steps and narrow paths. Rail to lawn.

57 NEW 121 ERSKINE HILL, NW11

Hampstead Garden Suburb, London, NW11 6HU. Mike & Heather Collins. *Nr A406 & A1. Tube: Golders Green. H2 Hail & Ride bus from Golders Green to garden, or 13, 460, 102 buses to Temple Fortune (10 mins walk). Garden is located at the bottom end of Erskine Hill.* **Sun 1 July (1-6). Adm £4, chd free. Home-made teas. Also open 18 Dorchester Gardens.**

Primarily a large romantic rose garden containing different areas of interest, incl a newly acquired extension, planted with a variety of new trees, shrubs and perennials. This garden is host to a variety of reclaimed materials incl some interesting stone ornaments, pots and salvage. Designed to be dog friendly, it is also a people's garden where one can party, play or relax.

59 NEW 12 FAIRFIELD ROAD, N8

HORNSEY, N8 9HG. Christine Lane. *Tube: Finsbury Park and then W3 (Weston Park stop) or W7 (Crouch End Broadway) alternatively Archway and then 41 bus (Crouch End Broadway) it's then a short walk.* **Sun 20 May (2-5.30). Adm £3.50, chd free. Also open 19 Coolhurst Road.**

This peaceful, secluded garden backs onto the Picturehouse cinema. Created on two levels and with year-round interest, it is packed with a variety of trees, shrubs and flowers, as well as succulents, palms and bamboos. A woodland garden with sculptures, a cobbled Zen garden and a raised pond - made by a Vietnamese family - create different atmospheres while seating provides places to contemplate.

60 ◆ FENTON HOUSE, NW3

Hampstead Grove, Hampstead, NW3 6SP. National Trust, www.nationaltrust.org.uk. *300yds from Hampstead tube. Entrances: Top of Holly Hill & Hampstead Grove.* **For NGS: Evening opening Tue 12 June (6.30-7.30). Adm £10. Pre-booking essential, please visit www.ngs.org.uk or phone 01483 211535 for information & booking. Wine. For other opening times and information, please visit garden website.**

Join the Gardener-in-Charge for a special evening tour. Andrew Darragh who brings over 10yrs experience from Kew to Fenton House will explore this timeless 1½ acre walled garden. Laid out over 3 levels, and featuring formal areas, a small sunken rose garden, a 300yr old orchard and kitchen garden, Andrew will present the garden and the changes he has made.

GROUP OPENING

61 FOREST HILL GARDENS GROUP, SE23

Forest Hill, London, SE23 3BP. *Off S Circular (A205) behind Horniman Museum & Gardens. Station: Forest Hill, 10 mins walk. Buses: 176, 185, 312, P4.* **Sun 20 May (1-6). Combined adm £7, chd free. Teas available at 53 Ringmore Rise.** Donation to St Christopher's Hospice and Marsha Phoenix Trust.

7 CANONBIE ROAD
June Wismayer.

THE COACH HOUSE, 3 THE HERMITAGE
Pat Rae.

HILLTOP, 28 HORNIMAN DRIVE
Frankie Locke.

27 HORNIMAN DRIVE
Rose Agnew, 020 8699 7710, roseandgraham@talktalk.net. **Visits also by arrangement Apr to Sept small groups welcome.**

53 RINGMORE RISE
Valerie Ward.

Five very different gardens on the highest hill in SE London with spectacular views over London and the South Downs. The gardens are within a short walk of each other, help available (for a small donation) for those with mobility problems. See an evolving plantswoman's garden, with prairie planting in the sunny dry garden contrasting with a watery fern garden. Wander in an eclectic country style garden with a small meadow, an ever changing story trail for children, and new chicken breeds. Delight in an artist's studio in an C18th courtyard filled with sculptures and plants and feed the resident robins! Enjoy an embroidery of a garden with vibrant colours and breathtaking views. Unwind with delicious cakes and listen to music from a talented duo amid the drifting pastel hues of the tea lady's garden inspired by Beth Chatto – and Mary Berry! Great views everywhere. Plants for sale: 27 Horniman Drive and 7 Canonbie Rd. Teas: 53 Ringmore Rise. Admission tickets are available at Hilltop, 28 Horniman Drive.

62 9 FURLONG ROAD, N7

Islington, London, N7 8LS. Nigel Watts & Tanuja Pandit. *Close to Highbury & Islington tube station. Tube & Overground: Highbury & Islington, 3 mins walk along Holloway Rd, 2nd L. Furlong Rd joins Holloway Rd & Liverpool Rd. Buses: 43, 271, 393.* **Sun 13 May (2-6). Adm £3, chd free. Home-made teas. Also open 13 College Cross, N1.**
Award winning small garden designed by Karen Fitzsimon which makes clever use of an awkwardly shaped plot. Curved lines are used to complement a modern extension. Raised beds contain a mix of tender and hardy plants to give an exotic feel and incl loquat, banana, palm, cycad and tree fern. Contrasting traditional front garden. Featured in Small Family Gardens and Modern Family Gardens by Caroline Tilston.

63 GARDEN BARGE SQUARE AT DOWNINGS ROADS MOORINGS, SE1

31 Mill Street, London, SE1 2AX. Mr Nick Lacey. *5 mins walk from Tower Bridge. Mill St off Jamaica Rd, between London Bridge & Bermondsey stns, Tower Hill also nearby. Buses: 47, 188, 381, RV1.* **Sun 20 May (2-5). Adm £4, chd free. Home-made teas.** Donation to RNLI.
Series of seven floating barge gardens connected by walkways and bridges. Gardens have an eclectic range of plants for yr-round seasonal interest. Marine environment: suitable shoes and care needed. Small children must be closely supervised.

64 ◆ THE GARDEN MUSEUM, SE1

Lambeth Palace Road, London, SE1 7LB. The Garden Museum, www.gardenmuseum.org.uk. *E side of Lambeth Bridge. Tube: Lambeth North, Vauxhall, Waterloo. Buses: 507 Red Arrow from Victoria or Waterloo mainline & tube stns, also 3, 77, 344.* **For NGS: Sat 8 Sept (10.30-4). Adm £5, chd free. Light refreshments.** For other opening times and information, please visit garden website.
Britain's only Museum of Gardens re-opened in spring 2017 after a £6.5 million refurbishment. The centre piece of a new extension will be a new garden designed by Dan Pearson as a contemporary re-interpretation of plant collectors' lust for plants, inspired by the life of John Tradescant, who is buried here. Please note that this will be a newly-planted emerging garden. The new extension incl a new cafe. The Museum curates three major exhibitions each year on the art and design of gardens, and has over fifty events in its public programme. The Museum is accessible for wheelchair users via ramps and access lift.

65 NEW 74 GLENGALL ROAD, IG8

Woodford Green, IG8 0DL. Mr & Mrs J Woolliams. *5 mins walk from Woodford Central line, off Snakes Lane West. Buses nearby incl 275,179,W13 & 20. No parking restrictions on Suns.* **Sun 13 May (2-5). Adm £3.50. Home-made teas.**
A secluded S-facing cottage style garden, developed over 25 years for yr-round interest. Areas incl 2 lawns, a rock garden, small wildlife pond with bog garden, shade borders and a gravel garden, linked by several paths. Throughout are mixtures of trees shrubs perennials bulbs bamboos grasses and climbers. Some steps but mostly wheelchair accessible.

67 69 GLOUCESTER CRESCENT, NW1

Camden, London, NW1 7EG. Sandra Clapham, 020 7485 5764, set69@gloscres.com. *Between Regent's Park & Camden Town tube station. Tube: Camden Town 2 mins, Mornington Crescent 10 mins. Metered parking in Oval Rd.* **Visits by arrangement May to Oct.**
Delightful little cottage front garden, opening with No. 70 upon request. It shows what can be done with a small front garden as a lovely alternative to a concrete parking space. Ursula Vaughan Williams lived here and the very old iceberg rose at the front, the yellow roses, the border of London pride and the Crinum powellii Rosea lily in a pot are all inherited from her. Many plants have been added since, incl a bed of tomatoes and a delicious 20yr old grape vine, trained up and along the balcony, that produced 8lbs of grape jelly in 2015 & 2017!

66 70 GLOUCESTER CRESCENT, NW1

London, NW1 7EG. Lucy Gent, 07531 828752 (texts only), gent.lucy@gmail.com. *Between Regent's Park & Camden Town tube station. Tube: Camden Town 2 mins, Mornington Crescent 10 mins. Metered parking in Oval Rd.* **Sun 3 June (2-5.30), also open Royal College of Physicians' Medicinal Garden. Sun 5 Aug (2.30-5.30). Adm £3.50, chd free. Visits also by arrangement Apr to Oct groups 30 max.**
Here is an oasis in Camden's urban density, where resourceful planting outflanks challenges of space and shade. June open day alongside other distinctive local gardens while an August opening shows how wonderful the month can be in a town garden.

68 20 GOLDHAZE CLOSE, IG8

Woodford Green, IG8 7LE. Jenny Richmond. *Off A1009 Broadmead Rd, Orchard Estate Bus Stop for W14 then forward and L into Underwood Rd and L then R into Goldhaze Cl. Tube: Woodford Station.* **Sun 29 July, Sun 5 Aug (12.30-5). Adm £4.50, chd free. Home-made teas.**
100ft L-shaped landscaped garden bursting with over 100 plants grown in different types of conditions. A huge 35 yr-old eucalyptus resembles a mature oak with beautiful bark. Paths lined with a strawberry tree, roses, campsis, penstemons, crocosmia and variety of other plants. Vegetables (in pots grown from seed in a greenhouse) leads to a secret decked garden for relaxation.

69 GOLF COURSE ALLOTMENTS, N11

Winton Avenue, London, N11 2AR. GCAA Haringey, www.golfcourseallotments.co.uk. *Junction of Winton Av & Blake Rd. Tube: Bounds Green. Buses: 102, 184, 299 to Sunshine Garden Centre, Durnsford Rd. Through park to Bidwell Gdns. Straight on up Winton Ave. No cars on site.* **Sun 2 Sept (1-4.30). Adm £4, chd free. Home-made teas and light lunches.**

Large, long established allotment with over 200 plots, some organic. Maintained by culturally diverse community growing wide variety of fruit, vegetables and flowers. Picturesque corners and quirky sheds - a visit feels like being in the countryside. Autumn Flower and Produce Show on Sun 3 Sep features prize winning horticultural and domestic exhibits and beehives. Tours of best plots. Fresh allotment produce, chutneys, jams, honey, cakes and light refreshments for sale. Wheelchair access to main paths only. Gravel and some uneven surfaces. WC incl disabled.

70 GORDON ROAD ALLOTMENTS, N3

Gordon Road, Finchley, London, N3 1EL. Judy Woollett, www.finchleyhorticulturalsociety.org.uk. *Finchley Central. 10 mins walk from Finchley Central tube. 326 bus. Parking in Gordon Rd & adjacent st. No parking on site.* **Mon 27 Aug (1.30-5). Adm £3.50, chd free. Home-made teas.**

Founded in 1940 to promote the interests of gardeners throughout Finchley with over 70 plots. Allotments comprise a mixture of traditional plots and raised beds for those with physical disabilities and for children from local schools. Also a thriving apiary with several bee hives producing local honey for sale. Tours of best plots. Seasonal vegetables on sale incl perennial flowers. Wheelchair access on main paths only. Disabled WC.

71 21 GOSPATRICK ROAD, N17

London, N17 7EH. Matthew Bradby, 020 8352 2354, mattbradby@hotmail.com. *Nearest underground station Turnpike Lane or Wood Green, overland station Bruce Grove. Bus routes 144, 217, 231, 444 to Gospatrick Rd, or 123, 243 to Waltheof Ave, or 318 to Gt Cambridge Rd.* **Sat 7 July (2-6). Adm £3.50, chd free. Home-made teas. Visits also by arrangement May to Sept, groups welcome. Evening visits available week days and weekends. Wine optional.**

Diverse 40 metre plot with lawn dominated by large weeping willow, giving dappled shade over fan palms, grasses, ferns and climbers. Patio with exotics in pots. Fruit and vegetable garden with large banana plant, grapevine, olive, climbing roses, greenhouse and goldfish pond. Mainly organic and managed for nature, this is a very tranquil and welcoming garden. Home-made wine and preserves for sale.

72 17 GREENSTONE MEWS, E11

Wanstead, London, E11 2RS. Mr & Mrs S Farnham, 07761 476651, farnhamz@yahoo.co.uk. *Wanstead. Tube: Snaresbrook or Wanstead, 5 mins walk. Bus: 101, 308, W12, W14 to Wanstead High St. Greenstone Mews is accessed via Voluntary Place which is off Spratt Hall Road.* **Visits by arrangement May to Sept for groups refreshment can be provided. Drink of tea or coffee is included in the admission price. Adm £5. Light refreshments.**

Coloured Slate paved garden (20ft x 17ft). Height provided by a mature strawberry tree. Sunken reused bath now a fishpond surrounded by climbers clothing fences underplanted with herbs, vegetables, shrubs and perennials grown from cuttings. Ideas aplenty for small space gardening. Regret garden unsuitable for children. Wheelchair access through garage. Limited turning space.

73 NEW 40 GREENWAYS, BR3

Beckenham, BR3 3NQ. N Dooley and C Murray. *Garden is located on the corner of Greenways and Uplands, close to the triangular green.* **Sun 1 July (2-5.30). Adm £3.50, chd free. Home-made teas. Also open 12 Overbrae.**

Two contrasting garden spaces. The tapering 70ft rear garden, redesigned in 2015, is planted in a mediterranean style, gives all year interest and is wildlife friendly. Features include olive trees, grasses, thyme bed, unusual insect hotel/screen, pond and sculptures and areas to relax/dine. The front garden has fruit trees and small meadow surrounded by newly replanted borders in coloured 'rooms'.

74 7 THE GROVE, N6

Highgate Village, London, N6 6JU. Mr Thomas Lyttelton, 07713 638161. *Between Highgate West Hill & Hampstead Lane. Tube: Archway or Highgate. Buses: 143, 210, 214 and 271.* **Sun 18 Feb (11-3). Light refreshments. Sun 8 Apr (2-5.30); Sun 10 June (2-6). Home-made teas. Adm £5, chd free. Visits also by arrangement, refreshments on request.** Donation to The Harington Scheme.

Half-acre garden designed for yr round interest making a tapestry of greens and yellows. A wild garden with mature trees giving a woodland feel. Large lawn, perfect for teas. Brilliant for hide and seek, Pooh-sticks and young explorers. Water garden, 20 paths, vistas and views galore. Snowdrops in February. Exceptional camellias and magnolia in the spring. Hot soup incl with entry for Snowdrop openings. Cup of tea incl with entry for Spring/Summer openings.

75 24 GROVE PARK, SE5

Camberwell, SE5 8LH. Clive Pankhurst, www.alternative-planting.blogspot.com. *Chadwick Rd end of Grove Park. Stns: Peckham Rye or Denmark Hill, both 10 mins walk. Easy bus from Vauxhall (185) or Elephant and Castle (176, 40). Good street parking.* **Sun 2 Sept (2-5.30). Adm £3.50, chd free. Home-made teas.**

An exotic jungle of lush big leafed plants, ponds and Southeast Asian influences. Towering paulownias, bananas, dahlias, tetrapanax and exotica transport you to the tropics. Huge hidden garden created from buying the bottom halves of two neighbouring gardens gives unexpected size. Lawn and lots of hidden corners give spaces to sit and enjoy. Renowned for delicious home-made cake.

76 NEW 58 HALLIFORD STREET, N1

London, N1 3NQ. Jennifer Tripp Black. *Canonbury. Tube: Highbury & Islington or Essex Rd. From Essex Road, house numbers consecutive on LH side by third speed bump.* **Sun 24 June (2-6). Combined adm with 41 Ecclesbourne Road £5.50, chd free. Light refreshments.**

An English country garden in the heart of Islington. Lush planting: cytisus battandieri 'Yellow Tail' tree, two apple trees, one quince. Roses: bush and climbing, clematis, rhododendrons, exotic palms, cannas, abutilons, heucheras, salvias, cordelines. Small greenhouse, antique pergola, pots containing hosta collection and window boxes. The front garden welcomes with special roses and agapanthus.

77 ◆ HAMPTON COURT PALACE, KT8

East Molesey, KT8 9AU. Historic Royal Palaces, www.hrp.org.uk. *Follow brown tourist signs on all major routes. Junction of A308 with A309 at foot of Hampton Court Bridge.* **For NGS: Evening opening Thur 19 Apr, Thur 12 July (6-8). Adm £12, chd free. Pre-booking essential, please visit www.ngs.org.uk or phone 01483 211535 for information & booking. Wine.** For other opening times and information, please visit garden website.

Take the opportunity to join 2 special NGS private tours, after the wonderful historic gardens have closed to the public. Spring Walk around the Garden 19th April 2018 and Mid-Summer abundance 12th July 2018 in the wonderful gardens of Hampton Court Palace. Some un-bound gravel paths.

GROUP OPENING

78 HAMPTON HILL GARDENS, TW12

Hampton Hill, TW12 1DW. Bernard Wigginton. *3m from Twickenham. 4m from Kingston-upon-Thames. Between A312 (Uxbridge Rd) & A313 (Park Rd). Bus: 285 from Kingston stops on Uxbridge Rd, Windmill Rd Stop. Stn: Fulwell 15 mins walk.* **Sat 26, Sun 27 May (2-5). Combined adm £5, chd free. Home-made teas at 30 St James's Road and 16 Links View Road.**

18 CRANMER ROAD
Bernard Wigginton.

16 LINKS VIEW ROAD
Guy & Virginia Lewis.

30 ST JAMES'S ROAD
Jean Burman.

WAYSIDE
Mr Steve Croft.

4 gardens of diverse interest in an attractive West London suburb. With the backdrop of St James's Church spire, 18 Cranmer Rd is a colourful garden with herbaceous and exotic borders and a WW2 air raid shelter transformed as rockery and water garden with azaleas, helianthemums and foliage plants. The SE facing garden at 30 St James's Rd is subdivided into 5 rooms. Decking with seating leads to ponds surrounded by grasses and shrubs and an African themed thatched exterior sitting room. Wayside, 25 St James's Rd, is a large urban garden divided into several areas, the entire garden is planted to attract wildlife with 2 wildlife ponds, mixed herbaceous borders, water feature, urns and pots. 16 Links Rd has many interesting features and luxurious planting by plantaholic owner. Partial wheelchair access.

79 77 HANDSWORTH ROAD, N17

London, N17 6DB. Serge Charles. *Seven Sisters/Turnpike Lane 15 mins walk from either station or take W4 bus from T Lane, alight Broadwater Lodge stop. 230 bus first stop Philip Lane L into Handsworth Rd. Free parking.* **Sun 3 June (2-6). Adm £3, chd free. Also open 159 Higham Road.**

Narrow front garden is home to bamboos, roses and clematis which screen a secret knot garden of box. Container planted trees incl olive, mimosa and myrtle. Shady path, planted with a wide range of rare and unusual ferns and shade tolerant plants leads to a tiny back garden where the bamboos reach 25ft underplanted with tree ferns. Many other interesting plants and features inc sculptures. Featured in Ham & High.

80 37 HAROLD ROAD, E11

Leytonstone, London, E11 4QX. Dr Matthew Jones Chesters. *Tube: Leytonstone exit L subway 5 mins walk. Overground: Leytonstone High Rd 5 mins walk. Buses: 257 & W14. Parking at station or limited on street.* **Sun 29 July (1-5). Adm £4, chd free. Home-made teas.**

50ft x 60ft pretty corner garden arranged around 7 fruit trees. Fragrant climbers, woodland plants and shade-tolerant fruit along north wall. Fastigiate trees protect raised vegetable beds and herb rockery. Long lawn bordered by roses and perennials on one side; prairie plants on the other. Patio with raised pond, palms and rhubarb. Planting designed to produce fruit, fragrance and lovely memories.

Plant list and garden plan available. Home-made cakes and preserves.

81 12 HAYWOOD CLOSE, HA5

Pinner, HA5 3LQ. Brenda & Roy Jakes, 0208 868 6638, brendamjakes@gmail.com. *Approx ½m from Pinner Met Line Stn. off Elm Park Rd. From Northwood, Stanmore, Harrow & Watford head towards Pinner Green & look for signs. Haywood Close is narrow; we suggest parking in Elm Park Rd.* **Sun 10 June (2-5). Adm £4, chd free. Home-made teas including gluten free cakes. Visits also by arrangement May to Aug for groups of between 5 and 15. Tea, coffee and cakes available by prior arrangement.**
Suburban garden recently created by enthusiastic, plantaholic owner. Herbaceous perennial borders surround oval lawn. The garden contains over 100 varieties of roses and clematis, a covered rose walk, gazebo, sink garden, pleached hornbeam trees with box collars and a small fruit and vegetable garden. Seating areas and summer house to rest and relax. Most of garden wheelchair accessible.

82 31 HENDON AVENUE, N3

Finchley, London, N3 1UJ. Sandra Tomaszewska. *Finchley Central. 15 mins walk from Finchley Central Tube. Buses: 326 & 143. Car: 5 mins from A1 via Hendon Ln. No parking restrictions on Sun.* **Sun 3 June (2-6). Adm £4, chd free. Home-made teas.**
An extensive garden with mature trees, shrubs and perennials divided into areas. Herbaceous beds in semi shade, a raised triangular bed with lavender, agapanthus and roses. Two arches, draped with grapevines, wisteria, kiwi and clematis, guide you into a tranquil, white garden and a wildlife pond, lead to tropical and Mediterranean beds with olive, bean and fig trees, palms, bamboos and cannas. Refreshments served from the pool house; relax by the pool in the tropical garden. Partial wheelchair access.

83 159 HIGHAM ROAD, N17

Downhills Park, Tottenham, N17 6NX. Jess Kitley & Sally Gray. *Tube: Turnpike Lane then 15 mins walk/W4 alight Higham Rd or Seven Sisters then 41 bus alight Philip Lane, walk up through Downhills Park. Buses 341, 230,41,W4. Free parking on Higham Rd.* **Sun 3 June (2-6). Adm £4, chd free. Home-made teas. Also open 77 Handsworth Road. Cream teas and Prosecco.**
Transformed 5 years ago, this sloping 80'x30' garden backs onto woodland. It is subtly terraced, incorporating sculptural elements amongst perennials, shrubs and trees. The pond, dug into clay, harnesses natural springs mitigating constant flooding. There are various areas to sit and contemplate, each with a unique character of its own, where you can appreciate the planting and enjoy the wildlife. Featured in the 'Ham & High'.

84 HIGHWOOD ASH, NW7

Highwood Hill, Mill Hill, NW7 4EX. Mr & Mrs R Gluckstein. *Totteridge & Whetstone on Northern line, then bus 251 stops outside - Rising Sun/Mill Hill stop. By car: A5109 from Apex Corner to Whetstone. Garden located opp The Rising Sun PH.* **Sun 13 May (2-6). Adm £5, chd free. Home-made teas.**
Created over the last 50yrs, this 3¼ acre garden features rolling lawns, two large interconnecting ponds with koi, herbaceous and shrub borders and a modern gravel garden. A garden for all seasons with many interesting plants and sculptures. A country garden in London. Featured in Garden News. Partial access for wheelchairs, lowest parts too steep.

20 Beechwood Avenue

85 THE HOLME, NW1

Inner Circle, Regents Park, NW1 4NT. Lessee of The Crown Commission. *In centre of Regents Park on The Inner Circle. Within 15 mins walk from Great Portland St or Baker St Underground Stations, opp Regents Park Rose Garden Cafe.* **Sat 30 June, Sun 1 July, Sat 4, Sun 5 Aug (2.30-5.30). Adm £5, chd free.**

4 acre garden filled with interesting and unusual plants. Sweeping lakeside lawns intersected by islands of herbaceous beds. Extensive rock garden with waterfall, stream and pool. Formal flower garden with unusual annual and half hardy plants, sunken lawn, fountain pool and arbour. Gravel paths and some steps which gardeners will help wheelchair users to negotiate.

86 33 HUDDLESTON ROAD, N7

London, N7 0AD. Gilly Hatch & Tom Gretton. *5 mins from Tufnell Park Tube. Tube: Tufnell Park. Buses: 4, 134, 390 to Tufnell Park. Follow Tufnell Park Rd to 3rd rd on R.* **Sun 24 June (2-6.30). Adm £3.50, chd free. Home-made teas.**

The rambunctious front garden weaves together perennials, grasses and ferns, while the back garden makes a big impression in a small space. After 40yrs, the lawn is now a wide curving path, a deep sunny bed on one side, mixing shrubs and perennials in an ever changing blaze of colour, on the other, a screen of varied greens and textures. This flowery passage leads to a secluded sitting area. Exhibition of paintings and hand-made prints by Gilly Hatch, with 10% of sales going to the NGS.

87 1A HUNGERFORD ROAD, N7

London, N7 9LA. David Matzdorf, davidmatzdorf@blueyonder.co.uk, www.growingontheedge.net. *Between Camden Town & Holloway. Tube: Caledonian Rd. Buses: 17, 29, 91, 253, 259, 274, 390 & 393. Parking free on Sundays.* **Sun 17 June (12-6). Adm £3, chd free. Also open 60 & 62 Hungerford Road. Visits also by arrangement Apr to Oct.**

Unique eco house with walled, lush front garden in modern exotic style, densely planted with palms, acacia, bamboo, ginger lilies, bananas, ferns, yuccas, abutilons and unusual understorey plants. Floriferous and ambitious green roof resembling Mediterranean or Mexican hillside, planted with yuccas, dasylirions, agaves, aloes, flowering shrubs, euphorbias, grasses, alpines, sedums and aromatic herbs. Sole access to roof is via built in ladder. Garden and roof each 50ft x 18ft.

88 60 & 62 HUNGERFORD ROAD, N7

London, N7 9LP. John Gilbert, Lynne Berry & Frances Pine. *Between Camden Town & Holloway. Tube: Caledonian Rd, 6 mins walk. Buses: 29 & 253 to Hillmarton Rd stop in Camden Rd. Also 17, 91, 259, 393 to Hillmarton Rd. 10 to York Way.* **Sun 17 June (2-6). Adm £5, chd free. Tea. Also open 1a Hungerford Road.**

Joint opening of two contrasting gardens behind a Victorian terrace. No. 62 is a densely planted mature garden designed to maximise space for planting and create several different sitting areas, views and moods. Professional garden designer's own garden. No 60 is a family garden with a large lawn and a good range of shrubs, flowering perennials and trees. Together they form an inspiring oasis.

89 THE HURLINGHAM CLUB, SW6

Ranelagh Gardens, London, SW6 3PR. The Members of the Hurlingham Club, www.hurlinghamclub.org.uk. *Main gate at E end of Ranelagh Gardens. Tube: Putney Bridge (110yds). NB: No onsite parking. Meter parking on local streets & restricted parking on Sats (9-5).* **Sat 19 May (10-5). Adm £5, chd free. Light refreshments in the Napier Servery in the East Wing.**

Rare opportunity to visit this 42 acre jewel with many mature trees, 2 acre lake with water fowl, expansive lawns and a river walk. Capability Brown and Humphry Repton were involved with landscaping. The gardens are renowned for their roses, herbaceous and lakeside borders, shrubberies and stunning bedding displays. The riverbank is a haven for wildlife with native trees, shrubs and wild flowers. Garden Tours at 11am and 2pm - ticketed event, tickets available at entrance.

90 HURST HOUSE, IG8

1 Broomhill Walk, Woodford Green, IG8 9HF. Nicola & Nicolas Munday, www.hursthousewoodford.com. *On Woodford Green nr statue of Sir Winston Churchill. Private rd directly in front of house for drop off & pick up only. Parking in nearby rds. 15 mins walk from S Woodford Central Line Station.* **Mon 7 May (2-5). Adm £5, chd free. Light refreshments.**

Large, tranquil walled garden behind Queen Anne house. Well structured with York stone balustraded terrace leading to formal lawn and rose garden separated by an informal glade. Many of the trees and shrubs incl a weeping silver pear tree and handkerchief tree date back to 1954 to designs by Percy Cane (a well known Essex born designer). Garden accessed by gentle slopes and mainly level.

91 9 IMBER PARK ROAD, KT10

Esher, KT10 8JB. Jane & John McNicholas, 020 8398 0801, jane_mcnicholas@hotmail.com. *½m from centre of Esher. From the A307, turn into Station Rd which becomes Ember Lane. Go past Esher train station on R. Take 3rd rd on R into Imber Park Rd.* **Sun 24 June (1-5). Adm £3.50, chd free. Home-made teas. Visits also by arrangement May to Aug, groups 10+.**

An established cottage style garden, designed and maintained by the owners who are passionate about gardening and plants. The garden is S-facing, with well stocked, colourful herbaceous borders containing a wide variety of perennials, evergreen and deciduous shrubs, a winding lawn area and a small garden retreat. Featured in Garden News Magazine.

92 23 IMPERIAL ROAD, N22

London, N22 8DE. Kate Gadsby. *Off Bounds Green Rd between Bounds Green Tube & Wood Green Tube. 5 mins from Alexandra Palace mainline.* **Sun 30 Sept (12-4). Adm £3.50, chd free. Home-made teas.**

Tiny back garden overflowing with interesting and unusual plants where an inventive and inspiring approach to planting, has created a surprising number of perspectives. A late September opening to show how many varieties of aster can be fitted into a very small space. Semi covered deck allows enjoyment in sun and rain.

93 THE INNER AND MIDDLE TEMPLE GARDENS, EC4

Crown Office Row, Inner Temple, London, EC4Y 7HL. The Honourable Societies of the Inner and Middle Temples, www.innertemple.org.uk/www.middletemple.org.uk. *Entrance: Main Garden Gate on Crown Office Row, access via Tudor Street gate or Middle Temple Lane gate.* **Tue 19 June (11.30-3). Adm £50. Pre-booking essential, please visit www.ngs.org.uk or phone 01483 211535 for information & booking. Light refreshments.**

Inner Temple Garden is a haven of tranquillity and beauty with sweeping lawns, unusual trees and charming woodland areas. The well known herbaceous border shows off inspiring plant combinations from early spring through to autumn. The award winning gardens of Middle Temple are comprised of a series of courtyards and one larger formal garden. Each courtyard has its own character and continues to offer peaceful respite from the bustle of central London as they have for centuries. **Adm incl conducted tour of the gardens by Head Gardeners. Light lunch in Middle Hall, one of the finest examples of an Elizabethan hall in the country.** Please advise in advance if wheelchair access is required.

GROUP OPENING

94 KEW GREEN GARDENS, TW9

Kew, TW9 3AH. *NW side of Kew Green. Tube: Kew Gardens. Mainline stn: Kew Bridge. Buses: 65, 391. Entrance via riverside.* **Sun 27 May (2-5). Combined adm £6, chd free. Evening opening Sun 3 June (6-8). Combined adm £8, chd free. Teas in St Anne's Church (May). Wine at Gardens (June).**

65 KEW GREEN
Giles & Angela Dixon.

67 KEW GREEN
Lynne & Patrick Lynch.

69 KEW GREEN
John & Virginia Godfrey.

71 KEW GREEN
Mr & Mrs Jan Pethick.

73 KEW GREEN
Sir Donald & Lady Elizabeth Insall.

Five long gardens behind a row of C18 houses on the Green, close to the Royal Botanic Gardens. These gardens feature the profusely planted and traditional borders of a mature English country garden, and contrast formal gardens, terraces and lawns, laid out around tall old trees, with wilder areas and woodland and wild flower planting. One has an unusual architect designed summerhouse, while another offers the surprise of a modern planting of espaliered miniature fruit trees. There is also a water feature.

Macmillan and the National Garden Scheme, partners for more than 30 years

95 NEW 57 KING EDWARD ROAD, EN5

Barnet, EN5 5AU. Ms Pam Mitchell. *New Barnet. High Barnet tube, 15 mins walk. Bus 263 and others to Everyman Cinema. Turn up Potters Lane opposite BP Garage then 1st left. Plenty of free parking. Entry also via Meadway if coming from Nth.* **Sun 15 July (2-6). Adm £4, chd free. Home-made teas.**

When we bought this property 3 years ago, the garden was a sloping wilderness covered with brambles and tree stumps. While the builders were busy renovating the house we worked on transforming the garden. The only thing left from the original is the large Bramley Apple tree.

96 KING HENRY'S WALK GARDEN, N1

11c King Henry's Walk, London, N1 4NX. Friends of King Henry's Walk Garden, www.khwgarden.org.uk. *Buses incl: 21, 30, 38, 56, 141, 277. Behind adventure playground on KHW, off Balls Pond Rd.* **Mon 7 May (2-4.30). Adm £3.50, chd free. Home-made teas.** Donation to Friends of KHW Garden.

Vibrant ornamental planting welcomes the visitor to this hidden oasis and leads you into a verdant community garden with secluded woodland area, beehives, wildlife pond, wall trained fruit trees, and plots used by local residents to grow their own fruit and vegetables. Disabled WC.

10 York Road

97 LAMBETH PALACE, SE1

Lambeth Palace Rd, London, SE1 7JU. The Church Commissioners, www.archbishopofcanterbury.org. *Entrance via Main Gatehouse facing Lambeth Bridge. Station: Waterloo. Tube: Westminster, Vauxhall all 10 mins walk. Buses: 3, C10, 77, 344, 507.* **Evening opening Mon 21 May, Mon 18 June (5.30-8). Adm £5, chd free. Wine.**

Lambeth Palace has one of the oldest and largest private gardens in London. It has been occupied by Archbishops of Canterbury since 1197. Formal courtyard boasts historic White Marseilles fig planted in 1556. Parkland style garden features mature trees, woodland and native planting, orchard and pond. There is a formal rose terrace, summer gravel border, scented chapel garden and active beehives. Tours will be available. Ramped path to rose terrace, disabled WC.

98 NEW 16 LANDELLS ROAD, SE22

East Dulwich, London, SE22 9PG. Clare Bawcutt. *Entrance to garden is via a gate in Plough Lane which runs behind the property.* **Sun 27 May (2-5). Adm £3.50, chd free.**

A mature cherry tree provides a canopy to this compact (14m x 5m) Victorian terrace oasis. Stepping stones and a brick pathway allow you to explore modern country style planting and an impressive spring display of alliums and peonies. Side return displays delicate succulents and pretty terracotta planters. Shaded area with foxgloves and a variety of ferns.

99 12 LANSDOWNE ROAD, W11

London, W11 3LW. The Lady Amabel Lindsay. *Tube: Holland Park. Buses: 12, 88, 94, 148, GL711, 715 to Holland Park, 4 mins walk up Lansdowne Rd.* **Thur 10 May (2.30-6.30). Adm £5, chd free. Light refreshments. Soft drinks.**

A country garden in the heart of London. An old mulberry tree, billowing borders, rambling Rosa banksiae, and a greenhouse of climbing pelargoniums. Partial wheelchair access to level paved surfaces.

100 42 LATIMER ROAD, E7

Forest Gate, E7 0LQ. Janet Daniels. *8 mins walk from Forest Gate or Wanstead Park stn. From Forest Gate cross to Sebert Rd, then 3rd rd on L.* **Sun 22 July (11-4). Adm £3.50, chd free. Home-made teas.**

Passionate plant collector's garden in two separate areas. First (90ft x 15ft) has an abundance of baskets, climbers, shrubs, fruit trees and ponds. Step down to large secret garden (70ft x 30ft) containing exuberant borders, wildlife pond with gunnera and walnut tree. Unusual and exotic plants and other quirky features. Wildlife friendly. Summerhouse full of collectables, dinky toys and collection of old wooden tools.

101 84 LAVENDER GROVE, E8

Hackney, E8 3LS. Anne Pauleau, a.pauleau@hotmail.co.uk. *50m off junction between Lansdowne Drive and Lavender Grove.* **Sun 24 June (2-5). Adm £3, chd free. Home-made teas. Visits also by arrangement Mar to Sept.**

Courtyard garden with backdrop of bamboos and palms, foil to clipped shrubs leading to wilder area mingling roses, lilies, alliums, grasses, clematis, poppies, star jasmine and jasmine. A very highly scented garden with rampant ramblers and billowing vegetation. Children's quiz offered with prize on completion.

102 2 LITTLEBURY ROAD, SW4

Clapham, SW4 6DN. Jack Wallington & Christopher Anderson, www.jackwallington.com. *2 mins from Clapham High Street station, 4 mins walk from Clapham North & Clapham Common. From main High St, head down Clapham Manor St, turn R down Voltaire Rd past leisure centre. Take 1st L on Littlebury Rd, house on R.* **Sun 9 Sept (12-5). Adm £3.50, chd free. Home-made teas.**

Small garden, creatively packed with bright colours and interesting plants. Features a living wall of 50 fern species, a micro-pond, tropical plants and quirky indoor plants. In July colour comes from monad, clematis, acanthus, salvia and aliums. September opening sees Dahlias in triumphant, unmissable glory. Owned by a garden designer/writer who uses his garden as a trial ground for new ideas. Fern wall planned and constructed by the owners to house their collection of rare and unusual fern species. Plants in every part of the house, from the front, through rooms and out to the garden. Cut flowers from Jack's allotment.

103 49 LOFTUS ROAD, W12

London, W12 7EH. Emma Plunket, emma@plunketgardens.com, www.plunketgardens.com. *Shepherds Bush or Shepherds Bush Market tube, train or bus to Uxbridge Rd. Free street parking.* **Evening opening Thur 14 June (5.30-8). Adm £4, chd free. Wine. Visits also by arrangement May to Sept.**

Professional garden designer, Emma Plunket, opens her acclaimed walled garden. Richly planted, it is the ultimate hard working city garden with all year structure and colour; fruit, vegetables and herbs. Set against a backdrop of trees, it is unexpectedly open and peaceful. Garden plan, plant list and advice available.

104 NEW 2 LONSDALE SQUARE, N1

London, N1 1EN. Jenny Kingsley. *Barnsbury. Tube: Highbury & Islington or Angel. Along Liverpool Rd, walk up Richmond Ave. 1st R, entrance via passageway on R.* **Sun 13 May (2.30-5.30). Adm £2.50, chd free. Also open Malvern Terrace Gardens.**

One could describe our garden as a person: small, unpretentious and attractively formed by yew and box hedges, and faithful beds with hellebores, fatsia, erysimum, euonymous, euphorbia and the lively climbing roses, star jasmine and solanium. Planters with olive trees, herbs and pansies are fine companions, mauve, white and emerald favoured colours. She walks on cobblestones, a most tranquil soul. Teas at Malvern Terrace Gardens N1 1HR.

GROUP OPENING

105 LOWER CLAPTON GARDENS, E5

Hackney, London, E5 0RL. *12 mins walk from Hackney Central or Hackney Downs stns. Buses 38, 55, 106, 253, 254 or 425, alight Lower Clapton Rd.* **Sun 20 May (2-6). Combined adm £5, chd free. Home-made teas at 16 Powerscroft Rd.**

8 ALMACK ROAD
Philip Lightowlers.

16 POWERSCROFT ROAD
Elizabeth Welch.

77 RUSHMORE ROAD
Penny Edwards.

Lower Clapton is an area of mid Victorian terraces sloping down to the River Lea. This group of gardens reflect their owner's tastes and interests. 77 Rushmore Rd features a fruit and vegetable garden and wildlife pond. At 16 Powerscroft Rd we have a S facing garden with a raised pond, space for meditation and mixed borders. 8 Almack Rd is a long thin garden with two different rooms, one cool and peaceful the other with hot colours and tropical foliage.

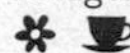

GROUP OPENING

106 LYNDHURST SQUARE GROUP, SE15

Lyndhurst Square, London, SE15 5AR. Group Gardens. *Overground to Peckham Rye station; numerous bus routes.* **Sun 17 June (1.30-5). Combined adm £5, chd free. Home-made teas at 5 Lyndhurst square.** Donation to MIND, Mental Health Charity.

5 LYNDHURST SQUARE
Martin Lawlor & Paul Ward.

6 LYNDHURST SQUARE
Iain Henderson & Amanda Grygelis.

7 LYNDHURST SQUARE
Pernille Ahlström & Barry Joseph.

Three very attractive gardens open in this small, elegant square of 1840s listed villas located in Peckham SE London. Each approx 90ft x 50ft has its own shape and style as the Square curves in a U shape. No. 5, the design combines Italianate and Gothic themes with roses, lavender, olives, euphorbia and ferns within yew and box parterres. Plants for sale here. No. 6 is an up to date family garden given drama with architectural plants. A wisteria pergola frames the vegetables bordered by espaliered apples. Check out the treehouse! Simplicity, Swedish style, is key at No. 7, with roses and raised beds, framed by yew hedges.

107 16 MAIDA WAY, E4

Chingford, E4 7JL. Clare & Steve Francis. *1m from Chingford town centre off Kings Head Hill. Maida Way is a cul-de-sac off Maida Avenue that can be accessed via Kings Head Hill or Sewardstone Road.* **Sun 1 July (1-5). Adm £4, chd free. Light refreshments.**

Three distinct areas. Walled patio with raised beds of ferns, climbers, hostas and patio planters. Steps up to middle garden with a large koi pond, seating area, acers, shrubs, herbaceous plants, grasses and grapevine. Top garden reached via archway in a the bay hedge. Kitchen garden with raised beds of fruit trees and bushes, herbs and vegetables. Numerous retro artefacts creatively upcycled. Wheelchair access to patio area only.

GROUP OPENING

108 MALVERN TERRACE GARDENS, N1

Malvern Terrace, London, N1 1HR. *Barnsbury, Islington. Malvern Terrace is off Thornhill Rd (nr The Albion PH) between Hemingford Rd & Liverpool Rd.* **Sun 13 May (2.30-5.30). Combined adm £4, chd free. Home-made teas. Also open 13 College Cross, N1.**

Group of unique 1830s terrace houses built on the site of Thomas Oldfield's dairy and cricket field. Cottage style front gardens in cobbled cul-de-sac - a peaceful oasis in the heart of London. Live music.

109 4 MANNINGTREE ROAD, HA4

Ruislip, HA4 0ES. Costas Lambropoulos & Roberto Haddon. *Manningtree Road is just off Victoria Road, 10 mins walk from South Ruislip tube station.* **Sun 29 July (2-6). Adm £4, chd free. Home-made teas.**

Compact garden with an exotic feel that combines hardy architectural plants with more tender ones. A feeling of a small oasis incl plants like Musa Basjoo, Ensette Montbelliardii, tree ferns, black bamboo etc. Potted mediterranean plants on the patio incl a fig tree and two olive trees.

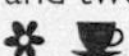

110 53 MANOR ROAD, N16

Stoke Newington, N16 5BH. Jonathan Trustram. *Nr Stoke Newington station & Heathland Rd 106 bus stop.* **Evening opening Sun 10 June (4-8.30). Sun 9 Sept (1-5). Adm £3.50, chd free. Home-made teas. Also jams and chutneys for sale from the Decent Hard-Working Family Preserves Co.**

Big garden for London, thickly enclosed by ivy, roses and jasmine, crowded with plants, many unusual: eryngiums, thalictrums, salvias, pelargoniums, eucomis, inulas, lilies, indigofera, azara, myrtle. Small sculptural rock garden. Soft fruit. Lots of poorly policed self-seeders. Organic credentials finally lost in 30 years war against slugs. Featured in Ham and High.

GROUP OPENING

111 MAPLEDENE GARDENS, E8

Mapledene Road, Hackney, E8 3JW. *7 mins walk from 67, 149, 242, 243 bus stop on Middleton Rd, 10 mins from 30, 38, 55 stops on Dalston Lane. 7 mins from Haggerston Overground or 10 mins walk through London Fields from Mare St buses.* **Sun 3 June (2-6). Combined adm £5, chd free.**

53 MAPLEDENE ROAD
Tigger Cullinan, 020 7249 3754, tiggerine8@blueyonder.co.uk. **Visits also by arrangement May to Aug for groups of 20 max.**

55 MAPLEDENE ROAD
Amanda & Tony Mott.

61 MAPLEDENE ROAD
Katja & Ned Staple.

NEW 63 MAPLEDENE ROAD
Helen Hunsperger & Simon Mathews.

With much the same space, these 4 strongly contrasting N-facing neighbouring gardens have very different design intentions and styles. 53 is an established plantaholic's garden, with jewel-like planting where clematis take pride of place. 55 is a garden with Moorish influenced terrace leading to a wildlife garden planted to attract birds, butterflies and bees. 61 is a newly planted family garden with large open lawn, wildflower meadow and delicate, ethereal planting and 63 has a romantic feel with repeat planting of roses, hydrangeas and box balls.

112 MARIE CURIE HOSPICE, HAMPSTEAD, NW3

Lyndhurst Gardens, London, NW3 5NS. Arlene Main. *Nearest tube: Belsize Park. Buses: 46, 268 & C11 all stop nr Hospice.* **Sun 24 June (2-5.30). Adm £3.50, chd free. Home-made teas.**

This peaceful and secluded two part garden surrounds the Marie Curie Hospice, Hampstead. A garden tended to by dedicated volunteers makes for a wonderful space for patients to enjoy the shrubs and seasonal colourful flowers. The garden has seating areas for relaxation either in the shade or in the sunshine with a great views of the garden, and in company with squirrels running through the trees.

113 27 MENELIK ROAD, NW2

West Hampstead, NW2 3RJ. C Klemera, cklemera@hotmail.com. *E of Shoot up Hill , N of Mill Lane. From Kilburn tube, buses 16, 32,189, 316, 332 to Mill Lane on Shoot up Hill, then walk Minster Rd to Menelik Rd at end. Or, from W. Hampstead tube, C11 bus (direction Brent Cross) to Menelik Rd stop.* **Sun 1 July (2-5.30). Adm £4, chd free. Home-made teas in the drive at the entrance. Visits also by arrangement Apr to Sept groups 10+ with guided information by owner. Tea and cake available.**

A garden full of surprises and humour. A 30yr old Trachycarpus overlooks many exotic plants of strong shape, texture and colour. Discover a cloud pruned tree in the oriental corner from your seat in the tea house. Topiary pops up from the tapestry of flowers and the piazza is secluded by bay and banana trees, often in flower. Paths lead you between lush foliage to brush your senses! New additions annually.

114 41 MILL HILL ROAD, W3

London, W3 8JE. Marcia Hurst, 020 8992 2632 or 07989 581940, marcia.hurst@sudbury-house.co.uk. *Tube: Acton Town, cross zebra crossing, bear right, Mill Hill Rd second right off Gunnersbury Lane. Many local Buses and London Overground.* **Evening opening Fri 6 July (7-9). Combined adm with 65 Mill Hill Road £6, chd free. Wine. Sun 5 Aug (2-6). Combined adm with 65 Mill Hill Road £5, chd free. Home-made teas. Visits also by arrangement June to Aug no min, max 20.**

120ft x 40ft garden. A surprisingly large and sunny garden, with lavender and hornbeam hedges, herbaceous planting and climbers, incl unusual and rare plants as the owner is a compulsive plantaholic. Good in July and August, with many salvias, clematis, dahlias and late flowering hardy and half hardy annuals. Lots of space to sit and enjoy the garden. A good selection of the plants growing in the garden are for sale in pots with planting and growing advice from the knowledgable owner. Featured in the Daily Mail Weekend Magazine.

115 65 MILL HILL ROAD, W3

London, W3 8JF. Anna Dargavel, 07802 241965, annadargavel@mac.com. *Tube: Acton Town, turn R, Mill Hill Rd on R off Gunnersbury Lane.* **Evening opening Fri 6 July (7-9). Combined adm with 41 Mill Hill Road £6. Wine. Sun 5 Aug (2-6). Combined adm with 41 Mill Hill Road £5. Home-made teas. Visits also by arrangement June to Aug groups 20 max.**
Garden designer's own garden. A secluded and tranquil space, paved, with changes of level and borders. Sunny areas, topiary, a greenhouse and interesting planting combine to provide a wildlife haven. A pond and organic principles are used to promote a green environment and give a stylish walk to a studio at the end of the garden.

116 27 NASSINGTON ROAD, NW3

Hampstead, London, NW3 2TX. Lucy Scott-Moncrieff. *From Hampstead Heath rail stn & bus stops at South End Green, go up South Hill Pk, then Parliament Hill, R into Nassington Rd.* **Sun 10 June (2-6). Adm £5, chd free. Home-made teas.**
Double width town garden planted for colour and to support wildlife. Spectacular ancient wisteria, prolific roses; herbs and unusual fruit and vegetables in with the flowers. The main feature is a large eco pond with colourful planting in and out of the water, and lots of mini-beasts. Pots and planters, arches, bowers, view of allotments and very peaceful location give a rural feel in the city. Pond dipping for newts and mini beasts all afternoon. Live music from the Secret Life Sax Quartet from 4:30 to 5:30pm. Cakes incl lemon drizzle made with lemons from the garden and gluten free cakes; teas incl rose hips from the garden but also real tea.

118 15 NORCOTT ROAD, N16

Stoke Newington, N16 7BJ. Amanda & John Welch. *Buses: 67, 73, 76, 106, 149, 243, 393, 476, 488. Clapton & Rectory Rd mainline stns. One way system: by car approach from Brooke Rd which crosses Norcott Rd, garden in S half of Norcott Rd.* **Sun 16 Sept (12-4). Adm £3.50, chd free. Home-made teas.**
A large (for London) walled garden. Developed by the present owners over the past thirty-five years, it has a pond, aged fruit trees and an abundance of herbaceous plants. For those loyal visitors used to our garden in early summer a complete change – we've decided to risk September, with an earlier opening time, untidy but generally glorious with michaelmas daisies, heleniums, dahlias.

119 26 NORMANDY AVENUE, EN5

Barnet, EN5 2JA. Derek Epstein & Jo Vargas. *Tube: High Barnet then 5 mins walk. Buses: 34, 184, 84, 107, 307, 263, 326, 234. Ample parking. Normandy Ave is opp QE Girls School with Old Court House on corner.* **Sun 1 July (2-6). Adm £3.50, chd free. Home-made teas.**
120ft garden with three water features, two lawns, two 1920s garden buildings, two terraces, 40 pots, woodland walk, a veggie patch, sculptures and ornaments. A host of plants including roses, hydrangeas, begonias, shrubs. Some of our sculpture and pottery will be on display. Sit on one of the terraces, in the lovely summerhouse, or by the pond while you enjoy tea and our delicious cakes.

120 5 NORTHAMPTON PARK, N1

London, N1 2PP. Andrew Bernhardt & Anne Brogan. *Backing on to St Paul's Shrubbery, Islington. 5 mins walk from Canonbury stn, 10 mins from Highbury & Islington Tube (Victoria Line) Bus: 30, 277, 341, 476.* **Evening opening Fri 29 June (6-9). Sat 30 June (2-6). Tea. Adm £3, chd free. Evening opening 29 June: Prosecco. Afternoon opening 30 June: Teas, strawberries and cream.**
Early Victorian S-facing walled garden, (1840's) saved from neglect and developed over the last 22yrs. Arches, palms, box and yew hedging frame the cool North European blues, whites and greys moving to splashes of red/orange Mediterranean influence. The contrast of the cool garden shielded by a small park creates a sense of seclusion from its inner London setting.

121 OAK FARM/ HOMESTEAD, EN2

Cattlegate Road, Crews Hill, Enfield, EN2 9DS. Genine & Martin Newport. *5 mins. from M25 J24 & J25. Follow yellow signs. Few mins walk from Crews Hill station. Opp Warmadams. Entrance in Homestead.* **Sun 13 May (12-5). Adm £4.50, chd free. Light refreshments.**

From pig farm to pastoral idyll spanning 3 acres, reclaimed over 30yrs. Romantic woodland glade, burgeoning arboretum, relaxed planting around sloping lawns, stone ornaments. Walled garden leads to vegetable plot, greenhouse, chickens, small orchard. Martin built the house, Genine the gardens. Enjoy joint inspirational herculean labour of love. In the barn there will be an exhibition of quilts made by a group that are local and use the barn for charity purposes.

122 NEW 46 OLLERTON ROAD, N11

New Southgate, N11 2LA. Mr & Mrs J Richardson. *Close to North circular. Tube: Bounds Green then 10 mins walk direction, N circular corner of Evesham Rd.* **Sun 15, Sun 22 July (2-5.30). Adm £3.50, chd free. Home-made teas.**

A paved garden that has been created from scratch in just 3yrs. Its owner has created raised flower beds out of reclaimed wooden tracks and has managed to create an oasis of calm and tranquility by using Hollyhocks and other tall plants. A lovely pergola covered in vines makes for a shady spot to sit and enjoy the garden. Artist studio will be open showing the owners paintings.

123 ORMELEY LODGE, TW10

Ham Gate Avenue, Richmond, TW10 5HB. Lady Annabel Goldsmith. *From Richmond Park exit at Ham Gate into Ham Gate Ave, 1st house on R. From Richmond A307, after 1½m, past New Inn on R. At T-lights turn L into Ham Gate Ave.* **Sun 17 June (3-6). Adm £5, chd free. Tea.**

Large walled garden in delightful rural setting on Ham Common. Wide herbaceous borders and box hedges. Walk through to orchard with wild flowers. Vegetable garden, knot garden, aviary and chickens. Trellised tennis court with roses and climbers. A number of historic stone family dog memorials. Dogs not permitted.

124 4 ORMONDE ROAD, HA6

Moor Park, Northwood, HA6 2EL. Hasruty & Yogesh Patel. *Approx 5m from J17 & 18, M25; 6½m from J5, M1. From Batchworth Lane take Wolsey Rd exit at mini r'about. Ormonde Rd is 2nd turning on L. Ample parking on Ormonde Rd & surrounding rds.* **Sun 13 May (2-5). Adm £4.50, chd free. Cream teas.**

Beautifully planted frontage entices visitors to a large rear garden. A calm oasis enclosed by mature hedging. A rare variegated flowering tulip tree provides dappled shade alongside rhododendrons, peonies, magnolias and diverse acers. Lavender hues of phlox foam along the raised patio. There is much interest throughout the whole garden due to attention paid to successional planting.

125 12 OVERBRAE, BR3

Beckenham, BR3 1SX. Mrs Alix Branch. *Off Worsley Bridge Road, nr Kent Cricket Ground. Nearest stations, Beckenham Junction, Lower Sydenham or Beckenham Hill. Each approx 1m Bus 352.* **Sun 1 July (2-5). Adm £3.50, chd free. Light refreshments. Also open 40 Greenways.**

Medium sized suburban garden with a small woodland area that won Bromley in Bloom. Lots of summer colour in beds, hanging baskets and pots. Box hedge has been clipped in form of Loch Ness Monster (guaranteed friendly). Large collection of cacti and succulents add interest and variety. Some steep slopes require care.

126 PADDOCK ALLOTMENTS & LEISURE GARDENS, SW20

51 Heath Drive, Raynes Park, SW20 9BE. Paddock Horticultural Society. *Bus:57, 131, 200 to Raynes Pk station then 10 min walk or bus 163. 152 to Bushey Rd 7 min walk; 413, 5 min walk from Cannon Hill Lane. Street parking.* **Sat 16 June (12-5). Adm £3.50, chd free. Light refreshments.**

An allotment site not to be missed, over 150 plots set in 5½ acres. Our tenants come from diverse communities growing a wide range of flowers, fruits and vegetables, some plots are purely organic others resemble English country gardens. Winner of London in Bloom Best Allotment. Plants, jams and produce for sale. Display of arts and crafts by members of the Paddock Hobby Club. Ploughmans lunch available. Paved and grass paths, mainly level.

127 11 PARK AVENUE NORTH, N8

Crouch End, London, N8 7RU. Mr Steven Buckley & Ms Liz Roberts. *Tube: Finsbury Park & Turnpike Lane, nearest bus stop W3, 144, W7.* **Sun 24 June (11.30-6). Adm £4, chd free. Home-made teas.**

An exotic 250ft T-shaped garden, threaded through what was once an Edwardian orchard. Dramatic, mainly spiky, foliage dominates, with the focus on palms, agaves, dasylirions, aeoniums, tree ferns, nolinas, cycads, bamboo, yuccas, cacti and several hundred types of succulent. Aloes are a highlight. Fruit trees include banana, peach and apricot. Rocks and terracotta pots lend a Mediterranean accent.

128 18 PARK CRESCENT, N3

Finchley, N3 2NJ. Rosie Daniels, 020 8343 3270. *Tube: Finchley Central. Buses: 82 to Victoria Park, also 125, 460, 626, 683. Walk from Ballards Lane into Etchingham Pk Road, 2nd L Park Crescent.* **Sun 17 June (2-6). Adm £4, chd free. Home-made teas. Visits also by**

arrangement June & July, groups min 10, max 16.
Constantly evolving, charming small garden designed and densely planted by owner. Roses and clematis in June and salvias, rudbeckia, helenium and some new grasses in July. Small pond, tub water feature and bird haven. Stepped terrace with lots of pots. New glass installations and sculptures by owner. Hidden seating with view through garden. Secluded, peaceful, restorative. Children's treasure hunt. Extensive collection of clematis.

129 3 THE PARK N6

off Southwood Lane, London, N6 4EU. Mr & Mrs G Schrager, 020 8348 3314, buntyschrager@gmail.com. *3 mins from Highgate tube, up Southwood Lane. The Park is 1st on R. Buses: 43, 134, 143, 263.* **Sun 20 May (2.30-5.30). Adm £3.50, chd free. Home-made teas. Also open 33 Wood Vale. Visits also by arrangement Apr to June, small groups welcome.**
Established large garden with informal planting for colour, scent and bees. Pond with fish, frogs and tadpoles. Tree peonies, Crinodendron hookerianum and Paulownia. Plants, tea and home-made jam for sale. Children particularly welcome - a treasure hunt with prizes!

GROUP OPENING

130 NEW PARK ROAD GARDENS, W4

London, W4 3HH. *Arrive by overground train at Chiswick Stn, follow Park Rd (opp the stn, N side) for approx ½m north.* **Evening opening Sun 24 June (6-8.30). Combined adm £8, chd free. Wine.**

NEW 34 PARK ROAD
Simon Lockett.

36 PARK ROAD
Meyrick & Louise Chapman.

NEW 45 PARK ROAD
Helen Morris.

NEW 57 PARK ROAD
Simon & Alison Hosken.

These four gardens are all within 100 metres of each other on the northern end of Park Road. They offer a range of design from contemporary formal through romantic to mediterranean. Each one, however, offers an expansiveness that is rare in London gardens and all blend a concern for plantsmanship with design and successfully include the wider environment. Partial wheelchair access to all gardens.

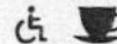

131 4 PARK VILLAGE EAST (TOWER LODGE GARDENS), NW1

Regents Park, London, NW1 7PX. Eveline Carn, 07831 136069, evelinecbcarn@icloud.com. *Tube: Camden Town or Mornington Crescent 7 mins. Bus: C2 or 274 3 mins. Opp The York & Albany, just off junction of Parkway/Prince Albert Rd.* **Evening opening Sat 26 May (5.30-8.30). Adm £6, chd free. Wine. Sun 3 June (2.30-6). Adm £5, chd free. Home-made teas. Also open 70 Gloucester Crescent. Visits also by arrangement with home-made teas, coffee and cakes, or drinks and canapés, any size group welcome.**
An unexpectedly large, tranquil garden behind a John Nash house, screened by trees and descending over 3 terraces with stepped ponds to the original foundations of the Regents Canal. Emphasis on shape, texture and bold foliage in strong landscape architecture. Areas of new planting. Open again in June alongside two other unique local gardens. Tree hung swing. Sculpture. Secret Life Saxophone Quartet will perform on Saturday 26 May from 6.45pm.

132 174 PECKHAM RYE, SE22

East Dulwich, London, SE22 9QA. Mr & Mrs Ian Bland. *Stn: Peckham Rye. Buses: 12, 37, 63, 197, 363. Overlooks Peckham Rye Common from Dulwich side.* **Sun 10 June (2.30-5.30). Adm £3.50, chd free. Home-made teas. Also open 4 Cornflower Terrace.** Donation to St Christopher's Hospice.
An oasis of calm along Peckham Rye. Every year sees something new as the garden evolves. It is densely planted with a wide variety of contrasting foliage. Unusual plants with interesting colour and texture are combined with old favourites. It remains easy care and child friendly. Garden originally designed by Judith Sharpe. Home-made cakes are a must and the plant sale attracts enthusiasts. Easy wheelchair access via side alley.

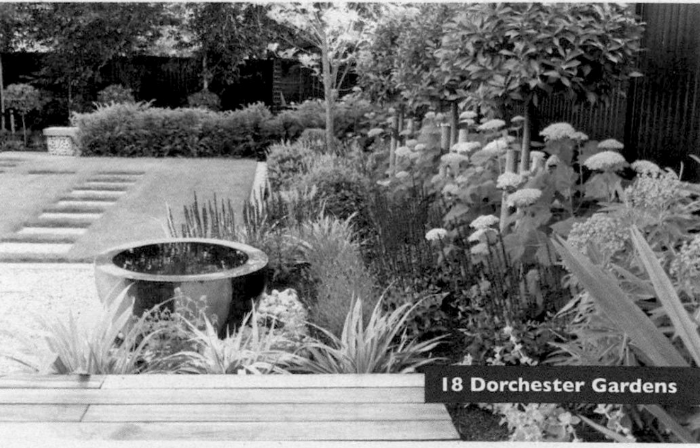

18 Dorchester Gardens

133 PETERSHAM HOUSE, TW10

Petersham Road, Petersham, Richmond, TW10 7AA. Francesco & Gael Boglione, 020 8940 5230, info.richmond@petershamnurseries.com, www.petershamnurseries.com. *Stn: Richmond, then 65 bus to Dysart PH. Entry to garden off Petersham Rd, through nursery. Parking very limited on Church Lane.* **Sun 22 Apr (10-4). Adm £4, chd free. Visits also by arrangement in Apr.**

Broad lawn with large topiary, generously planted double borders. Productive vegetable garden with chickens. Adjoins Petersham Nurseries with extensive plant sales, shop and café serving lunch, tea and cake.

134 18 PETTITS BOULEVARD, RM1

Rise Park, Romford, RM1 4PL. Peter & Lynn Nutley. *From M25 take A12 towards London, turn R at Pettits Lane junction then R again into Pettits Blvd or Romford Stn then 103 or 499 bus to Romford Fire Stn and follow NGS signs.* **Sat 23, Sun 24 June (1-5). Adm £3.50, chd free. Home-made teas.**

A garden 80ft x 23ft on three levels with an ornamental pond, patio area with shrubs and perennials, many in pots. A large eucalyptus tree leads to a woodland themed area with many ferns and hostas. There are agricultural implements and garden ornaments giving a unique and quirky feel to the garden. There are also tranquil seating areas situated throughout. Agricultural implements on show. Havering In Bloom winner.

135 4 PIERMONT GREEN, SE22

East Dulwich, London, SE22 0LP. Janine Wookey. *Triangle of green facing Peckham Rye at the Honor Oak Rd end. Stns: Peckham Rye & Honor Oak. Buses: 63 & 363 (pass the door) & 12. No parking on Green but free parking on side streets nearby.* **Sun 10 June (2-5.30). Combined adm with 4 Cornflower Terrace £5, chd free. Home-made teas. Also open 174 Peckham Rye.**

Given a new look last summer, this L-shaped garden will open in June for the first time with a rather different look parading roses, irises and flowering shrubs. The gravel garden has libertia, crambe maritima and dierama in full swing. Crambe maritima in the white border will be on high and bananas in the shady edible corner will have uncurled their fronds. Live music in the garden.

136 470 PINNER ROAD, HA5

Pinner, HA5 5RR. Nitty Chamcheon. *N Harrow Station, L to T-lights, L at next T-lights, cross to be on Pinner Rd. L - 3rd house from T-lights. Parking: Pinner Rd & George V Av - yellow lines stop after 15 yds.* **Sun 16 Sept (2-6). Adm £4, chd free. Home-made teas.**

Once (18yrs ago) a back yard with just a lawn in the first half and the second half a jungle with a very mature apple and pear tree; now a beautiful garden. A path passing through fruit and vegetable garden to the secret log cabin after a bridge over the pond with waterfall in front of a tree house in the pear tree. An attempt has been made to extend the season as far as possible.

137 153 PORTLAND ROAD, BR1

Bromley, BR1 5AY. Lucia & Simon Parnell. *Off Burnt Ash Lane between Sundridge Park & Grove Park BR stns. From Burnt Ash Lane (at the Toyota showroom) turn into New Street Hill, proceed up hill. Turn L into Portland Road, house is second on the right.* **Sun 5 Aug (2-5.30). Adm £4, chd free. Home-made teas. Pimms.**

Beautifully maintained, this award winning garden is entered via mature front garden. Continue through to a densely planted canvas of lush greenery. Central pathway framed by Buxus. Impressive Redwood structure with Wisteria, Clematis, grasses and seating. Borders with Tree Ferns, Acers, Anemone. Pond. Greenhouse. 4 composters. Quirky garden shed with seating. Live music by Guitarist. Kent made honey for sale. Awarded Silver Gilt and Gold Certificates by The London Garden Society.

138 57 PREBEND GARDENS, W6

Stamford Brook, London, W6 0XT. Jennifer Taylor. *Tube: 2 min walk from Stamford Brook station. Buses: 27, 94, 190, 237, 267, 391, H91 all 3-4 mins walk. Drivers: approach from Bath Rd. Street parking available.* **Evening opening Wed 1, Sat 4 Aug (5.30-8). Adm £4, chd free. Light refreshments.**

Colourful courtyard garden (55 x 25 ft). Professionally designed and planted 5 years ago but constantly evolving. Changes of level, hot bed, pergola, seating areas, alpine garden atop bike shed. Unusual varieties of hydrangea, salvia and pelargonium. Many established plants in pots with underplanting, incl a clementine tree. Ever seen a Buddha's hand? Now is your chance! Awarded 1st Prize - Kensington Gardeners Club.

GROUP OPENING

139 PRINCES AVENUE GARDENS, N10

Muswell Hill, N10 3LS. *Buses: 43 & 134 from Highgate tube; also W7, 102, 144, 234, 299. Princes Ave opp M&S in Muswell Hill Broadway, or John Baird PH in Fortis Green.* **Sun 13 May (2-6). Combined adm £4, chd free. Home-made teas.**

17 PRINCES AVENUE
Patsy Bailey & John Rance.

28 PRINCES AVENUE
Ian & Viv Roberts.

In a beautiful Edwardian avenue in the heart of Muswell Hill Conservation Area, two very different gardens reflect the diverse life styles of their owners. The charming garden at No 17 is designed for relaxing and entertaining . Although south facing it is shaded by large surrounding trees - among which is a ginko. The garden features a superb hosta and fern display. No 28 is a well established traditional garden reflecting the charm typical of the era. Mature trees, shrubs, mixed borders and woodland garden creating an oasis of calm just off the bustling Broadway.

GROUP OPENING

140 RAILWAY COTTAGES, N22

2 Dorset Road, Alexandra Palace, London, N22 7SL. *Tube: Wood Green, 10 mins walk. Overground: Alexandra Palace, 3 mins. Buses W3, 184. 3 mins. Free parking in local streets on Suns.* **Sun 1 July (2-5.30). Combined adm £4.50, chd free. Home-made teas at 2 Dorset Rd.**

2 DORSET ROAD
Jane Stevens, janestevens_london@yahoo.co.uk.
Visits also by arrangement July & Aug for groups 4+.

4 DORSET ROAD
Mark Longworth.

14 DORSET ROAD
Cathy Brogan.

22 DORSET ROAD
Mike & Noreen Ainger.

24A DORSET ROAD
Eddie & Jane Wessman.

A row of historical railway cottages, tucked away from the bustle of Wood Green nr Alexandra Palace, takes the visitor back in time. The tranquil country style garden at 2 Dorset Rd flanks three sides of the house. Hawthorne topiary by the original owner and clipped hedges contrast with climbing roses, clematis, honeysuckle, abutilon, grasses and ferns. Trees include mulberry, quince, fig, apple and a mature willow creating an interesting shady corner with a pond. There is an emphasis on scented flowers that attract bees and butterflies and the traditional medicinal plants found in cottage gardens. No 4 is a pretty secluded woodland garden (accessed through the rear of no 2), and sets off the sculptor owners figurative and abstract work. There are three front gardens open for view. No 14. An informal, organic, bee friendly garden, planted with fragrant and useful herbs, flowers and shrubs. No 22 is nurtured by the grandson of the original railway worker occupant. A lovely place to sit and relax and enjoy the varied planting. No.24a reverts to the potager style cottage garden with raised beds overflowing with vegetables and flowers.

141 RICHARD HOUSE CHILDREN'S HOSPICE, E16

Richard House Drive, Beckton, E16 3RG. Richard House Children's Hospice, www.richardhouse.org.uk. *DLR to Royal Albert, follow footpath, cross Royal Albert Way, 1st L Stansfeld Way 2nd L Richard House Drive. Car: postcode for SatNav not reliable, enter Richard House Drive.* **Sun 20 May (12-4). Adm £3.50, chd free. Tea.**

A series of individual areas around the hospice designed for children, young people, their families and others' enjoyment. Drought tolerant area with silver leaved plants (Save the Water) transferred from Chelsea Flower Show in 2001. Also one of a few sensory gardens in East London incl grassy mounds (Telly Tubby). Bulbs in spring. Shrubs and a mature fig tree. Small interesting woodland walk. Level grounds, with wheelchair accessible woodland path and other ramps as necessary.

142 26 RINGWOOD AVENUE, N2

London, N2 9NS. Ms J Rickards, www.jilaynerickards.com. *Nearest Tube: East Finchley, 10-15 mins walk. Bus: 102, 234, 5-10 mins walk.* **Sun 20 May (2-5.30). Adm £4, chd free. Light refreshments. Tea, coffee, cold drinks and home made cakes available.**

Garden Designer's own private contemporary garden open for 2018 only. Water features provide calm reflective surfaces while also reflecting the changes in ground level. Harmonious use of materials creating a fabulous indoor/outdoor transition. Relaxed meticulous shady woodland planting with backdrop of magnificent mature Oaks. Floriferous front garden. Featured in various publications incl Homes and Gardens, The English Garden and The Garden.

143 NEW ROOFTOPVEGPLOT, W1

122 Gt Titchfield Street, London, W1W 6ST. Miss Wendy Shillam, http://www.rooftopvegplot.com. *Fitzrovia. Located on the 5th floor, flat roof of a private house. Ring the doorbell marked Shillam & Smith to be let into the building.* **Sat 14, Sun 15 July (11-4). Adm £5, chd free. Home-made teas. Cakes and drinks using garden ingredients where possible. Pre-booking essential, please phone 01483 211535 to book.**

A nutritional garden, where fruit and veg grow amongst complementary flowers in six inches of soil, in raised beds on a flat roof. This is a tiny garden, so tours are restricted to six persons. Home made cakes and growing and nutritional tips from Wendy Shillam, a keen environmentalist with an extensive knowledge of green nutrition. Tomatoes and cucumber growing in a greenhouse. Grapevine from Le Moulin Gif-sur-Yvette, France. Elder, Jasmine, Japanese wineberry. Potatoes. Edible honeysuckle (Henrii) Salads, artichokes, garlic, annuals, roses, marigolds, nasturtiums, hyssop, sweet and garden peas, climbing beans and courgettes. Featured in Daily Mail Weekend, Plant Your Own Urban Farm, by Constance Craig Smith. TV Britain's Best Gardens with Alan Titchmarsh, My Tiny Vegplot by Lia Leendertz London Garden Book A-Z Abigail Willis Herb Society Journal.

144 ROYAL COLLEGE OF PHYSICIANS' MEDICINAL GARDEN, NW1

11 St Andrews Place, London, NW1 4LE. Royal College of Physicians of London, www.garden.rcplondon.ac.uk. *Tubes: Great Portland St & Regent's Park. Garden is one block N of station exits, on Outer Circle opp SE corner of Regent's Park.* **Sun 3 June (2-5). Adm £5, chd free. Also open 4 Park Village East NW1 (Tower Lodge Gardens). Visits also by arrangement, with refreshments by prior request.**

One of three distinctive gardens opening in NW1 on Sunday 3 June. Here are 1100 different plants used in medicines around the world and throughout history: plants named after physicians and plants which make modern medicines. Unique beds with the plants used medicinally in the College's Pharmacopoeia of 1618. Guided tours by physicians explaining the uses of the plants, their histories and stories about them. Books about the plants in the medicinal garden will be on sale. The award winning College building will also be open for visitors. Wheelchair ramps at steps.

145 ROYAL TRINITY HOSPICE, SW4

30 Clapham Common North Side, London, SW4 0RN. Royal Trinity Hospice, www.royaltrinityhospice.org.uk. *Tube: Clapham Common. Buses: 35, 37, 345, 137 stop outside.* **Sun 8 Apr, Sun 20 May, Sun 2 Sept (10-4.30). Adm £3, chd free. Home-made teas.**

Royal Trinity's beautiful, award winning gardens play an important therapeutic role in the life and function of Royal Trinity Hospice. Over the years, many people have enjoyed our gardens and today they continue to be enjoyed by patients, families and visitors alike. Set over nearly 2 acres, they offer space for quiet contemplation, family fun and make a great backdrop for events. Picnics welcome. Ramps and pathways.

146 NEW 79 ROYSTON AVENUE, E4

CHINGFORD, E4 9DE. Paul & Christine Lidbury, 07972 002634, lidders.beer@ntlworld.com. *From A406 Crooked Billet r'about take A112 towards Chingford. Continue 0.5m, across T-lights (Morrison's), Royston Ave is 3rd turn on R. Bus 97, 158, 215, 357 (Leonard Rd or Ainslie Wood Rd stops).* **Mon 28 May (12-6). Adm £3.50, chd £1. Tea/coffee and homemade cakes. Quality home-brewed beer tastings available. Visits also by arrangement May to Oct.**

A 55 x 19ft urban garden with over 600 different varieties of plants - a great many in containers, including collections of Hostas, Acers, and Sempervivums. An oasis for local birds and wildlife with two small ponds and insect habitats with further interest provided by ornaments, sculptures and artwork, where words of gardening wisdom abound. Not suitable for young children.

147 7 ST GEORGE'S ROAD, TW1

St Margarets, Twickenham, TW1 1QS. Richard & Jenny Raworth, 020 8892 3713, jraworth@gmail.com, www.raworthgarden.com. *1½m SW of Richmond. Off A316 between Twickenham Bridge & St Margarets r'about.* **Evening opening Sat 2 June (6-8). Adm £6, chd free. Wine. Visits also by arrangement May to Aug for groups 10+.**

Exuberant displays of Old English roses and vigorous climbers with unusual herbaceous perennials. Massed scented crambe cordifolia. Pond with bridge converted into child safe lush bog garden and waterfall. Large N-facing luxuriant conservatory with rare plants and climbers. Pelargoniums a speciality. Sunken garden Pergola covered with climbing roses and clematis. Water feature and fernery.

148 87 ST JOHNS ROAD, E17

London, E17 4JH. Andrew Bliss. *15 mins walk from W'stow tube/ overground or 212/275 bus. Alight at St Johns Rd stop. 10 mins walk from Wood St overground. Very close to N Circular.* **Sun 5 Aug (1.30-5.30). Adm £3.50, chd £0.50. Home-made teas.**

My garden epitomises what can be achieved with imagination, design and colour consideration in a small typical terraced outdoor area. Its themes are diverse and incl a fernery, Jardin Majorelle, a water feature and 3 individual seating areas. All enhanced with circles, mirrors and over planting to create an atmosphere of tranquility within an urban environment.

149 27 ST PETERS SQUARE, W6

London, W6 9NW. Oliver Leigh Wood, oliverleighwood@hotmail.com. *Tube to Stamford Brook exit station & turn S down Goldhawk Rd. At T-lights cont ahead into British Grove. Entrance to garden at 50 British Grove 100 yds on L.* **Sun 6 May (2-6). Adm £4, chd free. Home-made teas. Visits also by arrangement Apr to July.**

This long, secret space, is a plantsman's eclectic semi-tamed wilderness. Created over the last 10yrs it contains lots of camellias, magnolias and fruit trees. Much of the hard landscaping is from skips and the whole garden is full of other people's unconsidered trifles of fancy incl a folly and summer house.

150 19 ST PETER'S STREET, N1

Islington, London, N1 8JD. Adrian Gunning. *Angel, Islington. Tube: Angel. Bus: Islington Green.* **Sun 20 May (2.30-5.30). Adm £3.50, chd free. Also open Diespeker Wharf.**

Charming secluded town garden with climbing roses, trees, shrubs, climbers, pond, patio with containers, and a gazebo with a trompe l'oeil mural.

151 57 ST QUINTIN AVENUE, W10

London, W10 6NZ. Mr H Groffman, 020 8969 8292. *Less than 1mile from Ladbroke Grove or White City tube. Buses: 7, 70, 220 all to North Pole Rd. Free parking on Sundays.* **Sun 8, Sun 22 July (2-6). Adm £5, chd free. Home-made teas. Visits also by arrangement July & Aug, refreshments by advance arrangement.**

A 30ft x 40ft walled garden with a wide selection of plant material incl evergreen and deciduous shrubs for foliage effects. Patio area mainly furnished with bedding material, colour themed. Focal points throughout. Refurbished with new plantings and special features. Garden theme this year is commemoration of the Centenary of the end of World War 1. Annual themed carpet bedding display complemented by patio colour scheme. Clever use of mirrors. Winner of 12 Garden Awards.

152 5 ST REGIS CLOSE, N10

Alexandra Park Road, Muswell Hill, London, N10 2DE. Ms S Bennett & Mr E Hyde, 020 8883 8540, suebearlh@yahoo.co.uk. *Tube: Bounds Green then 102 or 299 bus, or E. Finchley take 102. Alight St Andrews Church. 134 or 43 bus stop at end of Alexandra Pk Rd, follow arrows.* **Sun 29 Apr, Sun 17 June, Sun 22 July (2-6.30). Adm £4, chd free. Home-made teas. Visits also by arrangement Apr to Oct for groups 10+. Home-made teas/light refreshments.**

Cornucopia of sensual delights. Artist's garden famous for architectural features and delicious cakes. New Oriental Tea House. Baroque temple, pagodas, Raku tiled mirrored wall conceals plant nursery. American Gothic shed overlooks Liberace Terrace and stairway to heaven. Maureen Lipman's favourite garden, combines colour, humour, trompe l'oeil with wildlife friendly ponds, waterfalls, weeping willow, lawns, abundant planting. A unique experience awaits! Open studio with ceramics and prints. Mega plant sale. Featured in RHS The Garden Magazine, Matthew Biggs. Photos Nicola Stocken. TV More 4 Gardens Great and Small. Wheelchair access to all parts of garden unless waterlogged.

153 NEW 22 SHIRLEY AVENUE, SM1

Sutton, SM1 3QT. Clare & Ken Brain. *Rail Carshalton St then short walk. The Carshalton Rd (A232) runs parallel with Westmead Rd and Shirley Ave is approached via Browning Ave.* **Sun 24 June (1-5). Adm £3.50, chd free. Light refreshments.**

A small very colourful garden created by the owners over the past 45 years. South facing, with a variety of plants including acers, wisteria, roses and mixed herbaceous. A small pond, greenhouse and summerhouse add variety and overall effect is a garden whose interest outweighs its size. Regret wheelchairs not possible because of narrow access along side entrance.

154 SOUTH LONDON BOTANICAL INSTITUTE, SE24

323 Norwood Road, London, SE24 9AQ. South London Botanical Institute, www.slbi.org.uk. *Mainline stn: Tulse Hill. Buses: 68, 196, 322 & 468 stop at junction of Norwood & Romola Rds.* **Sun 22 Apr (2-5). Adm £3.50, chd free. Home-made teas.** Donation to South London Botanical Institute.

London's smallest botanical garden, densely planted with 500 labelled species grown in a formal layout of themed borders. Wildflowers flourish beside medicinal herbs. Carnivorous, scented, native and woodland plants are featured, growing among rare trees and shrubs. Spring highlights including mosses, unusual bulbs and flowering trees. The fascinating SLBI building is also open.

155 41 SOUTHBROOK ROAD, SE12

Lee, London, SE12 8LJ. Barbara & Marek Polanski, 020 8333 2176, polanski101@yahoo.co.uk. *Southbrook Rd is situated off S Circular, off Burnt Ash Rd. Train: Lee & Hither Green, both 10 mins walk. Bus: P273, 202.* **Sat 9, Sun 10 June (2-5.30). Adm £3.50, chd free. Home-made teas. Visits also by arrangement May to Aug (2-5.30) groups up to 15.**

Developed over 14yrs, this large garden has a formal layout, with wide mixed herbaceous borders full of colour and interest, surrounded by mature trees, framing sunny lawns, a central box parterre and an Indian pergola. Ancient pear trees festooned in June with clouds of white kiftsgate and rambling rector roses. Discover fish and damselflies in 2 lily ponds. Many places to sit and relax. Enjoy refreshments in a small classical garden building with interior wall paintings, almost hidden by roses climbing way up into the trees. Orangery. The garden has featured in a number of Gardening Magazines, Bises a Japanese publication, notably it was garden of the week in Garden News, and in 'Show Me Your Garden' on Sky1. Side access available for standard wheelchairs.

156 SOUTHWOOD LODGE, N6

33 Kingsley Place, Highgate, N6 5EA. Mr & Mrs C Whittington, 020 8348 2785, suewhittington@hotmail.co.uk. *Tube: Highgate then 6 mins uphill walk along Southwood Lane. 4 min walk from Highgate Village along Southwood Lane. Buses: 143, 210, 214, 271.* **Sun 13 May (2-5.30). Adm £4, chd free. Home-made teas. Visits also by arrangement Apr to July, lunches (for 10+) or teas (any number) by arrangement.**

Densely planted garden hidden behind C18 house (not open). Unusual plants preferred, many propagated for sale. Ponds, waterfall, frogs, toads, newts. Many topiary shapes formed from self sown yew trees. Sculpture carved from three trunks of a massive conifer which became unstable in a storm. Hard working greenhouse! Only one open day this year so visits by appointment especially welcome. Featured in First Ladies of Gardening by Heidi Howcroft and Marianne Majerus. Toffee hunt for children. Secret Life Sax Quartet will perform in the garden from 2.30pm.

GROUP OPENING

157 SPITALFIELDS GARDENS, E1

London, E1 6QE. *Nr Spitalfields Market. 10 mins walk from Aldgate E Tube & 5 mins walk from Liverpool St stn. Overground: Shoreditch High St - 3 mins walk.* **Sat 16 June (11-4). Combined adm £14, chd free. Home-made teas at Town House, 5 Fournier Steet.**

26 ELDER STREET
The Future Laboratory.

20 FOURNIER STREET
Ms Charlie de Wet.

29 FOURNIER STREET
Juliette Larthe.

21 PRINCELET STREET
Marianne & Nicholas Morse.

37 SPITAL SQUARE
Society for the Protection of Ancient Buildings.

21 WILKES STREET
Rupert Wheeler.

NEW **23 WILKES STREET**
Juliet McKoen.

A collection of hidden treasures behind some of the finest merchants and weavers houses in Spitalfields. It is fitting to visit the courtyard of the Society for the Protection of Ancient Buildings (SPAB) at 37 Spital Square, founded by William Morris in 1877. The other gardens incl. one in nearby Elder Street, two in Wilkes Street, one in Princelet Street and two in Fournier Street. Visitors will be enchanted by how each garden owner has adapted their modest pocket of green to complement an historic house. Vegetables, herbs, layered vertical and ground beds with 'very English planting', ornamental pots, statuary and architectural artefacts greet you. The area has fertile roots: once a field beside the 12th century St Mary's Spital priory. In the17th century French Huguenots brought their silkweaving skills to the area and built the elegant houses with lofts. The herbalist physician Nicholas Culpeper set up a pharmacy in Spitalfields, using herbs collected nearby. Walk back in time!

158 STOKES HOUSE, TW10

Ham Street, Ham, Richmond, TW10 7HR. Peter & Rachel Lipscomb, 020 8940 2403, rlipscomb@virginmedia.com. *2m S of Richmond off A307. Trains & tube to Richmond & train to Kingston which link with 65 bus stopping at Ham Common.* **Sun 3 June (1-5). Adm £4, chd free. Home-made teas. Visits also by arrangement Apr to Oct, garden groups and overseas visits 10+ welcome.**

Originally an orchard, this ½ acre walled country garden surrounding Georgian house (not open) is abundant with roses, clematis and perennials. There are mature trees incl ancient mulberries and wisteria. The yew hedging, pergola and box hedges allow for different planting schemes throughout the year. Supervised children are welcome to play on the slide and swing. Herbaceous borders, brick garden, wild garden, large compost area and interesting trees. Many plants for sale. Teas, garden tour, history of house and area for group visits. Interview and film for Austrian TV network. Wheelchair access via double doors from street with 2 wide steps. Unfortunately no access for larger motorised chairs.

159 STONEY HILL HOUSE, SE26

Rock Hill, London, SE26 6SW. Cinzia & Adam Greaves. *Off Sydenham Hill. Train: Sydenham, Gipsy Hill or Sydenham Hill (closest) stations. Buses: To Crystal Palace, 202 or 363 along Sydenham Hill. House at end of cul-de-sac on L coming from Sydenham Hill.* **Sun 20 May (2-6). Adm £4.50, chd free. Home-made teas.**

Garden and woodland of approx 1 acre providing a secluded secret green oasis in the city. Paths meander through mature rhododendron, oak, yew and holly trees, offset by pieces of contemporary sculpture. The garden is on a slope and a number of viewpoints set at different heights provide varied perspectives. The planting in the top part of the garden is fluid and flows seamlessly into the woodland. Fresalca, a wonderful saxophone quartet, will be playing for the afternoon. Swings and woodland tree-house.

160 72 TANFIELD AVENUE, NW2

London, NW2 7RT. Mr Orod Ohanians, 07887853090. *Nearest station: Neasden - Jubilee line then 10 mins walk; or various bus routes to Neasden Parade or Tanfield Ave.* **Sun 17 June (12-5.30). Adm £3.50, chd free. Cream teas. Visits also by arrangement in June.**

Garden designed to be a 'mini botanical garden', packed with many exotic plants from China, New Zealand, Australia, Chile, central America, Middle East, Mediterranean, S Africa and Britain. Plants carefully chosen to survive, with a bit of care, in the British climate and complemented by rocks, pond, waterfall and bog garden. Over 400 species of plants. There is nothing like this garden anywhere. Many unusual plants that must be seen to appreciate. Small collection of cacti on exhibit. The garden contains many large rocks and sculptures.

NPC

161 93 TANFIELD AVENUE, NW2

Dudden Hill, London, NW2 7SB. Mr James Duncan Mattoon, 020 8830 7410. *Dudden Hill - Neasden. Nearest station: Neasden - Jubilee line then 10 mins walk; or various bus routes to Neasden Parade or Tanfield Ave.* **Sun 29 July (2-6). Adm £4, chd free. Home-made teas. Visits also by arrangement May to Sept for groups 30 max.**

Professional plantsman's petite hillside paradise! Arid/tropical deck with panoramic views of Wembley and Harrow, descends through Mediterranean screes and warm sunny slopes, to subtropical oasis packed with many rare and exotic plants e.g. Hedychium, Plumbago, Punica, Puya. To rear, jungle shade terrace and secret summer house offer cool respite on sunny days. Previous garden was Tropical Kensal Rise (Doyle Gardens) featured on BBC2 Open Gardens and in Sunday Telegraph. This garden was in Garden Answers Magazine and garden of the week in Garden News magazine!

162 NEW 31 TRELAWN ROAD, SW2

London, SW2 1DH. Mr Mark Simmons. *Brixton Tube, turn R along Effra Road towards Sainsbury's. Walk past the PC World and Trelawn Road 1st St on L. Buses 2, 3, 37, 196 & 415.* **Sun 10 June (2-5.30). Adm £3, chd free. Home-made teas. Also open Brixton Water Lane Gardens.**

A small city garden, only four years old, and designed to give the illusion of space, with a winding path and hidden vistas. Crammed with plants and dominated by perennials, roses and a crevice garden. There is no lawn, but several seating areas from which to contemplate the space.

163 TRUMPETERS HOUSE & SARAH'S GARDEN, TW9

Richmond, TW9 1PD. Baroness Van Dedem. *Richmond riverside. 5 mins walk from Richmond Station via Richmond Green in Trumpeter's Yard. Parking on Richmond Green & Old Deer Park car park only.* **Sun 10 June (2-5). Adm £5, chd free. Home-made teas.**

The 2 acre garden is on the original site of Richmond Palace. Long lawns stretch from the house to banks of the River Thames. There are clipped yews, a box parterre and many unusual shrubs and trees, a rose garden and oval pond with carp. The ancient Tudor walls are covered with roses and climbers. Discover Sarah's secret garden behind the high walls. Wheelchair access on grass and gravel.

164 NEW TUDOR HERBALIST GARDEN, NW3

37 Christchurch Hill, Hampstead, NW3 1LA. Paul & Hazelanne Lewis. *7 mins from Hampstead Underground, 10 mins from Hampstead Heath Overground Stn. L out of Hampstead Underground, L into Flask Walk, straight to Christchurch Hill, and R to 37. From Hampstead Heath Stn, walk uphill bearing L onto South End Rd and Willow Rd at Horse trough.* **Sun 8 July (12-5). Adm £3.50, chd free. Home-made teas.**

A narrow informal garden with a SW aspect, developed to meet the requirements of a Tudor Herbalist re-enactor. The garden is on four levels. The first level is predominantly flower beds with herbs being introduced progressively on the second and third levels. The informal layout means that herbs mix with plants like the mature Melianthus and Clematis climb over other plants. Entrance is via basement staircase.

165 NEW 51 TWEEDMOUTH ROAD, E13

Plaistow, London, E13 9HT. Cary Rajinder Sawhney. *10 mins walk from Plaistow District Line and Hammersmith & City Line stn. From Stratford stn 15 mins by bus (262,479). Balaam St stop. Parking free Sunday currently.* **Sun 19 Aug (1-5). Adm £3.50, chd £1. Light refreshments.**

Hidden away in the East End of London - a micro tropical garden with formal islamic garden accents in terms of design and Asian influences including Indian vegetables grown for foliage. Plantains meld with Black Mulberry, Loquat, Windmill palms and ginger and many other species in this secret 10m x 4m plot, including canal-style pond. The garden access is via the house only and has some low single steps.

166 NEW 24 TWYFORD AVENUE, N2

East Finchley, London, N2 9NJ. Rachel Lindsay and Jeremy Pratt. *Twyford Avenue runs parallel to Fortis Green, between East Finchley and Muswell Hill. Tube: Northern line to East Finchley. Bus 102 stops at end of road. Buses 102, 143, 234 and 263 to East Finchley. Buses 43, 143, 144, 234 to Muswell Hill. Garden signposted from Fortis Green.* **Sun 15 July (2-6). Adm £4, chd free. Home-made teas.**

A very sunny, 120 foot south-facing garden, planted for colour. Brick-edged borders and over-flowing containers packed with masses of traditional herbaceous and perennial cottage garden plants and shrubs. Shady area at the bottom evolving as much by happy accident as by design. Uneven ground in places. Water feature Greenhouse bursting with cuttings. Lots of places to sit and think, chat or doze.

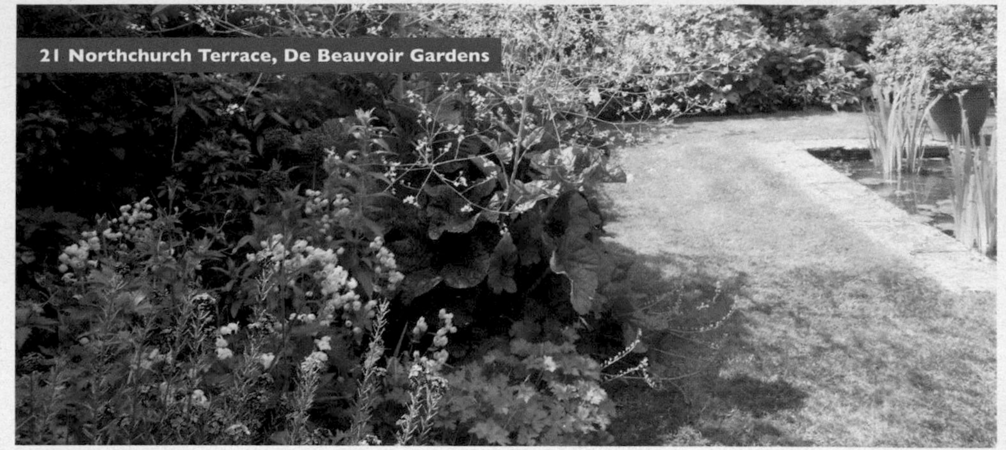
21 Northchurch Terrace, De Beauvoir Gardens

167 7 UPPER PHILLIMORE GARDENS, W8

Kensington, London, W8 7HF. Mr B Ritchie. *From Kensington High St turn into Phillimore Gdns or Campden Hill Rd; entrance at rear in Duchess of Bedford Walk.* **Sun 22 Apr (2.30-6.30). Adm £3.50, chd free. Light refreshments.**

Last chance to visit this lovely mature garden which was planned on different levels to create areas of varied character and mood. Pergola with Italian fountain and fishpond, lawn with borders leading to sunken garden with rockery. Groundcover and mature trees make a secluded haven in C London. Flowering shrubs and a fine display of spring bulbs. Plenty of seating to sit and enjoy a cup of tea!

168 NEW VICTORIA LODGE, E18

Hermitage Walk, Snaresbrook, E18 2BN. Lucy St Ville. *A six mins walk from Snaresbrook stn on the Central Line.* **Sat 30 June (2-5). Adm £4, chd free. Home-made teas.**

Enter this large London garden through a re-claimed Victorian iron pergola, past a colourful mixed bed to a relaxed fire pit. Shady ferns, next to a small rill created from cattle troughs, leads to a walkway cut through the mature rhododendrons. At the far end, sheltered by a high Victorian wall, is a wildlife garden, including a corten steel pond, bee friendly planting and secluded seating area.

169 1 WADES GROVE, N21

London, N21 1BH. C & K Madhvani. *Tube: Southgate then W9 to Winchmore Hill Green then short walk. Train: Winchmore Hill then short walk via Wades Hill.* **Sun 3 June (2-6). Adm £3, chd free. Home-made teas.**

Tiny secluded space in charming peaceful cul-de-sac as featured on the TV series presented by Dee Hart Dyke and Miranda Hart, All Gardens Great and Small. Views divided by selection of mature and young trees. Planting loose and naturalistic. Focus on scented plants, edibles, ground and wall coverings. Designed to encourage wildlife. Interesting use of recycled materials. Visitors welcome to explore tranquil adjoining Quaker gardens (free) via secret entrance.

170 208 WALM LANE, THE GARDEN FLAT, NW2

London, NW2 3BP. Miranda & Chris Mason, www.thegardennw2.co.uk. *Tube: Kilburn. Garden at junction of Exeter Rd & Walm Lane. Buses: 16, 32, 189, 226, 245, 260, 266, 316 to Cricklewood Broadway, then consult A-Z.* **Sun 3 June (2-6). Adm £3.50, chd free. Home-made teas.**

Tranquil oasis of green. Meandering lawn with island beds, curved and deeply planted borders of perennials, scented roses and flowering shrubs. An ornamental fishpond with fountain. Shaded mini woodland area of tall trees underplanted with rhododendrons, ferns, hostas and lily of the valley with winding path from oriental inspired summerhouse to secluded circular seating area. Live music and raffle prizes. 'Garden of the week' in Garden News, 'Beautiful Gardens' feature in Garden Answers.

171 THE WATERGARDENS, KT2

Warren Road, Kingston-upon-Thames, KT2 7LF. The Residents' Association. *1m E of Kingston. From Kingston take A308 (Kingston Hill) towards London; after approx ½m turn R into Warren Rd.* **Sun 13 May, Sun 14 Oct (2-4.30). Adm £5, chd free.**

Japanese landscaped garden originally part of Coombe Wood Nursery, planted by the Veitch family in the 1860s. Approx 9 acres with ponds, streams and waterfalls. Many rare trees which, in spring and autumn, provide stunning colour. For the tree lover this is a must see garden. Gardens attractive to wildlife.

172 WEST LODGE PARK, EN4

Cockfosters Road, Hadley Wood, EN4 0PY. Beales Hotels, 020 8216 3904, headoffice@bealeshotels.co.uk, www.bealeshotels.co.uk/westlodgepark. *1m S of Potters Bar. On A111. J24 from M25 signed Cockfosters.* **Sun 13 May (2-5); Sun 21 Oct (1-4). Adm £5, chd free. Visits also by arrangement May to Oct.**

Open for the NGS for over 30yrs, the 35 acre Beale Arboretum consists of over 800 varieties of trees and shrubs, incl National Collection of Hornbeam cultivars (Carpinus betulus) and National collection of Swamp Cypress (Taxodium). Network of paths through good selection of conifers, oaks, maples and mountain ash - all specimens labelled. Beehives and 2 ponds. Stunning collection within the M25. Guided tours available. Breakfasts, morning coffee/biscuits, restaurant lunches, light lunches, dinner all served in the hotel. Please see website.

NPC

173 29 WEST PARK ROAD, TW9

Kew Gardens, Richmond, TW9 4DA. Silvia & Francesca Doria. *Exit Kew Gardens Station; 4th house (end of terrace) on left on West Park Rd. Garden entrance to R of house.* **Sun 3 June (2-6). Combined adm with 31 West Park Road £5, chd free.**

Landscaped garden in the Edwardian style, with rose arches and traditional Portland stone and brick paving floor layout. The garden was designed and implemented by Roger Lang of Mike Bayon Garden Design in September 2014.

174 31 WEST PARK ROAD, TW9

Kew, Richmond, TW9 4DA. Anna Anderson. *Just by Kew Gardens stn.* **Sun 3 June (2-6). Combined adm with 29 West Park Road £5, chd free.**

Modern botanical garden with an oriental twist. Emphasis on foliage and an eclectic mix of plants, reflecting pool and rotating willow screens which provide varying views or privacy. Dry bed, shady beds, mature trees and a private paved dining area with dappled light and shade. Featured in Weekly Garden News, Amateur Gardening.

175 12 WESTERN ROAD, E13

Plaistow, E13 9JF. Elaine Fieldhouse, 020 8470 3681, fhouse@btinternet.com. *Stn: Upton Park, 3mins walk. Buses: 58, 104, 330, 376. No parking restrictions on Suns.* **Sun 27 May (1-5). Adm £4. Home-made teas. Gluten free/vegan options available. Visits also by arrangement May to Sept.**

Urban oasis, 85ft garden designed and planted by owners. Relying heavily on evergreen, ferns, foliage and herbaceous planting. Rear of garden leads directly onto a 110ft allotment and a half allotment adjoining it - part allotment, part extension of the garden - featuring topiary, medlar tree, mulberry tree, 2 ponds, small fruit trees, raised beds and small iris collection.

176 NEW 33 WEYMAN ROAD, SE3

Blackheath, London, SE3 8RY. Kevin & Cosetta Lawlor. *Weyman Rd is off Shooters Hill Rd. Stns: Kidbrooke or Blackheath. Bus: 178 from Kidbrooke stn, 89 from Blackheath stn, 386 from Greenwich. Free parking in Weyman Rd.* **Sun 24 June (2-5.30). Adm £3.50, chd free. Home-made teas. Also open Blackheath Gardens.**

A small but immaculate garden, that is as pretty as a picture in a wonderfully colour co-ordinated melange of pinks, whites, purples and blues. Divided into rooms to entice the visitor on, this is a couples' joint effort with hard and soft landscaping that offers unexpected delights round every corner. The garden finishes with a stunning display of succulents and an alpine rockery and waterfall.

177 WHITE COTTAGE, BR5

Crockenhill Road, Kevington, BR5 4ER. John Fuller & Alida Burdett, 01689 875134, alidaburdett@aol.com. *Kevingtom. Crockenhill Rd is B258. Garden at junction with Waldens Rd.* **Sun 10 June (1-5). Adm £5, chd free. Home-made teas. Visits also by arrangement June to Aug.**

Traditional box, clipped hedging and reclaimed materials give structure to this informal garden surrounding a Victorian gardener's cottage. Colour themed beds contain grasses, perennials, shrubs and fruit trees. There is a small but productive vegetable garden, a pond, rare chickens and bees. Wildlife promotion is a priority. Plenty of places to sit and enjoy the garden. Home-made produce using fruit and vegetables grown in the garden available for sale. Majority of garden accessible by wheelchair.

178 WHITGIFT SCHOOL, CR2

Haling Park, South Croydon, CR2 6YT. Romano Maccioni, www.whitgift.co.uk. *Train: South Croydon then 5 mins walk. Buses: 119, 197, 312, 466. School entrance on Nottingham Rd.* **Sun 20 May (1-5). Adm £4, chd free. Home-made teas.**

Whitgift Gardens are a series of fascinating, well-maintained gardens in a number of original styles within the extensive grounds of the School, all of which help to provide a stimulating environment for students. The Gardening Team are on a mission to make sure there isn't another school garden as excellent as this to be found in the UK. The popular Water Gardens underwent refurbishment in 2017. Wildlife and birds (wallabies, flamingos, peacocks in an enclosed area) are a feature of the School grounds. Most garden areas accessible by wheelchair. The Andrew Quadrangle can be accessed, but non accessible steps within the garden.

180 74 WILLIFIELD WAY, NW11

London, NW11 6YJ. David Weinberg, 020 8201 9052, davidwayne@hotmail.co.uk. *H2 bus from Golders Green Stn which will stop outside the house.* **Sun 24 June (2-6). Adm £4, chd free. Cream teas. cream teas. Visits also by arrangement May to Aug telephone for appointment.**

A very peaceful English country garden packed with herbaceous borders and perfumed rose beds with wonderful containers to the patio area with a beautiful handmade lead fountain. A haven of tranquillity to be enjoyed. A large variety of herbacious plants together with highly perfumed roses to the side and back flower beds together with a central white rose bed complimented by several different climbing roses.A beautiful lead fountain to the patio area. Wheelchair access to patio area only.

179 86 WILLIFIELD WAY, NW11

Hampstead Garden Suburb, NW11 6YJ. Diane Berger, 020 8455 0455, dianeberger@hotmail.co.uk. *1m N of Golders Green. Car: A1 & A406 to Henley's Corner into Finchley Rd. Tube: Golders Green, then H2 bus to Willifield Way. Buses 82, 102, 460 to Temple Fortune, walk along Hampstead Way, turn L at The Orchard.* **Sun 22 July (2-6). Adm £4, chd free. Home-made teas. Visits also by arrangement June to Sept min 8, max 20 visitors.**

Beautiful & constantly evolving cottage garden with year round interest. Screened by a huge black bamboo, a wildlife pond surrounded by primulas & rodgersia, opens out to spectacularly colourful deep herbaceous beds, crammed with a dazzling array of perennials & grasses. Clematis & wisteria clad pergola leads to a secret decked area surrounded by mature shrubs, trees, ferns & other shade lovers. Winner of Suburb in Bloom, Winner of London Gardens Society: Best Large Back Garden. Featured in 'Garden News' and 'Garden Answers' magazines 2017. Wheelchair access to front lawn only.

181 61 WOLSEY ROAD, KT8

East Molesey, KT8 9EW. Jan & Ken Heath, janheath61@gmail.com. *Less than 10 mins walk from Hampton Court Palace & stn.* **Sun 10 June (2-6). Adm £4, chd free. Home-made teas. Visits also by arrangement June & July e.g. groups may consider a visit to our garden to relax after visiting Hampton Court Flower Show.**

Romantic, secluded and peaceful garden of two halves designed and maintained by the owners. Part is shaded by two large copper beech trees with woodland planting. The second reached through a beech arch has cottage garden planting, pond and wooden obelisks covered with roses and sweet peas. Beautiful octagonal gazebo overlooks pond plus a new oak framed summerhouse designed and built by the owners. Extensive seating throughout the garden to sit quietly and enjoy your tea and cake, either in the cool shade of the gazebo under the copper beech trees, relaxing in the summerhouse or enjoying the full sunshine elsewhere in the garden.

79 Royston Avenue

182 33 WOOD VALE, N10

Highgate, N10 3DJ. Mona Abboud, 020 8883 4955, monaabboud@hotmail.com, www.monasgarden.co.uk. *Tube: Highgate, 10 mins walk. Buses: W3, W7 to top of Park Rd.* **Sun 20 May (1.30-5.30). Adm £3.50, chd free. Light refreshments. Visits also by arrangement May to Aug, visits by appointment particularly welcome.**

This 100m-long unique and award winning garden is home to the Corokia National Collection along with a great number of other unusual Australasian, Mediterranean and exotic plants complemented by perennials and grasses which thrive thanks to 250 tons of topsoil, gravel and compost brought in by wheelbarrow. Emphasis on structure, texture, shapes and contrasting foliage. Garden featured in TV programme 'All Gardens

Great and Small'. Article 'Corokia in Cultivation' published in edition of RHS 'The Plantsman' written, with photographs, by garden owner Mona Abboud.

183 7 WOODBINES AVENUE, KT1

Kingston-upon-Thames, KT1 2AZ. Mr Tony Sharples & Mr Paul Cuthbert. *Take K2, K3, 71 or 281 bus. From Surbiton, bus stop outside Waitrose & exit bus Kingston University Stop. From Kingston, walk or get the bus from Eden Street (opp Heals).* **Sun 15 July (1-6). Adm £4, chd free. Light refreshments.**

We have created a winding path through our 70ft garden with trees, evergreen structure, perennial flowers and grasses. Deep borders create depth, variety, texture and interest around the garden. We like to create a garden party so feel welcome to stay as long as you like.

184 21 WOODLAND RISE, N10

London, N10 3UP. Jill Pack & Ian Potts. *Close to Highgate Wood. Tube: Highgate, 10-15 mins walk. Bus 43 or 134 to Cranley Gardens stop. Off Muswell Hill Rd.* **Sun 17 June (2-5.30). Adm £3, chd free. Home-made teas. Also open 5 St Regis Close.**

A verdant N facing terraced garden that has been transformed by the owners from a rather ordinary space into one that is tranquil and inspiring. Hard landscaping, incl a small pond, is softened with naturalistic planting and many unusual varieties of trees, shrubs and perennials including ferns and some beautiful small trees such as Indigofera, Malus transitoria and Cornus 'Gloria Birkett'.

185 10 WOODSIDE AVENUE, N6

London, N6 4SS. Sheila & Anthony Rabin. *½m from East Finchley underground station.* **Sun 5 Aug (2-6). Adm £3.50, chd free. Home-made teas.**

An attractive densely planted suburban garden created from scratch 3yrs ago. Large herbaceous perennial borders give colour from April to October. A good contrast with shade loving area and terraced patio with alpine planting.

186 1 YORK CLOSE, W7

Hanwell, W7 3JB. Tony Hulme & Eddy Fergusson. *By road only, entrance to York Close via Church Rd. Nearest station Hanwell mainline. Buses E3, 195, 207.* **Sat 30 June (2-6). Adm £6, chd free. Sun 1 July (2-6). Adm £5, chd free.**

Tiny quirky, prize winning garden extensively planted with eclectic mix incl hosta collection, many unusual and tropical plants. Plantaholics paradise. Many surprises in this unique and very personal garden. Pimms on Saturday (incl in adm), Prosecco on Sunday for a donation!

187 NEW 10 YORK ROAD

London, N21 2JL. Androulla & Harry Tsappas. *Winchmore Hill. Buses: 329 from Wood Green to Enfield stops at Ridge Library. 2 mins walk. W8 also stops by Ridge library.* **Sun 17 June (2-6). Adm £4, chd free. Home-made teas.**

Newly planted garden of only 3 years. Featuring catalpa, acacia, olive and tree fern. Generous borders are planted with colourful perennials. The garden has a pretty dainty look and is inspired by cottage gardens. There is a large pond with fish, a summer house and wood choppers enclave. An array of wildlife such as frogs butterflies and bees are encouraged.

188 38 YORK ROAD, W5

Ealing, W5 4SG. Nick & Elena Gough, www.thedistinctivegardener.com. *Northfields & South Ealing Tube - 5 mins. Buses: E3, 65. 5 mins. Free parking in local streets. Off Northfield Av & South Ealing Rd.* **Sun 22 July (2-6). Adm £4, chd free. Home-made teas.**

A hidden oasis full of surprises and built on several different levels. This walled corner garden was restored and expanded by its present owners, having been acquired in 2014. There are a number of beautiful and diverse areas within it, all of which add to its special atmosphere, incl a woodland dell path, circular sun terrace, large pond with waterfalls and flower filled parterre. Featured in EalingToday.co.uk, 'Is this Ealing's most beautiful Garden?'.

189 ZEN GARDEN AT JAPANESE TEMPLE, W3

Three Wheels, 55 Carbery Avenue, London, W3 9AB. Reverend Prof K T Sato, www.threewheels.org.uk. *Tube: Acton Town 5 mins walk, 200yds off A406.* **Sat 2, Sun 3, Sat 23, Sun 24 June (2-5). Adm £3, chd free. Matcha tea and sweets. Japanese tea ceremony demonstration.**

Pure Japanese Zen garden (so no flowers) with 12 large and small rocks of various colours and textures set in islands of moss and surrounded by a sea of grey granite gravel raked in a stylised wave pattern. Garden surrounded by trees and bushes outside a cob wall. Oak framed wattle and daub shelter with Norfolk reed thatched roof. Japanese tea ceremony demonstration and talks on the Zen garden between 3-4pm. Buddha Room open to public. Featured in Time Out London, Evening Standard Online, Absolute London.

The National Garden Scheme and Perennial, helping gardeners when they are in need

NORFOLK

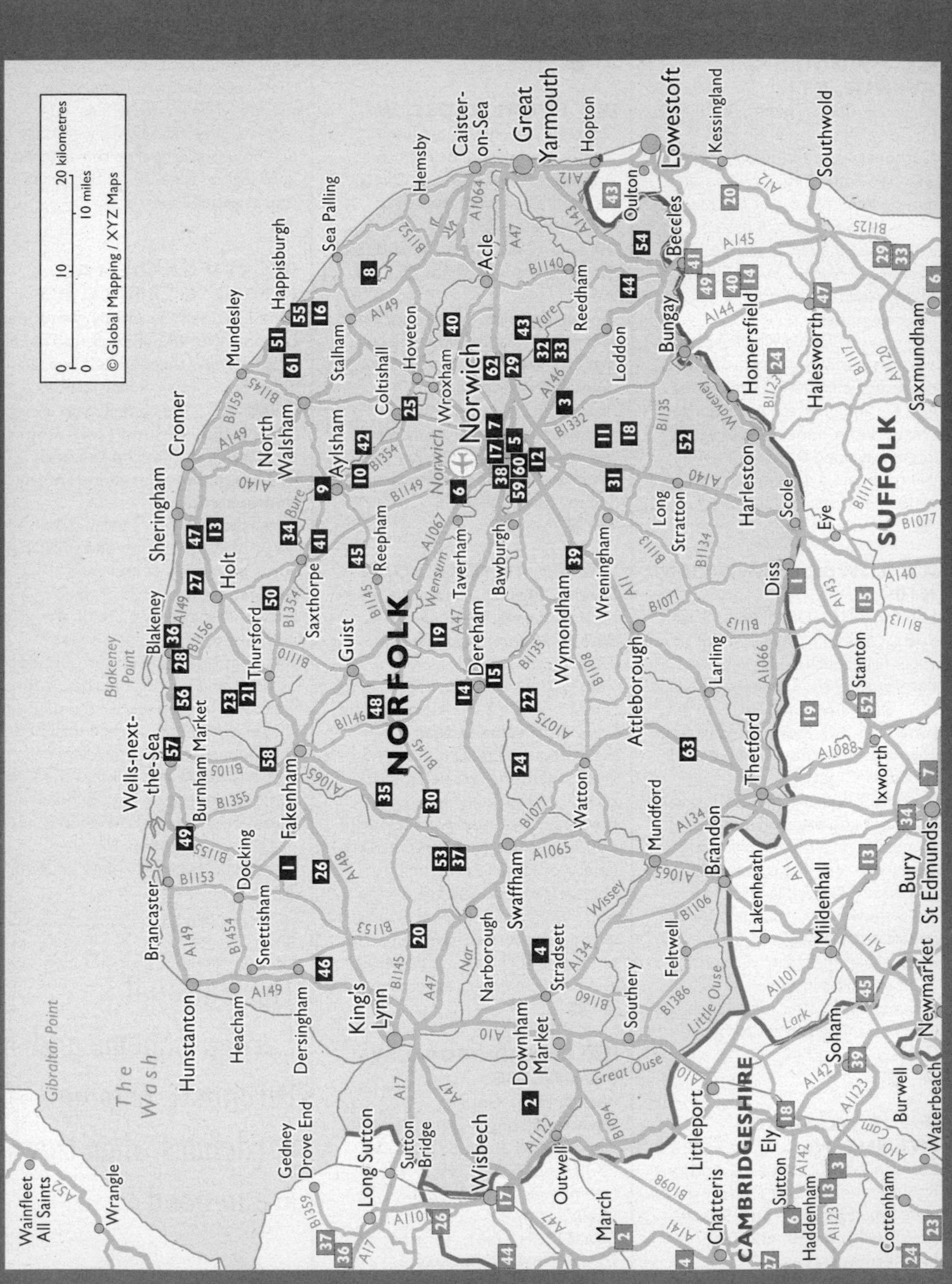

0 10 20 kilometres
0 10 miles
© Global Mapping / XYZ Maps
NORFOLK
SUFFOLK
CAMBRIDGESHIRE
The Wash
Gibraltar Point
Blakeney Point
Great Yarmouth
Caister-on-Sea
Hemsby
Sea Palling
Happisburgh
Mundesley
Cromer
Sheringham
Blakeney
Wells-next-the-Sea
Burnham Market
Brancaster
Hunstanton
Heacham
Dersingham
Snettisham
Docking
Fakenham
Thursford
Holt
North Walsham
Stalham
Aylsham
Coltishall
Hoveton
Wroxham
Acle
Norwich
Reepham
Saxthorpe
Guist
Taverham
Bawburgh
Dereham
Swaffham
Narborough
King's Lynn
Downham Market
Stradsett
Wymondham
Wreningham
Attleborough
Watton
Mundford
Brandon
Thetford
Larling
Long Stratton
Harleston
Loddon
Reedham
Bungay
Beccles
Oulton
Lowestoft
Hopton
Kessingland
Southwold
Halesworth
Homersfield
Saxmundham
Diss
Scole
Eye
Stanton
Ixworth
Bury St Edmunds
Mildenhall
Lakenheath
Feltwell
Southery
Outwell
Wisbech
Sutton Bridge
Long Sutton
Gedney Drove End
Wrangle
Wainfleet All Saints
March
Chatteris
Littleport
Ely
Sutton
Haddenham
Cottenham
Soham
Newmarket
Burwell
Waterbeach
Great Ouse
Little Ouse
Wensum
Bure
Yare
Waveney
Wissey
Nar
Lark
Cam

Norfolk is a lovely low-lying county, predominantly agricultural with a relatively small population.

Visitors come to Norfolk because they are attracted to the peaceful countryside, the medieval churches, the coastal area and the large network of rivers and waterways of the Broads. Norwich the capital is a fine city.

Our garden owners are a loyal group; Sandringham, one of the original gardens to open for the scheme has been supporting us continuously since 1927. Several gardens have been opening their gates for over 50 years, whilst others will be opening for the very first time. The variety is enormous from those of the large estates and manor houses, to the smaller cottages, courtyards and town gardens. Located throughout the county, styles vary too from the old and traditional, to the contemporary and naturalistic.

So why not come and experience for yourself the rich tapestry of big skies, rural countryside and beautiful gardens.

Below: **Dale Farm**

Volunteers

County Organiser
Julia Stafford Allen
01760 755334
julia.staffordallen@ngs.org.uk

County Treasurer
Neil Foster
01328 701288
neilfoster@lexhamestate.co.uk

Publicity
Graham Watts
01362 690065
graham.watts@ngs.org.uk

Social Media
Claire Reinhold
01485 576221
reinholdclaire@googlemail.com

Photographer
Simon Smith
01362 860530
simon.smith@ngs.org.uk

Booklet Co-ordinator
Sally Bate
07881 907735
sally.bate@ngs.org.uk

New Gardens Organiser
Fiona Black
01692 650247
fiona.black@ngs.org.uk

Assistant County Organisers
Isabel Cator
01603 270748
isabel@markcator.co.uk

Nick Collier
07733 108443
nick.collier@ngs.org.uk

Jennifer Dyer
01263 761811
jennifer.dyer.16@outlook.com

Sue Guest
01362 858317
guest63@btinternet.com

Sue Roe 01603 455917
sue@cliveandsue.plus.com

OPENING DATES

All entries subject to change. For latest information check **www.ngs.org.uk**

Map locator numbers are shown to the right of each garden name.

February

Snowdrop Festival

Saturday 17th
Horstead House 25

Sunday 25th
Bagthorpe Hall 1
Chestnut Farm 13

March

Sunday 4th
Chestnut Farm 13

Sunday 11th
◆ Raveningham Hall 44

Saturday 17th
◆ East Ruston Old Vicarage 16

Sunday 18th
Gayton Hall 20

April

Sunday 1st
Wretham Lodge 63

Monday 2nd
Wretham Lodge 63

Sunday 8th
16 Witton Lane 62

Sunday 15th
◆ Mannington Hall 34

Sunday 22nd
The Old House 40

May

Monday 7th
Witton Hall 61

Sunday 13th
NEW Kelling Hall 27

Thursday 17th
◆ Sheringham Park 47

Saturday 19th
NEW Sundial Farm 52

Sunday 20th
Blickling Lodge 9
Holme Hale Hall 24
Lexham Hall 30

Tuesday 22nd
◆ Stody Lodge 50

Sunday 27th
Bank House 2
Warborough House 56

June

Festival Weekend

Sunday 3rd
NEW Barton Bendish Hall 4
The Merchants House 36
Oulton Hall 41

Thursday 7th
◆ Sheringham Park 47

Saturday 9th
Kettle Hill 28
167 Norwich Road 39

Sunday 10th
Bolwick Hall 10
NEW Elm House 18
High House Gardens 22
167 Norwich Road 39

Wednesday 13th
High House Gardens 22

Saturday 16th
NEW Stanley House 49

Sunday 17th
Elsing Hall Gardens 19
Walcott House 55
Wells-Next-The-Sea Gardens 57
West Barsham Hall 58

Thursday 21st
◆ Mannington Hall 34

Sunday 24th
Manor House Farm, Wellingham 35
Oxnead Hall 42
NEW 30 West Parade 59
NEW 29 West Parade 60

Saturday 30th
The Bear Shop 5

July

Sunday 1st
The Bear Shop 5
Bishop's House 7
Chestnut Farm 13

Sunday 8th
9 Bellomonte Crescent 6
Salle Park 45
NEW Tyger Barn 54

Saturday 14th
Black Horse Cottage 8

Sunday 15th
Black Horse Cottage 8

Saturday 21st
Suil Na Mara 51

Sunday 22nd
Dunbheagan 15
68 Elm Grove Lane 17
Suil Na Mara 51

Saturday 28th
NEW 6 Lower Road 32
NEW 8 Lower Road 33

Sunday 29th
Brick Kiln House 11
Dale Farm 14
Holme Hale Hall 24
NEW 6 Lower Road 32
NEW 8 Lower Road 33

August

Wednesday 1st
Lexham Hall 30

Sunday 5th
The Long Barn 31
Minns Farm Barns 37
North Lodge 38
Tudor Lodgings 53

Sunday 12th
North Lodge 38

Sunday 26th
Bank House 2

September

Saturday 8th
NEW Greenways 21

Sunday 9th
NEW Greenways 21
High House Gardens 22

Wednesday 12th
High House Gardens 22

Sunday 30th
◆ Hindringham Hall 23

October

Saturday 13th
◆ East Ruston Old Vicarage 16

Sunday 14th
NEW Silverstone Farm 48

Sunday 21st
The Barn Arboretum 3

By Arrangement

Bank House 2
Brick Kiln House 11
NEW 21 Broadhurst Road 12
Chestnut Farm 13
Dale Farm 14
Dunbheagan 15
NEW Elm House 18
Gayton Hall 20
Holme Hale Hall 24
Lake House 29
Plovers Hill 43
Suil Na Mara 51
West Barsham Hall 58
Wretham Lodge 63

The Queen's Nursing Institute founded the National Garden Scheme over 90 years ago

THE GARDENS

1 BAGTHORPE HALL

Bagthorpe, Bircham, PE31 6QY. Mr & Mrs D Morton, 01485 578528, dgmorton@hotmail.com. *3½m N of East Rudham, off A148. King's Lynn to Fakenham. At East Rudham L opp The Crown, 3½m, hamlet of Bagthorpe. Farm buildings on L, wood on R, white gates set back from rd, top of drive.* **Sun 25 Feb (11-4). Adm £4, chd free. Home-made soups made with organic vegetables from the farm, home-made cakes & teas.**

Snowdrops carpeting a circular woodland walk, returning through the walled and main garden. Some access for wheelchairs in the garden, but not the woodland walk.

2 BANK HOUSE

Middle Drove, Marshland St James, PE14 8JT. Teresa Lovick & Andrew Stephens, 07950 362221, teresajoylovick@gmail.com. *A1122 in Outwell turn onto Langhorn's Lane at Crown Motel. Bear L onto Marsh Rd. R onto Stow Rd for 5 mins. Turn L at sign onto Middle Drove. Cross bridge with T-lights. Parking on L in paddock.* **Sun 27 May, Sun 26 Aug (10-4). Adm £3.50, chd free. Home-made teas. Visits also by arrangement May & June for groups of 10 to 30.**

An exuberant and established 2 acre garden. Range of growing conditions from damp shade to dry gravel: veg and fruit areas, ornamental grass garden, bog garden, new pond, formal lawn, mixed borders, patios, terraces and variety of secret spaces. Year-round interest but especially a range of primulas, irises and roses peaking May-July. Grasses and dahlias in August. An oasis in the Fens! Due to large amount of gravel paths and changes of level, we regret this garden has no wheelchair access.

3 THE BARN ARBORETUM

Spur Lane, Framingham Earl, Norwich, NR14 7SA. Mr James Colman. *3m SE of Norwich. From A47 take A146 for 1½m. Turn R at Old Feathers signed Framingham Pigot Business Centre. Follow the signs to Poringland after 1m the entrance is on L.* **Sun 21 Oct (10-3). Adm £5, chd free. Tea.**

The Arboretum at Framingham currently some 14 hectares, lies on the south slope of a 50 metre hill from which there are extensive views to the north east across some ornamental ponds built in the C18, and towards Great Yarmouth and the sea. In the middle distance St Andrew's church, Framingham Pigot is framed.

4 NEW BARTON BENDISH HALL

Fincham Road, Barton Bendish, King's Lynn, PE33 9DL. The Barton Bendish Gardening Team. *5m E of Downham Market off A1122. On entering Barton Bendish follow yellow signs to field parking.* **Sun 3 June (11-5). Adm £4, chd free. Home-made teas.**

Traditional 10 acre country estate garden. Woodland drive, orchard, kitchen garden with soft fruits, espaliered fruit trees, vegetables, and a Thomas Messenger style glasshouse full of scented pelargoniums. Walled herb and cut flower garden. Herbaceous borders, south facing terrace with open views onto the wider farmed landscape. The Hall is C17 although not open to the public. Some wheelchair access.

5 THE BEAR SHOP

Elm Hill, Norwich, NR3 1HN. Robert Stone. *Norwich City Centre. From St Andrews, L to Princes St, then L to Elm Hill. Garden at side of shop through large wooden gate & along alleyway.* **Sat 30 June, Sun 1 July (11-4). Adm £3, chd free. Home-made teas.**

Considered to be based on a design by Gertrude Jekyll, a small terraced garden behind a C15 house in the historic Cathedral Quarter of Norwich. Enjoy the tranquillity of the riverside. Wheel chair access is limited to the upper level of the garden.

6 9 BELLOMONTE CRESCENT

Drayton, Norwich, NR8 6EJ. Wendy & Chris Fitch. *5m N of Norwich. Turn off A1067 at Drayton Xrds. Drive past front of Red Lion Pub towards church. Access through gate back of churchyard or continue 1st exit r'about to School Rd, 1st L turn to Bellomonte Crescent.* **Sun 8 July (11-5). Adm £3, chd free. Home-made teas.**

On approx ¼ acre plot the garden, lovingly created from scratch by the owners, is a mix of traditional and more exotic mediterranean planting. A large deck overlooks main lawn with planted pergolas and arbour. Views across to Drayton church gives interest and privacy. Terraced upper garden with fruit and vegetables and secluded courtyard area. Home-made cakes and plants for sale. No wheelchair access to upper levels.

7 BISHOP'S HOUSE

Bishopgate, Norwich, NR3 1SB. The Bishop of Norwich, www.dioceseofnorwich.org/gardens. *City centre. Located in the city centre near the Law Courts & The Adam & Eve Pub.* **Sun 1 July (1-5). Adm £3, chd free. Home-made teas.**

4 acre walled garden dating back to the C12. Extensive lawns with specimen trees. Borders with many rare and unusual shrubs. Spectacular herbaceous borders flanked by yew hedges. Rose beds, meadow labyrinth, kitchen garden, woodland walk and long border with hostas and bamboo walk. Popular plant sales. Gravel paths and some slopes.

With your support we can help raise awareness of Carers Trust and unpaid carers.

8 BLACK HORSE COTTAGE

The Green, Hickling, Norwich, NR12 0YA. Yvonne Pugh. *3m E of Stalham. Turn E off A149 at Catfield, turn L onto Heath Rd, 1½m to centre of Hickling village. Next to The Greyhound Inn (Good food!).* **Sat 14, Sun 15 July (12-5). Adm £4.50, chd free. Home-made teas.**

Thatched house with traditional barn ½m from Hickling Broad. Plantsman's garden over 2 acres professionally redesigned. Spacious borders and islands with diverse range of characterful planting. Particular emphasis on achieving full year round interest. Wide range of managed mature specimen trees. Many long two-way vistas. Wide mown walkways through large meadow. Various sitting opportunities!

9 BLICKLING LODGE

Blickling, Norwich, NR11 6PS. Michael & Henrietta Lindsell. *½m N of Aylsham. Leave Aylsham on old Cromer rd towards Ingworth. Over hump back bridge & house is on R.* **Sun 20 May (2-5.30). Adm £5, chd free.**

Georgian house (not open) set in 17 acres of parkland including cricket pitch, mixed border, walled kitchen garden, yew garden, woodland/water garden.

10 BOLWICK HALL

Marsham, NR10 5PU. Mr & Mrs G C Fisher. *8m N of Norwich off A140. From Norwich, heading N on A140, just past Marsham take 1st R after Plough Pub, signed 'By Road' then next R onto private drive to front of Hall.* **Sun 10 June (1-5). Adm £5, chd free. Home-made teas.**

Landscaped gardens and park surrounding a late Georgian hall. The original garden design is attributed to Humphry Repton. The current owners have rejuvenated the borders, planted gravel and formal gardens and clad the walls of the house in old roses. Enjoy a woodland walk around the lake as well as as stroll through the working vegetable and fruit garden with its double herbaceous border. Please ask at gate for wheelchair directions.

11 BRICK KILN HOUSE

Priory Lane, Shotesham, Norwich, NR15 1UJ. Jim & Jenny Clarke, jennyclarke@uwclub.net. *6m S of Norwich. Shotesham All Saints Church may be approached from Poringland, Stoke Holy Cross or Saxlingham Nethergate. Priory Lane in 200m from church on R on Saxlingham Rd.* **Sun 29 July (11-5). Adm £5, chd free. Home-made teas. Visits also by arrangement May to Sept.**

2 acre country garden with a large terrace, lawns and colourful herbaceous boarders. There is an intimate rose garden, garden sculptures and a stream running through a diversely planted wood. Parking in field but easy access to brick path.

12 NEW 21 BROADHURST ROAD

Eaton Rise, Norwich, NR4 6RD. David & Beverly Woods, 07909 504769, dwoods054@icloud.com. *1m S of Norwich. Take A140 S from Norwich city centre to outer ring rd T-lights. Stay on A140 & Broadhurst Rd is 3rd turning on R opp tennis courts.* **Visits by arrangement July & Aug up to 10 visitors. Adm £3, chd free. Home-made teas.**

Around the world in 80 steps! This south facing suburban garden takes you from the Mediterranean to Japan. Mature trees from adjoining gardens create a 'borrowed landscape' feel. Olive trees, lavenders, palms, Japanese maples, pines and tree ferns in an unusual planting layout. Interesting topiary and stones throughout the garden. Drive and garden paths are mainly gravel.

13 CHESTNUT FARM

Church Road, West Beckham, Holt, NR25 6NX. Mr & Mrs John McNeil Wilson, 01263 822241, judywilson100@gmail.com. *2½m S of Sheringham. On A148 opp Sheringham Park entrance. Take the rd signed BY WAY TO WEST BECKHAM, about ¾m to the Village Sign and garden.* **Sun 25 Feb, Sun 4 Mar (11-4); Sun 1 July (11-5). Adm £5, chd free. Light refreshments. Visits also by arrangement Feb to Aug for groups of 10-40. Conducted tours offered, refreshments by request.**

Mature three acre garden with a lifetimes collection of plants, including many unusual ones. In Spring over 90 different varieties of Snowdrops, and large drifts of crocus, together with seasonal flowering shrubs and bulbs. Later the colourful borders come into their own, including Cornus capitata and kousa and many other flowering trees and shrubs. Creating a new woodland garden for 2018. Display of garden sculpture by local blacksmith Toby Winterbourne. Featured on Mustard TV Radio Norfolk Travelquest. Wheelchair access tricky if wet.

14 DALE FARM

Sandy Lane, Dereham, NR19 2EA. Graham & Sally Watts, 01362 690065, grahamwatts@dsl.pipex.com. *16m W of Norwich. 12m E of Swaffham. From A47 take B1146 signed to Fakenham, turn R at T-junction, ¼m turn L into Sandy Lane (before pelican crossing).* **Sun 29 July (11-5). Adm £4.50, chd free. Home-made teas. Visits also by arrangement June & July groups of 10+.**

2 acre plant lover's garden with a large spring-fed pond. Over 1000 plant species and varieties featured in exuberantly planted borders and waterside gardens. These incl a collection of 110 species and varieties of hydrangea. Vegetable plot, fruit trees, naturalistic planting areas, gravel garden and sculptures. Gravel drive and some grass paths. Wide range of plants for sale incl many hydrangeas.

15 DUNBHEAGAN

Dereham Road, Westfield, NR19 1QF. Jean & John Walton, 01362 696163, jandjwalton@btinternet.com. *2m S of Dereham. From Dereham take A1075 towards Shipdham. L into Westfield Rd at Vauxhall Garage. At Xrds ahead into country lane, becomes Dereham Rd.* **Sun 22 July (12.30-5). Adm £4.50, chd free. Home-made teas. Visits also by arrangement June & July groups no minimum.**

Relax and enjoy walking among extensive borders and island beds - a riot of colour all Summer. Includes unique 'heaven and hell' and a vibrant hot border. Vast collection of rare, unusual and more recognisable plants in this ever changing plantsman's garden. If you love flowers, you'll love it here. We aim for the WOW factor. Sculptures by Toby Winterbourn. Featured in Nick Bailey's book 365 Days of Colour, Sarah Wint's Sunshine over Clover, Garden Answers magazine and Norfolk magazine. Music during the afternoon. Recent article in local press. Gravel driveway.

16 ◆ EAST RUSTON OLD VICARAGE

East Ruston, Norwich, NR12 9HN. Alan Gray & Graham Robeson, 01692 650432, erovoffice@btconnect.com, www.eastrustonoldvicarage.co.uk. *3m N of Stalham. Turn off A149 onto B1159 signed Bacton, Happisburgh. After 2m turn R 200yds N of East Ruston Church (ignore sign to East Ruston).* **For NGS: Sat 17 Mar, Sat 13 Oct (12-5.30). Adm £8.50, chd £1. Light refreshments. For other opening times and information, please phone, email or visit garden website.**

32 acre exotic coastal garden incl traditional borders, exotic garden, desert wash, sunk garden, topiary, water features, walled and Mediterranean gardens. Many rare and unusual plants, stunning plant combinations, wild flower meadows, old-fashioned cornfield, vegetable and cutting gardens.

NPC

17 68 ELM GROVE LANE

Norwich, NR3 3LF. Selwyn Taylor, www.selwyntaylorgarden.co.uk. *1¾m N of Norwich city centre. Proceed from Norwich city centre to Magdalen St, to Magdalen Rd, bear L to St. Clements Hill turn L into Elmgrove Lane. No.68 is at bottom on R.* **Sun 22 July (11-4). Adm £4, chd free. Home-made teas. Selection of delicious home-made cakes, including gluten free.**

This extended living/working space is the owner's endeavour to redefine a suburban garden and to provide inspiration when viewed from his studio window. Aesthetic values, initially took precedent over gardening know-how, but over 30 years a more balanced approach has resulted in an eclectic array of informal planting, rich in colour and form and full of surprises.

18 NEW ELM HOUSE

The Green, Saxlingham Nethergate, Norwich, NR15 1TH. Mrs Linda Woodwark, lyncwpoppyland@live.co.uk. *8m S of Norwich. From Norwich take A140 to Ipswich, at Newton Flotman turn L at sign post to Saxlingham Nethergate, continue to the end of the rd, turn R & travel through the village, follow NGS signs.* **Sun 10 June (11.30-5). Adm £4, chd free. Light refreshments. Visits also by arrangement June to Sept after 5.30pm weekdays. Anytime weekends.**

A family country garden whose owner loves plants. There are several island beds, 2 long autumn borders, filled with herbaceous perennials and shrubs, an arbour and a natural wildlife pond for ducks and moorhens. There is also a paddock / play area for children, chickens and 3 goats and a vegetable area complete with fruit trees. There is a certain amount of wheelchair access.

19 ELSING HALL GARDENS

Elsing Hall, Hall Road, Elsing, NR20 3DX. Patrick Lines & Han Yang Yap, www.elsinghall.com. *6km NW of Dereham. From A47 take the N Tuddenham exit. From A1067 take the turning to Elsing opp the Bawdeswell Garden Centre. Follow NGS signs to the garden.* **Sun 17 June (1-4). Adm £5, chd free. Home-made teas.**

C15 fortified manor house (not open) with working moat. 10 acre gardens and 10 acre park surrounding the house. Significant collection of old roses, walled garden, formal garden, marginal planting, Gingko avenue, viewing mound, moongate, interesting pineturn and terraced garden.

Tyger Barn

20 GAYTON HALL

Gayton, Kings Lynn, PE32 1PL. Viscount & Viscountess Marsham, 01485 528432, ciciromney@icloud.com. *6m E of King's Lynn. Gayton is situated on B1145; R on B1153. R down Back St 1st entrance on L.* **Sun 18 Mar (1-5). Adm £5, chd free. Home-made teas. Visits also by arrangement Feb to Oct conducted tours for groups of 12+.**

This rambling semi-wild 20 acre water garden, has over 2m of paths, and contains lawns, lakes, streams, bridges and woodland. In the traditional and waterside borders are primulas, astilbes, hostas, lysichiton and gunneras. A variety of unusual trees many of which are labelled, and shrubs have been planted over the years. There is an abundance of spring bulbs. Wheelchair access to most areas, paths are gravel and grass.

21 NEW GREENWAYS

Blacksmiths Lane, Hindringham, Fakenham, NR21 0QB. Gerry Maelzer & Anne Callow. *Close to village centre. A148 Holt to Fakenham Road, turn by Crawfish Pub at Thursford, follow rd for approx 2m, Blacksmiths Lane 1st L after village hall. Parking at village hall.* **Sat 8, Sun 9 Sept (11-4). Adm £4, chd free. Light refreshments.**

A special garden set in one acre with a meandering stream, a self seeding gravel garden and island beds with trees, shrubs and perennials providing constant colour and interest. This is a garden designed with wild life in mind. Look for the quirky fish pond and wild life pond. A small area for vegetables. And no garden would be complete without our resident chickens and ducks!

22 HIGH HOUSE GARDENS

Blackmoor Row, Shipdham, Thetford, IP25 7PU. Susan & Fred Nickerson. *6m SW of Dereham. Take the airfield or Cranworth Rd off A1075 in Shipdham. Blackmoor Row is signed.* **Sun 10, Wed 13 June, Sun 9, Wed 12 Sept (2-5.30). Adm £4.50, chd free. Home-made teas.**

3 acre plantsman's garden developed and maintained by the current owners, over the last 40 years. Garden consists of colour themed herbaceous borders with an extensive range of perennials, box edged rose and shrub borders, woodland garden, pond and bog area, orchard and small arboretum. Plus large vegetable garden. Gravel paths.

23 ◆ HINDRINGHAM HALL

Blacksmiths Lane, Hindringham, NR21 0QA. Mr & Mrs Charles Tucker, 01328 878226, info@hindringhamhall.org, www.hindringhamhall.org. *7m from Holt/Fakenham/Wells. Turn off A148 between Holt & Fakenham at Crawfish Pub. Drive into Hindringham (2m). Turn L into Blacksmiths Lane.* **For NGS: Sun 30 Sept (10-4). Adm £5, chd free. Home-made teas. For other opening times and information, please phone, email or visit garden website.**

Tudor Manor House surrounded with complete C12 moat. Working Walled Vegetable Garden, Victorian Nut Walk, Medieval Fishponds, Formal beds, Bog and Stream gardens. The garden has something of interest throughout the year continuing well into autumn. Apart from the beautiful gardens surrounding the Tudor Hall visitors have access to the 3 acres of medieval fishponds with explanatory signs. Described by most visitors as 'a natural' english garden. Tea Room and Plant Sales. Featured in Gardens Illustrated and Landscape Magazine. Suitable for wheelchairs able to cope with gravel paths.

24 HOLME HALE HALL

Holme Hale, Thetford, IP25 7ED. Mr & Mrs Simon Broke, 01760 440328, simon.broke@hotmail.co.uk. *6m E of Swaffham, 8m W of Dereham, 5m N of Watton. 2m S of Necton off A47 main rd. 1m E of Holme Hale Village.* **Sun 20 May, Sun 29 July (12-4). Adm £6, chd free. Home-made teas in Tea Rooms back of Holme Hale Hall, close to car park, available 12 till 4. Savoury and sweet options, also gluten free. Visits also by arrangement Apr to Aug coach parties very welcome.**

Noted for its spring display of tulips and alliums, historic wisteria plus mid and late summer flowering. Walled kitchen garden and front garden designed and planted in 2000 by Chelsea winner Arne Maynard. The garden incorporates herbaceous borders, trained fruit, vegetables and traditional greenhouse. The garden was rejuvenated by Arne Maynard in 2016/17 with brand new herbaceous borders. Parkland, Water Feature, 1832 Dovecote. Listed Buildings. Featured in Country Life, Arne Maynard books. Eastern Daily Press. Wheelchair access available to the Front Garden, Kitchen Garden and tearoom.

25 HORSTEAD HOUSE

Mill Road, Horstead, Norwich, NR12 7AU. Mr & Mrs Matthew Fleming. *6m NE of Norwich on North Walsham rd, B1150. Down Mill Rd opp the Recruiting Sargeant Pub.* **Sat 17 Feb (11-4). Adm £4, chd free. Home-made teas.**

Millions of beautiful snowdrops carpet the woodland setting with winter flowering shrubs. A stunning feature are the dogwoods growing on a small island in R Bure, which flows through the garden. Small walled garden. Wheelchair access to main snowdrop area.

26 ◆ HOUGHTON HALL WALLED GARDEN

Bircham Road, New Houghton, King's Lynn, PE31 6UE. The Cholmondeley Gardens Trust, 01485 528569, info@houghtonhall.com, www.houghtonhall.com. *11m W of Fakenham. 13m E of King's Lynn. Signed from A148.* For

opening times and information, please phone, email or visit garden website.
The award-winning, five acre Walled Garden includes a spectacular double-sided herbaceous border, rose parterre, Mediterranean garden, and kitchen garden with arches and espaliers of apples and pears. There are also glasshouses and antique statues and fountains. Plants on sale. Gravel and grass paths. Electric buggies available for use in the walled garden.

27 NEW KELLING HALL

Holt Road, Kelling, Holt, NR25 7EW. Mr & Mrs Widdowson, 01263 712201, stay@kelling-estate.co.uk, www.kelling-estate.co.uk. *2m NE of Holt, head through High St, follow Cromer Rd past BP petrol station, after 300 metres turn L onto Kelling Rd. Continue & follow signs.* **Sun 13 May (11-4). Adm £5, chd free. Cream teas at Holt Garden Centre.**
In NGS for first time in 55yrs. The owners of Holt Garden Centre invite you to walk the lower gardens and woods of Kelling Hall on their private estate. There is a wonderful bluebell walk, spring bulbs, Saxon/Roman ruins on an island, ponds, lakes and beautiful mature woods, a meadow with views to the sea. Holt Garden Centre discount voucher included in entry fee (T&C's apply). www.holtgardencentre.co.uk and The Pheasant Hotel, www.pheasanthotelnorfolk.co.uk both are part of the Kelling Estate.

28 KETTLE HILL

The Downs, Langham Road, Blakeney, NR25 7PN. Mrs R Winch. *½ m from Blakeney off the B1156 to Langham.* **Sat 9 June (11.30-4). Adm £5, chd free. Home-made teas.**
A garden with herbaceous borders, wild flower meadows and a secret garden. Stunning rose garden and grass paths through woods, a real treat for any garden lover. Excellent views across Morston to the sea, framed by lavender, roses and sky. Gardens have been developed by the owner with design elements from George Carter and Tamara Bridge. Garden Featured in County Life. Gravel drive way and lawns but hard paving near the house. Ramps are situated around the garden making all except the wood accessible for wheelchairs.

29 LAKE HOUSE

Postwick Lane, Roman Drive, Brundall, NR13 5LU. Mrs Janet Muter, 01603 712933. *5m E of Norwich. On A47; take Brundall turn at r'about. Turn R into Postwick Lane at T-junction.* **Visits by arrangement Jan to Oct refreshments by arrangement. Adm £5, chd free.**
In the centre of Brundall Gardens, a series of ponds descends through a wooded valley to the shore of a lake. Steep paths wind through a variety of shrubs and flowers in season, which attract many kinds of rare birds, dragonflies and mammals. Water features, great variety of bird life, dragonflies, pond life and forest trees.

30 LEXHAM HALL

nr Litcham, PE32 2QJ. Mr & Mrs Neil Foster, www.lexhamestate.co.uk. *2m W of Litcham. 6m N of Swaffham off B1145.* **Sun 20 May, Wed 1 Aug (11-5). Adm £6, chd free. Home-made teas.**
Parkland with lake and river walks around C17/18 Hall (not open). Formal garden with terraces, yew hedges, roses and mixed borders. Traditional kitchen garden with crinkle crankle wall. A garden with all year round interest; in May rhododendrons, azaleas, camellias and magnolias dominate the 3 acre woodland garden, and August sees the many walled garden borders at their peak. Vegetables and fruit trees, many espaliered. A reed thatched summerhouse, with windows and door. A 15' wisteria clad 'Dome' is the centrepiece in the walled garden with trellis backed parallel borders.

31 THE LONG BARN

Flordon Road, Newton Flotman, Norwich, NR15 1QX. Mr & Mrs Mark Bedini. *6m S of Norwich along A140. Leave A140 in Newton Flotman towards Flordon. Exit Newton Flotman & approx 150 yards beyond 'passing place' on L, turn L into drive. Note that SatNav does not bring you to destination.* **Sun 5 Aug (11-5.30). Adm £5, chd free. Home-made teas. Coffee, sausage rolls and soft drinks as well as homemade cakes and tea served all day.**
Beautiful setting with new haha! creating 'infinity' views across ancient parkland. Delightful Mediterranean influences throughout large paved courtyard, outdoor pool and unique walled group of 4 venerably gnarled olive trees. Herbaceous borders, tiered lawns and woodland garden set around a stunning barn conversion in parkland setting with woodland walks to a stretch of the little river Tas.

32 NEW 6 LOWER ROAD

Rockland St. Mary, Norwich, NR14 7HS. Philip & Harriet Halstead. *8m SE of Norwich. From Norwich A146 past A47 junction take 1st L signed RSM. Continue through Bramerton & RSM, park at Staithe car park opp New Inn.* **Sat 28, Sun 29 July (11-5). Combined adm with 8 Lower Road £5, chd free. Home-made teas.**
The garden is about half an acre on a gentle east-facing slope with lovely views towards the River Yare. Garden rooms with voluptuous planting, fruit trees and vegetables. Mature shrubs and hedges provide a backdrop to herbaceous and annual planting. The pond and wilder areas of the garden provide a habitat for wildlife. An exhibition of our artwork in the studio. Partial wheelchair access. Side track to studio, garden has an access ramp and some hard surfaces, gravel paths form main route around garden.

33 NEW 8 LOWER ROAD

Rockland St. Mary, Norfolk, Norwich, NR14 7HS. Roger & Caroline Brooks. *From Norwich A146 past A47 junction take 1st L signed RSM. Continue through Bramerton & RSM, park at Staithe car park opp New Inn.* **Sat 28, Sun 29 July (11-5). Combined adm with 6 Lower Road £5, chd free. Home-made teas at 6 Lower Road, coffee, home-made cakes and scones.**

We moved into our bungalow 3 years ago. The garden, which is relatively compact, had been neglected for many years and is still a work in progress. Wheelchair access limited.

34 ◆ MANNINGTON HALL

Mannington, Norwich, NR11 7BB. The Lord & Lady Walpole, 01263 584175, admin@walpoleestate.co.uk, www.manningtongardens.co.uk. *18m NW of Norwich. 2m N of Saxthorpe via B1149 towards Holt. At Saxthorpe/Corpusty follow signs to Mannington.* **For NGS: Sun 15 Apr (11-4). Home-made teas. Evening opening Thur 21 June (6-8.30). Adm £6, chd free.** For other opening times and information, please phone, email or visit garden website.

20 acres feature shrubs, lake, trees and roses. Heritage rose and period gardens. Borders. Sensory garden. Extensive countryside walks and trails. Moated manor house and Saxon church with C19 follies. Wild flowers and birds. The Greedy Goose tearooms offer home made locally sourced food with light lunches and home made teas. Gravel paths, one steep slope.

35 MANOR HOUSE FARM, WELLINGHAM

nr Fakenham, Kings Lynn, PE32 2TH. Robin & Elisabeth Ellis, 01328 838227, libby.elliswellingham@gmail.com, www.manor-house-farm.co.uk. *7m W from Fakenham. 8m E from Swaffham, ½m off A1065 N of Weasenham. Garden is beside the church.* **Sun 24 June (11-5). Adm £6, chd free. Home-made teas.**

Charming 4 acre country garden surrounds an attractive farmhouse: Formal quadrants with obelisks. 'Hot spot' of grasses and gravel. Small arboretum with unusual specimen trees. Pleached lime walk, vegetable parterre and rose tunnel. Unusual 'Taj' garden with old-fashioned roses, tree peonies, lilies and a pond. Good selection of herbaceous plants. Walled garden. Small herd of Formosan Sika deer. Featured in Country Life Magazine Eastern Daily Press Norfolk Magazine Mail on Saturday. Some wheelchair access. Area of gravel and a few steps negotiable with assistance.

36 THE MERCHANTS HOUSE

Blakeney, Holt, NR25 7NT. Mr & Mrs David Marris. *Centre of Blakeney Village. Garden located N of A149 (New Road) up Little Lane in Blakeney.* **Sun 3 June (1-5). Adm £5, chd free. Home-made teas.**

2 acres of walled secret garden with terrace, woodland walk, parterre, shrub borders, orchard, kitchen garden, herbaceous border and ice house. Dogs on leads. Most of the garden is suitable for wheelchairs.

37 MINNS FARM BARNS

Castle Acre, Castle Acre, King's Lynn, PE32 2AA. Geoff & Kate Hunnam. *Located in the centre of the village opp the church.* **Sun 5 Aug (11-5). Combined adm with Tudor Lodgings £6, chd free.**

Just over an acre in size and developed over 16 years from a previous cattle yard and small paddock, the garden surrounds a stone and flint barn where wisteria and roses climb the walls. The courtyard is informal, allowing plants to seed and tumble in a controlled way. The flower beds in the former padddock are surrounded by box hedging, and the planting is exuberant with plenty of colour.

38 NORTH LODGE

51 Bowthorpe Road, Norwich, NR2 3TN. Bruce Bentley & Peter Wilson. *1½m W of Norwich City Centre. Turn into Bowthorpe Rd off Dereham Rd, garden 150 metres on L. By bus: 5, 21, 22, 23, 23A/B, 24 & 24A from City centre, Old Catton, Heartsease, Thorpe & most of W Norwich. Parking available outside.* **Sun 5, Sun 12 Aug (11-5). Adm £4, chd free. Home-made teas.**

Town garden of almost ⅕ acre on difficult triangular plot surrounding Victorian Gothic Cemetery Lodge (not open). Strong structure and attention to internal vista with Gothic conservatory, formal ponds and water features, Oriental water garden, classical temple and 80ft deep well! Predominantly herbaceous planting. Self-guided walk around associated historic parkland cemetery also available. House extension won architectural award. Slide show of house and garden history. Wheelchair access possible but difficult. Sloping gravel drive followed by short, steep, narrow, brickweave ramp. WC not easily wheelchair accessible.

39 167 NORWICH ROAD

Wymondham, NR18 0SJ. Rachel & Richard Dylong. *¾m N of Wymondham centre A11 to Wymondham. Take exit, straight to Waitrose & turn L at r'about. Garden on R after ¼m* **Sat 9, Sun 10 June (10-4). Adm £3.**

In our ¼-acre town garden, created from a blank canvas 12 years ago, meandering pathways round a circular lawn to a secluded tropical haven, on to a sunken pergola, greenhouse with cacti collection and fruit and vegetable plot. We love to recycle and experiment

40 THE OLD HOUSE

Ranworth, NR13 6HS. The Hon Mrs Jacquetta Cator. *9m NE of Norwich. Nr South Walsham, below historic Ranworth Church.* **Sun 22 Apr (11-5). Adm £5, chd free. Home-made teas.**

Attractive linked and walled gardens alongside beautiful, peaceful Ranworth inner broad. Bulbs, shrubs,

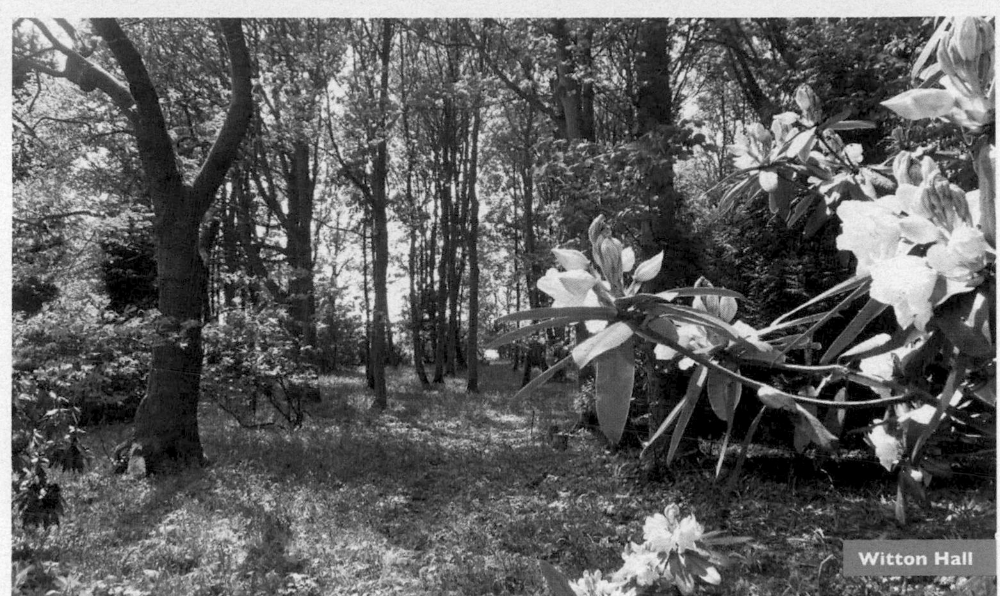
Witton Hall

potager and mown rides through arboretum where dogs may be walked on leads (dogs not allowed in garden itself). Spectacular views of the church and the broad. Some rough grass and gravel.

♿ ☕

41 OULTON HALL

Oulton, Aylsham, NR11 6NU. Bolton Agnew. *4m W of Aylsham. From Aylsham take B1354. After 4m turn L for Oulton Chapel, Hall ½m on R. From B1149 (Norwich/Holt rd) take B1354, next R, Hall ½m on R.* **Sun 3 June (1-5). Adm £5, chd free. Home-made teas.**

C18 manor house (not open) and clocktower set in 6-acre garden with lake and woodland walks. Chelsea designer's own garden - herbaceous, Italian, bog, water, wild, verdant, sunken and parterre gardens all flowing from one tempting vista to another. Developed over 16yrs with emphasis on structure, height and texture, with a lot of recent replanting in the contemporary manner. First opening since major fire destroyed house in March 2015. Restoration now complete.

♿ ☕

42 OXNEAD HALL

Oxnead, Norwich, NR10 5HP. Mr & Mrs David Aspinall. *3m from Aylsham. From Norwich take A140 to Cromer. After Aylsham turn R to Burgh-next-Aylsham. After Burgh take R turn at next Xrds signed Brampton & Buxton .After the Oxnead sign take 1st L.* **Sun 24 June (11-5). Adm £5, chd free. Home-made teas.**

The 14 acre gardens were laid out by the Pastons between 1580 and 1660 and are largely intact. The design consists of a series of Italianate courtyards and terraces which are embellished with statuary. The gardens are undergoing renovation with guidance from George Carter and now incl a parterre, viewing mound, water garden, lake, herbaceous borders, walled kitchen garden, and woodland. There are slopes to most parts of the garden, but some areas cannot be accessed by wheelchair.

♿ 🛏 ☕

43 PLOVERS HILL

Buckenham Road, Strumpshaw, NR13 4NL. Jan Saunt, 01603 714587, sauntjan@gmail.com. *9m E of Norwich. Off A47 at Brundall continuing through to Strumpshaw village. Turn R 300yds past The Huntsman, then take 1st R, at T-junction . Plovers Hill is 1st on R up the hill.* **Visits by arrangement May to Sept. Adm £5, chd free. Home-made teas.**

1 acre garden of contrasts, small C18 house (not open) with RIBA award winning orangery. Formal lawn hedged with yew and lesser species, huge mulberry, gingko, and Japanese bitter orange, herbaceous borders with a range of varied plants and spring bulbs. Kitchen garden with orchard and soft fruits. Garden sculptures. Water feature. Cast aluminium silver birches. Wheelchair access to main part of garden, some gentle steps to teas.

♿ 🐕 ✿ ☕

Gardens are at the heart of hospice care

Chestnut Farm

© Marcus Harpur

44 ◆ RAVENINGHAM HALL

Raveningham, Norwich, NR14 6NS. Sir Nicholas & Lady Bacon, 01508 548480, barbara@raveningham.com, www.raveningham.com. *14m SE of Norwich. 4m from Beccles off B1136.* **For NGS: Sun 11 Mar (11-4). Adm £5, chd free. Light refreshments. For other opening times and information, please phone, email or visit garden website.**

Traditional country house garden in a glorious parkland setting. Restored Victorian conservatory and walled kitchen garden. Herbaceous borders, newly planted stumpery. An arboretum was established after the 1987 gale and a lake to mark the Millennium. There is also a Time Garden inspired by Sir Francis Bacon, a herb garden and a rose garden. Sculpture by Susan Bacon throughout the Garden. February snowdrops are followed by daffodils and narcissus and other spring bulbs and flowering shrubs. In May there are meadow flowers and the herbaceous borders fill out. The summer months showcase the walled kitchen garden and the agapanthus for which the garden is known. There are gravelled paths around the Garden which allow wheelchair access. Access to the Tea Room is through the courtyard entrance.

♿ 🐕 ✽ 🚌 ☕

45 SALLE PARK

Salle, Reepham, NR10 4SF. Sir John White, www.salleestategardens.com. *1m NE of Reepham. Off B1145, between Cawston & Reepham.* **Sun 8 July (10-4). Adm £4, chd free. Home-made teas in The Orangery.**

Fully productive Victorian kitchen garden with original vine houses, double herbaceous borders, ice house, and Norfolk Heritage Fruit orchard. Formal Georgian pleasure gardens with yew topiary, rose gardens and lawns and newly planted Orangry. Some bark chip paths.

♿ 🐕 ☕

46 ◆ SANDRINGHAM GARDENS

Sandringham, PE35 6EH. Her Majesty The Queen, 01485 545408, visits@sandringhamestate.co.uk, www.sandringhamestate.co.uk. *6m NW of King's Lynn. By gracious permission, the House, Museum & Gardens will be open. Follow the brown & white tourist signs from A148 & A149.* **For opening times and information, please phone, email or visit garden website.**

60 acres of glorious gardens, woodland and lakes, with rare plants and trees. Colour and interest throughout the year with sheets of spring-flowering bulbs, avenues of rhododendrons and azaleas, beds of lavender and roses, and dazzling autumn colour. Donations are given from the Estate to various charities. Open daily from Easter Saturday to end of October except for a period at the end of July. Gravel paths (not deep), long distances - please telephone or visit website for our Accessibility Guide.

♿ ✽ 🚌 ☕

47 ◆ SHERINGHAM PARK

Wood Farm Visitors Centre, Upper Sheringham, NR26 8TL. National Trust, 01263 820550, sheringhampark@nationaltrust.org.uk, www.nationaltrust.org.uk/sheringham. *2m SW of Sheringham. Access for cars off A148 Cromer to Holt Rd, 5m W of Cromer, 6m E of Holt, signs in Sheringham town.* **For NGS: Thur 17 May, Thur 7 June (10-5). For other opening times and information, please phone, email or visit garden website.**

80 acres of species rhododendron, azalea and magnolia. Also numerous specimen trees incl handkerchief tree. Viewing towers, waymarked walks, sea and parkland views. No admission charge to Sheringham Park, car park charge £5.70 for non NT members Special walkway and WCs for disabled. 1½ m route is accessible for wheelchairs, mobility scooters available to hire.

♿ 🐕 ✽ 🚌 ☕

48 NEW SILVERSTONE FARM

North Elmham, Dereham, NR20 5EX. George Carter Design Limited, georgecartergardens.co.uk. *Nearer to Gateley than North Elmham. From North Elmham church head N to Guist. Take 1st L onto Great Heath Rd. L at T-junction. Take 1st R signed Gateley, Silverstone Farm is 1st drive on L by a wood.* **Sun 14 Oct (1-4.30). Adm £5, chd free. Home-made teas.**

Garden belonging to George Carter described by the Sunday Times as 'one of the 10 best garden designers in Britain'. 1830s farmyard and formal gardens in 2 acres. Inspired by C17 formal gardens, the site consists of a series of interconnecting rooms with framed views and vistas designed in a simple palette of evergreens and deciduous trees and shrubs such as available in that period. Books by the owner for sale. Featured in many articles and books including: Barbara Segall, 'Secret Gardens of East Anglia', 'Garden Magic: Making the Ordinary Extraordinary', Country Life, The English Garden, Gardens Illustrated. Level site mostly wheelchair accessible.

49 NEW STANLEY HOUSE

Herrings Lane, Burnham Market, King's Lynn, PE31 8DW. Mrs Barbara Cartwright. *In the centre of Burnham Market. 11m from Fakenham, 7m from Wells next the Sea. Off the B1105. Parking available in nearby public car park with WC.* **Sat 16 June (2-5.30). Adm £3, chd free. Home-made teas.**

Created just 18 months ago this is a small garden designed around a newly built house. A mix of contemporary and traditional, the contained site comprises a formal parterre with a modern twist, patio area, raised vegetable beds, and a neat lawn, and demonstrates what can be achieved within a short time and in a compact site. Very limited wheelchair access.

50 ◆ STODY LODGE

Melton Constable, NR24 2ER. Mr & Mrs Charles MacNicol, 01263 860572, enquiries@stodyestate.co.uk, www.stodylodgegardens.co.uk. *16m NW of Norwich, 3m S of Holt. Off B1354. Signed from Melton Constable on Holt Rd. For SatNav NR24 2ER. Gardens signed as you approach.* **For NGS: Tue 22 May (1-5). Adm £6, chd free. Home-made teas. For other opening times and information, please phone, email or visit garden website.**

Spectacular gardens with one of the largest concentrations of rhododendrons and azaleas in East Anglia. Created in the 1920s, the gardens also feature magnolias, camellias, a variety of ornamental and specimen trees, late daffodils, tulips and bluebells. Expansive lawns and magnificent yew hedges. Woodland walks and 4 acre Water Gardens filled with over 2,000 vividly-coloured azalea mollis. Home-made teas provided by selected local and national charities. Access to most areas of the garden. Gravel paths to Azalea Water Gardens with some uneven ground.

51 SUIL NA MARA

North Walsham Road, Bacton, Norwich, NR12 0LG. Bill & Bev Kerr, 01692 652386, billkerr1@btinternet.com. *19m N of Norwich on N Norfolk coast. Take the N Walsham to Bacton rd. We are just past the Coastguard Station in Pollard St. From Mundesley & Walcott direction garden on R just as you enter Pollard St.* **Sat 21, Sun 22 July (10.30-5). Adm £4, chd free. Light refreshments. Tea, coffee, cake. Visits also by arrangement June to Sept no min number.**

This ¼ acre exotic garden incorporates more than 250 plant varieties in an unusual mix of lush semi tropical planting meets Norfolk Coast meets Industrial and rural decay. Set in a series of garden rooms the striking architectural plants mixed with beachcombed wood, rusty metal and unusual water features all provides plenty to look at and enjoy. Often described as a 'Tardis' of a garden! Featured in EDP Norfolk magazine. Sorry all paths are gravelled and are difficult for wheelchair/mobility access.

52 NEW SUNDIAL FARM

Shelton Green, Shelton, Norwich, NR15 2SQ. Ally & John Hodgson. *12m S of Norwich. From A140 take B1527 towards Hempnall. Turn R towards Fritton. Cross the common & take 1st L (Alburgh Rd).* **Sat 19 May (11-5). Adm £4, chd free. Home-made teas.**

3 acre family garden with charming features including giant topiary faces, a secret garden and a pond. There is a new ornamental cutting and vegetable garden with greenhouse, extensive perennial planting, a hazel walk and orchards. The journey through the garden mixes open areas of light and more secluded, shady places to create interesting contrasts. The atmosphere is relaxed yet playful. Wheelchair access may be difficult as there are some steps and different surfaces, but help can be called upon if needed.

53 TUDOR LODGINGS

Castle Acre, King's Lynn, PE32 2AN. Gus & Julia Stafford Allen. *4m N of Swaffham off A1065 Swaffham to Fakenham. Situated on L as you come into the village with parking in the field below the house.* **Sun 5 Aug (11-5). Combined adm with Minns Farm Barns £6, chd free. Home-made teas in the Barn.**

The C15 house (not open), incorporates part of the Norman earthworks, and has beautiful views towards the R Nar. The 2 acre garden contains C18 dovecote, abstract topiary, lawns and a 'Mondrian' knot garden. Ornamental grasses and hot border. Productive fruit cage dominates the vegetable garden. A natural wild area includes a shepherd's hut and informal pond. Bantams and Ducks. EDP. Wheelchair access is limited but some areas possible please ask for assistance beforehand. Disabled WC.

54 NEW **TYGER BARN**
Wood Lane, Aldeby, Beccles, NR34 0DA. Julianne Fernandez. *Approx 1m from Toft Monks. From A143 towards Great Yarmouth at Toft Monks turn R into Post Office Lane opp White Lion Pub, after ¼m turn L into Wood Lane. After ½m Tyger Barn is 2nd house on L.* **Sun 8 July (11-5). Adm £5, chd free. Light refreshments.**
A 'work in progress', started in 2007 on the site of a former farmyard, the garden incl extensive densely planted borders with hot, exotic and 'ghost' themes, a secret cottage garden, wild flower swathes and colonies of bee orchids. A traditional hay meadow and ancient woodland provide a beautiful setting. Garden is mainly level, but is divided by a shingle drive which wheelchairs without wide wheels will find difficult to cross.

55 **WALCOTT HOUSE**
Walcott Green, Walcott, Norwich, NR12 0NU. Mr & Mrs Nick Collier. *3m N of Stalham. Off the Stalham to Walcott rd (B1159).* **Sun 17 June (12-5). Adm £4, chd free. Light refreshments.**
A young garden with emphasis on formal structure around the house and a traditional set of Norfolk farm buildings. These provide a series of connecting gardens which, through a south facing garden wall, lead to further gardens of clipped box, pleached hornbeam, fruit trees and roses. All set within recently planted woodland and specimen trees providing avenues and vistas. Small single steps to negotiate when moving between gardens in the yards.

56 **WARBOROUGH HOUSE**
2 Wells Road, Stiffkey, NR23 1QH. Mr & Mrs J Morgan. *13m N of Fakenham, 4m E of Wells-Next-The-Sea on A149 in the centre of village. Please DO NOT park in main rd as this causes congestion. Parking is available & signed at garden entrance. Coasthopper bus stop outside garden.* **Sun 27 May (1-5). Adm £5, chd free.**
7 acre garden on a steep chalk slope, surrounding C19 house (not open) with views across the Stiffkey valley and to the coast. Woodland walks, formal terraces, shrub borders, lawns and walled garden create a garden of contrasts. Garden slopes steeply in parts. Paths are gravel, bark chip or grass. Disabled parking allows access to garden nearest the house and teas.

Funds from National Garden Scheme gardens help Macmillan support thousands of people every year

GROUP OPENING

57 **WELLS-NEXT-THE-SEA GARDENS**
Wells-Next-The-Sea, NR23 1DP. *10m N of Fakenham. All gardens near Coasthopper 'Burnt Street' or 'The Buttlands' bus stops. Car-parking for all 4 gardens also in Market Lane area.* **Sun 17 June (11-5). Combined adm £5, chd free. Light refreshments.**

CAPRICE
Clubbs Lane. David & Joolz Saunders.

NEW **FICKLINGS BARN, 4 MARSH LANE**
Steve & Jane Barber.

7 MARKET LANE
Hazel Ashley.

POACHER COTTAGE
Burnt St. Roger & Barbara Oliver.

Wells-next-the-Sea is a small, friendly coastal town on the glorious North Norfolk Coast: popular with families, walkers and bird watchers. The harbour has shops, cafes, fish and chips, while a mile along The Run lies Wells Beach, served by a narrow gauge railway. The four town gardens, though small, demonstrate a variety of design and planting approaches incorporating herbaceous borders, 'cottage', shrubs and fruit. The route around the four gardens takes in the Parish Church of St Nicholas, the High Street with its beautiful once-shop windows and the tree lined Georgian green square, The Buttlands. New garden in the group for 2018. Two gardens with 'rooms'. One with small alpine section. Wheelchair access at all gardens EXCEPT Ficklings Barn. The garden at Ficklings Barn is on different levels so wheelchair access very difficult.

58 **WEST BARSHAM HALL**
Fakenham, NR21 9NP. Mr & Mrs Jeremy Soames, 01328 863519, susannasoames@gmail.com. *3m N of Fakenham. From Fakenham take A148 to Cromer then L on B1105 to Wells. After ½m L again to Wells. After 1½m R The Barshams & West Barsham Hall.* **Sun 17 June (11-5). Adm £6, chd free. Cream teas. Morning coffee and light refreshments, afternoon cream teas. Visits also by arrangement May to Sept groups welcome.**
Large garden with lake, approx 10 acres. Mature yew hedging and sunken garden originally laid out by Gertrude Jeykll. Swimming pool garden, shrub borders, kitchen garden with herbaceous borders, fruit cage, cutting garden and bog garden. Separate old fashioned cottage garden also open. Some slopes and gravel paths.

59 NEW **30 WEST PARADE**
Norwich, NR2 3DW. Anna Walker. *½m from Norwich city centre, off Earlham Rd. Nos 29 & 30 are at the far end of cul-de-sac. No on-street parking, 2 hour bays available in adjacent streets. By bus 26 from City Centre.* **Sun 24 June (11.30-5.30).**

Combined adm with 29 West Parade £5, chd free. Home-made teas and cakes incl gluten free.

30 West Parade is a recently established family garden. There are large mixed borders, unusual trees, shrubs and climbers/rambling roses and lavender lined paths, all encouraging bees and other wildlife. Secluded courtyard area with some exotic planting, as well as enclosed dining areas and a large lawn. Gravel drives/paths and some steps at no 30 make wheelchair access challenging but not impossible.

60 NEW 29 WEST PARADE

Norwich, NR2 3DN. Tony Hufton. *West Parade is ½m W of Norwich centre off Earlham Road. 29 & 30 are at the far end of cul-de-sac. No parking in West Parade, bays are available in adjacent streets. By Bus 26 from City Centre.* **Sun 24 June (11.30-5). Combined adm with 30 West Parade £5, chd free. Home-made teas and cakes incl gluten free.**

29 West Parade is a walled Victorian town garden which has been developed over the last 20 years. There are some rare and unusual plants, flower borders, box and yew hedging, espaliered fruit, several fine specimen trees, medlar, small meadow area and vegetable plot. Features include flint walls and a WWII air raid shelter. Gravel paths - wheelchair access challenging but not impossible.

61 WITTON HALL

Old Hall Road, North Walsham, NR28 9UF. Sally Owles. *3½m from North Walsham. From North Walsham take Happisburgh Rd or Byway to Edingthorpe Rd off North Walsham bypass. Situated nr to Bacton Woods.* **Mon 7 May (12-4). Adm £3, chd free. Light refreshments.**

A natural woodland garden. Walk past the handkerchief tree and wander through carpets of English bluebells, rhododendrons and azaleas. Walk from the garden down the field to the church. Stunning views over farmland to the sea. Sensible footwear required as deer, rabbits and badgers inhabit this garden! Witton Park laid out by Humphrey Repton. Wheelchair access difficult if wet.

62 16 WITTON LANE

Little Plumstead, NR13 5DL. Sally Ward & Richard Hobbs. *5m E of Norwich. Take A47 to Yarmouth, 1st exit after Postwick, turn L to Witton Green & Gt Plumstead, then 1st R into Witton Lane for 1½m. Garden on L.* **Sun 8 Apr (11-4). Adm £3, chd free.**

An 'Aladdin's Cave' for the alpine and woodland plant enthusiast. Tiny garden with wide range of rare and unusual plants will be of great interest with its species tulips, daffodils, scillas, dog's tooth violets, other bulbous plants and many trilliums and wood anemones. A garden for the plant specialist. National Collection of Muscari. Plants for sale and refreshments. Not suitable for wheelchair access due to narrow gravel paths.

NPC

63 WRETHAM LODGE

East Wretham, IP24 1RL. Mr Gordon Alexander & Mr Ian Salter, 01953 498997. *6m NE of Thetford. A11 E from Thetford, L up A1075, L by village sign, R at Xrds then bear L.* **Sun 1, Mon 2 Apr (11-5). Adm £5, chd free. Home-made teas in Church. Visits also by arrangement Apr to Sept.**

10 acre garden surrounding former Georgian rectory (not open). In spring masses of species tulips, hellebores, fritillaries, daffodils and narcissi; bluebell walk and small woodland walk. Topiary pyramids and yew hedging lead to double herbaceous borders. Shrub borders and rose beds (home of the Wretham Rose). Traditionally maintained walled garden with fruit, vegetables and perennials.

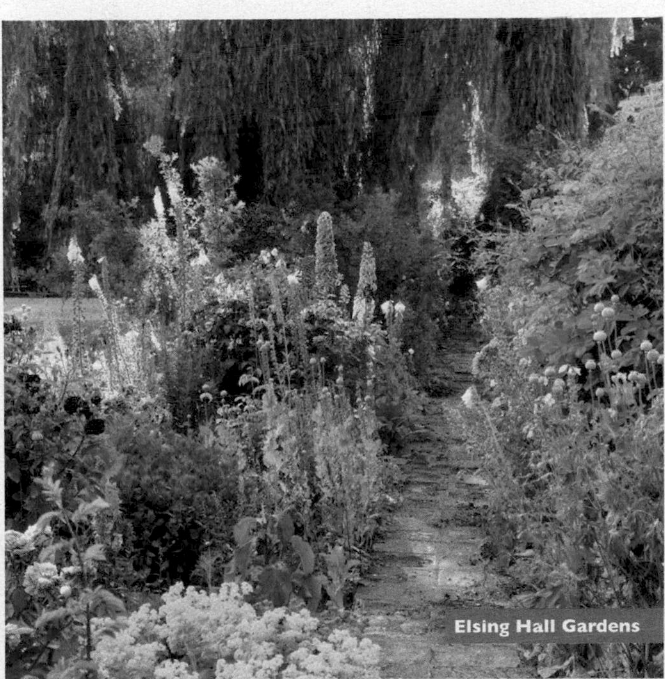

Elsing Hall Gardens

NORTH EAST

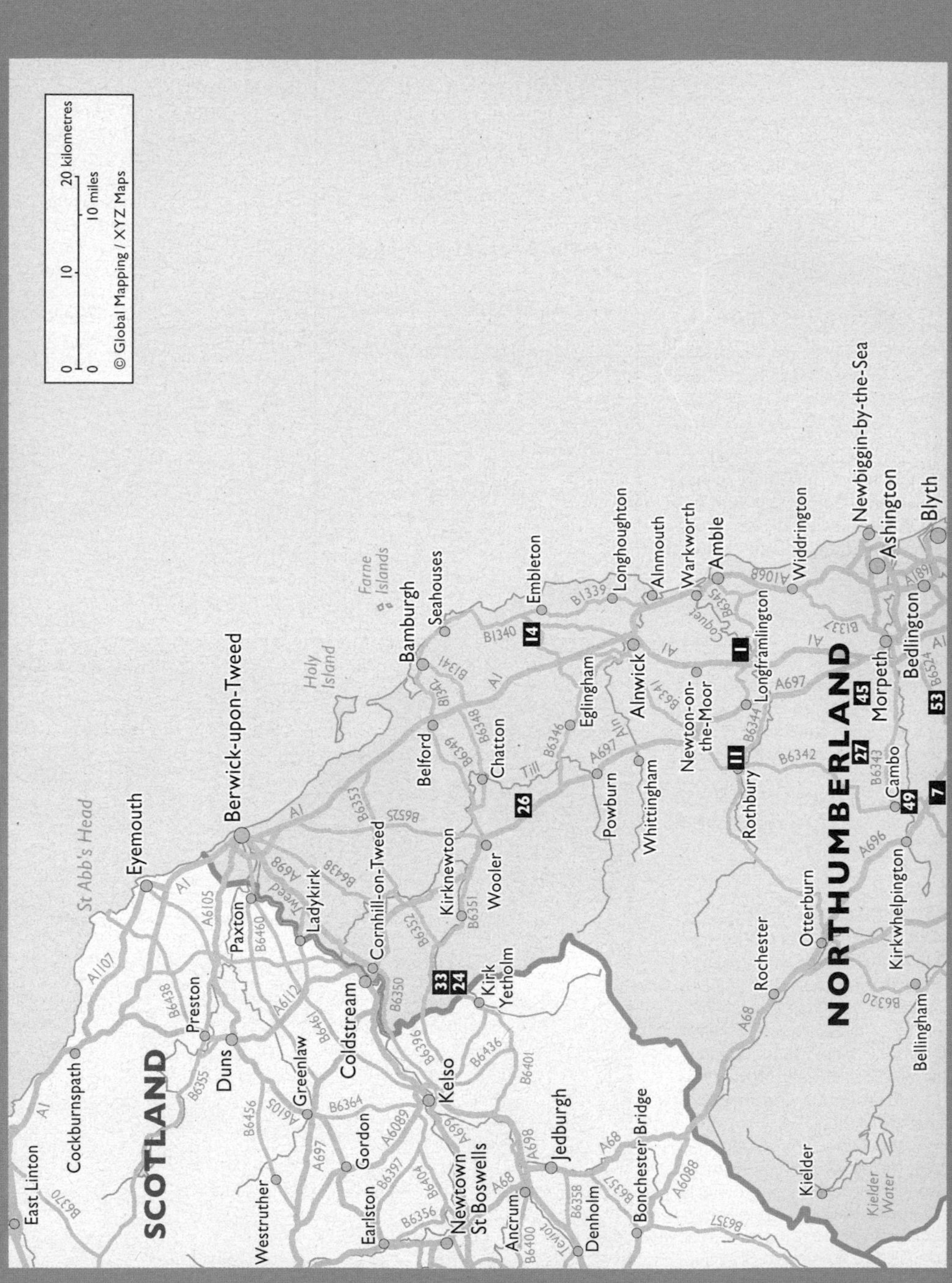

0 10 20 kilometres
0 10 miles
© Global Mapping / XYZ Maps
SCOTLAND
NORTHUMBERLAND
St Abb's Head
Eyemouth
Berwick-upon-Tweed
Holy Island
Farne Islands
Bamburgh
Seahouses
Embleton
Longhoughton
Alnmouth
Warkworth
Amble
Widdrington
Newbiggin-by-the-Sea
Ashington
Blyth
Bedlington
Morpeth
Longframlington
Newton-on-the-Moor
Alnwick
Eglingham
Chatton
Belford
Powburn
Whittingham
Rothbury
Cambo
Kirkwhelpington
Otterburn
Rochester
Bellingham
Kielder
Kielder Water
Wooler
Kirknewton
Kirk Yetholm
Cornhill-on-Tweed
Ladykirk
Paxton
Coldstream
Preston
Duns
Cockburnspath
East Linton
Greenlaw
Westruther
Gordon
Earlston
Kelso
Newtown St Boswells
Ancrum
Jedburgh
Denholm
Bonchester Bridge
Tweed
Till
Aln
Coquet
Teviot
A1
A68
A697
A698
A699
A696
A6105
A6112
A6089
A6088
A1107
A1068
B6355
B6438
B6460
B6461
B6456
B6364
B6397
B6404
B6356
B6400
B6358
B6357
B6401
B6436
B6396
B6350
B6352
B6351
B6525
B6353
B6349
B6348
B6346
B6341
B6344
B6342
B6343
B6345
B6320
B6524
B1337
B1339
B1340
B1341
B1342
B6370
14
1
11
26
27
45
49
53
7
33
24

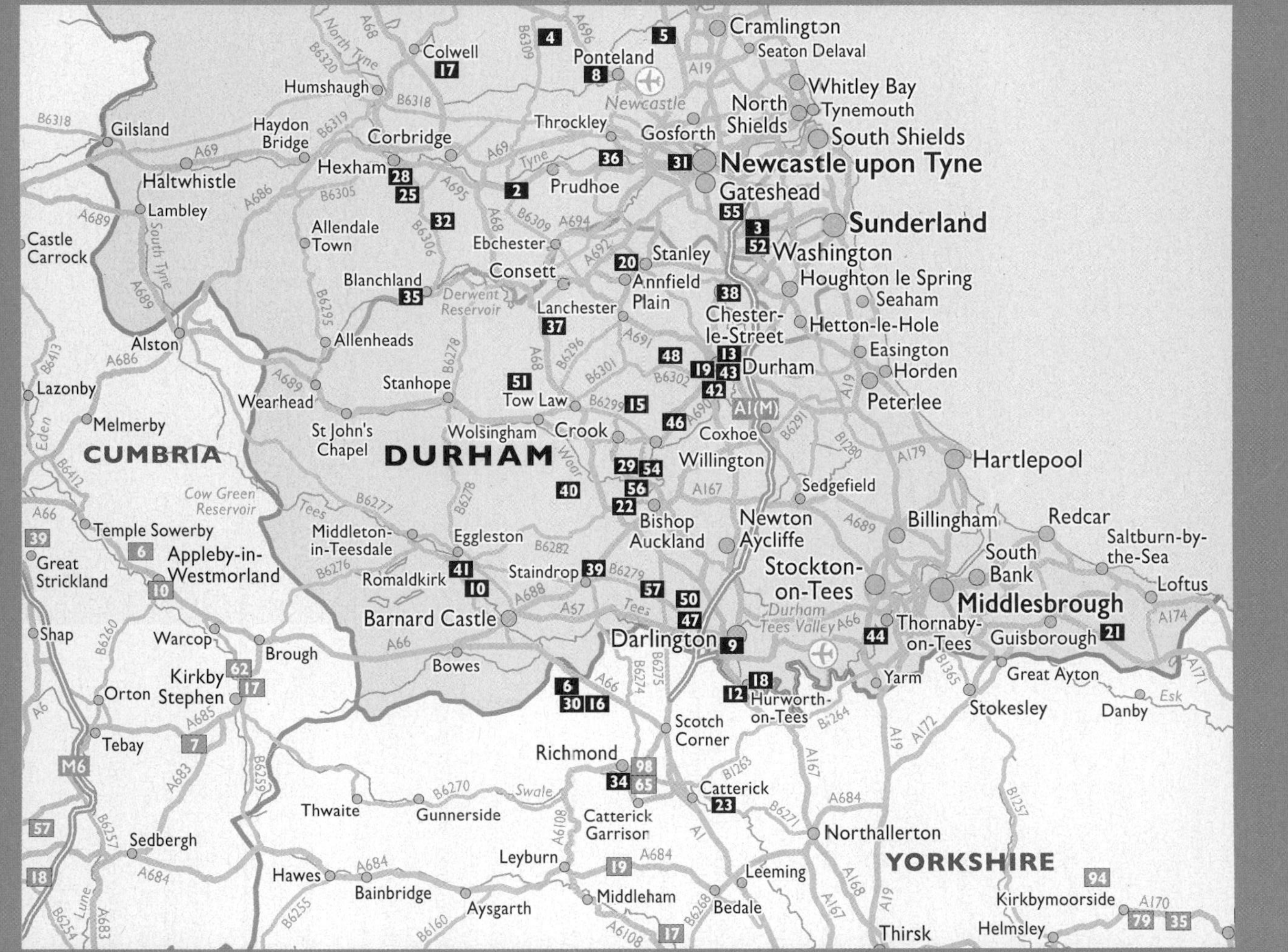
Cramlington
Seaton Delaval
Colwell
Ponteland
Newcastle
Humshaugh
Whitley Bay
North Shields
Tynemouth
South Shields
Gilsland
Haydon Bridge
Corbridge
Throckley
Gosforth
Hexham
Prudhoe
Newcastle upon Tyne
Gateshead
Haltwhistle
Lambley
Sunderland
Castle Carrock
Allendale Town
Ebchester
Stanley
Washington
Consett
Annfield Plain
Houghton le Spring
Blanchland
Derwent Reservoir
Seaham
Lanchester
Chester-le-Street
Hetton-le-Hole
Alston
Allenheads
Easington
Durham
Horden
Lazonby
Stanhope
Wearhead
Tow Law
Peterlee
Melmerby
St John's Chapel
Wolsingham
Crook
Coxhoe
CUMBRIA
DURHAM
Hartlepool
Willington
Cow Green Reservoir
Sedgefield
Bishop Auckland
Newton Aycliffe
Billingham
Redcar
Temple Sowerby
Middleton-in-Teesdale
Eggleston
Saltburn-by-the-Sea
Great Strickland
Appleby-in-Westmorland
South Bank
Staindrop
Stockton-on-Tees
Romaldkirk
Loftus
Middlesbrough
Barnard Castle
Durham Tees Valley
Shap
Warcop
Thornaby-on-Tees
Darlington
Guisborough
Brough
Bowes
Great Ayton
Kirkby Stephen
Yarm
Orton
Hurworth-on-Tees
Stokesley
Danby
Scotch Corner
Tebay
Richmond
Catterick
Thwaite
Gunnerside
Catterick Garrison
Northallerton
Sedbergh
Leyburn
YORKSHIRE
Hawes
Leeming
Bainbridge
Middleham
Kirkbymoorside
Aysgarth
Bedale
Thirsk
Helmsley
North Tyne
South Tyne
Tyne
Eden
Tees
Wear
Swale
Lune
Esk
A1
A1(M)
M6
A19
A66
A68
A69
A167
A171
A174
A179
A684
A689
A696
A6108
B6309
B6318
B6275
B6274
B1257
B1365

Volunteers

County Durham
County Organiser
Iain Anderson
01325 778446
iain.anderson@ngs.org.uk

County Treasurer
Sue Douglas
07712 461002
pasm.d@btinternet.com

Booklet Co-ordinator
Sheila Walke
07837 764057
sheila.walke@ngs.org.uk

Assistant County Organisers
Gill Knights
01325 483210
gillianknights55@gmail.com

Dorothy Matthews
01833 627025
matthews.dorothy@googlemail.com

Gill Naisby
01325 381324
gillnaisby@gmail.com

Gill Sullivan
gill.sullivan1956@btinternet.com

Sue Walker
01325 481881
walker.sdl@gmail.com

Northumberland & Tyne and Wear
County Organiser
& Booklet Coordinator
Maureen Kesteven
01914 135937
kestevenmaureen@gmail.com

County Treasurer
David Oakley 07941 077594
david.oakley@ngs.org.uk

Publicity
Susie White 07941 077595
susie@susie-white.co.uk

Maxine Eaton 077154 60038
acottagegardener@gmail.com

Assistant County Organisers
Natasha McEwen 07917 754155
natashamcewengd@aol.co.uk

Liz Reid 01914 165981
lizreid52@ntlworld.com

David Young 01434 600699
davyoung0601@me.com

County Durham: an unsung county.

At the heart of this once industrial land lies the medieval city of Durham. The city is a fascinating blend of ancient and modern, respecting the heritage and traditions of its forefathers whilst embracing changing lifestyles and culture.

This epitomises the county as a whole; old, industrial sites and coal mines have been sensitively cleared to restore the land to its original 'green' beauty.

Set amongst this varied and beautiful countryside are gardens which open their gates for the NGS.

So, stand amongst the rare and unusual plants at 14 Grays Terrace and be amazed by the spectacular view of Durham Cathedral, or visit the wonderful and imaginative hidden garden that has been created behind the working forge at Ravensworth.

Northumberland is a county rich in history with sturdy castles, stunning coastline and a wild landscape threaded with sheltered valleys.

Gardeners have learnt how to make the most of the land; terracing hillsides, enhancing the soil and often using the wonderful architecture as a backdrop, such as at Lilburn Tower.

Garden owners have managed to create gardens whatever the conditions. At Blagdon the solution has been to plant within an old quarry, and at Wallington to use a long narrow valley for shelter.

An eclectic range of gardens open for the NGS. Each reflects the style and character of their owners, with the extra attraction of home-made teas and plant sales.

Below: **The Beacon**

OPENING DATES

All entries subject to change. For latest information check www.ngs.org.uk

Map locator numbers are shown to the right of each garden name.

February

Snowdrop Festival

Sunday 25th
◆ Crook Hall & Gardens 13

April

Saturday 21st
◆ Wallington 49

Friday 27th
◆ Cragside 11

May

Sunday 6th
Southlands 44

Sunday 13th
Hillside Cottages 22
Thornton Hall Gardens 47

Sunday 20th
Blagdon 5

Sunday 27th
Croft Hall 12
Lilburn Tower 26

Monday 28th
Woodbine House 54

June

Festival Weekend

Saturday 2nd
Ushaw College 48

Sunday 3rd
24 Bede Crescent 3
◆ Washington Old Hall 52

Sunday 10th
107 Coniscliffe Road 9
Oliver Ford Garden 37

Croft Hall

Saturday 16th
◆ Wallington 49

Sunday 17th
Broaches Farm 6
Harperley Hall Farm 20
NEW Lowbridge House 30
◆ Mindrum Garden 33

Saturday 23rd
Middle Grange 32
Ravensford Farm 40

Sunday 24th
The Beacon 2
Longwitton Hall 27
Romaldkirk Gardens 41

Saturday 30th
Fallodon Hall 14
Gardens On The Green 18
Warrenfell 51
Woodlands 55

July

Sunday 1st
Cotherstone Village Gardens 10
Marie Curie Hospice Newcastle on Tyne 31
Warrenfell 51
◆ Whalton Manor Gardens 53

Thursday 5th
Woodlands 55

Friday 6th
The Fold 15

Saturday 7th
The Fold 15
NEW Kirky Cottage 24

Sunday 8th
St Margaret's Allotments 43

Wednesday 11th
Coldcotes Moor Farm 8

Saturday 14th
◆ Raby Castle 39

Sunday 15th
Bichfield Tower 4
Gardener's Cottage Plants 17

Sunday 22nd
Kiplin Hall 23
Newbiggin House 35
No. 2 Ferndene 36
Woodside House 56

Sunday 29th
Lambshield 25
St Cuthbert's Hospice 42

August

Saturday 4th
NEW Woodside, Killerby 57

Sunday 5th
Coldcotes Moor Farm 8
NEW Heather Holm 21
Loughbrow House 28
4 Stockley Grove 46

Sunday 12th
Capheaton Hall 7

Sunday 19th
Mr Yorke's Walled Garden 34
NEW Walworth Gardens 50

September

Sunday 23rd
Harperley Hall Farm 20

By Arrangement

Acton House 1
The Beacon 2
24 Bede Crescent 3
Broaches Farm 6
Coldcotes Moor Farm 8
The Fold 15
The Forge 16
14 Grays Terrace 19
Harperley Hall Farm 20
Hillside Cottages 22
NEW Kirky Cottage 24
Lambshield 25
Lilburn Tower 26
Loughbrow House 28
10 Low Row 29
NEW Lowbridge House 30
Middle Grange 32
No. 2 Ferndene 36
25 Park Road South 38
Ravensford Farm 40
Stanton Fence 45
4 Stockley Grove 46
Thornton Hall Gardens 47
Ushaw College 48
Warrenfell 51
Woodlands 55
Woodside House 56

THE GARDENS

1 ACTON HOUSE

Felton, Morpeth, NE65 9NU. Mr Alan & Mrs Eileen Ferguson, Head Gardener 07779 860217, jane@actonhouseuk.com. *N of Morpeth. On old A1 N of Felton, take turning to Acton, follow rd for ½m until fork & follow sign to Acton House.* **Visits by arrangement May to Aug for groups of 6+. Adm £5, chd free.**

This stunning walled garden has structure, colour and variety of planting, with abundant herbaceous perennials and different grasses. Planted in the spring of 2011, it has sections devoted to fruit and vegetables, David Austin rose borders, standard trees and climbers spreading over the brick walls. There are additional mixed borders, a ha-ha, and developing woodland planting, in total extending over 5 acres. Herbaceous perennial plantings include species and varieties favoured by butterflies and bees.

2 THE BEACON

10 Crabtree Road, Stocksfield, NE43 7NX. Derek & Patricia Hodgson, 01661 842518, patandderek@btinternet.com. *12m W of Newcastle upon Tyne. From A69 follow signs into village. Station & cricket ground on L . Turn R into Cadehill Rd then 1st R into Crabtree Rd (cul de sac) Park on Cadehill.* **Sun 24 June (2-5.30). Adm £5, chd free. Cream teas. Visits also by arrangement May to Sept groups of 10+.**

This garden illustrates how to make a cottage garden on a steep site with loads of interest at different levels. Planted with acers, roses and a variety of cottage garden and formal plants. Water runs gently through it and there are tranquil places to sit and talk or just reflect. Stunning colour and plant combinations. Wildlife friendly - numerous birds, frogs, newts, hedgehogs. Haven for butterflies and bees. Featured in The Northumbrian Magazine. Steep, so not wheelchair friendly but wheelchair users have negotiated the drive and enjoyed the view of the main garden.

3 24 BEDE CRESCENT

Washington, NE38 7JA. Sheila Brookes, 0191 417 9702, sheilab24@hotmail.co.uk. *From WOH, past Cenotaph, 600yds up Village Lane past R C Church, & Black Bush Pub. Follow NGS sign through cut to Town Centre, into Bede Crescent, end house of 5, facing grassed oval.* **Sun 3 June (1-4). Adm £2, chd free. Also open Washington Old Hall. Obtain ticket at Washington Old Hall. Visits also by arrangement June to Sept small groups only. No refreshments, but local Pubs and cafes in Village.**

A lesson in how to make a small shady place colourful and interesting. Small 'courtyard style' garden, with central paved area, surrounded by borders containing shrubs and box balls for year round structure, and packed with colourful Astilbes, lilies and clematis for summer impact. Small patio front garden, with gravel border planted with box balls and containerised shrubs. Opens in conjunction with Washington Old Hall. Access into paved 'courtyard garden' via a side gate, (which should accommodate a small wheelchair, although not a wide entrance).

4 BICHFIELD TOWER

Belsay, Newcastle Upon Tyne, NE20 0JP. Lesley & Stewart Manners, 075114 39606, lesleymanners@gmail.com, www.bitchfieldtower.co.uk. *Private rd off B6309, 4m N of Stamfordham and SW of Belsay village.* **Sun 15 July (1-4). Adm £5, chd free. Home-made teas in the carriage house garden and building.**

The 6 acre maturing garden in it's 4th year of rejuvenation. Set around a Medieval Pele Tower, there is an impressive stone water feature, large trout lake,mature woodland, Pear Orchard, and 2 Walled gardens. Extensive herbaceous borders, prairie borders and contemporary grass borders. Delicious home-made teas provided by the 6th Morpeth Scout Group in the carriage house garden and building. Historic building, tennis court, woodlands, fairy walk for kids, sculpture walk throughout the grounds, croquet lawn and set, trout lake, pop-up shops of local businesses.

5 BLAGDON

Seaton Burn, NE13 6DE. Viscount Ridley, www.blagdonestate.co.uk. *5m S of Morpeth on A1. 8m N of Newcastle on A1, N on B1318, L at r'about (Holiday Inn) & follow signs to Blagdon. Entrance to parking area signed.* **Sun 20 May (1-4.30). Adm £5, chd free. Home-made teas.**

Unique 27 acre garden encompassing formal garden with Lutyens designed 'canal', Lutyens structures and walled kitchen garden. Valley with stream and various follies, quarry garden and woodland walks. Large numbers of ornamental trees and shrubs planted over many generations. National Collections of Acer, Alnus and Sorbus. Trailer rides around the estate (small additional charge) and stalls selling local produce. Partial wheelchair access.

NPC

6 BROACHES FARM

Dalton, Richmond, DL11 7HW. Mr & Mrs Hutchinson, 01833 621369, jude1@myfwi.co.uk. *7m W of Scotch Corner. From Scotch Corner on A66 W, 7m turn L at The Rokeby Inn. After ½m turn L to Dalton. Farm on L after 1m.* **Sun 17 June (12-6). Combined adm with Low Bridge House £6, chd free. Home-made teas in the barn. Visits also by arrangement June to Aug any number of visitors.**

In 1996 this wonderful garden was a field. It now includes 2 ponds, one with koi, stream, bog garden and wooded area. Mixed colourful borders are full of herbaceous perennials. Informal and naturalistic, this is a rural idyll. Abundant wildlife incl kingfishers, dippers, wagtails, frogs and toads. Lots of seating areas including summerhouse and gazebo.

7 CAPHEATON HALL

Capheaton, Newcastle Upon Tyne, NE19 2AB. William & Eliza Browne-Swinburne, 01830530159, capheatonhall@gmail.com, www.capheatonhall.co.uk/accomodation. *24m N of Newcastle off A696. From S turn L onto Silver Hill rd signed Capheaton. From N, past Wallington/Kirkharle junction, turn R.* **Sun 12 Aug (2-5). Adm £5, chd free. Home-made teas.**

Set in parkland, Capheaton Hall has magnificent views over the Northumberland countryside. Formal ponds sit south of the house, which has an C18 conservatory, and a walk to a Georgian folly of a chapel. The outstanding feature is the very productive walled garden, at its height in late summer, mixing colourful vegetables, espaliered fruit with annual and perennial flowering borders. Walled Kitchen Garden; fruit and vegetable production; Victorian glasshouse and conservatory;.

8 COLDCOTES MOOR FARM

Ponteland, Newcastle Upon Tyne, NE20 0DF. Ron & Louise Bowey, info@theboweys.co.uk. *Off A696 N of Ponteland. From S, leave Ponteland on A696 towards Jedburgh, after 1m take L turn marked 'Milbourne 2m'. After 400yds turn L into drive.* **Pre-booking essential for these two dates. Wed 11 July, Sun 5 Aug (1-5). Adm £8, chd free. Tea, coffee and cake incl in adm. Please email kestevenmaureen@gmail.com, or phone 01914 135937 to book, max 40 visitors. Visits also by arrangement June to Aug for groups of 10+, adm incl tea/coffee and cake.**

The garden, landscaped grounds and woods cover around 15 acres. The wooded approach opens out to lawned areas surrounded by ornamental and woodland shrubs and trees. A courtyard garden leads to an ornamental walled garden, beyond which is an orchard, vegetable garden, flower garden and rose arbour. To the south the garden looks out over a lake and field walks, with woodland walk to the west. Small children's play area. WI Life, Hexham Courant. Most areas can be accessed though sometimes by circuitous routes or an occasional step. WC access involves three steps.

9 107 CONISCLIFFE ROAD

Darlington, DL3 7ET. Jill Jackson. *2m from A1 near town centre. From A1 S, L at r'about, L next r'about R onto Coniscliffe Rd. Follow signs towards Barnard Castle A167 from town centre /ring rd and this is Coniscliffe Rd. Please park in nearby streets.* **Sun 10 June (2-4). Adm £3, chd free. Cream teas.**

This is a small garden designed for a wildlife loving wheelchair user and features a pond, a patch of meadow, huge bug palace, numerous bird feeders and living brush pile. In addition vegetables shares the borders with the flowers. There are some weeds as the rule is if the bees butterflies and bugs love it, it stays. The garden owner is a wheelchair user so access is fine but it is a slope with sloped paths, not all on the flat.

GROUP OPENING

10 COTHERSTONE VILLAGE GARDENS

Cotherstone, Barnard Castle, DL12 9QW. *4m NW of Barnard Castle. On B6277 Middleton-in-Teesdale to Barnard Castle road. Gardens are spread throughout the village. Home made teas at three points in the village.* **Sun 1 July (11.30-4.30). Combined adm £5, chd free. Home-made teas in village hall and two gardens.**

A warm welcome awaits you in this traditional and historic Teesdale village. The village is bounded on two sides by the Balder and Tees rivers. A wide variety of country gardens (and allotments) are opening. Look out for some great Teesdale views as you walk between them. Visitors can help themselves to herbs from the pick your own boxes spread throughout the village. The village is on the Teesdale Way footpath and there are many picturesque walks in and around the locality. Cotherstone and the surrounding area is a beautiful place for walking. There are 2 Pubs, and a shop in the village where refreshments can also be obtained. Owing to the variety of gardens and allotments some may not be accessible for wheelchair users.

Thornton Hall Gardens

Donations from the National Garden Scheme help Parkinson's UK care for more people

11 ◆ CRAGSIDE

Rothbury, NE65 7PX.
National Trust, 01669 620333, cragside@nationaltrust.org.uk, www.nationaltrust.org.uk/cragside. *13m SW of Alnwick. (B6341); 15m NW of Morpeth (A697).* **For NGS: Fri 27 Apr (10-4). Adm £14.30, chd £7.20. For other opening times and information, please phone, email or visit garden website.**

The Formal Garden is in the 'High Victorian' style created by the 1st Lord and Lady Armstrong. Incl orchard house, carpet bedding, ferneries, Italian terrace and Rose borders. The largest sandstone Rock Garden in Europe with its tumbling cascades. Extensive grounds of over 1000 acres famous for rhododendrons in June, large lakes and magnificent conifer landscape. The House, mainly the design of Norman Shaw, with its very fine arts and crafts interiors is worth a separate visit. Limited wheelchair access to formal garden.

12 CROFT HALL

Croft-on-Tees, DL2 2TB. Mr & Mrs Trevor Chaytor Norris. *3m S of Darlington. On A167 to Northallerton, 6m from Scotch Corner. Croft Hall is 1st house on R as you enter village from Scotch Corner.* **Sun 27 May (2-5). Adm £5, chd free. Home-made teas.**

A lovely lavender walk leads to a Queen Anne-fronted house (not open) surrounded by a 5 acre garden, comprising a stunning herbaceous border, large fruit and vegetable plot, two ponds and wonderful topiary arched wall. Pretty rose garden and mature box Italianate parterre are beautifully set in this garden offering peaceful, tranquil views of open countryside. Wheelchair access, some gravel paths.

13 ◆ CROOK HALL & GARDENS

Sidegate, Durham City, DH1 5SZ. Maggie Bell, 0191 384 8028, info@crookhallgardens.co.uk, www.crookhallgardens.co.uk. *Centre of Durham City. Crook Hall is short walk from Durham's Market Place. Follow the tourist info signs. Pay and display parking available at entrance.* **For NGS: Sun 25 Feb (10-5). Adm £7.50, chd £5. For other opening times and information, please phone, email or visit garden website.**

Described in Country Life as having 'history, romance and beauty'. Intriguing medieval manor house surrounded by 4 acres of fine gardens. Visitors can enjoy magnificent cathedral views from the 2 walled gardens. Other garden 'rooms' incl the silver and white garden. An orchard, moat pool, maze and Sleeping Giant give added interest! Refreshments in the Tea Room (main building) and the Café (entrance building). Wheelchair accessible and disabled WC.

14 FALLODON HALL

Alnwick, NE66 3HF. Mr & Mrs Mark Bridgeman, 01665 576252, luciabridgeman@gmail.com, www.bruntoncottages.co.uk. *5m N of Alnwick, 2m off A1. From the A1 turn onto the B6347 signed Christon Bank & Seahouses. Turn into the Fallodon gates after exactly 2m, at Xrds. Follow drive for 1m.* **Sat 30 June (2-5). Adm £5, chd free. Home-made teas in stable yard.**

Extensive, well established garden, including a 30 metre border, finishing beside a hot greenhouse and bog garden. The late C17 walls of the kitchen garden surround cutting and vegetable borders and the fruit greenhouse. The sunken garden from 1898 has been replanted by Natasha McEwen. Woodlands, pond and arboretum extend over 10 acres to explore. Renowned home-made teas in stable yard, and plant sale. House and gardens used for filming 'Downton Abbey' and Alexander Armstrong's music videos and photographs for his CD. Partial wheelchair access.

Newbiggin House

© Val Corbett

15 THE FOLD

High Wooley, Stanley Crook, DL15 9AP. Mr & Mrs G Young, 01388 768412, gfamyoung@gmail.com. *Turn R at Xrds in Brancepeth, opp turn to Castle, drive 3m along the single track rd until you reach the junction on bend with the main rd. Entrance 100yards on L.* **Fri 6, Sat 7 July (10.30-4.30). Adm £4, chd free. Home-made teas. Visits also by arrangement May to Sept groups of 10+.**

Garden, approx ½ acre created over 20 years in an area that had been extensively mined. It stands at 700ft and enjoys splendid views over countryside. Herbaceous borders, alpine bed, island beds, ponds, numerous mature trees and small roof garden. Wide range of plants, mostly perennials, many grown from seed and cuttings. Emphasis on colour, harmony and texture to create all year interest. Featured in Garden World. No disabled access as steep slopes and gravel paths.

16 THE FORGE

Ravensworth, Richmond, DL11 7EU. Mr & Mrs Peter & Enid Wilson, 01325 718242, enid.wilson@btconnect.com. *7m N of Richmond. Travel 5½m W on A66 from Scotch Corner. Turn L to Ravensworth & follow NGS signs.* **Visits by arrangement May to July groups or individuals are most welcome. Adm £3, chd free. Cream teas and home-made cakes.**

The Blacksmith's Secret Garden - the garden is hidden from view behind The Forge House and Forge Cottage. It has two small wildlife ponds with natural stone features and a meadow. There are a number of unusual plants i.e. Dactylorhiza, Garden Orchids and Arisaema. Featured in Northern Echo, Teesdale Mercury, Amateur Gardener. Wheelchair access across gravel path.

17 GARDENER'S COTTAGE PLANTS

Gardener's Cottage, Bingfield, Newcastle Upon Tyne, NE19 2LE. Andrew Davenport, www.gcplants.co.uk. *6m N of Corbridge. From N turn L off A68 signed Bingfield, after approx. 0.6m turn L at T junction, garden on R approx. 0.9m. From S turn R off A68 signed Bingfield, garden on R approx. 1.8m.* **Sun 15 July (11-4). Adm £3, chd free. Variety of home-made cakes and scones.**

This compact (¼ acre) experimental garden and nursery provides an education in organic and sustainable gardening. Organic vegetable, fruit, herb and floral gardens show the use of mulching, hen assisted composting and other ideas from the garden's inventive creator. Pollinator friendly wild flowers thrive amongst cultivated varieties in a range of attractive ornamental borders.

GROUP OPENING

18 GARDENS ON THE GREEN

Hurworth-on-Tees, Darlington, DL2 2JA. *2m SE of Darlington. Follow main road through Hurworth Place. Off A66 - follow signs to Hurworth.* **Sat 30 June (11-4). Combined adm £5, chd free.**

A variety of village gardens of different sizes and aspects on the village green. . These include a courtyard garden and formal and cottage gardens. There are lovely views of the River Tees from some gardens. Two of the gardens are previous winners in the Darlington in Bloom competition. The village of Hurworth has three inviting and historical pubs should you wish to combine your garden visit with lunch.

19 14 GRAYS TERRACE

Redhills, Durham, DH1 4AU. Mr Paul Beard, 0191 5972849, pauljofraeard@yahoo.co.uk. *Just off A167 on W side of Durham. ½m S of A167 / A691 r'about, turn L into Redhills Lane. When road turns R with no entry sign, Grays Terrace is ahead. No.14 is at the very end.* **Visits by arrangement Apr to Aug. Adm by donation.**

A steeply sloping garden of about ⅔ acre with a superb view over Durham Cathedral, Castle and surroundings. Very informal garden; no bedding and a significant wild area. Planting is mixed with interest throughout the year. Many unusual and rare plants. Particularly knowledgeable owner who is happy to escort groups round the garden. Not suitable for wheelchairs.

20 HARPERLEY HALL FARM

Harperley, Stanley, DH9 9UB. Gary McDermott, 01207 233318, enquiries@harperleyhallfarmnurseries.co.uk, www.harperleyhallfarmnurseries.co.uk. *Leave A1 J63. At r'about exit A693 for Stanley, for 5m, over 3 r'abouts. take R turn top of bank, turn R @ T then L for Tanfield Ind Est follow signs. From Durham A691 Consett follow yellow signs.* **Sun 17 June, Sun 23 Sept (10-4). Adm £3, chd free. Home-made teas. Visits also by arrangement Mar to Sept groups welcome daytime or evenings.**

The garden is attached to an award winning specialist plant nursey (5 Chelsea Gold Medals and winner of the RHS Presidents Award 2015) It is being developed around large ponds and is filled with Primulas, incl Primula 'Inverewe' and P pulverulenta Bartleys Hybrid, Meconopsis, incl M 'Lingholm', M quintuplinervia, M cookei and the very rare M punicea 'Sichuan Silk'. The garden is in a tranquil setting and a flock of Rainbow and other Lorikeet fly at liberty around the garden. The garden and owner have been featured in the RHS Garden magazine and on BBC Chelsea Flower Show. The majority of the garden and nursery can be accessed by wheelchair users, but there are some slopes and irregular pathways.

21 NEW HEATHER HOLM

Stanghow Road, Stanghow, Saltburn-By-The-Sea, TS12 3JU. Arthur & June Murray. *Stanghow is 5 km E of Guisborough on A171. Turn L at Lockwood Beck (signed Stanghow) Heather Holm is on the R past the crossroads.* **Sun 5 Aug (12-4). Adm £4, chd free. Home-made teas.**

At 700 feet above sea level on the edge of the North Yorkshire Moors, Stanghow has won numerous RHS Gold awards for Best Small Village, winning again in 2017, and was a Champion among Champions in the 2013 Britain in Bloom competition. Heather Holm has extensive topiary which adds form and structure to this ¼ acre garden. Featured in Coastal View and Moor News. Wheelchair access to viewing deck only.

GROUP OPENING

22 HILLSIDE COTTAGES

Low Etherley, Bishop Auckland, DL14 0EZ. Mary Smith, Eric & Delia Ayres, 01388 832727, mary@maryruth.plus.com. *Off the B6282 in Low Etherley, nr Bishop Auckland. To reach the gardens walk down the track opp number 63 Low Etherley. Please park on main rd. Limited disabled parking at the cottages.* **Sun 13 May (1.30-5). Combined adm £4, chd free. Home-made teas. Visits also by arrangement Mar to Nov.**

1 HILLSIDE COTTAGE
Eric & Delia Ayres.

2 HILLSIDE COTTAGE
Mrs M Smith.

The gardens of these two C19 cottages offer contrasting styles. At Number 1, grass paths lead you through a layout of trees and shrubs including many interesting specimens. Number 2 is based on island beds and has a cottage garden feel with a variety of perennials among the trees and shrubs and also incl a wild area, vegetables and fruit. Both gardens have ponds and water features. This year we are opening to show off spring flowers and Rhododendrons. There are steps in both gardens.

23 KIPLIN HALL

nr Scorton, Richmond, North Yorkshire, DL10 6AT. Kiplin Hall Trustees, www.kiplinhall.co.uk. *Between Richmond & Northallerton on B6271. Approx 5m E of A1. Due to its upgrade, we are unable to give precise directions from the A1 at time of going to print. Please consult maps or internet for up-to-the-minute directions.* **Sun 22 July (10-5). Adm £5.90, chd £3.20. Cream teas. Home baking, lunches and teas using fresh garden produce. Hot/cold drinks, wine, beer.**

Fabulous lake views, gardens, woodland and parkland. These beautiful grounds, once in decline, are being restored to their former beauty in this lovely setting. Topiary surrounds the White and Rose Gardens. Perennial and Hot Borders, Knot and Sensory Gardens. Mayflies dance in the Bog Garden and the Walled Garden is once more productive. From snowdrops to glorious autumn colours, this garden is a joy! Wheelchair access. The gardens close to the house and Walled Garden are accessible. Coaches must be booked in advance.

24 NEW KIRKY COTTAGE

12 Mindrum Farm Cottages, Mindrum, TD12 4QN. Mrs Ginny Fairfax. *6m SW of Coldstream. 9m NW of Wooler on B6352. 4m N of Yethlome village.* **Sat 7 July (10-5.30). Adm £3, chd free. Home-made teas. Visits also by arrangement for groups of 10+**

Ginny Fairfax is known as the creator of the fabulous Mindrum Garden. Five years ago she began creating a new garden at Kirky Cottage. This is a gravel garden in cottage garden style, with her favourite plants from Mindrum and many others, which have matured beautifully. It is an abundant garden, full of interesting plants.

25 LAMBSHIELD

Hexham, NE46 1SF. David Young, 01434 600699, davyoung0601@me.com. *2m S of Hexham. Take the B6306 from Hexham. After 1.6m turn R at chevron sign. Lambshield drive is 2nd on L after 0.6m.* **Sun 29 July (1-4.30). Adm £5, chd free. Home-made teas. Visits also by arrangement May to Aug for groups of 8+.**

2 acre country garden with strong structure and exciting plant combinations, begun in 2010 around a working farm. Distinct areas and styles with formal herbaceous, grasses, contemporary planting, cottage garden, pool and orchard. Cloud hedging, pleached trees, and topiary create a backdrop to colourful and exuberant planting. Modern sculpture. Oak building and fencing by local craftsmen. Featured in The Northumbrian Magazine. Level ground but gravel paths not suitable for wheelchairs.

26 LILBURN TOWER

Alnwick, NE66 4PQ. Mr & Mrs D Davidson, 01668 217291, davidson309@btinternet.com. *3m S of Wooler. On A697.* **Sun 27 May (2-5). Adm £5, chd free. Home-made teas. Visits also by arrangement May to Sept groups of 6+.**

10 acres of magnificent walled and formal gardens set above river; rose parterre, topiary, scented garden, Victorian conservatory, wild flower meadow. Extensive fruit and vegetable garden, large glasshouse with vines. 30 acres of woodland with walks. Giant lilies, meconopsis around pond garden. Rhododendrons and azaleas. Also ruins of Pele Tower, and C12 church. Partial wheelchair access.

27 LONGWITTON HALL

Longwitton, Morpeth, NE61 4JJ. Michael & Louise Spriggs. *2m N of Hartburn off B6343. Entrance at east end of Longwitton village.* **Sun 24 June (12-4). Adm £5, chd free. Home-made teas.**

6 acre historic site with glorious views to the south. Sheltered, mature garden, with specimen trees and acers, currently being redeveloped with new borders. Circular rose garden, crescent shaped pool surrounded by foliage plants, 'standing stone' feature and a rhododendron and azalea glade leading to newly planted laburnum tunnel. Tree peonies and yew walk. Good wheelchair access.

28 LOUGHBROW HOUSE

Hexham, NE46 1RS.
Mrs K A Clark, 01434 603351, patriciaclark351@btinternet.com. *1m S of Hexham on B6306. Dipton Mill Rd. Rd signed Blanchland, ¼m take R fork; then ¼m at fork, lodge gates & driveway at intersection.* **Sun 5 Aug (2-5). Adm £5, chd free. Home-made teas. Visits also by arrangement.**

A real country house garden with sweeping, colour themed herbaceous borders set around large lawns. Unique Lutyens inspired rill with grass topped bridges and climbing rose arches. Part walled kitchen garden and paved courtyard. Bog garden with pond. Developing new border and rose bed. Wild flower meadow with specimen trees. Woodland quarry garden with rhododendrons, azaleas, hostas and rare trees. Home-made jams and chutneys for sale.

29 10 LOW ROW

North Bitchburn, Crook, DL15 8AJ. Mrs Ann Pickering, keightleyann@yahoo.co.uk. *3m NW of Bishop Auckland. From Bishop Auckland take A689 (N) to Howden-le-Wear. R up bank before petrol stn, 1st R in village at 30mph sign. Park in the village.* **Visits by arrangement for individuals and groups of 20 max. Adm by donation.**

Unusual, original and truly organic, rambling garden: 90% grown from seeds and cuttings. Created without commercially bought plants or expense. Environmentally friendly. A haven for wildlife! Sloping garden with a myriad of paths and extensive views over the Wear Valley. Colour yr-round from snowdrops to autumn leaves. Knowledgeable garden owner who will make your visit one to remember. Open all yr except Tuesdays. Book by phone or e-mail. Refreshment offered in adjacent Pub. Featured in the Weekend Guardian. This garden is on a sloping and sometimes steep site.

30 NEW LOWBRIDGE HOUSE

Dalton, Richmond, DL11 7FB. Mrs Clarissa Milbank, 01833 621228, clarissamilbank@btinternet.com. *From W turn R off A66 at Rokeby Inn. In 1½m turn L to Dalton. Straight over Xrds. 100yds. Lowbridge House is on L. From E 6½m from Scotch Corner on A66 take L turn to Dalton. L at Xrds 100yds on L is Lowbridge House.* **Sun 17 June (12-6). Combined adm with Broaches Farm £6, chd free. Light refreshments on patio area by pond. Ice cream, tray bakes, hot drinks & squash. Visits also by arrangement June to Aug price upon application. Refreshments offered according to numbers booked.**

Rural setting with wonderful panoramic views of local countryside. Garden consists of mixed borders, roses and sweet peas. Large pond (small lake) stocked with ghost carp and trout, with natural planting including candelabra primulas and wild flower banks. Island has ducks, coots and moorhens nesting. Patio area suitable for wheelchairs . Woodland and streamside walk with dippers and kingfishers. First opening for NGS. Most areas are accessible with care.

31 MARIE CURIE HOSPICE NEWCASTLE ON TYNE

Marie Curie Hospice, Marie Curie Drive, Newcastle Upon Tyne, NE4 6SS. Marie Curie Organisation, www.mariecurie.org.uk/help/hospice-care/hospices/newcastle/about. *The Hospice is in West Newcastle just off Elswick rd. At the bottom of a housing estate. The turning is between MA brothers & Dallas Carpets.* **Sun 1 July (2-4.30). Adm by donation. Light refreshments served in our Garden Café.**

The landscaped gardens of the purpose-built Marie Curie Hospice overlook the Tyne and Gateshead and offer a beautiful, tranquil place for patients and visitors to sit and chat. Rooms open onto a patio garden with gazebo and fountain. There are climbing roses, evergreens and herbaceous perennials.The garden is well maintained by volunteers. Come and see the work NGS funding helps make possible. Plant sale and refreshments available. The Hospice and Gardens are wheelchair accessible.

32 MIDDLE GRANGE

Slaley, Hexham, NE47 0AA.
Sir Michael & Lady Darrington, 01434 673440, darringtondesign@hotmail.com. *5m S of Hexham. From Riding Mill, entrance is on RHS approx 0.4m along. From Hexham entrance is on L approx 0.3m along. Please leave cars at roadside & walk up drive.* **Sat 23 June (1.30-5). Adm £5, chd free. Home-made teas. Visits also by arrangement May & June well behaved children and dogs on leads welcome.**

Hidden garden combining well executed design, traditional features and varied planting. Gravel garden, pond, large hexagonal pergola, lawn with borders and imposing 3 tier terrace topped by a seating area - all feature mature, colourful interesting planting of superb quality. Meadow area leads to a view across the countryside. Once farm land, this is now a secret herbaceous heaven! Tea and homemade cakes for sale. We hope to have the local school band in attendance. Featured in The Northumbrian and Amateur Gardening. Please contact owners prior to visit if wheelchair access is required.

33 ◆ MINDRUM GARDEN

Mindrum, Northumberland, TD12 4QN. Mr & Mrs T Fairfax, 01890 850228, tpfairfax@gmail.com, www.mindrumestate.com. *6m SW of Coldstream, 9m NW of Wooler. Off B6352, 4m N of Yetholm. 5m from Cornhill on Tweed. Disabled parking close to house.* **For NGS: Sun 17 June (2-5). Adm £5, chd free. Home-made teas.** **For other opening times and information, please phone, email or visit garden website.**

7 acres of romantic planting with old fashioned roses, violas, hardy perennials, lilies, herbs, scented shrubs, and intimate garden areas flanked by woodland and river walks. Glasshouses with vines, jasmine. Large hillside limestone rock garden with water leading to a pond, delightful stream, woodland and wonderful views across Bowmont valley. Large plant sale, mostly home grown. Partial wheelchair access due to landscape. Wheelchair accessible WC available.

34 MR YORKE'S WALLED GARDEN

Cravengate, Richmond, DL10 4RE. Mr & Mrs Dennis & Marcia McLuckie, 01748 825525, marcia@yorkshirecountryholidays.co.uk. *5 min walk from Richmond Market Place. Third of way down Cravengate on rd out to Leyburn. From Market Place go up Finkle St, past Black Lion into cobbled Newbiggin. L into Cravengate. Garden on R. No parking at the garden.* **Sun 19 Aug (1-5.30). Adm £5, chd free. Home-made teas, cakes and scones, tea and coffee.**

Charming C18 walled garden, redesigned with herbaceous border, ponds, mature trees, standard and climbing roses, vegetable garden, fruit trees, lawns and grassy paths. This is a garden in change and work has progressed since the garden opened for the NGS last year. The owners continue clearing it of brambles, self-sets and weeds to further enhance this one acre pleasant, tranquil town garden. Fabulous views of Richmond Castle and Culloden Tower, which may be open on the day please check. Featured in Yorkshire Life, Darlington and Stockton Times, Yorkshire Post, Richmondshire Today. The garden is on a hill. Main grass paths accessible with a wheelchair, but they are quite steep.

35 NEWBIGGIN HOUSE

Blanchland, DH8 9UD. Mrs A Scott-Harden. *12m S of Hexham. From Blanchland village take Stanhope Rd. ½m along narrow rd follow yellow signs up tarmac drive into car park.* **Sun 22 July (2-5). Adm £5, chd free. Cream teas.**

5-acre landscaped garden at 1000ft, started in 1996 and maturing beautifully. Enjoy old-fashioned herbaceous borders, peonies, shrubs, roses, bog and wild gardens incl a wild rose walk. Magnificent collection of unusual trees and shrubs. The garden is still being developed and there are new plants and features to enjoy. Partial wheelchair access.

36 NO. 2 FERNDENE

2 Holburn Lane Court, Holburn Lane, Ryton, NE40 3PN. Maureen Kesteven, 0191 413 5937, kestevenmaureen@gmail.com, https://www.facebook.com/northeastgardenopenforcharity/. *In Ryton Old Village, 8m W of Gateshead. Off B6317, on Holburn Lane in Old Ryton Village. Park in Co-op carpark on High St, cross rd & walk through Ferndene Park following yellow signs.* **Sun 22 July (1-4.30). Adm £5, chd free. Home-made teas. Pizzas from wood fired oven and prosecco. Visits also by arrangement Mar to Aug groups of 10+.**

¾ acre garden, developing since 2009, surrounded by trees. Informal areas of herbaceous perennials, more formal box bordered area, sedum roof, wildlife pond, cutting, bog and fern gardens. Willow work. Early interest - hellebores, snowdrops, daffodils, bluebells and tulips. Summer interest from wide range of flowering perennials. 1½ acre mixed broadleaf wood. 2018 new gravel garden. Pizzas (cooked in wood fired oven) and prosecco.

37 OLIVER FORD GARDEN

Longedge Lane, Rowley, Consett, DH8 9HG. Bob & Bev Tridgett, www.gardensanctuaries.co.uk. *5m NW of Lanchester. Signed from A68 in Rowley. From Lanchester take rd towards Sately. Garden will be signed as you pass Woodlea Manor.* **Sun 10 June (1-5). Adm £4, chd free. Home-made teas.**

A peaceful, contemplative 3 acre garden developed and planted by the owner and BBC Gardener of the Year as a space for quiet reflection. Arboretum specialising in bark, stream, wildlife pond and bog garden. Semi-shaded Japanese maple and dwarf rhododendron garden. Rock garden and scree bed. Insect nectar area, orchard and 1½ acre meadow. Annual wild flower area. Terrace and ornamental kitchen garden,. Has a number of sculptures around the garden. Unfortunately not suitable for wheelchairs.

38 25 PARK ROAD SOUTH

Chester le Street, DH3 3LS. Mrs A Middleton, 0191 388 3225, midnot2@gmail.com. *4m N of Durham. Located at S end of A167 Chester-le-St bypass rd. Precise directions provided when booking visit.* **Visits by arrangement May to July. Adm £3, chd free. Light refreshments.**

A stunning town garden with all year round interest. Herbaceous borders with unusual perennials, grasses, shrubs surrounding lawn and paved area. Courtyard planted with foliage and small front gravel garden. The garden owner is a very knowledgeable plantswoman who enjoys showing visitors around her inspiring garden. No minimum size of group. Plants for sale.

39 ◆ RABY CASTLE

Staindrop, Darlington, DL2 3AH. Lord Barnard, 01833 660202, admin@rabycastle.com, www.rabycastle.com. *12m NW of Darlington, 1m N of Staindrop. On A688, 8m NE of Barnard Castle.* **For NGS: Sat 14 July (11-5). Adm £7.50, chd £3.50. Light refreshments in the Raby Castle Stables Tearoom. For other opening times and information, please phone, email or visit garden website.**

Raby Castle is one of the founding gardens of the NGS and has been opening for charity since 1927. C18 walled gardens set within the grounds of Raby Castle. Designers such as Thomas White and James Paine have worked to establish the gardens, which now extend to 5 acres, displaying herbaceous borders, old yew hedges, formal rose gardens and informal heather and conifer gardens. Tearoom is located just outside the entrance gate to the Walled Gardens. Assistance will be needed for wheelchairs.

40 RAVENSFORD FARM

Hamsterley, DL13 3NH. Jonathan & Caroline Peacock, 01388 488305, caroline@ravensfordfarm.co.uk. *7m W of Bishop Auckland. From A68 at Witton-le-Wear turn off W to Hamsterley. Go through village & turn L just before tennis courts at west end.* **Sat 23 June (2-5). Adm £4, chd free. Home-made teas. Visits also by arrangement Mar to Oct please confirm numbers for catering and parking in good time.**

This nearly three-acre garden offers colour and interest throughout the year. Beyond the large lawn and herbaceous beds are two ponds, a sunken garden, a wood with shade-loving plants, an orchard with children's play house and swings, and a good number of unusual plants, shrubs and trees. On NGS day we sell plants, we serve home-made teas, and Northumbrian pipers provide the background music. Some gravel, so assistance will be needed for wheelchairs. Assistance dogs only in the garden, but others okay in the field.

GROUP OPENING

41 ROMALDKIRK GARDENS

Teesdale, DL12 9DZ. *6m NW of Barnard Castle. On B6277, 2m S of Eggleston.* **Sun 24 June (1-5.30). Combined adm £4, chd free. Home-made teas in The Reading Room, opp Rose and Crown Hotel.**

A group of 8 gardens of great variety. Most gardens are clustered around the village greens. Some are a short walk/drive to the edge of the village. Romaldkirk is an interesting, old, traditional village with a water pump, stocks and attractive church of St Romald. Some gardens are typical cottage gardens with herbaceous borders, another larger garden includes a pond and grotto, one has lawns, rockery and interesting shrubs. Another garden which is well established has an attractive design of lawns, lake, herbaceous borders, trees and shrubs. Wheelchair access to some gardens.

42 ST CUTHBERT'S HOSPICE

Park House Road, Durham, DH1 3QF. Paul Marriott, CEO, www.stcuthbertshospice.com. *1m SW of Durham City on A167. Turn into Park House Rd, the Hospice is on the L after bowling green car park. Parking available.* **Sun 29 July (11-4). Adm £4, chd free. Home-made teas and cakes. Hot and cold drinks, served in the Victorian style greenhouse.**

5 acres of mature gardens surround this CQC outstanding-rated Hospice. In development since 1988, the gardens are cared for by volunteers. Incl a Victorian-style greenhouse and large vegetable, fruit and cut flower area. Lawns surround smaller scale specialist planting, and areas for patients and visitors to relax. Woodland area with walks, and an 'In Memory' garden with stream. New sensory garden. Plants and produce for sale. We are active participants in Northumbria in Bloom and Britain in Bloom, with several awards in recent years, including overall winner in 2015 for the Care/ Residential /Convalescent Homes / Day Centre / Hospices category. Almost all areas are accessible for wheelchairs.

Lambshield

ALLOTMENTS

43 ST MARGARET'S ALLOTMENTS

Margery Lane, Durham, DH1 4QU. *From A1 take A690 to City Centre/ Crook. Straight ahead at T-lights after 4th r'about. 10mins walk from bus or rail station.* **Sun 8 July (2-5). Combined adm £4, chd free. Home-made teas in hall adjacent to allotments.**

5 acres of 82 allotments against the spectacular backdrop of Durham Cathedral. This site has been cultivated since the Middle Ages, and was saved from development 25yrs ago, allowing a number of enthusiastic gardeners to develop plots which display a great variety of fruit, vegetables and flowers. Guided tours available. Many unusual vegetables. Display of creative and fun competitions for plot holders. The site has some steep and narrow paths.

44 SOUTHLANDS

The Avenue, Eaglescliffe, Stockton-On-Tees, TS16 9AS. Ian Waller. *1½m from Yarm on A135. JA66 signed A135 Stockton West/Yarm. South towards Yarm for approx 1½ m past Preston Park. From Yarm on A135 for 1½ m passing Golf Course. The Avenue is opposite junction to Railway Station.* **Sun 6 May (2-5.30). Adm £5, chd free. Light refreshments, cakes and scones.**

South facing High Victorian Gardens created by Sir Samuel and Lady Sadler. Elevated site with sloping lawns, herbaceous borders, orchards and woodland areas. A natural stream runs through this 10 acre garden with a miniature lake and island. Established Rhododendrons and Azaleas, specimen trees with ginko, maples, beech, pines and redwoods. Coaching house (serving teas), Bothy, old Greenhouse and fountain. Last opened in 1957 for NGS. Steeply sloping site.

45 STANTON FENCE

Stanton, Morpeth, NE65 8PP. Sir David & Lady Kelly, 01670 772236, stantonfence@hotmail.com. *5m NW of Morpeth. Nr Stanton on the C144 between Pigdon & Netherwitton. OS map ref NZ 13588.* **Visits by arrangement May & June for groups of 10+. Adm £5, chd free.**

Contemporary 4.7 acre country garden designed by Chelsea Gold Medal winner, Arabella Lennox-Boyd, in keeping with its rural setting. A strong underlying design unites the different areas from formal parterre and courtyard garden to orchard, wild flower meadows and woodland. Romantically planted rose covered arbours and long clematis draped pergola walk. Nuttery, kitchen garden and greenhouse. Delightful views. Wheelchair access for those chairs that can use mown paths as well as hard paving.

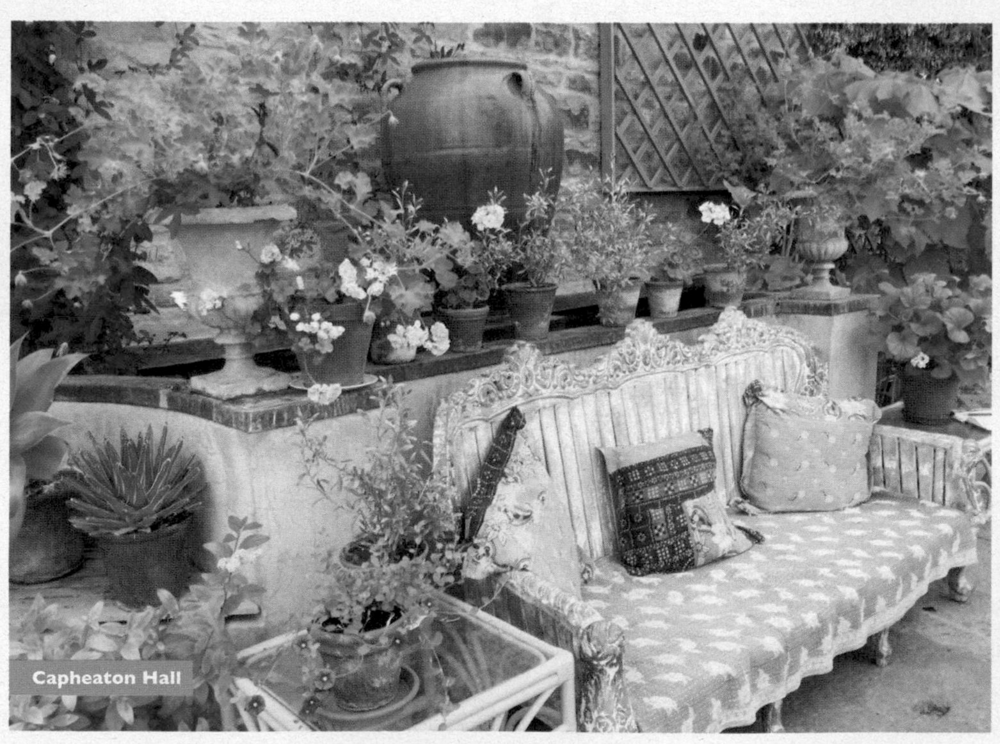

Capheaton Hall

46 4 STOCKLEY GROVE

Brancepeth, DH7 8DU. Mr & Mrs Bainbridge, 079439 40708, fabb63@sky.com. *5m W of Durham City. Situated on the A690 between Durham & Crook. There is no parking available in Stockley Grove. From Durham direction turn L at village Xrds & park at castle at end of rd. Lifts to the garden will be available if required.* **Sun 5 Aug (1-5). Adm £4, chd free. Home-made teas. Visits also by arrangement May to Sept.**

A stunning ½ acre garden with inspirational planting to provide yr-round colour and interest. Landscaped with hidden grassy paths with many unusual trees, shrubs and plants incl wildlife pond, rockery area and water features. Rockery currently being extended. 4 times winners of The Beautiful Durham Competition.

47 THORNTON HALL GARDENS

Staindrop Road, Darlington, DL2 2NB. Michael & Sue Manners, 07713 508222, info@thorntonhallgardens.co.uk, www.thorntonhallgardens.co.uk. *On B6279 Staindrop Rd. 3m W of Darlington.* **Sun 13 May (1-4). Adm £7, chd £1. Home-made teas. Visits also by arrangement May to July.**

C16 Grade I listed hall (not open). 2 walled gardens with Elizabethan raised borders, separate vegetable garden. Plantsman's garden with emphasis on colour-themed borders, plant associations, form and foliage. Unusual perennials, interspersed with interesting trees and shrubs in mixed herbaceous borders. Large collection of tulips, auriculas, roses, clematis. Wildlife and ornamental ponds. For other opening times and information, please phone, email or visit garden website.

48 USHAW COLLEGE

Woodland Road, Durham, DH7 9BJ. The Trustees of Ushaw College, 0191 3738500, meet@ushaw.org, www.ushaw.org. *3m W of Durham City. From A167 N of Neville's Cross turn on to minor road signed Bearpark & Ushaw College. The College entrance is signed to the R in 2½ m.* **Sat 2 June (10-4). Adm £4, chd free. Home-made teas in the College. Visits also by arrangement for 10+.**

Part of the 50 acre landscape within open countryside around Ushaw College, the gardens were originally laid out in 1840 in front of the Georgian house and feature a formal rhododendron garden with herbaceous borders and rose beds. Extensive renovations to the garden have been under way for the last 3 years and continue, with some wild areas, a former pond, and extensive areas of woodland. Wheelchair access to concentric paths, but not to more overgrown areas.

49 ◆ WALLINGTON

Cambo, NE61 4AR. National Trust, 01670 773600, simon.thompson@nationaltrust.org.uk, www.nationaltrust.org.uk/wallington. *12m W of Morpeth 20m NW Newcastle. From N B6343; from S via A696 from Newcastle, 6m W of Belsay, B6342 to Cambo.* **For NGS: Sat 21 Apr, Sat 16 June (10-5). Adm £14.50, chd £7.30. Light refreshments at Courtyard Cafe. For other opening times and information, please phone, email or visit garden website.**

Magical walled, terraced garden with herbaceous and mixed borders. Packed with colour. Edwardian conservatory with unusual plants. 100 acres of woodland. Pleasure grounds, river and lakes. Set in a stunning landscape, with opportunities for walking and cycling. House dates from 1688. Wheelchair access limited to top terrace in Walled Garden but elsewhere possible with care and support.

GROUP OPENING

50 NEW WALWORTH GARDENS

Darlington, DL2 2LY. *Approx 5m W of Darlington on A68 or ½ m E of Piercebridge on A67. Follow brown signs to Walworth Castle Hotel. Just up the hill from the Castle entrance, follow NGS yellow signs down private track. Tickets & Teas at Quarry End.* **Sun 19 Aug (1-5). Combined adm £5.50, chd free. Home-made teas.**

NEW **THE ARCHES**
Stephen & Becky Street-Howard.

NEW **THE DOVECOTE**
Tony & Ruth Lamb.

QUARRY END
Iain & Margaret Anderson.

Enjoy 3 very different gardens in this new group opening.
Quarry End is a 1½ acre woodland garden developed over 18 years on the site of an ancient quarry. It incorporates a newly developed woodland, a wide variety of trees, shrubs, perennials, a fernery and ornamental vegetable plot. The site includes an 18c ice house. Not all the garden is wheelchair accessible, some steep and rough paths. The Arches and The Dovecote are both in a 6 year old complex of converted C19 listed barns.
The Dovecote has 3 areas. A japanese garden with a Koi pond and a large collection of specimen Acers, a thriving vegetable garden with imaginative planting to maximise crops from a small area, and an english garden with lawn, flower border and a chicken run. In contrast the 1 acre garden at The Arches comprises an orchard, a large vegetable garden, a wild life pond, an ornamental garden and a new arboretum. There is also a large play area available so bring the family! Some areas of the Quarry End garden are not accessible, though the main garden area is.

51 WARRENFELL

2 Filter Cottages, Tunstall Reservoir, Wolsingham, Bishop Auckland, DL13 3LX. Fran Toulson, 01388 528392, warrenfell@btinternet.com. *Weardale. On western edge of Wolsingham village turn by Wolsingham School, signed to Tunstall Reservoir. No through Road. Garden 2m on R below dam wall.* **Sat 30 June, Sun 1 July (10.30-4). Adm £3.50, chd free. Home-made teas. Visits also by arrangement Apr to Sept.**

The garden, started 2012, is just over 650ft in approx ¼ acre. A stunning location, lots of birdlife. Combine with a walk at the reservoir? The garden has a lot to interest in a small space. Some unusual plants in borders with shrubs, perennials, roses, peonies and an alpine garden added 2015. Pergola and arbour. Kitchen garden with raised beds, espaliered apples and pears. Small wild flower area. Visits also by arrangement. Besides the summer the garden is particularly attractive in the spring with colour not only from Spring bulbs and hellebores but also many spring flowering Alpines. The garden was featured in Garden News and Living North magazines.

52 ◆ WASHINGTON OLD HALL

The Avenue, Washington Village, NE38 7LE. National Trust, 0191 416 6879, www.nationaltrust.org.uk/washingtonoldhall. *7m SE of Newcastle upon Tyne. From A19 onto A1231, from A1 exit J64 onto A195 in both cases stay on the road until you pick up brown signs to Washington Old Hall.* **For NGS: Sun 3 June (1-4). Adm by donation. Light refreshments. Also open 24 Bede Crescent. For other opening times and information, please phone or visit garden website.**

The picturesque stone manor house and its gardens provide a tranquil oasis in an historic setting. It contains a formal Jacobean garden with box hedging borders around evergreens and perennials, vegetable garden, wild flower nut orchard with bee hives. Places to sit out and enjoy a picnic. Enjoy cakes, snacks and ice cream in the cafe. A private garden in the village also open. Map and entry tickets purchased at the NGS SUPER SALE plant stall. Accessible café in the lower gardens (hot and cold drinks, cake, snacks and ice cream) SUPER SALE of NGS garden owners' plants. Designated parking spaces. Accessible WC located in lower gardens via outdoor lift. All formal paths accessible .

53 ◆ WHALTON MANOR GARDENS

Whalton, Morpeth, NE61 3UT. Mr T R P S Norton, 01670 775205, gardens@whaltonmanor.co.uk, www.whaltonmanor.co.uk. *5m W of Morpeth. On the B6524, the house is at E end of the village & will be signed.* **For NGS: Sun 1 July (2-5). Adm £5, chd free. Home-made teas. For other opening times and information, please phone, email or visit garden website.**

The historic Whalton Manor, altered by Sir Edwin Lutyens in 1908, is surrounded by 3 acres of magnificent walled gardens, designed by Lutyens with the help of Gertrude Jekyll. The gardens have been developed by the Norton family since the 1920s and incl extensive herbaceous borders, 30yd peony border, rose garden, listed summerhouses, pergolas and walls, festooned with rambling roses and clematis. Partial wheelchair access, some stone steps.

Your visit helps fund 389 Marie Curie Nurses

54 WOODBINE HOUSE

22 South View, Hunwick, Crook, DL15 0JW. Stewart Irwin & Colin Purvis. *On main road through the village opposite village green. B6286 off A689 Bishop Auckland - Crook or A690 Durham - Crook. On street parking, entrance to the rear of the property RHS of house.* **Mon 28 May (1-5). Adm £3.50, chd free. Home-made teas, all refreshments are home-made.**

The garden is approx a quarter of an acre, divided into two, one half used as a vegetable garden with large greenhouse. The other half of the garden is lawn with well stocked (and some unusual planting) herbaceous borders and small pond. Bees are kept in the vegetable garden. Wheelchair access to refreshment area but paths in garden are not wide enough for wheelchairs.

55 WOODLANDS

Peareth Hall Road, Springwell Village, Gateshead, NE9 7NT. Liz Reid, 07719 875750, lizreid52@ntlworld.com. *3½m N Washington Galleries. 4m S Gateshead town centre. On B1288 turn opp Guide Post PH (NE9 7RR) onto Peareth Hall Rd. Continue for ½m passing 2 bus stops on L. Third drive on L past Highbury Ave.* **Sat 30 June, Thur 5 July (1.30-4.30). Adm £3, chd free. Home-made teas, beer and wine available. Visits also by arrangement groups of 10+.**

Mature garden on a site of approx one seventh acre- quirky, with tropical themed planting and Caribbean inspired bar. A fun garden with colour throughout the year, interesting plants, informal beds and borders, pond area and decks.

56 WOODSIDE HOUSE

Witton Park, Bishop Auckland, DL14 0DU. Charles & Jean Crompton, 01388 609973, ctjcrompton@gmail.com, www.woodsidehousewittonpark.com. *2m N of Bishop Auckland. From Bishop Auckland take A68*

to Witton Park. In village DO NOT follow SatNav. park on main st, walk down track next to St Pauls Church. **Sun 22 July (1-4.30). Adm £5, chd free. Home-made teas. Visits also by arrangement Apr to Sept for groups of 10+. Coaches welcome.**
Stunning 2 acre, mature, undulating garden full of interesting trees, shrubs and plants. Superbly landscaped (by the owners) with island beds, flowing herbaceous borders, an old walled garden, rhododendron beds, fernery, 3 ponds, grass bed and vegetable garden. Delightful garden full of interesting and unusual features: much to fire the imagination. Winner of Bishop Auckland in Bloom. featured in Sunday Telegraph, Garden News and local press. Partial wheelchair access.

57 NEW WOODSIDE, KILLERBY

North Lane, Killerby, Darlington, DL2 3UH. Dr Satinder Faulkner. *Killerby sits between Summerhouse & Ingleton. We can offer parking in our fields & if ground very wet, vehicles can also park on the main road in Killerby village & walk the ¼m up North Lane.* **Sat 4 Aug (1-6). Adm £5, chd free. Home-made teas.**
Woodside is set in 12 acres of which 2 acres have been developed into garden. The owner had a stroke 31 years ago yet has designed and executed the works mostly single handedly. The garden includes prairie bed, woodland beds, rose garden, over 100 trees, a wood, wildlife pond, vegetable and cut flower beds and from 2018 will run horticultural therapy for adults with disability. The garden sits mostly on one level although paths in the woods are narrow for wheelchair access.

Your visit helps the Queen's Nursing Institute to champion excellence in community nursing

Gardens on the Green

NORTHAMPTONSHIRE

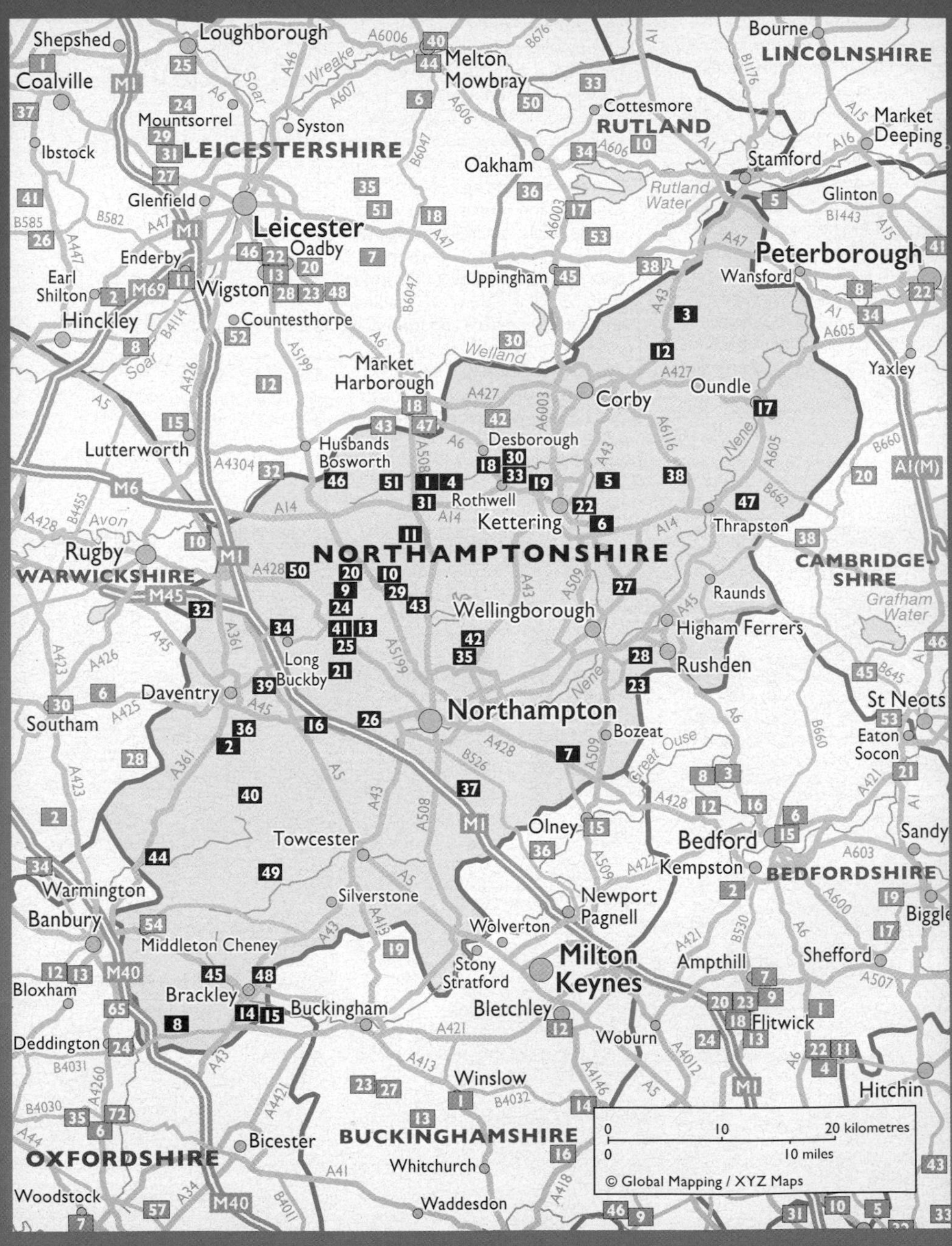

The county of Northamptonshire is famously known as the 'Rose of the Shires', but is also referred to as the 'Shire of Spires and Squires', and lies in the East Midlands area of the country bordered by eight other counties.

Take a gentle stroll around charming villages with thatch and stone cottages and welcoming inns. Wander around stately homes, discovering art treasures and glorious gardens open for the National Garden Scheme: Kelmarsh Hall, Holdenby House, Castle Ashby, Cottesbrooke Hall and Boughton House. In contrast visit some village groups, which include small imaginatively designed gardens.

Explore historic market towns such as Oundle and Brackley in search of fine footwear, antiques and curiosities. Or visit wildlife sanctuaries such as Sulby Gardens with 12 acres of interesting flora and fauna.

The serenity of our waterways will delight, and our winding country lanes and footpaths will guide you around a rural oasis, far from the pressures of modern living, where you can walk knee-deep in bluebells and snowdrops in spring at gardens such as Greywalls and Bosworth House, or view the late autumn colours of Boughton House.

Our first garden opens in February and the final opening occurs in November, giving a glimpse of gardens throughout the seasons.

Volunteers

County Organisers
David Abbott
01933 680363
d_j_abbott@btinternet.com

Gay Webster
01604 740203
gay.webster6@gmail.com

County Treasurer
Michael Heaton
01604 846032
ngs@mimomul.co.uk

Publicity
David Abbott
(as above)

Booklet Coordinators
David Abbott
(as above)

Michael Heaton
(as above)

Assistant County Organisers
Lindsey Cartwright
01327 860056
lindsey@loisweedon.net

Philippa Heumann
01327 860142
pmheumann@gmail.com

Geoff Sage
01788 510334
geoffsage256@btinternet.com

Left: **136 High Street**

OPENING DATES

All entries subject to change. For latest information check **www.ngs.org.uk**

Map locator numbers are shown to the right of each garden name.

February

Snowdrop Festival

Sunday 18th
Bosworth House 4

Sunday 25th
◆ Boughton House 5
67-69 High Street 27

March

Sunday 4th
Greywalls 23
NEW Winwick Manor 50

April

Sunday 8th
Flore Gardens 16
◆ Kelmarsh Hall & Gardens 31

Sunday 15th
Bosworth House 4
Briarwood 6
The Old Vicarage 39

Sunday 22nd
◆ Cottesbrooke Hall Gardens 10
◆ The Old Rectory, Sudborough 38

Thursday 26th
Sulby Gardens 46

Sunday 29th
Charlton Gardens 8
◆ Deene Park 12
Guilsborough Gardens 24

May

Sunday 6th
Great Brington Gardens 21

Monday 7th
Titchmarsh House 47

Sunday 20th
NEW Badby Gardens 2
NEW Evenley Gardens 14
◆ Evenley Wood Garden 15
◆ Kelmarsh Hall & Gardens 31
Old Rectory, Quinton 37
Titchmarsh House 47

Sunday 27th
NEW Newnham Gardens 36

June

Festival Weekend

Sunday 3rd
67-69 High Street 27
Preston Capes and Little Preston Gardens 40
NEW Winwick Manor 50

Saturday 9th
Titchmarsh House 47

Sunday 10th
Foxtail Lilly 17
Harpole Gardens 26
Kilsby Gardens 32
Spratton Gardens 43
Weedon Lois & Weston Gardens 49

Thursday 14th
Sulby Gardens 46

Saturday 16th
Flore Gardens 16

Sunday 17th
Flore Gardens 16
Rosearie-de-la-Nymph 42

Sunday 24th
Arthingworth Open Gardens 1
67-69 High Street 27
Rosearie-de-la-Nymph 42
Turweston Gardens 48

Saturday 30th
NEW The Wooden Owl 51

July

Sunday 1st
◆ Castle Ashby Gardens 7
◆ Steane Park 45
NEW The Wooden Owl 51

Sunday 8th
NEW Moulton College Horticulture Unit 35
Ravensthorpe Gardens 41

Saturday 14th
East Haddon Hall 13
◆ Haddonstone Show Gardens 25

Sunday 15th
East Haddon Hall 13
◆ Haddonstone Show Gardens 25
◆ Holdenby House Gardens 29
NEW 16 Leys Avenue 33

Sunday 22nd
Blatherwycke Estate 3
Long Buckby Gardens 34

Sunday 29th
Froggery Cottage 18
136 High Street 28
Hostellarie 30

August

Thursday 2nd
Sulby Gardens 46

Sunday 12th
Dale Farm 11
The Green Patch 22

September

Sunday 2nd
Old Rectory, Quinton 37

Sunday 9th
◆ Coton Manor Garden 9

October

Thursday 11th
Sulby Gardens 46

Friday 12th
Sulby Gardens 46

Sunday 14th
Briarwood 6

Sunday 21st
◆ Boughton House 5

By Arrangement

Bosworth House 4
Briarwood 6
The Close, Harpole Gardens 26
Dripwell House, Guilsborough Gardens 24
Foxtail Lilly 17
Froggery Cottage 18
Glendon Hall 19
Gower House 20
Greywalls 23
67-69 High Street 27
Hostellarie 30
19 Manor Close, Harpole Gardens 26
Pytchley House, Kilsby Gardens 32
Ravensthorpe Nursery, Ravensthorpe Gardens 41
4 Skinyard Lane, Long Buckby Gardens 34
The Spring House 44
Titchmarsh House 47
Wisteria House, Long Buckby Gardens 34
NEW The Wooden Owl 51

Your support helps Carers Trust to provide more help to unpaid carers

THE GARDENS

GROUP OPENING

1 ARTHINGWORTH OPEN GARDENS

Arthingworth, nr Market Harborough, LE16 8LA. *6m S of Market Harborough. From Market Harborough via A508, after 4m take L to Arthingworth. From Northampton, A508 turn R just after Kelmarsh.* **Sun 24 June (1.30-5.30). Combined adm £5, chd free. Home-made teas at village hall.**

Arthingworth has been welcoming NGS visitors for more than 8 yrs. It is a village affair, with 8 to 9 gardens opening and 2 pop-up tearooms with home baked cakes. We now have some regulars who keep us on our toes and we love it. Come and enjoy the diversity, we aim to give visitors an afternoon of discovery. Our gardens have been chosen because they are all different in spirit, and tended by young and weathered gardeners. We have gardens with stunning views, traditional with herbaceous borders and vegetables, walled, and artisan. The village is looking forward to welcoming you. St Andrew's church Grade listed II* open. The village is next to the national cycle path. Wheelchair access to some gardens.

GROUP OPENING

2 NEW BADBY GARDENS

Badby, Daventry, NN11 3AR. *3m S of Daventry on E-side of A361.* **Sun 20 May (2-6). Combined adm £5, chd free. Teas & home-made cakes in St Mary's Church.**

THE OLD HOUSE
Mr & Mrs Robert Cain.

SHAKESPEARES COTTAGE
Sarah & Jocelyn Hartland-Swann.

SOUTHVIEW COTTAGE
Alan & Karen Brown.

NEW **THREEWAYS COTTAGE**
Richard Green.

TRIFIDIA
Colin & Shirley Cripps.

Delightful hilly village with attractive old houses of golden-coloured Hornton stone set around a C14 church and two village greens. No through traffic. There are five gardens of differing styles: a wisteria-clad thatched cottage (not open) with a sloping garden and modern sculptures; a traditional garden featuring a spectacular view across fields to Badby Wood; a recently restored sloping garden filled with interesting features and looking across a babbling brook; an elevated garden with views over the village; and a hillside garden focussing on unusual and interesting plants that aim for yr-round interest, with a conservatory and vegetable garden. Teas and delicious home-made cakes are available in St Mary's Church, close to all five gardens. We look forward to welcoming you to our lovely village!

3 BLATHERWYCKE ESTATE

Blatherwycke, Peterborough, PE8 6YW. Mr George. *Blatherwycke is signed off the A43 between Stamford & Corby. Follow road through village & the gardens entrance is immed next to the large river bridge.* **Sun 22 July (11-4). Adm £4, chd free. Home-made teas.**

Blatherwycke Hall demolished in the 1940s, its grounds and gardens lost until now! In April 2011 we started the renovation of the derelict 4 acre walled gardens. So far a large kitchen garden, wall trained fruit trees, extensive herbaceous borders, seasonal beds, parterre, pleaching orchard, and wild flower meadows have been built, planted and sown. Also a very large arboretum is being planted. Grass and gravel paths, some slopes and steps with ramps.

4 BOSWORTH HOUSE

Oxendon Road, Arthingworth, Nr Market Harborough, LE16 8LA. Mr & Mrs C E Irving-Swift, 01858 525202, irvingswift@btinternet.com. *From the phone box, when in Oxendon Rd, take the little lane with no name, 2nd to the R.* **Sun 18 Feb (12-4); Sun 15 Apr (2-6). Adm £3, chd free. Home-made teas at village hall. Visits also by arrangement May to Aug for groups of 15+. Guided visit by Cecile Irving-Swift for 1½ hours £4, or with home-made cake £7.**

Just under 3 acres, almost completely organic garden and paddock with fabulous panoramic views. Early in the season a pleasing display of snowdrops, wood anemones, fritillaries, daffodils, bluebells and tulips. The garden also incl herbaceous borders, orchard, cottage garden with greenhouse, vegetable garden, herbs and strawberries, and little spinney. There is a magnificent Wellingtonia. Partial wheelchair access.

Threeways Cottage, Badby Gardens

5 ◆ BOUGHTON HOUSE

Geddington, Kettering, NN14 1BJ. Duke of Buccleuch & Queensberry, KBE, 01536 515731, clister@buccleuch.com, www.boughtonhouse.org.uk. *3m NE of Kettering. From A14, 2m along A43 Kettering to Stamford, turn R into Geddington, house entrance 1½m on R.* **For NGS: Sun 25 Feb, Sun 21 Oct (11-3). Adm £6, chd £3. Light refreshments in C18 Stable Block. For other opening times and information, please phone, email or visit garden website.**

The Northamptonshire home of the Duke and Duchess of Buccleuch. The garden opening incl opportunities to see the historic walled kitchen garden and herbaceous border incl the newly created sensory and wildlife gardens. The wilderness woodland will open for visitors to view the spring flowers or the autumn colours. As a special treat the garden originally created by Sir David Scott (cousin of the Duke of Buccleuch) will also be open.

6 BRIARWOOD

4 Poplars Farm Road, Barton Seagrave, Kettering, NN15 5AF. William & Elaine Portch, 01536 522169, elaine.portch@yahoo.com, www.elainechristian-gardendesign.co.uk. *1½m SE of Kettering Town Centre. J10 off A14 turn onto Barton Rd (A6) towards Wicksteed Park. R into Warkton Lane, after 200 metres R into Poplars Farm Rd.* **Sun 15 Apr (10-4); Sun 14 Oct (11-3). Adm £4.50, chd free. Light refreshments. Visits also by arrangement Apr to Oct.**

A garden for all seasons with quirky original sculptures and many faces. Firstly, a south aspect lawn and borders containing bulbs, shrubs, roses and rare trees with yr-round interest; hedging, palms, climbers, a wildlife, fish and lily pond, terrace with potted bulbs and unusual plants in odd containers. Secondly, a secret garden with summerhouse, small orchard, raised bed potager and greenhouse. Crafts for sale and children's quiz. Featured in Garden News and Northamptonshire Telegraph.

7 ◆ CASTLE ASHBY GARDENS

Castle Ashby, Northampton, NN7 1LQ. Earl Compton, 01604 695200, petercox@castleashby.co.uk, www.castleashbygardens.co.uk. *6m E of Northampton. 1½m N of A428, turn off between Denton & Yardley Hastings. Follow brown tourist signs (SatNav will take you to the village, look for brown signs).* **For NGS: Sun 1 July (10-5.30). Adm £7, chd £1. For other opening times and information, please phone, email or visit garden website.**

35 acres within a 10,000 acre estate of both formal and informal gardens, incl Italian gardens with orangery and arboretum with lakes, all dating back to the 1860s, as well as a menagerie which includes meerkats and marmosets. Play area, tearooms and gift shop. Gravel paths within gardens.

GROUP OPENING

8 CHARLTON GARDENS

Banbury, OX17 3DR. *7m SE of Banbury, 5m W of Brackley. From B4100 turn off N at Aynho, or from A422 turn off S at Farthinghoe. Parking at village hall.* **Sun 29 Apr (2-5.30). Combined adm £5, chd free. Home-made teas at Walnut House.**

CHARLTON LODGE
Mr & Mrs Andrew Woods.

THE CROFT
Mr & Mrs R D Whitrow.

WALNUT HOUSE
Sir Paul & Lady Hayter.

Pretty stone village with a selection of gardens large and small, incl a cottage garden with colourful planting, interesting corners and lovely views; a large garden behind C17 farmhouse (not open) with colour themed borders, separate small gardens; and a large terraced garden with a 140ft long herbaceous border and raised bed vegetable patch, overlooking a lake.

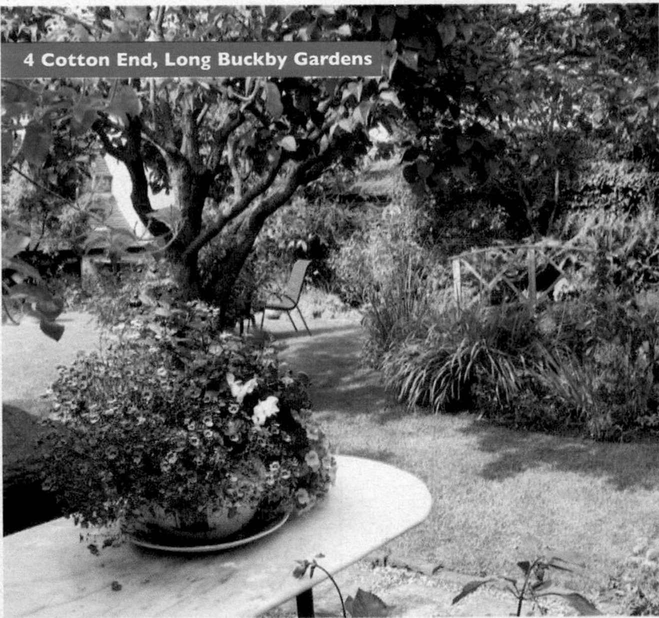

4 Cotton End, Long Buckby Gardens

9 ◆ COTON MANOR GARDEN

Coton, Northampton, NN6 8RQ. Mr & Mrs Ian Pasley-Tyler, 01604 740219, www.cotonmanor.co.uk. *10m N of Northampton, 11m SE of Rugby. From A428 & A5199 follow tourist signs.* **For NGS: Sun 9 Sept (12-5.30). Adm £7, chd £2.50. Light refreshments at Stableyard Cafe. For other opening times and information, please phone or visit garden website.**

10 acre garden set in peaceful countryside with old yew and holly hedges and extensive herbaceous borders, containing many unusual plants. One of Britain's finest throughout the season, the garden is at its most magnificent in September, and is an inspiration as to what can be achieved in late summer. Adjacent specialist nursery with over 1000 plant varieties propagated from the garden. Partial wheelchair access as some paths are narrow and the site is on a slope.

10 ◆ COTTESBROOKE HALL GARDENS

Cottesbrooke, NN6 8PF. Mr & Mrs A R Macdonald-Buchanan, 01604 505808, welcome@cottesbrooke.co.uk, www.cottesbrooke.co.uk. *10m N of Northampton. Signed from J1 on A14. Off A5199 at Creaton, A508 at Brixworth.* **For NGS: Sun 22 Apr (2-5.30). Adm £7, chd £4. Tea, coffee & home-made cakes. For other opening times and information, please phone, email or visit garden website.**

Award-winning gardens by Geoffrey Jellicoe, Dame Sylvia Crowe, James Alexander Sinclair and more recently Arne Maynard. Formal gardens and terraces surround Queen Anne house with extensive vistas onto the lake and C18 parkland containing many mature trees. Wild and woodland gardens, which are exceptional in spring, a short distance from the formal areas. Partial wheelchair access as paths are grass, stone and gravel. Access map identifies best route.

11 DALE FARM

Maidwell, Northampton, NN6 9JE. Mr & Mrs D Keir. *A508 from Northampton. In Maidwell take 1st L, opp the road to Draughton. After 1m take the R fork by a tree, to the house. Park only in field (signed), not on the access road or verges.* **Sun 12 Aug (11-4). Adm £4, chd free. Home-made teas in the summerhouse.**

Dale Farm is a 2 acre garden, with formal hedging and trees. Flower borders near the house and secluded vegetable garden with cutting flowers. The garden has lovely views over the surrounding countryside, including the neighbouring stone barn.

12 ◆ DEENE PARK

Corby, NN17 3EW. Mr & Mrs Robert & Charlotte Brudenell, 01780 450278, admin@deenepark.com, www.deenepark.com. *6m N of Corby. Off A43 between Stamford & Corby.* **For NGS: Sun 29 Apr (12-5). Adm £6, chd £3. Light refreshments in Old Kitchen Tea Room. For other opening times and information, please phone, email or visit garden website.**

Interesting garden set in beautiful parkland. Large parterre with topiary designed by David Hicks echoing the C16 decoration on the porch stonework, long mixed borders, old fashioned roses, Tudor courtyard, White Garden and Golden Garden. Lake and waterside walks with rare mature trees in natural garden. Wheelchair access available to main features of garden.

13 EAST HADDON HALL

Main Street, East Haddon, Northampton, NN6 8BU. Mr & Mrs John Beynon. *Located in the centre of the village, nr the church.* **Sat 14, Sun 15 July (11-5). Combined adm with Haddonstone Show Gardens £5, chd free. Home-made teas in Haddonstone Show Gardens.**

First opened for the NGS in 1928 and now restored by the present owners. 8 acres of parkland surrounding a Grade I listed Georgian house (not open) with extensive lawns, mature specimen trees and lovely views. More formal planting surrounds the house with many exuberantly planted containers.

GROUP OPENING

14 NEW EVENLEY GARDENS

Evenley, Brackley, NN13 5SG. *From Brackley 1m S on A43. Gardens situated on Broad Lane, the village green & Church Lane. Follow signs around the village. Tickets cover entry to all gardens & are available at each garden.* **Sun 20 May (2-6). Combined adm with Evenley Wood Garden £6, chd free. Home-made teas in St George's Church.**

NEW **CHRISTMAS COTTAGE**
Stuart & Wendy Freestone.

NEW **15 CHURCH LANE**
Carrie & Kevin O'Regan.

NEW **FINCH COTTAGE**
Cathy & Chris Ellis.

Evenley is a charming village situated approx 1m south of Brackley off the A43. It has a central village green surrounded by many period houses (not open), an excellent village shop and The Red Lion Pub which offers first class food and a warm welcome. Evenley gardens are a mix of established gardens and those being developed over the past five years. They all have large mixed borders with established shrubs and trees. There are also orchards and vegetable gardens in some. Partial wheelchair access to gardens across gravel drives and narrow paths to reach some areas.

15 ◆ EVENLEY WOOD GARDEN

Evenley, Brackley, NN13 5SH. Nicola Taylor, 07789 514468, grannyno1@yahoo.co.uk, www.evenleywoodgarden.co.uk. *¾m S of Brackley. Turn off at Evenley r'about on A43 & follow signs within the village to the garden which is situated off the Evenley & Mixbury road.* **For NGS: Sun 20 May (2-6). Combined adm with Evenley Gardens £6, chd free. Picnics welcome.** For other opening times and information, please phone, email or visit garden website.

This 60 acre privately owned woodland garden contains a large and notable collection of trees, shrubs, bulbs, and more. Its unusual band of acid soil, in what is a predominantly alkaline area, allows the cultivation of plants which do not usually thrive in this location; including rhododendrons, camellias, and magnolias. Please take care as all paths are grass.

GROUP OPENING

16 FLORE GARDENS

Flore, Northampton, NN7 4LQ. *Off A45 2m W of M1 J16. Free car park NN7 4LS (Do Not Use The By-Pass). Garden map provided. Coaches, please phone 01327 341225 for parking.* **Sun 8 Apr (2-6); Sat 16, Sun 17 June (11-6). Combined adm £5, chd free. Home-made teas in Chapel School Room (Apr). Coffee & teas in Church and light lunches & teas in Chapel School Room (June).** Donation to All Saints Church & United Reform Church, Flore.

24 BLISS LANE
John & Sally Miller.
Open on all dates

BUTTERCUP COTTAGE
Mrs Elizabeth Chignell.
Open on Sat 16, Sun 17 June

THE CROFT
John & Dorothy Boast.
Open on all dates

THE GARDEN HOUSE
Edward & Penny Aubrey-Fletcher.
Open on Sat 16, Sun 17 June

THE OLD BAKERY
John Amos & Karl Jones, www.johnnieamos.co.uk.
Open on all dates

PRIVATE GARDEN OF BLISS LANE NURSERY
Christine & Geoffrey Littlewood.
Open on all dates

ROCK SPRINGS
Tom Higginson & David Foster.
Open on all dates

RUSSELL HOUSE
Peter Pickering & Stephen George, 01327 341734, peterandstephen@btinternet.com.
Open on all dates

17 THE GREEN
Mrs Wendy Amos.
Open on Sat 16, Sun 17 June

Flore gardens have been open since 1963 as part of the Flore Flower Festival and the partnership with the NGS started in 1992. Flore is an attractive village with views over the Upper Nene Valley. We have a varied mix of gardens, developed by friendly, enthusiastic and welcoming owners. Our gardens range from the traditional to the eccentric providing yr-round interest. There are greenhouses, gazebos and summerhouses, with seating providing opportunities to rest while enjoying the gardens. In spring there are early flowering perennials, interesting trees, shrubs, and bulbs in pots and border drifts. There is planting for all situations from shade to full sun. June gardens open in association with Flore Flower Festival. The gardens incl formal and informal designs with lots of roses, clematis and many varieties of trees, shrubs, perennials, herbs, fruit and some vegetables. Featured on ITV News Anglia (17 June 2017). Partial wheelchair access to most gardens, some assistance may be required.

17 FOXTAIL LILLY

41 South Road, Oundle, PE8 4BP. Tracey Mathieson, 01832 274593, foxtaillilly41@gmail.com, www.foxtail-lilly.co.uk. *1m from Oundle town centre. From A605 at Barnwell Xrds take Barnwell Rd, 1st R to South Rd.* **Sun 10 June (11-5). Adm £4, chd free. Home-made teas. Visits also by arrangement May to Sept for groups of 60 max.**

A cottage garden where perennials and grasses are grouped creatively together amongst gravel paths, complementing one another to create a natural look. Some unusual plants and quirky oddities create a different and colourful informal garden. Lots of flowers for cutting, and a shop in the barn. New meadow pasture turned into new cutting garden.

18 FROGGERY COTTAGE

85 Breakleys Road, Desborough, NN14 2PT. Mr John Lee, 01536 760002, froggerycottage@hotmail.com, www.froggerycottage.com. *6m N of Kettering. 5m S of Market Harborough. Signed off A6 & A14.* **Sun 29 July (11.30-5). Combined adm with Hostellarie £3, chd free. Home-made teas, a gluten free option & light lunches. Visits also by arrangement May to Sept for groups of 4+.**

1 acre plantsman's garden full of rare and unusual plants. NCCPG Collection of 435 varieties of penstemons incl dwarfs and species. Mediterranean and water gardens with large herbaceous borders. Artifacts on display incl old ploughs and garden implements. Penstemon workshops throughout the day. Featured in Gardens Illustrated (2017).

NPC

19 GLENDON HALL

Kettering, NN14 1QE. Rosie Bose, 01536 711732, rosiebose@googlemail.com. *1½m E of Rothwell. A6003 to Corby (A14 J7) W of Kettering, turn L onto Glendon Rd signed Rothwell, Desborough, Rushton. Entrance*

1½m on L past turn for Rushton. **Visits by arrangement for groups of 25 max. Adm £3, chd free.**

Mature specimen trees, topiary, box hedges, and herbaceous borders stocked with many unusual plants. Large walled kitchen gardens with glasshouse, and a shaded area well stocked with ferns. Some gravel and slopes, but wheelchair access via longer route.

♿ ✿ 🚌 ☕

20 GOWER HOUSE

Guilsborough, Northampton, NN6 8PY. Ann Moss, 01604 740140, cattimoss@aol.com. *Off High St by The Witch & Sow Pub, through pub car park.* **Visits by arrangement May & June for combined visit with Dripwell House only.**

Although Gower House garden is small, it is closely planted with specimen trees, shrubs, perennials, orchids, thyme lawn, wild flowers and alpines; some rare or unusual, with foliage colour being important. Several seating areas designed for elderly relatives incorporating recycled materials. Soft fruit and vegetable garden shared with Dripwell is an important part of our gardening.

☕

GROUP OPENING

21 GREAT BRINGTON GARDENS

Northampton, NN7 4JJ. *7m NW of Northampton. Off A428 Rugby Rd. From Northampton, 1st L turn past main gates of Althorp. Free parking. Programmes & maps available at car park.* **Sun 6 May (11-5). Combined adm £5, chd free. Home-made teas & cakes in Parish Church & morning coffee & lunches in Reading Room.**

FOLLY HOUSE
Sarah & Joe Sacarello.

15 HAMILTON LANE
Mr & Mrs Robin Matthews.

NEW **63 MAIN STREET**
Kim Robinson & Michael Carter.

ROSE COTTAGE
David Green & Elaine MacKenzie.

THE STABLES
Mrs A George.

SUNDERLAND HOUSE
Mrs Margaret Rubython.

YEW TREE HOUSE
Mrs Joan Heaps.

Great Brington is proud of its nearly 25 yr association with the NGS and arguably one of the most successful one day scheme events in the county. This year we offer seven gardens open to view including one new garden which has never been accessible to the public. Our gardens provide superb quality and immense variety; many of the gardens continue to evolve each year and most are designed, planted and maintained by their owners on a scale which is eminently practical and rewarding. Our particularly picturesque, predominately stone and thatch village is well worth a day out in its own right, and its configuration is perfect for the occasion; compact, self-contained, circular and virtually flat. On offer on the day, including our memorable gardens; a warm welcome, free car parking, programmes and maps, morning coffee, lunches and teas, plant stalls and a local history exhibition. Small coaches of groups up to 26 max welcome by prior arrangement only, please call 01604 770939.

✿ 🚌 ☕

22 THE GREEN PATCH

Valley Walk, Kettering, NN16 0LU. Sue McKay. *Junction of Valley Walk & Margret Rd, signed from A4300 Stamford Rd.* **Sun 12 Aug (11.30-2.30). Adm £3, chd free. Light refreshments.**

The Green Patch is a 2½ acre, Green Flag award-winning community garden, situated on the edge of Kettering. We have hens, ducks, beehives, ponds, children's play area, orchard and so much more. We rely on our wonderful volunteers to make our friendly and magical garden the warm and welcoming place it is. Run by the environmental charity Groundwork Northamptonshire. Sandwiches, cakes and drinks on sale - bring a blanket for a picnic. Wheelchair access and disabled WC facilities.

♿ 🐕 ✿ 🚌 ☕

23 GREYWALLS

Farndish, NN29 7HJ. Mrs P M Anderson, 01933 353495, greywalls@dbshoes.co.uk. *2½m SE of Wellingborough. A609 from Wellingborough, B570 to Irchester, turn to Farndish by cenotaph. House adjacent to church.* **Sun 4 Mar (12-3). Adm £3.50, chd free. Light refreshments. Visits also by arrangement. Coaches welcome.**

2 acre mature garden surrounding old vicarage (not open). Over 100 varieties of snowdrops, drifts of hardy cyclamen and hellebores. Alpine house and raised alpine beds. Water features and natural ponds with views over open countryside. Rare breed hens and 2 rescue donkeys.

♿ ✿ 🚌 ☕

Buttercup Cottage, Flore Gardens

The Old Vicarage

GROUP OPENING

24 GUILSBOROUGH GARDENS

High Street, Guilsborough, NN6 8RA. *10m NW of Northampton. 10m E of Rugby. Between A5199 & A428. J1 off A14. Car parking in field on Hollowell Rd out of Guilsborough. Information & maps from village hall, next to primary school.* **Sun 29 Apr (1-5.30). Combined adm £6, chd free. Home-made teas in village hall.**

DRIPWELL HOUSE
Mr J W Langfield & Dr C Moss, 01604 740140, cattimoss@aol.com.
Visits also by arrangement May & June for combined visit with Gower House.

FOUR ACRES
Mark & Gay Webster.

THE GATE HOUSE
Mike & Sarah Edwards.

GUILSBOROUGH HOUSE
Mr & Mrs John McCall.

OAK DENE
Mr & Mrs R A Darker.

THE OLD HOUSE
Richard & Libby Seaton Evans.

THE OLD VICARAGE
John & Christine Benbow.

Enjoy a warm welcome in this village with its very attractive rural setting of rolling hills and reservoirs. Seven varied village gardens, from a flower arranger's small garden surrounding a modern house (not open), to large gardens with sweeping lawns, mature trees and beautiful views. There is plenty of room to sit and relax and picnics can be spread out in the car park field. Several of us are interested in growing fruit and vegetables, and walled kitchen gardens and a potager are an important part of our gardening. Plants both rare and unusual from our plantsmen's gardens are for sale, a true highlight here. Dripwell House has opened for the NGS since 1986, originally an individual garden and is a destination in its own right. There is thus a lot to see and visitors find that they need the whole afternoon. No wheelchair access at Dripwell and The Gate House. No dogs at Oak Dene.

25 ◆ HADDONSTONE SHOW GARDENS

The Forge House, Church Lane, East Haddon, Northampton, NN6 8DB. Haddonstone Ltd, 01604 770711, info@haddonstone.co.uk, www.haddonstone.com. *7m NW of Northampton. Brown tourism signs from A428. Located in centre of village, nr church & opp school.* **For NGS: Sat 14, Sun 15 July (11-5). Combined adm with East Haddon Hall £5, chd free. Home-made teas.** For other opening times and information, please phone, email or visit garden website.

See classic Haddonstone garden ornaments in the beautiful setting of the walled manor gardens incl planters, fountains, statues, bird baths, sundials, balustrades and follies. Garden is on different levels with roses, clematis, climbers, herbaceous, ornamental flowers, topiary, specimen shrubs and trees. New additions: designs from Sir John Soane's Museum and busts of Capability Brown and Repton. The gardens incorporate planting, structures and ornaments used at the company's acclaimed Chelsea Flower Show exhibits. Wheelchair access to all key features of main garden.

GROUP OPENING

26 HARPOLE GARDENS

Harpole, NN7 4BX. *On A45 4m W of Northampton towards Weedon. Turn R at The Turnpike Hotel into Harpole. Village maps given to all visitors.* **Sun 10 June (1-6). Combined adm £5, chd free. Home-made teas at The Close.**

BRYTTEN-COLLIER HOUSE
James & Lucy Strickland.

THE CLOSE
Michael Orton-Jones, 01604 830332, michael@orton-jones.com. **Visits also by arrangement June & July for groups of 10+.**

14 HALL CLOSE
Marion & Charley Oliver.

19 MANOR CLOSE
Caroline & Andy Kemshed, 01604 830512, carolinekemshed@live.co.uk. **Visits also by arrangement from Mon 11 June for one week only.**

THE OLD DAIRY
David & Di Ballard.

We welcome everyone to join in the Harpole Gardens experience. Visit us and you will delight in varied gardens of all shapes, sizes and content. Harpole is an attractive village which is renowned for its annual Scarecrow Festival (2nd weekend of Sept), well worth a visit! Amongst our various garden structures you will find a summerhouse, a treehouse, a vine-covered pergola and plenty of seating for the weary. We have herbaceous borders, luxuriant lawns, water features, including several ponds. You will see mixed borders with plants for both shade and sun, mature trees, herbs, vegetables and alpines. You will be able to enjoy views over neighbouring farmland and perhaps best of all delicious home-made teas! Wheelchair access at Brytten-Collier House, The Close and The Old Dairy only.

Perennial, supporting horticulturalists since 1839

27 67-69 HIGH STREET

Finedon, NN9 5JN. Mary & Stuart Hendry, 01933 680414, sh_archt@hotmail.com. *6m SE Kettering. Garden signed from A6 & A510 junction.* **Sun 25 Feb (11-3); Sun 3, Sun 24 June (2-6). Adm £3.50, chd free. Soup & roll in Feb (incl in adm). Cream teas in June. Visits also by arrangement Feb to Sept.**

Constantly evolving ⅓ acre rear garden of C17 cottage (not open). Early spring garden with snowdrops and hellebores, summer and autumn mixed borders, and many obelisks and containers, kitchen garden, herb bed, rambling roses, at least 60 different hostas, all giving varied interest from Feb through to Oct. Large selection of home raised plants for sale (all proceeds to NGS). Well behaved dogs welcome. Look at the NGS website and twitter @NorthantsNGS for pop-up public openings in late May/ June.

28 136 HIGH STREET

Irchester, Wellingborough, NN29 7AB. Mr & Mrs Ade & Jane Parker. *At end of High St, about ½m before junction with A45.* **Sun 29 July (12-4). Adm £3.50, chd free. Home-made teas.**

½ acre garden with various different borders including those planted for shade, sun and bee friendly situations. Alpine houses, raised beds and planted stone sinks. Wildlife pond. Seasonally planted tubs.

29 ◆ HOLDENBY HOUSE GARDENS

Holdenby House, Holdenby, Northampton, NN6 8DJ. Mr & Mrs James Lowther, 01604 770074, office@holdenby.com, www.holdenby.com. *6m NW of Northampton. From A5199 or A428 between East Haddon & Spratton. Follow brown tourist signs.* **For NGS: Sun 15 July (1-5). Adm £5, chd free. Cream teas.** For other opening times and information, please phone, email or visit garden website.

Holdenby has an historic Grade I listed garden. The inner garden incl Rosemary Verey's renowned Elizabethan Garden and Rupert Golby's Pond Garden and long borders. There is also a delightful walled kitchen garden with original Victorian greenhouse. Away from the formal gardens the terraces of the original Elizabethan Garden are still visible, one of the best preserved examples of their kind. Victorian Tea Room. The estate includes gravel paths.

30 HOSTELLARIE

78 Breakleys Road, Desborough, NN14 2PT. Stella Freeman, stelstan78@aol.com. *6m N of Kettering. 5m S of Market Harborough. From church & war memorial turn R into Dunkirk Ave, then 3rd R. From cemetery L into Dunkirk Ave, then 4th L.* **Sun 29 July (11.30-5). Combined adm with Froggery Cottage £3, chd free. Home-made teas & a gluten free option. Visits also by arrangement June & July for groups of 10-25.**

Over 180ft long town garden. Divided into rooms of different character; courtyard garden with a sculptural clematis providing shade, colour themed flower beds, ponds and water features, cottage gardens and gravel borders, clematis and roses, all linked by lawns and grass paths. The collection of hostas, over 50 different varieties, are taking up more space each year and are the pride of the garden.

31 ◆ KELMARSH HALL & GARDENS

Main Road, Kelmarsh, Northampton, NN6 9LY. The Kelmarsh Trust, 01604 686543, enquiries@kelmarsh.com, www.kelmarsh.com. *Kelmarsh is 5m S of Market Harborough & 11m N of Northampton. From A14, exit J2 & head N towards Market Harborough on the A508.* **For NGS: Sun 8 Apr, Sun 20 May (11-5). Adm £6, chd £3.50. The tea room offers light lunches, cream teas & cakes.** For other opening times and information, please phone, email or visit garden website.

Kelmarsh Hall is an elegant Palladian house set in glorious Northamptonshire countryside with highly regarded gardens, which are the work of Nancy Lancaster, Norah Lindsay and Geoffrey Jellicoe. Hidden gems incl an orangery, sunken garden, long border, rose gardens and, at the heart of it all, a historic walled garden. Highlights throughout the seasons incl fritillaries, tulips, roses and dahlias. In spring 2018, Kelmarsh Hall will be opening their exciting Heritage Lottery Funded project 'Tunnelling through the Past'. The recently restored laundry and servant's quarters will be opened to the public, creating the incredible opportunity to experience life 'below stairs' in a country house. Featured in the Telegraph '30 of the Best Late-Season Gardens to visit before Autumn Sets in' (Aug 2017) and The Times '20 Great Gardens - the Best Places to Visit this Summer' (June 2017). Blue badge disabled parking is available close to the Visitor Centre entrance. Paths are loose gravel, wheelchair users advised to bring a companion.

The National Garden Scheme is Hospice UK's largest single funder

GROUP OPENING

32 KILSBY GARDENS

Kilsby Village, CV23 8XP. *5m SE of Rugby. 6m N of Daventry on A361. The road through village is the B4038.* **Sun 10 June (2-6). Combined adm £5, chd free. Home-made teas at Kilsby Village Hall.**

NEW **ORCHARD HOUSE**
Barbara & Frank Almond.

PYTCHLEY GARDENS
Kathy Jenkins & Neighbours.

PYTCHLEY HOUSE
Mr & Mrs T F Clay, 01788 822373, tomfclay@gmail.com.
Visits also by arrangement June to Sept.

RAINBOW'S END
Mr & Mrs J Madigan.

NEW **17 RUGBY ROAD**
Margaret Couldrey.

Kilsby is a stone and brick village with historic interest, home of St Faith's Church dating from the C12. The village was the site of one of the first skirmishes of the Civil War in 1642, and also gave its name to Stephenson's nearby lengthy rail tunnel built in the 1830s. Four large, and several attractive patio gardens will be open this year, all within easy walking distance. Comments from 2016 said 'Kilsby is a particularly friendly village', so please come and see us. Partial wheelchair access to most gardens. Narrow access to Pytchley Gardens.

33 NEW 16 LEYS AVENUE

Desborough, Kettering, NN14 2PY. Mr & Mrs Keith & Beryl Norman. *6m N of Kettering, 5m S of Market Harborough. From church & War Memorial turn R into Dunkirk Ave & 5th R into Leys Ave.* **Sun 15 July (2-6.30). Adm £3, chd free. Light refreshments.**

A town garden with two water features plus a stream and a pond flanked by a 12ft clinker built boat. There are five raised beds which are planted with vegetables, dahlias and chrysanthemums. A patio lined with acers has two steps down to a gravel garden with paved paths. Mature trees and acers give the garden yr-round structure and interest. Access by two steps from patio to main garden.

GROUP OPENING

34 LONG BUCKBY GARDENS

Northampton, NN6 7RE. *8m NW of Northampton, midway between A428 & A5. Long Buckby is signed from A428 & A5. 10 mins from J18 M1. Long Buckby train station is ½m from centre of the village.* **Sun 22 July (1-6). Combined adm £5, chd free. Home-made teas at Lawn Cottage.**

25 BERRYFIELD
Mandy Morley & Jane Harrison.

3 COTTON END
Roland & Georgina Wells.

4 COTTON END
Sue & Giles Baker.

THE GROTTO
Andy & Chrissy Gamble.

7 HIGH STACK
Tiny & Sheila Burt.

LAWN COTTAGE, 36 EAST STREET
Michael & Denise Nichols.

10 LIME AVENUE
June Ford.

4 SKINYARD LANE
William & Susie Mitchell, 01327 843426, mitchewi52@gmail.com.
Visits also by arrangement May to Sept for groups of 10-25.

WISTERIA HOUSE
David & Clare Croston, 07771 911892, dad.croston@gmail.com.
Visits also by arrangement May to Sept for gardening groups.

WOODCOTE VILLA
Sue & Geoff Woodward.

Ten gardens in the historic villages of Long Buckby and Long Buckby Wharf. Varying in size and style, from courtyard and canal side to cottage garden, some are established and others evolving. They incl water features, pergolas, garden structures, chickens and pigs, but the stars are definitely the plants. Bursting with colour, visitors will find old favourites and the unusual, used in a variety of ways; trees, shrubs, perennials, climbers, annuals, fruit and vegetables. Our award-winning local museum will also be open. Of course there will be teas and plants for sale to complete the visit. Full or partial wheelchair access to all gardens, except 4 Skinyard Lane.

35 NEW MOULTON COLLEGE HORTICULTURE UNIT

Holcot Site (Gate 3), Pitsford Road, Moulton, NN3 7RR. Moulton College, www.moulton.ac.uk. *Horticulture Unit via the Garden Centre. Turn off A43 Northamton to Kettering Rd at small r'about to Overstone Rd. In village centre follow yellow signs. The car park is on the Pitsford Rd out of the village.* **Sun 8 July (10-4). Adm £5, chd free. Tea, coffee & cake.**

Moulton College started life as an agricultural college and has a strong horticultural dept. There are show gardens, allotments, a 2½ hectare millenium arboretum, more formal areas around the original 1920s buildings and interesting specimen trees, maintained by the students, in an attractive rural setting. Wide tarmac path from carpark to village centre via arboretum.

GROUP OPENING

36 NEW NEWNHAM GARDENS

Newnham, Daventry, NN11 3HF. *2m S of Daventry on B4037 between the A361 & A45. Continue to the centre of the village & follow signs for the car park, just off the main village green.* **Sun 27 May (11-5). Combined adm £5, chd free. Light lunches in village hall & drinks & cakes in the church.**

THE BANKS
Sue & Geoff Chester, www.suestyles.co.uk.

NEW **THE COTTAGE**
Jacqueline Minor.

HILLTOP
David & Mercy Messenger.

NEW **KEY COTTAGE**
David & Janet Woodford.

WREN COTTAGE
Mr & Mrs Jim Dorkins.

Five lovely gardens set in a beautiful ancient village cradled between the gentle hills of south Northamptonshire. The varied gardens, set around traditional village houses (not open), look enchanting at this special time of year and include a long-standing NGS opener and two brand new openings for 2018. Spend the day with us enjoying the gardens, buying plants, strolling around the old village lanes, visiting our C14 church and its exhibitions and indulging yourself with tasty light lunches and scrumptious refreshments and cakes. Please note that the village and gardens are hilly in parts and while most gardens are accessible, others may be more restricted

37 OLD RECTORY, QUINTON

Preston Deanery Road, Quinton, Northampton, NN7 2ED. Alan Kennedy & Emma Wise, quintonoldrectory.com. *M1 J15, 1m from Wootton towards Salcey Forest. House is next to the church.* **Sun 20 May, Sun 2 Sept (11-5). Adm £5, chd free. Teas & light lunches.**

A beautiful contemporary 3 acre rectory garden designed by multi award-winning designer, Anoushka Feiler. Taking the Old Rectory's C18 history and its religious setting as a key starting point, the main garden at the back of the house has been divided into six parts; a kitchen garden, glasshouse and flower garden, a woodland menagerie, a pleasure garden, a park and an orchard. Elements of C18 design such as formal structures, parterres, topiary, long walks, occasional seating areas and traditional craft work have been introduced, however with a distinctly C21 twist through the inclusion of living walls, modern materials and features, new planting methods and abstract installations. Wheelchair access, but there are gravel paths.

38 ◆ THE OLD RECTORY, SUDBOROUGH

Kettering, NN14 3BX. Mr & Mrs G Toller, 01832 734085, contact@theoldrectorygardens.co.uk, www.theoldrectorygardens.co.uk. *8m NE of Kettering. Exit 12 off A14. Village just off A6116 between Thrapston & Brigstock. Free private parking in a small paddock adjacent to the house.* **For NGS: Sun 22 Apr (11-5). Adm £7, chd free. Home-made teas & cake.**
For other opening times and information, please phone, email or visit garden website.

A charming 3 acre village garden situated next to a church, including extensive herbaceous borders, a rose garden, gravel border and highly regarded potager, designed by Rosemary Verey. This is a garden for all seasons with early spring bulbs, a wide variety of old roses, tree peonies, standard Lycianthes Rantonnetii, a small lily pond and charming woodland walk alongside Harpers Brook. Set in a tranquil conservation area with stunning views and setting. Partial wheelchair access as some gravel paths. Guide dogs welcome.

The National Garden Scheme is the largest single funder of Macmillan

39 THE OLD VICARAGE

Daventry Road, Norton, Daventry, NN11 2ND. Mr & Mrs Barry & Andrea Coleman. *Norton is about 2m E of Daventry, 11m W of Northampton. From Daventry follow signs to Norton for 1m. On A5 N from Weedon follow road for 3m, take L turn signed Norton. On A5 S take R at Xrds signed Norton, 6m from Kilsby. Garden is R of All Saints Church.* **Sun 15 Apr (1-4). Adm £4, chd free. Home-made teas in the orangery.**

Based upon a traditional but once faded vicarage layout, the garden aims to be lively and colourful throughout the yr, using a few of the original yews, pines and laurels as a seasonal framework. The garden's heritage incl a carpet of snowdrops in winter, and irrepressible primroses in spring. After yrs of taming and shaping the garden, it now is quietly developing a little touch of drama. The interesting C14 church of All Saints will be open to visitors.

GROUP OPENING

40 PRESTON CAPES AND LITTLE PRESTON GARDENS

Little Preston, Daventry, NN11 3TF. *6m SW of Daventry. 13m NE of Banbury. 3m N of Canons Ashby. Preston Capes and Little Preston are ½m apart.* **Sun 3 June (1-5). Combined adm £5, chd free. Home-made cakes & teas at Old West Farm from 1-5.**

CITY COTTAGE
Mrs Gavin Cowen.

LADYCROFT
Mervyn & Sophia Maddison.

THE MANOR
Mr Graham Stanton.

NORTH FARM
Mr & Mrs Tim Coleridge.

OLD WEST FARM
Mr & Mrs Gerard Hoare.

A selection of five differing gardens in the beautiful unspoilt south Northamptonshire ironstone villages, most with a backdrop of fantastic views of the surrounding countryside. Gardens range from small contemporary, through to classical country style with old fashioned roses and borders. Features include attractive village with local sandstone houses and cottages (not open), Norman church and wonderful views. Partial wheelchair access to some parts of the gardens.

GROUP OPENING

41 RAVENSTHORPE GARDENS

Ravensthorpe, NN6 8ES. *7m NW of Northampton. Signed from A428. Wigley Cottage is in The Hollows off Bettycroft.* **Sun 8 July (1.30-5.30). Combined adm £5, chd free. Home-made teas at village hall.**

33 GUILSBOROUGH ROAD
Mr & Mrs Tim & Deborah Hogben.

RAVENSTHORPE NURSERY
Mr & Mrs Richard Wiseman, 01604 770548, ravensthorpenursery@hotmail.com.
Visits also by arrangement May to Sept.

TREETOPS
Ros & Gordon Smith.

WIGLEY COTTAGE
Mr & Mrs Dennis Patrick.

Attractive village in Northamptonshire uplands near to Ravensthorpe reservoir and Top Ardles Wood Woodland Trust, which have bird watching and picnic opportunities. Established and developing gardens set in beautiful countryside displaying a wide range of plants, many of which are available from the Nursery. Offering inspirational planting, quiet contemplation, beautiful views, water features, gardens encouraging wildlife and a flower arranger's garden. Partial wheelchair access to Wigley Cottage.

42 ROSEARIE-DE-LA-NYMPH

55 The Grove, Moulton, Northampton, NN3 7UE. Peter Hughes, Mary Morris, Irene Kay, Steven Hughes & Jeremy Stanton. *N of Northampton town. Turn off A43 at small r'about to Overstone Rd. Follow NGS signs in village. The garden is on the Holcot Rd out of Moulton.* **Sun 17, Sun 24 June (11-5). Adm £4.50, chd free.**

We have been developing this romantic garden for about 10 yrs and now have over 1800 roses, incl English, French and Italian varieties. Many unusual water features and specimen trees. Roses, scramblers and ramblers climb into trees, over arbours and arches. Collection of 95 Japanese maples. Butterfly rearing unit. Sorry, no refreshments available. Mostly flat, but there is a standard width doorway to negotiate.

Dripwell House, Guilsborough Gardens

33 Guilsborough Road, Ravensthorpe Gardens

GROUP OPENING

43 SPRATTON GARDENS

Smith Street, Spratton, NN6 8HP. *6½ m NNW of Northampton. On A5199 between Northampton & Welford. S from J1, A14. Car Park at Spratton Hall School with close access to gardens.* **Sun 10 June (11-5). Combined adm £6, chd free.**

THE COTTAGE
Mr & Mrs Andrew Elliott.

DALE HOUSE
Fiona & Chris Cox, 01604 846458, fionacox19@aol.com.

FORGE COTTAGE
Daniel & Jo Bailey.

THE GRANARY
Margo Lerin.

11 HIGH STREET
Philip & Frances Roseblade.

MULBERRY COTTAGE
Michael & Morley Heaton.

STONE HOUSE
John Forbear.

1 WILLOW CLOSE
Mr & Mrs Ken & Lorraine Bennett.

9A YEW TREE LANE
John Hunt.

As well as attractive cottage gardens alongside old Northampton stone houses, Spratton also has unusual gardens, including showing good use of a small area; one dedicated to encouraging wildlife; a highly structured courtyard shrub garden; a newly renovated garden; mature gardens with fruit trees and herbaceous borders, one with a 300 yr old Holm Oak and miniature Shetland ponies looking on, surrounded by beautiful views of the agricultural landscape. There will be a 'Bug Hunt' for children. Tea, cakes and rolls will be available in the Norman St. Andrew's Church with additional displays of the Pocket Park, which is just a short walk away. The King's Head Pub will be open, lunch reservations recommended.

44 THE SPRING HOUSE

Mill Lane, Chipping Warden, Banbury, OX17 1JZ. Mr F Tuthill, 01295 660059, francisttuthill@gmail.com. *Chipping Warden is a village on A361 approx 8m NE of Banbury. The Spring House is on Mill Lane which leads off A361.* **Visits by arrangement Mar to June. Adm £5, chd free. Home-made teas.**

Large garden of 3¾ acres with wonderful trees and bog garden. The garden, originally part of The Court House garden until The Spring House was built in the 1960s, was designed by the renowned landscape designer Kitty Lloyd Jones (responsible also for Greys Court, Achamore House on the Isle of Gigha and Upton House in Warwickshire).

45 ◆ STEANE PARK

Brackley, NN13 6DP. Lady Connell, 01280 705899, www.steanepark.co.uk. *2m from Brackley towards Banbury. On A422, 6m E of Banbury.* **For NGS: Sun 1 July (11-5). Adm £4.50, chd free. Cream teas. For other opening times and information, please phone or visit garden website.**

The garden was in an extremely dilapidated and overgrown state; over the past 24 yrs we have tried to recapture its original glory. There are beautiful trees in 80 acres of parkland, old waterway and fish ponds, 1620 church in grounds. The gardens are constantly being updated in sympathy with old stone house and church. Amongst many features and attractions there is the The Monet Bridge, built by a craftsman from Suffolk. It was delivered in several pieces and constructed on-site with the aid of a lot of ropes, getting wet and crossed fingers, but the end result looks magnificent! Partial wheelchair access.

The National Garden Scheme is Marie Curie's largest single funder

46 SULBY GARDENS

Sulby, Northampton, NN6 6EZ. Mrs Alison Lowe. *16m NW of Northampton, 2m NE of Welford off A5199. Past Wharf House Hotel, take 1st R signed Sulby. After R & L bends, turn R at sign for Sulby Hall Farm. Turn R at junction, garden is 1st L. Parking limited, no vans or buses please.* **Thur 26 Apr, Thur 14 June, Thur 2 Aug (2-5); Thur 11 Oct (1-4); Fri 12 Oct (11-4). Adm £4, chd free. Home-made teas.**
Interesting and unusual property, on the Leicestershire border between Welford and Husbands Bosworth, covering 12 acres comprising working Victorian kitchen garden, orchard, and late C18 icehouse, plus species-rich nature reserve incl woodland, feeder stream to River Avon, a variety of ponds and established wild flower meadows. Open Day features incl April: snakeshead fritillaries, cowslips, bluebells. June: flower meadows in full bloom. Aug: butterflies, dragonflies, aquatic plants. Oct: two-day Apple Event, labelled display of apples, new season's Sulby Gardens Apple Juice, and apple-themed cakes. Regular plant sales. Featured on BBC Radio Leicester (Sept 2017). CPRE Award Winner 2017. NB: Children welcome but under strict supervision because of deep water.

47 TITCHMARSH HOUSE

Chapel Street, Titchmarsh, NN14 3DA. Sir Ewan & Lady Harper, 01832 732439, ewan@ewanh.co.uk, www.titchmarsh-house.co.uk. *2m N of Thrapston. 6m S of Oundle. Exit A14 at junction signed A605, Titchmarsh signed as turning E towards Oundle & Peterborough.* **Mon 7, Sun 20 May (2-6); Sat 9 June (12.30-5). Adm £4, chd free. Teas at parish church (May). BBQ lunch & teas at village fete (June). Visits also by arrangement Apr to June.**
4½ acres extended and laid out since 1972. Special collections of magnolias, spring bulbs, iris, peonies and roses with many rare trees and shrubs. Walled ornamental vegetable garden and ancient yew hedge. Some newly planted areas; please refer to the website. Wheelchair access to most of the garden without using steps. No dogs.

GROUP OPENING

48 TURWESTON GARDENS

Brackley, NN13 5JY. *2m E of Brackley. A43 from M40 J10. On Brackley bypass turn R on A422 towards Buckingham, ½m turn L signed Turweston.* **Sun 24 June (2-5.30). Combined adm £3, chd free. Home-made teas at Turweston House.**

TURWESTON HOUSE
Mr & Mrs C Allen.

NEW **TURWESTON LODGE**
Mr & Mrs B P Collins.

TURWESTON MILL
Mr Harry Leventis.

Charming unspoilt stone built village in a conservation area. Three very different beautiful gardens. The Mill with bridges over the millstream and a spectacular waterfall, wildlife pond and a kitchen garden. At Turweston House there are landscaped gardens with borders, woodlands, lake and parkland and Turweston Lodge with a lovely cottage garden and spectacular rambling roses. Some gravel and slopes, but generally good access.

Your visit has already helped 600 more people gain access to a Parkinson's nurse

GROUP OPENING

49 WEEDON LOIS & WESTON GARDENS

Weedon Lois, Towcester, NN12 8PJ. *7m W of Towcester. 7m N of Brackley. Turn off A43 at Towcester, towards Abthorpe & Wappenham where you turn R for Weedon Lois. Or turn off A43 at Brackley, follow signs to Helmdon & Weston.* **Sun 10 June (2-5.30). Combined adm £5, chd free. Home-made teas in Baptist Chapel, Weston.**

THE GARDENER'S COTTAGE
Mrs Sitwell.

HILLSIDE
Mrs Karen Wilcox.

LOIS WEEDON HOUSE
Lady Greenaway.

OLD BARN
Mr & Mrs John Gregory.

RIDGEWAY COTTAGE
Jonathan & Elizabeth Carpenter.

4 VICARAGE RISE
Ashley & Lindsey Cartwright.

Two adjacent villages in south Northamptonshire with a handsome Medieval church in Weedon Lois. The extension churchyard contains the graves of the poets Dame Edith Sitwell and her brother Sir Sacheveral Sitwell who lived in Weston Hall. There are four gardens in Weedon Lois, including a large, well established garden with wonderful views and a water garden; a plantsman garden, lovingly developed over the last thirty years; a recently developed garden with rediscovered stone terracing, both structural and cottage style planting and an ornamental pond; and a large garden with woodland planting, herbaceous borders and a productive vegetable garden surrounded by a wavy hedge. In Weston there are two gardens, one newly created with roses, a wild flower area and orchard, and a charming cottage garden with beds, borders and semi-mature trees.

50 NEW WINWICK MANOR

Winwick, Northampton, NN6 7PD. Anthony Gross & Richard Slade. *E of J18 of the M1 Winwick lies 1½m on the N-side of the A428 between the villages of Crick & West Haddon.* **Sun 4 Mar (12-4.30); Sun 3 June (12-6). Adm £6, chd free. Lunches & home-made teas.**

First opened for the NGS in 1930 when the then owner of the manor owned the whole of Winwick. The gardens cover approx 8 acres and includes formal areas, woodlands and open views of the rural countryside. Early opening features masses of snowdrops and daffodils. Some areas of the garden have steps.

51 NEW THE WOODEN OWL

10A The Green, Clipston, Market Harborough, LE16 9RS. Mrs Julie Connell, 01858 525336, j.connell118@btinternet.com. *Clipston is on the Daventry, West Haddon, Naseby Market Harborough road. Approx 15m W of Kettering, NW of Northampton & SSE of Leicester. Off A14 J1 the A5199 go to Naseby then Clipston. Off A14 J2 the A508 go to Kelmarsh then Clipston.* **Sat 30 June (2-5); Sun 1 July (11-5). Adm £4, chd free. Cream teas with home-made scones & cakes. Visits also by arrangement Mar to Dec for groups of 15+.**

A garden in the making around owner's new house (not open), built in the stableyard of The Maltings, the garden the owner opened for the NGS for 10 yrs. The garden is within the owner's old plantsman's garden, full of unusual plants, shrubs, clematis. Many different fruit trees and bushes, vegetables and a new water garden. This will be a garden with great interest, especially to those people who used to visit The Maltings. It will be interesting to see how it develops over the coming yrs. Most of the garden is wheelchair friendly.

The Wooden Owl

NOTTINGHAMSHIRE

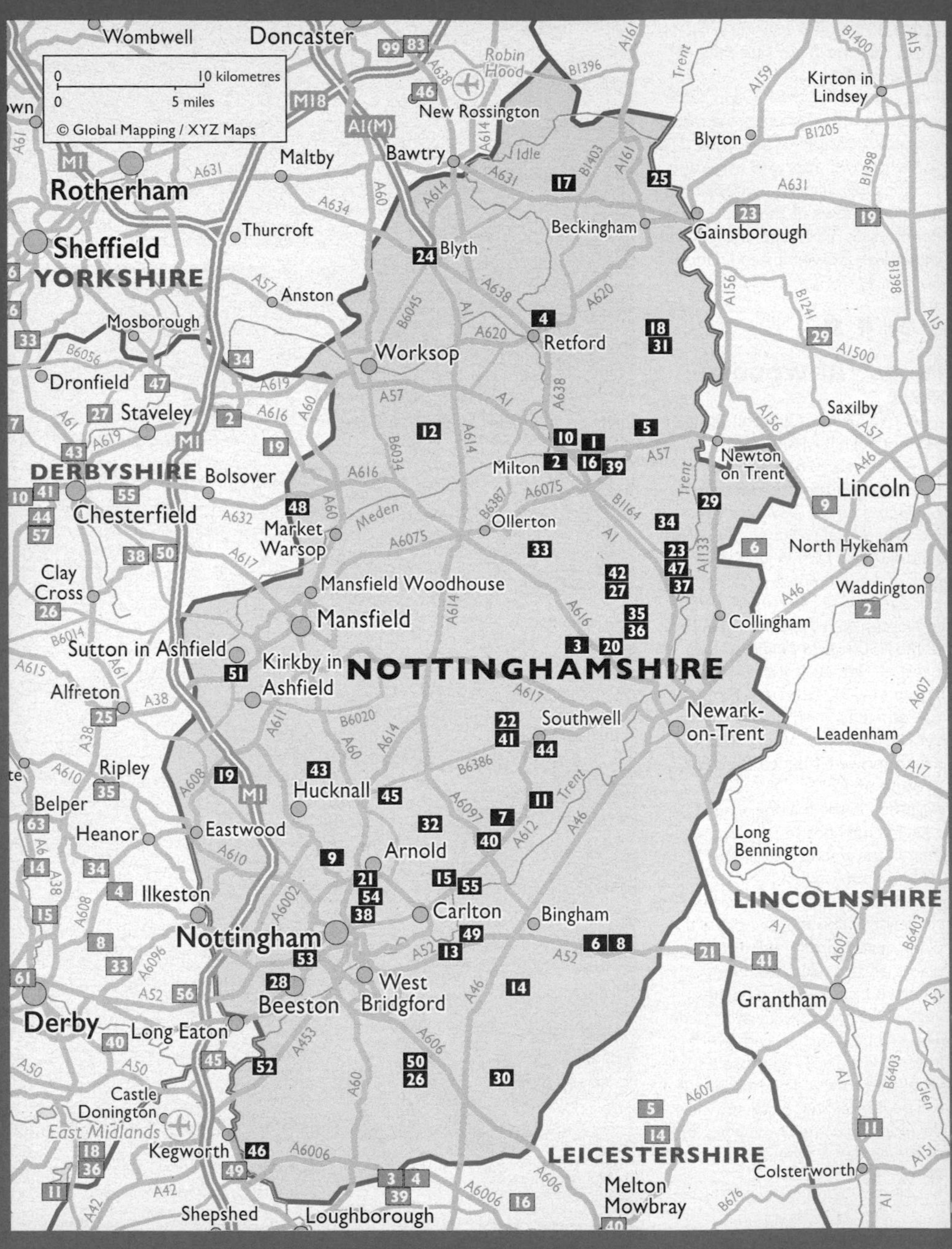

Nottinghamshire is best known as Robin Hood country. His legend persists and his haunt of Sherwood Forest, now a nature reserve, contains some of the oldest oaks in Europe. The Major Oak, thought to be 800 years old, still produces acorns.

Civil War battles raged throughout Nottinghamshire, and Newark's historic castle bears the scars. King Charles I surrendered to the Scots in nearby Southwell after a night at The Saracen's Head, which is still an inn today.

The Dukeries in the north of the county provide an unmatched landscape of lakes, parks and woods, so called because four dukes lived there, and their estates were contiguous. The dukes are gone, but their estates at Clumber, Thoresby and Welbeck continue to offer a pre-industrial haven in a thickly populated county.

Oaks in Sherwood, apples in Southwell (where the original Bramley tree still stands) and 100 kinds of rhubarb in the ducal kitchen garden at Clumber Park – they await your visit.

Volunteers

County Organiser
Georgina Denison
01636 821385
campden27@aol.com

County Treasurer
Nicola Cressey
01159 655132
nicola.cressey@gmail.com

Publicity
Julie Davison
01302 719668
jandp2@icloud.com

Social Media
Malcolm Turner
01159 222831
malcolm.turner14@btinternet.com

Booklet Co-ordinators
Malcolm and Wendy Fisher
0115 966 4322
wendy.fisher111@btinternet.com.

Assistant County Organisers
Judy Geldart
01636 823832
judygeldart@gmail.com

Beverley Perks
01636 812181
perks.family@talk21.com

Mary Thomas
01509 672056
nursery@piecemealplants.co.uk

Andrew Young
01623 863327
andrew.young@ngs.org.uk

Left: **5 Burton Lane**

OPENING DATES

All entries subject to change. For latest information check **www.ngs.org.uk**

Map locator numbers are shown to the right of each garden name.

February

Snowdrop Festival

Sunday 11th
The Beeches 2

Sunday 18th
Woodpeckers 55

Wednesday 21st
The Beeches 2

Sunday 25th
Church Farm 10
Ellicar Gardens 17
Holmes Villa 25

March

Sunday 4th
◆ Hodsock Priory Gardens 24
Woodpeckers 55

April

Sunday 8th
Broadlea 5

Sunday 15th
◆ Felley Priory 19
Normanton Hall 34

Sunday 22nd
Capability Barn 7

May

Sunday 6th
The Old Vicarage 41

Sunday 13th
38 Main Street 32
◆ Norwell Nurseries 36
Woodpeckers 55

Sunday 20th
Capability Barn 7
Church House 11
Floral Media 20
6 Hope Street 28
Ivy Bank Cottage 29

Sunday 27th
The Chimes 9
Papplewick Hall 43
Patchings Art Centre 45

Monday 28th
Holmes Villa 25
The Old Hall 40

June

Festival Weekend

Sunday 3rd
5 Burton Lane 6

Sunday 10th
Askham Gardens 1
NEW Beesthorpe Hall Farm 3
The Chimes 9

Saturday 16th
Halam Gardens and Wildflower Meadow 22

Sunday 17th
Hopbine Farmhouse, Ossington 27
Ossington House 42
Riseholme, 125 Shelford Road 49
NEW Spring Bank House 51
Thrumpton Hall 52

Sunday 24th
Bolham Manor 4
Kinoulton Gardens 30
Norwell Gardens 35
6 Weston Close 54

Wednesday 27th
Norwell Gardens 35

Saturday 30th
The Old Vicarage 41

July

Sunday 1st
East Markham Gardens 16
National Holocaust Centre and Museum 33

Sunday 8th
Cropwell Butler Gardens 14
The Glade 21
National Holocaust Centre and Museum 33
6 Weston Close 54

Saturday 14th
◆ Clumber Park Walled Kitchen Garden 12

Sunday 15th
National Holocaust Centre and Museum 33
Rhubarb Farm 48

Sunday 22nd
Cornerstones 13
Home Farm House, 17 Main Street 26
National Holocaust Centre and Museum 33
Rose Cottage 50

Sunday 29th
The Elms 18
5a High Street 23
Lodge Mount 31
National Holocaust Centre and Museum 33
NEW Norwood 37

August

Saturday 4th
Oak Barn Exotic Garden 39

Sunday 5th
NEW Nottinghamshire Hospice 38

Sunday 12th
The Old Vicarage 41

Sunday 19th
University Park Gardens 53

Sunday 26th
The Poplars 47

Monday 27th
5 Burton Lane 6
Cedarwood 8

September

Sunday 2nd
NEW Spring Bank House 51

October

Sunday 7th
Oak Barn Exotic Garden 39

Sunday 14th
◆ Norwell Nurseries 36

Sunday 21st
◆ Norwell Nurseries 36

By Arrangement

The Beeches 2
Broadlea 5
5 Burton Lane 6
Capability Barn 7
Church Farm 10
Cornerstones 13
Dumbleside 15
Ellicar Gardens 17
The Elms 18
Home Farm House, 17 Main Street 26
Lodge Mount 31
The Manor, East Markham Gardens 16
Normanton Hall 34
NEW Norwood 37
The Old Vicarage 41
Park Farm 44
Piecemeal 46
The Poplars 47
Rhubarb Farm 48
Riseholme, 125 Shelford Road 49
6 Weston Close 54

Clumber Park Walled Kitchen Garden

THE GARDENS

GROUP OPENING

1 ASKHAM GARDENS

Markham Moor, Retford, NG22 0RP. *6m S of Retford. On A638, in Rockley village turn E to Askham or on A57 at East Markham turn N to Askham.* **Sun 10 June (2-6). Combined adm £4, chd free. Home-made teas at Manor Lodge.**

DOVECOTE COTTAGE
Mrs C Slack.

NEW **MANOR LODGE**
Mr & Mrs K Bloom.

NURSERY HOUSE
Mr & Mrs D Bird.

Variety of pleasant English village gardens, with a flower festival in the church. Nursery House is a plantsman's garden, secluded and private, with every plant meticulously labelled; waterfall and well stocked pond. Dovecote Cottage is an enchanting terraced cottage garden with roses on the walls, perennial beds and attractive raised fish pond. Manor Lodge is a large garden, opposite the church with many summer houses and extensive lawns. Deep gravel at Nursery House. Steep slopes at Dovecote Cottage.

2 THE BEECHES

The Avenue, Milton, Newark, NG22 0PW. Margaret & Jim Swindin, 01777 870828, james91.swindin@mypostoffice.co.uk. *1m S A1 Markham Moor. Exit A1 at Markham Moor, take Walesby sign into village (1m). From Main St, L up The Avenue.* **Sun 11, Wed 21 Feb (11-4). Adm £3, chd free. Home-made teas. Teas £2. Visits also by arrangement Feb to Apr groups min 6, max 40.**

One acre garden full of colour and interest to plant enthusiasts looking for unusual and rare plants. Spring gives some 250 named snowdrops together with hellebores and early daffodils. The lawn is awash with crocus, fritillarias, anemones, narcissi and cyclamen. Large vegetable garden on raised beds. Lovely views over open countryside. Newcastle Mausoleum (adjacent) open. Local guides present history. Some slopes and gravel paths - seats in garden.

3 NEW BEESTHORPE HALL FARM

Caunton, Newark, NG23 6AT. Pamela & Peter Littlewood. *On the Maplebeck rd. ½ way between Caunton and Maplebeck. From A616 at Caunton take the Maplebeck/ Eakring rd. 1m farm on R. 2 fields off the rd.* **Sun 10 June (1-5). Adm £3.50, chd free. Home-made teas.**

Country garden with extensive views, large gravel garden, meadow and wildlife pond. Beautifully planted.

4 BOLHAM MANOR

Bolham Way, Bolham, Retford, DN22 9JG. Pam & Butch Barnsdale. *1m from Retford. A620 Gainsborough Rd from Retford, turn L onto Tiln Lane, signed 'A620 avoiding low bridge'. At sharp R bend take rd ahead to Tiln then L Bolham Way.* **Sun 24 June (12-4). Adm £3.50, chd free. Home-made teas.**

This is a much loved 3 acre garden with mature and interesting specimen trees and wildflower borders, vibrant herbaceous borders and varied and interesting terraced planting leading down to the ponds and cave. Wander across the croquet lawn to the old orchard with its magnificent climbing roses and relax with homemade teas. Partial wheelchair access to parts of garden.

5 BROADLEA

North Green, East Drayton, Retford, DN22 0LF. David & Jean Stone, 01777248315, Davidr.stone@btinternet.com. *Broadlea. From A1 take A57 E towards Lincoln. East Drayton is signed L off A57, approx 2m from A1. North Green runs N from church. Garden last gate on R.* **Sun 8 Apr (2-5). Adm £3, chd free. Home-made teas. Tea and cakes £1.50. Visits also by arrangement in Apr no limit on group size.**

Our aim in this 1 acre garden is to have interest throughout the yr and attract wildlife. There is plenty to see, woodland walk, many perennials, shrubs and spring bulbs. Large pond is a haven for wildlife and a kitchen garden together with wild bank and dyke add attraction to the formal vistas. Partial wheelchair access.

6 5 BURTON LANE

Whatton in the Vale, NG13 9EQ. Ms Faulconbridge, 01949 850942, jpfaulconbridge@hotmail.co.uk, www.ayearinthegardenblog.wordpress.com. *3m E of Bingham. Follow signs to Whatton from A52 between Bingham & Elton. Garden nr Church in old part of village. Follow yellow NGS signs.* **Sun 3 June (1.30-5). Adm £3.50, chd free. Mon 27 Aug (1.30-5). Combined adm with Cedarwood £5, chd free. Home-made teas. For combined opening with Cedarwood refreshments at 5 Burton Lane. Visits also by arrangement May to Sept refreshments at additional cost by arrangement.**

Modern cottage garden which is productive and highly decorative. We garden organically and for wildlife. The garden is full of colour and scent from spring to autumn. Several distinct areas, incl fruit and vegetables. Large beds are filled with over 500 varieties of plants with paths through so you can wander and get close. Also features seating, gravel garden, pond, shade planting and sedum roof. Historic church, attractive village with walks. Garden News 'Garden of the Week', Garden Answers feature, Nottingham Evening Post, Newark advertiser.

7 CAPABILITY BARN

Gonalston Lane, Hoveringham, NG14 7JH. Malcolm & Wendy Fisher, 01159 664322, wendy.fisher111@btinternet.com, www.capabilitybarn.com *8m NE of Nottingham. A612 from Nottingham through Lowdham. Take 1st R into Gonalston Lane. 1m on L.* **Sun 22 Apr, Sun 20 May (12-4.30). Adm £3.50, chd free. Home-made teas. Visits also by arrangement Apr to June adm £6 incl refreshments Min 15 visitors.**

Later dates this year for new selection of plants in imaginatively planted, large country garden. Tulips mingle with daffs/wisteria adorns barn front - erythroniums/primulas/ pulmonaria in long borders together with Rhodo/azaleas/apple blossom star in May. Herbaceous lupins/ delphs/more plus veg/fruit and newly re-planted front complete the picture. Come enjoy! Extensive collection of dahlias and flowering begonias.

8 CEDARWOOD

Burton Lane, Whatton in the Vale, NG13 9EQ. Louise Bateman. *3m E of Bingham. Cedar-clad bungalow situated in the old part of Whatton in the Vale just around the corner from local church.* **Mon 27 Aug (1.30-5). Combined adm with 5 Burton Lane £5, chd free. Home-made teas at 5 Burton Lane opposite.**

Cedarwood is a ⅓ acre plantswoman's garden developed over the last 13yrs. It is planted for yr-round colour and plants are chosen for their attractiveness to wildlife as well as people. It incl mixed borders, formal pond, bog garden, raised alpine bed and cedar alpine greenhouse. The rose garden has been replaced by a formal area focusing on foliage. Featured in Garden Answers magazine. Most of the garden has gravel paths and some small steps. Plenty of seating available to rest for the less able.

9 THE CHIMES

37 Glenorchy Crescent, Heronridge, NG5 9LG. Stan & Ellen Maddock. *4m N of Nottingham. A611 towards Hucknall onto Bulwell Common. Turn R at Tesco Top Valley up to island. Turn L 100 yds. 1st L then 2nd L onto Glenorchy Crescent to bottom.* **Sun 27 May, Sun 10 June (12-5). Adm £3, chd free.**

We would like to invite you to pass through our archway and into our own little oasis on the edge of a busy city. Come and share our well-stocked although small garden, full of roses, peonies, lilies and much more. Visit us and be surprised. We look forward to seeing you.

10 CHURCH FARM

Church Lane, West Drayton, Retford, DN22 8EB. Robert & Isobel Adam, 01777838250, robertadam139@btinternet.com. *A1 exit Markham Moor. A638 Retford 500 yrds signed West Drayton. 1m Church Lane, 1st R past church. Ample parking in farm yard.* **Sun 25 Feb (12-4). Adm £3, chd free. Light refreshments in church next door. Visits also by arrangement in Feb.**

The garden is essentially a spring garden and a little on the wild side. We have a small woodland area which is carpeted with many snowdrops, aconites and cyclamen which have seeded into the adjoining churchyard, with approx 180 named snowdrops growing in island beds. Limited amount of snowdrops and miniature iris for sale. Featured on BBC radio Nottingham, and in local papers and magazines.

11 CHURCH HOUSE

Hoveringham, NG14 7JH. Alex & Sue Allan. *6m NE of Nottingham. Next to church hall in village.* **Sun 20 May (1-5). Adm £3.50, chd free.**

Small, walled, cottage-style garden with herbaceous borders, auricula theatre, Japanese area and vegetable plot. This charming garden offers a delightful setting in which to relax and is packed with ideas for those gardeners with limited space.

12 ◆ CLUMBER PARK WALLED KITCHEN GARDEN

Clumber Park, Worksop, S80 3AZ. National Trust, 01909 476592, clumberpark@nationaltrust.org.uk, www.nationaltrust.org.uk/clumber-park. *4m S of Worksop. From main car park or main entrance follow directions to Walled Kitchen Garden.* **For NGS: Sat 14 July (10-5). Adm £4. For other opening times and information, please phone, email or visit garden website.**

Beautiful 4 acre walled kitchen garden, growing unusual and old varieties of vegetables and fruits. Herbs and flower beds, incl the magnificent 400ft double herbaceous borders. 450ft glasshouse with grapevines. Museum of gardening tools. Soft fruit garden, rose garden. Garden has been awarded National Collection status for its collection of culinary rhubarbs (over 130 varieties) and regional (Nottinghamshire, Derbyshire, Lincolnshire, Leicestershire, Yorkshire) apples (72 varieties). Refreshments at Garden Tea House next to Walled Kitchen Garden or at Café in the Park. Gravel paths and slopes.

NPC

13 CORNERSTONES

15 Lamcote Gardens, Radcliffe-on-Trent, Nottingham, NG12 2BS. Judith & Jeff Coombes, 0115 8458055, judithcoombes@gmail.com, www.cornerstonesgarden.co.uk. *4m E of Nottingham. From A52 take Radcliffe exit at RSPCA junction, then 2nd L just before hairpin bend.* **Sun 22 July (1.30-5). Adm £3.50, chd free. Home-made teas. Visits also by arrangement July & Aug for groups 15+ mid July to mid August. Adm £7 incl introduction and refreshments.**

Plant lovers' garden, approaching ½ acre. Flowing colour themed and specie borders, with rare, exotic and unusual plants, provide a wealth of colour and interest, whilst the unique fruit and vegetable garden generates an abundance of produce. Bananas, palms, fernery, fish pond, bog garden, lovely summerhouse area and greenhouse. Enjoy tea and delicious home-made cake in a beautiful setting. To be featured in Garden News as Garden of the Month in summer 2018. Wheelchair access but some bark paths and unfenced ponds.

GROUP OPENING

14 CROPWELL BUTLER GARDENS

Cropwell Butler, NG12 3AA. *10m E of Nottingham. From Nottingham, keep on A52 E (towards Grantham) until R turn to village near Radcliffe on Trent. From A52/A46 r'about, follow signs to village. Maps with garden locations available in each garden.* **Sun 8 July (1-5). Combined adm £5, chd free. Home-made teas in Cropwell Butler Village Hall.**

REDLAND HOUSE
Mrs Shelagh Barnes.

VILLAGE HOUSE
Neil & Paddy Gledson.

Redland House garden has been nurtured under a flower arranger's eye and incl colourful borders containing a variety of shrubs, trees and perennials, a woodland walk, new fernery and iris bed. Some gravel paths. Village House is a ¼ acre 'English' garden with colour-themed borders full of shrubs and herbaceous perennials supplemented with annuals in two areas. Terrace with vine-clad pergola and a small, productive vegetable area. Narrow access and steps. Wheelchair access at Redland House only.

Rose Cottage

15 DUMBLESIDE

17 Bridle Road, Burton Joyce, NG14 5FT. Mr P Bates, 01159 313725, cpbates2015@gmail.com. *5m NE of Nottingham. The Bridle Road is an unsurfaced, single track, R hand fork off Lambley Lane. Leave passengers at our gate and park 50 yards beyond where the rd branches 3 ways.* **Visits by arrangement Feb to Oct talk and guided tours. Refreshments on request when booking (extra cost). Adm £4, chd free. Home-made teas.**

Gorgeous 2 acres of varied habitat. Stream with primulas, iris, tree ferns and the like; 50yds of mixed herbaceous borders; gardening in grass with wild flowers, Spring and Autumn bulbs; woodland walks of massed cyclamen, snowdrops & anemones and a nice sunny raised gravel bed for alpines and small plants. Plant lovers' delight! Steep slopes towards stream therefore partial access only for wheelchairs.

GROUP OPENING

16 EAST MARKHAM GARDENS

Church Street, East Markham, Newark, NG22 0SA. Anne Beeby, anne.beeby@sky.com. *East Markham Newark NG22 0SA. 7m S of Retford. Take A1 Markham Moor r'about exit for A57 Lincoln. Turn at East Markham junction & follow signs for the church.* **Sun 1 July (1-5). Combined adm £5, chd free. Home-made teas in the grounds of The Manor.**

THE MANOR
Ms Christine Aldred, 01777 872719, clownsca@yahoo.co.uk. **Visits also by arrangement.**

NORWOOD COTTAGE
Anne Beeby.

OAK BARN EXOTIC GARDEN
Simon Bennett & Laura Holmes. (See separate entry)

NEW **SPRINGFIELD HOUSE**
Graham & Sue White.

All gardens are situated in the close proximity of the beautiful St John the Baptist church in the lovely village of East Markham. Each garden is very different and will give visitors the opportunity to experience and appreciate their individuality- Norwood Cottage - a typical cottage garden incorporating roses, perennials, interesting foliage plants and many interesting nooks any crannies. The Manor - an extensive coloured theme garden on various levels, incl a sunken garden and pond. Adjacent to the church and beautiful views of the surrounding countryside. Oak Barn - a densely planted exotic oasis incorporating lush green unusual foliage plants tree ferns and many more. This unusual garden explodes into life in the summer. Springfield House -the garden is a spring/summer garden designed to complement the property. Recently added paved patio area, Rose garden and arches leading into the garden incorporating herbaceous borders. Wheelchair access to some parts of the gardens only.

Oak Barn Exotic Garden, East Markham Gardens

17 ELLICAR GARDENS

Carr Road, Gringley-on-the-Hill, Doncaster, DN10 4SN. Will & Sarah Murch, 01777 817218, sarah@ellicargardens.co.uk, www.ellicargardens.co.uk. *Gringley-on-the-Hill. Approx 2m outside village of Gringley on the Hill. Turn onto Leys Lane, drive out of village, over canal, Ellicar Gardens on L on Carr Rd, opp cream house.* **Sun 25 Feb (12-4). Combined adm with Holmes Villa £4.50, chd free. Home-made teas in Walkeringham Village Hall. Visits also by arrangement Feb to Oct for groups 10+ during term times.**

This vibrant, naturalistic family garden is a haven for garden lovers, wildlife enthusiasts and children. Sweeping borders with new perennials and grasses grow alongside wild flowers and specimen trees. Beautiful in winter and vibrant in summer, highlights incl a winter garden, hellebores, gravel garden, old roses, orchard and natural pool. Children love exploring the school garden and willow maze. New perennials and grasses, late season borders and colour, old roses, over 250 young specimen trees, wildlife garden, winter garden, natural pool, rare breed pets. Featured in The English Garden, Garden News, Daily Mail, The Telegraph, Gardenista Sourcebook, Country Homes and Interiors, BBC TV Gardener's World,. Some uneven surfaces, grass and gravel paths.

18 THE ELMS

Main Street, North Leverton, DN22 0AR. Tim & Tracy Ward, 01427 881164, tracyrward@gmail.com. *5m E of Retford, 6m SW of Gainsborough. From Retford take rd to Leverton for 5m, into North Leverton with Habblesthorpe.* **Sun 29 July (1-5). Adm £3, chd free. Home-made teas. Also open Lodge Mount. Visits also by arrangement July to Sept.**

This garden is very different, creating an extension to the living space. Inspiration comes from Mediterranean countries, giving a holiday feel. Palms, bamboos and bananas, along with other exotics, create drama and yet make a statement true to many gardens, that of peace and calm. North Leverton Windmill may be open for visitors. Garden fully viewable, limited wheelchair access onto decked and tiled areas.

19 ◆ FELLEY PRIORY

Underwood, NG16 5FJ. Ms Michelle Upchurch for the Brudenell Family, 01773 810230, michelle@felleypriory.co.uk, www.felleypriory.co.uk. *8m SW of Mansfield. Off A608 ½m W M1 J27.* **For NGS: Sun 15 Apr (10-4). Adm £6, chd free. Light refreshments. For other opening times and information, please phone, email or visit garden website.**

Garden for all seasons with yew hedges and topiary, snowdrops, hellebores, herbaceous borders and rose garden. There are pergolas, a white garden, small arboretum and borders filled with unusual trees, shrubs, plants and bulbs. The grass edged pond is planted with primulas, bamboo, iris, roses and eucomis. Bluebell woodland walk. Orchard with extremely rare daffodils.

20 FLORAL MEDIA

Norwell Road, Caunton, Newark, NG23 6AQ. Mr & Mrs Steve Routledge, 01636 636283, info@floralmedia.co.uk, www.floralmedia.co.uk. *Take Norwell Rd from Caunton. Approx ½m from Caunton on L.* **Sun 20 May (10-4). Adm £3.50, chd free. Home-made teas.**

A beautifully well maintained country garden. Beds overflowing with a variety of roses, shrubs and flowers. A gravel/oriental garden, wildlife pond, vegetable, herb and fruit garden. Through the archway entrance, you will find a relaxing purple/white planting scheme. This garden has many different rooms for you to indulge in! New for 2018, wild flower meadow leading to a new seating area. A local folk group called The Jolly Beggars will be playing music throughout the afternoon. Full wheelchair access incl disabled WC.

21 THE GLADE

2a Woodthorpe Avenue, Woodthorpe, Nottingham, NG5 4FD. Tony Hoffman. *3m N of Nottingham. A60 Mansfield Rd from Nottingham. After Sherwood shops turn R at T-lights by Woodthorpe Park into Woodthorpe Drive. 2nd L into Woodthorpe Av.* **Sun 8 July (1-5). Combined adm with 6 Weston Close £5, chd free.**

Exquisite medium sized garden developed over 8yrs on the site of a former Great Western Railway track with very free draining soil which allows Mediterranean plants to thrive. Feature plants incl tree ferns, 30ft high bamboos, fan palms, acers and other shrubs rarely seen. The railway arch, enclosed in trellis work, provides shade for a variety of ferns and hostas.

GROUP OPENING

22 HALAM GARDENS AND WILDFLOWER MEADOW

Nr Southwell, NG22 8AX. *Village gardens within walking distance of one another. Hill's Farm wildflower meadow is a short drive of ½m towards Edingley village, turn R at brow of hill as signed.* **Sat 16 June (1-5). Combined adm £5.50, chd free. Home-made teas at The Old Vicarage, Halam.**

HILL FARM HOUSE
Victoria Starkey.

HILL'S FARM
John & Margaret Hill.

THE OLD VICARAGE
Mrs Beverley Perks.
(See separate entry)

Unusual mix of a very popular beautiful, well-known, organic, rural plant lovers' garden with bounteous roses, clematis, campanula and lots else with sweeping lawns, lots of pond life; a small wrap-around cottage garden and a 6 acre wildflower meadow - part of an organic farm - visitors can be assured of an inspiring discussion with the farmer; passionate about the benefits of this method of farming for our environment. 12th Century Church open - surrounded by freely planted, attractive churchyard - all welcome to enjoy this peaceful haven in English rural village setting. Newark and Southwell Advertisers Garden News.

23 5A HIGH STREET

Sutton-on-Trent, Newark, NG23 6QA. Kathryn & Ian Saunders. *6m N of Newark. Leave A1 at Sutton on Trent , follow Sutton signs. L at Xrds. 1st R turn (approx 1m) onto Main Street. 2nd L onto High Street. Garden 50 yds on R. Park on road or in Old England hotel car park.* **Sun 29 July (12-5). Combined adm with Norwood £4, chd free. Light refreshments.**

This hidden plot started as a field 30 years ago. Trees form a frame for this plantsman's garden. Ponds run through the area which ranges from tropical to naturalistic. 600 named plants incl over 100 types of fern in the woodland areas. Herbaceous borders add a riot of colour. Ornamental grass borders and succulents add further interest. All shown off to great effect by well manicured lawns.

24 ◆ HODSOCK PRIORY GARDENS

Blyth, Worksop, S81 0TY. Sir Andrew & Lady Buchanan, 01909 591204, info@snowdrops.co.uk, www.snowdrops.co.uk. *North Nottinghamshire. 4m N of Worksop off B6045. M1 J30 or 31 & close to A1(M). Blyth-Worksop rd approx 2m from A1M. Well signed locally. Ample free parking.* **For NGS: Sun 4 Mar (10-4). Adm £5, chd £1. Light refreshments.** For other opening times and information, please phone, email or visit garden website.

Enjoy a leisurely walk through a surprisingly fragrant winter garden and woodland before having coffee, lunch or tea in our cafes. Snowdrops, aconites, irises, cornus, honeysuckles and hellebores also on display. Free daily history talk by the campfire. Bacon sandwiches cooked in the wood. Wrap up warm and wear outdoor clothes and boots. Hodsock Snowdrops open daily from Sat 10th Feb to Sun 4th March (10-4). Whispering Woodfolk Theatre w/e 16-18 Feb 2018. Shortbreaks available in our B&B. Featured in English Garden, RHS Garden Magazine and Country Life. Some paths difficult for wheelchairs when wet.

Donations from the National Garden Scheme enable Perennial to care for horticulturalists

25 HOLMES VILLA

Holmes Lane, Walkeringham, Gainsborough, DN10 4JP. Peter & Sheila Clark. *4m NW of Gainsborough. A620 from Retford or A631 from Bawtry/Gainsborough & A161 to Walkeringham then towards Misterton. Follow NGS signs for 1m. Plenty of parking. Reserved disabled parking.* **Sun 25 Feb (12-4). Combined adm with Ellicar Gardens £4.50, chd free. Mon 28 May (1-5). Adm £2.50, chd free. Home-made teas in Walkeringham Village Hall next to the Fox & Hounds pub on the main A161 Walkeringham.**

1¾ acre plantsman's garden offering yr-round interest and inspiration starting with carpets of snowdrops, mini daffodils, hellebores and spring bulbs. Unusual collection of plants and shrubs for winter. Come and be surprised at the different fragrant and interesting plants in early spring. Places to sit and ponder, gazebos, arbours, wildlife pond, hosta garden, old tools on display and scarecrows. A flower arranger's artistic garden.

26 HOME FARM HOUSE, 17 MAIN STREET

Keyworth, Nottingham, NG12 5AA. Graham & Pippa Tinsley, 01159 377122, Graham_Tinsley@yahoo.co.uk, www.homefarmgarden.wordpress.com. *7m S of Nottingham. Follow signs for Keyworth from A60 or A606 & head for church. Garden about 50yds down Main St. Parking on the street or at village hall or Bunny Lane car parks.* **Sun 22 July (1-5). Combined adm with Rose Cottage £4, chd free. Visits also by arrangement June to Aug.**

A large garden hidden behind old farmhouse in the village centre with views over open fields. Many trees incl cedars, limes, oaks and chestnuts which, with high beech and yew hedges, create hidden places to be explored. Old orchard, ponds, turf mound, rose garden, winter garden and old garden with herbaceous borders. Pergolas with wisteria, ornamental vine and roses. Interesting and unusual perennials for sale by Piecemeal Plants (www.piecemealplants.co.uk). Access via gravel yard. Some steps and slopes.

27 HOPBINE FARMHOUSE, OSSINGTON

Hopbine Farmhouse, Main Street, Ossington, NG23 6LJ. Mr & Mrs Geldart. *From A1 N take exit marked Carlton, Sutton-on-Trent, Weston etc. At T-Junction turn L to Kneesall. Drive 2m to Ossington. In village turn R to Moorhouse & park in field.* **Sun 17 June (2-5). Combined adm with Ossington House £4, chd free. Home-made teas at The Hut, Ossington.**

A small but full garden with interesting and unusual plants. The large border has collections of salvia, clematis and cranesbills. A diamond bed planted in 2016 with unusual colour combinations has excelled itself with vigorous growth. The small and intimate walled garden which faces North has a white wall of Clematis Summer Snow, Ghislaine de Feligonde and Hydrangea Petiolaris. Some narrow paths.

28 6 HOPE STREET

Beeston, Nottingham, NG9 1DR. Elaine Liquorish. *From M1 J25, A52 for Nottm. After 2 r'abouts, turn R for Beeston at The Nurseryman (B6006). Beyond hill, turn R into Bramcote Dr. Third turn on L into Bramcote Rd, then immediately R into Hope St.* **Sun 20 May (1.30-5.30). Adm £3, chd free. Home-made teas.**

A small garden packed with a wide variety of plants providing flower and foliage colour year round. Collections of alpines, bulbs, mini, small and medium size hostas, ferns, grasses, carnivorous plants, succulents, perennials, shrubs and trees. A pond and a greenhouse with subtropical plants. Troughs and pots. Home made crafts. There is a small step down into the front part of the garden and a step up into the greenhouse.

29 IVY BANK COTTAGE

The Green, South Clifton, Newark, NG23 7AG. David & Ruth Hollands. *12m N of Newark. From S, exit A46 N of Newark onto A1133 towards Gainsborough. From N, exit A57 at Newton-on-Trent onto A1133 towards Newark.* **Sun 20 May (1-5). Adm £3, chd free. Home-made teas.**

A traditional cottage garden, with herbaceous borders, fruit trees incl a Nottinghamshire Medlar, vegetable plots, and many surprises, incl a stumpery, a troughery, dinosaur footprints and even fairies! Many original features: pigsties, double privy and a wash house. Children can search for animal models and explore inside the shepherd's van. Seats around and a covered refreshment area.

GROUP OPENING

30 KINOULTON GARDENS

Nottingham, NG12 3EL. s.ahammond@btinternet.com. *8m SE of West Bridgford. Off A46 at junction with A606. Follow rd signs into village. Bishops Cottage is just a few hundred yards after the Village Hall on the right and Lindy Edge is on the left after the canal and Church.* **Sun 24 June (1-5). Combined adm £5, chd free. Home-made teas in Kinoulton Village Hall.**

BISHOPS COTTAGE
Ann Hammond.

LINDY EDGE
Mrs Jan Osbond.

Bishops Cottage is a large, mature, cottage garden with mixed herbaceous borders with an emphasis on scent and colour coordination where possible. A wildlife pond and open views over the countryside. Plants for sale. Lindy Edge is an artisan garden created through imaginative planting and design with twists and turns providing surprises around every corner. Fruit and vegetables in raised beds. Plants and original art for sale. Bishops Cottage has gravel drive and Lindy Edge has some steps.

31 LODGE MOUNT

Town Street, South Leverton, Retford, DN22 0BT. Mr A Wootton-Jones, 07427 400848, a.wj@live.co.uk. *4m E of Retford. Opp Miles Garage on Town Street.* **Sun 29 July (1-5). Adm £3, chd free. Home-made teas. Also open The Elms. Visits also by arrangement June & July.**

Originally a field, much of the ½ acre garden, although planned on paper for yrs, was landscaped within a few months during 2012 in order to fulfill an ambition following Helen Wootton-Jones' terminal diagnosis. Following organic principles, an orchard and large vegetable and fruit plots are complemented by an area of unusual perennial edibles, and helpful plants, with a view to self sufficiency. Clematis, roses, and climbers provide fragrance and a feeling of enclosure/peacefulness. Helen's aunt also had cancer and the garden was specifically designed to open for the NGS to raise money for cancer charities.

32 38 MAIN STREET

Woodborough, Nottingham, NG14 6EA. Martin Taylor & Deborah Bliss. *Turn off Mapperley Plains Rd at sign for Woodborough. Alternatively, follow signs to Woodborough off A6097 (Epperstone bypass). Property is between Park Av & Bank Hill.* **Sun 13 May (1-5). Adm £3.50, chd free. Home-made teas.**

Varied ⅓ acre. Bamboo fenced Asian species area with traditional outdoor wood fired Ofuro bath, herbaceous border, raised rhododendron bed, vegetables, greenhouse, pond area and art studio and terrace.

33 NATIONAL HOLOCAUST CENTRE AND MUSEUM

Acre Edge Road, Laxton, Newark, NG22 0PA. Janet Mills, www.holocaust.org.uk. *Take A614 from Nottingham. At Ollerton r'about take 4th exit A6075 signed Tuxford. On leaving Boughton turn sharp R signed Laxton. Disabled parking & WC.* **Sun 1, Sun 8, Sun 15, Sun 22, Sun 29 July (10-4.30). Adm £3, chd free. Light refreshments in the museum cafe.**

The Memorial Garden is set in an acre of beautifully landscaped countryside and provides an important counterpoint to the museum. Over 1200 scented white roses have been planted, many of them dedicated by Holocaust survivors and their families. Each rose has an inscribed plaque helping visitors to understand that the victims are not just a catalogue of statistics but human beings, with names. Visitors are welcome to visit the Museum and exhibitions (separate charge). Refreshments incl sandwiches, home-made soup and cakes.

34 NORMANTON HALL

South Street, Normanton-on-Trent, NG23 6RQ. His Honour John & Mrs Machin, 01636822780. *3m SE of Tuxford. Leave A1 at Sutton Carlton/Normanton-on-Trent junction. Turn L onto B1164 in Carlton. In Sutton-on-Trent turn R at Normanton sign. Go through Grassthorpe, turn L at Normanton sign.* **Sun 15 Apr (2-6). Adm £3, chd free. Home-made teas. Visits also by arrangement Apr & May.**

3 acres with mature oak, lime beech and yew and recently planted trees. Vegetable area. New plantings of bulbs, rhododendrons and a camellia walk. Arboretum planted with unusual, mainly hardwood trees which are between three and twelve years old. Also specimen oaks and beech. Fine established trees and recently planted arboretum of specimen oaks and beech. All surfaces level from car park.

GROUP OPENING

35 NORWELL GARDENS

Newark, NG23 6JX. *6m N of Newark. Halfway between Newark & Southwell. Off A1 at Cromwell turning, take Norwell Rd at bus shelter. Or off A616 take Caunton turn.* **Sun 24 June (1-5). Evening opening Wed 27 June (6.30-9). Combined adm £4.50, chd free. Home-made teas in Village Hall (24 June) and Norwell Nurseries (27 June).**

THE BAKEHOUSE
Peter & Linda Jones.

FAUNA FOLLIES
Mr Roy Pilgrim.

NORTHFIELD FARM
Mr & Mrs D Adamson.

NORWELL ALLOTMENT / PARISH GARDENS
Norwell Parish Council.

♦ NORWELL NURSERIES
Andrew & Helen Ward.
(See separate entry)

THE OLD MILL HOUSE, NORWELL
Mr & Mrs M Burgess.

SOUTHVIEW COTTAGE
Margaret & Les Corbett.

NEW **WILLOUGHBY HOUSE**
Mrs Suzannah Edward-Jones.

This is the 21st yr that Norwell has opened a range of different, very appealing gardens all making superb use of the beautiful backdrop of a quintessentially English countryside village. It incl a garden and nursery of national renown and the rare opportunity to walk around vibrant allotments with a wealth of gardeners from seasoned competition growers to plots that are substitute house gardens, bursting with both flower colour and vegetables in great variety. To top it all there are a plethora of breathtaking village gardens showing the diversity that is achieved under the umbrella of a cottage garden description! The beautiful medieval church and its peaceful churchyard with grass labyrinth will be open for quiet contemplation.

36 ♦ NORWELL NURSERIES

Woodhouse Road, Norwell, NG23 6JX. Andrew & Helen Ward, 01636 636337, wardha@aol.com, www.norwellnurseries.co.uk. *6m N of Newark halfway between Newark & Southwell. Off A1 at Cromwell turning, take rd to Norwell at bus stop. Or from A616 take Caunton turn.* **For NGS: Sun 13 May, Sun 14, Sun 21 Oct (2-5). Adm £2.50, chd free. Home-made teas. Opening with Norwell Gardens on Sun 24, Wed 27 June. For other opening times and information, please phone, email or visit garden website.**

Jewel box of over 2,500 different, beautiful and unusual plants sumptuously set out in a one acre plantsman's garden incl shady garden with orchids, woodland gems, cottage garden borders, alpine and scree areas. Pond with opulently planted margins. Extensive herbaceous borders and effervescent colour themed beds. Innovative Grassoretum (like an arboretum but for grasses). New borders every year. Nationally renowned nursery open with over 1,000 different rare plants for sale. Autumn opening features UK's largest collection of hardy chrysanthemums for sale and the National Collection of Hardy Chrysanthemums. New borders incl the National Collection Of Astrantias. Grass paths, no wheelchair access to woodland paths.

NPC

37 NEW NORWOOD

Carlton Lane, Sutton-On-Trent, Newark, NG23 6PH. Linda Cobb & Danny Mellor, 07979550654, cobb.linda999@gmail.com. *Enter the village of Carlton on Trent via the A1 make your way to Old North Rd, turn onto main St and you will find Carlton Lane on the sharp bend.* **Sun 29 July (12-5). Combined adm with 5a High Street £4, chd free. Visits also by arrangement Oct & Nov group between 2 and 10 people.**

The quirky oriental themed garden with its tea room has been an ongoing project for more than 35 yrs. We welcome you to wander down the gravel paths to discover a variety of ferns and palms alongside native and none native plants. Take a peep in the cave and look in the nooks and crannies of the stone built walls where you will find a few surprises and we are sure to find something of interest.

38 NEW NOTTINGHAMSHIRE HOSPICE

384 Woodborough Road, Nottingham, NG3 4JF. Nottinghamshire Hospice, http://www.nottshospice.org. *Located on the B684, Woodborough Rd, served by the bus route number 45, Sky Blue Line, from the city centre towards Mapperley. No public parking allowed onsite, plenty of on-street parking.* **Sun 5 Aug (1-4). Adm £3, chd free. Light refreshments.**

Large enclosed area, with various protected trees, shrubs, planting, rockeries and lawn. Within our garden there is a beautiful pond and water feature. There are raised vegetable beds, and a terraced area. Some sloping areas, with steps. The garden is designed to be a relaxing space and give therapeutic benefit to hospice patients. You are very welcome to bring your own picnic to enjoy.

39 OAK BARN EXOTIC GARDEN

Oak Barn Church Street, East Markham, Newark, NG22 0SA. Simon Bennett & Laura Holmes, www.facebook.com/OakBarn1. *From A1 Markham Moor junction take A57 to Lincoln. Turn R at Xrds into E Markham. L onto High St & R onto Plantation Rd. Enter farm gates at T-Junction, garden located on L.* **Evening opening Sat 4 Aug (6-9). Light refreshments. Sun 7 Oct (12-4). Home-made teas.**

Adm £3, chd free. Opening with East Markham Gardens on Sun 1 July.
On entering the Oak Lych style gate you will be met with the unexpected dense canopy of greenery and tropical foliage. The hidden paths lead to the newly built Jungle Hut and large bespoke greenhouse which houses our growing collection of tender plants which are bedded out on mass between the bright flowers and colourful foliage of the more hardy specimens. Private visits and plant sales by arrangement.

40 THE OLD HALL

Church Lane, Lowdham, Nottingham, NG14 7BQ. Mr & Dr Stewart. *On the R of Church Lane, which is a turning off Ton Lane (same side of the bypass in Lowdham as World's End Pub). The lane is found by following the sign to St Mary's Church.* **Mon 28 May (1-5). Adm £4, chd free. Home-made teas.**
A gorgeous lime tree avenue leads to The Old Hall which is centrally located in this large garden comprises a mound from the original Ludham Castle left of the drive surrounded on 3 sides by a moat. Daffodils adorn the drive in Spring. The Hall is Wisteria clad as well as a pergola of late white Wisteria. Vegetable garden with raised beds and formal yew hedges divide our elegant garden.

41 THE OLD VICARAGE

Halam Hill, Halam, NG22 8AX. Mrs Beverley Perks, 01636 812181, perks.family@talk21.com. *1m W of Southwell. Please park diagonally into beech hedge on verge with speed interactive sign or in village - a busy road so no parking on roadside.* **Sun 6 May (1-5); Sat 30 June (1-4.30); Sun 12 Aug (1-5). Adm £4, chd free. Home-made teas. Opening with Halam Gardens and Wildflower Meadow on Sat 16 June. Visits also by arrangement Apr to Aug for groups 15+, guided tour/history of gdn incl.**

Riseholme, 125 Shelfrod Road

Celebrating 21 yrs since major planting transformation. Single handed labour of love has grown out of hillside pony paddocks into much admired landscape gardens. One-time playground for children, a source of shared pleasure from village openings incl 16 yrs for NGS (unfortunately this is likely to be our last). An artful eye for design/texture/colour and love of unusual plants. Using natural landscape to advantage entices exploration round all corners. Beautiful C12 Church open only short walk into the village or across field through attractively planted churchyard - rare C14 stained glass window. Featured in Newark/Southwell Advertiser Garden News. Gravel drive - undulating levels as on a hillside - plenty of cheerful help available.

42 OSSINGTON HOUSE

Moorhouse Road, Ossington, Newark, NG23 6LD. Georgina Denison. *10m N of Newark, 2m off A1. From A1 N take exit marked Carlton, Sutton-on-Trent, Weston etc. At T-junction turn L to Kneesall. Drive 2m to Ossington. In village turn R to Moorhouse & park in field next to Hopbine Farmhouse.* **Sun 17 June (2-5). Combined adm with Hopbine Farmhouse, Ossington £4, chd free. Home-made teas in The Hut, Ossington.**
Vicarage garden redesigned in 1960 and again in 2014. Chestnuts, lawns, formal beds, woodland walk, poolside planting. Orchard, kitchen garden. Terraces, yews, grasses. Ferns, herbaceous perennials, roses. Disabled parking available in drive to Ossington House.

43 PAPPLEWICK HALL

Blidworth Waye, Papplewick, Nottinghamshire, NG15 8FE. J R Godwin-Austen Esq, www.papplewickhall.co.uk. *7m N of Nottingham. 300 yards out N end of Papplewick village, on B683 (follow signs to Papplewick from A60 & B6011). Free parking at Hall.* **Sun 27 May (2-5). Adm £4, chd free. Donation to St James' Church.**
This historic, mature, 8 acre garden, mostly shaded woodland, abounds with rhododendrons, hostas, ferns, and spring bulbs. Suitable for wheelchair users, but sections of the paths are gravel.

44 PARK FARM

Crink Lane, Southwell, NG25 0TJ. Ian & Vanessa Johnston, 01636 812195, v.johnston100@gmail.com. *1m SE of Southwell. From Southwell town centre go down Church St, turn R on Fiskerton Rd & 200yds up hill turn R into Crink Lane. Park Farm is on 2nd bend.* **Visits by arrangement Apr to Aug guided tour additional 50p per person. Adm £3.50, chd free.**
3 acre garden remarkable for its extensive variety of trees, shrubs and perennials, many rare or unusual. Long colourful herbaceous borders, roses, woodland garden, alpine/scree garden and a large wildlife pond. Spectacular views of the Minster across a wildflower meadow and ha-ha. Photographs and descriptions can be accessed in the blog of 90 gardens in the NGS scheme www.thegardengateisopen.blog.

45 PATCHINGS ART CENTRE

Oxton Road, Calverton, Nottingham, NG14 6NU. Chas & Pat Wood, www.patchingsartcentre.co.uk. *N of Nottingham city take A614 towards Ollerton. Turn R on to B6386 towards Calverton and Oxton. Patchings is on L before turning to Calverton. Brown tourist directional signs.* **Sun 27 May (10.30-3.30). Adm £3, chd free. Light refreshments at Patchings Cafe.**

Patchings Art Centre is 30 years old. In celebration additional areas and walks have been created within the 50 acres of wild flower, woodland and meadow landscapes. The aim is to inspire and encourage artists to paint in the open, whilst providing enjoyment and tranquility for visitors. The day also incl a variety of free art and craft activities with links to the grounds and gardens. Four exhibition galleries, featuring paintings, photography, jewellery, ceramics and glass. Card gallery, gift shop and art materials. Studio artists in residence. Patchings Cafe. In the Pavilion - free 'have a go' opportunity, being creative with a variety of painting and craft materials. Grass paths, with some undulations and uphill sections accessible to wheelchairs with help. Please enquire for assistance.

46 PIECEMEAL

123 Main Street, Sutton Bonington, Loughborough, LE12 5PE. Mary Thomas, 01509 672056, nursery@piecemealplants.co.uk. *2m SE of Kegworth (M1 J24). 6m NW of Loughborough. Almost opp St Michael's Church & Sutton Bonington Hall at the north end of the village.* **Visits by arrangement June to Aug for groups min 4, max 10. For 10+ please contact to discuss. Tea and biscuits available. Adm £3, chd free.**

Pots of (mainly terracotta) pots! Up to 400 housing large collection of shrubs, climbers, perennials and even a few trees! Many unusual and not fully hardy. All in a tiny, sheltered walled garden. Focus is on distinctive form, foliage shape and colour combination - providing interest from spring to autumn. Collection of ferns around well. Conservatory housing tender plants. A jungle by midsummer! Featured in Garden News.

47 THE POPLARS

60 High Street, Sutton-on-Trent, Newark, NG23 6QA. Sue & Graham Goodwin-King, 01636 821240. *7m N of Newark. Leave A1 at Sutton/Carlton/ Normanton-on-Trent junction. In Carlton turn L onto B1164. Turn R into Hemplands Lane then R into High St. 1st house on R. Limited parking.* **Sun 26 Aug (1-5). Adm £3.50, chd free. Home-made teas. Visits also by arrangement June to Aug for groups 10+.**

Mature ½ acre garden on the site of a Victorian flower nursery, now a series of well planted areas each with its own character. Exotics courtyard with late summer colour. Iron balcony overlooking pond and oriental style gravel garden. 'Jungle' with thatched shack. Black and white garden. Woodland area. Walled potager. Fernery and hidden courtyard. Lawns, borders and charming sitting places. Some gravel paths and shallow steps, but most areas accessible.

48 RHUBARB FARM

Hardwick Street, Langwith, Mansfield, NG20 9DR. Community Interest Company, www.rhubarbfarm.co.uk. *On NW border of Nottinghamshire in village of Nether Langwith. From A632 in Langwith, by bridge (single file traffic) turn up steep Devonshire Drive. N.B. Turn off SatNav. Take 2nd L into Hardwick St. Rhubarb Farm at end. Parking to R of gates.* **Sun 15 July (10-4.30). Adm £2.50, chd free. Cream teas. Delicious cream teas and locally made cakes/biscuits. Visits also by arrangement Apr to Nov min group size 15.**

52 varieties of fruit and vegetables organically grown not only for sale but for therapeutic benefit. This 2 acre social enterprise provides training and volunteering opportunities to 50 ex offenders, drug and alcohol misusers, and people with mental and physical ill health and learning disability. Timed tours at 10.30am, 12.30pm and 2.30pm. 3x 65ft polytunnels, outdoor classroom, willow domes and willow arches, 100 hens, sensory garden, outdoor pizza ovens, comfrey bed and comfrey fertiliser factory, composting toilet. Chance to meet and chat with volunteers with a variety of needs, who come to gain skills, confidence and training. Local media - Mansfield 102.3FM, The Chad newspaper, and the Derbyshire Times. Main path down site suitable for wheelchairs but bumpy. Not all of site accessible, or easy for wheelchairs. Composting toilet wheelchair accessible.

49 RISEHOLME, 125 SHELFORD ROAD

Radcliffe on Trent, NG12 1AZ. John & Elaine Walker, 01159 119867. *4m E of Nottingham. From A52 follow signs to Radcliffe. In village centre take turning for Shelford (by Co-op). Approx ¾m on L.* **Sun 17 June (1.30-5). Adm £3, chd free. Home-made teas. Visits also by arrangement June to Sept for groups 10+. Adm £3.50, refreshments extra.**

Imaginative and inspirational is how the garden has been described by visitors. A huge variety of perennials, grasses, shrubs and trees combined with an eye for colour and design. Jungle area with exotic lush planting contrasts with tender perennials particularly salvias thriving in raised beds and in gravel garden with stream. Unique and interesting objects complement planting. Featured in Saturday Telegraph gardening section. Gravel drive and paths may prove difficult for wheelchairs.

50 ROSE COTTAGE

81 Nottingham Road, Keyworth, Nottingham, NG12 5GS. Richard & Julie Fowkes. *7m S of Nottingham.*

Follow signs for Keyworth from A606. Garden (white cottage) on R 100yds after Sainsburys. From A60, follow Keyworth signs & turn L at church, garden is 400yds on L. **Sun 22 July (1-5). Combined adm with Home Farm House, 17 Main Street £4, chd free. Home-made teas. Vegan and gluten free options available.**

Small cottage garden packed full with colourful, bee friendly, informal planting. A sedum roof, mosaics, water features, and a brick well all add unique interest. There is a decked seating area and summerhouse. A wildlife stream meanders down to a pond and bog garden. The woodland area leads to the fruit, veg and a herb spiral. Art studio will be open. Paintings and art cards designed by Julie will be on sale.

51 NEW SPRING BANK HOUSE

Kirkby Road, Sutton-in-Ashfield, NG17 1GH. Mr Peter Robinson. *From Mansfield take A38 to Sutton-in-Ashfield. Turn R on to Station Rd, turn L on to High Pavement and continue on to Kirkby Rd.* **Sun 17 June, Sun 2 Sept (12-5). Adm £3, chd free. Home-made teas.**

After purchasing the house in 2012 a mass clearance was needed before a new garden could take shape. Help was enlisted for the preparation and layout of new beds and in structural design. The garden evolved as work progressed without a firm plan, which enabled a personal vision to be realised in the planting. A collection of rare and unusual plants had been selected over the preceding two years. Coaches may be possible but will need to park elsewhere.

52 THRUMPTON HALL

Thrumpton, NG11 0AX. Miranda Seymour, www.thrumptonhall.com. *7m S of Nottingham. M1 J24 take A453 towards Nottingham. Turn L to Thrumpton village & cont to Thrumpton Hall.* **Sun 17 June (1.30-4.30). Adm £5, chd free. Home-made teas.**

2 acres incl lawns, rare trees, lakeside walks, flower borders, rose garden and box bordered sunken herb garden, all enclosed by C18 ha-ha and encircling a Jacobean house. Garden is surrounded by C18 landscaped park and is bordered by a river. Rare opportunity to visit Thrumpton Hall (separate ticket). Jacobean mansion, unique carved staircase, Great Saloon, State Bedroom, Priest's Hole.

53 UNIVERSITY PARK GARDENS

Nottingham, NG7 2RD. University of Nottingham, www.nottingham.ac.uk/estates/grounds/. *Approx 4m SW of Nottingham city centre & opp Queens Medical Centre. NGS visitors: Please purchase admission tickets in the Millennium Garden (in centre of campus), signed from N & W entrances to University Park & within internal road network.* **Sun 19 Aug (12-4). Adm £3.50, chd free. Light refreshments at Lakeside Arts Centre.**

University Park has many beautiful gardens incl the award winning Millennium garden with its dazzling flower garden, timed fountains and turf maze. Also the huge Lenton Firs rock garden, the dry garden and the Jekyll garden. During summer, the walled garden is alive with exotic plantings. In total, 300 acres of landscape and gardens. Picnic area, cafe, walking tours, accessible minibus to feature gardens within campus. Plants for sale in Millennium garden. Some gravel paths and steep slopes.

54 6 WESTON CLOSE

Woodthorpe, Nottingham, NG5 4FS. Diane & Steve Harrington, 01159 857506, mrsdiharrington@gmail.com. *3m N of Nottingham. A60 Mansfield Rd. Turn R at T-lights into Woodthorpe Drive. 2nd L Grange Road. R into The Crescent. R into Weston Close. Please park on The Crescent.* **Sun 24 June (1-5). Adm £3, chd free. Sun 8 July (1-5). Combined adm with The Glade £5, chd free. Home-made teas. incl gluten free. Visits also by arrangement June to Aug for groups 10+. Adm £5 incl tea & cake.**

Set on a substantial slope with 3 separate areas, dense planting creates a full, varied yet relaxed display incl many scented roses, clematis and a collection of over 60 named mature hostas in the impressive colourful rear garden. Large plant sale packed with good value home propagated plants. Occasional craft stalls. Featured in Garden News and Garden Answers.

55 WOODPECKERS

35 Lambley Lane, Burton Joyce, Nottingham, NG14 5BG. Lynn & Mark Carr. *6m N of Nottingham. In Burton Joyce, turn off A612 (Nottingham to Southwell rd) into Lambley Lane, turn L onto private drive to access gardens. Ample parking Lambley Lane.* **Sun 18 Feb, Sun 4 Mar (10.30-3); Sun 13 May (11.30-5). Adm £4, chd free. Home-made teas. Local Brownies providing cakes and refreshments.**

4 acres of mature woodland and formal gardens with spectacular views over Trent Valley. Carpets of snowdrops at Feb/March opening. 500 rhododendrons/azaleas in May. Scented rose tunnel/wisteria arbour. Balustrade terrace for teas. Glade with 200yr old cedars overlooking ponds, waterfalls and croquet lawn. Bog garden and sunken area below ha-ha, then onwards to ancient well. Gravel and grass paths, steep slopes but no access for wheelchair/disabled as snowdrops down steep slopes - some visible from terrace.

The National Garden Scheme is the largest single funder of the Queen's Nursing Institute

OXFORDSHIRE

In Oxfordshire we tend to think of ourselves as one of the most landlocked counties, right in the centre of England and furthest from the sea.

We are surrounded by Warwickshire, Northamptonshire, Buckinghamshire, Berkshire, Wiltshire and Gloucestershire, and, like these counties, we benefit from that perfect British climate which helps us create some of the most beautiful and famous gardens in the world.

Many gardens open in Oxfordshire for the National Garden Scheme between spring and late-autumn. Amongst these are the perfectly groomed college gardens of Oxford University, and the grounds of stately homes and palaces designed by a variety of the famous garden designers such as William Kent, Capability Brown, Rosemary Verey, Tom Stuart-Smith and the Bannermans of more recent fame.

But we are also a popular tourist destination for our honey-coloured mellow Cotswold stone villages, and for the Thames which has its spring near Lechlade. More villages open as 'groups' for the National Garden Scheme in Oxfordshire than in any other county, and offer tea, hospitality, advice and delight with their infinite variety of gardens.

All this enjoyment benefits the excellent causes that the National Garden Scheme supports.

Volunteers

County Organiser
Marina Hamilton-Baillie
01367 710486
marina_hamilton_baillie@hotmail.com

County Treasurer
David White
01295 812679
davidwhite679@btinternet.com

Publicity
Priscilla Frost
01608 810578
info@oxconf.co.uk

Social Media
Lara Cowan
lara.cowan@ngs.org.uk

Petra Hoyer Millar
01869 338156
petra.hoyermillar@ngs.org.uk

Photographer
Alexandra Davies
07833 461120
hello@alexandrajdavies.co.uk

Booklet Co-ordinator
Petra Hoyer Millar
(as above)

Assistant County Organisers
Lynn Baldwin
01608 642754
elynnbaldwin@gmail.com

Lara Cowan
(as above)

Petra Hoyer Millar
(as above)

John & Joan Pumfrey
01189 722848
joanpumfrey@lineone.net

Charles & Lyn Sanders
01865 739486
sandersc4@hotmail.com

Left: Yew Tree Cottage, East Hagbourne Gardens

OPENING DATES

All entries subject to change. For latest information check **www.ngs.org.uk**

Map locator numbers are shown to the right of each garden name.

February

Snowdrop Festival

Sunday 11th
Stonehaven 73

Sunday 18th
Hollyhocks 40

March

Sunday 11th
Monks Head 57

Sunday 25th
Trinity College 75

April

Monday 2nd
Church Farm Field 20
Kencot Gardens 45

Sunday 8th
Ashbrook House 2
Broughton Poggs & Filkins Gardens 14
Buckland Lakes 15
Hilltop Cottage 39
Magdalen College 51
Upper Green 77
Wadham College 78

Thursday 12th
Monks Head 57

Sunday 15th
Lime Close 50
◆ Waterperry Gardens 79

Sunday 22nd
The Old Vicarage, Bledington 63

Saturday 28th
50 Plantation Road 66

Sunday 29th
◆ Broughton Grange 13
Old Boars Hill Gardens 59
50 Plantation Road 66

May

Saturday 5th
50 Plantation Road 66

Sunday 6th
50 Plantation Road 66

Monday 7th
Denton House 26
Monks Head 57
Sparsholt Manor 70

Wednesday 9th
NEW Kingham Lodge 47

Sunday 13th
Headington Gardens 37

Saturday 19th
Ridgeway 68

Sunday 20th
NEW Brightwell-cum-Sotwell Gardens 10
The Grove 35
The Old Mill 60
Ridgeway 68

Sunday 27th
Barton Abbey 6
Meadow Cottage 52
Westwell Manor 81

Monday 28th
Church Farm Field 20
Friars Court 31

June

Festival Weekend

Sunday 3rd
Bolters Farm 9
Failford 29
Lime Close 50
116 Oxford Road 64
Steeple Aston Gardens 72
Wayside 80
Whitehill Farm 83

Saturday 9th
NEW Deddington Gardens 24

Sunday 10th
Charlbury Gardens 17
NEW Chestlion Manor 18
Cumnor Village Gardens 23
East Hagbourne Gardens 28
NEW Foxington 30
Iffley Gardens 44
Langford Gardens 49
Wheatley Gardens 82

Thursday 14th
Wootton Gardens 85

Friday 15th
Asthall Manor 3

Saturday 16th
NEW Swerford Park 74

Sunday 17th
Blewbury Gardens 8
Hilltop Cottage 39
NEW Kingston Blount Gardens 48
Middleton Cheney Gardens 54
The Old Vicarage, Bledington 63
NEW Swerford Park 74
Upper Green 77

Sunday 24th
Brize Norton Gardens 11
NEW Cobb House 21
Corpus Christi College 22
68 Hurst Rise Road 42
86 Hurst Rise Road 43
Midsummer House 55
Sibford Gardens 69
Woolstone Mill House 84

Saturday 30th
◆ Blenheim Palace 7

July

Sunday 1st
Chalkhouse Green Farm 16
Mill Barn 56

Sunday 8th
Dorchester Gardens 27
Green and Gorgeous 33
Wadham College 78

Sunday 15th
◆ Broughton Grange 13
Ham Court 36

Sunday 22nd
◆ Broughton Castle 12
Merton College Oxford Fellows' Garden 53

Sunday 29th
Trinity College 75

August

Sunday 19th
Radcot House 67

Sunday 26th
Aston Pottery 4

Monday 27th
Aston Pottery 4

September

Sunday 2nd
Bannisters 5
Bolters Farm 9
Hollyhocks 40
Mill Barn 56
Upper Green 77

Sunday 9th
Ashbrook House 2

Sunday 16th
◆ Broughton Grange 13
◆ Waterperry Gardens 79

October

Sunday 7th
Radcot House 67

Kingham Lodge

February 2019

Sunday 17th
Hollyhocks 40

By Arrangement

Appleton Dene 1
Ashbrook House 2
Barton Abbey 6
Bolters Farm 9
Carter's Yard, Sibford Gardens 69
Chivel Farm 19
103 Dene Road 25
Denton House 26
Failford 29
NEW Foxington 30
The Grange 32
Green and Gorgeous 33
Greenfield Farm 34
Hearns House 38
Hollyhocks 40
Home Close 41
10 Kennett Road 46
Lime Close 50
Meadow Cottage 52
Mill Barn 56
Monks Head 57
NEW 16 Oakfield Road 58
Old Rectory 61
The Old Vicarage 62
The Old Vicarage, Bledington 63
40 Osler Road, Headington Gardens 37
116 Oxford Road 64
Placketts 65
Primrose Gardens, Steeple Aston Gardens 72
64 Spring Road 71
Uplands, Old Boars Hill Gardens 59
Upper Green 77
Wayside 80
Wheatley Gardens 82
Whitehill Farm 83

THE GARDENS

1 APPLETON DENE

Yarnells Hill, Botley, Oxford, OX2 9BG. Mr & Mrs A Dawson, 07701 000977, annrobe@aol.com. *3m W of Oxford. Take W road out of Oxford, through Botley Rd, pass under A34, turn L into Westminster Way, Yarnells Hill 2nd on R, park at top of hill. Walk 200 metres.* **Visits by arrangement May to Sept for small groups, booked in advance. Home-made teas and floral demo.**

Beautiful secluded garden set in a hidden valley bordered by woods and a field. The ¼ acre garden on a steeply sloping site surrounds a mature tulip tree. There is a skillfully incorporated level lawn area overlooked by deep borders incl a wide variety of plants for long seasonal interest. A small cut flower allotment ½ m from the garden is also available to visit. Featured in Garden News and Garden Answers.

2 ASHBROOK HOUSE

Blewbury, OX11 9QA. Mr & Mrs S A Barrett, 01235 850810, janembarrett@me.com. *4m SE of Didcot. Turn off A417 in Blewbury into Westbrook St. 1st house on R. Follow yellow signs for parking in Boham's Rd.* **Sun 8 Apr, Sun 9 Sept (2-5.30). Adm £4, chd free. Light refreshments. Visits also by arrangement Apr to Sept.**

The garden where Kenneth Grahame read Wind in the Willows to local children and where he took inspiration for his description of the oak doors to Badger's House. Come and see, you may catch a glimpse of Toad and friends in this 3½ acre chalk and water garden, in a beautiful spring line village. In spring the banks are a mass of daffodils and in late summer the borders are full of unusual plants.

3 ASTHALL MANOR

Asthall, Burford, OX18 4HW. Rosanna Pearson, www.onformsculpture.co.uk/asthall-manor. *3m E of Burford. Going from Witney to Burford on A40, turn R at r'about. Coming from Chipping Norton, come through Shipton-under-Wychwood & Swinbrook. The nearest bus stop (a 10 min walk) is on route 233.* **Evening opening Fri 15 June (6-9). Adm £7.50, chd free. Wine.**

6 acres of dramatic planting surround this C17 Cotswolds manor house (not open), once home to the Mitford family. The gardens, designed by I & J Bannerman in 1998, offer 'a beguiling mix of traditional and contemporary' as described by the Good Gardens Guide. Exuberant scented borders, sloping box parterres, wild flowers, a gypsy wagon, a turf sculpture and a hidden lake all contribute to the mix. Partial wheelchair access.

4 ASTON POTTERY

Aston, Bampton, OX18 2BT. Mr Stephen Baughan, www.astonpottery.co.uk. *On the B4449 between Bampton & Standlake. 4m S of Witney.* **Sun 26, Mon 27 Aug (12-5). Adm £5, chd free. Light refreshments in the café.**

5 stunning borders flower from June until November, set around Aston Pottery's Gift Shop and Cafe. Featuring a 72 metre hornbeam walk with summerhouse and 200 perennials, 80 metre hot bank with kniphofia, alstroemeria, cannas, salvias, a double dahlia border with over 600 dahlias, agapanthus and asters and a border full of over 5000 annuals. Featured in The Telegraph and Country Living magazine.

5 BANNISTERS

Middle Street, Islip, Kidlington, OX5 2SF. Wendy Price. *2m E of Kidlington & approx 5m N of Oxford. From A34, exit Bletchingdon & Islip. B4027 direction Islip, turn L into Middle St, beside Great Barn.* **Sun 2 Sept (2-5.30). Combined adm with Hollyhocks £5, chd free.**

Perennials and grasses, naturalistic planting contrasted with trained fruit trees and shrubs. A contemporary interpretation of an old garden. Gravel paths and some shallow steps.

6 BARTON ABBEY

Steeple Barton, OX25 4QS. Mr & Mrs P Fleming, 07731 413985. *8m E of Chipping Norton. On B4030, ½m from junction of A4260 & B4030.* **Sun 27 May (2-5). Adm £5, chd free. Home-made teas. Visits also by arrangement May to Aug.**

15 acre garden with views from house (not open) across sweeping lawns and picturesque lake. Walled garden with colourful herbaceous borders, separated by established yew hedges and espalier fruit, contrasts with more informal woodland garden paths with vistas of specimen trees and meadows. Working glasshouses and fine display of fruit and vegetables.

7 ◆ BLENHEIM PALACE

Woodstock, OX20 1PX. His Grace the Duke of Marlborough, 01993 810530, operations@blenheimpalace.com, www.blenheimpalace.com. *8m N of Oxford. Bus: S3 Oxford-Chipping Norton, alight Woodstock.* **For NGS: Sat 30 June (10-6). Adm £4, chd £2. For other opening times and information, please phone, email or visit garden website.**

Blenheim Gardens, originally laid out by Henry Wise, incl the formal Water Terraces and Italian Garden by Achille Duchêne, Rose Garden, Arboretum, and Cascade. The Secret Garden offers a stunning garden paradise in all seasons. Blenheim Lake, created by Capability Brown and spanned by Vanburgh's Grand Bridge, is the focal point of over 2,000 acres of landscaped parkland. The Pleasure Gardens complex incl the Herb and Lavender Garden and Butterfly House. Other activities incl the Marlborough Maze, adventure play area, giant chess and draughts. Some gravel paths, terrain can be uneven in places, incl some steep slopes. Dogs allowed in park only.

GROUP OPENING

8 BLEWBURY GARDENS

Blewbury, OX11 9QB. *4m SE of Didcot. On A417. Follow yellow signs for car parks.* **Sun 17 June (2-6). Combined adm £5, chd free. Home-made teas at Blewbury Manor, all proceeds to the NGS.**

BLEWBURY MANOR
Mr & Mrs M R Blythe.

BROOKS END
Jean & David Richards.

GREEN BUSHES
Phil Rogers.

HALL BARN
Malcolm & Deirdre Cochrane.

STOCKS
Norma & Richard Bird.

As celebrated by Rachel de Thame in Gardener's World, five gardens will open, in a charming downland village. Blewbury Manor with moat and 10 acre garden. Features incl a parterre, flower garden, herbaceous and mixed borders, pergola, vegetable and herb garden, stream planting, woodland, lake, sunken gravel garden, and courtyard. Brooks End a 1960s bungalow with colour themed beds, damp border, hidden garden, small orchard, shady border, greenhouse and vegetable garden. Green Bushes a garden created by plant lover Rhon Rogers over many years, around C15 cottage. The garden continues to be nurtured and developed by Phil with colour themed borders, ponds and poolside planting, ferns, pleached limes and roses. Hall Barn has 4 acres with traditional herbaceous borders, kitchen garden, croquet lawn, C16 dovecote, thatched cob wall and chalk stream. Stocks an early cruck-constructed thatched cottage, surrounded by densely planted lime tolerant herbaceous perennials offering tiers of colour yr-round. Plant stall in the car park by Edulis Plant Nursery. Featured in Waitrose Garden magazine (Summer 2017). Wheelchair access to most gardens.

9 BOLTERS FARM

Chilson, Pudlicote Lane, Chipping Norton, OX7 3HU. Robert & Amanda Cooper, 07778 476517, art@amandacooper.co.uk. *Centre of Chilson village. On arrival in the hamlet of Chilson, heading N, we are the last in an old row of cottages on R with old white gates. Please drive past & park considerately on the L in the lane.* **Sun 3 June, Sun 2 Sept (2-5.30). Adm £5, chd free. Tea & gluten free options. Visits also by arrangement Mar to Sept for groups of 20 max.**

Donation to Hands Up Foundation.

A cherished old cottage garden restored over the last 10 yrs. Tumbly moss covered walls and sloping lawns down to a stream with natural planting and character. Wheelchairs have to negotiate sloping deep gravel!

GROUP OPENING

10 NEW BRIGHTWELL-CUM-SOTWELL GARDENS

Kingston Blount, Wallingford, OX10 0RW. *2m W of Wallingford. Parking in village centre or village hall. From Wallingford, 1st entry into village, through S bends, Dobsons & Priory on L. Rose Cottage close by. From Didcot, 1st entry into village, past Red Lion.* **Sun 20 May (1-5.30). Combined adm £5, chd free. Home-made teas in cottage garden, 50yds away.**

DOBSONS
Anne Salisbury.

THE PRIORY
Trish Scroggs.

NEW **ROSE COTTAGE**
James & Jane Davys.

Ancient village with many timber-framed and thatched cottages. Three differing gardens (houses not open) from formal to semi-formal. Dobsons has C16 origins; gardens surrounded by brick and flint walls that were dated by members of the Dobson family. Pretty, old walled garden restored over last 5 yrs with yr-round interest. Three distinct areas separated by beech hedges; formal lawn with herbaceous border, orchard being regenerated with trees under-planted with daffodils; a box knot garden. The Priory, a beautiful Tudor s-facing house with small Italianate gravel garden leading to larger pretty walled garden with herbaceous plants and rose beds. A plantswoman's garden with many interesting specimens. Rose Cottage a C19 red brick house surrounded by traditional cottage gardens. The front has a rose border and Japanese themed area, while the rear walled garden has deep herbaceous borders with views to the church next door. Garden has two patios with ornamental shrubberies on different levels. Partial wheelchair access as there are a few small steps and gentle slopes.

GROUP OPENING

11 BRIZE NORTON GARDENS

Brize Norton, OX18 3LY. www.bncommunity.org/ngs. *3m SW of Witney. Brize Norton Village, S of A40, between Witney & Burford. Parking at Elderbank Hall and Mason Arms in Burford Rd. Coaches welcome with plenty of parking nearby.* **Sun 24 June (1-6). Combined adm £5, chd free. Light refreshments at Elderbank Village Hall & Grange Farm.**

BARNSTABLE HOUSE
Mr & Mrs P Butcher, www.ourgarden.org.uk.

17 CHICHESTER PLACE
Mr & Mrs D Howard.

CHURCH FARM HOUSE
Philip & Mary Holmes.

CLUMBER
Mr & Mrs S Hawkins.

GRANGE FARM
Mark & Lucy Artus.

MIJESHE
Mr & Mrs M Harper.

PAINSWICK HOUSE
Mr & Mrs T Gush.

NEW **ROOKERY FARM**
Ian & Fiona Roberts.

ROSEDALE
Mr & Mrs S Finlayson.

NEW **91 STATION ROAD**
Bev & Phil Tyrell.

95 STATION ROAD
Mr & Mrs P A Timms.

STONE COTTAGE
Mr & Mrs K Humphris.

Doomsday village on the edge of the Cotswold's offering a number of gardens open for your enjoyment. You can see a wide variety of planting incl ornamental trees, herbaceous borders, ornamental grasses and traditional fruit and vegetable gardens. Features incl a Mediterranean style patio, courtyard garden, water features, plus gardens where you can just sit, relax and enjoy the day. Plants will be available for sale at individual gardens. A Flower Festival will take place in the Brize Norton St Britius Church. Partial wheelchair access to some gardens.

12 ◆ BROUGHTON CASTLE

Banbury, OX15 5EB. Martin Fiennes, 01295 276070, info@broughtoncastle.com, www.broughtoncastle.com. *2½m SW of Banbury. On Shipston-on-Stour road (B4035).* **For NGS: Sun 22 July (2-4.30). Adm £5, chd £5. Light refreshments.** For other opening times and information, please phone, email or visit garden website.
1 acre; shrubs, herbaceous borders, walled garden, roses, climbers seen against background of C14-C16 castle surrounded by moat in open parkland. House also open (additional charge).

13 ◆ BROUGHTON GRANGE

Wykham Lane, Broughton, Banbury, OX15 5DS. S Hester, www.broughtongrange.com. *¼m out of village. From Banbury take B4035 to Broughton. Turn L at Saye & Sele Arms Pub up Wykham Lane (one way). Follow road out of village for ¼m. Entrance on R.* **For NGS: Sun 29 Apr, Sun 15 July, Sun 16 Sept (10-5). Adm £8, chd free. Home-made teas.** For other opening times and information, please visit garden website.
An impressive 25 acres of gardens and light woodland in an attractive Oxfordshire setting. The centrepiece is a large terraced walled garden created by Tom Stuart-Smith in 2001. Vision has been used to blend the gardens into the countryside. Good early displays of bulbs followed by outstanding herbaceous planting in summer. Formal and informal areas combine to make this a special site incl newly laid arboretum with many ongoing projects.

Chestlion Manor

GROUP OPENING

14 BROUGHTON POGGS & FILKINS GARDENS

Lechlade, GL7 3JH. www.filkins.org.uk. *3m N of Lechlade. 5m S of Burford. Just off A361 between Burford & Lechlade on the B4477. Map of the gardens available.* **Sun 8 Apr (2-6). Combined adm £5.50, chd free. Home-made teas in Filkins Village Hall.**

NEW **ANSTRUTHER**
Julian & Caroline Alder.

BROUGHTON HALL
Karen & Ian Jobling.

BROUGHTON POGGS MILL
Charlie & Avril Payne.

THE CORN BARN
Ms Alexis Thompson.

FIELD COTTAGE
Peter & Sheila Gray.

FILKINS ALLOTMENTS
Filkins Allotments.

FILKINS HALL
Filkins Hall Residents.

LITTLE PEACOCKS
Colvin & Moggridge.

PEACOCK FARMHOUSE
Pauline & Peter Care.

PIGEON COTTAGE
Lynne Savege.

PIP COTTAGE
G B Woodin.

3 THE COACH HOUSE
Peter & Brenda Berners-Price.

NEW **WELL COTTAGE**
Christiaan Richards & Michelle Woodworth.

13 gardens and flourishing allotments in these beautiful and vibrant Cotswold stone twin villages. Scale and character vary from the grand landscape setting of Filkins Hall and the equally extensive but more intimate Broughton Hall, to the small but action packed Pigeon Cottage and The Tallot. Broughton Poggs Mill has a rushing mill stream with an exciting bridge; Pip Cottage combines topiary, box hedges and a fine rural view. In these and the other equally exciting gardens horticultural interest abounds. Features incl plant stall by professional local nursery, Swinford Museum of Cotswolds tools and artefacts, and Cotswold Woollen Weavers. Many gardens have gravel driveways, but most are suitable for wheelchair access. Most gardens welcome dogs on leads.

15 BUCKLAND LAKES

Nr Faringdon, SN7 8QW. The Wellesley Family. *3m NE of Faringdon. Buckland is midway between Oxford (14m) & Swindon (15m), just off the A420. Faringdon 3m, Witney 8m. Follow the yellow NGS signs which will lead you to driveway & car park by St Mary's Church.* **Sun 8 Apr (2-5). Adm £5, chd free. Home-made teas at Memorial Hall.** Donation to RWMT (community bus).

Descend down wooded path to two large secluded lakes with views over undulating historic parkland, designed by Georgian landscape architect Richard Woods. Picturesque mid C18 rustic icehouse, cascade with iron footbridge, thatched boathouse and round house, and renovated exedra. Many fine mature trees, drifts of spring bulbs and daffodils amongst shrubs. Norman church adjoins. Cotswold village. Children must be supervised due to large expanse of unfenced open water.

16 CHALKHOUSE GREEN FARM

Chalkhouse Green, Kidmore End, Reading, RG4 9AL. Mr & Mrs J Hall, www.chgfarm.com. *2m N of Reading, 5m SW of Henley-on-Thames. Situated between A4074 & B481. From Kidmore End take Chalkhouse Green Rd. Follow NGS yellow signs.* **Sun 1 July (2-6). Adm £3, chd free. Cream teas.**

1 acre garden and open traditional farmstead. Herbaceous borders, herb garden, shrubs, old fashioned roses, trees incl medlar, quince and mulberries, walled ornamental kitchen garden. New cherry orchard. Rare breed farm animals incl British White cattle, Suffolk Punch horses, donkeys, Berkshire pigs, chickens, ducks and turkeys. Plant and jam stall, donkey and pony rides, swimming in covered pool, trailer rides, farm trail, heavy horse and bee display. Partial wheelchair access.

GROUP OPENING

17 CHARLBURY GARDENS

Charlbury, OX7 3PP. *6m SE of Chipping Norton. Large Cotswold village on B4022 Witney-Enstone Rd.* **Sun 10 June (2-5). Combined adm £5, chd free. Home-made teas in St Mary's Church.**

NEW **CLOVER PATCH**
Dr & Mrs J Goves.

GOTHIC HOUSE
Mr & Mrs Andrew Lawson.

THE PRIORY GARDEN
Dr D El Kabir & Colleagues.

Three varied gardens in the centre of this large Cotswold village, in the context of traditional stone houses. New for 2018, Clover Patch, a ½ acre garden with a newly formed cutting garden to the front; a small fruit, vegetable and propagating area with raised beds leading to lawns, a water garden and shady woodland area to the rear. Gothic House with ⅓ acre walled garden designed with sculpture and colour in mind. New area of planted squares replaces lawn. False perspective, pleached lime walk, trellis, terracotta containers. The Priory Garden has 1 acre of formal terraced topiary gardens with Italianate features. Foliage colour schemes, shrubs, parterres with fragrant plants, old roses, water features, sculpture and inscriptions aim to produce a poetic, wistful atmosphere. Arboretum of over 3 acres borders the River Evenlode and incl wildlife garden and pond.

18 NEW CHESTLION MANOR

Chestlion Lane, Bourton Road, Clanfield, Bampton, OX18 2PA. Louise Johnson. *3m S of Carterton. Chestlion Lane is off A4020 Bourton Rd in the village of Clanfield.* **Sun 10 June (2-5). Adm £5, chd free. Home-made teas.**

The garden surrounding the house (not open), has been planted since the new owners took on the house 7 yrs ago. The garden to the rear of the house, has approx ¾ acre of mixed planting, with many blowsy roses adorning the walls and soft romantic planting in borders. There is a circular meditative garden and a round pond along with a productive kitchen, cutting garden, greenhouse and herb garden. There is a boat house and pond outside the walled area and a newly planted wild flower meadow (work in progress) with a fruit tree avenue and a hornbeam avenue leading to the back entrance.

19 CHIVEL FARM

Heythrop, OX7 5TR. Mr & Mrs J D Sword, 01608 683227, rosalind.sword@btinternet.com. *4m E of Chipping Norton. Off A361 or A44.* **Visits by arrangement May to Sept, with adm dependent on group size. Light refreshments.**

Beautifully designed country garden with extensive views, designed for continuous interest that is always evolving. Colour schemed borders with many unusual trees, shrubs and herbaceous plants. Small formal white garden and a conservatory.

20 CHURCH FARM FIELD

Church Lane, Epwell, Banbury, OX15 6LD. Mrs D V D Castle. *7½m W of Banbury on N side of Epwell village.* **Mon 2 Apr, Mon 28 May (2-6). Adm £2, chd free. Home-made teas.**

Woods, arboretum with wild flowers (planting started 1992), over 90 different trees and shrubs in 4½ acres. Paths cut through trees for access to various parts. Lawn tennis court and croquet lawns. Light refreshments (weather permitting).

21 NEW COBB HOUSE

Church Close, Bampton, OX18 2LW. Dame Pippa Harris & Richard McBrien. *Approx ½m N of Bampton's market square via A4095. Turn L into Church View, then 1st R into Church Close. Cobb House is on the corner, opp St Mary's Church.* **Sun 24 June (2-5). Adm £5, chd free. Tea.**

Cobb House is a Cotswold stone rectory (not open), built between 1640-1740 and set within the historic village of Bampton. The owners have gradually developed the garden over the past nine years, most recently under the guidance of designer Christopher Masson. The garden is approximately an acre, including herbaceous borders, roses, shrubs and parterre. Partial wheelchair access as gravel drive and paths.

22 CORPUS CHRISTI COLLEGE

Merton Street, Oxford, OX1 4JF. Domestic Bursar, www.ccc.ox.ac.uk. *Entrance from Merton St.* **Sun 24 June (2-6). Adm £2, chd free. Home-made teas in College Hall.**

David Leake, the College gardener since 1979, avoiding chemicals and sprays, has created a marvellous wild garden by blending a huge range of wild and cultivated flowers into a vivid, yet harmonious, landscape. In amongst beautiful buildings and with wonderful views of Christ Church meadows from the mound beside the ancient town wall, the Corpus garden is a real treasure. The garden incl one slope.

GROUP OPENING

23 CUMNOR VILLAGE GARDENS

Leys Road, Cumnor, Oxford, OX2 9QF. *4m W of central Oxford. From A420, exit for Cumnor & follow B4017 into the village. Parking on road & side roads, behind PO, or behind village hall in Leys Rd. Additional parking in Bertie & Norreys Rd.* **Sun 10 June (2-6). Combined adm £5, chd free. Home-made teas in United Reformed Church Hall, Leys Road.**

36 BERTIE ROAD
Esther & Neil Whiting.

10 LEYS ROAD
Penny & Nick Bingham.

41 LEYS ROAD
Philip & Jennie Powell.

STONEHAVEN
Dr Dianne & Prof Keith Gull.
(See separate entry)

1 THE WINNYARDS
Brenda & Roy Darnell.

Five gardens of varying styles in attractive village setting. 10 Leys Road, long narrow cottage garden with a wide variety of shrubs and trees with many interesting and unusual perennials. 41 Leys Road, ¾ acre plot including C16 cottage (not open) with flower and fruit garden, orchard, large vegetable garden, mature trees and wild flowers. 1 The Winnyards, a medium sized garden planted for yr-long interest, plus a water feature, pergola and open views across a meadow. 36 Bertie Road, a small professionally designed garden, structured layout of three rooms, pergola, raised vegetable bed, relaxed planting style with emphasis on form and texture. Stonehaven, front garden partially gravelled, side courtyard has pots, rear garden overlooks meadows. Unusual plants, many with black or bronze foliage, old apple trees, wildlife pond. Japanese influence. Wheelchair access to 1 The Winnyards and 36 Bertie Road. Partial access to Stonehaven due to pebbles. WC facilities in United Reformed Church Hall.

GROUP OPENING

24 NEW DEDDINGTON GARDENS

Castle Street, Deddington, Banbury, OX15 0TE. *Deddington is about 6m S of Banbury on the A4260 Oxford to Banbury road.* **Sat 9 June (2-5.30). Combined adm £5, chd free. Home-made teas.**

NEW CASTLE END HOUSE
Petra Hoyer Millar.

NEW RUSHALL HOUSE
Lynda Lake-Stewart.

SATIN LANE ALLOTMENTS
Deddington Allotment Society.

Beautiful ironstone village on the edge of the Cotswolds. Deddington is centred around a charming, bustling market place, church and chapel square. Two lovely village gardens and the flourishing village allotments are opening their gates to visitors this year. All are in close proximity, located to the east of the village. Castle End House, a new garden now three years in the making; one acre dry-stone walled garden, featuring formal lawns, ha-ha, substantial herbaceous borders, terraced orchard, woodland garden and (in development) herb garden. Rushall House, delightful small walled garden containing intensively planted perennial beds to cover all seasons and filled with family plant and sculpture treasures. Satin Lane Allotments are a thriving community treasure, established in 1925. The site accommodates 47 beautiful individual plots that have been worked over generations. Satin Lane Allotments and Castle End House are featured on the Oxonian Gardener blog and online guide Gardenista.

25 103 DENE ROAD

Headington, Oxford, OX3 7EQ. Mr & Mrs Steve & Mary Woolliams, 01865 764153, stevewoolliams@gmail.com. *S Headington nr Nuffield. Dene Rd accessed from The Slade from the N, or from Hollow Way from the S. Both access roads are B4495. Garden on sharp bend.* **Visits by arrangement Apr to Sept for groups of 10 max, children very welcome. Adm £3, chd free. Home-made teas.**

A surprising eco-friendly garden with borrowed view over the Lye Valley Nature Reserve. Lawns, a wild flower meadow, pond and large kitchen garden are incl in a suburban 60ft x 120ft sloping garden. Fruit trees, soft fruit and mixed borders of shrubs, hardy perennials, grasses and bulbs, designed for seasonal colour. This garden has been noted for its wealth of wildlife incl a variety of birds and butterflies and other insects, incl the rare Brown Hairstreak butterfly and the rare Currant Clearwing moth.

26 DENTON HOUSE

Denton, Oxford, OX44 9JF. Mr & Mrs Luke, 01865 874440, waveney@jandwluke.com. *In a valley between Garsington & Cuddesdon.* **Mon 7 May (1.30-6). Adm £5, chd free. Home-made teas. Visits also by arrangement May to Oct for any group size up to 30 max. Refreshments on request.**

Large walled garden surrounds a Georgian mansion (not open), with shaded areas, walks, topiary and many interesting mature trees. Large lawns and herbaceous borders and rose beds. The windows in the wall were taken in 1864 from Brasenose College Chapel and Library. Wild garden and a further walled fruit garden.

GROUP OPENING

27 DORCHESTER GARDENS

Dorchester-On-Thames, Wallingford, OX10 7HZ. *Off A4074 or A415 signed to Dorchester. Parking at Old Bridge Meadow, at SE end of Dorchester Bridge. Disabled parking at 26 Manor Farm Road (OX10 7HZ). Tickets available at each garden.* **Sun 8 July (2-5). Combined adm £5, chd free. Home-made teas in the tearoom at Abbey Guesthouse.**

26 MANOR FARM ROAD
David & Judy Parker.

6 MONKS CLOSE
Leif & Petronella Rasmussen.

7 ROTTEN ROW
Michael & Veronica Evans.

Three contrasting gardens in a historic village surround the Medieval abbey, the scene of many Midsomer Murders. 26 Manor Farm Road (OX10 7HZ) was part of an old, neglected garden which now has a formal lawn and planting, vegetable garden and greenhouse. Children should be accompanied. From the yew hedge down towards the River Thame which often floods in winter, is an apple orchard underplanted with spring bulbs. 6 Monks Close (OX10 7JA) is idyllic and surprising. A small spring-fed stream and sloping lawn surrounded by naturalistic planting runs down to a monastic fish pond. Bridges over this deep pond lead to the River Thame with steep banks, children should be accompanied. 7 Rotten Row (OX10 7LJ) is Dorchester's lawnless garden, a terrace with borders leads to a lovely geometric garden supervised by a statue of Hebe. Access is from the allotments. Wheelchair access to 26 Manor Farm Road, partial access to other gardens.

GROUP OPENING

28 EAST HAGBOURNE GARDENS

East Hagbourne, OX11 9LN. *½m S of Didcot. Enter village via B4016, or from A417 through West Hagbourne & Coscote. Cycle path 44.* **Sun 10 June (2-5). Combined adm £5, chd free. Home-made teas. The Fleur de Lys Pub is also open for food and drinks.**

BOTTOM BARN
Mr Colin & Dr Jean Millar.

BUCKELS
Felicity Topping.

NEW **THE GABLES**
Sally & Bill Barksfield.

5 HIGGS CLOSE
Mrs Jenny Smith.

KINGFISHER HOUSE
Mr & Mrs Robert & Nicola Ainger.

LIME TREE COTTAGE
Jane & Robin Bell.

LIME TREE FARM
Mrs Erica Bevan.

NEW **LITTLE THATCH**
Mark Granger & Chris Beverley.

NEW **YEW TREE COTTAGE**
Sarah Beynon.

Pretty Domesday village, timber frame and local clunch stone houses. Open every 3 yrs. Follow main road or explore pretty alleyways to visit 9 gardens; Bottom Barn, in the shadow of the C12 church, with topiary and perennial planting around a converted C18 barn; Lime Tree Farm, a picturesque village garden and orchard, separated by Hakkas Brook; Lime Tree Cottage with water plants, mature trees, and secret garden; Buckels, a sculptured walled garden with cypresses, box, heritage fruit trees and herbs; 5 Higgs Close, a colourful garden with herbaceous borders, small pond and vegetable patch; Kingfisher House, a family garden with mixed herbaceous planting. New for 2018: Little Thatch, a cottage garden with a stream, pond planting, perennials, lavender beds, and kitchen garden; The Gables, a garden full of colour with roses, perennials, lavender, box and trees; Yew Tree Cottage, a secluded garden to the front of a thatched cottage (not open) with roses, clematis and honeysuckle. Features include access to wildflower meadow, plant sales and refreshments, along with a beautiful C12 church

29 FAILFORD

118 Oxford Road, Abingdon, OX14 2AG. Miss R Aylward, 01235 523925, aylwardsdooz@hotmail.co.uk. *118 is on the LH-side of Oxford Rd when coming from Abingdon Town, or on the RH-side when approaching from the N. Entrance to this garden is via 116 Oxford Road.* **Sun 3 June (11-4). Combined adm with 116 Oxford Road £4, chd free. Home-made teas. Visits also by arrangement May to Sept for groups up to 20 max. Refreshments on request.**
A town garden that won Abingdon in Bloom 'Best Large Back Garden' competition. An extension of the home the garden has both formal and informal areas. Features incl walkways through shaded areas, arches, kitchen garden, grasses, roses, topiaries, acers, hostas and heucheras. A wide variety of planting, all within an area 570 sq ft. Partial wheelchair access due to gravel areas, narrow pathways and uneven surfaces.

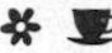

30 NEW FOXINGTON

Britwell Salome, Watlington, OX49 5LG. Mrs Mary Roadnight, 01491 612418, mary@foxington.co.uk. *At Red Lion Pub take turning to Britwell Hill. After 350yds turn into drive on L.* **Sun 10 June (2-6). Adm £5, chd free. Home-made teas. Visits also by arrangement Mar to Oct.**
Stunning views to the Chiltern Hills provide a wonderful setting for this impressive garden, remodelled in 2009. Patio, heather and gravel gardens enjoy this view, whilst the back and vegetable gardens are more enclosed. The relatively new planting is maturing well and the area around the house (not open) is full of colour. There is a orchard, a flock of white doves and vintage tractors. Well behaved dogs are welcome. They must be kept on a lead at all times as there are many young wild animals in the garden, wildflower meadow, wood and neighbouring fields. There are no steps and the paths in the garden are smooth. The paths through the wildflower meadow and orchard are firm and level.

31 FRIARS COURT

Clanfield, OX18 2SU. Charles Willmer, www.friarscourt.com. *5m N of Faringdon. On A4095 Faringdon to Witney. ½m S of Clanfield.* **Mon 28 May (2-6). Adm £4, chd free. Cream teas.**
Three acres of formal and informal gardens are within the remaining arms of a C16 moat, which partially surrounds the large C17 Cotswold stone manor house. Bridges span the moat and beyond the gardens is a woodland walk. A museum detailing the history of Friars Court is located in the old Coach House. A level path goes around the main gardens but some areas may not be accessible to wheelchair users.

32 THE GRANGE

Berrick Road, Chalgrove, OX44 7RQ. Mrs Vicky Farren, 01865 400883, vickyfarren@mac.com. *12m E of Oxford & 4m from Watlington, off B480. The entrance to The Grange is at the grass triangle between Berrick Rd & Monument Rd.* **Visits by arrangement June to Nov. Adm £5, chd free. Home-made teas on request (additional £3 pp).**
11 acre plot with an evolving garden including herbaceous borders and a field turned to prairie with many grasses inspired by the Dutch style. There is a lake with bridges and a planted island, a brook running through the garden, wild flower meadow, a further pond, arboretum, an old orchard and partly walled vegetable garden. There is deep water and bridges may be slippery when wet. Partial wheelchair access due to grass paths in many areas, bridges, island and steps.

The National Garden Scheme is committed to helping unpaid carers

33 GREEN AND GORGEOUS

Little Stoke, Wallingford, OX10 6AX. Rachel Siegfried, 07977 445041, www.greenandgorgeousflowers.co.uk. *3m S of Wallingford. Off B4009 between N & S Stoke, follow single track road down to farm.* **Sun 8 July (12-5). Adm £3.50, chd free. Home-made teas. Visits also by arrangement June to Aug for groups of 15-40 max.**

6 acre working flower farm next to River Thames. Cut flowers (many unusual varieties) in large plots and polytunnels, planted with combination of annuals, bulbs, perennials, roses and shrubs, plus some herbs, vegetables and fruit to feed the workers! Flowers selected for scent, novelty, nostalgia and naturalistic style. Floristry demonstrations. Short grass paths, large concrete areas.

34 GREENFIELD FARM

Christmas Common, Nr Watlington, OX49 5HG. Andrew & Jane Ingram, 01491 612434, andrew@andrewbingram.com. *4m from J5 of M40, 7m from Henley. J5 M40, A40 towards Oxford for ½m, turn L signed Christmas Common. ¾m past Fox & Hounds Pub, turn L at Tree Barn sign.* **Visits by arrangement June to Sept for groups of 6+. Adm £4, chd free.**

10 acre wild flower meadow surrounded by woodland, established 18 yrs ago under the Countryside Stewardship Scheme. Traditional Chiltern chalkland meadow in beautiful peaceful setting with 100 species of perennial wild flowers, grasses and 5 species of orchids. ½m walk from parking area to meadow. Opportunity to return via typical Chiltern beechwood.

35 THE GROVE

North Street, Middle Barton, Chipping Norton, OX7 7BZ. Ivor & Barbara Hill. *7m E Chipping Norton. On B4030, 2m from junction A4260 & B4030, opp Carpenters Arms Pub. Parking in street.* **Sun 20 May (1.30-5). Adm £3, chd free. Home-made teas.**

Mature informal plantsman's ⅓ acre garden, planted for yr-round interest around C19 Cotswold stone cottage (not open). Numerous borders with wide variety of unusual shrubs, trees and hardy plants; several species weigela syringa viburnum and philadelphus. Pond area, well stocked greenhouse. Plant list and garden history available. Home-made preserves for sale. Wheelchair access to most of garden.

36 HAM COURT

Ham Court Farm, Weald, Bampton, OX18 2HG. Emma Bridgewater & Matthew Rice. *Drive through the village towards Clanfield. The drive is on the R, exactly opp Weald St.* **Sun 15 July (10-4). Adm £5, chd free. Tea.**

Ham Court was once the gate house of a major C14 castle. Emma Bridgewater and Matthew Rice found it with no garden at all and have been making painfully slow progress in the project of putting this to rights. Beginning by digging a moat, planting thousands of trees, hiding thousands of tonnes of rubble and laying down the plans for their future garden. Now a productive kitchen garden and a lot of bright flowers. This is a garden in development, no two years are the same. Come early as delicious teas run out quick!

GROUP OPENING

37 HEADINGTON GARDENS

Old Headington, OX3 9BT. *2m E from centre of Oxford. After T-lights in the centre of Headington heading towards Oxford, take the 2nd turn on R into Osler Rd. Gardens at end of road in Old Headington, and in Beech Rd nearby.* **Sun 13 May (2-6). Combined adm £5, chd free. Home-made teas.**

NEW **11 BEECH ROAD**
Lucy Capel.

THE COACH HOUSE
David & Bryony Rowe.

MONCKTON COTTAGE
Julie Harrod & Peter McCarter, 01865 751471, petermccarter@msn.com.

40 OSLER ROAD
Nicholas & Pam Coote, 07804 932748, pamjcoote@gmail.com.
Visits also by arrangement May to Aug.

RUSKIN COLLEGE
Ruskin College, www.ruskincrinklecrankle.org/.

7 ST ANDREWS ROAD
Monique Halloran.

9 STOKE PLACE
Clive Hurst.

WHITE LODGE
Catharine Macksmith.

Situated above Oxford, Headington is an old village with high stone walls, narrow lanes and a Norman church. The 8 gardens offer wide variety. 40 Osler Road is a well-established garden with an Italian theme brimming with exotic planting. White Lodge provides a large park-like setting for a Regency property where visitors can linger and picnic. The Coach House combines a formal setting with hedges, flowers and lawn and a courtyard with a water garden. 9 Stoke place has a traditional lawn and mixed border on one side and a formal garden on the other. The walled vegetable garden in the grounds of Ruskin College incorporates a Grade II listed Crinkle Crankle Wall. Monckton Cottage is a walled, woodland garden with a meadow area, intriguing topiary, and unusual plants. 7 St Andrews Road is a small town garden with mixed borders and a unique water feature. New this year, 11 Beech Road is a recently planted garden in its first full season. Partial wheelchair access to most gardens due to gravel paths and steps.

38 HEARNS HOUSE

Gallowstree Common, RG4 9DE. John & Joan Pumfrey, 01189 722848, joanpumfrey@lineone.net. *5m N of Reading, 5m W of Henley. From A4074 turn E at Cane End.* **Visits by arrangement May to Aug with introductory talk by the owner and open studio. Adm £4, chd free. Home-made teas.**
An inspiration for artists and gardeners with unusual hard landscaping, sculpture and indigenous and exotic planting designed to suit specific areas including dry shade under trees, a hot bank and a low maintenance courtyard. New for 2018 is a wild flower area and a display of the National Collection of brunnera and omphalodes. The nursery is full of wonderful plants propagated from the garden. Within the 2 acres is an almost entirely paved walled garden with many self-seeding plants to give a pretty effect with low maintenance. Groups of gardeners and artists are welcome to enjoy/ paint inspirational hard landscaping and planting. Grass lawn access generally, with occasional single steps at terrace.

♿ 🐕 ✿ NPC ☕

39 HILLTOP COTTAGE

Horton-cum-Studley, Oxford, OX33 1AU. Professor Sarah Randolph. *Centre of village on main road. Enter village, R up Horton Hill, Hilltop Cottage on L at the top. Two disabled spaces in lay-by opp, other parking at bottom of hill.* **Sun 8 Apr, Sun 17 June (2-5). Combined adm with Upper Green £5, chd free. Home-made teas at Studley Barn (Apr), Upper Green (June).**
Plantaholic's large cottage garden, with productive vegetable plot, soft fruit and ornamentals. Beds incl herbaceous, shrubbery and prairie look. Small trees incl Acer griseum, Sorbus spp, silver-leaved shrubs. Colour in April, shrubs and a wide range of bulbs; in June, early perennials in a rich herbaceous border, shrub roses, frothy pink shrubbery. Featured as 'Garden of the Week' in Garden News (8 Apr 2017). Path with shallow steps.

♿ ☕

40 HOLLYHOCKS

North Street, Islip, Kidlington, OX5 2SQ. Avril Hughes, 01865 377104, ahollyhocks@btinternet.com. *3m NE of Kidlington. From A34, exit Bletchingdon & Islip. B4027 direction Islip, turn L into North St.* **Sun 18 Feb (1.30-5). Adm £3, chd free. Sun 2 Sept (2-5.30). Combined adm with Bannisters £5, chd free. Home-made teas. 2019: Sun 17 Feb. Visits also by arrangement Feb to Oct for groups up to 25 max.**
Plantswoman's small Edwardian garden brimming with yr-round interest, especially planted to provide winter colour, scent and snowdrops. Divided into areas with bulbs, herbaceous borders, roses, clematis, shade and woodland planting especially Trillium, Podophyllum and Arisaema, late summer salvias and annuals give colour. There are several alpine troughs as well as lots of pots around the house (not open). Some steps into the garden.

✿ ☕

41 HOME CLOSE

Southend, Garsington, OX44 9DH. Ms M Waud & Dr P Giangrande, 01865 361394. *3m SE of Oxford. N of B480, opp Garsington Manor.* **Visits by arrangement Apr to Sept. Refreshments on request. Adm £4, chd free.**
2 acre garden with listed house (not open) and listed granary. Unusual trees and shrubs planted for yr-round effect. Terraces, walls and hedges divide the garden and the planting reflects a Mediterranean interest. Vegetable garden and orchard. 1 acre mixed tree plantation with fine views.

42 68 HURST RISE ROAD

Oxford, OX2 9HH. Stephen & Anne Wright. *W side of Oxford. Take Botley interchange off A34 from N or S. Follow signs for Oxford & then turn R at Botley T-lights, opp MacDonalds & follow NGS yellow signs.* **Sun 24 June (2-6). Combined adm with 86 Hurst Rise Road £4, chd free.**
West facing town garden on clay, tiered to accommodate sloping site and divided into a series of rooms. Herbaceous borders and shrubs planted for yr-round interest, with a particular focus on roses. Range of intimate seating areas with views and raised vegetable beds. Partial wheelchair access.

43 86 HURST RISE ROAD

Cumnor Hill, Oxford, OX2 9HH. Ms P Guy & Mr L Harris. *W side of Oxford. Take Botley interchange off A34 from N or S. Follow signs for Oxford & then turn R at Botley T-lights, opp MacDonalds & follow NGS yellow signs.* **Sun 24 June (2-5.30). Combined adm with 68 Hurst Rise Road £4, chd free.**
A small town garden designed and planted by the owners in 2013. Good use of a 40ft x 40ft space brimming with herbaceous perennial plants, roses, clematis, shrubs and small trees. Seasonal use of containers and hanging baskets incl tender succulents. An unusual stone water feature, two raised beds packed with interesting plants, an arch and pergola all add to a plantaholic's garden. Partial wheelchair access as path is partly pebble.

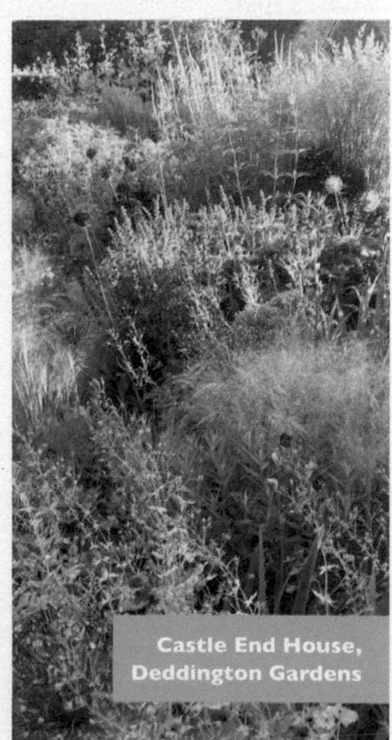

Castle End House, Deddington Gardens

GROUP OPENING

44 IFFLEY GARDENS

Iffley, Oxford, OX4 4EF. *2m S of Oxford. Within Oxford's ring road, off A4158 Iffley road, from Magdalen Bridge to Littlemore r'about, to Iffley village. Map provided at each garden.* **Sun 10 June (2-6). Combined adm £5, chd free. Home-made teas in village hall.**

17 ABBERBURY ROAD
Mrs Julie Steele.

NEW **24 ABBERBURY ROAD**
Ged & Jill Guinness.

25 ABBERBURY ROAD
Rob & Bridget Farrands.

29 ABBERBURY ROAD
Sarah North & Andrew Rathmell.

86 CHURCH WAY
Helen Beinart & Alex Coren.

122 CHURCH WAY
Sir John & Lady Elliott.

THE MALT HOUSE
Helen Potts.

THE THATCHED COTTAGE
Martin & Helen Foreman.

Secluded old village with renowned Norman church, featured on cover of Pevsner's Oxon Guide. Visit 8 gardens ranging in variety and style from the large Malt House garden and a thatched C17 cottage garden to mixed family gardens with shady borders and vegetable. Varied planting throughout the gardens including herbaceous borders, shade loving plants, roses, fine specimen trees and plants in terracing. Features incl water features, formal gardens, vegetable gardens, small lake and Thames riverbank. Plant Sale at 17 Abberbury Road. Wheelchair access to some gardens only.

GROUP OPENING

45 KENCOT GARDENS

Kencot, Lechlade, GL7 3QT. *5m NE of Lechlade. E of A361 between Burford & Lechlade. Village maps available.* **Mon 2 Apr (2-6). Combined adm £5, chd free. Home-made teas at village hall.**

THE ALLOTMENTS
Amelia Carter Trust.

BELHAM HAYES
Mr Joseph Jones.

THE GARDENS
Bridget Shirley.

HILLVIEW HOUSE
John & Andrea Moss.

IVY NOOK
Gill & Wally Cox.

KENCOT HOUSE
Tim & Katie Gardner.

THE MALTINGS
Mrs Jay Mathews.

MANOR FARM
Henry & Kate Fyson.

The Allotments tended by 8 people, with vegetables, flowers and fruit. Belham Hayes a mature cottage garden with mixed herbaceous borders, two old fruit trees, with an emphasis on scent and colour coordination. The Gardens a ⅓ acre garden with plentiful bulbs in spring. Mature front garden with 2 old apples trees and a newly planted rear garden. Hillview House, a 2 acre garden, lime tree drive, shrubs, borders, spring flowers ongoing planting of flower borders and vegetables. Ivy Nook with spring flowers, shrubs, rockery, small pond, waterfall, magnolia and fruit trees. Kencot House with a Gingko tree and shrubs that provides a backdrop to spring bulbs which bloom in abundance in this 2 acre walled garden. The Maltings a small cottage garden with herb wheel, pots and mature trees. Manor Farm, a 2 acre walled garden with bulbs, wood anemones, fritillaria in mature orchards, old English fruit trees, pleached lime walk, 130 yr old yew ball, Black Hamburg vine. Pigs and chickens. Plant sale at Manor Farm. No wheelchair access to The Allotments.

46 10 KENNETT ROAD

Headington, Oxford, OX3 7BJ. Linda & David Clover, 01865 765881, lindaclover@yahoo.co.uk. *2m E of Oxford in Central Headington. S of London Rd between New High St, with Shark to the W & Windmill Rd to the E. Parking in Old High St (Waitrose) or St Leonard's Rd (off Windmill Rd).* **Visits by arrangement for groups of 8 max. Adm £4, chd free. Light refreshments.**

Small suburban garden planted for yr-round interest. Spring snowdrops and hellebores, summer cottage garden planting, autumn colours and winter evergreens in a simply planned space on sandy subsoil, where small lawns provide a focus for the surrounding borders. Tiny pond has a quiet fernery and the glasshouse encourages cacti and succulents; a collection of auriculas and alpines brave the weather.

47 NEW KINGHAM LODGE

West End, Kingham, Chipping Norton, OX7 6YL. Christopher Stockwell. *From Kingham Village, West St turns into West End at tree in middle of road, bear R & you will see black gates for Kingham Lodge immed on L.* **Wed 9 May (10-5). Adm £5, chd free. Home-made lunches & teas.**

Many ericaceous plants not normally seen in the Cotswolds grow on 5 acres of garden, planted over 2 decades on sand over gravel. Big display of rhododendron, laburnum arch and azaleas. Formal 150 metre border, backed with trellis, shaded walks with multi-layered planting, an informal quarry pond, formal mirror pond, massive pergola, parterre and unique Islamic garden. Sculpture show from 5-13 May. Featured in Country Life and in regional news bulletins.

GROUP OPENING

48 NEW KINGSTON BLOUNT GARDENS

Brook Street, Kingston Blount, Chinnor, OX39 4RZ. *4m S of Thame. 2m E of J6, M40 on B4009 towards Princes Risborough. 1st L in Kingston Blount, go 300yds, follow signs for parking at field opp Town Farm Cottage. Limited disabled parking at property.* **Sun 17 June (2-5.30). Combined adm £4, chd free. Home-made teas.**

NEW **6 BENNETTS YARD**
Ms Emma Rogers.

NEW **BROOKSIDE**
Rosie & Peter Hetherington.

NEW **CORNERSTONE**
Richard & Rosemary Webb.

NEW **TOWN FARM COTTAGE**
Mr & Mrs J Clark, 07971 436504, theresa@townfarmcottage.co.uk, www.townfarmcottage.co.uk.

NEW **YEW COTTAGE**
Pat Isherwood.

Attractive small village at the foot of the Chilterns, with 5 gardens ranging from quite small to very large, all located in Brook Street. Enjoy the wild flowers whilst strolling round the lake at Town Farm Cottage, a 1½ acre garden featuring large rockery, herbaceous shrubbery, pergola, and scree planting. 6 Bennetts Yard, a plantswoman's small hidden gem, with rockery, herbaceous border and delightful pots. Cornerstone has fruit trees together with a small white shaded area at the front. To the rear there is a herbaceous border and standard roses around a fountain. Beyond a robinia hedge there is a productive vegetable plot. Yew Cottage, a cottage garden, bee and butterfly friendly, with many self-seed flowers. Brookside, a thatched listed cottage (not open), by a stream and surrounded by a well-stocked garden with herbaceous plants, roses and flowering shrubs set apart from a small orchard and vegetable plot.

GROUP OPENING

49 LANGFORD GARDENS

Lechlade, GL7 3LF. *6m S of Burford A361 towards Lechlade. 1½m E of Filkins. Large free car park in village. Maps of gardens available.* **Sun 10 June (2-6). Combined adm £6, chd free. Home-made teas at Pember House & village hall.**

BAKERY COTTAGE
Mr & Mrs R Robinson.

BAY TREE COTTAGE
Mr & Mrs R Parsons.

BRIDGEWATER HOUSE
Mr & Mrs T R Redston.

5 CHURCH LANE
Derek & Pat Potter.

1 COOKS FARM COTTAGES
Mr & Mrs M Clark.

CORKSCREW COTTAGE
Fiona Gilbert.

COTSWOLD BUNGALOW
John & Hilary Dudley.

COTSWOLD COTTAGE
Mr & Mrs Tom Marshall.

THE CROWN
Mr & Mrs D Evans.

THE FORGE
Chris King & Jum Beyazchuman.

THE GRANGE
Mr & Mrs J Johnston.

KEMPS YARD
Mr & Mrs R Kemp.

LIME TREE COTTAGE
Diane & Michael Schultz.

LOCKEY HOUSE
Ms Sophie Hanson.

LOWER FARM HOUSE
Mr & Mrs Templeman.

NEW **MEADOW VIEW**
Linda Moore.

THE OLD BAKERY
Mr & Mrs G Edwards.

THE OLD SCHOOL
David Freeman.

THE OLD VICARAGE
Mr & Mrs C Smith.

PEMBER HOUSE
Mr & Mrs J Potter.

ROSEFERN COTTAGE
Mrs D Lowden.

SPRINGFIELD
Mr & Mrs M Harris.

STONECROFT
Christine Apperley.

WELLBANK
Sir Brian & Lady Pomeroy.

WELLBANK HOUSE
Mr & Mrs Robert Hill.

Langford is a charming small Cotswold village with both the important Grade I listed St Matthew's Church and a splendid pub where lunch is available. 25 gardens will be open, with a delightful mix from large formal to small cottage gardens. Ancient Cotswold stone walls provide a backdrop for many old variety roses. Our plant stall has a large range of local plants and shrubs. Live music in Pember House garden during the afternoon, as well as village teas, and a church floral display add to an enjoyable day for everyone. Some gardens have gravel paths so wheelchair access may vary.

50 LIME CLOSE

35 Henleys Lane, Drayton, Abingdon, OX14 4HU. M C de Laubarede, mail@mclgardendesign.com. *2m S of Abingdon. Henleys Lane is off main road through Drayton.* **Sun 15 Apr, Sun 3 June (2-5.30). Adm £5, chd free. Cream teas. Visits also by arrangement for groups of 10+.** Donation to CLIC Sargent Care for Children.

4 acre mature plantsman's garden with rare trees, shrubs, perennials and bulbs. Mixed borders, raised beds, pergola, unusual topiary and shade borders. Herb garden by Rosemary Verey. Listed C16 house (not open). Cottage garden by MCL Garden Design, focusing on colour combinations and an iris garden with 100 varieties of tall bearded irises. Winter bulbs. New arboretum with exotic trees planted in 2016.

51 MAGDALEN COLLEGE

Oxford, OX1 4AU. Magdalen College, www.magd.ox.ac.uk. *Entrance in High St.* **Sun 8 Apr (1-6). Adm £6, chd £5. Light refreshments in the Old Kitchen.**

60 acres incl deer park, college lawns, numerous trees 150-200 yrs old; notable herbaceous and shrub plantings. Magdalen meadow where purple and white snake's head fritillaries can be found is surrounded by Addison's Walk, a tree lined circuit by the River Cherwell developed since the late C18. Ancient herd of 60 deer. Press bell at the lodge for porter to provide wheelchair access.

52 MEADOW COTTAGE

Christmas Common, Watlington, OX49 5HR. Mrs Zelda Kent-Lemon, 01491 613779, zelda_kl@hotmail.com. *1m from Watlington. Coming from Oxford M40 to J6. Turn R & go to Watlington. Turn L up Hill Rd to top. Turn R after 50yds, turn L into field.* **Sun 27 May (12-5). Adm £5, chd free. Home-made teas. Visits also by arrangement Feb to Sept.**

1¾ acre garden adjoining ancient bluebell woods created by the owner from 1995 onwards, with many areas to explore. A professionally designed vegetable garden, large composting areas, wild flower garden and pond, old and new fruit trees, many shrubs, much varied hedging and large areas of lawn. Indigenous trees, and C17 barn (not open). Wonderful snowdrops in February, and during the month of May visit the bluebell woodland and treehouse. Partial wheelchair access as gravel driveway and lawns.

53 MERTON COLLEGE OXFORD FELLOWS' GARDEN

Merton Street, Oxford, OX1 4JD. Merton College, 01865 276310. *Merton St runs parallel to High St.* **Sun 22 July (10-5). Adm £5, chd free.**

Ancient mulberry, said to have associations with James I. Specimen trees, long mixed border, recently established herbaceous bed. View of Christ Church meadow.

GROUP OPENING

54 MIDDLETON CHENEY GARDENS

Middleton Cheney, Banbury, OX17 2ST. *3m E of Banbury. From M40 J11 follow A422 signed Middleton Cheney. Map available at all gardens.* **Sun 17 June (1-6). Combined adm £5, chd free. Home-made teas at Peartree House.**

CHURCH COTTAGE
David & Sue Thompson.

CROFT HOUSE
Richard & Sandy Walmsley.

GLEBE BARN
John & Verena Childs.

19 GLOVERS LANE
Michael Donohoe & Jane Rixon.

38 MIDWAY
Margaret & David Finch.

PEARTREE HOUSE
Roger & Barbara Charlesworth.

14 QUEEN STREET
Brian & Kathy Goodey.

SPRINGFIELD HOUSE
Lynn & Paul Taylor.

Large village with C13 church with renowned William Morris stained glass. 8 open gardens with a variety of sizes, styles and maturity. Of the smaller gardens, one contemporary garden contrasts formal features with colour-filled beds, borders and exotic plants. Another modern garden has flowing curves that creates an elegant, serene feeling. One features cottage and Mediterranean planting with summerhouse and statuary. A mature small front and back garden is planted profusely and feels like an intimate haven. A garden that has evolved through family use feature rooms and dense planting. The larger gardens incl a thatched barn conversion with a garden; everything you would expect from a greenhouse, to vegetables, to chickens. Another continues with its renovation of a long lost garden, along with restoring areas of orchard, beds and borders. A third has an air of mystery with hidden corners and an extensive water feature weaving its way throughout the garden.

55 MIDSUMMER HOUSE

Woolstone, Faringdon, SN7 7QL. Anthony & Penny Spink. *7m W & 7m S of Faringdon. Woolstone is a small village off B4507, below Uffington White Horse Hill.* **Sun 24 June (2-6). Combined adm with Woolstone Mill House £6, chd free. Home-made teas.**

On moving to Midsummer House three years ago, new owners created the garden using herbaceous plants brought with them from their previous home at Woolstone Mill House. Herbaceous border, parterre with new topiary, and espaliered Malus Everest. Opening with Woolstone Mill House which is now owned by their son, renowned landscape architect Justin Spink.

56 MILL BARN

25 Mill Lane, Chalgrove, OX44 7SL. Pat Hougham, 01865 890020, pat@gmec.co.uk. *12m E of Oxford. Chalgrove is 4m from Watlington off B480. Mill Barn is in Mill Lane on the W of Chalgrove, 300yds S of Lamb Pub. Parking in lane or gravel entrance yard.* **Sun 1 July, Sun 2 Sept (2-4.30). Adm £4, chd free. Light refreshments. Visits also by arrangement May to Sept.**

Mill Barn has an informal cottage garden with a variety of flowers, shrubs and fruit trees including medlar, mulberry and quince in sunny and shaded beds. Rose arches and a pergola lead to a vegetable plot surrounded by a cordon of fruit trees all set in a mill stream landscape.

57 MONKS HEAD

Weston Road, Bletchingdon, OX5 3DH. Sue Bedwell, 01869 350155, bedwell615@btinternet.com.

Approx 4m N of Kidlington. From A34 take B4027 to Bletchingdon, turn R at Xrds into Weston Rd. **Sun 11 Mar, Thur 12 Apr (2-5); Mon 7 May (2-5.30). Adm £3, chd free. Home-made teas. Visits also by arrangement.**
Plantaholics' garden for all year interest. Bulb frame and alpine area, greenhouse. Changes evolving all the time.

58 NEW 16 OAKFIELD ROAD

Carterton, OX18 3QN. Karen & Jason Cammish, 01993 841066, jakacam@ntlworld.com. *Off A40 Oxford W bound Carterton & Brize Norton junction. Go past RAF Brize Norton main gate, head for town center. Through T-lights, take 3rd L Foxcroft Dr. Follow road around to T-junction, then turn R into Oakfield Rd.* **Visits by arrangement for one weekend only on Sat 11 & Sun 12 Aug. Please contact for staggered appointment times. Adm £4, chd free. Tea, cake & light refreshments.**
A tropical inspired garden that incorporates good use of the small space. Overflowing with palms, bamboo, cannas, tree ferns, hedychiums, tetrapanax papyrifera 'rex', and colocasia. Small wooden walkway leading to a decked area with hot tub and thatched gazebo with seating. Also small pond, lawn, patio area with pots and greenhouse, all in an area of approx 10 metres x 12 metres. Partial wheelchair access on patio area only.

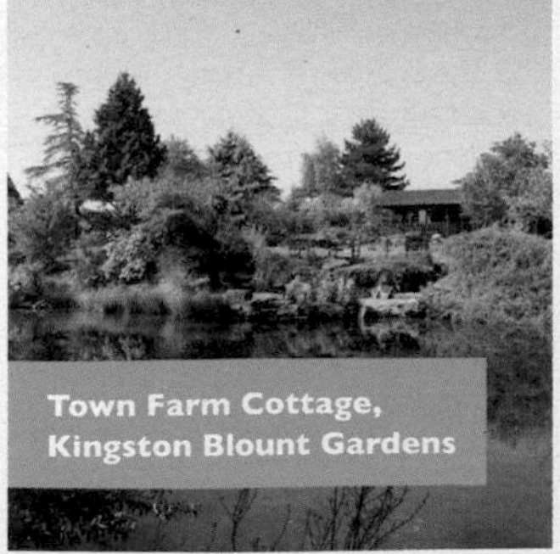
Town Farm Cottage, Kingston Blount Gardens

GROUP OPENING

59 OLD BOARS HILL GARDENS

Jarn Way, Boars Hill, Oxford, OX1 5JF. Charles & Lyn Sanders. *3m S of Oxford. From S ring road towards A34 at r'about follow signs to Wootton & Boars Hill. Up Hinksey Hill take R fork. 1m R into Berkley Rd to Old Boars Hill.* **Sun 29 Apr (2-6). Combined adm £5, chd free. Home-made teas at Uplands.**

NEW HOLLY TREE HOUSE
Jillian Morrow.

UPLANDS
Charles & Lyn Sanders, 01865 739486, sandersc4@hotmail.com. **Visits also by arrangement Mar to Oct.**

WHITSUN MEADOWS
Jane & Nigel Jones.

Three delightful gardens in a semi-rural conservation area with views over Oxford. Each garden has a different setting. Uplands a southerly facing garden full of colour and an extensive range of plants for all seasons. Whitsun Meadows has a magical backdrop with a mixture of mature Scots pine, English oak, acer and cherry. Against this the owners have developed an interesting mixture of herbaceous borders, hosta beds, gravel gardens and a wild flower meadow defined by a curving cleft chestnut post and rail fencing, all on a pleasingly level site of 2 acres. New for 2018, Holly Tree House, a beautiful landscaped garden of flowers, shrubs and mature trees, on three levels down the side of a hill including seasonal interest and seating at each level. Follow pathways to discover sculptures by local and national artists, fragrant rose beds, water features and a tucked away 1 acre cottage garden.

60 THE OLD MILL

Berry Lane, Blewbury, Didcot, OX11 9QJ. Dermot & Helen Mathias. *Turn off A417 in Blewbury into Westbrook St & follow yellow signs for parking in village hall. Limited disabled parking at house, please phone 01235 850359 to reserve a space.* **Sun 20 May (2-5.30). Adm £4, chd free. Home-made teas.**
3 acre garden bounded by streams on three sides with unusual trees, mill pond and further ponds. Mixed borders, vegetable and soft fruit garden, further acre with small orchard in wild flower field, cutting garden and vegetable plot.

61 OLD RECTORY

Salford, Chipping Norton, OX7 5YL. Mr & Mrs N M Chambers, 01608 643969. *Small village on A44, approx 3m W of Chipping Norton.* **Visits by arrangement Feb to Oct for groups of 10 max. Adm £4, chd free.**
1½ acre garden with yr-round interest. Early flowering shrubs and bulbs, some snowdrops, mixed borders and old roses. Small orchard and vegetable garden. Salford Inn open for lunch from 12.00-2.30pm (closed on Mondays). Partial wheelchair access. No dogs.

62 THE OLD VICARAGE

Aston Rowant, Watlington, OX49 5ST. Julian & Rona Knight, 01844 351315, jknight652@aol.com. *Between Chinnor & Watlington, off B4009. From M40 J6, take B4009 towards Chinnor & Princes Risborough. After 1m, turn L signed Aston Rowant Village only.* **Visits by arrangement June to Sept for groups of 10-30. Tea & home-made cake, or wine & snacks. Adm £4, chd free.**
Romantic, 1¾ acre vicarage garden, lovingly rejuvenated and enjoyed by the present family. Centered around a croquet lawn surrounded by beds brimming with shrubs and herbaceous plants, hot bed and roses. Lushly planted pond leading through a pergola overflowing with roses and clematis, to a tranquil green garden. Small vegetable and cutting garden.

63 THE OLD VICARAGE, BLEDINGTON

Main Road, Bledington, Chipping Norton, OX7 6UX. Sue & Tony Windsor, 01608 658525, tony.g.windsor@gmail.com. *6m SW of Chipping Norton. 4m SE of Stow-on-the-Wold. On the main street B4450 through Bledington. Not next to church.* **Sun 22 Apr (11-5); Sun 17 June (1-6). Adm £4, chd free. Visits also by arrangement Apr to July for groups up to 35 max. Refreshments on request.**

1½ acre garden around a late Georgian vicarage (1843) not open. Borders and beds filled with spring bulbs, hardy perennials, shrubs and trees. Informal rose garden with over 300 David Austin roses. Small pond and vegetable garden. Paddock with trees, shrubs and herbaceous border. Planted for yr-round interest. Gravel driveway and gently sloped garden.

64 116 OXFORD ROAD

Abingdon, OX14 2AG. Mr & Mrs P Aylward, 01235 523925, aylwardsdooz@hotmail.co.uk. *116 Oxford Road is on the RH-side if coming from A34 N exit, or on the LH-side after Picklers Hill, turn if approaching from Abingdon town centre.* **Sun 3 June (11-4). Combined adm with Failford £4, chd free. Home-made teas. Visits also by arrangement May to Sept for groups up to 20 max. Refreshments on request.**

New town garden opening for its second year, a creation that started in July 2014. The garden is wedge-shaped, 70ft x 37ft wide at the bottom and 80ft in length. The challenge was it had to be interesting and look as though it had been there for many years. It incorporates quirky features, raised beds, lawns, herbaceous borders and a diverse collection of plants and trees. Access by gravel driveway.

65 PLACKETTS

High Street, Adderbury, Banbury, OX17 3LS. Dr D White, 01295 812679. *Enter village after 300yds garden on L. From Bloxham, garden straight ahead as you pass Tithe Barn in village.* **Visits by arrangement June to Aug for groups up to 25 max.**

Queen Anne cottage (not open); ⅕ acre walled garden and sheltered gravel courtyard. Main garden exposed and sunny with views. Many tulips, euphorbias, primulas, anemones. Numerous clematis and paeonies. Partial wheelchair access, some gravel to cross.

66 50 PLANTATION ROAD

Oxford, OX2 6JE. Philippa Scoones. *Central Oxford. N on Woodstock Rd take 2nd L. Coming into Oxford on Woodstock Rd turn R after Leckford Rd. No disabled parking nr house.* **Sat 28, Sun 29 Apr, Sat 5, Sun 6 May (2-6). Adm £3.50, chd free. Home-made teas.**

Surprisingly spacious city garden designed in specific sections. N-facing front garden, side alley filled with shade loving climbers. S-facing rear garden with hundreds of tulips in spring, unusual trees incl Mount Etna Broom, conservatory, terraced area and secluded water garden with water feature, woodland plants and alpines.

67 RADCOT HOUSE

Radcot, OX18 2SX. Robin & Jeanne Stainer, www.radcothouse.com. *1¼m S of Clanfield. On A4095 between Witney & Faringdon, 300yds N of Radcot bridge.* **Sun 19 Aug, Sun 7 Oct (2-6). Adm £5, chd free. Home-made teas.**

Approx 3 acres of dramatic yet harmonious planting in light and shade, formal pond, fruit and vegetable cages. Convenient seating at key points enables relaxed observation and reflection. Extensive use of grasses and unusual perennials and interesting sculptural surprises. Spectacular autumn display.

68 RIDGEWAY

Lincombe Lane, Boars Hill, Oxford, OX1 5DZ. John & Viccy Fleming, www.facebook.com/RidgewayOpenGarden/. *Between Oxford & Abingdon. Off Foxcombe Rd & Fox Lane between A34 Hinksey Hill r'about & B4017 Wootton to Abingdon road. Nearly opp Fox Pub.* **Sat 19, Sun 20 May (2-5). Adm £4, chd free. Light refreshments.**

Developed since 2004 to provide yr-round interest, this ¾ acre garden on sandy soil has some rare shrubs and plants. The intricate design incl 2 alpine beds, a fruit garden, a vegetable garden and multiple borders with varied planting. Paths are gravel and woodchip.

GROUP OPENING

69 SIBFORD GARDENS

Sibford Gower, OX15 5RX. *7m W of Banbury. Nr the Warwickshire border, S of B4035, in centre of village nr Wykham Arms Pub.* **Sun 24 June (2-6). Combined adm £7, chd free. Home-made teas at Sibford Gower Village Hall (opp the church).**

BUTTSLADE HOUSE
James & Sarah Garstin.

CARTER'S YARD
Sue & Malcolm Bannister, 01295 780365, sebannister@gmail.com. **Visits also by arrangement May to Oct for groups of 5+, guided by the owner.**

HOME CLOSE
Graham & Carolyn White.

LARKSPUR
Ivan & Veronique Tyrrell.

STICKLEYS HOUSE
Stephen Gomersall.

In two charming small villages of Sibford Gower and Sibford Ferris, off the beaten track with thatched stone cottages, five contrasting gardens ranging from an early C20 Arts and Crafts house (not open) and garden, to varied cottage gardens bursting with bloom, interesting planting and some unusual plants. No wheelchair access to Carter's Yard, partial access to Buttslade House and Home Close.

70 SPARSHOLT MANOR
Wantage, OX12 9PT. Sir Adrian & Lady Judith Swire. *3½m W of Wantage. Off B4507 Ashbury Rd.* **Mon 7 May (2-6). Adm £4, chd free.**
Lakes and wildfowl; ancient boxwood wilderness with walkways and summer borders. Wheelchair access to most of the garden.

71 64 SPRING ROAD
Abingdon, OX14 1AN. Mrs Janet Boulton, 01235 524514, j.boulton89@btinternet.com, www.janetboulton.co.uk. *S Abingdon from A34 take L turn after police station into Spring Rd. Minute's drive to number 64 on L.* **Visits by arrangement May to Sept for limited numbers only. Adm £6, chd free.**
An artist's garden (4½ x 30½ metres) behind a Victorian terrace house, narrow with steps. Predominantly green it contains numerous sculptures with inscriptions relating to art, history and the human spirit.

GROUP OPENING

72 STEEPLE ASTON GARDENS
Steeple Aston, OX25 4SP. *14m N of Oxford, 9m S of Banbury. ½m E of A4260.* **Sun 3 June (1-6). Combined adm £6, chd free. Home-made teas in village hall.**

ACACIA COTTAGE
Jane & David Stewart.

NEW **CEDAR COTTAGE**
Robert Scott.

COMBE PYNE
Chris & Sally Cooper.

KRALINGEN
Mr & Mrs Roderick Nicholson.

THE LONGBYRE
Mr Vaughan Billings.

THE POUND HOUSE
Mr & Mrs R Clarke.

PRIMROSE GARDENS
Richard & Daphne Preston, 01869 340512, richard.preston5@btopenworld.com. **Visits also by arrangement Feb to Sept. Refreshments on request.**

TOUCHWOOD
Gary Norris.

Steeple Aston, often considered the most easterly of the Cotswold villages, is a beautiful stone built village with gardens that provide a huge range of interest. A stream meanders down the hill as the landscape changes from sand to clay. The 8 open gardens incl; small floriferous cottage gardens, large landscaped gardens, natural woodland areas, ponds and bog gardens, and themed borders. No wheelchair access at Primrose Gardens.

73 STONEHAVEN
6 High Street, Cumnor, Oxford, OX2 9PE. Dr Dianne & Prof Keith Gull. *4m from central Oxford. Exit to Cumnor from the A420. In centre of village opp PO. Parking at back of PO.* **Sun 11 Feb (2-5). Adm £3, chd free. Opening with Cumnor Village Gardens on Sun 10 June.**
Front, side and rear garden of a thatched cottage (not open). Front is partly gravelled and side courtyard has many pots. Rear garden overlooks meadows, with old apple trees underplanted with ferns, wildlife pond, unusual plants, many with black or bronze foliage, planted in drifts and repeated throughout the garden. Planting has mild Japanese influence; rounded, clipped shapes interspersed with verticals. Snowdrops in February. There are two pubs in the village serving food; The Bear & Ragged Staff and The Vine. Gravel drive to access garden.

74 NEW **SWERFORD PARK**
nr Chipping Norton, OX7 4AT. Mr & Mrs J W Law. *4m NE of Chipping Norton. Just off A361 to Banbury. ½m W of Swerford Church. Approach along front drive where signed, parking at rear only.* **Sat 16, Sun 17 June (2-6). Adm £6, chd free. Home-made teas.**
In extensive parkland setting with lakeside walk, garden of Georgian house (not open), overlooks spectacular wooded valley with series of lakes linked by waterfalls.

75 TRINITY COLLEGE
Broad Street, Oxford, OX1 3BH. Paul Lawrence, Head Gardener, www.trinity.ox.ac.uk. *Central Oxford. Entrance in Broad St.* **Sun 25 Mar, Sun 29 July (1-5). Adm £2.50, chd free. Home-made teas in dining hall.**
Historic main College gardens with specimen trees incl aged forked catalpa, spring bulbs, fine long herbaceous border and handsome garden quad originally designed by Wren. President's Garden surrounded by high old stone walls, mixed borders of herbaceous, shrubs and statuary. Fellows' Garden, small walled terrace, herbaceous borders and water feature formed by Jacobean stone heraldic beasts. Award-winning Lavender Garden and walk-through rose arbour.

76 ◆ UNIVERSITY OF OXFORD BOTANIC GARDEN

Rose Lane, Oxford, OX1 4AZ. University of Oxford, 01865 286690, www.botanic-garden.ox.ac.uk. *1m E of Oxford city centre. Bottom of High St in central Oxford, on banks of the River Cherwell by Magdalen Bridge & opp Magdalen College Tower.* **For opening times and information, please phone or visit garden website.**

The Botanic Garden contains plants that originate from all over the world. It is one of the most biodiverse collections of plants per acre globally. These plants are grown in 7 glasshouses, water and rock gardens, large herbaceous border, walled garden and every available space. In total there are around 5,000 different plants to see. Features incl glasshouses, systematic beds, National Collection of hardy Euphorbia species, herbaceous border, the Merton borders, biodiversity hotspot collections, fruit and vegetable collection. Gravel paths.

16 Oakfield Road

77 UPPER GREEN

Brill Road, Horton cum Studley, Oxford, OX33 1BU. Susan & Peter Burge, 01865 351310, sue.burge@ndm.ox.ac.uk, www.uppergreengarden.co.uk. *6½m NE of Oxford. Enter village, turn R up Horton Hill. At T-junction turn L into Brill Rd. Upper Green 250yds on R, 2 gates before pillar box. Roadside parking.* **Sun 8 Apr, Sun 17 June (2-5). Combined adm with Hilltop Cottage £5, chd free. Sun 2 Sept (2-5). Adm £4, chd free. Home-made teas at Studley Barn (Apr), Upper Green (June & Sept). Visits also by arrangement Feb to Sept for groups of up to 20 max.** Donation to The British Skin Foundation.

Mature ½ acre garden with gravel area, mixed borders, potager, bog area and pond. Variety of snowdrops. Spring colour with marsh marigolds, hellebores, euphorbias, fritillaries and other bulbs. Perennials, ferns, grasses and shrubs provide yr-round interest. Old apple trees support rambling roses. Plant lists. Sculptures by Sophie Thompson. Gravel drive limits wheelchair access.

78 WADHAM COLLEGE

Parks Road, Oxford, OX1 3PN. The Warden & Fellows. *Central Oxford. Wadham College gardens are accessed through the main entrance of the College on Parks Rd.* **Sun 8 Apr, Sun 8 July (2-5). Adm £2, chd free.**

5 acres, best known for trees, spring bulbs and mixed borders. In Fellows' main garden, fine ginkgo and *Magnolia acuminata*; bamboo plantation; in Back Quadrangle very large *Tilia tomentosa* 'Petiolaris'; in Mallam Court white scented garden est 1994; in Warden's garden an ancient tulip tree; in Fellows' private garden, Civil War embankment with period fruit tree cultivars, recently established shrubbery with unusual trees and ground cover amongst older plantings.

79 ◆ WATERPERRY GARDENS

Waterperry, Wheatley, OX33 1JZ. School of Economic Science, 01844 339226, office@waterperrygardens.co.uk, www.waterperrygardens.co.uk. *7½m from Oxford city centre. From E M40 J8, from N M40 J8a. Follow brown tourist signs. For SatNav please use OX33 1LA.* **For NGS: Sun 15 Apr, Sun 16 Sept (10-5.30). Adm £7.95, chd free. Light refreshments in the teashop (10-5). For other opening times and information, please phone, email or visit garden website.**

Waterperry gardens are extensive, well-maintained and full of interesting plants. From The Virgin's Walk with its shade-loving plants to the long classical herbaceous border, brilliantly colourful from late May until Oct. The Mary Rose Garden illustrates modern and older roses, and the formal garden is neatly designed and colourful, with a small knot garden, herb border and wisteria tunnel. Newly redesigned walled garden, river walk, statues and pear orchard. Riverside walk may be inaccessible to wheelchair users if very wet.

NPC

80 WAYSIDE

82 Banbury Road, Kidlington, OX5 2BX. Margaret & Alistair Urquhart, 01865 460180, alistairurquhart@ntlworld.com. *5m N of Oxford. On R of A4260 travelling N through Kidlington.* **Sun 3 June (2-6). Adm £3, chd free. Tea. Visits also by arrangement May & June.**

¼ acre garden shaded by mature trees. Mixed border with some rare and unusual plants and shrubs. A climber clothed pergola leads past a dry gravel garden to the woodland garden with an extensive collection of hardy ferns. Conservatory and large fern house with a collection of unusual species of tree ferns and tender exotics. Important collection of hardy garden ferns. Partial wheelchair access.

81 WESTWELL MANOR

Westwell, Nr Burford, OX18 4JT. Mr Thomas Gibson. *2m SW of Burford. From A40 Burford-Cheltenham, turn L ½m after Burford r'about signed Westwell. After 1½m at T-junction, turn R & Manor is 2nd house on L.* **Sun 27 May (2.30-6). Adm £5, chd free.** Donation to St Marys Church, Westwell.

7 acres surrounding old Cotswold manor house (not open), with knot garden, potager, shrub roses, herbaceous borders, topiary, earth works, moonlight garden, auricula ladder, rills and water garden.

✽

GROUP OPENING

82 WHEATLEY GARDENS

High Street, Wheatley, OX33 1XX. 01865 875022, echess@hotmail.co.uk. *5m E of Oxford. Leave A40 at Wheatley, turn into High St. Gardens at W end of High St, S side.* **Sun 10 June (2-6). Combined adm £5, chd free. Cream teas at The Manor House. Visits also by arrangement Mar to July.**

BREACH HOUSE GARDEN
Liz Parry.

CATCHMOLE COTTAGE
Catherine Lane.

THE MANOR HOUSE
Mrs Elizabeth Hess.

THE STUDIO
S & A Buckingham.

Four adjoining gardens in the historic coaching village of Wheatley. Catchmole Cottage garden has been developed over 30 yrs to provide sanctuary for wildlife, birds, insects and slow-worms. Surrounded by ancient walls and high shrubs the garden is a frost pocket so is planted with hardy perennials, shrubs and ferns. Breach House Garden has an established main area with extensive shrubs and perennials, a more contemporary reflective space and a wild meadow with ponds. The Studio, cottage style walled garden developed from previous farmyard. Herbaceous borders, climbing roses and clematis, shrubs, vegetable plot and fruit trees. The Manor House is a 1½ acre garden surrounding an Elizabethan manor house (not open). Formal box walk, herb garden, cottage garden with rose arches and a shrubbery with old roses. A romantic oasis. All in all a lovely collection of gardens set in the heart of the busy village of Wheatley. Various musical events. Wheelchair access with assistance, although there are gravel paths, two shallow steps and grass.

♿ 🐕 ✽ ☕

83 WHITEHILL FARM

Widford, Burford, OX18 4DT. Mr & Mrs Paul Youngson, 01993 822894, anneyoungson@btinternet.com. *1m E of Burford. From A40 take road signed Widford. Turn R at the bottom of the hill, 1st house on the L with ample car parking.* **Sun 3 June (2-6). Adm £4, chd free. Home-made teas. Visits also by arrangement May to Aug for groups of 10+ only.**

2 acres of hillside gardens and woodland with spectacular views overlooking Burford and Windrush valley. Informal plantsman's garden built up by the owners over 20 yrs. Herbaceous and shrub borders, ponds and bog area, old fashioned roses, ground cover, ornamental grasses, bamboos and hardy geraniums. Large cascade water feature, pretty tea patio and wonderful Cotswold views.

🐕 ✽ ☕

84 WOOLSTONE MILL HOUSE

Woolstone, Faringdon, SN7 7QL. Mr & Mrs Justin Spink. *7m W of Wantage. 7m S of Faringdon. Woolstone is a small village off B4507, below Uffington White Horse Hill.* **Sun 24 June (2-6). Combined adm with Midsummer House £6, chd free. Home-made teas.**

Redesigned by new owner, garden designer Justin Spink in 2015, this 1½ acre garden has large mixed perennial beds, and small gravel, cutting, kitchen and bog gardens. Topiary, medlars and old fashioned roses. Treehouse with spectacular views to Uffington White Horse and White Horse Hill. C18 millhouse and barn (not open). Partial wheelchair access.

♿ 🚌 ☕

GROUP OPENING

85 WOOTTON GARDENS

Wootton, OX13 6DP. *Wootton is 3m SW of Oxford. From the Oxford ring road S, take the turning to Wootton. Parking for all gardens at the Bystander Pub & on the road.* **Thur 14 June (2-5.30). Combined adm £5, chd free. Tea.**

60 BESSELSLEIGH ROAD
Mrs Freda East.

22 SANDLEIGH ROAD
Mr & Mrs Peter & Jennie Debenham.

35 SANDLEIGH ROAD
Mrs Hilal Baylav Inkersole.

3 inspirational small gardens, all with very different ways of providing a personal joy. 60 Besselsleigh Road has 'The Deadwood Stage' with toadstools and a secret garden with many creatures to find. 22 Sandleigh Road is a wildlife friendly garden packed with cottage garden favourites beside brick paths. A kitchen garden is complete with chickens and a beach hut! 35 Sandleigh Road is a mature garden, laid to lawn on two levels. Grown mostly from cuttings the garden is brimming with vibrant flowers, pond-side planting and mature shrubs. Partial wheelchair access.

♿ ✽ ☕

SHROPSHIRE

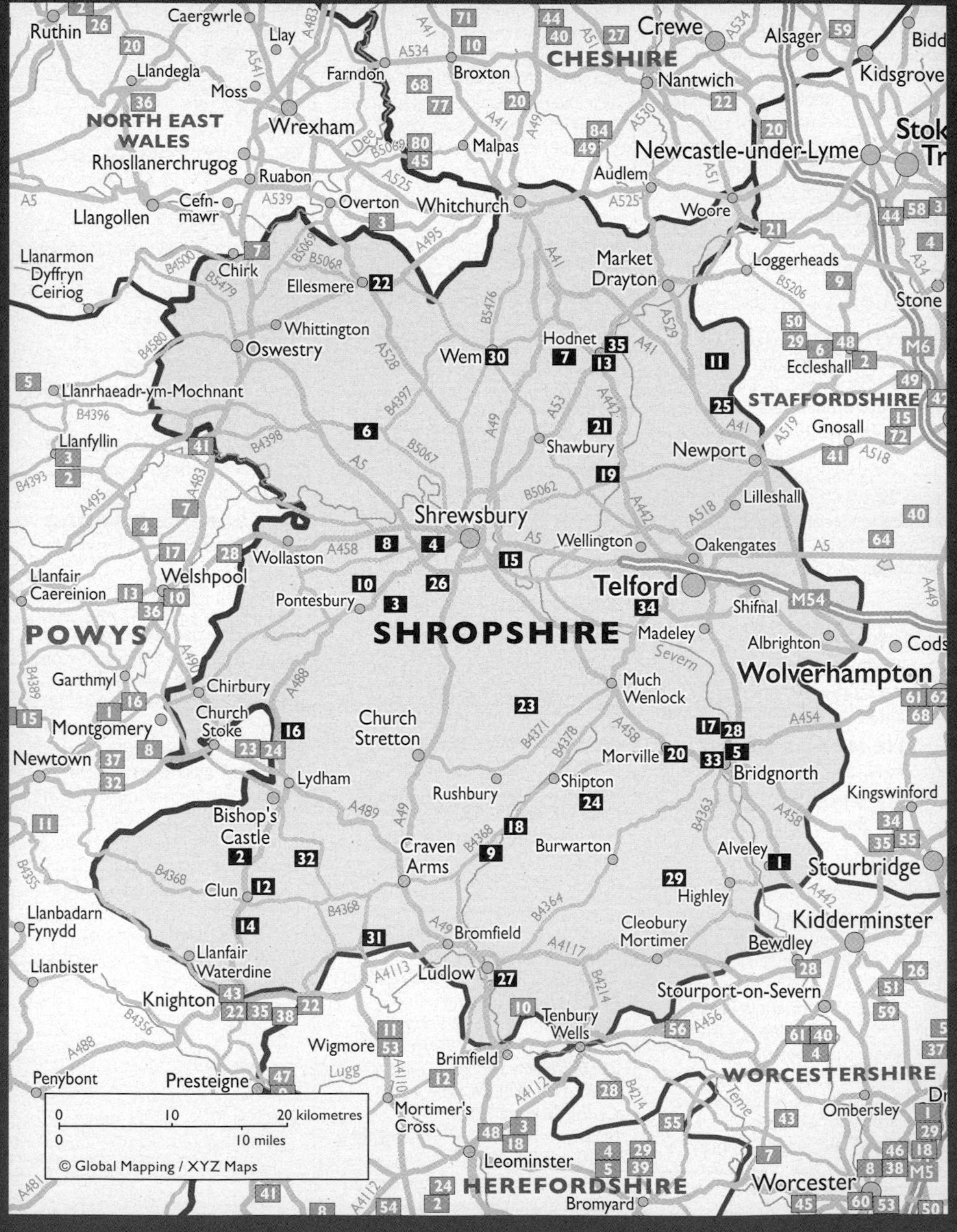

CHESHIRE
NORTH EAST WALES
POWYS
SHROPSHIRE
STAFFORDSHIRE
WORCESTERSHIRE
HEREFORDSHIRE
Ruthin
Caergwrle
Llay
Llandegla
Moss
Wrexham
Farndon
Broxton
Crewe
Alsager
Kidsgrove
Nantwich
Malpas
Audlem
Newcastle-under-Lyme
Rhosllanerchrugog
Ruabon
Overton
Whitchurch
Woore
Llangollen
Cefn-mawr
Llanarmon Dyffryn Ceiriog
Chirk
Ellesmere
Market Drayton
Loggerheads
Stone
Whittington
Oswestry
Wem
Hodnet
Eccleshall
Llanrhaeadr-ym-Mochnant
Llanfyllin
Shawbury
Newport
Gnosall
Lilleshall
Shrewsbury
Wellington
Oakengates
Wollaston
Welshpool
Llanfair Caereinion
Pontesbury
Telford
Shifnal
Madeley
Albrighton
Wolverhampton
Severn
Garthmyl
Chirbury
Much Wenlock
Church Stoke
Montgomery
Church Stretton
Newtown
Morville
Bridgnorth
Lydham
Rushbury
Shipton
Kingswinford
Bishop's Castle
Craven Arms
Burwarton
Alveley
Stourbridge
Clun
Highley
Kidderminster
Llanbadarn Fynydd
Bromfield
Cleobury Mortimer
Bewdley
Llanfair Waterdine
Llanbister
Ludlow
Stourport-on-Severn
Knighton
Tenbury Wells
Wigmore
Brimfield
Penybont
Presteigne
Lugg
Mortimer's Cross
Teme
Ombersley
Leominster
Worcester
Bromyard
0 10 20 kilometres
0 10 miles
© Global Mapping / XYZ Maps

One of England's best kept secrets and one of the least populated areas in the country, Shropshire has a lot to offer visitors.

Our county has stunning gardens, majestic estates, interesting towns, history both modern and new (Shropshire was home to the ancient tribes of Mercia and also the birthplace of modern industry at Ironbridge), wonderful natural beauties such as the 'Blue Remembered Hills' that the poet A. E. Housman epitomised, and Shropshire is the self-proclaimed 'foodie' capital of Britain.

Above all, Shropshire's gardens are a must for the visitor. Generous garden owners and volunteers across the county have many open gardens, ranging from large estates to small, beautifully designed town gardens.

We hope 2018 will be another successful year where many garden openers welcome dogs and children and provide wonderful home-made teas and raise money for our very important charities.

Volunteers

County Organiser
Allison Walter
01743 627900
allison.walter@ngs.org.uk

County Treasurer
Suzanne Stevens
01588 660314
harrystevens@btconnect.com

Publicity
Victoria Kirk
01743 821429
victoria.kirk@ngs.org.uk

April Jones
april.jones@ngs.org.uk

Booklet Co-ordinator
Fiona Chancellor
01952 507675
fionachancellor@btinternet.com

Talks Organiser
Chris Neil
01743 821651

Assistant County Organisers
Sue Griffiths
sue.griffiths@btinternet.com

Sheila Jones
smaryjones@icloud.com

Louise Roberts
louroberts@btinternet.com

Left: Wollerton Old Hall

OPENING DATES

All entries subject to change. For latest information check **www.ngs.org.uk**

Extended openings are shown at the beginning of the month.

Map locator numbers are shown to the right of each garden name.

February

Snowdrop Festival

Sunday 18th
Millichope Park 18

April

Sunday 8th
Edge Villa 10

Friday 13th
8 Westgate Villas 33

Sunday 15th
8 Westgate Villas 33

Tuesday 24th
Brownhill House 6

May

Sunday 6th
Lyndale House 17
Millichope Park 18

Monday 7th
Ruthall Manor 24

Saturday 12th
Upper Shelderton House 31

Sunday 13th
The Citadel 7
Guilden Down Cottage 12
Oteley 22
Upper Shelderton House 31

Friday 18th
Ruthall Manor 24
◆ Wollerton Old Hall 35

Saturday 19th
Edge Villa 10
Ruthall Manor 24

Sunday 20th
Ancoireán 1
Delbury Hall Walled Garden 9
Longner Hall 15
Stanley Hall 28

Tuesday 22nd
Brownhill House 6

Sunday 27th
Walcot Hall 32

Monday 28th
Walcot Hall 32

Wednesday 30th
Goldstone Hall Gardens 11

June

Festival Weekend

Saturday 2nd
NEW Cruckfield House 8

Sunday 3rd
NEW 2 School Cottages 26
Windy Ridge 34

Friday 8th
Ruthall Manor 24

Saturday 9th
Ruthall Manor 24

Sunday 10th
Delbury Hall Walled Garden 9
Hodnet Hall Gardens 13
Morville Hall Gardens 20

Saturday 16th
Stottesdon & District Open Gardens 29

Sunday 17th
Preen Manor 23
Stottesdon & District Open Gardens 29

Saturday 23rd
Secret Garden 27

Sunday 24th
Delbury Hall Walled Garden 9

Tuesday 26th
Brownhill House 6

Wednesday 27th
Goldstone Hall Gardens 11

July

Sunday 1st
NEW Lower Brookshill 16
NEW 2 School Cottages 26

Saturday 7th
NEW Cruckfield House 8
Ruthall Manor 24

Sunday 8th
Ruthall Manor 24
Windy Ridge 34

Wednesday 11th
Goldstone Hall Gardens 11
Oakgate Nursery & Garden Centre 21

Sunday 15th
Delbury Hall Walled Garden 9
Sambrook Manor 25

Sunday 22nd
Sunningdale 30

Wednesday 25th
Goldstone Hall Gardens 11

August

Wednesday 1st
Goldstone Hall Gardens 11

Sunday 12th
Sambrook Manor 25
Windy Ridge 34

Wednesday 15th
Goldstone Hall Gardens 11

Sunday 19th
Delbury Hall Walled Garden 9
Edge Villa 10

Wednesday 29th
Goldstone Hall Gardens 11

September

Sunday 2nd
Windy Ridge 34

Wednesday 5th
Goldstone Hall Gardens 11

Sunday 9th
48 Bramble Ridge 5
Sunningdale 30

Saturday 15th
Ruthall Manor 24

Sunday 16th
Ruthall Manor 24

October

Sunday 14th
Millichope Park 18

By Arrangement

Ancoireán 1
NEW Argoed House 2
Avocet 3
Bowbrook Allotment Community 4
Brownhill House 6
The Citadel 7
NEW Cruckfield House 8
Edge Villa 10
Goldstone Hall Gardens 11
Guilden Down Cottage 12
The Hollies 14
NEW Lower Brookshill 16
Lyndale House 17
Moortown 19
Oteley 22
Preen Manor 23
Ruthall Manor 24
Sambrook Manor 25
Secret Garden 27
Sunningdale 30
Walcot Hall 32
Windy Ridge 34

Your visit helps Marie Curie work night and day in people's homes

THE GARDENS

1 ANCOIREÁN
24 Romsley View, Alveley, WV15 6PJ. Judy & Peter Creed, 01746 780504, pdjc@me.com. *6m S Bridgnorth off A442 Bridgnorth to Kidderminster rd. N from Kidderminster turn L just after Royal Oak PH. S from Bridgnorth turn R after Squirrel Pub. Take 3rd turning on R & follow NGS signs.* **Sun 20 May (1-5). Adm £4, chd free. Home-made teas. Visits also by arrangement May & June 20+.**
Natural garden layout on several levels, developed over 30yrs, with a large variety of herbaceous plants and shrubs, water features, wooded area with bog garden containing numerous varieties of ferns and hostas, and colourful alpine scree. Features, wooded area, stumpery, ornamental grass border and Spring bulb collection, clematis collection, acer and azalea beds. Selection of plants, bird and insect boxes for sale. Close to Severn Valley Railway and Country Park and Dudmaston Hall NT.

2 NEW ARGOED HOUSE
Bryn, Bishops Castle, SY9 5LE. Roger & Jane Fairweather, 01588 630663, janefairweather1@icloud.com. *Bishop's Castle A488 S for 3m. Take lane on R "Bryn 1, Cerfn Einion 2, Mainstone 3" for ½m past Captain's Coppice. At fork go right up hill. Garden 200yds on L. Email for map.* **Visits by arrangement May to July for individuals and groups of 20 max. Adm £4, chd free. Home-made teas.**
1 acre garden approx. 700ft high, nestled amongst hills and surrounded by woods. The front garden was professionally landscaped in 2002 with large beds of spring bulbs, perennial plants and shrubs, living willow structures and a sizeable pond with informal planting. This opens out into a sloping mown areas with specimen trees. To the rear, the garden goes uphill and is left for wild flowers.

3 AVOCET
3 Main Road, Plealey, Shrewsbury, SY5 0UZ. Malc & Jude Mollart, 01743 791743, malcandjude@btinternet.com. *6m SW of Shrewsbury. From A5 take A488 signed Bishops Castle, approx ½m past Lea Cross Tandoori turn L signed Plealey. In ¾m turn L, garden on R. SatNav unreliable!* **Visits by arrangement Apr to Aug individuals or groups. Adm £4, chd free. Home-made teas.**
Cottage style garden with modern twists owned by plantaholics and shared with wildlife. Designed around a series of garden compartments and for year round interest. Features include a wildlife pool, mixed borders, seaside garden, gravel garden, succulents, trained fruit trees, and sculpture. Children are welcome. Countryside views and walks from the garden. The garden was featured in the launch edition of the 'My Shrewsbury' magazine.

ALLOTMENTS

4 BOWBROOK ALLOTMENT COMMUNITY
Mytton Oak Road, Shrewsbury, SY3 5BT. Bowbrook Allotment Community, 01743 363605, pete-haycox@hotmail.co.uk, bowbrookallotments.wordpress.com. *On western edge of Shrewsbury between A5 Bypass & Royal Shrewsbury Hospital. From A5 Shrewsbury Bypass take B4386 (Mytton Oak Road) towards Shrewsbury, following signs to Royal Shrewsbury Hospital. The allotment entrance is ½m from A5 r'about, on R, opp Oak Lane.* **Visits by arrangement May to Sept groups of 10+ (but less than 10 may be accepted). Adm £5, chd free. Light refreshments. Tea/Coffee and Cakes provided for visitors incl in adm**
Recipient of RHS National Certificate of Distinction, this 5 acre site, comprising 93 plots, displays wide ranging cultivation methods. The site has featured on BBC TV, local radio programmes and in several magazines. Members cultivate organically with nature in mind using companion planting and attracting natural predators. Green spaces flourish throughout and include Gardens of the 4 Seasons, orchards, and many wildlife features including wild flower meadows and pond. Children are encouraged to be part of the community and have their own special places such as a story telling willow dome, willow tunnel, sensory garden and turf spiral. See how the Contemplation Garden and the Prairie Garden have developed. Wheelchair access possible with care. Generally flat wide grass paths allow access to all the main areas of the site, although paths may be bumpy!

5 48 BRAMBLE RIDGE
Bridgnorth, WV16 4SQ. Chris & Heather. *From Bridgnorth N on B4373 signed Broseley. 1st on R Stanley Lane, 1st R Bramble Ridge. From Broseley S on B4373, nr Bridgnorth turn L into Stanley Lane, 1st R Bramble Ridge.* **Sun 9 Sept (12.30-5.30). Adm £4, chd free. Light refreshments.**
Steep garden with many steps, part wild, part cultivated, terraced in places and overlooking the Severn valley with views to High Rock and Queens Parlour. Described by some as fascinating and full of interest; the garden incl shrubs, perennials, small vegetable plot, herbs, wildlife pond and summerhouse. Full of interesting plants. Roughly 88 steps from the front of the house to the very top of the garden.

6 BROWNHILL HOUSE

Ruyton XI Towns, Shrewsbury, SY4 1LR. Roger & Yoland Brown, 01939 261121, brownhill@eleventowns.co.uk, www.eleventowns.co.uk. *9m NW of Shrewsbury on B4397. On the B4397 in the village of Ruyton XI Towns.* **Tue 24 Apr, Tue 22 May, Tue 26 June (1.30-5). Adm £4, chd free. Home-made teas. Visits also by arrangement May to July individuals or groups.**

"Has to be seen to be believed". A unique hillside garden (over 700 steps) bordering R Perry. Wide variety of styles and plants from formal terraces to woodland paths, plus large kitchen garden. Lawn area redeveloped in 2017 with new statues. Kit cars on show.

7 THE CITADEL

Weston-under-Redcastle, SY4 5JY. Mr Beverley & Mrs Sylvia Griffiths, 01630 685204, griffiths@thecitadelweston.co.uk, www.thecitadelweston.co.uk. *12m N of Shrewsbury on A49. At Xrds turn for Hawkstone Park, through village of Weston-under-Redcastle, ¼m on R beyond village.* **Sun 13 May (2-5). Adm £5, chd free. Home-made teas. Visits also by arrangement April to June groups of 10+.**

Imposing castellated house (not open) stands in 4 acres. Mature garden, with fine trees, rhododendrons, azaleas, acers and camellias. Herbaceous borders; walled potager and Victorian thatched summerhouse provide added interest. Paths meander around and over sandstone outcrop at centre.

8 NEW CRUCKFIELD HOUSE

Shoothill, Ford, Shrewsbury, SY5 9NR. Geoffrey Cobley, 01743 850222. *5m W of Shrewsbury. A458, turn L towards Shoothill.* **Sat 2 June, Sat 7 July (2-6). Adm £6, chd free. Home-made teas. Visits also by arrangement May to July min group 25+.**

3 acre romantic S-facing garden, formally designed, informally and intensively planted with a great variety of unusual herbaceous plants Nick's garden, with many species trees and shrubs, surrounds a large pond with bog and moisture-loving plants. Ornamental kitchen garden with pretty outbuildings. Rose and peony walk. Courtyard fountain garden and large shrubbery and extensive clematis collection. Topiary, large rockery and lily pond.

9 DELBURY HALL WALLED GARDEN

Delbury Hall Estate, Mill Lane, Diddlebury, Craven Arms, SY7 9DH. Mr & Mrs Rallings, www.myndhardyplants.co.uk. *8m W of Craven Arms. 1m off B4368, Craven Arms to Bridgnorth, through village of Diddlebury, turn R at Mynd Hardy Plants sign.* **Sun 20 May, Sun 10, Sun 24 June, Sun 15 July, Sun 19 Aug (11-5). Adm £4, chd free. Home-made teas.**

A two acre early Victorian Walled Garden with large herbaceous borders, a herb garden, shrubbery, demonstration vines and very old fruit trees. In addition there is a large Penstemon and Hemerocallis collection. The gardens of Delbury Hall will be accessible unless a private function is being held. Please check our website for details. Gravel and grass paths.

10 EDGE VILLA

Edge, nr Yockleton, SY5 9PY. Mr & Mrs W F Neil, 01743 821651, billfneil@me.com. *6m SW of Shrewsbury. From A5 take either A488 signed to Bishops Castle or B4386 to Montgomery for approx 6m then follow NGS signs.* **Sun 8 Apr, Sat 19 May, Sun 19 Aug (2-5). Adm £4, chd free. Home-made teas. Visits also by arrangement Apr to Aug group 10+.**

Two acres nestling in South Shropshire hills. Self-sufficient vegetable plot. Chickens in orchard, foxes permitting. Large herbaceous borders. Dewpond surrounded by purple elder, irises, candelabra primulas and dieramas. Large selection of fragrant roses. Teas in sheltered courtyard. Wendy House and Teepee for children. Some German and French spoken. Some gravel paths.

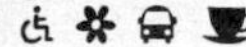

Lower Brookshill

11 GOLDSTONE HALL GARDENS

Goldstone, Market Drayton, TF9 2NA. Mr John Cushing, 01630 661202, enquiries@goldstonehall.com, www.goldstonehall.com. *5m N of Newport on A41. Follow brown signs from Hinstock. From Shrewsbury A53, R for A41 Hinstock & follow brown signs.* **Wed 30 May, 27 June, 11, 25 July, 1, 15, 29 Aug, 5 Sept (2-5). Adm £4.50, chd free. Home-made teas. Visits also by arrangement June to Sept for groups of 10+.**

5 acres with highly productive beautiful kitchen garden. Unusual vegetables and fruits - Large Polytunnel with Alpine strawbs, Heritage toms and crammed with salad, chillies, celeriac. Roses in Walled Garden from May, Double herbaceous at its best July and August but Sedums and Roses stunning in September. Teas in Pavilion with cakes created by Award Winning Chef. Lawn aficionados will enjoy the Stripes. Good Food Guide listed restaurant AA Red Star Country House Hotel Good Hotel Guide listed. Majority of garden can be accessed on gravel and lawns.

12 GUILDEN DOWN COTTAGE

Guilden Down, Clun, Craven Arms, SY7 8NZ. Mike Black & Sue Wilson, 01588 640124, sue.guilden@gmail.com, https;//m.facebook.com/teaontheway. *In Clun Signs for YHA. Continue 1m up hill. Past cottages on L. At farm bear R through farm buildings. 100 yds at end of road .Garden on L.* **Sun 13 May (2-6). Adm £5, chd free. Home-made teas. Guilden Down Cottage also operates as a tea garden under the name of TEA on the WAY. Visits also by arrangement Apr to July.**

With spectacular views, this one acre organic garden has been developed over the past 14 years to be in harmony and its surroundings. Divided into many rooms, there are vibrant herbaceous borders and terraces, rose trellises and a large vegetable plot. Our wild garden includes a natural pond, living willow structures, wild flower orchard, trees, shrubs and planted borders. Partial wheelchair access, front garden only but worth it for the views.

13 HODNET HALL GARDENS

Hodnet, Market Drayton, TF9 3NN. Sir Algernon & The Hon Lady Heber-Percy, www.hodnethallgardens.org. *5½m SW of Market Drayton. 12m NE Shrewsbury. At junction of A53 & A442.* **Sun 10 June (12-5). Adm £7, chd £1. Light refreshments.**

60 acre landscaped garden with series of lakes and pools; magnificent forest trees, great variety of flowers, shrubs providing colour throughout season. Unique collection of big-game trophies in C17 tearooms. Kitchen garden. For details please see website and Facebook page. Maps are available to show access for our less mobile visitors.

NPC

14 THE HOLLIES

Rockhill, Clun, SY7 8LR. Pat & Terry Badham, 01588 640805, patbadham@btinternet.com. *10m W of Craven Arms. 8m S of Bishops Castle. From A49 Craven Arms take B4368 to Clun. Turn L onto A488 continue for 1½m. Bear R signed Treverward. After 50 yards turn R at Xrds, property is 1st on L.* **Visits by arrangement July to Sept individuals / groups of 1-20. Adm £4, chd free. Refreshments in Clun..**

A garden of approx 2 acres at 1000ft which was started in 2009. Features include a kitchen garden with raised beds and fruit cage. Large island beds and borders with perennials, shrubs and grasses, specimen trees. Wildlife dingle with stream. Wheelchair access is available to the majority of the garden over gravel and grass.

15 LONGNER HALL

Atcham, Shrewsbury, SY4 4TG. Mr & Mrs R L Burton. *4m SE of Shrewsbury. From M54 follow A5 to Shrewsbury, then B4380 to Atcham. From Atcham take Uffington rd, entrance ¼m on L.* **Sun 20 May (2-5). Adm £4, chd free. Home-made teas.**

A long drive approach through parkland designed by Humphry Repton. Walks lined with golden yew through extensive lawns, with views over Severn Valley. Borders containing roses, herbaceous and shrubs, also ancient yew wood. Enclosed walled garden containing mixed planting, garden buildings, tower and game larder. Short woodland walk around old moat pond. 1 acre walled garden currently being restored now open to visitors. Woodland walk not suitable for wheelchairs.

16 NEW LOWER BROOKSHILL

Shelve, Minsterley, Shrewsbury, SY5 0JW. Patricia & Robin Oldfield, 01588 650137, robin.oldfield@live.com. *3m N of Lydham on the A488. Take turn to Nind & after ½m sharp L & follow narrow rd for another ½m. No access from Shelve.* **Sun 1 July (2-6). Adm £4, chd free. Home-made teas. Visits also by arrangement in May max 30.**

10 acres of mainly hillside garden and woods (bluebells in May) in the Shropshire Hills ANOB with borrowed views over and down a valley. The start of the River West Onny meanders through the property. Begun in 2010 from a largely derelict stony site at 950ft, it includes a 'pocket' park, four ponds, mixed borders and lawns. Sensible footwear recommended. Not suitable for wheelchairs.

17 LYNDALE HOUSE

Astley Abbotts, Bridgnorth, WV16 4SW. Bob & Mary Saunders, montyspot@me.com. *2m out of Bridnorth off B4373. From High Town Bridgnorth take B4373 Broseley Rd for 1½m, then take lane signed Astley Abbotts & Colemore Green.* **Sun 6 May (2-5). Adm £4, chd free. Light refreshments. Visits also by arrangement May to July for 10 visitors, plus 2 months notice.**

Large 1½ acre garden which has evolved over 20yrs. Terrace with roses, alliums and iris surrounded by box hedging. Specimen trees planted in large lawn. Hundreds of tulips for spring colour. Clematis walk to pool. Courtyard planted with scented violas. Greenhouse full of streptocarpus. Large rockery and scree bed and all surrounded by the beautiful Shropshire countryside. Topiary garden, waterfall to pool, many unusual trees. Please ask owner about wheelchair friendly access.

18 MILLICHOPE PARK

Munslow, Craven Arms, SY7 9HA. Mr & Mrs Frank Bury, www.wildegoosenursery.co.uk. *8m NE of Craven Arms. off B4368 Craven Arms to Bridgnorth Rd. Nr Munslow then follow yellow signs.* **Sun 18 Feb (2-5); Sun 6 May (1-6); Sun 14 Oct (2-5). Adm £5, chd free. Home-made teas in the walled garden tea room.**

Historic landscape gardens covering 14 acres with lakes, cascades dating from C18, woodland walks and wildflowers. Snowdrops in February, Bluebells and Violas in May, Roses and Autumn colour in October. Also open the Walled Garden at Millichope, an exciting restoration project bringing the walled gardens and C19 glasshouses back to life. opportunity to see the Bouts Viola collection. UK's largest collection of hardy, perennial, scented violas. Many varieties for sale during the May opening. Wildegoose nursery and the walled garden at Millichope will also be open. As featured in House and Garden Magazine.

19 MOORTOWN

nr Wellington, TF6 6JE. Mr David Bromley, 01952 770205. *8m N of Telford. 5m N of Wellington. Take B5062 signed Moortown 1m between High Ercall & Crudgington.* **Visits by arrangement in June groups 10+. Adm £5, chd free.**

Approx 1-acre plantsman's garden. Here may be found the old-fashioned, the unusual and even the oddities of plant life, in mixed borders of 'controlled' confusion. Has gardened for over 50 years and for 32 years for NGS.

GROUP OPENING

20 MORVILLE HALL GARDENS

Bridgnorth, WV16 5NB. *3m W of Bridgnorth. On A458 at junction with B4368.* **Sun 10 June (2-5). Combined adm £6, chd free. Home-made teas in Morville Church.**

THE COTTAGE
Mrs A Nichol-Smith.

THE DOWER HOUSE
Dr Katherine Swift.

1 THE GATE HOUSE
Mr & Mrs Rowe.

2 THE GATE HOUSE
Mrs G Medland.

MORVILLE HALL
The National Trust.

SOUTH PAVILION
Mr & Mrs B Jenkinson.

An interesting group of gardens that surround a beautiful Grade I listed mansion (not open). The Cottage has a pretty walled cottage garden with plenty of colour.
The Dower House is a horticultural history lesson about Morville Hall which incl a turf maze, cloister garden, Elizabethan knot garden, C18 canal garden, Edwardian kitchen garden and more. It is the setting of Katherine Swift's bestselling book 'The Morville Hours', and the sequel 'The Morville Year'. 1 and 2 The Gate House are cottage-style gardens with colourful borders, formal areas, lawns and wooded glades. The 4-acre Morville Hall (NT) garden has a parterre, medieval stew pond, shrub borders and large lawns, all offering glorious views across the Mor Valley.
South Pavilion features new thoughts and new designs in a small courtyard garden. Mostly level ground, but plenty of gravel to negotiate.

21 OAKGATE NURSERY & GARDEN CENTRE

Ellerdine Heath, nr Telford, TF6 6RL. Oakgate Garden Centre, www.oakgatenursery.co.uk. *Signed A53 between Shawbury & Hodnet A442 Between Shawbirch & Hodnet.* **Wed 11 July (10-4). Adm £5, chd free. Coffee and slice of cake incl in adm.**

The owners Philip and Valerie Newington moved to Shropshire 30yrs ago from Chobham, Surrey, when the complete site was a Pick Your Own Farm. Over the years the garden has been transformed to what it is today, a delightful haven of trees, shrubs, herbaceous and seasonal bedding. All dug by hand incl 2 ponds by Philip. The gardens are still maintained by the family who live on site but welcome visitors who enjoy the peaceful setting relaxing in our tearoom overlooking the pond. Limited wheelchair access.

22 OTELEY

Ellesmere, SY12 0PB. Mr R K Mainwaring, 01691 622514. *1m SE of Ellesmere. Entrance out of Ellesmere past Mere, opp Convent nr to A528/495 junction.* **Sun 13 May (2-5). Adm £5, chd free. Home-made teas. Visits also by arrangement for 10+.**

10 acres running down to The Mere. Walled kitchen garden, architectural features, many old interesting trees despite recent storms, rhododendrons, azaleas, wild woodland walk and views across Mere to Ellesmere. First opened in 1927 when NGS first started. Wheelchair access if dry.

Ruthall Manor

23 PREEN MANOR

Church Preen, SY6 7LQ. Mr & Mrs J Tanner, katytanner@msm.com. *6m W of Much Wenlock. From A458 Shrewsbury to Bridgnorth rd turn off at Harley follow signs to Kenley & Church Preen. From B4371 Much Wenlock to Church Stretton road go via Hughley to Church Preen.* **Sun 17 June (2-5). Adm £6, chd free. Home-made teas. Visits also by arrangement May to July for groups of 10+.**

6-acre garden on site of Cluniac monastery and Norman Shaw mansion. Kitchen, chess, water and wild gardens. Fine trees in park; woodland walks. Developed for over 30yrs with changes always in progress.

24 RUTHALL MANOR

Ditton Priors, Bridgnorth, WV16 6TN. Mr & Mrs G T Clarke, 01746 712608, clrk608@btinternet.com. *7m SW of Bridgnorth. Ruthall Rd signed nr garage in Ditton Priors. See yellow arrows.* **Mon 7, Fri 18, Sat 19 May, Fri 8, Sat 9 June, Sat 7, Sun 8 July, Sat 15, Sun 16 Sept (1-6). Adm £5, chd free. Home-made teas. Light meals by arrangement. Visits also by arrangement Apr to Oct light refreshments on request.**

Offset by a mature collection of specimen trees, the garden is divided into intimate sections, carefully linked by winding paths. The front lawn flanked by striking borders, extends to a gravel, art garden and ha-ha. Clematis and roses scramble through an eclectic collection of wrought-iron work, unique pottery and secluded seating. A stunning horse pond features primulas, iris and bog plants. Lots of lovely shrubs to see. Jigsaws for sale Bring or buy. Collecting box some days if wet. Wheelchair access to most parts.

25 SAMBROOK MANOR

Sambrook, Newport, TF10 8AL. Mrs E Mitchell, 01952 550256, sambrookmanor@gmail.com. *Between Newport & Ternhill. 1m off A41 in the village of Sambrook.* **Sun 15 July, Sun 12 Aug (12.30-5). Adm £4, chd free. Home-made teas. Visits also by arrangement May to Aug for groups of 10+.**

The garden surrounds the early C18 manor house (not open) and contains a wide selection of herbaceous plants and roses. Features incl a waterfall down to a pond and various acers. A new development leading to the river along the edge of the garden is filled with a variety of shrubs and trees. Plants on sale from Barlow Nurseries.

26 NEW 2 SCHOOL COTTAGES

Hook-a-Gate, Shrewsbury, SY5 8BQ. Andrew Roberts. *From B4380 Roman Rd in Shrewsbury by cemetery take the Longden rd island. 1.8m past school's continue to the village Hook-a-Gate. Garden is situated on L past Hill Side Nursery. Parking at Nursery.* **Sun 3 June, Sun 1 July (1-5). Adm £4, chd free. Home-made teas.**

A new 3 acre garden set on a slope with steps and inclines. A mixture of various herbaceous beds, shrubs, trees, sunken garden and formal planting. Orchard, vegetable, soft fruit cage, greenhouse, chickens and pigs. Large oriental garden with surprises leading you to pasture with wildlife-friendly hedging and spectacular views of the Welsh Hills. Continues to woodland walk with stream and arboretum.

27 SECRET GARDEN

21 Steventon Terrace, Steventon New Road, Ludlow, SY8 1JZ. Mr & Mrs Wood, 01584 876037, carolynwood2152@yahoo.co.uk. *Park & Ride if needed, stops outside garden.* **Sat 23 June (12.30-5). Adm £3.50, chd free. Home-made teas, cakes, coffee and ice cream. Visits also by arrangement refreshments if requested.**

½-acre of very secret S-facing garden, Developed over 30yrs with enthusiasm creativity and the love of gardening by the present owners. Divided up into different sections rose garden herbaceous borders koi fish pond with gazebo, summer house poly tunnel and chickens Mediterranean style terrace garden with views of the Shropshire hills. 2017 heart of England in bloom Chairmans award. Featured in Shropshire Star, Ludlow advertiser, Shropshire Life and Britain in bloom with RHS Heart of England in bloom Chairmans Award.

28 STANLEY HALL

Bridgnorth, WV16 4SP. Mr & Mrs M J Thompson. *½m N of Bridgnorth. Leave Bridgnorth by N gate B4373; turn R at Stanley Lane. Pass Golf Course Club House on L & turn L at Lodge.* **Sun 20 May (2-6). Adm £4, chd free. Home-made teas.**

Drive ½m with rhododendrons, fine trees and pools. Restored ice-house. Woodland walks. Also open Dower House (Mr & Mrs Colin Wells)

4 acre woodland and shrub garden with contemporary sculpture and walled vegetable garden. The Granary (Mr & Mrs Jack Major) Small trellis garden with flowers in hanging baskets and herbaceous borders and South Lodge (Mr Tim Warren) Cottage hillside garden.

GROUP OPENING

29 STOTTESDON & DISTRICT OPEN GARDENS

Stottesdon, Kidderminster, DY14 8TZ. Stottesdon Garden Committee. *Between Bridgnorth & Cleobury Mortimer. Stottesdon is signed on B4364 between Bridgnorth & Ludlow & B4363 between Bridgnorth & Cleobury Mortimer. B4194 from Bewdley joins B4363 4m from Stottesdon. Postcode for SatNav DY14 8TZ.* **Sat 16, Sun 17 June (11-5). Combined adm £6, chd free. Home-made teas in garden of the Old Fox and Hounds. Light lunches, tea, coffee, soft drinks and traditional afternoon teas.**

Located in unspoilt Shropshire countryside near the Clee Hills, up to 15 village gardens in Stottesdon and Chorley are open to the visitor to enjoy. Some have stunning views. There are at least 2 new ones and a re-opening. Many are traditional or modern interpretations of the cottage garden, containing fruit, vegetables and livestock. Some have been developed for outdoor living, one for wheelchair use and one for low maintenance. There are 2 contrasting vegetable gardens; one devoted to the principles of permaculture and the other to the rearing of champion vegetables. The largest garden is two thirds of an acre, a serene garden, evolved over 4 decades, that blends into the surrounding woodland. Allow plenty of time to visit them all. Take refreshments on the old bowling green, whilst admiring the new garden at the Old Fox and Hounds, and play a game of skittles. A competition, called A Garden Fit for a Gnome, will be held and will be judged by garden visitors. Dogs on leads please. Coaches by prior arrangement. A light lunch menu will be available in the Tea Garden and traditional afternoon teas will be served from 3pm. Most gardens have some wheelchair access. Those gardens not suitable for wheelchair access will be listed.

30 SUNNINGDALE

9 Mill Street, Wem, Shropshire, SY4 5ED. Mrs Susan Griffiths, 01939 236733, sue.griffiths@btinternet.com. *Town centre. Wem is on B5476. Parking in public car park Barnard St. The property is opp the purple house below the church.* **Sun 22 July (10-4), Sun 9 Sept (11-4). Adm £3, chd free. Home-made teas.**

2 School Cottages

Visits also by arrangement Feb to Nov.
A good half acre town garden. A wildlife haven for squirrels, voles, and a huge variety of birds including nesting gold crests. The addition of excellent nectar rich plants means that butterflies and other pollinators are in abundance. Interesting plantings with rare plants and many interesting sculptural elements. Koi pond and natural stone waterfall rockery. Antique and modern sculpture. Sound break yew walkway. Large perennial borders Rare plants. Although the garden is on the level there are a number of steps mostly around the pond area Paths are in the main gravel or flags it has a flat lawn.

31 UPPER SHELDERTON HOUSE

Shelderton, Clungunford, Craven Arms, SY7 0PE. Andrew Benton & Tricia McHaffie, 01547 540525. *Between Ludlow & Craven Arms. Heading from Shrewsbury to Ludlow on A49, take 1st R after Onibury railway crossing. Take 3rd R signed Shelderton. After approx 2½ m the house is on L. Garden will be signed.* **Sat 12, Sun 13 May (2-5). Adm £4, chd free. Home-made teas.**
Set in a stunning tranquil position, our naturalistic and evolving 6½ acre garden was originally landscaped in 1962. Most of the trees, azaleas and rhododendrons were planted then. There is a wonderful new kitchen garden designed and planted by Jayne and Norman Grove. Ponds and woodland walk encourage wildlife. A large sweeping lawn leads in various directions revealing a multitude of colourful rhododendron and azaelea beds ponds a varied collection of trees and a very productive kitchen garden. There are plenty of tranquil seating areas from which to enjoy a moment in our garden.

32 WALCOT HALL

Lydbury North, SY7 8AZ. Mr & Mrs C R W Parish, 01588 680570, secretary@walcothall.com, www.walcothall.com. *4m SE of Bishop's Castle. B4385 Craven Arms to Bishop's Castle, turn L by Powis Arms, in Lydbury North.* **Sun 27, Mon 28 May (1.30-5.30). Adm £4, chd free. Home-made teas. Visits also by arrangement May to July for groups of 15+.**
Arboretum planted by Lord Clive of India's son, Edward. Cascades of rhododendrons, azaleas amongst specimen trees and pools. Fine views of Sir William Chambers' Clock Towers, with lake and hills beyond. Walled kitchen garden; dovecote; meat safe; ice house and mile-long lakes. Outstanding ballroom where excellent teas are served. Russian wooden church, grotto and fountain now complete and working; tin chapel. Relaxed borders and rare shrubs. Lakeside replanted, and water garden at western end re-established. The garden adjacent to the ballroom is accessible via a sloping bank, as is the walled garden and arboretum.

33 8 WESTGATE VILLAS

Salop Street, Bridgnorth, WV16 4QX. Bill & Marilyn Hammerton. *From A458 Bridgnorth bypass, at Ludlow Rd r'about take rd into Bridgnorth signed town centre. At T-junction (possible parking at council offices here) turn R, garden is 100yds on L past Victoria Road.* **Evening opening Fri 13 Apr (7-9.30). Adm £5, chd free. Wine. Sun 15 Apr (2-5.30). Adm £4, chd free. Tea. 13 April: Canapés 15 April: Cake.**
Town garden having formal Victorian front garden with box hedging and water feature. Back garden has a shade border, patios with seating and potted plants, a lawn and small knot garden, together with a strong oriental influence incl Japanese style teahouse, Zen garden, Chinese style pebble path, moongate sculpture, prayer flags and basalt sett and gravel hard landscaping. Wine, canapes, music and garden lighting incl at evening opening. Our garden was used by Alan Titchmarsh as an inspirational garden for a Japanese garden he was building in 'Love Your Garden' series (shown 19.7.2017). Featured in Shropshire Magazine & local press. Partial wheelchair access.

34 WINDY RIDGE

Church Lane, Little Wenlock, Telford, TF6 5BB. George & Fiona Chancellor, 01952 507675, fionachancellor@btinternet.com. *2m S of Wellington. Follow signs for Little Wenlock from N (J7, M54) or E (off A5223 at Horsehay). Parking signed. Do not rely on SatNav.* **Sun 3 June, Sun 8 July, Sun 12 Aug, Sun 2 Sept (12-5). Adm £5, chd free. Home-made teas. Visits also by arrangement May to Sept suitable for coaches.**
'Stunning' and 'inspirational' are how visitors frequently describe this multi-award-winning ⅔ acre village garden. The strong design and exuberant colour-themed planting (over 1000 species, mostly labelled) offer a picture around every corner. The grass and perennial gravel garden has created a lot of interest and versions are now appearing in gardens all over the country! Some gravel paths but help available.

35 ◆ WOLLERTON OLD HALL

Wollerton, Market Drayton, TF9 3NA. Lesley & John Jenkins, 01630 685760, info@wollertonoldhallgarden.com, www.wollertonoldhallgarden.com. *4m SW of Market Drayton. On A53 between Hodnet & A53-A41 junction. Follow brown signs.* **For NGS: Fri 18 May (12-5). Adm £7, chd £1. Light refreshments, lunches and, wine.** For other opening times and information, please phone, email or visit garden website.
4-acre garden created around C16 house (not open). Formal structure creates variety of gardens each with own colour theme and character. Planting is mainly of perennials, the large range of which results in significant collections of salvias, clematis, crocosmias and roses. Ongoing lectures by Gardening Celebrities including Chris Beardshaw, and other garden designers and personalities. For refreshments, food is freshly prepared in the Tea Room for each open day. Home-cooked, hot and cold lunches which have a reputation for quality. Free Head Gardener's Walks. Partial wheelchair access.

SOMERSET, BRISTOL AREA & SOUTH GLOUCESTERSHIRE incl BATH

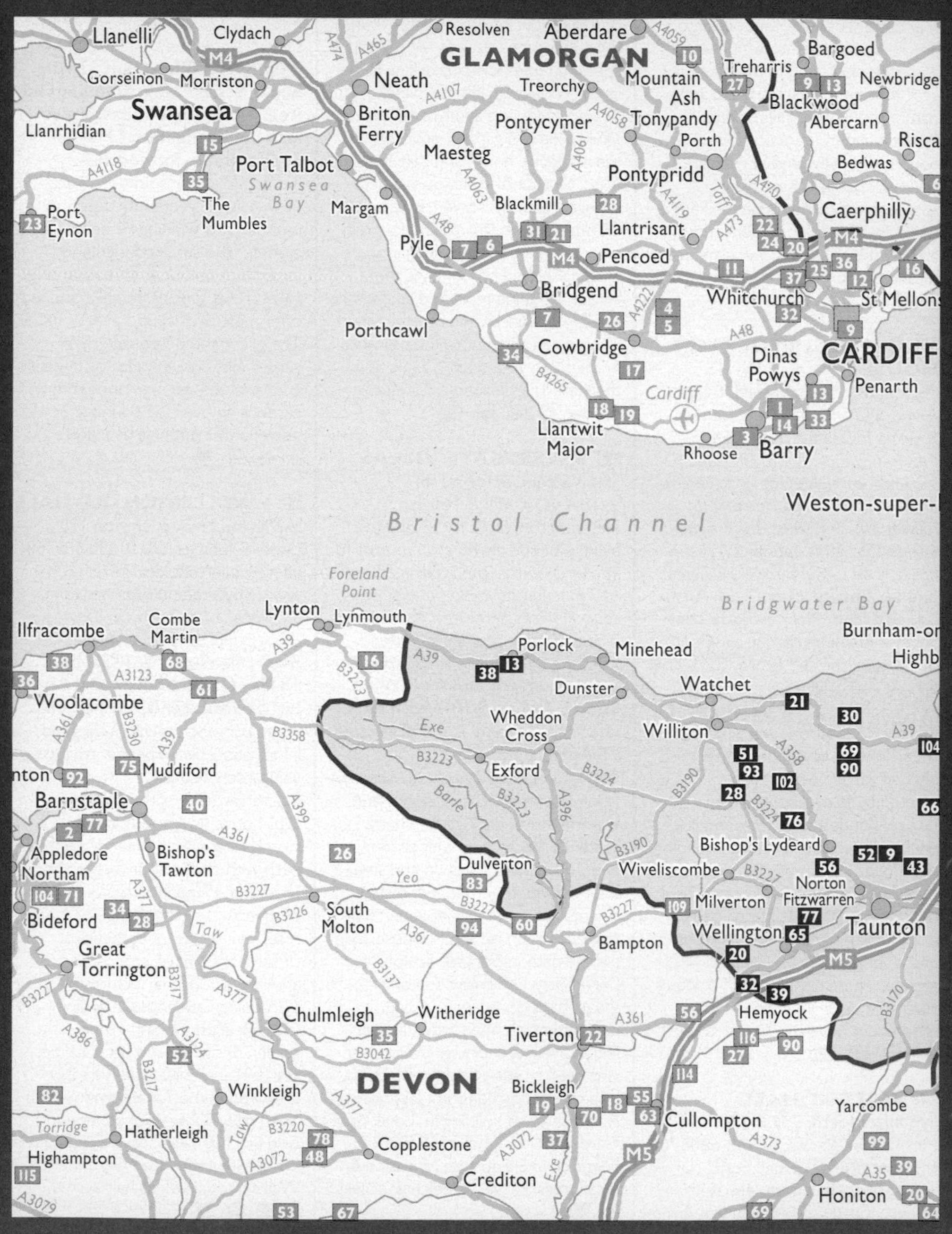

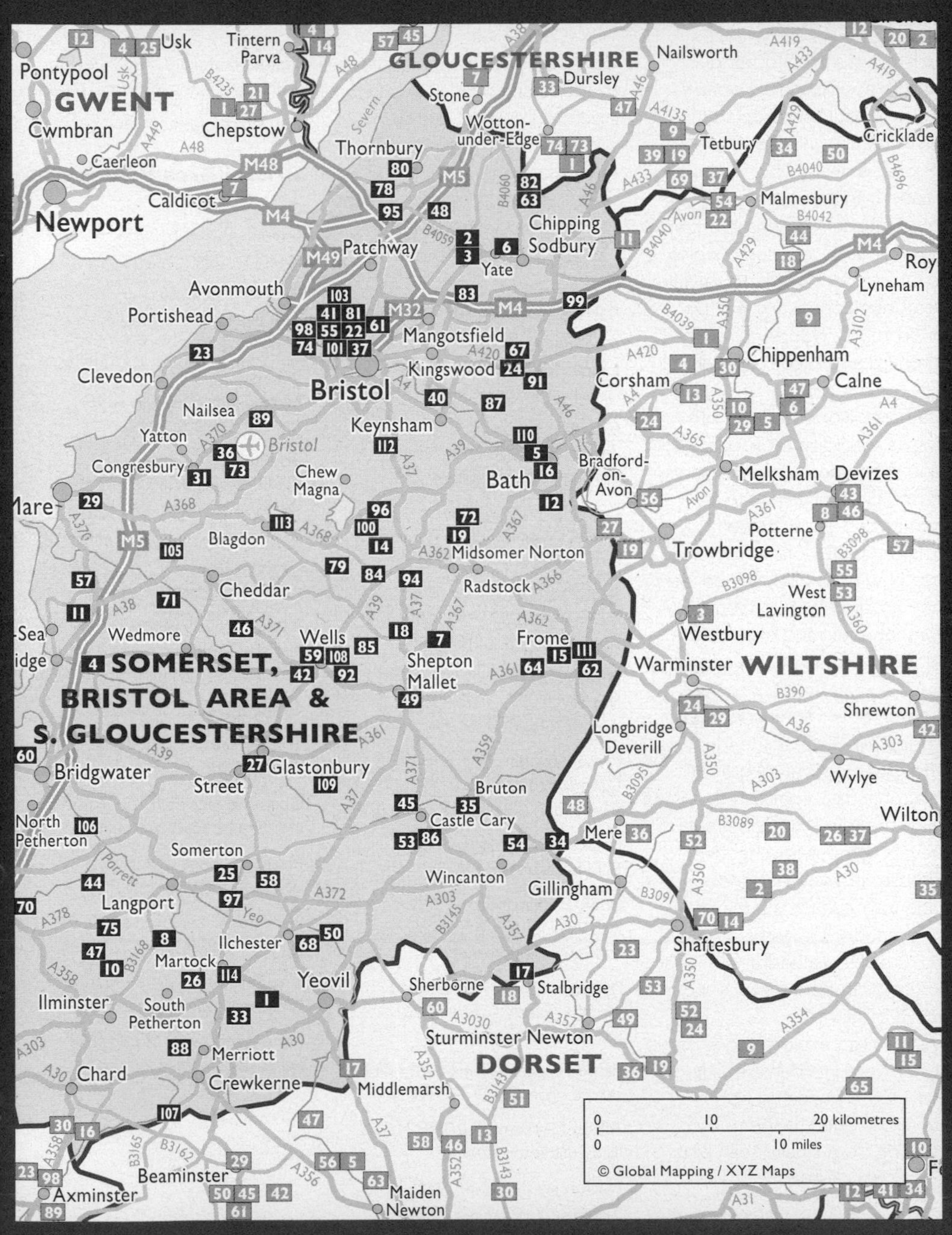
GLOUCESTERSHIRE
GWENT
SOMERSET, BRISTOL AREA & S. GLOUCESTERSHIRE
WILTSHIRE
DORSET
Usk
Tintern Parva
Pontypool
Cwmbran
Chepstow
Caerleon
Caldicot
Newport
Thornbury
Stone
Dursley
Nailsworth
Wotton-under-Edge
Tetbury
Cricklade
Malmesbury
Chipping Sodbury
Yate
Patchway
Avonmouth
Portishead
Mangotsfield
Kingswood
Bristol
Clevedon
Nailsea
Yatton
Congresbury
Keynsham
Chew Magna
Bath
Bradford-on-Avon
Corsham
Chippenham
Calne
Lyneham
Melksham
Devizes
Potterne
Trowbridge
Blagdon
Midsomer Norton
Radstock
Cheddar
Wedmore
Wells
Shepton Mallet
Frome
Westbury
West Lavington
Warminster
Shrewton
Longbridge Deverill
Wylye
Wilton
Bridgwater
Street
Glastonbury
Bruton
Castle Cary
Mere
North Petherton
Somerton
Wincanton
Gillingham
Langport
Ilchester
Shaftesbury
Martock
Yeovil
Sherborne
Stalbridge
Ilminster
South Petherton
Sturminster Newton
Merriott
Chard
Crewkerne
Middlemarsh
Beaminster
Axminster
Maiden Newton
0 10 20 kilometres
0 10 miles
© Global Mapping / XYZ Maps

Somerset, Bristol, Bath and South Gloucestershire make up an NGS 'county' of captivating contrasts, with castles and countryside and wildlife and wetlands, from amazing cities to bustling market towns, coastal resorts and picturesque villages.

Bristol's stunning location and famous landmarks offer a wonderful backdrop to our creative and inspiring garden owners who have made tranquil havens and tropical back gardens in urban surroundings. The surrounding countryside is home to gardens featuring contrasting mixtures of formality, woodland, water, orchard and kitchen gardens.

Bath is a world heritage site for its Georgian architecture and renowned for its Roman Baths. Our garden visitors can enjoy the quintessentially English garden of Bath Priory Hotel with its billowing borders and croquet lawn, or venture further afield and explore the hidden gems in nearby villages.

Somerset is a rural county of rolling hills such as the Mendips, the Quantocks and Exmoor National Park contrasted with the low-lying Somerset Levels. Famous for cheddar cheese, strawberries and cider; agriculture is a major occupation. It is home to Wells, the smallest cathedral city in England, and the lively county town of Taunton.
Visitors can explore more than 150 diverse gardens, mostly privately owned and not normally open to the public ranging from small urban plots to country estates.

Gardens on windswept hilltops, by the seaside, hidden in lush green countryside, in idyllic villages as well as communal town allotments are all to be visited, as well as historic gardens designed by Gertrude Jekyll, Margery Fish and Harold Peto.

Somerset Volunteers

County Organiser
Laura Howard 01460 282911
laura.howard@ngs.org.uk

County Treasurer
Sue Youell 01984 656741
braglands@hotmail.com

Publicity
Roger Peacock 01275 341584
barum@blueyonder.co.uk

Social Media
Bill Hodgson 07711 715311
somersetngs@outlook.com

Photographer
Sue Sayer 07773 181891
suesayer58@hotmail.com

Presentations
Dave & Prue Moon 01373 473381
davidmoon202@btinternet.com

Booklet Co-ordinator
Bill Hodgson (as above)

Booklet Distributor
Ash Warne 07548 889705
ashwarne@btinternet.com

Assistant County Organisers
Marsha Casely 07854 882616
marjac321@hotmail.com

Patricia Davies-Gilbert 01823 412187
pdaviesgilbert@btinternet.com

Alison Highnam 01258 821576
allies1@btinternet.com

Marion Jay 01643 841486
marion.jay@icloud.com

Judith Stanford 01761 233045
judithstanford.ngs@hotmail.co.uk

Ash Warne (as above)

Bristol Area Volunteers

County Organiser
Su Mills 01454 615438
susanlmills@gmail.com

County Treasurer
Ken Payne 01275 333146
kg.payne@outlook.com

Publicity
Myra Ginns 01454 415396
m.ginns1@btinternet.com

Booklet Co-ordinator
Bill Hodgson 07711 715311
somersetngs@outlook.com

Booklet Distributor
Graham Guest 01275 472393
gandsguest@btinternet.com

Assistant County Organisers
Angela Conibere 01454 413828
aeconibere@hotmail.com

Graham Guest (as above)

Tracey Halladay 07956 784838
thallada@icloud.com

Christine Healey 01454 612795
christine.healey@uwclub.net

Margaret Jones 01225 891229
ian@weircott.plus.com

Jeanette Parker 01454 299699
jeanette_parker@hotmail.co.uk

Jane Perkins 01454 414570
janekperkins@gmail.com

Irene Randow 01275 857208
irene.randow@sky.com

OPENING DATES

All entries subject to change. For latest information check **www.ngs.org.uk**

Map locator numbers are shown to the right of each garden name.

February

Snowdrop Festival

Saturday 3rd
◆ Elworthy Cottage 28

Sunday 4th
◆ Elworthy Cottage 28
Rock House 78
Vine House 103

Sunday 11th
Hanham Court 40
Rock House 78
◆ Sherborne Garden 84

Monday 12th
◆ Sherborne Garden 84

Saturday 17th
◆ East Lambrook Manor Gardens 26

Sunday 18th
Nynehead Court 65

Thursday 22nd
Southfield Farm 89

March

Tuesday 6th
◆ Hestercombe Gardens 43

Tuesday 13th
Lower Shalford Farm 54

Thursday 22nd
Southfield Farm 89

Friday 23rd
Tormarton Court 99

Sunday 25th
NEW The Flax Barn 33
Rock House 78

April

Monday 2nd
◆ Elworthy Cottage 28
Rock House 78

Saturday 7th
Truffles 100

Sunday 8th
Fairfield 30
Truffles 100

Tuesday 10th
◆ Elworthy Cottage 28

Sunday 15th
Algars Manor 2
Algars Mill 3
Lucombe House 55
Rose Cottage 79
◆ The Yeo Valley Organic Garden at Holt Farm 113

Tuesday 17th
◆ Elworthy Cottage 28

Thursday 19th
Bath Priory Hotel 5
Sparrows 90

Saturday 21st
◆ Barrington Court
◆ The Walled Gardens of Cannington 104

Sunday 22nd
◆ The Walled Gardens of Cannington 104

Sunday 29th
Watcombe 105
Wayford Manor 107

May

Thursday 3rd
◆ Elworthy Cottage 28

Saturday 5th
Hillcrest 44

Sunday 6th
NEW The Flax Barn 33
Hillcrest 44

Thursday 10th
Forest Lodge 34
◆ Kilver Court Gardens 49

Friday 11th
Little Yarford Farmhouse 52

Saturday 12th
Little Yarford Farmhouse 52
Lower Shalford Farm 54

Sunday 13th
◆ East Lambrook Manor Gardens 26
Little Yarford Farmhouse 52
◆ Midney Gardens 58
◆ Milton Lodge 59

Monday 14th
Little Yarford Farmhouse 52

Sunday 20th
◆ Court House 21
4 Haytor Park 41
The Old Vicarage, Over Stowey 69
Rendy Farm 77
◆ University of Bristol Botanic Garden 101
Watcombe 105

Wednesday 23rd
Laughing Water 50
The Old Vicarage, Over Stowey 69

Saturday 26th
25 Chaucer Road 16
NEW Stoneleigh Down 95

Sunday 27th
Babbs Farm 4
25 Chaucer Road 16
Hanham Court 40
St Monica Trust 81
NEW Stoneleigh Down 95

Monday 28th
Babbs Farm 4
◆ Elworthy Cottage 28
Hanham Court 40

Tuesday 29th
Wellfield Barn 108

Wednesday 30th
Vellacott 102

Thursday 31st
◆ Elworthy Cottage 28
Vellacott 102

June

Festival Weekend

Saturday 2nd
◆ East Lambrook Manor Gardens 26
NEW ◆ Homeacres 45

Sunday 3rd
14 Eskdale Close 29
Fernbank 31
Greystones 37
NEW ◆ Homeacres 45
◆ Milton Lodge 59
16 Montroy Close 61
The Old Vicarage, Ruishton 70

Monday 4th
The Old Vicarage, Ruishton 70

Tuesday 5th
◆ Elworthy Cottage 28
◆ Hestercombe Gardens 43

Wednesday 6th
Church Farm House 18

Thursday 7th
Watcombe 105

Saturday 9th
NEW Halsecombe House and Halsecombe Cottage 38
Isle Abbotts Gardens 47
Lower Cockhill Farmhouse 53
The Old Rectory, Doynton 67
Reeds Court 76
South Cary House 86

Sunday 10th
9 Catherston Close 15
Church Farm House 18
NEW Halsecombe House and Halsecombe Cottage 38
Isle Abbotts Gardens 47
Lower Cockhill Farmhouse 53
Lydeard House 56
Model Farm 60
Penny Brohn UK 74
Reeds Court 76
South Cary House 86
84 Weymouth Road 111

Wednesday 13th
Goblin Combe House 36

Thursday 14th
Forest Lodge 34

Friday 15th
9 Catherston Close 15
Tormarton Court 99

Saturday 16th
Boweys 9
Brewery House 12

The Dairy 23
Laughing Water 50
Lympsham Gardens 57
The Old Vicarage, Weare 71
NEW St Arilda's House 80
Westbrook House 109
Weston Village Gardens 110

Sunday 17th
Boweys 9
9 Catherston Close 15
Crete Hill House Gardens 22
The Dairy 23
Lympsham Gardens 57
The Old Vicarage, Weare 71
NEW St Arilda's House 80
Sparrows 90
Stogumber Gardens 93
Weston Village Gardens 110

Monday 18th
Boweys 9

Wednesday 20th
Vellacott 102

Thursday 21st
◆ Special Plants 91
Vellacott 102

Sunday 24th
◆ Stoberry Garden 92
Swift House 98
Vine House 103

Tuesday 26th
◆ Elworthy Cottage 28

Saturday 30th
NEW Little Hintock 51

July

Sunday 1st
Gants Mill & Garden 35
◆ Milton Lodge 59
Nunney Gardens 64
Nynehead Court 65

Thursday 5th
◆ Elworthy Cottage 28

Saturday 7th
◆ Barrington Court

Sunday 8th
Brent Knoll Gardens 11
Honeyhurst Farm 46

Monday 9th
Honeyhurst Farm 46

Tuesday 10th
Muriel Jones Field Allotments 62

Thursday 12th
9 Catherston Close 15
◆ Elworthy Cottage 28

Sunday 15th
Doynton House 24
NEW Northend House 63
NEW The School Yard 82
Stowey Gardens 96

Thursday 19th
◆ Special Plants 91

Saturday 21st
Boweys 9
Old Orchard 66

Sunday 22nd
Benter Gardens 7
Boweys 9
◆ Court House 21
Fernhill 32
Hangeridge Farmhouse 39
Old Orchard 66

Monday 23rd
Boweys 9

Wednesday 25th
◆ Ston Easton Park 94

Saturday 28th
◆ Cothay Manor & Gardens 20
Park Cottage 73

Sunday 29th
Sutton Hosey Manor 97

August

Saturday 4th
Park Cottage 73

Sunday 5th
◆ Jekka's Herbetum 48

Sunday 12th
◆ Elworthy Cottage 28
Parish's House 72

Thursday 16th
◆ Special Plants 91

Sunday 19th
Fernhill 32

Sunday 26th
Babbs Farm 4

Monday 27th
Babbs Farm 4
◆ Elworthy Cottage 28

Thursday 30th
◆ Elworthy Cottage 28

September

Saturday 1st
NEW Stoneleigh Down 95

Sunday 2nd
NEW Stoneleigh Down 95

Thursday 6th
◆ Kilver Court Gardens 49

Sunday 9th
Beechwell House 6

Thursday 13th
Bath Priory Hotel 5

Friday 14th
◆ Midney Gardens 58

Saturday 15th
◆ The Walled Gardens of Cannington 104
Whitewood Lodge 112

Sunday 16th
The Red Post House 75
◆ The Walled Gardens of Cannington 104

Thursday 20th
◆ Special Plants 91

October

Thursday 11th
Nynehead Court 65

Sunday 14th
NEW The Flax Barn 33

Thursday 18th
◆ Special Plants 91

February 2019

Sunday 3rd
Rock House 78

Sunday 10th
Rock House 78
◆ Sherborne Garden 84

Monday 11th
◆ Sherborne Garden 84

Sunday 17th
◆ East Lambrook Manor Gardens 26

By Arrangement

Abbey Farm 1
Babbs Farm 4
Ball Copse Hall, Brent Knoll Gardens 11
Benter Gardens 7
Bowdens Farm 8
Boweys 9
Bradon Farm 10
Brewery House 12
Broomclose 13
NEW Cameley House 14
Cherry Bolberry Farm 17
Church Farm House 18
NEW Coldharbour Cottage 19
The Dairy 23
East End Farm 25
NEW Elmcroft 27
Forest Lodge 34
Hangeridge Farmhouse 39
4 Haytor Park 41
Henley Mill 42
Hillcrest 44
Honeyhurst Farm 46
Knoll Cottage, Stogumber Gardens 93
Laughing Water 50
Little Yarford Farmhouse 52
Lucombe House 55
Nynehead Court 65
The Old Rectory, Limington 68
The Old Vicarage, Over Stowey 69
The Old Vicarage, Weare 71
Parish's House 72
The Red Post House 75
Rock House 78
Rose Cottage 79
Serridge House 83
Sole Retreat 85
Somerset Lodge Garden, Nunney Gardens 64
South Kelding 87
South Street Allotment 88
Sparrows 90
Sutton Hosey Manor 97
Tormarton Court 99
Vellacott 102
Watcombe 105
Waverley 106
Wellfield Barn 108
Westbrook House 109
Whitewood Lodge 112
Yews Farm 114

THE GARDENS

1 ABBEY FARM

Montacute, TA15 6UA. Elizabeth McFarlane, 01935 823556, ct.fm@btopenworld.com. *4m from Yeovil. Follow A3088, take slip rd to Montacute, turn L at T-junction into village. Turn R between Church & King's Arms (no through rd).* **Visits by arrangement May to July. Groups of 10 +. Adm £5, chd free. Light refreshments.**

2½ acres of mainly walled gardens on sloping site provide the setting for Cluniac Medieval Priory gatehouse. Interesting plants incl roses, shrubs, grasses, clematis. Herbaceous borders, white garden, gravel garden. Small arboretum. Pond for wildlife - frogs, newts, dragonflies. Fine mulberry, walnut and monkey puzzle trees. Seats for resting. Restored Grade 2 listed dovecote. Gravel area and one steep slope.

2 ALGARS MANOR

Station Rd, Iron Acton, BS37 9TB. Mrs B Naish. *9m N of Bristol, 3m W of Yate/Chipping Sodbury. Turn S off Iron Acton bypass B4059, past village green and past White Hart PH, 200yds, then over level crossing. No access from Frampton Cotterell via lane; ignore SatNav. Parking at Algars Manor.* **Sun 15 Apr (2-5). Combined adm with Algars Mill £5, chd free. Home-made teas.**

2 acres of woodland garden beside River Frome, mill stream, native plants mixed with collections of 60 magnolias and 70 camellias, rhododendrons, azaleas, eucalyptus and other unusual trees and shrubs. Daffodils and other early spring flowers. Partial wheelchair access only, gravel paths, some steep and uneven slopes.

3 ALGARS MILL

Frampton End Rd, Iron Acton, Bristol, BS37 9TD. Mr & Mrs John Wright. *9m N of Bristol, 3m W of Yate/Chipping Sodbury. (For directions see Algars Manor).* **Sun 15 Apr (2-5). Combined adm with Algars Manor £5, chd free. Home-made teas.**

2 acre woodland garden bisected by R Frome; spring bulbs, shrubs; very early spring feature (Feb-Mar) of wild Newent daffodils. 300-400yr-old mill house (not open) through which millrace still runs.

4 BABBS FARM

Westhill Lane, Bason Bridge, Highbridge, TA9 4RF. Sue & Richard O'Brien, 01278 793244, www.babbsfarm.co.uk. *1½m E of Highbridge, 1½m SSE of M5 exit 22. Turn into Westhill Lane off B3141 (Church Rd), 100yds S of where it joins B3139 (Wells-Highbridge rd).* **Sun 27, Mon 28 May, Sun 26, Mon 27 Aug (2-5). Adm £5, chd free. Home-made teas. Visits also by arrangement May to Aug.**

¾ acre plantsman's garden in Somerset Levels, gradually created out of fields surrounding old farmhouse over last 20 yrs and still being developed. Trees, shrubs and herbaceous perennials planted with an eye for form and shape in big flowing borders. Various ponds (formal and informal), box garden, patio area and conservatory.

◆ BARRINGTON COURT

Barrington, Ilminster, TA19 0NQ. National Trust, 01460 241938, barringtoncourt@nationaltrust.org.uk, www.nationaltrust.org.uk. *5m NE of Ilminster. In Barrington village on B3168. Follow brown NT signs.* **For NGS: Sat 21 Apr, Sat 7 July (10.30-5). Adm £11.92, chd £6. Light refreshments at Strode Dining & Tearoom, lunches also served.** For other opening times and information, please phone, email or visit garden website.

Well known garden constructed in 1920 by Col Arthur Lyle from derelict farmland (C19 cattle stalls still exist). Gertrude Jekyll suggested planting schemes for the layout. Paved paths with walled rose and iris, white and lily gardens, large kitchen garden. The kitchen garden has been in continuous production for over 90yrs. Some paths a little uneven.

5 BATH PRIORY HOTEL

Weston Rd, Bath, BA1 2XT. Jane Moore, Head Gardener, 01225 331922, info@thebathpriory.co.uk, www.thebathpriory.co.uk. *Close to centre of Bath. Metered parking in Royal Victoria Park. No 4, 14, 39 and 37 buses from City centre. Please note: Disabled parking only in Hotel grounds.* **Thur 19 Apr, Thur 13 Sept (2-5). Adm £3, chd free. Home-made teas.**

Discover 3 acres of mature walled gardens. Quintessentially English, the garden has billowing borders, croquet lawn, wild flower meadow and ancient specimen trees. Spring is bright with tulips and flowering cherries; autumn alive with colour. Perennials and tender plants provide summer highlights while the kitchen garden supplies herbs, fruit and vegetables to the restaurant. Gravel paths and some steps.

6 BEECHWELL HOUSE

51 Goose Green, Yate, BS37 5BL. Tim Wilmot, www.beechwell.com. *10m NE of Bristol. From Yate centre, go N onto Church Ln. After ½m turn L onto Greenways Rd then R onto Church Ln. After 300yds take R fork, garden 100yds on L.* **Sun 9 Sept (1-5). Adm £3.50, chd free. Home-made teas.**

Enclosed, level, subtropical garden created over last 29 yrs and filled with exotic planting, incl palms (over 6 varieties), tree ferns, yuccas, agaves and succulent bed, rare shrubs, bamboos, bananas, and other architectural planting. Wildlife pond and koi pond. C16 40ft deep well. Featured in Amateur Gardening magazine 2017 and on BBC Garden Rescue 2017 as a featured garden. Some narrow pathways.

GROUP OPENING

7 BENTER GARDENS

Benter, Oakhill, Radstock, BA3 5BJ. 01761 232605, alex@crossmanassociates.co.uk. *Between the villages of Chilcompton, Stratton on Fosse and Oakhill, narrow lanes. A37, from Bristol and Shepton Mallet, turn to gardens by village shop in Gurney Slade. Follow lane for approx 1m, R at grass triangle before incline. From Bath A367, after Stratton on Fosse, 2nd R to Benter.* **Sun 22 July (10-5). Combined adm £5, chd free. Home-made teas at Fire Engine House. Visits also by arrangement July & Aug please confirm visitor numbers and refreshments 2 weeks prior to visit.**

COLLEGE BARN
Alex Crossman & Jen Weaver.

FIRE ENGINE HOUSE
Patrick & Nicola Crossman.

Two contrasting gardens in beautiful, rural setting. The garden at Fire Engine House is mature and established, with lawns, generous borders and narrow, enticing paths; through a garden door and tumble-down bothy is a small orchard and arboretum. College Barn garden is 4 yrs old and draws upon the surrounding meadows and woods with hazel and hornbeam hedges, swathes of perennials and prairie planting with ornamental grasses. Intimate walled garden filled with vegetables, herbs, flowers and fruit. Peace and tranquillity surrounds. Featured in regional press and radio.

Your visit to a garden will help more people be cared for by a Parkinson's nurse

8 BOWDENS FARM

Hambridge, Langport, TA10 0BP. Mary Lang, 01458 251225, Lang61@btinternet.com. *10m E of Taunton. In Curry Rivel turn off A378 by Shell garage to Hambrige (B3168) Continue for 1m, 50yds past Hambridge village sign take 1st L signed Bowdens Farm.* **Visits by arrangement June & July for groups of 10+. Adm £5, chd free. Home-made teas.**
Peaceful garden with stunning views. 2 acres incl 6 yr old formal garden with mixed herbaceous borders, old fashioned roses, box, yew and pergola smothered in climbers. Lily covered pond with drifts of wild orchid and flag iris, self seeded herb garden and pretty courtyard garden. Productive kitchen garden and seating on lawns amongst maturing trees. Mostly wheelchair access.

9 BOWEYS

Church Lane, Kingston St Mary, TA2 8HR. Mr N Palfrey & Ms Geraldine Campbell, 01823 451868, www.country-matters.co.uk. *2½m N of Taunton. Close to church in village, please use church car park. Disabled parking at Boweys.* **Sat 16, Sun 17, Mon 18 June, Sat 21, Sun 22, Mon 23 July (2-5). Adm £4.50, chd free. Home-made teas. Visits also by arrangement.**
Mature cottage garden, fascinating stonework, water and topiary with imaginative planting completed after 22years, weeds welcome occasionally. Garden and buildings designed for wildlife as much as for the owners. Summerhouse finalised, gazebo enclosed. About 500 nest boxes for Insects, birds and bats. A reclaimed Paradise. Partial wheelchair access via gravel paths, paved slopes.

10 BRADON FARM

Isle Abbotts, Taunton, TA3 6RX. Mr & Mrs Thomas Jones, deborahjstanley@hotmail.com. *Take turning to Ilton off A358. Bradon Farm is 1½m out of Ilton on Bradon Lane.* **Visits by arrangement June to Aug for groups of 10 - 100. Adm £5, chd free. Home-made teas.**
Classic formal garden created in recent years, demonstrating the effective use of structure. Much to see incl parterre, knot garden, pleached lime walk, formal pond, herbaceous borders, orchard and wildflower planting. Featured in Visit Somerset, Somerset County Gazette, Western Gazette, Somerset Life.

GROUP OPENING

11 BRENT KNOLL GARDENS

Highbridge, TA9 4DF. *2m N of Highbridge. Off A38 & M5 J22. From M5 take A38 N (Cheddar etc) first L into Brent Knoll.* **Sun 8 July (12-5). Combined adm £7, chd free. Light refreshments at Ball Copse Hall, also cream teas.**

BALL COPSE HALL
Mrs S Boss & Mr A J Hill, 01278 760301, susan.boss@gmail.com. **Visits also by arrangement Mar to Oct.**

LABURNUM COTTAGE
Catherine Weber.

WOODBINE FARM
Mrs Samantha Jackson.

The distinctive hill of Brent Knoll, an iron age hill fort, is well worth climbing 449ft for the 360° view of surrounding hills incl Glastonbury Tor and the Somerset Levels. Lovely C13 church renowned for its bench ends. Ball Copse Hall: S-facing Edwardian house (not open) on lower slopes of Knoll. Front garden maturing well with curving slopes and paths. Ha-ha, wild area and kitchen garden. Views to Quantock and Polden Hills. Kitchen garden enclosed by crinkle crankle wall. Flock of Soay sheep. Laburnum Cottage: ½ acre garden developed over 15 yrs with over 100 varieties of hemerocallis (day lilies) incl many unusual forms and spider types. Large, sweeping borders with mixed plantings of shrubs and herbaceous plants.

Woodbine Farm: a quintessential English garden. Many very old, established climbers in old walled gardens and on house, incl roses, wisteria and clematis. Large herbaceous border. Cottage garden with hydrangeas, fruit and herbs. Paddock with huge lavender beds. Wheelchair access in all gardens, some restricted.

12 BREWERY HOUSE

Southstoke, Bath, BA2 7DL. John & Ursula Brooke, 01225 833153, jbsouthstoke@gmail.com. *2½ m S of Bath. A367 Radstock Rd from Bath. At top of dual carriageway turn L onto B3110. Straight on at double r'about. Next R into Southstoke.* **Sat 16 June (2-5). Adm £3.50, chd free. Cream teas. Visits also by arrangement May to Aug, please ring for parking arrangements and timings. Teas can be arranged on request.**

¾ acre garden in centre of village with splendid views to S over rolling countryside. Long established walled garden with fine, mature trees, shrubs and climbers. The mature planting gives a sense of mystery as one explores the contrast of colours, shapes and the unusual variety of species. Wheelchair access restricted to lower part of garden.

13 BROOMCLOSE

Porlock, Minehead, TA24 8NU. David & Nicky Ramsay, 01643 862078, davidjamesramsay@gmail.com. *Off A39 on Porlock Weir Rd, between Porlock and West Porlock. From Porlock take rd signed to Porlock Weir. Leave houses of Porlock behind, pass 3 fields, we are 1st drive on L. NB Some SatNavs direct wrongly from Porlock - beware.* **Visits by arrangement Apr to Sept. Groups or individuals welcome. Adm £4, chd free. Home-made teas.**

Large, varied garden set around early 1900s Arts and Crafts house overlooking the sea. Original stone terraces, Mediterranean garden, long borders, copse, camellia walk, meadow with bee hives and vegetable garden. Maritime climate favours unusual sub-tropical trees, shrubs and herbaceous plants. Featured as 'Garden of the Week' in Garden News.

14 NEW CAMELEY HOUSE

Cameley, Temple Cloud, Bristol, BS39 5AJ. Fiona & Jonathan Hayward 01761 451111, flodden@btconnect.com. *10m from Bristol, Bath and Wells. In Temple Cloud turn off A37 onto Cameley Road/Cameley Lane. 1½ m on L.* **Visits by arrangement between mid April & May for groups 10-30 (smaller groups considered). Adm £5, chd free. Home-made teas.**

3 acre garden surrounding C18 Strawberry Hill Gothic house (not open). An established garden on a sloping site developed and re-planted by owners over the last 8 years. The Cam Brook runs through the garden with woodland including ginkgo and tulip trees. Borders with tulips, hellebores, geums, camassias and magnolias. White garden. Cherry orchard with topiary and sculpture. Alpine troughs. Limited wheelchair access.

15 9 CATHERSTON CLOSE

Frome, BA11 4HR. Dave & Prue Moon. *15m S of Bath. Town centre W towards Shepton Mallet (A361). R at Sainsbury's r'about, follow lane for ½ m. L into Critchill Rd. Over Xrds, 1st L Catherston Close.* **Sun 10 June (12-5). Combined adm with 84 Weymouth Road £6, chd free. Fri 15, Sun 17 June, Thur 12 July (12-5). Adm £4, chd free.**

What a surprise around the corner in waiting, a small town garden which has grown to ⅓ acre! Colour-themed shrub and herbaceous borders, pond, patios, pergolas and wild meadow areas lead to wonderful far reaching views. Productive vegetable and fruit garden with greenhouse. Exhibition of garden photography by the garden owner, from near and far, displayed in summerhouse. Gold winner Frome-in-Bloom. Featured in Amateur Gardener, Somerset Gardens Trust, regional press and radio. Several shallow steps, gravel paths. Please note shorter opening times of 84 Weymouth Road on 10 June.

16 25 CHAUCER ROAD

Bath, BA2 4QX. Tina Payne. *From centre of Bath follow signs to Radstock (A367) along Wellsway to Bear Flat. At T-lights by The Bear PH take any road to L and these will take you to junction with Chaucer Road.* **Sat 26, Sun 27 May (1-5). Adm £3, chd free. Home-made teas.**

Compact town garden designed by present owners which has achieved Bath In Bloom gold and silver gilt awards. A courtyard of potted plants surrounded by attractive colour co-ordinated herbaceous borders leads to the next levels which include small fish pond, resident tortoise and vegetable section. Garden is open to coincide with the Bear Flat Artists weekend.

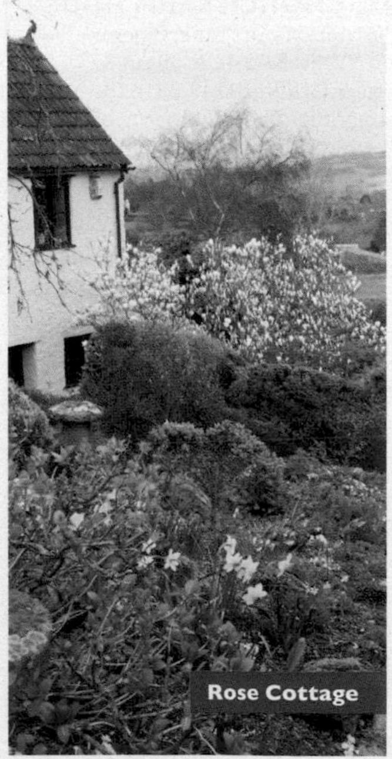

Rose Cottage

17 CHERRY BOLBERRY FARM

Furge Lane, Henstridge, BA8 0RN. Mrs Jenny Raymond, 01963 362177, cherrybolberryfarm@tiscali.co.uk. *6m E of Sherborne. In centre of Henstridge, R at small Xrds signed Furge Lane. Continue straight up lane, over 2 cattle grids, garden at top of lane on R.* **Visits by arrangement in June for groups of 10+. Adm £5, chd free. Home-made teas.**

40 yr-old award winning, owner designed and maintained, 1 acre garden planted for yr-round interest with wildlife in mind. Colour themed island beds, shrub and herbaceous borders, unusual perennials and shrubs, old roses and an area of specimen trees. Lots of hidden areas, brilliant for hide and seek! Vegetable and flower cutting garden, greenhouses, nature ponds. Wonderful extensive views. Garden surrounded by our dairy farm which has been in the family for nearly 100 years. You will see Jersey cows, sheep, horses and hens!

18 CHURCH FARM HOUSE

Turners Court Lane, Binegar, nr Wells, BA3 4UA. Susan & Tony Griffin, 01749 841628, smgriffin@beanacrebarn.co.uk, www.beanacrebarn.co.uk. *5m NE of Wells. From Wells B3139 NE for 4½ m, turn R signed Binegar, yellow NGS sign at Xrds. From A37 in Gurney Slade at George Inn follow sign to Binegar, past church, at Xrds NGS sign.* **Wed 6, Sun 10 June (11-4.30). Adm £4, chd free. Visits also by arrangement June & July any number very welcome.**

Wrapped around an old farmhouse are 2 walled gardens planted in contemporary cottage style, roses and clematis on walls and unusual perennials in deep borders give interest all seasons. South garden has progressive colourist design. The ever expanding insect friendly planting in the gravel of the old farmyard creates an interesting display of form and colour often with self-seeded surprises! A very good example of a cottage garden using unusual as well as traditional plants. Featured in Mendip Times, local press and radio. Gravel forecourt, 2 shallow steps.

19 NEW COLDHARBOUR COTTAGE

Radford Hill, Radford, Radstock, BA3 2XU. Ms Amanda Cranston, 01761 470600, amanda.cranston@yahoo.co.uk. *Bath & NE Somerset. South of Bath, please ask for directions when booking.* **Visits by arrangement Apr to Sept for adults and children over 13 yrs. Adm £5, chd £2.50. Light refreshments. Please confirm visitor numbers 2 weeks prior to visit.**

¾ acre rural garden with mature trees, wild areas, vegetable garden and open lawns and borders with secluded seating areas. Interesting out-buildings, hen house, small ponds and stumpery. Pretty lavender and rose path in summer. Designed to attract wildlife all year round and a quiet and informal space for calm enjoyment and reflection. Quiet garden for relaxation, enjoyment and reflection. Dementia groups and carers particularly welcome. Wheelchair access to grassed areas may be weather-dependant. Some narrow and uneven paths.

20 ◆ COTHAY MANOR & GARDENS

Greenham, Wellington, TA21 0JR. Mrs Alastair Robb, 01823 672283, cothaymanor@btinternet.com, www.cothaymanor.co.uk. *5m SW of Wellington. 7m off M5 via A38, signed Greenham, follow brown signs for Cothay Manor & Gardens. See website for more detailed directions.* **For NGS: Sat 28 July (2-5). Adm £7.80, chd £3.90. Cream teas.** For other opening times and information, please phone, email or visit garden website.

Few gardens are as evocatively romantic as Cothay. Laid out in 1920s and replanted in 1990s within the original framework, Cothay encompasses a rare blend of old and new. Plantsman's paradise set in 12 acres of magical gardens. Small nursery and tea room. Sorry no dogs or picnicing in gardens. House tour 3.00pm (separate admission cost). Partial wheelchair access, gravel paths.

21 ◆ COURT HOUSE

East Quantoxhead, TA5 1EJ. East Quantoxhead Estate (Hugh Luttrell Esq), 01278 741271, hugh_luttrell@yahoo.co.uk. *12m W of Bridgwater. Off A39, house at end of village past duck pond. Enter by Frog Street (Bridgwater/Kilve side from A39). Car park £1 in aid of church.* **For NGS: Sun 20 May, Sun 22 July (2-5). Adm £5, chd free. Cream teas.** For other opening times and information, please phone or email.

Lovely 5 acre garden, trees, shrubs (many rare and tender), herbaceous and 3 acre woodland garden with spring interest and late summer borders. Traditional kitchen garden (chemical free). Views to sea and Quantocks. Gravel, stone and some mown grass paths.

22 CRETE HILL HOUSE GARDENS

Cote House Lane, Durdham Down, Bristol, BS9 3UW. John Burgess. *2m N of Bristol city centre/3m S J16 M5. A4018 Westbury Rd from city centre, L at White Tree r'about, R into Cote Rd, continue into Cote House Lane across the Downs. 2nd house on L. Parking on street.* **Sun 17 June (1-5). Adm £3.50, chd free. Home-made teas.**

C18 house in hidden corner of Bristol. Mainly SW facing garden, 80'x40', with shaped lawn, heavily planted traditional mixed shrub, rose, clematis and herbaceous borders. Pergola with climbers, terrace with pond, several seating areas. Tranquil semi-walled area on 2 levels with shady planting. Roof terrace (40 steps) with far reaching views to Wales.

23 THE DAIRY

Clevedon Road, Weston-in-Gordano, Bristol, BS20 8PZ. Mrs Christine Lewis, 01275 849214, chris@dairy.me.uk. *Weston-in-Gordano is on B3124 Portishead to Clevedon rd. Find Parish Church on main rd and take lane down side of churchyard for 200m.* **Sat 16, Sun 17 June (2-5). Adm £5, chd free. Home-made teas. Visits also by arrangement May to Sept.**

The garden surrounds a barn conversion and has been developed from concrete milking yards and derelict land. Once the site of Weston in Gordano Manor House, the ambience owes much to the use of medieval stone which had lain undiscovered in the land for over 2 centuries. Changes of level, with steps and gravel paths, make wheelchair access difficult.

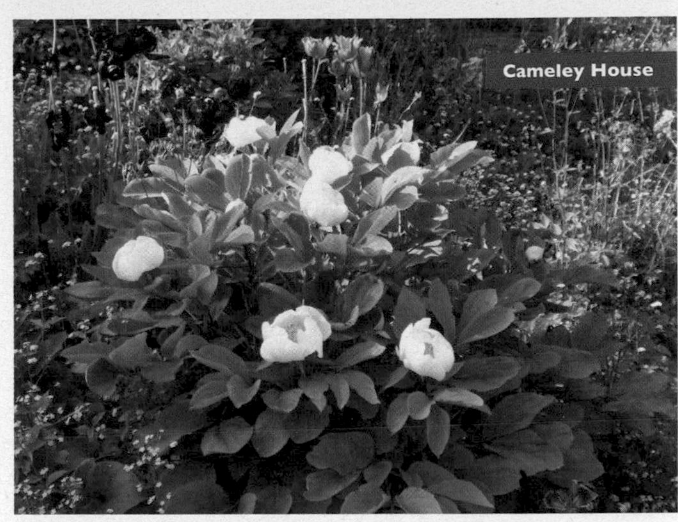

Cameley House

24 DOYNTON HOUSE

Bury Lane, Doynton, Bristol, BS30 5SR. Frances & Matthew Lindsey-Clark. *5m S of M4 J18, 6m N of Bath, 8m E of Bristol. Doynton is NE of Wick (turn off A420 opp Bath Rd) and SW of Dyrham (signed from A46). Doynton House is at S end of Doynton village, opp Culleysgate/Horsepool Lane. Park in signed field.* **Sun 15 July (1-5). Adm £5, chd free. Home-made teas.**

A variety of garden areas separated by old walls and hedges. Mixed borders, wall planting, parterre, rill garden, walled vegetable garden, cottage beds, pool garden, dry garden, spring garden, peach house and greenhouse. Bees. Chickens. Meadow area being prepared and sown 17-18. Paths are of hoggin, stone and gravel. The grade of the gravel makes it a hard push in places but all areas are wheelchair accessible.

25 EAST END FARM

Pitney, Langport, TA10 9AL. Mrs A M Wray, 01458 250598. *2m E of Langport. Please telephone for directions.* **Visits by arrangement in June. Adm £3.50, chd free.**

Approx ⅓ acre. Timeless small garden of many old-fashioned roses in beautiful herbaceous borders set amongst ancient listed farm buildings. Mostly wheelchair access.

26 ◆ EAST LAMBROOK MANOR GARDENS

Silver Street, East Lambrook, TA13 5HH. Mike & Gail Werkmeister, 01460 240328, enquiries@eastlambrook.com, www.eastlambrook.com. *2m N of South Petherton. Follow brown tourist signs from A303 South Petherton r'about or B3165 Xrds with lights N of Martock.* **For NGS: Sat 17 Feb, Sun 13 May, Sat 2 June (10-5). Adm £6, chd free. Tea. 2019: Sun 17 Feb.** For other opening times and information, please phone, email or visit garden website.

The quintessential English cottage garden created by C20 gardening legend Margery Fish. Plantsman's paradise with old-fashioned and contemporary plants grown in a relaxed and informal manner to create an extraordinary garden of great beauty and charm. With noted collections of snowdrops, hellebores and geraniums and the excellent specialist Margery Fish Plant Nursery. Also open 1 Feb - 31 Oct, Tues to Sat and BH Mons plus Suns in Feb and May to July; (10-5). Featured on BBC Gardeners' World. Main features not accessible to wheelchair users due to narrow paths and steps.

27 NEW ELMCROFT

11 The Roman Way, Glastonbury, BA6 8AB. Mrs Joanna Cobb, 01458 832178, ericjoanna@waitrose.com. *From Glastonbury town centre take A361 Fishers Hill in direction Shepton Mallet. Turn R at top of hill onto Butleigh Rd and immed R onto Tor View Ave for The Roman Way.* **Visits by arrangement Mar to Oct. Information sheets incl garden plan. Individuals/ groups up to 20. Adm £3, chd free. Light refreshments. Cakes and biscuits with gluten free choices.**

Situated on legendary Wearyall Hill with stunning views of Glastonbury Tor and Somerset Levels, this once neglected garden has been transformed by art historian Joanna into an intriguing and varied series of rooms. Incorporating all of the elements and senses, here is space for exploration, inspiration, conversation and quiet contemplation. Artists and photographers most welcome. Winner of Glastonbury in Bloom 2017

28 ◆ ELWORTHY COTTAGE

Elworthy, Taunton, TA4 3PX. Mike & Jenny Spiller, 01984 656427, mike@elworthy-cottage.co.uk, www.elworthy-cottage.co.uk. *12m NW of Taunton. On B3188 between Wiveliscombe and Watchet.* **For NGS: Sat 3, Sun 4 Feb, Mon 2, Tue 10, Tue 17 Apr, Thur 3, Mon 28, Thur 31 May, Tue 5, Tue 26 June, Thur 5, Thur 12 July, Sun 12, Mon 27, Thur 30 Aug (11-5). Adm £3.50, chd free. Visits also by arrangement Apr – Sept and also Feb for snowdrops.** For other opening times and information, please phone, email or visit garden website.

1 acre plantsman's garden in tranquil setting. Island beds, scented plants, clematis, unusual perennials and ornamental trees and shrubs to provide yr-round interest. In spring, pulmonarias, hellebores and more than 300 varieties of snowdrops. Planted to encourage birds, bees and butterflies, lots of birdsong. Wild flower areas, decorative vegetable garden, living willow screen. Stone ex-privy and pigsty feature. Garden attached to plantsman's nursery, open at the same time.

29 14 ESKDALE CLOSE

Weston-super-Mare, BS22 8QG. Janet & Adrian Smith. *1½m E of WsM town centre. From M5 J21, B3440 to town centre, L at Corondale Rd, R into Garsdale Rd. Take footpath next to number 37.* **Sun 3 June (1.30-4.30). Adm £3, chd free. Home-made teas. Also open Fernbank.**

Informal garden with plenty of seating to relax in and enjoy the various areas and styles of planting. Mediterranean area leads to patio and lawn, partly enclosed by a tall border. Pond and collection of conifers on raised rockery. Archway leading to vegetable and fruit garden. Awarded best large garden in Weston Horticultural Society's Weston in Bloom 2017. No wheelchair access to vegetable patch.

30 FAIRFIELD

Stogursey, Bridgwater, TA5 1PU. Lady Acland Hood Gass. *7m E of Williton. 11m W of Bridgwater. From A39 Bridgwater to Minehead rd turn N. Garden 1½m W of Stogursey on Stringston rd. No coaches.* **Sun 8 Apr (2-5). Adm £4, chd free. Home-made teas.**

Woodland garden with bulbs, shrubs and fine trees. Paved maze. Views of Quantocks and sea. Featured in Daily Telegraph & Shepton Mallet Journal.

31 FERNBANK

High Street, Congresbury, BS49 5JA. Julia Thyer, www.juliathyer.blogspot.co.uk. *Midway between Weston-super-Mare and Bristol. From T-lights on A370 at Ship & Castle, turn into High St (B3133 to Churchill). Garden 100yds on R. Drop off only. Park at Ship & Castle, side streets or car park N of river.* **Sun 3 June (10.30-5). Adm £4, chd free. Home-made teas. Also open 14 Eskdale Close. Yummy cakes, cream teas and gluten free.**

Enter an alternative universe behind Victorian house within conservation area of 'The kindest village in Britain'. Quirky ⅓ acre garden with lots of surprises. Explore the potager, greenhouse, potting shed, Wendy house, lily ponds and banks of potted plants. Type poetry in a beach hut, lounge on a blanket on the lawn. Quiz for kids. Delicious teas in conservatory accompanied by birdsong. Enjoy! Narrow gates, and some gravel paths make wheelchair access very difficult. A few intrepid explorers have made it to the lawn and patio.

32 FERNHILL

Whiteball, Wellington, TA21 0LU. Peter & Audrey Bowler, www.sampfordarundel.org.uk/fernhill. *3m W of Wellington. At top of Whiteball hill on A38 on L going West, just before dual carriageway, parking on site.* **Sun 22 July, Sun 19 Aug (2-5). Adm £3.50, chd free. Home-made teas.**

In approx 2 acres, a delightful garden to stir your senses, with a myriad of unusual plants and features. Intriguing almost hidden paths leading through English roses and banks of hydrangeas. Scenic views stretching up to the Blackdowns and its famous monument. Truly a Hide and Seek garden ..... for all ages. Well stocked herbaceous borders, octagonal pergola and water garden with slightly wild boggy area. Wheelchair access to terrace and other parts of garden from drive.

33 NEW THE FLAX BARN

Broadmead Lane, Norton Sub Hamdon, TA14 6SS. Mrs Jayne English. *1.2m SE from A303. From A303 take A356 SE towards Crewkerne. After 0.7mile L to Norton-sub-Hamdon. After 0.5m L into Broadmead Lane, no through road. The Flax Barn is 50 yds on L set back from rd.* **Sun 25 Mar, Sun 6 May, Sun 14 Oct (11-4). Adm £5, chd free. Light refreshments served in The Pink Palace in garden, where colourful patchwork quilts will also be on display.**

A modern masterpiece hosting herbaceous perennials, ornamental grasses, spring bulbs, crocus lawn, assortments of alliums and agapanthus and much more! Wend your way past a pond, sculptures, shrubs, circular lawns and then take a breath, maybe even a cup of tea, in an opulent rotating orb. Garden is SW facing and newly landscaped from old orchard. Wheelchair accessible.

34 FOREST LODGE

Pen Selwood, BA9 8LL. Mr & Mrs James Nelson, 07974 701427, lucillanelson@gmail.com. *1½m N of A303, 3m E of Wincanton. Leave A303 at B3081 (Wincanton to Gillingham rd), up hill to Pen Selwood, L towards church. ½m, garden on L - low curved wall and sign saying Forest Lodge Stud.* **Thur 10 May, Thur 14 June (2.30-4.30). Adm £5, chd free. Home-made teas. Visits also by arrangement Mar to Oct**

for groups of 5+. Donation to Heads Up Wells, Balsam Centre Wincanton.
3 acre mature garden with many camellias and rhododendrons in May. Lovely views towards Blackmore Vale. Part formal with pleached hornbeam allée and rill, part water garden with lake. Wonderful roses in June. Unusual spring flowering trees such as Davidia involucrata, many beautiful cornus. Interesting garden sculpture. Wheelchair access to front garden only, however much of garden viewable from there.

35 GANTS MILL & GARDEN

Gants Mill Lane, Bruton, BA10 0DB. Elaine & Greg Beedle. *½m SW of Bruton. From Bruton centre take Yeovil rd, A359, under railway bridge, 100yds uphill, fork R down Gants Mill Lane. Parking for wheelchair users.* **Sun 1 July (2-5). Adm £6, chd free. Home-made teas.**
¾ acre garden. Clematis, rose arches and pergolas, streams, ponds, waterfalls. Riverside walk to top weir, delphiniums, day lilies, 100+ dahlia varieties, vegetable, soft fruit and cutting flower garden. Garden is overlooked by the historic watermill, open on NGS day. Firm wide paths round garden. Narrow entrance to mill not accessible to wheelchairs. WC.

36 GOBLIN COMBE HOUSE

Plunder Street, Cleeve, Bristol, BS49 4PQ. Hilary Burn. *10m S of Bristol. A370, turn L onto Cleeve Hill Rd before Lord Nelson Inn; 300m L onto Plunder St, 1st drive on R. Parking just beyond Plunder St turning. On main bus route.* **Wed 13 June (1.30-5). Adm £4, chd free. Home-made teas.**
2 acre terraced garden with stunning views. Interesting collection of trees, mixed shrubs and herbaceous borders, surrounded by orchards, fields with wild flowers and woodlands. Many different climbing and rambling roses. Uneven and steep paths, very slippery when wet.

37 GREYSTONES

Hollybush Lane, Bristol, BS9 1JB. Mr & Mrs P Townsend. *2m N of Bristol city centre, close to Durdham Down in Bristol, backing onto the Botanic Garden. A4018 Westbury Rd, L at White Tree r'about, L into Saville Rd, Hollybush Lane 2nd on R. Narrow lane, parking limited, recommended to park in Saville Rd.* **Sun 3 June (2-5). Adm £3.50, chd free. Home-made teas.**
Peaceful garden with places to sit and enjoy a quiet corner of Bristol. Interesting courtyard with raised beds and large variety of conifers and shrubs leads to secluded garden of contrasts - from sun drenched beds with olive tree and brightly coloured flowers to shady spots, with acers, hostas and a fern walk. Small apple orchard, espaliered pears and koi pond. Paved footpath provides level access to all areas.

38 NEW HALSECOMBE HOUSE AND HALSECOMBE COTTAGE

Parsons Hill, Porlock, Minehead, TA24 8QP. Dr Judy Baxter. *On top of Porlock Hill. Follow A39 through Porlock and up Porlock Hill to top of tree line. When road bends sharply R, take L farm track, follow to end. For SatNav, use postcode TA24 8QH. Parking in adjacent field (parking in drive only for those with mobility issues).* **Sat 9, Sun 10 June (1-5). Adm £5, chd free. Home-made teas at the stables, Halsecombe House.**
Set on top of Porlock Hill with outstanding views of Welsh coast, the Bristol Channel and surrounding Exmoor hills, a breathtaking location. Lawns on different levels, all with sweeping views of surrounding countryside. Of special interest are the series of ponds and reed beds, richly stocked with bulrushes, reeds, irises, kingcups and home to herons, ducks, butterflies and dragonflies. Fine examples of Exmoor drystone walls throughout both gardens. House is circled by generously sized beds and the Cottage is more ornamental with many rare plants. Regret no wheelchair access.

39 HANGERIDGE FARMHOUSE

Wrangway, Wellington, TA21 9QG. Mrs J M Chave, 07812 648876, hangeridge@hotmail.co.uk. *2m S of Wellington. Off A38 Wellington bypass signed Wrangway. 1st L towards Wellington monument, over motorway bridge 1st R.* **Sun 22 July (2-5). Adm £3, chd free. Home-made teas. Visits also by arrangement May to Aug for groups of 10+.**
Rural fields and mature trees surround this 1 acre informal garden offering views of the Blackdown and Quantock Hills. Magnificent hostas and heathers, colourful flower beds, cascading wisteria and roses and a trickling stream. Relax with home made refreshments on sunny or shaded seating admiring the views and birdsong.

40 HANHAM COURT

Ferry Road, Hanham Abbots, BS15 3NT. Hanham Court Gardens, www.hanhamcourtgardens.co.uk. *5m E of Bristol centre. Old Bristol Rd A431 from Bath, through Willsbridge (past Queen's Head), L at mini r'about, down Court Farm Rd for 1m. Drive entrance on sharp L bend between signs on Court Farm Rd.* **Sun 11 Feb (11-4); Sun 27, Mon 28 May (12-5). Adm £5, chd free. Home-made teas.**
Hanham Court Gardens develop this rich mix of bold formality, water, woodland, orchard, meadow and kitchen garden with emphasis on scent, structure and romance, set amid a remarkable cluster of manorial buildings between Bath and Bristol. Partial wheelchair access. Caution: dense gravel paths throughout and some steep landscape.

41 4 HAYTOR PARK

Bristol, BS9 2LR. Mr & Mrs C J Prior, 07779 203626, p.l.prior@gmail.com. *3m NW of Bristol city centre. From A4162 Inner Ring Rd take turning into Coombe Bridge Ave, Haytor Park is 1st on L. Please no parking in Haytor Park.* **Sun 20 May (1-5). Adm £3, chd free. Visits also by arrangement May to Aug for groups 10-30.**

Explore the changes to a garden that seems never-ending. Linger awhile on hidden seats, observe multi-layered planting through many arches. Find dragons in nooks or frogs in a pond, pots on a patio, ferns in cool, secret spaces and plants from all over the world.

42 HENLEY MILL

Henley Lane, Wookey, BA5 1AW. Peter & Sally Gregson, 01749 676966, millcottageplants@gmail.com, www.millcottageplants.co.uk. *2m W of Wells, off A371 towards Cheddar. Turn L into Henley Lane, 50 yds turn L through stone pillars, continue to the end of drive. Henley Mill is on R of building, garden visitor entry through garage doors.* **Visits by arrangement Apr to Sept. Teas/refreshments by arrangement, pls confirm numbers and refreshments req'd 2 wks prior to visit. Adm £5, chd free.**

2½ acres beside R Axe. Scented garden with roses, hydrangea borders, shady folly garden and late summer borders with grasses and perennials. Zig-zag boardwalk at river level. Kitchen and cutting garden. Rare Japanese hydrangeas and new Chinese epimediums. We have been collecting the Benton bearded irises bred by Cedric Morris. Some may well be in flower in May/June. Collections of Hydrangea serrata and Chinese epimediums. Featured in regional press and radio. Garden is on one level but paths can get a bit muddy after heavy rain.

43 ◆ HESTERCOMBE GARDENS

Cheddon Fitzpaine, Taunton, TA2 8LG. Hestercombe Gardens Trust, 01823 413923, info@hestercombe.com, www.hestercombe.com. *4m N of Taunton, less than 6m from J25 of M5. Follow brown tourist signs. SatNav postcode TA2 8LQ.* **For NGS: Tue 6 Mar, Tue 5 June (10-4). Adm £11.80, chd £5.90. Light refreshments in Stables Café offering light lunches, teas and cakes with indoor and covered courtyard seating.** For other opening times and information, please phone, email or visit garden website.

Georgian landscape garden designed by Coplestone Warre Bampfylde, Victorian terrace and shrubbery and stunning exquisite example of Lutyens/Jeykll designed formal garden. These together make up 50 acres of woodland walks, temples, terraces, pergolas, lakes and cascades. Hestercombe House is also now open comprising a contemporary art gallery and second-hand book shop. Restored watermill and barn, lesser horseshoe bats, historic house and family garden trails. Gravel paths, steep slopes, steps. All abilities route marked. Tramper mobility scooter available, booking required.

44 HILLCREST

Curload, Stoke St. Gregory, Taunton, TA3 6JA. Charles & Charlotte Sundquist, 01823 490852, chazfix@gmail.com. *At top of Curload. From A358 turn L along A378, then branch L to North Curry and Stoke St. Gregory. L ½m after Willows & Wetlands centre. Hillcrest is 1st on R with parking directions.* **Sat 5, Sun 6 May (1.30-5). Adm £4, chd free. Home-made teas. Visits also by arrangement Apr to July (incl late afternoon/early evening).**

The garden boasts stunning views of the Somerset Levels, Burrow Mump and Glastonbury Tor, but even on a hazy day this 5 acre garden offers plenty of interest. Woodland walks, varied borders, flowering meadow and several ponds; also kitchen garden, greenhouses, orchards and unique standing stone as focal point. Most of garden is level. Long gently sloping path through flower meadow to lower pond and wood.

45 NEW ◆ HOMEACRES

Alhampton, Shepton Mallet, BA4 6PZ. Mr Charles Dowding, 07922 719765, charles@charlesdowding.co.uk, https://www.charlesdowding.co.uk/. *1m from Castle Cary rail station, signs to Homeacres nr Alhampton Inn. Up narrow no-through road 150m from the village main road. Please park carefully in village, short walk to garden, 3rd on L after pretty chapel. Disabled drop-off at property.* **For NGS: Sat 2, Sun 3 June (12-4.30). Adm £5, chd free.** For other opening times and information, please phone, email or visit garden website.

⅓ acre market and teaching garden; I conduct trials into different ways of growing plants, incl dig/no dig, no rotation, using different composts, all signed. Wide range of vegetables outside and under cover, fruit trees, flower borders and intensive composting system of 7 bays. No dig means healthy plants and fewer weeds, very noticeable in the vegetables and flowers. Internationally acclaimed no dig organic vegetable garden, prolific vegetables and flowers of excellence, author of many books. Featured on TV and radio, BBC Gardeners World and in Gardening Which? Wheelchair access to garden only. No steps anywhere but neither WC accessible by wheelchair. Well behaved dogs on short leads welcome.

46 HONEYHURST FARM

Honeyhurst Lane, Rodney Stoke, Cheddar, BS27 3UJ. Don & Kathy Longhurst, 01749 870322, donlonghurst@btinternet.com, www.ciderbarrelcottage.co.uk. *4m E of Cheddar. From A371 between Wells and Cheddar, turn into Rodney*

Stoke signed Wedmore. Pass church on L and continue for almost 1m. **Sun 8, Mon 9 July (2-5). Adm £3.50, chd free. Home-made teas. Cream teas. Visits also by arrangement Apr to Oct for groups of 10 to 40.**

⅔ acre part walled rural garden with babbling brook and 4 acre traditional cider orchard, with views. Specimen hollies, copper beech, paulownia, yew and poplar. Pergolas, arbour and numerous seats. Mixed informal shrub and perennial beds with many unusual plants. Many pots planted with shrubs, hardy and half-hardy perennials. Level, grass and some shingle.

GROUP OPENING

47 ISLE ABBOTTS GARDENS

Church Street, Isle Abbotts, Isle Abbotts, nr Ilminster, TA3 6RJ. *4m N of Ilminster. All gardens located on Church St. Parking will be signed.* **Sat 9, Sun 10 June (2-5.30). Combined adm £5, chd free. Home-made teas in village hall. Teas, coffees and delicious home-made cakes.**

GREGGS
Jenny Byrom.

MONKS ORCHARD
Maureen & David Bradshaw.

NEW **MONKS THATCH**
Mr Derold Page.

Historic village dating from Saxon times, located on edge of Somerset Levels with many thatched stone cottages. C13 Grade I listed church is described as 'The Jewel in the Crown of Somerset Churches'. Open church tower. 3 well-established unique gardens with many exquisite herbaceous borders. Greggs: ⅓-acre garden of many parts, shrubs, borders and vegetable beds joined by winding paths. Monks Orchard: ¾-acre garden developed over 14 yrs. Many large mixed borders with lots of unusual plants. Stunning views. Plants for sale propagated from garden. Monks Thatch: Front garden is a charming Elizabethan style topiary herb garden with water features and gazebo. At the rear is a seductive, private exotic paradise water garden with boardwalk, bridge, spiral courtyard and tropical planting. Wheelchair access to 2 gardens.

48 ◆ JEKKA'S HERBETUM

Shellards Lane, Alveston, Bristol, BS35 3SY. Mrs Jekka McVicar, 01454 418878, sales@jekkasherbfarm.com, www.jekkasherbfarm.com. *7m N of M5 J16 or 6m S from J14 of M5. 1m off A38 signed Itchington. From M5 J16, A38 to Alveston, past church turn R at junction signed Itchington. M5 J14 on A38 turn L after T-lights to Itchington.* **For NGS: Sun 5 Aug (10-4). Adm £5, chd free. Home-made teas.** For other opening times and information, please phone, email or visit garden website.

Jekka's Herbetum is a living herb encyclopaedia displaying the largest collection of culinary herbs in the UK. A wonderful resource for plant identification for the gardener and a gastronomic experience for chefs and cooks. Wheelchair access possible however terrain is rough from car park to Herbetum.

49 ◆ KILVER COURT GARDENS

Kilver Street, Shepton Mallet, BA4 5NF. Roger & Monty Saul, 01749 340410, info@kilvercourt.com, www.kilvercourt.com. *Directly off A37 rd to Bath, opp cider factory in Shepton Mallet.* **For NGS: Thur 10 May, Thur 6 Sept (9.30-4). Adm £5, chd £2.50. Light refreshments in Sharpham Pantry Restaurant & Harlequin Café. Children under 6 yrs free entry.** For other opening times and information, please phone, email or visit garden website.

Kilver Court Gardens in Somerset is the perfect day out for those looking to explore a little known treasure. Today, the gardens, which have appeared on BBC Gardeners' World, are like stepping into another world - a peaceful oasis away from modernity. Featured in The English Garden, Your County magazine, regional publications and radio. Some slopes, rockery not accessible for wheelchairs but can be viewed. Disabled parking in lower car park.

50 LAUGHING WATER

Weir Lane, Yeovilton, Yeovil, BA22 8EU. Peter & Joyce Warne, 01935 841933, p.j.warne@btinternet.com. *2m from A303, 7m N of Yeovil. Leave A303 signed Ilchester, take B3151 dir RNAS Yeovilton, take Bineham Lane, signed Yeovilton village, Laughing Water last house on R at end of village. Park at weir just past house.* **Wed 23 May (2-5); Sat 16 June (11.30-4.30). Adm £3.50, chd free. Home-made teas. Visits also by arrangement May & June for groups, min 8, max 30, day or eve.**

½ acre+ garden hidden behind Grade II listed house (not open). A mature garden, remodelled since 2011, it reflects the owner's love of flowers and foliage with sweeping grass paths through mixed beds of shrubs, herbaceous perennials, annuals and bulbs. Floriferous from early spring through to autumn frosts. Large wildlife pond and ornamental water features. Picturesque weir (after which the house is named) on river 20 mtrs past house. Fleet Air Arm Memorial Church, with C13 Nave, in village worth a visit. Limited wheelchair access.

The National Garden Scheme and Perennial, helping gardeners when they are in need

Little Yarford Farmhouse

51 NEW LITTLE HINTOCK

Higher Vellow, near Stogumber, Taunton, TA4 4JH. Julian Spicer & Christopher Legrove. *1.5m from A358 between Taunton (15m) and Minehead (12m). On Vellow Road halfway between Stogumber and Lower Vellow.* **Sat 30 June (12-6). Adm £3, chd free. Home-made teas.**

A quirky and rather wild garden. From streamside orchard with summerhouse, climbing to small flower garden in front of C17 stone cottage, then wooded hillside with roses growing through the trees and lovely views across peaceful hills. One acre in all, incl new areas being tamed. Cobbles, steps and some steep paths.

52 LITTLE YARFORD FARMHOUSE

Kingston St Mary, Taunton, TA2 8AN. Brian Bradley, 01823 451350, yarford@ic24.net. *1½m W of Hestercombe, 3½m N of Taunton. From Taunton on Kingston St Mary rd. At 30mph sign turn L at Parsonage Lane. Continue 1¼m W, to Yarford sign. Continue 400yds. Turn R up concrete rd.* **Fri 11 May (11-5). Light refreshments. Sat 12, Sun 13 May (2-5). Cream teas. Mon 14 May (11-5). Light refreshments. Adm £5, chd free. Weekdays incl, coffee, soup, bread & cheese. Visits also by arrangement Apr to Oct day or eve - clubs, friends, art, health and well-being groups.**

This unusual garden embraces a C17 house (not open) overgrown with climbing plants. A wealth of aquatic plants in 3 ponds. Of special interest is the finest tree collection in Taunton Deane, 300+ rare and unusual cultivars (listed on NGS website), both broad leaf and conifer: the trees that Bamfylde Warre would have planted at Hestercombe had they been available. Guided tree tours at 2 & 3.30. The 5 acres are a delight to both artist and plantsman. 'An inspirational, magical experience'. An exercise in landscaping and creating views both within the garden and without to the vale and the Quantock Hills. 5 acres. On Google maps. Mostly wheelchair access.

53 LOWER COCKHILL FARMHOUSE

Cockhill, Castle Cary, BA7 7NZ. David Curtis & Biddy Peppin. *1m SW of Castle Cary. From Station Rd Castle Cary turn down Torbay Rd, at bend take rd signed North Barrow for 1m. From South St (B3152) take South Cary Lane and at bottom of hill turn L.* **Sat 9, Sun 10 June (2-5.30). Combined adm with South Cary House £5, chd free. Teas at South Cary House.**

Artist's small semi-walled garden in farm setting; courtyard, overflowing long borders planted for colour, contrasting shape and height, with self-seeding welcomed. Pyramidal yews, box-edging and espaliered fruit trees for structure. Climbing roses, fan-trained cherry and pears. Narrow paths, no grass. Professional artist's studio open. Some narrow uneven paths in garden, one step up into studio;.

54 LOWER SHALFORD FARM

Shalford Lane, Charlton Musgrove, Wincanton, BA9 8HE. Mrs Suki Posnett. *Shalford Lane. 2m NE of Wincanton. Leave A303 at Wincanton go N on B3081. Turn R for Shalford Village ½m on L.* **Tue 13 Mar (10-3). Adm £4, chd free. Sat 12 May (10-4). Adm £5, chd free. Light refreshments.**

Fairly large open garden with extensive lawns and wooded surroundings. Small winterbourne stream running through with several stone bridges. Walled rose/parterre garden, hedged herbaceous garden and several ornamental ponds. Work is in constant progress. Very good village plant sale on same day in May. Partial wheelchair access.

55 LUCOMBE HOUSE

12 Druid Stoke Ave, Stoke Bishop, Bristol, BS9 1DD. Malcolm Ravenscroft, 01179 682494, famrave@gmail.com. *4m NW of Bristol centre. On L at top of Druid Hill. Garden on R 200m from junction.* **Sun 15 Apr (2-5.30). Adm £3.50, chd free. Home-made teas. Visits also by arrangement Apr to Sept.**

A Garden for Tree Lovers of all ages!! In addition to the 250 yr old Lucombe Oak - now registered as one of the most significant trees in the South West - there are over 30 mature English trees planted together with ferns and bluebells to create an urban woodland. Also, there are semi formal flowering beds and an untouched wild area. A landscape gardener will be available to answer questions. Rough paths in woodland area, 2 steps to patio.

56 LYDEARD HOUSE

West Street, Bishops Lydeard, Taunton, TA4 3AU. Mrs Colin Wilkins. *5m NW of Taunton. A358 Taunton to Minehead, do not take 1st 3 R turnings to Bishops Lydeard but 4th signed to Cedar Falls. Follow signs to Lydeard House.* **Sun 10 June (2-5.30). Adm £4.50, chd free. Light refreshments.**

4 acre garden with C18 origins and many later additions. Sweeping lawns, lake overhung with willows, canal running parallel to Victorian rose-covered pergola, along with box parterre, chinoiserie-style garden, recent temple folly and walled vegetable garden plus wonderful mature trees. Plants for sale. Children must be supervised because of very deep water. Deep gravel paths and steps may cause difficulty for wheelchairs but most features accessible by lawn.

GROUP OPENING

57 LYMPSHAM GARDENS

Church Road, Lympsham, Weston-super-Mare, BS24 0DT. *5m S of Weston-super-Mare and 5m N of Burnham on Sea. 2m M5 J22. Entrance to both gardens from main gates of Manor at junction of Church Rd and Lympsham Rd.* **Sat 16, Sun 17 June (2-5). Combined adm £5, chd free. Cream teas.**

CHURCH FARM
Andy & Rosemary Carr.

LYMPSHAM MANOR
James & Lisa Counsell.

At the picturesque heart of the village of Lympsham is C15 church of St Christopher. The Manor, built as the rectory 200 years ago, and C17 Church Farm are next to the church and connected to each other by a side gate. The Manor is a Gothic pinnacled, castellated rectory manor house with 2 octagonal towers (not open), set in 10 acres of formal and semi-formal garden, surrounded by paddocks and farmland. Main features are its carefully preserved, fully working Victorian kitchen garden and greenhouse, arboretum of trees from all parts of the world, large stocked fish pond and beautiful old rose garden. Old outside Victorian privy. Church Farm's ¾ acre informal country garden surrounds the farmhouse. Well-stocked herbaceous border, shrub lined paths, raised cut-flower beds and small courtyard garden.

58 ◆ MIDNEY GARDENS

Mill Lane, Midney, Somerton, TA11 7HR. David Chase & Alison Hoghton, 01458 274250, www.midneygardens.co.uk. *1m SE of Somerton. 100yds off B3151. From Podimore r'about on A303 take A372. After 1m R on B3151 towards Street. After 2m L on bend into Mill Lane.* **For NGS: Sun 13 May, Fri 14 Sept (11-5). Adm £5, chd free. Home-made teas. Cream teas also available.** For other opening times and information, please phone or visit garden website.

1.4 acre plantsman's garden, where unusual planting combinations, interesting use of colour, subtle themes and a natural flowing style create a garden full of variety and inspiring ideas. Increasingly known for it's wildlife friendly planting. Incl seaside garden, white garden, kitchen garden, woodland walk, wildlife pond and undercover world gardens. Nursery offers herbaceous perennials, alpines, herbs and grasses.

The Queen's Nursing Institute founded the National Garden Scheme over 90 years ago

59 ◆ MILTON LODGE

Old Bristol Road, Wells, BA5 3AQ. Simon Tudway Quilter, 01749 672168, www.miltonlodgegardens.co.uk. *½m N of Wells. From A39 Bristol-Wells, turn N up Old Bristol Rd; car park 1st gate on L signed.* **For NGS: Sun 13 May, Sun 3 June, Sun 1 July (2-5). Adm £5, chd free. Tea. Discount/prepaid vouchers not valid on NGS open days. Children under 14 free.** For other opening times and information, please phone or visit garden website.

Mature Grade II terraced garden. Sloping land transformed into architectural terraces with profusion of plants capitalising on views of Wells Cathedral and Vale of Avalon. 1960, garden was lovingly restored to its former glory, orchard replaced with collection of ornamental trees. Cross Old Bristol Rd to 7 acre woodland garden, the Combe, a natural peaceful contrast to formal garden of Milton Lodge. This garden opened for the NGS in 1962. Featured in The Telegraph, Your County, regional press and radio. Unsuitable for wheelchairs/pushchairs or those with limited mobility due to slopes and differing levels.

60 MODEL FARM

Perry Green, Wembdon, Bridgwater, TA5 2BA. Mr & Mrs Dave & Roz Young, 01278 429953, daveandrozontour@hotmail.com, www.modelfarm.com. *4m from J23 of M5. Follow Brown signs from r'about on A39 2m W of Bridgwater.* **Sun 10 June (2-5.30). Adm £4, chd free. Home-made teas.**

4 acres of flat gardens to S of Victorian country house. Created from a field in last 8 yrs and still being developed. A dozen large mixed flower beds planted in cottage garden style with wildlife in mind. Wooded areas, lawns, wildflower meadows and wildlife pond. Plenty of seating throughout the gardens. Lawn games including croquet.

61 16 MONTROY CLOSE

Henleaze, BS9 4RS. Sue & Rod Jones. *3½ m N of Bristol city centre. From Bristol, on B4056 continue past all Henleaze shops, R into Rockside Dr (opp Eastfield Inn). Up hill, across Xrds into The Crescent. Montroy Close is 3rd turning on L.* **Sun 3 June (2-5.30). Adm £3.50, chd free. Home-made teas in the tearoom, overlooking the garden. Tea, coffee & home-made lemonade and cakes.**
Large SW-facing town garden on corner plot. 20 ft stream, informal pond with pebble beach, pergola and seats. Lawn with curving flower beds incl ferns, shrubs, perennials, climbers, small rock garden with water feature, unusual partitioned greenhouse with alpine bench. 8ft wide arch with climbers. Hanging baskets and many pots of fuchsias. Width of gateway: 79cm.

62 MURIEL JONES FIELD ALLOTMENTS

Birchill Lane, Feltham, Frome, BA11 5ND. Frome Allotment Association. *15m S of Bath. On Frome by-pass (take A361). At r'about exit B3092 signed Blatchbridge. Drive approx ½m towards Frome, turn R into Birchill Lane. Continue to allotments, parking on R.* **Tue 10 July (11-5). Adm £4.50, chd free. Home-made teas.**
98 pretty allotments on a charming 5 acre site, displaying a range of gardening styles from the traditional to a more relaxed approach. A rural setting on the outskirts of Frome with views of Longleat Forest across the river and into the trees and Cley Hill in the distance. Flowers, fruit and vegetables in abundance. Visitors are welcome to bring a picnic. Featured in Kitchen Garden Magazine, regional publications and radio. Viewing area over allotments designated for wheelchair users. Accessible WC.

63 NEW NORTHEND HOUSE

3 High Street, Wickwar, Wotton-Under-Edge, GL12 8NE. John Addison & Julie Cragg. *12m N of Bristol. Between T-lights at N end of High Street. If using SatNav please note High Street Wickwar not High Street Wotton under Edge. Parking in village - please park respectfully and consider our neighbours.* **Sun 15 July (1-5). Combined adm with The School Yard £5, chd free. Home-made teas in village hall.**
Victorian walled garden of approximately a third of an acre, run on organic principles. Mature shrubs and informally planted perennial borders designed to attract bees and butterflies. Wildlife pond with small stream.

GROUP OPENING

64 NUNNEY GARDENS

Nunney, nr Frome, BA11 4NP. *3m S of Frome. Nunney Catch, A361 between Frome and Shepton Mallet, follow signs to Nunney (1m). In market sq, follow yellow arrows.* **Sun 1 July (11.30-4). Combined adm £6, chd free. Teas at The Miller's House.**

THE MILLER'S HOUSE
Caroline Toll.

SOMERSET LODGE GARDEN
Lord & Lady Watson, 01373 836740, karenwatsonkw@yahoo.co.uk.
Visits also by arrangement Apr & May, please confirm group number 2 weeks prior to agreed visit date.

The Miller's House owner describes herself as an untidy gardener who falls for a plant and then finds a suitable place to put it! Set in a small valley with the main garden above a deep mill pond. Planted mainly with perennials and shrubs with an eye to butterfly attraction and perfume. Rockeries, borders, small terraced vegetable patch; water plants and wild paddock along the valley between the leat and Nunney Brook. Care needed in wild area of garden, wet and uneven surfaces, stout footwear advised. Somerset Lodge, created from rough pasture some 20 years ago by artist owner and first time gardener. Formal yew and box topiaries, stunning avenue of standard roses, rare hawthorn orchard, wildflower meadow covered with drifts of blue and white camassias in spring, long wisps of white Rosa Nevada enhanced by flowering pear trees Nevalis make an interesting and contrasting garden. Adjoining farm yard converted from cattle barn to an attractive courtyard with a strong Mediterranean feel. Miller's Hse, small steps to top garden accessible to visitors with restricted mobility, part of remaining garden/ millpond can be viewed from here. No wheelchair access at Somerset Lodge. Dogs welcome on short leads.

65 NYNEHEAD COURT

Nynehead, Wellington, TA21 0BN. Nynehead Care Ltd, 01823 662481, nyneheadcare@aol.com, www.nyneheadcare@aol.com. *Small village on outskirts of Wellington. M5 J26 B3187 towards Wellington. R on r'about marked Nynehead & Poole, follow lane for 1m, take Milverton turning at fork.* **Sun 18 Feb, Sun 1 July, Thur 11 Oct (2-4.30). Adm £6.50, chd free. Home-made teas in Orangery. Visits also by arrangement Feb to Dec.**
English Heritage garden of historic interest. The house and gardens were owned by the Sandford family up till 1902, after which time it was let, finally becoming a residential care home for the elderly in 1940 (one of the oldest in the county). The gardens as we see them today were completed during the victorian period. A garden tour, approx 45mins, will be conducted by Justin Cole, Head Gardener, at 2pm. Visitors can also explore freely using leaflets available. Snowdrops at Feb opening. Autumn tree colours and sweet chestnuts for picking in Oct. Limited wheelchair access: cobbled yards, gentle slopes, chipped paths.

66 OLD ORCHARD

Goathurst, Bridgwater, TA5 2DF. Mr Peter Evered. *4m SW of Bridgwater or 2½m W of North Petherton. Close to church. Park in field at Northern end of village 500yds from garden.* **Sat 21, Sun 22 July (2-5). Adm £3.50, chd free. Home-made teas.**

¼ acre cottage style garden in centre of village. Planted to complement the cottage with over 100 clematis viticella interplanted with a range of shrubs, herbaceous perennials, annuals and bulbs. The planting gives all yr colour and interest on all 4 sides of cottage. Limited wheelchair access.

67 THE OLD RECTORY, DOYNTON

18 Toghill Lane, Doynton, Bristol, BS30 5SY. Edwina & Clive Humby, **www.doyntongardens.tumblr.com.** *At heart of village of Doynton, between Bath and Bristol. Follow Toghill Lane up from The Holy Trinity Church about 500 metres, around cricket field to car park field. Signs to garden.* **Sat 9 June (11-4). Adm £4, chd free. Home-made teas.**

Doynton's Grade II-listed Georgian Rectory's walled garden and extended 15 acre estate. Renovated over 12 yrs, it sits within AONB. Garden has diversity of modern and traditional elements, fused to create an atmospheric series of garden rooms. It is both a landscaped and large kitchen garden, featuring a canal, vegetable plots, fruit cages and tree house. Partial wheelchair access, some narrow gates and uneven surfaces.

68 THE OLD RECTORY, LIMINGTON

Church St, Limington, Yeovil, BA22 8EQ. John Langdon & Paul Vintner, 01935 840127, jdlpv@aol.com. *2m E of Ilchester. From A303 exit on A37 to Yeovil/ Ilchester. At 1st r'about L to Ilchester/Limington. 2nd R to Limington. Continue 1½m and house is immediately past church on R. Please park on drive.* **Visits by arrangement May to Sept daytime or evening for groups. Adm £5, chd free. Tea, coffee, cold drinks, cream teas and ploughman' lunches available by prior arrangement.**

Romantic walled gardens of 1½ acres. Formal parterres, herbaceous borders. Many unusual shrubs and trees incl 200 yr-old lucombe oak, liriodendron, laburnocytisus, trochdendron, leycesteria and poncirus. A variety of peaceful seating areas where refreshments can be taken. Previously featured in The English Garden, Somerset Life, Mendip Times. Gravel drive, one gentle slope only into rerouted garden.

69 THE OLD VICARAGE, OVER STOWEY

Over Stowey, Bridgwater, TA5 1HA. Mrs Sally Jago, 01278 733354, jagosally@gmail.com. *10m W of Bridgwater. A39 from Bridgwater, L fork at Cottage Inn to Over Stowey. Over Xrds, opp church, car park in field.* **Sun 20 May (2.30-5.30); Wed 23 May (2.30-6). Adm £5, chd free. Cream teas. If wet, refreshments in stables or if dry, on top lawn. Visits also by arrangement Apr to June for groups, max 30. Evening visits by arrangement.**

Set in the beautiful Quantock Hills, and developed from an original 1-acre garden to nearly 3 acres. A quirky garden with a huge, eclectic variety of shrubs, trees, grasses, agapanthus, sub-tropical palms, phormiums, exotic ornaments, together with an arboretum, large pond and willow arbour. Original dry stone ha-ha, built in 1780 by Rev William Holland and discovered by owner 25 years ago! A truly loved space. 'A garden is never finished' is the owner's mantra and each year new projects are in hand; this year's is a thatched tree house for the grandchildren. Due to steep slopes, upper part of garden has only partial wheelchair access.

70 THE OLD VICARAGE, RUISHTON

Church Lane, Ruishton, Taunton, TA3 5LL. Mr & Mrs Andrew Lukes. *Opp St George's church through white gates.* **Sun 3, Mon 4 June (2-5). Adm £4, chd free. Home-made teas.**

2nd year of opening for NGS, a new garden in progress. Much of the 1 acre plot was field but is now laid out and brimming with potential. Traces of old garden still in evidence with plenty of new beds incorporated. Lovely terrace overlooks compact formal lawns and pretty walled garden with attractive rope roses and herbaceous beds. Sweeping lawns lead to wildlife area with pond.

71 THE OLD VICARAGE, WEARE

Sparrow Hill Way, Weare, Axbridge, BS26 2LE. Trish & Jeremy Gibson, 01934 732731, trishgibson50@gmail.com, **www.oldvicaragegardeners.com.** *2.8m SW of Axbridge. Turn off A38 in Lower Weare, signed Wedmore, Weare. Turn L opp school into Sparrow Hill Way. Continue 0.3m. Garden on R on corner of Coombe Lane.* **Sat 16, Sun 17 June (2-5.30). Adm £4, chd free. Home-made teas. Visits also by arrangement May to Sept for groups of 6-20.**

From outside you'd expect a traditional Old Vicarage garden but, inside its surrounding tall hedges, you discover a very different contemporary look with relaxed country-style planting and design. Around Georgian outbuildings with terraces and courtyards, there's a stream garden and vegetable plot, all set in undulating lawns. Inside the delightful Old Barn, you'll find art and garden sculpture. Partial wheelchair access. Some gravel paths, steps and steep slopes. No disabled WC.

72 PARISH'S HOUSE

Hook Hill, Timsbury, Bath, BA2 0ND. Jackie Hamblen (Gardener), 07956 022016, jackieparishhouse@gmail.com. *On B3115 North Road to Hook Hill entrance on R or from Camerton/ Tunley take Timsbury exit at mini r'about, follow rd bend R. Garden is at E edge of village.* **Sun 12 Aug (2-5). Adm £5, chd free. Light refreshments. Visits also by arrangement Apr to Oct for groups of 10+ days or evenings, conducted tours.**

8-acre garden surrounding Regency house (not open) with beautiful views across open countryside. Lawns sweep down to ha-ha. Colour themed herbaceous and shrub borders. Elegant water feature. Arboretum of specimen trees and more recently planted acer glade. New woodland walk taking you from native British woodland to more exotic woodland planting. Walled kitchen garden: vegetables, fan trained and cordoned fruit trees of significant age and cut flower beds. Parts of the garden are being developed so we invite you to share our vision, anticipation and excitement! Featured in Bath Life.

73 PARK COTTAGE

Wrington Hill, Wrington, Bristol, BS40 5PL. Mr & Mrs J Shepherd. *Halfway between Bristol & Weston S Mare. 10m S of Bristol on A370 at Cleeve turn L onto Cleeve Hill Rd continue 1½ miles; car park in field on R approx 50m from garden on L.* **Sat 28 July, Sat 4 Aug (11-5). Adm £4, chd free. Home-made teas provided by Wrington Pop-Up Vintage Café, proceeds to Weston Hospicecare.**

Follow every path! Take a colourful journey through 1¼ acres of this 'Alice in Wonderland' herbaceous perennial flower garden celebrating its 25th year. Divided by high hedges are many different areas including the potager, jungle garden, rainbow border, white garden and 90ft double herbaceous borders. A large Victorian-style greenhouse displays tender plants. Come and join the party! Countryside views and plenty of seating. Sorry no dogs and no WC. Mostly good wheelchair access, some narrow bark chip paths. Narrow flagstone bridge with steps.

74 PENNY BROHN UK

Chapel Pill Lane, Pill, North Somerset, BS20 0HH. Penny Brohn UK, 01275 370076, ian.riddell@pennybrohn.org.uk, www.pennybrohn.org.uk. *4m W of Bristol. Off A369 Clifton Suspension Bridge to M5 (J19 Gordano Services). Follow signs to Penny Brohn UK and to Pill/Ham Green (5 mins).* **Sun 10 June (10-4). Adm £4, chd free. Light refreshments.**

3½ acre tranquil garden surrounds Georgian mansion with many mature trees, wild flower meadow, flower garden, cedar summerhouse, fine views from historic gazebo overlooking River Avon, courtyard gardens with water features. Garden is maintained by volunteers and plays an active role in the Charity's Living Well with Cancer approach. Plants, teas, music and plenty of space to enjoy a picnic. Gift shop. Tours of centre to find out more about the work of Penny Brohn UK. Some gravel and grass paths.

75 THE RED POST HOUSE

Fivehead, Taunton, TA3 6PX. The Rev Mervyn & Mrs Margaret Wilson, 01460 281558. *10m E of Taunton. On the corner of A378 and Butcher's Hill, opp garage. From M5 J25, take A358 towards Langport, turn R at T-lights at top of hill onto A378. Garden is at Langport end of Fivehead.* **Sun 16 Sept (2-5). Adm £3.50, chd free. Home-made teas. Visits also by arrangement Apr to Oct parking mainly in road.**

⅓ acre walled garden with shrubs, borders, trees, circular potager, topiary. We combine beauty and utility. Further 1½ acres with various planting, lawn, orchard and vineyard. Plums, 40 apple and 20 pear. Apples and pears should be bearing fruit. Mown paths, longer grass. Views aligned on Ham Hill. Summerhouse with sedum roof, belvedere. Garden in its present form developed over last 14 yrs. Paths are gravel and grass, belvedere is not wheelchair accessible. Dogs on leads.

76 REEDS COURT

Lydeard St. Lawrence, Taunton, TA4 3RX. Ben Mack. *12m NW of Taunton. From Taunton take A358 towards Minehead, 4m outside Taunton take L turn signed B3224 Lydeard St. Lawrence. After 2m turn R into lane signed Lydeard St Lawrence.* **Sat 9, Sun 10 June (11-5). Adm £3.50, chd free. Tea.**

A series of gardens within a garden. Approx 1½ acres. Structured but wild, with striking yet subtle planting. Meander through the different rooms to discover a wealth of colour, scents, shapes and foliage. Partial wheelchair access with some quite steep slopes so you need a strong assistant!

77 RENDY FARM

Oake, Taunton, TA4 1BB. Mr & Mrs N Popplewell. *1m from Oake PO and shop on road from Oake to Nynehead.* **Sun 20 May (1-5). Adm £4, chd free. Home-made teas.**

3 acre garden with formal walled front garden, raised vegetable beds, greenhouse and polytunnel enclosed by hornbeam, box and yew hedging. Decorative fruit and cut flower beds, meadow with large wild pond and orchard with stream running through, marked by pollarded willows. New Shepherd's Hut Garden. Regret no wheelchair access.

78 ROCK HOUSE

Elberton, BS35 4AQ. Mr & Mrs John Gunnery, 01454 413225. *10m N of Bristol. 3½m SW Thornbury. From Old Severn Bridge on M48 take B4461 to Alveston. In Elberton, take 1st turning L to Littleton-on-Severn and turn immed R.* **Sun 4, Sun 11 Feb, Sun 25 Mar, Mon 2 Apr (11-4). Adm £3.50, chd free.**

2019: Sun 3, Sun 10 Feb. Visits also by arrangement for small groups.
2 acre garden. Pretty woodland vistas with many snowdrops and daffodils, some unusual. Spring flowers, cottage garden plants and roses. Old yew tree and pond. Limited wheelchair access.

79 ROSE COTTAGE

Smithams Hill, East Harptree, Bristol, BS40 6BY. Bev & Jenny Cruse, 01761 221627, bandjcruse@gmail.com. *5m N of Wells, 15m S of Bristol. From B3114 turn into High St in EH. L at Clock Tower and immed R into Middle St, up hill for 1m. From B3134 take EH rd opp Castle of Comfort, continue 1½m. Car parking in field opp cottage.* **Sun 15 Apr (2-5). Adm £4.50, chd free. Home-made teas. in aid of St Laurence Church. Visits also by arrangement Apr to June.**
1-acre hillside cottage garden with panoramic views over Chew Valley. Garden carpeted with primroses, spring bulbs and hellebores. Bordered by stream and established mixed hedges. Gravel garden. Scented arbour and plenty of seating areas to enjoy the views and teas, as well as the music of the Congresbury Brass Band. Wildlife area and pond in corner of car park field. Featured in Mendip Times, regional press and radio. Limited wheelchair access, hillside setting.

80 NEW ST ARILDA'S HOUSE

Kington, Thornbury, Bristol, BS35 1NQ. Carolyn & Tom Frost. *Leave Thornbury out of Castle St turning L into Kington Lane. Continue towards Oldbury, St Arild's House is approx 1½m on L. Follow signs for parking.* **Sat 16, Sun 17 June (2-5). Adm £5, chd free. Home-made teas.**
Approx ¾-acre garden in traditional English style. Walled garden with many split sections incl rose beds, herbaceous, shrubs and mature trees. Vegetable garden and small orchard outside walled area. Featured in local Gazette and Forward magazine.

81 ST MONICA TRUST

Cote Lane, Westbury on Trym, Bristol, BS9 3UN. St Monica Trust. *A4018 towards Bristol from M5/ Cribbs Causeway, St Monica Trust is on R, just before start of Durdham Downs.* **Sun 27 May (10.30-3). Adm £5, chd free. Light refreshments. Teas, cold drinks and cakes.**
The gardens of the St Monica Trust retirement community are a mix of old established borders and new planting. The tree collection, documented in a tree guide, is extensive and impressive, with many unusual specimens. The scented garden is the centrepiece of the gardens and provides yr-round interest. The ponds and woodland wildlife areas benefit from being closed to traffic, and are home to a wide range of bird, mammal and insect species.

82 NEW THE SCHOOL YARD

2 High Street, Wickwar, Wotton-under-Edge, GL12 8NE. Jeanette & Tony Parker. *12m N of Bristol. Between T-lights at N end of High Street. If using SatNav please note High Street Wickwar not High Street Wotton under Edge. Parking in village - please park respectfully and consider our neighbours.* **Sun 15 July (1-5). Combined adm with Northend House £5, chd free. Home-made teas in village hall.**
Garden arranged around a former Victorian school. Vegetable plot with large greenhouse. Raised beds edged by espalier and step-over fruit trees. Terraced flower garden with variety of trees and shrubs. Mediterranean courtyard. Ancient yew tree and olive tree in courtyard area. Variety of English apples and pear trees. Article in WI Life magazine due for publication Summer 2018. Limited wheelchair access, gravel paths and steps.

83 SERRIDGE HOUSE

Henfield Rd, Coalpit Heath, BS36 2UY. Mrs J Manning, 01454 773188. *9m N of Bristol. On A432 at Coalpit Heath T-lights (opp church), turn into Henfield Rd. R at PH, ½m small Xrds, garden on corner with Ruffet Rd, park on Henfield Rd.* **Visits by arrangement July & Aug for groups of 12-70. Adm £5, chd free. Adm incl home made teas/ evening visits with a glass of wine.**
2½ acre garden with mature trees, heather and conifer beds, island beds mostly of perennials, woodland area with pond. Colourful courtyard with old farm implements. Lake views and lakeside walks. Unique tree carvings. Mostly flat grass and concrete driveway. Wheelchair access to lake difficult.

84 ◆ SHERBORNE GARDEN

Litton, Radstock, BA3 4PP. Mrs Pamela Southwell, 01761 241220. *15m S of Bristol. 15m W of Bath, 7m N of Wells. On B3114 Chewton Mendip to Harptree rd, ½m past The Litton (PH).* **For NGS: Sun 11, Mon 12 Feb (11-4). Adm £4, chd free. Tea/coffee and home-made biscuits. 2019: Sun 10, Mon 11 Feb.** For other opening times and information, please phone.
4½ acre gently sloping garden with small pinetum, holly wood and many unusual trees and shrubs. Cottage garden leading to privy. 3 ponds linked by wadi and rills with stone and wooden bridges. Snowdrops and hellibores. Hosta walk leading to pear and nut wood. Rondel and gravel gardens with grasses and phormiums. Collections of day lilies, rambling and rose species. Good labelling. Plenty of seats. Garden open for private visits and parties. Grass and gentle slopes.

85 SOLE RETREAT

Haydon Drove, Haydon, nr West Horrington, Wells, BA5 3EH. Jane Clisby, 01749 672648/07790 602906, janeclisby@aol.com, www.soleretreat.co.uk. *3m NE of Wells. From Wells take B3139 towards the Horringtons and keep on main road for 3m. L into Haydon Drove and Sole Retreat Reflexology, signed, garden 50yds on L.* **Visits by arrangement July & Aug, groups of 10+ car sharing is advisable. Adm £4.50, chd free. Tea. Please confirm numbers and refreshments required 2 weeks prior to agreed date.**

What a challenge to garden at 1000' on the Mendip Hills AONB but this has been described as 'stepping into a piece of paradise'. Laid out with tranquillity and healing in mind, garden is full of old favourites set in ⅓ acre. 10 differing areas within dry stone walls and raw face bedrock incl herbaceous borders, labyrinth, water feature, vegetable plot, contemplation garden and new Gothic corner. Tranquil, contemplation garden with corners for mindful thinking. Featured in regional press and radio. Some gravel, narrow paths.

86 SOUTH CARY HOUSE

South Street, Castle Cary, BA7 7ES. Sally Walford. *For South St, from Station Rd turn L then R onto B3152 into Castle Cary, turn R down high street, pass church on R onto South St. The house has black rails and is opp local pub.* **Sat 9, Sun 10 June (2-5). Combined adm with Lower Cockhill Farmhouse £5, chd free. Cream teas.**

Approx 1 acre of gardens in grounds of Grade II listed Georgian house. A newly constructed garden in development, semi walled garden with small woodand walk with views of Lodge Hill, specimen trees, rose gardens, box-edging, colour border and pots and extensive lawns. Wheelchair access by arrangement.

87 SOUTH KELDING

Brewery Hill, Upton Cheyney, Bristol, BS30 6LY. Barry & Wendy Smale, 0117 9325145, wendy.smale@yahoo.com. *Halfway between Bristol and Bath. Upton Cheyney lies ½m up Brewery Hill off A431 just outside Bitton. Detailed directions and parking arrangements given when appt made. Restricted access means pre-booking essential.* **Visits by arrangement May to Sept, max 30. Adm £4.50, chd free. Home-made cakes and tea/coffee are an additional £2.50 per person.**

7 acre hillside garden offering panoramic views from its upper levels, with herbaceous and shrub beds, prairie-style scree beds, orchard, native copses and small arboretum grouped by continents. Large wildlife pond, boundary stream and wooded area featuring shade and moisture-loving plants. In view of slopes and uneven terrain this garden is unsuitable for disabled access.

88 SOUTH STREET ALLOTMENT

Hinton St George, TA17 8SE. John Studley, 07831 489391, johnstudley12@talktalk.net. *N of A30 Crewkerne-Chard; S of A303 Ilminster Town Rd. At r'about signed Lopen & Merriott, then R to Hinton St George. Approx 500yds in southerly direction from X-rds, past last houses. Entrance signed on L.* **Visits by arrangement May to Aug. Refreshments by arrangement.**

This is my 5th year on the 30x10m allotment situated at Hinton St George. I have an agriculture background and have always been very enthusiastic about growing crops. My aim is to grow a broad variety of vegetables, soft fruit, apples and pears. Light and fairly neutral soil type, hence needing plenty of organic matter to hold moisture and nutrients. 6.2x4m polytunnel and 3.7x2.4m greenhouse. Not suitable for wheelchairs.

89 SOUTHFIELD FARM

Farleigh Rd, Backwell, Bristol, BS48 3PE. Pamela & Alan Lewis. *6m S of Bristol. On A370, 500yds after George Inn towards WsM. Farm directly off main rd on R, large car park.* **Thur 22 Feb, Thur 22 Mar (11-3). Adm £4, chd free. Home-made teas.**

2 acre owner-designed garden of rooms. Mixed shrub and herbaceous borders. Much winter colour and scent. Aconites, heathers, snowdrops, hellebores and more. Courtyards, terrace, orchard, vegetable and herb gardens. Paths through native meadow to woodland garden and large wildlife pond with bird hides. Indoor tearooms in old stable yard. Wheelchair access to most areas on grass paths. Some gravel and steps.

90 SPARROWS

Over Stowey, Bridgwater, TA5 1HA. Mrs Annie Shoosmith, 01278 733595, Annie@annieshoo.com. *8m W of Bridgwater. Take A39 from Bridgwater to Minehead. After 8m at Cottage Inn, fork L to Over Stowey. Straight over 2 Xrds. Park in field on L before church. Walk west.* **Thur 19 Apr (2-5.30); Sun 17 June (2-6). Adm £5, chd free. Home-made teas. Visits also by arrangement Apr to June for groups, please phone.**

Shaded cottage garden, full of interesting and unusual shrubs and plants. 3 very old copper beeches shade a collection of ferns and woodland plants; a path leads you to the middle lawn, then to a pretty view of the foothills of the Quantocks. Sit and have a cup of tea in one of the many nooks and crannies. Small vegetable and working area. Partial wheelchair access, phone in advance.

91 ◆ SPECIAL PLANTS

Greenway Lane, Cold Ashton, SN14 8LA. Derry Watkins, 01225 891686, derry@specialplants.net, www.specialplants.net. *6m N of Bath. From Bath on A46, turn L into*

Greenways Lane just before r'about with A420. **For NGS: Thur 21 June, Thur 19 July, Thur 16 Aug, Thur 20 Sept, Thur 18 Oct (11-5). Adm £5, chd free. Home-made teas.** For other opening times and information, please phone, email or visit garden website.
Architect-designed ¾ acre hillside garden with stunning views. Started autumn 1996. Exotic plants. Gravel gardens for borderline hardy plants. Black and white (purple and silver) garden. Vegetable garden and orchard. Hot border. Lemon and lime bank. Annual, biennial and tender plants for late summer colour. Spring fed ponds. Bog garden. Woodland walk. Allium alley. Free list of plants in garden.

92 ◆ STOBERRY GARDEN

Stoberry Park, Wells, BA5 3LD. Frances & Tim Young, 01749 672906, stay@stoberry-park.co.uk, www.stoberryhouse.co.uk. *½m N of Wells. From Bristol - Wells on A39, L into College Rd and immed L through Stoberry Park, signed.* **For NGS: Sun 24 June (2-5.30). Adm £5, chd free. Home-made teas. Please confirm visitor nos and refreshments req'd for by arrangement visits 2 weeks prior to booked date.** For other opening times and information, please phone, email or visit garden website.
Open By Arrangement 1 April to 30 Sept, please confirm your visit is to support the National Garden Scheme when booking.. With breathtaking views over Wells Cathedral, this 6 acre family garden planted sympathetically within its landscape provides stunning combinations of vistas accented with wildlife ponds, water features, sculpture, 1½ acre walled garden, gazebo, and lime walk. Colour and interest every season; spring bulbs, irises, salvias, wild flower circles, new meadow walk and fernery. Featured in Telegraph Travel Supplement, National Garden Magazines, BBC TV, Gardens of Somerset, Somerset Life and regional press and radio. Regret no wheelchair access.

GROUP OPENING

93 STOGUMBER GARDENS

Station Road, Stogumber, TA4 3TQ. *11m NW of Taunton. 3m W of A358. Signed to Stogumber, W of Crowcombe. Village maps given to all visitors.* **Sun 17 June (2-6). Combined adm £6, chd free. Home-made teas in village hall.**

BRAGLANDS BARN
Simon & Sue Youell.

BROOK HOUSE
Jan & Jonathan Secker-Walker.

CRIDLANDS STEEP
Audrey Leitch.

HIGHER KINGSWOOD
Fran & Tom Vesey.

KNOLL COTTAGE
Elaine & John Leech, 01984 656689, john@Leech45.com, www.knoll-cottage.co.uk. **Visits also by arrangement June to Sept.**

NEW **ORCHARD DEANE**
Brenda & Peter Wilson.

POUND HOUSE
Barry & Jenny Hibbert.

7 delightful and very varied gardens in picturesque village at edge of Quantocks. 3 surprisingly large gardens in village centre, one semi-wild garden, and 3 very large gardens on outskirts of village, with many rare and unusual plants. Conditions range from waterlogged clay to well-drained sand. Walled garden, ponds, bog gardens, rockery, vegetable and fruit gardens, collection of over 80 different roses, even an apple orchard. Fine views of surrounding countryside. Dogs on leads allowed in 6 gardens. Wheelchair access to main features of all gardens.

94 ◆ STON EASTON PARK

Ston Easton, Radstock, BA3 4DF. Ston Easton Ltd, 01761 241631, reception@stoneaston.co.uk, www.stoneaston.co.uk. *On A37 between Bath & Wells. Entrance to Park through high metal gates set back from main road, A37, in centre of village, opp bus shelter.* **For NGS: Wed 25 July (10.30-4). Adm £4.50, chd free. Refreshments in hotel. Booking essential for lunch and/ or full afternoon tea, please phone 01761 241631 to make reservation.** For other opening times and information, please phone, email or visit garden website.
A hidden treasure in the heart of the Mendips, do come and see for yourself. Walk through the glorious parkland of the historic Repton landscape, along the quietly cascading River Norr. Productive walled Victorian kitchen garden, octagonal rose garden, stunning herbaceous border, fruit cage and orchard. July brings clematis, magnolias and early roses with the start of planting unusual vegetable seed, not forgetting the famous loofahs. Deep gravel paths, steep slopes, shallow steps.

95 NEW STONELEIGH DOWN

Upper Tockington Road, Tockington, Bristol, BS32 4LQ. Su & John Mills. *12m N of Bristol. On LH side of Upper Tockington Road when travelling from Tockington towards Olveston. Set back from the road up a gravel drive. Parking in village. Disabled drop off in the drive.* **Sat 26, Sun 27 May, Sat 1, Sun 2 Sept (1-5). Adm £4, chd free. Home-made teas.**
Redesigned in 2014 by the current owners. The garden has been densely planted with a wide variety of trees, shrubs and bulbs for year-round interest and continues to be developed. Approaching ⅔ acre, the south-facing gardens' curved gravel pathways connect the themed areas that flow into each other: sub-tropical, wildlife and oriental ponds, seasonal planting. Gravel paths. Steps into courtyard.

GROUP OPENING

96 STOWEY GARDENS

Stowey, Bishop Sutton, Bristol, BS39 5TL. *10m W of Bath. Stowey Village on A368 between Bishop Sutton and Chelwood. From Chelwood r'about take A368 to Weston-s-Mare. At Stowey Xrds turn R to car park, 150 yards down lane, ample off road parking opp Dormers.* **Sun 15 July (2-6). Combined adm £5, chd free. Home-made teas at Stowey Mead; pedestrian entrance for teas via lower gate on A368, Stowey Xrds, entrance to R of seat, diagonally opposite lane to Dormers.**

DORMERS
Mr & Mrs G Nicol.

◆ MANOR FARM
Richard Baines & Alison Fawcett, 01275 332297.

STOWEY MEAD
Mr Victor Pritchard.

A broad spectrum of interest and styles developing year on year. Flower-packed beds, borders and pots, roses, topiary, hydrangeas, exotic garden, many unusual trees and shrubs, orchards, vegetables, ponds, specialist sweet peas, lawns and ha ha. Abundant collection of mature trees and shrubs. Seating areas for enjoyment of some wonderful views from each garden. Something of interest for everyone, all within a few minutes walk of car park and with natural progression from one to another. Home made teas at Stowey Mead. Plant sales at Dormers. Well behaved dogs on short leads welcome. Featured in Somerset Life, Mendip Times, regional press and radio. Wheelchair access restricted in places, many grassed areas in each garden. Limited disabled parking at each garden which will be signed.

97 SUTTON HOSEY MANOR

Long Sutton, TA10 9NA. Roger Bramble, 0207 3906700, rbramble@bdbltd.co.uk. *2m E of Langport, on A372. Gates N of A372 at E end of Long Sutton.* **Sun 29 July (2.30-6). Adm £5, chd £2. Home-made teas. Visits also by arrangement.**

3 acres, of which 2 walled. Lily canal through pleached limes leading to amelanchier walk past duck pond; rose and juniper walk from Italian terrace; judas tree avenue; ptelea walk. Ornamental potager. Drive-side shrubbery. Music by Young Musicians Symphony Orchestra.

98 SWIFT HOUSE

9 Lyndale Avenue, Stoke Bishop, Bristol, BS9 1BS. Mark & Jane Glanville, **www.bristolgarden.weebly.com.** *NW Bristol - 4m from city centre. 2m from M5 J18 Portway (A4). Turn into Sylvan Way. At lights take R onto Shirehampton Rd. After ¾m turn R into Sea Mills Lane. Lyndale Ave is 2nd rd on L - we're half way up.* **Sun 24 June (2-5). Adm £3, chd free.**

We've designed our city garden to look beautiful, provide fruit and vegetables and to be a haven for wildlife. Plants are grown to provide food and shelter throughout the year, with the emphasis on flowers that are nectar rich. We also have the largest colony of swifts nesting in Bristol. Nest boxes with inbuilt cameras. Swift cards, DVD's and plants for sale.

99 TORMARTON COURT

Church Road, Tormarton, GL9 1HT. Noreen & Bruce Finnamore, 01454 218236, home@thefinnamores.com. *3m E of Chipping Sodbury, off A46 at J18 M4. Follow signs to Tormarton from A46 then follow signs for car parking.* **Fri 23 Mar, Fri 15 June (10-3.30). Adm £5, chd free. Home-made teas. Visits also by arrangement limited availability for groups of 12+, weekdays (10-3), refreshments by prior arrangement.**

11 acres of formal and natural gardens in stunning Cotswold setting. Features incl roses, herbaceous, kitchen garden, Mediterranean garden, mound and natural pond. Extensive walled garden, spring glade and meadows with young and mature trees.

100 TRUFFLES

Church Lane, Bishop Sutton, Bristol, BS39 5UP. Sally Monkhouse. *10m W of Bath. On A368 Bath to Weston-super-Mare rd. Take rd opp PO/stores uphill towards Top Sutton/Hinton Blewett. 1st R into Church Lane. Please park on road, one level disabled parking place at top of drive.* **Sat 7, Sun 8 Apr (1-5). Adm £4.50, chd free. Delicious home-made refreshments.**

2 acres, a surprising and relaxing large garden with views. Formal and wildlife planting linked with meandering paths, lots of sturdy seating. Magical wooded valley, stream, snowdrops with lots of spring bulbs everywhere. Wildlife pond, dragon flies, flower meadows, varied flower beds, some sculpture and hens. Unique ¼ acre kitchen garden with several 21 ft long x 4 ft wide waist high raised beds. Drop off at house available before parking on nearby road. Slope up to the house, grass and gravel paths for partial wheelchair access.

101 ◆ UNIVERSITY OF BRISTOL BOTANIC GARDEN

Stoke Park Road, Stoke Bishop, Bristol, BS9 1JG. University of Bristol Botanic Garden, 0117 4282041, botanic-gardens@bristol.ac.uk, www.bristol.ac.uk/Botanic-Garden. *¼m W of Durdham Downs. Located in Stoke Bishop next to Durdham Downs 1m from city centre. After crossing the Downs to Stoke Hill, Stoke Park Rd is first on R.* **For NGS: Sun 20 May (10-5). Adm £6, chd free. Light refreshments. Hot and cold drinks, sandwiches,**

cakes and ice cream. For other opening times and information, please phone, email or visit garden website. Donation to University of Bristol Botanic Garden.
Exciting contemporary botanic garden with organic flowing network of paths which lead visitors through collections of Mediterranean flora, rare native, useful plants (incl European and Chinese herbs) and those that illustrate plant evolution. Large floral displays illustrating pollination/flowering plant evolution. Glasshouses, home to giant Amazon waterlily, tropical fruit and medicine plants, orchids, cacti and unique sacred lotus collection. Open at other times by arrangement. Special tours of garden throughout day A science exhibit hosted by PhD students from the School of Biological Sciences explains some of the pioneering work being undertaken into how insect pollinators select flowers and how flowers use a variety of features to attract pollinators. Wheelchair available to borrow from Welcome Lodge. Wheelchair friendly route through garden available upon request, also accessible WC.
♿ ✿ 🚌 ☕

102 VELLACOTT

Lawford, Crowcombe, TA4 4AL. Kevin & Pat Chittenden, 01984 618249, kevinchit@hotmail.co.uk. *9m NW of Taunton. Off A358, signed Lawford. For directions please phone.* **Wed 30, Thur 31 May, Wed 20, Thur 21 June (2-5). Adm £3.50, chd free. Home-made teas. Visits also by arrangement May to Sept, 25 max.**
Large informal garden on S-facing slope with splendid views of the Quantock and Brendon Hills. Profusely planted with a wide selection of herbaceous perennials, shrubs and trees. Restored shepherd's hut sits in small orchard and wildflower area - a tranquil place to enjoy the surroundings. The overall aim is for the garden to blend into the beautiful countryside. Featured in Exmoor Magazine.
✿ 🚌 ☕

103 VINE HOUSE

Henbury Road, Henbury, Bristol, BS10 7AD. Pippa Atkinson. *2m from M5 J17. From M5 J17 head to Bristol Centre. At 3rd r'about, R to Blaise. L at end of Crow Lane. 1st house on R.* **Sun 4 Feb (11-3). Sun 24 June (1.30-4.30). Light refreshments. Adm £4, chd free. Regret no refreshments available on 4th February.**
1½ acres of garden behind listed Georgian house. Mature trees, shrubs, herbaceous borders, rock stream and gunnera. Garden originally planted in 1940's for yr-round interest by the Hewer family, and features many unusual plants and trees. Limited wheelchair access. Some paths around upper area of garden.
♿ 🐕 ☕

104 ◆ THE WALLED GARDENS OF CANNINGTON

Church Street, Cannington, TA5 2HA. Bridgwater College, 01278 655042, walledgardens@bridgwater.ac.uk, www.canningtonwalledgardens.co.uk. *3m NW of Bridgwater. On A39 Bridgwater-Minehead rd - at 1st r'about in Cannington 2nd exit, through village. War memorial, 1st L into Church Street then 1st L.* **For NGS: Sat 21, Sun 22 Apr, Sat 15, Sun 16 Sept (10-5). Adm £5, chd free. Light refreshments.** For other opening times and information, please phone, email or visit garden website.
Within the grounds of a medieval Priory, the Gardens have undergone extensive redevelopment over the last few years. Classic and contemporary features incl National Collections of Deschampsia and Santolina, stunning blue garden, sub-tropical walk, hot herbaceous border with large botanical glasshouse incl aquaponics system. Gravel paths. Motorised scooter can be borrowed free of charge (only one available).
♿ 🐕 ✿ 🚌 NPC ☕

105 WATCOMBE

92 Church Road, Winscombe, BS25 1BP. Peter & Ann Owen, 01934 842666, peter.o@which.net. *12m SW of Bristol, 3m N of Axbridge. 100 yds after Yellow Signs on A38 turn L, (from S), or R. (from N) into Winscombe Hill. After 1m reach 'The Square'. Watcombe on*

The Flax Barn

L after 150yds. **Sun 29 Apr, Sun 20 May, Thur 7 June (2-5.30). Adm £4, chd free. Home-made cakes and cream teas, gluten-free available. Visits also by arrangement Apr to June, any size group welcome.**
¾-acre mature Edwardian garden with colour-themed, informally planted herbaceous borders. Strong framework separating several different areas; pergola with varied wisteria, unusual topiary, box hedging, lime walk, pleached hornbeams, cordon fruit trees, 2 small formal ponds and growing collection of clematis. Many unusual trees and shrubs. Small vegetable plot. Some steps but most areas accessible by wheelchair with minimal assistance.

106 WAVERLEY
Moorland, Bridgwater, TA7 0AT. Ash & Alison Warne, 01278 691058, ashwarne@btinternet.com. *On Somerset Levels, with easy access 3m from J24, M5. Please phone for directions & parking advice.* **Visits by arrangement in June for any numbers, from 1 - 25, day or eve. Phone to discuss any catering arrangements for your visit. Adm £3.50, chd free. Home-made teas.**
Started in 2010, this ⅓ acre garden is packed with informal arrangements of shrubs, trees and perennials. Flooded to a depth of 3ft for 3 weeks in Feb 2014, this garden demonstrates the resilience of nature in bouncing back after adversity. Over 75 roses and 20 clematis vie for space amongst 20 different young trees. Some 12 different species of bamboo thrive. Paths allow access to all areas. Gravel access drive. All paths are level, most paved, some wood chip/gravel.

107 WAYFORD MANOR
Wayford, Crewkerne, TA18 8QG. Wayford Manor. *3m SW of Crewkerne. Turn N off B3165 at Clapton, signed Wayford or S off A30 Chard to Crewkerne rd, signed Wayford.* **Sun 29 Apr (2-5). Adm £5, chd £2.50. Home-made teas.**
The mainly Elizabethan manor (not open) mentioned in C17 for its 'fair and pleasant' garden was redesigned by Harold Peto in 1902. Formal terraces with yew hedges and topiary have fine views over W Dorset. Steps down between spring-fed ponds past mature and new plantings of magnolia, rhododendron, maples, cornus and, in season, spring bulbs, cyclamen, giant echium. Primula candelabra, arum lily, gunnera around lower ponds.

108 WELLFIELD BARN
Walcombe Lane, Wells, BA5 3AG. Virginia Nasmyth, 01749 675129. *½m N of Wells. From A39 Bristol to Wells rd turn R at 30 mph sign into Walcombe Lane. Entrance at 1st cottage on R, parking signed.* **Tue 29 May (11.30-4.30). Adm £4.50, chd free. Home-made teas. Visits also by arrangement June & July, max 29 seat coach on site. For by arrangement visits please book refreshments in advance.**
½-acre garden, created over 21yrs from concrete farmyard. Ha-ha, wonderful views, pond, lawn, mixed borders, formal sunken garden, hydrangea bed, grass walks and interesting young and semi-mature trees. Structured design integrates house and garden with landscape. New areas under development. Special interest plants are the hardy geranium family, shown on BBC Gardeners World with Carol Klein. Featured in regional press and radio. Moderate slopes in places, some gravel paths.

109 WESTBROOK HOUSE
West Bradley, BA6 8LS. Keith Anderson & David Mendel, 01458 850604, andersonmendel@aol.com. *4m E of Glastonbury. From A361 at W Pennard follow signs to W Bradley (2m) From A37 at Wraxall Hill follow signs to W Bradley (2m).* **Sat 16 June (11-6). Adm £4.50, chd free. Visits also by arrangement Apr to Sept for groups 10 - 30.** Donation to West Bradley Church.
4 acres comprising 3 distinct gardens with formal layout around house which leads to meadow and orchard with spring bulbs, species roses and lilacs. Planting and layout began 2004. Feature in Landscape Magazine.

GROUP OPENING

110 WESTON VILLAGE GARDENS
Weston, Bath, BA1 4AS. *W side of Bath, approx 8m S of J18 on M4. From city centre follow signs for the Royal United Hospital. Past main entrance on Combe Park, turn 1st R into Weston Lane, then 1st L and then immed L again into Weston Park.* **Sat 16, Sun 17 June (2-5). Combined adm £5, chd free. Home-made teas at Glenfield, Weston Park.**

94 BROADMOOR LANE
Liz & Peter Winney.

GLENFIELD
Mrs Sue Haskins.

INGLESIDE
Christine & Stephen Brook.

NEW **SAVILE HOUSE**
Rod & Jill Anderson.

4 gardens tucked away in a village community. 94 Broadmoor Lane: large SW facing sloping garden with beautiful views up to Kelston Round Hill. Herbaceous borders, roses, clematis and wisteria. Terracing and raised vegetable garden, soft fruit, rockery with alpines. Glenfield: 1 acre. Formal design with series of rooms with scented and colour-themed plants. Herb garden, woodland walk, pastel sunken garden, kitchen garden, exuberant rose pergola. Ingleside: Revamped garden with new hard landscaping and fresh planting, herbaceous borders, pond, fernery, vegetable plot and greenhouse. Savile House: 1-acre newly designed and planted garden with herbaceous, parterre and fountain, Mediterranean terrace with arbour, summerhouse

with reflecting pool and wild flower garden. Only partial access to all gardens due to steps and level changes.

✽ ☕

Stoneleigh Down

111 84 WEYMOUTH ROAD

Frome, BA11 1HJ. Amanda Relph. *Parking in road outside house, alternatively use nearby car park in Badcox.* **Sun 10 June (1-4). Combined adm with 9 Catherston Close £6, chd free.**

Seasoned NGS garden openers opening a garden designed and planted by Simon Relph. The garden is open to celebrate his life. Architectural design of metal arches and geometrical raised beds surround raised pond. Many sculptured features by their son Alex Relph and other artists. Carefully chosen shrubs surround walled garden. Fern area, roses and camellias surround central courtyard. Raised vegetable beds, greenhouse and soft fruits. Featured in Wiltshire Garden Trust, regional press and radio. Paved paths, 3 small steps. Please note longer opening times of 9 Catherston Close on 10 June.

♿

112 WHITEWOOD LODGE

Norton Lane, Whitchurch, Bristol, BS14 0BU. Guy & Selena Norfolk, 07753 322318, selena.gray@btopenworld.com. *S of Bristol off A37 Wells Rd. Leave Bristol on A37 Wells rd. Pass Whitchurch Village into green belt, R down Norton Lane for approx 1m, garden on R. Parking in field behind house.* **Sat 15 Sept (1-4). Adm £4, chd free. Home-made teas. Visits also by arrangement Mar to Oct for groups of 6-10 weekends or evenings.**

¾ acre garden developed over 30yrs from field. Pond, orchard, herb area, woodland walk and mature trees and beds. Minimal use of chemicals in the garden, which aims to provide an ecologically friendly and sustainable environment. Many seats in different parts of garden from which to enjoy the wonderful views of Maes Knoll, an ancient hill fort. Featured in Garden News (Garden of the Week). The article described the evolution of the garden over 30 years and the move to a chemical free and wildlife friendly garden. Partial wheelchair access, gravel paths and some steps.

🐕 ☕

113 ◆ THE YEO VALLEY ORGANIC GARDEN AT HOLT FARM

Bath Road, Blagdon, BS40 7SQ. Mr & Mrs Tim Mead, 01761 461425, gardens@yeovalley.co.uk, www.yeovalleyorganicgarden.co.uk. *12m S of Bristol. Off A368. Entrance is approx ½m outside Blagdon towards Bath, on L, then follow garden signs past dairy.* **For NGS: Sun 15 Apr (2-5). Adm £5, chd free. Light refreshments. For other opening times and information, please phone, email or visit garden website.**

One of only a handful of ornamental gardens that is Soil Association accredited, 6.5 acres of contemporary planting, quirky sculptures, bulbs in their thousands, purple palace, glorious meadow and posh vegetable patch. Great views, green ideas. Events, workshops and exhibitions held throughout the year - see website for further details. Level access to the café, around garden some grass paths, some uneven bark and gravel paths. Accessibility map available at ticket office.

✽ ☕

114 YEWS FARM

East Street, Martock, TA12 6NF. Louise & Fergus Dowding, 01935 822202, fergus.dowding@btinternet.com, www.louise.dowding.co.uk. *Turn off main road through village at Market House, onto East St, past PO, garden 150 yards on R, 50m before Nag's Head.* **Visits by arrangement June & July for groups of 20-50. Adm £6, chd free. Tea. Glass of fine home-made cider to all with a healthy constitution and aged over 18.**

Theatrical planting in large walled garden. Outsized plants in jungle garden. Sculptural planting for height, shape, leaf and texture. Self-seeded gravel garden, box and bay ball border, espalier apples, eclectic cloud pruning, much block planting. Farmyard garden where hens do the weeding. Working organic kitchen garden. Hens, pigs, orchard and active cider barn - the full monty! We grow the Martock broad bean, the only known survivor of a medieval variety of broad bean. Visitors may throw Beauty of Bath apples to the pigs. Child friendly garden. Mostly wheelchair access.

♿ 🚌 ☕

STAFFORDSHIRE

Birmingham & West Midlands

Staffordshire, Birmingham and part of the West Midlands is a landlocked 'county', one of the furthest from the sea in England and Wales.

It is an NGS 'county' of surprising contrasts, from the 'Moorlands' in the North East, the 'Woodland Quarter' in the North West, the 'Staffordshire Potteries' and England's 'Second City' in the South East, with much of the rest of the land devoted to agriculture, both dairy and arable.

The garden owners enthusiastically embraced the NGS from the very beginning, with seven gardens opening in the inaugural year of 1927, and a further thirteen the following year.

The county is the home of the National Memorial Arboretum, the Cannock Chase Area of Outstanding Natural Beauty and part of the new National Forest.

There are many large country houses and gardens throughout the county with a long history of garden-making and with the input of many of the well known landscape architects.

Today, the majority of NGS gardens are privately owned and of modest size. However, a few of the large country house gardens still open their gates for NGS visitors.

Volunteers

County Organiser
John & Susan Weston
01785 850448
john.weston@ngs.org.uk

County Treasurer
Brian Bailey
01902 424867
brian.bailey@ngs.org.uk

Publicity
Graham & Judy White
01889 563930
graham&judy.white@ngs.org.uk

Booklet Co-ordinator
Peter Longstaff
01785 282582
peter.longstaff@ngs.org.uk

Assistant County Organisers
Jane Cerone
01827 873205
janecerone@btinternet.com

Ken & Joy Sutton
01889 590631
suttonjoy2@gmail.com

Sheila Thacker
01782 791244
metbowers@gmail.com

Left: 'John's Garden' at Ashwood Nurseries

OPENING DATES

All entries subject to change. For latest information check **www.ngs.org.uk**

Map locator numbers are shown to the right of each garden name.

January

Wednesday 17th
◆ The Trentham Estate 58

March

Sunday 18th
The Beeches 5
23 St Johns Road 52
29 St John's Road 53

Sunday 25th
The Beeches 5

Wednesday 28th
◆ The Trentham Estate 58

April

Sunday 8th
The Beeches 5
Millennium Garden 39

Thursday 19th
23 St Johns Road 52

Sunday 22nd
'John's Garden' at Ashwood Nurseries 34

Saturday 28th
Wild Thyme Cottage 65

May

Wednesday 2nd
High Trees 31

Sunday 6th
Hall Green Gardens 28
Keeper's Cottage; Bluebell Wood 35
Yew Tree Cottage 72

Monday 7th
Keeper's Cottage; Bluebell Wood 35

Wednesday 9th
◆ Birmingham Botanical Gardens 7

Thursday 10th
Yew Tree Cottage 72

Saturday 12th
NEW Barlaston Hall 4

Sunday 13th
NEW Barlaston Hall 4
NEW Cats Whiskers 14
NEW 45 Trafalgar Road 57

Wednesday 16th
High Trees 31

Friday 18th
23 St Johns Road 52
29 St John's Road 53

Saturday 19th
NEW White Wood Lodge 63

Sunday 20th
The Beeches 5
Courtwood House 20
Dorset House 22
89 Marsh Lane 37
Millennium Garden 39
Tanglewood Cottage 55
NEW White Wood Lodge 63

Wednesday 23rd
The Secret Garden 54

Sunday 27th
The Old Dairy House 44

Monday 28th
Bridge House 11
22 Greenfield Road 27
The Old Dairy House 44

June

Friday 1st
Coley Cottage 18
The Secret Garden 54

Festival Weekend

Sunday 3rd
The Garth 25
The Pintles 49
NEW 49 The Plantation 56
19 Waterdale 61
12 Waterdale 62

Friday 8th
23 St Johns Road 52

Saturday 9th
Colour Mill 19

Sunday 10th
Ashcroft and Claremont 2
◆ Castle Bromwich Hall Gardens 13
NEW Chapel House 15
◆ Middleton Hall 38
Wild Wood Lodge 66

Monday 11th
◆ Middleton Hall 38

Wednesday 13th
Bankcroft Farm 3
◆ The Trentham Estate 58

Saturday 16th
The Beeches 5
2 Woodland Crescent 68

Sunday 17th
Coley Cottage 18
The Secret Garden 54
Woodbrooke Quaker Study Centre 67
2 Woodland Crescent 68
NEW Woodside Farm 70

Wednesday 20th
Bankcroft Farm 3
5 East View Cottages 24

Friday 22nd
Yarlet House 71

Sunday 24th
NEW 21 Alexandra Drive 1
Brooklyn 12
5 East View Cottages 24
The Garth 25
Mitton Manor 40
The Mount, Coton, Gnosall 41
NEW 15 New Church Road 43
The Pintles 49

Wednesday 27th
Bankcroft Farm 3

July

Every Thursday to Thursday 19th
Yew Tree Cottage 72

Sunday 1st
344 Chester Road 16
Grafton Cottage 26
Hall Green Gardens 28
Marie Curie Hospice Garden 36
Pereira Road Gardens 47
19 Waterdale 61
12 Waterdale 62

Friday 6th
22 Greenfield Road 27

Sunday 8th
NEW 21 Alexandra Drive 1
Bournville Village 8

Sunday 15th
NEW 21 Alexandra Drive 1
Grafton Cottage 26
NEW Holmefield & Newfields Farm 32
NEW The Mount at Creswell 42
NEW Woodside Farm 70

Saturday 21st
NEW Pershall Farm Cottage 48
41 Twentylands 59

Sunday 22nd
Dorset House 22
The Old Vicarage 45
NEW Pershall Farm Cottage 48
56 St Agnes Road 51
Vernon House 60
The Wickets 64
Yew Tree Cottage 72

Sunday 29th
The Beeches 5
198 Eachelhurst Road 23
Grafton Cottage 26

August

Wednesday 1st
The Secret Garden 54

Sunday 5th
Grafton Cottage 26

Wednesday 8th
Coley Cottage 18

THE GARDENS

1 NEW 21 ALEXANDRA DRIVE

Yoxall, Burton-On-Trent, DE13 8PL. Mr & Mrs Paul Shum. *9m SW of Burton On Trent. Located on A515. Easily accessible from A38 at Lichfield or Burton On Trent, can also be accessed via the A50 at Sudbury.* **Sun 24 June, Sun 8, Sun 15 July (11-5). Adm £3.50, chd free. Home-made teas.**
A plant lovers dream, full of colour and perfume. Every inch packed with wide varieties of roses, clematis, sanguisorba, lilies and thalictrum between many other different plants. Also featuring wooden arches and large Indian sandstone patio. A hidden gem-the more you look, the more you will find. Slightly sloping grassed area.

GROUP OPENING

2 ASHCROFT AND CLAREMONT

Eccleshall, ST21 6JP. *7m W of Stafford. J14 M6. At Eccleshall end of A5013 the garden is 100 metres before junction with A519. On street parking nearby. Note: Some Satnavs give wrong directions.* **Sun 10 June (2-5). Combined adm £4, chd free. Home-made teas at Ashcroft.**

ASHCROFT
Peter & Gillian Bertram.

26 CLAREMONT ROAD
Maria Edwards.

Two gardens as different as Monet's soft pastel colours are to Vincent's bright sunflowers. Ashcroft is a 1 acre wildlife-friendly garden, pond and covered courtyard. Rooms flow seamlessly around the Edwardian house. Herb bed, treillage, greenhouse with raised beds. Find the topiary peacock that struts in the gravel bed. In the woodland area Gollum lurks in the steps of the ruin. Claremont is a small town garden its design based on feng shui principles. Manicured lawns, herbaceous borders, shrubs, perennials and annuals. Constantly evolving with colour and new features, maintaining interest throughout the year. Come and be inspired! Maria is happy to explain the principles of feng shui in garden layout. Teas in aid of Katherine House Hospice. Tickets, teas and plants available at Ashcroft. Wheelchair access at Ashcroft only.

3 BANKCROFT FARM
Tatenhill, Burton-on-Trent, DE13 9SA. Mrs Penelope Adkins. *2m SW of Burton-on-Trent. Take Tatenhill Rd off A38 Burton-Branston flyover. 1m, 1st house on L approaching village. Parking on farm.* **Wed 13, Wed 20, Wed 27 June (2-5). Adm £3, chd free.**
Lose yourself for an afternoon in our 1½-acre organic country garden. Arbour, gazebo and many other seating areas to view ponds and herbaceous borders, backed with shrubs and trees with emphasis on structure, foliage and colour. Productive fruit and vegetable gardens, wildlife areas and adjoining 12 acre native woodland walk. Picnics welcome. Gravel paths.
♿

4 NEW BARLASTON HALL
Queen Marys Drive, Barlaston, Stoke-On-Trent, ST12 9AT. James & Carol Hall. *From A34 turn towards Barlaston. Over level Xing, turn L at village green. Cont straight on, the hall is on L. Limited parking except for blue badge holders. Parking available by village green.* **Sat 12, Sun 13 May (2-5). Adm £4, chd free. Light refreshments.**
A 3½ acre garden containing a double herbaceous border, woodland walk containing many spring flowers and interesting mature trees, walled vegetable garden and wild flower meadow. Wheelchair access to most areas.
♿ ☕

5 THE BEECHES
Mill Street, Rocester, ST14 5JX. Ken & Joy Sutton, 01889 590631, suttonjoy2@gmail.com. *5m N of Uttoxeter. On B5030 from Uttoxeter turn R at 2nd r'about into village by JCB factory. At Red Lion Pub & mini r'about take rd signed Mill Street. Garden 250 yds on R. Parking at JCB Academy Sat & Suns only.* **Sun 18, 25 Mar, Sun 8 Apr (11-4). Adm £3, chd free. Tea. Sun 20 May, Sat 16 June, Sun 29 July, Sun 2 Sept (1.30-5). Adm £4, chd free. Home-made teas. Visits also by arrangement May to Aug min charge £80 if less than 20 people. Tea extra.**
A stunning plant lover's garden of ⅔ acre with countryside views, Box garden, shrubs, rhododendrons and azaleas, vibrant colour-themed herbaceous borders, scented roses, clematis and climbing plants, fruit trees, pools, late flowering perennials, vegetable and soft fruit garden. Perennials cut back and shrubs pruned to reveal an under planting of spring jewels from bulbs, hellebores and early perennials (March opening). Partial wheelchair access.
♿ ✽ 🚌 ☕

6 BIRCH TREES
Copmere End, Eccleshall, ST21 6HH. Susan & John Weston, 01785 850448, johnweston123@btinternet.com. *1½m W of Eccleshall. On B5026, turn at junction signed Copmere End. After ½m straight across Xrds by Star Inn.* **Sun 26, Mon 27 Aug (1.30-5). Adm £3.50, chd free. Home-made teas. Also open Pershall Farm Cottage. Visits also by arrangement July & Aug, groups of 10 - 30.**
Surprising ½ acre SW-facing sun trap hidden from the road which takes advantage of the 'borrowed landscape' of the surrounding countryside. Take time to explore the pathways between the island beds which contain many unusual herbaceous plants, grasses and shrubs; also vegetable patch, stump bed, alpine house, orchard and water features.
♿ ✽ ☕

7 ◆ BIRMINGHAM BOTANICAL GARDENS
Westbourne Road, Edgbaston, B15 3TR. Birmingham Botanical & Horticultural Society, 0121 454 1860, admin@birminghambotanicalgardens.org.uk, www.birminghambotanicalgardens.org.uk. *1½m SW of the centre of Birmingham. From J6 M6 take A38(M) to city centre. Follow underpasses signed Birmingham West to A456. At Fiveways island turn L onto B4217 (Calthorpe Rd) signed Botanical Gardens.* **For NGS: Wed 9 May (10-7). Adm £7.50, chd £5.25. Light snacks & refreshments in Terrace Pavilion tearoom. For other opening times and information, please phone, email or visit garden website.**
Extensive botanical garden set in a green urban environment with a comprehensive collection of plants from throughout the world growing in the glasshouses and outside. Four stunning glasshouses take you from tropical rainforest to arid desert. Fifteen acres of beautiful landscaped gardens. Roses, alpines, perennials, rare trees and shrubs. Playground, Children's Discovery Garden, Gallery, Gift Shop. Gardens open every day of the year except Christmas Day and Boxing Day.
♿ ✽ 🚌 ☕

GROUP OPENING

8 BOURNVILLE VILLAGE
Birmingham, B30 1QY. Bournville Vilage Trust, www.bvt.org.uk. *Gardens spread across 1,000 acre estate. Walks of up to 30 mins between some. Map supplied on day.* **Sun 8 July (11-5). Combined adm £6, chd free. Home-made teas at various locations. Light meals, additional parking & comfort facilities: Wyevale Garden Centre, Rowheath Pavilion, Weoley Hill Village Hall.**

NEW 103 BOURNVILLE LANE
B30 1LH. Mrs Jennifer Duffy.

19 GREEN MEADOW ROAD
B29 4DD. Mr & Mrs Robert & Annette Booth.

82 HAY GREEN LANE
B30 1UP. Mr Tony Walpole & Mrs Elsie Wheeler.

32 KNIGHTON ROAD
B31 2EH. Mrs Anne Ellis & Mr Lawrence Newman.

NEW 40 MIDDLE PARK ROAD
B29 4BJ. Ms Anna De Ville and Mr Chris Elsom.

143 OAK FARM ROAD
B30 1ET. Sue Harris.

Bournville Village is showcasing: a once-overgrown and now restored urban cottage garden; a north-facing ⅕ acre informal garden; a jungle meets cottage style garden and a fun garden. New for 2017: a densely planted garden with bulbs, perennials, shrubs & annuals for all-year interest, bordering one of Bournville's spinneys. Bournville is famous for it's large gardens, outstanding open spaces and of course it's chocolate factory! Free information sheet/ map available on the day. Gardens spread across the 1,000 acre estate, with walks of up to 30 minutes between sites. For those with a disability, full details of access are available on the NGS and Bournville Village Trust (BVT) websites: www.ngs.org.uk or www.bvt.org.uk. Visitors with particular concerns with regards to access are welcome to call BVT on 0300 333 6540 or email: CommunityAdmin@bvt.org.uk. Music and singing available across a number of sites. Please check on the day. Press release by BVT to be made 2 weeks before event. Approx. date of release 22 June 2018. Visitors with disabilities are advised to check before travelling.

9 THE BOWERS

Church Lane, Standon, Eccleshall, ST21 6RW. Maurice & Sheila Thacker, 01782 791244, metbowers@gmail.com. *5m N of Eccleshall. Take A519 & at Cotes Heath turn L signed Standon. After 1m turn R at Xrds by church, into Church Lane ½m on L.* **Visits by arrangement July & Aug groups of 10+. Adm £3, chd free. Home-made teas.**

This cottage style garden is reopening following a 2 year break. The garden has had a considerable make over but still retains a large collection of clematis and colourful borders throughout. Some gravel paths may prove difficult.

10 BREAKMILLS

Hames Lane, Newton Regis, Tamworth, B79 0NH. Mr Paul Horobin, 07966 531239. *Approx 5m N of Tamworth & 3m S of M42 J11. Signed from B5493, Hames Lane is a single track lane near the Queens Head Pub. Disabled parking at the house, other visitors please follow parking signs or park in village centre.* **Visits by arrangement in July for groups of 12+. Adm £4.50, chd free. Home-made teas.**

Just under 2 acres of low maintenance garden featuring small tropical area, island beds, shale area for grasses. Pond, man made stream, vegetable patch and mature trees. Originally a paddock area, trees planted some 15-20 yrs ago but garden really developed over the last 5yrs and still a work in progress. Lots of seating areas to enjoy both the fun aspects of our garden and the surrounding countryside. Larger grassed area may be difficult for wheelchairs on very wet days but access to long drive and eating area in all conditions.

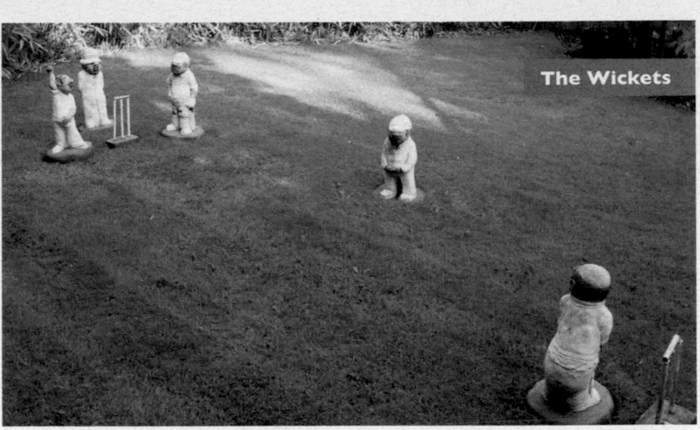

The Wickets

11 BRIDGE HOUSE

Dog Lane, Bodymoor Heath, B76 9JD. Mr & Mrs J Cerone, 01827 873205, janecerone@btinternet.com. *5m S of Tamworth. From A446 at Belfry Island take A4091 to Tamworth, after 1m turn R onto Bodymoor Heath Lane & continue 1m into village, parking in field opp garden.* **Mon 28 May, Mon 27 Aug (2-5). Adm £4, chd free. Home-made teas. Visits also by arrangement May to Sept for groups 5-30.**

1 acre garden surrounding converted public house. Divided into smaller areas with a mix of shrub borders, azalea and fuchsia, herbaceous and bedding, orchard, kitchen garden with large greenhouse and wild flower meadow. Pergola walk, formal fish pool, pond, bog garden and lawns. Kingsbury Water Park and RSPB Middleton Lakes Reserve located within a mile.

12 BROOKLYN

Gratton Lane, Endon, Stoke-on-Trent, ST9 9AA. Janet & Steve Howell. *4m W of Leek. 6m from Stoke-on-Trent on A53 turn at Black Horse Pub into centre of village, R into Gratton Lane 1st house on R. Parking signed in village.* **Sun 24 June (12-5). Adm £3.50, chd free. Cream teas.**

A cottage garden in the picturesque old village of Endon. Pretty front garden overflows with roses geraniums and astrantias, box surrounds a central sundial. Rear garden features shady area with hostas and ferns, small waterfall and pond. Steps lead to rear lawn, large well stocked borders and summerhouse. Several seating areas with village and rural views. Enjoy tea and cake in the potting shed. Traditional cottage garden in village location.

13 ◆ CASTLE BROMWICH HALL GARDENS

Chester Road, Castle Bromwich, Birmingham, B36 9BT. Castle Bromwich Hall & Gardens Trust, 0121 749 4100, admin@cbhgt.org.uk, www.castlebromwichhallgardens.org.uk. *4m East of Birmingham centre. 1m J5 M6 (exit N only).* **For NGS: Sun 10 June (12.30-4.30). Adm £4.50, chd £1. Light refreshments.** For other opening times and information, please phone, email or visit garden website.

10 acres of restored C17/18 walled gardens attached to a Jacobean manor (now a hotel) just minutes from J5 of M6. Formal yew parterres, wilderness walks, summerhouses, holly maze, espaliered fruit and wild areas. Visitor Centre open for light refreshments in addition to cream teas on the lawn. Paths are either lawn or rough hoggin - sometimes on a slope. Most areas generally accessible, rough areas outside the walls difficult when wet.

♿ 🐕 ✿ 🚗 ☕

14 NEW CATS WHISKERS

42 Amesbury Rd, Moseley, Birmingham, B13 8LE. Dr Alfred & Mrs Michele White. *Opposite back of Moseley Hall Hospital. Past Edgbaston Cricket ground straight on at r'about & up Salisbury Rd. Amesbury Rd 1st on R.* **Sun 13 May (1.30-5). Combined adm with 45 Trafalgar Road £5, chd free. Wine.**

A plantsman's garden developed over the last 38 years but which has kept its 1923 landscape. The front garden whilst not particularly large is full of interesting trees and shrubs ; the rear garden is on 3 levels with steps leading to a small terrace and further steps to the main space. At the end of the garden is a pergola leading to the vegetable garden and greenhouse. Back garden is not suitable for wheelchairs as there are two flights of steps.

✿ ☕

Gardens are at the heart of hospice care

15 NEW CHAPEL HOUSE

Coton Clanford, Stafford, ST18 9PE. Mr Richard Clamp, 01785 282958, richardhclamp@aol.com. *2m W of J14 M6. From M6 J14 take A5013 to Eccleshall, in 1½m L onto B5405 to Woodseaves, in ¼m L to Seighford. After 1m 3rd L onto Bunns Bank/Clanford Lane. Continue for 1m.* **Sun 10 June (12-4). Adm £4, chd free. Visits also by arrangement May to July 25 maximum.**

Mature country garden in rural location, with 3 distinct areas. Multiple boarders bring colour and foliage in late Spring in the formal garden. The vegetable and fruit garden provides ample produce and feature a small herb bed; while a woodland area creates a natural habitat for wildlife, including a pond. A number of seating areas around the garden provide quiet spots to enjoy the tranquility.

☕

16 344 CHESTER ROAD

Boldmere, Sutton Coldfield, B73 5BU. Mr & Mrs David & Hilary Godbehere. *4m NW of Birmingham City Centre. J6 M6, take Gravelly Hill Rd to 6 Ways, Summer Rd & then Gravelly Lane. Turn L onto Chester Rd, Boldmere, located between Lake House Rd & Sycamore Rd. Parking in nearby side rds.* **Sun 1 July (12-4.30). Adm £3.50, chd free. Home-made teas. Teas and cakes.**

Urban oasis with pond and waterfall, raised beds, multiple pathways threading through garden, unusual plants and tropical area. Refreshments and cakes. Wheelchair access possible but not easy.

✿ ☕

17 CHURCH COTTAGE

Aston, Stone, ST15 0BJ. Andrew & Anne Worrall. *1m S of Stone. North side of St Saviour's Church, Aston. Go S 150 metres on A34 after junction with A51. Turn L at Aston Village Hall. 200 metres down lane into churchyard for parking.* **Thur 16 Aug (12-4.30). Adm £3, chd free. Home-made teas.**

An acre of cottage garden with large pond, waterfall and stream. More than 60 trees, small orchard and wild flowers. Dahlias by award-winning grower Dave Bond. Views across the R Trent. Quiet seating. Wheelchair access to refreshments but only to a small part of the garden.

🐕 ☕

18 COLEY COTTAGE

Coley Lane, Little Haywood, Stafford, ST18 0UU. Yvonne Branson, 01889 882715, yvonnebranson@outlook.com. *5m SE of Stafford. A51 from Rugeley or Weston signed Little Haywood. ½m from Seven Springs. A513 Coley Lane from Red Lion Pub past Back Lane, 100yds on L opp red post box.* **Fri 1, Sun 17 June, Wed 8 Aug (11-4.30). Adm £3, chd free. Home-made teas in the garden. Visits also by arrangement June to Aug pre bookings 10+.**

A plant lover's cottage garden, full of subtle colours and perfume, every inch packed with plants. Clematis and old roses covering arches, many hostas and agapanthus, a wildlife pool, all designed to attract birds and butterflies. This garden is now 10yrs old, trees, roses and herbaceous planting has become well established. Visited by radio Stoke. Featured in Gardeners News. Wheelchair access front garden only.

🐕 ✿ 🚗 ☕

19 COLOUR MILL

Winkhill, Leek, ST13 7PR. Bob & Jackie Pakes, 01538 308680, jackie.pakes@icloud.com, www.colourmill.webplus.net. *7m E of Leek. Follow A523 from either Leek or Ashbourne, look for NGS signs on the side of the main rd*

which will direct you down to Colour Mill. **Sat 9 June, Thur 23 Aug (1.30-5). Adm £3.50, chd free. Home-made teas. Visits also by arrangement June to Aug.**
¾ acre S-facing garden, created in the shadow of a former iron foundry, set beside the delightful R Hamps frequented by kingfisher and dipper. Informal planting in a variety of rooms surrounded by beautiful 7ft beech hedges. Large organic vegetable patch complete with greenhouse and polytunnel. Maturing trees provide shade for the interesting seating areas. Newly acquired willow area beside river.

20 COURTWOOD HOUSE

3 Court Walk, Betley, CW3 9DP. Mike Reeves. *6m S of Crewe. On A531 toward Keele & Newcastle under Lyme or from J16 off M6, pickup A531 off A500 on Nantwich rd, into village by Betley Court.* **Sun 20 May (12.30-5.30). Adm £3, chd free. Light refreshments.**
Small L-shaped, walled garden, which is designed as a walk-through sculpture. Mainly shrubs with structures and water features, hidden spaces and seating areas, with strong shapes and effects utilising a wide range of materials, incl. a synthetic lawn. Small art gallery with acrylic paintings by owner for sale.

21 NEW ◆ DOROTHY CLIVE GARDEN

Willoughbridge, Market Drayton, TF9 4EU. Willoughbridge Garden Trust, 01630 647237, info@dorothyclivegarden.co.uk, www.dorothyclivegarden.co.uk. *3m SE of Bridgemere Garden World. From M6 J15 take A53 W bound, then A51 N bound midway between Nantwich & Stone, near Woore.* **For NGS: Sat 13, Sun 14 Oct (10-5.30). Adm £3.50, chd £2. Light refreshments.** For other opening times and information, please phone, email or visit garden website.
12 informal acres, incl superb woodland garden, alpine scree, gravel garden, fine collection of trees and spectacular flower borders. Renowned in May when woodland quarry is brilliant with rhododendrons. Waterfall and woodland planting. Laburnum Arch in June. Creative planting has produced stunning summer borders. Large Glasshouse. Spectacular autumn colour. Much to see, whatever the season. The Dorothy Clive Tea rooms will be open throughout the weekend for refreshments, lunch and afternoon tea. Plant sales, Gift room Picnic area and children's play area for a wide age range. Regular features on Radio Stoke and Radio Shropshire. Articles in Staffordshire Life and other gardening publications. Wheelchairs are available to book through the tea rooms. Disabled parking is available near Disabled toilets on both upper and lower car parks.

22 DORSET HOUSE

68 Station Street, Cheslyn Hay, WS6 7EE. Mary & David Blundell, 01922 419437, david.blundell@talktalk.net. *2m SE of Cannock J11 M6 A462 towards Willenhall. L at island. At next island R into 1-way system (Low St), at T junction L into Station St. A5 Bridgetown L to island, L Coppice St. R into Station St.* **Sun 20 May, Sun 22 July (11-5). Adm £3, chd free. Home-made teas. Visits also by arrangement May to July groups of 10+.**
Step back in time with a visit to this inspirational ½-acre garden which incorporates country cottage planting at its very best. Unusual rhododendrons, acers, shrubs and perennials planted in mixed borders. Clematis-covered arches and hidden corners with water features including stream and wildlife pool all come together to create a haven of peace and tranquillity. Featured in local papers.

23 198 EACHELHURST ROAD

Walmley, Sutton Coldfield, B76 1EW. Jacqui & Jamie Whitmore. *5mins N of Birmingham. M6 J6, A38 Tyburn Rd to Lichfield, continue to T-lights at Lidl & continue on Tyburn Rd, at island take 2nd exit to destination rd.* **Sun 29 July (12.30-4.30). Adm £3, chd free. Home-made teas.**
A long garden approx 210ft x 30ft divided by arches and pathways. Plenty to explore incl wildlife pond,corner arbour, cottage garden and hanging baskets leading to formal garden with box-lined pathways, well, stocked borders, gazebo and chicken house then through to raised seating area, overlooking Pype Hayes golf course, with summer house and bar and Mediterranean plants.

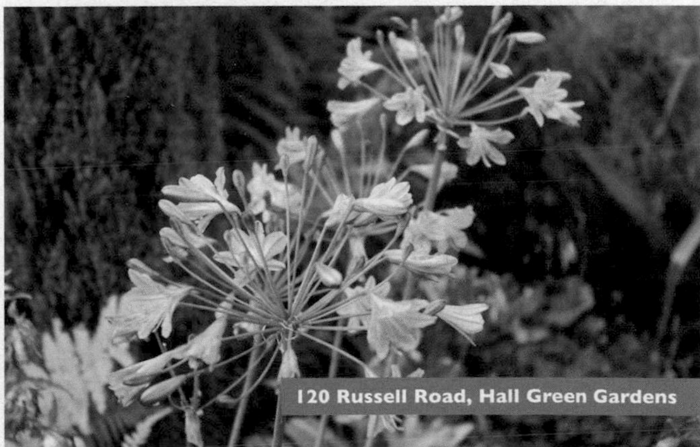
120 Russell Road, Hall Green Gardens

24 5 EAST VIEW COTTAGES

School Lane, Shuttington, nr Tamworth, B79 0DX. Cathy Lyon-Green, 01827 892244, cathyatcorrabhan@hotmail.com, www.ramblinginthegarden.wordpress.com. *2m NE of Tamworth. From Tamworth, Amington Rd or Ashby Rd to Shuttington. From M42 J11, B5493 for Seckington & Tamworth; signed L turn to Shuttington. Pink house nr top of School Lane. Parking signed, disabled at house.* **Wed 20 June (11-4); Sun 24 June (12-6). Adm £4, chd free. Home-made teas. Visits also by arrangement in July min charge (excl teas) £60 if less than 15.**

Plantlover's garden: deceptive, quirky and full of surprises. Informally planted themed borders, cutting beds, woodland, woodland edge borders, shrub border, stream, water features, sitooterie, folly and many artefacts. Roses, clematis, hostas, perennials, foliage and annual fillers. Benches and seating areas to contemplate the garden and birdlife or enjoy homemade cake. "A wonderful hour's wander".

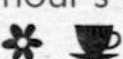

25 THE GARTH

2 Broc Hill Way, Milford, Stafford, ST17 0UB. Mr & Mrs David Wright, 01785 661182, anitawright1@yahoo.co.uk, www.anitawright.co.uk. *4½m SE of Stafford. A513 Stafford to Rugeley rd; at Barley Mow turn R (S) to Brocton; L after ½m.* **Sun 3, Sun 24 June (2-6). Adm £3, chd free. Cream teas. Visits also by arrangement.**

½ acre garden of many levels on Cannock Chase AONB. Acid soil loving plants. Series of small gardens, water features, raised beds. Rare trees, island beds of unusual shrubs and perennials, many varieties of hosta and ferns. Varied and colourful foliage, summerhouse, arbours and quiet seating to enjoy the garden. Ancient sandstone caves.

26 GRAFTON COTTAGE

Barton-under-Needwood, DE13 8AL. Margaret & Peter Hargreaves, 01283 713639. *6m N of Lichfield. Leave A38 for Catholme S of Barton, follow sign to Barton Green, L at Royal Oak, ¼m.* **Sun 1, Sun 15, Sun 29 July, Sun 5 Aug (11.30-5). Adm £4, chd free. Home-made teas. Visits also by arrangement June to Aug min adm £80 if less than 20 people.** Donation to Alzheimer's Research Trust.

A visitor commented 'your garden is a delight, the colours, planting, association of form all are excellent one of the best gardens we have seen. Admired over 25 years. Coloured themed borders with unusual herbaceous plants and perfume from old fashioned Roses, Sweet peas, violas, dianthus, phlox and lilies. Particular interests are viticella clematis, salvia, penstemon, cottage garden annuals and use of foliage plants, pelargonium, parterre and babbling brook. Featured on BBC Gardeners World. Numerous press articles.

27 22 GREENFIELD ROAD

Stafford, ST17 0PU. Alison & Peter Jordan, 01785 660819, alison.jordan2@btinternet.com. *3m S of Stafford. Follow the A34 out of Stafford towards Cannock. 2nd L onto Overhill Rd. 1st R into Greenfield Rd.* **Mon 28 May (11-5). Adm £3, chd free. Cream teas. Evening opening Fri 6 July (6-9). Adm £4, chd free. Wine. Adm incl glass of wine. Visits also by arrangement May to Aug for groups min 20, adm incl cream tea.**

Suburban garden created in the last 6 years, working towards all year round interest. In spring interesting bulbs, in May stunning azaleas and rhododendrons, June onwards interesting perennials and grasses. A garden that shows being diagnosed with Parkinson's needn't stop you creating a peaceful place to sit, ponder and enjoy.

GROUP OPENING

28 HALL GREEN GARDENS

Hall Green, Birmingham, B28 8SQ. *Off A34, 3m city centre, 6m from M42 J4. From CIty Centre start at Russell Rd B28 8SQ, from M42 start at Boden Rd B28 9DL, Hall Green.* **Sun 6 May, Sun 1 July (1-5.30). Combined adm £5, chd free. Home-made teas at 111 Southam Rd.**

42 BODEN ROAD
Mrs Helen Lycett.
Open on all dates

16 BURNASTON ROAD
Howard Hemmings & Sandra Hateley, 0121 624 1488, howard.hemmings@blueyonder.co.uk.
Open on all dates
Visits also by arrangement May to July.

37 BURNASTON ROAD
Mrs Carolyn Wynne-Jones, 0121 608 2397, markwynne-jones@blueyonder.co.uk.
Open on all dates
Visits also by arrangement May to July.

36 FERNDALE ROAD
Mrs E A Nicholson, 0121 777 4921.
Open on all dates
Visits also by arrangement Apr to July no min, max 30.

63 GREEN ROAD
Mr & Mrs A Wilkes, 01217770510.
Open on all dates
Visits also by arrangement Apr to July.

120 RUSSELL ROAD
Mr David Worthington, 0121 624 7906, hildave@hotmail.com.
Open on all dates
Visits also by arrangement Apr to July groups up to 30. Teas incl in adm.

NEW **87 SOUTHAM ROAD**
Mrs Sarah Moss.
Open on all dates

111 SOUTHAM ROAD
Ms Val Townend & Mr Ian Bate.
Open on all dates

19 STAPLEHURST ROAD
Mrs Sheena Terrace.
Open on Sun 6 May

A group of diverse suburban gardens. 42 Boden Rd: Large restful garden, mature trees, cottage borders, seating areas and small vegetable area.
16 Burnaston Rd: Quirky garden with children's quiz. 37 Burnaston Rd: Tranquil garden, curving borders, perennials, shade areas, soft fruit and vegetables.
36 Ferndale Rd: Florist's large suburban garden, ponds and waterfalls, and fruit garden. 63 Green Rd: Eccentric's north facing wildlife friendly garden.
120 Russell Rd: Plantsman's garden, formal raised pond and hosta collection and unusual perennials, container planting. 87 Southam Rd: Mature garden with deep, sunny herbaceous borders.
111 Southam Rd: Mature garden with well defined areas including ponds, white garden, rescue hens and a majestic cedar. 19 Staplehurst Rd: Shady garden with mature trees, pond, cottage style borders. Some gardens have limited access. Telephone for more information or consult the NGS website.

Funds from National Garden Scheme gardens help Macmillan support thousands of people every year

29 HEATH HOUSE
Offley Brook, Eccleshall, ST21 6HA. Dr D W Eyre-Walker, 01785 280318, neyrewalker@btinternet.com. *3m W of Eccleshall. From Eccleshall take B5026 towards Woore. At Sugnall turn L, after 1½m turn R immed by stone garden wall. After 1m straight across Xrds. Use Satnav, mobile phones do not work locally.* **Visits by arrangement Apr to Sept. Adm £5, chd free. Refreshments available for small numbers..**
1½ acre country garden of C18 miller's house in lovely valley setting, overlooking mill pool. Plantsman's garden containing many rare and unusual plants in borders, bog garden, woodland, alpine house, raised bed and shrubberies and incl slowly expanding collection of hardy terrestrial orchids. Vegetable garden now converted to wild flower meadow. Wheelchair access difficult with only partial access.

30 HIDDEN GEM
15 St Johns Road, Pleck, Walsall, WS2 9TJ. Maureen & Sid Allen, 07825 804670, maureenallen42@gmail.com. *2m W of Walsall. Off J10 M6. Head for Walsall on A454 Wolverhampton Rd. Turn R into Pleck Rd A4148 then 4th R into St Johns Rd.* **Visits by arrangement July to Sept groups of 10 to 30 max. Adm £3, chd free.**
Situated between two busy motorway junctions. Come and visit our 'Hidden Gem.' What a surprise! A long narrow pretty garden, lovely foliage in June, pretty perennials, shrubs, trees, lush tropical plants from July onwards. Japanese area with stream. Shady walk with ferns, into pretty gravel garden lots of wildlife. Very relaxing atmosphere. WHAT A GEM!

31 HIGH TREES
18 Drubbery Lane, nr Longton Park, ST3 4BA. Peter & Pat Teggin. *5m S of Stoke-on-Trent. Off A5035, midway between Trentham Gardens & Longton. Opp Longton Park.* **Wed 2, Wed 16 May (1-4). Adm £3.50, chd free. Cream teas.**
A pretty, perfumed hidden garden. Colourful herbaceous plants juxtapose to create a rich woven tapestry of spires, flats and fluffs interwoven with structure planting and focal points. An ideas garden continuing to inspire, evoking orderly diversity. All within two minutes walk of a Victorian park.

32 NEW HOLMEFIELD & NEWFIELDS FARM
Sheen, Buxton, SK17 0HW. Connie Chafer & Sean Whittaker, Margaret & John Gould. *Approx 10m S of Buxton. A515 Buxton/ Ashboune rd. Take B5054 through Hartington after approx 2m take 1st R signed Sheen & Longnor.* **Sun 15 July (12-4.30). Adm £5, chd free. Home-made teas.**
Two neighbouring gardens in the Peak District National Park, Holmfield -Young cottage style garden created over the past four years with large beds filled with a wide variety of plants, shrubs ,seating areas to sit and contemplate the garden and panoramic views. Newfields Farm -12 years old medium sized garden with colourful herbaceous borders, large koi pool, working greenhouse and seating areas.

33 IDLEROCKS FARM
Hilderstone Road, Spot Acre, nr Stone, ST15 8RP. Barbara Dixon, 01889 505450. *3m E of Stone. From Stone take A520 to Meir Heath, turn R onto B5066 towards Hilderstone, farm 1½m on R. ½m drive with parking in the field by house.* **Visits by arrangement Feb to Aug also Feb for snowdrops. Adm £3, chd free. Home-made teas, cakes and coffee.**
Medium sized garden set in farmland and woodland, 800ft above sea level. Long herbaceous border, wildlife pond, views across the Trent Valley to the Wrekin and Clee Hills.

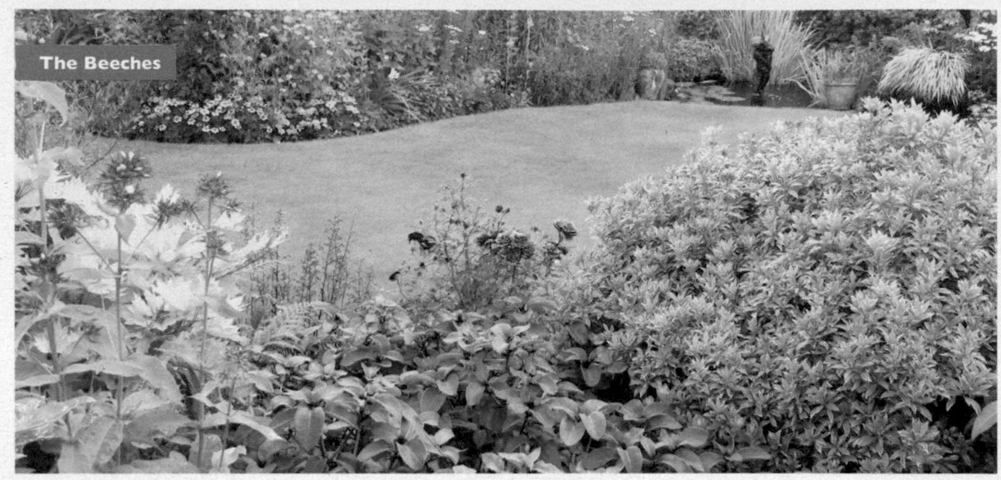
The Beeches

34 'JOHN'S GARDEN' AT ASHWOOD NURSERIES

Ashwood Lower Lane, Ashwood, nr Kingswinford, DY6 0AE. John Massey, www.ashwoodnurseries.com. *5m S of Wolverhampton. 1m past Wall Heath on A449 turn R to Ashwood along Doctor's Lane. At T-junction turn L. Park at Ashwood Nurseries.* **Sun 22 Apr (10-4). Adm £5, chd free. Light refreshments at adjacent Tea Room at Ashwood Nurseries.**

A stunning private garden adjacent to Ashwood Nurseries, it has a huge plant collection and many innovative design features in a beautiful canal-side setting. There are informal beds, woodland dells, a South African border, rock garden, fern stump garden and wildlife meadow. Fine displays of grasses, herbaceous perennials and clematis together with a notable collection of hydrangeas. Tea Room, Garden Centre and Gift Shop at adjacent Ashwood Nurseries. Coaches are by appointment only. Disabled access difficult if very wet.

NPC

35 KEEPER'S COTTAGE; BLUEBELL WOOD

24 Greensforge Lane, Stourton, Stourbridge, DY7 5BB. Peter & Jenny Brookes, 07974 454503, peter@brookesmedia.com. *2m NW of Stourbridge. At junction of A449 & A458 at Stourton, take Bridgnorth Rd (A458) westward, after ½m turn R into Greensforge Lane. Keeper's Cottage ½m on R.* **Sun 6, Mon 7 May (11-3). Adm £4, chd free. Home-made teas. Gluten-free and diabetic bakes available. Visits also by arrangement in May. Visits will be restricted to the bluebell season and will have to be arranged around owners' work.**

This stunning bluebell wood adorns the banks of a river deep in the South Staffordshire countryside, yet only a few miles from the conurbation. In May, the bluebells form a beautiful carpet, sweeping through the natural woodland and down to the river, the site of ancient nail making. It is a quintessentially English landscape which can only be glimpsed for a few short weeks of the year. Local newspapers and local radio. The woods contain steep pathways, totally unsuitable for wheelchairs.

36 MARIE CURIE HOSPICE GARDEN

Marsh Lane, Solihull, B91 2PQ. Mrs Do Connolly, www.mariecurie.org.uk/westmidlands. *Close to J5 M42 to E of Solihull Town Centre. Leave M42 at J5 & travel towards Solihull on A41. Take slip rd toward Solihull to join B4025 & after island take 1st R onto Marsh Lane. Marie Curie Hospice is on R.* **Sun 1 July (11-4). Adm £3.50, chd free. Home-made teas.**

The gardens include two large, formally laid out patients' gardens (including a ball fountain water feature), indoor courtyards, a vegetable plot, a long border adjoining the car park, gardens and a beautiful wildlife and pond area at the rear of the hospice. The volunteer gardening team hope that the gardens provide a peaceful and comforting place for patients, their visitors and staff.

37 89 MARSH LANE

Solihull, B91 2PE. Mrs Gail Wyldes. *½m from Solihull town centre. A41 from M42 J5. Turn sharp L at 1st T-lights. Garden on R. Parking 400 metres further along Marsh Lane at Solihull Cricket Club by mini r'about & Marie Curie car park further along.* **Sun 20 May (2-5). Adm £3.50, chd free. Home-made teas.**

Suburban Oasis. Trees, shrubs and herbaceous planting for all year interest with emphasis on leaf shape and structure. Wildlife pond, bog garden, water features, african style gazebo, gravel gardens, shady places and sunny seating areas. Patio with pergola and raised beds. Hostas and ferns abound.

The garden is continually evolving with new plants and features. Wheelchair access - small step from patio to the main back garden and paths may be a little narrow.

38 ◆ MIDDLETON HALL

Tamworth, B78 2AE. Middleton Hall Trust, 01827 283095, enquiries@middleton-hall.co.uk, www.middleton-hall.co.uk. *4m S of Tamworth, 2m N J9 M42. On A4091 between The Belfry & Drayton Manor.* **For NGS: Sun 10, Mon 11 June (11-4). Adm £5.50, chd free. Light refreshments in our Courtyard Centre. For other opening times and information, please phone, email or visit garden website.**

Our formal gardens form part of the 42 estate of the Grade II* Middleton Hall, the C17 home of naturalists Sir Francis Willoughby and John Ray. The formal gardens are made up of two walled gardens a Glade and an Orchard. The Walled gardens contain a variety of herbaceous and seasonal planting with specimen plants that have a botanical and/or historical significance to our site. Bake 180 Coffee Shop will also be open serving lunches and other light refreshments. Wheelchair access - walled garden paths are paved, Glade and Orchard paths are grass. No access to 1st floor of the Hall and Nature Trail.

39 MILLENNIUM GARDEN

London Road, Lichfield, WS14 9RB. Carol Cooper. *1m S of Lichfield. Off A38 along A5206 towards Lichfield ¼m past A38 island towards Lichfield. Park in field on L. Yellow signs on field gate.* **Sun 8 Apr, Sun 20 May (1-5). Adm £3.50, chd free.**

2-acre garden with mixed spring bulbs in the woodland garden and host of golden daffodils fade slowly into the summer borders in this English country garden. Designed with a naturalistic edge and with the environment in mind. A relaxed approach creates a garden of quiet sanctuary with the millennium bridge sitting comfortably, with its surroundings of lush planting and mature trees. Well stocked borders give shots of colour to lift the spirit and the air fills with the scent of wisterias and climbing roses. A stress free environment awaits you at the Millennium Garden.

40 MITTON MANOR

Mitton, Penkridge, Stafford, ST19 5QW. Mrs E A Gooch, info@mittonmanor.co.uk, , www.mittonmanor.co.uk. *2m W of Penkridge. Property is on Whiston Rd. Parking in field before house. No parking for coaches.* **Sun 24 June (11.30-4.30). Adm £5, chd free. Cream teas. Visits also by arrangement Apr to Sept groups of 20+. Full catering menu available. Deposit of full entry fee required on booking.**

This 7-acre country garden was started in 2001 and has been developed from an overgrown wilderness. The garden surrounds a Victorian manor (not open) and contains rooms of different styles, formal box/topiary, prairie planting and natural woodland bordered by a stream. Stunning vistas, water features and sculpture. New potager opening in 2018. Live music at Alice's Tea Party. Many levels, narrow and gravel paths. Wheelchair users will need assistance.

41 THE MOUNT, COTON, GNOSALL

Stafford, ST20 0EQ. Andrew & Celia Payne, 01785 822253, ac.payne@waitrose.com. *8m W of Stafford. From Stafford take A518 W towards Newport/Telford. Go through Gnosall, over canal. Garden on edge of Gnosall Village on L of A518.* **Sun 24 June (2-5). Adm £3.50, chd free. Home-made teas. Visits also by arrangement June & July for groups of 10+.**

Richly planted wildlife friendly garden with large collection of unusual plants set in ¾ acre. Divided into areas, incl a wild flower meadow, cottage garden and vegetable plot, highlights consist of over 100 different hosta varieties, many colourful hardy geraniums, bamboos and a huge Kiftsgate rose. The plant stall will have over 40+ varieties of hosta for sale plus other interesting plants. Teas in aid of Macmillan Cancer Support.

42 NEW THE MOUNT AT CRESWELL

Creswell Drive, Stafford, ST18 9QS. Mr & Mrs Robert Williams. *NW of Stafford. Off A5013, Creswell Grove, 400 metres from J14, M6. Towards Eccleshall. Look for large iron gates, signed The Mount, Private Drive. Head to the bottom of the drive, fork L.* **Sun 15 July (11-5). Adm £4, chd free. Home-made teas.**

A secret oasis formerly part of a walled kitchen garden. The front is mainly given to lawns, mature trees, and summer bedding. A small secluded courtyard garden, leads onto lawn and very relaxed herbaceous borders, stream leading to two ponds, boardwalk, 'woodland' walk, beautiful agapanthus, lilies and summer bedding. Enjoy tea and cakes served from the summerhouse.

43 NEW 15 NEW CHURCH ROAD

Sutton Coldfield, B73 5RT. Owen & Lloyd Watkins. *4½m NW of Birmingham city centre. Take A38M then A5127 to 6 Ways r'about, take 2nd exit then bear L Summer Rd then Gravelly Lane over Chester Rd to Boldmere Rd, 5th R New Church Rd.* **Sun 24 June (12-4). Adm £3.50, chd free. Light refreshments.**

A garden created and recreated, evolving over 7 years. From the patio a recently extended pond takes centre stage. Varied planting including herbaceous borders, shade loving plants, tree ferns and bamboo, a rockery and woodland area. Rear of the garden has raised vegetable beds, fruit trees and chickens. Wheelchair access with assistance, please note some areas may not be accessible. Several steps.

44 THE OLD DAIRY HOUSE

Trentham Park, Stoke-on-Trent, ST4 8AE. Philip & Michelle Moore. *S edge of Stoke-on-Trent. Next to Trentham Gardens. Off Whitmore Rd. Please follow NGS signs or signs for Trentham Park Golf Club. Parking in church car park.* **Sun 27, Mon 28 May (1-5). Adm £3, chd free. Home-made teas.**

Grade 2 listed house (not open) designed by Sir Charles Barry forms backdrop to this 2-acre garden in parkland setting. Shaded area for rhododendrons, azaleas plus expanding hosta and fern collection. Mature trees, 'cottage garden' and long borders. Narrow brick paths in vegetable plot. Large courtyard area for teas. Wheelchair access - some gravel paths but lawns are an option.

45 THE OLD VICARAGE

Fulford, nr Stone, ST11 9QS. Mike & Cherry Dodson. *4m N of Stone. From Stone A520 (Leek). 1m R turn to Spot Acre & Fulford, turn L down Post Office Terrace, past village green/Pub towards church. Parking signed on l.* **Sun 22 July (1-5). Adm £4, chd free. Home-made teas.**

1½ acres of formal sloping garden around Victorian house. Sit on the terrace or in the summerhouse to enjoy home-made cakes and tea amongst mature trees, relaxed herbaceous borders, roses and a small pond. Move to the organic vegetable garden with raised beds, fruit cage and very big compost heaps! In complete contrast, easy walk around the natural setting of a two-acre reclaimed lake planted with native species designed to attract wildlife. Waterfall, jetty, fishing hut, acer and fern glade plus young arboretum provide more interest. Featured in Weekend Telegraph. Children will enjoy meeting the chickens and horses. Wheelchair access to most areas.

46 PAUL'S OASIS OF CALM

18 Kings Close, Kings Heath, Birmingham, B14 6TP. Mr Paul Doogan, 0121 444 6943, gardengreen18@hotmail.co.uk. *4m from city centre. 5m from M42 J4. Take A345 to Kings Heath High St then B4122 Vicarage Rd. Turn L onto Kings Rd then R to Kings Close.* **Visits by arrangement May to Aug groups max 15. Adm £2.50, chd free. Cream teas.**

Garden cultivated from nothing into a little oasis. Measuring 18ft x 70ft. It's small but packed with interesting and unusual plants, water features and 7 seating areas. It's my piece of heaven. Council land which I have had permission to garden has been featured in the Sunday Mirror.

GROUP OPENING

47 PEREIRA ROAD GARDENS

Harborne, Birmingham, B17 9JN. *Between Gillhurst Rd & Margaret Grove, ¼m from Hagley Rd or ½m from Harborne High St.* **Sun 1 July (1.30-5). Combined adm £5, chd free. Home-made teas at Pereira Road allotments, accessed via driveway between 31 and 33 Pereira Road or through 55 Pereira Road. Drinks and homemade cakes plus jams and vegetables on sale.**

14 PEREIRA ROAD
Mike Foster.

48 PEREIRA ROAD
Rosemary Klem & Julie Werrett.

50 PEREIRA ROAD
Peg Peil.

55 PEREIRA ROAD
Emma Davies & Martin Commander.

Group of 4 different urban gardens. No.14 a well established suburban garden with mixed herbaceous and shrub borders. Wildlife-friendly with 2 ponds and wild flower area. Ongoing alterations provide new areas of interest each year. No 48 has recently been relandscaped to create a terraced garden with steps linking a patio, herbaceous and shrub planting and koi carp pond and a vegetable garden. No. 50 is a plantaholic's paradise with over 1000 varieties, many rare, incl fruits, vegetables, herbs, grasses and large bed of plants with African connections. Over 100 varieties on sale - see how they grow. No. 55 is a sloping garden, incl gravelled beds with mixed planting, grasses and a pond. All gardens have steps. In July, free admission to Harborne Nature Reserve and Pereira Road allotments incl. The gardens of both 14 and 50 were featured in Amateur Gardening. No 14 was also used as an example of a wild life friendly garden in the first series of BBC1's Instant Gardener programme.

48 NEW PERSHALL FARM COTTAGE

Pershall, Eccleshall, ST21 6NE. Wendy Johnson. *1m W of Eccleshall. From Eccleshall Xrds, take High St towards Loggerheads (B5026). In 1m turn L into Pershall.* **Sat 21, Sun 22 July (1.30-5). Sun 26, Mon 27 Aug (1.30-5). Adm £3, chd free. Home-made teas. Also open Birch Trees.**

South facing country garden designed for entertaining with herbaceous borders and water feature. Low hedge takes full advantage of the borrowed agricultural landscape of the Sow River valley with distant view of Eccleshall Church tower.

49 THE PINTLES

18 Newport Road, Great Bridgeford, Stafford, ST18 9PR. Peter & Leslie Longstaff, 01785 282582, peter.longstaff@ngs.org.uk. *J14 M6 take A5013 towards Eccleshall. In Great Bridgeford turn L onto B5405. Car park on L after ¼ min Village Hall car park.* **Sun 3, Sun 24 June (1.30-5). Adm £3, chd free. Home-made teas. Visits also by arrangement June & July for**

groups of 10+.
Located in the village of Great Bridgeford this traditional semi-detached house has a medium sized wildlife friendly garden designed to appeal to many interests. There are two greenhouses, over 500 cacti and succulents, orchids, vegetable and fruit plot, wildlife pond, weather station, and hidden woodland shady garden. Plenty of outside seating to enjoy the home made cakes and refreshments. Featured in Amateur Gardening. Steps or small ramp into main garden.

50 ROWLEY HOUSE FARM

Croxton, Stafford, ST21 6PJ. Tony & Beryl Roe, 01630 620248. *4m W of Eccleshall. Between Eccleshall & Loggerheads on B5026. At Wetwood Xrds turn for Fairoak. Take 1st L turn & continue for ¾m.* **Visits by arrangement June & July. Max 50 visitors.**
Quiet country garden, part reclaimed from farm rick-yard. Shrub roses in orchard, soft fruits, vegetables and water feature incl. Extensive views towards the Wrekin and Welsh hills from adjacent land at 570ft, with plantings of 130 varieties of 7 species of ilex, various corylus and specimen trees. Small water feature. Teas in aid of St. Paul's Church. Croxton. Wheelchair access - ground firm when dry.

51 56 ST AGNES ROAD

Birmingham, B13 9PN. Michael & Alison Cullen. *3m from city centre. From Moseley T-lights take St Mary's Row which becomes Wake Green Rd. After ½m turn R into St Agnes Rd and L at the church. Number 56 is approx 200 metres on L.* **Sun 22 July (1-5.30). Adm £3, chd free.**
Immaculately maintained, medium-sized, urban garden with curving borders surrounding a formal lawn punctuated with delicate acers and contemporary sculpture. Seating by a Victorian-style fish pond with a fountain and waterfall offers a peaceful setting to enjoy the tranquillity of this elegant garden.

52 23 ST JOHNS ROAD

Rowley Park, Stafford, ST17 9AS. Fiona Horwath, 07908 918181, fiona_horwath@yahoo.co.uk. *½m S of Stafford Town Centre. Just a few minutes from J13 M6, towards Stafford. After approx 2m turn L into St. John's Rd after bus-stop.* **Sun 18 Mar (2-5). Combined adm with 29 St John's Road £5, chd free. Home-made teas. Thur 19 Apr (2-5). Adm £4, chd free. Home-made teas. Evening opening Fri 18 May (6.30-9). Combined adm with 29 St John's Road £7, chd free. Wine. Fri 8 June (2-5). Adm £4, chd free. Home-made teas. Wine and nibbles incl in adm Friday 18 May. Visits also by arrangement Mar to Sept groups of 10+.**
Pass through the black and white gate of this Victorian house into a part-walled gardener's haven. Bulbs and shady woodlanders in Spring and masses of herbaceous plants and climbers. Sit and enjoy home-made cakes by the pond or Victorian-style greenhouse. Gardener is keen Hardy Plant Society member and sows far too many seeds, so always something good for sale! Our new outdoor kitchen is great for refreshments! The waterlily wildlife pond remains - with the greenhouses - the beating heart of the garden. A growing interest in alpines is leading to a proliferation of troughs. Whilst ferns, the quiet green stars of shady areas are also increasing in number! Featured in Staffordshire Life and Weekend Telegraph.

53 29 ST JOHN'S ROAD

Rowley Park, Stafford, ST17 9AP. Mrs Carol Shanahan, 07831 453130, shanahanfamily@hotmail.com. *1m from Stafford town centre, 2m from M6 J13. 2m on A449 to Stafford from M6 J13, turn L through the gates into St Johns Rd. From Stafford A449 towards Wolverhampton, 1st R after railway bridge. Private Park, please park considerately.* **Sun 18 Mar (2-5). Combined adm with 23 St Johns Road £5, chd free. Home-made teas. Evening opening Fri 18 May (6.30-9). Combined adm with 23 St Johns Road £7, chd free. Wine. May opening incl a glass of wine and nibbles. Visits also by arrangement Mar to Sept groups of 10+.**
Against a backdrop of mature Hornbeams there are 2 acres of informal garden made up of many complementary areas. View the wooded 'dingly dell', colourful terraces, abundant kitchen garden, bronze armillary, water features, circular lawns plus the roses and clematis that scramble through the trees. Don't miss the working area of the garden for the most upmarket compost bins – all made from decking. The majority of the garden is accessible by wheelchair and there are ramps at most of the steps.

54 THE SECRET GARDEN

3 Banktop Cottages, Little Haywood, ST18 0UL. Derek Higgott & David Aston, 01889 883473, poshanddeks@gmail.com. *5m SE of Stafford. A51 from Rugeley or Weston signed Little Haywood A513 Stafford Coley Lane, Back Lane R into Coley Grove. Entrance 50 metres on L.* **Wed 23 May (11-4). Adm £4. Fri 1, Sun 17 June, Wed 1 Aug (11-4). Adm £4, chd free. Home-made teas. Visits also by arrangement May to Aug.**
Wander past the other cottage gardens and through the evergreen arch and there before you a fantasy for the eyes and soul. Stunning garden approx ½ acre, created over the last 30yrs. Strong colour theme of trees and shrubs, underplanted with perennials, 1000 bulbs and laced with clematis; other features incl water, laburnum and rose tunnel and unique buildings. Is this the jewel in the crown? Raised gazebo with wonderful views over untouched meadows and Cannock Chase. Wheelchair access - some slopes.

55 TANGLEWOOD COTTAGE

Crossheads, Colwich, Stafford, ST18 0UG. Dennis & Helen Wood, 01889 882857, shuvitdog@gmail.com. *5m SE of Stafford. A51 Rugeley/Weston R into Colwich. Church on L school on R, under bridge R into Crossheads Lane follow railway approx ¼ m (it does lead somewhere). Parking signed on grass opp brick kiln cottage.* **Sun 20 May (10.30-3). Adm £3, chd free. Light lunches and home made cakes. Visits also by arrangement May to July for groups 15+. Catering requirements on request, home-made cakes and lunches.**

A tranquil country cottage garden. Including koi carp pool, vegetables, fruit, chickens, and an array of wonderful perennials. Meander through the different rooms. sit in the courtyard and enjoy Helen's home-made fayre - cakes and meals. Year on year people spend many hours relaxing with us and don't forget Charlie the parrot - be warned he can be naughty! Art/jewellery/crafts/book sales. Annual HPS Plant fair usually on same weekend. Past Staffordshire in bloom winners Best large garden winners. Lots of gravel paths, people with walking sticks seem to manage quite well. Wheelchairs would have difficulty.

56 NEW 49 THE PLANTATION

Pensnett, Brierley Hill, DY5 4RT. Dave & Kath Baker. *Brierley Hill. From Russells Hall Hospital, take Pensnett High St (A4101) to Kingswinford. After 1½ m turn L into The Plantation. Please park with consideration.* **Sun 3 June, Sun 2 Sept (11-5.30). Adm £3, chd free. Home-made teas.**

Small suburban garden 60 ft x 30 ft with lots of roses, hemerocallis, well stocked borders and fruit trees. Greenhouse with tomatoes, cucumbers and grape vine. Productive vegetable garden.

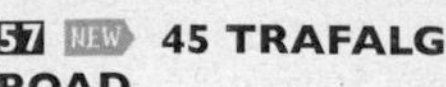

57 NEW 45 TRAFALGAR ROAD

Moseley, Birmingham, B13 8BJ. Mr & Mrs David & Linda Isgrove. *Don't follow SatNav at the end: it takes you into a Close nearby. Watch out for yellow signs to our house (45 Trafalgar Rd) which is opposite number 24.* **Sun 13 May (1.30-5). Combined adm with Cats Whiskers £5, chd free. Home-made teas.**

Mature grape arbour looks down onto the lawn and two very different mature herbaceous borders, one north-facing and one south. Unusual curved hedge adds perspective inviting exploration of the beautiful pond and bog garden that lie beyond. Hard landscaping scavenged from Moseley buildings provides a 'potted' history of the built environment. Look out for intriguing bricks embedded with a Star of David. Wheelchair access onto top patio but to get to lawn and rest of garden there is either a steep ramp 31ins (79cms) wide or a series of low steps.

58 ◆ THE TRENTHAM ESTATE

Stone Road, Stoke-on-Trent, ST4 8JG. Michael Walker, 01782 646646, enquiry@trentham.co.uk, www.trentham.co.uk. *M6 J15. Well signed on r'about, A34 with A5035.* **For NGS: Wed 17 Jan, Wed 28 Mar (10-10.30am). Adm £6, chd free. Evening opening Wed 13 June, Wed 19 Sept (5.30-6). Adm £6.25, chd free. For other opening times and information, please phone, email or visit garden website.**

Trentham Gardens has undergone a major programme of restoration which has both revealed the historic landscape designed by Capability Brown and is replenishing this with vast new contemporary plantings of annuals, perennials, trees and shrubs. NGS Special Openings with Trenthams' Head of Garden and Estate, Michael Walker, and Garden Team Manager, Carol Adams, will provide a complimentary tour of the recently revealed areas around Browns mile long lake at 10am Wed 17 Jan and 28 March, and at 5.30pm 13 June and 19 Sept.

59 41 TWENTYLANDS

Rolleston-on-Dove, Burton-on-Trent, DE13 9AJ. Maureen & Joe Martin, 01283 520208, joe.martin11@btinternet.com. *3m E of Tutbury. At r'about on Tutbury by-pass A511 take 1st exit, continue through Rolleston-on-Dove, past Scout HQ. Twentylands on R, opp the Jinny Inn. From A38 take turn off to Stretton continue to Rolleston.* **Sat 21 July (1-5.30). Adm £3, chd free. Light refreshments. Visits also by arrangement May to Sept min 6 max 20. Teas.**

Small back garden. Every corner used and packed with plants. Herbaceous borders with fruit trees and shrubs. Herb corner, fernery, bog garden with many candelabra primula, in Spring, and other bog plants. Chinese garden with chess pavilion and bonsai, water features, small pond with lilys, wood carvings, greenhouses, Water harvesting and composting systems. living roof. Tutbury Castle, Blue Cross Horse Sanctuary and Jinny Nature Trail nearby. Wheelchair access to patio overlooking garden.

60 VERNON HOUSE

26, Vernon Road, Edgbaston, Birmingham, B16 9SH. Dr & Mrs Steve & Chris Smith. *2m W of Birmingham city centre. Take the A456 (Hagley Rd). If arriving from E (Birmingham) turn R in to Portland Rd, then 2nd R onto Vernon Rd. If arriving from W (M5) turn L in to Rotton Park Rd, then 2nd R (exit 3) onto Vernon Rd.* **Sun 22 July (12-4.30). Adm £3.50, chd free. Light refreshments.**

A large (over ⅓ acre) but secluded city garden framed by mature trees. There are extensive lawns and herbaceous borders with a wide range of planting creating several distinct areas. Decks, pergolas and patios offer a variety of places to sit and reflect. Featuring an ornamental koi pond, a wildlife pond with bog garden, a unique holly hedge and an original Victorian conservatory. Three small steps up to patio areas and a further 3 steps to access main garden.

61 19 WATERDALE

Compton, Wolverhampton, WV3 9DY. Anne & Brian Bailey, 01902 424867, m.bailey1234@btinternet.com, www.facebook.com/pages/Garden-of-Surprises/165745816926408. *1½m W of Wolverhampton city centre. From Wolverhampton Ring Rd take A454 towards Bridgnorth for 1m. Waterdale is on L off A454 Compton Rd West.* **Sun 3 June, Sun 1 July (12.30-5.30). Combined adm with 12 Waterdale £5, chd free. Home-made teas. Visits also by arrangement May to Aug for groups of 10-35.**

A romantic garden of surprises, which gradually reveals itself on a journey through deep, lush planting, full of unusual plants. From the sunny, flower filled terrace, a ruined folly emerges from a luxuriant fernery and leads into an oriental garden, complete with tea house. Towering bamboos hide the way to the gothic summerhouse and mysterious shell grotto. Winner of Daily Mail National Garden Competition. Summerhouse and grotto featured in 'Amazing Spaces - Shed of the Year' TV programme. Filmed for Gardeners' World TV series.

62 12 WATERDALE

Compton, Wolverhampton, WV3 9DY. Mr & Mrs Colin Bennett. *1½m W of Wolverhampton city centre. From Wolverhampton Ring Rd take A454 towards Bridgnorth for 1m. Waterdale is on the L off A454 Compton Rd West.* **Sun 3 June, Sun 1 July (12.30-5.30). Combined adm with 19 Waterdale £5, chd free.**

A riot of colour welcomes visitors to this quintessentially English garden. The wide central circular bed and side borders overflow with classic summer flowers, including the tall spires of delphiniums, lupins, irises, campanula, poppies and roses. Clematis tumble over the edge of the decked terrace, where visitors can sit among pots of begonias and geraniums to admire the view over the garden.

63 NEW WHITE WOOD LODGE

Sich Lane, Yoxall, Burton-On-Trent, DE13 8NS. Mr & Mrs Michael &Victoria Riley, 01543 472262, vicki-riley@hotmail.com. *From A38 Lichfield or Derby. Exit for Barton under Needwood, straight through village in direction of Yoxall. After little India on R go straight for 2m. Sich Lane 1st R. 1m down lane to Lodge.* **Sat 19, Sun 20 May, Sun 12, Sun 19 Aug (12-4.30). Adm £4, chd free. Cream teas. Visits also by arrangement May to Aug.**

With panoramic views of stunning Staffordshire countryside, this garden offers a collection of various mature shrubs and flowers. Including hanging baskets and unusual planters with all their spectacular colours, hosta and rose beds, a large pond filled with carp, Peter Rabbit vegetable and herb garden, mediterranean patio, wandering peacocks and a tearoom serving Peggy Porschen recipe cakes. Full disabled access to tearoom and WC. Most of paths have free access for wheelchairs.

The Old Vicarage

64 THE WICKETS

47 Long Street, Wheaton Aston, ST19 9NF. Tony & Kate Bennett, 01785 840233, ajtonyb@talktalk.net. *8m W of Cannock, 10m N of Wolverhampton, 10m E of Telford. M6 J12 W towards Telford on A5; 3m R signed Stretton; 150yds L signed Wheaton Aston; 2m L; over canal, garden on R or at Bradford Arms on A5 follow signs.* **Sun 22 July, Thur 23, Sun 26 Aug (1.30-5). Adm £3, chd free. Home-made teas. Visits also by arrangement July & Aug.**
There's a delight around every corner and lots of quirky features in this most innovative garden. Its themed areas include a fernery, grasses bed, hidden gothic garden, succulent theatre, cottage garden beds and even a cricket match! It will certainly give you ideas for your own garden as you sit and enjoy our acclaimed tea and cake. Wheelchair access - two single steps in garden and 2 gravel paths.

Donations from the National Garden Scheme help Parkinson's UK care for more people

65 WILD THYME COTTAGE

Woodhouses, Barton Under Needwood, Burton-On-Trent, DE13 8BS. Ray & Michele Blundell. *B5016 Midway between villages of Barton & Yoxall. From A38 through Barton Village B5016 towards Yoxall. Or from A513 at Yoxall centre take Town Hill sign for Barton. Garden is at Woodhouses, approx 2m from either village.* **Sat 28 Apr, Sat 27 Oct (10.30-4.30). Adm £4, chd free. Light refreshments.**
The garden surrounds a self built timber frame house now 20 years old and extends to ⅓ acre. There is a collection of over 120 Japanese Maples with other rare semi mature White bark Birch trees, shrubs and herbaceous perennials. Newly developed large beds of Ornamental grasses with taller perennials. Specialist growers of Zantedeschia (Arum Lily's). Plants sales. Newly constructed Lychgate entrance. Ornamental grasses. Rare trees and shrubs. Featured in Daily Mail and Gardeners World. Partial wheelchair access on gravel and grass.

66 WILD WOOD LODGE

Bushton Lane, Anslow, Burton-On-Trent, DE13 9QL. Richard & Dorothy Ward, 01283 812100, poplarsfarm@breathe.com. *Bushton Lane is signed in centre of village. Wild Wood Lodge is ¼m down Bushton Lane.* **Sun 10 June, Sun 12 Aug (1.30-5). Adm £3.50, chd free. Home-made teas. Visits also by arrangement June to Sept any numbers welcome.£6 per head incl tea/coffee and cakes.**
Covering approx 2 acre it consists of a productive orchard with apples,pears and plums. A Soft Fruit Garden with Raspberries and Strawberries etc., a wide selection of vegetables on raised beds, colourful herbaceous borders, shrubs, ornamental trees, wild life pond and fishing lake. The Garden was overall winner in the Staffs. Agricultural Societies Farm Garden Competition 2016. Teas in aid of Notts City Hospital Leukaemia Appeal. Level garden, wide paths.

67 WOODBROOKE QUAKER STUDY CENTRE

1046 Bristol Road, Selly Oak, B29 6LJ. Woodbrooke Quaker Study Centre, 0121 472 5171, enquiries@woodbrooke.org.uk, www.woodbrooke.org.uk. *6m SW of Birmingham. On A38 Bristol Rd, S of Selly Oak, opp Witherford Way.* **Sun 17 June (1-4). Adm £5, chd free. Tea. Visits also by arrangement June to Sept.**
George Cadbury's former home, which includes a lake, wild area, herbaceous borders, herb garden and a walled garden, the whole area extending to 10 acres. Very fine variety of trees. Our Head Gardener and other staff will be on hand to help visitors to identify the key garden features and make the most of their visit. Garden tours and short talks will be available. Freshly baked cakes and hot drinks will be available to purchase. Some paths may be unsuitable for wheelchair access depending on the weather.

68 2 WOODLAND CRESCENT

Finchfield, Wolverhampton, WV3 8AS. Mr & Mrs Parker, 01902 332392, alisonparker1960@hotmail.co.uk. *2m SW of Wolverhampton City centre. From Inner Ring Rd take A41 W to Tettenhall. At junction with A459 turn L onto Merridale Rd. Straight over Bradwell Xrds then R onto Trysull Rd. 3rd R onto Coppice Rd & 1st R onto Woodland Crescent.* **Sat 16, Sun 17 June (11.30-5). Adm £3, chd free. Home-made teas and cakes. Visits also by arrangement June & July. Groups of 10 to 25 welcome.**
A semi-detached townhouse garden 120 x 25 ft, every inch packed with perennials, trees, shrubs, roses, hostas and clematis. Wildlife pond and nesting boxes to attract birds. Productive vegetable and fruit garden. Informal style but clipped box and topiary add some formality.

19 Waterdale

GROUP OPENING

69 WOODLEIGHTON GROVE GARDENS

Woodleighton Grove, Uttoxeter, ST14 8BX. 01889 563930, graham&judy.white@ngs.org.uk. *SE of Uttoxeter. From Uttoxeter take B5017 (Marchington). Go over Town Bridge, 1st exit at r'about, then 3rd exit at r'about into Highwood Rd, After ¼m turn R.* **Visits by arrangement only, between 11 Jun & 13 Jul, min 12 persons Adm £7 (which includes Refreshments).**

At the end of a quiet cul-de-sac in the Staffordshire market town of Uttoxeter, two next door neighbours will be delighted to welcome visitors to their intriguing and highly acclaimed Woodleighton Grove Gardens. For 2018, the gardens will not be holding any Public Open Days, but will still accept bookings from Clubs, Organisations, Societies etc., for Private Group Visits by Arrangement. Featured on ITV Central and BBC Radio Derby.

70 NEW WOODSIDE FARM

Clamgoose Lane, Kingsley Moor, Stoke-On-Trent, ST10 2EG. Mr & Mrs Garry & Alison Szafranski, 07841 501666, garry.szafranski@btinternet.com. *Approx 3m N of the market town of Cheadle. Access to Clamgoose Lane via A52 is preferable then Woodside Farm is approx 400m on L. Can also be accessed via A522 follow the lane for about 1m. Garden on R.* **Sun 17 June, Sun 15 July, Sun 19 Aug (11.30-4). Adm £4, chd free. Home-made teas. Visits also by arrangement May to Sept £4 pp. Min charge £80 if less than 20 people. Teas extra.**

Situated along a quite lane is a 3 acre garden developed over the last 10 years featuring a wild flower meadow with newly planted specimen trees that leads on past the chicken and pig enclosures into the large ornamental vegetable garden and cut flower beds large herbaceous border and newly planted orchard. The house is fronted by a bustling cottage garden and box parterre with ornamental pond. Parking is in the adjoining field and there are some gravel paths.

71 YARLET HOUSE

Yarlet, Stafford, ST18 9SD. Mr & Mrs Nikolas Tarling. *2m S of Stone. Take A34 from Stone towards Stafford, turn L into Yarlet School & L again into car park.* **Fri 22 June (9.30-1.30). Adm £4, chd free. Home-made teas.** Donation to Staffordshire Wildlife Trust.

4 acre garden with extensive lawns, walks, lengthy herbaceous borders and traditional Victorian box hedge. Water gardens with fountain and rare lilies. Sweeping views across Trent Valley to Sandon. Victorian School Chapel. 9 hole putting course. Boules pitch. Yarlet School Art Display. Gravel paths.

72 YEW TREE COTTAGE

Podmores Corner, Long Lane, White Cross, Haughton, ST18 9JR. Clive & Ruth Plant, 07591 886925, pottyplantz@aol.com. *4m W of Stafford. Take A518 W Haughton, turn R Station Rd (signed Ranton) 1m, then turn R at Xrds ¼m on R.* **Sun 6 May (2-5); Thur 10 May (11-4). Every Thur 5 July to 19 July (11-4). Sun 22 July (2-5). Adm £3.50, chd free. Home-made teas. Visits also by arrangement May to July.**

Hardy Plant Society member's garden brimming with unusual plants. All-yr-round interest incl Meconopsis, Trillium, and Arisaema. National Collection Dierama flowering in July. ½-acre incl gravel, borders, vegetables and plant sales area. Covered courtyard with oak-timbered vinery to take tea in if the weather is unkind, and seats in the garden for lingering on sunny days. Wheelchair access - level access, grass and paved paths, some narrow and some gravel.

NPC

SUFFOLK

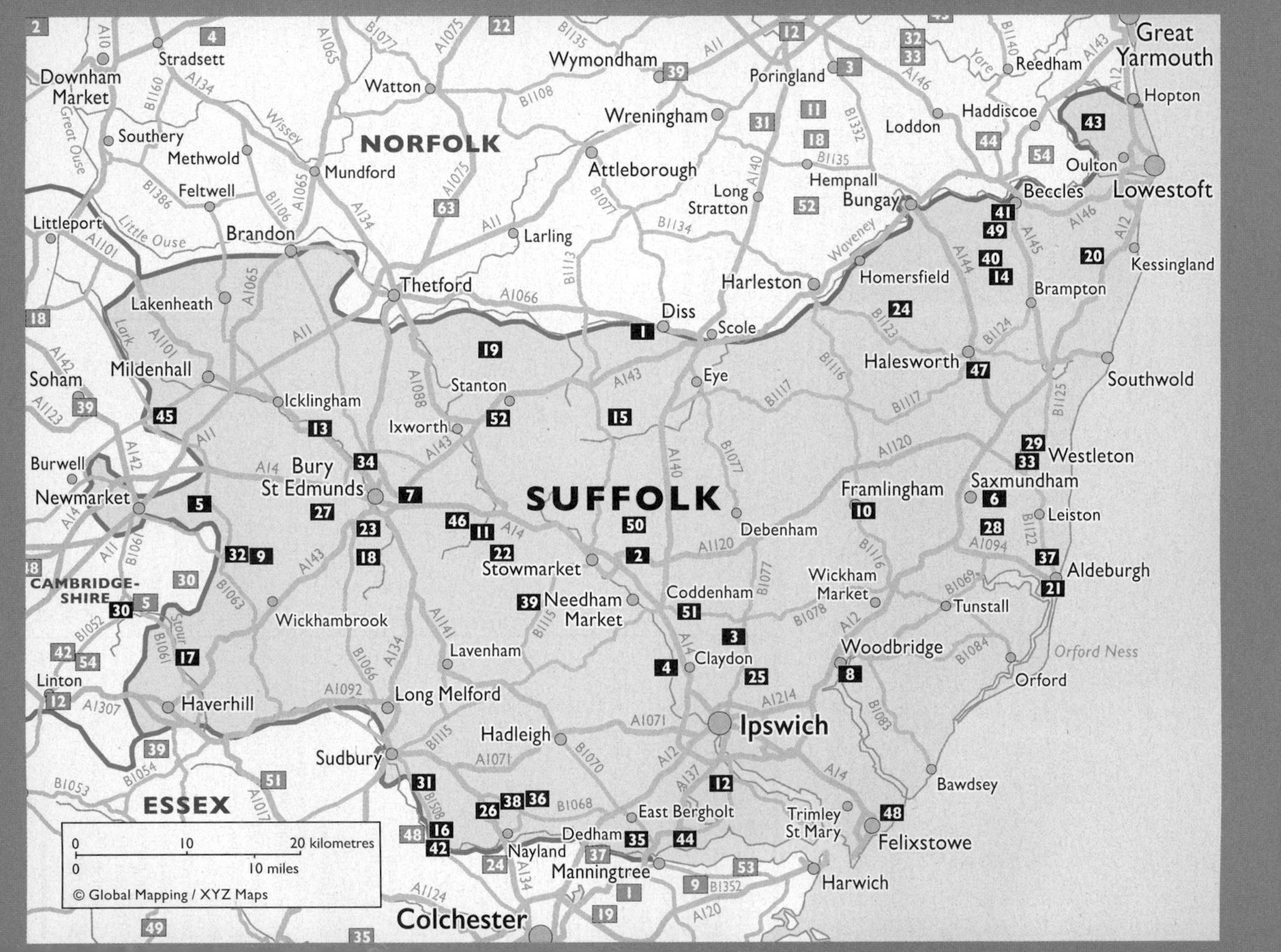

SUFFOLK
NORFOLK
ESSEX
CAMBRIDGE-SHIRE
Great Yarmouth
Hopton
Lowestoft
Kessingland
Southwold
Westleton
Leiston
Aldeburgh
Orford Ness
Orford
Saxmundham
Tunstall
Bawdsey
Felixstowe
Harwich
Woodbridge
Wickham Market
Framlingham
Halesworth
Brampton
Beccles
Oulton
Reedham
Haddiscoe
Loddon
Bungay
Homersfield
Hempnall
Poringland
Harleston
Long Stratton
Scole
Diss
Eye
Debenham
Coddenham
Claydon
Ipswich
Trimley St Mary
East Bergholt
Dedham
Manningtree
Nayland
Colchester
Hadleigh
Needham Market
Stowmarket
Wymondham
Wreningham
Attleborough
Larling
Thetford
Stanton
Ixworth
Bury St Edmunds
Lavenham
Long Melford
Sudbury
Wickhambrook
Haverhill
Watton
Mundford
Brandon
Icklingham
Lakenheath
Mildenhall
Methwold
Feltwell
Stradsett
Southery
Downham Market
Littleport
Soham
Burwell
Newmarket
Linton
Great Ouse
Little Ouse
Lark
Wissey
Waveney
Yare
Stour
0 10 20 kilometres
0 10 miles
© Global Mapping / XYZ Maps

Suffolk has so much to offer – from charming coastal villages, ancient woodlands and picturesque valleys – there is a landscape to suit all tastes.

Keen walkers and cyclists will enjoy Suffolk's low-lying, gentle countryside, where fields of farm animals and crops reflect the county's agricultural roots.

Stretching north from Felixstowe, the county has miles of Heritage Coast set in an Area of Outstanding Natural Beauty. The Suffolk coast was the inspiration for composer Benjamin Britten's celebrated work, and it is easy to see why.

To the west and north of the county are The Brecks, a striking canvas of pine forest and open heathland, famous for its chalky and sandy soils – and one of the most important wildlife areas in Britain.

A variety of gardens to please everyone open for Suffolk NGS, so come along on an open day and enjoy the double benefit of a beautiful setting and supporting wonderful charities.

Volunteers

County Organiser
Jenny Reeve
01638 715289
jenny.reeve@ngs.org.uk

County Treasurer
David Reeve
01638 715289
dreeve43@gmail.com

Publicity
Jenny Reeve
(as above)

Booklet Co-ordinator
Adrian Simpson-James
01502 710555
adriansimpsonjames@gmail.com

Assistant County Organisers
Gilly Beddard
01394 450468
gbedd@btinternet.com

Frances Boscawen
01728 638768
francesboscawen@gmail.com

Michael Cole
01473 272920
michael.m.d.cole@btinternet.com

Yvonne Leonard
01638 712742
yj.leonard@btinternet.com

Jake Lovick
07957 111935
jlovick@hotmail.com

Marie-Anne Mackenzie
01728 831155
marieanne_mackenzie@yahoo.co.uk

Barbara Segall
01787 312046
barbara@bsegall.com

Peter Simpson
01787 249845
bergholt2002@btopenworld.com

Left: **Freston House**

OPENING DATES

All entries subject to change. For latest information check **www.ngs.org.uk**

Map locator numbers are shown to the right of each garden name.

February

Snowdrop Festival

Sunday 18th
◆ Blakenham Woodland Garden 4
Gable House 14

March

Sunday 11th
Woodwards 51

Sunday 25th
The Laburnums 24

April

Monday 2nd
Woodwards 51

Sunday 8th
Great Thurlow Hall 17
◆ The Place for Plants, East Bergholt Place Garden 35

Sunday 15th
Cattishall Farmhouse 7
Helyg 19

Sunday 22nd
Ousden House 32

Sunday 29th
◆ Blakenham Woodland Garden 4
Moat House 27
◆ The Place for Plants, East Bergholt Place Garden 35

May

Sunday 6th
NEW Mulberry House, Westleton 29
Rosedale 42

Sunday 13th
NEW Cumberland House 8
◆ Fullers Mill Garden 13
NEW Hawstead Place 18
NEW Horsecroft Hall 23
Street Farm 45
41 Westmorland Road 48

Sunday 20th
The Priory 38

Sunday 27th
Berghersh Place 3
NEW Freston House 12

Monday 28th
Holm House 22
Leaven Hall 26
Woodwards 51

June

Festival Weekend

Saturday 2nd
◆ Wyken Hall 52

Sunday 3rd
Great Thurlow Hall 17
◆ Wyken Hall 52

Wednesday 6th
◆ Somerleyton Hall Gardens 43

Sunday 10th
Drinkstone Park 11
Wood Farm, Gipping 50

Sunday 17th
NEW Moor Farm 28

Saturday 23rd
Larks' Hill 25

Sunday 24th
Old Rectory House 31
5 Parklands Green 34
Priors Oak 37

July

Sunday 1st
Drinkstone Park 11
NEW Spinners Lodge 44

Saturday 7th
NEW Paget House 33
White House Farm 49

Sunday 8th
NEW Paget House 33
Woodwards 51

Sunday 15th
Drinkstone Park 11
Redisham Hall 40

Sunday 22nd
Great Bevills 16
NEW 5 Ringsfield Road 41

Tuesday 24th
Woodwards 51

Sunday 29th
Batteleys Cottage 1
Rosedale 42

August

Saturday 4th
Gislingham Gardens 15

Sunday 5th
Gislingham Gardens 15
Henstead Exotic Garden 20
Trinity House 46

Tuesday 14th
Woodwards 51

Sunday 26th
Woodwards 51

Monday 27th
Holm House 22

September

Sunday 2nd
Leaven Hall 26
Wenhaston Grange 47

Sunday 9th
11 Brookside 5
By the Crossways 6

Sunday 16th
Heron House 21

Saturday 22nd
The Old Rectory 30

October

Sunday 7th
◆ Fullers Mill Garden 13
◆ The Place for Plants, East Bergholt Place Garden 35

By Arrangement

Batteleys Cottage 1
Bays Farm 2
11 Brookside 5
By the Crossways 6
Dip-on-the-Hill 9
28 Double Street 10
Drinkstone Park 11
Gable House 14
Helyg 19
Heron House 21
Larks' Hill 25
Moat House 27
NEW Paget House 33
5 Parklands Green 34
Polstead Mill 36
Priors Oak 37
1 Redbricks 39
Redisham Hall 40
41 Westmorland Road 48
White House Farm 49
Wood Farm, Gipping 50
Woodwards 51

Your visit helps fund 389 Marie Curie Nurses

THE GARDENS

1 BATTELEYS COTTAGE

The Ling, Wortham, Diss, IP22 1ST. Mr & Mrs Andy & Linda Simpson, 07949 204820, lindaruth11@gmail.com. *3m W of Diss. Turn signed from A143 Diss/Bury Rd at Wortham. By church turn R at T-junction. At top of hill turn L. Go down hill & round sharp L corner.* **Sun 29 July (1-5.30). Adm £4, chd free. Home-made teas. Visits also by arrangement May to July refreshments available for groups on request.**

A varied one acre garden planted for abundance in all seasons. Formality and informality, a mix of winding bark paths, light and shade, secluded spots to sit, new vistas at every turn. Fitting into its rural setting, it supports a wealth of bird life. There is a diversity of planting in densely planted borders as well as pots, sculptures, meadow, ponds, stream and vegetable areas to inspire you. Wheelchair access to most parts of the garden, gravel, grass and bark paths.

2 BAYS FARM

Forward Green, Earl Stonham, Stowmarket, IP14 5HU. Richard & Stephanie Challinor, 01449 711286, stephanie@baysfarmsuffolk.co.uk, www.baysfarmgardens.co.uk. *3½m E of Stowmarket. J50 A14, take A1120 direction Stowupland. Proceed through Stowupland on A1120 for 1m, at sharp L bend turn R signed Broad Green. 1st house on R.* **Visits by arrangement Apr to Sept refreshments will be available for groups whatever the size. Adm £3.50, chd free. Light refreshments.**

Bays Farm is an all year interest garden and will be opening only for groups during 2018. Groups large or small are encouraged to call or email to visit at any time during the year when it suits them. Visitors will see for themselves how this true plantsman's garden changes from month to month in not only the formal flower beds but also the progress in the greenhouses, kitchen gardens and orchard. Formal gardens designed by Chelsea Gold Medal winner, Xa Tollemache of Helmingham Hall and recently redesigned moat. Gravel paths, uneven surfaces.

3 BERGHERSH PLACE

Berghersh Drive, Witnesham, Ipswich, IP6 9EZ. Mr & Mrs T C Parkes. *Farm entrance on bend of B1077 N of Witnesham village. Approx 1m S of Ashbocking Xrds. Concrete drive entrance on sharp bend so please drive slowly. Turn in between North Lodge & Berghersh House.* **Sun 27 May (12-5). Adm £4, chd free. Home-made teas.**

Peaceful walled and hedged gardens surround elegant Regency house (not open) among fields above the Fynn Valley. Circular walk from the farm buildings, around house with lawns and mature trees to a pretty view of the valley. Mound, ponds, bog area and orchard paddock. Informal family garden with shrub and perennial beds. Garden created over last 20 years by current owner. Parking for elderly and disabled at end of farmyard close to family garden. Most areas are accessible to disabled visitors.

4 ◆ BLAKENHAM WOODLAND GARDEN

Little Blakenham, Ipswich, IP8 4LZ. M & M Blakenham, 07760 342131, www.blakenhamwoodlandgarden.org.uk. *4m NW of Ipswich. Follow signs at Little Blakenham, 1m off B1113 or go to Blakenham Woodland Garden web-site.* **For NGS: Sun 18 Feb, Sun 29 Apr (10-5). Adm £4, chd £2. Home-made teas, tea, coffee, cakes & plant sales are available on NGS days only.** For other opening times and information, please phone or visit garden website.

Beautiful 6 acre woodland garden with variety of rare trees and shrubs, Chinese rocks and landscape sculpture. Lovely in spring with snowdrops, daffodils, camellias, magnolias and bluebells followed by roses in early summer. Woodland Garden open from 1 March to 31 July. Donations to NGS on NGS days. For groups of ten or more on other days ring 07789 268552 for special arrangements. Partial wheelchair access.

Paget House

5 11 BROOKSIDE

Moulton, Newmarket, CB8 8SG. Elizabeth Goodrich & Peter Mavroghenis, 07973 622136, goodrichelizabeth1@gmail.com. *Near the Packhorse Bridge & Pub. 3m due E of Newmarket on B1085.* **Sun 9 Sept (2-5). Adm £4, chd free. Home-made teas. Visits also by arrangement June to Oct.**

1½ acres over 4 levels. Traditional hedges, mature trees and roses at the front while rear garden landscaped in contemporary style. Lower terrace with water feature and fig trees. Terraced beds with ornamental grasses, knot garden, hosta courtyard. Metal retaining wall to former paddock, many specimen trees, apple espalier bordered greenhouse with kitchen garden, apples and vines.

6 BY THE CROSSWAYS

Kelsale, Saxmundham, IP17 2PL. Mr & Mrs William Kendall, 077678 24923, miranda@bythecrossways.co.uk. *2m NE of Saxmundham, just off Clayhills Rd. ½m N of town centre, turn R to Theberton on Clayhills Rd. After 1½m, 1st L to Kelsale, then turn L immed after white cottage.* **Sun 9 Sept (11-4). Adm £4, chd free. Home-made teas. We also offer soft drinks, tea and coffee. Visits also by arrangement May to Sept for groups of 10 during the week.**

3 acre wildlife garden designed as a garden within an organic farm, where wilderness areas lie next to productive beds. Large semi-walled vegetable and cutting garden, a spectacular crinkle-crankle wall. Extensive perennial planting, grasses and wild areas. Set around the owner's Edwardian family home built by suffragist ancestor. The garden is mostly flat, with paved or gravel pathways around the main house, a few low steps and extensive grass paths and lawns.

7 CATTISHALL FARMHOUSE

Cattishall, Great Barton, Bury St. Edmunds, IP31 2QT. Mrs J Mayer, 07738 936496, joannamayer42@googlemail.com. *3m NE of Bury St Edmunds. Approach Great Barton from Bury on A143 take 1st R turn to church. If travelling towards Bury take last L turn to church as you leave the village. At church bear R & follow lane to Farmhouse on R.* **Sun 15 Apr (1-5). Adm £4, chd free. Home-made teas.**

Approx 2 acre farmhouse garden enclosed by a flint wall and mature beech hedge laid mainly to lawns with both formal and informal planting and large herbaceous border. There is an abundance of roses, small wildlife pond and recently developed kitchen garden incl a wild flower area and fruit cages. Chickens, bees and a boisterous Labrador also live here. Generally flat with some gravel paths. The occasional small step.

8 NEW CUMBERLAND HOUSE

17 Cumberland Street, Woodbridge, IP12 4AH. John & Lindi Carrington. *Town centre; 6 min walk from station car park (parking charge) via Quay Street. Exit A12 at r'about southern end of Woodbridge Bypass onto B1438 (Ipswich Rd) towards Woodbridge town centre. Follow signs to station car park IP12 4AJ 1½m. no parking in Cumberland Street.* **Sun 13 May (12-5). Adm £4, chd free. Home-made teas.**

This large south facing walled garden to the rear of Grade 2* listed Cumberland House (not open) is well hidden in the town centre conservation area. Mature specimen trees (including Arbutus, Japanese cherries, Mulberry, Judas tree) and established flowering shrubs provide shady planting areas in contrast to the new drought tolerant planting schemes. A flower arranger's garden.

9 DIP-ON-THE-HILL

Ousden, Newmarket, CB8 8TW. Geoffrey & Christine Ingham, 01638 500329, gki1000@cam.ac.uk. *5m E of Newmarket; 7m W of Bury St Edmunds. From Newmarket: 1m from junction of B1063 & B1085. From Bury St Edmunds follow signs for Hargrave. Parking at village hall. Follow NGS sign at the end of the lane.* **Visits by arrangement May to Sept 15 max. Adm £4.50, chd free. Home-made teas.**

Approx one acre in a dip on a S-facing hill based on a wide range of architectural/sculptural evergreen trees, shrubs and groundcover: pines; grove of Phillyrea latifolia; 'cloud pruned' hedges; palms; large bamboo; ferns; range of kniphofia and croscosmia. Visitors may wish to make an appointment when visiting gardens nearby.

10 28 DOUBLE STREET

Framlingham, IP13 9BN. Mr & Mrs David Clark, clarkdn@btinternet.com. *250yrds from Market Hill (main square) Framlingham opp Church. Leave square from top L into Church St. Double St is 100yds on R. Car parking in main square & near to Framlingham Castle.* **Visits by arrangement May to July groups of 10+. Adm £3.50, chd free. Tea.**

A town garden featuring roses together with a wide range of perennials and shrubs. Conservatory, greenhouse, gazebo, summerhouse and terrace full of containers all add interest to the garden. Good views of Framlingham's roofscape. Fine shingle access drive with two ramps.

11 DRINKSTONE PARK

Park Road, Drinkstone, Bury St. Edmunds, IP30 9ST. Michael & Christine Lambert, 01359 272513, chris@drinkstonepark.co.uk, www.drinkstonepark.co.uk. *6m from Bury St Edmunds. E on A14 J46 turn L and the R for Drinkstone. W*

on A14 J46 turn R for Drinkstone. Turn into Park Rd. We are not in the village. Park Rd is parallel to the road that runs through the village. **Sun 10 June, Sun 1, Sun 15 July (1-5). Adm £4, chd free. Home-made teas. Visits also by arrangement May to July refreshments on request to suit group.**
Three acre garden with wildlife pond formal Koi pond, herbaceous borders, orchard, woodland and wildlife area, large productive vegetable plot with poly tunnel and greenhouses. Some gravel paths.

12 NEW FRESTON HOUSE

The Street, Freston, Ipswich, IP9 1AF. Mr & Mrs Andrew & Judith Whittle, www.frestonhouse.co.uk. *Go under the Orwell Bridge from Ipswich towards Holbrook. At the junction for Holbrook & Woolverstone, turn sharp R signed Freston. After 300m, turn L into a no through road.* **Sun 27 May (12-5). Adm £5, chd free. Home-made teas.**
20-acre garden and large Georgian rectory set in parkland, planted from 2006 onwards by the current owners. Individual colour-themed, roomed gardens, cottage garden and formal long borders with mass plantings of hundreds of shrubs and perennials. A one-acre kitchen garden, wildlife pond, winter garden, gravel garden and woodlands with over 1,000 varieties of hostas and other shade-loving plants. One of the largest collections of hostas in the country. Several roomed, coloured-themed gardens, large winter garden. Some gravel paths.

13 ◆ FULLERS MILL GARDEN

West Stow, IP28 6HD. Perennial, 01284 728888, fullersmillgarden@perennial.org.uk, www.fullersmillgarden.org.uk. *6m NW of Bury St Edmunds. Turn off A1101 Bury to Mildenhall Rd, signed West Stow Country Park, go past Country Park continue for ¼m, garden entrance on R. Sign at entrance.* **For NGS: Sun 13 May, Sun 7 Oct (2-5). Adm £4.50, chd free. Light refreshments. For other opening times and information, please phone, email or visit garden website.**
An enchanting 7 acre garden on the banks of the river Lark. A beautiful site with light dappled woodland and a plantsman's paradise of rare and unusual shrubs, perennials and marginals planted with great natural charm. Euphorbias and lilies are a particular feature with the late flowering colchicums, including many rare varieties, being of great interest in Autumn. Tea, coffee and soft drinks. Home-made cakes. Partial wheelchair access around garden.

14 GABLE HOUSE

Halesworth Road, Redisham, Beccles, NR34 8NE. John & Brenda Foster, 01502 575298, gablehouse@btinternet.com. *5m S of Beccles. A144 S from Bungay, L at St Lawrence School, 2m to Gable House. Or A12 Blythburgh, A145 to Beccles, Brampton Xrd L to Station Rd. 3m on is garden.* **Sun 18 Feb (11-4.30). Adm £4, chd free. Warming soups available and home-made teas. Visits also by arrangement June to Sept 10+.** Donation to St Peter's Church, Redisham.
We have a large collection of snowdrops, cyclamen, hellebores and other flowering plants for the Snowdrop Day in February. Many bulbs and plants will be for sale. Hot soup and home made teas available. Greenhouses contain rare bulbs and tender plants. Featured in Suffolk magazine and East Anglian Daily Times.

GROUP OPENING

15 GISLINGHAM GARDENS

Mill Street, Gislingham, IP23 8JT. *4m W of Eye. Gislingham 2½m W of A140. 9m N of Stowmarket, 8m S of Diss. Disabled parking at Ivy Chimneys.* **Sat 4, Sun 5 Aug (11-4.30). Combined adm £4, chd free. Home-made teas at Ivy Chimneys. Teas cakes and soft drinks.**

HAREBELLS
Jenny & Darrel Charles.

IVY CHIMNEYS
Iris & Alan Stanley.

2 varied gardens in a picturesque village with a number of Suffolk timbered houses. Ivy Chimneys is planted for yr round interest with ornamental trees, some topiary, exotic borders and fishpond set in an area of Japanese style. Wisteria draped pergola supports a productive vine. Also a separate ornamental vegetable garden. New for 2014 fruit trees in the front garden. Harebells, 150 yards further down Mill Street from Ivy Chimneys, was a new build property in 2013 and the garden has since been developed from scratch. The garden has a feature round lawn edged by colour themed borders. A walk through pergola leads to a productive area incl a greenhouse and raised vegetables beds, a wildlife pond and views over open countryside. Partial wheelchair access.

16 GREAT BEVILLS

Sudbury Road, Bures, CO8 5JW. Mr & Mrs G T C Probert. *4m S of Sudbury. Just N of Bures on the Sudbury rd B1508.* **Sun 22 July (2-5.30). Adm £4, chd free. Home-made teas.**
Overlooking the Stour Valley the gardens surrounding an Elizabethan manor house are formal and Italianate in style with Irish yews and mature specimen trees. Terraces, borders, ponds and woodland walks. A short drive away from Bevills visitors may wish to also see the 13thc St Stephen's Chapel with wonderful views of the Old Bures Dragon recently re-created by the owner. Woodland walks give lovely views over the Stour Valley. Gravel paths.

17 GREAT THURLOW HALL

Great Thurlow, Haverhill, CB9 7LF. Mr George Vestey. *12m S of Bury St Edmunds, 4m N of Haverhill. Great Thurlow village on B1061 from Newmarket; 3½m N of junction with A143 Haverhill/Bury St Edmunds rd.* **Sun 8 Apr, Sun 3 June (2-5). Adm £4, chd free. Home-made teas and cakes are available in Church.**

13 acres of beautiful gardens set around the River Stour, the banks of which are adorned with stunning displays of daffodil and narcissi together with blossoming trees in spring. Herbaceous borders, rose garden and extensive shrub borders come alive with colour from late spring onwards, there is also a large walled kitchen garden and arboretum.

18 NEW HAWSTEAD PLACE

Bull Lane, Pinford End, Bury St. Edmunds, IP29 5NU. Mr & Mrs R. Brown, www.suffolkbarn.co.uk. *On A143 take a L down Sharpes Lane in Horringer. At the end of Sharpes Lane the Hawstead Place drive is directly in front of you. Go down the drive & follow the signs for the Suffolk Barn.* **Sun 13 May (11-5). Combined adm with Horsecroft Hall £5, chd free. Home-made teas.**

The garden consists of a Kitchen garden, the back walled garden which is abundant with tulips and Narcissi and a small walled garden with shrubs and perennial borders. Late spring colour is provided by bulbs, tulips, alliums and camassias. The front lawn overlooks the parkland and two small borders. No steps so wheelchairs are possible and we have a disabled toilet.

19 HELYG

Thetford Road, Coney Weston, Bury St. Edmunds, IP31 1DN. Jackie & Briant Smith, 01359 220106, briant@broadsspirituality.org.uk. *From Barningham Xrds/shop turn off the B1111 towards Coney Weston & Knettishall Country Park. Helyg will be found on the L behind some large willow trees after approx 1m.* **Sun 15 Apr (2-5). Adm £3.50, chd free. Cream teas. Visits also by arrangement Apr to Sept groups 8 +.**

Just under half an acre of garden being developed for ease of maintenance and including several novel features. There is a woodland walk, raised flower and vegetable beds, small orchard, wildlife area and ponds, all planted with spring bulbs as well as a small rose garden, a lawned area and a large greenhouse. There is a composting toilet but this is not wheelchair accessible. Teas in aid of MIND. Most of the garden is wheelchair accessible with a variety of surfaces including concrete slab, gravel and wood-chip paths.

20 HENSTEAD EXOTIC GARDEN

Church Road, Henstead, Beccles, NR34 7LD. Andrew Brogan, www.hensteadexoticgarden.co.uk. *Equal distance between Beccles, Southwold & Lowestoft approx 5m. 1m from A12 turning after Wrentham (signed Henstead) very close to B1127.* **Sun 5 Aug (11-4). Adm £4, chd £1. Home-made teas.**

2 acre exotic garden featuring 100 large palms, 20+ bananas and 200 bamboo plants. 2 streams, 20ft tiered walkway leading to Thai style wooden covered pavilion. Mediterranean and jungle plants around 3 large ponds with fish. Suffolk's most exotic garden. Featured in Daily Telegraph, Daily Mail, London Metro, Saga Magazine, Gardeners World, Winner Alan Titchmarsh Britain's Best Garden.

21 HERON HOUSE

Aldeburgh, IP15 5EP. Mr & Mrs Jonathan Hale, 01728 452200, jonathanrhhale@aol.com. *At the southeastern junction of Priors Hill Rd & Park Rd. Last house on Priors Hill Rd on R, at the junction where it rejoins Park Rd.* **Sun 16 Sept (2-5). Adm £5, chd free. Visits also by arrangement May to Oct parking available.**

2 acres with views over coastline, river and marshes. Unusual trees, herbaceous beds, shrubs and ponds with waterfall in large rock garden, stream and bog garden. Interesting attempts to grow half hardy plants in the coastal micro-climate. Partial wheelchair access.

22 HOLM HOUSE

Garden House Lane, Drinkstone, Bury St. Edmunds, IP30 9FJ. Mrs Rebecca Shelley. *7m SE of Bury St Edmunds. Coming from the E exit A14 at J47, from the W J46. Follow signs to Drinkstone, then Drinkstone Green. Turn into Rattlesden Road & look for Garden House Lane. Then it is first house on L.* **Mon 28 May, Mon 27 Aug (11.30-4.30). Adm £5, chd free. Home-made teas.**

7 different areas to see: lawn with mature trees and Holm Oaks; formal garden with topiary, box hedging and borders with year round interest; rose garden; woodland walk with hellebores, camellias, rhododendrons and bulbs; cut flower garden with greenhouse and cutting beds; large kitchen garden with impressive greenhouse; and Mediterranean courtyard with mature olive tree. + Brand new lake and woodland. Much of the garden is wheelchair accessible, but not the kitchen garden.

23 NEW HORSECROFT HALL

Horsecroft, Bury St. Edmunds, IP29 5NY. Mrs Sarah Wells. *From Bury St Edmunds follow the B1066 towards Whepsted, pass Gypsy Lane on L then approx 0.25km further on take the first entrance on your L. Parking will be signed.* **Sun 13 May (11-5). Combined adm with Hawstead Place £5, chd free. Home-made teas at Hawstead Place.**

Extensive lawns sweep around the east and south sides of The Hall and the formal gardens are separated from the adjacent park land by a ha-ha. The sizeable garden has formal beds, including a shrub bank and a partially walled kitchen garden. A woodland walk surrounds a wild flower meadow and there are a number of ponds, including an ancient carp lake said to feed the monks from the Abbey. Partial wheelchair access.

24 THE LABURNUMS

The Street, St James South Elmham, Halesworth, IP19 0HN. Mrs Jane Bastow. *6m W of Halesworth, 7m E of Harleston & 6m S of Bungay. Parking at nearby village hall. For disabled parking please phone to arrange. Yellow signs from 8m out.* **Sun 25 Mar (11-5). Adm £4.50, chd free. Light refreshments. Hot/cold drinks, cakes and hot soup.**

The 1 acre garden is 25 year old and is packed with annuals, perennials, shrubs and trees and thousands of bulbs.Spring 2015 saw an extra 5,000 Snowdrops planted. The large pond has been completely refurbished and restocked with fish and plants. All year round colour ,spring bulbs, Hellebores and so much more. The conservatory houses citrus and many tender plants. Plant stall with a variety of plants and bulbs. Newly restored pond and sunken garden. Daffodil walk and thousands of Snowdrops. Featured in local newspapers and magazines, local radio. Gravel drive. Partial wheelchair access to front garden. Steps to sunken garden. Concrete path in back garden.

25 LARKS' HILL

Clopton Road, Tuddenham St Martin, IP6 9BY. Mr John Lambert, 01473 785248, jrlambert@talktalk.net. *3m NE of Ipswich. From Ipswich take B1077, go through village, take the Clopton Rd to the L, after 300 metres at the brow of the hill you will see the house. Follow the car parking signs.* **Sat 23 June (1.30-5). Adm £5, chd free. Home-made teas. Our Big Shed Café can comfortably seat thirty or so and there is additional seating outside. Sit and talk and plan what to do next. Visits also by arrangement Apr to Sept groups of 15+.**

The gardens of eight acres comprise woodland, a newly-planted conifer garden, and formal areas, and fall away from the house to the valley floor. A hill within a garden and in Suffolk at that! Hilly garden with a modern castle keep with an interesting and beautiful site overlooking the gentle Fynn valley and the village beyond. A fossil of a limb bone from a Pliosaur that lived at least sixty million years ago was found in the garden in 2013. The discovery was reported in the national press but its importance has been recognised world-wide. A booklet is available to purchase giving all the details.

Spinners Lodge

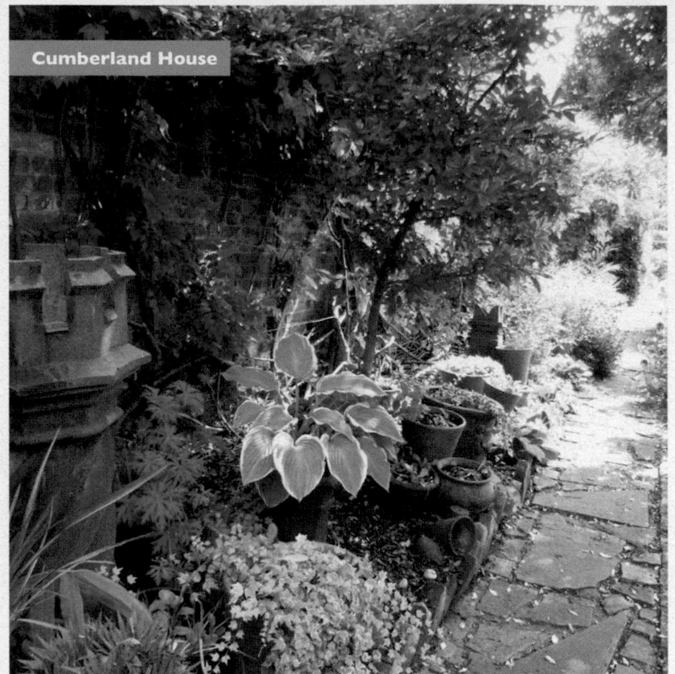
Cumberland House

26 LEAVEN HALL

Nayland Road, Leavenheath, Colchester, CO6 4PU. Mr & Mrs Mark Ellis, 01787 210579, leavenhall@btinternet.com, www.leavenhall.com. *6m W of Colchester, Essex. Off A134 in Leavenheath between church & Hare and Hounds Pub.* **Mon 28 May, Sun 2 Sept (2-5). Adm £4, chd free. Home-made teas.**

A long gravel drive leads to the wisteria and rose clad C17 house set amid 15 acres of meadows and gardens. Walled garden and a huge pond/bog garden/woodland with lawns and mature trees. There is a working vegetable/cut flower garden and peach, nectarine and apricots by the pool. Chickens, horses and pigs live here too! Featured in The Garden Magazine and Suffolk Magazine. B&B. Gravel paths, some steps by the pond and woodchips in veg/woodland areas. Grass fairly flat and can be used to reach all areas.

27 MOAT HOUSE

Little Saxham, Bury St. Edmunds, IP29 5LE. Mr & Mrs Richard Mason, 01284 810941, rnm333@live.com. *2m SW of Bury St Edmunds. Leave A14 at J42 – leave r'about towards Westley. Through Westley Village, at Xrds R towards Barrow/Saxham. After 1.3m turn L down track. (follow signs).* **Sun 29 Apr (1-5). Adm £5, chd free. Home-made teas. Suzanne's home made cakes.**

Visits also by arrangement Apr to Sept groups welcome - min 20 up to 50.

Set in a 2 acre historic and partially moated site. This tranquil mature garden has been developed over 20yrs. Bordered by mature trees the garden is in various sections incl a sunken garden, rose and clematis arbours, herbaceous borders with hydrangeas and alliums surrounded by box hedging, small arboretum. A Hartley Botanic greenhouse erected and new partere created in 2017. Featured in mamy local and national magazines.

28 NEW MOOR FARM

Friston, Saxmundham, IP17 1NH. Mr & Mrs Michael Mahony. *Moor Farm is accessed from B1121 Saxmundham Rd between Friston & Sternfield, 3m N of Snape Maltings, 5m NW of Aldeburgh & 2m SE of Saxmundham. Ample parking available at the garden.* **Sun 17 June (11-5). Adm £5, chd free. Home-made teas. There will be some tables and chairs for teas and a picnic area in the wild flower meadow.**

Large garden comprising a number of distinct areas from formal to wild with two large connected ponds and a wildlife pond. Formal gardens include lawns bordered by yew, box or beech hedging with beds featuring a variety of perennials and roses. There is woodland, a wild flower meadow and an orchard. The garden also features an avenue of hornbeams , a 'Monet' bridge over the pond and an orangery. Partial wheelchair access, gravel drive and some mown paths.

29 NEW MULBERRY HOUSE, WESTLETON

Darsham Road, Westleton, Saxmundham, IP17 3AH. Barbara Buckley & Hillas Smith. *Westleton village is approx. 2m off A12 turnoff at Yoxford heading toward the sea. It is well signed. Please park around the village & green as there is no parking at the house.* **Sun 6 May (12-5). Adm £4, chd free. Home-made teas.**

This is a completely new garden for our new home. The contemporary house in the centre of a traditional Suffolk village sits in a great space. We want to create a garden to do the architecture, the landscape and the village setting justice. It is a contemporary garden with a traditional cottage garden twist designed to be viewed as much from inside the house as from any point in the garden. Two pubs in the village do lunches. The White Horse and The Crown. Most of the garden is wheelchair accessible, there are some gravel paths but no steps. I am sorry there is no disabled parking at the property.

30 THE OLD RECTORY

Hall Lane, Brinkley, CB8 0SB. Mr & Mrs Mark Coley. *Hall Lane is a turning off Brinkley High St. At the end of Hall Lane, white gates on the R.* **Sat 22 Sept (1.30-5.30). Adm £3.50, chd free. Home-made teas in Brinkley Village Hall.**
Two acre garden started in 1973. Interesting trees showing autumn colour planted to supplement beech, yew and chestnut already there. Mixed Herbaceous borders designed for late season interest with dahlias, michaelmas daisies, japanese anemones and hydrangea. Spectacular display of cyclamen hederifolium. Tradtional Potager with box hedges. A small woodland area is still being developed. Limited wheelchair access.

31 OLD RECTORY HOUSE

Kedington Hill, Little Cornard, Sudbury, CO10 0PD. Jane & David Mann. *2½m outside Sudbury off B1508 Bures Rd. From Bures Rd follow signs to Little Cornard Parish Church. Garden is approx ½m up the lane on L. Parking opp.* **Sun 24 June (2-5). Adm £4, chd free. Home-made teas.**
An Informal country garden surrounded by meadows which are managed to encourage floral diversity and wildlife. Take a pleasant stroll through the grasses and wild flowers on seasonally mown paths. The garden includes a walled vegetable and fruit garden and greenhouse, a clipped box parterre, herbaceous borders, old roses, ponds, woodland and specimen trees. Wheelchair access - some slopes and uneven ground. Loose gravel in places.

32 OUSDEN HOUSE

Ousden, Newmarket, CB8 8TN. Mr & Mrs Alastair Robinson. *Newmarket 6m, Bury St Edmunds 8m. Ousden House stands at the west end of the village next to the Church.* **Sun 22 Apr (2-5.30). Adm £5, chd free. Home-made teas.**
A large spectacular garden with fine views over the surrounding country. Herbaceous borders, rose garden and lawns leading to Spring woodland, and lake. Additional special features include a long double crinkle-crankle yew hedge leading from the clock tower and a moat garden densely planted with hellebores,flowering shrubs and moisture loving plants. Tea is served in the house with log fires. Extensive garden on various levels not suitable for wheelchairs or people who find difficulty in walking.

33 NEW PAGET HOUSE

Back Road, Middleton, Saxmundham, IP17 3NY. Julian & Fiona Cusack, 01728 649060, julian.cusack@btinternet.com. *From A12 at Yoxford take B1122 towards Leiston. Turn L after 1.2m at Middleton Moor. After 1m enter Middleton village & drive straight ahead into Back Road.* **Sat 7, Sun 8 July (10.30-5). Adm £4, chd free. Visits also by arrangement Apr to Aug.**
The garden, started in 2012, is a wildlife friendly garden with formal planting, an orchard, a vegetable plot and areas of woodland. There are layered hedges, a pond supporting amphibians and dragonflies, a wild flower meadow and an abstract garden sculpture by local artist Paul Richardson. We record over 40 bird species each year and a good showing of butterflies and wild flowers including orchids. Gravel drive and mown paths.

34 5 PARKLANDS GREEN

Fornham St Genevieve, Bury St. Edmunds, IP28 6UH. Mrs Jane Newton, newton.jane@talktalk.net. *2m Northwest of Bury St Edmunds off B1106. Plenty of parking on the green.* **Sun 24 June (11-4). Adm £4, chd free. Home-made teas. Visits also by arrangement May to Sept.**
1½ acres of gardens developed since the 1980s for all year interest. There are mature and unusual trees and shrubs and riotous herbaceous borders. Explore the maze of paths to find 4 informal ponds, a tree house, the sunken garden, greenhouses and woodland walks. Partial wheelchair access only.

35 ◆ THE PLACE FOR PLANTS, EAST BERGHOLT PLACE GARDEN

East Bergholt, CO7 6UP. Mr & Mrs Rupert Eley, 01206 299224, sales@placeforplants.co.uk, www.placeforplants.co.uk. *2m E of A12, 7m S of Ipswich. On B1070 towards Manningtree, 2m E of A12. Situated on the edge of East Bergholt.* **For NGS: Sun 8, Sun 29 Apr (2-5). Adm £7, chd free. Sun 7 Oct (1-5). Adm £6, chd free. Home-made teas.** For other opening times and information, please phone, email or visit garden website.
20-acre garden originally laid out at the turn of the last century by the present owner's great grandfather. Full of many fine trees and shrubs, many seldom seen in East Anglia. A fine collection of camellias, magnolias and rhododendrons, topiary, and the National Collection of deciduous Euonymus. Partial Wheelchair access in dry conditions - it is advisable to telephone before visiting.

Your visit helps the Queen's Nursing Institute to champion excellence in community nursing

36 POLSTEAD MILL

Mill Lane, Polstead, Colchester, CO6 5AB. Mrs Lucinda Bartlett, 01206 265969, lucyofleisure@hotmail.com. *Between Stoke by Nayland & Polstead on the R Box. From Stoke by Nayland take rd to Polstead - Mill Lane is 1st on L & Polstead Mill is 1st house on R.* **Visits by arrangement May to Sept for groups of 10+. Adm £6.50, chd free. Home-made teas. A range of refreshments available from coffee and biscuits to full cream teas and even light lunches..**

The garden has been developed since 2002, it has formal and informal areas, a wild flower meadow and a large productive kitchen garden. The R Box runs through the garden and there is a mill pond, which gives opportunity for damp gardening, while much of the rest of the garden is arid and is planted to minimise the need for watering. Partial wheelchair access.

♿ ✿ ☕

37 PRIORS OAK

Leiston Road, Aldeburgh, IP15 5QE. Mrs Trudie Willis, 01728 452580, trudie.willis@dinkum.free-online.co.uk, www.sites.google.com/site/priorsoakbutterflygarden. *1m N of Aldeburgh on B1122. Garden on L opp RSPB Reserve.* **Sun 24 June (2-6). Adm £5, chd free. Home-made teas. Visits also by arrangement May to Sept.**

10-acre wildlife and butterfly garden. Ornamental salad and vegetable gardens with companion planting. Herbaceous borders, ferns and Mediterranean plants. Pond and wild flower acid grassland with a small wood. Skirting the wood are 100 buddleia in eccess of 30 varieties forming a perfumed tunnel. Very tranquil and fragrant garden with grass paths and yearly interest. Rich in animal and bird life. Specialist butterfly garden, as seen in SAGA magazine,and Horticulture in USA renovated railway carriages, tortoise breeding, donkeys, wildlife walks. Coaches or private visits by arrangement only.

♿ ✿ ☕

38 THE PRIORY

Stoke by Nayland, Colchester, CO6 4RL. Mr & Mrs H F A Engleheart. *5m SW of Hadleigh. Entrance on B1068 to Sudbury (NW of Stoke by Nayland).* **Sun 20 May (2-5). Adm £5, chd free. Home-made teas.**

Interesting 9 acre garden with fine views over Constable countryside; lawns sloping down to small lakes and water garden; fine trees, rhododendrons and azaleas; walled garden; mixed borders and ornamental greenhouse. Wide variety of plants. Wheelchair access over most of garden, some steps.

♿ 🐕 ✿ 🚌 ☕

39 1 REDBRICKS

Worlds End Lane, Buxhall, Stowmarket, IP14 3ED. Mr Steve Pryke, Thebuxhallgardener@hotmail.com. *5m SW of Stowmarket. From A14 take exit 50 southbound to Stowmarket. Follow A1120, turn L into A1308, then R into B1115. Follow B1115 to Great Finborough then follow NGS signs.* **Visits by arrangement May to Sept for groups of 10 to 35. Adm £4.50, chd free. Home-made teas.**

A distinctive garden of one and half acres in a rural setting. Includes several large perennial beds planted in a naturalistic style, a mature seasonal pond, a newly developed bog garden, a recently established wildlife pond, semi-formal low maintenance drought tolerant north and south facing gardens, vegetable beds, greenhouse, summerhouse, and mixed orchard.

🐕 ✿ ☕

40 REDISHAM HALL

Redisham Rd, Redisham, nr Beccles, NR34 8LZ. The Palgrave Brown Family, 01502 575894, sarah.hammond7@hotmail.co.uk. *5m S of Beccles. From A145, turn W on to Ringsfield-Bungay rd. Beccles, Halesworth or Bungay, all within 5m.* **Sun 15 July (2-6). Adm £4.50, chd free. Home-made teas. Visits also by arrangement June to Aug groups 10 min.**

C18 Georgian house (not open). 5-acre garden set in 400 acres parkland and woods. Incl 2-acre walled kitchen garden (in full production) with peach house, vinery and glasshouses. Lawns, herbaceous borders, shrubberies, ponds and mature trees. Sorry No Dogs. Redisham Hall has been opening it's gardens for the NGS for over 50 yrs. The garden has lots of gravel paths and there are lawned slopes. Wheelchair access is possible with assistance. Parking is on uneven parkland.

♿ ✿ ☕

41 NEW 5 RINGSFIELD ROAD

Beccles, NR34 9PQ. Jan & Mark Oakley. *Next to Sir John Leman High School, Beccles. Signed from Beccles town centre & the Bungay Rd/London Road T-lights.* **Sun 22 July (11-5). Adm £4, chd free. Home-made teas. Including gluten free cakes.**

Stepping around the side of this lovely Arts and Crafts home, you'll discover an acre of gorgeous colour themed garden. The herbaceous beds and borders harmonise beautifully, with sumptuous purples, cool pastels and hot scarlet collections. As you wander through the garden you'll find fun topiary and some fine specimen trees. Please park nearby at Sir John Leman High School NR34 9PG. Disabled parking and level access to the rear of the property in Ashmans Road.

♿ ✿ ☕

Mulberry House, Westleton

© Marcus Harpur

42 ROSEDALE
40 Colchester Road, Bures, CO8 5AE. Mr & Mrs Colin Lorking. *6m SE of Sudbury. From Colchester take B1508. After 10m garden on L as you enter the village, from Sudbury B1508 after 5m garden on R.* **Sun 6 May, Sun 29 July (12-5.30). Adm £3, chd free. Home-made teas.**
Approx one-third of an acre plantsman's garden developed over the last 24 years, containing many unusual plants, herbaceous borders and pond. For the May opening see a super collection of peonies and for the July opening a stunning collection of approx 60 Agapanthus in full flower.

43 ◆ SOMERLEYTON HALL GARDENS
Somerleyton, NR32 5QQ. Lord Somerleyton, 01502 734901, info@somerleyton.co.uk, www.somerleyton.co.uk. *5m NW of Lowestoft. From Norwich (30mins) - on the B1074, 7m SE of Great Yarmouth (A143). Coaches should follow signs to the rear west gate entrance.* **For NGS: Wed 6 June (10-5). Adm £6.95, chd £4.90. For other opening times and information, please phone, email or visit garden website.**
12½ acres of beautiful gardens contain a wide variety of magnificent specimen trees, shrubs, borders and plants providing colour and interest throughout the yr. Sweeping lawns and formal gardens combine with majestic statuary and original Victorian ornamentation. Highlights incl the Paxton glasshouses, pergola, walled garden and famous yew hedge maze. House and gardens remodelled in 1840s by Sir Morton Peto. House created in Anglo-Italian style with lavish architectural features and fine state rooms. All areas of the gardens are accessible, path surfaces are gravel and can be a little difficult after heavy rain. Wheelchairs available on request.

44 NEW SPINNERS LODGE

The Street, Brantham, Manningtree, CO11 1PN. Mr & Mrs Gary Calver. *From A14 take J56 on A137 towards Manningtree - follow A137 to Brantham - go up the hill pass the Brantham Bull pub on L on corner.. Spinners Lodge is 4 doors past the pub.* **Sun 1 July (10.30-5). Adm £3, chd free. Home-made teas.**

Stunning backdrop with countryside views over the River Stour - The garden has shrubs, patio with planters and collection of fuchsias, herb garden, grasses area, wildlife pond and alpine area, pebbled water feature, wisteria/grape vine pergola leading to long border and pergola with collection of fragrant roses leading into a secret garden area with shrubs and plants, vegetable and fruit area. Scenic views. Brantham Bull offers refreshments and full menu for those wishing to stay on after your visit. Wheelchairs can get onto patio/terrace area - we can provide ramp to lawn pathway but no wheelchair access to other garden areas. Disabled parking.

45 STREET FARM

North Street, Freckenham, IP28 8HY. David & Clodagh Dugdale. *3m W of Mildenhall. From Newmarket, follow signs to Snailwell, & Chippenham & then onto Freckenham.* **Sun 13 May (11-5). Adm £4, chd free. Home-made teas.**

Approx 1 acre of landscaped garden, with several mature trees. The garden includes a water cascade, pond with island and a number of bridges. Formal rose garden, rose pergola and hornbeam walk. Gravel paths with steps and slopes.

46 TRINITY HOUSE

Rectory Gardens, Beyton, Bury St. Edmunds, IP30 9UZ. Barbara & Graham Jones. *6m E of Bury St Edmunds. From West, A14 exit J46, then R at Green L at White Horse into Church Rd. After ½m park at Church on L. Follow signs for garden. From East, J46 follow Rd to White Horse, then as above.* **Sun 5 Aug (11-5). Adm £3, chd free. Home-made teas in Church Hall adjacent to Car Park. Tea, Coffee and soft drinks with home made cakes and biscuits.**

Peaceful village garden surrounded by mature trees. Meandering paths wind around beds of hydrangea, ferns and not-often seen perennials, along with several unusual trees. Fruiting Kiwi vine and climbing hydrangeas adorn the house walls. Fish Pond with lillies, rill, bog bed and tucked away 'frog' pond. Summerhouse, conservatory with exotic plants, and seating areas offer vistas over the garden. Main entrance to garden from car-park a little uneven. Access also available through Rectory Gardens, follow signs but care needed - no path on road.

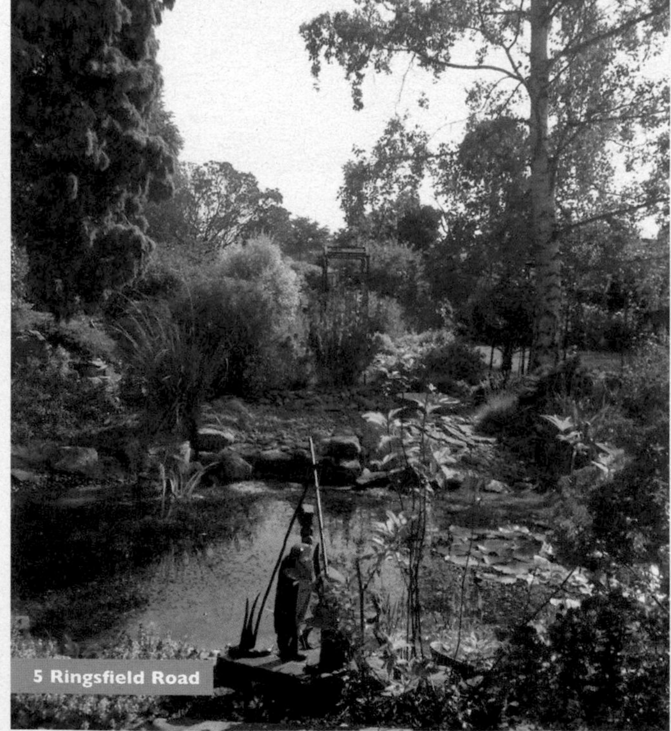

5 Ringsfield Road

47 WENHASTON GRANGE

Wenhaston, Halesworth, IP19 9HJ. Mr & Mrs Bill Barlow. *Turn SW from A144 between Bramfield & Halesworth. Take the single track rd (signed Walpole 2) Wenhaston Grange is approx ½m, at the bottom of the hill on L.* **Sun 2 Sept (11-4). Adm £5, chd free. Home-made teas.**

Over 3 acres of varied gardens on a long established site which has been extensively landscaped and enhanced over the last 15 yrs. Long herbaceous borders, old established trees and a series of garden rooms created by beech hedges. Levels and sight lines have been carefully planned. The garden is on a number of levels, with steps so wheelchair access would be difficult.

48 41 WESTMORLAND ROAD

Felixstowe, IP11 9TJ. Mr & Mrs Mick & Diane Elmes, 01394 284647, dianeelmes@talktalk.net. *Enter Felixstowe on A154. At r'about take 1st exit then turn R into*

Beatrice Avenue. L to High Road East. Proceed to Clifflands Car Park & turn L. Follow signs No. 41 is on the corner of Wrens Park. **Sun 13 May (11-5). Adm £4, chd free. Light refreshments. Cakes and savouries with a selection of drinks. Visits also by arrangement Jan to Oct for groups up to 20.**

We moved into this house in 2009 since when we have recovered the garden by taking down 21 leylandii trees and various other dead trees. It is now a perennial garden(over 400 different types of perennial plants) with interesting and eclectic features. All main areas wheelchair accessible.

♿ 🐕 ☕

49 WHITE HOUSE FARM

Ringsfield, Beccles, NR34 8JU. James & Jan Barlow, (gardener) 07780 901233, coppertops707@aol.com. *2m SW of Beccles. From Beccles take B1062 to Bungay, after 1¼ turn L signed Ringsfield. Continue for approx 1m. Parking opp church. Garden 300yds on L.* **Sat 7 July (10-4.30). Adm £4, chd free. Light refreshments. Cakes and savoury flans. Visits also by arrangement May to Sept, Tuesday - Friday, daytime or evening, not wk/ends.**

Tranquil park-type garden approx 30 acres, bordered by farmland and with fine views. Comprising formal areas, copses, natural pond, woodland walk, vegetable garden and orchard. Picnickers welcome. NB The pond and beck are unfenced. Partial wheelchair access to the areas around the house.

♿ 🐕 ✿ ☕

50 WOOD FARM, GIPPING

Back Lane, Gipping, Stowmarket, IP14 4RN. Mr & Mrs R Shelley, 07809 503019, els@maritimecargo.com. *From A14 take A1120 to Stowupland, Turn L opp Petrol Station, Turn R at T- junction, follow for approx 1m turn L at Allards Farm Shop, then imm R & follow for 1m along country lane. Wood Farm is on L.* **Sun 10 June (2-5). Adm £4, chd free. Cream teas. Large Party Barn with Facilities. Visits also by arrangement May to July for groups of 10+.**

Wood Farm is an old farm with ponds, orchards and a magnificent 8 acre wild flower meadow (with mown paths) bordered with traditional hedging, trees and woodland. The large cottage garden was created in 2011 with a number of beds planted with flowers, vegetables and topiary. Wildlife is very much encouraged in all parts of the garden (particularly bees and butterflies). Partial wheelchair access.

♿ 🐕 ✿ ☕

The National Garden Scheme is Hospice UK's largest single funder

51 WOODWARDS

Blacksmiths Lane, Coddenham, Ipswich, IP6 9TX. Marion & Richard Kenward, 01449 760639, richardwoodwards@btinternet .com. *7m N of Ipswich. From A14 turn onto A140, after ¼m take B1078 towards Wickham Market, Coddenham is on route. Coaches please use postcode IP6 9PS. Ample parking for coaches.* **Sun 11 Mar, Mon 2 Apr, Mon 28 May, Sun 8, Tue 24 July, Tue 14, Sun 26 Aug (10.30-5). Adm £3.50, chd free. Home-made teas. Visits also by arrangement Mar to Sept groups from 2 to 100+. Entrance fee £6 to include teas.**

Award winning S facing gently sloping garden of 1½ acres, overlooking the rolling Suffolk countryside. Designed and maintained by owners for yr-round colour and interest, lots of island beds, well stocked with 1000s of bulbs, shrubs and perennials, vegetable plot, display of 100+ hanging baskets for spring and summer. Well kept lawns, with large mature trees. More than 25000 bulbs have been planted over the last 3yrs for our spring display. Featured in East Anglian Daily Times, Suffolk and Norfolk Life, Suffolk Magazine and Garden News.

♿ 🐕 ✿ 🚌 ☕

52 ◆ WYKEN HALL

Stanton, IP31 2DW. Sir Kenneth & Lady Carlisle, 01359 250262, kenneth.carlisle@wykenvineyards.co.uk, www.wykenvineyards.co.uk. *9m NE of Bury St Edmunds. Along A143. Follow signs to Wyken Vineyards on A143 between Ixworth & Stanton.* **For NGS: Sat 2 June (10-6). Light refreshments in restaurant and cafe. Sun 3 June (10-6). Wine in restaurant and cafe. Adm £4, chd free. For other opening times and information, please phone, email or visit garden website.**

4-acres, with knot and herb garden, old-fashioned rose garden, kitchen and wild garden, nuttery, pond, gazebo and maze; herbaceous borders and old orchard. Woodland walk, vineyard. Restaurant and shop. Vineyard. Booking in the restaurant for lunch: 01359 250287. Farmers' Market on Saturdays 9-1.

♿ ✿ ☕

SURREY

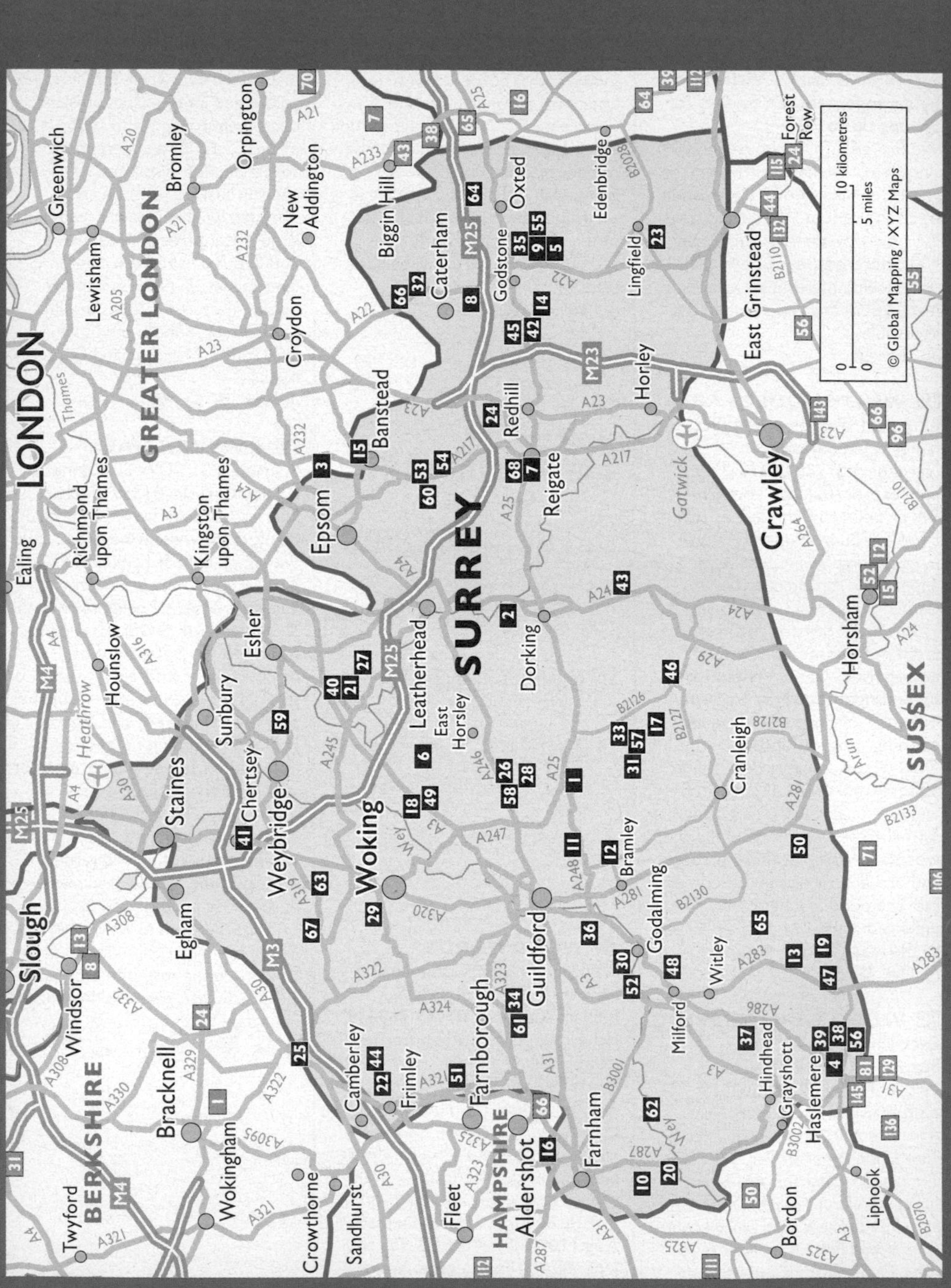

LONDON
GREATER LONDON
SURREY
BERKSHIRE
HAMPSHIRE
SUSSEX
Greenwich
Lewisham
Bromley
Orpington
Croydon
New Addington
Biggin Hill
Caterham
Godstone
Oxted
Edenbridge
Lingfield
East Grinstead
Forest Row
Richmond upon Thames
Kingston upon Thames
Ealing
Hounslow
Heathrow
Slough
Windsor
Staines
Egham
Sunbury
Chertsey
Weybridge
Esher
Epsom
Banstead
Redhill
Reigate
Horley
Gatwick
Crawley
Leatherhead
East Horsley
Dorking
Horsham
Woking
Guildford
Bramley
Godalming
Cranleigh
Milford
Witley
Hindhead
Grayshott
Haslemere
Liphook
Bordon
Farnham
Aldershot
Farnborough
Frimley
Camberley
Fleet
Sandhurst
Crowthorne
Wokingham
Bracknell
Twyford
Thames
Wey
Arun
© Global Mapping / XYZ Maps
10 kilometres
5 miles

As a designated Area of Outstanding Natural Beauty, it's no surprise that Surrey has a wealth of gardens on offer.

With its historic market towns, lush meadows and scenic rivers, Surrey provides the ideal escape from the bustle of nearby London.

Set against the rolling chalk uplands of the unspoilt North Downs, the county prides itself on extensive country estates with historic houses and ancient manors. Visitors are inspired by the breathtaking panorama from Polesden Lacey, lakeside views at The Old Croft or timeless terraces at Albury Park.

Surrey is the heartland of the NGS at Hatchlands Park and the RHS at Wisley, both promoting a precious interest in horticulture. Surrey celebrates a landscape coaxed into wonderful vistas by great gardeners such as John Evelyn, Capability Brown and Gertrude Jekyll.

With many eclectic gardens to visit, there's certainly plenty to treasure in Surrey.

Below: The Chalet

Volunteers

County Organiser
Margaret Arnott
01372 842459
m.a.arnott@btinternet.com

County Treasurer
Jean Thompson
01483 425633
norney.wood@btinternet.com

Publicity
Barbara Brooks
01428 687767
barbarabrooks@btinternet.com

Public Relations
Maxine Dyer
maxine.dyer@ngs.org.uk

Booklet Production
Barbara Brooks
(as above)

Booklet Co-ordinator
Keith Lewis
01737 210707
kandelewis@ntlworld.com

Assistant County Organisers
Anne Barnes
01306 730196
spurfold@btinternet.com

Barbara Brooks
(as above)

Penny Drew
01252 792909
penelopedrew@yahoo.co.uk

Di Grose
01883 742983
di.grose@godstone.net

Annie Keighley
01252 838660
annie.keighley12@btinternet.com

Keith Lewis
(as above)

Caroline Shuldham
01932 596960
c.m.shuldham@btinternet.com

Jean Thompson
(as above)

OPENING DATES

All entries subject to change. For latest information check **www.ngs.org.uk**

Extended openings are shown at the beginning of the month.

Map locator numbers are shown to the right of each garden name.

February

Snowdrop Festival

Sunday 11th
◆ Gatton Park 24

March

Saturday 17th
Timber Hill 63

Sunday 18th
Albury Park 1

Sunday 25th
◆ Vann 65

April

Sunday 1st
Caxton House 7
The Chalet 8

Monday 2nd
Coverwood Lakes 17

Sunday 8th
The Chalet 8
Coverwood Lakes 17
Timber Hill 63

Sunday 15th
Coverwood Lakes 17
◆ Vann 65

Monday 16th
◆ Vann 65

Tuesday 17th
◆ Vann 65

Wednesday 18th
◆ Vann 65

Thursday 19th
◆ Dunsborough Park 18

Sunday 22nd
41 Shelvers Way 53
Springwood House 56

Sunday 29th
◆ Hatchlands Park 26
Springwood House 56

May

Saturday 5th
The Garth Pleasure Grounds 23
57 Westhall Road 66

Sunday 6th
Chestnut Cottage 10
Coverwood Lakes 17
The Garth Pleasure Grounds 23
Malabar 38
57 Westhall Road 66

Monday 7th
◆ Vann 65

Tuesday 8th
◆ Vann 65

Wednesday 9th
◆ Vann 65

Thursday 10th
◆ Vann 65

Friday 11th
◆ Ramster 47
◆ Vann 65

Saturday 12th
NEW Dyers House 19
Hall Grove School 25
◆ Vann 65
Westways Farm 67

Sunday 13th
NEW Dyers House 19
26 The Fairway 22
Roe Deer Farm 48
Stuartfield 59
◆ Vann 65
Westways Farm 67

Saturday 19th
56 Copse Avenue 16

Sunday 20th
Chilworth Manor 11
56 Copse Avenue 16
◆ Dunsborough Park 18
Knowle Grange 31
The Manor House 39
◆ Titsey Place Gardens 64

Monday 21st
Chauffeur's Flat 9

Tuesday 22nd
Chauffeur's Flat 9

Wednesday 23rd
Chauffeur's Flat 9

Thursday 24th
Chauffeur's Flat 9

Friday 25th
Chauffeur's Flat 9

Saturday 26th
Chauffeur's Flat 9

Sunday 27th
Chauffeur's Flat 9
Chestnut Cottage 10
The Old Croft 43
Shieling 54
Spurfold 57

Monday 28th
15 The Avenue 3
Fairmile Lea 21
Moleshill House 40
The Old Croft 43

June

Festival Weekend

Saturday 2nd
15 The Avenue 3
Monks Lantern 41

Sunday 3rd
53 Commonfield Road 15
26 The Fairway 22
High Clandon Estate Vineyard 28
The Therapy Garden 61

Saturday 9th
7 Rose Lane 49

Sunday 10th
Lark Rise 33
The Old Rectory 45
Shackleford Garden Safari 52

Saturday 16th
The Coach House 13
NEW 9 Landscape Road 32
NEW Little Court House 35

Sunday 17th
2 Chinthurst Lodge 12
The Coach House 13
Horsell Group Gardens 29
NEW 9 Landscape Road 32
NEW Little Court House 35
◆ Loseley Park 36
Lower House 37
◆ Titsey Place Gardens 64
◆ Vann 65

Monday 18th
Chauffeur's Flat 9

Tuesday 19th
Chauffeur's Flat 9

Wednesday 20th
Chauffeur's Flat 9
2 Chinthurst Lodge 12

Thursday 21st
Chauffeur's Flat 9

Friday 22nd
Ashleigh Grange 2
Chauffeur's Flat 9

Saturday 23rd
Chauffeur's Flat 9

Sunday 24th
Ashleigh Grange 2
Chauffeur's Flat 9

Monday 25th
The Bothy 5

Tuesday 26th
The Bothy 5

Wednesday 27th
Ashleigh Grange 2
The Bothy 5

Thursday 28th
The Bothy 5

Friday 29th
The Bothy 5

Saturday 30th
Bardsey 4
The Bothy 5

July

Sunday 1st
Bardsey 4
The Bothy 5
Pratsham Grange 46

Saturday 7th
16 Hurtmore Chase 30
Southlands Lodge 55
Woodbury Cottage 68

Sunday 8th
16 Hurtmore Chase 30
Southlands Lodge 55
Woodbury Cottage 68

Saturday 21st
Earleywood 20

Sunday 22nd
Earleywood 20
Heathside 27
◆ Titsey Place Gardens 64

Saturday 28th
Bardsey 4
35 Tadorne Road 60

Sunday 29th
Bardsey 4
35 Tadorne Road 60

August

Sunday 5th
41 Shelvers Way 53

Saturday 11th
NEW 69 Salisbury Grove 51

Sunday 12th
Heathside 27

Sunday 19th
Pratsham Grange 46
◆ Titsey Place Gardens 64

September

Saturday 1st
Coldharbour House 14

Sunday 2nd
Coldharbour House 14
The Therapy Garden 61

Saturday 8th
Woodbury Cottage 68

Sunday 9th
53 Commonfield Road 15
◆ Dunsborough Park 18
Woodbury Cottage 68

Tuesday 11th
Woodbury Cottage 68

October

Sunday 7th
Albury Park 1

Sunday 14th
Coverwood Lakes 17

November

Sunday 4th
Timber Hill 63

By Arrangement

Ashleigh Grange 2
15 The Avenue 3
Bardsey 4
Bridge End Cottage 6
Caxton House 7
2 Chinthurst Lodge 12
The Coach House 13
Coldharbour House 14
53 Commonfield Road 15
56 Copse Avenue 16
Coverwood Lakes 17
NEW Dyers House 19
The Garth Pleasure Grounds 23
Heathside 27
NEW Linton 34
Malabar 38
Moleshill House 40
Monks Lantern 41
Odstock 42
Old Knowles 44
The Old Rectory 45
Pratsham Grange 46
Saffron Gate 50
NEW 69 Salisbury Grove 51
41 Shelvers Way 53
Shieling 54
Spurfold 57
Stuart Cottage 58
The Therapy Garden 61
Tilford Cottage 62
Timber Hill 63
Westways Farm 67
Woodbury Cottage 68

THE GARDENS

1 ALBURY PARK

Albury, GU5 9BH. Trustees of Albury Estate. *5m SE of Guildford. From A25 take A248 towards Albury for ¼m, then up New Rd, entrance to Albury Park immed on L.* **Sun 18 Mar, Sun 7 Oct (2-5). Adm £4.50, chd free. Home-made teas.**
14 acre pleasure grounds laid out in 1670s by John Evelyn for Henry Howard, later 6th Duke of Norfolk. ¼m terraces, fine collection of trees, lake and river. Gravel path and slight slope.

2 ASHLEIGH GRANGE

Off Chapel Lane, Westhumble, RH5 6AY. Clive & Angela Gilchrist, 01306 884613, ar.gilchrist@btinternet.com. *2m N of Dorking. From A24 at Boxhill/ Burford Bridge follow signs to Westhumble. Through village & L up drive by ruined chapel (1m from A24).* **Evening opening Fri 22 June (6-8). Adm £6, chd free. Wine. Sun 24, Wed 27 June (2-5.30). Adm £4, chd free. Home-made teas. Visits also by arrangement May to July (sorry, no access for coaches). Donation to Barnardo's.**
Plant lover's chalk garden on 3½ acre sloping site in charming rural setting with delightful views. Many areas of interest incl rockery and water feature, raised ericaceous bed, prairie style bank, foliage plants, woodland walk, fernery and folly. Large mixed herbaceous and shrub borders planted for dry alkaline soil and widespread interest.

3 15 THE AVENUE

Cheam, Sutton, SM2 7QA. Jan & Nigel Brandon, 020 8643 8686, n.brandon@imperial.ac.uk. *1m SW of Sutton. By car; exit A217 onto Northey Av, 2nd R into The Avenue. By train; 10 mins walk from Cheam station. By bus; use 470.* **Mon 28 May (1-5). Adm £5, chd free. Home-made teas. Evening opening Sat 2 June (6-9). Adm £8, chd £3. Wine. Visits also by arrangement May to July for groups min 10, max 35.**
A contemporary garden designed by RHS Chelsea Gold Medal Winner, Marcus Barnett. Four levels divided into rooms by beech hedging and columns; formal entertaining area, lawn and wildflower meadow. Over 100 hostas hug the house. Silver birch, cloud pruned box, ferns, grasses, tall bearded irises, contemporary sculptures. Lit for evening opening. A wine/beer/soft drink and snacks are included in the entry fee for the evening opening on June 2nd. Contemporary sculpture. Partial wheelchair access, terraced with steps; sloping path provides view of whole garden but not all accessible.

The National Garden Scheme is the largest single funder of Macmillan

4 BARDSEY

11 Derby Road, Haslemere, GU27 1BS. Maggie & David Boyd, 01428 652283, maggie.boyd@live.co.uk, www.bardseygarden.co.uk. *¼m N of Haslemere station. Turn off B2131 (which links A287 to A286 through town) 400yds W of station into Weydown Rd, 3rd R into Derby Rd, garden 400yds on R.* **Sat 30 June, Sun 1, Sat 28, Sun 29 July (1-5). Adm £5, chd free. Home-made teas. Visits also by arrangement June & July for groups 10+.**

Unexpected 2 acre garden in the heart of Haslemere. Several distinct areas containing scent, colour, texture and movement. Stunning pictorial meadow within an ilex crenata parterre. Prairie planted border provides a modern twist. Large productive fruit and vegetable garden. Natural ponds and bog gardens. Several unusual sculptures. Bee hive and bug hotel. Ducks and chickens supply the eggs for cakes. Classic MGs on parade. Home-made produce stall. Glass sculptures by Wendy Stafford for sale. Featured in Surrey life magazine. Saturday telegraph. First third of garden level, other two thirds sloping.

5 THE BOTHY

Tandridge Court, Tandridge Lane, Oxted, RH8 9NJ. Diane & John Hammond, 07785612478, dhammo@hotmail.co.uk. *5 mins from J6 of M25, towards Oxted. From N, at r'about on A25 between A22 & Oxted go S into Tandridge Lane, after ¼m follow signs. From S, N up Tandridge Lane from Ray Lane, on exiting Tandridge Village follow signs.* **Mon 25, Tue 26, Wed 27, Thur 28, Fri 29 June (11-4). Evening opening Sat 30 June, Sun 1 July (5-9). Wine. Adm £5, chd free. Refreshments in aid of St Peters Church, Tandridge and Cornwall Hedgehog Rescue, Falmouth.**

A 1 ½ acre hillside garden on 5 levels. Accessed by steps and slopes, creating varying views, with specimen trees, incl a Sequoia, Acers and Banana. Explore wild banks, perennial beds, woodland and relaxing areas. Along with a productive kitchen garden with fruit trees, fruit cage and large greenhouse. Each level contains either water features, garden artwork, chickens and more. The garden entrance is down a number of steps and on different levels and therefore it is unsuitable for people with mobility issues.

6 BRIDGE END COTTAGE

Ockham Lane, Ockham, GU23 6NR. Clare & Peter Bevan, 01483 479963, c.fowler@ucl.ac.uk. *Nr RHS Gardens, Wisley. At Wisley r'about turn L onto B2039 to Ockham/Horsley. After ½m turn L into Ockham Lane. House ½m on R. From Cobham go to Blackswan Xrds.* **Visits by arrangement June & July groups 30 max. Adm £5, chd free. Home-made teas in the garden room.**

A two acre country garden with different areas of interest, incl perennial borders, mature trees, pond and streams, small herb parterre, fruit trees and a vegetable patch. An adjacent two acre field was sown with perennial wild flower seed in May 2013 and has flowered well in June. In recent years the flowering in July has become more varied. Large perennial wildflower meadow. Partial wheelchair access.

7 CAXTON HOUSE

67 West Street, Reigate, RH2 9DA. Bob Bushby, 01737 243158 / 07836201740, Bob.bushby@sky.com. *On A25 towards Dorking, approx ¼m W of Reigate. Parking on Rd or past Black Horse PH on Flanchford Rd.* **Sun 1 Apr (2-5). Adm £5, chd free. Cream teas. Visits also by arrangement Apr to Sept for groups 10+.**

Lovely large spring garden with Arboretum, 2 well stocked ponds, large collection of hellebores and spring flowers. Pots planted with colourful displays. Interesting plants. Small Gothic folly built by owner. Herbaceous borders with grasses, perennials, spring bulbs, and parterre. New bed with wild daffodils, and prairie style planting in summer. Antique dog cart completes the picture 7 Acres. Wheelchair access to most parts of the garden.

8 THE CHALET

Tupwood Lane, Caterham, CR3 6ET. Miss Lesley Manning & Mr David Gold. *½m N of M25 J6. Exit J6 off M25 onto A22 to N. After ½m take sharp 1st L, or follow signs from Caterham. Ample free parking. Disabled access via top gate.* **Sun 1, Sun 8 Apr (11-4.30). Adm £5, chd free. Home-made teas.** Donation to St Catherine's Hospice.

55 acres. Carpets of tens of thousands of daffodils; lakes, ornamental ponds, koi pond and waterfall. Ancient woodlands, grasslands and formal garden. Large planted terraces. Beautiful Victorian mansion (not open). Woodland and garden trail. On view, a limited edition Blue Train Bentley, a Phantom Rolls Royce and a helicopter plus the oldest FA Cup and other trophies. Featured in Caterham Independent, County Border News. Partial wheelchair access, some steep slopes. 3 large unfenced ponds.

9 CHAUFFEUR'S FLAT

Tandridge Lane, Tandridge, RH8 9NJ. Mr & Mrs Richins. *2m E of Godstone. 2m W of Oxted. Turn off A25 at r'about for Tandridge. Take 2nd drive on L past church. Follow arrows to circular courtyard.* **Daily Mon 21 May to Sun 27 May (10-5). Daily Mon 18 June to Sun 24 June (10-5). Adm £5, chd free. Home-made teas (Sats & Suns only).**

Enter a 1½ acre tapestry of magical secret gardens with magnificent views. Touching the senses, all sure footed visitors may explore the many surprises on this constantly evolving exuberant escape from reality. Imaginative use of recycled materials creates an inspired variety of ideas, while wild and specimen plants reveal an ecological haven.

10 CHESTNUT COTTAGE

15 Jubilee Lane, Boundstone, Farnham, GU10 4SZ. Mr & Mrs David Wingent. *2½m SW of Farnham. At A31 r'about take A325 - Petersfield, ½m bear L. At r'about into School Hill, ½m over staggered Xrds into Sandrock Hill Rd, 4th turn R after PH.* **Sun 6, Sun 27 May (2-5.30). Adm £4, chd free. Home-made teas.**

½ acre secret garden created on different levels, with mature rhododendrons, azaleas, acers, herbaceous border all set in a sylvan setting. A particular feature of the garden is a pergola supporting a 24ft long wisteria. Attractive gazebo copied from the original National Trust's Hunting Lodge in Odiham. Visitors say wherever you sit there is a completely different vista. Plant expert John Negus will be in attendance.

11 CHILWORTH MANOR

Halfpenny Lane, Chilworth, Guildford, GU4 8NN. Mia & Graham Wrigley. *3½m SE of Guildford. From centre of Chilworth village turn into Blacksmith Lane. 1st drive on R on Halfpenny Lane.* **Sun 20 May (11-5). Adm £6, chd free. Home-made teas.**

Extensive grounds of lawns and mature trees surrounding C17/C18 manor house on C11 monastic site. Substantial C18 terraced walled garden developed by Sarah, Duchess of Marlborough, with herbaceous borders, topiary and fruit trees. Original monastic stewponds integrated with Japanese themed and woodland garden. Paddock home to alpacas. Plenty of space for visitors to explore and relax or participate in accompanied walks in this peaceful garden. Garden and Tree Walks at 12 noon, 1.30pm, 2.30pm and 4pm. NEW for 2018 -Tasting of Chilworth Manor Rose Wine throughout the day.

12 2 CHINTHURST LODGE

Wonersh Common, Wonersh, Guildford, GU5 0PR. Mr & Mrs M R Goodridge, 01483 535108, michaelgoodridge@ymail.com. *4m S of Guildford. From A281 at Shalford turn E onto B2128 towards Wonersh. Just after Waverley sign, before village, garden on R.* **Sun 17, Wed 20 June (11-5). Adm £5, chd free. Home-made teas. Visits also by arrangement May to July for groups 10+.**

One acre yr-round enthusiast's atmospheric garden, divided into rooms. Herbaceous borders, dramatic white garden, specimen trees and shrubs, gravel garden with water feature, small kitchen garden, fruit cage, two wells, ornamental ponds, herb parterre and millennium parterre garden, as featured in Period Homes and Interiors and Surrey Life. Some gravel paths, which can be avoided.

13 THE COACH HOUSE

The Green, Chiddingfold, Godalming, GU8 4TU. Mr & Mrs S Brooks, 01428 687767, barbarabrooks@btinternet.com. *7M S of Godalming. Eastern corner of village green. Parking around village green or along Pickhurst Rd.* **Sat 16, Sun 17 June (1-5). Adm £5, chd free. Home-made teas. Visits also by arrangement May & June for groups 10+ No coaches.**

Garden designer's garden comprising one acre walled garden and additional courtyards, designed by the owners and created since 2013. Lawns divided into areas by trees and borders filled with perennials, shrubs and roses. A courtyard rose garden, wildflower meadow, white garden and kitchen garden provide varied interest. Stumpery added recently. Featured in The English Garden, Period Living, Surrey Life.

Chauffeur's Flat

14 COLDHARBOUR HOUSE

Coldharbour Lane, Bletchingley, Redhill, RH1 4NA. Mr Tony Elias, 01883 742685, eliastony@hotmail.com. *Coldharbour Lane off Rabies Heath Rd ½m from A25 at Bletchingley & 0.9m from Tilburstow Hill Rd. Park in field & walk down to house.* **Sat 1, Sun 2 Sept (1-5). Adm £5, chd free. Home-made teas. Visits also by arrangement Apr to Oct for groups 10+.**

This 1½ acre garden offers breathtaking views to the South Downs. Originally planted in the 1920's, it has since been adapted and enhanced. Several mature trees and shrubs incl a copper beech, a Canadian maple, magnolias, azaleas, rhododendrons, camellias, wisterias, fuschias, hibiscus, potentillas, mahonias, a fig tree and a walnut tree.

15 53 COMMONFIELD ROAD

Banstead, SM7 2JR. Jennifer Russell, 01737 379510, jenniferlindarussell@hotmail.co.uk. *From A217 turn into Winkworth Rd, then 1st turning on L after mini r'about. Parking on rd, please do not block neighbours drives.* **Evening opening Sun 3 June (5.30-8.30). Adm £5, chd £2. Wine. Sun 9 Sept (11-3.30). Adm £3, chd free. Home-made teas. A glass of wine free with entrance ticket on evening opening. All refreshments in aid of Cancer Research. Visits also by arrangement Apr to Sept teas for Cancer Research.**

An interesting cottage garden of curvaceous beds with layered plantings of small trees, shrubs, perennials, bulbs and grasses to give a succession of highlights. Enter through a rose covered arch to be inspired. If you have a garden and want to take away some ideas, you are welcome. A small male voice choir will be singing at the June evening opening. The garden featured in Surrey Life, Discover the county's hidden Gems, and Gorgeous Gardens in Surrey Life. Small wheelchairs; lots of seating areas for less mobile.

16 56 COPSE AVENUE

Farnham, GU9 9EA. Lyn & Jimmy James, 01252 323473, lynandjimmy@virginmedia.com. *Approx 1½m N of Farnham. At Shepherd & Flock r'about take A325 to Farnborough. At 2nd r'about take Weybourne exit. At T-lights turn L onto Upper Weybourne Lane. Turn R onto Oakland Avenue. At T-Junction turn L.* **Sat 19, Sun 20 May (2-5). Adm £4, chd free. Home-made teas. Visits also by arrangement May & June for groups 10+.**

A fascinating and unusual one acre garden in a residential area. The garden was originally landscaped in the late 1960s following the plans of a Chelsea Flower Show garden, but was subsequently allowed to become very overgrown. The present owners have restored many of the original features and are adding innovative areas of planting and interest. Accessible for wheelchairs but some steep steps and uneven paths.

17 COVERWOOD LAKES

Peaslake Road, Ewhurst, GU6 7NT. The Metson Family, 01306 731101, coverwoodfarm@coverwoodlakes.co.uk, www.coverwoodlakes.co.uk. *7m SW of Dorking. From A25 follow signs for Peaslake; garden ½m beyond Peaslake on Ewhurst rd.* **Mon 2, Sun 8, Sun 15 Apr, Sun 6 May, Sun 14 Oct (11-5). Adm £6, chd free. Light refreshments. Visits also by arrangement Apr to Sept for groups of 15 plus. Group refreshments can be discussed.**

14 acre landscaped garden in stunning position high in the Surrey Hills with 4 lakes and bog garden. Extensive rhododendrons, azaleas and fine trees. 3½ acre lakeside arboretum. Marked trail through the 180 acre working farm with Hereford cows and calves, sheep and horses, extensive views of the surrounding hills. Light refreshments, incl home produced beef burgers, gourmet coffee and home-made cakes.

18 ◆ DUNSBOROUGH PARK

Ripley, GU23 6AL. Baron & Baroness Sweerts de Landas Wyborgh, 01483 225366, office@sweerts.com, www.dunsboroughpark.com. *6m NE of Guildford. Entrance across Ripley Green via The Milkway past cricket green on R & playground on L, round corner to double brown wooden gates.* **For NGS: Thur 19 Apr (3.30-7); Sun 20 May, Sun 9 Sept (11.30-3.30). Adm £7, chd free. Home-made teas. For other opening times and information, please phone, email or visit garden website.**

6 acres of walled gardens redesigned by Penelope Hobhouse and Rupert Golby – a box hedged parterre showcasing spectacular tulip displays in April; different garden rooms; lush herbaceous borders with standard wisterias; 70ft Ginkgo hedge; Rose Walk; ancient mulberry tree; Italian Garden; potager; water garden and folly bridge. Enjoy Roses and Peonies in June and Dahlias in September. Festival of Tulips. Amazing tulip meadow display. Wild meadow with poppies and cornflowers. Sept: Over 50 varieties of Dahlias 50cm-2.5m. Produce for sale when available.

19 NEW DYERS HOUSE

Pickhurst Road, Chiddingfold, Godalming, GU8 4TG. Mr and Mrs Nicholas Allen, 07970378797, jane.allen01@me.com. *6m south of Godalming. 1¼ miles out of Chiddingfold on Pickhurst Road. Parking in field.* **Sat 12, Sun 13 May (2-6). Adm £4.50, chd free. Home-made teas. Teas in aid of Friends of St Mary's Church. Visits also by arrangement Apr to June visits for groups of 8+ by arrangement.**

Approximately 2 acre family garden established over the last 30 years, extended and designed by enthusiastic owners. Year round interest, colour themed borders, fruit trees, bulbs, large Banksia rose climbs over the house. Vegetable garden, fruit cage and 17th century barn.

20 EARLEYWOOD

Hamlash Lane, Frensham, Farnham, GU10 3AT. Mrs Penny Drew. *3m S of Farnham just off A287. From A31 Farnham take A287 to Frensham. R 1st turn passed Edgeborough School. From A3, N on A287 to Frensham. Parking available, More House School Lower Car Park top of Hamlash Lane.* **Sat 21, Sun 22 July (11-5). Adm £5, chd free. Home-made teas.**

Award winning, ½ acre garden with colourful shrubberies, unusual trees and mixed borders throughout. Wide variety of summer flowering shrubs, particularly hydrangeas, together with herbaceous perennials in colour themed borders - vibrant reds and yellows and cool pinks and blues - also shady areas with groundcover and shade loving plants. Productive greenhouse. John Negus, well known horticulturalist, gardening writer and broadcaster will be in the garden to answer gardening questions during the weekend. Also demonstration of lavender weaving and craft items for sale. Article in Surrey Life. Disabled drop off at front gate, short gravel drive then level lawns throughout.

21 FAIRMILE LEA

Portsmouth Road, Cobham, KT11 1BG. Steven Kay. *2m NE of Cobham. On Cobham to Esher rd. Access by lane adjacent to Moleshill House & car park for Fairmile Common woods.* **Mon 28 May (2-5). Combined adm with Moleshill House £6, chd free.**

Large Victorian sunken garden fringed by rose beds and lavender with a pond in the centre. An old acacia tree stands in the midst of the lawn. Interesting planting on a large mound camouflages an old underground air raid shelter. Caged vegetable garden. Formality adjacent to wilderness.

22 26 THE FAIRWAY

Camberley, GU15 1EF. Jacky Sheppard. *1½m from M3 J4. Follow signs to Frimley Pk Hosp. At r'about take 3rd exit B311 Chobham Rd. Cont on B311 L at 2nd r'about. 1st L into Fairway.* **Sun 13 May, Sun 3 June (11-4). Adm £4, chd free. Light refreshments.**

Spring and summer is the ideal time to see the azaleas, rhododendrons and heathers that surround the house. Bulbs, primroses and winter hellebores give ground cover beneath the shrubs. Climbers and a variety of plants continue a theme to make way for summer flowering. A new water feature has been added, with other additions to the garden including a new flowering centre bed with a pergola. Small area at back of garden not easily accessed by wheelchair.

23 THE GARTH PLEASURE GROUNDS

Newchapel Road, Lingfield, RH7 6BJ. Mr Sherlock & Mrs Stanley, ab_post@yahoo.com, , www.oldworkhouse.webs.com. *From A22 take B2028 by Mormon Temple to Lingfield. The Garth is on L after 1½m, opp Barge Tiles. Parking: Gun Pit Road and limited space for disabled at Barge Tiles.* **Evening opening Sat 5 May (4-6). Sun 6 May (2-6). Adm £5, chd free. Home-made teas. Visits also by arrangement May & June please email a few weeks in advance.**

Mature 9 acre Pleasure Grounds created by Walter Godfrey in 1919 present an idyllic setting surrounding the former parish workhouse refurbished in Edwardian style. The formal gardens, enchanting nuttery, a spinney with many mature trees and a pond attract wildlife. Wonderful bluebells in spring. The woodland gardens and beautiful borders full of colour and fragrance for yr-round pleasure. Many areas of interest incl pond, woodland garden, formal gardens, spinney with large specimen plants incl 500yr old oak and many architectural features designed by Walter H Godfrey. Partial wheelchair access in woodland, iris and secret gardens.

24 ◆ GATTON PARK

Rocky Lane, Merstham, RH2 0TW. Royal Alexandra & Albert School, 01737 649068, events@gatton-park.org.uk, www.gattonpark.com. *3m NE of Reigate. 5 mins from M25 J8 (A217) or from top of Reigate Hill, over M25 then follow sign to Merstham. Entrance off Rocky Lane accessible from Gatton Bottom or A23 Merstham.* **For NGS: Sun 11 Feb (11-4). Adm £5, chd free. Light refreshments at Gatton Hall. Tea/coffee & cake. Soup and roll lunch. For other opening times and information, please phone, email or visit garden website.**

Gatton Park is the core 250 acres of the estate originally laid out by Capability Brown. Gatton also boasts a Japanese garden, rock and water garden and Victorian parterre nestled within the sweeping parkland. Stunning displays of snowdrops and aconites in February. Free activities for children. Tea, cake, soup and rolls available on the day.

25 HALL GROVE SCHOOL

London Road (A30), Bagshot, GU19 5HZ. Mr & Mrs A R Graham, www.hallgrove.co.uk. *6m SW of Egham. M3 J3, follow A322 1m until sign for Sunningdale A30, 1m E of Bagshot, opp Longacres garden centre, entrance at footbridge. Ample car parking.* **Sat 12 May (2-5). Adm by donation. Home-made teas.**

Formerly a small Georgian country estate, now a co-educational preparatory school. Grade II listed house (not open). Mature parkland with specimen trees. Historical features incl ice house, old walled garden under restoration, heated peach wall, lake, woodland walks, rhododendrons and azaleas. Live music at 3pm.

26 ◆ HATCHLANDS PARK
East Clandon, Guildford, GU4 7RT. National Trust, 01483 222482, hatchlands@nationaltrust.org.uk, www.nationaltrust.org.uk/hatchlands-park. *4m E of Guildford. Follow brown signs to Hatchlands Park (NT).* **For NGS: Sun 29 Apr (10-4). Adm £7.50, chd £3.75. Light refreshments.** For other opening times and information, please phone, email or visit garden website.
Garden and park designed by Repton in 1800. Follow one of the park walks to the stunning bluebell wood in spring (2.5km/1.7m round walk over rough and sometimes muddy ground). In autumn enjoy the changing colours on the long walk. Partial wheelchair access to parkland, rough, undulating terrain, grass and gravel paths, dirt tracks, cobbled courtyard. Tramper booking essential.

27 HEATHSIDE
10 Links Green Way, Cobham, KT11 2QH. Miss Margaret Arnott & Mr Terry Bartholomew, 01372 842459, m.a.arnott@btinternet.com. *1½m E of Cobham. Through Cobham A245, 4th L after Esso garage into Fairmile Lane. Straight on into Water Lane. Links Green Way 3rd turning on L.* **Sun 22 July, Sun 12 Aug (1-5). Adm £4, chd free. Home-made teas. Visits also by arrangement.**
⅓ acre terraced, plantsman's garden, designed for yr-round interest. Gorgeous plants all set off by harmonious landscaping. Urns and obelisks aid the display. Two ponds and four water features add tranquil sound. A contemporary parterre and various topiary shapes add formality. Stunning colour combinations excite. Beautiful new glasshouse housing the exotic. Many inspirational ideas. Situated 5 miles from RHS Wisley. Featured in Surrey Life & Garden News.

28 HIGH CLANDON ESTATE VINEYARD
High Clandon, East Clandon, Guildford, GU4 7RP. Mrs Sibylla Tindale, www.highclandon.co.uk. *A3 Wisley junction, L for Ockham/ Horsley for 2m to A246. R for Guildford for 2m, then 100yds past landmark Hatchlands NT, turn L into Blakes Lane straight up through gates High Clandon to vineyard entrance. Extensive parking in our woodland area.* **Sun 3 June (11-4). Adm £6, chd free. Home-made teas. Our High Clandon Cuvée 2013 vintage sparkling wine will be available at £6/glass in the Glass Barn.**
Views, gardens, sculptures, vineyard in beautiful Surrey Hills AONB. 6 acres. Panoramic views to London, water features, Japanese garden, wildflower meadow, truffière, apiary, vineyard producing gold-award, vintage-only English sparkling wine, High Clandon Cuvée. Overall winner of Cellar Door of the Year. Sculptures in the Vineyard by noted artists. Percentage of sales to Cherry Trees charity. Atmospheric Glass Barn used for wine tastings and art exhibitions. Sparkling wine tasting available at extra charge of £6 per glass. Featured in Daily Telegraph.

GROUP OPENING

29 HORSELL GROUP GARDENS
Horsell, Woking, GU21 4XA. *1½m W of Woking in Village of Horsell. Leave M25 at J11. Take A320 signed Woking then A3046 signed Chobham after approx 1m at r'about turn L signed Horsell, with parking on Village Green outside Cricketers PH.* **Sun 17 June (12-5). Combined adm £5, chd free. Home-made teas.**

BIRCH COTTAGE
Celia & Mel Keenan.

3-4 BIRCH COTTAGES
Mr & Mrs Freeman.

HORSELL ALLOTMENTS
Horsell Allotments Association, www.horsellalots.wordpress.com.

2 gardens and an award winning allotment in the village of Horsell which is on the edge of the Common, famously mentioned in HG Wells's War of the Worlds. 3-4 Birch Cottages is full of charm with an interesting courtyard with rill. Walk down this long garden through into a series of rooms with topiary and attractive planting and many specimen roses. Birch Cottage is a Grade II listed cottage with a box hedge style knot garden, a chinese slate courtyard with planted pots and hanging baskets, a canal water feature and an active white dove dovecote, surrounded with an abundance of planting. Horsell Allotments have over 100 individual plots growing a variety of unusual flowers and vegetables, many not seen in supermarkets, 2 working beehives with informative talks from their owners. Allotments are bumpy and 3-4 Birch Cottage are flat, Birch Cottage, has gravel and steps but wheelchair visitors can see main garden.

30 16 HURTMORE CHASE
Hurtmore, Godalming, GU7 2RT. Mrs Ann Bellamy. *4m SW of Guildford. From Godalming follow signs to Charterhouse & cont about ¼m beyond Charterhouse School. Or from A3 take Norney, Shackleford & Hurtmore turn off & proceed E for ½m.* **Sat 7, Sun 8 July (11-5). Adm £4, chd free. Light refreshments.**
A secluded medium sized (approx ¼ acre) garden comprised mainly of a large lawn divided into discrete areas by shrubs, trees and flowerbeds with a high degree of colour. On the bungalow side of the lawn there is a patio area with hanging baskets, troughs and planted pots with fuchsias being a speciality. In the opposite corner there is a shaded arbour bordered by hostas. Kerb height step up from patio to lawn so minor assistance may be required for wheelchairs.

31 KNOWLE GRANGE

Hound House Road, Shere, Guildford, GU5 9JH. Mr P R & Mrs M E Wood. *8m S of Guildford. From Shere (off A25), through village for ¾m. After railway bridge, cont 1½m past Hound House on R (stone dogs on gateposts). After 100yds turn R at Knowle Grange sign, go to end of lane.* **Sun 20 May (11-4.30). Adm £6, chd free. Home-made teas.**
80 acre idyllic hilltop position. Extraordinary and exciting 7 acre gardens, created from scratch since 1990 by Marie-Elisabeth Wood, blend the free romantic style with the strong architectural frame of the classical tradition. Walk the rural 1m Bluebell Valley Unicursal Path of Life and discover its secret allegory. Featured on Austrian and German TV gardening program. Deep unfenced pools, high unfenced drops.

32 NEW 9 LANDSCAPE ROAD

Warlingham, CR6 9JB. Wendy Riches. *3 miles N of M25 J6, take A22 London. First r'about, 4th exit to Warlingham, turn L at top of hill into Landscape Rd (NB 1:4 hill - avoid via Whyteleafe).* **Sat 16, Sun 17 June (2-5). Adm £3.50, chd free. Home-made teas. Donations to Emmanuel Church Hall, Croydon.**
Set in a ⅓ of an acre and designed by Chris Beardshaw, the garden has a heavy clay soil. Divided into separate spaces by pleached lime trees, yew and beech hedges. Mixed borders with dense herbaceous perennials, climbing and shrub roses. A formal pond. Productive fruit and veg patch with raised beds and greenhouse. Old coach house and terrace for tea and cake.

33 LARK RISE

Franksfield, Peaslake, Guildford, GU5 9SS. Sarah & Peter Copping. *8m SE of Guildford or 6.8m from Dorking along A25. From Peaslake Stores go N on Peaslake Lane; go around sharp L bend (rd now Pursers Lane) & take next R into Hoe Lane. Go steep uphill & turn R into Franksfield then R again. Signs to parking in field.* **Sun 10 June (11-4.30). Adm £5, chd free. Home-made teas.**
A tranquil one acre garden created over many years to provide different areas of interest incl informal perennial borders set within formal yew hedging; wisteria clad pergola; a meadow surrounding a natural pond; productive vegetable plot with small greenhouse; spring garden with rhododendrons, ferns and spring flowers. Interesting sculptures to discover and a surprising variety of mature trees. Disabled drop off arrangements possible. Gravel driveway, few steps but most of garden accessible via lawns.

34 NEW LINTON

Guildford Road, Normandy, Guildford, GU3 2AR. Mrs A Adey, 01483 232477, ann.adey80@gmail.com. *SW of Guildford. Take A323 (direction Aldershot) At the entrance of Normandy pass 2 sharp road bends. Turn L immed after the 2nd one to Wells Lane (parking). Linton is 4th house on main rd (LHS).* **Visits by arrangement May to Aug for groups of 3-10 visitors, and visitors with dogs. All visits between 10:00 and 17:00. Adm £3, chd free. Tea. coffee and biscuits available at a small charge.**
Linton is a bungalow with inspiring gardens on 3 sides, designed by the owner over 23 years. It offers an opportunity to view what can be achieved in a small garden, the rear being only 12m x 9m (40ft x 30ft). Enjoy a surprising diversity of colourful shrubs, roses, clematis and herbaceous plants, growing in harmony. Ideas for raising fruits and vegetables in containers offered.

35 NEW LITTLE COURT HOUSE

Jackass Lane, Tandridge, Oxted, RH8 9NH. Jane and Graham King. *2m from J6 on M25. Head S on A22 from J6, L onto A25 towards Oxted, at mini-r'about right onto Tandridge Lane, 1st R onto Jackass Lane.* **Sat 16, Sun 17 June (1-5). Adm £4, chd free. Home-made teas.**
¾ acre garden created from scratch in beautiful country setting. Small courtyard style front garden, gate through to charming terraced rear garden with lawn, herbaceous borders, wisteria and rose covered pergola, archway through to wider area of garden and further to kitchen garden with greenhouse, fruit trees, raised cutting and veg beds.

36 ◆ LOSELEY PARK

Guildford, GU3 1HS. Mr & Mrs M G More-Molyneux, 01483 304440/405112, pa@loseleypark.co.uk, www.loseleypark.co.uk. *4m SW of Guildford. For SatNav please use GU3 1HS Stakescorner Lane.* **For NGS: Sun 17 June (11-5). Adm £5, chd free. Cream teas. Tea Room located just outside the gardens.** For other opening times and information, please phone, email or visit garden website.
Delightful 2½ acre walled garden. Award winning rose garden (over 1,000 bushes, mainly old fashioned varieties), extensive herb garden, fruit/flower garden, white garden with fountain, and spectacular organic vegetable garden. Magnificent vine walk, herbaceous borders, moat walk, ancient wisteria and mulberry trees. Refreshments available in our tea room.

The National Garden Scheme is Marie Curie's largest single funder

37 LOWER HOUSE

Bowlhead Green, Godalming, GU8 6NW. Mrs Georgina Harvey. *Just over 1m off A3 from Thursley/ Bowlhead Green junction. From A3 follow signs to Bowlhead Green. From A286 Brook turn N into Park Lane then 1st R into Beech Hill. At Xrds follow signpost to Lower House after 300yds stay R. Field parking.* **Sun 17 June (11-5). Adm £6, chd free. Home-made teas.**

A mature garden mainly planted thirty years ago with many ericaceous plants, trees, shrubs, roses, perennials, bulbs and a comprehensive kitchen garden. Lawns and narrow paths winding through plantings. A topiary garden with a small pond and water feature. Daffodils & spring bulbs start the year followed by azaleas, rhododendrons, roses, hydrangeas and glorious autumn colour. Home-made teas served in the Orchard. Alternative routes avoiding steps for wheelchairs users although some paths could be narrow.

38 MALABAR

Holdfast Lane, Haslemere, GU27 2EY. Beryl & Tony Bishop, 01428 661486, beryl.bishop@clara.co.uk. *Off B2136 Petworth Rd from Haslemere High St. Turn L in to Holdfast Lane, well before Lythe Hill Hotel. Parking in field opp. Please drop off disabled passengers before parking.* **Sun 6 May (11.30-5). Adm £5, chd free. Home-made teas. Visits also by arrangement Mar to Nov groups 6+.**

2½ acre country garden bounded by mature oaks with climbing hydrangeas, clematis and roses. Undulating lawns bordered by colourful planting of unusual shrubs, rhododendrons, and azaleas. Bluebells, hellebores, primulas, lily of the valley and wood anemones throughout. Tranquil bark chipped level woodland walks with natural archways give a host of different vistas. Bring your children and see how many owls they can find. Paths are wide and firm.

39 THE MANOR HOUSE

Three Gates Lane, Haslemere, GU27 2ES. Mr & Mrs Gerard Ralfe. *1m NE of Haslemere. From Haslemere centre take A286 towards Milford. Turn R after Museum into Three Gates Lane. At T-Junction turn R into Holdfast Lane. Car park on R.* **Sun 20 May (12-5). Adm £5, chd free. Home-made teas.**

Described by Country Life as 'The hanging gardens of Haslemere', The Manor House gardens are in a valley of the Surrey Hills. One of Surrey's inaugural NGS gardens, fine views, 6 acres, water gardens.

40 MOLESHILL HOUSE

The Fairmile, Cobham, KT11 1BG. Penny Snell, pennysnellflowers@btinternet.com, , www.pennysnellflowers.co.uk. *2m NE of Cobham. On A307 Esher to Cobham Rd next to free car park by A3 bridge, at entrance to Waterford Close.* **Mon 28 May (2-5). Combined adm with Fairmile Lea £6, chd free. Visits also by arrangement May to July for groups 15+.**

Romantic garden. Short woodland path leads from dovecote to beehives. Informal planting contrasts with formal topiary box and garlanded cisterns. Colourful courtyard and pots, conservatory, fountains, bog garden. Pleached avenue, circular gravel garden replacing most of the lawn. Gipsy caravan garden, green wall and stumpery. New espaliered crab apples. Chickens. Music at Moleshill House, teas at Fairmile Lea. Garden 5 mins from Claremont Landscape Garden, Painshill Park and Wisley, also adjacent to excellent dog walking woods. Featured on Swedish and Austrian TV.

41 MONKS LANTERN

Ruxbury Road, Chertsey, KT16 9NH. Mr & Mrs J Granell, 01932 569578, janicegranell@hotmail.com. *1m NW from Chertsey. M25 J11, signed A320/Woking. R'about 2nd exit A320/Staines, straight over next r'about. L onto Holloway Hill,*

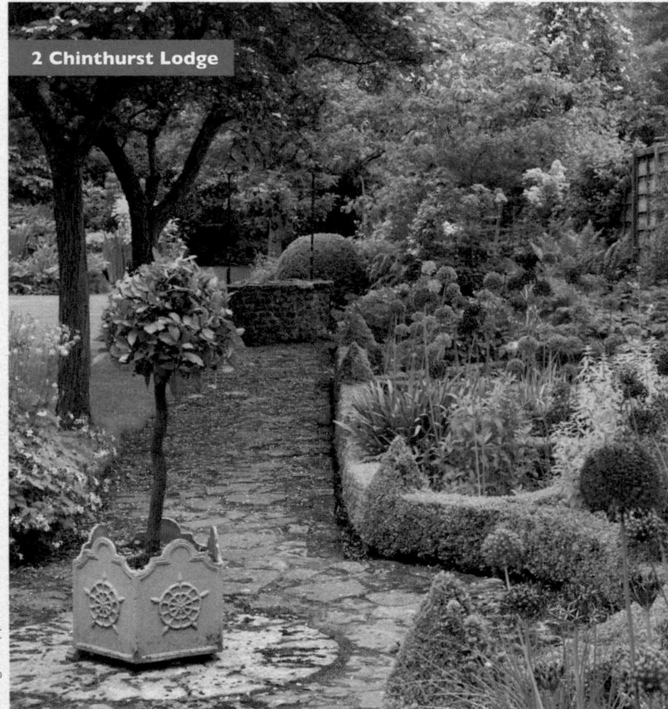

2 Chinthurst Lodge

R Hardwick Lane. ½m, R over motorway bridge, on Almners then Ruxbury Rd. **Sat 2 June (1-5). Adm £4, chd free. Wine. Light refreshments. Visits also by arrangement May to Aug for groups 10 - 15 max.**
A delightful garden with borders arranged with colour in mind: silvers and white, olive trees, nicotiana and senecio blend together. Large rockery and an informal pond. A weeping silver birch leads to the oranges and yellows of a tropical bed, with large bottle brush, hardy palms, and fatsia japonica. There is a display of hostas, cytisus battandieri and a selection of grasses in an island bed. Aviary with small finches. For wheelchair access, park on gravel drive to front of house, side access to garden, no steps, flat lawn.

42 ODSTOCK

Castle Square, Bletchingley, RH1 4LB. Averil & John Trott, 01883 743100. *3m W of Godstone. Just south of A25 in Bletchingley. At top of village nr Red Lion PH.* **Visits by arrangement May to Sept for groups 10+. Adm £5. Tea/coffee and home made cake available by prior arrangement.**
⅔ acre plantsman's garden maintained by owners and developed for yr-round interest. Special interest in grasses, climbers and dahlias. A no dig, low maintenance vegetable garden. Featured in Surrey Life. Short gravel drive. Main lawn suitable for wheelchairs but some paths may be too narrow.

43 THE OLD CROFT

South Holmwood, Dorking, RH5 4NT. David & Virginia Lardner-Burke, www.lardner-burke.org.uk. *2m S of Dorking. From Dorking A24 S for 2m, L to Leigh/Brockham into Mill Rd. ½m on L, 2 free NT car parks on Holmwood Com. Access 600yds along woodland walk. Follow signs.* **Sun 27, Mon 28 May (2-6). Adm £5, chd free. Home-made teas.**
Beautiful 5 acre garden with many diverse areas of natural beauty, giving a sense of peace and tranquillity. Stunning vistas incl lake, bridge, pond fed by natural stream running over rocky weirs, bog gardens, roses, perennial borders, elevated viewing hide, tropical bamboo maze, curved pergola of rambling roses, unique topiary buttress hedge, many specimen trees and shrubs. Visitors return again and again. Featured in Surrey Life. **For direct access for disabled and elderly visitors please phone 01306 888224.**

44 OLD KNOWLES

150 Upper Chobham Road, Camberley, GU15 1ET. The Hobbs Family, hobbsgreta@btinternet.com. *2½m from M3 J4. Follow signs to Frimley Pk Hosp. At r'about take 3rd exit B311 Chobham Rd. Cont on. Please park on Upper Chobham Rd (B311) nr Prior Rd, outside drive to Old Knowles.* **Visits by arrangement in May, Sats to Weds only. Parking is available on the Upper Chobham Road. Adm £3.50, chd free. Home-made teas.**
Take tea on the broad terrace and enjoy a stunning panorama of Douglas pines, bright azaleas, mature rhododendrons and an oriental surprise. Period sunken rose garden and birch copse offer space to wander or sit in shade. Children are welcome to tumble on our family friendly lawn. Care required near poolside.

45 THE OLD RECTORY

Sandy Lane, Brewer Street, Bletchingley, RH1 4QW. Mr & Mrs A Procter, 01883 743388 or 07515 394506, trudie.y.procter@googlemail.com. *Top of village nr Red Lion PH, turn R into Little Common Lane then R Cross Rd into Sandy Lane. Parking nr house, disabled parking in courtyard.* **Sun 10 June (11-4.30). Adm £5, chd free. Home-made teas. Visits also by arrangement Mar to Sept please phone/email for bookings.**
Georgian Manor House (not open). Quintessential Italianate topiary garden, statuary, box parterres, courtyard with columns, water features, antique terracotta pots. Much of the 4 acre garden is the subject of ongoing reclamation. This incl the ancient moat, woodland with fine specimen trees, rill, sunken and exotic garden under construction. The largest Tulip Tree in the UK. Featured in Magazines Town and Country, Topiaries The journal of the European Boxwood and Topiary Society. Gravel paths.

46 PRATSHAM GRANGE

Tanhurst Lane, Holmbury St Mary, RH5 6LZ. Alan & Felicity Comber, 01306 621116, alancomber@aol.com. *12m SE of Guildford, 8m SW of Dorking. From A25 take B2126. After 4m turn L into Tanhurst Lane. From A29 take B2126. Before Forest Green turn R on B2126 then 1st R to Tanhurst Lane.* **Sun 1 July, Sun 19 Aug (1-5). Adm £5, chd free. Home-made teas. Visits also by arrangement July & Aug.**
5 acre garden overlooked by Holmbury Hill and Leith Hill. Features incl 2 ponds joined by cascading stream, extensive scented rose and blue hydrangea beds. Also herbaceous borders, cutting flower garden, white and yellow beds. South garden replanted over last 3 years. Some slopes and gravel paths. Deep ponds.

47 ◆ RAMSTER

Chiddingfold, Surrey, GU8 4SN. Mr & Mrs Paul Gunn, 01428 654167, office@ramsterhall.com, www.ramsterevents.com. *Ramster is on A283 1½m south of Chiddingfold, large iron gates on right, the entrance is signed from the road.* **For NGS: Fri 11 May (10-5). Adm £7.50, chd free. Light refreshments. For other opening times and information, please phone, email or visit garden website.**
A stunning, mature woodland garden set in over 20 acres, famous for its rhododendron and azalea collection and its carpets

of bluebells in Spring. Enjoy a peaceful wander down the woodland walk, explore the bog garden with its stepping stones, or relax in the tranquil enclosed tennis court garden. The teahouse open every day while the garden is open, serving delicious cakes and sandwiches. Ramster appeared on BBC Gardeners' World. The teahouse is wheelchair accessible, some paths in the garden are suitable for wheelchairs.

48 ROE DEER FARM

Portsmouth Road, Godalming, GU7 2JT. Lucy & Justin Gurney. *Godalming/Milford border next to Squire's Garden Centre (GU8 5HL). Please drive through Squire's garden centre car park towards the 'Pick your own'. Turn R & enter through back gate. No entrance from main road.* **Sun 13 May (11-5). Adm £6, chd free. Home-made teas.**
A diverse and varied 17 acre garden incl mature woodlands has been created over the past 10yrs by the present owners. Views through to the parkland setting can be seen from many of the formal and informal areas creating a garden full of interest throughout the seasons. Lawn terraces lead you to naturally planted woodland walks, a kitchen garden, dingly-dell and a pirate ship! Families welcome and children invited to board the pirate ship and see the ducks and chickens. Please be aware of open water features and swimming pool. Level access for wheelchairs and buggies. Some gravel paths and woodland paths may become difficult to traverse after rain.

49 7 ROSE LANE

Ripley, Woking, GU23 6NE. Mindi McLean, 01483 223200, info@broadwaybarn.com, www.broadwaybarn.com. *Just off Ripley High St on Rose Lane, 3rd house on L next to shoe repair shop.* **Sat 9 June (10-4). Adm £3.50, chd free. Home-made teas.**
7 Rose Lane is a small but perfectly formed village centre garden behind an historic listed cottage. It has 3 rooms - a traditional perennial flower garden laid to lawn; a vegetable and fruit garden with Agriframe orchard and a working garden with greenhouse, compost bins and shed. It is a perfect example of how to make the most of a cottage garden. Monthly Ripley Farmers Market and Grapes and Grain Drinks Festival held on 9 June (9am-4pm).

50 SAFFRON GATE

Tickners Heath, Alfold, Cranleigh, GU6 8HU. Mr & Mrs D Gibbison, 01483 200219, clematis@talk21.com. *Between Alfold & Dunsfold. A281 between Guildford & Horsham approx 8m turn at Alfold crossways follow signs for Dunsfold. Do not turn at A281 T-lights for Dunsfold (wrong road).* **Visits by arrangement Apr to July normally groups of 10+. Evening visits possible during summer months. Home-made teas.**
This garden is a plant lovers paradise, colour for most of the year, many unusual plants and a plethora of clematis of all shapes and sizes as featured in the RHS garden magazine. Arbor with many varieties of climbers. A productive vegetable garden. Garden was subject of a lecture given at Great Dixter. Photos used in RHS Garden magazine. Disabled drop off point.

51 NEW 69 SALISBURY GROVE

Mytchett, Camberley, GU16 6DA. Juliette Derwent, 07702 241921, juliette@mycraftedgarden.co.uk, www.mycraftedgarden.co.uk. *At double r'bout in Mytchett, follow signs for Basingstoke Canal Centre, turn L into Salisbury Grove. From Brookwood/Pirbright, go past Canal Centre, over bridge, turn R before double r'about.* **Sat 11 Aug (11-5). Adm £3, chd free. Light refreshments. Visits also by arrangement June to Sept small groups possible.**
On the Surrey/Hampshire/Berkshire border, My Crafted Garden is a small garden with a difference. Full of garden art/crafts and terracotta pots, there is so much to see. A garden would not be a garden without the plants and My Crafted Garden specialises in acers and grasses, amongst others. There is also a bus shelter (yes really!) and a raised fish pond. Garden decorations are for sale. Close to Mytchett Canal Centre & Canalside Walks.

GROUP OPENING

52 SHACKLEFORD GARDEN SAFARI

Godalming, GU8 6AY. *5m SW of Guildford. Go to centre of Shackleford Village which is ½m towards Elstead from A3 Hurtmore/Shackleford junction. Follow signs for parking.* **Sun 10 June (10.30-5). Combined adm £10, chd free.**

NEW ALDRO SCHOOL
Mr James Hanson.

DOLPHIN HOUSE
Mr & Mrs C Bell.

HEADLANDS
David & Jackie Sowerbutts.

NORNEY WOOD
Mr & Mrs R Thompson, www.norneywood.co.uk.
D

Enjoy a leisurely Sunday visiting three inspirational gardens and the private grounds of Aldro preparatory school, in the village of Shackleford in the Surrey Hills, finishing with tea and cake at Norney Wood. Three of the gardens have opened previously and Aldro School is opening its gates for the first time under the NGS. Meet the owners, headmaster and gardeners and hear their stories, from the creation of a new garden to the conservation of historic areas within a modern context. Meander through the naturalistic planting, meadow and woodland of Headlands. See the historical walls and the sophisticated and richly planted borders of Dolphin House. For the first time, enter the gates of Aldro School that includes a 20th century garden with features by Gertrude Jekyll. And finally, relax in the gardens of Norney Wood amidst the heavenly scented Gertrude Jekyll roses to enjoy delicious home-made teas. Follow signs for parking to start your visit at either Headlands or Dolphin House. Surrey Hills village, historic buildings and structures, country gardens, contemporary landscaping, woodland, ancient trees, formal and informal water features, Society of Garden Designer gardens. Partial wheelchair access available at most gardens. Gravel paths, steps and slopes.

---

53 41 SHELVERS WAY

Tadworth, KT20 5QJ. Keith & Elizabeth Lewis, 01737 210707, kandelewis@ntlworld.com. *6m S of Sutton off A217. 1st turning on R after Burgh Heath T-lights heading S on A217. 400yds down Shelvers Way on L.* **Sun 22 Apr, Sun 5 Aug (2-5.30). Adm £5, chd free. Home-made teas. Visits also by arrangement Apr to Aug for groups 10+.**

Visitors say 'one of the most colourful back gardens in Surrey'. In spring, a myriad of small bulbs with specialist daffodils and many pots of colourful tulips. Choice perennials follow, with rhododendrons and azaleas. Cobbles and shingle support grasses and self sown plants with a bubble fountain. Annuals, phlox and herbaceous plants ensure colour well into September. A garden for all seasons.

54 SHIELING

The Warren, Kingswood, Tadworth, KT20 6PQ. Drs Sarah & Robin Wilson, 01737 833370, sarahwilson@doctors.org.uk. *Kingswood Warren Estate. Off A217, gated entrance just before church on southbound side of dual carriageway after Tadworth r'about . ¾m walk from Station. Parking on The Warren or by church on A217.* **Sun 27 May (11-5). Adm £5, chd free. Home-made teas. Visits also by arrangement May & June.**

One acre garden restored to its original 1920s design. Formal front garden with island beds and shrub border. Unusual large rock garden and mixed borders with collection of beautiful slug free hostas and uncommon perennials. The rest is a woodland garden with acid loving plants and some old and interesting trees and shrubs. Plant list provided for visitors. Gravel drive and some narrow paths in back garden. Otherwise grass and paths easy for wheelchairs.

55 SOUTHLANDS LODGE

Southlands Lane, Tandridge, Oxted, RH8 9PH. Colin David & John Barker. *3m from J6 of M25. From Tandridge Village head S down hill for ¼m to T-junction with Southlands Lane. Turn L along Southlands Lane, approx ¼m to Southlands Lodge entrance gate.* **Evening opening Sat 7, Sun 8 July (5.30-9). Adm £4, chd free. Wine.**

A surprising garden, on the edge of a woodland, enjoying open views of adjacent fields. Formal and informal areas are scaled to compliment a late Georgian gatehouse. Mass planting offsets selected specimens, mostly chosen for their pollen and nectar that helps sustain the resident honey bees. An enclosed vegetable garden with greenhouse, a flock of Shetland sheep and chickens also feature. The garden contains a working apiary of 10 beehives.

56 SPRINGWOOD HOUSE

85 Petworth Road, Haslemere, GU27 3AX. Mr & Mrs Ian Bateson. *1m E of Haslemere. Entrance to property is almost opp junction of Holdfast Lane with Petworth Road. Postcode for SatNav brings you approx 300yds W entrance.* **Sun 22, Sun 29 Apr (11-4). Adm £5, chd free. Home-made teas.**

Wooded walkway with large amount of native bluebells at the end of April, and 24 small wooden bridges following spring-fed stream. 3 large ponds with further bridges set in parkland type garden, waterfalls connecting the ponds which contain fish and also three small islands. Two large fields with walkways round the perimeter, and an orchard. Bridge walkway is narrow and bare earth, step of 2-3 inches at each bridge. At end of walk there is a steep path, return if necessary.

57 SPURFOLD

Radnor Road, Peaslake, Guildford, GU5 9SZ. Mr & Mrs A Barnes, 01306 730196, spurfold@btinternet.com. *8m SE of Guildford. A25 to Shere then through to Peaslake. Pass Village stores & L up Radnor Rd.* **Sun 27 May (11-5.30). Adm £6, chd free. Home-made teas. Visits also by arrangement May to July, home-made teas (day), wine (eve). Group refreshments can be discussed.**

2½ acres, large herbaceous and shrub borders, formal pond with Cambodian Buddha head, sunken gravel garden with topiary box and water feature, terraces, beautiful lawns, mature rhododendrons and azaleas, woodland paths, and gazebos. Garden contains a collection of Indian elephants and other objets d'art. Topiary garden created 2010 and new formal lawn area created in 2012. Garden featured in Period Living magazine.

58 STUART COTTAGE

Ripley Road, East Clandon, GU4 7SF. John & Gayle Leader, 01483 222689, gayle@stuartcottage.com, www.stuartcottage.com. *4m E of Guildford. Off A246 or from A3 through Ripley until r'about, turn L & cont through West Clandon until T-lights, then L onto A246. East Clandon 1st L.* **Visits by arrangement May to Sept for groups of 15+. Home-made teas. Suitable refreshments by arrangement for groups.**

Walk in to this tranquil partly walled ½ acre garden to find an oasis of calm. Beds grouped around the central fountain offer floral continuity through the seasons with soft harmonious planting supported by good structure with topiary, a rose/clematis walk and wisteria walk. Outside the wall is the late border with its vibrant colours and fun planting. A small orchard and decorative organic kitchen garden with central iron structure supporting apple trees.

59 STUARTFIELD

113 Silverdale Avenue, Walton-on-Thames, KT12 1EQ. Caroline Ingram MBE & Kevin Ingram. *1.3m S of Walton-on-Thames. From A3, A245 to Walton. R B365 Seven Hills Rd. At 2nd r'about A317 to Walton. L next r'about B365 Ashley Rd. Silverdale Av 2nd on L.* **Sun 13 May (11-4). Adm £5, chd free. Home-made teas.**

An inspiring garden that takes you to different parts of the world, whether through New Zealand tree ferns, Japanese acers, or a Moroccan inspired summerhouse. A mature garden with planting inspired by the tropics, as well as the challenges of shade. The garden was extensively redesigned by Joe Swift of Gardener's World fame. There is also a pond and many sculptural features to enjoy.

60 35 TADORNE ROAD

Tadworth, KT20 5TF. Rod & Thelma Lay. *6m S of Sutton, 3m N of M25 J8. On A217 to large r'about. Take B2220 signed Tadworth. Tadorne Rd 2nd on R.* **Sat 28, Sun 29 July (1.30-5.30). Adm £4, chd free. Home-made teas.**

Colourful, curvaceous garden with lots of variety and hidden corners. We have bright herbaceous borders, shrubby island beds, flower covered pergolas, wildlife pond, secluded seating areas, potager style vegetable plot, pebble patch, wild woodland corner and varied patio display – all in ⅓ acre! Delicious home-made teas served in plant filled conservatory. Gravel drive at entrance.

61 THE THERAPY GARDEN

Manor Fruit Farm, Glaziers Lane, Normandy, Guildford, GU3 2DT. The Centre Manager, 01483 813846, info@thetherapygarden.org, www.thetherapygarden.org. *SW of Guildford. Take A323 travelling from Guildford towards Aldershot, turn L into Glaziers Lane in centre of Normandy village opp War Memorial. The Therapy Garden is 200yds on L.* **Sun 3 June, Sun 2 Sept (11-4). Adm £5, chd free. Light refreshments. Visits also by arrangement Apr to Sept for groups or single visitors.**

The Therapy Garden is a horticulture and education charity that uses gardening to generate positive change for adults and teenagers living with learning difficulties and mental health challenges. Our gardens are designed for accessibility incl wheelchair friendly pathways, raised vegetable and flower beds, sensory areas and quiet spaces. The Therapy Garden is a registered charity that provides social and therapeutic horticulture to different groups in the local community. Light lunches, salads and sandwiches, teas, coffees and cakes all available. The Therapy Garden featured on ITV's 'Love Your Garden'. Paved pathways throughout the garden, many with substantial handrails.

62 TILFORD COTTAGE

Tilford Road, Tilford, GU10 2BX. Mr & Mrs R Burn, 01252 795423 or 07712 142728, rodburn@tiscali.co.uk, www.tilfordcottagegarden.co.uk. *3m SE of Farnham. From Farnham station along Tilford Rd. Tilford Cottage opp Tilford House. Parking by village green.* **Visits by arrangement Apr to Sept. Adm £6, chd free. Groups 6+**

Artist's garden designed to surprise, delight and amuse. Formal planting, herb and knot garden. Numerous examples of topiary combine beautifully with the wild flower river walk. Japanese and water gardens, hosta beds, rose, apple and willow arches, treehouse and fairy grotto all continue the playful quality especially enjoyed by children. Dogs on lead please. Local pub within walking distance. Partial wheelchair access. Some gravel paths and steep slopes.

63 TIMBER HILL

Chertsey Road, Chobham, GU24 8JF. Nick & Lavinia Sealy, 01932 873875, nicksealy@chobham.net, www.timberhillgarden.co.uk. *4m N of Woking. 2½m E of Chobham & ⅓m E of Fairoaks aerodrome on A319 (N side). 1¼m W of Ottershaw, J11 M25.* **Sat 17 Mar, Sun 8 Apr, Sun 4 Nov (11-3.30). Adm £5, chd free. Home-made teas. Visits also by arrangement Feb to June.**

Beautifully kept 15 acre park like garden and woodland with views to N Downs. Fine oaks, liquidambar and liriodendron. Early witch hazel walk, a sea of snowdrops and species crocus; beech, cherry, maples, acers, over 200 camellias and magnolias. Drifts of spring narcissi, daffodils and stunning camassias, tulips in borders; bluebells/azaleas in May; early roses in June. Fine autumn colour. A garden for all seasons! Nature and wildlife trails for children. Refreshments served in beautiful old Surrey barn. Delicous home-made cakes and tea served in beautiful old Surrey barn **For**

other information and events, please telephone or see garden website .

♿ 🐕 ✿ ☕

64 ◆ TITSEY PLACE GARDENS

Titsey, Oxted, RH8 0SA. The Trustees of the Titsey Foundation, 01273 407007, tom.hayes@struttandparker.com, www.titsey.org. *3m N of Oxted. A25 between Oxted & Westerham. Follow brown signs to Titsey Estate from A25 at Limpsfield or see website directions.* **For NGS: Sun 20 May, Sun 17 June, Sun 22 July, Sun 19 Aug (11-5). Adm £5, chd £1.** For other opening times and information, please phone, email or visit garden website.

One of the largest surviving historic estates in Surrey. Magnificent ancestral home and gardens of the Gresham family since 1534. Walled kitchen garden restored early 1990s. Golden Jubilee rose garden. Etruscan summer house adjoining picturesque lakes and fountains. 15 acres of formal and informal gardens in idyllic setting within the M25. Tearooms with delicious home-made teas served between 12:30-5 on open days. Last admissions to gardens at 4pm, gardens close at 5pm. Dogs allowed in picnic area, car park and woodland walks. Disabled car park alongside tearooms.

♿ ☕

65 ◆ VANN

Hambledon, GU8 4EF. Mrs M Caroe, 01428 683413, vann@caroe.com, www.vanngarden.co.uk. *6m S of Godalming. A283 to Lane End, Hambledon. On NGS days only, follow yellow Vann signs for 2m. Please park in the field, not in the road. At other times follow the website instructions.* **For NGS: Sun 25 Mar (11-5); Sun 15, Mon 16, Tue 17, Wed 18 Apr (10-6). Mon 7 May (2-6). Home-made teas. Daily Tue 8 May to Sun 13 May (10-6). Sun 17 June (10-6). Adm £6.50, chd free. N.B. Home-made teas Mon 7 May only.** For other opening times and information, please phone, email or visit garden website.

5 acre English Heritage registered garden surrounding Tudor and William and Mary house (not open) with Arts and Crafts additions by W D Caröe incl a Bargate stone pergola. At the front, brick paved original cottage garden; to the rear, newly dredged lake, yew walk with rill and Gertrude Jekyll water garden. Snowdrops and hellebores, spring bulbs, spectacular Fritillaria in Feb/March. Island beds, crinkle crankle wall, orchard with wild flowers. Vegetable garden. Gertrude Jekyll water garden and spring bulbs. Open by appointment. Featured in Life in Haslemere 'Vann Glorious'. Water garden paths not suitable for wheelchairs, but many others are. Please ring prior to visit to request disabled parking.

♿ ✿ 🚌 ☕

66 57 WESTHALL ROAD

Warlingham, CR6 9BG. Robert & Wendy Baston. *3m N of M25. M25, J6, A22 London, at Whyteleafe r'about, take 3rd R, under railway bridge, turn immed R into Westhall Rd.* **Sat 5, Sun 6 May (2-5). Adm £3.50, chd free. Home-made teas. Free top ups on tea and coffee.** Donation to Warlingham Methodist Church.

Reward for the sure footed – many steep steps to 3 levels! Swathes of tulips and alliums. Mature kiwi and grape vines. Mixed borders. Raised vegetable beds. Box, bay, cork oak and yew topiaries. Amphitheatre of potted plants on lower steps. Stunning views of Caterham and Whyteleafe from top garden. Featured in Surrey Life Magazine.

🐕 ✿ ☕

67 WESTWAYS FARM

Gracious Pond Road, Chobham, GU24 8HH. Paul & Nicky Biddle, 01276 856163, nicolabiddle@rocketmail.com. *4m N of Woking. From Chobham Church proceed over r'about towards Sunningdale, 1st Xrds R into Red Lion Rd to junction with Mincing Lane.* **Sat 12, Sun 13 May (11-4.30). Adm £4, chd free. Home-made teas. Visits also by arrangement May & June for groups min 10, max 50.**

6 acre garden surrounded by woodlands planted in 1930s with mature and some rare rhododendrons, azaleas, camellias and magnolias, underplanted with bluebells, lilies and dogwood; extensive lawns and sunken pond garden. Working stables and sandschool. Lovely Queen Anne House (not open) covered with listed *Magnolia grandiflora*. Victorian design glasshouse. New planting round garden room.

♿ 🐕 ✿ 🚌 ☕

68 WOODBURY COTTAGE

Colley Lane, Reigate, RH2 9JJ. Shirley & Bob Stoneley, 01737 244235. *1m W of Reigate. M25 J8, A217 (Reigate). Immed before level crossing turn R into Somers Rd, cont as Manor Rd. At end turn R into Coppice Lane & follow signs to car park. Do not come up Colley Lane from A25.* **Sat 7, Sun 8 July, Sat 8, Sun 9, Tue 11 Sept (1-5). Adm £4, chd free. Home-made teas. Visits also by arrangement July to Oct groups 10+.**

Cottage garden just under ¼ acre. It is stepped on a slope, enhanced by its setting under Colley Hill and the North Downs. We grow a colourful diversity of plants incl perennials, annuals and tender ones. A particular feature throughout the garden is the use of groups of pots containing unusual and interesting plants. The garden is colour themed and is still rich and vibrant in September.

✿ ☕

Donations from the National Garden Scheme enable Perennial to care for horticulturalists

SUSSEX

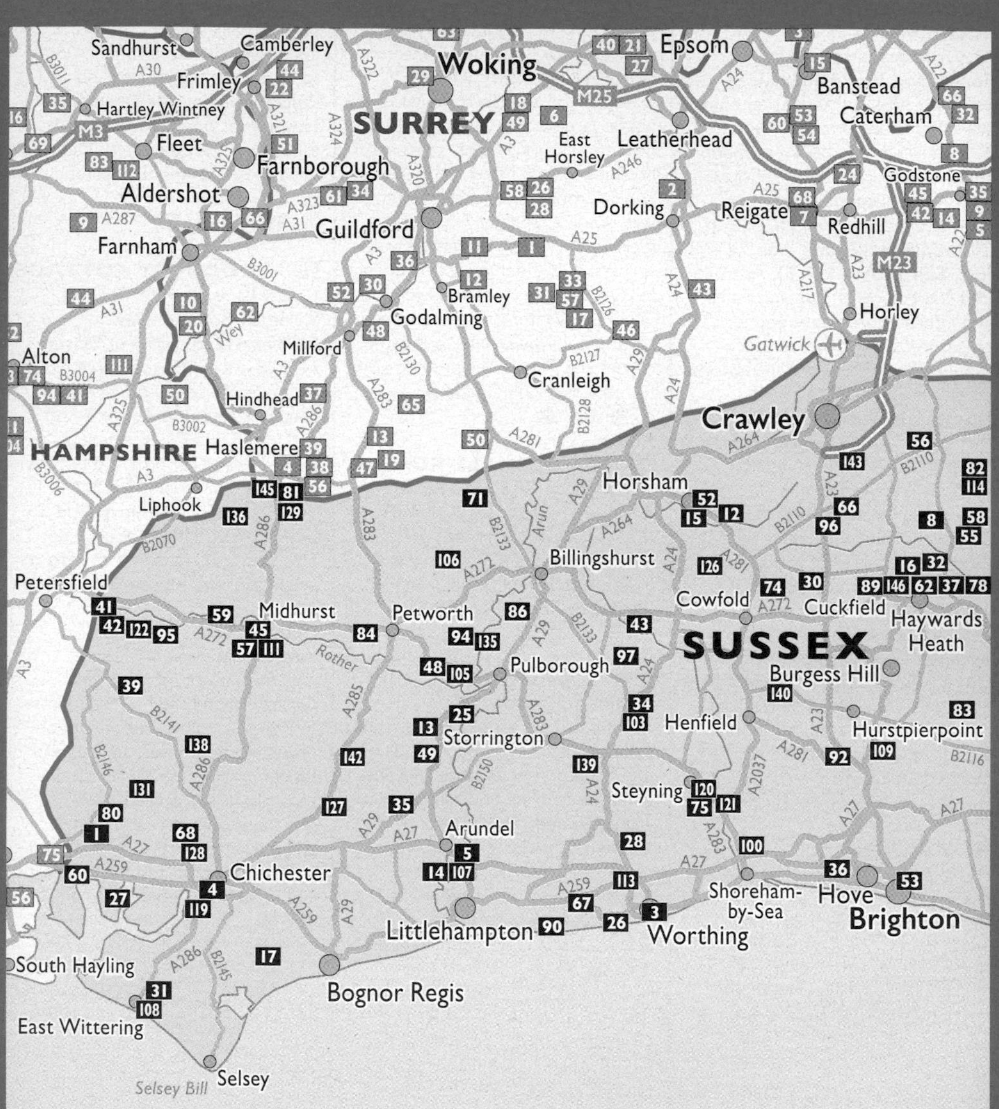

SURREY
HAMPSHIRE
SUSSEX
Sandhurst
Camberley
Woking
Epsom
Frimley
Banstead
Hartley Wintney
Caterham
Fleet
East Horsley
Leatherhead
Farnborough
Aldershot
Godstone
Dorking
Reigate
Guildford
Redhill
Farnham
Bramley
Godalming
Horley
Millford
Gatwick
Alton
Cranleigh
Hindhead
Crawley
Haslemere
Liphook
Horsham
Billingshurst
Petersfield
Midhurst
Petworth
Cowfold
Cuckfield
Haywards Heath
Pulborough
Burgess Hill
Henfield
Hurstpierpoint
Storrington
Steyning
Arundel
Chichester
Shoreham-by-Sea
Hove
Brighton
Littlehampton
Worthing
South Hayling
Bognor Regis
East Wittering
Selsey
Selsey Bill
Wey
Arun
Rother

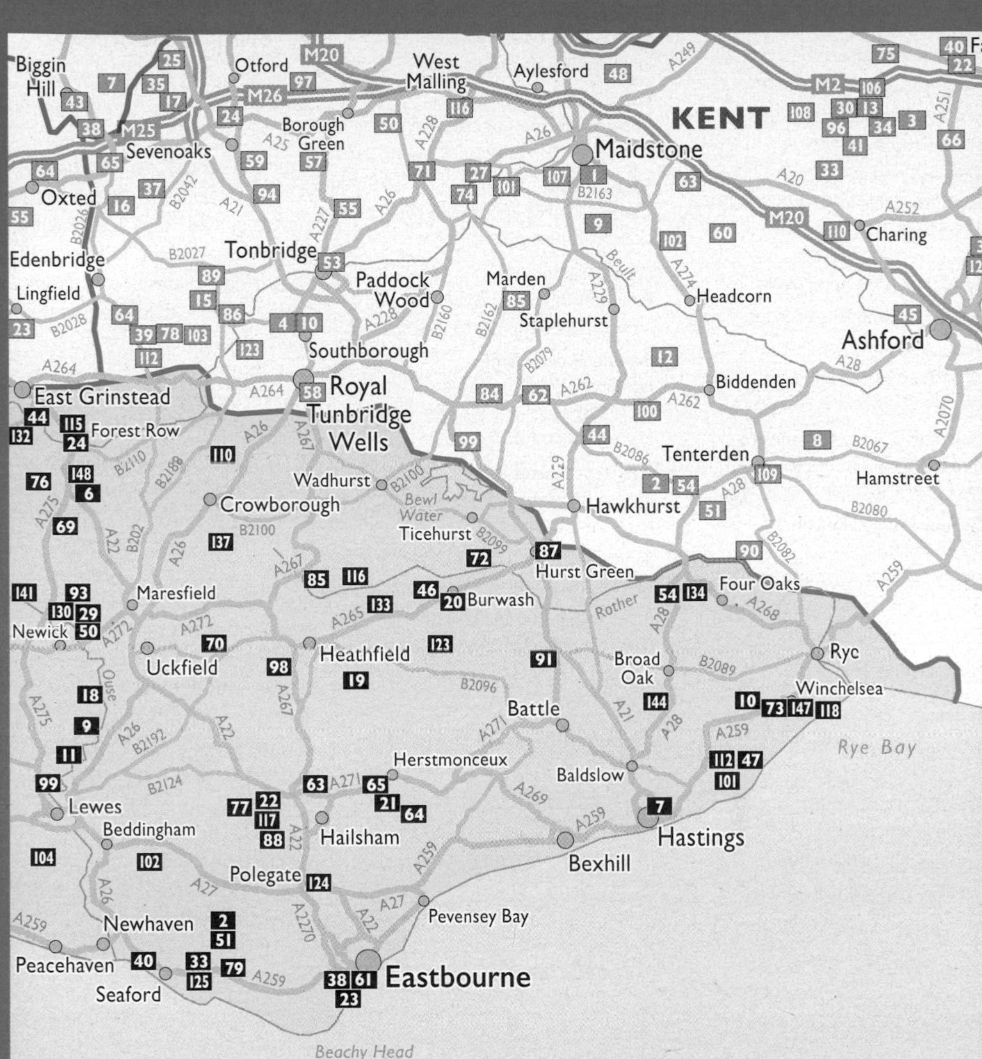
KENT
Biggin Hill
Otford
West Malling
Aylesford
Maidstone
Sevenoaks
Borough Green
Oxted
Edenbridge
Lingfield
Tonbridge
Paddock Wood
Marden
Staplehurst
Headcorn
Charing
Ashford
Southborough
Royal Tunbridge Wells
East Grinstead
Forest Row
Biddenden
Tenterden
Hamstreet
Wadhurst
Bewl Water
Ticehurst
Crowborough
Hawkhurst
Hurst Green
Maresfield
Newick
Burwash
Four Oaks
Rother
Uckfield
Heathfield
Broad Oak
Rye
Winchelsea
Battle
Rye Bay
Herstmonceux
Baldslow
Lewes
Beddingham
Hailsham
Hastings
Bexhill
Polegate
Newhaven
Pevensey Bay
Peacehaven
Seaford
Eastbourne
Beachy Head
Ouse
Beult
0 10 kilometres
0 5 miles
© Global Mapping / XYZ Maps

East & Mid Sussex Volunteers

County Organiser, Booklet & Advertising Co-ordinator
Irene Eltringham-Willson
01323 833770
irene.willson@btinternet.com

County Treasurer
Andrew Ratcliffe 01435 873310
anratcliffe@gmail.com

Publicity
Geoff Stonebanks 01323 899296
ngseastsussex@gmail.com

Twitter
Liz Warner 01273 586050
liz@elizabethwarnergardendesign.com

Photographer
Liz Seeber 01323 639478
lizseeber@btinternet.com

Assistant County Organisers
Jane Baker 01273 842805
jane.baker47@btinternet.com

Michael & Linda Belton
01797 252984
belton.northiam@gmail.com

Linda Field 01323 720179
lindafield3@gmail.com

Diane Gould 01825 750300
lavenderdgould@gmail.com

Aideen Jones 01323 899452
sweetpeasa52@gmail.com

Susan Laing 01444 892500
splaing@btinternet.com

Sarah Ratcliffe 01435 873310
sallyrat@btinternet.com

Geoff Stonebanks (as above)

Liz Warner (as above)

David Wright 01435 883149
david.wright101@btinternet.com

West Sussex Volunteers

County Organiser
Patty Christie 01730 813323
sussexwestngs@gmail.com

County Treasurer
Liz Collison 01903 719245
liz.collison@ngs.org.uk

Publicity
Position Vacant. For details please contact Patty Christie (as above)

Social Media
Claudia Pearce 07985 648216
claudiapearce17@gmail.com

Photographer
Judi Lion 07810 317057
judilion.ngs@gmail.com

Booklet Advertising
Ian Gregory
01903 892433
id.gregory@btinternet.com

Assistant County Organisers
Teresa Barttelot 01798 865690
tbarttelot@gmail.com

Sanda Belcher 01428 723259
sandambelcher@gmail.com

Lesley Chamberlain 07950 105966
chamberlain_lesley@hotmail.com

Sue Foley 01243 814452
suefoley@mac.com

Elizabeth Gregory 01903 892433
elizabethgregory1@btinternet.com

Peter & Terri Lefevre 01403 256002
teresalefevre@outlook.com

Jane Lywood 07852 684488
jmlywood@aol.com

Judi Lion (as above)

Carrie McArdle 01403 820272
carrie.mcardle@btinternet.com

Claudia Pearce (as above)

Fiona Phillips 01273 462285
fiona.h.phillips@btinternet.com

Susan Pinder 01403 820430
nasus.rednip@gmail.com

Diane Rose 07789 565094
dirose8@me.com

Sussex is a vast county with two county teams, one covering East and Mid Sussex and the other covering West Sussex.

Over 80 miles from west to east, Sussex spans the southern side of the Weald from the exposed sandstone heights of Ashdown Forest, past the broad clay vales with their heavy yet fertile soils and the imposing chalk ridge of the South Downs National Park, to the equable if windy coastal strip.

Away from the chalk, Sussex is a county with a largely wooded landscape with imposing oaks, narrow hedged lanes and picturesque villages. The county offers much variety and our gardens reflect this. There is something for absolutely everyone and we feel sure that you will enjoy your garden visiting experience - from rolling acres of parkland, country and town gardens, to small courtyards and village trails. See the results of the owner's attempts to cope with the various conditions, discover new plants and talk with the owners about their successes.

Many of our gardens are open by arrangement, so do not be afraid to book a visit or organise a visit with your local gardening or U3A group.

Should you need advice, please e-mail ngseastsussex@gmail.com for anything relating to East and Mid Sussex or sussexwestngs@gmail.com for anything in West Sussex.

OPENING DATES

All entries subject to change. For latest information check **www.ngs.org.uk**

Extended openings are shown at the beginning of the month.

Map locator numbers are shown to the right of each garden name.

February

Snowdrop Festival

By Arrangement
Pembury House 109

Sunday 11th
Manor of Dean 84

Sunday 18th
◆ Highdown Gardens 67
Sandhill Farm House 122

Sunday 25th
The Old Vicarage 103

March

Friday 2nd
The Garden House 53

Saturday 10th
Cissbury 28

Sunday 11th
◆ King John's Lodge 72

Sunday 18th
Manor of Dean 84

Saturday 24th
Butlers Farmhouse 21

Sunday 25th
Butlers Farmhouse 21

April

Monday 2nd
The Old Vicarage 103

Saturday 7th
Oakleigh Cottage 98

Sunday 8th
Dachs 34
Oakleigh Cottage 98
Shalford House 129

Saturday 14th
Rymans 119
Winchelsea's Secret Gardens 147

Sunday 15th
Dachs 34
Newtimber Place 92
Rymans 119
Shepherds Cottage 131

Monday 16th
Copyhold Hollow 32
Shepherds Cottage 131

Tuesday 17th
Bignor Park 13

Saturday 21st
Cookscroft 31
The Garden House 53
Sandhill Farm House 122

Sunday 22nd
The Garden House 53
Manor of Dean 84
Parsonage Farm 106
Penns in the Rocks 110
Sandhill Farm House 122

Tuesday 24th
Copyhold Hollow 32

Wednesday 25th
Fittleworth House 48

Saturday 28th
Banks Farm 9
Burwash Hidden Gardens 20
Down Place 39

Sunday 29th
Banks Farm 9
Blue Jays 15
◆ Clinton Lodge 29
Down Place 39
Offham House 99
Peelers Retreat 107

May

Every Wednesday
Fittleworth House 48

Thursday 3rd
Fairlight End 47

Saturday 5th
◆ King John's Lodge 72

Sunday 6th
◆ King John's Lodge 72
Mountfield Court 91
NEW Stanley Farm 136

Monday 7th
Copyhold Hollow 32
NEW 70 Dale View 36

Wednesday 9th
◆ Sheffield Park and Garden 130
Wych Warren House 148

Saturday 12th
Holly House 69
The Moongate Garden 90
Stone Cross House 137

Sunday 13th
Champs Hill 25
Cookscroft 31
Ham Cottage 58
Hammerwood House 59
Holly House 69
The Moongate Garden 90
The Old Vicarage 103
Stone Cross House 137

Tuesday 15th
Bignor Park 13
Copyhold Hollow 32

Wednesday 16th
Balcombe Gardens 8
Cookscroft 31

Thursday 17th
The Apuldram Centre 4

Friday 18th
Caxton Manor 24
2 Quarry Cottages 115

Saturday 19th
96 Ashford Road 7
Caxton Manor 24
NEW Harlands Gardens 62
2 Quarry Cottages 115

Sunday 20th
Aldsworth House 1
NEW Harlands Gardens 62
Legsheath Farm 76
Peelers Retreat 107
Penns in the Rocks 110
Sennicotts 128
Shalford House 129

Monday 21st
Sennicotts 128

Tuesday 22nd
Aldsworth House 1

Wednesday 23rd
The Walled Garden At Tilgate Park 143

Thursday 24th
The Apuldram Centre 4
The Walled Garden At Tilgate Park 143

Friday 25th
Copyhold Hollow 32

Saturday 26th
96 Ashford Road 7
54 Elmleigh 45
◆ The Priest House 114
NEW 71 Stonerock Cottage 138

Sunday 27th
The Beeches 11
54 Elmleigh 45
NEW 71 Stonerock Cottage 138
Upwaltham Barns 142

Monday 28th
54 Elmleigh 45
Great Lywood Farmhouse 55
Upwaltham Barns 142

Wednesday 30th
◆ Highdown Gardens 67
NEW Oaklands Farm 97

Thursday 31st
The Apuldram Centre 4

June

Every Wednesday
Fittleworth House 48

Friday 1st
Great Lywood Farmhouse 55

Festival Weekend

Saturday 2nd
Lordington House 80
Lowder Mill 81
Waterworks & Friends 144

Sunday 3rd
Dittons End 38
Great Lywood Farmhouse 55
NEW Guillards Oak Gardens 57
Hardwycke 61
Lordington House 80
Lowder Mill 81
Offham House 99
Sedgwick Park House 126
NEW Sienna Wood 132

Tuesday 5th
NEW Guillards Oak Gardens 57

Wednesday 6th
Rolfs Farm 116

Thursday 7th
The Apuldram Centre 4

Friday 8th
NEW 1 Pest Cottage 111

Saturday 9th
51 Carlisle Road 23
Durford Mill House 42
54 Elmleigh 45
Mayfield Gardens 85
Old Vicarage 102

Sunday 10th
Ashdown Park Hotel 6
Beauchamps 10
Bignor Park 13
51 Carlisle Road 23
Dale Park House 35
Durford Mill House 42
54 Elmleigh 45
Herstmonceux Parish Trail 65
◆ High Beeches Woodland and Water Garden 66
Mayfield Gardens 85
NEW Mill Hall Farm 89
Peelers Retreat 107
NEW 1 Pest Cottage 111
Sayerland House 124

Monday 11th
◆ Clinton Lodge 29

Wednesday 13th
4 Hillside Cottages 68
Rolfs Farm 116

Thursday 14th
The Apuldram Centre 4
Bradness Gallery 18
Chidmere Gardens 27
Elphicks Cottage 46
Town Place 141

Friday 15th
Elphicks Cottage 46

Saturday 16th
Balcombe Gardens 8
Channel View 26
Cookscroft 31
Down Place 39
◆ King John's Lodge 72
Rymans 119
Winchelsea's Secret Gardens 147

Sunday 17th
Channel View 26
Down Place 39
◆ King John's Lodge 72
NEW Meadow Farm 86
The Old Vicarage 103
Rymans 119
Seaford Gardens 125
Selhurst Park 127

Tuesday 19th
◆ Alfriston Clergy House 2
Driftwood 40

Thursday 21st
Town Place 141

Friday 22nd
Parsonage Farm 106

Saturday 23rd
Burwash Hidden Gardens 20
Durford Abbey Barn 41
54 Elmleigh 45
◆ Herstmonceux Castle Gardens and Grounds 64
Luctons 82
North Hall 93
NEW Pett Village Gardens 112
◆ The Priest House 114
Sandhill Farm House 122

Sunday 24th
Ambrose Place Back Gardens 3
Durford Abbey Barn 41
54 Elmleigh 45
Foxglove Cottage 52
Luctons 82
North Hall 93
NEW Pett Village Gardens 112
Sandhill Farm House 122
Town Place 141

Monday 25th
◆ Clinton Lodge 29
1 Rose Cottage 117

Tuesday 26th
Luctons 82

Thursday 28th
The Long House 79

Friday 29th
Cupani Garden 33
◆ St Mary's House Gardens 121

Saturday 30th
◆ St Mary's House Gardens 121

July

Sunday 1st
NEW Bowley Farm 17
NEW 70 Dale View 36
North Springs 94
33 Peerley Road 108
Town Place 141

Thursday 5th
NEW Old Stonelynk Edge 101

Saturday 7th
Fletching Secret Gardens 50
Holly House 69

Sunday 8th
Foxglove Cottage 52
NEW Hellingly Parish Trail 63
Holly House 69
Peelers Retreat 107
Town Place 141

Tuesday 10th
Driftwood 40

Wednesday 11th
Wych Warren House 148

Friday 13th
Cupani Garden 33

Saturday 14th
54 Elmleigh 45

Sunday 15th
54 Elmleigh 45
Saffrons 120

Monday 16th
Copyhold Hollow 32

Wednesday 18th
NEW Oaklands Farm 97
South Grange 134
The Walled Garden At Tilgate Park 143

Thursday 19th
Saffrons 120
The Walled Garden At Tilgate Park 143

Saturday 21st
The Hundred House 70
Ouse Valley To The Coast Trail 104

Sunday 22nd
NEW East Grinstead Town Gardens 44
4 Hillside Cottages 68
The Hundred House 70
Ouse Valley To The Coast Trail 104
NEW Park Lodge 105

Tuesday 24th
Driftwood 40

Friday 27th
Cupani Garden 33

Saturday 28th
The Beeches 11
54 Elmleigh 45
Ham Cottage 58
The Moongate Garden 90

Sunday 29th
The Beeches 11
54 Elmleigh 45
Ham Cottage 58
The Moongate Garden 90

Monday 30th
◆ Clinton Lodge 29

August

Wednesday 1st
Cupani Garden 33

Sunday 5th
Driftwood 40
Manor of Dean 84

Thursday 9th
◆ Merriments 87

Friday 10th
NEW South Binns, Swife Lane 133

Saturday 11th
Butlers Farmhouse 21
NEW South Binns, Swife Lane 133

Sunday 12th
Butlers Farmhouse 21
Camberlot Hall 22
Champs Hill 25
Colwood House 30

Saturday 18th
Camberlot Hall 22
Holly House 69
Limekiln Farm 77

Sunday 19th
NEW 70 Dale View 36
Holly House 69
Limekiln Farm 77
Malthouse Farm 83

Wednesday 22nd
Malthouse Farm 83

Saturday 25th
4 Ben's Acre 12

Monday 27th
Durrance Manor 43
The Old Vicarage 103

September

Saturday 1st
Follers Manor 51
South Grange 134

Sunday 2nd
Follers Manor 51
Grove Farm House 56
Jacaranda 71
South Grange 134

Thursday 6th
Chidmere Gardens 27

Sunday 9th
Parsonage Farm 106
◆ Sussex Prairies 140

Friday 14th
◆ Sarah Raven's Cutting Garden 123

Saturday 15th
Rymans 119

Sunday 16th
The Moongate Garden 90
Peelers Retreat 107
Rymans 119

Saturday 22nd
King's Leap 73
Rye View 118
Sandhill Farm House 122

Sunday 23rd
◆ High Beeches Woodland and Water Garden 66
◆ King John's Lodge 72
◆ Nymans 96
Sandhill Farm House 122

October

Monday 1st
◆ Borde Hill Garden 16

Sunday 14th
The Old Vicarage 103

Wednesday 17th
◆ Great Dixter House, Gardens & Nurseries 54

By Arrangement

Aldsworth House 1
The Beeches 11
4 Ben's Acre 12
4 Birch Close 14
Blue Jays 15
Bradness Gallery 18
Brightling Down Farm 19
Butlers Farmhouse 21
51 Carlisle Road 23
Champs Hill 25
Channel View 26
Colwood House 30
Cookscroft 31
Copyhold Hollow 32
Cupani Garden 33
Dachs 34
Dale Park House 35
47 Denmans Lane 37
Dittons End 38
Down Place 39
Driftwood 40
Durford Mill House 42
Durrance Manor 43
54 Elmleigh 45
Fairlight End 47
Fittleworth House 48
Five Oaks Cottage 49
Foxglove Cottage 52
The Garden House 53
Great Lywood Farmhouse 55
Ham Cottage 58
Harbourside 60
Hardwycke 61
4 Hillside Cottages 68
Holly House 69
Jacaranda 71
Laroche, 43 Coombe Drove 75
Legsheath Farm 76
NEW Lindfield Jungle 78
The Long House 79
Lordington House 80
Luctons 82
Malthouse Farm 83
Manor of Dean 84
The Moongate Garden 90
North Hall 93
Nyewood House 95
NEW Oaklands Farm 97
Old Erringham Cottage 100
The Old Vicarage 103
Peelers Retreat 107
33 Peerley Road 108
Pembury House 109
Penns in the Rocks 110
6 Plantation Rise 113
144 Rodmell Avenue, Ouse Valley To The Coast Trail 104
1 Rose Cottage 117
Rymans 119
Saffrons 120
Sandhill Farm House 122
Sayerland House 124
Sedgwick Park House 126
Shepherds Cottage 131
South Grange 134
NEW Springs Hanger 135
NEW 71 Stonerock Cottage 138
Sullington Old Rectory 139
Town Place 141
46 Westup Farm Cottages, Balcombe Gardens 8
Whitehanger 145
5 Whitemans Close 146
Winterfield, Balcombe Gardens 8

4 Ben's Acre

THE GARDENS

1 ALDSWORTH HOUSE

Emsworth Common Road, Aldsworth, PO10 8QT. Tom & Sarah Williams, darmady1@btinternet.com. *6m W of Chichester. From Havant follow signs to Stansted House until Emsworth Common Rd, stay on this road until Aldsworth. From Chichester B2178/B2146 follow road through Funtington to Aldsworth.* **Sun 20, Tue 22 May (11-5). Adm £5, chd free. Light refreshments, home-made cakes & cream teas. Visits also by arrangement Feb to May for groups of 10+ (or min charge £50).**

6 acre tranquil family garden being adapted to modern needs by plantaholic owners with enthusiastic help from two terriers. Unusual trees, shrubs, perennials, ancient apple trees, magnolias, roses and over 100 peonies. Beautiful views over National Park. Carpets of spring bulbs including snowdrops, crocuses, daffodils, bluebells and fritillaries. Two arboretums and two gravel gardens. Children's quiz. Short DVD showing the garden and family in the 1930s.

2 ◆ ALFRISTON CLERGY HOUSE

Alfriston, BN26 5TL. National Trust, 01323 871961, alfriston@nationaltrust.org.uk, www.nationaltrust.org.uk/alfriston. *4m NE of Seaford. Just E of B2108, in Alfriston village, adjoining The Tye & St Andrew's Church. Bus: RDH 125 from Lewes, Autopoint 126 from Eastbourne & Seaford.* **For NGS: Tue 19 June (10.30-4.30). Adm £5.60, chd £2.80. For other opening times and information, please phone, email or visit garden website.**

Enjoy the scent of roses; admire the vegetable garden and orchard in a tranquil setting with views across the River Cuckmere. Visit this C14 thatched Wealden hall house, the first building to be acquired by the NT in 1896. Our gardener will be available to talk to you about the garden. Partial wheelchair access.

GROUP OPENING

3 AMBROSE PLACE BACK GARDENS

Richmond Road, Worthing, BN11 1PZ. *Worthing Town Centre. Entry points: Ambrose Villa, corner Portland Rd & Richmond Rd; No 4 Ambrose Place opp Worthing Library.* **Sun 24 June (10-5). Combined adm £6, chd free. Home-made teas & cakes at Ambrose Villa & 5 Ambrose Place. Please note all gardens closed 1-2pm.**

3 AMBROSE PLACE
Michael & Claire Victory.

4 AMBROSE PLACE
Graham & Terri Heald.

5 AMBROSE PLACE
Sue Owen.

8 AMBROSE PLACE
Steve & Claire Hughes.

9 AMBROSE PLACE
Anna Irvine.

10 AMBROSE PLACE
Marie Pringle.

11 AMBROSE PLACE
Stephen & Carolyn Bailey.

12 AMBROSE PLACE
Peter May.

13 AMBROSE PLACE
Malcolm & Hilary Leeves.

14 AMBROSE PLACE
Andrew & Kristen Dryden.

AMBROSE VILLA
Mark & Christine Potter.

The highly acclaimed back gardens of Ambrose Place have been described as a horticultural phenomenon and for 2018, 11 gardens will be open for visitors. Behind a classic Regency terrace, itself the architectural jewel of Worthing, the gardens have a rich panoply of styles, plantings and layouts, drawing inspiration from such exotic diversity as Morocco, Provence and the Alhambra, to the more traditional sources of the English cottage and Victorian gardens. All within the typically limited space of a terrace. A variety of imaginative water features add to the charm and attraction for all gardeners and prove that small can be beautiful. Do come and enjoy our special spaces. Featured on BBC Sussex Radio Dig-it programme, in the Worthing Herald & West Sussex Gazette. Very limited wheelchair access to all gardens.

4 THE APULDRAM CENTRE

Appledram Lane South, Apuldram, Chichester, PO20 7PE. The Apuldram Centre, www.apuldram.org. *1m S of A27. Follow A259 Fishbourne & turn into Appledram Lane South.* **Thur 17, Thur 24, Thur 31 May, Thur 7, Thur 14 June (11-3). Adm £4, chd free. Light refreshments.**

Award-winning Wildlife and Sensory Garden. Winding pathway sensitively planted with bee loving plants, all grown from seed, which leads to a tranquil pond and bog garden. Full of surprises, this garden encompasses many interesting features incl sculptures and other art works created by our adult trainees with learning difficulties. Teas, coffees, light lunches and home-made cakes served in the café until 4pm. Booking is advised for larger groups wanting to use the café facilities. Local produce incl our home-made apple juice, local honey, plants, bird boxes and bug boxes for sale in the shop. WC on-site. Wheelchair access throughout Sensory Garden. Restricted access to working greenhouses and vegetable plots.

5 ◆ ARUNDEL CASTLE & GARDENS - THE COLLECTOR EARL'S GARDEN

Arundel, BN18 9AB. Arundel Castle Trustees Ltd, 01903 882173, visits@arundelcastle.org, www.arundelcastle.org. *In the centre of Arundel, N of A27.* **For opening times and information,**

please phone, email or visit garden website.
Ancient castle. Family home of the Duke of Norfolk. 40 acres of grounds and gardens. The Collector Earl's Garden with hot subtropical borders and wild flowers. English herbaceous borders. Stumpery. Wild flower garden, 2 restored Victorian glasshouses with exotic fruit and vegetables. Walled flower and organic kitchen gardens. C14 Fitzalan Chapel white garden.

6 ASHDOWN PARK HOTEL
Wych Cross, East Grinstead, RH18 5JR. Mr Kevin Sweet, 01342 824988, reservations@ashdownpark.co.uk, www.elitehotels.co.uk. *6m S of East Grinstead. Turn off A22 at Wych Cross T-lights.* **Sun 10 June (1-5). Adm £5, chd free. Light refreshments.**
186 acres of parkland, grounds and gardens surrounding Ashdown Park Hotel. Our Secret Garden is well worth a visit with many new plantings. Large number of deer roam the estate and can often be seen during the day. Enjoy and explore the woodland paths, quiet areas and views. Featured in Sussex Life and local press. Some gravel paths and uneven ground with steps.

7 96 ASHFORD ROAD
Hastings, TN34 2HZ. Lynda & Andrew Hayler. *From A21 (Sedlescombe Rd N) towards Hastings, take 1st exit on r'about A2101, then 3rd on L.* **Sat 19, Sat 26 May (1-5). Adm £3, chd free.**
Small (100ft x 52ft) Japanese inspired front and back garden. Full of interesting planting, with many acers, azaleas and bamboos. Over 100 different hostas, many miniature. Lower garden with greenhouse and raised beds. Also an attractive Japanese Tea House.

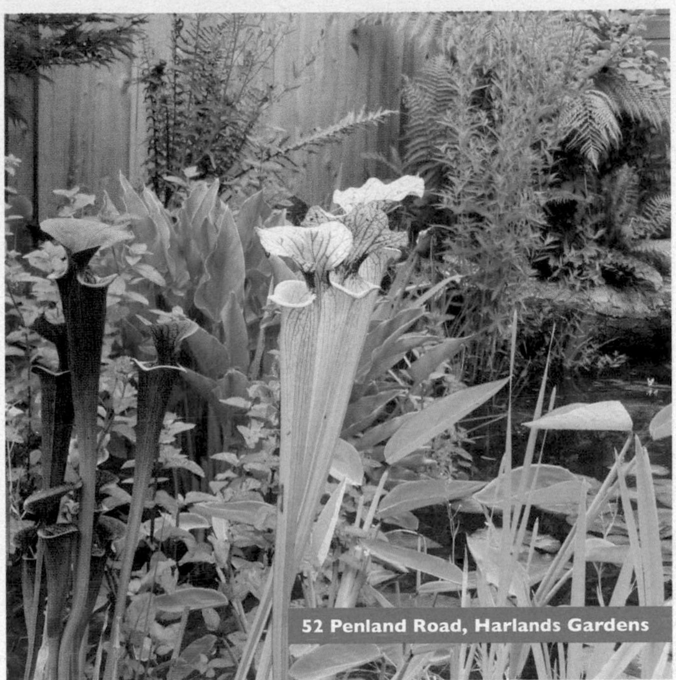
52 Penland Road, Harlands Gardens

GROUP OPENING

8 BALCOMBE GARDENS
Balcombe, RH17 6JJ. *Follow B2036 N from Cuckfield for 3m. ¼m N of Balcombe Station, turn L immed before Balcombe Primary School (signed) for ¾m. From N, take J10A from M23 & follow S for 2½m.* **Wed 16 May, Sat 16 June (12-5). Combined adm £6, chd free. Home-made teas at Stumlet.**

NEW **STUMLET**
Oldlands Avenue, RH17 6LW. Max & Nicola Preston Bell.

46 WESTUP FARM COTTAGES
London Road, RH17 6JJ. Chris Cornwell, 01444 811891, chris.westup@btinternet.com. **Visits also by arrangement Apr to Sept, minimum £10.**

WINTERFIELD
Oldlands Avenue, RH17 6LP. Sue & Sarah Howe, 01444 811380, sarahjhowe_uk@yahoo.co.uk. **Visits also by arrangement May to July for groups of 4+.**

Balcombe is in a designated AONB. Traceable back to the Saxons, the village contains 55 listed buildings incl C15 parish church of St Mary's. Nearby is the famous Ouse Valley Viaduct, ancient woodlands, lake, millpond and reservoir. Within this setting there are three quite different gardens that will appeal to plant lovers. They are full of variety and interest. No 46 is a classic cottage garden with borders, trees, shrubs, vegetables and a new herb garden amidst the countryside of the High Weald. In the village, Winterfield is a country garden packed with uncommon shrubs and trees, and a wildlife area. Whereas nearby Stumlet is a garden changing from being a space for boys to play, to becoming a peaceful area with sitting places and calming views, plus a vegetable garden. Winterfield featured on Austrian TV (2017). Wheelchair access at Winterfield and Stumlet.

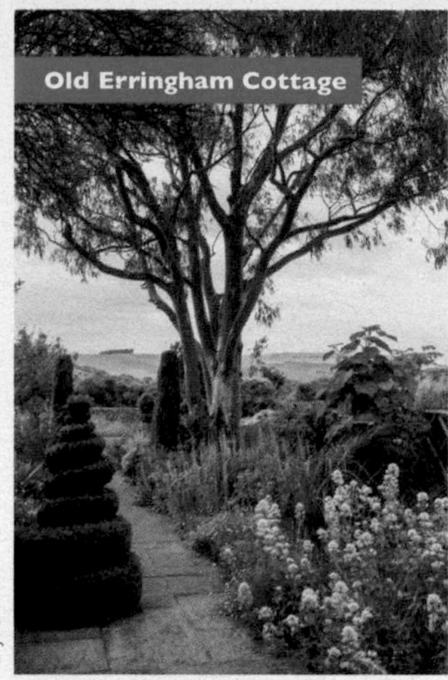
Old Erringham Cottage

9 BANKS FARM

Boast Lane, Barcombe, Lewes, BN8 5DY. Nick & Lucy Addyman. *From Barcombe Cross follow signs to Spithurst & Newick. 1st road on R into Boast Lane towards the Anchor Pub. At sharp bend carry on into Banks Farm.* **Sat 28, Sun 29 Apr (11-4). Adm £5, chd free. Home-made teas.**

9 acre garden set in rural countryside. Extensive lawns and shrub beds merge with the more naturalistic woodland garden set around the lake. An orchard, vegetable garden, ponds and a wide variety of plant species add to an interesting and very tranquil garden.

10 BEAUCHAMPS

Float Lane, Udimore, Rye, TN31 6BY. Matty & Richard Holmes. *3m W of Rye. 3m E of Broad Oak Xrds. Turn S off B2089 down Float Lane ½m.* **Sun 10 June (2-5). Adm £5, chd free. Home-made teas.**

Set in beautiful countryside, our lovely mature cottage garden features many unusual herbaceous plants, shrubs and trees, including Cornus controversa Variegata and Crinodendron hookerianum. Small areas of woodland, kitchen garden, orchard and wildflower meadow. An exceptionally wide range of excellent home propagated plants for sale, many of them to be seen flowering in the garden. Full wheelchair access, except after any recent rainfall.

11 THE BEECHES

Church Road, Barcombe, Lewes, BN8 5TS. Sandy Coppen, 01273 401339, sand@thebeechesbarcombe.com, www.thebeechesbarcombe.com. *From Lewes, A26 towards Uckfield for 3m, turn L signed Barcombe. Follow road for 1½m, turn L signed Hamsey & Church. Follow road for approx ½m & parking on the R in a field.* **Sun 27 May, Sat 28, Sun 29 July (2-5). Adm £5, chd free. Home-made teas. Visits also by arrangement June to Aug for groups of 10-16 max. Teas, and wine for early eve visits.**

C18 walled garden with cut flowers, vegetables, salads and fruit. Separate orchard and rose garden. Herbaceous borders and hot border. There are two ponds, one with a willow house. Extensive lawns and a C18 barn. A hazel walk is being developed. Featured on BBC4 A Year In An English Garden (23 Oct 2017). Some of the ground is a little bumpy but everything is accessible without steps.

12 4 BEN'S ACRE

Horsham, RH13 6LW. Pauline Clark, 01403 266912, brian.clark8850@yahoo.co.uk. *E of Horsham. A281 via Cowfold, after Hilliers Garden Centre, turn R by Tesco, St Leonards Rd-Comptons Ln. 5th R Heron Way at r'about, 2nd L Glebe Cres, 1st L Ben's Acre. From N A264-B2195, 1st exit Comptons Ln.* **Sat 25 Aug (1-5). Adm £4.50, chd free. Home-made teas. Visits also by arrangement late June to end Aug, for groups of 15-35. Refreshments on request. Garden groups most welcome.**

Our garden (100ft x45ft) creates an illusion of spaciousness by good use of steps and terracing to give impressive views around the garden. Visitors comment on our interesting plants and their colour combinations, calling it inspirational and a visual delight. Featuring a summerhouse, ponds, rockery, topiary and pots of succulents. Many seating areas around the garden to enjoy your cake and pot of tea. Just 15 mins from Nymans NT garden. Visit us at YouTube Pauline & Brian's Sussex Garden.

13 BIGNOR PARK

Pulborough, RH20 1HG. The Mersey Family, www.bignorpark.co.uk. *5m S of Petworth & Pulborough. Well signed from B2138. Nearest villages Sutton, Bignor & West Burton. Approach from the E, directions & map available on website.* **Tue 17 Apr, Tue 15 May, Sun 10 June (2-5). Adm £5, chd free. Home-made teas.**

11 acres of peaceful garden to explore with magnificent views of the South Downs. Interesting trees, shrubs, wild flower areas, with swathes of daffodils in spring. The walled flower garden has been replanted with herbaceous borders. Temple, Greek loggia, Zen pond and unusual sculptures. Former home of romantic poet Charlotte Smith, whose sonnets were inspired by Bignor Park. Spectacular Cedars of Lebanon and rare Holm Oak. Wheelchair access to shrubbery and croquet lawn, gravel paths in rest of garden and steps in stables quadrangle.

14 4 BIRCH CLOSE

Arundel, BN18 9HN. Elizabeth & Mike Gammon, 01903 882722, e.gammon@talktalk.net. *1m S of Arundel. From A27 & A284 r'about at W end of Arundel take Ford Rd. After ½m turn R into Maxwell Rd & follow signs.* **Visits by arrangement in May for groups of 10+. Light refreshments on request. Adm £3.50, chd free.**

⅓ acre of woodland garden on edge of Arundel. Wide range of mature trees and shrubs with many hardy perennials. Emphasis on extensive selection of spring flowers and clematis with over 100 incl 12 montana. All in a tranquil setting with secluded corners, meandering paths and plenty of seating. Partial wheelchair access to approx half of garden.

15 BLUE JAYS

Chesworth Close, Horsham, RH13 5AL. Stella & Mike Schofield, 01403 251065. *5 mins walk SE of St Mary's Church, Horsham. From A281 (East St) L down Denne Rd, L to Chesworth Lane, R to Chesworth Close. Garden at end of close. 4 disabled spaces, other parking in local streets & Denne Rd car park.* **Sun 29 Apr (12.30-5). Adm £4, chd free. Home-made teas. Visits also by arrangement Apr to July for groups of 8+. Refreshments on request.** Donation to The Badger Trust.

Wooded 1 acre garden with rhododendrons, camellias and azaleas. Candelabra primulas and ferns edge the River Arun. Primroses and spring bulbs border woodland path and stream. Cordylines, gunneras, flower beds, a pond, a fountain and formal rose garden set in open lawns. Arch leads to a vegetable plot and orchard bounded by the river. Large WW2 pill box in the orchard; visits inside with short talk are available. Wheelchair access to most areas.

16 ◆ BORDE HILL GARDEN

Borde Hill Lane, Haywards Heath, RH16 1XP. Borde Hill Garden Ltd, 01444 450326, info@bordehill.co.uk, www.bordehill.co.uk. *1½m N of Haywards Heath. 20 mins N of Brighton, or S of Gatwick on A23 taking exit 10a via Balcombe.* **For NGS: Mon 1 Oct (10-5). Adm £9.50, chd £6.35. Light refreshments.** For other opening times and information, please phone, email or visit garden website.

Rare plants and stunning landscapes make Borde Hill Garden the perfect day out for horticultural enthusiasts, families and those who love beautiful countryside. Enjoy tranquil outdoor rooms, woodland walks, playgrounds, picnic areas, home-cooked food and events throughout the season. Wheelchair access to 17 acres of formal garden. Dogs welcome on leads.

17 NEW BOWLEY FARM

Bowley Lane, South Mundham, Chichester, PO20 1NB. Tim Clarke. *From r'about by Walnut Tree Pub in Runcton, take Mill Lane exit which leads into Runcton Lane. Follow to next junction, branch L into Bowley Lane & follow to the end of the lane.* **Sun 1 July (2-5). Adm £5, chd free. Home-made teas.**

Lying south east of cathedral city, Chichester, the ever peaceful location is a haven to garden birds, ducks and wild fowl who gather daily around the many tall and wild grasses and camouflage. The magical gardens are a mix of countless exquisite perennials, shrubs and roses, all connected by handmade stone paths, peacefully sitting under the hang-dog leaves of a magnificent willow. Drenched from corner to corner in flowers, the original walled garden is a few paces from the main lawn reached by one of the bedecked rose arches. Topiary features in the gardens as well as arches with climbing and rambling roses. Regret no wheelchair access due to the gradient of the lawns, the bridges and the lake.

18 BRADNESS GALLERY

Spithurst Road, Spithurst, Barcombe, BN8 5EB. Michael Cruickshank & Emma Burnett, 01273 400606, emma@bradnessgallery.com, www.bradnessgallery.com. *5m N of Lewes. Bradness Gallery lies midway between Barcombe & Newick in Spithurst. Free parking in field. Disabled parking will be available outside the gallery.* **Thur 14 June (2-5.30). Adm £4, chd free. Home-made teas. Visits also by arrangement Apr to Oct.**

Delightful and tranquil mature, organic, wildlife garden with trees, scented shrubs, old roses, herbaceous borders and wild garden planting. A wooded stream flows along the bottom and two large ponds are home to wild ducks, dragonflies and frogs. Also raised beds for vegetables, herbs and cut flowers. Surrounded by fields and cows. Delicious home-made teas and cakes and a lovely tearoom for rainy days. The gallery will be open showing original paintings, prints, cards and hand painted lampshades by the owners. Wheelchair access to the upper part of the garden. Sloping and uneven ground to the ponds and stream.

19 BRIGHTLING DOWN FARM

Observatory Road, Dallington, TN21 9LN. Val & Pete Stephens, 07770 807060 / 01424 838888, valstephens@icloud.com. *1m from Woods Corner. At Swan Pub at Woods Corner, take road opp signed Brightling. Take 1st L signed Burwash & almost immed, turn into 1st driveway on L.* **Visits by arrangement May to Oct for groups of 10-30. Adm £8, chd free. Home-made teas.**

The garden has several different areas incl a Zen garden, water garden, walled vegetable garden with two large greenhouses, herb garden, herbaceous borders and a new woodland walk. The garden makes clever use of grasses and is set amongst woodland with stunning countryside views. Winner of the Society of Garden Designers award. Featured in Country Living (Oct 2017). Most areas can be accessed with the use of temporary ramps.

The National Garden Scheme is the largest single funder of the Queen's Nursing Institute

GROUP OPENING

20 BURWASH HIDDEN GARDENS

Burwash, TN19 7EN. *Burwash is on the A265, 3m W of junction with A21 at Hurst Green; 6m E of Heathfield. Parking planned for Swan Meadow sports field, subject to weather conditions, follow signs from High St. Tickets & map at entry points: Bowzell & Mandalay (Apr); Church House, Longstaffes & Mandalay (June).* **Sat 28 Apr (2-5). Combined adm £4, chd free. Sat 23 June (2-5). Combined adm £6, chd free. Home-made teas in Swan Meadow Sports Pavilion, Ham Lane.**

BOWZELL
Shirley Viney.
Open on Sat 28 Apr

 **BRAMDEAN**
Fiona Barkley.
Open on Sat 28 Apr

CHURCH HOUSE
Rosemary & Graham Sendall.
Open on Sat 23 June

FARLEY HOUSE
Ian & Nancy Craston.
Open on Sat 28 Apr

IVY HOUSE
Louise Lidington.
Open on Sat 23 June

LIME COTTAGE
Shelagh Bedford-Turner.
Open on Sat 23 June

LINDEN COTTAGE
Philip & Anne Cutler.
Open on Sat 23 June

LONGSTAFFES
Dorothy & Paul Bysouth.
Open on Sat 23 June

MANDALAY
David & Vivienne Wright.
Open on all dates
D

MOUNT HOUSE
Richard & Lynda Maude-Roxby.
Open on Sat 23 June

3 PROSPECT COTTAGES
Mary Clarke.
Open on Sat 23 June

We're all intrigued by a hidden garden aren't we? Here in our beautiful village in the High Weald AONB the gardens are well concealed from public view located mainly behind centuries-old listed properties. They vary in style and planting, and range in size from a few square meters to three acres. Located on and around the picturesque High St, all are within a level and easy walking distance of each other. For the first time we have a spring opening with four gardens open, and in late June eight gardens will be open. We have three new gardens this year; a potter's small, quirky garden, and two gardens with extensive views over unspoiled Wealden countryside. Restricted wheelchair access to rear gardens as mainly terraced properties, access possible to five gardens.

21 BUTLERS FARMHOUSE

Butlers Lane, Herstmonceux, BN27 1QH. Irene Eltringham-Willson, 01323 833770, irene.willson@btinternet.com, www.butlersfarmhouse.co.uk. *3m E of Hailsham. Take A271 from Hailsham, go through village of Herstmonceux, turn R signed Church Rd then approx 1m turn R. Do not use SatNav!* **Sat 24, Sun 25 Mar (2-5). Adm £3.50, chd free. Sat 11, Sun 12 Aug (2-5). Adm £6, chd free. Home-made teas. Jazz in the garden in Aug. Visits also by arrangement Mar to Oct with refreshments provided.**

Lovely rural setting for 1 acre garden surrounding C16 farmhouse with views of South Downs. Pretty in spring with daffodils, hellebores and primroses. Mainly herbaceous with rainbow border, small pond and Cornish inspired beach corners. Restored to former glory, as shown in old photographs, but with a few quirky twists such as a poison garden, secret jungle garden and some naturalistic areas. Relax and listen to live jazz in the garden in Aug. Most of garden accessible by wheelchair.

22 CAMBERLOT HALL

Camberlot Road, Lower Dicker, Hailsham, BN27 3RH. Nicky Kinghorn. *500yds S of A22 at Lower Dicker, 4½m N of A27 Drusillas r'about. From A27 Drusillas r'about through Berwick Station to Upper Dicker & L into Camberlot Rd after The Plough Pub, we are 1m on the L. From the A22 we are 500yds down Camberlot Rd on the R.* **Sun 12 Aug (2-5). Afternoon tea & cake. Evening opening Sat 18 Aug (5-8). Wine & nibbles. Adm £5, chd free.**

A 3 acre country garden with a lovely view across fields and hills to the South Downs. Created from scratch over the last 6 yrs with all design, planting and maintenance by the owner. Lavender lined carriage driveway, naturalistic border, vegetable garden, shady garden, mini annual meadow, newly planted 30 metre white border and exotic garden. Wildflower meadow in development. Gravel drive and some uneven ground.

23 51 CARLISLE ROAD

Eastbourne, BN21 4JR. Mr & Mrs N Fraser-Gausden, 01323 722545, n.fg@sky.com. *200yds inland from seafront (Wish Tower), close to Congress Theatre.* **Sat 9, Sun 10 June (2-5). Adm £3, chd free. Home-made teas. Visits also by arrangement May & June.**

Small walled, s-facing garden (82ft x 80ft) with mixed beds intersected by stone paths and incl small pool. Profuse and diverse planting. Wide selection of shrubs, old roses, herbaceous plants and perennials mingle with specimen trees and climbers. Constantly revised planting to maintain the magical and secluded atmosphere. Has featured in many garden magazines over the years and won a number of awards.

24 CAXTON MANOR

Wall Hill, Forest Row, RH18 5EG. Adele & Jules Speelman. *1m N of Forest Row, 2m S of East Grinstead. From A22 take turning to Ashurstwood, entrance on L after ⅓m, or 1m on R from N.* **Fri 18,**

Sat 19 May (2-5). Adm £5, chd free. Home-made teas. Donation to St Catherine's Hospice, Crawley. Delightful 5 acre Japanese inspired gardens planted with mature rhododendrons, azaleas and acers surrounding large pond with boathouse, massive rockery and waterfall, beneath the home of the late Sir Archibald McIndoe (house not open). Japanese tea house and Japanese style courtyard. **Also open 2 Quarry Cottages (separate admission).**

25 CHAMPS HILL

Waltham Park Road, Coldwaltham, Pulborough, RH20 1LY. Mr & Mrs David Bowerman, 01798 831205, mary@thebct.org.uk. *3m S of Pulborough. On A29 turn R to Fittleworth into Waltham Park Rd, garden 400 metres on R.* **Sun 13 May, Sun 12 Aug (2-5). Adm £5, chd free. Tea. Visits also by arrangement Mar to Aug for groups of 10+.**
Champs Hill has been developed around three disused sand quarries since 1960. The woodlands are full of beautiful rhododendrons and azaleas, but the most striking feature is the collection of heathers in August. The garden also has some interesting sculptures and stupendous views.

26 CHANNEL VIEW

52 Brook Barn Way, Goring-by-Sea, Worthing, BN12 4DW. Jennie & Trevor Rollings, 01903 242431, tjrollings@gmail.com. *1m W of Worthing, nr seafront. Turn S off A259 into Parklands Ave, L at T-junction into Alinora Cres. Brook Barn Way is immed on L.* **Sat 16, Sun 17 June (2-5). Adm £5, chd free. Home-made teas. Visits also by arrangement May to Sept for groups of 10-25.**
A seaside Tudor cottage garden blending traditional, antipodean and subtropical plants. Dense planting, secret rooms and intriguing sight-lines, with brick and flint paths inlaid with thundereggs radiating from a wildlife pond. Shady viewpoints, sunny patios, insect friendly flowers and unusual structures supporting over a hundred roses, clematis and other climbers. Numerous planted hanging baskets and containers, sinuous beds packed with flowers and foliage, with underplanting to ensure a 3-D experience. Lots of unusual plants for sale. Featured in Garden News magazine, Worthing Herald, Worthing Journal, and Goring Guide in 2017. Partial wheelchair access.

27 CHIDMERE GARDENS

Chidham Lane, Chidham, Chichester, PO18 8TD. Jackie & David Russell, www.chidmerefarm.com. *6m W of Chichester on A259. Turn into Chidham Lane, continue until a RH-bend, followed by a 2nd RH-bend. Chidmere Gardens is on the L immed after the large village pond.* **Thur 14 June, Thur 6 Sept (2-5). Adm £5, chd free. Home-made teas.**
Wisteria clad C15 house (not open) surrounded by yew and hornbeam hedges situated next to Chidmere pond; a natural wildlife preserve approx 5 acres. Garden incl formal rose garden, well stocked herbaceous borders, contemporary borders and 8 acres of orchards with wide selection of heritage and modern varieties of apples, pears and plums. Partial wheelchair access.

28 CISSBURY

Nepcote Lane, Findon, Worthing, BN14 0SR. Geoffrey & Etta Wyatt, www.cissbury.com. *5m N of Worthing in the hamlet of Nepcote, Findon. From A24 S follow signs to Worthing. Only turn L at the sign for Nepcote. After about 100 metres at the sharp LH-corner, turn R into Cissbury's driveway.* **Sat 10 Mar (10-4). Adm £4, chd free. Home-made teas.**
Set in its own parkland and grounds in the SDNP with views towards Cissbury Ring and the sea. Spectacular drifts of daffodils and snowdrops. Cedar trees and a holm oak hedge line the drive; by the pond is a metasequoia glyptostroboides. Walled kitchen garden with plots let out to Findon Gardening Club. Original L-shaped greenhouse featuring cork screw winding gear, still in partial working order. Wheelchair access from the car park, around the house and walled garden.

The Long House

29 ◆ CLINTON LODGE

Fletching, TN22 3ST. Lady Collum, 01825 722952, garden@clintonlodge.com, www.clintonlodgegardens.co.uk. *4m NW of Uckfield. Clinton Lodge is situated in Fletching High St, N of Rose & Crown Pub. Off road parking provided. It is important visitors do not park in street. Parking available from 1pm.* **For NGS: Sun 29 Apr, Mon 11, Mon 25 June, Mon 30 July (2-5.30). Adm £6, chd free. Home-made teas.** For other opening times and information, please phone, email or visit garden website. Donation to local charities.

6 acre formal and romantic garden overlooking parkland with old roses, William Pye water feature, double white and blue herbaceous borders, yew hedges, pleached lime walks, copy of C17 scented herb garden, Medieval style potager, vine and rose allée, wild flower garden. Canal garden, small knot garden, shady glade and orchard. Caroline and Georgian house (not open).

30 COLWOOD HOUSE

Cuckfield Lane, Warninglid, RH17 5SP. Mrs Rosy Brenan, 01444 461352. *6m W of Haywards Heath, 6m SE of Horsham. Entrance on B2115 (Cuckfield Lane). From E, N & S, turn W off A23 towards Warninglid for ¾m. From W come through Warninglid village.* **Sun 12 Aug (1.30-4.30). Adm £5, chd free. Home-made teas. Visits also by arrangement May to Sept for groups of 8+.** Donation to Seaforth Hall.

12 acres of garden with mature and specimen trees from the late 1800s, lawns and woodland edge. Formal parterre, rose and herb gardens. 100ft terrace and herbaceous border overlooking flower rimmed croquet lawn. Cut turf labyrinth and forsythia tunnel. Water features, statues and gazebos. Pets' cemetery. Giant chessboard. Lake with island and temple. The garden has gravel paths and some slopes.

31 COOKSCROFT

Bookers Lane, Earnley, Chichester, PO20 7JG. Mr & Mrs J Williams, 01243 513671, williams.cookscroft330@btinternet.com, www.cookscroft.co.uk. *6m S of Chichester. At end of Birdham Straight A286 from Chichester, take L fork to East Wittering B2198. 1m on before sharp bend, turn L into Bookers Lane, 2nd house on L. Parking available.* **Sat 21 Apr, Sun 13, Wed 16 May (11-4). Light refreshments. Evening opening Sat 16 June (5-9). Wine. Adm £5, chd free. Visits also by arrangement Apr to Sept for groups of up to 30 max.**

This is a garden for all seasons which delights the visitor. Started in 1988, it features cottage, woodland and Japanese style gardens, water features and borders of perennials with a particular emphasis on southern hemisphere plants. Unusual plants for the plantsman to enjoy, many grown from seed. The differing styles of the garden flow together making it easy to wander anywhere. The garden has grass paths and unfenced ponds.

32 COPYHOLD HOLLOW

Copyhold Lane, Borde Hill, Haywards Heath, RH16 1XU. Frances Druce, 01444 413265, ngs@copyholdhollow.co.uk, www.copyholdhollow.co.uk. *2m N of Haywards Heath. Follow signs for Borde Hill Gardens. With Borde Hill Gardens on L over brow of hill, take 1st R signed Ardingly. Garden ½m. If the drive is full, please park in the lane.* **Mon 16, Tue 24 Apr, Mon 7, Tue 15, Fri 25 May, Mon 16 July (12-4). Adm £4, chd free. Home-made teas. Visits also by arrangement Apr to Aug for groups of 4+.**

A different NGS experience in 2 north-facing acres. The cottage garden surrounding C16 house (not open) gives way to steep slopes up to woodland garden: a challenge to both visitor and gardener. Species primulas a particular interest of the owner. Stumpery, dizzy crow's nest viewing platform. Not a manicured plot but with a relaxed attitude to gardening, an inspiration to visitors.

33 CUPANI GARDEN

8 Sandgate Close, Seaford, BN25 3LL. Dr D Jones & Ms A Jones OBE, 01323 899452, sweetpeasa52@gmail.com, www.cupanigarden.com. *From A259 follow signs to Alfriston, E of Seaford. Turn R into Hillside Ave, L into Hastings Ave, R into Deal Close & R into Sandgate Close. Bus route 12A from Brighton & Eastbourne to Hillside Ave. A walk down narrow pathway (twitten) & garden on R.* **Fri 29 June, Fri 13, Fri 27 July, Wed 1 Aug (12-5). Adm £4.50, chd free. Light refreshments. Opening with Seaford Gardens on Sun 17 June. Visits also by arrangement June to Aug for groups of 6+. Lunch or afternoon tea incl.**

Cupani is a green and tranquil haven with a delightful mix of trees, shrubs and perennial borders in different themed beds. Courtyard garden, gazebo, summerhouse, water features, sweet pea obelisks, huge range of plants in all seasons. Plenty of places to sit and enjoy, either in the shade or under cover. New projects underway each year to provide variety for visitors. See TripAdvisor reviews. Delicious afternoon tea and a good range of lunches, phone in advance for any special dietary needs (always vegetarian options). Plants, jams, books and china for sale. Featured in Sussex Life, Garden News and local press. Although mostly flat, the garden is not suitable for wheelchairs. Steps to courtyard and steep steps to WC.

34 DACHS

Spear Hill, Ashington, RH20 3BA. Bruce Wallace, 01903 892466, wallacebuk@aol.com. *Approx 6m N of Worthing. From A24 at Ashington onto B2133 Billingshurst Rd, R into Spear Hill. We are the 1st house, garden runs along Billingshurst Rd. Do not go up Spear Hill as we are at the bottom.* **Sun 8, Sun 15 Apr (2.30-5.30). Adm £4.50, chd free. Home-made teas. Visits also by arrangement Apr to July for day or eve visits. Happy to give talks to groups and gardening tips.**

A waterlogged field turned into a beautiful garden of about 2 acres incl white garden, bog area and stream. Over 250 varieties of daffodil and narcissus some more added each year. AGM varieties for sale. Free gifts for children to encourage them to grow things. A number of plants for sale at economical prices incl daffodils. Featured in Sussex Life. Disabled parking by house on tarmac drive and access the rear patio by ramp. No steps.

35 DALE PARK HOUSE

Madehurst, Arundel, BN18 0NP. Robert & Jane Green, 01243 814260, robertgreen@farming.co.uk. *4m W of Arundel. Take A27 E from Chichester or W from Arundel, then A29 (London) for 2m, turn L to Madehurst & follow red arrows.* **Sun 10 June (2-5). Adm £4.50, chd free. Home-made teas. Visits also by arrangement May to July for any size group.**

Set in parkland within the SDNP, enjoying magnificent views to the sea. Come and relax in the large walled garden which features an impressive 200ft herbaceous border. There is also a sunken gravel garden, mixed borders, a small rose garden, dreamy rose and clematis arches, interesting collection of hostas, foliage plants and shrubs, an orchard and kitchen garden. Wheelchair access not easy.

36 NEW 70 DALE VIEW

Hove, BN3 8LB. Chris & Tony Butland-Steed. *1m from Hove junction of A27. From the Hove junction of A27, at the r'about take A2038 towards Hove. Continue down to mini-r'about by Grenadier Pub & take 2nd exit into West Way. Dale View is 1st L after zebra crossing.* **Mon 7 May, Sun 1 July, Sun 19 Aug (11-5). Adm £5, chd free. Home-made teas.**

Star of Channel 4's Gogglebox, Chris Butland-Steed and husband Tony have completely re-landscaped their garden (100ft by 50ft) over the last 3 yrs. It shows lush and full planting across several zones and seating areas. Surrounded by mature trees, highlights incl herbaceous borders, fountain, rose garden, shady garden and terraced raised beds, with interest from spring through to late autumn.

37 47 DENMANS LANE

Lindfield, Haywards Heath, RH16 2JN. Sue & Jim Stockwell, 01444 459363, jamesastockwell@aol.com, www.lindfield-gardens.co.uk/47denmans-lane. *Approx 1½m NE of Haywards Heath town centre. From Haywards Heath train station follow B2028 signed Lindfield & Ardingly for 1m. At T-lights turn L into Hickmans Lane, then after 100 metres take 1st R into Denmans Lane.* **Visits by arrangement Mar to Oct for groups of 10-40. Adm £8, chd free. Home-made teas incl. Evening visits with wine & canapes, or combined visits with Lindfield Jungle or 5 Whitemans Close on request.**

A beautiful and tranquil 1 acre garden created by the owners, Sue and Jim Stockwell, over the past 20 yrs. The garden is divided into different areas planted for interest throughout the yr. Spring bulbs and woodland flowers from Feb to May followed by azaleas, rhododendrons, alliums, roses, and herbaceous perennials. The garden also incl ponds, vegetable and fruit gardens. NB: Deep water. Most of the garden accessible by wheelchair, but some areas involve steep slopes.

38 DITTONS END

Southfields Road, Eastbourne, BN21 1BZ. Mrs Frances Hodkinson, 01323 647163. *Town centre, ⅓m from train station. Off A259 in Southfields Rd. House directly opp Dittons Rd. 3 doors from NGS open garden Hardwycke.* **Sun 3 June (11-5). Combined adm with Hardwycke £5, chd free. Home-made teas at Hardwycke. Visits also by arrangement May to Sept.**

Lovely well maintained, small town garden. At the back, a very pretty garden (35ft x 20ft) with small lawn area, patio surrounded by a selection of pots and packed borders with lots of colour. In the front a compact lawn with colourful borders (25ft x 18ft). No steps.

39 DOWN PLACE

South Harting, Petersfield, GU31 5PN. Mr & Mrs D M Thistleton-Smith, 01730 825374, selina@downplace.co.uk. *1m SE of South Harting. B2141 to Chichester, turn L down unmarked lane below top of hill.* **Sat 28, Sun 29 Apr, Sat 16, Sun 17 June (2-6). Adm £4, chd free. Home-made & cream teas. Visits also by arrangement Apr to July for groups of 15+.** Donation to The Friends of Harting Church.

7 acre hillside, chalk garden on the north side of the South Downs with fine views of surrounding countryside. Extensive herbaceous, shrub and rose borders on different levels merging into natural wild flower meadow renowned for its collection of native orchids. Fully stocked vegetable garden and greenhouses. Spring flowers and blossom. Amazing natural wild meadow. Substantial top terrace and borders accessible to wheelchairs.

The National Garden Scheme is committed to helping unpaid carers

40 DRIFTWOOD

4 Marine Drive, Bishopstone, Seaford, BN25 2RS. Geoff Stonebanks & Mark Glassman, 01323 899296, geoffstonebanks@gmail.com, www.driftwoodbysea.co.uk. *A259 between Seaford & Newhaven. Turn L into Marine Drive from Bishopstone Rd, 2nd on R. Please park carefully in road, but not on bend beyond house.* **Tue 19 June, Tue 10, Tue 24 July, Sun 5 Aug (11-5). Adm £5, chd free. Visits also by arrangement June to Aug for groups of 1+, incl guided tour by owner. Lunch or afternoon tea can be incl.**

Monty Don said in his introduction to Driftwood on BBC 2 Gardeners' World in Sept 2016, 'It's a small garden by the sea (112ft x 40ft) with inspired planting and design'. Sunday Telegraph said 'Geoff's enthusiasm is catching, and he and his amazing garden deserve every visitor that makes their way up his enchanting garden path'. This is a real must see garden say many TripAdvisor visitors - awarded Certificate of Excellence 2017 for over 60, 5-star reviews. Large selection of home-made cakes and savoury items available, all served on vintage china, on trays in the garden. Visitors from China, Japan, Austria, Belgium and South America in 2017. In 2017 featured in Coast magazine (Aug) and Country Gardener magazine (June). Listed Great British Gardens Website and much coverage in local newspapers and monthly piece in Garden News magazine. Steep drive with handrail, narrow paths and many levels with steps, but help readily available on-site or call ahead before visit.

41 DURFORD ABBEY BARN

Petersfield, GU31 5AU. Mr & Mrs Lund. *3m from Petersfield. Situated on the S side of A272 between Petersfield & Rogate, 1m from the junction with B2072. Limited parking by house.* **Sat 23, Sun 24 June (2-5.30). Adm £4, chd free. Home-made teas.**

With lovely views across open countryside to the South Downs, this 1 acre garden is set around a converted barn in the National Park. It has distinct levels and areas incl cottage garden with roses and herbaceous borders, a natural pond, shady vine covered pergola, productive vegetable terrace, lawns and shrubberies, prairie border, and seating placed to soak up the views. Partial wheelchair access as some areas have quite steep grass slopes to negotiate.

42 DURFORD MILL HOUSE

West Harting, Petersfield, GU31 5AZ. Mrs Sue Jones, 01730 821125, sdurford@btinternet.com. *3m E of Petersfield. Turn off A272 between Petersfield & Rogate, signed Durford Mill & the Hartings. From Chichester into South Harting past village shop on L, take 1st L to West Harting, continue for 2½m.* **Sat 9, Sun 10 June (2-5.30). Adm £4, chd free. Cream teas. Visits also by arrangement Apr to July for groups up to 30 max.**

Come and relax in our peaceful mill garden with its meandering stream and quiet places to sit. Wander along the paths and over the bridges among the flowers, shrubs and beautiful trees. Finishing up with delicious home-made cakes and tea. Wheelchair access to main garden and tea area.

43 DURRANCE MANOR

Smithers Hill Lane, Shipley, RH13 8PE. Gordon & Joan Lindsay, 01403 741577, galindsay@gmail.com. *7m SW of Horsham. A24 to A272 (S from Horsham, N from Worthing), turn W towards Billingshurst. Approx 1¾m, 2nd L Smithers Hill Lane signed to Countryman Pub. Garden 2nd on L.* **Mon 27 Aug (2-6). Adm £5, chd free. Home-made teas. Visits also by arrangement Apr to Oct.**

This 2 acre garden surrounding a Medieval hall house (not open) with Horsham stone roof, enjoys uninterrupted views over a ha-ha of the South Downs and Chanctonbury Ring. There are Japanese inspired gardens, a large pond, wild flower meadow and orchard, colourful long borders, hosta walk, and vegetable garden. There is a Monet style bridge over a pond with waterlilies.

The Moongate Garden

© Judi Lion

GROUP OPENING

44 NEW EAST GRINSTEAD TOWN GARDENS

East Grinstead, RH19 4DD. *7m E of Crawley on A264 & 14m N of Uckfield on A22. Map will be provided at all properties.* **Sun 22 July (1-5). Combined adm £6, chd free. Home-made teas at 29 Mill Way & 16 Musgrave Avenue.**

NEW **71 GARDEN WOOD ROAD**
RH19 1RX. Carol & Roger Hawkins.

NEW **27 MILL WAY**
RH19 4DD. Jeff Dyson.

NEW **29 MILL WAY**
RH19 4DD. Dee & Richard Doyle.

NEW **16 MUSGRAVE AVENUE**
RH19 4BS. Carole & Bob Farmer.

NEW **26 THE STENNINGS**
RH19 1PF. Mary & Roy Birmingham.

Gardens to lift the spirits and make you smile! These town gardens are all past winners of East Grinstead in Bloom Best Front Garden. The back gardens have quite different styles. Most are established, displaying a mix of planting incl shrubs, perennials, and annuals, with tubs and baskets. The enthusiastic owners are keen propagators, growing from seed, cuttings and plugs, sharing their surplus plants. 26 The Stennings has an interesting collection of bonsai and 16 Musgrave Avenue a vegetable garden. Plant sales will be available at 27 Mill Way and 16 Musgrave Avenue. The Town Council hanging baskets and planting are not to be missed. For steam train fans, the Bluebell Railway starts nearby. Full wheelchair access at 26 The Stennings, partial access at other gardens.

---

45 54 ELMLEIGH

Midhurst, GU29 9HA.
Wendy Liddle, 07796 562275, wendyliddle@btconnect.com.
¼m W of Midhurst off A272. Reserved disabled parking at the top of the drive, please phone on arrival for assistance. **Sat 26, Sun 27, Mon 28 May, Sat 9, Sun 10, Sat 23, Sun 24 June, Sat 14, Sun 15, Sat 28, Sun 29 July (10-5). Adm £3.50, chd free. Home-made teas & cream teas. Visits also by arrangement May to Sept. Coaches please drop off visitors, then park in Midhurst Coach Park.**

⅓ acre property with terraced front garden, leading to a heavily planted rear garden with majestic 100 yr old Black Pines. Shrubs, perennials, packed with interest around every corner, giving all season colours. Many raised beds, numerous sculptures, vegetables in boxes, a greenhouse, pond, and bog garden. Hedgehogs in residence, supporter of Sidlesham Animal Sanctuary. Child friendly. Come and enjoy the peace and tranquillity in this award-winning garden.

46 ELPHICKS COTTAGE

Spring Lane, Burwash, TN19 7HU. Lorna Chernajosvky. *200yds L down Spring Lane from Burwash High St. 6m E of Heathfield on A265, Spring Lane L after petrol station. From Hurst Green take A265, 4m W through Burwash passing shops & pub. Turn R 200yds after car sales room into Spring Lane.* **Thur 14, Fri 15 June (1-5). Adm £4, chd free. Home-made teas.**

2 acre site surrounding 300 yr old cottage (not open). Formal front garden with knot garden contrasts with areas of naturalistic planting. On different levels with steep paths in places. A tranquil unfenced ¼ acre lake with island is stocked with carp and rudd. Woodland was cleared of 200 Scots pine trees in 2013 and replanting is currently underway.

47 FAIRLIGHT END

Pett Road, Pett, Hastings, TN35 4HB. Chris & Robin Hutt, 07774 863750, chrishutt@fairlightend.co.uk, www.fairlightend.co.uk. *4m E of Hastings. From Hastings take A259 to Rye. At White Hart Beefeater turn R into Friars Hill. Descend into Pett village. Park in village hall car park, opp house.* **Thur 3 May (2-5). Adm £5, chd free. Opening with Pett Village Gardens on Sat 23, Sun 24 June. Visits also by arrangement May to Sept for groups of 10+.** Donation to Pett Village Hall.

Gardens Illustrated, June 2016, said 'The 18th century house is at the highest point in the garden with views down the slope over abundant borders and velvety lawns that are punctuated by clusters of specimen trees and shrubs. Beyond and below are the wild flower meadows and the ponds with a backdrop of the gloriously unspoilt Wealden landscape'. As seen on ITV's 'Love your Garden' with Alan Titchmarsh (2017). Steep paths, gravelled areas, unfenced ponds.

D

48 FITTLEWORTH HOUSE

Bedham Lane, Fittleworth, Pulborough, RH20 1JH. Edward & Isabel Braham, 01798 865074, marksaunders66.com@gmail.com. *2m E, SE of Petworth. Midway between Petworth & Pulborough on the A283 in Fittleworth, turn into lane by sharp bend signed Bedham. Garden is 50yds along on the L.* **Every Wed 25 Apr to 27 June (2-5). Adm £5, chd free. Home-made teas. Visits also by arrangement Apr to July for groups of 5+.**

3 acre tranquil country garden featuring working walled kitchen garden with long herbaceous borders and a wide range of fruit and vegetables. Large glasshouse and old potting shed, mixed flower borders, rose beds, rhododendrons and lawns. Magnificent 112ft tall cedar overlooks wisteria covered Grade II listed Georgian house (not open). Wildlife pond, wild garden, long grass areas and spring bulbs. New for 2018 are a brand new fountain and newly restored old potting shed. The garden sits on a gentle slope but is accessible for wheelchairs and buggies. Non-disabled WC.

49 FIVE OAKS COTTAGE

Petworth, RH20 1HD. Jean & Steve Jackman, 07939 272443, jeanjackman@hotmail.com. *5m S of Pulborough. SatNav does not work! To ensure best route, we will provide printed directions at the time of booking.* **Visits by arrangement 23 July-31 July & 27 Aug-2 Sept for groups of 5-35, from 9.30am to 8.30pm. Adm £5, chd free. Happy to do tea & cakes or wine & nibbles.**

An acre of delicate jungle surrounding an Arts and Crafts style cottage (not open), owned by artists and founders of The Floral Fringe Fair. Stunning views of the South Downs from an unconventional garden, which is designed to encourage maximum wildlife. Knapweed meadow on clay attracting clouds of butterflies in July, two small ponds and lots of seating.

GROUP OPENING

50 FLETCHING SECRET GARDENS

High Street, Fletching, Uckfield, TN22 3SS. *4m NW of Uckfield. Follow signs to Church Farm, Church St, TN22 3SP for parking. For Holmesdale Oast park on Bell Lane, TN22 3YB, approx ½m N from the High St (take R at junction into Bell Lane, cont ½m).* **Sat 7 July (12-5). Combined adm £6, chd free. Home-made teas at 4 Corner Cottages.**

4 CORNER COTTAGES
Mrs Jackie Pateman.

NEW **HOLMESDALE OAST**
Susanna Martin.

STONES
Belinda & David Croft.

NEW **4 WHITES COTTAGES**
Philip & Joy Burchell.

In the heart of the picturesque village of Fletching, near the historic church are three small, welcoming cottage style gardens, each with their own character. 4 Corner Cottages where home-made teas will be served, is a small restful garden, tucked behind the High St, with a pond, small white border and more. Stunning views across farmland to Sheffield Park. The garden at Stones is packed with interest in a relatively small space. Colourful hanging baskets and pots, vegetable plot, fruiting kiwi climber, cardoon bed and mistletoe. The edge of the garden is wild to provide habitat for birds and wildlife. 4 Whites Cottages has much packed into it, incl soft fruit, cottage flowers, shrubs and herbs plus an observatory. Holmesdale Oast is a pleasant surprise. Situated out of main village, down a track, this cottage garden with a difference has a deep restored Oast pond, and a sandstone restored bridge which is not to be missed. 4 Whites Cottages featured in Sussex Living & The Argus. Partial wheelchair access to some parts of the gardens.

51 FOLLERS MANOR

White Way, Alfriston, BN26 5TT. Geoff & Anne Shaw, anne.shaw1@hotmail.com, www.follersmanor.co.uk. *½m S of Alfriston. From Alfriston uphill towards Seaford. Park on L in paddock before garden. Garden next door to old Alfriston Youth Hostel immed before road narrows. Visitors with walking difficulties drop at gate.* **Sat 1, Sun 2 Sept (12-5). Adm £6, chd free. Home-made teas.**

Contemporary garden designed by Ian Kitson attached to C17 listed historic farmhouse. Entrance courtyard, sunken garden, herbaceous displays, wildlife pond, wild flower meadows, woodland area and beautiful views of the South Downs. Winner of Sussex Heritage Trust Award and three awards from the Society of Garden Designers; Best Medium Residential Garden, Hard Landscaping and, most prestigious, the Judges Award. New for 2018, a newly designed area of the garden by original designer Ian Kitson. We have no idea what he will come up with so all very exciting judging by his previous efforts. Featured in numerous worldwide magazines and also a number of appearances on TV shows.

52 FOXGLOVE COTTAGE

29 Orchard Road, Horsham, RH13 5NF. Peter & Terri Lefevre, 01403 256002, teresalefevre@outlook.com. *From Horsham Station, over bridge (signed Crawley) at r'about 3rd exit, 1st R Sterling Way, at end turn L, then 1st R Orchard Rd. From A281, Clarence Rd at end, turn R, at end turn L, street parking.* **Sun 24 June, Sun 8 July (1-5). Adm £4, chd free. Home-made teas. Visits also by arrangement June & July for groups of 10+.**

Unusual 150ft x 50ft plantaholic's garden with a plethora of planted containers, quirky vintage finds and gardenalia. Gravel and bark paths are interspersed by planting areas encompassing sun drenched and shady borders, with plenty of seating dotted about. A beach inspired summerhouse and decking are flanked by a water feature; the end of the garden is dedicated to propagation, cut flowers and fruit growing.

53 THE GARDEN HOUSE

5 Warleigh Road, Brighton, BN1 4NT. Bridgette Saunders & Graham Lee, 07729 037182, contact@gardenhousebrighton.co.uk, www.gardenhousebrighton.co.uk. *1½m N of Brighton Pier. The Garden House can be found 1½m N of seafront, 1st L off Ditching Rd, past T-lights. Paid street parking available. London Road Station is a short walk away & buses 46 & 26 stop nearby.* **Fri 2 Mar (12-4). Adm £5.50, chd free. Sat 21, Sun 22 Apr (11.30-4). Adm £5, chd free. Hot soup & bread, mulled cider, tea & coffee (Mar). Home-made teas (Apr). Visits also by arrangement Apr to Sept for groups of 10+.**

Tucked away in the heart of the city this really is a secret garden, in Victorian times a market garden. The garden is organic and gives interest all yr-round, supporting cut flowers, vegetables, fruit, old climbing roses and a pond. Many of the plants have been propagated by the garden owner, and the garden has unique features using many recycled materials. Garden produce and plants for sale.

54 ◆ GREAT DIXTER HOUSE, GARDENS & NURSERIES

Northiam, TN31 6PH. Great Dixter Charitable Trust, 01797 253107, office@greatdixter.co.uk, www.greatdixter.co.uk. *8m N of Rye. Off A28 in Northiam, follow brown signs.* **For NGS: Wed 17 Oct (1-5). Adm £5, chd free. Light refreshments. For other opening times and information, please phone, email or visit garden website.**

Designed by Edwin Lutyens and Nathaniel Lloyd. Christopher Lloyd made the garden one of the most experimental and constantly changing gardens of our time, a tradition now being carried on by Fergus Garrett. Clipped topiary, wild flower meadows, the famous long border, pot displays, exotic garden and more. The garden in autumn is of particular note.

55 GREAT LYWOOD FARMHOUSE

Lindfield Road, Ardingly, RH17 6SW. Richard & Susan Laing, 01444 892500, splaing@btinternet.com. *2½m N of Haywards Heath. Between Lindfield & Ardingly on B2028. From Lindfield, after ¾m turn L down signed paved track. 1st house on R, car park beyond house.* **Mon 28 May, Fri 1, Sun 3 June (2-6). Adm £6, chd free. Home-made teas. Visits also by arrangement May & June for groups of 10+, no coaches.**

Approx 1½ acre garden surrounding C17 Sussex farmhouse (not open). The extensive but accessible and gentle terracing provides immediate views of many different aspects of the garden and distant views towards the South Downs. There are garden seats on every level making this a garden in which to rest and enjoy the countryside. Wheelchair access possible, some slopes and short grass.

56 GROVE FARM HOUSE

Paddockhurst Road, Turners Hill, RH10 4SF. Mr & Mrs Piers Gibson. *¼m W of Turners Hill on B2110. The garden is on the edge of the village of Turners Hill; entrance is on the Paddockhurst Rd (B2110), ¼m W of village Xrds.* **Sun 2 Sept (1-5). Adm £7.50, chd free. Home-made teas.**

A welcome return to the NGS for this gorgeous, 4 acre classic terraced garden with views of South Downs. The garden includes a circular yew maze, ha-ha, lime walk, herb and vegetable gardens, shrub and herbaceous borders, and a pond in a woodland setting. Garden extends over a series of terraces, has several flights of steps.

GROUP OPENING

57 NEW GUILLARDS OAK GARDENS

Guillards Oak, Midhurst, GU29 9JZ. *Leave Midhurst on the A272 towards Petersfield. Guillards Oak is the wide opening on the L, halfway up the hill before the pelican crossing. Purchase ticket for all gardens at Garden House, 49 Guillards Oak.* **Sun 3, Tue 5 June (2-6). Combined adm £5, chd free. Home-made teas at Garden House, 49 Guillards Oak.**

NEW GARDEN HOUSE, 49 GUILLARDS OAK
Mr & Mrs David Christie.

NEW 14 GUILLARDS OAK
Mrs Jill Emery.

NEW 38 GUILLARDS OAK
Mr & Mrs Mike & Pam Nobes.

Three very different gardens on the same road in the old market town of Midhurst. No 14 owned by a plants woman crammed with many interesting and colourful plants. The garden is on several levels, accessed by steps so is not suitable for wheelchair access. No 38 is owned by the winner of Midhurst in Bloom. The upper level with patio and seating area, has a bed planted with a riot of colour and the lower level, accessed by several steps, has a fish pond stocked with Koi Carp and Goldfish and is fed by a little waterfall. No 49, Garden House, is one-third of the original house. The garden has a formal design but is very informally planted by a real 'plantaholic' and is always being developed. There are two shallow steps from the road onto the patio, and three down onto the lawn.

58 HAM COTTAGE

Hammingden Lane, Highbrook, Ardingly, RH17 6SR. Peter & Andrea Browne, 01444 892746, aegbrowne@btinternet.com, www.hamcottage.com. *5m N of Haywards Heath. On B2028 1m S of Ardingly turn into Burstow Hill Lane. Signed to Highbrook, then follow NGS signs.* **Sun 13 May, Sat 28, Sun 29 July (2-5). Adm £5, chd free. Home-made teas. Visits also by arrangement May to Sept.**

8 acre garden created from agricultural land during the last 20 yrs by the present owners. The garden is now well established with yr-round colour bursting from the many borders, large bog garden and winter garden. A gentle stream flows down over waterfalls into a bluebell carpeted wood. Above the arboretum there is an amphitheatre within an old sandstone quarry. Wheelchair access to most of the garden with assistance.

Visit a garden and support hospice care in your local community

59 HAMMERWOOD HOUSE

Iping, Midhurst, GU29 0PF. Mr & Mrs M Lakin. *3m W of Midhurst. Take A272 from Midhurst, approx 2m outside Midhurst turn R for Iping. From A3 leave for Liphook, follow B2070, turn L for Milland & Iping.* **Sun 13 May (1.30-5). Adm £5, chd free. Home-made teas.** Donation to Iping Church.

Large s-facing garden with lots of mature shrubs incl camellias, rhododendrons and azaleas. An arboretum with a variety of flowering and fruit trees. The old yew and beech hedges give a certain amount of formality to this traditional English garden. Tea on the terrace is a must with the most beautiful view of the South Downs. For the more energetic there is a woodland walk. Partial wheelchair access as garden is set on a slope.

60 HARBOURSIDE

Prinsted Lane, Prinsted, Southbourne, PO10 8HS. Ann Moss, 01243 370048, ann.moss8@btinternet.com. *6m W of Chichester. A27 to Tesco r'about onto A259 W, after 2nd r'about take 2nd L. Chinese Restaurant on corner, follow lane until forced to turn R at Scout Hut & car park. House next door with old boat in front garden.* **Visits by arrangement for groups of 12-30. Various refreshment options, please call and discuss. Adm £4.50, chd free.**

Award-winning coastal garden takes you on a journey through garden styles from around the world. Visit France, Holland, New Zealand and Japan. View and enjoy tree ferns, topiary, shady area, secret woodland parlor, potager, containers, unusual shrubs and plants, silver birch walk, herbaceous borders, art and crafts, seaside garden, blue and white area, all yr-round colour and interest. Piped music. Wheelchair access to most of the garden, after 10ft of gravel at the garden entrance.

61 HARDWYCKE

Southfields Road, Eastbourne, BN21 1BZ. Lois Machin, 01323 729391, loisandpeter@yahoo.co.uk. *Centre of Eastbourne, Upperton. A259 towards Eastbourne, Southfields Rd on R just before junction with A2270 (Upperton Rd). Limited parking, public car park (pay) in Southfields Rd.* **Sun 3 June (11-5). Combined adm with Dittons End £5, chd free. Home-made teas. Visits also by arrangement Apr to Sept for groups of 10-25. Refreshments on request.**

Delightful s-facing town garden mainly of chalky soil, with many usual and unusual plants. Separate vegetable garden with restored 1920s summerhouse. Wide selection of shrubs incl fifty types of clematis. L-shaped garden that has two spaces 70ft x 50ft and 18ft x 50ft. Wheelchair access with care, two slight steps to rear garden area.

GROUP OPENING

62 NEW HARLANDS GARDENS

Penland Road, Haywards Heath, RH16 1PH. *Follow the yellow signs from Balcombe Rd or Milton Rd & Bannister Way (Sainsbury's). Bus stop on Bannister Way (Route 30, 31, 39 & 80). Gardens within 5 min easy walk from train station & bus stop.* **Sat 19, Sun 20 May (1-5). Combined adm £5, chd free. Home-made teas at 27 Turners Mill Road.**

NEW **52 PENLAND ROAD**
Karen & Marcel van den Dolder.

NEW **55 PENLAND ROAD**
Steve & Lisa Williams.

NEW **5 SUGWORTH CLOSE**
Lucy & Brian McCully.

NEW **27 TURNERS MILL ROAD**
Sam & Derek Swanson.

An eclectic mix of town gardens designed, built and maintained by busy people who love and enjoy their gardens. We comprise awkward shapes and differing gradients and are designed with relaxation and socialisation in mind. Our gardens offer rich cottage-style planting schemes, varied ponds, delightful courtyards, practical kitchen gardens and habitats for wildlife. Look out for interesting pots and carnivorous plants. Adjacent woodland provides beautiful walks (maybe muddy) to extend your visit. Roadside parking is readily available. Park once to visit all gardens. Plants sale at 52 Penland Road. Find out more at www.facebook.com/Harlands-Gardens-269271216906342/. The nearby quaintly English villages of Cuckfield and Lindfield are worthy of a visit. Partial wheelchair access to all gardens.

GROUP OPENING

63 NEW HELLINGLY PARISH TRAIL

Hellingly, Hailsham, BN27 4EZ. *All gardens are close together, 2 of the gardens & tea venue are within the bounds of the churchyard with the remaining 3 just outside. Yellow signs will direct you to the church.* **Sun 8 July (2-5). Combined adm £5, chd free. Home-made teas in St. Peter & St. Paul Parish Church.**

NEW **ASH CROFT**
Gillian Chubb.

NEW **BROADVIEW**
Gill Riches.

NEW **1 CHURCH LANE**
Josephine Brown.

NEW **PRIORS COTTAGE**
Pat Booth.

NEW **PRIORS GRANGE**
Sylvia Stephens.

There are five examples of cottage gardens and tea at the parish church on this trail, all within walking distance of each other. The village can be reached on the 51 bus from Eastbourne. The Cuckoo Cycle Trail is nearby. Two of the gardens are in Grade II listed cottages (not open) and the Grade I listed church are within the bounds of the only complete Circ (Celtic) in Sussex. Parking is available in surrounding streets and lanes in the village. WC at church.

64 ◆ HERSTMONCEUX CASTLE GARDENS AND GROUNDS

Herstmonceux, Hailsham, BN27 1RN. Bader International Study Centre, Queen's University (Canada), 01323 833816, c_harber@bisc.queensu.ac.uk, www.herstmonceux-castle.com. *Located between Herstmonceux and Pevensey on the Wartling Rd. From Herstmonceux take A271 to Bexhill, 2nd R signed Castle. Do not use SatNav.* **For NGS: Sat 23 June (10-6). Adm £6, chd £3. Cream teas & light lunches in Chestnuts Tearoom.** For other opening times and information, please phone, email or visit garden website.

Herstmonceux is renowned for its magnificent moated castle set in beautiful parkland and superb Elizabethan walled gardens, leading to delightful discoveries such as our rhododendron, rose and herb gardens and onto our woodland trails. Take a slow stroll past the lily covered lakes to the 1930s folly and admire the sheer magnificence of the castle. The Gardens & Grounds first opened for the NGS in 1927. Partial wheelchair access to formal gardens.

GROUP OPENING

65 HERSTMONCEUX PARISH TRAIL

Hailsham, BN27 4JF. *4m NE of Hailsham. 5m S of Heathfield or Herstmonceux. The trail can start at Cowbeech House in Cowbeech Village, opp the Merrie Harriers Pub or at any other garden listed. Map of the trail will be provided. Please note: this is not a walking trail.* **Sun 10 June (12-5). Combined adm £6, chd free. Teas & BBQ lunch at The Windmill.**

2 ACRES
BN27 4RS. Di Tate.

THE ALLOTMENTS, STUNTS GREEN
BN27 4PP. Chris Reed.

COWBEECH HOUSE
BN27 4JF. Mr Anthony Hepburn.

1 ELM COTTAGES
BN27 4RT. Audrey Jarrett.

MONTANA
BN27 1RG. Paul & Caroline Lucas.

NEW **THE WINDMILL**
BN27 4RT. Windmill Hill Windmill Trust

Five gardens and a historic Windmill will open as part of the Herstmonceux Parish Trail this yr. Cowbeech House, a place to linger, has an exciting range of water features in the garden and dates back to 1731. The Allotments comprise 54 allotments growing a huge variety of traditional and unusual crops. 2 Acres has mature trees and a large pond with fish, and is on the same site as Lime Cross Nursery with a free Pinetum to visit. A short ½m stroll or drive into Windmill Hill brings you to 1 Elm Cottages, a stunning cottage garden packed full of edible and flowering plants you cannot afford to miss. Montana is a romantic garden with beautiful planting that cascades down a grassy bank. The Windmill, is a restored Mill and will be the venue for teas and a lovely BBQ lunch.

66 ◆ HIGH BEECHES WOODLAND AND WATER GARDEN

High Beeches Lane, Handcross, Haywards Heath, RH17 6HQ. High Beeches Gardens Conservation Trust, 01444 400589, gardens@highbeeches.com, www.highbeeches.com. *5m NW of Cuckfield. On B2110, 1m E of A23 at Handcross.* **For NGS: Sun 10 June, Sun 23 Sept (1-5). Adm £8.50, chd £2. Light refreshments in the High Beeches Tea Room.** For other opening times and information, please phone, email or visit garden website.

25 acres of enchanting landscaped woodland and water gardens with spring daffodils, bluebells and azalea walks, many rare and beautiful plants, an ancient wild flower meadow and glorious autumn colours. Picnic area. National Collection of Stewartias.

Bradness Gallery

67 ◆ HIGHDOWN GARDENS

33 Highdown Rise, Littlehampton Road, Goring-by-Sea, Worthing, BN12 6FB. Worthing Borough Council, 01903 501054, highdown.gardens@adur-worthing.gov.uk, www.highdowngardens.co.uk. *3m W of Worthing. Off the A259 approx 1m from Goring-by-Sea Train Station.* **For NGS: Sun 18 Feb (10-4). Adm £5, chd free. Wed 30 May (10-6). Adm by donation.** For other opening times and information, please phone, email or visit garden website.

Created by Sir Frederick Stern and situated on downland countryside in a chalk pit, Highdown features a wide collection of plants, with many raised from seed brought from China by great collectors like Wilson, Farrer and Kingdon-Ward. In spring and early summer, a colourful succession of bulbs such as snowdrops, crocus, anemones and daffodils are followed by paeonies and bearded iris. New for 2018, we are proud to be part of the National Garden Scheme's February Snowdrop Festival. Spring bulb tours will be conducted by the Head Gardener and team throughout the day for an additional £2.50 per person. Partial wheelchair access to hillside garden with mainly grass paths.

NPC

68 4 HILLSIDE COTTAGES

Downs Road, West Stoke, Chichester, PO18 9BL. Heather & Chris Lock, 01243 574802, chlock@btinternet.com. *3m NW of Chichester. From A286 at Lavant, head W for 1½m, nr Kingley Vale.* **Wed 13 June (11-4); Sun 22 July (2-5). Adm £3.50, chd free. Home-made teas. Visits also by arrangement June to Aug.**

Garden 120ft x 27ft in a rural setting, densely planted with mixed borders and shrubs. Large collection of roses, mainly New English shrub roses; walls, fences and arches covered with mid and late season clematis; baskets overflowing with fuchsias. A profusion of colour and scent in a well maintained small garden.

69 HOLLY HOUSE

Beaconsfield Road, Chelwood Gate, Haywards Heath, RH17 7LF. Mrs Deirdre Birchell, 01825 740484, db@hollyhousebnb.co.uk, www.hollyhousebnb.co.uk. *7m E of Haywards Heath. From Nutley village on A22 turn off at Hathi Restaurant signed Chelwood Gate 2m. Chelwood Gate Village Hall on R, Holly House is opp.* **Sat 12, Sun 13 May, Sat 7, Sun 8 July, Sat 18, Sun 19 Aug (2-5). Adm £4.50, chd free. Home-made teas. Visits also by arrangement May to Aug.**

An acre of English garden providing views and cameos of plants and trees round every corner with many different areas giving constant interest. A fish pond and a wildlife pond beside a grassy area with many shrubs and flower beds. Among the trees and winding paths there is a cottage garden which is a profusion of colour and peace. Exhibition of paintings and cards by owner. Garden accessible by wheelchair in good weather, but it is not easy.

70 THE HUNDRED HOUSE

Pound Lane, Framfield, TN22 5RU. Dr & Mrs Michael Gurney. *4m E of Uckfield. From Uckfield take B2102 through Framfield. 1m from centre of village turn L into Pound Lane, then ¾m on R. Disabled parking is close by the entrance gate.* **Sat 21, Sun 22 July (2-5). Adm £5, chd free. Home-made teas.**

Delightful garden with panoramic views set in the grounds of the historic The Hundred House (not open). Fine stone ha-ha. 1½ acre garden with mixed herbaceous borders, productive vegetable garden, greenhouse, ancient yew tree, pond area with some subtropical plants, secret woodland copse and orchard. Beech hedge, field and butterfly walk, Silver Birch (jacquemontii) grove under development. Home grown plants, vegetables and fruit for sale.

71 JACARANDA

Chalk Road, Ifold, RH14 0UE. Brian & Barbara McNulty, 01403 751532, bmcn0409@icloud.com. *1m S of Loxwood. From A272/A281 take B2133 (Loxwood). ½m S of Loxwood take Plaistow Rd, then 3rd R into Chalk Rd. Follow signs for parking & garden. Wheelchair users can park in driveway.* **Sun 2 Sept (2-5). Adm £4, chd free. Home-made teas. Visits also by arrangement Apr to Oct for groups of 25 max.**

A plant lover's garden created by the owners from a bare plot. Curving borders take you on a journey around the garden. Trees with interesting bark, many unusual shrubs and a variety of hosta displays, together with perennials, roses, climbers and bulbs, combine to make this a garden for all seasons. The vegetable area has a large raised bed, a greenhouse and herbs plus a hanging potting bench.

72 ◆ KING JOHN'S LODGE

Sheepstreet Lane, Etchingham, TN19 7AZ. Jill Cunningham, 01580 819220, harry@kingjohnsnursery.co.uk, www.kingjohnsnursery.co.uk. *2m W of Hurst Green. A265 Burwash to Etchingham. Turn L before Etchingham Church into Church Lane which leads into Sheepstreet Lane after ½m. Turn L after 1m.* **For NGS: Sun 11 Mar, Sat 5, Sun 6 May, Sat 16, Sun 17 June, Sun 23 Sept (11-5). Adm £5, chd free. Home-made teas & lunches in the tearoom of King John's Nursery.** For other opening times and information, please phone, email or visit garden website.

4 acre romantic garden for all seasons surrounding an historic listed house (not open). Formal garden with water features, rose walk and wild garden and pond. Rustic bridge to beds of woodland perennials, large herbaceous borders, old shrub roses and secret garden. Further 4 acres of meadows and fine trees. Nursery, shop, small children's soft play. In 2017 we featured twice on Songs of Praise. Garden is mainly

flat. Stepped areas can usually be accessed from other areas. No disabled WC.

73 KING'S LEAP

Castle Street, Winchelsea, TN36 4HU. Philip Kent. *2m W of Rye, 8m E of Hastings. Park in streets around the church TN36 4EB & follow signs. Opening with Rye View, 600yds apart.* **Sat 22 Sept (1-5). Combined adm with Rye View £4, chd free. Opening with Winchelsea's Secret Gardens on Sat 14 Apr.**

Large cottage-style garden comprising mixed beds, woodland border and rockery, all packed with plants for yr-round colour and interest. Refreshments available locally.

75 LAROCHE, 43 COOMBE DROVE

Bramber, Steyning, BN44 3PW. Lynne Broome, 01903 814170, lynnecbroome@gmail.com. *From Bramber Castle r'about, take Clays Hill signed Steyning, turn 2nd L into Maudlin Lane, after 100 metres, turn R into Coombe Drove. Garden at top of road.* **Visits by arrangement 14 Feb to end of March & in June for groups of 10+. If group is smaller, you can join another group. Adm £4, chd free. Home-made teas.**

⅓ acre garden situated on lower slope of the South Downs. Very wide variety of plants, many unusual. Portland stone terracing, with a small but steep woodland path with many snowdrops, hellebores, aconites and cyclamen in spring. In summer the garden bursts into colour with a white bed, hot bed, an array of containers, hanging baskets and a beautiful pergola covered in roses and clematis. Due to steep slope and steps, wheelchair access only to lower lawn.

76 LEGSHEATH FARM

Legsheath Lane, nr Forest Row, RH19 4JN. Mr & Mrs M Neal, legsheath@btinternet.com. *4m S of East Grinstead. 2m W of Forest Row, 1m S of Weirwood Reservoir.* **Sun 20 May (1.30-4.30). Adm £5, chd free. Home-made teas. Visits also by arrangement Apr to Aug for groups of 15+.** Donation to Holy Trinity Church, Forest Row.

Legsheath was first mentioned in Duchy of Lancaster records in 1545. It was associated with the role of Master of the Ashdown Forest. Set high in the Weald, it has far reaching views of East Grinstead and Weirwood Reservoir. The garden covers 11 acres with a spring fed stream feeding ponds. There is a magnificent davidia, rare shrubs, embothrium, many different varieties of meconopsis, abutilons.

77 LIMEKILN FARM

Chalvington Road, Chalvington, Hailsham, BN27 3TA. Dr J Hester & Mr M Royle. *10m N of Eastbourne. Nr Hailsham. Turn S off A22 at Golden Cross & follow the Chalvington Rd for 1m. The entrance has white gates on the LH-side. Disabled parking space close to the house, other parking 100 metres further along road.* **Sat 18, Sun 19 Aug (2-5). Adm £5, chd free. Home-made teas in the Oast House.**

The garden was designed in the 1930s when the house was owned by Charles Stewart Taylor, MP for Eastbourne. It has not changed in basic layout since then. The planting aims to reflect the age of the C17 property (not open) and original garden design. The house and garden are mentioned in Virginia Woolf's diaries of 1929, depicting a dilapidated charm that still exists today. Flint walls enclose the main lawn, herbaceous borders and rose garden. There is a vegetable garden, informal pond, secret garden, mature and newly planted specimen trees and late flowering annuals and dahlias.

78 NEW LINDFIELD JUNGLE

16 Newton Road, Lindfield, Haywards Heath, RH16 2ND. Tim Richardson & Clare Wilson, 01444 484132, info@lindfieldjungle.co.uk, www.lindfieldjungle.co.uk. *Approx 1½m NE of Haywards Heath town centre. Take B2028 signed Lindfield into the village. Turn R onto Lewes Rd, turn L onto Chaloner Rd, & turn R into Chaloner Close. Garden is located at the far end, please use postcode RH16 2NH.* **Visits by arrangement June to Oct for groups of up to 12 max. Adm £8, chd free. Home-made teas incl. Visits can be combined with 47 Denmans Lane or 5 Whitemans Close.**

A surprising, intimate garden, approx 17metres x 8metres. Transformed since 1999 into an atmospheric jungle oasis planted for tropical effect. Lush and exuberant with emphasis on foliage and hot colours that develop through the seasons. From the planter's terrace enjoy the winding path through lillies, cannas, ginger and bamboo, to the tranquil sundowner's deck over hidden pools. Join Tim & Clare for tiffin!

79 THE LONG HOUSE

The Lane, Westdean, Nr Seaford, BN25 4AL. Robin & Rosie Lloyd, 01323 870432, rosiemlloyd@gmail.com, www.thelonghousegarden.co.uk. *3m E of Seaford, 6m W of Eastbourne. From A27 follow signs to Alfriston then Litlington, Westdean 1m on L. From A259 at Exceat, L on Litlington Rd, ¼m on R. Free parking in the village.* **Thur 28 June (2-5). Adm £5, chd free. Home-made teas. Visits also by arrangement May to July for groups of 10+.**

The Long House's 1 acre garden is in the idyllic South Downs hamlet of Westdean. Lavenders, hollyhocks, roses, wild flower meadow, long perennial border, water folly and pond. 'A classic cottage garden... we enjoyed it as much as Sissinghurst' said Austrian visitors. The one thing everyone remarks on is the romantic and very special atmosphere of The Long House garden. Situated on The South Downs Way in the SDNP. Featured in Period Living (Sept 2017). Gravel forecourt at entrance, some slopes and steps.

80 LORDINGTON HOUSE

Lordington, Chichester, PO18 9DX. Mr & Mrs John Hamilton, 01243 375862, hamiltonjanda@btinternet.com. *7m W of Chichester. On W side of B2146, ½m S of Walderton, 6m S of South Harting. Enter through white railings.* **Sat 2, Sun 3 June (1.30-4.30). Adm £4.50, chd free. Home-made teas. Visits also by arrangement in June, regret no coaches.**

Early C17 house (not open) and walled gardens in SDNP. Clipped yew and box, lawns, borders and fine views. Vegetables, fruit and poultry in old kitchen garden. Carpet of daffodils in spring. Nearly 100 roses planted since 2008. Various trees both mature and young. Lime avenue planted in 1973 to replace elms. Overlooks Ems valley, farmland and wooded slopes of South Downs, all in AONB. Gravel paths, some uneven paving and slopes.

81 LOWDER MILL

Bell Vale Lane, Fernhurst, Haslemere, GU27 3DJ. Anne & John Denning, 01428 644822, anne@denningconsultancy.co.uk, www.lowdermill.com. *1½m S of Haslemere. Follow A286 out of Midhurst towards Haslemere, through Fernhurst & take 2nd R after Kingsley Green into Bell Vale Lane. Lowder Mill is approx ½m on R.* **Sat 2 June (11-5.30); Sun 3 June (10.30-5.30). Adm £4.50, chd £2. Home-made tea and cake served overlooking the lake.**

C17 mill house and former mill set in 3 acre garden. The garden has been restored with the help of Bunny Guinness. Interesting assortment of container planting, forming a stunning courtyard between house and mill. Streams, waterfalls, innovative and quirky container planting around the potting shed and restored greenhouse. Raised vegetable garden. Rare breed chickens and ducks, as well as resident kingfishers. Extensive plant stall, mainly home propagated. Choir singing on Sun. Featured in Country Life, Country Living, Sussex Life, and Chichester Observer.

82 LUCTONS

North Lane, West Hoathly, East Grinstead, RH19 4PP. Drs Hans & Ingrid Sethi, 01342 810085, ingrid@sethis.co.uk. *4m SW of East Grinstead, 6m E of Crawley. Off minor road between Turners Hill & Forest Row. Nr Church, Cat Inn & Priest House. Car parks in village.* **Sat 23 June (1-5), also open The Priest House. Sun 24, Tue 26 June (1-5). Adm £5, chd free. Home-made teas. Visits also by arrangement June to Aug for groups of 10-30.**

A very varied 2 acre Gertrude Jekyll style garden, with box parterre, topiary, acclaimed herbaceous borders, swathes of spotted orchids, wild flowers in the orchard, chickens, greenhouses, large vegetable and fruit garden, croquet lawn, herb garden, and a huge number of plants. Admired by overseas garden tour visitors, and cared for lovingly by the Indian owner, a partition refugee.

83 MALTHOUSE FARM

Streat Lane, Streat, Hassocks, BN6 8SA. Richard & Helen Keys, 01273 890356, helen.k.keys@btinternet.com. *2m SE of Burgess Hill. From r'about between B2113 & B2112 take Folders Lane & Middleton Common Lane E; after 1m, R into Streat Lane, garden is ½m on R. Ample parking on grass verge.* **Sun 19, Wed 22 Aug (2-5.30). Adm £5, chd free. Home-made teas. Visits also by arrangement Apr to Oct for groups of 10+.**

Rural 5 acre garden with stunning views to South Downs. Garden divided into separate rooms, box parterre and borders with glass sculpture, herbaceous and shrub borders, mixed border for seasonal colour and kitchen garden. Orchard leading to partitioned areas with grass walks, snail mound, birch maze and willow tunnel. Wildlife farm pond with planted surround. Featured in Country Life (8 Nov 2017), Sussex Life and Architectural Digest. Wheelchair access possible although some steps. Caution if wet as much access is across grass.

84 MANOR OF DEAN

Tillington, Petworth, GU28 9AP. Mr & Mrs James Mitford, 07887 992349, emma@mitford.uk.com. *3m W of Petworth. From Petworth towards Midhurst on A272, pass Tillington & turn R onto Dean Lane following NGS signs. From Midhurst on A272 towards Petworth past Halfway Bridge, turn L following NGS signs.* **Sun 11 Feb (2-4); Sun 18 Mar, Sun 22 Apr, Sun 5 Aug (2-5). Adm £4.50, chd free. Home-made teas. Visits also by arrangement Feb to Sept for groups of 15+, regret no coaches.**

Traditional English garden, approx 3 acres with herbaceous borders, a variety of early flowering bulbs, snowdrops, spring bulbs, grass walks and grass steps. Walled kitchen garden with fruit, vegetables and cutting flowers. Lawns, rose garden and informal areas with views of the South Downs. Garden under a long-term programme of improvements. Rhubarb for sale in April and dahlias for sale in August. Garden on many levels with old steps and paths making it unsuitable for buggies or wheelchairs.

GROUP OPENING

85 MAYFIELD GARDENS

Mayfield, TN20 6AB. *10m S of Tunbridge Wells. Turn off A267 into Mayfield. Parking is available in the village & field parking at Hoopers Farm, TN20 6BD. A detailed map will be available at each of the gardens.* **Sat 9, Sun 10 June (1-5). Combined adm £6, chd free. Home-made teas at Hoopers Farm & The Oast.**

HOOPERS FARM
Andrew & Sarah Ratcliffe.

MAY COTTAGE
M Prall.

MEADOW COTTAGE
Adrian & Mo Hope.

MULBERRY
M Vernon.

OAKCROFT
Nick & Jennifer Smith.

THE OAST
Mike & Tessa Crowe.

NEW **SHALDON**
William & Phyllida de Salis.

SOUTH STREET PLOTS
Val Buddle.

Mayfield is a beautiful Wealden village with tearooms, an old pub and many interesting historical connections. The gardens to visit are all within walking distance of the village centre. They vary in size and style, including colour themed, courtyard and cottage garden planting, wildlife meadows and fruit and vegetable plots. There are far reaching, panoramic views over the beautiful High Weald. Partial wheelchair access to some gardens; see leaflet on the day for details.

---

86 NEW MEADOW FARM

Blackgate Lane, Pulborough, RH20 1DF. Charles and Vanessa Langdale. *5m N of Pulborough. From Pulborough take A29 N. Just outside Pulborough L into Blackgate Lane signed to Toat. Continue on road for 1½m. At sign for Scrase Farms keep going straight. Look out for parking signs on R.* **Sun 17 June (2-5). Adm £4, chd free. Home-made teas.**

Approx 1 acre garden built from scratch over the last 10 years. Hot colour-schemed beds at the front lead into a small shrubbery and then onto double borders with a formal pond. A pleached hornbeam avenue takes the eye out to the West Sussex countryside. The walled garden provides fruit, cut flowers and vegetables for the family. This leads in turn to the orchard with bees and a hazelnut walk. Unfortunately, the gravel drive and paths at the front and the uneven ground in the orchard mean that it is hard for wheelchairs to gain access.

87 ◆ MERRIMENTS

Hawkhurst Road, Hurst Green, TN19 7RA. Lucy Cross, 01580 860666, info@merriments.co.uk, www.merriments.co.uk. *Off A21, 1m N of Hurst Green. On A229 Hawkhurst Rd. Situated between Hurst Green & Hawkhurst 300yds on R from A21.* **For NGS: Thur 9 Aug (10-4.30). Adm £8, chd free.** **For other opening times and information, please phone, email or visit garden website.**

Beautiful 4 acre garden with colour themed borders set amongst the rolling countryside of East Sussex. Seamlessly blending its large borders of inspiring planting evolved through the seasons from spring pastels to the fiery autumn hues of the many trees, all on a gently sloping s-facing site with good parking and easy access. There are a number of benches in the garden to allow visitors to enjoy the atmosphere of this special ever-evolving garden. There are many unusual plants most of which are sold in the plant centre; there is also a great shop, restaurant serving home-made lunches and teas. Dogs are welcome on leads. Wheelchairs available from the shop.

88 ◆ MICHELHAM PRIORY

Upper Dicker, Hailsham, BN27 3QS. Sussex Archaeological Society, 01323 844224, www.sussexpast.co.uk. *3m W of Hailsham. A22 N from Eastbourne, exit L to Arlington Rd W. 1⅙m turn R, Priory on R after approx 300yds.* **For opening times and information, please phone or visit garden website.**

The stunning 7 acre gardens at Michelham Priory (open to the public) are enclosed by England's longest water-filled moat, which teams with wildlife and indigenous waterlilies. Cloister and Physic gardens weave together features of medieval gardening. Over 40 yrs of developments have created a variety of features incl herbaceous borders, orchard, kitchen garden and tree lined Moat Walk. The gardens have 80,000 daffodils that create a blaze of colour from early spring onwards.

89 NEW MILL HALL FARM

Whitemans Green, Cuckfield, Haywards Heath, RH17 5HX. Kate & Jonathan Berry. *2½m E of A23, junction with B2115. Driveway on N-side B2115 at W-end of Burrell Cottages. No parking at house as narrow driveway with no passing places. Please park in free car park on S-side & walk 150yds.* **Sun 10 June (12.30-5). Adm £5, chd free. Home-made teas.**

2½ acre garden that begun in March 2012. N-facing long view sloping down to pond with lilies, irises, sanguisorba (deep water). Long border with young trees and herbaceous plants incl cercidiphyllum, catalpa aurea, Metasequoia Gold Rush, cornus, acers and pulmonarias, daylilies, phlox, penstemon and brunnera, climbing roses, clematis and golden hop. Fruit and vegetable garden. Victorian underground water cistern. Plants for sale. Garden is generally bumpy with sloping lawn. No wheelchair access to WC.

Macmillan and the National Garden Scheme, partners for more than 30 years

90 THE MOONGATE GARDEN

6 Elm Avenue, East Preston, Littlehampton, BN16 1HJ. Helen & Derek Harnden, 07870 324654, derek@shiningmylight.plus.com. *Over railway crossing from A259, continue straight onto Golden Ave. Turn R into Elm Ave, within 110 metres.* **Sat 12, Sun 13 May, Sat 28, Sun 29 July (11-4); Sun 16 Sept (12-4). Adm £5, chd free. Home-made teas. Visits also by arrangement May to Sept for groups of 20+. If your group is smaller, do ask to join another group.**

S-facing garden 50 x 15 metres, in its third year. A stunning Purbeck stone wall with moongate bisects the garden, creating two distinct halves. Within these, there are several sections including contemporary fish pond with stainless steel waterfall, a Hobbit house, circular lawns surrounded by herbaceous borders with a variety of grasses and trees for yr-round interest. Spectacular alliums in May, Japanese area, vegetables, fruit cage, grasses, stumpery and fernery. Featured on BBC Gardener's World (19 Jul 2017). Wheelchair access through large gate on left side of house, with direct access to garden on flat paving.

91 MOUNTFIELD COURT

Robertsbridge, TN32 5JP. Mr & Mrs Simon Fraser. *3m N of Battle. On A21 London-Hastings; ½m NW from Johns Cross.* **Sun 6 May (2-5). Adm £5, chd free. Home-made teas.**

3 acre wild woodland garden; bluebell lined walkways through exceptional rhododendrons, azaleas, camellias, and other flowering shrubs; fine trees and outstanding views. Beautiful paved herb garden.

92 NEWTIMBER PLACE

Newtimber, BN6 9BU. Mr & Mrs Andrew Clay, 01273 833104, andy@newtimberholidaycottages.co.uk, www.newtimberplace.co.uk. *7m N of Brighton. From A23 take A281 towards Henfield. Turn R at small Xrds signed Newtimber in approx ½m. Go down Church Lane, garden is at end of lane on L.* **Sun 15 Apr (2-5.30). Adm £5, chd free. Home-made teas.**

Beautiful C17 moated house (not open). Gardens and woods full of bulbs and wild flowers in spring. Herbaceous border and lawns. Moat flanked by water plants. Mature trees, wild garden, ducks, chickens and fish. Wheelchair access across lawn to some of garden, tearoom and WC.

93 NORTH HALL

North Hall Lane, Sheffield Green, Uckfield, TN22 3SA. Celia & Les Everard, 01825 791103, indigodogs@yahoo.co.uk. *1½m NW of Fletching village. 6m N of Uckfield. From A272 turn N at Piltdown or N Chailey. From A275 turn E at Sheffield Green into North Hall Lane.* **Sat 23, Sun 24 June (2-5.30). Adm £4, chd free. Home-made teas. Visits also by arrangement mid April to May for groups of 10-20. June to mid July for groups of 10-40.**

This quintessential cottage garden surrounding a C16 house (not open) is planted to please the senses. Owner maintained, inspired by Hardy Plant Society membership, the planting is dense and varied in a palette of soft colours. Flowing themed island beds and a moated terrace add to the many other cottage garden features. Wildlife and self-seeding encouraged. Home grown plants and scrumptious teas.

94 NORTH SPRINGS

Bedham, nr Fittleworth, RH20 1JP. Mr & Mrs R Haythornthwaite. *Between Fittleworth & Wisborough Green. From Wisborough Green take A272 towards Petworth. Turn L into Fittleworth Rd signed Coldharbour & proceed 1½m. From Fittleworth take Bedham Lane off A283 & proceed for approx 3m NE. Limited parking.* **Sun 1 July (1-6). Adm £4.50, chd free. Home-made teas.**

Hillside garden with beautiful views surrounded by mixed woodland. Focus on structure with a wide range of mature trees and shrubs. Stream, pond and bog area. Abundance of roses, clematis, hostas, rhododendrons and azaleas.

95 NYEWOOD HOUSE

Nyewood, Petersfield, GU31 5JL. Mr & Mrs C J Wright, 01730 821563, s.warren.wright@gmail.com. *4m E of Petersfield. From A272 at Rogate take South Harting Rd for 1½m. Turn L at pylon towards South Downs Manor. Nyewood House 2nd on R over cattle grid.* **Visits by arrangement May to July for groups of 20+. Various refreshment options.**

Victorian country house garden with stunning uninterrupted views of the South Downs. 3 acres comprising formal gardens with rose walk and arbours, pleached hornbeam, colour themed herbaceous borders, shrub borders, lily pond and fully stocked kitchen garden with greenhouse. Wooded area featuring spring flowers followed by wild orchids and wild flowers. Wonderful, extended views of the South Downs. Refreshments include morning coffee and cake or biscuits, home-made tea, cream teas or wine and nibbles. Gravel drive.

96 ◆ NYMANS

Staplefield Road, Handcross, RH17 6EB. National Trust, 01444 405250, nymans@nationaltrust.org.uk, www.nationaltrust.org.uk/nymans. *4m S of Crawley. On B2114 at Handcross signed off M23/A23 London-Brighton road. Metrobus 271 & 273 stop nearby.* **For NGS: Sun 23 Sept (10-5). Adm £12.60, chd £6.50. Light refreshments. For other opening times and information, please phone, email or visit garden website.**

A garden lovers' home for all seasons, with an extensive yet intimate garden set around a romantic house and ruins. Some level pathways. See full access statement on the Nymans website.

NPC

97 NEW OAKLANDS FARM

Hooklands Lane, Shipley, Horsham, RH13 8PX. Zsa & Stephen Roggendorff, zedrog@roggendorff.co.uk. *S of A272, R at Countryman Pub, follow yellow signs N of A24 Ashington. Head along Billingshurst Rd, take 1st R signed Shipley, garden 2m outside of Shipley village.* **Wed 30 May, Wed 18 July (11-6). Adm £5, chd free. Visits also by arrangement Apr to July.**

Country garden designed by Nigel Philips. Approached from a small lane, along an oak lined drive leading to the house and farm. The drive opens out to an enclosed courtyard with pleached hornbeam and yew. The herbaceous borders are filled with summer colours. Small orchard beyond the tennis court and wild meadow area with views into the fields. Vegetable garden with raised beds, and greenhouse. Gravel and brick paths, large lawn area and grassy paths.

98 OAKLEIGH COTTAGE

Back Lane, Cross in Hand, TN21 0ND. Mr & Mrs Simons. *2m from Heathfield. 1m off A267 at Cross in Hand. Back Lane runs behind Oak Showroom. We are 1m down Back Lane on the L, opp Kees Farm where you might wish to park.* **Sat 7, Sun 8 Apr (11-4.30). Adm £5, chd free. Home-made teas.** Donation to Lymphoma Association.

Pretty cottage garden with a variety of habitats in ¾ acre. In spring, orchard full of daffodils, secret camellia garden, colourful shrubbery, woodland garden and many kinds of hellebore. Also large herbaceous borders with a garden bank of bee-friendly flowers all year. Plants from the garden for sale and tea, coffee, soft drinks and home-made cakes available. Wheelchair access to main areas of garden.

99 OFFHAM HOUSE

The Street, Offham, Lewes, BN7 3QE. Mr S Goodman and Mr & Mrs P Carminger. *2m N of Lewes on A275. Offham House is on the main road (A275) through Offham between the filling station & the Blacksmiths Arms.* **Sun 29 Apr, Sun 3 June (1-5). Adm £5, chd free. Tea & home-made cake.**

Romantic garden with fountains, flowering trees, arboretum, double herbaceous border, long peony bed. 1676 Queen Anne house (not open) with well knapped flint facade. Herb garden and walled kitchen garden with glasshouses, coldframes, chickens, guinea fowl, sheep and friendly pig.

100 OLD ERRINGHAM COTTAGE

Steyning Road, Shoreham-By-Sea, BN43 5FD. Fiona & Martin Phillips, 01273 462285, fiona.h.phillips@btinternet.com. *2m N of Shoreham by Sea. From A27 Shoreham flyover take A283 towards Steyning. Take 2nd R into private lane. Follow sharp LH-bend at top, house on L.* **Visits by arrangement mid May to early July for groups of 10+. If your group is smaller, ask if you can join another group. Adm £5, chd free.**

Plantsman's garden set high on the South Downs with panoramic views overlooking the Adur valley. 1⅓ acres with flower meadow, stream bed and ponds, formal and informal planting areas with over 600 varieties of plants. Very productive fruit and vegetable garden with glasshouses. Many plants grown from seed and coastal climate gives success with tender plants. Part of house dates from 1480 (not open).

Sussex Prairies

© Nicola Harthoorn

101 NEW OLD STONELYNK EDGE

63 Battery Hill, Fairlight, Hastings, TN35 4AP. Joe & Kerry Gentleman. *5m E of Hastings. On the Ore to Cliff End main road at the junction with Warren Rd. 101 bus stops close by. Parking limited & on the main road.* **Thur 5 July (1-5). Adm £5, chd free. Light refreshments.**

Large, well established garden with variety of shrubs and borders. Small wildlife pond with waterfall. Various flower beds and lawn sloping steeply down to sizeable fish pond with a bridge leading to woodland walk and a variety of shady seating areas. A number of steps to access the front garden, and sloping rear garden. Not suitable for wheelchairs or those with reduced mobility.

102 OLD VICARAGE

The Street, Firle, Lewes, BN8 6NR. Mr & Mrs Charlie Bridge. *Off A27 5m E of Lewes. Signed from main road.* **Sat 9 June (1-4). Adm £5, chd free. Cream teas.**

Garden originally designed by Lanning Roper in the 1960s. 4 acre garden with lots of different rooms, set around a Regency vicarage (not open) with wonderful Downland views. Features a walled garden with vegetable parterre and flower borders, wild flower meadow, pond, pleached limes and over 100 roses. Partial wheelchair access as some areas may be difficult.

103 THE OLD VICARAGE

The Street, Washington, RH20 4AS. Sir Peter & Lady Walters, 07766 761926, meryl.walters@me.com. *2½m E of Storrington, 4m W of Steyning. From Washington r'about on A24 take A283 to Steyning. 500yds R to Washington. Pass Frankland Arms, R to St Mary's Church.* **Sun 25 Feb (10.30-3); Mon 2 Apr (10.30-4); Sun 13 May, Sun 17 June, Mon 27 Aug (10.30-4.30); Sun 14 Oct (10.30-3). Adm £5, chd free. Home-made teas. Gluten free cakes & biscuits available. Visits also by arrangement Feb to Oct for groups of 10+.**

Gardens of 3½ acres set around 1832 Regency house (not open). The front, formally laid out with topiary, wide lawn, mixed border, and contemporary water sculpture. The rear, features new and mature trees from C19, herbaceous borders, water garden and stunning uninterrupted views of the North Downs. Also Japanese garden with waterfall and pond, a large copse, stream, treehouse and stumpery. Architectural stumpery new for 2017 and extended for 2018, plus 2000 tulips have been planted for spring as well as 10,000 mixed bulbs in the new meadow area. In progress a new Italianate gazebo with green oak columns and led roof. Featured in Sussex Life (Autumn 2017), as well as many previous articles. Wheelchair access to the front garden, but the rear garden is on a slope.

GROUP OPENING

104 OUSE VALLEY TO THE COAST TRAIL

Swanborough, BN7 3PE. *Visitors can start at any of the 5 gardens listed.* **Sat 21, Sun 22 July (1-5). Combined adm £6, chd free. Home-made teas.**

12 AINSWORTH AVENUE
BN2 7BG. Jane & Chris Curtis.

CATTLEGATE
BN7 3PE. Caroline Courtauld.

5 OLD COASTGUARD COTTAGES
BN9 9EH. Corrina & Gill Weaver.

144 RODMELL AVENUE
BN2 8PJ. Sue & Ray Warner, 01273 305137, suwarner@xeonflux.com.
Visits also by arrangement in Aug for groups of 2-20.

SKYSCAPE
BN2 7BG. Lorna & John Davies.

Five uniquely different Sussex gardens flowing from the Ouse Valley down to the coast! Cattlegate in Swanborough has a small garden surrounding a white modernist house (not open), with a spectacular view as painted by the artist Eric Ravilious. Down on the coast see an amazing coastal garden on a slope at 5 Old Coastguard Cottages. Further along to Saltdean, see 144 Rodmell Avenue, a fun jungle garden, 65ft x 36ft, but appearing larger with winding paths meandering through lush jungle and insect friendly planting, listen out for the parrots squawking in the trees! Then in Ovingdean, see Skyscape at 46 Ainsworth Avenue, a 250ft s-facing rear garden on a sloping site with fantastic views of South Downs and sea. Also 12 Ainsworth Avenue, a small coastal garden begun in 2014 and still developing. Pergola, arches and arbor strategically positioned to provide privacy and a choice of places to sit with different aspects, even a glimpse of the sea. No wheelchair access at 144 Rodmell Avenue & 5 Old Coastguard Cottages and partial access at other gardens.

105 NEW PARK LODGE

Bedham Lane, Fittleworth, Pulborough, RH20 1JH. Mark & Louise Saunders. *3m SE of Petworth. Midway between Petworth & Pulborough on the A283, turn off into lane signed Bedham on sharp bend by the church.* **Sun 22 July (2-5). Adm £4, chd free. Home-made teas.**

½ acre head gardener's cottage garden, mixing formal and informal, cultivated and wild garden. Hedges divide the garden, mixed borders and roses, summerhouse, chickens. Also open with the working walled kitchen garden and glasshouse from Fittleworth House next door. Virtually all on flat ground, easily accessible to wheelchairs.

106 PARSONAGE FARM

Kirdford, RH14 0NH. David & Victoria Thomas. *5m NE of Petworth. From centre of Kirdford (before church) turn R through village towards Balls Cross, past Foresters*

Pub on R. Entrance on L, just past R turn to Plaistow. For SatNav use RH14 0NG. **Sun 22 Apr, Fri 22 June, Sun 9 Sept (2-6). Adm £6, chd free. Home-made teas.**
Major garden in beautiful setting developed over 20 yrs with fruit theme and many unusual plants. Formally laid out on grand scale with long vistas; C18 walled garden with borders in apricot, orange, scarlet and crimson; topiary walk; pleached lime allée; tulip tree avenue; rose borders; large vegetable garden with trained fruit; turf amphitheatre; lake; informal autumn shrubbery and jungle walk.

107 PEELERS RETREAT

70 Ford Road, Arundel, BN18 9EX. Tony & Lizzie Gilks, 01903 884981, timespan70@tiscali.co.uk, www.peelersretreat.co.uk. *1m S of Arundel. At Chichester r'about take exit to Ford & Bognor Regis onto Ford Rd. We are situated close to Maxwell Rd, Arundel.* **Sun 29 Apr, Sun 20 May, Sun 10 June, Sun 8 July, Sun 16 Sept (2-5). Adm £4, chd free. Home-made teas. Visits also by arrangement Apr to Sept for groups of 2-24.**
This beautiful garden has been designed to create a paradise in which to entertain and relax in. A concentrated effort has been made by two talented owners to incorporate their own eye-catching woodland sculptures including 'Joey the war horse', 'Wee Brodie' our stag, and Athena the owl in flight catching her prey and featuring our latest addition, two boxing hares. Exhibition of historical artefacts or hand-crafted garden ornaments. We featured in Amateur Gardening magazine (Autumn 2017) and The Bell magazine. Restricted wheelchair access due to our narrow side entrance, regret no motorised wheelchairs.

108 33 PEERLEY ROAD

East Wittering, PO20 8PD. Paul & Trudi Harrison, 01243 673215, stixandme@aol.com. *7m S of Chichester. From A286 take B2198 to Bracklesham. Turn R into Stocks Lane, L at Royal British Legion into Legion Way. Follow road round to Peerley Rd. No 33 is halfway along.* **Sun 1 July (12-4). Adm £2.50, chd free. Visits also by arrangement May to Oct for groups of up to 20 max.**
Small seaside garden 65ft x 32ft, 110yds from the sea. Packed full of ideas and interesting plants using every inch of space to create rooms and places for adults and children to play. A must for any suburban gardener. Specialising in unusual plants that grow well in seaside conditions with advice on coastal gardening.

109 PEMBURY HOUSE

Ditchling Road (New Road), Clayton, Hassocks, BN6 9PH. Nick & Jane Baker, 01273 842805, jane.baker47@btinternet.com, www.pemburyhouse.co.uk. *6m N of Brighton, off A23. On B2112, 110yds from A273. Parking for groups at house. Please car share. Overflow parking at village green, BN6 9PJ; then enter by Cinder Track & back gate. Good public transport service.* **Visits by arrangement Feb & Mar for groups of 10-30. Individuals can be added to groups. Walking groups welcome. Adm £9, chd free, incl home-made teas.**
Depending on the vagaries of the season, hellebores and snowdrops are at their best in last 2 weeks of Feb and early March. It is a country garden, tidy but not manicured. There is always work in progress on new areas. Winding paths give a choice of walks through 2 acres of owner maintained garden, which is in, and enjoys views of the SDNP. Wellies, macs and winter woolies advised. Featured in Sky 1 TV garden series, Japanese TV, Gardeners World, and numerous UK and European magazines.

110 PENNS IN THE ROCKS

Groombridge, Tunbridge Wells, TN3 9PA. Mr & Mrs Hugh Gibson, 01892 864244, www.pennsintherocks.co.uk. *7m SW of Tunbridge Wells. On B2188 Groombridge to Crowborough road, just S of Xrd to Withyham. For SatNav use TN6 1UX which takes you to the white drive gates, through which you should enter the property.* **Sun 22 Apr, Sun 20 May (2-6). Adm £6, chd free. Home-made teas. Visits also by arrangement.**
Large garden with spectacular outcrop of rocks, lake, C18 temple and woods. Daffodils, bluebells, azaleas, magnolias and tulips. Old walled garden with herbaceous borders, roses and shrubs. Part C18 house (not open). Walls recently restored by Richard and Columba Strachey. Restricted wheelchair access. No disabled WC. Dogs on lead in park only.

111 NEW 1 PEST COTTAGE

Carron Lane, Midhurst, GU29 9LF. Jennifer Lewin. *W edge of Midhurst behind Carron Lane Cemetery. Free parking at recreation ground at top of Carron Lane. Short walk on woodland track to garden, please follow signs.* **Evening opening Fri 8 June (4-7). Sun 10 June (2-6). Adm £4, chd free. Light refreshments.**
This edge of woodland, architects' studio garden of approx ¾ acre sits on a sloping sandy site. Designed to support wildlife and bio-diversity, a series of outdoor living spaces, connected with informal paths through lightly managed areas, creates a charming secret world tucked into the surrounding common land. The garden spaces have made a very small house (not open) into a hospitable family home. Architects garden studio open with exhibition boards. Track access and sloping site makes the garden unsuitable for wheelchairs or restricted mobility.

GROUP OPENING

112 NEW PETT VILLAGE GARDENS

Pett Road, Pett, Hastings, TN35 4HB. *4m E of Hastings. From Hastings take A259 to Rye. At White Hart Beefeater turn R into Friars Hill. Descend into Pett village. Park in village hall car park.* **Sat 23, Sun 24 June (11-5). Combined adm £6, chd free. Home-made teas at Fairlight End.** Donation to Pett Village Hall.

NEW **AMBLESIDE**
David & Jackie Richards.

NEW **BREANROSS**
Tim & Libby Rothwell.

FAIRLIGHT END
Chris & Robin Hutt.
(See separate entry)

NEW **FRENCH COURT FARMHOUSE**
Suzie Gibbons, 07701 096210
suzie@flowerpowerpictures.com

Pett is the last village in the Sussex Weald before it sweeps down to meet the English Channel a mile away. Four gardens are opening in Pett Village in 2018, three opening for the NGS for the first time. The variety in the gardens, all within walking distance of each other, is extensive and intriguing. Two gardens cover 3 acres and two are more compact. Features include magnificent views over surrounding landscape and secret gardens enclosed by woodland. Pett has two excellent village pubs. Wheelchair access to all gardens. French Court Farmhouse, down an off road track, has three disabled parking spaces.

113 6 PLANTATION RISE

Worthing, BN13 2AH. Nigel & Trixie Hall, 01903 262206, trixiehall@btinternet.com. *2m from seafront on outskirts of Worthing. A24 meets A27 at Offington r'about. Turn into Offington Lane, 1st R into The Plantation, 1st R again into Plantation Rise.* **Visits by arrangement Mar to Sept for groups of 4-20, incl home-made teas. Adm £5, chd free.**

Our garden is 70' x 80' with pond, summerhouse, folly, flower decked pergolas over patios, 9 silver birches, plus evergreen shrubs, azaleas, rhododendrons and acers. Heathers in spring, and a profusion of roses, clematis and perennials in August, all to ensure year round colour and interest. We are also in the Worthing Eco programme in September. My favourite feature are the birch trees. The variety is Tristus, which is semi pendula. The garden has some steps. WC available on request.

114 ◆ THE PRIEST HOUSE

North Lane, West Hoathly, RH19 4PP. Sussex Archaeological Society, 01342 810479, priest@sussexpast.co.uk, www.sussexpast.co.uk. *4m SW of East Grinstead. Turn E to West Hoathly, 1m S of Turners Hill at Selsfield Common junction on B2028. 2m S turn R into North Lane, garden ¼m.* **For NGS: Sat 26 May (10.30-5.30). Home-made teas. Sat 23 June (10.30-5.30). Also open Luctons. Adm £2, chd free. For other opening times and information, please phone, email or visit garden website.**

C15 timber framed farmhouse with cottage garden on acid clay. Large collection of culinary and medicinal herbs in a small formal garden and mixed with perennials and shrubs in exuberant borders. Long established yew topiary, box hedges and espalier apple trees provide structural elements. Traditional fernery and stumpery, recently enlarged with a small secluded shrubbery and gravel garden. Adm to Priest House Museum £1 for NGS visitors.

115 2 QUARRY COTTAGES

Wall Hill Road, Ashurst Wood, East Grinstead, RH19 3TQ. Mrs Hazel Anne Archibald. *1m S of East Grinstead. From N turn L off A22 from East Grinstead, garden adjoining John Pears Memorial Ground. From S turn R off A22 from Forest Row, garden on R at top of hill.* **Fri 18, Sat 19 May (2-5). Adm £3.50, chd free. Home-made teas.**

Peaceful little garden that has evolved over 40 yrs by present owners. A natural sandstone outcrop hangs over an ornamental pond; mixed borders of perennials and shrubs with specimen trees. Many seating areas tucked into corners. Highly productive vegetable plot. Terrace round house. Florist and gift shop in barn. **Also open Caxton Manor (separate admission).**

116 ROLFS FARM

Witherenden Road, Mayfield, TN20 6RP. Kate Langdon. *2m E of Mayfield (approx 5 mins). On Witherenden Rd, we are ½m from Mayfield end of road. Do not follow SatNav to postcode. Long, narrow, uneven driveway downhill through woods.* **Wed 6, Wed 13 June (10-3). Adm £4, chd free. Home-made teas.**

Very different from the usual NGS garden! Large wildlife friendly garden (no boundary fences to encourage visiting wildlife) with wildflower meadows, hazel trees, and clipped box hedging. Large orchard next to the garden. Tom Stuart-Smith designed modern meadow garden. Two ponds, small vegetable garden, and informal, naturalistic planting throughout. Uneven grass paths, sensible shoes please. Sorry, no wheelchair access as steep uneven driveway, and many steps in garden.

117 1 ROSE COTTAGE

Chalvington Road, Golden Cross, Nr Hailsham, BN27 3SS. Chris & Jackie Burgess, 01825 872753, burgess.clan24@gmail.com, www.rosecottagegarden.co.uk. *Approx 11m N of Eastbourne. Travelling N on the A22, turn L into Chalvington Rd immed S of Golden Cross Pub. Our property is the 1st on the R, approx 100yds after leaving the A22.* **Mon 25 June (11-5). Adm £4, chd free. Home-made teas. Visits also by arrangement May to Aug for groups.**

A cottage garden with densely planted borders. Roses, honeysuckles and clematis, plus a wide range of perennials viewed as you walk along meandering paths, some ending with secluded seating. Colour themed borders planted for yr-round interest. Fruit cage, large productive greenhouse and several raised vegetable beds (including two trial 'no dig' beds) add interest. Plants propagated by owners will be on sale. Pots of tea and home-made cakes served on pretty china, with delightful tablecloths. Featured in Sussex Life (June 2017). No wheelchair access.

118 RYE VIEW

The Strand, Winchelsea, TN36 4JY. Howard Norton & David Page. *2m W of Rye, 8m E of Hastings. Park in streets around the church TN36 4EB & follow signs. Walk 600yds downhill to garden. No parking at the garden but drop-off possible at entrance, email david@ryeview.net for more info.* **Sat 22 Sept (1-5). Combined adm with King's Leap £4, chd free. Opening with Winchelsea's Secret Gardens on Sat 14 Apr.**

Riverside views over Rye Marsh. A blend of formal and informal planting with a collection of bamboos, grasses and many unusual shrubs. Bulbs and spring foliage in April. Asters, grasses, dahlias, autumn colour in September. Refreshments available locally. Article in RHS 'The Garden' (May 2017).

119 RYMANS

Apuldram, Chichester, PO20 7EG. Mrs Michael Gayford, 01243 783147, suzanna.gayford@btinternet.com. *1m S of Chichester. Take Witterings Rd, at 1½m SW turn R signed Dell Quay. Turn 1st R, garden ½m on L.* **Sat 14, Sun 15 Apr, Sat 16, Sun 17 June (2-5); Sat 15 Sept (2.30-5); Sun 16 Sept (2-5). Adm £5, chd free. Home-made teas. Visits also by arrangement Apr to Sept for groups of 10+.**

Walled and other gardens surrounding lovely C15 stone house (not open); bulbs, flowering shrubs, roses, ponds, and potager. Many unusual and rare trees and shrubs. In late spring the wisterias are spectacular. The heady scent of hybrid musk roses fills the walled garden in June. In late summer the garden is ablaze with dahlias, sedums, late roses, sages and Japanese anemones. Featured in Guardian gardening supplement (Spring 2017). No wheelchair access.

120 SAFFRONS

Holland Road, Steyning, BN44 3GJ. Tim Melton & Bernardean Carey, 01903 810082, tim.melton@btinternet.com. *6m NE of Worthing. Exit r'about on A283 at S end of Steyning bypass into Clays Hill Rd. 1st R into Goring Rd, 4th L into Holland Rd. Park in Goring Rd & Holland Rd.* **Sun 15, Thur 19 July (2-5.30). Adm £5, chd free. Home-made teas. Visits also by arrangement in July for groups of 10+.**

A stylish garden of textural contrasts and rich colour. The herbaceous beds are furnished with agapanthus, spiky eryngiums, salvias, alliums and fragrant lilies. A broad lawn is surrounded by borders with Japanese maples, rhododendrons, hydrangeas and specimen trees interspersed with ferns and grasses. A fruit cage, vegetable beds and fruit trees comprise the productive area of the garden. Photograph of the garden selected for Hallmark's Gorgeous Floral Gardens 2018 wall calendar. Wheelchair access difficult in very wet conditions.

121 ◆ ST MARY'S HOUSE GARDENS

Bramber, BN44 3WE. Roger Linton & Peter Thorogood, 01903 816205, info@stmarysbramber.co.uk, www.stmarysbramber.co.uk. *1m E of Steyning. 10m NW of Brighton in Bramber village off A283.* **For NGS: Fri 29, Sat 30 June (2-5.30). Adm £6, chd free. Light refreshments. For other opening times and information, please phone, email or visit garden website.**

5 acres incl formal topiary, large prehistoric *Ginkgo biloba*, and magnificent *Magnolia grandiflora* around enchanting timber-framed Medieval house (not open for NGS). Victorian 'Secret Gardens' incl splendid 140ft fruit wall with pineapple pits, Rural Museum, Terracotta Garden, Jubilee Rose Garden, King's Garden and circular Poetry Garden. Woodland walk and Landscape Water Garden. In the heart of the SDNP. Level paths throughout.

The Walled Garden at Tilgate Park

122 SANDHILL FARM HOUSE

Nyewood Road, Rogate, Petersfield, GU31 5HU. Rosemary Alexander, 07551 777873, r.a.alexander@talk21.com, www.rosemaryalexander.co.uk. *4m SE of Petersfield. From A272 Xrds in Rogate take road S signed Nyewood & Harting. Follow road for approx 1m over small bridge. Sandhill Farm House on R, over cattle grid.* **Sun 18 Feb (12-3). Adm £4, chd free. Sat 21, Sun 22 Apr, Sat 23, Sun 24 June, Sat 22, Sun 23 Sept (2-5). Adm £5, chd free. Home-made teas. Visits also by arrangement Feb to Oct for groups of 10+. Gardening Clubs welcome.**

Front and rear gardens broken up into garden rooms incl small kitchen garden. Front garden incl small woodland area planted with early spring flowering shrubs, ferns and bulbs; topiary and white garden, large leaf border and terraced area. Rear garden has mirror borders, small decorative vegetable garden, red border, and grasses border. Home of author and principal of The English Gardening School. The garden has gravel paths and a few steps not easily negotiated in a wheelchair.

123 ◆ SARAH RAVEN'S CUTTING GARDEN

Perch Hill Farm, Willingford Lane, Robertsbridge, Brightling, TN32 5HP. Sarah Raven, 01424 838000, school@thecuttinggarden.com, www.sarahraven.com. *7m SW of Hurst Green. From Burwash turn off A265 by church & memorial, follow road for 3m. From Woods Corner take road opp Swan Inn, take 1st L, go uphill & take 1st L again. Parking is in a field (uneven ground possible).* **For NGS: Fri 14 Sept (9.30-4). Adm £5, chd free. Tea, coffee & cake served all day. Lunch available from 12.15.** For other opening times and information, please phone, email or visit garden website.

Sarah's inspirational, productive 2 acre working garden with different garden rooms incl large cut flower garden, vegetable and fruit garden, salads and herbs area, plus two ornamental gardens. We have some steps and gravel paths so wheelchair access is difficult in these areas.

124 SAYERLAND HOUSE

Sayerland Lane, Polegate, BN26 6QP. Penny & Kevin Jenden, 07789 992348, penny@jenden.net. *2m S of Hailsham, 1m N of Polegate. At Cophall r'about on A27 take A22, turn L at 1st turning (100yds). Follow through Bay Tree Lane, turn sharp L into Sayerland Lane. From N on A22 turn L into Bay Tree Lane before r'about.* **Sun 10 June (2-6). Adm £5, chd free. Home-made teas. Visits also by arrangement July to Sept for groups of up to 10 max.**

Romantic, rambling, 5 acre garden surrounding listed C15 house (not open). Several distinct garden areas. Walled garden with colour themed borders, rose garden, ponds, organic kitchen and cutting garden, hot beds and shade beds, all with naturalistic feel. Wild woodland area. Many mature shrubs and specimen trees incl Tulip tree.

GROUP OPENING

125 SEAFORD GARDENS

Seaford, BN25 3LL. *Start at any garden. All will be signed from the A259 & maps are available at each garden for the trail. 12a bus route goes to Seaford. 3 gardens are close together but this is not a walking trail.* **Sun 17 June (12-5). Combined adm £6, chd free. Home-made teas and lunches.**

34 CHYNGTON ROAD
BN25 4HP. Dr Maggie Wearmouth & Richard Morland.

CUPANI GARDEN
Dr D Jones & Ms A Jones OBE. (See separate entry)

HIGH TREES
83 Firle Road, BN25 2JA. Tony & Sue Luckin.

LAVENDER COTTAGE
69 Steyne Road, BN25 1QH. Christina & Steve Machan.

NEW **SEAFORD COMMUNITY GARDEN**
East Street, BN25 1AD. Seaford Community Garden, www.seaford-sussex.co.uk/scg/.

Five unique gardens opening for Seaford Gardens group this year. Seaford Community Garden is new and provides an interesting space from members of the community to come together and share a gardening experience. High Trees is a beautiful garden with interesting plants, ferns and grasses, plus a woodland garden. Lavender Cottage is a flint walled garden with a coastal and kitchen garden, terraced bank, and views of Seaford Head from the balcony. 34 Chyngton Road is divided into garden rooms with pastels, hot beds, a small meadow, Japanese inspired courtyard and a prairie. Cupani Garden is a green and tranquil haven with a delightful mix of planting. Home-made teas at High Trees and Lavender Cottage. Lunches and teas at Cupani. Partial wheelchair access to 34 Chyngton Road, Lavender Cottage and the Community Garden. Some gardens allow dogs on leads.

126 SEDGWICK PARK HOUSE

Sedgwick Park, Horsham, RH13 6QQ. Clare Davison, 01403 734930, clare@sedgwickpark.com, www.sedgwickpark.co.uk. *1m S of Horsham off A281. A281 towards Cowfold, Hillier Garden Center on R, then 1st R into Sedgwick Lane. At end of lane enter N gates of Sedgwick Park or W gate via Broadwater Lane, from Copsale or Southwater off A24.* **Sun 3 June (12-5). Adm £5, chd free. Home-made teas. Visits also by arrangement May to Sept for tours of house and gardens.**

Parkland, meadows and woodland. Formal gardens by Harold Peto featuring 20 interlinking ponds, impressive water garden known as The White Sea. Large Horsham stone terraces and lawns look out onto clipped yew hedging and specimen trees. Well stocked herbaceous borders, set in the grounds of Grade II listed Ernest George Mansion. One of the finest views of the South Downs, Chanctonbury Ring and Lancing Chapel. Turf labyrinth and organic vegetable garden. Featured in Sussex Life (2017). Garden has uneven paving, slippery when wet; unfenced ponds and swimming pool.

127 SELHURST PARK

Halnaker, Chichester, PO18 0LZ. Richard & Sarah Green. *8m S of Petworth. 4m N of Chichester on A285.* **Sun 17 June (2-5). Adm £4.50, chd free. Home-made teas.**
Come and explore the varied gardens surrounding a beautiful Georgian flint house (not open) approached by a Chestnut avenue. The flint walled garden has a mature 160ft herbaceous border with unusual planting along with rose, hellebore and hydrangea beds. Pool garden with exotic palms and grasses divided from a formal knot and herb garden by Espalier apples. Kitchen and walled fruit garden. Wheelchair access to walled garden, partial access to other areas.

128 SENNICOTTS

West Broyle, Chichester, PO18 9AJ. Mr & Mrs James Rank, www.sennicotts.com. *2m NW of Chichester. White gates diagonally opp & W of the junction between Salthill Rd & the B2178.* **Sun 20, Mon 21 May (9.30-4). Adm £4, chd free. Home-made teas in the walled garden.**
Historic gardens set around a Regency villa (not open) with views across mature Sussex parkland to the South Downs. Working walled kitchen and cutting garden. Lots of space for children and a warm welcome for all.

129 SHALFORD HOUSE

Square Drive, Kingsley Green, GU27 3LW. Sir Vernon & Lady Ellis. *2m S of Haslemere. Just S of border with Surrey on A286. Square Drive is at brow of hill to the E. Turn L after approx ¼m & follow road to R at bottom of hill.* **Sun 8 Apr, Sun 20 May (2-5.30). Adm £5, chd free. Home-made teas.**
Highly regarded 10 acre garden designed and created from scratch over last 24 yrs. Beautiful hilly setting with streams, ponds, waterfall, sunken garden, good late borders, azaleas and walled kitchen garden. Wild flower meadow with orchids, prairie style plantation and stumpery merging into further 7 acre woodland. Additional 30 acre arboretum with beech, rhododendrons, bluebells, ponds and specimen trees.

130 ◆ SHEFFIELD PARK AND GARDEN

Uckfield, TN22 3QX. National Trust, 01825 790231, sheffieldpark@nationaltrust.org.uk, www.nationaltrust.org.uk/sheffieldpark. *10m S of East Grinstead. 5m NW of Uckfield; E of A275.* **For NGS: Wed 9 May (10-5). Adm £11, chd £5.50. Light refreshments in Coach House Tearoom. For other opening times and information, please phone, email or visit garden website.**
Magnificent 120 acres (40 hectares) landscaped garden laid out in C18 by Capability Brown and Humphry Repton. Further development in early yrs of this century by its owner Arthur G Soames. Centrepiece is original lakes with many rare trees and shrubs. Beautiful at all times of the year, but noted for its spring and autumn colours. National Collection of Ghent azaleas. Natural play trail for families on South Park. Large number of Champion Trees, 87 in total. Garden largely accessible for wheelchairs, please call for information.

NPC

131 SHEPHERDS COTTAGE

Milberry Lane, Stoughton, Chichester, PO18 9JJ. Jackie & Alan Sherling, 07795 388047, milberrylane@gmail.com. *9⅙m NW Chichester. Off B2146, next village after Walderton. Cottage is near telephone box & beside St Mary's Church. No parking in lane beside house.* **Sun 15, Mon 16 Apr (11-4). Adm £5, chd free. Home-made teas. Visits also by arrangement Apr to June for groups of 10+.**
A compact terraced garden using the borrowed landscape of Kingley Vale in the South Downs. The s-facing flint stone cottage (not open) is surrounded by a Purbeck stone terrace with lush planting schemes. The upper beds are planted with a profusion of tulips, alliums, roses, verbascum, and lilies. A small orchard (under-planted with meadow), lawns, yew hedges, ilex balls and drifts of wind grass provide structure and yr-round interest. Many novel design ideas for a small garden. Ample seating throughout the garden to enjoy the views. Lunches and WC at the Hare & Hound Pub, a 5 min walk away. In 2017, featured on Alan Titchmarsh's 'Love Your Garden' (June), and in Gardens Illustrated (Oct). Not suitable for wheelchairs or people with mobility issues.

D

132 NEW SIENNA WOOD

Coombe Hill Road, East Grinstead, RH19 4LY. Belinda & Brian Quarendon. *1m W of East Grinstead, off B2110 East Grinstead to Turners Hill. Garden is ½m down Coombe Hill Rd on L.* **Sun 3 June (12-5). Adm £5, chd free. Home-made teas.**

Meander our peaceful 3½ acre garden, lovely lakeside walk and 6 acre ancient woodland behind. Start at the herbaceous borders surrounding the croquet lawn, through the formal rose garden to the lawns and summer borders; then down through the arboretum to the lake and back through the vegetable garden. Many unusual trees and shrubs. Child friendly with children's nature trail, treehouse and play area. Possible sighting of wild deer including white deer. Partial wheelchair access to many parts of the garden.

133 NEW SOUTH BINNS, SWIFE LANE

Broad Oak, Heathfield, TN21 8UX. Carole Franks. *N off A265 between Heathfield & Burwash. 3m E of Heathfield, turn N into Swife Lane, road forks at ½m keep R. Go downhill to junction with Foxhole Lane, then 20 metres South Binns on R, white gates to drop off, field parking nearby.* **Fri 10, Sat 11 Aug (2-5.30). Adm £5, chd free. Home-made teas.**

Approx 2½ acres in High Weald with rural views. Sloping garden with ponds and stream, woodland walk, exuberant flower garden, orchard, wildflower meadow, formal parterre, vegetable and fruit garden, and greenhouse. Sculptures and seating throughout garden. Tea terrace and plants for sale. Steps and uneven paths make it unsuitable for wheelchairs. No dogs.

134 SOUTH GRANGE

Quickbourne Lane, Northiam, Rye, TN31 6QY. Linda & Michael Belton, 01797 252984, belton.northiam@gmail.com. *Between A268 & A28, approx ½m E of Northiam. From Northiam centre follow Beales Lane into Quickbourne Lane, or Quickbourne Lane leaves A286 approx ½m S of A28 & A286 junction. Disabled parking at front of house.* **Wed 18 July (2-5). Home-made teas. Sat 1, Sun 2 Sept (11-5). Light refreshments. Adm £5, chd free. Sandwiches made to order (Sept only). Visits also by arrangement Apr to Oct for groups of 20 max.**

Hardy Plant Society members' garden, so a wide variety of trees, shrubs, perennials and pots arranged into a complex garden display for yr-round colour and interest. Raised vegetable beds, wildlife pond, orchard with rose arbour, soft fruit cage and living gazebo. House roof runoff diverted to storage and pond. Small area of wildwood. We try to maintain varied habitats for most of the creatures that we share the garden with, hoping that this variety will keep the garden in good heart. Home propagated plants for sale. Article in Sussex Life (Sept 2017). Hard paths through much of the garden, but steps up to patio and WC.

135 NEW SPRINGS HANGER

Bedham Lane, Bedham, Pulborough, RH20 1JP. Mr & Mrs I Anderson, 07539 773164, janegog@hotmail.co.uk. *Situated between Wisborough Green & Fittleworth. SatNav does not always work! To ensure best route, please ring or email & printed directions will be provided. Limited parking for 4 cars max.* **Visits by arrangement mid Feb to end Oct for groups up to 8 max. Adm £8 (or min charge £60), incl tour and home-made teas.**

Mainly woodland in nature, this is a sloping young garden of approx 7 acres, planted from 1994 and still under development. Incl a wide variety of unusual trees and shrubs underplanted and a sizeable collection of magnolias. Herbaceous border, vegetable garden, glasshouse, exotic and other areas of informal planting. Beehives. Fine views to the south and east. This garden is for the sure-footed plantsman, capable of steps and slopes.

136 NEW STANLEY FARM

Highfield Lane, Liphook, GU30 7LW. Bill & Emma Mills. *For SatNav please use GU30 7LN, which takes you to Highfield Lane & then follow NGS signs. Track to Stanley Farm is 1m.* **Sun 6 May (12-5). Adm £5, chd free. Home-made teas.**

1 acre garden created over the last 15 yrs around an old West Sussex farmhouse (not open), sitting in the midst of its own fields and woods. The formal garden incl a kitchen garden with heated glasshouse, orchard, espaliered wall trained fruit, lawn with ha-ha, and cutting garden. A motley assortment of animals incl sheep, donkeys, chickens, ducks and geese. Bluebells flourish in the woods, so feel free to bring dogs and a picnic, and take a walk after visiting the gardens. Tea and cakes served in the courtyard. Wheelchair access via a ramp to view main part of the garden. Difficult access to woods due to muddy, uneven ground.

137 STONE CROSS HOUSE

Alice Bright Lane, Crowborough, TN6 3SH. Mr & Mrs D A Tate. *1½m S of Crowborough Cross. At Crowborough T-lights (A26) turn S into High St & shortly R onto Croft Rd. Over 3 mini-r'abouts to Alice Bright Lane. Garden on L at next Xrds.* **Sat 12, Sun 13 May (2-5). Adm £5, chd free. Home-made teas.**

Beautiful 9 acre country property (not open) with gardens containing a delightful array of azaleas, acers, rhododendrons and camellias, interplanted with an abundance of spring bulbs. The very pretty cottage garden has interesting examples of topiary and unusual plants. Jacob sheep graze the surrounding pastures. Mainly flat and no steps. Gravel drive. No WC available.

138 NEW 71 STONEROCK COTTAGE

Chilgrove Park Road, Chilgrove, Chichester, PO18 9NA. Michele Roads, 01243 535394, roads.michele@gmail.com. *Off B2141 S of the White Horse Pub. Take lane signed Farm B&B & follow signs.* **Sat 26, Sun 27 May (2-5). Adm £3.50, chd free. Home-made teas. Visits also by arrangement in May for groups of 10.**

Small cottage garden positioned at foot of South Downs, within the SDNP, edged by woodland and fields with lovely open views across the countryside. Colourful densely planted borders with annuals and perennials and new shaded wildflower meadow area.

139 SULLINGTON OLD RECTORY

Sullington Lane, Storrington, Pulborough, RH20 4AE. Oliver & Mala Haarmann. Mark Dixon, Head Gardener, 07795 568343, mark@sullingtonoldrectory.com. *Traveling S on A24 take 3rd exit on Washington r'about. Proceed to Xrds on A283 for Sullington Lane & Water Lane. Take L onto Sullington Lane & garden located at the top.* **Visits by arrangement in July for groups of 10+, incl tour with Head Gardener. If group is smaller, ask if you can join another. Adm £5, chd free. Home-made teas.**

With a backdrop of stunning views of the South Downs, the naturalistic style of this country garden sits well into the surrounding landscape. Many areas to enjoy incl potager, orchard, herb garden, pleached lime walk, perennial borders and moist meadow. With a strong framework of established trees and shrubs, new plantings and areas under development. Home-made teas at Sullington Manor Farm's tudor barn £5 per person. Wheelchair access to most areas.

140 ◆ SUSSEX PRAIRIES

Morlands Farm, Wheatsheaf Road (B2116), Henfield, BN5 9AT. Paul & Pauline McBride, 01273 495902, morlandsfarm@btinternet.com, www.sussexprairies.co.uk. *2m NE of Henfield on B2116 Wheatsheaf Rd (also known as Albourne Rd). Follow Brown Tourist signs indicating Sussex Prairie Garden.* **For NGS: Sun 9 Sept (11-5). Adm £8, chd free. Home-made teas. For other opening times and information, please phone, email or visit garden website.**

Exciting prairie garden of approx 8 acres planted in the naturalistic style using 60,000 plants and over 1600 different varieties. A colourful garden featuring a huge variety of unusual ornamental grasses. Expect layers of colour, texture and architectural splendour. Surrounded by mature oak trees with views of Chanctonbury Ring and Devil's Dyke on the South Downs. Permanent sculpture collection and exhibited sculpture throughout the season. Rare breed sheep and pigs. Featured in Waitrose Garden magazine (May) and the Daily Mail. Gravel at entrance. Woodchip paths in borders not accessible, but plenty of flat garden for both wheelchairs and mobility scooters. Disabled WC.

141 TOWN PLACE

Ketches Lane, Freshfield, Sheffield Park, RH17 7NR. Anthony & Maggie McGrath, 01825 790221, mcgrathsussex@hotmail.com, www.townplacegarden.org.uk. *5m E of Haywards Heath. From A275 turn W at Sheffield Green into Ketches Lane for Lindfield. 1¾m on L.* **Thur 14, Thur 21, Sun 24 June, Sun 1, Sun 8 July (2-6). Adm £6, chd free. Cream teas. Visits also by arrangement June & July for groups of 20+.**

A stunning 3 acre garden with a growing international reputation for the quality of its design, planting and gardening. Set round a C17 Sussex farmhouse (not open), the garden has over 600 roses, herbaceous borders, herb garden, topiary inspired by the sculptures of Henry Moore, ornamental grasses, an 800 year old oak, potager, and a unique 'ruined' Priory Church and Cloisters, in hornbeam.

142 UPWALTHAM BARNS

Upwaltham, GU28 0LX. Roger & Sue Kearsey. *6m S of Petworth. 6m N of Chichester on A285.* **Sun 27, Mon 28 May (1.30-5.30). Adm £4.50, chd free. Home-made teas. Donation to St Mary's Church.**

Unique farm setting transformed into a garden of many rooms. Entrance is a tapestry of perennial planting to set off C17 flint barns. At the rear is a walled, terraced garden redeveloped and planted with an abundance of unusual plants, we are always adding something new. Beautiful inner courtyard and seating area for tea, coffee and great home-made cakes. Extensive vegetable garden. Roam at leisure, relax and enjoy. Features incl lovely views of the South Downs and a C12 Shepherds Church (open to visitors). Partial access with some gravel paths.

143 THE WALLED GARDEN AT TILGATE PARK

Tilgate Drive, Tilgate, Crawley, RH10 5PQ. Crawley Borough Council, www.friendsoftilgatepark.co.uk. *SE Crawley. Leave M23 at J11. From r'about follow A23 Brighton Rd for short distance. Turn R at sign to Tilgate Park. Disabled parking at entrance of the walled garden, other car park 150 metres away. Coach parking by arrangement.* **Evening opening Wed 23, Thur 24 May, Wed 18, Thur 19 July (6.30-9). Adm £7, accompanied children under 16 free. No concessions. Cash only. Glass of wine & canapés incl.**

A chance to explore the walled garden and heritage grounds of Tilgate Park with the Head Gardener, Nick Hagon at different times of the year. The azaleas, camellias, candelabra primulas plus the rhododendron collection make a colourful impact in May. In July the tour focuses on the walled garden, the specimen trees planted in centuries past and parkland. Talk begins at 7pm at the Walled Garden. Wheelchair access within the walled garden.

Down Place

© Judi Lion

GROUP OPENING

144 WATERWORKS & FRIENDS

Broad Oak & Brede, TN31 6HG. *Waterworks Cots Brede, off A28 by church & opp Red Lion Pub, ¾m at end of lane. Woodlands & Sculdown on B2089 Chitcombe Rd, W off A28 at Broad Oak Xrds. Start at any garden, a map will be provided.* **Sat 2 June (10.30-4). Combined adm £5, chd free. Home-made teas at Sculdown.**

SCULDOWN
TN31 6EX. Mrs Christine Buckland.

4 WATERWORKS COTTAGES
TN31 6HG. Mrs Kristina Clode, www.kristinaclodegardendesign.co.uk.
D

WOODLANDS
TN31 6EU. Mr George Terry.
D

An opportunity to visit 3 unique gardens and discover the Brede Steam Giants 35ft Edwardian water pumping engines and Grade II listed pump house located behind 4 Waterworks Cottages. Garden designer Kristina Clode created her wildlife friendly garden at 4 Waterworks Cottages over the last 8 yrs. Delightful perennial wildflower meadow, pond, wisteria covered pergola and mixed borders packed full of unusual specimens with yr-round interest and colour. Woodlands is an intensely colourful back garden in 3 sections, also designed by Kristina Clode. Mixed borders, lawn and pleached hornbeam hedge, leading to a formal quartered box edged garden with filigree gazebo, spiral topiary and vibrant planting. Framed view to the perennial wildflower meadow beyond. Sculdown's garden is dominated by a very large wildlife pond formed as a result of iron-ore mining over 100 yrs ago. The stunning traditional cottage provides a superb backdrop for several colourful herbaceous borders and poplar trees. Plants for sale at 4 Waterworks Cottages. WC only available at Brede Steam Giants, regret no disabled facilities and assistance dogs only (free entry, donations encouraged). Wheelchair access at Sculdown (please park in the flat area at the top of field) and in the front garden of Waterworks Cottages only.

145 WHITEHANGER

Marley Lane, Haslemere, GU27 3PY. David & Lynn Paynter, 07774 010901, l.paynter@btopenworld.com. *3m S of Haslemere. Take the A286 Midhurst road from Haslemere & after approx 2m turn R into Marley Lane (opp Hatch Lane). After 1m turn into drive shared with Rosemary Park Nursing Home.* **Visits by arrangement June to Sept for groups of 10-35. Refreshments incl tea & cake (day), wine (eve).**

Set in 6 acres on the edge of the SDNP surrounded by NT woodland, this rural garden was started in 2012 when a new Huf house was built on a derelict site. Now there are lawned areas with beds of perennials, a serenity pool with Koi carp, a wild flower meadow, a Japanese garden, a sculpture garden, a woodland walk and a large rockery.

146 5 WHITEMANS CLOSE

Cuckfield, Haywards Heath, RH17 5DE. Shirley Carman-Martin, 01444 473520, shirleycarmanmartin@gmail.com. *1m N of Cuckfield. On B2036 signed Balcombe, Whitemans Close is 250yds from r'about on LH-side. Parking on road. Buses stop at Whitemans Green, where there is also a large car park.* **Visits by arrangement June & July for groups of up to 12 max. Adm £8, chd free. Home-made teas incl. Visits can be combined with 47 Denmans Lane or Lindfield Jungle.**

A garden visit for plant lovers. This relatively small cottage garden is packed full of exciting and unusual plants. The enthusiastic Hardy Plant Society member will take the group around the garden whilst talking about the most interesting and noteworthy plants. There will be time to explore the garden after tea, coffee and cake. Much enjoyed by previous groups. Flower beds overflowing with gorgeous plants in colour schemed borders, small, but productive vegetable garden, collection of echeveria and sempervivum and half hardy plants too. Sorry, but rear garden unsuitable for wheelchairs owing to steps.

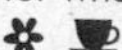

GROUP OPENING

147 WINCHELSEA'S SECRET GARDENS

Winchelsea, TN36 4EJ. *2m W of Rye, 8m E of Hastings. Purchase ticket for all gardens at first garden visited; a map will be provided showing gardens & location of teas.* **Sat 14 Apr (1-5.30); Sat 16 June (11-5). Combined adm £6, chd free. Home-made teas.**

THE ARMOURY
Mr & Mrs A Jasper.
Open on Sat 16 June

BACKFIELDS END
Sandra & Peter Mackenzie Smith.
Open on Sat 16 June

CLEVELAND HOUSE
Mr & Mrs J Jempson.
Open on all dates

CLEVELAND PLACE
Sally & Graham Rhodda.
Open on all dates

KING'S LEAP
Philip Kent.
Open on Sat 14 Apr
(See separate entry)

LOOKOUT COTTAGE
Mary & Roger Tidyman.
Open on Sat 16 June

MAGAZINE HOUSE
Susan & Stuart Stradling.
Open on Sat 16 June

THE ORCHARDS
Brenda & Ralph Courtenay.
Open on Sat 16 June

PERITEAU HOUSE
Dr & Mrs Lawrence Youlten.
Open on all dates

RYE VIEW
Howard Norton & David Page.
Open on Sat 14 Apr
(See separate entry)

SOUTH MARITEAU
Robert & Sheila Holland.
Open on Sat 16 June

2 STRAND PLAT
Mr & Mrs Anthony & Gillian Tugman.
Open on Sat 16 June

THE WELL HOUSE
Alice Kenyon.
Open on all dates

Many styles, large and small, secret walled gardens, spring bulbs, herbaceous borders and more, in the beautiful setting of the Cinque Port of Winchelsea. Explore the town with its magnificent church and famous medieval merchants' cellars. Information at winchelsea.com and winchelseachurch.co.uk. Enquiries to david@ryeview.net, 01797 226524. If you are bringing a coach please let us know. Guided tours of cellars on mornings of 14 April and 16 June, booking essential 07596 182874. See winchelsea.com/cellar-tours. Wheelchair access to four gardens in April and five in June; see map provided on the day for details.

148 WYCH WARREN HOUSE

Wych Warren, Forest Row, RH18 5LF. Colin King & Mary Franck. *1m S of Forest Row. Proceed S on A22, track turning on L, 100 metres past 45mph warning triangle sign. Or 1m N of Wych Cross T-lights track turning on R. Go 400 metres across golf course till the end.* **Wed 9 May (2-5). Home-made teas. Evening opening Wed 11 July (5-9). Wine. Adm £4, chd free.**
6 acre garden in Ashdown Forest, AONB, much of it mixed woodland. Perimeter walk around property (not open). Delightful and tranquil setting with various aspects of interest, as works in progress incl a large pond, bog garden, Mediterranean and exotic garden and mixed herbaceous borders. Fine specimen trees and shrubs, rhododendrons and azaleas, lovely stonework. Much to please the eye! From the terrace beautiful views and refreshments available. Partial wheelchair access by tarmac track to the kitchen side gate.

The Beeches

WARWICKSHIRE

For Birmingham & West Midlands see Staffordshire

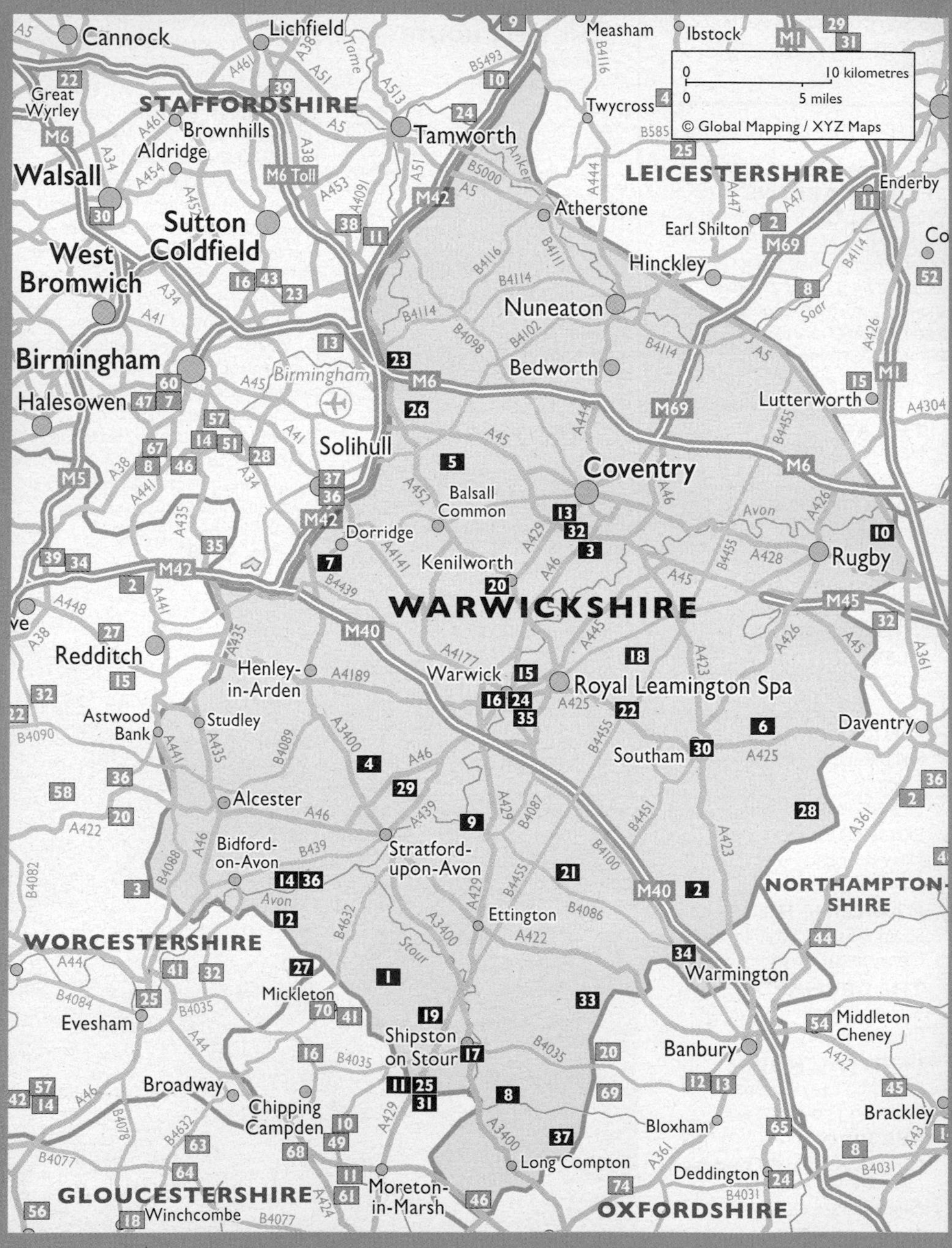

This county – say 'Worrick-sher' – is a landlocked county, with a small capital town, a fashionable spa and plenty of quintessentially English villages.

There are also many welcoming Tudor beams and pretty stone 'foodie' pubs, and many varieties of plants and trees, depending on the soil type, all year round. Undulating countryside takes you from the edge of the Cotswolds in the south to the Evesham Vale in the west, up to the hillside of Atherstone in the north and on to Rugby and the farming land of the east. The gardens of Warwickshire are as varied as its landscape; gardens of every shape and size welcome visitors in aid of the National Garden Scheme.

Today, Warwickshire has a new theme for a new century – Tourism. Inspired by our old poacher William Shakespeare at Stratford-upon-Avon, the Bard's fans flock to Warwickshire from all over the world to delight in theatre, history and castles. But Warwickshire's gardens are also well worth a visit, being wonderfully varied in size and style, and all lovingly-looked after by very generous owners.

So next time you are visiting Warwickshire be sure to bring your Garden Visitor's Handbook with you, and enjoy the wonderful gardens our county has to offer!

Volunteers

County Organiser
Brenda Boardman
07769 913686
brenboardman@me.com

County Treasurer
Liz Watson
01926 512307
liz.watson@talktalk.net

Publicity
Lily Farrah
07545 560298
lily.farrah@ngs.org.uk

Social Media
Sal Renwick
01564 770215
sal.renwick@blueyonder.co.uk

Booklet Co-ordinator
Hugh Thomas
01926 423063
hughthomas1203@gmail.com

Assistant County Organisers
Elspeth Napier
01608 666278
elspethmjn@gmail.com

David Ruffell
01926 316456
de.ruffell@btinternet.com

Liz Watson
01926 512307
liz.watson@talktalk.net

Left: Felly Lodge, Pebworth Gardens

OPENING DATES

All entries subject to change. For latest information check **www.ngs.org.uk**

Extended openings are shown at the beginning of the month.

Map locator numbers are shown to the right of each garden name.

February

Snowdrop Festival

Saturday 10th
Elm Close 14

Sunday 11th
Elm Close 14

Saturday 17th
◆ Hill Close Gardens 16

Sunday 18th
Court House 11

March

Saturday 31st
◆ Bridge Nursery 6

April

Every Saturday and Sunday
◆ Bridge Nursery 6

Monday 2nd
◆ Bridge Nursery 6

Sunday 8th
Stretton-on-Fosse Gardens 31

Sunday 15th
Broadacre 7

May

Every Saturday and Sunday
◆ Bridge Nursery 6

Sunday 6th
Packington Hall 26

Monday 7th
◆ Bridge Nursery 6
Earlsdon Gardens 13

Saturday 26th
Ilmington Gardens 19

Sunday 27th
Ilmington Gardens 19
Pebworth Gardens 27

Monday 28th
◆ Bridge Nursery 6
Pebworth Gardens 27

June

Every Saturday and Sunday
◆ Bridge Nursery 6

Festival Weekend

Saturday 2nd
Hunningham Gardens 18
Tysoe Gardens 33

Sunday 3rd
Hunningham Gardens 18
Tysoe Gardens 33

Thursday 7th
Mallory Court Hotel 22

Sunday 10th
Dorsington Gardens 12
Lighthorne Gardens 21
Maxstoke Castle 23
Styvechale Gardens 32

Sunday 17th
Honington Gardens 17
Kenilworth Gardens 20
Warmington Gardens 34
Whichford & Ascott Gardens 37

Saturday 23rd
Welford-on-Avon & District Gardens 36

Sunday 24th
Berkswell Gardens 5
Old Beams 25
Welford-on-Avon & District Gardens 36

Tuesday 26th
Mallory Court Hotel 22

Wednesday 27th
NEW Admington Hall 1

Friday 29th
Priors Marston Manor 28

Saturday 30th
Priors Marston Manor 28

The Master's Garden, Warwick Gardens

July

Every Saturday and Sunday
◆ Bridge Nursery 6

Sunday 1st
Avon Dassett Gardens 2
Burmington Grange 8
NEW Snitterfield Gardens 29
NEW Southam Gardens 30

Saturday 21st
Guy's Cliffe Walled Garden 15

Sunday 22nd
◆ Avondale Nursery 3

Sunday 29th
◆ The Mill Garden 24
NEW Warwick Gardens 35

August

Every Saturday and Sunday
◆ Bridge Nursery 6

Sunday 5th
NEW Bearley Gardens 4

Sunday 19th
◆ Avondale Nursery 3

Friday 24th
◆ Charlecote Park 9

Monday 27th
◆ Bridge Nursery 6

September

Every Saturday and Sunday to Sunday 23rd
◆ Bridge Nursery 6

Saturday 1st
◆ Hill Close Gardens 16

Sunday 2nd
Burmington Grange 8

By Arrangement

10 Avon Carrow, Avon Dassett Gardens 2
Broadacre 7
Clifton Hall Farm 10
Court House 11
16 Delaware Road, Styvechale Gardens 32
Elm Close 14
Fieldgate, Kenilworth Gardens 20
2 The Hiron, Styvechale Gardens 32
The Motte, Hunningham Gardens 18

THE GARDENS

1 NEW ADMINGTON HALL

Admington, Shipston-on-Stour, CV36 4JN. Mark & Antonia Davies. *6m NW of Shipston-on-Stour. From Ilmington, follow signs to Admington. Approx 2m, turn R to Admington by Polo Ground. Continue 1m & follow NGS parking signs into field on L.* **Wed 27 June (10.30-4.30). Adm £7.50, chd free. Home-made teas.**

A continually evolving 8 acre garden with an established structure of innovative planning and planting. An extensive collection of fine and mature specimen trees provide the essential core structure to this traditional country garden. Features include a lush broad lawn, orchard, white garden, large walled garden, wild-flower meadow and extensive modern topiary. This is a garden in motion.

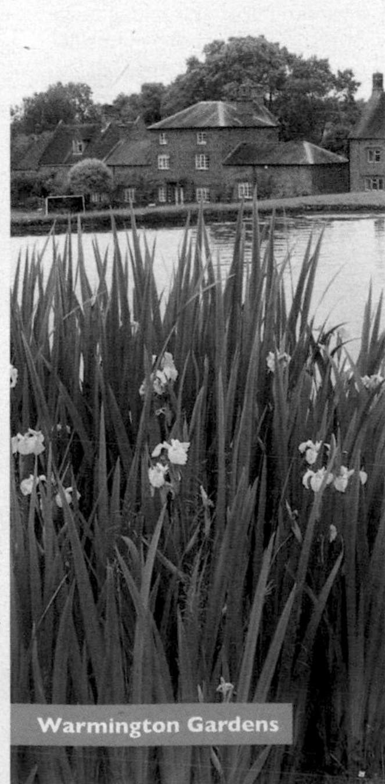

Warmington Gardens

GROUP OPENING

2 AVON DASSETT GARDENS

Southam, CV47 2AE. *7m N of Banbury. From M40 J12 turn L & L again onto the B4100, following signs to Herb Centre & Gaydon. Take 2nd L into village (signed). Park in village & at cemetery car park at the top of the hill.* **Sun 1 July (1-5). Combined adm £7, chd free. Home-made teas at The Limes.**

10 AVON CARROW
Anna Prosser, annaatthecarrow@btopenworld.com.
Visits also by arrangement Apr to Sept (excl Sun 1 July) for groups of 5+.

11 AVON CARROW
Mick & Avis Forbes.

THE COACH HOUSE
Diana & Peter Biddlestone.

THE EAST WING, AVON CARROW
Christine Fisher & Terry Gladwin.

NEW **FAIRWINDS**
Mr & Mrs Walter & Jenny Sherriff.

HILL TOP FARM
Mrs N & Mr D Hicks.

THE LIMES
John & Diane Anderson.

NEW **THE NEW RECTORY**
Mrs Victoria Pick.

OLD MILL COTTAGE
Mike & Jill Lewis.

OLD ORCHARD HOUSE
Steven & Tracey Bianciardi.

THE OLD RECTORY
Lily Hope-Frost.

POPPY COTTAGE
Bob & Audrey Butler.

THE THATCHES
Trevor & Michele Gill.

Pretty Hornton stone village sheltering in the lee of the Burton Dassett hills, well wooded with parkland setting and The Old Rectory mentioned in Domesday Book. Wide variety of gardens including kitchen gardens, cottage, gravel and tropical gardens. Range of plants incl alpines, herbaceous, perennials, roses, climbers and shrubs. The gardens are along the main road through the village which is up a relatively steep hill. Features incl book sale, plant sales, tombola and historic church open. Wheelchair access to most gardens.

3 ◆ AVONDALE NURSERY

at Russell's Nursery, Mill Hill, Baginton, CV8 3AG.
Mr Brian Ellis, 02476 673662, enquiries@avondalenursery.co.uk, www.avondalenursery.co.uk. *3m S of Coventry. At junction of A45 & A46 take slip road to Baginton, 1st L to Mill Hill, opp Old Mill Inn.* **For NGS: Sun 22 July, Sun 19 Aug (11-4). Adm £3, chd free. Light refreshments in Potting Shed Cafe at Russell's Nursery.**
For other opening times and information, please phone, email or visit garden website.

Vast array of flowers and ornamental grasses, incl National Collections of *Anemone nemorosa*, *Sanguisorba* and *Aster novae-angliae*. Choc-a-bloc with plants, our Library Garden is a well labelled reference book illustrating the unusual, exciting and even some long-lost treasures. Adjacent nursery is a plantaholic's delight! Big collections of *Helenium, Crocosmia, Sanguisorba* and ornamental grasses, and the garden will be looking at its best in July and August! Featured in Country Living magazine (Mar 2017). 'Passionate Gardeners' article on our National Collection of *Anemone nemorosa* (wood anemones).

The National Garden Scheme and Perennial, helping gardeners when they are in need

GROUP OPENING

4 NEW BEARLEY GARDENS

Snitterfield Road, Bearley, Stratford-upon-Avon, CV37 0EX. *Bearley Village 3m N of Stratford-upon-Avon via Snitterfield or off the A3400. Signed car park is located on Snitterfield Rd in a field at the eastern end of the village. Ticket & map available on the day.* **Sun 5 Aug (2-5.30). Combined adm £6, chd free. Home-made teas.**

NEW APPLE TREE COTTAGE
Mrs Rozanne Chapman.

NEW BROADYARD
Brian & Brenda Young.

NEW 15 CHERRY LANE
Fiona & Adrian Starr.

NEW TRADE WINDS
Martin & Jenny Ridehalgh.

NEW WOODLANDS BARN
Andrew & Elizabeth Gorsuch.

NEW WOODLANDS HOUSE
Graham & Sue Adcock.
D

The village of Bearley, with a population of 700+, is notable for C12 St Mary's Church, a veteran oak, award-winning Bearley Vineyard, and nearby the longest aqueduct in England. The slightly acid soil is fairly heavy clay. At the eastern end of the village Woodlands House looks out over an outstanding garden created by the owners, one being a garden designer. Next door at Woodlands Barn the emphasis is on environmental sustainability and a wide range of organically-grown vegetables. A 10 min walk leads via The Green to 15 Cherry Lane, where the newly redesigned garden shows a refreshing, contemporary approach. In the Church Lane 'loop' nearby is charming Apple Tree Cottage garden, while at Trade Winds further round, a number of sculptures enhance a spacious arrangement of mature trees and shrubs framing rural views and reflecting the owners' artistic skills. Next door at Broadyard is a haven for birds where new areas open up as you explore among fine trees and other features. Partial wheelchair access as several gardens have grass pathways (may be difficult in wet weather) and gravel driveways.

GROUP OPENING

5 BERKSWELL GARDENS

Berkswell, Coventry, CV7 7BB. *7m W of Coventry. A452 to Balsall Common & follow signs to Berkswell. Tickets & maps available at the village Reading Room (CV7 7BB) & also at each garden. Car necessary to visit all gardens.* **Sun 24 June (11-6). Combined adm £7, chd free. Light refreshments at Beehive Cottage, Eardley Cottage, 248 Station Road & Yew Tree Barn.**

NEW BEEHIVE COTTAGE
Sophie & Graham Lock.

BROOKSIDE HOUSE
Shirley & Frank Rounthwaite.

145 DUGGINS LANE
Mary & Edward Cotterrell.

EARDLEY COTTAGE
June & Bob Smitten.

FAIRWAYS
Tom Bunt & Janet Lloyd-Bunt.

HOLLY LODGE
Anne & Alastair Dymond.

THE PINES
Mr & Mrs C Davis.

SQUIRRELS JUMP
Brian & Jenny Harris.

248 STATION ROAD
Caroline & Paul Joyner.

YEW TREE BARN
Angela & Ken Shaw.

Berkswell is a beautiful village dating back to Saxon times with a C12 Norman church and has several C16 and C17 buildings including the pub and old Museum. In 2014 and 2015 the village was awarded Gold in the RHS Britain in Bloom campaign, plus a special RHS award in 2014 for the Best Large Village in the Heart of England. The gardens provide great variety with fine examples of small and large, formal and informal, wild, imaginatively planted herbaceous borders and productive vegetable gardens. Something for everyone and plenty of ideas to take home. Plants for sale at some gardens. Also open to visitors is the C12 Norman church with a garden. Wheelchair access to some gardens.

6 ◆ BRIDGE NURSERY

Tomlow Road, Napton, Southam, CV47 8HX. Christine Dakin & Philip Martino, 01926 812737, chris.dakin25@yahoo.com, www.bridge-nursery.co.uk. *3m E of Southam. Brown tourist sign at Napton Xrds on A425 Southam to Daventry road.* **For NGS: Every Sat and Sun 31 Mar to 23 Sept (10-4). Mon 2 Apr, Mon 7, Mon 28 May, Mon 27 Aug (10-4). Adm £3, chd free. Light refreshments.** For other opening times and information, please phone, email or visit garden website.

Clay soil? Don't despair. Here is a garden full of an exciting range of plants which thrive in hostile conditions. Grass paths lead you round borders filled with many unusual plants. Features incl a pond and a bamboo grove complete with panda! A peaceful haven for wildlife and visitors. Visits also by arrangement, groups welcome, all proceeds to the NGS.

7 BROADACRE

Grange Road, Dorridge, Solihull, B93 8QA. John Woolman, 07818 082885, jw234567@gmail.com, www.broadacregarden.org. *Approx 3m SE of Solihull. On B4101 opp Railway Pub. Plenty of parking available.* **Sun 15 Apr (2-6). Adm £5, chd free. Home-made teas.** **Visits also by arrangement for any group size.**

Broadacre is a semi-wild garden, managed organically. Attractively landscaped with pools, lawns and trees, beehives, and adjoining stream and wild flower meadows. Bring stout footwear to follow the nature trail. Dorridge Cricket Club is on-site (the bar will be open). Lovely venue for a picnic. Dogs and children are welcome. Excellent country pub, The Railway at the bottom of the drive.

Apple Tree Cottage, Bearley Gardens

8 BURMINGTON GRANGE

Cherington, Shipston-on-Stour, CV36 5HZ. Mr & Mrs Patrick Ramsay. *2m E of Shipston-on-Stour. Take Oxford Rd (A3400) from Shipston-on-Stour, after 2m turn L to Burmington, go through village & continue for 1m, turn L to Willington & Barcheston, on sharp L bend turn R over cattle grid.* **Sun 1 July, Sun 2 Sept (2-6). Adm £5, chd free. Home-made teas.**

Interesting plantsman's garden extending to about 1½ acres, set in the rolling hills of the North Cotswolds with wonderful views over unspoilt countryside. The garden is well developed considering it was planted 15 yrs ago. Small vegetable garden, beautiful sunken rose garden with herbaceous and shrub borders. Orchard and tree walk with unusual trees.

9 ◆ CHARLECOTE PARK

Wellesbourne, Warwick, CV35 9ER. National Trust, 01789 470277, charlecote.park@nationaltrust.org.uk, www.nationaltrust.org.uk/charlecote-park. *5m E of Stratford-upon-Avon, 6m S of Warwick, 1m W of Wellesbourne. J15 of M40 take A429 towards Cirencester, then signs for Charlecote Park. From Stratford-upon-Avon B4086 towards Wellesbourne, then signs for Charlecote Park.* **For NGS: Evening opening Fri 24 Aug (6-8). Adm £10, chd free. Drinks & canapés. Private tour of gardens led by the Park & Garden Manager. Pre-booking essential, please phone to book (25 places).** For other opening times and information, please phone, email or visit garden website.

Charlecote Park has been home to the Lucy family for more than 800 yrs. The gardens incl a formal parterre, woodland walk, herbaceous border and wider parkland which is a Capability Brown landscape offering picturesque views across the River Avon. A herd of fallow deer has been in the park since Tudor times. Charlecote Park was one of the first gardens to open in support of NGS back in 1927. House not open. Gravel paths around the grounds.

10 CLIFTON HALL FARM

Lilbourne Road, Clifton-upon-Dunsmore, Rugby, CV23 0BB. Robert & Jenny Spencer, 07717 650837, Jenny.ruth.spencer@gmail.com. *2m E of Rugby. From Clifton Church take Lilbourne Rd out of village. 1st farm on R, just past the 30mph limit.* **Visits by arrangement for groups of 6+. Adm £5, chd free. Home-made teas.**

A feast of flowers down on the farm. A garden blossoming with emerald lawns and billowing borders. Silvery foliage, pond, waving grasses and 'pop' plants all there for a yr-round display. The different garden areas incl a jungle area, pool area with a bridge across, and small arboretum, together with a display of old farm machinery, providing a variety of interest. A few gravel areas.

11 COURT HOUSE

Stretton-on-Fosse, GL56 9SD. Christopher White, 01608 663811, mum@star.co.uk. *Off A429 between Moreton-in-Marsh & Shipston-on-Stour. Located in centre of village, next to the church.* **Sun 18 Feb (11-2.30). Adm £5, chd free. Opening with Stretton-on-Fosse Gardens on Sun 8 Apr.**

Visits also by arrangement Feb to Oct.

4 acre garden with yr-round interest and colour. Extensive and varied spring bulbs and garden of winter interest. Herbaceous borders, spring beds, fernery, recently redesigned and restored walled kitchen garden. Rose garden, pond area and paddocks established with wild flowers. Newly planted winter garden. Featured in Cotswold Life. Wheelchair access is not impossible, but difficult with a gravel drive.

GROUP OPENING

12 DORSINGTON GARDENS

Dorsington, CV37 8AR. *6m SW of Stratford-upon-Avon. On B439 from Stratford turn L to Welford-on-Avon, then R to Dorsington. Disabled parking available, please follow signs.* **Sun 10 June (12-5). Combined adm £6, chd free. Home-made teas in the village (signed on the day).**

NEW **ABERFOYLE COTTAGE**
Mr & Mrs Roger & Jenny Waller.

1 GLEBE COTTAGES
Mr & Mrs A Brough.

NEW **HIGHFIELD HOUSE**
Mr & Mrs Derek & Dawn Richardson.

MEADOW HOUSE
Margaret Lindsay.

THE OLD RECTORY
Mrs C.M. Phillips.

WELFORD PASTURES COTTAGE
Annie & John Daly.

Dorsington is a tranquil hamlet mentioned in the Domesday book, with a conservation area at its heart. You can visit a varied selection of gardens, ranging from extensive mature gardens to small cottage gardens. Each garden has the distinctive touch of their individual owners, so enjoy the abundant herbaceous borders, mature trees, neatly kept lawns, fruit and vegetable gardens, but do not forget to visit our lovely marquee for a splendid home-made tea. Additional village gardens will open on the day. The Garden of Heroes and Villains may also be opening on Sun 10 June, exclusively to NGS Dorsington Gardens group opening only. Please look at the NGS website www.ngs.org.uk early June for further details.

GROUP OPENING

13 EARLSDON GARDENS

Coventry, CV5 6FS. *Turn towards Coventry at A45 & A429 T-lights. Take 3rd L into Beechwood Ave, continue ½m to St Barbara's Church at Xrds with Rochester Rd. Maps & tickets at St Barbara's Church Hall.* **Mon 7 May (11-4). Combined adm £4, chd free. Light refreshments at St Barbara's Church Hall.**

43 ARMORIAL ROAD
Gary & Jane Flanagan.

NEW **27 HARTINGTON CRESCENT**
Mr & Mrs David & Judith Bogle.

40 HARTINGTON CRESCENT
Viv & George Buss.

114 HARTINGTON CRESCENT
Liz Campbell & Denis Crowley.

40 RANULF CROFT
Mr & Mrs Spencer & Sue Swain.

54 SALISBURY AVENUE
Pam Moffit.

2 SHAFTESBURY ROAD
Ann Thomson & Bruce Walker.

23 SPENCER AVENUE
Susan & Keith Darwood.

27 SPENCER AVENUE
Helene Devane.

Varied selection of town gardens from small to more formal with interest for all tastes incl a mature garden with deep borders bursting with spring colour; a large garden with extensive lawns and an array of rhododendrons, azaleas and large mature trees; densely planted town garden with sheltered patio area and wilder woodland; and a surprisingly large garden offering interest to all ages! There is also a pretty garden set on several levels with hidden aspect; a large peaceful garden with water features and vegetable plot; a large mature garden in peaceful surroundings; and a plantaholic's garden with a large variety of plants, clematis and small trees.

14 ELM CLOSE

Welford-on-Avon, CV37 8PT. Eric & Glenis Dyer, 01789 750793, glenisdyer@gmail.com. *5m SW of Stratford, off B4390. Elm Close is between Welford Garage & The Bell Inn, roadside parking.* **Sat 10, Sun 11 Feb (1.30-3.30). Adm £3, chd free. Home-made teas. Opening with Welford-on-Avon & District Gardens on Sat 23, Sun 24 June. Visits also by arrangement for groups of 10-30. Adm £3 per head or min £30. Refreshments by prior request only.**

Drifts of snowdrops, aconites, erythroniums and hellebores in spring are followed by species peonies, sumptuous tree peonies, herbaceous peonies and delphiniums. Colourful Japanese maples, daphnes and cornus are underplanted with hostas, heucheras, and brunneras. Then agapanthus, salvias and hydrangeas extend the seasons, with hundreds of clematis providing yr-round colour. Gravel front drive slightly sloping, garden mainly flat.

15 GUY'S CLIFFE WALLED GARDEN

Coventry Road, Guy's Cliffe, Warwick, CV34 5FJ. Sarah Ridgeway, www.guyscliffewalledgarden.org.uk. *Behind Hintons Nursery in Guy's Cliffe, Warwick (use Hintons car park). Guy's Cliffe is on the A429, between North Warwick & Leek Wootton.* **Sat 21 July (10-3.30). Adm £3, chd free. Home-made teas.**

A Grade II listed garden of special historic interest, having been the kitchen garden for Guy's Cliffe House. The garden dates back to the mid-1700s. Restoration work started 4 yrs ago; using plans from the early C19, the garden layout has already been reinstated and the beds, once more, planted with fruit, flowers and vegetables incl many heritage varieties. Glasshouses awaiting restoration. Original C18 walls. Exhibition of artefacts discovered during restoration.

16 ◆ HILL CLOSE GARDENS
Bread and Meat Close, Warwick, CV34 6HF. Hill Close Gardens Trust, 01926 493339, centremanager@hcgt.org.uk, www.hillclosegardens.com.
Town centre. Follow signs to the racecourse. Entry from Friars St onto Bread and Meat Close. Car park by entrance next to racecourse. 2 hrs free parking. Disabled parking outside the gates. **For NGS: Sat 17 Feb (11-4); Sat 1 Sept (11-5). Adm £4, chd £1. Light refreshments in Visitor Centre.**
For other opening times and information, please phone, email or visit garden website.
Restored Grade II* Victorian leisure gardens comprising 16 individual hedged gardens, 8 brick summerhouses. Herbaceous borders, heritage apple and pear trees, C19 daffodils, over 100 varieties of snowdrops, many varieties of asters and chrysanthemums. Heritage vegetables. Plant Heritage border, auricula theatre, and Victorian style glasshouse. Children's garden. Wheelchair available, please book in advance by phone. Access route indicated on plan of the gardens.
NPC

The Queen's Nursing Institute founded the National Garden Scheme over 90 years ago

GROUP OPENING

17 HONINGTON GARDENS
Shipston-on-Stour, CV36 5AA.
1½ m N of Shipston-on-Stour. Take A3400 towards Stratford-upon-Avon then turn R signed Honington. **Sun 17 June (2-5.30). Combined adm £6, chd free. Home-made teas.**

HONINGTON GLEBE
Mr & Mrs J C Orchard.

HONINGTON HALL
B H E Wiggin.

THE MALTHOUSE
Mr & Mrs R Hunt.

THE OLD COTTAGE
Liz Davenport.

THE OLD HOUSE
Mr & Mrs I F Beaumont.

SHOEMAKERS COTTAGE
Christopher & Anne Jordan.

C17 village, recorded in Domesday, entered by old toll gate. Ornamental stone bridge over the River Stour and interesting church with C13 tower and late C17 nave after Wren. Six super gardens. 2 acre plantsman's garden consisting of rooms planted informally with yr-round interest in contrasting foliage and texture, lily pool and parterre. Extensive lawns and fine mature trees with river and garden monuments. Secluded walled cottage garden with roses, and a structured cottage garden formally laid out with box hedging and small fountain. Small, developing garden created by the owners with informal mixed beds and borders. Wheelchair access to most gardens.

The Whichford Pottery, Whichford & Ascott Gardens

GROUP OPENING

18 HUNNINGHAM GARDENS

Hunningham, Leamington Spa, CV33 9DS. *6m NE of Leamington Spa, 8m SW of Rugby, 7m S of Coventry. Just off the Fosse Way (B4455), or take B4453 from Leamington through Weston-under-Wetherley, then turn R to Hunningham, signed car park in village.* **Sat 2, Sun 3 June (1-5.30). Combined adm £5, chd free. Home-made teas.**

GLENCOVE
Mr & Mrs S Shackleton.

NEW **HUNNINGHAM HILL FARM**
Jonathan Hofstetter.

5 LEIGH TERRACE
Rob & Lynn Parsons.

THE MOTTE
Margaret & Peter Green, 01926 632903, pjgreen8232@gmail.com.
Visits also by arrangement May to Aug for groups of up to 20 max. Home-made teas on request.

THE OLD HALL
Nicholas & Rona Horler.

SANDY ACRE
David & Janis Tait.

Hunningham, a hamlet nestling in the countryside close to the River Leam with St Margaret's church dating in part to the C13. Six gardens in varied styles, with more open on the day. A plant lover's garden brimming with woodland plants, tender perennials, unusual shrubs and trees, new fruit and vegetable plot and a plant filled conservatory. Newly formed garden with pleached hornbeam avenue, parterre with feature sculpture, panoramic views, wooded areas, cut flower garden and new holm oak circle. Large partly walled garden with mature shrubs and trees surrounding the Old Hall. Newly created large cottage garden with attractive herbaceous borders, hard landscaping features and vegetable plot. Hedged cottage garden with herbaceous perennials, fruit and vegetable areas. Lastly new for 2018 a garden set high on the hill with views across the Shire, with herbaceous planting, walled vegetable garden, natural pond, orchard and wildflower meadow. Views across the River Leam from some of the gardens. Good plant sale. Tea, coffee and home-made cakes in St Margaret's Church, Parish Room from 1pm. Visit Hill Top Farm Shop & Café or the Red Lion Pub.

GROUP OPENING

19 ILMINGTON GARDENS

Ilmington, CV36 4LA. 01608 682230. *8m S of Stratford-upon-Avon. 8m N of Moreton-in-Marsh. 4m NW of Shipston-on-Stour off A3400. 3m NE of Chipping Campden.* **Sat 26, Sun 27 May (2-6.30). Combined adm £7, chd free. Cream teas in Ilmington Community Shop, Upper Green (Sat) & at the village hall (Sun).** Donation to Warwickshire & Northamptonshire Air Ambulance.

THE BEVINGTONS
Mr & Mrs N Tustain.

CHERRY ORCHARD
Mr Angus Chambers.

FROG ORCHARD
Mr & Mrs Jeremy Snowden.

GRUMP COTTAGE
Mr & Mrs Martin Underwood.

ILMINGTON MANOR
Mr Martin Taylor.

PARK FARM HOUSE
Mike & Lesley Lane.

RAVENSCROFT
Mr & Mrs Clasper.

STUDIO COTTAGE
Sarah Hobson.

NEW **7 WILKINS WAY**
Mr & Mrs Steve & Pam Routly.

Ilmington is an ancient hillside Cotswold village 2m from the Fosse Way with two good pubs and splendid teas at the village hall. Buy your ticket at Ilmington Manor (next to the Red Lion Pub); wander the 3 acre gardens with fish pond. Then walk to the upper green behind the village hall to tiny Grump Cottage's small stone terraced suntrap. Up Grump St to Ravenscroft's large sculpture filled sloping vistas commanding the hilltop. Walk to nearby Frog Lane, view cottage gardens at Park Farm House, Cherry Orchard, Frog Orchard, and Studio Cottage. Then to the Bevingtons many chambered cottage garden at the bottom of Vallenders Lane near the church and manor ponds. Also visit the delightful newly planted cottage garden of 7 Wilkins Way, on the Armscote Rd on the north eastern fringe of the village. The Ilmington Morris Men performing round the village on Sun 27 May only.

GROUP OPENING

20 KENILWORTH GARDENS

Kenilworth, CV8 1BT. *Fieldgate Lane off A452. Tickets & maps available at all gardens. Parking available at Abbey Fields. Street parking on Fieldgate Lane (limited), Siddley Avenue & Beehive Hill.* **Sun 17 June (12-5). Combined adm £6, chd free. Home-made teas at St Nicholas Parochial Hall.**

BEEHIVE HILL ALLOTMENTS
Madeleine Sexton.

NEW **CAPESTHORNE**
Mr & Mrs T Brayson.

FIELDGATE
Liz & Bob Watson, 01926 512307, liz.watson@talktalk.net.
Visits also by arrangement May to Sept for groups of 5-30.

14C FIELDGATE LANE
Mrs Sandra Aulton.

1 FIELDGATE LAWN
Andrew Clough.

NEW **3 FIELDGATE LAWN**
Gerry Rutter.

7 FIELDGATE LAWN
Simon Cockell.

NEW **OAKWOOD HOUSE**
Mrs Jan Kenyon.

ST NICHOLAS PAROCHIAL HALL
St Nicholas Church.

NEW **1 SIDDELEY AVENUE**
Clare Wightman.

Kenilworth was historically a very important town in Warwickshire. It has one of England's best castle ruins and plenty of pubs and good restaurants. This year we welcome four new gardens on Fieldgate Lane and Siddeley Avenue to the group making ten gardens in all, providing great variety. There are small and large gardens, formal, contemporary and cottage styles with trees, shrubs, herbaceous borders, ponds and more intimate, wildlife friendly areas, plus plenty of vegetables at the allotments. Many of the gardens have won Gold in the Kenilworth in Bloom garden competition. Partial wheelchair access to most of the gardens.

GROUP OPENING

21 LIGHTHORNE GARDENS

Lighthorne, Warwick, CV35 0AR. *10m S of Warwick. Lighthorne will be signed from the Fosse Way & B4100.* **Sun 10 June (1.30-5). Combined adm £6, chd free. Home-made teas at the village hall.**

1 CHURCH HILL COURT
Irene Proudman.

4 CHURCH HILL COURT
Carol Schofield.

THE OLD RECTORY
The Hon Lady Butler.

THE PADDOCK
Martin & Lesley Thornton.

SMITHY COTTAGE
Paul & Josette Tait.

TAWTON
David Copson & Maureen Thomson.

Lighthorne is a compact, pretty village between the Fosse Way and the B4100, with a charming church (open), pub and village hall. The six gardens opening are within easy reach on foot. At The Old Rectory the garden is sheltered by old stone walls clothed with roses and dominated by two magnificent copper beeches. Some gardens are small and some larger but all are interesting and different. Partial wheelchair access to some of the gardens.

22 MALLORY COURT HOTEL

Harbury Lane, Leamington Spa, CV33 9BQ. Mrs Sarah Baker, General Manager, 01926 330214, reception@mallory.co.uk, www.mallory.co.uk. *3½m S of Leamington Spa, just off the B4087, between Whitnash & Bishop's Tachbrook.* **Thur 7 June (3-5). Evening opening Tue 26 June (5-8). Adm £10, chd free. Drinks & canapés. Private tour of gardens led by the Group Estate Manager. Pre-booking essential, please phone to book (30 places for each opening).**

Mallory Court is a breathtakingly beautiful country house hotel set in 10 acres of gardens that incl sweeping lawns, a croquet lawn, rose gardens, herbaceous borders and beds of seasonal flower displays. A range of herbs, vegetables and soft fruits are grown yr-round in the hotel's kitchen gardens for use in the restaurant.

23 MAXSTOKE CASTLE

Coleshill, B46 2RD. Mr & Mrs M C Fetherston-Dilke. *2½m E of Coleshill. E of Birmingham, on B4114. Take R turn down Castle Lane, Castle drive 1¼m on R.* **Sun 10 June (11-5). Adm £7.50, chd £5. Home-made teas.**

Approx 5 acres of garden and grounds with herbaceous, shrubs and trees in the immediate surroundings of this C14 moated castle. No wheelchair access to house.

24 ◆ THE MILL GARDEN

55 Mill Street, Warwick, CV34 4HB. Julia (née Measures) Russell & David Russell, www.visitwarwick.co.uk/placeofinterest/the-mill-garden. *Off A425 beside old castle gate, at the bottom of Mill St. Disabled parking & drop off only, use nearby St Nicholas car park.* **For NGS: Sun 29 July (1-5). Combined adm with Warwick Gardens £6, chd free.** For other opening times and information, please visit garden website.

This garden lies in a magical setting on the banks of the River Avon beneath the walls of Warwick Castle. Winding paths lead round every corner to dramatic views of the castle and ruined Medieval bridge. This informal cottage garden is a profusion of plants, shrubs and trees. Beautiful all year. In 2017 the garden won first prize in the Warwick in Bloom competition for the best garden open to the public and was awarded Certificate of Excellence from Trip Advisor. Open daily 1st April to 31st October 9am-6pm. Partial wheelchair access. Not suitable for electric wheelchairs or large pushchairs.

25 OLD BEAMS

Stretton-on-Fosse, Moreton-in-Marsh, GL56 9SG. Mrs Hilary Fossey. *Off A429 between Moreton-in-Marsh & Shipston-on-Stour. Located in centre of village, two doors down from the church. Parking at village hall.* **Sun 24 June (2-5.30). Adm £3.50, chd free. Cream teas in village hall. Opening with Stretton-on-Fosse Gardens on Sun 8 Apr.**

Walled cottage garden on a slope, not very large, but densely planted with hardy perennials and traditional cottage garden plants. Small lawn with seating available, surrounded by rockery and mixed low planting. A vegetable garden and fruit cage are followed by a gravelled area with hostas in pots and a bed of ericas and ferns A great deal to interest plant lovers. Cuttings willingly supplied wherever possible!

26 PACKINGTON HALL

Meriden, nr Coventry, CV7 7HF. Lord & Lady Aylesford. *Midway between Coventry & Birmingham on A45. Entrance 400yds from Stonebridge Island towards Coventry. For SatNav please use CV7 7HE.* **Sun 6 May (2-5). Adm £5.50, chd free. Home-made teas.** Packington is the setting for an elegant Capability Brown landscape. Designed from 1750 in 100 acres of parkland which sweeps down to a lake incl 1762 Japanese bridge. Delicious WI teas on the terrace or in The Pompeiian Room if wet. No wheelchair access to gardens.

GROUP OPENING

27 PEBWORTH GARDENS

Stratford-upon-Avon, CV37 8XZ. *9m SW of Stratford-upon-Avon. On B439 at Bidford turn S towards Honeybourne, after 3m turn L at Xrds signed Pebworth.* **Sun 27, Mon 28 May (1-6). Combined adm £7, chd free. Home-made teas at Pebworth Village Hall (no lunches available).**

BANK HOUSE
Clive & Caroline Warren.

EDGEFIELD, 4 ORCHARD CLOSE
Mr & Mrs G Grainger.

1 ELM CLOSE
Mr & Mrs G Keyte.

FELLY LODGE
Maz & Barrie Clatworthy.

IVYBANK
Mr & Mrs R Davis.
NPC

JASMINE COTTAGE
Ted & Veronica Watson.

THE KNOLL
Mr & Mrs K Wood.

MAPLE BARN
Mr & Mrs Richard & Wendi Weller.

MEON COTTAGE
David & Sally Donnison.

NEW **OAK HOUSE**
Sue Jordan.

ORCHARD HOUSE
David & Susan Lees.

PETTIFER HOUSE
Mr & Mrs Michael Veal.

PRIMROSE HILL
Richard & Margaret Holland.

4 WESLEY GARDENS
Anne & Mike Johnson.

For the second year running Pebworth has won the Heart of England in Bloom, winning Gold and Category Winner for Best Village 2017, and awarded Silver Gilt in the National Finals of RHS Britain in Bloom 2017. The village is topped by St Peter's Church which came joint 2nd in Worcestershire Best Kept Churchyard 2017. It has a large ring of ten bells, unusual for a small rural church. Pebworth is a delightful village with thatched cottages and properties young and old. There are a variety of garden styles from cottage gardens to modern, walled and terraced gardens. This year we have 14 gardens opening, with scrumptious tea and cakes provided by the Pebworth WI. No wheelchair access to several of the gardens.

28 PRIORS MARSTON MANOR

The Green, Priors Marston, CV47 7RH. Dr & Mrs Mark Cecil. *8m SW of Daventry. Off A361 between Daventry & Banbury at Charwelton. Follow sign to Priors Marston approx 2m. Arrive at T-junction with war memorial on R. Manor on L. Follow yellow signs to car parking.* **Fri 29 June (11-6); Sat 30 June (2-6). Adm £5, chd free. Home-made teas. Fri 29 June incl an indoor Bonhams Valuation Day (11-2), suggested donation £2 per item, proceeds to NGS.**
Arrive in Priors Marston village and explore the manor gardens. Greatly enhanced by present owners to relate back to a Georgian manor garden and pleasure grounds. Wonderful walled kitchen garden provides seasonal produce and cut flowers for the house. Herbaceous flower beds and a sunken terrace with water feature by William Pye. Lawns lead down to the lake around which you can walk amongst the trees and wildlife, with stunning views up to the house and garden aviary. Sculpture on display. Partial wheelchair access.

GROUP OPENING

29 NEW SNITTERFIELD GARDENS

Stratford-upon-Avon, CV37 0QA. *5 mins from J15 M40. Follow A46. Turn R into Kings Lane. Follow NGS signs. Parking & Tickets at The Grove CV37 0QA & Ingon Grange CV37 0QF. Tickets also at The Hill Cottage CV37 0QA & Taxus CV37 0JY.* **Sun 1 July (1-5). Combined adm £6, chd free. Home-made teas at Ingon Grange & in the village.**

NEW **BEVERLEY COTTAGE**
Yvonne & Peter Spilman.

NEW **FERNBANK**
Hâf Briggs.

NEW **THE GROVE**
Anna & Peter Turner.

NEW **THE HILL COTTAGE**
Gillie & Paul Waldron, 01789 731830, info@thehillcottage.co.uk, www.thehillcottage.co.uk.

NEW **INGON GRANGE**
Margaret & Rodney Watkins.

NEW **JOINER'S COTTAGE**
Vikki & Duncan Parker.

NEW **SHERBOURNE HOUSE**
Graham & Ann Barker.

NEW **TAXUS**
Sally & Andy Hopkinson.

For your pleasure eight gardens will open for the first time in 2018 for the NGS. Explore the wide variety of sizes, styles, aspects, features and specialities, from a quiet courtyard with tinkling water to extended grounds with a ha-ha. We offer you woodland walks with majestic trees and far-reaching views. Borders to brood over, pristine perennials, island bed ideas, grand gravel gardens and secret paths. Gazebos to gaze from, containers galore, vibrant vegetables, whimsical wild flowers and peaceful ponds. Even donkeys and peacocks await you in our gardens ranging from the formal to the laid-back, the intimate to the grand. Enjoy!

GROUP OPENING

30 NEW SOUTHAM GARDENS

Southam, CV47 0JL. *Close to the centre of Southam. On the A423 approx 15m S of Coventry & 15m N of Banbury. Also on A425 approx 8m E of Leamington Spa & 8m W of Daventry. Plenty of free street parking. Tickets from 4 Warwick Place.* **Sun 1 July (11-5). Combined adm £4, chd free. Ploughman's lunches & home-made teas at Beech Loft.**

NEW 59 BANBURY ROAD
Rhona Baker.

NEW BEECH LOFT
Jacky Graham.

NEW 4 WARWICK PLACE
Lesley & Jeff Smith.

Southam is a small market town mentioned in the Domesday Book as Sucham. The centre of the town is a conservation area. There are three very different gardens to visit. 4 Warwick Place incorporates the garage roof into the rear garden, which is packed with plants. The steep bank at the side of the house has a variety of ground cover plants, and the front garden has many drought tolerant plants. Beech Loft, 5 Warwick Road has a delightful cobbled courtyard with baskets and troughs, leading to a walled rear garden arranged as individual rooms, with trees, box hedges and perennials. The newly discovered deep well has running water at the bottom! 59 Banbury Road is a garden designed to be explored, with a woodland walk, wild corner and hidden organic vegetable patch. There is a well with a working hand pump, a fire pit and a wildlife friendly pond. Clematis and roses abound! Partial wheelchair access at 4 Warwick Place and Beech Loft. Gravel driveway at 59 Banbury Road.

GROUP OPENING

31 STRETTON-ON-FOSSE GARDENS

Stretton-on-Fosse, GL56 9SD. *Off A429 between Moreton-in-Marsh & Shipston-on-Stour. Two gardens in the centre of the village. Court House is next to the church, Old Beams a few doors away.* **Sun 8 Apr (2-5.30). Combined adm £6, chd free. Home-made teas at Court House.**

COURT HOUSE
Christopher White.
(See separate entry)

OLD BEAMS
Mrs Hilary Fossey.
(See separate entry)

Court House is a continually evolving, 4 acre garden with yr-round interest and colour. Extensive and varied spring bulbs. Herbaceous borders, fernery, recently redesigned and restored walled kitchen garden. Rose garden, newly planted winter garden, pond area and paddocks which are gradually being established with wild flowers. Old Beams is a walled cottage garden on a slope with traditional cottage garden plants, small lawn, rockery, fruit cage and vegetable garden.

GROUP OPENING

32 STYVECHALE GARDENS

Baginton Road, Coventry, CV3 6FP. *The gardens are located on the s-side of Coventry close to A45. Tickets & map available on the day from West Orchard United Reformed Church, The Chesils, CV3 6FP. Advance tickets available from suepountney@btinternet.com.* **Sun 10 June (11-5). Combined adm £4, chd free. Light refreshments throughout the day & hot bacon or sausage batches from 11-2.** Donation to Coventry Myton Hospice.

11 BAGINTON ROAD
Ken & Pauline Bond.

164 BAGINTON ROAD
Fran & Jeff Gaught.

59 THE CHESILS
John Marron & Richard Bantock.

16 DELAWARE ROAD
Val & Roy Howells,
02476 419485,
valshouse@hotmail.co.uk.
Visits also by arrangement May to Sept with 2 The Hiron.

2 THE HIRON
Sue & Graham Pountney,
02476 502044,
suepountney@btinternet.com.
Visits also by arrangement May to Sept with 16 Delaware Road.

177 LEAMINGTON ROAD
Barry & Ann Suddens.

8 THE SPINNEY
Professor Michael & Eleni Tovey.

A collection of lovely, mature, suburban gardens, each one different in style and size. Come and enjoy the imaginatively planted herbaceous borders, spectacular roses, water features, fruit and vegetable patches, cottage garden planting and shady areas, something for everyone and plenty of ideas for you to take home. Relax in the gardens and enjoy the warm, friendly welcome you will receive from us all. There will be refreshments available and plants for sale in some of the gardens. Other gardens will be open on the day. A vehicle will be required to visit 8 The Spinney, but a garden well worth the trip; an easy 10 min drive from the ticket office. The gardens open include the winner of the 2017 Daily Mail National Garden Competition.

With your support we can help raise awareness of Carers Trust and unpaid carers

GROUP OPENING

33 TYSOE GARDENS

Middle and Upper Tysoe, Warwick, CV35 0SE. *W of A422, N of Banbury (9m). E of A3400 & Shipston-on-Stour (4m). N of A4035 & Brailes (3m). Parking on the recreation ground CV35 0SE. Entrance tickets & maps at the village hall. Free bus.* **Sat 2, Sun 3 June (2-6). Combined adm £6, chd free. Home-made teas in Tysoe Village Hall & cold drinks at Garden Cottage.**

DINSDALE HOUSE
Julia & David Sewell.

GARDEN COTTAGE & WALLED KITCHEN GARDEN
Sue & Mike Sanderson.

NEW **HOME FARM**
Marcus & Carol Lymbery.

IVYDALE
Sam & Malcolm Littlewood.

KERNEL COTTAGE
Christine Duke.

LAUREL HOUSE
Damaris & Michael Appleton.

THE OLD BUTCHER'S HOUSE
Sue & Gerald Hart.

SMARTSWELL COTTAGE
Jan & Colin Lumley.

THE WILLOWS
Alan & Ethel Birkbeck.

Tysoe, an original Hornton stone village divided into three parts sits at the foot of the north-eastern edge of the Cotswold Hills near the site of the Battle of Edgehill. The gardens making up this group in Middle Tysoe are diverse in character of house, planting, size and style. As early summer openers there is always a huge question mark over what will or will not be in bloom on the two days that we open. A lottery for the visitors and gardeners alike! But what Tysoe always offers is a happy atmosphere, some glorious gardens, a good walk round the village or if you prefer, a free bus ride, and a jolly good tea made by the large band of bakers, mostly WI members, living in the village. A warm welcome awaits you in this buzzy, energetic, friendly village and gardening community. Partial wheelchair access.

GROUP OPENING

34 WARMINGTON GARDENS

Banbury, OX17 1BU. *5m NW of Banbury. Take B4100 N from Banbury, after 5m turn R across short dual carriageway into Warmington. From N take J12 off M40 onto B4100.* **Sun 17 June (2-5). Combined adm £6, chd free. Home-made teas at village hall.**

NEW **2 CHAPEL STREET**
c/o Mark Broadbent, Group Coordinator.

NEW **3 COURT CLOSE**
Mr & Mrs C J Crocker.

NEW **GOURDON**
Jenny Deeming.

NEW **GREENWAYS**
Mark Broadbent.

NEW **LANTERN HOUSE**
Peter Harburn.

THE MANOR HOUSE
Mr & Mrs G Lewis.

NEW **THE ORCHARD**
Mike Cable.

SPRINGFIELD HOUSE
Jenny & Roger Handscombe, 01295 690286, jehandscombe@btinternet.com.

NEW **UNDEREDGE**
Alison & Nick Jackson.

1 THE WHEELWRIGHTS
Ms E Bunn.

Warmington is a charming historic village, mentioned in the Doomsday Book, situated at the north-east edge of the Cotswolds in a designated AONB. There is a large village green with a pond overlooked by an Elizabethan Manor House. There are other historic buildings including St Michael's Church, The Plough Inn and Springfield House all dating from the C16 or before. There is a mixed and varied selection of gardens to enjoy during your visit to Warmington. These include the formal knot gardens and topiary of The Manor House, cottage and courtyard gardens, terraced gardens on the slopes of Warmington Hill and orchards containing local varieties of apple trees. Some gardens will be selling home-grown plants. WC at village hall, along with delicious home-made cakes, and hot and cold drinks. Warmington is on a hill with many steps and gravel driveways which could be difficult for wheelchairs.

Mallory Court Hotel

GROUP OPENING

35 NEW WARWICK GARDENS

Warwick, CV34 6PQ. *The Master's Garden is in the town centre. Other gardens are to the SE, down Castle Hill & Banbury Rd. Park in St Nicholas Car Park or in nearby Myton Fields, but not in Archery Fields or Mill St. Map will be provided on the day.* **Sun 29 July (1-5). Combined adm with The Mill Garden £6, chd free. Home-made teas at Brethren's Kitchen at Lord Leycester Hospital & at St Nicholas Church.**

NEW 4 ARCHERY FIELDS
David & Sally Howells.

◆ THE MASTER'S GARDEN
The Governors, 01926 491422, info@lordleycester.com, www.lordleycester.com.

NEW THE OAK HOUSE
Peter Freeman & Glynis Hovell.

Four outstanding gardens in the centre and south of Warwick, all different in character. Historical interest, award-winning excellence and views to die for. At their best in late-summer. An unusual opportunity to see the River Avon and the Castle from both sides of the river. The Mill Garden is a nationally known garden at the foot of Warwick Castle, with exceptionally rich planting. 4 Archery Fields is modernistic in style, with many rare plants. The Oak House garden runs colourfully down to the river opposite The Mill Garden. The Master's Garden is a beautiful recreation of a historic garden site. See detailed descriptions on the website. Planting, views, historical associations.

GROUP OPENING

36 WELFORD-ON-AVON & DISTRICT GARDENS

Welford-on-Avon, CV37 8PT. *5m SW of Stratford-upon-Avon. Off B4390.* **Sat 23, Sun 24 June (2-5). Combined adm £5, chd free. Home-made teas in village hall.**

ASH COTTAGE
Mr & Mrs Peter & Sue Hook.

ELM CLOSE
Eric & Glenis Dyer.
(See separate entry)

THE OLD RECTORY
Frank Kennedy.

6 QUINEYS LEYS
Mr & Mrs Gordon & Penny Whitehurst.

In addition to its superb position on the river, with serene swans, dabbling ducks and resident herons, Welford-on-Avon has a beautiful church and a selection of pubs serving great food. Just down the road is a highly popular farm shop selling seasonal fruit and vegetables. With its great variety of house styles, including an abundance of beautiful cottages with thatched roofs and chocolate-box charisma, Welford also has many keen gardeners. The gardens that open for the NGS range from small to large, from established to newly designed and planted, and include some with fruit and vegetable plots and wild areas.

GROUP OPENING

37 WHICHFORD & ASCOTT GARDENS

Whichford & Ascott, Shipston-on-Stour, CV36 5PP. *6m SE of Shipston-on-Stour. Taking the A3400, the turning to Whichford & Ascott is equidistant between Chipping Norton & Shipston-on-Stour. From Banbury & villages to the NE, take the Hook Norton & Whichford road from Bloxham. Free car parking opp the church & in Ascott.* **Sun 17 June (2-5.30). Combined adm £6, chd free. Home-made teas at Knights Place.**

ASCOTT LODGE
Charlotte Copley.

BELMONT HOUSE
Robert & Yoko Ward.

KNIGHT'S PLACE
Mrs Derek Atkins.

THE OLD RECTORY
Peter & Caroline O'Kane.

PLUM TREE COTTAGE
Janet Knight.

WHICHFORD HILL HOUSE
Mr & Mrs John Melvin.

THE WHICHFORD POTTERY
Jim & Dominique Keeling, www.whichfordpottery.com.

This group of gardens reflects a range of several garden types and sizes. The two villages are in an AONB. They nestle within a dramatic landscape of hills, pasture and woodland, which is used to picturesque effect by the garden owners. Fine lawns, mature shrub planting and much interest to plantsmen provide a peaceful visit to a series of beautiful gardens. Many incorporate the inventive use of natural springs, forming ponds, pools and other water features. Classic cottage gardens contrast with larger and more classical gardens which adopt variations on the traditional English garden of herbaceous borders, climbing roses, yew hedges and walled enclosures. Other amenities are the C12 church, the internationally renowned pottery, and a pub serving meals. Good press coverage in local press. Partial wheelchair access as some gardens are on sloping sites.

Gardens are at the heart of hospice care

WILTSHIRE

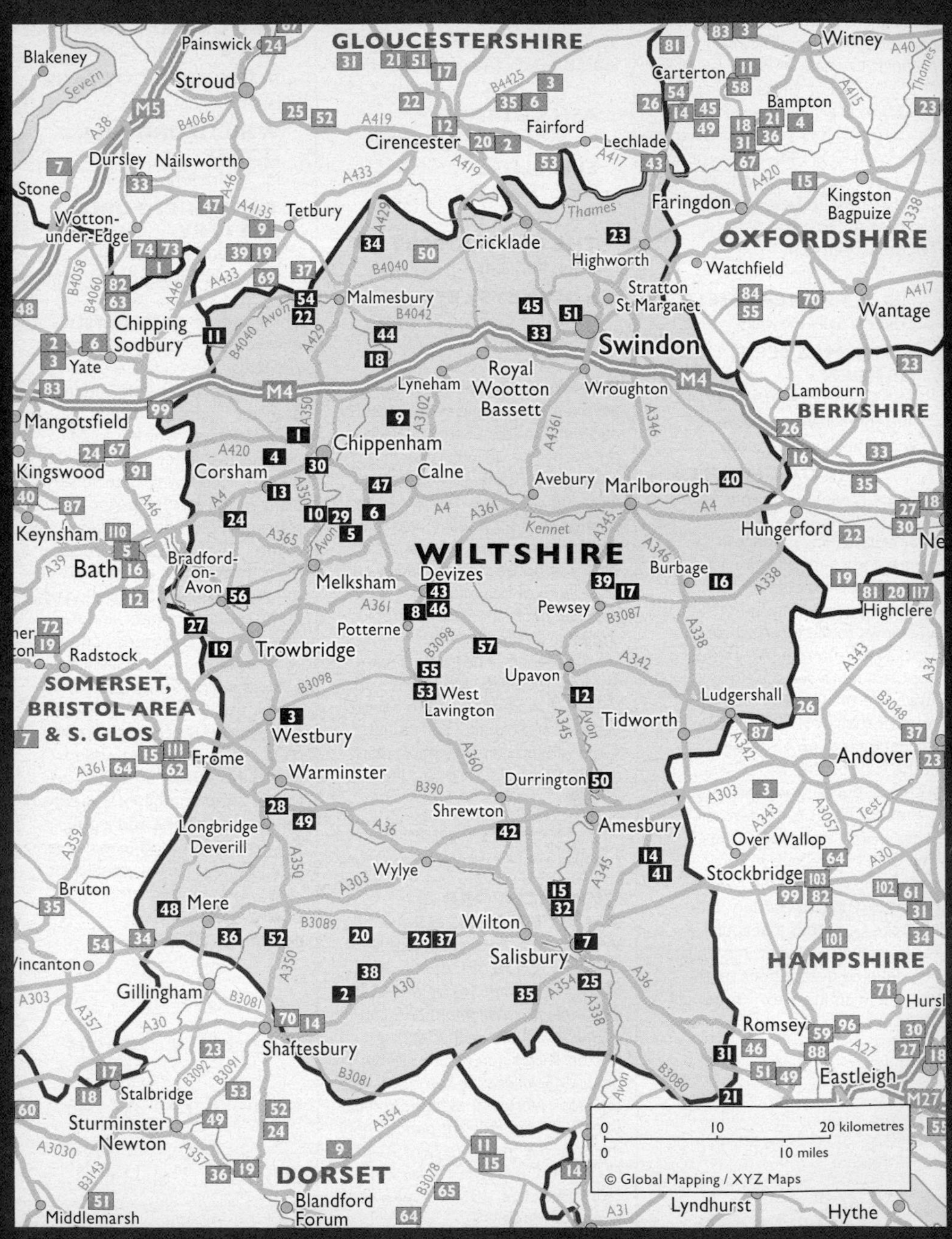
GLOUCESTERSHIRE
OXFORDSHIRE
BERKSHIRE
WILTSHIRE
SOMERSET, BRISTOL AREA & S. GLOS
HAMPSHIRE
DORSET
Stroud
Cirencester
Swindon
Chippenham
Malmesbury
Marlborough
Devizes
Trowbridge
Salisbury
Bath
0 10 20 kilometres
0 10 miles
© Global Mapping / XYZ Maps

Wiltshire, a predominantly rural county, covers 1,346 square miles and has a rich diversity of landscapes, including downland, wooded river valleys and Salisbury Plain.

Chalk lies under two-thirds of the county, with limestone to the north, which includes part of the Cotswolds Area of Outstanding Natural Beauty. The county's gardens reflect its rich history and wide variety of environments.

Gardens opening for the National Garden Scheme include the celebrated landscape garden of Stourhead and large privately owned gems such as Broadleas, Oare House and Cadenham Manor, and more modest properties that are lovingly maintained by the owners, such as Mitre Cottage and North Cottage.

The season opens with the snowdrops at Lacock Abbey and continues with fine spring gardens like Fonthill House and Corsham Court.

A wide selection of gardens, large and small, are at their peak in the summer. There are also town gardens, a new village opening at Hannington, allotments, manor houses and a Chinese garden at Beggars Knoll. There is something to delight the senses from February to September.

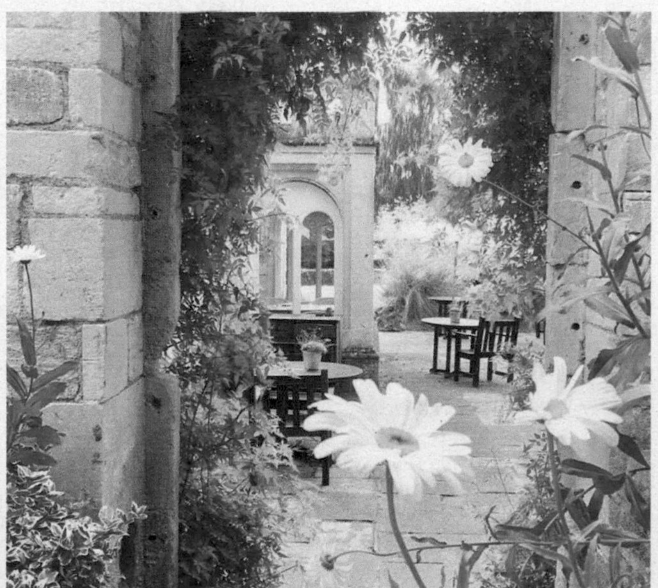

Volunteers

County Organiser
Annabel Dallas
01672 520266
annabel.dallas@btinternet.com

County Treasurer
Sean Magee
01666 880009
spbmagee@gmail.com

Publicity
& Booklet Co-ordinator
Tricia Duncan
01672 810443
tricia@windward.biz

Social Media
Marian Jones
01249 657400
marian.jones@ngs.org.uk

Assistant County Organiser
Suzie Breakwell
01985 850297
suzievb@me.com

Sarah Coate
01722 782365
sarah.coate@woodfordvalley.net

Jo Hankey
01722 742472
rbhankey@gmail.com

Shirley Heywood
01985 844486
shirleyheywood@btinternet.com

Tracey Mosley
01249 782515
traceyemosley1@gmail.com

Diana Robertson
01672 810515
diana@broomsgrovelodge.co.uk

Left: Woolley Grange Hotel

OPENING DATES

All entries subject to change. For latest information check **www.ngs.org.uk**

Map locator numbers are shown to the right of each garden name.

February

Snowdrop Festival

Saturday 24th
◆ Lacock Abbey Gardens 29

March

Sunday 18th
Fonthill House 20

Thursday 22nd
NEW The Meadows 36

Friday 23rd
NEW The Meadows 36

Sunday 25th
Biddestone Manor 4

April

Sunday 8th
◆ Corsham Court 13

Sunday 15th
Broadleas House Gardens 8
Cottage in the Trees 14

Saturday 21st
Job's Mill 28

Sunday 22nd
◆ Corsham Court 13
NEW Foxley Manor 22
◆ Stourhead Garden 48

Wednesday 25th
Hazelbury Manor Gardens 24

Friday 27th
◆ Bowood Woodland Gardens 6

Sunday 29th
Allington Grange 1
Horatio's Garden 25
◆ Iford Manor 27
Oare House 39
◆ Waterdale House 52

May

Sunday 6th
Little Durnford Manor 32

Sunday 13th
Purton House 45

Wednesday 16th
Bowden Park 5

Sunday 20th
Ark Farm 2
Broadleas House Gardens 8
◆ Twigs Community Garden 51

Thursday 24th
Windmill Cottage 55

Friday 25th
Windmill Cottage 55

Saturday 26th
Job's Mill 28

Sunday 27th
Cottage in the Trees 14
Trantor House 50

June

Festival Weekend

Saturday 2nd
Trantor House 50

Sunday 3rd
Cantax House 10
Crofton Lock House 16
Forest Cottage 21
Hazelbury Manor Gardens 24
Hyde's House 26
Trantor House 50

Wednesday 6th
NEW Cadenham Manor 9

Saturday 9th
West Lavington Manor 53

Sunday 10th
Chisenbury Priory 12
◆ Lydiard Park Walled Garden 33
North Cottage 38
The Old Mill 40

Thursday 14th
Windmill Cottage 55

Friday 15th
Pear Cottage 43
1 Southview 46
Windmill Cottage 55

Sunday 17th
Manor Farm 34

Sunday 24th
Cottage in the Trees 14
Dauntsey Gardens 18
NEW Hannington Village Gardens 23
Lavender Gardens 31
North Cottage 38
Oare House 39
NEW The Old Rectory, Boscombe 41

Thursday 28th
Whatley Manor 54

Saturday 30th
Dane Brook 17

July

Sunday 1st
Broadleas House Gardens 8
Dane Brook 17

Saturday 7th
Pear Cottage 43
1 Southview 46

Sunday 8th
NEW Braemar Lodge 7
NEW Cherry Orchard Barn 11
Duck Pond Barn 19
Mitre Cottage 37
84 Studley Lane 47

Wednesday 11th
Manor House, Stratford Tony 35

Thursday 12th
Windmill Cottage 55

Friday 13th
Windmill Cottage 55

Sunday 22nd
◆ Twigs Community Garden 51

Saturday 28th
Dane Brook 17

Sunday 29th
Crofton Lock House 16
Dane Brook 17
130 Ladyfield Road & Allotments 30

August

Sunday 5th
Crofton Lock House 16

Friday 10th
NEW Woolley Grange Hotel 56

Saturday 11th
NEW Woolley Grange Hotel 56

Sunday 19th
The Old Mill 40

Wednesday 22nd
Manor House, Stratford Tony 35

September

Thursday 6th
NEW The Meadows 36

Friday 7th
NEW The Meadows 36

Wednesday 12th
Hazelbury Manor Gardens 24

February 2019

Saturday 23rd
◆ Lacock Abbey Gardens 29

By Arrangement

Beggars Knoll Chinese Garden 3
Biddestone Manor 4
Broadleas House Gardens 8
Cottage in the Trees 14
The Court House 15
Crofton Lock House 16
Dane Brook 17
Duck Pond Barn 19
Manor House, Stratford Tony 35
North Cottage 38
The Old Rectory, Winterbourne Stoke 42
The Pound House 44
84 Studley Lane 47
NEW Sutton Veny House Nursing Home 49
Trantor House 50
West Lavington Manor 53
Windmill Cottage 55
NEW Woolley Grange Hotel 56
Wudston House 57

THE GARDENS

1 ALLINGTON GRANGE
Allington, Chippenham, SN14 6LW. Mrs Rhyddian Roper, www.allingtongrange.com. *2m W of Chippenham. Take A420 W from Chippenham. 1st R signed Allington Village, entrance 1m up lane on L.* **Sun 29 Apr (2-5). Adm £4, chd free. Home-made teas.**
Informal country garden of approx 1½ acres, around C17 farmhouse (not open) with yr-round interest and a diverse range of plants. Many early spring bulbs. Mixed and herbaceous borders, colour themed; white garden with water fountain. Pergola lined with clematis and roses. Walled potager. Small orchard with chickens. Wildlife pond with natural planting. Mainly level with ramp into potager. Dogs on leads.

2 ARK FARM
Old Wardour, Tisbury, Salisbury, SP3 6RP. Mrs Miranda Thomas. *Old Wardour is 2m from Tisbury. Drive down High Street and on, past station, take 1st R. Follow signs to Old Wardour Castle.* **Sun 20 May (2-5). Adm £4, chd free. Home-made teas.**
Informal hidden gardens in beautiful setting with small wooded area, pond, water plants, lakeside walk, views of Old Wardour castle. This is a very difficult garden for wheelchairs. Not advised!

3 BEGGARS KNOLL CHINESE GARDEN
Newtown, Westbury, BA13 3ED. Colin Little & Penny Stirling, 01373 823383, silkendalliance@talktalk.net. *1m SE of Westbury. Turn off B3098 at White Horse Pottery, up hill towards the White Horse for ¾m. Parking at end of drive for 10-12 cars.* **Visits by arrangement June & July group max 24, but smaller numbers and individuals are welcome. Visits incl guided tour. Adm £5.50, chd free. Tea and home-made cake £3.50. We already have quite a reputation for the homemade cakes - especially the walnut and coffee cake.**
Inspirational 1 acre plantsman's garden on chalk hillside, divided up into a series of Chinese rooms. The colourful plantings include many rare Chinese trees, shrubs and flowers, set against a backdrop of Chinese pavilions and gateways. Intricate mosaic pavements wind around ponds and rocks. A large potager with flower-filled borders houses chickens. Spectacular views to the Mendips.

4 BIDDESTONE MANOR
Chippenham Lane, Biddestone, SN14 7DJ. Rosie Harris, Head Gardener, 01249 713211. *5m W of Chippenham. On A4 between Chippenham & Corsham turn N. From A420, 5m W of Chippenham, turn S. Use car park.* **Sun 25 Mar (2-5). Adm £5, chd free.**
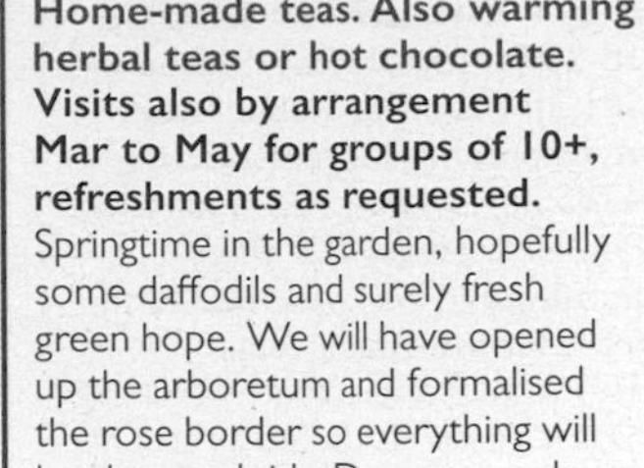
Home-made teas. Also warming herbal teas or hot chocolate. Visits also by arrangement Mar to May for groups of 10+, refreshments as requested.
Springtime in the garden, hopefully some daffodils and surely fresh green hope. We will have opened up the arboretum and formalised the rose border so everything will be clean and tidy. Do come and see us before the wilderness returns, please check NGS website or phone 01249 713211 if it has been wet. Wheelchair access to most parts, a few steps, help always available.

5 BOWDEN PARK
Lacock, Chippenham, SN15 2PP. Bowden Park Estate. *10 mins from Chippenham. Entrance via Top Lodge at top of Bowden Hill, between A342 at Sandy Lane and A350 in Lacock.* **Wed 16 May (11-4). Adm £5, chd free. Light refreshments.**
22 acre private garden within surrounding parkland. Pleasure garden, water garden, working kitchen garden with formal lawns and grotto. Rhododendrons and azaleas in flower.

6 ◆ BOWOOD WOODLAND GARDENS
Calne, SN11 9PG. The Marquis of Lansdowne, 01249 812102, reception@bowood.org, www.bowood.org. *3½m SE of Chippenham. Located off J17 M4 nr Bath & Chippenham. Entrance off A342 between Sandy Lane & Derry Hill Villages. Follow brown tourist signs. For SatNav please use SN11 9PG.* **For NGS: Fri 27 Apr (11-6). Adm £6, chd free.** For other opening times and information, please phone, email or visit garden website.
This 60 acre woodland garden of azaleas, magnolias, rhododendrons and bluebells is one of the most exciting of its type in the country. From the individual flowers to the breathtaking sweep of colour formed by hundreds of shrubs, this is a garden not to be missed. The Woodland Gardens are located 2m from Bowood House and Garden.

Cantax House

7 NEW BRAEMAR LODGE

18-20 Stratford Road, Salisbury, SP1 3JH. Charles Hubberstey, www.braemarlodgecare.co.uk. *A345 off Salisbury ring rd, Stratford Rd 2nd L, garden 300 yards on L.* **Sun 8 July (2-5). Adm £3, chd free. Home-made teas.**

This vibrant and colourful Nursing Home garden is tucked all around the building. Paths lead through the Butterfly Walk, down past our small orchard, along the Woodland Walk, to the main courtyard garden of roses, clematis and perennials. Plenty of seating with a tea house by the Rose Garden. All main garden areas are wheelchair accessible, there is a sloping, rolled gravel path to the garden.

8 BROADLEAS HOUSE GARDENS

Devizes, SN10 5JQ. Mr & Mrs Cardiff, 01380 722035, karincardiff@btinternet.com. *1m S of Devizes. From Hartmoor Rd turn L into Broadleas Park, follow rd for 350 metres then turn R into estate. Please note, there is no access from A360 Potterne Rd.* **Sun 15 Apr, Sun 20 May, Sun 1 July (2-5.30). Adm £5, chd free. Home-made teas. Visits also by arrangement Mar to Sept contact via email in first instance.**

6 acre garden of hedges, herbaceous borders, rose arches, bee garden and orchard stuffed with good plants. It is overlooked by the house and arranged above the small valley garden which is crowded with magnolias and rhododendrons, cornus and hydrangeas. Wheelchair access to upper garden only, some gravel and narrow grass paths.

9 NEW CADENHAM MANOR

Foxham, Chippenham, SN15 4NH. Victoria & Martin Nye. *B4069 from Chippenham or M4 J17 through Sutton Benger, turn R in Christian Malford and L in Foxham. From A3102 turn L from Calne or R from Lyneham (NW) at Xrds between Hilmarton and Goatacre.* **Wed 6 June (2-5). Adm £10, chd free. Pre-booking essential, please visit www.ngs.org.uk or phone 01483 211535 for information & booking. Home-made teas.** Donation to Horatio's Garden.

The glorious 4 acre garden comprises a series of rooms around a listed manor and dovecot. Divided by yew hedges and moats, the rooms are furnished with specimen trees, mixed borders, plus fountains and statues to focus the eye. Vegetable garden, herb garden and water garden in old canal. June's highlights are a spectacular range of old roses and the peony walk. This is a very private garden rarely open to the public.

10 CANTAX HOUSE

Lacock, SN15 2JZ. Andrew & Deborah van der Beek, www.deborahvanderbeek.com. *3m S of Chippenham. Off A350 between Chippenham & Melksham. Please use signed public car park if possible (except disabled). Entrance to garden in Cantax Hill.* **Sun 3 June (2-6). Adm £5, chd free. Cream teas.** Donation to Amnesty International.

Queen Anne former vicarage (not open). Medium-sized garden of colour, pattern and scent straddling the Bide Brook. Designed and maintained by sculptor owner for 29yrs; both common and unusual plants incl wild flower sports; hornbeam spire, yew castle and other topiary; old orchard wildflower garden; sculpture by owner and friends. In lovely old village featured in many films. House front featured in Cranford, BBC Emma and Harry Potter (Slughorn's house).

11 NEW CHERRY ORCHARD BARN

Cherry Orchard Lane, Luckington, SN14 6NZ. Paul Fletcher and Tim Guard. *Note that Cherry Orchard Barn is ¾m before the centre of SN14 6NZ, at a T junction. Passing the Barn is ill-advised, as turning rapidly becomes difficult.* **Sun 8 July (1.30-5). Adm £5, chd £3. Home-made teas.**

Charming 1-acre garden created over past 4 yrs from the corner of a field, with open views of the surrounding countryside. Containing 7 rooms, 3 of which are densely planted with herbaceous perennials, each with individual identities and colour themes. The garden is described by visitors as a haven of tranquillity. Largely level access to all areas of the garden. Some gravel paths.

12 CHISENBURY PRIORY

East Chisenbury, SN9 6AQ. Mr & Mrs John Manser. *3m SW of Pewsey. Turn E from A345 at Enford then N to E Chisenbury, main gates 1m on R.* **Sun 10 June (2-6). Adm £5, chd free. Tea.**

Medieval Priory with Queen Anne face and early C17 rear (not open) in middle of 5 acre garden on chalk. Mature garden with fine trees within clump and flint walls, herbaceous borders, shrubs, roses. Moisture loving plants along mill leat, carp pond, orchard and wild garden, many unusual plants. Featured in Country Life 2017.

13 ◆ CORSHAM COURT

Corsham, SN13 0BZ. Lord Methuen, 01249 701610, staterooms@corsham-court.co.uk, www.corsham-court.co.uk. *4m W of Chippenham. Signed off A4 at Corsham.* **For NGS: Sun 8, Sun 22 Apr (2-5.30). Adm £5, chd £2.50. For other opening times and information, please phone, email or visit garden website.**

Park and gardens laid out by Capability Brown and Repton. Large lawns with fine specimens of ornamental trees surround the Elizabethan mansion. C18 bath house hidden in the grounds. Spring bulbs, beautiful lily pond with Indian bean trees, young arboretum and stunning collection of magnolias. Wheelchair (not motorised) access to house, gravel paths in garden.

14 COTTAGE IN THE TREES

Tidworth Rd, Boscombe Village, nr Salisbury, SP4 0AD. Karen & Richard Robertson, 01980 610921, robertson909@btinternet.com. *7m N of Salisbury. Turn L off A338 just before Social Club. Continue past church, turn R after bridge to Queen Manor, cottage 150yds on R.* **Sun 15 Apr, Sun 27 May (1.30-5). Adm £3, chd free. Sun 24 June (1.30-5). Combined adm with The Old Rectory, Boscombe, £6, chd free. Home-made teas. Visits also by arrangement Apr to June for groups of 10+.**

Enchanting ½ acre cottage garden, immaculately planted with water feature, raised vegetable beds, small wildlife pond and gravel garden. Spring bulbs, hellebores and pulmonarias give a welcome start to the season, with pots and baskets, roses and clematis. Mixed borders of herbaceous plants, dahlias, grasses and shrubs giving all-yr interest.

15 THE COURT HOUSE

Lower Woodford, SP4 6NQ. Mr & Mrs J G Studholme, 01722 782237, joestudholme@icloud.com. *6m S of Amesbury. Driving S on Woodford Valley rd (parallel to A360 & A345) The Court House is 2nd house on L after Lower Woodford village sign.* **Visits by arrangement May to July no min number, max 30. Adm £5, chd free. Light refreshments by arrangement.**

4½ acre garden on banks of River Avon. Herbaceous borders, waterside planting, yew hedges, rambler roses and wild flowers. Unusual trees. Ancient site of Bishop's Palace when Salisbury Cathedral was at Old Sarum. Tree house. Garden developed by present owners over past 27 years. Most of garden is flat, with wheelchair access over lawns and mown grass paths.

16 CROFTON LOCK HOUSE

Crofton, Great Bedwyn, Marlborough, SN8 3DW. Michael & Jenny Trussell, 01672 870674, jennytrussell@hotmail.com. *Lock 62, K&A Canal, Crofton, 1m W of Great Bedwyn. 4m W of Hungerford. Signs from A4 at Great Bedwyn turning, and from A338 at East Grafton. Limited parking. Garden 8 - 10 mins walk along towpath.* **Sun 3 June, Sun 29 July, Sun 5 Aug (1.30-5.30). Adm £3.50, chd free. Home-made teas. Gluten free cakes available. Visits also by arrangement May to Aug for groups of 20 max.** Donation to Wiltshire Air Ambulance.

¾ acre garden in idyllic setting around 200 yr old, off grid lock keeper's cottage. Garden comprises herbaceous beds designed with a painter's eye to provide riotous colour, sculptural form, and an abundance of wildlife from spring to autumn; at rear a small orchard, collection of apple and soft fruit trees, raised vegetable beds, artists' studio (open) and restored privy. There is no access by car. Wheelchairs have to be pushed along the tow path.

17 DANE BROOK

Milkhouse Water, Pewsey, SN9 5JX. Mr & Mrs P Sharpe, 01672 562620, gill.sharpe@modini.co.uk. *1m NE of Pewsey. From Pewsey take B3087 Burbage Rd. After approx ¾m turn L to Milkhouse Water. Dane Brook is 1st on R after railway bridge.* **Sat 30 June, Sun 1, Sat 28, Sun 29 July (12.30-5). Adm £5, chd free. Home-made teas. Gluten free available. Visits also by arrangement June to Aug groups of 20 max.** Donation to Veterans Outreach Support.

Approx 1 acre of gardens, incl herbaceous beds, shrubs, trees, semi formal garden, roses, oxbow pond with planted banks and thatched summerhouse. Tree lined river walk runs the length of the garden, leading to shrubbery. Also lawns and paved areas with planted containers. Far reaching views from paddocks. Small craft stall with handmade gifts and accessories, home-made sweets, jams, chutney, fresh laid eggs. Rare breed sheep, horses and vintage tractor. Wheelchair accessible in dry weather with exception of pond and stream areas.

Hazelbury Manor Gardens

GROUP OPENING

18 DAUNTSEY GARDENS

Church Lane, Dauntsey, Chippenham, SN15 4HW. *5m SE of Malmesbury. Approach via Dauntsey Rd from Gt Somerford, 1¼ m from Volunteer Inn Great Somerford.* **Sun 24 June (1-5). Combined adm £6, chd free. Home-made teas at Idover House.**

THE COACH HOUSE
Col & Mrs J Seddon-Brown.

DAUNTSEY PARK
Mr & Mrs Giovanni Amati, 01249 721777, enquiries@dauntseyparkhouse.co.uk.

THE GARDEN COTTAGE
Miss Ann Sturgis.

IDOVER HOUSE
Mr & Mrs Christopher Jerram.

NEW **THE OLD COACH HOUSE**
Tony & Janette Yates.

THE OLD POND HOUSE
Mr & Mrs Stephen Love.

This group of 6 gardens, centred around the historic Dauntsey Park Estate, ranges from the Classical C18 country house setting of Dauntsey Park, with spacious lawns, old trees and views over the River Avon, to mature country house gardens and traditional walled gardens. Enjoy the formal rose garden in pink and white, old fashioned borders and duck ponds at Idover House, and the quiet seclusion of The Coach House with its thyme terrace and gazebos, climbing roses and clematis. Here, mop-headed pruned crataegus prunifolia line the drive. The Garden Cottage has a traditional walled kitchen garden with organic vegetables, apple orchard, woodland walk and yew topiary. Meanwhile the 2 acres at The Old Pond House are both clipped and unclipped! Large pond with lilies and fat carp, and look out for the giraffe and turtle. The Old Coach House is a small garden with perennial plants, shrubs and climbers.

19 DUCK POND BARN

Church Lane, Wingfield, Trowbridge, BA14 9LW. Janet & Marc Berlin, 01225 777764, janet@berlinfamily.co.uk. *On B3109 from Frome to Bradford on Avon, turn opp Poplars PH into Church Lane. Duck Pond Barn is at end of lane. Big field for parking.* **Sun 8 July (2-5). Adm £4, chd free. Light refreshments. Visits also by arrangement May to Aug.**
Garden of 1.6 acres with large duck pond, lawns, ericaceous beds, orchard, vegetable garden, big greenhouse, spinney and wild area of grass and trees. Large dry stone wall topped with flower beds with rose arbour. New addition of 3 ponds linked by a rill in the flower garden. Set in farmland and mainly flat. Coach parties please ring in advance for catering purposes.

20 FONTHILL HOUSE

Tisbury, SP3 5SA. The Lord Margadale of Islay, www.fonthill.co.uk/gardens. *13m W of Salisbury. Via B3089 in Fonthill Bishop. 3m N of Tisbury.* **Sun 18 Mar (12-5). Adm £6, chd free. Light refreshments. Sandwiches and cakes, all proceeds to NGS.**
Large woodland garden. Daffodils, rhododendrons, azaleas, shrubs, bulbs; magnificent views; formal gardens. The gardens have been extensively redeveloped under the direction of Tania Compton and Marie-Louise Agius. The formal gardens are being continuously improved with new designs, exciting trees, shrubs and plants. Beckford Bottle Shop will have a stall selling wine. Partial wheelchair access.

21 FOREST COTTAGE

Bramshaw, Lyndhurst, SO43 7JN. Norah Dunn. *Nr Landford, off A36 between Salisbury and Southampton. From A36 take B3079 through Landford and into the New Forest. Take L turn towards Newbridge. Forest Cottage is on L after 300 yds.* **Sun 3 June (1-5). Adm £3, chd free. Home-made teas are available at two nearby gardens, Oaklands and Waldrons, 2 miles away at Brook. (see Hampshire).**
A large, peaceful garden in the New Forest, developed from a paddock in 1997. Cottage garden areas contrast with shrubs and trees forming wandering pathways and open spaces. Two ponds encourage a wide variety of wildlife, and a wildflower meadow behind has many wild orchids.

22 NEW FOXLEY MANOR

Foxley, Malmesbury, SN16 0JJ. Richard and Louisa Turnor. *about 2m W of Malmesbury. 10 mins from J17 on M4. Turn towards Malmesbury/Cirencester, then towards Norton and follow signs for the Vine Tree, follow road to T-junction in Foxley village, signed from here.* **Sun 22 Apr (11-5). Adm £5, chd free. Home-made teas.**
Yew hedges divide lawns, borders, rose garden, lily pond and a newer wild area with a natural swimming pond shaded by a Liriodendron. Views through large Turkey Oaks to farmland beyond. Small courtyard gravel garden. Sculptures are sited throughout the gardens. Regret steps and gravel paths make this unsuitable for wheelchairs.

GROUP OPENING

23 NEW HANNINGTON VILLAGE GARDENS

Hannington, Swindon, SN6 7RP. *Off B4019 Blunsdon to Highworth Rd by the Freke Arms. Park behind the Jolly Tar PH, tickets from Quarry Bank, 14 Queens Road.* **Sun 24 June (12-5). Combined adm £5, chd free. Home-made teas in Hannington Village Hall.**

NEW **BUTLER'S COTTAGE**
Mr & Mrs John & Karen Mayell.

NEW **QUARRY BANK**
Paul Minter & Michael Weldon.

NEW **ROSE COTTAGE**
Mr & Mrs Keith & Ruth Scholes.

NEW **STEP COTTAGE**
Mr & Mrs J Clarke.

YORKE HOUSE GARDEN
Mrs Catherine Bozeat.

Hannington has a dramatic hilltop position and the views into and out of the village resulted in it being made a very large conservation area. The C12 church stands apart from the settlement which has a Jacobean Manor House and many other listed buildings. Large and small gardens in a variety of styles. Many of the gardens follow the brow of the hill and afford stunning views of the upper Thames Valley and the surrounding farm land which is crossed by footpaths and bridleways. Limited wheelchair access as many gardens are on steep hills and feature steps.

24 HAZELBURY MANOR GARDENS

Wadswick, Box, SN13 8HX. Mr L Lacroix. *5m SW of Chippenham, 5m NE of Bath. From A4 at Box, A365 to Melksham, at Five Ways junction L onto B3109 towards Corsham; 1st L in ¼ m, drive immed on R.* **Wed 25 Apr (11-3). Sun 3 June (1-5). Home-made teas. Wed 12 Sept (11-3). Adm £5, chd free. Teas on Sunday opening only.**
8 Acres of Grade II landscaped organic gardens set around C15 fortified manor (not open). Edwardian garden consisting of yew hedges, topiary, pleached beech, and laburnum tunnel. Large variety of plants fill 5000 square metres of planting; many of which are native or herbal. Vegetable gardens, orchards, megalithic circle and wild flowers extend beyond the formal gardens.

25 HORATIO'S GARDEN

Duke of Cornwall Spinal Treatment Centre, Salisbury Hospital NHS Foundation Trust, Odstock Road, Salisbury, SP2 8BJ. Horatio's Garden Charity, www.horatiosgarden.org.uk. *1m from centre of Salisbury. Please park in car park 8 or 10.* **Sun 29 Apr (1-4). Adm £5, chd free. Home-made teas. Tea and delicious cakes - made by Horatio's Garden volunteers - will be served in the Garden Room.** Donation to Horatio's Garden.
Award winning hospital garden which opened in Sept 2012 and was designed by Cleve West for patients with spinal cord injury at the Duke of Cornwall Spinal Treatment Centre. Built from donations given in memory of Horatio Chapple who was a volunteer at the centre in his school holidays. Low limestone walls, which represent the form of the spine, divide densely planted beds and double as seating. Everything in the garden has been designed to benefit patients during their long stays in hospital. Garden is run by Head Gardener and team of volunteers. At 3pm there will be a talk about therapeutic gardens by Charity Chair Dr Olivia Chapple & Head Gardener, Stephen Hackett. 3 Society of Garden Designers Awards 2015 and Bali Award 2014. Cleve West has 8 RHS gold medals, incl Best in Show at Chelsea Flower Show in 2011 and 2012. Featured in RHS The Garden & BBC Gardeners' World. Fully accessible to wheelchairs.

26 HYDE'S HOUSE

Dinton, SP3 5HH. Mr George Cruddas. *9m W of Salisbury. Off B3089 nr Dinton Church on St Mary's Rd.* **Sun 3 June (2-5). Adm £5.50, chd free. Home-made teas at Thatched Old School Room with outside tea tables.**
3 acres of wild and formal garden in beautiful situation with series of hedged garden rooms. Numerous shrubs, flowers and borders, all allowing tolerated wild flowers and preferred weeds, while others creep in. Large walled kitchen garden, herb garden and C13 dovecote (open). Charming C16/18 Grade I listed house (not open), with lovely courtyard. Every year varies. Free walks around park and lake. Steps, slopes, gravel paths and driveway.

27 ◆ IFORD MANOR

Bradford-on-Avon, BA15 2BA. Mr Cartwright-Hignett, 01225 863146, info@ifordmanor.co.uk, www.ifordmanor.co.uk. *7m S of Bath. Off A36, brown tourist sign to Iford 1m. Or from Bradford-on-Avon or Trowbridge via Lower Westwood Village (brown signs). Campervans should call ahead for directions avoiding narrow lanes.* **For NGS: Sun 29 Apr (11-4). Adm £6, chd £5.20. Home-made teas. Tea room also serves home-made cream teas, cakes, ice cream, fresh coffee and selection of specialist teas. Please note no lunches available.** For other opening times and information, please phone, email or visit garden website.
Very romantic award-winning, Grade I listed Italianate garden famous for its tranquil beauty. Home to Edwardian architect and designer Harold Peto 1899-1933. Garden is characterised by steps, terraces, sculpture and magnificent rural views. (House not open). 2018 sees the completion of a historic replant throughout the garden over the past decade. Housekeeper's cream teas and home-made cakes at weekends. Light refreshments in Loggia at other times. World famous Summer Arts festival June to Aug, www.ifordarts.org.uk. Please see website for wheelchair access details. Featured in The Times, The Australian, Wiltshire Life, Bath Life and Manolo: The Boy Who Made Shoes for Lizards film. Please see website for wheelchair access details.

Funds from National Garden Scheme gardens help Macmillan support thousands of people every year

28 JOB'S MILL

Five Ash Lane, Crockerton, Warminster, BA12 8BB. Lady Silvy McQuiston. *1½m S of Warminster. Down lane E of A350, S off A36 r'about.* **Sat 21 Apr (2-5); Sat 26 May (2-5.30). Adm £4.50, chd free. Home-made teas.**

Delightful 5 acre garden through which River Wylye flows. Laid out on many levels surrounding old converted water mill. Water garden, herbaceous border, vegetable garden, orchard, riverside and woodland walks and secret garden. Grass terraces designed by Russell Page. Bulbs and Erythronium in the spring and perhaps the tallest growing wisteria?

29 ◆ LACOCK ABBEY GARDENS

High Street, Lacock, Chippenham, SN15 2LG. National Trust, 01249 730459, lacockabbey@nationaltrust.org.uk, www.nationaltrust.org.uk/lacock. *3m S of Chippenham. Off A350. Follow NT signs. Use public car park (parking fee).* **For NGS: Sat 24 Feb (10.30-5.30). Adm £6, chd £3. Light refreshments in courtyard tea room. Several pubs and tea rooms in village. 2019: Sat 23 Feb.** For other opening times and information, please phone, email or visit garden website.

Woodland garden with carpets of aconites, snowdrops, crocuses and daffodils. Botanic garden with greenhouse, medieval cloisters and magnificent trees. Mostly level site, some gravel paths.

30 130 LADYFIELD ROAD & ALLOTMENTS

Ladyfield Road, Chippenham, SN14 0AP. Philip & Pat Canter and Chippenham Town Council. *1m SW of Chippenham. Between A4 Bath and A420 Bristol rds. Signed off B4528 Hungerdown Lane which runs between A4 & A420.* **Sun 29 July (1.30-5.30). Adm £4, chd free. Light refreshments.**

Very pretty small garden with more than 40 clematis, climbing roses and small fish pond. Curved neat edges packed with colourful herbaceous plants and small trees. 2 patio areas with lush lawn, pagoda and garden arbour. Also Hungerdown Allotments, 15 allotments owned by Chippenham Town Council. Featured in Garden News, Garden Answers and Amateur Gardening magazines. Wheelchair access to main path in garden and to allotments on main drive only.

31 LAVENDER GARDENS

Giles Lane, Landford, Salisbury, SP5 2BG. Mr Michael Hayward, www.newforestlavender.com. *11m from Southampton, 11m from Salisbury on A36. From Salisbury: Village landmark on A36 Royal Jaipur Indian restaurant approx 1m turn L. From Southampton landmark The Shoe Inn approx 1m turn R.* **Sun 24 June (9.30-5). Adm £2, chd free. NGS day: cream teas, cakes and light lunches.**

Small lavender field with adjacent cottage and annual garden. Mostly grass pathways in garden area. Cottage plants, lavender, herbs and roses. Tearoom, nursery and gift shop open Wed - Sun (10-4). Wheelchair access from car park to tea room and plant sales area. Remainder of access level grassed area. Disabled WC.

32 LITTLE DURNFORD MANOR

Little Durnford, Salisbury, SP4 6AH. The Earl & Countess of Chichester. *3m N of Salisbury. Just N beyond Stratford-sub-Castle. Remain to E of R Avon at road junction at Stratford Bridge and continue towards Salterton for ½m heading N. Entrance on L just past Little Durnford sign.* **Sun 6 May (2-5). Adm £4, chd free. Home-**

Manor House, Stratford Tony

made teas in cricket pavilion within grounds.
Extensive lawns with cedars, walled gardens, fruit trees, large vegetable garden, small knot and herb gardens. Terraces, borders, sunken garden, water garden, lake with islands, river walks, labyrinth walk. Little Durnford Manor is a substantial grade II listed, C18 private country residence (not open) built of an attractive mix of Chilmark stone and flint. Camels, alpacas, llama, pigs, pygmy goats, donkeys and sheep are all grazing next to the gardens. Gravel paths, some narrow. Steep slope and some steps.

33 ◆ LYDIARD PARK WALLED GARDEN

Lydiard Tregoze, Swindon, SN5 3PA. Swindon Borough Council, 01793 466664, lydiardpark@swindon.gov.uk, www.lydiardpark.org.uk. *3m W Swindon, 1m from J16 M4. Follow brown signs from W Swindon.* **For NGS: Sun 10 June (10-4). Adm £3, chd £2. Light refreshments in Coach House Tea Rooms.** For other opening times and information, please phone, email or visit garden website.
Beautiful ornamental C18 walled garden. Trimmed shrubs alternating with individually planted flowers and bulbs incl rare daffodils and tulips, sweet peas, annuals and wall-trained fruit trees. Unique features incl well and sundial. Wide level paths, no steps.
NPC

34 MANOR FARM

Crudwell, Malmesbury, SN16 9ER. Mr & Mrs J Blanch. *4m N of Malmesbury on A429. Heading N on A429 in Crudwell, turn R signed to Eastcourt. Farm entrance is on L 200m after end of speed limit sign.* **Sun 17 June (11-5). Adm £5, chd free. Home-made teas.**
Set within Cotswold stone walls and with a backdrop of Crudwell church lies a half acre garden with a further 5 acres of mini parkland ideal for a Sunday afternoon stroll. The garden is divided by box and yew hedges to create different areas both formal and informal. Herbaceous borders, old fashioned roses, catmint are grown among fountains and extensive lawns.

35 MANOR HOUSE, STRATFORD TONY

Stratford Tony, Salisbury, SP5 4AT. Mr & Mrs Hugh Cookson, 01722 718496, lucindacookson@stratfordtony.co.uk, www.stratfordtony.co.uk. *4m SW of Salisbury. Take minor rd W off A354 at Coombe Bissett. Garden on S after 1m. Or take minor rd off A3094 from Wilton signed Stratford Tony and racecourse.* **Wed 11 July, Wed 22 Aug (2-5). Adm £5, chd free. Home-made teas. Visits also by arrangement May to Oct, refreshments and tours by arrangement for garden groups of 10+.**
Varied 4 acre garden with all yr interest. Formal and informal areas. Small lake fed from R Ebble, waterside planting, herbaceous borders with colour from spring to late autumn. Pergola-covered vegetable garden, parterre garden, orchard, shrubberies, roses, specimen trees, winter colour and structure, many original contemporary features and places to sit and enjoy the downland views. Some gravel.

36 NEW THE MEADOWS

Limpers Hill, Mere, BA12 6BB. Mr K Potts. *½m S of Mere off A303. From centre of Mere, past Walton's Post Office, after Walnut Tree Inn turn L into Southbrook, The Meadows is ½m on R. Limited parking on rd.* **Thur 22, Fri 23 Mar, Thur 6, Fri 7 Sept (11-5). Adm £3, chd free.**
Small garden developed over past 3 yrs for yr-round interest. A good demonstration of the potential of a restricted space. In early spring the focus is on small bulbs; in September, salvias, phlox, anemones, a pond, even a young dawn redwood, witch hazels and liquidambars.

37 MITRE COTTAGE

Snow Hill, Dinton, SP3 5HN. Mrs Beck. *9m W of Salisbury. From B3089 turn up Snowhill by shop. From Wylye bear L at fork by church.* **Sun 8 July (2-6). Adm £3.50, chd free.**
'Mitre cottage exemplifies what can be achieved in ¾ of an acre without looking contrived or over designed. Well chosen and often unusual plants are balanced at this time of the year by effusive plantings of old fashioned roses and perennials. Set on a slight hillside, paths lead enticingly from one area to another.' Daily Telegraph July 2016. A water feature is a recent addition to the garden.

38 NORTH COTTAGE

Tisbury Row, Tisbury, SP3 6RZ. Jacqueline & Robert Baker, 01747 870019, baker_jaci@yahoo.co.uk. *12m W of Salisbury. From A30 turn N through Ansty, L at T-junction, towards Tisbury. From Tisbury take Ansty road. Car park entrance nr junction signed Tisbury Row.* **Sun 10, Sun 24 June (11.30-5). Adm £4, chd free. Home-made light lunches and afternoon teas. Visits also by arrangement June & July for groups of 10+.**
On leaving car park, walk past vegetables and through wild flowers to reach house and gardens. Although small there is much variety to find. Garden is divided with lots to explore as each part differs in style and feel. From the intimacy of the garden go out to see the orchard, find the ponds, walk the coppice wood and see the rest of the smallholding. Ceramics, wooden furniture and handicrafts all made by garden owners, including creations from their own sheep's wool for sale. Exciting metal work sculpture exhibition. Large variety of plants for sale.

39 OARE HOUSE

Rudge Lane, Oare, nr Pewsey, SN8 4JQ. Sir Henry Keswick. *2m N of Pewsey. On Marlborough Rd (A345).* **Sun 29 Apr, Sun 24 June (2-6). Adm £5.50, chd free. Home-made teas. Home-made cakes.** Donation to The Order of St John.

1740s mansion house later extended by Clough Williams Ellis in 1920s (not open). The formal gardens originally created around the house have been developed over the years to create a wonderful garden full of many unusual plants. Current owner is very passionate and has developed a fine collection of rarities. Garden is undergoing a renaissance but still maintains split compartments each with its own individual charm; traditional walled garden with fine herbaceous borders, vegetable areas, trained fruit, roses and grand mixed borders surrounding formal lawns. The Magnolia garden is wonderful in spring with some trees dating from 1920s, together with strong bulb plantings. Large arboretum and woodland with many unusual and champion trees. In spring and summer there is always something of interest, with the glorious Pewsey Vale as a backdrop. Partial wheelchair access.

40 THE OLD MILL

Ramsbury, SN8 2PN. Annabel & James Dallas. *8m NE of Marlborough. From Marlborough head to Ramsbury. At The Bell PH follow sign to Hungerford. Garden behind yew hedge on R 100yds beyond The Bell.* **Sun 10 June, Sun 19 Aug (2-6). Adm £5, chd £5. Home-made teas.**

Water running through a multitude of channels no longer drives the mill but provides a backdrop for whimsical garden of pollarded limes and naturalistic planting. Paths meander by streams and over small bridges. Vistas give dramatic views of downs beyond. Potager style kitchen garden and separate cutting garden provide a more formal contrast to the relaxed style elsewhere. Limited wheelchair access as gravel paths and bridges.

41 NEW THE OLD RECTORY, BOSCOMBE

Tidworth Road, Boscombe, Salisbury, SP4 0AB. Helen and Peter Sheridan. *7m N of Salisbury on A338. From Salisbury, 2nd L turning after Earl of Normanton PH, just S of Boscombe Social Club and Black Barn.* **Sun 24 June (1.30-5). Combined adm with Cottage in the Trees £6, chd free. Single garden admission £4.**

The elegant gardens of this period property feature a traditional walled garden with herbaceous borders and vegetable beds, contrasting with a parkland of sweeping lawns, mature trees and flowering shrubs. Wheelchair access, though ground may be soft after rain and paths are gravel.

42 THE OLD RECTORY, WINTERBOURNE STOKE

Church Street, Winterbourne Stoke, Salisbury, SP3 4SW. Mr & Mrs J Dutton, 01980 621247, olivia.dutton@outlook.com. *10m NW of Salisbury. 3m W of Stonehenge. Follow Church Street (turning on S side of A303 opp Solstice Rest PH & garage) over small bridge. Entrance gates on L just after yellow salt bin.* **Visits by arrangement Apr to Sept for groups of 10+. Adm £5, chd free. Home-made teas.**

3 acre garden in idyllic setting surrounding Georgian rectory with lovely views. Mirrored herbaceous perennial borders with abundant colour Apr-Oct, with backdrop of mature and specimen trees, contrast with wildflower areas. 120ft west-facing wall with climbing roses and clematis; parterre with 100+ roses; orchard; ornate trellis and cottage garden planting around pool; croquet lawn with pergola.

43 PEAR COTTAGE

28 Pans Lane, Devizes, SN10 5AF. Mary & Paul Morgan. *From Devizes Mkt Pl go S (Long St). At r'about go L (Southbroom) & R at r'about - Pans Ln. Park in road or roads nearby.* **Fri 15 June, Sat 7 July (2-5). Combined adm with 1 Southview £6, chd free.**

A 'jewel of a small garden' choc full of interest all yr. Spiral paths and low hedges, with alpines, hellebores, perennials, peonies in the front. Vibrant exotic patio at the back, steps up to quirky topiary, roses, grasses, clematis, herbs, fruit. Timber greenhouse. Beyond is a tranquil wild garden with trees, perennials, alliums, willow arbour and pond with toads, newts, frogs and dragonflies. Many places in Devizes for lunches and teas. 10 mins level walk, plenty of parking in town. Garden has won Devizes & Roundway in Bloom Awards 2016 & 2017 in 3 categories, back garden, single container and hanging basket. Wheelchair access to front garden and rear patio only.

44 THE POUND HOUSE

Little Somerford, Chippenham, SN15 5JW. Mr & Mrs Michael Baines, 01666 823212, squeezebaines@yahoo.com. *2m E of Malmesbury on B4024. In village turn S, leave church on R. Car park on R before railway bridge.* **Visits by arrangement May to July all groups welcome. Teas £2 per person. Adm £5, chd free. Home-made teas.**

Large well planted garden surrounding former rectory attached to C17 house. Mature trees, hedges and spacious lawns. Well stocked herbaceous borders, roses, shrubs, pergola, parterre, swimming pool garden, water, ducks, chickens, alpacas and horses. Raised vegetable garden and lots of places to sit. A beautiful English garden!

45 PURTON HOUSE

Church End, Purton, Swindon, SN5 4EB. Mrs Myf Barker. *Turn off Purton High St towards St Mary Church into Church St. At tithe barn L into Church End, after about 300 metres car park on R opp Purton Organics sign (shop open).* **Sun 13 May (12-5). Adm £5, chd free. Cream teas.**

This is something different. A large organically managed garden with beautiful specimen trees and

Georgian house. Used as wedding venue. The huge ancient plane tree by the lake (formerly monastic carp ponds) is home to a fairy garden. Walled garden with many old varieties of fruit trees, soft fruit and vegetables. NB some weeds as garden is in mid restoration. Interesting sculptures. Possible wheelchair access to lawn areas although some rough ground.

46 1 SOUTHVIEW

Wick Lane, Devizes, SN10 5DR. Teresa Garraud. *From Devizes Mkt Pl go S (Long St). At r'about go L (Southbroom) & R at r'about - Pans Lane, continue over bridge turn R at r'about (Wick Ln). Gdn on R. Park in road or roads nearby.* **Fri 15 June, Sat 7 July (2-5). Combined adm with Pear Cottage £6, chd free.**
An atmospheric small town garden that leads you through many different, fascinating areas as it seems to go on and on. A plantswoman's garden with mature topiary and trees including acers and a Cercis canadensis setting off colourful shrub/herbaceous borders and a multitude of large pots on the patios featuring unusual herbaceous plants, giving delightful contrasts in colour and texture. Many places in Devizes for lunches & teas. 10 mins level walk, plenty of parking in town.

48 ♦ STOURHEAD GARDEN

Stourton, Warminster, BA12 6QD. National Trust, 01747 841152, stourhead@nationaltrust.org.uk, www.nationaltrust.org.uk/stourhead. *3m NW of Mere on B3092. Follow NT signs, the property is very well signed from all main roads incl A303.* **For NGS: Sun 22 Apr (9-6). Adm £18.30, chd £9.20. Admission incl house and garden.** For other opening times and information, please phone, email or visit garden website.
One of the earliest and greatest landscape gardens in the world, creation of banker Henry Hoare in 1740s on his return from the Grand Tour, inspired by paintings of Claude and Poussin. Planted with rare trees, rhododendrons and azaleas over last 250yrs. Wheelchair access, buggy available.

47 84 STUDLEY LANE

Studley, Calne, SN11 9NH. Stephen Cox, 01249 812968, stephencox.gardentrust@gmail.com, www.stephencoxgarden.simplesite.com. *Just off A4 between Chippenham & Calne. From A4 at Studley Xrds turn off opp Derry Hill & Bowood turning. Garden 1st R in lane. Purple fence/gates. Park in private car park or lane.* **Sun 8 July (2-6). Adm £3, chd free. Home-made teas. Visits also by arrangement June to Aug for groups, max 40. Student groups for art & nature studies also welcome.**
Created from a field is a small, quirky garden of rooms: orchard, vegetables, dwarf conifers, dianthus, roses, fuchsias, grasses, exotics, coastal, heathers, herbarium, alpines, cottage, specimen trees. All divided by lawns, paths, walls and arches. Fish pond, fountains, waterfall, wetland and beach. Life size stone statues, 30 plaques of garden wisdom. Relax in 18 seating areas and five arbours. Garden map. Educational literature for visitors.

49 NEW SUTTON VENY HOUSE NURSING HOME

Sutton Veny, Warminster, BA12 7BJ. Mrs Christina Bila, 01985 840224, www.suttonvenyhouse.com. *Outskirts of Sutton Veny village on Bishopstrow Rd. Look for gatehouse and green sign.* **Visits by arrangement in June. Adm by donation. Home-made teas in Drawing Room or Sensory Garden.**
22 acres of grounds including several formal garden areas, a woodland walk and landscaped grounds. Formal gardens surround the house and incl a number of seating areas with views of extensive landscaped gardens from this vantage point. Easily accessible by wheelchair from the front car park. Woodland walk and landscaped areas are accessible although ground will be too rough for most wheelchair users.

50 TRANTOR HOUSE

Hackthorne Road, Durrington, SP4 8AS. Mrs Jane Turner, 01980 655101. *10m N of Salisbury. Turn off A345 (signed Village Centre) onto Hackthorne Rd. Approx 200 yds on L.* **Sun 27 May (12-5), also open Cottage in the Trees. Sat 2, Sun 3 June (12-5). Adm £4, chd free. Visits also by arrangement May to July.**
Border Oak timber framed house on country lane surrounded by approx ⅔ acre of both formal and informal gardens. Attractive mixed and herbaceous colour themed borders, rose garden, wildlife pond and stream. Summerhouse, raised vegetable beds and wildflower meadow. Chickens. Sloping garden with steps.

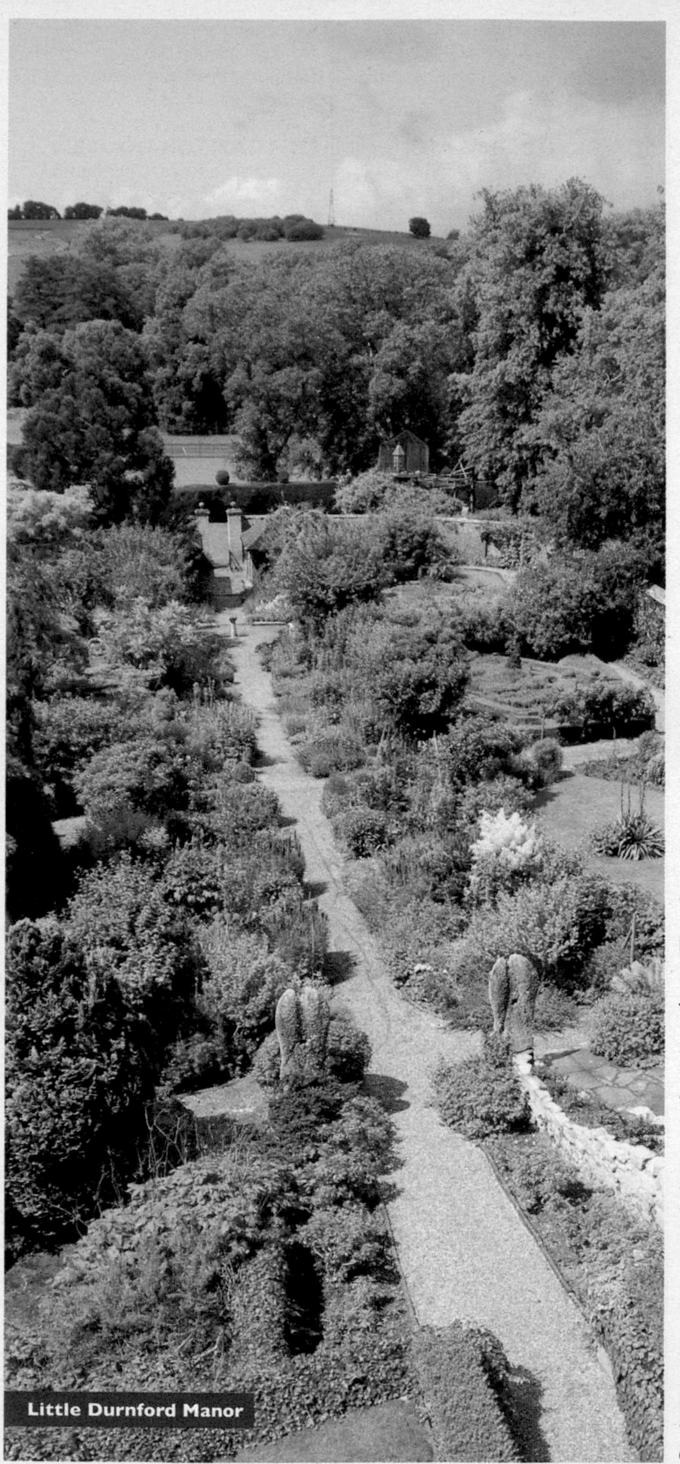

Little Durnford Manor

51 ◆ TWIGS COMMUNITY GARDEN

Manor Garden Centre, Cheney Manor, Swindon, SN2 2QJ. TWIGS, 01793 523294, twigs.reception@gmail.com, www.twigscommunitygardens.org.uk. *From Gt Western Way, under Bruce St Bridges onto Rodbourne Rd. 1st L at r'about, Cheney Manor Industrial Est. Through estate, 2nd exit at r'about. Opp Pitch & Putt. Signs on R to Manor Garden Centre.* **For NGS: Sun 20 May, Sun 22 July (1-5). Adm £3, chd free. Home-made teas. Excellent hot and cold lunches available at Olive Tree café within Manor Garden centre adj to Twigs.** For other opening times and information, please phone, email or visit garden website.

Delightful 2 acre community garden, created and maintained by volunteers. Features incl 7 individual display gardens, ornamental pond, plant nursery, Iron Age round house, artwork, fitness trail, separate kitchen garden site, Swindon beekeepers and the haven, overflowing with wild flowers. Featured in Garden Answers & Wiltshire Life magazine and on Great British Gardens website. In Top 100 Attractions in South West England. Most areas wheelchair accessible. Disabled WC.

52 ◆ WATERDALE HOUSE

East Knoyle, SP3 6BL. Mr & Mrs Julian Seymour, 01747 830262. *8m S of Warminster. N of East Knoyle, garden signed from A350. Do not use SatNav.* **For NGS: Sun 29 Apr (2-6). Adm £5, chd free. Home-made teas.** For other opening times and information, please phone.

4 acre mature woodland garden with rhododendrons, azaleas, camellias, maples, magnolias, ornamental water, bog garden, herbaceous borders. Bluebell walk. Shrub border created by storm damage, mixed with agapanthus and half hardy salvias. Sensible footwear essential due to difficult surfaces, parts of garden very wet. Partial wheelchair access.

53 WEST LAVINGTON MANOR

1 Church Street, West Lavington, SN10 4LA. Andrew Doman, andrewdoman01@gmail.com. *6m S of Devizes, on A360. House opp White St, where parking available.* **Sat 9 June (11-6). Adm £10, chd free. Light refreshments. Home-made teas and lunch provided by West Lavington Youth Club. Visits also by arrangement for groups of 10+ any weekday.** Donation to West Lavington Youth Club.

5 acre walled garden first established in C17 by John Danvers who brought Italianate gardens to the UK. Herbaceous border, redeveloped Japanese garden, new rose garden, orchard and arboretum with some outstanding specimen trees all centred around a trout stream and duck pond. White Birch grove and walk along southern bank of the stream. Picnics welcome. Only limited areas of garden accessible by wheelchair.

54 WHATLEY MANOR

Twatley, Malmesbury, SN16 0RB. Christian & Alix Landolt, www.whatleymanor.com. *4m W of Malmesbury. From A429 at Malmesbury take B4040 signed Sherston. Manor 2m on L.* **Thur 28 June (2-7). Adm £5, chd free. Tea, coffee and home-made cake in The Loggia Garden. The Hotel will also be open for lunch and full afternoon tea.**

12 acres of English country gardens with 26 distinct rooms each with a strong theme based on colour, scent or style. Original 1920s plan inspired the design and combines classic style with more contemporary touches; including specially commissioned sculpture. Dogs must be on a lead at all times.

55 WINDMILL COTTAGE

Kings Road, Market Lavington, SN10 4QB. Rupert & Gill Wade, 01380 813527. *5m S of Devizes. Turn E off A360 1m N of West Lavington, 2m S of Potterne. At top of hill turn L into Kings Rd, L into Windmill Lane after 200yds. Limited parking on site, ample parking nearby.* **Thur 24, Fri 25 May, Thur 14, Fri 15 June, Thur 12, Fri 13 July (2-5). Adm £4, chd free. Home-made teas. Visits also by arrangement May to July for groups of 4+. Refreshments by arrangement.**

1 acre cottage style, wildlife friendly garden on greensand. Mixed beds and borders with long season of interest. Roses on pagoda, large vegetable patch for kitchen and exhibition at local shows, greenhouse. Whole garden virtually pesticide free for last 20yrs. Small bog garden by wildlife pond. Secret glade with prairie. Grandchildren's little wood and annual flower meadow in July. Majority of garden accessible. Some soft and gravel parts.

56 NEW WOOLLEY GRANGE HOTEL

Woolley Green, Bradford-on-Avon, BA15 1TX. Woolley Grange Hotel, 01225 864705, info@woolleygrangehotel.co.uk, www.woolleygrangehotel.co.uk. *1m NE of Bradford-on-Avon. Just off B3105 at Woolley Green.* **Fri 10, Sat 11 Aug (10-5). Adm £5, chd free. Cream teas in garden on open days. On other days refreshments served in Restaurant or Orangery. Visits also by arrangement May to Sept for groups of 5+.**

Beautiful 14 acre garden with mixed borders, pond, orchard and a wildlife garden. The Victorian walled garden has been restored and is fully productive, and a gang of Indian runner ducks roam free keeping the slugs at bay. Lots to do for the children incl White Witch's House and Woolley Sheep Trail. All set against the stunning backdrop of this Jacobean manor house hotel. Lots of play areas for children. Garden staff available for help & advice. Walled Garden produce is grown for the hotel restaurant, open to the public for lunches, teas and evening meals. Several steps around the gardens, but walled garden is accessible to wheelchairs.

57 WUDSTON HOUSE

High Street, Wedhampton, Devizes, SN10 3QE. David Morrison, 01380 840965, djm@piml.co.uk. *Wedhampton lies on N side of A342 approx 4m E of Devizes. House half way up High Street, Parking signed.* **Visits by arrangement June to Sept for groups of 10-30. Adm £10, chd free. Light refreshments.**

The garden of Wudston House was started in 2010 following completion of the house. It consists, inter alia, of formal gardens round the house, a perennial meadow, pinetum and an arboretum. Nick Macer and James Hitchmough, who has pioneered the concept of perennial meadows, have been extensively involved in aspects of the garden, which is still developing. Partial wheelchair access.

Braemar Lodge

WORCESTERSHIRE

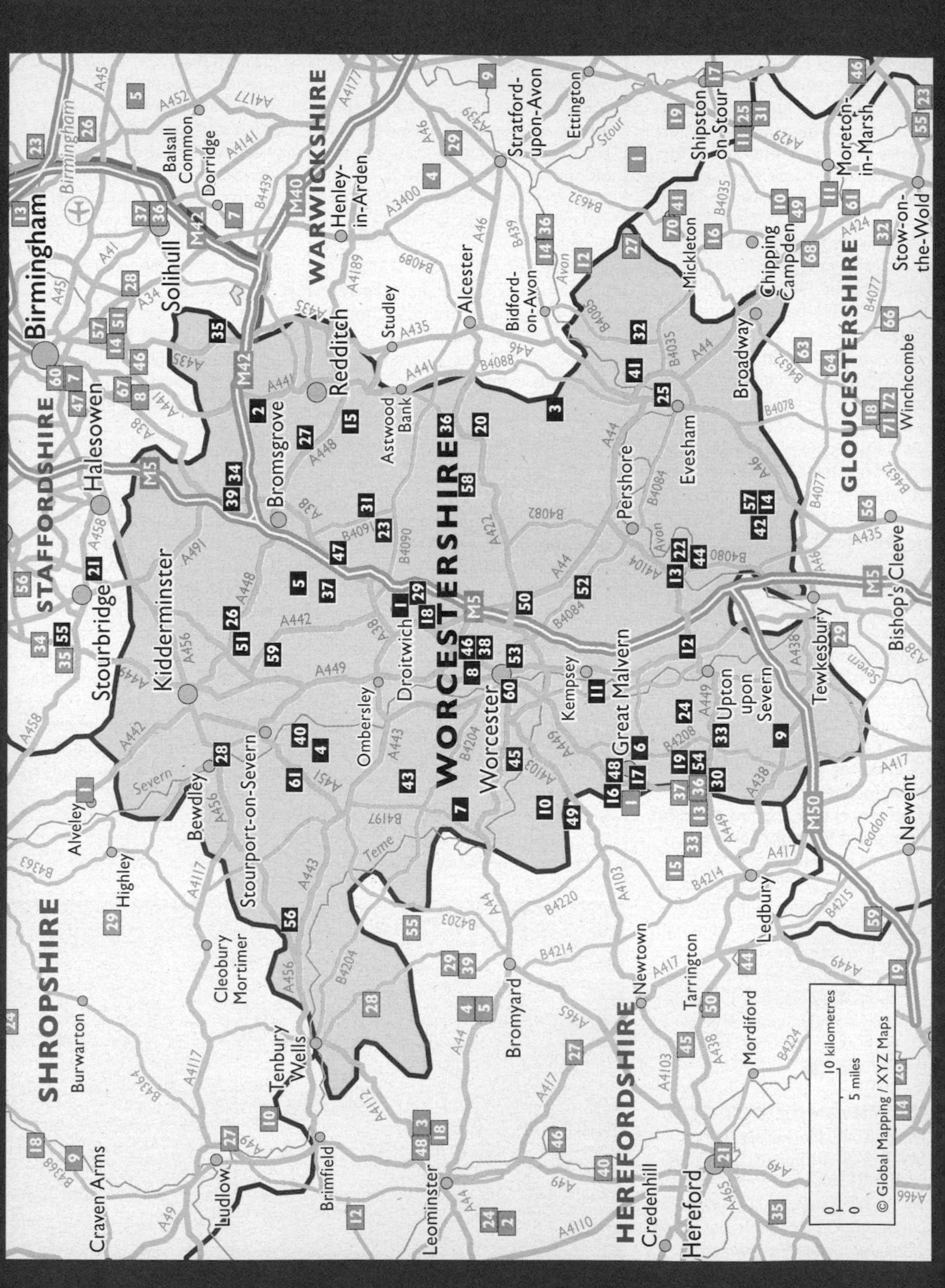

Worcestershire has something to suit every taste, and the same applies to its gardens.

From the magnificent Malvern Hills, the inspiration for Edward Elgar, to the fruit orchards of Evesham which produce wonderful blossom trails in the spring, and from the historic city of Worcester, with its 11th century cathedral and links to the Civil War, to the numerous villages and hamlets that are scattered throughout the county, there is so much to enjoy in this historic county.

Worcestershire is blessed with gardens created by celebrated gardeners such as Capability Brown to ordinary amateur gardeners, and the county can boast properties with grounds of over one hundred acres to small back gardens of less than half an acre, but all have something special to offer.

Visitors to Worcestershire's NGS gardens will find some with wonderful arrays of plants, trees and vegetables, while others show the owners' creativity or sense of fun. There are gardens with significant historical interest and some with magnificent views. We also have a number of budding artists involved with the Scheme, and a few display their works of art on garden open days.

Worcestershire's garden owners guarantee visitors beautiful gardens, some real surprises and a warm welcome.

Volunteers

County Organiser
David Morgan
01214 453595
meandi@btinternet.com

County Treasurer
Lynn Glaze
01386 751924
lynnglaze@cmail.co.uk

Publicity
Pamela Thompson
01886 888295
peartree.pam@gmail.com

Advertising & Booklet Co-ordinator
Alan Nokes
01214 455520
alan.nokes@ngs.org.uk

Assistant County Organisers
Brian Bradford
07816 867137
brianbradford101@outlook.com

Below: The Cottage, 3 Crumpfields Lane

OPENING DATES

All entries subject to change. For latest information check **www.ngs.org.uk**

Map locator numbers are shown to the right of each garden name.

February

Snowdrop Festival

Sunday 11th
Brockamin 11

March

Every Friday from Friday 9th to Friday 23rd
◆ Little Malvern Court 30

Sunday 18th
Brockamin 11

Friday 30th
◆ Spetchley Park Gardens 50

April

Saturday 7th
NEW The River School Worcester 46

Sunday 8th
24 Alexander Avenue 1
Bylane 12
White Cottage & Nursery 58

Sunday 15th
Bridges Stone Mill 10

Saturday 21st
Morton Hall 36
The Walled Garden 53
◆ Whitlenge Gardens 59

Sunday 22nd
◆ Whitlenge Gardens 59

Monday 23rd
NEW Lovells Vineyard 33

Wednesday 25th
The Walled Garden 53

Saturday 28th
Shuttifield Cottage 49

Sunday 29th
Hiraeth 29

May

Every Wednesday
Badge Court 5

Saturday 5th
Hewell Grange 27
New House Farm, Elmbridge 37

Sunday 6th
1 Church Cottage 13
Hewell Grange 27
New House Farm, Elmbridge 37
Whitcombe House 57
White Cottage & Nursery 58

Monday 7th
1 Church Cottage 13
◆ Little Malvern Court 30

Saturday 12th
Oak Tree House 39
Shuttifield Cottage 49

Sunday 13th
Shuttifield Cottage 49

Saturday 19th
NEW Redwood 45

Sunday 20th
NEW 3 Oakhampton Road 40
NEW Redwood 45

Thursday 24th
5 Beckett Drive 8

Saturday 26th
Shuttifield Cottage 49

Sunday 27th
Brockamin 11
Bylane 12
1 Church Cottage 13
White Cottage & Nursery 58
68 Windsor Avenue 60

Monday 28th
1 Church Cottage 13
Rothbury 48
White Cottage & Nursery 58
68 Windsor Avenue 60

June

Every Wednesday
Badge Court 5

Festival Weekend

Saturday 2nd
The Barton 7
Pershore Gardens 44

Sunday 3rd
The Barton 7
Pear Tree Cottage 43
Pershore Gardens 44
Whitcombe House 57

Saturday 9th
Eckington Gardens 22
◆ Hanbury Hall & Gardens 23
Hanley Swan NGS Gardens 24
Shuttifield Cottage 49

Sunday 10th
Birtsmorton Court 9
Eckington Gardens 22
◆ Hanbury Hall & Gardens 23
Hanley Swan NGS Gardens 24

Wednesday 13th
47 High Street 28

Saturday 16th
NEW Long Hyde House 32
◆ Whitlenge Gardens 59

Sunday 17th
Hiraeth 29
◆ Whitlenge Gardens 59

Saturday 23rd
Alvechurch Gardens 2
The Cottage, 3 Crumpfields Lane 15
Worralls Mill 61

Sunday 24th
24 Alexander Avenue 1
Alvechurch Gardens 2
Astley Towne House 4
The Cottage, 3 Crumpfields Lane 15
Cowleigh Lodge 16
David's Garden 18
Rothbury 48
Worralls Mill 61

Monday 25th
NEW Lovells Vineyard 33

Saturday 30th
24 Croft Bank 17
◆ Harvington Hall 26
The Lodge 31
NEW Long Hyde House 32

July

Every Wednesday
Badge Court 5

Sunday 1st
Bylane 12
24 Croft Bank 17
◆ Harvington Hall 26
The Lodge 31
◆ Spetchley Park Gardens 50
NEW Wharf House 56

Saturday 7th
NEW North Worcester Gardens 38

Sunday 8th
NEW North Worcester Gardens 38

Saturday 14th
Westacres 55

Sunday 15th
24 Alexander Avenue 1
David's Garden 18
Westacres 55

Wednesday 18th
47 High Street 28

Thursday 19th
NEW 3 Oakhampton Road 40

Sunday 22nd
Hiraeth 29
Rothbury 48

Sunday 29th
Astley Towne House 4
Cowleigh Lodge 16

August

Wednesday 1st
5 Beckett Drive 8

Saturday 4th
Offenham Gardens 41

Sunday 5th
Offenham Gardens 41

Saturday 11th
NEW The River School Worcester 46
Shuttifield Cottage 49

Sunday 12th
Marlbrook Gardens 34

Wednesday 15th
47 High Street 28

Tuesday 21st
NEW 3 Oakhampton Road 40

Sunday 26th
Astley Towne House 4
1 Church Cottage 13
Pear Tree Cottage 43

Monday 27th
Astley Towne House 4
1 Church Cottage 13

September

Saturday 1st
Morton Hall 36
New House Farm, Elmbridge 37

Sunday 2nd
Bylane 12
New House Farm, Elmbridge 37

Wednesday 5th
NEW 3 Oakhampton Road 40

Saturday 8th
6 Dingle End 20

Saturday 15th
◆ Whitlenge Gardens 59

Sunday 16th
◆ Whitlenge Gardens 59

Sunday 23rd
Brockamin 11

Monday 24th
NEW Lovells Vineyard 33

By Arrangement

24 Alexander Avenue 1
Ashley 3
Badge Court 5
Barnard's Green House 6
The Barton 7
5 Beckett Drive 8
Brockamin 11
1 Church Cottage 13
Conderton Manor 14
The Cottage, 3 Crumpfields Lane 15
Cowleigh Lodge 16
24 Croft Bank 17
David's Garden 18
The Dell House 19
6 Dingle End 20
Eckington Gardens 22
Hanley Swan NGS Gardens 24
47 High Street 28
Hiraeth 29
The Lodge 31
NEW Long Hyde House 32
Marlbrook Gardens 34
74 Meadow Road 35
New House Farm, Elmbridge 37
Oak Tree House 39
Overbury Court 42
Pear Tree Cottage 43
NEW The River School Worcester 46
Round Hill Garden, Marlbrook Gardens 34
Shuttifield Cottage 49
The Tynings 52
223 Wells Road 54
Westacres 55
Whitcombe House 57
White Cottage & Nursery 58
19 Winnington Gardens, Hanley Swan NGS Gardens 24

THE GARDENS

1 24 ALEXANDER AVENUE

Droitwich Spa, WR9 8NH. Malley & David Terry, 01905 774907, terrydroit@aol.com. *1m S of Droitwich. Droitwich Spa towards Worcester A38. Or from M5 J6 to Droitwich Town centre.* **Sun 8 Apr (2-5); Sun 24 June, Sun 15 July (2-5.30). Adm £3.50, chd free. Visits also by arrangement Apr to Sept.**

Beautifully designed giving feeling of space and tranquillity. 100+ clematis varieties interlacing high hedges. Borders with rare plants and shrubs. Sweeping curves of lawns and paths to woodland area with shade-loving plants. Drought-tolerant plants in S-facing gravel front garden. Alpine filled troughs. April spring bulbs and alpines, July clematis colourful mixed shrub and herbaceous borders. Partial wheelchair access.

Redwood

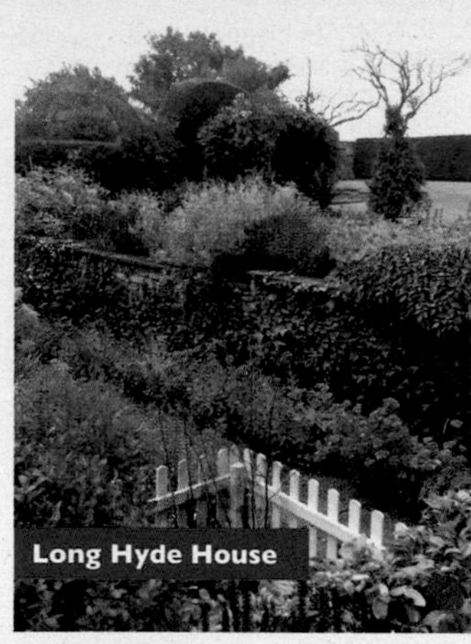
Long Hyde House

GROUP OPENING

2 ALVECHURCH GARDENS

Red Lion Street, Alvechurch, B48 7LF. Group Co-ordinator Philip Aubury. *3m N of Redditch, 3m NE of Bromsgrove. NGS Gardens are signed from all roads into Alvechurch village. Pick up your map when you pay at your first garden.* **Sat 23, Sun 24 June (1-6). Combined adm £5, chd free. Light refreshments at Old Rectory Cottage.**

NEW **18 BEAR HILL**
Joanne & Mark Winson.

NEW **69 BIRMINGHAM ROAD**
Anna & Andy Ingram.

28 CALLOW HILL ROAD
Martin & Janet Wright.

CORNER HOUSE
Janice Wiltshire.

NEW **THE MOAT HOUSE**
Mr & Mrs Mike & Tracy Fallon.

THE OLD SWAN
Ray & Norma Yarnell.

RECTORY COTTAGE
Celia Hitch, 0121 445 4824, celia@rectorycottage-alvechurch.co.uk.

4 SNAKE LANE
Jason & Paul Emery.

76 TANYARD LANE
Dianne & Barry Court.

Large village - much new development but interesting core - buildings spanning medieval to Edwardian church on hill with a selection of lovely gardens ranging from a riverside rectory with waterfall to a corner plot 'gardened' for wildlife. There's a professionally landscaped terraced garden and a cottage garden with lots of colour in pots and a wrap-around informal garden. Sloped garden with potted plants and shrubs, and a garden with wooden bridge, decking and pebbled areas. Around the gardens there are rose beds, shrubberies, herbaceous beds and fruit and vegetable gardens. Last but not least many gardens include sculptures. Not all gardens are wheelchair accessible.

3 ASHLEY

Low Road, Church Lench, Evesham, WR11 4UH. Roy & Betty Bowron, 01386 871347, bettybowz@gmail.com. *6m N of Evesham. In centre of Church Lench take Low Rd N at junction with Main Street. Ashley is 4th property on R.* **Visits by arrangement Apr to Aug groups max 12. Adm £3.50, chd free. Home-made teas.**

Sloping garden with steps down to lawn, garden pond with plants and fish. Mixed flower beds, greenhouse and vegetable garden. Large pergola with climbing roses, and shaded section with semi-exotic plants which incl tree ferns, other ferns, banana plants, etc. Plants on the large patio incl sago palms, bird of paradise (strelitzia), Hawaiian Palm, agaves and various other plants.

4 ASTLEY TOWNE HOUSE

Astley, DY13 0RH. Tim & Lesley Smith, www.astleytownehousesubtropicalgarden.co.uk. *3m W of Stourport-on-Severn. On B4196 Worcester to Bewdley Road.* **Sun 24 June, Sun 29 July, Sun 26, Mon 27 Aug (12.30-4.30). Adm £5, chd free. Home-made teas.**

2½ acres garden of a Grade II listed timber building (not open) incl sub-tropical planting. Stumpery garden with tree ferns and woodland temple. Mediterranean garden, tree house, revolving summerhouse and underground grotto with shell mosaics and water features. A recent addition is 'Mr McGregor's' vegetable garden. Featured on and in More4 All Gardens Great and Small, Daily Mail, Radio Times and Radio 2. Partial wheelchair access.

5 BADGE COURT

Purshull Green Lane, Elmbridge, Droitwich, WR9 0NJ. Stuart & Diana Glendenning, 01299 851216, dianaglendenning1@gmail.com. *5m N of Droitwich Spa. 2½m from J5 M5. Turn off A38 at Wychbold down side of the Swan Inn. Turn R into Berry Lane. Take next L into Cooksey Green Lane. Turn R into Purshull Green Lane. Garden is on L.* **Evening opening every Wed 1 May to 31 July (5.30-8.30). Adm £5, chd free. Visits also by arrangement May to July 10+ outside school hours.**

Tudor house (not open) set in over 2 acres of garden which includes a large pool, aquaponic fish tanks, topiary garden, rockery, orchard (with 16 varieties of apple trees) formal lawns and borders, large vegetable garden with soft fruits, aviary, greenhouses and terrace where teas are served. Also within the curtilage is the Garden House with cottage garden.

6 BARNARD'S GREEN HOUSE

Hastings Pool, Poolbrook Road, Malvern, WR14 3NQ. Mrs Sue Nicholls, 01684 574446. *1m E of Malvern. At junction of B4211 & B4208.* **Visits by arrangement Feb to Oct any number welcome. Adm £4, chd free. Light refreshments.**

With a magnificent backdrop of the Malvern Hills, this 1½ acre old-fashioned garden is a plantsman's paradise. The main feature is a magnificent cedar. 3 herbaceous and 2 shrub borders, rose garden, red and white and yellow borders, an evergreen and hydrangea bed,

2 rockeries, pond, sculptures and vegetable garden. Good garden colour throughout the year. Was the home of Charles Hastings - founder of the British Medical Association (1794-1866). Dogs on leads.

7 THE BARTON

Berrow Green, Martley, WR6 6PL. David & Vanessa Piggott, 01886 822148, v.piggott@btinternet.com. *1m S of Martley. On B4197 between Martley & A44 at Knightwick, corner of lane to Broadheath. Parking at Admiral Rodney Pub opp.* **Sat 2, Sun 3 June (1-5). Adm £4, chd free. Home-made teas. Visits also by arrangement in June groups of between 10 & 20.**

This ½ acre cottagey garden full of colour and texture contains unusual shrubs and billowing herbaceous planting. Paths wind through colour-themed gardens, gravel and grass beds. Roses, clematis and unusual climbers decorate pergolas and trellises. Terracotta-decorated walls enclose a vegetable plot and new tender bed. Visitors comments 'Best private garden I've seen.' ' So unusual and beautiful.'. Book sale. Featured in Garden News.

8 5 BECKETT DRIVE

Northwick, Worcester, WR3 7BZ. Jacki & Pete Ager, 01905 451108, agers@outlook.com. *1½m N of Worcester city centre. Cul-de-sac off A449 Ombersley Rd directly opp Grantham's Autocare, 1m S of Claines r'about on A449.* **Thur 24 May (2-5). Adm £3, chd free. Home-made teas. Evening opening Wed 1 Aug (6-9). Adm £4, chd free. Wine. Opening with North Worcester Gardens on Sat 7, Sun 8 July. Visits also by arrangement May to July groups or societies between 10 & 30.**

An extraordinary town garden on the northern edge of Worcester packed with different plants and year-round interest guaranteed to give visitors ideas and inspiration for their own gardens. Over the past 14 years visitors have enjoyed the unique and surprising features of this garden which has many planting schemes for a variety of situations. Plants at bargain prices and delicious home-made teas.

9 BIRTSMORTON COURT

Birtsmorton, nr Malvern, WR13 6JS. Mr & Mrs N G K Dawes. *7m E of Ledbury. Off A438 Ledbury/Tewkesbury rd.* **Sun 10 June (2-6). Adm £6, chd free. Home-made teas.**

10 acre garden surrounding beautiful medieval moated manor house (not open). White garden, built and planted in 1997 surrounded on all sides by old topiary. Potager, vegetable garden and working greenhouses, all beautifully maintained. Rare double working moat and waterways including Westminster Pool laid down in Henry VII's reign to mark the consecration of the knave of Westminster Abbey. Ancient yew tree under which Cardinal Wolsey reputedly slept in the legend of the Shadow of the Ragged Stone. No dogs.

10 BRIDGES STONE MILL

Alfrick Pound, WR6 5HR. Sir Michael & Lady Perry. *6m NW of Malvern. A4103 from Worcester to Bransford r'about, then Suckley Rd for 3m to Alfrick Pound.* **Sun 15 Apr (2-5.30). Adm £6, chd free. Home-made teas.**

Once a cherry orchard adjoining the mainly C19 flour mill, this is now a 2½ acre all-year-round garden laid out with trees, shrubs, mixed beds and borders. The garden is bounded by a stretch of Leigh Brook (an SSSI), from which the mill's own weir feeds a mill leat and small lake. A newly completed traditional Japanese garden and an ornamental vegetable 'potager' complete the scene. Wheelchair access by car to courtyard.

11 BROCKAMIN

Old Hills, Callow End, Worcester, WR2 4TQ. Margaret Stone, 01905 830370, stone.brockamin@btinternet.com. *5m S of Worcester. ½m S of Callow End on the B4424, on an unfenced bend, turn R into the car-park signed Old Hills. Walk towards the houses keeping R.* **Sun 11 Feb (11-4). Light refreshments. Sun 18 Mar, Sun 27 May, Sun 23 Sept (2-5). Home-made teas. Adm £3, chd free. Visits also by arrangement Feb to Oct for groups of 10+.**

An informal 1½ acre garden adjacent to common land. Mixed borders contain a wide variety of hardy perennials, including Plant Heritage National Collections of Symphyotrichum (Aster) novae-angliae and some Hardy Geraniums. Flowering starts with spring bulbs, including a collection of snowdrops. There is a seasonal pond and kitchen garden. The garden also contains a good collection of Pulmonarias. An access path reaches a large part of the garden.

NPC

12 BYLANE

Worcester Road, Earls Croome, WR8 9DA. Shirley & Fred Bloxsome. *1m N of Upton on Severn turning. On main A38 directly past Earls Croome Garden Centre, signed Bridle Way. Directly behind Earls Croome Garden Centre, turn down bridle way to park.* **Sun 8 Apr, Sun 27 May, Sun 1 July, Sun 2 Sept (1-5). Adm £3, chd free. Light refreshments.**

Herbaceous garden, paddock with wildlife pond, vegetable garden, and chickens, wood with mature trees and bluebells. Approximatley 2 acres in all. Plenty of seating areas and shelter if needed, very quiet and secluded.

Your visit helps fund 389 Marie Curie Nurses

13 1 CHURCH COTTAGE

Church Road, Defford, Worcester, WR8 9BJ. John Taylor & Ann Sheppard, 01386 750863, ann98sheppard@btinternet.com. *3m SW of Pershore. A4104 Pershore to Upton rd, turn into Harpley Rd, Defford, black & white cottage at side of church. Parking in village hall car park.* **Sun 6, Mon 7, Sun 27, Mon 28 May, Sun 26, Mon 27 Aug (11-5). Adm £3.50, chd free. Home-made teas. Visits also by arrangement Apr to Aug groups of 10 - 30.**

True countryman's ⅓ acre garden. Interesting layout. Japanese - style feature with 'dragons den'. Specimen trees; water features; perennial garden, vegetable garden; poultry and cider making. New small stream side bog garden. Wheelchair access to most areas.

14 CONDERTON MANOR

Conderton, nr Tewkesbury, GL20 7PR. Mr & Mrs W Carr, 01386 725389, carrs@conderton.com. *5½m NE of Tewkesbury. From M5 - A46 to Beckford - L for Overbury/Conderton. From Tewkesbury B4079 to Bredon - then follow signs to Overbury. Conderton from B4077 follow A46 directions from Teddington r'about.* **Visits by arrangement Mar to Nov individuals and groups welcome. 30 max. Light refreshments. Coffee and biscuits in the morning. Tea and biscuits/cakes in the afternoon Wine and snacks in the evening..**

7 acre garden, recently replanted in a contemporary style with magnificent views of Cotswolds. Flowering cherries and bulbs in spring. Formal terrace with clipped box parterre; huge rose and clematis arches, mixed borders of roses and herbaceous plants, bog bank and quarry garden. Many unusual trees and shrubs make this a garden to visit at all seasons. Visitors are particularly encouraged to come in spring and autumn. This is a garden/small arboretum of particular interest for tree lovers. The views towards the Cotswolds are spectacular and it provides a peaceful walk of about an hour. Some gravel paths and steps - no disabled WC.

15 THE COTTAGE, 3 CRUMPFIELDS LANE

Webheath, Redditch, B97 5PN. Victor Johnson, pjohnson889@btinternet.com. *From A448 through Redditch take slip rds signed to Headless Cross, at r'about take 3rd exit then follow NGS signs.* **Sat 23 June (10.30-5); Sun 24 June (11-4). Adm £5, chd free. Tea/coffee, cakes and soft drinks. Visits also by arrangement June & July for groups from 2 to 20.**

Established in 2012/13 a 1½- acre garden landscaped to provide 5 rooms on 4 levels stepped into a hillside. From the 2nd level are stunning views over Vale of Evesham. 2 water features, (1 in a cave) and places to sit and enjoy the wildlife. Wonderland can be found in meadow area of wild flowers. Most paths and steps have a handrail. Partial wheelchair access to levels 2 and 3 are accessible with able body escort (help available).

16 COWLEIGH LODGE

16 Cowleigh Bank, Malvern, WR14 1QP. Jane & Mic Schuster, 01684 439054, dalyan@hotmail.co.uk. *7m SW from Worcester, on the slopes of the Malvern Hills. From Worcester or Ledbury follow the A449 to Link Top. Take North Malvern Rd (behind Holy Trinity church), follow yellow signs. From Hereford take B4219 after Storridge church, follow yellow signs.* **Sun 24 June, Sun 29 July (11-5). Adm £4, chd free. Home-made teas. Visits also by arrangement June & July min 10, max 30.**

Just under an acre, the garden is on the slopes of the Malvern Hills and has been described by one visitor as 'quirky'! Formal rose garden, grass beds, bamboo walk, colour themed beds, nature path leading to a pond. Large vegetable plot and orchard with 'Michaels Mount' viewing platform overlooking the Severn Valley. Explore the poly tunnel and then relax with a cuppa and slice of homemade cake. This is the fourth year of opening of a developing and expanding garden - visitors from previous years will be able to see the difference! Lots of added interest with staddle stones, troughs, signs and other interesting artefacts. Slopes and steps throughout the garden. WC and refreshments.

17 24 CROFT BANK

Malvern, WR14 4DU. Andy & Cathy Adams, 01684 899405, andrewadams2005@yahoo.co.uk. *From Worcester on A449 to Gt Malvern. R onto B4232 signed Bromyard & West Malvern. Continue approx 1½m. Turn R at Elim College Conference centre onto Croft Bank. No 24 is on R.* **Sat 30 June, Sun 1 July (11-5). Adm £3.50, chd free. Home-made teas. Visits also by arrangement Apr to Aug open for groups and individuals (max 30).**

This half acre garden enjoys wonderful far reaching south and westerly views from high on the Malvern Hills. It continues to evolve with new projects each year. There are colourful flower borders for all seasons, vegetable beds, a small woodland area and bog garden as well as a studio containing artwork inspired by its surroundings. There are places to sit in sun, shade and shelter. This years new project is to construct a new gazebo. Come and see how it is coming along. Sloping areas and woodland walk not suitable for wheelchairs. Some steps.

18 DAVID'S GARDEN

Badgers Way, Ash Lane, Martin Hussingtree, Worcester, WR3 8TB. Sarah & David Beauchamp, 01905 340104, davidsnurseries0@tiscali.co.uk. *Parking at David's Nurseries, Martin Hussingtree & follow yellow signs from car park.* **Sun 24 June, Sun 15 July (11-4). Adm £4.50, chd free. Home-made teas. Visits also by arrangement June & July**

for groups of 10+.
After retiring from running the Garden Centre, David and Sarah followed their passion for plants dividing their garden into areas each with its own unique style and planting incl secluded fairy garden, romantic folly garden, beach garden and wildlife pond, herbaceous borders, vegetable garden, Potager and greenhouses with a collection of Streptocarpus. Japanese inspired garden and prairie are new additions. This 1½ acre garden has been created from scratch over the last 3 years. A viewing platform and Jungle Garden were added in 2017 and work is now underway to transform ½ acre of scrub land into a haven for birds, insects and bees. Most areas of the garden are wheelchair friendly.

19 THE DELL HOUSE

2 Green Lane, Malvern Wells, WR14 4HU. Kevin & Elizabeth Rolph, 01684 564448, stay@thedellhouse.co.uk, www.thedellhouse.co.uk. *2m S of Great Malvern. Behind former church on corner of Wells Rd & Green Lane just north of petrol station on A449 Wells Rd. Beware satnavs and Google often get incorrect location from postcode.* **Visits by arrangement Mar to Nov adm £4, child free. Individuals or groups up to 20. Combined adm with 223 Wells Road [200 yds] £7. Light refreshments.**
Two acre wooded hillside garden of the 1820s Dell House, a former rectory now a B&B. In the latter stages of recovery by new owners. Peaceful and natural, the garden contains many magnificent specimen trees including a Wellingtonia Redwood. Informal in style with spectacular tree carvings, meandering bark paths, historic garden buildings, garden railway and a paved terrace with distant views. The garden contains several tree carvings by Steve Elsby, and a variety of other sculptures by various artists. Wheelchair access limited. Parking is on gravel. Sloping bark paths, some quite steep.

20 6 DINGLE END

Inkberrow, Worcester, WR7 4EY. Mr & Mrs Glenn & Gabriel Allison, 01386 792039. *12m E of Worcester. A422 from Worcester. At the 30 sign in Inkberrow turn R down Appletree Lane then 1st L up Pepper St. Dingle End is 4th on R of Pepper St. Limited parking in Dingle End but street parking on Pepper St.* **Sat 8 Sept (11-5). Adm £3, chd free. Home-made teas. Visits also by arrangement Apr to Sept groups min 6, max 26.**
Over 1 acre garden with formal area close to the house opening into a flat area featuring a large pond, stream and weir with apple orchard and woodland area. Large vegetable garden incl an interesting variety of fruits. Garden designed for wildlife. Ducks, giant redwood tree. Refreshments for pre arranged groups can be tailored by arrangement e.g. soup and sandwiches, tea and cakes etc. Wheelchair access - slopes alongside every terrace.

GROUP OPENING

22 ECKINGTON GARDENS

Brook House, Manor Rd, Eckington, WR10 3BH. Group Coordinator Lynn Glaze, 01386 751924, lynnglaze@cmail.co.uk. *4 gardens - 1 in Manor Rd, 2 in or close to New Rd/ Nafford Rd, 3rd 1m out on Nafford Rd. A4104 Pershore to Upton & Defford, L turn B4080 to Eckington. In centre, by war memorial turn R for Brook House & L for other gardens.* **Sat 9, Sun 10 June (11-5). Combined adm £6, chd free. Home-made teas at Brook House on Saturday; at Nafford House on Sunday. Visits also by arrangement May to Sept could be all or some of the gardens depending on dates/ availability. Price will reflect availability.**

BROOK HOUSE
George & Lynn Glaze.

HILLTOP
Richard & Margaret Bateman.

MANTOFT
Mr & Mrs M J Tupper.

NAFFORD HOUSE
Janet & John Wheatley.

4 very diverse gardens; cottage garden and koi fish pond; formal walled garden; hilltop garden with' windows' in formal hedging and natural wooded garden sloping down to the riverside. Set in/close to lovely village of Eckington with riverside parking and picnic site. Brook House - acre of cottage style planting with koi carp pond and new summer house/patio area. Mantoft - formal walled garden with fish pond, topiary and dew pond, with ducks and geese. Hedges and stone paths, gazebo overlooking garden and new dovecote. Hilltop - 1 acre with sunken garden/ pond, rose garden, herbaceous borders and formal hedging with 'windows' and views over extensive countryside. Nafford House - 2 acre mature natural garden/ wood with slopes to River Avon, formal gardens around the house and magnificent wisteria. Mantoft featured in Cotswold Life. Some wheelchair access issues at all gardens esp. Nafford House - see NGS website for details.

The River School, Worcestershire

23 ◆ HANBURY HALL & GARDENS

School Road, Hanbury, Droitwich, WR9 7EA. National Trust, 01527 821214, hanburyhall@nationaltrust.org.uk, www.nationaltrust.org.uk/hanburyhall. *4m E of Droitwich. From M5 exit 5 follow A38 to Droitwich; from Droitwich 4m along B4090.* **For NGS: Sat 9, Sun 10 June (10-5). Adm £12.60, chd £6.30.** For other opening times and information, please phone, email or visit garden website.

The early eighteenth century gardens and park at Hanbury Hall are a rare example of the work of Royal Designer, George London. The pre-eminent Gardener of his time, his creations provided soothing, order in a chaotic world and initiated the later English Landscape Movement. Servants Hall Tea-Room - hot lunches, tea and cake. Stableyard Cafe for take away snacks and drinks. Chambers Tea-Room for traditional afternoon tea. Buggy available to bring visitors from the car park to the front of the property and wheelchairs are available to borrow from the house.

♿ ✿ 🚌 ☕

GROUP OPENING

24 HANLEY SWAN NGS GARDENS

Hanley Swan, Worcester, WR8 0DJ. Group Co-ordinator Brian Skeys, 01684 311297, brimfields@icloud.com. *5m E of Malvern, 3m NW of Upton upon Severn, 9m S of Worcester & M5. From Worcester/Callow End take B4424 to Hanley Castle then turn R. From Upton upon Severn B4211 to Hanley Castle turn L. From Malvern/Ledbury from A449 take B4209. Signed from village Xrds.* **Sat 9, Sun 10 June (1-5). Combined adm £6, chd free. Cream teas at 19 Winnington Gardens. Visits also by arrangement June to Sept for groups of 10-30. Number of gardens depends on availability which price will reflect.**

CHASEWOOD
Mrs Sydney Harrison, 01684 310527, Sydneyharrison@btinternet.com.
🛏

MEADOW BANK
Mrs Lesley Stroud & Mr Dave Horrobin, 01684 310917, Dave@meadowbankhs.freeserve.co.uk.
🛏

THE PADDOCKS
Mr & Mrs N Fowler.

19 WINNINGTON GARDENS
Brian & Irene Skeys, 01684311297, brimfields@icloud.com. **Visits also by arrangement May to Sept individual up to 10 please contact one week before.**

20 WINNINGTON GARDENS
Mr & Mrs Pete & Tina Sauntson.

NEW **YEW TREE COTTAGE**
Mr & Mrs David & Margaret Read.

6 gardens different in style in Hanley Swan. Chasewood has lavender and old fashioned roses. A gravel garden with an Iris and Thyme walk. A collection of Bonsai and Coach Built Prams. Yew Tree Cottage is a C17 cottage within a cottage garden, with a vegetable garden at the rear. Meadow Bank, a modern interpretation of a cottage garden, with a hot border, Dahlias grown for show, Iris and Auriculas. The Paddocks is a wildlife garden with ponds, a tadpole nursery, mixed borders, cacti and succulents. Developed since 2011 when their son 'gave them back the football pitch' and a curved patio was built, 20 Winnington Gardens has an octagonal greenhouse, water features and decorative details with colourful beds and planters providing year round colour. 19 Winnington Gardens is a garden of rooms. Mixed borders enclosed with climbing roses, a small oriental garden, fruit trees, raised herb bed with a special standard gooseberry bush and a collection of vintage garden tools. Entrance tickets from Chasewood. Four gardens access too narrow for wheelchairs and mobility scooters. One with access and one partial access with gravel paths.

✿ ☕

26 ◆ HARVINGTON HALL

Harvington, Kidderminster, DY10 4LR. The Roman Catholic Archdiocese of Birmingham, 01562 777846, harvingtonhall@btconnect.com, www.harvingtonhall.com. *3m SE of Kidderminster. ½m E of A450 Birmingham to Worcester Rd & approx ½m N of A448 from Kidderminster to Bromsgrove.* **For NGS: Sat 30 June, Sun 1 July (11.30-5). Adm £3.50, chd £1.50. Light refreshments.** For other opening times and information, please phone, email or visit garden website.

Romantic Elizabethan moated manor house with charming walled gardens and a small Elizabethan-style herb garden, all tended by volunteers. Tours of the Hall, which contain secret hiding places and rare wall paintings, are also available. Visitor Centre, Tea Room serving light lunches, homemade cakes, and hot and cold beverages, shop and WC. Wheelchair access to gardens and ground floor of Malt House Visitor Centre.

♿ ✿ 🚌 ☕

27 HEWELL GRANGE

Hewell Lane, Tardebigge, Redditch, B97 6QS. HMP Hewell. *2m NW of Redditch. HMP Hewell is situated on B4096. For SatNav use B97 6QQ. Follow signs to Grange Resettlement Unit. Visitors must book in advance via email (address below). This is a prison with booking and security procedures to be followed.* **Sat 5, Sun 6 May (9.30-4). Adm £5, chd free. Home-made teas. Visitors must be pre booked by email to roy.jones01@hmps.gsi.gov.uk before arrival, No booking will result in no entry as this is a working Prison.**

C18 landscape park and lake by

Lancelot Brown, modified c1812 by Humphery Repton. Blubells, lake and Repton bridge, formal garden, water tower, rock garden and mature woodland. Not a flower garden. Visitors will be escorted in small groups. Tour may be over 60 mins and visitors must be able to walk for this length of time. Uneven surfaces so sensible walking footwear is essential. Lakeside walk and bluebell walk a chance to see a historic garden not normally open to the public. Please Note - All visits have to have been booked prior to date for security reasons. There is no wheelchair access to the Gardens.

28 47 HIGH STREET

Bewdley, DY12 2DJ. Simon & Penny Smith, 07850 089988, simon@rhwork.co.uk. *In centre of Bewdley. No parking at premises - public parking in either Dog Lane or Gardners Meadow car parks within 500 yards of the property.* **Evening opening Wed 13 June, Wed 18 July, Wed 15 Aug (6-9). Adm £3.50, chd free. Wine. Adm incl one free glass of locally produced beer or wine (or a soft drink if preferred) and a range of olives & snacks. Visits also by arrangement May to Sept visitors are welcome by prior arrangement individually or in groups up to 20.**

This small garden is to the rear of a listed town house, only 120 ft long. The owners have tried to use every inch of space to create outside living space and maximum summer long interest. Intensively planted mixed borders link the house, with its hosta bed, wall mounted planters and hot garden specimens, to a contemporary designed upper terrace with summerhouse, pizza oven and copper lined rills. Attached at the rear of the garden is one of only a handful of air raid shelters still in existence in the area.

29 HIRAETH

30 Showell Road, Droitwich, WR9 8UY. Sue & John Fletcher, 07752 717243 or 01905 778390, sueandjohn99@yahoo.com. *1m S of Droitwich. On The Ridings estate. Turn off A38 r'about into Addyes Way, 2nd R into Showell Rd, 500yds on R. Follow the yellow signs!* **Sun 29 Apr, Sun 17 June, Sun 22 July (2-5). Adm £3.50, chd free. Home-made teas. Visits also by arrangement Apr to Sept for groups of 10-30.**

Third acre gardens, front, rear contain many plant species, cottage, herbaceous, hostas, ferns, 300yr old Olive Tree, pool, waterfall, oak sculptures, metal animals etc inc giraffes, elephant, birds. An oasis of colours in a garden not to be missed described by visitor as 'A haven on the way to Heaven'. Excellent tea, coffee, cold drinks, home-made cakes and scones served with china cups, saucers, plates, tea-pots and coffee-pots - silver service! Partial wheelchair access.

30 ◆ LITTLE MALVERN COURT

Little Malvern, WR14 4JN. Mrs T M Berington, 01684 892988, littlemalverncourt@hotmail.com, www.littlemalverncourt.co.uk. *3m S of Malvern. On A4104 S of junction with A449.* **For NGS: Every Fri 9 Mar to 23 Mar (2-5). Adm £5, chd free. Mon 7 May (2-5). Adm £7, chd £1. Tea & biscuits available in March. Homemade teas May BH.** For other opening times and information, please phone, email or visit garden website.

10 acres attached to former Benedictine Priory, magnificent views over Severn valley. Garden rooms and terrace around house designed and planted in early 1980s; chain of lakes; wide variety of spring bulbs, flowering trees and shrubs. Notable collection of old-fashioned roses. Topiary hedge and fine trees. The May Bank Holiday - Flower Festival in the Priory Church. Partial wheelchair access.

31 THE LODGE

off Holmes Lane, Dodderhill Common, Hanbury, Bromsgrove, B60 4AU. Mark & Lesley Jackson, 07860 794736, mnljack@aol.com. *1m N of Hanbury Village. 3½m E from M5 J5, on A38 at the Hanbury Turn Xrds, take A4091 S towards Hanbury. After 2½m turn L into Holmes Lane, then IMMEDIATE L again into dirt track. Car Park (Worcs Woodland Trust) on L.* **Sat 30 June, Sun 1 July (11-4). Adm £3, chd free. Home-made teas, cake, coffee, soft drinks served 11am - 4pm. Visits also by arrangement June to Aug refreshments available by prior arrangement.**

A one and half acre garden attached to a part C16 black and white house (not open) with 3 lawned areas, new traditional greenhouse, various beds plus stunning views from Dodderhill Common over the North Worcestershire countryside. Small display of classic cars plus other cars of interest. Garden is wheelchair accessible, disabled parking within grounds, toilets not wheelchair accessible. No dogs.

32 NEW LONG HYDE HOUSE

Long Hyde Road, South Littleton, Evesham, WR11 8TH. David & Linda Lamb, 01386 834697. *From the Badsey r'about on A46, follow B4035 towards Bretforton, then L on B4085 to The Littletons approx 1.7m. L onto Long Hyde Rd. Garden on L opp playing field.* **Sat 16, Sat 30 June (2-5.30). Adm £5, chd free. Cream teas. Visits also by arrangement in June.**

Beautiful 1 acre traditional garden in Vale of Evesham with stunning views of Cotswolds. Formal rose garden, clipped box hedging, herb garden with 2 ponds, large vegetable area, extensive borders, giant chess set with dark planting and variety of baskets and tubs. Honey locust tree dominates main lawn, raised patios and seating areas. Wide paths and disabled parking.

33 NEW LOVELLS VINEYARD

Garrett Bank, Welland, Malvern, WR13 6NF. Cathie Rolinson, www.lovellsvineyard.co.uk/garden. *4m from Upton Upon Severn; 4m from Great Malvern. In the centre of Welland Village. At the Xrds in village on B4208 parallel to the Malvern Hills.* **Mon 23 Apr, Mon 25 June, Mon 24 Sept (11-3.30). Adm £4.50, chd free. Refreshments available will be tea/coffee and cake or a wine tasting.**

Long drive with Scotch Pines leads to 3 acres of garden and small wooded area with mature trees. Garden mostly lawns with small fruit orchard, borders and vegetable plot plus nine acres of established vineyard with red and white grapes. House (not open) dates to 1700's. Vineyard produces award-winning white, rose and sparkling wines which are available for sale. Visitors will be offered either tea/coffee and cake/biscuit or a chance to taste one of the wines. Gravel on drive but rest of gardens grass, no steps apart from one step into barn/shop area. Friendly dogs on leads welcome.

♿ 🐕 ☕

GROUP OPENING

34 MARLBROOK GARDENS

Braces Lane, Marlbrook, Bromsgrove, B60 1DY. Group Co-ordinator Alan Nokes, 0121 445 5520, alan.nokes@ngs.org.uk. *2m N of Bromsgrove. 1m N of M42 J1, follow B4096 signed Rednal, turn L at Xrds into Braces Lane. 1m S of M5 J4, follow A38 signed Bromsgrove, turn L at T-lights into Braces Lane. Parking available.* **Sun 12 Aug (1.30-5.30). Combined adm £5, chd free. Home made Teas in both gardens. Visits also by arrangement July & Sept for groups of 10+ Viewing for one or both gardens. Oak Tree House will also open during May & June.**

OAK TREE HOUSE
Di & Dave Morgan.
(See separate entry)

ROUND HILL GARDEN
Lynn & Alan Nokes, www.roundhillgarden.weebly.com.
Visits also by arrangement July to Sept, groups of 10+

Two unique and stunning gardens, each have opened individually in their own right. Experience the contrasting styles, Round Hill Garden a traditional garden with a twist into the exotic and unusual. Rear garden divided into four distinct areas, Mediterranean, Patio/pond, Lawn with borders and islands and vegetable garden with raised beds and greenhouses. Oak Tree House a plantswoman's cottage garden with views over open fields. Past the twisted rail, through the arch leads to a garden packed full of shrubs and herbaceous planting with grass paths weaving in and out. Both gardens overflowing with plants for sun and shade, also ponds, water features, patios, artifacts and sculptures. Recognised for excellence, with many articles over the years published in national papers/gardening magazines. Continually evolving, many repeat visitors enjoy sharing with us their new discoveries. Art displays at both gardens by garden owners. Garden Quiz for children. Both gardens ideal for art groups. Round Hill Garden featured in Amateur Gardening, Garden News and short listed down to 12 gardens from over 2000 entries in Daily Mail National Garden competition.

✿ 🚌 ☕

35 74 MEADOW ROAD

Wythall, B47 6EQ. Joe Manchester, 01564 829589, joe@cogentscreenprint.co.uk. *4m E of Alvechurch. 2m N from J3 M42. On A435 at Becketts Farm r'about take rd signed Earlswood/Solihull. Approx 250 metres turn L into School Drive, then L into Meadow Rd.* **Visits by arrangement May to Aug. Adm £3, chd free. Light refreshments.**

Has been described one of the most unusual urban garden dedicated to woodland, shade-loving plants. 'Expect the unexpected' in a few tropical and foreign species. Meander through the garden under the majestic pine, eucalyptus and silver birch. Sit and enjoy the peaceful surroundings and see how many different ferns and hostas you can find.

✿ 🚌 ☕

36 MORTON HALL

Morton Hall Lane, Holberrow Green, Redditch, B96 6SJ. Mrs A Olivieri, www.mortonhallgardens.co.uk. *In the centre of Holberrow Green, at a wooden bench around a tree, turn up Morton Hall Lane. Follow the NGS signs to the gate opposite Morton Hall Farm.* **Sat 21 Apr, Sat 1 Sept (10-4). Adm £7, chd free.**

One of Worcestershire's best kept secrets. Perched atop an escarpment with breath taking views, hidden behind a tall hedge, lies a unique garden of outstanding beauty. A garden for all seasons, it features one of the country's largest fritillary spring meadows, sumptuous herbaceous summer borders, a striking potager, a majestic woodland rockery and an elegant Japanese Stroll Garden with tea house. For other garden openings please see website. Featured in English Garden Magazine, Gardens Illustrated, 2018, in preparation Country Life, 2018.

🚌

37 NEW HOUSE FARM, ELMBRIDGE

Elmbridge Lane, Elmbridge, WR9 0DA. Charles & Carlo Caddick, 01299 851249, Carlocaddick@hotmail.com. *2½m N of Droitwich Spa. A442 from Droitwich to Cutnall Green. Take lane opp Chequers Pub. Go 1m to T-junction. L towards Elmbridge Green/Elmbridge (past church & hall). At T-junction go R into Elmbridge Lane, garden on L.* **Sat 5, Sun 6 May, Sat 1, Sun 2 Sept (2-4.30). Adm £4, chd free.**

Home-made teas. Visits also by arrangement May to Sept.
This charming one acre garden surrounding an early C19 farm house (not open) has a wealth of rare trees and shrubs under planted with unusual bulbs and herbaceous plants. Special features are the topiary and perry wheel, natural pond, dry garden, rose garden, and small courtyard retreat. Exotics for sun and shade. Plants for sale.

GROUP OPENING

38 NEW NORTH WORCESTER GARDENS

5 Beckett Drive, Worcester, WR3 7BZ. Jacki & Pete Ager. *Northwick, Worcester. Two gardens, one at 5 Beckett Drive - 1½ m N of Worcester centre. Cul-de-sac off A449 Ombersley Rd & 1m S of Claines r'about on A449. Second at 10 Lucerne Close, WR3 7NA off Old Northwick Lane.* **Sat 7, Sun 8 July (2-5). Combined adm £4, chd free. Home-made teas. Homemade ice cream for sale at 5 Beckett Drive.**

5 BECKETT DRIVE
Jacki & Pete Ager.
(See separate entry)

NEW 10 LUCERNE CLOSE
Mark & Karen Askwith.

Two town gardens on the northern edge of Worcester both packed with a wide variety of plants. Roses are a speciality at Lucerne Close with unique landscaping enhancing the planting at Beckett Drive. These two gardens are guaranteed to give visitors ideas and inspiration. Plants at bargain prices and homemade ice cream at Beckett Drive and delicious home made cake and teas available at Lucerne Close.

39 OAK TREE HOUSE

504 Birmingham Road, Marlbrook, Bromsgrove, B61 0HS. Di & Dave Morgan, 0121 445 3595, meandi@btinternet.com. *On A38 midway between M42 J1 & M5 J4. When open individually park in old A38 - R fork 250 yds N of garden or small area in front of Marlbrook Pub car park 200 yds S.* **Evening opening Sat 12 May (5-9). Adm £4, chd free. Wine. Opening with Marlbrook Gardens on Sun 12 Aug. Visits also by arrangement May to Aug groups of 10+.**
Plantswoman's cottage garden overflowing with plants, pots and interesting artifacts. Secluded patio with plants and shrubs for Spring, small pond and waterfall. Plenty of seating, separate wildlife pond, water features, alpine area, rear open vista. Scented plants, hostas, dahlias and lilies. Conservatory with art by owners. Visitor HS said: "Such a wonderful peaceful oasis". Open as single garden by arrangement May/June and part of Marlbrook Gardens or as single garden July/Aug.

40 NEW 3 OAKHAMPTON ROAD

Stourport-On-Severn, DY13 0NR. Sandra & David Traynor. *Between Astley Cross & Kings Arms Public Houses. From Stourport follow A451 Dunley Rd towards Worcester. Approx 1600 yds turn L into Pearl Lane. Take 4th R into Red House Rd, past the Kings Arms Pub, and next L into Oakhampton Rd.* **Evening opening Sun 20 May, Thur 19 July, Tue 21 Aug, Wed 5 Sept (5-8.30). Adm £3.50, chd free. Wine.**
Beginning in March 2016 our plan was to put together a garden with a decidedly tropical feel to include palms from around the world, with tree ferns, bananas and as many other strange and unusual plants from warmer climes that would normally be considered difficult to grow here, as well as a pond and small waterfall. Not a large garden but you'll be surprised what can be done with a small space! Some narrow paths.

69 Birmingham Road, Alvechurch Gardens

GROUP OPENING

41 OFFENHAM GARDENS

Main Street, Offenham, WR11 8QD. *Approaching Offenham on B4510 from Evesham, L into village signed Offenham & ferry ¾m. Follow road round into village. Park in Village Hall car park opp Church. Walk to gardens from car park.* **Sat 4, Sun 5 Aug (11-5). Combined adm £5, chd free. Home-made teas.**

DECHMONT
Angela & Paul Gash.

FORGE HOUSE
Mr & Mrs Rob & Maggie Watts.

LANGDALE
Sheila & Adrian James, www.adrianjames.org.uk.

WILLOWAY
Stephen & Linda Pitts.

Offenham is a picturesque village in the heart of the Vale of Evesham, with thatched cottages and traditional maypole. Four gardens of diverse interests from traditional to plantsman and exotic. Langdale is a plant lover's garden designed for all year round interest. Surrounding a formal rill are relaxed borders in a variety of styles leading down to a productive vegetable garden and naturalistic planting. Willoway, an oasis of sound and colour, is initially hidden by the traditional front garden. A corridor of Hostas leads the visitor to the patio, an extensive Streptocarpus collection, a lush carpet of lawn and via a bamboo curtain to the oriental area. With a mature walnut tree Dechmont features box topiary, patio areas, year round interest from conifers, shrubs and acers, colour from bulbs, perennials, annuals, clematis and roses set within curved borders. Forge House is a newly created garden with exciting tropical exotics set amongst more traditional plants.

42 OVERBURY COURT

Overbury, GL20 7NP. Sir Bruce & Lady Bossom, 01386 725111(office), pa@overburyenterprises.co.uk. *5m NE of Tewkesbury. Village signed off A46. Turn off village rd beside the church. Park by the gates & walk up the drive.* **Visits by arrangement Mar to Oct for groups of 10+. Adm £4.50, chd free. No refreshments available on site.**

Georgian house 1740 (not open); landscaped garden of same date with stream and pools; daffodil bank and grotto. Plane trees, yew hedges; shrubs; cut flowers; coloured foliage; gold and silver, shrub rose borders. Norman church adjoins garden. Close to Whitcombe and Conderton Manor. Some slopes, while all the garden can be viewed, parts are not accessible to wheelchairs.

43 PEAR TREE COTTAGE

Witton Hill, Wichenford, Worcester, WR6 6YX. Pamela & Alistair Thompson, 01886 888295, peartree.pam@gmail.com, www.peartreecottage.me. *13m NW of Worcester & 2m NE of Martley. From Martley, take B4197. Turn R into Horn Lane then take 2nd L signed Witton Hill. Keep L & Pear Tree Cottage is on R at top of hill.* **Sun 3 June (12-6.30); Sun 26 Aug (2-10). Adm £5, chd free. Home-made teas. Wine served after 6pm in Aug. Visits also by arrangement May to Aug all visitors in any numbers are always VERY welcome. Please call first.**

A Grade II listed black and white cottage (not open) SW-facing gardens and far reaching views across orchards to Abberley Clock Tower. The ¾ acre gardens comprise of gently sloping lawns with mixed and woodland borders, shade and plenty of strategically placed seating. The garden exudes a quirky and humorous character with the odd surprise and even includes a Shed of the Year Runner Up 2017! 'Garden by Twilight' evenings are very popular. Trees, shrubs and sculptures are softly uplit and the garden is filled with 100's of candles and nightlights (weather permitting!) Visitors are invited to listen to the owls and watch the bats whilst enjoying a glass of wine. Featured on TV's Channel 4, and in local society magazines, gardening journals and many newspapers both national and local. Partial wheelchair access.

GROUP OPENING

44 PERSHORE GARDENS

Pershore, WR10 1BG. Group Co-ordinator Jan Garratt, www.visitpershore.co.uk. *On B4084 between Worcester & Evesham, & 6m from exit 7 on M5. There is also a train station to the north of the town.* **Sat 2, Sun 3 June (1-5). Combined adm £5, chd free.**

Each year about twenty gardens open in Pershore. This small town has been opening gardens as part of the NGS for 50 years, almost continuously. In those days the open gardens were in the Georgian heart of the town but now, gardens open from all over the town. Some gardens are surprisingly large, well over an acre, while others are courtyard gardens. All have their individual appeal and present great variety. This keeps it fresh and interesting for returning visitors. The wealth of pubs, restaurants and cafes offer ample opportunities for refreshment while the Abbey and the River Avon are some of the many points of interest in this market town. Tickets with a map are valid for both days and are available in advance from the Tourist Information and 'Blue' in Broad Street and on the day at Number 8 Community Arts Centre in the High Street or any open garden. Refreshments available in PHs and cafes in the town. Wheelchair access to some gardens.

45 NEW REDWOOD

Cotheridge, Worcester, WR6 5LZ. Margaret & Max Pardoe. *3m W of Worcester. Take A44 from Worcester & follow signs for Bromyard & Leominster. ¼m beyond Laylock's Garden Centre turn L signed Cotheridge Church. Parking in field adjacent to the church.* **Sat 19, Sun 20 May (2-5). Adm £3.50, chd free. Home-made teas.**
Plant enthusiasts 1 acre garden overlooking lake, with lovely views. Garden with mature trees including a magnificent Wellingtonia Redwood with a 40ft girth. Numerous borders bursting with shrubs and a wide variety of hardy perennials to suit many growing conditions including dry shade and lakeside planting. Large selection of reasonably priced plants for sale including unusual perennials.

46 NEW THE RIVER SCHOOL-WORCESTER

Rose Bank, Claines, Worcester, WR3 7ST. Christian Education Trust-Worcester, 01905 454496, bill222saunders@btInternet.com, www.riverschool.co.uk. *2.4m N of Worcester City Centre. At J6 M5, take A449 signed for Kidderminster, turn off at 1st turning marked for Blackpole. Turn R to Fernhill Heath & at T-junction with A38 turn L. The school is ½m on R.* **Sat 7 Apr, Sat 11 Aug (9.30-5). Adm £5, chd free. Light refreshments in School Gym adjacent to the Walled Garden. Visits also by arrangement Mar to Oct for groups of 12+ outside school hours.**
Worcester's 'Heligan' - the lost Horticultural Teaching College garden that is being brought back to life. For 35 years after WW2 the site was known as Oakfield Teacher Training College for Horticulture. (OTTC-H) Such was its reputation that visitors came from 58 different countries and at least 8 other Horticultural Colleges were founded by people inspired by OTTC-H. The estate features a number of less common shrubs and trees as well as a forest school pond area.

47 ◆ RIVERSIDE GARDENS AT WEBBS

Wychbold, Droitwich, WR9 0DG. Webbs of Wychbold, 01527 860000, www.webbsdirect.co.uk. *2m N of Droitwich Spa. 1m N of M5 J5 on A38. Follow tourism signs from M5.* For opening times and information, please phone or visit garden website.
2½ acres. Themed gardens incl Colour spectrum, tropical and dry garden, Rose garden, vegetable garden area, seaside garden, bamboozelum, Contemplation and self sufficient Garden. New Wave gardens opened 2004, is home to our new hobbit house and includes natural seasonal interest with grasses and perennials. This area is also home to beehives which produce honey for our own food hall. The New Wave Garden was slightly changed over 2014 to become more of a natural wildlife area. There are willow wigwams made for children to play in. This area now incl a bird hide and new in 2016 the Hobbit house. Open all yr except Christmas, Boxing Day and Easter Sun. Our New Wave Gardens area has grass paths which are underlaid with mesh so people with heavy duty wheelchairs can be taken around.

48 ROTHBURY

5 St Peters Road, North Malvern, WR14 1QS. John Bryson, Philippa Lowe & David. *7m W of M5 J7 (Worcester). Turn off A449 Worcester to Ledbury Rd at B4503, signed Leigh Sinton. Almost immed take the middle rd (Hornyold Rd). St Peter's Rd is ¼m uphill, 2nd R.* **Mon 28 May (8.30-5); Sun 24 June, Sun 22 July (11-5). Adm £3, chd free. Light refreshments. Continental breakfast on 28 May 8.30am to 11am. All openings; fresh coffee, pots of tea, filled rolls, homemade cakes inc. gluten free, cream teas.**
Set on slopes of Malvern Hills, ⅓ acre plant-lovers' garden surrounding Arts and Crafts house (not open), created by owners since 1999. Herbaceous borders, rockery, wildlife pond, vegetables, small orchard, containers. Magnificent Eucryphia glutinosa in July. A series of hand-excavated terraces accessed by sloping paths and steps. Views and seats. Facebook: Rothbury NGS Garden. Partial wheelchair access. One very low step at entry, one standard step to main lawn and one to WC. Decking slope to top lawn.

49 SHUTTIFIELD COTTAGE

Birchwood, Storridge, WR13 5HA. Mr & Mrs David Judge, 01886 884243, judge.shutti@btinternet.com. *8m W of Worcester. Turn R off A4103 opp Storridge Church to Birchwood. After 1¼m L down steep tarmac drive. Please park on roadside at the top of the drive but drive down if walking is difficult (150 yards).* **Sat 28 Apr, Sat 12, Sun 13, Sat 26 May, Sat 9 June, Sat 11 Aug (1.30-5). Adm £5, chd free. Home-made teas. Visits also by arrangement Apr to Sept subject to the availability of the Owners, by email or telephone.**
Superb position and views. Unexpected 3-acre plantsman's garden, extensive herbaceous borders, primula and stump bed, many unusual trees, shrubs, perennials, colour-themed for all-yr interest. Walks in 20-acre wood with ponds, natural wild area. Anemones, bluebells, rhododendrons and azaleas are a particular spring feature. Large old rose garden with many spectacular climbers. Good garden colour throughout the yr. Small deer park, vegetable garden. Wildlife ponds, wild flowers and walks in 20 acres of ancient woodland. Some sloping lawns and steep paths in wooded area.

Perennial, supporting horticulturalists since 1839

50 ◆ SPETCHLEY PARK GARDENS

Spetchley, Worcester, WR5 1RS. Mr John Berkeley, 01905 345106, enquiries@spetchleygardens.co.uk, www.spetchleygardens.co.uk. *2m E of Worcester. On A44, follow brown signs.* **For NGS: Fri 30 Mar, Sun 1 July (11-6). Adm £7, chd £2.50. Light refreshments.** For other opening times and information, please phone, email or visit garden website.
Surrounded by glorious countryside lays one of Britain's best-kept secrets. Spetchley is a garden for all tastes and ages, containing one of the biggest private collections of plant varieties outside the major botanical gardens and weaving a magical trail for younger visitors. Spetchley is not a formal paradise of neatly manicured lawns or beds but rather a wondrous display of plants, shrubs and trees woven into a garden of many rooms and vistas. Plant sales, gift shop and tea room. Annual Specialist Plant Fair will be held on Sun 22 April. Gravel paths.

51 ◆ STONE HOUSE COTTAGE GARDENS

Church Lane, Stone, DY10 4BG. James & Louisa Arbuthnott, 07817 921146, louisa@shcn.co.uk, www.shcn.co.uk. *2m SE of Kidderminster. Via A448 towards Bromsgrove, next to church, turn up drive.* For opening times and information, please phone, email or visit garden website.
A beautiful and romantic walled garden adorned with unusual brick follies. This acclaimed garden is exuberantly planted and holds one of the largest collections of rare plants in the country. It acts as a shop window for the adjoining nursery. Open Wed to Sat late March to early Sept 10-5. Partial wheelchair access.

52 THE TYNINGS

Church Lane, Stoulton, Worcester, WR7 4RE. John & Leslie Bryant, 01905 840189, johnlesbryant@btinternet.com. *5m S of Worcester; 3m N of Pershore. On the B4084 (formerly A44) between M5 J7 & Pershore. The Tynings lies beyond the church at the extreme end of Church Lane. Ample parking.* **Visits by arrangement June to Sept. Adm £4, chd free. Light refreshments.**
Acclaimed plantsman's ½-acre garden, generously planted with a large selection of rare trees and shrubs. Features incl specialist collection of lilies, many unusual climbers and rare ferns. The colour continues into late summer with dahlia, berberis, euonymus and tree colour. Surprises around every corner. You will not be disappointed. Lovely views of adjacent Norman Church and surrounding countryside. Plants labelled and plant lists available. Featured in Garden News.

53 THE WALLED GARDEN

6 Rose Terrace, off Fort Royal Hill, Worcester, WR5 1BU. William & Julia Scott. *Close to the City centre. ½m from Cathedral. Via Fort Royal Hill, off London Rd (A44). Park on 1st section of Rose Terrace & walk the last 20yds down track.* **Sat 21, Wed 25 Apr (1-5). Adm £4, chd free. Tea.**
This C19 Walled Kitchen Garden, reawakened in 1995 is a peaceful oasis near the centre of Worcester. A tapestry of culinary and medicinal herbs, fruit of all sorts including medlar, mulberry and quince, vegetables and flowers are all grown organically. History is at the centre of the rescue and evolution of this enclosed garden. Featured in Kitchen Garden magazine.

54 223 WELLS ROAD

Malvern, WR14 4HF. Brian & Elaine Hitchens, 01684 897716, brianhitchens281@btinternet.com. *2½m S of Great Malvern. On A449 - shared drive with 225 Wells Road.* **Visits by arrangement Apr to Nov adm £4, child free. Groups up to 20 max. Combined adm with Dell House [200 yds] £7. Light refreshments.**
½ acre garden developed over the last five years on the eastern slope of the Malvern Hills. The front is closely planted with shade loving plants such as hostas together with camellias, magnolias rhododendrons and foliage plants such as tree ferns, palms, etc. The rear comprises lawns, mixed borders and small formal pool complex. It has scarce and tender shrubs and herbaceous perennials. Unsuitable for wheelchairs.

55 WESTACRES

Wolverhampton Road, Prestwood, Stourbridge, DY7 5AN. Mrs Joyce Williams, 01384 877496, Koijoy62@yahoo.co.uk. *3m W of Stourbridge. A449 in between Wall Heath (2m) & Kidderminster (6m). Ample parking Prestwood Nurseries (next door).* **Sat 14, Sun 15 July (11-4). Adm £4, chd free. Home-made teas. Visits also by arrangement June to Sept minimum 60 mins, max 4 hours. Min group 10 visitors.**
¾-acre plant collector's garden with unusual plants and many different varieties of acers, hostas, shrubs. Woodland walk, large koi pool. Covered tea area with home-made cakes. Come and see for yourselves, you won't be disappointed. Described by a visitor in the visitors book as 'A garden which we all wished we could have, at least once in our lifetime'. Garden is flat. Disabled parking.

56 NEW WHARF HOUSE

Newnham Bridge, Tenbury Wells, WR15 8NY. Gareth Compton & Matthew Bartlett. *Off the A456 in hamlet of Broombank, between Mamble & Newnham Bridge. Garden signed. Do not rely on SatNav.* **Sun 1 July (10-4). Adm £5, chd free. Home-made teas.**
A developing 2 acre country garden, set around an C18 house and out buildings (not open). Mixed herbaceous borders with some colour theming including 'hot' beds and yellow bed; white garden; double border; courtyards; stream, vegetable garden. The garden is on several levels, with very limited wheelchair

access and some uneven paths. Parking 600 yards from garden.

57 WHITCOMBE HOUSE

Overbury, Tewkesbury, GL20 7NZ. Faith & Anthony Hallett, 01386 725206, faith.hallett1@gmail.com. *9m S of Evesham, 5m NE Tewkesbury. Leave A46 at Beckford to Overbury (2m). Or B4080 from Tewkesbury through Bredon/Kemerton (5m). Or small lane signed Overbury at r'about junction A46, A435 & B4077. Approx 5m from J9 M5.* **Sun 6 May, Sun 3 June (2-5). Adm £4, chd free. Tea. Visits also by arrangement Apr to Sept and evening visits (with wine) also possible.**

A dramatic, alluring, classical English cottage garden. Wafting, changing colours on rainbow watch,framed over arch and bent against ubiquous stonewalls. Sit by the Captains bridge, near brook banked with primula, astilbe geranium. Pastel coloured borders with rose, potentilla, smilicinia, acers and shrubbery bits. Be led down the paths of dreams and themes: the joy of plant seekers! For easiest wheelchair access please contact us in advance for details.

58 WHITE COTTAGE & NURSERY

Earls Common Road, Stock Green, Inkberrow, B96 6SZ. Mr & Mrs S M Bates, 01386 792414, smandjbates@aol.com, whitecottage.garden. *2m W of Inkberrow, 2m E of Upton Snodsbury. A422 Worcester to Alcester, turn at sign for Stock Green by Red Hart Pub, 1½m to T-junction, turn L 500 yds on the L.* **Sun 8 Apr, Sun 6, Sun 27, Mon 28 May (11-4.30). Adm £3.50, chd free. Visits also by arrangement Apr to Sept groups and individuals welcome.**

2 acre garden with large herbaceous and shrub borders, island beds, stream and bog area. Spring meadow with 100's of snakes head fritillaries. Formal area with lily pond and circular rose garden. Alpine rockery and new fern area. Large collection of interesting trees incl Nyssa Sylvatica, Parrotia persica, and Acer 'October Glory' for magnificent Autumn colour and many others. Nursery open most Thursdays from 10.30-5pm please check. Gravel drive to the gate but it is manageable for wheelchair users.

59 ◆ WHITLENGE GARDENS

Whitlenge Lane, Hartlebury, DY10 4HD. Mr & Mrs K J Southall, 01299 250720, keith.southall@creativelandscapes.co.uk, www.whitlenge.co.uk. *5m S of Kidderminster, on A442. A449 Kidderminster to Worcester L at T-lights, A442 signed Droitwich, over island, ¼m, 1st R into Whitlenge Lane. Follow brown signs.* **For NGS: Sat 21, Sun 22 Apr, Sat 16, Sun 17 June, Sat 15, Sun 16 Sept (10-5). Adm £3.50, chd £1.50. Light refreshments in adacent tea rooms.** For other opening times and information, please phone, email or visit garden website.

3 acre show garden of a professional designer incorporating a large variety of trees, shrubs etc. features include a Twisted brick pillar pergola, Moongate as featured on TV, waterfalls, ponds and streams. Mystic features of the Green Man, 'Sword in the Stone' and cave fernery. Walk the turf labyrinth and take refreshments in The Garden 'Design Studio' tearoom. 2½ metre high curved reclaim brick and solid oak Moongate with 4 cascading waterfalls, deck walk through giant Gunnera leaves, Camomile paths through herb gardens, 400 sq metre grass labyrinth, play and pet corner. Locally sourced home-made food in tearoom, extensive plant nursery. mix of hard pathways, gravel pathways and lawn.

60 68 WINDSOR AVENUE

St Johns, Worcester, WR2 5NB. Roger & Barbara Parker. *W area of Worcester, W side of R Severn. Off the A44 to Bromyard. Into Comer Rd, 3rd L Into Laugherne Rd, 3rd L into Windsor Ave, at bottom in Cul-de-sac. Limited parking, please park courteously on road sides, car share if possible.* **Sun 27, Mon 28 May (1-5). Adm £4.50, chd free. Tea, cake and soft drinks also available.**

Almost one acre garden divided into three areas, situated behind a 1930's semi detached house in a cul-de-sac. Visitors are amazed and comment on size of garden and the tranquility! The garden includes bog gardens, flower beds, 'oriental' area, vegetable patch, five greenhouses and a Koi pond plus three other ponds each in very different styles. We also have chickens and Ornamental Pheasants. Gravel paths are everywhere.

61 WORRALLS MILL

Netherton Lane, Abberley, DY13 0UL. Mr & Mrs B J Merriman. *3m SW of Stourport-on-Severn. From Stourport on Severn take Gt Witley rd over R Severn. Continue to sign for Dunley on L, take 2nd turn on R Heightington tel box on corner, top of lane, turn L.* **Sat 23, Sun 24 June (11-5.30). Adm £5, chd free. Light refreshments. Tea, coffee and home-made cakes.**

Old water mill, brook runs through garden. Large trees, oak, ash, shrubs and red bridge at front of house. Back of house, terracing, hot bed, mixed borders, pergola to 'jungle', bamboo, fatsia etc. Fish pond; large pool (wildlife) in what was once mill race bog; garden stream; old woodland. Approx ¼m long, 2 acres. Partial wheelchair access, gravel paths and some steps.

Your visit helps the Queen's Nursing Institute to champion excellence in community nursing

YORKSHIRE

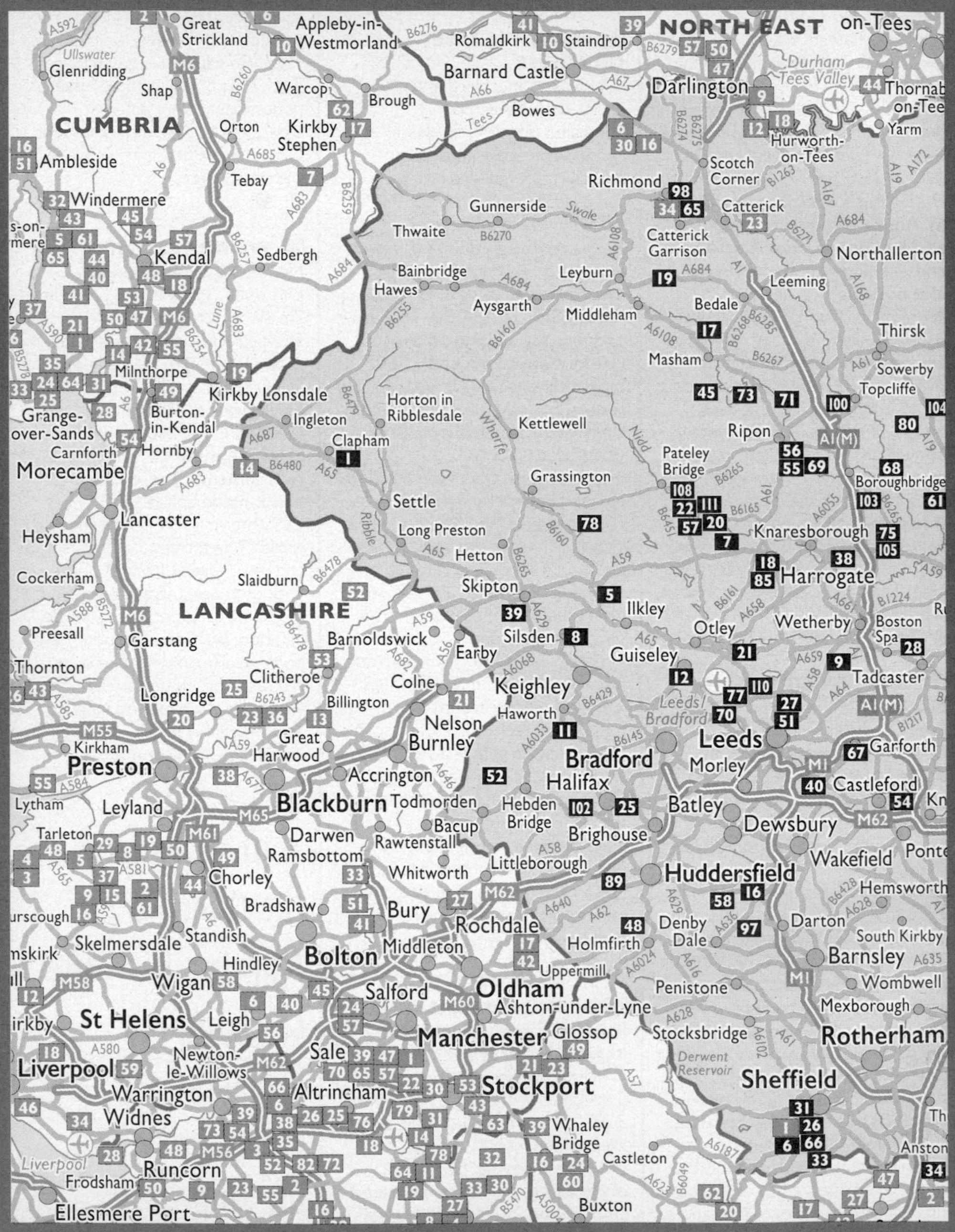

0 10 20 kilometres
0 10 miles
© Global Mapping / XYZ Maps
YORKSHIRE
LINCOLNSHIRE
Middlesbrough
Saltburn-by-the-Sea
Hinderwell
Guisborough
Sandsend
Whitby
Great Ayton
Stokesley
Danby
Sleights
Robin Hood's Bay
Goathland
Burniston
Scalby
Scarborough
West Ayton
Kirkbymoorside
Pickering
Eastfield
Helmsley
Snainton
Filey
Filey Bay
Oswaldkirk
Hunmanby
Hovingham
Brandsby
Malton
Norton
Flamborough Head
Flamborough
Easingwold
North Grimston
Bridlington
Sledmere
Langtoft
Burton Agnes
Bridlington Bay
Shipton
Stamford Bridge
Haxby
Fridaythorpe
Driffield
Skipsea
York
Bainton
Hutton Cranswick
Fulford
Pocklington
Hornsea
Hayton
Brandesburton
Market Weighton
Aldbrough
Cawood
Holme-on-Spalding-Moor
Beverley
Barlby
Bubwith
Cottingham
Bilton
Selby
North Cave
South Cave
Kingston upon Hull
Howden
Hedon
Withernsea
North Ferriby
Hessle
Snaith
Goole
Barton-upon-Humber
Patrington
Easington
Winterton
Thorne
Crowle
Scunthorpe
Immingham
Askern
Hatfield
Humberside
Grimsby
Spurn Head
Bentley
Bottesford
Cleethorpes
Epworth
Brigg
Laceby
Doncaster
Humberston
Waltham
Caistor
Robin Hood
Blyton
Kirton in Lindsey
North Somercotes
Bawtry
Ludborough
Maltby
Gainsborough
Binbrook
Market Rasen
Louth
Mablethorpe
Retford
Maltby le Marsh
Worksop
Dunholme
Alford
Newton on Trent
Saxilby
Wragby
Nettleham

Volunteers

County Organisers

East Yorks
Helen Marsden
01430 860222
jerryhelen@btinternet.com

North Yorks – Cleveland, Hambleton, Richmond, Rydale & Scarborough
Hugh Norton
01653 628604
hughnorton0@gmail.com

South & West Yorks & North Yorks - Craven, Harrogate, Selby & York
Bridget Marshall BEM
01423 330474
biddymarshall@btinternet.com

County Treasurer
Angela Pugh
01423 330456
amjopugh@clannet.co.uk

Publicity
Jane Cooper 01484 604232
jane.cooper@ngs.org.uk

Booklet Advertising
John Plant
01347 888125
plantjohnsgarden@btinternet.com

By Arrangement Visits
Penny Phillips
01937 834970
penny.phillips@ngs.org.uk

Clubs & Societies
Penny Phillips (as above)

Assistant County Organisers

East Yorks
Ian & Linda McGowan
01482 896492
adnil_magoo@yahoo.com

Hazel Rowe 01430 861439
hrowe@uwclub.net

Natalie Verow 01759 368444
natalieverow@aol.com

North Yorks
Gillian Mellor 01723 891636
gill.mellor@btconnect.com

Josephine Marks 01845 501626
carlton331@btinternet.com

Judi Smith 01765 688565
lowsutton@hotmail.co.uk

West & South Yorks
Deborah Bigley 01423 330727
debsandbobbigley@btinternet.com

Felicity Bowring 01729 823551
f.bowring@gmail.com

Veronica Brook 01423 340875
veronicabowring@me.com

Rosie Hamlin 01302 535135
rosiehamlin@aol.com

Jane Hudson 01924 840980
janehudson42@btinternet.com

© Clive Nicholls

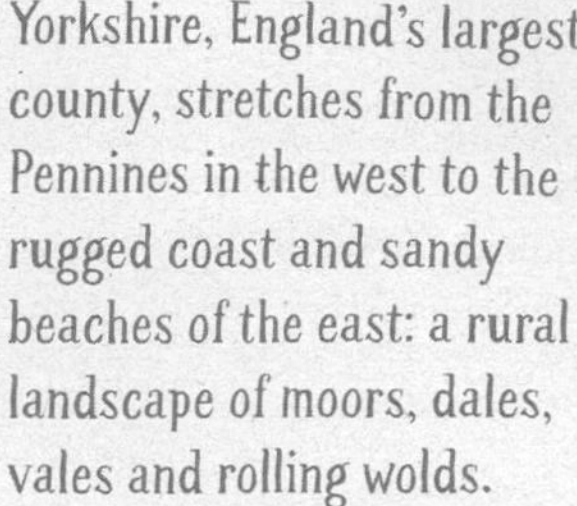

Yorkshire, England's largest county, stretches from the Pennines in the west to the rugged coast and sandy beaches of the east: a rural landscape of moors, dales, vales and rolling wolds.

Nestling on riverbanks lie many historic market towns, and in the deep valleys of the west and south others retain their 19th century industrial heritage of coal, steel and textiles.

The wealth generated by these industries supported the many great estates, houses and gardens throughout the county. From Hull in the east, a complex network of canals weaves its way across the county, connecting cities to the sea and beyond.

The Victorian spa town of Harrogate with the RHS garden at Harlow Carr, or the historic city of York with a minster encircled by Roman walls, are both ideal centres from which to explore the gardens and cultural heritage of the county.

We look forward to welcoming you to our private gardens - you will find that most of them open not only on a specific day, but also 'by arrangement' for groups and individuals - we can help you to get in touch.

Left: **Hunmanby Grange**

OPENING DATES

All entries subject to change. For latest information check **www.ngs.org.uk**

Extended openings are shown at the beginning of the month.

Map locator numbers are shown to the right of each garden name.

February

Snowdrop Festival

Sunday 18th
Devonshire Mill 24
Fawley House 32

Wednesday 21st
Austwick Hall 1

Sunday 25th
Bridge Farm House 10

March

Saturday 10th
NEW Primrose Bank Nursery 81

Sunday 11th
NEW Primrose Bank Nursery 81

Sunday 25th
◆ Constable Burton Hall Gardens 19

April

Sunday 8th
Clifton Castle 17
Ellerker House 29
Goldsborough Hall 38

Sunday 15th
Barnville 2

Sunday 22nd
The Circles Garden 16

Monday 30th
Himalayan Garden & Sculpture Park 45

May

Sunday 6th
Highfield Cottage 43
The Orchard 77
◆ RHS Garden Harlow Carr 85

Monday 7th
The Old Vicarage 75

Sunday 13th
Low Hall 57
◆ Stillingfleet Lodge 96
Warley House Garden 102
Woodlands Cottage 108

Wednesday 16th
Beacon Hill House 5
◆ Parcevall Hall Gardens 78
Warley House Garden 102

Sunday 20th
Fawley House 32
The Red House 83
Rustic Cottage 87
Scape Lodge 89
Tamarind 99

Wednesday 23rd
◆ Land Farm 52

Sunday 27th
Beacon Garth 4
Creskeld Hall 21
Highfield Cottage 43
◆ Jackson's Wold 50
Penny Piece Cottages 79
Rewela Cottage 84
1 School Lane 90
NEW 113 Southfield 95

June

Festival Weekend

Saturday 2nd
Hunmanby Grange 49
Old Sleningford Hall 73
Shiptonthorpe Gardens 92

Sunday 3rd
Brookfield 11
Clifton Castle 17
Ellerker Manor 30
Hunmanby Grange 49
Millrace Garden 67
◆ Norton Conyers 71
Old Sleningford Hall 73
Shiptonthorpe Gardens 92
NEW The Villa 101
◆ The Yorkshire Arboretum 112

Wednesday 6th
Well House 103
Whixley Gardens 105

Thursday 7th
Skipwith Hall 93

Friday 8th
◆ Shandy Hall Gardens 91

Wednesday 13th
NEW 39 The Drive 27
NEW Midendale 63
Pilmoor Cottages 80

Sunday 17th
◆ Dove Cottage Nursery Garden 25
NEW 3 Embankment Road 31
Glaramara 36
The Manor House 60
NEW Midendale 63
The Ridings 86
Rustic Cottage 87
Yorke House 111

Saturday 23rd
Linden Lodge 53
Omega 76

Sunday 24th
Birstwith Hall 7
34 Dover Road 26
Fernleigh 33
NEW Glencoe House 37
◆ Jackson's Wold 50
Linden Lodge 53
Omega 76
NEW Willow Cottage 107

Wednesday 27th
Sleightholmedale Lodge 94

Friday 29th
◆ Shandy Hall Gardens 91

Saturday 30th
Linden Lodge 53

July

Sunday 1st
3 Church Walk 15
Daneswell House 23
Havoc Hall 42
2 Hollin Close 46
Millgate House 65
Myton Grange 68
NEW The Old Vicarage 74
NEW Primrose Bank Nursery 81
Tamarind 99
Wyedale 109

Wednesday 4th
Brookfield 11
The Grange 39
Grasmere 40
◆ Land Farm 52

Saturday 7th
Cawood Gardens 13
Linden Lodge 53

Sunday 8th
NEW Briar Bank 9
Cawood Gardens 13
Dacre Banks & Summerbridge Gardens 22
NEW Honey Head 48
Millgate House 65
The Nursery 72

Wednesday 11th
Grasmere 40
The Nursery 72

Saturday 14th
Sue Proctor Plants Nursery Garden 97

Sunday 15th
NEW The Coach House 18
Queensgate & Kitchen Lane Allotments 82
Sue Proctor Plants Nursery Garden 97

Wednesday 18th
Grasmere 40

Friday 20th
Manor Farm 59

Sunday 22nd
Cow Close Cottage 20
◆ Dove Cottage Nursery Garden 25
Goldsborough Hall 38
54 Hollym Road 47
◆ Thornycroft 100

Wednesday 25th
Grasmere 40

Millgate House

© Susie White

Sunday 29th
NEW 90 Bents Road 6
Daneswell House 23
Grasmere 40
The Jungle Garden 51
Little Eden 54
Rewela Cottage 84

August

Wednesday 1st
◆ Land Farm 52
2 Newlay Grove 70

Thursday 2nd
Whyncrest 106

Friday 3rd
Whyncrest 106

Sunday 5th
14 Chellsway 14
Littlethorpe Gardens 55
NEW The Villa 101

Wednesday 8th
The Grange 39

Sunday 12th
NEW East Wing, Newton Kyme Hall 28
Millrace Garden 67
Sleightholmedale Lodge 94

Saturday 18th
Mansion Cottage 62

Sunday 19th
◆ Dove Cottage Nursery Garden 25
Little Eden 54
Mansion Cottage 62
Scape Lodge 89

Sunday 26th
Fernleigh 33
Pilmoor Cottages 80

September

Saturday 1st
Bramble Croft 8

Sunday 9th
Littlethorpe Manor 56

Sunday 16th
◆ Stillingfleet Lodge 96

February 2019

Sunday 17th
Fawley House 32

By Arrangement

Barnville 2
Basin Howe Farm 3
Birstwith Hall 7
Bramble Croft 8
Bridge Farm House 10
Butterfield Heights 12
Cawood Gardens 13
3 Church Walk 15
Cobble Cottage, Whixley Gardens 105
Cow Close Cottage 20
Dacre Banks & Summerbridge Gardens 22
Daneswell House 23
34 Dover Road 26
Ellerker Manor 30
Fawley House 32
Fernleigh 33
Firvale Allotment Garden 34
Friars Hill 35
NEW Glencoe House 37
The Grange 39
Grasmere 40
Greencroft, Littlethorpe Gardens 55
Greenwick Farm 41
Highfield Cottage 43
Hillside 44
The Jungle Garden 51
Linden Lodge 53
Little Eden 54
Littlethorpe Manor 56
Low Hall 57
Lower Crawshaw 58
The Manor House 61
Mansion Cottage 62
115 Millhouses Lane 66
The Nursery 72
The Old Vicarage 75
The Orchard 77
Penny Piece Cottages 79
Pilmoor Cottages 80
NEW Primrose Bank Nursery 81
Rewela Cottage 84
The Ridings 86
Rustic Cottage 87
Scape Lodge 89
Skipwith Hall 93
Sue Proctor Plants Nursery Garden 97
Swale Cottage 98
The White House 104
Whixley Gardens 105
Whyncrest 106
NEW Willow Cottage 107
Woodlands Cottage 108
Yorke House 111

THE GARDENS

1 AUSTWICK HALL

Town Head Lane, Austwick, Settle, LA2 8BS. James E Culley & Michael Pearson, 015242 51794, austwickhall@austwick.org, www.austwickhall.co.uk. *5m W of Settle. Leave the A65 to Austwick. Pass the PO on R, Gamecock Inn on L. Take 1st L onto Town Head Lane. Parking on Town Head Lane.* **Wed 21 Feb (12-4). Adm £4, chd free. Light refreshments.**

Set in the dramatic limestone scenery of the Dales the garden nestles into a steeply wooded hillside. Extensive drifts of common single and double snowdrops are an impressive sight with examples of over 50 other varieties. Sculptures along the trail add further interest. Woodland paths may be slippery in wet weather so sensible footwear is recommended.

2 BARNVILLE

Wilton, Nr Pickering, YO18 7LE. Bill & Liz Craven, 07867 503242, lizcraven40@gmail.com. *4m E of Pickering. On main A170, travelling from Pickering towards Scarborough, enter village of Wilton. Turn R. House on L in 200yrds.* **Sun 15 Apr (12-5). Adm £3.50, chd free. Home-made teas. Members of Wilton Village Hall provide and serve home-baked cakes and cream teas in the garden. Visits also by arrangement Apr to Oct for groups of 10+, adm £5.50 incl light refreshments.**

Over an acre of hidden gardens on the edge of the North York Moors. Unusual plants make a garden for all seasons: Winter is coloured by cyclamen, snowdrop, hellebore and witchhazel. Spring, magnolia and azalea shelter naturalised bulbs, trillium and erythronium. Summer's cool green foliage highlights allium, agapanthus and foxtail lilies. Autumn brings a blaze of coloured foliage, berries and flowers. Proceeds from refreshments are in aid of Wilton Village Hall Proceeds from plant sales are in aid of, a charity close to our hearts, Greyhound Gap. Lower garden unsuitable for wheelchairs in wet, but level stone paths in upper gardens. Access to sunken garden via steps - can be viewed from above.

3 BASIN HOWE FARM

Cockmoor Road, Sawdon, Scarborough, YO13 9EG. Richard & Heather Mullin, 01723 850180, info@basinhowefarm.co.uk, www.basinhowefarm.co.uk. *Turn off A170 between Scarborough & Pickering at Brompton by Sawdon follow sign to Sawdon. Basin Howe Farm 1½m above Sawdon village on the L.* **Visits by arrangement May to Aug (not Sats) Groups and couples welcome too. Adm £5, chd free. Tea, coffee and cakes for groups by arrangement.**

These gardens have a lovely atmosphere. 3 acres of garden with box parterre with seasonal planting and koi pond, herbaceous borders, wildlife pond and elevated viewing deck with Pod summer house and a number of sculptures. Orchard and woodland, ferns, lawns and shrubs. Paved seating areas but gravel paths. Basin Howe is high above the Wolds and has a Bronze Age Burial Mound. Maintained by owners. Winner of a Gold Award in Yorkshire in Bloom 4 years running. Wheelchair Access is possible to most areas but a helper is required. Access is via gravel paths and grass.

4 BEACON GARTH

Redcliff Road, Hessle, Hull, HU13 0HA. Ivor & June Innes. *4½m W of Hull. Follow signs for Hessle Foreshore. Parking available in foreshore car park followed by a short walk up Cliff Rd. Enter the garden through the double gates on Redcliff Rd.* **Sun 27 May (12-5.30). Combined adm with 113 Southfield £6, chd free. Home-made teas.**

Edwardian, Arts and Crafts House (mentioned in Pevsner's Guide to Hull) and S-facing garden set in 3½ acres, in an elevated position overlooking the Humber. Stunning sunken rock garden with bulbs and specimen trees, hostas and ferns. Mature trees, large lawns and herbaceous borders. Gravel paths, haha, box hedges and topiary. Child friendly; children's play area. Teas served in main hallway of house. Partial wheelchair access.

5 BEACON HILL HOUSE

Langbar, Ilkley, LS29 0EU. Mr & Mrs H Boyle. *4m NW of Ilkley. 1¼m SE of A59 at Bolton Bridge.* **Wed 16 May (1.30-5). Adm £4.50, chd free. Home-made teas.** Donation to Riding for the Disabled.

Delightful but steep walks with long distance views take you up through the woodland which shelters this seven acre garden. Although nearly 1000ft above sea level and adjacent to a grouse moor, many unusual trees and shrubs grow here. Spring is the showiest time for this garden with its magnolias and rhododendrons. Small kitchen garden and orchard, pond, some original Victorian features. No wheelchair access.

6 NEW 90 BENTS ROAD

Bents Green, Sheffield, S11 9RL. Mrs Hilary Hutson. *3m SW of Sheffield. From Moore St r'about in Sheffield Centre (nr Waitrose), follow A625. After approx 3m turn R on to Bents Rd.* **Sun 29 July (10.30-4.30). Adm £3.50, chd free. Light refreshments. Refreshments also at 12 Ansell Road, S11 7PE - see NGS Derbyshire.**

Plantswoman's NE facing garden. Patio with alpine troughs for year-round interest, plus pots of colourful tropical plants in summer. Mixed borders surround a lawn, which leads to mature trees underplanted with shade-loving plants at end of garden. Many unusual and borderline-hardy species. Front garden peaks in summer with hot-coloured blooms. Featured in Sheffield Telegraph. Front garden and patio flat and accessible. Remainder of back garden accessed via 6 steps (with handrail), so unsuitable for wheelchairs.

7 BIRSTWITH HALL

High Birstwith, Harrogate, HG3 2JW. Sir James & Lady Aykroyd, 01423 770250, ladya@birstwithhall.co.uk. *5m NW of Harrogate. Between Hampsthwaite & Birstwith villages, close to A59 Harrogate/Skipton Rd.* **Sun 24 June (2-5). Adm £4.50, chd free. Home-made teas. Visits also by arrangement groups and small coaches welcome.**

Large 4 acre garden nestling in secluded Yorkshire dale with formal garden and ornamental orchard, extensive lawns, picturesque stream, large pond and Victorian greenhouse. Also home-made teas and refreshments for large groups.

8 BRAMBLE CROFT

Howden Road, Silsden, Keighley, BD20 0JB. Debbi Wilson, 01535 658032, deb2711@googlemail.com. *Next to Springbank Nursing Home, please park in Howden Rd.* **Sat 1 Sept (11-4). Adm £3.50, chd free. Light refreshments. Visits also by arrangement May to Sept for small groups please telephone.**

Bramble's small hidden hillside artist's garden full of colour, texture and newly developed borders includes perennials, ferns, climbers, grasses, topiary and sculptures, lies on the edge of Silsden village. Wildlife encouraged with pond, bird and insect boxes. Original paintings are on show and for sale in the new tranquil garden room. Terrace and outdoor covered dining patio. Seating available. WC. Light lunches, cakes and hot drinks. Featured in Amateur Garden Magazine. No dogs please as we have our own.

9 NEW BRIAR BANK

Mill Lane, Bardsey, Leeds, LS17 9AN. Freya Skilton. *Bardsey cum Rigton - 8m NE of Leeds, 4m S of Wetherby. A1 J45 follow signs A58 towards Leeds. After Bardsey T-lights take 1st L. From (A58) Leeds take 2nd R In Bardsey.* **Sun 8 July (11-4). Adm £3.50, chd free. Light refreshments and home-made cakes.**

Steep steps access this sloping hillside garden with bold prairie planting melding into the landscape of fields behind. Narrow wood edged paths meander through colourful borders with indigenous wild flowers, plants for shade and roses underplanted with geraniums and herbaceous perennials. Seating areas make the most of the elevation, encouraging you to pause and take in the views beyond.

10 BRIDGE FARM HOUSE

Long Lane, Great Heck, Selby, DN14 0BE. Barbara & Richard Ferrari, 01977 661277, barbaraferrari@mypostoffice.co.uk. *6m S of Selby, 3m E M62 J34. At M62 J34 take A19 to Selby, at r'about turn E towards Snaith on A645. Before Snaith turn R at T-lights, L at T-junction onto Main St, past Church, to T-junction, cross to car park.* **Sun 25 Feb (12-4). Adm £3.50, chd free. Light refreshments in church (opp). Visits also by arrangement February and March.**

2 acre garden divided by hedges into separate areas planted with unusual and interesting plants. All yr interest starts with hellebores, winter shrubs and over 150 named snowdrops. Long double mixed borders; bog, with orchids; gravel garden, with grasses and pond; interesting trees. Hens; compost heaps and wildlife areas. Wheelchair access easiest by front gate, please ask.

11 BROOKFIELD

Jew Lane, Oxenhope, Keighley, BD22 9HS. Mrs R L Belsey. *5m SW of Keighley. From Keighley take A629 (Halifax) Fork R A6033 towards Haworth & Oxenhope turn L at Xrds into village. Turn R (Jew Lane) at bottom of hill.* **Sun 3 June, Wed 4 July (1.30-5). Adm £4, chd free. Home-made teas.**

An intimate 1 acre garden with steps and paths leading down to a large pond with an island, mallards and wild geese also greylags. Many varieties of Primula, candelabra and florindae and Dactylorrhiza majalis which have seeded into the lower lawn around a small pond with stream; azaleas and rhododendrons. Unusual trees and shrubs in a series of island beds, screes, greenhouse and conservatory. 'Round and Round the Garden' children's quiz.

12 BUTTERFIELD HEIGHTS

4 Park Crescent, Guiseley, Leeds, LS20 8EL. Vicky Harris, 078521 63733, vickyharris1951@gmail.com. *11m NW of Leeds. From Guiseley A65 (Otley-Leeds) A6038 towards Shipley (Bradford Rd). Park Crescent ½m on L. Park on Bradford Rd.* **Visits by arrangement July to Sept for groups of 10+. Adm £5, chd free. Cream teas.**

Garden completely restored over 20 years but retaining and enhancing the original 1930's landscaping. Mixed planting of unusual shrubs, perennials and mature trees now undergoing further transitions as the owners try to reduce their garden workload. Statuesque planting creates a riot of colour while topiary features and tall perennials add to the character of the garden at the height of summer. Tree carving and Fairy Post Office (with gifts). Featured in Garden News, Yorkshire Post. Garden on three levels with some steep steps and gravel paths.

GROUP OPENING

13 CAWOOD GARDENS

Cawood, nr Selby,
YO8 3UG. 01757 268571,
dave-judyjones@hotmail.co.uk.
On B1223 5m N of Selby & 7m SE of Tadcaster. Between York & A1 on B1222. Village maps given at all gardens. **Sat 7, Sun 8 July (12-5). Combined adm £6, chd free. Home-made teas at 9 Anson Grove & 21 Great Close. Visits also by arrangement June & July.**

9 ANSON GROVE
Tony & Brenda
Finnigan, 01757 268888,
beeart@ansongrove.co.uk.

21 GREAT CLOSE
David & Judy Jones,
01757 268571,
dave-judyjones@hotmail.co.uk.

THE PIGEONCOTE
Maria Parks & Angela
Darlington, 01757 268661,
mariaparks@gmail.com.

These three contrasting gardens in an attractive historic village are linked by a pretty riverside walk to the C11 church and Memorial garden and across the Castle Garth to the remains of Cawood Castle. 9 Anson Grove is a small garden with tranquil pools and secluded sitting places. Narrow winding paths and raised areas give views over oriental-style pagoda, bridge and Zen garden. 21 Great Close is a flower arranger's garden, designed and built by the owners. Interesting trees and shrubs combine with herbaceous borders incl many grasses. Two ponds are joined by a stream, winding paths take you to the vegetable garden and summerhouse, then back to the colourful terrace for views across the garden and countryside beyond. The small walled garden, Pigeoncote at 2 Wistowgate is surrounded by historic C17 buildings. A balanced design of formal box hedging, cottage garden planting and creative use of grasses. Angled brick pathways lead to shaded seating areas with all day sunny views. Crafts and paintings on sale at 9 Anson Grove. Wheelchair access limited at 9 Anson Grove and 21 Great Close.

14 14 CHELLSWAY

Chellsway, Withernsea, HU19 2EN.
Neil & Caroline Ziemski. *15m E of Hull. Enter Withernsea on A1033, turn L onto B1362, 2nd L onto Carrs Meadow, L onto Beaconsfield R onto Chellsway.* **Sun 5 Aug (12-5). Adm £2.50, chd free. Light refreshments. Home made cakes, tea and coffee.**
Jungle garden with grass and gravel paths surrounded by hardy and tender plants. Collection of bamboo, bananas, gingers, palms, succulents and other exotic plants, combine to create a tropical effect rarely seen on the Yorkshire coast. An authentic jungle hut and various seating areas allow the visitor to see different aspects of the garden. Small pond and rockery area to see. www.hulldailymail.co.uk/news/property/ordinary-looking-house-amazing-secret-294367.

15 3 CHURCH WALK

Bugthorpe, York, YO41 1QL.
Barrie Creaser & David Fielding, 01759 368152,
barriecreaser@gmail.com.
Stamford Bridge to Bridlington rd, after 4m you will see the yellow direction arrows, for Bugthorpe. Park in the village outside the church. **Sun 1 July (10-4). Adm £3, chd free. Home-made teas. Also open Daneswell House. Refreshments available in both gardens. Visits also by arrangement June to Aug for 15 max.**
A garden created from scratch 16 years ago, surprisingly mature, with mixed borders and trees, water feature and pond. Raised vegetable garden and greenhouse. The lawn leads onto a paddock with views of open countryside, lots of seating to sit and enjoy the different vistas. Wheelchair access: garden accessible, but gravel in courtyard. Please contact owners prior to arrival to ensure access to garden by car.

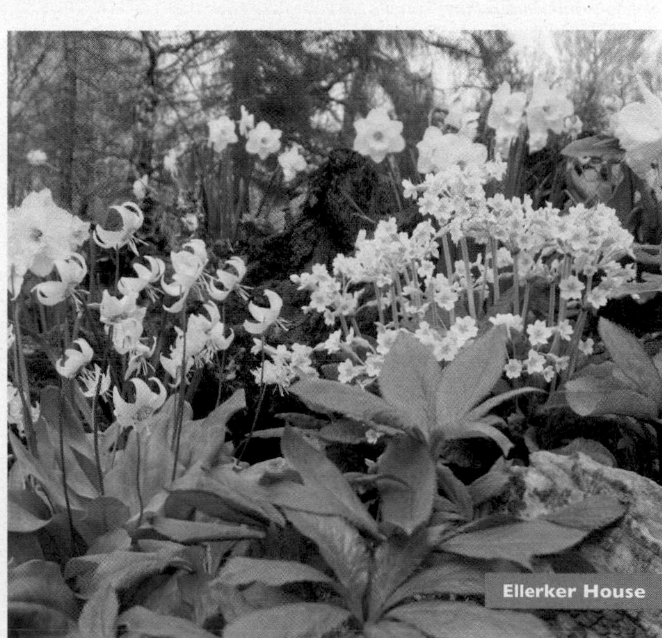

Ellerker House

16 THE CIRCLES GARDEN

8 Stocksmoor Road, Midgley, nr Wakefield, WF4 4JQ. Joan Gaunt. *Equidistant from Huddersfield, Wakefield & Barnsley, W of M1. Turn off A637 in Midgley at the Black Bull Pub (sharp bend) onto B6117 (Stocksmoor Rd). Please park on L adjacent to houses.* **Sun 22 Apr (1.30-4.30). Adm £3.50, chd free. Home-made teas.**

An organic and self-sustaining plantswoman's ½ acre garden on gently sloping site overlooking fields, woods and nature reserve opposite. Designed and maintained by owner. Interesting herbaceous, bulb and shrub plantings linked by grass and gravel paths, woodland area with mature trees, spring and summer meadows, fernery, greenhouse, fruit trees, viewing terrace with pots. Also, around 100 hellebores grown from my seed. South African plants, hollies, small bulbs are particular interests.

17 CLIFTON CASTLE

Ripon, HG4 4AB. Lord & Lady Downshire. *2m N of Masham. On rd to Newton-le-Willows & Richmond. Gates on L next to red telephone box.* **Sun 8 Apr, Sun 3 June (2-5). Adm £5, chd free. Home-made teas.**

Fine views, river walks, wooded pleasure grounds with bridges and follies. Cascades, wild flower meadow and C19 walled kitchen garden. Gravel paths and steep slopes to river.

18 NEW THE COACH HOUSE

Queens Road, Harrogate, HG2 0HB. Rachel Mann. *Harrogate Town Centre. At A61 Prince of Wales r'about turn W up B6162 Otley Rd. Queens Road is 3rd turning on R. Free parking on rd side or disc parking in adjacent rds (some parking discs available at garden).* **Sun 15 July (11-5). Adm £3.50, chd free. Home-made teas.**

Small but beautifully formed this front garden of a late C19 coach house is a true hidden gem concealed behind large Victorian houses. Every inch of space has been used resulting in a surprisingly well matured 8 year old garden, with trees, shrubs, perennials, a woodland corner, espalier fruit trees, raised vegetable beds. Wall art, vessels and sculptures add interest.

The Villa

19 ◆ CONSTABLE BURTON HALL GARDENS

Constable Burton, Leyburn, DL8 5LJ. Mr & Mrs D'Arcy Wyvill, 01677 450428, gardens@constableburton.com, www.constableburton.com. *3m E of Leyburn. Constable Burton Village. On A684, 6m W of A1, between the towns of Bedale & Leyburn.* **For NGS: Sun 25 Mar (12-5). Adm £5, chd free. Light Lunches and Teas.** For other opening times and information, please phone, email or visit garden website.

Large romantic garden with terraced woodland walks. Garden trails, shrubs, roses and water garden. Display of daffodils and over 6,500 tulips planted annually amongst extensive borders. Fine John Carr house (not open) set in splendour of Wensleydale countryside. Constable Burton Hall Gardens plays host to a magnificent Tulip Festival, on the first May Bank Holiday weekend. Sponsored by Chelsea award winning nursery Bloms Bulbs, over 6,500 traditional and new variant tulips are planted throughout the gardens.

20 COW CLOSE COTTAGE

Stripe Lane, Hartwith, Harrogate, HG3 3EY. William Moore & John Wilson, 01423 779813, cowclose1@btinternet.com. *8m NW of Harrogate. From A61(Harrogate-Ripon) at Ripley take B6165 to Pateley Bridge. 2m beyond Burnt Yates turn R signed Hartwith onto Stripe Lane. Parking available.* **Sun 22 July (10.30-4.30). Adm £4, chd free. Home-made teas. Visits also by arrangement in July group visits of 10+.**

⅔ acre country garden on sloping site with stream and far reaching views. Large borders with drifts of interesting, well-chosen, later flowering summer perennials and some grasses contrasting with woodland shade and streamside plantings. Gravel path leading to vegetable area. Courtyard area, terrace and seating with views of the garden. Orchard and ha-ha with steps leading to wild flower meadow. The lower part of the garden can be accessed via the orchard.

21 CRESKELD HALL

Arthington, Leeds, LS21 1NT. J & C Stoddart-Scott. *5m E of Otley. On A659 between Pool & Harewood.* **Sun 27 May (12-5). Adm £5, chd free. Home-made teas.**
Historic picturesque 3½ acre Wharfedale garden with beech avenue, mature rhododendrons and azaleas. Gravel path from terrace leads to attractive water garden with canals set amongst woodland plantings. Walled kitchen garden and flower garden. Specialist nurseries.

GROUP OPENING

22 DACRE BANKS & SUMMERBRIDGE GARDENS

Nidderdale, HG3 4EW. 01423 780456, pat@yorkehouse.co.uk, www.yorkehouse.co.uk. *4m SE Pateley Bridge, 10m NW Harrogate, 10m N Otley, on B6451 & B6165. Parking at each garden. Maps available to show garden locations.* **Sun 8 July (12-5). Combined adm £8, chd free. Home-made teas at Yorke House, Low Hall and Woodlands Cottage. Visits also by arrangement June & July for groups of 10 minimum.**

LOW HALL
Mrs P A Holliday.
(See separate entry)

RIVERSIDE HOUSE
Joy Stanton.
joy.stanton21@gmail.com

WOODLANDS COTTAGE
Mr & Mrs Stark.
(See separate entry)

YORKE HOUSE
Tony & Pat Hutchinson.
(See separate entry)

Dacre Banks and Summerbridge Gardens are situated in the beautiful countryside of Nidderdale and designed to take advantage of the scenic Dales landscape. The gardens are linked by an attractive walk along the valley and each may be accessed individually by car. Low Hall has a romantic walled garden set on different levels around the historic C17 family home (not open) with herbaceous borders, shrubs, climbing roses and tranquil water garden. Riverside House is a mysterious waterside garden on many levels, supporting shade-loving plants and incorporates a Victorian folly, fernery, courtyard and naturalistic riverside plantings. Woodlands Cottage is a garden of many rooms, with exquisite formal and informal plantings,which together with an attractive wild flower meadow harmonise with the boulder-strewn woodland. Yorke House has extensive colour-themed borders, fabulous waterside plantings of candelabra primula and a secluded millennium garden full of fragrant plants and rambling roses. Visitors welcome to use orchard picnic area at Yorke House. Featured in Radio York and Harrogate Advertiser. Partial wheelchair access at some gardens.

23 DANESWELL HOUSE

35 Main Street, Stamford Bridge, YO41 1AD. Brian & Pauline Clayton, 01759 371446, Pauline-clayton44@outlook.com. *7m E of York. On A166 at the E end of the village. Garden on your L as you leave the village towards Bridlington.* **Sun 1 July (10-4), also open 3 Church Walk. Sun 29 July (10-4). Adm £4, chd free. Cream teas. Visits also by arrangement July & Aug.**
A ¾ acre secluded garden that sweeps down to the R Derwent. It has tiered terraces, ponds, including a new pond with bridge, water feature, shrubs, borders. The garden attracts abundant wildlife. Teas are served at the top of the garden. This is a sloping garden down to river, however access is possible with care.

24 DEVONSHIRE MILL

Canal Lane, Pocklington, York, YO42 1NN. Sue & Chris Bond, 01759 302147, chris.bond.dm@btinternet.com, www.devonshiremill.co.uk. *1m S of Pocklington. Canal Lane, off A1079 at The Wellington Oak Pub.* **Sun 18 Feb (11-4.30). Adm £4, chd free. Home-made teas.**
Drifts of double snowdrops, hellebores and ferns surround the historic grade II listed water mill. Explore the two acre garden with mill stream, orchards, woodland, herbaceous borders, hen run and greenhouses. The old mill pond is now a vegetable garden with raised beds and a polytunnel. Over the past twenty years the owners have developed the garden on organic principles to encourage wildlife.

25 ◆ DOVE COTTAGE NURSERY GARDEN

Shibden Hall Road, nr Halifax, HX3 9XA. Kim & Stephen Rogers, 01422 203553, info@dovecottagenursery.co.uk, www.dovecottagenursery.co.uk. *1m E Halifax. From Halifax take A58 turn L signed Claremount, cont over bridge, cont ½m. J26 M62- A58 Halifax. Drive 4m. L turn at Paw Prints pet store down Tanhouse Hill, cont ½m.* **For NGS: Sun 17 June (10-4). Tea. Sun 22 July, Sun 19 Aug (10-4). Adm £3.50, chd free. For other opening times and information, please phone, email or visit garden website.**
Hedges and green oak gates enclose ⅓ acre sloping garden, generously planted by nursery owners over 20yrs. A beautiful mix of late summer perennials and grasses. Winding paths and plenty of seats incl a romantic tulip arbour. Garden open Wed-Sun from June. Plants for sale in nursery. Wildlife friendly. 'Considered good example of cottage garden' (Carole Klein thought so!). Appeared on Gardeners World.

The National Garden Scheme is Hospice UK's largest single funder

26 34 DOVER ROAD
Hunters Bar, Sheffield, S11 8RH. Marian Simpson, 079575 36248, marian@mjsimpson.plus.com. *1½m SW of city centre. From A61 (ring rd) A625 Moore St/Ecclesall Rd for approx 1m. Dover Rd on R.* **Sun 24 June (10-4). Adm £3.50, chd free. Home-made teas. Wide range of home made drinks and cakes. Visits also by arrangement May to Aug for groups of 10+.**
Colourful, small town garden packed with interest and drama, combining formality with exotic exuberance. Attractive alpine area replacing old driveway, many interesting containers and well-stocked borders. Conservatory, seating areas and lawns complement unusual plants and planting combinations. Featured on TV (Titchmarsh) Yorkshire Post, Radio Sheffield, local press, etc.

27 NEW 39 THE DRIVE
Roundhay, Leeds, LS8 1JQ. John & Judith Rothenberg. *N Leeds. Nr Roundhay Park. From A6120 N Leeds Ring Rd turn towards Leeds at Park Lane T-lights. Continue on Park Lane to junction with Street Lane. Turn L then 1st R (Old Park Rd). The Drive is 6th turning on R* **Wed 13 June (2-6). Adm £3.50, chd £1.**
Hidden from view is an unexpected, established garden with a mature collection of unusual trees and shrubs under planted with perennials and meadow. Narrow paths lead to a cutting garden, vegetables, fruit and orchard trees. Refreshments available at Roundhay Park and Tropical World.

28 NEW EAST WING, NEWTON KYME HALL
Croft Lane, Newton Kyme, Nr Boston Spa, LS24 9LR. Fiona & Chris Royffe, www.plantsbydesign.info. *2m from Tadcaster or Boston Spa. Follow directions for Newton Kyme from A659.* **Sun 12 Aug (11-5). Adm £3.50, chd free. Home-made teas.**
Small owner designed contemporary garden in dramatic setting creating a unique sense of place. Views of medieval ruins of Kyme Castle, St Andrews Church and C18 Fairfax family home Newton Kyme Hall (not open). Sculptural beech and yew hedges enclose spaces for features such as herb and cutting gardens, lawns and small meadow. Includes exhibition of garden design.

29 ELLERKER HOUSE
Everingham, York, YO42 4JA. Mrs R Los & Mr M Wright, www.ellerkerhouse.weebly.com. *15m SE of York. 5½m from Pocklington. Just out of the village heading towards Harswell.* **Sun 8 Apr (10-5). Adm £5, chd free. Light refreshments. delicious home made cakes with tea and coffee served all day, savouries served over lunch time.**
This garden is 5 acres with many fine old trees, lawns surrounded by colour themed herbaceous borders planted with unusual plants and shrubs for all year colour and interest. Daffodils planted around the lake amongst the stumpery also spring bulbs, alpines and Hellebores. 11 acres of woodland thatched breeze hut. RARE PLANT FAIR many different plant stalls selling a variety of unusual plants. Featured in the Telegraph, Yorkshire life, living magazine and Waitrose magazine. Most of the garden in accessible by wheelchair.

30 ELLERKER MANOR
Cave Lane, Ellerker, Brough, HU15 2DX. Philip & Sally Bean, 01430 423035, Pmegabean@aol.com. *From the S Cave exit on A63 turn towards West End S Cave & the lorry sign to Ellerker. At T-junction, turn L. Garden on L after Ellerker Village sign.* **Sun 3 June (11-5). Adm £4, chd free. Home-made teas. Visits also by arrangement May & June.**
A village garden belonging to the previous owners of Saltmarshe Hall. The garden has good trees and shrubs, borders packed with herbaceous plants and bulbs. Climbers grow on trellis. The pretty potager has vegetables and flowers. A less structured part of the garden has ponds and wild flower area. Final year of opening. Teas in aid of Ellerker church. Gravel driveway, and wheelchairs would need to be pushed across grass, but most of the garden can be seen.

31 NEW 3 EMBANKMENT ROAD
Broomhill, Sheffield, S10 1EZ. Charlotte Cummins. *1½m W of city centre, 7½m from J33 M1. A61 ring rd follow A57 to Manchester. In Broomhill turn R onto Crookes Rd, 1st R on to Crookesmoor Rd. Embankment Rd is 2nd on L.* **Sun 17 June (10-5). Adm £3.50, chd free. Home-made teas.**
Compact city garden. Cottage styled planting, with well stocked borders of interesting and carefully selected herbaceous perennials. Patio with steps leading to elevated lawn, raised vegetable beds and garden. Clipped boxes, hostas and lavender bed with alliums in the front garden. Collections of astrantias, ferns, heucheras and over 100 different varieties of hostas. Home grown plants for sale.

32 FAWLEY HOUSE
7 Nordham, North Cave, HU15 2LT. Mr & Mrs T Martin, 01430 422266, louisem200@hotmail.co.uk, www.nordhamcottages.co.uk. *15m W of Hull. L at J38 on M62E. L at '30' & signs: Wetlands & Polo. At L bend, R into Nordham. Fawley's on RHS. Car park further ahead. From Beverley, B1230 to N Cave. R after church. Over bridge. Car park*

ahead. **Sun 18 Feb (11-3); Sun 20 May (12-5). Adm £5, chd free. Home-made teas. Refreshments in the stone cottage with log fires in February, also in May if necessary! 2019: Sun 17 Feb. Visits also by arrangement Feb to Oct for groups of 10+, adm £10 to incl home-made tea.**

Tiered, 2½ acre garden with lawns, mature trees, formal hedging and gravel pathways. Lavender beds, mixed shrub/herbaceous borders, and hot double herbaceous borders. Apple espaliers, pears, soft fruit, produce and herb gardens. Terrace with pergola and vines. Sunken garden with white border. Woodland with naturalistic planting and spring bulbs. Quaker well, stream and spring area with 3 bridges, ferns and hellebores near mill stream. Beautiful snowdrops and aconites early in year. Treasure Hunt for children. Self catering accommodation at Nordham Cottages see website. Partial wheelchair access to top of garden and terrace on pea gravel. Sloping paths thereafter.

33 FERNLEIGH

9 Meadowhead Avenue, Meadowhead, Sheffield, S8 7RT. Mr & Mrs C Littlewood, 01142 747234, littlewoodchristine@gmail.com. *4m S of Sheffield city centre. From Sheffield city centre. A61, A6102, B6054 r'about, exit B6054. 1st R Greenhill Ave, 2nd R. From M1 J33, A630 to A6102, then as above.* **Sun 24 June, Sun 26 Aug (11-5). Adm £3.50, chd free. Light refreshments and home-made cakes. Visits also by arrangement June to Aug groups of 10 to 30.**

Plantswoman's ⅓ acre cottage style garden. Large variety of unusual plants set in differently planted sections to provide all-yr interest. Seating areas to view different aspects of garden. Auricula theatre, patio, gazebo and greenhouse. Miniature log cabin with living roof and cobbled area with unusual plants in pots. Sempervivum, alpine displays and wildlife 'hotel'. Wide selection of home grown plants for sale. Animal Search for children. Featured in Sheffield Telegraph and Star, Active 8 Magazine Daily Telegraph.

ALLOTMENTS

34 FIRVALE ALLOTMENT GARDEN

Winney Hill, Harthill, nr Worksop, S26 7YN. Don & Dot Witton, 01909 771366, donshardyeuphorbias@btopenworld.com, www.euphorbias.co.uk. *12m SE of Sheffield, 6m W of Worksop. M1 J31 A57 to Worksop. Turn R to Harthill. Allotments at S end of village, 26 Casson Drive at N end on Northlands Estate.* **Visits by arrangement Apr to July no min number. Adm £3, chd free. Home-made teas at 26 Casson Drive Harthill (S26 7WA).**

Large allotment containing 13 island beds displaying 500+ herbaceous perennials incl the National Collection of hardy Euphorbias with over 100 varieties flowering between March and October. Organic vegetable garden. Refreshments, WC, plant sales at 26 Casson Drive – small garden with mixed borders, shade and seaside garden.

NPC

35 FRIARS HILL

Sinnington, YO62 6SL. Mr & Mrs C J Baldwin, 01751 432179, friars.hill@abelgratis.co.uk. *4m W of Pickering. On A170.* **Visits by arrangement Mar to July individuals, couples and quite happy with groups of 10+. Adm £4, chd free.**

Plantswoman's 1¾ acre garden containing over 2500 varieties of perennials and bulbs, with yr-round colour. Early interest with hellebores, bulbs and woodland plants. Herbaceous beds. Hostas, delphiniums, old roses and stone troughs. Excellent Autumn colour.

36 GLARAMARA

Lambwath Lane, New Ellerby, Hull, HU11 5BT. Pam & Giles Hufford. *From Hull, leave A165 just before Skirlaugh, turn R onto Mulberry Lane. After 1½m, turn L on to Lambwath Lane. Glaramara is 200yds on L.* **Sun 17 June (10.30-4). Adm £3, chd free. Home-made teas.**

Wildlife haven on the highest point of the Holderness Plain. Steps leading to patio, lawn with borders and small pond. Archway to henhouse and willow windbreaks surrounded by too many trees and plants to list. Twisting pathways to the sleep house and secret garden. Small wooded area with gate leading to greenhouse, apiary, mixed fruit and vegetable plots with specimen trees.

Manor Farm

37 NEW GLENCOE HOUSE

Main Street, Bainton, Driffield, YO25 9NE. Liz Dewsbury, 01377 217592, efdewsbury@gmail.com. *6m SW of Driffield on A614. 10m N of Beverley on B1248 Malton Rd. The house is on the W side of A614 in centre of the village. Parking is around village or in lay-by 280m N of house towards the Bainton r'about.* **Sun 24 June (12-4.30). Adm £4, chd free. Home-made teas. Visits also by arrangement Feb to June.**

The 3 acre garden, with year round interest, is divided by hedges into 4 areas and has been developed over 40 years by the owner. Near to the house are the kitchen garden and roses, perennials and a Tulip tree in the cottage garden. A gate leads into a mown field with specimen trees. Native and unusual trees and a large wildlife pond have been established in the remaining 1.9 acres beyond. Wheelchair access to paved area in cottage garden but difficult elsewhere.

38 GOLDSBOROUGH HALL

Church Street, Goldsborough, HG5 8NR. Mr & Mrs M Oglesby, 01423 867321, info@goldsboroughhall.com, www.goldsboroughhall.com. *2m SE of Knaresborough. 3m W of A1M. Off A59 (York-Harrogate) carpark 300yds past pub on R.* **Sun 8 Apr (12-4); Sun 22 July (12-5). Adm £5, chd free. Cream teas. Light lunches, sandwiches and cakes. Donation to St Mary's Church.**

Previously opened for NGS from 1928-30 and now beautifully restored by present owners (re-opened in 2010). 12 acre garden and formal landscaped grounds in parkland setting and Grade II*, C17 house, former residence of the late HRH Princess Mary, daughter of George V and Queen Mary. Gertrude Jekyll inspired replanted 120ft double herbaceous borders and rose garden. Quarter-mile Lime Tree Walk planted by royalty in the 1920s, orchard, redesigned kitchen garden and a flower border featuring 'Yorkshire Princess' rose, named after Princess Mary. Regularly featured in local newspapers and magazines. Gravel paths and some steep slopes.

39 THE GRANGE

Carla Beck Lane, Carleton in Craven, Skipton, BD23 3BU. Mr & Mrs R N Wooler, 07740 639135, margaret.wooler@hotmail.com. *1½m SW of Skipton. Turn off A56 (Skipton-Clitheroe) into Carleton. Keep L at Swan Pub, continue to end of village then turn R into Carla Beck Lane.* **Wed 4 July, Wed 8 Aug (12-4.30). Adm £5, chd free. Cream teas. Visits also by arrangement July & Aug groups of 30+. Donation to Sue Ryder Care Manorlands Hospice.**

Over 4 acres set in the grounds of Victorian house (not open) with mature trees and panoramic views towards The Gateway to the Dales. The garden has been restored by the owners over the last 2 decades with many areas of interest being added to the original footprint. Bountiful herbaceous borders with many unusual species, rose walk, parterre, mini-meadows and water features. Large greenhouse and raised vegetable beds. Oak seating placed throughout the garden invites quiet contemplation - a place to 'lift the spirit'. Gravel paths and steps.

The National Garden Scheme is the largest single funder of Macmillan

40 GRASMERE

48 Royds Lane, Rothwell, LS26 0BH. Terry & Tina Cook, 011 328 24958, tinacook555@gmail.com. *5m S of Leeds, 6½m N of Wakefield. M62 J30 follow A642 towards Leeds. Turn L after 200yds (Royds School) Pennington Lane follow rd for 1m. Car parking at school opp or in rd nr Squash Club.* **Evening opening Wed 4, Wed 11, Wed 18, Wed 25 July (6-9). Light refreshments. Sun 29 July (1-5). Home-made teas. Adm £3.50, chd free. Visits also by arrangement July & Aug.**

Amongst old orchard trees is hidden a restful family suburban garden of ⅓ acre. Wildlife encouraged by many nesting boxes, ponds, wild flower area, log piles for hedgehogs and flowers to attract butterflies. Secluded summerhouse enclosed by colourful tapestry hedge and architectural planting. Pergola walkway leads to hidden vegetable garden. The garden is ever changing. Formal and wildlife ponds, wildlife habitat, pergola walkway. Featured on and in BBC Radio Leeds Garden Show, Local Publication Rothwell Record.

41 GREENWICK FARM

Huggate, York, YO42 1YR. Fran & Owen Pearson, 01377 288122, greenwickfarm@hotmail.com. *2m W of Huggate. From York on A166, turn R Im after Garrowby Hill, at brown sign for picnic area & scenic route. White wind turbine on drive.* **Visits by arrangement July & Aug refreshments to be agreed upon when visit is arranged. Adm £6, chd free. Home-made teas. Tea tables in conservatory & outside.**

1 acre woodland garden created 8yrs ago from disused area of the farm. Set in a large dell with many mature trees . Paths up the hillside through borders lead to terrace planted with Hydrangeas, many seating areas with spectacular views across wooded valley and the Wolds, small stumpery and new hot border. Herbaceous/shrub borders. Described by guests as a

The Old Vicarage, Whixley Gardens

graceful and very tranquil garden. Access for wheelchairs difficult, but good view of garden from hard standing outside house/tea area.

42 HAVOC HALL

York Rd, Oswaldkirk, York, YO62 5XY. David & Maggie Lis, 01439 788846, maggielis@me.com, www.havochall.co.uk. *21m N of York. On B1363, 1st house on R as you enter Oswaldkirk from S & last house on L as you leave village from N.* **Sun 1 July (1-5). Adm £5.50, chd free. Home-made teas.**
Started in 2009, comprising 8 areas incl knot, herbaceous, mixed shrub and flower gardens, courtyard, vegetable area and orchard, woodland walk and large lawned area with hornbeam trees and hedging. To the S is a 2 acre wild flower meadow and small lake. Extensive collection of roses, herbaceous perennials and grasses. See website for other opening times. Some steps but these can be avoided.

43 HIGHFIELD COTTAGE

North Street, Driffield, YO25 6AS. Debbie Simpson, 01377 256562, debbie@simpsonhighfield.karoo.co.uk. *30m E of York, 29m E of M62. Exit at A614/A166 r'about onto York Rd into Driffield. Carry straight until you reach the park with the Rose & Crown Pub opp. Highfield Cottage is the white detached house next to pub* **Sun 6, Sun 27 May (11-4). Adm £3.50, chd free. Cream teas. if weather permits. Unfortunately we haven't facilities for wet weather.**
Visits also by arrangement Apr to Sept will open by prior arrangement if possible. Please email.
A ¾ acre suburban garden bordered by mature trees and stream. Structure is provided by numerous yew and box topiary, a pergola and sculptures all created by and maintained by the owner. Something for everyone; lawns with island beds, mixed shrubs, fruit trees and herbaceous borders ensure year round interest. A natural and constantly evolving garden, described as 'magical' by NGS visitors. The garden is not suited to wheelchairs and access is uneven.

44 HILLSIDE

West End, Ampleforth, York, YO62 4DY. Sue Shepherd & Jon Borgia, 01439 788993, sue@sueandjon.net. *West End of Ampleforth village, 4m S of Helmsley. From A19, follow brown sign to Byland Abbey & continue to Ampleforth. From A170 take B1257 to Malton, after 1m turn R to Ampleforth. Roadside parking only. Please be considerate.* **Visits by arrangement June to Oct groups of 10+. Adm £5, chd free. Home-made teas.**
Half acre garden on a south facing slope. The design is evolving, based on informal planting and a wildlife friendly approach. Woodland and meadow areas. 2 ponds and drainage ditch with bog garden. Lawn rising up to summer house and deck with fine views of the Coxwold - Gilling Gap. Fruit trees and kitchen garden. All year round interest with an emphasis on autumn colour.

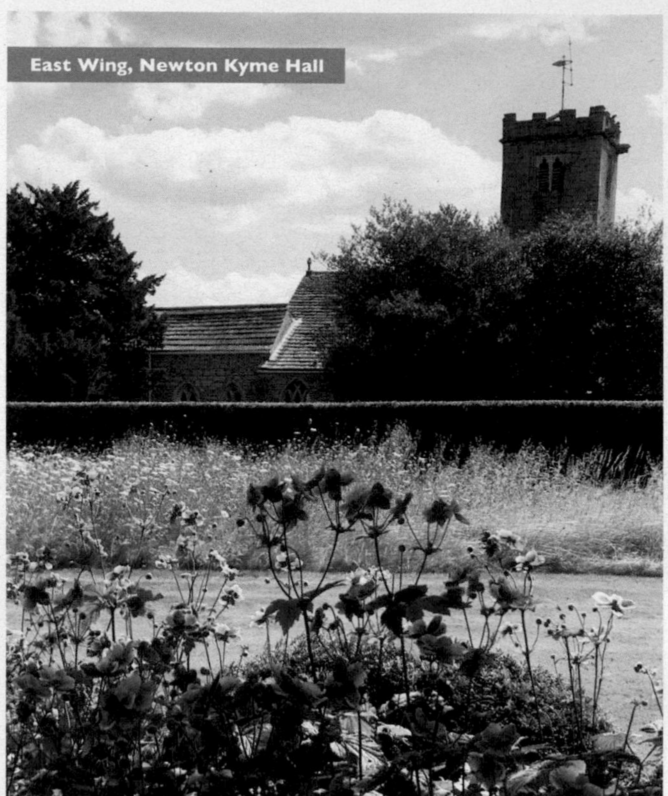
East Wing, Newton Kyme Hall

45 HIMALAYAN GARDEN & SCULPTURE PARK

Hutts Lane, Grewelthorpe, Ripon, North Yorkshire, HG4 3DA. Mr & Mrs Peter Roberts, www.himalayangarden.com. *5m NW of Ripon. From N: A1(M) J51 A684 (Bedale) then B6268 (Masham). From S: A1M J50 (Ripon) then A6108 (Masham) after North Stainley turn L (Mickley & Grewelthorpe). Follow garden signs.* **Mon 30 Apr (10-4). Adm £7.50, chd free. Chd under 12 free.**

A stunning hidden gem 30 acre woodland garden. Home to an extensive collection of rare Rhododendrons, Azaleas and Himalayan plants, set amongst plantings of showy hybrids. A rich tapestry of spring colour with streams meandering through valleys, teaming with arrays of plants and sculptures, leading down to peaceful lakes. Arboretum, Tearoom, Playground and Nursery. Group tours and talks available. 60 Contemporary Sculptures Himalayan Shelter Lakeside Pagoda Thatched Summer House Buddha Garden. Limited Wheelchair Access.

46 2 HOLLIN CLOSE

Rossington, nr Doncaster, DN11 0XX. Mr & Mrs Hann. *5m S of Doncaster. From J3 on M18 take A6182 signed Airport. At T-lights, A638 signed Bawtry turn R (Littleworth Lane) 5m N of Bawtry after T-lights signed Airport take next L (Littleworth Lane). Hollin Close is 2nd R.* **Sun 1 July (11-5). Combined adm with Tamarind, Bessacarr DN4 7AE £5, chd free. Home-made teas.**

⅓ acre terraced garden designed and maintained by owners with four themes on three levels. Cottage style herbaceous planting surrounds a circular lawn alongside a tranquil oriental garden. Steps lead to the greenhouse and Mediterranean gravel garden with sun-loving plants for bees and butterflies. Below lies a wildlife friendly small woodland glade with bug hotel, stumpery, fruit and ferns. 3 times winner of Doncaster in Bloom Best Private Residents Garden.

47 54 HOLLYM ROAD

Withernsea, HU19 2PJ. Mr Matthew Pottage. *23m E of Hull, 16m S of Hornsea. Enter Withernsea from A1033 onto Hollym Rd. From Hornsea, B1242 through town onto Hollym Rd.* **Sun 22 July (11-5). Adm £3, chd free. Cream teas. Gluten free cake available.**

Opening for its tenth and final year, this garden is brimming with colourful herbaceous perennials, roses, and masses of foliage plants including hostas and ferns. Unusual exotics feature here too, with many plants of New Zealand origin, all mixed into a magical setting with a pond, topiary hedge, meadow, cactus and succulent collection. Family home of Matthew Pottage, Curator of RHS Wisley. Excellent plantsman's display of plants and extensive plant sales. Unsuitable for wheelchairs after very wet weather as most of the garden is accessed via the lawn.

48 NEW HONEY HEAD

Wood Nook, Meltham, Holmfirth, HD9 4DU. Andrew Brass. *6m S of Huddersfield. Turn from A616 to Honley, through village then follow Meltham rd for 1m, turn L on Wood Nook Lane.* **Sun 8 July (10-4). Adm £3.50, chd free. Home-made teas.**

Set high on a Pennine hillside with panoramic views, Honey Head aspires to provide year round interest whilst attempting to be self sufficient in fruit, vegetables, cut flowers and plants. Formal gardens with interconnecting ponds lead to extensive kitchen gardens with greenhouses complemented by areas planted to encourage wildlife.

49 HUNMANBY GRANGE

Wold Newton, Driffield, YO25 3HS. Tom & Gill Mellor. *12½m SE of Scarborough. Hunmanby Grange home of Wold Top Brewery, between Wold Newton & Hunmanby on rd from Burton Fleming to Fordon.* **Sat 2, Sun 3 June (11-5). Adm £5, chd free. Light refreshments in Wold Top Brewery bar area. Field and Forage will also be catering in courtyard.**

3-acre garden created over the last 35 yrs from exposed open field, on top of Yorkshire Wolds nr coast. Hedges and fences now provide shelter from wind, making series of gardens with yr-round interest and seasonal highlights. In the Brewery courtyard is the water feature from The Welcome to Yorkshire Chelsea Garden - The Brewers Yard. The Wold Top Brewery will be open with catering from Field and Forage. There is plenty of space in the woodland with mown paths for children to play and explore. Steps can be avoided by using grass paths and lawns. Pond garden not completely accessible to wheelchairs but can be viewed from gateway.

50 ◆ JACKSON'S WOLD

Sherburn, Malton, YO17 8QJ. Mr & Mrs Richard Cundall, 07966 531995, jacksonswoldgarden@gmail.com, www.jacksonswoldgarden.com. *11m E of Malton, 10m SW of Scarborough. Signs only from A64. A64 Eastbound to Scarborough .R at T-lights in Sherburn, take the Weaverthorpe rd ,after 100 metres R fork to Helperthorpe & Luttons. 1m to top of hill, turn L at garden sign.* **For NGS: Sun 27 May, Sun 24 June (1-5). Adm £4, chd free. Home-made teas. For other opening times and information, please phone, email or visit garden website.**

2 acre garden with stunning views of the Vale of Pickering. Walled garden with mixed borders, numerous old shrub roses underplanted with unusual perennials. Woodland paths lead to further shrub and perennial borders. Lime avenue with wild flower meadow. Traditional vegetable garden with roses, flowers and framed by a Victorian greenhouse. Adjoining nursery. Tours by appointment. Featured in Saturday Telegraph.

51 THE JUNGLE GARDEN

76 Gledhow Wood Avenue, Roundhay, Leeds, LS8 1NX. Nick & Gill Wilson, 0113 266 5196, nick.wilson@thejunglegarden.uk, https://thejunglegarden.uk/. *4m NE of Leeds. A58 from Leeds for 3½m to Oakwood. Turn L onto Gledhow Lane & follow NGS signs.* **Sun 29 July (11-5). Adm £3.50, chd free. Visits also by arrangement June to Sept for groups of 10 to 30.**

Multi level garden with jungle style planting and accents of hot tropical colour. Boardwalks and bark paths. Crown lifted trees create overhead canopy. Walk under mad, huge Gunnera leaves. 2 ponds, walkway over lower pond and raised deck with seating overlooks upper pond. Elevated 'Jungle Lodge' and aerial walkway with views over the garden. Tea room at Tropical World at Roundhay Park (1m) parking limited. Featured on and in Monty Don's Big Dreams Small Spaces - BBC2. ITV Yorkshire - Calendar News. Gardeners Question Time - Radio 4. The Great British Garden Revival - BBC2. Daily Mail and Daily Express.

52 ◆ LAND FARM

Edge Lane, Colden, Hebden Bridge, HX7 7PJ. Mr J Williams, 01422 842260, lizwilliams7@btinternet.com, www.landfarmgardens.co.uk. *8m W of Halifax. At Hebden Bridge (A646) after 2 sets of T-lights take turning circle to Heptonstall & Colden. After 2¾m in Colden village turn R at Edge Lane 'no through rd'. In ¾ mile turn left down lane.* **For NGS: Wed 23 May, Wed 4 July, Wed 1 Aug (10-5). Adm £5, chd free. Home-made teas. For other opening times and information, please phone, email or visit garden website.**

An intriguing 6 acre upland garden within a sheltered valley, created entirely by the present owner over a period of 40 years. In that time the valley has been planted with 20,000 trees by friends, neighbours and myself, which has encouraged a habitat rich in bird and wildlife. Within the garden, vistas have been created around thought provoking sculpture. Meconopsis and cardiocrimum lilies. Latest addition is a half-acre highly individual moss garden. Open weekends and Bank Hol Mons May to end Aug. Partial wheelchair access, please telephone.

53 LINDEN LODGE

Newbridge Lane, nr Wilberfoss, York, YO41 5RB. Robert Scott & Jarrod Marsden, 07900 003538, rdsjsm@gmail.com. *10m E of York. From York on the A1079, ignore signs for Wilberfoss, take next turning signed Bolton village, after 1m at the Xrds, turn L onto Newbridge Lane, Linden Lodge is on R in 200m.* **Sat 23 June (12-4). Light refreshments. Sun 24 June (1-5). Cream teas. Sat 30 June, Sat 7 July (12-4). Light refreshments. Adm £4, chd free. Saturday garden openings, light lunches/cakes are served. Visits also by arrangement in June opening during the last 2 weeks of June min of 20 visitors.**

6 acres in all. 1 acre garden owner designed and constructed since 2000. Gravel paths edged with brick or lavender, many borders with unusual mixed herbaceous perennials, shrubs and feature trees. A wildlife pond, summer house, kitchen garden, glasshouse. Orchard and woodland area. Formal garden with pond and water feature. 5 acres of developing meadow, trees, pathways, hens and Shetland sheep. Plant sales. Featured in 100 Inspirational Gardens of England, The Yorkshire Post, Kitchen Garden, Amateur Gardening and Yorkshire Life. Gravel paths and shallow steps.

54 LITTLE EDEN

Lancaster Street, Castleford, WF10 2NP. Melvyn & Linda Moran, 01977 514275, melvynmoran609@btinternet .com. *2½m NW of M62 J32. A639 (Castleford) 1st r'about 2nd exit B6136. At hill top turn L at T-lights, next r'about straight on, then 3rd R (Elizabeth Drive) then 2nd L, then 3rd L.* **Sun 29 July, Sun 19 Aug (10-4.30). Adm £3.50, chd free. Home-made teas. Visits also by arrangement July & Aug, groups min 7.**

Plant lovers' small hidden oasis of unusual, tender, exotic and tropical plants in the midst of large housing estate. Trellis and archway festooned with climbers, colourful pots and hanging baskets. Herbaceous perennials, succulents, tree ferns, palms, bananas, pond and a decorative summerhouse. Find 'NGS Little Eden' on Facebook. Pontefract&Castleford Express.

GROUP OPENING

55 LITTLETHORPE GARDENS

Pottery Lane, Ripon, HG4 3LS. *1½m SE of Ripon. Off A61 bypass follow signs to Littlethorpe. Turn R at church. From Bishop Monkton follow signs to Ripon (Knaresborough Rd), turn R to Littlethorpe.* **Sun 5 Aug (12-5). Combined adm £6, chd free. Home-made teas at Greencroft.**

GREENCROFT
David & Sally Walden, 01765 602487, s-walden@talk21.com. **Visits also by arrangement, July to mid Aug. Refreshments available.**

KIRKELLA
Jacky Barber.

LITTLETHORPE HOUSE
Mr & Mrs James Hare.

Littlethorpe is a small village characterised by houses interspersed with fields. Greencroft is a ½ acre informal garden made by the owners. Special ornamental features incl gazebo, temple pavilions, formal pool, stone wall with mullions, and gate to rose pergola leading to a cascade water feature. Long herbaceous borders packed with colourful late flowering perennials, annuals and exotics culminate in circular garden with views through to large wildlife pond and surrounding countryside. Kirkella is a small garden recently created by plantswoman and flower arranger to give constant interest. Gravel garden to the front with Mediterranean feel. Densely planted hidden paved rear garden with decorative summerhouse; hostas, half-hardy perennials, salvias, succulents, desirable small slhrubs, many in pots and containers. A willow hedge conceals a small productive vegetable plot. Opposite is Littlethorpe House with expansive lawns, clipped topiary and yew hedges, roses and large mixed herbaceous and shrub borders.

56 LITTLETHORPE MANOR

Littlethorpe Road, Littlethorpe, Ripon, HG4 3LG. Mr & Mrs J P Thackray, www.littlethorpemanor.com. *Outskirts of Ripon nr racecourse. Ripon bypass A61. Follow Littlethorpe Rd from Dallamires Lane r'about to stable block with clock tower. Map supplied on application.* **Sun 9 Sept (1.30-5). Adm £6, chd free. Home-made teas. Visits also by arrangement May to Sept groups of 20+ Guided tours.**

11 acres. Walled garden based on cycle of seasons with box, herbaceous, roses, gazebo. Sunken garden with white rose parterre and herbs. Brick pergola with white wisteria, blue and yellow borders. Terraces with ornamental pots. Formal lawns with fountain pool, hornbeam towers and yew hedging. Box headed hornbeam drive with Aqualens water feature. Extensive perennial borders. Parkland with lake, late summer plantings and classical pavilion. Cut flower garden. Spring bulbs, annual meadow and winter garden. Tea,coffee, biscuits and cake £2.50 served in marquee. Wheelchair access - gravel paths, some steep steps.

57 LOW HALL

Dacre Banks, Nidderdale, HG3 4AA. Mrs P A Holliday, 01423 780230, 1pamelaholliday@gmail.com. *10m NW of Harrogate. On B6451 between Dacre Banks & Darley.* **Sun 13 May (1-5). Adm £4, chd free. Also open Woodlands Cottage. Home made cakes etc. Opening with Dacre Banks & Summerbridge Gardens on Sun 8 July. Visits also by arrangement May to Sept small groups of 3 or 4 and large groups up to 50. Teas by prior arrangement.**

Romantic walled garden set on differing levels designed to complement historic C17 family home (not open). Spring bulbs, rhododendrons; azaleas round tranquil water garden. Asymmetric rose pergola underplanted with auriculas and lithodora links orchard to the garden. Extensive herbaceous borders, shrubs and climbing roses give later interest. Bluebell woods and lovely countryside of the farm all round overlooking the R Nidd. 80% of garden can be seen from a wheelchair but access involves three stone steps.

58 LOWER CRAWSHAW

off Stringer House Lane, Emley, Huddersfield, HD8 9SU. Mr & Mrs Neil Hudson, 01924 840980, janehudson42@btinternet.com. *8m E of Huddersfield. Close to Emley Moor TV mast. J39 off the M1 from the N, J38 if from the S. Take Denby Dale Rd turning R to EMLEY. 1m beyond Emley village & short of TV mast turn R along Stringer House Lane.* **Visits by arrangement July & Aug groups of 15+. Home-made teas.**

Lovely large tranquil country garden, hidden away down a farm lane, with stunning views and surrounded by open fields and farmland. 2 large ponds fed by a natural stream form the heart of the garden. Relaxed and informal plantings of grasses and colourful later flowering perennials, old roses and rose arches, a small orchard, and ornamental trees, shrubs and some topiary. Partial wheelchair access.

59 MANOR FARM

Thixendale, Malton, YO17 9TG. Charles & Gilda Brader, 01377 288315, manorfarmthixendale@hotmail.com, www.manorfarmthixendale.co.uk. *10m SE of Malton. Through Birdsall up hill turn L at Xrds, drive for 3mto Thixendale. Turn off A166 for Thixendale, passed Robert Fuller Gallery. Turn L into Thixendale village, drive to Farm at end.* **Evening opening Fri 20 July (4-8). Adm £6, chd free. Home-made teas. Homemade cakes and scones, individual cream pavlovas, tea and coffee. Ice creams. Individual savouries. Wine and Prosecco.**

Borders packed with chalk loving perennials, many unusual. Shrubs and trees. Topiary shapes and terracotta pots throughout. Small knot garden by rockery, trellis and arbour. Summerhouse with formal pool but restrained planting in this area! Fallen tree stream and pond. Large lawns and pergolas. Garden room full of sun loving plants. Always new ideas and projects. Limited in several areas.

60 THE MANOR HOUSE

Main Street, Heslington, York, YO10 5EA. George Smith & Brian Withill, www.georgesmithflowers.com. *2m S York City Centre. The garden will supply a map on booking.* **Sun 17 June (2-5). Adm £15, chd free. Home-made teas. Pre-booking essential, please visit www.ngs,org.uk or phone 01483 211535 for information & booking. Adm includes homemade teas.**

Home of the world renowned flower arranger George Smith, this 3 acre garden reflects his painterly style of planting. Sub-divided by mellow walls it abounds with many surprises as each area is colour themed featuring herbaceous perennials, especially hostas and ferns. Exotic sheltered corners, ponds and a shaded woodland create a wildlife haven. The eye of the artist abounds and the effect is of a living flower arrangement with careful attention to plant associations. Refreshments with George Smith will be served in the tiled rustic loggia beneath his Old Granary Studio. House not open.

61 THE MANOR HOUSE

Main Street, Tollerton, York, YO61 1QQ. Dr Weland & Audrey Stone, 01347 838454, weland.stone@btinternet.com. *10m N of York off A19. Turn up Main Street from village green. House is 200 yards on R.* **Visits by arrangement May to Sept we can provide tea and biscuits or wine for up to approx 20. Adm £5, chd free. Light refreshments.**

An acre in village centre, developed over 45 years. Outbuildings and barn of old brick are covered with climbers. Various mixed borders, shrub rose and geranium bed, smaller areas of Hostas and Heathers. Vegetable bed behind yew hedge. Shaded front garden mainly for spring, Rear lawn dominated by fine Genista aetnensis in July. Tarmac drive and lawns.

62 MANSION COTTAGE

8 Gillus Lane, Bempton, Bridlington, YO15 1HW. Polly & Chris Myers, 01262 851404, chrismyers0807@gmail.com. *2m NE of Bridlington. From Bridlington take B1255 to Flamborough. 1st L at T-lights - Bempton Lane, turn 1st R into Short Lane then L at end. Continue - L fork at Church.* **Sat 18, Sun 19 Aug (10-4). Adm £4, chd free. Light refreshments. We serve lunch on both Sat and Sun, with a wide menu choice featuring the best of local produce incl teas, coffee and home-made cakes. Visits also by arrangement June to Aug, groups of 10+.**

Exuberant, lush, vibrant late perennial planting highlighted with grasses in this hidden, peaceful and surprising garden offering many views and features. Visitors' book comments 'A truly lovely garden and a great lunch', 'The garden is inspirational, a veritable oasis!' Delicious home made lunches, produce stalls and hand made soaps. Areas include a globe garden, mini hosta walk, 100 ft border, summerhouse, veggie plot, cuttery, late summer hot border, bee and butterfly border, decks and lawns. New for 2018, revamped ponds, a Japanese inspired area. No wheelchair access.

63 NEW MIDENDALE

76 Main Street, Gowdall, Goole, DN14 0AE. Mr & Mrs Peter & Pauline Lacy. *M62 J34 take A19 towards Selby approx 1m then R on to A645 towards Goole in approx 4½m turn L to Gowdall. Please note roadside parking only.* **Wed 13 June (1-5); Sun 17 June (11-4). Adm £4, chd free. Light refreshments. Tea, coffee, cold drinks and a selection of home made cakes.**

2 acre garden built on a disused railway track and started in 2003. Comprising of flower, rose, conifer beds, a vegetable garden with raised beds, greenhouse and a herb potager area. An interesting feature is 'Ironhenge' an unusual use of scrap metal. At the bottom of the garden there is a wild flower meadow, orchard, small stumpery and compost area. Plenty of seating around the garden. A variety of topiary plants for sale. Wheelchairs can access most areas of the garden but will require pushing over the gravelled area.

65 MILLGATE HOUSE

Millgate, Richmond, DL10 4JN. Tim Culkin & Austin Lynch, 01748 823571, oztim@millgatehouse.demon .co.uk, www.millgatehouse.com. *Centre of Richmond. House located at bottom of Market Place opp Barclays Bank. Just off corner of Market Place. Park in the Market Place no restrictions on Sunday.* **Sun 1, Sun 8 July (8-9.30). Adm £3.50, chd free.**

SE walled town garden overlooking R Swale. Although small, the garden is full of character, enchantingly secluded with plants and shrubs. Foliage plants incl ferns and hostas. Old roses, interesting selection of clematis, small trees and shrubs. RHS associate garden. Immensely stylish, national award-winning garden. Featured in GGG. Gardeners' World. Specialist collections of clematis, ferns, hostas and roses. MANY STEPS AND STEEP SLOPES SLIPPERY SURFACES.

66 115 MILLHOUSES LANE

Sheffield, S7 2HD. Sue & Phil Stockdale, 0114 236 5571, phil.stockdale@gmail.com. *Approx 4m SW of Sheffield City Centre. Follow A625 Castleton/Dore rd, 4th L after Prince of Wales Pub, 2nd L. OR take A621 Baslow Rd; after Tesco garage take 2nd R, then 1st L.* **Visits by arrangement May to Sept for groups of 10+. Adm £3.50, chd free. Home-made teas.**

Plantswoman's ⅓ acre south facing level cottage style garden, containing many choice and unusual perennials and bulbs, providing year round colour and interest. Large collection of 50+hostas, roses, peonies and clematis, together with unusual tender and exotic plants - aeoniums, echeverias, bananas etc. Seating areas throughout the garden. Wide range of home propagated plants for sale. Garden featured in full page article in the Sheffield Telegraph.

The National Garden Scheme is Marie Curie's largest single funder

67 MILLRACE GARDEN

84 Selby Road, Garforth, Leeds, LS25 1LP. Mr & Mrs Carthy, www.millrace-plants.co.uk. *5m E of Leeds. On A63 in Garforth. 1m from M1 J46, 3m from A1.* **Sun 3 June, Sun 12 Aug (1-5). Adm £4, chd free. Home-made teas.**

Overlooking a secluded valley, garden incl large herbaceous borders containing over 3000 varieties of perennials, shrubs and trees, many of which are unusual and drought tolerant. Ornamental pond, vegetable garden and walled terraces leading to wild flower meadow, small woodland, bog garden and wildlife lakes. 3 June cutting collecting opportunity. 12 Aug seed/cutting collecting opportunity. Art exhibition.

68 MYTON GRANGE

Myton On Swale, York, YO61 2QU. Nick & Annie Ramsden. *15m N of York. From the N go through Helperby on York Rd. After ½m follow yellow signs towards Myton. From the S leave A19 through Tollerton & Flawith. Turn L at Xrds following yellow signs.* **Sun 1 July (1-5). Adm £5, chd free. Home made afternoon teas and wine.**

This garden, attached to a Victorian farmhouse, once formed part of the Myton Estate. Extending to ¾ acre, the site is adjacent to the R Swale and includes a paved terrace garden; formal parterre; circular garden with mixed shrub and herbaceous border; lawn with topiary borders. There will also be guided tours throughout the day of the recently restored Victorian Stud Farm buildings.

69 ◆ NEWBY HALL & GARDENS

Ripon, HG4 5AE. Mr R C Compton, 01423 322583, info@newbyhall.com, www.newbyhall.com. *4m SE of Ripon. (HG4 5AJ for Sat Nav). Follow brown tourist signs from A1(M) or from Ripon town centre.* **For opening times and information, please phone, email or visit garden website.**

40 acres of extensive gardens and woodland laid out in 1920s. Full of rare and beautiful plants. Formal seasonal gardens, stunning double herbaceous borders to R Ure and National Collection of Cornus. Miniature railway and adventure gardens for children. Sculpture exhibition (open June - Sept). Free parking Licensed restaurant Shop and Plant Nursery. Wheelchair map available Disabled parking. Manual and electric wheelchairs available on loan, please call to reserve.

NPC

70 2 NEWLAY GROVE

Horsforth, Leeds, LS18 4LH. Kate & Chris van Heel. *4m NW Leeds city centre. From Leeds follow A65. Turn L down Newlay Lane (just before pelican crossing), then 2nd R onto Newlay Grove. House is 25 metres on L, limited parking near house (House is opp no 14).* **Wed 1 Aug (1-5). Adm £3.50, chd free. Light refreshments.**

Large, rear family garden within a third of an acre plot in quiet conservation area close to R. Aire. Landscaped over past 23 years, featuring late summer perennials, shrubs, pond and shade loving plants. Steps and slopes link lawns and paved terracing. Various seating areas allow viewing from different perspectives.

71 ◆ NORTON CONYERS

Wath, Ripon, HG4 5EQ. Sir James & Lady Graham, 01765 640333, info@nortonconyers.org.uk, www.nortonconyers.org.uk. *4m NW of Ripon. Take Melmerby & Wath sign off A61 Ripon-Thirsk. Go through both villages to boundary wall. Signed entry 300 metres on R.*

For NGS: Sun 3 June (2-5). Adm £6, chd free. Home-made teas. For other opening times and information, please phone, email or visit garden website.

Romantic mid C18 walled garden of interest to garden historians. Lawns, herbaceous borders, yew hedges, and Orangery with attractive pond. The garden retains essential features of its original C18th design with sympathetic planting in the English style. There are borders of gold and silver plants, of old fashioned peonies and irises in season. Visitors frequently comment on the tranquil and romantic atmosphere. For House opening dates and times see website. Unusual hardy plants for sale. Featured in Country Life. Most areas wheelchair accessible, gravel paths.

72 THE NURSERY

15 Knapton Lane, Acomb, York, YO26 5PX. Tony Chalcraft & Jane Thurlow, 01904 781691, janeandtonyatthenursery@hotmail.co.uk. *2½m W of York. From A1237 take B1224 direction Acomb. At r'about turn L (Beckfield Ln.), after 150 metres Turn L.* **Sun 8 July (1-5); Wed 11 July (2-7). Adm £3, chd free. Home-made teas. Visits also by arrangement Apr to Oct talks and tastings of fruit/vegetables may be possible depending on date of visit. Min 10 visitors.**

Hidden, attractive and productive 1-acre organic garden behind suburban house (not open). Wide range of top and soft fruit with over 100 fruit trees, many in trained form. Many different vegetables grown both outside and under cover incl a large 20m greenhouse. Productive areas interspersed with informal ornamental plantings providing colour and habitat for wildlife. The extensive planting of different forms and varieties of fruit trees make this an interesting garden for groups to visit by appointment at blossom and fruiting times in addition to the main summer openings. Featured on BBC Gardener's World in 2017.

73 OLD SLENINGFORD HALL

Mickley, nr Ripon, HG4 3JD. Jane & Tom Ramsden. *5m NW of Ripon. Off A6108. After N Stainley turn L, follow signs to Mickley. Gates on R after 1½m opp cottage.* **Sat 2, Sun 3 June (12-4). Adm £5, chd free. Home-made teas.**

A large English country garden and award winning permaculture forest garden. Early C19 house (not open) and garden with original layout; wonderful mature trees, woodland walk and Victorian fernery; romantic lake with islands, watermill, walled kitchen garden; beautiful long herbaceous border, yew and huge beech hedges. Several plant and other stalls. Picnics very welcome. Reasonable wheelchair access to most parts of garden. Disabled WC at Old Sleningford Farm next to the garden.

74 NEW THE OLD VICARAGE

North Frodingham, Driffield, YO25 8JT. Professor Ann Mortimer. *6m E of Driffield on B1249. From Driffield take B1249 E for approx 6m. The church is on L. Garden is opp. Entrance is on T-junction of rd to Emmotland & B1249. From North Frodingham take the B1249 W for ½m.* **Sun 1 July (11-5). Adm £4, chd free. Home-made teas.**

1½ acre plantsman's garden, owner developed over 20 years. 15 themed areas e.g. rose garden, jungle, desert, fountain, scented, kitchen gardens, glasshouses. Many classical statues, lots of unusual trees and shrubs, 1 large 2 small ponds, orchard, nuttery. Children's interest with 'jungle book' and wild animal statues. Neo-Jacobean revival house, built 1837, mentioned in Pevsner (not open). The land now occupied by the house and garden was historically owned by the family of William Wilberforce. Visitors are welcome to pick produce from the fruit cage and kitchen garden. Parking along the B1249. The jungle garden and the nuttery have stepping stone paths, which cannot be traversed by wheelchair. The steps can mainly be circumvented though.

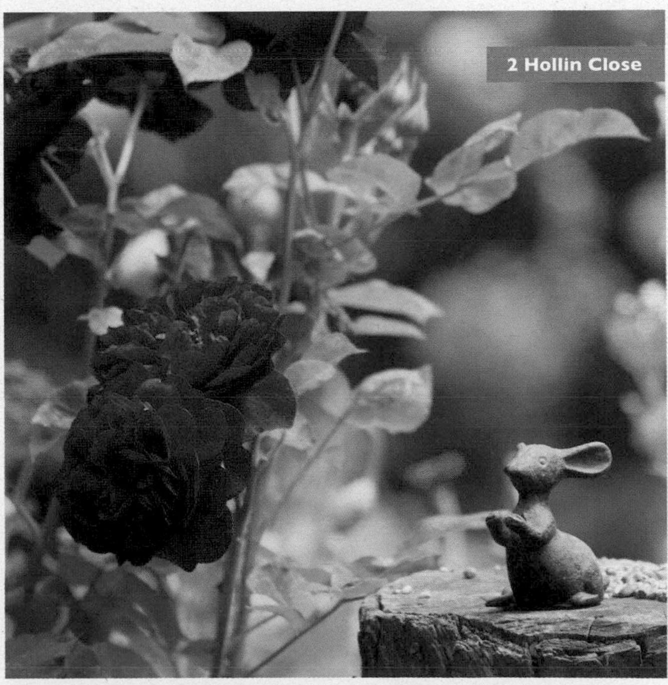

2 Hollin Close

75 THE OLD VICARAGE

Church Street, Whixley, YO26 8AR. Mr & Mrs Roger Marshall, biddymarshall@btinternet.com. *8m W of York, 8m E of Harrogate, 6m N of Wetherby. off A59 3m E of A1M Junction 47 (Postcode not for sat nav).* **Mon 7 May (2-5). Adm £5, chd free. Cream teas. Opening with Whixley Gardens on Wed 6 June. Visits also by arrangement May & June groups of 20+**

This delightful ¾ acre walled flower garden overlooks the deer park. The walls, house and various structures within the garden are festooned with climbers. Mixed borders, old roses, hardy and half-hardy perennials, topiary, bulbs and many hellebores give interest all year. Gravel and old brick paths lead to hidden seating areas creating the atmosphere of a romantic English garden. Partial wheelchair access due to gravelled surfaces and some steps.

76 OMEGA

79 Magdalen Lane, Hedon, HU12 8LA. Mr & Mrs D Rosindale. *6m E of Hull. Through to E Hull onto A1033. L into St Augustine's Gate through Market Place, immed R to Magdalen Gate, ahead to Magdalen Lane.* **Sat 23, Sun 24 June (12.30-5). Adm £3.50, chd free. Homemade Cream Teas, Full 3- tier afternoon tea can be pre-ordered. All cakes home-made.**

Front garden has box hedging and densely planted borders.Side garden has acers, ferns and planted troughs. The patio has planted containers. The back has herbaceous borders and a shady area. An arch leads to a small border, greenhouses. The newly planted willow dome is thriving. There are plants for sale in their hundreds. A full 'Afternoon Tea' can be booked in advance by telephone on or before the Wednesday prior to the open garden. Very large range of perennial plants for sale including minature hostas and large selection of succulents. Disabled access: the front garden can be viewed from the side (path too narrow for wheelchair). The side garden, patio with refreshments and the back garden have full access.

77 THE ORCHARD

4a Blackwood Rise, Cookridge, Leeds, LS16 7BG. Carol & Michael Abbott, 0113 2676764, michael.john.abbott@hotmail.co.uk. *5m N of Leeds centre. Off A660 (Leeds-Otley) N of A6120 Ring Rd. Turn L up Otley Old Rd. At top of hill turn L at T-lights (Tinshill Lane). Please park in Tinshill Lane.* **Sun 6 May (12-4.30). Adm £3.50, chd free. Light refreshments. Pop up cafe and cover for inclement weather. Visits also by arrangement, groups of 10+.**

⅓ acre plantswoman's hidden oasis. A wrap around garden of differing levels made by owners using stone found on site, planted for yr-round interest. Extensive rockery, unusual fruit tree arbour, oriental style seating area and Tea House, linked by grass paths, lawns and steps. Mixed perennials, hostas, ferns, shrubs, bulbs and pots amongst paved and pebbled areas. Best in area award Leeds in Bloom.

78 ◆ PARCEVALL HALL GARDENS

Skyreholme, Skipton, BD23 6DE. Walsingham College, 01756 720311, parcevallhall@btconnect.com, www.parcevallhallgardens.co.uk. *9m N of Skipton. Signs from B6160 Bolton Abbey-Burnsall rd or off B6265 Grassington-Pateley Bridge & at A59 Bolton Abbey r'about.* **For NGS: Wed 16 May (10-5). Adm £7, chd free. Light refreshments. For other opening times and information, please phone, email or visit garden website.**

The only garden open daily in the Yorkshire Dales National Park. 24 acres in Wharfedale sheltered by mixed woodland; terrace garden, rose garden, rock garden, ponds. Mixed borders, spring bulbs, tender shrubs and autumn colour. Tea rooms (contact no. 01756 720630) at the foot of the gardens. There is no wheelchair access in the garden as it is set on a steep hillside with uneven paths.

3 Church Walk

79 PENNY PIECE COTTAGES

41/43 Piercy End, Kirkbymoorside, York, YO62 6DQ. Mick & Ann Potter, 07890 870551, skimmers101@gmail.com. *Follow A170 to Kirkbymoorside at r'about turn up into Kirkby Main St approx 300yds on R. Street parking plus council car park at top of Main St.* **Sun 27 May (12-5). Adm £4, chd free. Home-made teas. Visits also by arrangement Apr to July, groups 10+.**

Hidden away off the main street in Kirkbymoorside is a romantic cottage garden. Now fully matured it offers a sunny circular gravel garden, lawns with island beds planted with mixed shrubs and border perennials . Gravel pathway leads to a brick garden, informal pond, bog garden and colourful herbaceous border. Wildlife pond and pretty wild flower meadow. Lots of places to sit and relax. Featured in the Daily Mail gardening suppliment.

80 PILMOOR COTTAGES

Pilmoor, nr Helperby, YO61 2QQ. Wendy & Chris Jakeman, 01845 501848, cnjakeman@aol.com. *20m N of York. From A1M J48. N end B'bridge follow rd towards Easingwold. From A19 follow signs to Hutton Sessay then Helperby. Garden next to mainline railway.* **Wed 13 June, Sun 26 Aug (12-5). Adm £3.50, chd free. Home-made teas. Visits also by arrangement June to Aug.**

A year round garden for Rail enthusiasts and Garden Visitors. A ride on the 71/4' Gauge railway runs through 2 acres of gardens and gives you the opportunity to view the garden from a different perspective. The journey takes you across water, through a little woodland area, past flower filled borders, and through a tunnel behind the rockery and water cascade. 1½ acre wild flower meadow and pond. Clock-golf putting green.

81 NEW PRIMROSE BANK NURSERY

Dauby Lane, Kexby, York, YO41 5LH. Mrs Sue Goodwill, 07774 944447, suegoodwill@yahoo.co.uk, www.primrosebank.co.uk. *4m E of York. At J of A64 & A1079 take rd signed to Hull, Travel 3m & just as entering Kexby, turn R onto Dauby Lane, signed for Elvington. From the E travel on A1079 towards York. Turn L in Kexby.* **Sat 10, Sun 11 Mar (11-4); Sun 1 July (11-5). Adm £4, chd free. Home-made teas. Includes designated area for dogs. Visits also by arrangement Feb to Sept groups of 10+. Please book refreshments when you book your group.**

Over 1 acre of rare and unusual plant varieties, shrubs and trees. Bulbs, Hellebores and flowering shrubs in spring, followed by planting for yr round interest. Courtyard garden, mixed borders, summer house and pond. Lawns, shade gdn, woodland garden with pond, stumpery, and shepherds' hut. Vegetable and herbs, orchard, poultry and Hebridean sheep. Dogs allowed in car park and designated tables at tearoom. Most areas of the garden are level and are easily accessible for wheelchairs and there is an accessible toilet.

ALLOTMENTS

82 QUEENSGATE & KITCHEN LANE ALLOTMENTS

Beverley, HU17 8NN. Beverley Town Council. *Outskirts of Beverley Town Centre. On A164 towards Cottingham, allotment site is before Victoria Rd, after double mini r'about & opp Beverley Grammar School.* **Sun 15 July (12-4). Adm £3, chd free. Tea.**

Varied allotment site of 85 plots, plus another 35 on Kitchen Lane, growing a wide variety of fruit, vegetables and flowers. Some allotment holders will be present to discuss their plots. Dogs on leads. Wide central grass pathway from which allotments can be viewed. Some can be accessed by wheelchairs.

83 THE RED HOUSE

17 Whin Hill Road, Bessacarr, Doncaster, DN4 7AF. Rosie Hamlin, www.pyjamagardenersyorks.com. *2m S of Doncaster. A638 South, L at T-lights for B1396, Whin Hill Rd is 2nd R. A638 North, R signed Branton B1396 onto Whin Hill.* **Sun 20 May (1-5). Combined adm with Tamarind £5, chd free. Home-made teas.**

Mature ⅔ acre garden. Dry shade a challenge but acid loving plants a joy. Fine acers, camellia, daphne, rhododendrons, kalmia and eucryphia. Terrace and rockery stepping stones lead past and through small woodland garden to lawn with modern orb-shaped rotating summerhouse, shrubs and young trees. White border conceals pond, compost and hens.

84 REWELA COTTAGE

Skewsby, YO61 4SG. John Plant & Daphne Ellis, 01347 888125, plantjohnsgarden@btinternet.com. *4m N of Sheriff Hutton, 15m N of York. After Sheriff Hutton, towards Terrington, turn L towards Whenby & Brandsby. Turn R just past Whenby to Skewsby. Turn L into village. 400yds on R.* **Sun 27 May, Sun 29 July (11-5). Adm £4, chd free. Home-made teas. Great cakes & scones, teas & coffees, soft drinks. Plus BBQ serving 100% Angus Beef-Burgers & Lincolnshire Sausages. WC. Visits also by arrangement May to July excluding June, min15 people in a single group.**

Situated in a lovely quiet country village, a little bit off the beaten track is one of Yorkshire little hidden treasures. Rewela Cottage was designed from a empty paddock, to be as labour saving as possible, using mainly unusual trees and shrubs offering interest all year, using foliage bark and berries, enhancing the well-designed structure. All unusual trees and shrubs have labels giving full descriptions, picture, and any cultivation notes incl propagation. Plant sales are specimens from garden. Many varieties of Heuchera, Heucherella and Tiarellas, Penstemon, Hostas, ferns and herbs for sale. WC. Featured on BBC's Gardeners World showing how an almost flower-free, foliage garden can be inspiring, and a small piece on Heucheras. Some gravel paths may be an effort for a wheelchair. Plenty of seats.

85 ◆ RHS GARDEN HARLOW CARR

Crag Lane, Harrogate, HG3 1QB. Royal Horticultural Society, 01423 565418, harlowcarr@rhs.org.uk, www.rhs.org.uk/harlowcarr. *1½m W of Harrogate town centre. On B6162 (Harrogate - Otley).* **For NGS: Sun 6 May (9.30-5). Adm £11.50, chd £5.75. For other opening times and information, please phone, email or visit garden website.**

One of Yorkshire's most relaxing yet inspiring locations! Highlights include spectacular herbaceous borders, streamside garden, alpines, scented and kitchen gardens. Lakeside Gardens, woodland and wild flower meadows. Betty's Cafe Tearooms, gift shop, plant centre and childrens play area incl tree house and log ness monster. Wheelchairs and mobility scooters available, advanced booking recommended.

86 THE RIDINGS

South Street, Burton Fleming, Driffield, YO25 3PE. Roy & Ruth Allerston, 01262 470489. *11m NE of Driffield. 11m SW of Scarborough. 7m NW of Bridlington. From Driffield B1249, before Foxholes turn R to Burton Fleming. From Scarborough A165 turn R to Burton Fleming.* **Sun 17 June (1-5). Combined adm with Rustic Cottage £6, chd free. Home-made teas. Single adm £3. Visits also by arrangement Apr to July.**

Secluded cottage garden with colour-themed borders surrounding neat lawns. Grass and paved paths lead to formal and informal areas through rose and clematis covered pergolas and arbours. Box hedging defines well stocked borders with roses, herbaceous plants and trees. Seating in sun and shade offer vistas and views. Potager, greenhouse and summerhouse. Terrace with waterfeature and farming bygones. Terrace, tea area and main lawn accessible via ramp.

87 RUSTIC COTTAGE

Front Street, Wold Newton, nr Driffield, YO25 3YQ. Jan Joyce, 01262 470710, janetmjoyce@icloud.com. *13m N of Driffield. From Driffield take B1249 to Foxholes (12m), take R turning signed Wold Newton. Turn L onto Front St, opp village pond, continue up hill, garden on L.* **Sun 20 May (12-4). Adm £4, chd free. Sun 17 June (12-4). Combined adm with The Ridings £6, chd free. Home-made teas at The Ridings, Burton Fleming, Sun 17 June. Single adm £4. Visits also by arrangement 20 max. Adm £4. Combined with Ridings adm £6. Refreshments at Ridings when both gardens are open.**

Plantswoman's cottage garden of much interest with many choice and unusual plants. Hellebores and bulbs are treats for colder months. Old-fashioned roses, fragrant perennials, herbs and wild flowers, all grown together provide habitat for birds, bees, butterflies and small mammals. It has been described as 'organised chaos'! The owner's 2nd NGS garden. Small dogs only.

88 ◆ SCAMPSTON WALLED GARDEN

Scampston Hall, Scampston, Malton, YO17 8NG. The Legard Family, 01944 759111, info@scampston.co.uk, www.scampston.co.uk/gardens. *5m E of Malton. ½m N of A64, nr the village of Rillington & signed Scampston only.* **For opening times and information, please phone, email or visit garden website.**

An exciting modern garden designed by Piet Oudolf. The 4-acre walled garden contains a series of hedged enclosures designed to look good throughout the year. The garden contains many unusual species and is a must for any keen plantsman. The Walled Garden is set within the grounds and parkland surrounding Scampston Hall. The Hall opens to visitors for a short period during the summer months. A newly restored Richardson conservatory at the heart of the Walled Garden re-opened as a Heritage and Learning Centre in 2015. The Walled Garden, Cafe and facilities are accessible for the disabled. Some areas of the Parkland and the first floor of Hall are harder to access.

89 SCAPE LODGE

11 Grand Stand, Scapegoat Hill, Golcar, Huddersfield, HD7 4NQ. Dr & Mrs David Smith, 01484 644320, elizabethrfsmith@btinternet.com. *5m W of Huddersfield. From J23 or 24 M62 follow signs to Rochdale. After Outlane village, 1st L. At top of hill, 2nd L. Parking at Scapegoat Hill Baptist Church (HD7 4NU) or in village. 5 mins walk to garden. 303/304 bus.* **Sun 20 May, Sun 19 Aug (1-5). Adm £3.50, chd free. Home-made teas. Visits also by arrangement June to Aug.** Donation to Mayor of Kirklees Charity.

⅓ acre contemporary country garden at 1000ft in the Pennines. Steeply sloping site with far-reaching views over the Colne Valley and out towards the Peak District. Gravel paths lead between mixed borders on many levels. Naturalistic planting for year round colour, with interesting plants. Steps lead to terraced kitchen and cutting garden. Gazebo, pond, shade garden, deck and places to sit.

90 1 SCHOOL LANE

Bempton, Bridlington, YO15 1JA. Mr Robert Tyas. *Close to the centre of the village. 3m N of Bridlington. From Brid take B1255 toward Flamborough. L at 1st T-lights. Follow Bempton Lane out of residential area then 2nd R onto Bolam Lane. Continue to end and garden is facing.* **Sun 27 May (10-4). Adm £3.50, chd free. Home-made teas.**

A village garden with many interesting features supported by planting for year round interest. Mixed borders and beds create a cottage garden feel at the front, whilst the rear boasts alpines presented in a variety of ways, including troughs, crevice rockery and a greenhouse display of Lewisia. Raised beds for veg, fruit trees and an expanding collection of unusual plants add further interest. Small vegetable area designed to maximise the space while the fruit trees and other features provide additional interest. Cottage style planting in front garden. Collection of Lewisia. All areas of the garden can be viewed from the wheelchair.

91 ◆ SHANDY HALL GARDENS

Coxwold, YO61 4AD. The Laurence Sterne Trust, 01347 868465, www.laurencesternetrust.org.uk/shandy-hall-garden.php. *N of York. From A19, 7m from both Easingwold & Thirsk, turn E signed Coxwold.* **For NGS: Fri 8, Fri 29 June (6.30-8am). Adm £3, chd free.** For other opening times and information, please phone or visit garden website.

Home of C18 author Laurence Sterne. 2 walled gardens, 1 acre of unusual perennials interplanted with tulips and old roses in low walled beds. In old quarry, another acre of trees, shrubs, bulbs, climbers and wild flowers encouraging wildlife, incl. over 420 recorded species of moths. Moth trap, identification and release. Wildlife garden. Wheelchair access to wild garden by arrangement.

GROUP OPENING

92 SHIPTONTHORPE GARDENS

Station Rd, Shiptonthorpe, York, YO43 3PQ. *2m NW of Market Weighton. Both gardens & VH are in the main village on the N of A1079.* **Sat 2, Sun 3 June (11-5). Combined adm £5, chd free. Home-made teas in the village hall.**

6 ALL SAINTS
Di Thompson.

WAYSIDE
Susan Sellars.

Two contrasting gardens offering different approaches to gardening style - 6 All Saints is an eclectic 'maze-like' garden with a mix of contemporary and cottage garden features; hidden corners, water features and pond. Wayside has interesting planting in different areas of the garden. Vegetable and fruit growing areas with greenhouse. Proceeds for teas to go to the village hall and church. Wheelchairs possible with help at 6 All Saints also at Wayside (narrow access and large gravel).

93 SKIPWITH HALL

Skipwith, Selby, YO8 5SQ. Mr & Mrs C D Forbes Adam, rosalind@escrick.com, , www.escrick.com/hall-gardens. *9m S of York, 6m N of Selby. From York A19 Selby, L in Escrick, 4m to Skipwith. From Selby A19 York, R onto A163 to Market Weighton, then L after 2m to Skipwith.* **Thur 7 June (1-4). Adm £5, chd free. Home-made teas. Visits also by arrangement May & June, groups of 10+.**

4-acre walled garden of Queen Anne house (not open). Extensive mixed borders and lawns, walled areas by renowned designer Cecil Pinsent. Recreated working kitchen garden with 15' beech hedge, pleached fruit, herb maze and pool. Woodland with specimen trees and shell house. Decorative orchard with espaliered and fan-trained fruit on walls. Italian Garden recently restored. Gravel paths.

♿ ✿ 🚘 ☕

94 SLEIGHTHOLMEDALE LODGE

Fadmoor, YO62 7JG. Patrick & Natasha James. *6m NE of Helmsley. Parking can be limited in wet weather. Garden is 1st property in Sleightholmedale, 1m from Fadmoor.* **Wed 27 June, Sun 12 Aug (2-6). Adm £5, chd free. Home-made teas.**

Hillside garden, walled rose garden and herbaceous borders with delphiniums, roses, verbascums in July. Species tulips and meconopsis in early June. Views over peaceful valley in N.Yorks Moors.

🐕 ☕

95 NEW 113 SOUTHFIELD

Southfield, Hessle, HU13 0ET. Michael & Nancy Baitson. *At r'about where A164 meets A15 go E onto A1105(to Hull). At 1st lights turn R onto Heads Lane. Cross Ferriby Rd at crossroads. Southfield is 2nd L.* **Sun 27 May (12-5.30). Combined adm with Beacon Garth £6, chd free. Home-made teas at Beacon Garth.**

A wrap round garden in ⅓ acre with a surprise at each corner. 2 water features, woodland pathway, unusual shrubs, a variety of Hellebores and Ferns. No lawn! The garden has been developed and maintained since 2003 by current owners. Changes are ongoing.

♿ ☕

96 ◆ STILLINGFLEET LODGE

Stewart Lane, Stillingfleet, York, YO19 6HP. Mr & Mrs J Cook, 01904 728506, vanessa.cook@stillingfleetlodgenurseries.co.uk, www.stillingfleetlodgenurseries.co.uk. *6m S of York. From A19 York-Selby take B1222 towards Sherburn in Elmet. In village turn opp church.* **For NGS: Sun 13 May, Sun 16 Sept (1-5). Adm £5, chd £1. Home-made teas. For other opening times and information, please phone, email or visit garden website.**

Organic, wildlife garden subdivided into smaller gardens, each based on colour theme with emphasis on use of foliage plants. Wild flower meadow and natural pond. 55yd double herbaceous borders. Modern rill garden. Rare breeds of poultry wander freely in garden. Adjacent nursery. Wildlife Day in June. Garden Courses run all summer see website. Featured in Yorkshire Post, The Garden and Daily Mail. Gravel paths and lawn. Ramp to cafe if needed. No disabled WC.

♿ ✿ 🚘 ☕

97 SUE PROCTOR PLANTS NURSERY GARDEN

69 Ings Mill Avenue, Clayton West, Huddersfield, HD8 9QG. Sue & Richard Proctor, 01484 866189, hostas@sueproctorplants.co.uk, www.sueproctorplants.co.uk. *9m NE of Holmfirth, 10m SW of Wakefield. Off A636 Wakefield/ Holmfirth. From M1 J39 in Clayton West Village turn L signed Clayton West, High Hoyland, then R signed Kaye's F & N School. Turn 1st R to Ings Mill Avenue.* **Sat 14, Sun 15 July (11-4). Adm £3.50, chd free. Light refreshments. Gluten free available. Visits also by arrangement May to July for groups of 10-30.**

Small, mainly sloping, suburban garden packed full of interest. Summer highlights include over 300 varieties of hostas and close plantings of flowering perennials with some rare and unusual plants. Shaded gravel and rock gardens show off acers, ferns and hostas, especially miniature hostas, the nursery specialism. The garden is close to the Kirklees Light Railway, Cannon Hall Country Park and Bretton Sculpture Park. A notable feature is our collection of hostas, one of the largest in the North of England, including the smallest miniature hostas, less than 4' in height to the world's largest 'Empress Wu'. A variety of half-hardy plants, especially climbers, flower throughout the summer. Partial wheelchair access and a graded path to the top of the garden.

🐕 ✿ ☕

98 SWALE COTTAGE

Station Road, Richmond, DL10 4LU. Julie Martin & Dave Dalton, 01748 829452, jmalandplan@btinternet.com. *Richmond town centre. On foot, facing bottom of Market Place, turn L onto Frenchgate, then R onto Station Rd. House 1st on R.* **Visits by arrangement May to Sept for groups of 10+. Adm £4, chd free. Teas and refreshments available in town centre nearby.**

½-acre urban oasis on steep site, with sweeping views and hidden corners. Several enclosed garden rooms on different levels. Mature herbaceous, rose and shrub garden with strong foliage interest. Magnificent yew and cedar. Organic vegetables and soft fruit and pond. Adjacent orchard and paddock with sheep.

☕

99 TAMARIND

2 Whin Hill Road, Bessacarr, Doncaster, DN4 7AE. Ken & Carol Kilvington. *2m S of Doncaster. Through Lakeside, past Dome on R turn R at Bawtry Rd T-lights, through pedestrian crossing & T-lights then 1st L. A638 N from Bawtry to Doncaster turn R signed Cantley-Branton (B1396).* **Sun 20 May (1-5). Combined adm with The Red House £5, chd free. Sun**

1 July (11-5). Combined adm with 2 Hollin Close, Rossington DN11 0XX £5, chd free. Light refreshments.
A ⅔ acre garden is level at the front with acers and interesting varied planting. Round lawn leads to a steeply terraced rear garden full of colour and differing styles. White border with dovecote and doves; hot border, rose garden, herbaceous, embankment, fern garden and rhododendron garden. Stream with waterfalls, ponds, rockery and bog garden, thatched summerhouse, patio. Steep steps. The front garden and rear lower patio is accessible to wheelchairs, from which most of the rear garden can be viewed. Steps to the rest of the garden.

100 ◆ THORNYCROFT
Rainton, nr Thirsk, YO7 3PH. Martin & Jill Fish, 01845 577157, martin@martinfish.com, www.martinfish.com. *1m E of A1(M) between Ripon & Thirsk. Approx 6m N of Boroughbridge, access to Rainton is from J48 or 50 of A1(M) or from A168 dual carriageway at Asenby or Topcliffe.* **For NGS: Sun 22 July (11-4.30). Adm £4, chd free. Home-made teas. For other opening times and information, please phone, email or visit garden website.**
A ¾ acre country garden created since 2009 comprising lawn areas, trees, shrubs and perennials and featuring some unusual plant specimens. Pergola, summerhouse and paved courtyard garden with container plants and raised beds. Orchard with mixture of heritage and modern varieties and an ornamental kitchen garden. Wooden greenhouse with decorative plants and productive poly-tunnel. BBC Radio gardening expert Martin Fish will be on hand to answer your gardening questions. The garden features regularly in Kitchen Garden and Garden News magazines, used for outside broadcasts for BBC Radio York and BBC Radio Nottingham. Photos for Martin and Jill's book 'Gardening on the Menu' were taken in the fruit and vegetable plot. Gravel drive and gravel paths in kitchen garden.

101 NEW THE VILLA
High Street, Hook, Goole, DN14 5PJ. Penny & John Settle. *Close to M62 J36 & J37. Approach Hook from A614 Boothferry Road along Westfield Lane around 'z' bend to Xrds where the village hall stands. Turn L, garden approx. 300yds down on R. Park on High St.* **Sun 3 June, Sun 5 Aug (11-4). Adm £3.50, chd free. Light refreshments.**
Acquired in 2011 in a derelict state, the garden has been constructed by the current owners to offer a variety of different areas incl. Mediterranean, bonsai and oriental, a pergola walkway, paved terraces, lawns, statues and a large variety of perennial shrubs, bamboo and ornamental grasses. In addition, there will be a display of work by local artists and plants grown in the garden for sale. The garden offers plenty of seating for visitors to sit and take in the tranquillity of this hidden gem.

102 WARLEY HOUSE GARDEN
Stock Lane, Warley, Halifax, HX2 7RU. Dr & Mrs P J Hinton, www.warleyhousegardens.com. *2m W of Halifax. Take A646 (towards Burnley) from Halifax centre. Go through large intersection after approx 1m. After further 1m take R turn up Windle Royd Lane. Signs will direct you from here. There is disabled parking on site, but limited to 4/5 vehicles.* **Sun 13, Wed 16 May (1-5). Adm £4, chd free. Home-made teas.**
Partly walled 2½ acre garden of demolished C18 House, renovated by the present owners. Rocky paths and Japanese style planting lead to lawns and lovely S-facing views. Alpine ravine planted with ferns and fine trees give structure to the developing woodland area. Drifts of shrubs, herbaceous plantings, wild flowers and heathers maintain constant seasonal interest. This is an historic garden, renovated after total neglect from 1945 to 1995. Spring planting is enhanced by many new rhododendrons and woodland planting. Partial wheelchair access to Japanese garden. Disabled access to WCs.

103 WELL HOUSE
Marton cum Grafton, YO51 9QJ. Glen Garnett. *2½m S of Boroughbridge. Turn off B6265 or A168 S of Boroughbridge.* **Wed 6 June (1-5). Combined adm with Whixley Gardens £6, chd free. Cream teas at The Old Vicarage, Whixley.**
On the outskirts of Grafton village, nestling under a hillside with long views to the White Horse and Hambleton hills, extending to 1½ acres, this garden was begun 37 years ago and is under constant change. A traditional English cottage garden, with herbaceous borders, climbing and rambling roses, and ornamental shrubs with a variety of interesting species. Paths lead to orchard with geese, ducks and chickens.

104 THE WHITE HOUSE
Husthwaite, YO61 4QA. Mrs A Raper, 01347 868688, audrey.husthwaite@btinternet.com. *5m S of Thirsk. Turn R off A19 signed Husthwaite. 1½m to centre of village opp parish church.* **Visits by arrangement any size group. Adm £6, chd free.**
Meet an enthusiastic plantswoman. Exchange ideas and visit a 1-acre country garden. Walled garden, conservatory, unusual plants and shrubs and interesting trees. Early season flowering of species and new intersectional pæonies. Collection of shrub roses and herbacious pæonies, alstromera and clematis. A garden for all seasons.

GROUP OPENING

105 WHIXLEY GARDENS

York, YO26 8AR. 01423 330474, biddymarshall@btinternet.com. *8m W of York, 8m E of Harrogate, 6m N of Wetherby. 3m E of A1(M) off A59 York-Harrogate. Signed Whixley.* **Wed 6 June (12-5). Combined adm with Well House, Grafton YO51 9QJ £6, chd free. Cream teas at The Old Vicarage. Visits also by arrangement May to July groups of 20+.**

COBBLE COTTAGE
John Hawkridge & Barry Atkinson, 01423 331419, john_barry44@outlook.com. **Visits also by arrangement only groups of 20+.**

THE OLD VICARAGE
Mr & Mrs Roger Marshall.
(See separate entry)

Attractive rural yet accessible village nestling on the edge of the York Plain with beautiful historic church and Queen Anne Hall (not open). The gardens are at opposite ends of the village with good footpaths. A plantsman's and flower arranger's garden at Cobble Cottage has views to the Hambleton Hills. Close to the church, The Old Vicarage, with a ¾-acre walled flower garden, overlooks the old deer park. The walls, house and various structures are festooned with climbers. Gravel and old brick paths lead to hidden seating areas creating the atmosphere of a romantic English garden.

Donations from the National Garden Scheme enable Perennial to care for horticulturalists

106 WHYNCREST

Bridlington Road, Hunmanby, Filey, YO14 9RS. Mrs Lieke Swann, 01723 890923, liekeswann@gmail.com. *Between Hunmanby & Reighton Nursery off A165 between Hunmanby Gap & Reighton. Exit A165, junction signed Reigthon Nurseries & Hunmanby, follow this rd for 200 yds, Whyncrest is on R. Parking on grass verge outside.* **Evening opening Thur 2, Fri 3 Aug (5.30-8.30). Adm £6, chd free. Adm incl. Wine/Juice. Visits also by arrangement July & Aug.**

Elevated garden with wow factor views across Filey Bay and beyond. The garden has been carefully designed, creating micro climate 'rooms' taking you from jungle garden to a pond garden with tropical planting and a huge waterfall, herbaceous borders and topiary shrubs. The collection of plants is varied, giving an all year interest from early spring with all its bulbs all the way into late autumn. Dogs on leads welcome.

107 NEW WILLOW COTTAGE

Beckside, Barmby Moor, York, YO42 4HA. Mrs Tez McCloskey, 07790 825110 or 07962 225600. *8m E of York just off A1079, 2m from Pocklington. Centre of village on village green. Parking is on Main street. Cut through church yard & turn R onto Beck Side.* **Sun 24 June (11-5). Adm £3.50, chd free. Also open Linden Lodge. Visits also by arrangement Apr to June.**

A white garden, north facing, small (just 300m2) but perfectly formed with several seating areas giving time to absorb the garden. Split into three sections and planted for scent. Patio with raised beds, shade area, and sunny lawn with borders summerhouse and home made greenhouse. Wheelchair access. Gravel drive and single step up to lawn.

108 WOODLANDS COTTAGE

Summerbridge, Nidderdale, HG3 4BT. Mr & Mrs Stark, 01423 780765, annstark@btinternet.com, www.woodlandscottagegarden.co.uk. *10m NW of Harrogate. On the B6165 W of Summerbridge.* **Sun 13 May (1-5). Adm £3.50, chd free. Home-made teas. Also open Low Hall. Opening with Dacre Banks & Summerbridge Gardens on Sun 8 July. Visits also by arrangement May to Aug.**

A one acre country garden created by its owners and making full use of its setting, which includes natural woodland with wild bluebells and gritstone boulders. There are several gardens within the garden, from a wild flower meadow and woodland rock-garden to a formal herb garden and herbaceous areas; also a productive fruit and vegetable garden. Gravel paths with some slopes.

109 WYEDALE

Ottringham Road, Keyingham, Hull, HU12 9RX. Mrs Angie & Mr J Woodmancy. *10m E of Hull. Enter Keyingham on A1033 Hull to Withernsea Rd, continue through village, garage on R, head towards mill. Parking on L at Eastend Nurseries, garden approx 70 yds on R.* **Sun 1 July (11-5). Adm £3.50, chd free. Home-made teas.**

An English Country garden, ¾ acre with far reaching views to Lincolnshire Wolds. Curved borders of herbaceous perennials, scented seating area with pinks, jasmin, philadelphus and herbs, wildlife pond. Gravel garden with grasses leading to pergola clothed in roses and clematis followed by cutting garden with interesting 'folly wall' wild life area leads to orchard. All areas have wheelchair access.

110 ◆ YORK GATE

Back Church Lane, Adel, Leeds, LS16 8DW. Perennial, 0113 267 8240, yorkgate@perennial.org.uk, www.yorkgate.org.uk. *5m N of*

Leeds. 2¼ m SE of Bramhope, signed from A660. Park in Church Lane in lay-by opp church & take public footpath through lovely churchyard to garden. For opening times and information, please phone, email or visit garden website.

An internationally acclaimed one acre masterpiece, widely recognised as one of the most innovative small gardens of the period. 14 garden rooms, reflecting the Arts & Crafts period are linked by delightful vistas. Enjoy the home baking in our tea room and browse the gift shop. Owned by Perennial, the charity that looks after gardeners and horticulturalists in times of need. Whether you're visiting individually, in smaller groups or with a coach party, new and returning visitors we'd love to welcome you. Groups please pre-book so we can arrange your personal introduction to the garden and its heritage, as well as your refreshments. Gravel paths make the garden unsuitable for wheelchairs and pushchairs.

111 YORKE HOUSE

Dacre Banks, Nidderdale, HG3 4EW. Tony & Pat Hutchinson, 01423 780456, pat@yorkehouse.co.uk, www.yorkehouse.co.uk. *4m SE of Pateley Bridge, 10m NW of Harrogate, 10m N of Otley. On B6451 near centre of Dacre Banks. Car park.* **Sun 17 June (11-5). Adm £5, chd free. Cream teas. Opening with Dacre Banks & Summerbridge Gardens on Sun 8 July. Visits also by arrangement June & July for groups of 10 minimum.**

Award-winning English country garden in the heart of Nidderdale. Designed as a series of distinct areas which flow naturally through 2 acres of ornamental garden. Colour-themed borders, fragrant millennium garden, woodland sanctuary and secluded seating areas. Natural ponds and stream with delightful waterside plantings. Flower arranger's garden with large collection of Hosta. Orchard picnic area. Winner Harrogate's Glorious Gardens. Radio York and Harrogate Advertiser. All main features accessible to wheelchair users.

112 ◆ THE YORKSHIRE ARBORETUM

Castle Howard, York, YO60 7BY. The Castle Howard Arboretum Trust, 01653 648598, visit@yorkshirearboretum.org, www.yorkshirearboretum.org. *15m NE of York. Off A64. Follow signs to Castle Howard then look for Yorkshire Arboretum signs at the obelisk r'about.* **For NGS: Sun 3 June (10-4.30). Adm £7, chd £3.50. Light refreshments at Roots, the Arboretum Cafe.** For other opening times and information, please phone, email or visit garden website.

A glorious, 120 acre garden of trees from around the world set in a stunning landscape of parkland, lakes and ponds. With walks and lakeside trails, tours, family activities, a woodland playground, cafè and gift shop we welcome visitors of all ages wanting to enjoy the space, serenity and beauty of this sheltered valley as well as those interested in our extensive collection of trees and shrubs. Internationally renowned collection of trees in a beautiful setting, accompanied by a diversity of wild flowers, birds, insects and other wildlife. Dogs on leads welcome. Not suitable for wheelchairs. Motorised all-terrain buggies are available on loan, please book 24hrs in advance on 01653 648598.

NPC

Swale Cottage

WALES

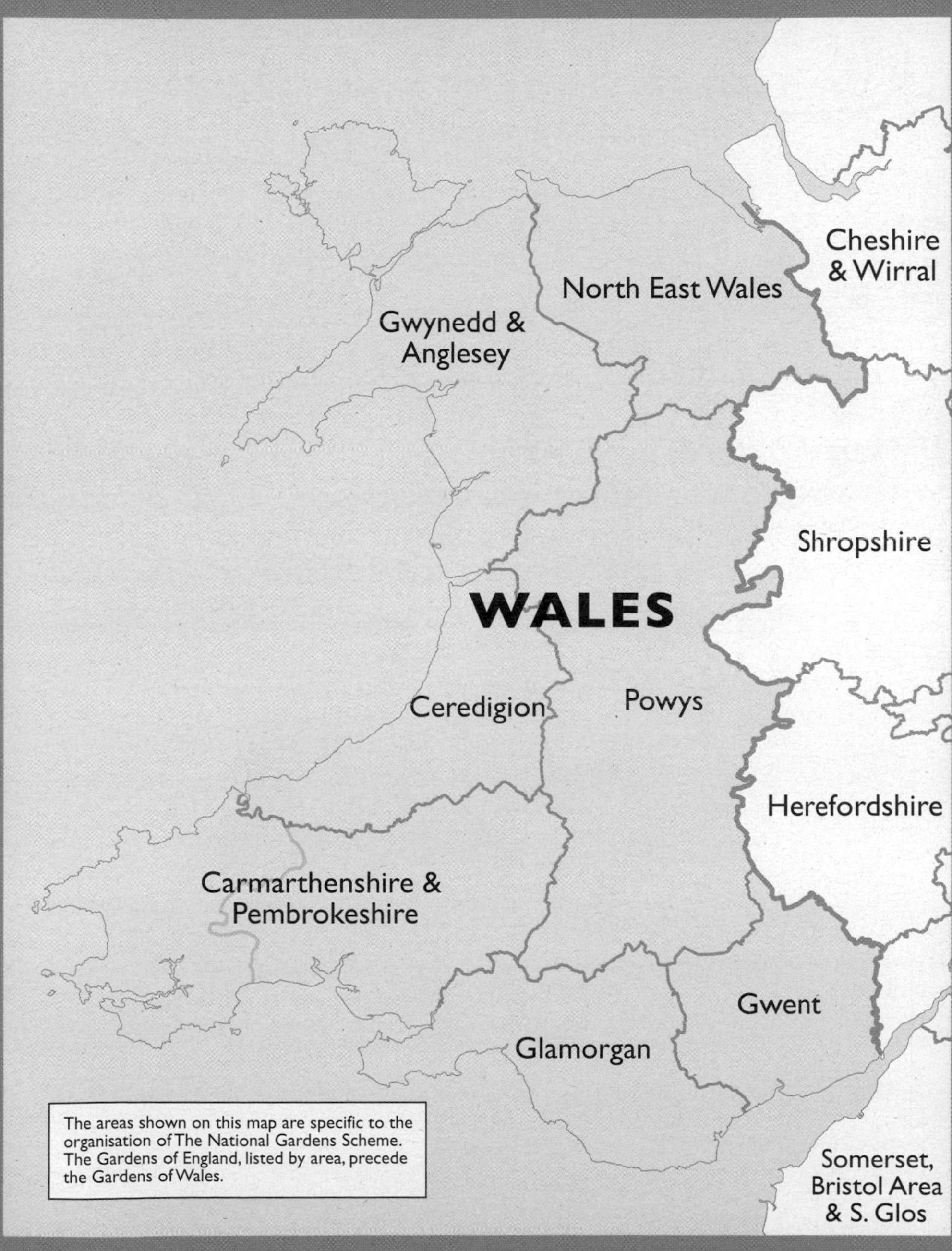

The areas shown on this map are specific to the organisation of The National Gardens Scheme. The Gardens of England, listed by area, precede the Gardens of Wales.

CARMARTHENSHIRE & PEMBROKESHIRE

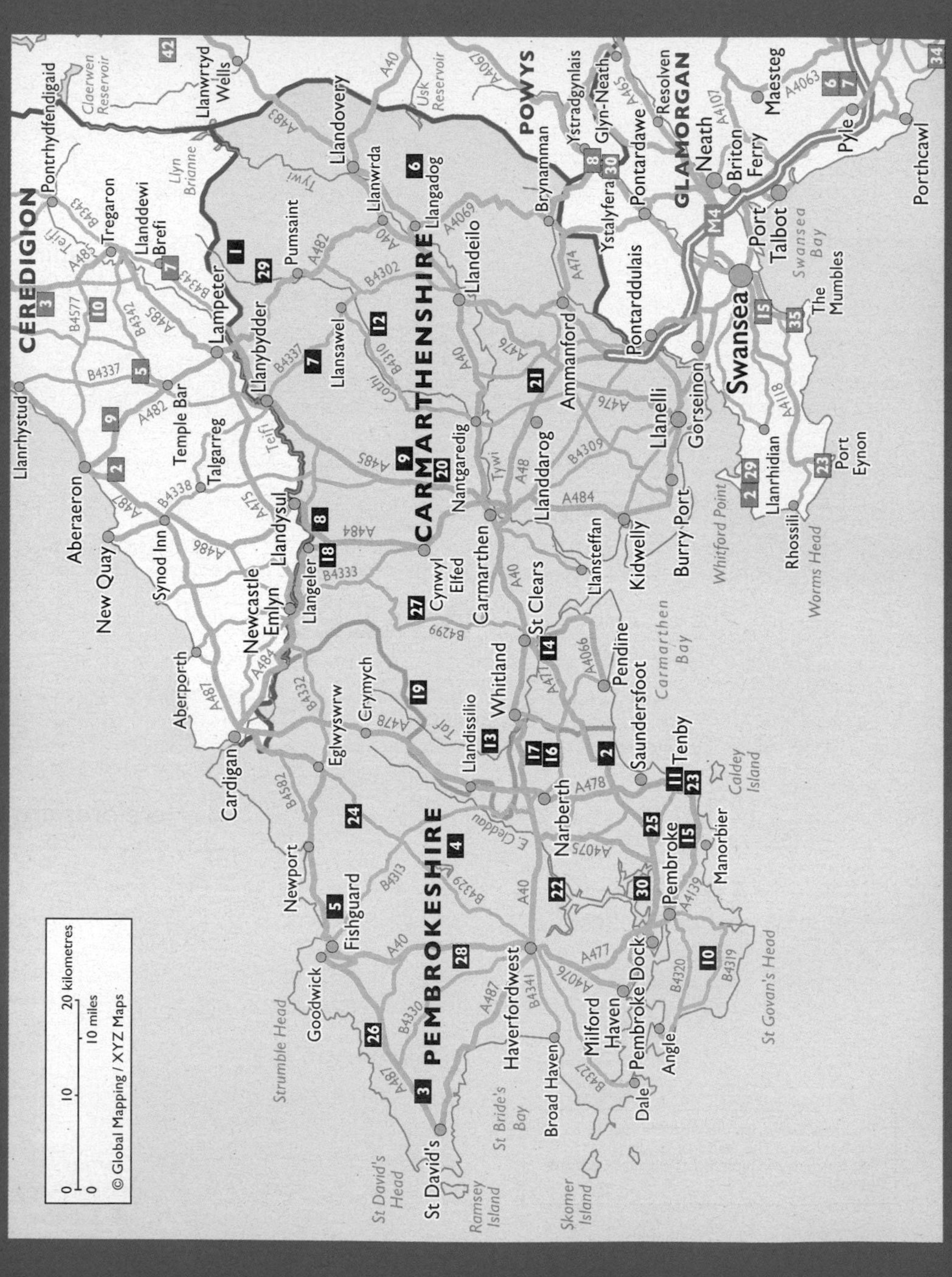

From the rugged Western coast and beaches to the foothills of the Brecon Beacons and Black Mountain, these counties offer gardens as varied as the topography and weather.

The remote and romantic gardens such as Bwlchau Duon, Gelli Uchaf and Pant-Y-Fedwen will delight with superb views and borrowed landscape, whilst in gardens such as The Retreat, Llwyngarreg, Panteg and Nantyietau, tender plants flourish. Each of our many gardens has something different to offer the visitor and many now welcome dogs as well as their owners!

Several fascinating gardens have restricted parking areas and so are only open 'By Arrangement'; the owners will be delighted to see you, but please do telephone first to arrange a visit. Most of our gardens also offer teas or light refreshments and what better way to enjoy an afternoon in a garden, where there is no weeding or washing up for you to do! We look forward to welcoming you to our gardens.

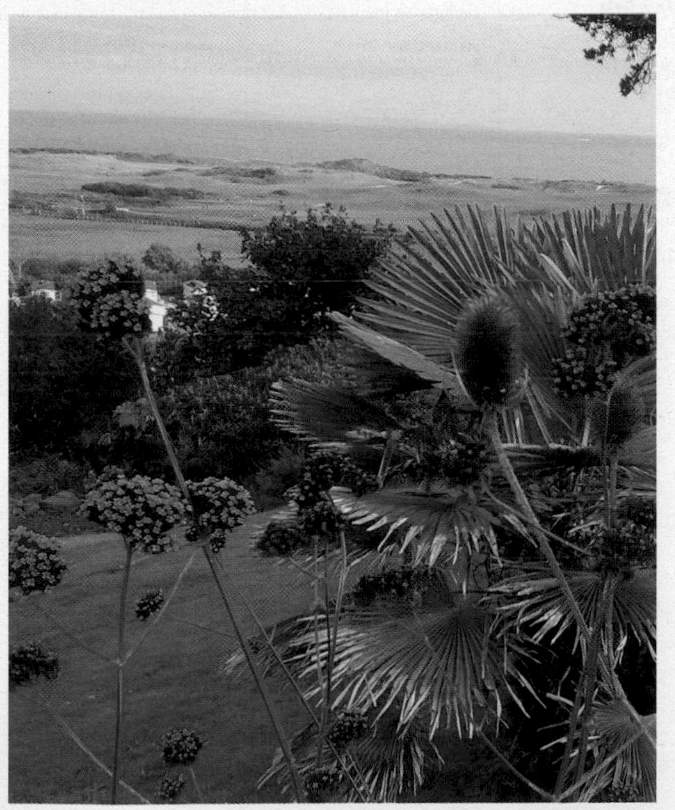

Volunteers

County Organisers
Jackie Batty
01437 741115
bathole2000@aol.com

County Treasurer
Christine Blower
01267 253334
cheahnwood@toucansurf.com

Assistant County Organisers
Elena Gilliatt
01558 685321

Liz and Paul O'Neill
01994 240717
lizpaulfarm@yahoo.co.uk

Ivor Stokes
01558 823233
ivor.t.stokes@btopenworld.com

Brenda Timms
01558 650187

Left: The Retreat

OPENING DATES

All entries subject to change. For latest information check **www.ngs.org.uk**

Extended openings are shown at the beginning of the month.

Map locator numbers are shown to the right of each garden name.

March

Sunday 25th
◆ Upton Castle Gardens 30

April

Sunday 1st
Llwyngarreg 13

May

Every day from Friday 4th to Thursday 17th
The Crystal Garden 3

Sunday 6th
◆ Dyffryn Fernant 5
Norchard 15
Treffgarne Hall 28

Saturday 12th
◆ Colby Woodland Garden 2

Sunday 13th
◆ Colby Woodland Garden 2

Sunday 20th
◆ Picton Castle & Gardens 22

Sunday 27th
Panteg 17

Monday 28th
The Old Rectory 16

June

Every Friday to Wednesday from Sunday 3rd to Sunday 17th
The Crystal Garden 3

Saturday 9th
NEW Glangwili Lodges 9

Sunday 10th
Gelli Mydog 6
NEW Glangwili Lodges 9
◆ Picton Castle & Gardens 22

Sunday 17th
Tradewinds 27

Saturday 23rd
Pant-y-Fedwen 18
NEW Pen-y-Garn 21

Sunday 24th
Bwlchau Duon 1
NEW Hayston Farmhouse 10
Llwyngarreg 13
NEW Pen-y-Garn 21

July

Every Friday to Wednesday from Sunday 1st to Sunday 15th
The Crystal Garden 3

Sunday 8th
NEW Heywood Lane Gardens 11
Llwyngarreg 13
NEW The Retreat 23

Sunday 15th
Pentresite 20

Sunday 22nd
Treffgarne Hall 28

Saturday 28th
Glandwr 8

Sunday 29th
Glandwr 8

August

Sunday 5th
◆ Dyffryn Fernant 5
Ty'r Maes 29

Sunday 19th
Tradewinds 27

September

Sunday 2nd
◆ Dyffryn Fernant 5

By Arrangement

Bwlchau Duon 1
The Crystal Garden 3
Cwm Pibau 4
Gelli Uchaf 7
Glandwr 8
Lan Farm 12
Llwyngarreg 13
NEW Nantyietau 14
The Old Rectory 16
Panteg 17
NEW Pencwm 19
Pentresite 20
NEW Pen-y-Garn 21
Rhyd-y-Groes 24
Rosewood 25
NEW Scotsborough House, Heywood Lane Gardens 11
Stable Cottage 26
Treffgarne Hall 28
Ty'r Maes 29

THE GARDENS

1 BWLCHAU DUON

Ffarmers, Llanwrda, Carmarthenshire, SA19 8JJ. Brenda & Allan Timms, 01558 650187, brendatimmsuk@gmail.com. *7m SE Lampeter, 8m NW Llanwrda. From A482 turn to Ffarmers. In Ffarmers, take lane opp Drovers Arms PH. Shortly after caravan site on L there is a very small Xrds, turn L into single track lane & follow NGS arrows.* **Sun 24 June (2-6). Adm £3.50, chd free. Home-made teas. Visits also by arrangement June to Aug.**

A 1 acre, ever evolving garden challenge, set in the foothills of the Cambrian Mountains at 1100ft. This is a plantaholics haven where borders are full of many unusual plants and lots of old favourites. There are raised vegetable gardens, a 100ft herbaceous border, recently planted natural bog areas, winding pathways through semi-woodland and magnificent views over the Cothi valley. Rare breed turkeys, chickens, geese and rabbits!

2 ◆ COLBY WOODLAND GARDEN

Amroth, Narberth, Pembrokeshire, SA67 8PP. National Trust, 01834 811885, www.nationaltrust.org.uk. *6m N of Tenby, 5m SE of Narberth. Follow brown tourist signs on coast rd & A477.* **For NGS: Sat 12, Sun 13 May (10-5). Adm £8, chd £4. Light refreshments in the Bothy Tearoom.** For other opening times and information, please phone or visit garden website.

8 acre woodland garden in a secluded valley with fine collection of rhododendrons and azaleas. Wildflower meadow and stream with rope swings and stepping stones for children to explore and play. Ornamental walled garden incl unusual gazebo, designed by Wyn Jones, with internal tromp

l'oeil. Incl in the *Register of Historic Parks and Gardens: Pembrokeshire*. Extensive play area for children incl den building and log climbing. Free family activities incl duck racing, pond dipping, campfire lighting etc. Children under 5, free entry. Full range of refreshments incl lunches. Partial access for wheelchair users.

3 THE CRYSTAL GARDEN

Golwg yr Ynys, Carnhedryn, St Davids, Pembrokeshire, SA62 6XT. Mrs Sue Clark, 01437 721082, sueclark132@gmail.com, www.thecrystalgarden.org.uk. *4m E of St Davids, 11m SW of Fishguard, 2m N of Solva. Village of Carnhedryn, off A487 between Fishguard & St Davids.* **Daily Fri 4 May to Thur 17 May (1-5). Every Fri to Wed 3 June to 17 June (1-5). Every Fri to Wed 1 July to 15 July (1-5). Adm £3.50, chd free. Tea. Visits also by arrangement Apr to Sept. Individuals or groups are very welcome, just ring first. Teas on request when booking.**

¾ acre garden for plantaholics with yr-round floral colour and foliage interest. Intriguing layout of sheltered rooms full of surprises packed with unusual shrubs, perennials and garden favourites. Ever changing outer garden. The garden never stands still. Specialities incl hebes and hydrangeas. A warm welcome awaits. Art wall, glazed visitor room. Appeared in Welsh Country magazine.

4 CWM PIBAU

New Moat, Clarbeston Road, Haverfordwest, Pembrokeshire, SA63 4RE. Mrs Duncan Drew, 01437 532454. *10m NE of Haverfordwest. 3m SW of Maenclochog. Off A40, take B4313 to Maenclochog, follow signs to New Moat, past church, then 2nd concealed drive on L, ½m rural drive.* **Visits by arrangement, please telephone first to ensure a welcome. Adm £3, chd free.**

5 acre woodland garden surrounded by old deciduous woodland and streams. Created in 1978, contains many mature, unusual shrubs and trees from Chile, New Zealand and Europe, set on S-facing hill. More conventional planting nearer house.

5 ◆ DYFFRYN FERNANT

Llanychaer, Fishguard, Pembrokeshire, SA65 9SP. Christina Shand & David Allum, 01348 811282, christina@dyffrynfernant.co.uk, www.dyffrynfernant.co.uk. *3m E of Fishguard, then ½m inland. A487 E 2m from Fishguard turn R towards Llanychaer at garden signs. ½m entrance is on L. Coming from direction of Dinas/Newport Pemb look for L turn off A487.* **For NGS: Sun 6 May, Sun 5 Aug, Sun 2 Sept (11-6). Adm £6, chd free. Home-made teas.** For other opening times and information, please phone, email or visit garden website.

Many differently planted areas in a 6 acre garden. 'Beautifully conceived small gardens brimming with rich, contemporary planting surround a glowing raspberry-fool coloured house, while a bog garden subtly gives way to a wetland valley floor. The best domestic garden in Wales.' Stephen Anderton, The Times. A Library for garden visitors incl a wide selection of books on gardening and art. Home-made teas on NGS days and for pre-booked groups. The Times number 1 of 20 Great Gardens, Country Homes and Interiors. Featured in print and online for Gardens Illustrated and on BBC Gardener's World.

6 GELLI MYDOG

Myddfai, Llandovery, Carmarthenshire, SA20 0JQ. Robert Lee & Barry Williams. *1.4m S of Myddfai. From Llandovery follow signs to Myddfai, approx 3m then follow yellow NGS signs. From Llangadog follow signs to Myddfai, approx 5m.* **Sun 10 June (12-5). Adm £4, chd free. Home-made teas.**

Approx 2 acre garden set in 9 acre grounds. Garden incl immaculate sweeping lawns, formal and informal herbaceous and shrub borders containing wide variety of plants. Recently completed stream side and pond gardens adjacent to restored wildlife meadows. Places to relax and enjoy the extensive views across the upland landscape. All main areas accessible by wheelchair.

7 GELLI UCHAF

Rhydcymerau, Llandeilo, Carmarthenshire, SA19 7PY. Julian & Fiona Wormald, 01558 685119, thegardenimpressionists@gmail.com, www.thegardenimpressionists.com. *5m SE of Llanybydder. 1m NW of Rhydcymerau. In Rhydcymerau on B4337 turn up Mountain Rd for Llanllwni (by BT phone box). After about 300yds turn R up farm track (uneven surface 10mph max please), cont ½m bearing R up hill at fork in track.* **Visits by arrangement : Sat 17, Sun 18 Feb, Sat 17, Sun 18 Mar, Sat 21, Sun 22 Apr. Booking times: 10.30am or 2.30pm only. Adm £4, chd free. Home-made teas.**

Complementing a C17 Longhouse and 11 acre smallholding this 1½ acre garden is mainly organic. Trees and shrubs are underplanted with collections of crocus, daffodils and snowdrops (200 cultivars). Diverse plantings incl colour filled perennial borders. Novel system for growing vegetables and fruit trees. Extensive views, seats to enjoy them. 6 acres of wildflower meadows, 2 ponds and stream. Snowdrop and daffodil collections. A magical and inspirational garden. Featured on BBC Gardeners World; Welsh Country Magazine and in Gardens Illustrated Magazine.

8 GLANDWR

Pentrecwrt, Llandysul, Carmarthenshire, SA44 5DA. Mrs Jo Hicks, 01559 363729, leehicks@btinternet.com. *15m N of Carmarthen, 2m S of Llandysul, 7m E of Newcastle Emlyn. On A486. At Pentrecwrt village, take minor rd opp Black Horse PH. After bridge keep L for ¼m. Glandwr is on R.* **Sat 28, Sun 29 July (11-5). Adm £3, chd free. Home-made teas. Visits also by arrangement, please phone first.**

Delightful easily accessed 1 acre cottage garden, bordered by a natural stream. Incl a rockery and colour themed beds. Enter the mature woodland, now transformed into an adventurous wander with plenty of shade loving plants, ground cover, interesting trees, shrubs and many surprises. Dogs permitted on leads.

9 NEW GLANGWILI LODGES

Llanllawddog, Carmarthenshire, SA32 7JE. Chris & Christine Blower. *7m NE of Carmarthen. Take A485 from Carmarthen. ¼m after Gwili Pottery on left in Pontarsais, turn R for Llanllawddog and Brechfa. ½m after Llanllawddog Chapel, rd bears sharply R, Glangwili Lodges 100yds on R.* **Sat 9, Sun 10 June (11-5). Adm £3.50, chd free. Light refreshments.**

Our 16 acre estate has a one acre enclosed walled garden, with rockeries, water features, flower and shrub beds, also a wisteria arbour, maples, magnolias and espalier fruit trees. Areas outside the wall, incl one acre of woodland, with stream, a 2 acre wildlife area, and a hedge tunnel containing a diverse collection of trees. There is also a productive vegetable garden and a polytunnel.

10 NEW HAYSTON FARMHOUSE

Merrion, Pembroke, Pembrokeshire, SA71 5EA. Mrs N Rogers, 01646 661462, haystonhouse@btinternet.com. *Take B4319 from Pembroke, follow signs to Castlemartin, go through St Petrox, once on straight road (B4319) take 4th L turn (signed to Thorne Chapel); entrance on R after approx. 500 yds.* **Sun 24 June (1-5). Adm £4, chd free. Home-made teas.**

Set in approx 2 acres, designed 15 years ago, consists of now mature yew, beech, hornbeam and lime hedges bordering lawns with spring flowers and shrubs, Herbaceous borders, vegetable garden with hips, haws and holly hedge. Orchard, formal walled garden and rectangular pond, sunken terrace with 2 sets of steps, pergola, raised stone beds and pots full of giant blue agapanthus. Seating areas.

GROUP OPENING

11 NEW HEYWOOD LANE GARDENS

Heywood Lane, Tenby Pembrokeshire, SA70 8BZ. *½m W of Tenby. From N (A478) R onto A4218, then R onto Serpentine Road, R into Heywood Lane. From S (B4318), bear L into Heywood Lane. Entry to the three gardens via Scotsborough House Garden drive. Street parking.* **Sun 8 July (1-5). Combined adm £5, chd free. Home-made teas in aid of Macmillan Cancer Support. Also open The Retreat.**

NEW THE GROVE
Rosemary Davies.

NEW SCOTSBOROUGH HOUSE
John and Shari Argent, 01834 842 077, shari.argent@gmail.com.
Visits also by arrangement June to Sept.

NEW WEST GROVE
Julius Rhys Davies.

Scotsborough House and The Grove were built on land owned by the Mayor, Aldermen and Burgesses of Tenby. This land, known as West Heywood Meadow, was used as a nursery garden where the Tenby Daffodil was first propagated. Scotsborough House Garden, with greenhouse buildings, walls and trees from the early 1900s, has varied planting incl. Blue Atlantic Cedars, beeches, woodland walk, acers, magnolias, many roses, *Hydrangea sargentiana*, an Edwardian grapevine and vegetable garden. The Grove and West Grove were restored to one property by the current owner of the Grove. The Grove Garden consists of land surrounding the original house and contains mature trees, incl. a Monkey Puzzle (*Araucaria*), manicured hedging, sculptures and seating areas in a tranquil setting. West Grove Garden has steep access, fabulous views, mature trees and secret gardens of interest to children. These three gardens, each with styles of their own, are linked by pathways, reflecting their historic connection. Partial wheelchair access.

12 LAN FARM

Talley, Llandeilo, Carmarthenshire, SA19 7BQ. Karen & David Thomas, 07950 178333, davidhuw@gmail.com. *10m N of Llandeilo. Talley is on B4302 between Llandeilo & Crugybar. In Talley follow signs to Abbey, passing it on R. Cont on single track lane for 2m. Drive to Lan, ¼m, on L, uneven surface, please take care.* **Visits by arrangement 11 June to 1 Aug. Teas on request when booking. Adm £3.50, chd free.**

Extremely rural 2 acre SW facing garden oasis 900ft above sea level that has been sympathetically developed to augment the countryside. There are spectacular borrowed views in all directions. Interesting planting with plenty of surprises incl a wildflower meadow, utilisation of old farm buildings, bog and Mediterranean areas. There is also a small lake that attracts a variety of wildlife. A remote and romantic garden!

13 LLWYNGARREG

Llanfallteg, Whitland, Carmarthenshire, SA34 0XH. Paul & Liz O'Neill, 01994 240717, lizpaulfarm@yahoo.co.uk, www.llwyngarreg.co.uk. *19m W of Carmarthen. A40 W from Carmarthen, turn R at Llandewi Velfrey, 2½m to Llanfallteg. Go through village, garden ½m further on: 2nd farm on R. Disabled car park in bottom yard on R.* **Sun 1 Apr, Sun 24 June, Sun 8 July (1.30-6). Adm £4.50, chd free. Home-made teas. Visits also by arrangement, please check phone message on the day.**

Llwyngarreg will delight plantsmen with its many rarities incl species Primulas, many bamboos with

Roscoeas, Hedychiums and Salvias extending the season through to riotous autumn colour. Trees and rhododendrons have been underplanted with perennials. New this year are a sunken garden for tender/exotic gems and extensive gravel terraces with formal raised pool. Springs meet to form a stream around the main garden, providing several bog gardens, colourful in spring and summer. Wildlife ponds, fruit and veg, composting, twig piles, numerous living willow structures. Partial wheelchair access.

14 NEW NANTYIETAU

New Mill Road, St Clears, Carmarthenshire, SA33 4HF. Matt Richards, 01994 231345, mattrichards320@gmail.com. *10m W of Carmarthen. Take the Laugharne turning off A40 then A4066 to Lower St Clears. Take first R after river bridge, continue for ½m along country lane, passing junction to R. Nantyietau is next house on L.* **Visits by arrangement June to Aug. Adm £4.**

A one acre garden with an eclectic mix of the unusual and traditional which reflects a passion for plants. Poultry, fish and other pets complete the quirky mix. Polytunnel and outbuildings with exotic and spiky plants squeezed into every corner. Limited parking. Regret no children.

15 NORCHARD

The Ridgeway, Manorbier, Tenby, Pembrokeshire, SA70 8LD. Ms H E Davies. *4m W of Tenby. From Tenby, take A4139 for Pembroke. ½m after Lydstep, take R at Xrds. Proceed down lane for ¾m. Norchard on R.* **Sun 6 May (2-6). Adm £5, chd free. Home-made teas.**

Historic gardens at medieval residence. Nestled in tranquil and sheltered location with ancient oak woodland backdrop. Strong structure with formal and informal areas incl early walled gardens with restored Elizabethan parterre and potager. 1½ acre orchard with old (many local) apple varieties. Mill and millpond. Extensive collections of roses, daffodils and tulips. Partial wheelchair access due to gravel paths. Access to potager via steps only.

16 THE OLD RECTORY

Lampeter Velfrey, Narberth, Pembrokeshire, SA67 8UH. Jane & Stephen Fletcher, 01834 831444, jane_e_fletcher@hotmail.com. *3m E of Narbeth. The Old Rectory is next to the church in the middle of Lampeter Velfrey. Parking in the church yard car park.* **Mon 28 May (1-5). Adm £3, chd free. Home-made teas. Visits also by arrangement May to Aug. Home-made teas on request.**

Historic approx 2 acre garden, sympathetically redesigned and replanted since 2009 and still being restored. Many unique trees, some over 300yrs old, wide variety of planting and several unique, architecturally designed buildings. Formal beds, mature woodland surrounding an old quarry with recently planted terraces and rhododendron bank. Newly planted meadow and orchard.

17 PANTEG

Llanddewi Velfrey, Narberth, Pembrokeshire, SA67 8UU. Mr & Mrs D Pryse Lloyd, 01834 860081, d.pryselloyd@btinternet.com. *Situated off main A40 in village of Llanddewi Velfrey. A40 from Carmarthen, after garage take 1st L. At next T-junction turn L. On R gateway with stone gate pillars which is ½m drive to Panteg.* **Sun 27 May (11-5). Adm £3, chd free. Visits also by arrangement Mar to Sept, groups 6+.**

Approached down a woodland drive, this tranquil, S-facing, large garden, surrounding a Georgian house (not open), has been developed since early 1990s. Plantsman's garden set off by lawns on different levels. Walled garden, wisteria covered pergola. Vegetable garden, camellia and azalea bank, wildflower woodland. Many rare shrubs and plants incl, *Embothrium, Eucryphia* and *Hoheria*.

18 PANT-Y-FEDWEN

Drefelin, Drefach Felindre, Llandysul, Carmarthenshire, SA44 5XB. Steven & Viki Harwood. *Drefach Felindre is signed from A484 approx 16m from Carmarthen & Cardigan, 5m from Newcastle Emlyn.* **Sat 23 June (11-5.30). Adm £3, chd free. Home-made teas.**

Re-opening after 3 years, a small front water garden with River Bargod running through, surrounded by lush architectural plantings. Hillside garden on 6 terraces behind house, informally managed, with unusual plants and various seating areas giving views over the valley. Quirky garden of about ⅓ acre, on 5 levels, culminating in a tranquil woodland garden. For the physically adept only. Arts and Crafts for sale in Workshop.

19 NEW PENCWM

Hebron, Whitland, Carmarthenshire, SA34 0JP. Lorna Brown, 01994 419471, lornambrown@hotmail.com. *10m N of Whitland. From A40 take St Clears exit and head N to Llangynin then on to Blaenwaun. Through village, after speed limit signs take 1st L. Over Xrds, 1¼m then 2nd lane on L marked Pencwm.* **Visits by arrangement Jan to Nov for groups of 5+. Adm £4, chd free. Hot and cold drinks and cakes. (Please request when booking).**

A secluded garden of about one acre set among large native trees, designed for year round interest and for benefit of wildlife. A wide variety of exotic specimen trees and shrubs, incl magnolias, rhododendrons, hydrangeas, bamboos and acers. Drifts of bluebells and other spring bulbs and good autumn colour. Incl boggy area and pond with appropriate planting.

20 PENTRESITE

Rhydargaeau Road, Carmarthen, SA32 7AJ. Gayle & Ron Mounsey, 01267 253928, gayle.mounsey@gmail.com. *4m N of Carmarthen. Take A485 heading*

N out of Carmarthen, once out of village of Peniel take 1st R to Horeb & cont for 1m. Turn R at NGS sign, 2nd house down lane. **Sun 15 July (2-5). Adm £3.50, chd free. Home-made teas. Visits also by arrangement May to Sept.**
1¼ acre garden developed over the last 9yrs with extensive lawns, colour filled herbaceous and mixed borders, on several levels. A bog garden and magnificent views of the surrounding countryside. There is now a new area planted with trees and gradually being filled with more herbaceous plants. This garden is south facing and catches the south westerly winds from the sea. Steep in places but possible for wheelchairs.

21 NEW PEN-Y-GARN

Foelgastell, Cefneithin, Llanelli, Carmarthenshire, SA14 7EU. Mary-Ann Nossent & Mike Wood, 07985077022, ma@penygarncottage.co.uk, www.penygarncottage.co.uk. *10m SE Carmarthen. A48 North take 1st L to Foelgastell R at T junction, 300 yds sharp L, 300 yards 1st gateway on L. A48 South NBGW turning, r'bout R to Porthyrhyd 1st L before T junction, less than 1m, 1st R & 300 yds on L.* **Sat 23, Sun 24 June (11-5). Adm £3.50, chd free. Home-made teas. Visits also by arrangement July to Sept. Teas on request when booking. Groups up to 10 max.**
1.3 acres set within a former old limestone quarry, the garden is on several levels with slopes and steps. Sympathetically developed to sit within the landscape, there are 5 distinct areas with a mixture of wild and cultivated plants. A shady area with woodland planting & wild ponds; kitchen garden; terraced borders with shrubs and herbaceous planting; lawns and pond; and a wild garden.

22 ◆ PICTON CASTLE & GARDENS

The Rhos, Haverfordwest, Pembrokeshire, SA62 4AS. Picton Castle Trust, 01437 751326, info@pictoncastle.co.uk, www.pictoncastle.co.uk. *3m E of Haverfordwest. On A40 to Carmarthen, signed off main rd.* **For NGS: Sun 20 May, Sun 10 June (10-5). Adm £7, chd £4. Light refreshments. Lunches and teas at Maria's Courtyard Restaurant.** For other opening times and information, please phone, email or visit garden website.
Mature 40 acre woodland garden with unique collection of rhododendrons and azaleas, many bred over decades, producing hybrids of great merit and beauty; rare and tender shrubs and trees incl *Magnolia*, myrtle, *Embothrium* and *Eucryphia*. Wild flowers abound. Walled garden with roses; fernery; herbaceous and climbing plants and large clearly labelled collection of herbs. Exciting art exhibitions and a wide range of seasonal events. Visit Maria's@Picton - our famous Spanish influenced restaurant. Some woodland walks unsuitable for wheelchair users.

23 NEW THE RETREAT

Retreat Road, Penally, Tenby, Pembrokeshire, SA70 7PL. Richard & Clare Rhys Davies. *1 mile SW of Tenby. Take A4139 to Pembroke. Turn R. after Kiln Park into Penally Village. Park in village & walk up Retreat Rd. or footpath. Strictly no parking or turning in Retreat Rd please.* **Sun 8 July (1-5.30). Adm £4, chd free. Also open Heywood Lane Gardens.**
Tucked away on a hill, up a private, single track road, backing onto meadows and bluebell woods, approx. one acre with panoramic sea views. Planting is an exuberant collection of cottage garden favourites punctuated by semi-tropicals, all billowing colourfully down the hillside from full sun into shadier areas. Hardy geraniums are a favourite with around 50 varieties at last count.

24 RHYD-Y-GROES

Brynberian, Crymych, Pembrokeshire, SA41 3TT. Jennifer & Kevin Matthews, 01239 891363. *12m SW of Cardigan. 5m W of Crymych, 16m NE of Haverfordwest, on B4329, ¾m downhill from cattlegrid (from Haverfordwest) & 1m uphill from signpost to Brynberian (from Cardigan).* **Visits by arrangement May to Aug groups of 20+. Refreshments on request when booking. Adm £4.50, chd £1.50.**
Colourful 4 acre country garden at 200m+ on exposed NE hillside. Dramatic, extensive views across upland bogs and moorland may be enjoyed from strategically placed seating. Exuberantly and skillfully planted to suit the varied conditions. Formal herbaceous borders, shrubbery, woodland area, bog, ornamental and natural meadow. Diverse plantings display what is possible without chemicals in this challenging environment. Featured in RHS The Garden Magazine.

25 ROSEWOOD

Redberth, Nr Tenby, Pembrokeshire, SA70 8SA. Keith Treadaway, 07855 192781 text only, keithatredberth@btinternet.com. *3m WSW of Kilgetty. On W side of village on old A477, now bypassed. Parking in field opp if dry, or on verge by side of rd if wet.* **Visits by arrangement Mar to Aug please request refeshments when booking. Contact by text or email only please. Adm £3.50, chd free. Light refreshments.**
Intimate well maintained ¼ acre garden, cleverly designed in different areas with long season of interest. Abundant colourful mixed plantings with exotic species and a collection of clematis, at its best in summer. There is a pergola with clematis and other climbers, as well as a good collection of Hemerocallis, grasses and ferns. A pond and bog garden were added recently. Partial wheelchair access.

26 STABLE COTTAGE

Rhoslanog Fawr, Mathry, Haverfordwest, Pembrokeshire, SA62 5HG. Mr Michael & Mrs Jane Bayliss, 01348 837712,

michaelandjane1954@michaelandjane.plus.com. *Rhoslanog, nr Mathry. Between Fishguard & St David's. Head W on A487 turn R at Square & Compass sign. ½m, past Chris Neale gallery, at hairpin take track L. Stable Cottage on L with block paved drive.* **Visits by arrangement May to Sept. Narrow access and very limited parking, max 5 cars. Adm £2.50, chd free. Refreshments available with prior notice (in aid of Withybush Cancer Day Unit).**
Garden extends to approx ⅓ of an acre. It is divided into several smaller garden types, with a seaside garden, small orchard and wildlife area, scented garden, small vegetable/kitchen garden, and two Japanese areas.

27 TRADEWINDS

Ffynnonwen, Pen-y-Bont, nr Trelech, Carmarthenshire, SA33 6PX. Stuart & Eve Kemp-Gee. *10m NW of Carmarthen. From A40 W of Carmarthen, take B4298 to Meidrim, then R onto B4299 towards Trelech. After 5m turn R at Tradewinds sign.* **Sun 17 June, Sun 19 Aug (11-5.30). Adm £3.50, chd free. Home-made teas.**
2½ acre plantsman's garden with abundance of herbaceous perennials, shrubs and trees giving yr-round interest. Mixed borders, natural streams and pond. Picturesque garden in tranquil setting. 100ft grass, 100ft herbaceous and 80ft conifer borders. The arboretum incl *Quercus cerris* 'Argenteovariegata', *Salix fargesii, Catalpa, Decaisnea* plus numerous rhododendrons, azaleas and hydrangeas. Stream banks planted with many moisture loving plants. Many rare and unusual plants to be seen. Art studio open.

28 TREFFGARNE HALL

Treffgarne, Haverfordwest, Pembrokeshire, SA62 5PJ. Martin & Jackie Batty, 01437 741115, bathole2000@aol.com. *7m N of Haverfordwest, signed off A40. Proceed up through village & follow rd round sharply to L, Hall ¼m further on L.* **Sun 6 May, Sun 22 July (1-5). Adm £4, chd free. Home-made teas. Visits also by arrangement, teas on request when booking.**
Stunning hilltop location with panoramic views: handsome Grade II listed Georgian house (not open) provides formal backdrop to garden of 4 acres with wide lawns and themed beds. A walled garden, with double rill and pergolas, is planted with a multitude of borderline hardy exotics. Also large scale sculptures, summer broadwalk, meadow patch, gravel garden, heather bed and stumpery. Planted for yr-round interest. The planting schemes are the owner's, and seek to challenge the boundaries of what can be grown in Pembrokeshire.

29 TY'R MAES

Ffarmers, Carmarthenshire, SA19 8JP. John & Helen Brooks, 01558 650541, johnhelen140@gmail.com. *7m SE of Lampeter. 8m NW of Llanwrda. 1½m N of Pumsaint on A482, opp turn to Ffarmers.* **Sun 5 Aug (1-5.30). Adm £4, chd free. Home-made teas. Visits also by arrangement, teas on request when booking.**
4 acre garden with splendid views. Herbaceous and shrub beds – formal design, exuberantly informal planting, full of cottage garden favourites and many unusual plants. Woodland garden with over 200 types of tree; wildlife and lily ponds; pergola, gazebos, post and rope arcade covered in climbers. Gloriously colourful from early spring till late autumn. Book and jewellery stalls. Some gravel paths.

30 ◆ UPTON CASTLE GARDENS

Cosheston, Pembroke Dock, Pembrokeshire, SA72 4SE. Prue & Stephen Barlow, 01646 689996, info@uptoncastle.com, www.uptoncastlegardens.com. *4m E of Pembroke Dock. 2m N of A477 between Carew & Pembroke Dock. Follow brown signs to Upton Castle Gardens through Cosheston.* **For NGS: Sun 25 Mar (11-4). Adm £4, chd free. Home-made teas. Home made soup. Refreshments in aid of St. Giles Chapel, Upton Castle.** For other opening times and information, please phone, email or visit garden website.
Lovely location in a tranquil valley leading to the upper reaches of the Cleddau estuary. 35 acres of mature gardens and arboretum; many rare trees and shrubs surrounding the C13 castle (not open) and C12 chapel. Spring flowering incl snowdrops, camellias, magnolias and rhododendrons. Also rose gardens, herbaceous borders, walled kitchen garden, wildflower meadow, woodland walks to estuary. Walk on the Wild Side: Woodland walks funded by C.C.W. and Welsh Assembly Government. Medieval chapel as featured on Time Team. Partial wheelchair access.

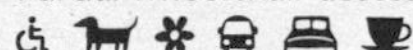

Heywood Lane Gardens

CEREDIGION

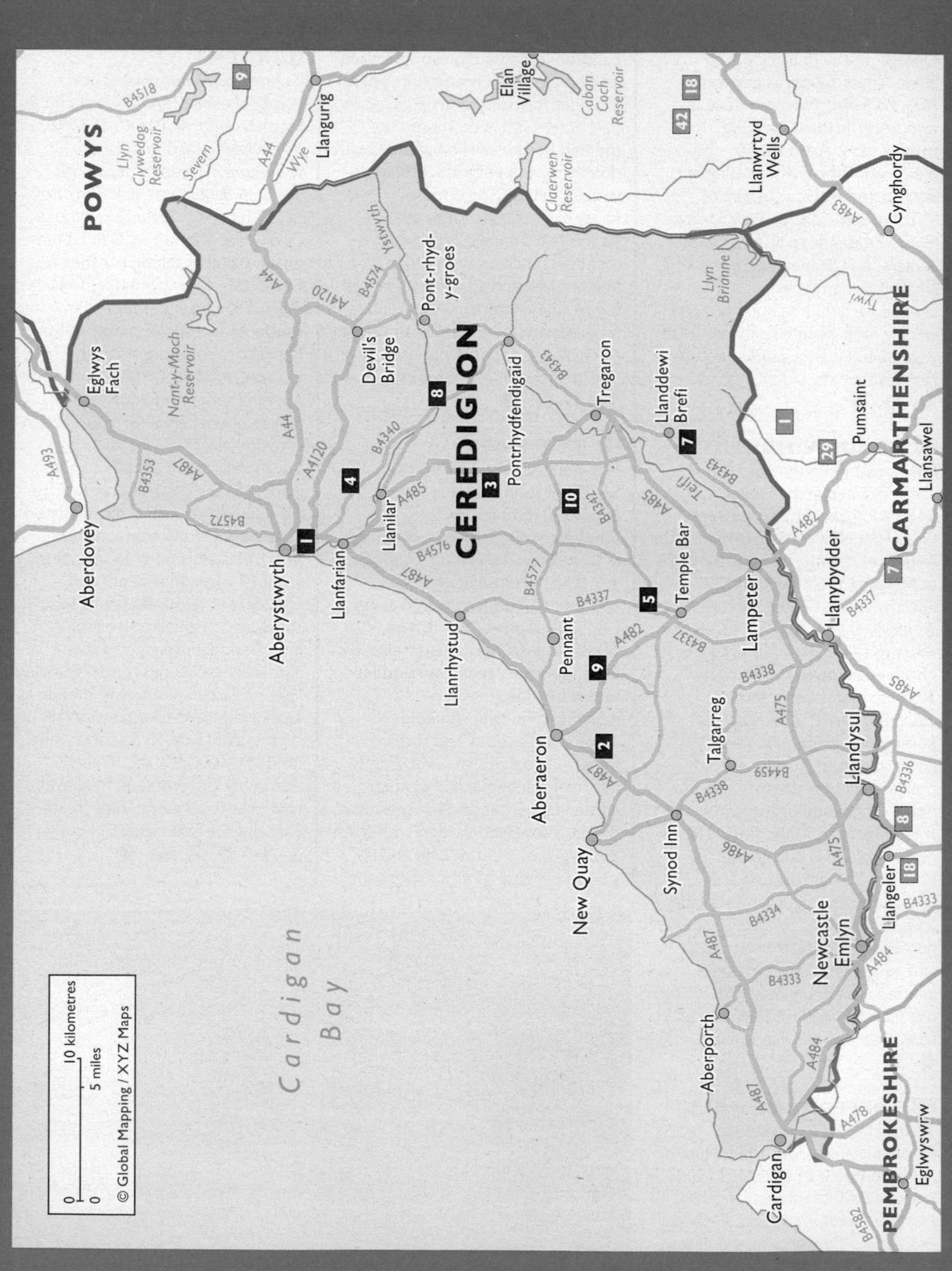
POWYS
CEREDIGION
CARMARTHENSHIRE
PEMBROKESHIRE
Cardigan Bay
Llangurig
Elan Village
Caban Coch Reservoir
Llanwrtyd Wells
Cynghordy
Llyn Clywedog Reservoir
Severn
Wye
Claerwen Reservoir
Pont-rhyd-y-groes
Ystwyth
Llyn Brianne
Tywi
Eglwys Fach
Nant-y-Moch Reservoir
Devil's Bridge
Pontrhydfendigaid
Tregaron
Llanddewi Brefi
Pumsaint
Llansawel
Aberdovey
Aberystwyth
Llanfarian
Llanilar
Teifi
Temple Bar
Lampeter
Llanybydder
Llanrhystud
Pennant
Aberaeron
Talgarreg
Llandysul
New Quay
Synod Inn
Newcastle Emlyn
Llangeler
Aberporth
Cardigan
Eglwyswrw
B4518
A44
A4120
B4574
B4343
A493
B4353
A487
B4572
B4340
A485
B4576
B4342
B4577
B4337
A482
A483
B4338
A475
B4459
A486
B4336
B4334
B4333
A484
A478
B4582
0 5 miles
0 10 kilometres
© Global Mapping / XYZ Maps

Ceredigion is a rural county and the second most sparsely populated in Wales.

Much of the land is elevated, particularly towards the east of the county. There are steep-sided wooded valleys, fast flowing rivers and streams, acres of moorland and a dramatic coast line with some lovely sandy beaches. From everywhere in the county there are breath taking views of the Cambrian Mountains and from almost everywhere views of the sea and glimpses of the stunning Cardigan Bay are visible.

The gardens in Ceredigion reflect this natural beauty and sit comfortably in the rugged scenery. There are some gardens that have been created with great imagination and enterprise from the barren water-soaked moorland, others have sensitively enhanced and embellished steep stony hillsides. Rhododendrons, azaleas and camellias thrive in the acid soil, and from April till June the gardens are awash with their bright jewel-like blossoms.

We have two gardens which are particularly family-friendly; both Bwlch y Geuffordd and Ty Glyn Walled Garden will provide children of all ages with hours of fun and adventure. There are a number of dedicated vegetable growers, you can see the fruits of their labours in the allotments in Aberaeron and Aberystwyth. In one small hilly, rock-strewn county, it is surprising how different the gardens are from each other, yet they have one thing in common; they are all created and tended with love, care and imagination.

Volunteers

County Organiser
Pat Causton
01974 272619
pat.causton30@gmail.com

County Treasurer
Steve Yeomans
01974 299370
s.j.yeomans@btinternet.com

Booklet Co-ordinator
Shelagh Yeomans
01974 299370
shelaghyeo@hotmail.com

Assistant County Organisers
Gay Acres
01974 251559
gayacres@aol.com

Lisa Raw-Rees
01545 570107
hywelrawrees@hotmail.com

Below: **Bwlch y Geuffordd Gardens**

OPENING DATES

All entries subject to change. For latest information check **www.ngs.org.uk**

Map locator numbers are shown to the right of each garden name.

May

Sunday 20th
Bwlch y Geuffordd 4

Sunday 27th
Arnant House 2

June

Thursday 21st
NEW National Botanic Garden of Wales 6

Sunday 24th
Ysgoldy'r Cwrt 10

July

Sunday 1st
Aberystwyth Allotments 1

Sunday 8th
Pantyfod 7

August

Saturday 4th
Penybont 8

Sunday 5th
Penybont 8

Sunday 12th
◆ Ty Glyn Walled Garden 9

By Arrangement

Arnant House 2
Bwlch y Geuffordd Gardens 3
Llanllyr 5
Penybont 8
Ysgoldy'r Cwrt 10

THE GARDENS

1 ABERYSTWYTH ALLOTMENTS

5th Avenue, Penparcau, Aberystwyth, SY23 1QT. Aberystwyth Town Council. *On S side of R Rheidol on Aberystwyth by-pass. From N or E, take A4120 between Llanbadarn & Penparcau. Cross bridge then take 1st R into Minyddol. Allotments ¼m on R.* **Sun 1 July (1-5). Adm £3.50, chd free. Home-made teas. Teas in aid of Duke of Edinburgh Award, Aberaeron School.**

There are 37 plots in total on 2 sites just a few yards from each other. The allotments are situated in a lovely setting alongside River Rheidol close to Aberystwyth. Wide variety of produce grown, vegetables, soft fruit, top fruit, flowers. Car parking available. For more information contact Brian Heath 01970 617112. Sample tastings from allotment produce. Grass and gravel paths.

2 ARNANT HOUSE

Llwyncelyn, Aberaeron, SA46 0HF. Pam & Ron Maddox, 01545 580083. *On A487, 2m S of Aberaeron. Next to Llwyncelyn Village Hall. Parking in lay-by opp house.* **Sun 27 May (12-5). Adm £3.50, chd free. Home-made teas. Visits also by arrangement Apr to Aug conducted tours offered.**

Garden created 17yrs ago from derelict ground. 1 acre, in Victorian style and divided into rooms and themes. Laburnum arch, wildlife ponds, rotunda and tea house. Wide, long borders full of perennial planting with a good variety of species, numerous statues and oddities to be discovered. Many attractive ornamental shrubs incl acers, magnolias and rhododendrons in May, plus about 50 different types of clematis. Also a good selection of hellebores, primulas and fritillaries. Partial wheelchair access. Garden is level, but help may be needed on gravel paths. Some paths are very narrow.

3 BWLCH Y GEUFFORDD GARDENS

Bronant, Aberystwyth, SY23 4JD. Mr & Mrs J Acres, 01974 251559, gayacres@aol.com, http://bwlch-y-geuffordd-gardens.myfreesites.net. *12m SE of Aberystwyth, 6m NW of Tregaron off A485. Take turning opp Bronant school for 1½m then L up ½m uneven track.* **Visits by arrangement any time (bar Tuesdays and Thursdays) but advisable to phone first, refreshments with 24hrs notice. Adm £4.50, chd £1. Tea.**

1000ft high, 3 acre, constantly evolving wildlife garden featuring a lake and several pools. There are a number of themed gardens, incl Mediterranean, cottage garden, woodland, oriental, memorial and jungle. An adventure garden for children, incl pond dipping and treasure hunt. Plenty of seating. Unique garden sculptures and buildings, incl a cave, temple, gazebo, jungle hut and willow den. Plus our wonderful Mad Hatters Tea Parties! Please check website for more details. Featured in Gardeners World magazine. Paths are gravel, and there are some steps.

4 BWLCH Y GEUFFORDD

New Cross, Aberystwyth, SY23 4LY. Manuel & Elaine Grande. *5m SE of Aberystwyth. Off A487, take B4340 to New Cross. Garden on R at bottom of small dip. Parking in lay-bys opp house.* **Sun 20 May (10.30-5). Adm £4, chd free. Home-made teas.**

Lovely sloping 1½ acre garden, views of the Cambrian mountains. Embraces it's natural features with different levels, 2 ponds, unusual shade loving plants, borders, bog gardens merging into carefully managed informal areas. Banks of rhododendrons, azaleas. Full of colourful perennials, flowering shrubs, mature trees, bluebells and climbing roses scrambling up the walls of the old stone buildings. Partial wheelchair access to lower levels around house. Some steps and steep paths further up.

5 LLANLLYR

Talsarn, Lampeter, SA48 8QB. Mr & Mrs Robert Gee, 01570 470900, lgllanllyr@aol.com. *6m NW of Lampeter. On B4337 to Llanrhystud.* **Visits by arrangement Apr to Oct. Adm £4, chd free. Tea.**
Large early C19 garden on site of medieval nunnery, renovated and replanted since 1989. Large pool, bog garden, formal water garden, rose and shrub borders, gravel gardens, laburnum arbour, allegorical labyrinth and mount, all exhibiting fine plantsmanship. Yr-round appeal, interesting and unusual plants.

6  NATIONAL BOTANIC GARDEN OF WALES

Middleton Hall, Llanarthne, SA32 8HG. National Botanic Garden of Wales, www.gardenofwales.org.uk. *Signed from A48, 4m W of Cross Hands, 8m E of Carmarthen. Or off the B4310 between Nantgaredig and Porthrhyd.* **Evening opening Thur 21 June (6-9). Adm £5, chd free. Light refreshments.**
568-acre estate in the hills overlooking Towy Valley, dedicated to science, education and leisure. Great Glasshouse with Mediterranean climates and interior landscape incl ravines, waterfalls and bridges. 240yd long herbaceous broadwalk, lakes, walled gardens, water discovery centre and woodland walks. Childrens play area. Has hosted BBC Television's Bargain Hunt, BBC Radio Gardeners' Question Time and Chris Evans Breakfast Show; S4C Prynhawn Da and Heno. All paths within the formal Garden area are wheelchair friendly.

7 PANTYFOD

Llanddewi Brefi, Tregaron, SY25 6PE. David & Susan Rowe, www.pantyfodgarden.co.uk. *About 3m S of Tregaron. From Llanddewi Brefi village square, take R fork past Community Centre. Go up hill, past Ffarmers turning on L, cont for approx ¾m. Pantyfod is on R.* **Sun 8 July (12-6). Adm £4, chd free. Home-made teas. Authentic Italian pizzas cooked to order in our wood-fired oven.**
Peaceful well established 3½ acre garden with lots of pathways through a wide variety of perennials, trees and shrubs, many unusual. Varying habitats incl terraces, woodland, mature trees, natural ponds. Hardy geraniums, candelabra primulas, Iris sibirica, grasses, rugosa roses. Wildlife friendly. Stunning, panoramic views of the Teifi Valley and mountains beyond. Authentic artisan wood-fired pizzas made using top quality Italian ingredients are served every Saturday all year round and other days by persuasion. Eat in the garden or take away. Please give 48hrs notice. Partial wheelchair access due to gravel paths, slopes and steps.

8 PENYBONT

Llanafan, Aberystwyth, SY23 4BJ. Norman & Brenda Jones, 01974 261737, tobrenorm@gmail.com. *9m SW of Aberystwyth. Ystwyth valley off B4340. Straight on from Aberystwyth, stay on B4340 for 9m via Trawscoed. R over stone bridge. ¼m up hill, turn R past row of cream houses.* **Sat 4, Sun 5 Aug (11-5.30). Adm £3.50, chd free. Home-made teas. Visits also by arrangement May to Sept please ring or email beforehand. Refreshments can be discussed.**
Penybont shows what can be achieved from a green field sloping site in just a few years. This exciting garden (about an acre) extended in 2016 is designed to compliment the modern building, its forest backdrop and panoramic views. Original design, rural location with stunning views of the Ystwyth valley and hill forts. 'Walking Country'. Partial wheelchair access because of sloping ground, gravel paths and lawn.

9 ◆ TY GLYN WALLED GARDEN

Ciliau Aeron, Lampeter, SA48 8DE. Ty Glyn Davis Trust, 07832970896, gardener@tyglyndavistrust.co.uk, www.tyglyndavistrust.co.uk. *3m SE of Aberaeron. Turn off A482 Aberaeron to Lampeter at Ciliau Aeron signed to Pennant. Entrance 700 metres on L.* **For NGS: Sun 12 Aug (12-5). Adm £4, chd free. Home-made teas. For other opening times and information, please phone, email or visit garden website.**
Secluded walled garden in beautiful woodland setting alongside River Aeron, developed specifically for special needs children. Terraced kitchen garden overlooks herbaceous borders, orchard and ponds with child orientated features and surprises amidst unusual shrubs and perennials. Planted fruit trees selected from former gardener's notebook of C19. Walled Garden, Children's play area. Access paths, lower garden and woodland walk accessible to wheelchairs.

10 YSGOLDY'R CWRT

Llangeitho, Tregaron, SY25 6QJ. Mrs Brenda Woodley, 01974 821542. *1½m N of Llangeitho. Llangeitho, turn L at school signed Penuwch. Garden 1½m on R. From Cross Inn take B4577 past Penuwch Inn, R after brown sculptures in field. Garden ¾m on L.* **Sun 24 June (11-5). Adm £4, chd free. Home-made teas. Visits also by arrangement Apr to Sept please give 24 hours notice for refreshments. £5 admission includes refreshments.**
One acre hillside garden, with 4 natural ponds which are a magnet for wildlife plus two new fish ponds. Areas of wildflower meadow, bog, dry and woodland gardens. Established rose walk. Rare trees, large herbaceous beds, acer collection, bounded by a mountain stream, with 2 natural cascades, and magnificent views. Shade bed with acers and azaleas. New large herbaceous bed with exotic grasses. Large Iris ensata and Iris laevigata collections in a variety of colours. Steeply sloping ground.

GLAMORGAN

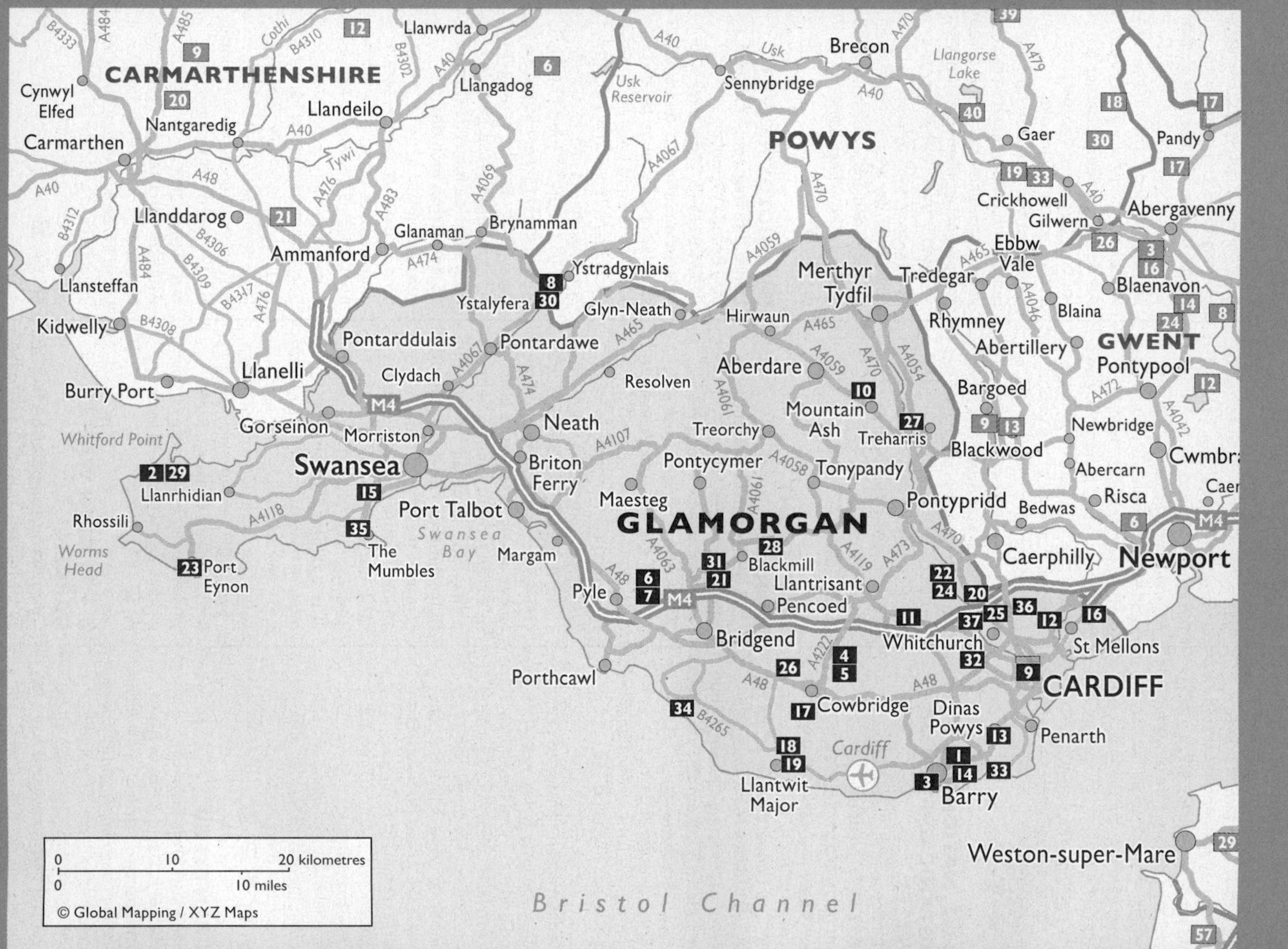
GLAMORGAN
POWYS
GWENT
CARMARTHENSHIRE
CARDIFF
Newport
Swansea
Bristol Channel
Swansea Bay
Weston-super-Mare
Abergavenny
Pandy
Crickhowell
Gilwern
Gaer
Blaenavon
Blaina
Pontypool
Newbridge
Abercarn
Risca
Caerphilly
Bedwas
Blackwood
Bargoed
Abertillery
Ebbw Vale
Tredegar
Rhymney
Merthyr Tydfil
Treharris
Pontypridd
Mountain Ash
Aberdare
Hirwaun
Tonypandy
Treorchy
Pontycymer
Maesteg
Llantrisant
Pencoed
Blackmill
Bridgend
Pyle
Porthcawl
Cowbridge
Llantwit Major
Whitchurch
St Mellons
Penarth
Dinas Powys
Barry
Cardiff
Brecon
Sennybridge
Llangorse Lake
Usk Reservoir
Usk
Llangadog
Llanwrda
Brynamman
Glanaman
Ystradgynlais
Glyn-Neath
Resolven
Neath
Briton Ferry
Port Talbot
Margam
Ystalyfera
Pontardawe
Clydach
Pontarddulais
Morriston
Gorseinon
Llanelli
The Mumbles
Ammanford
Llandeilo
Nantgaredig
Llanddarog
Carmarthen
Cynwyl Elfed
Llansteffan
Kidwelly
Burry Port
Whitford Point
Llanrhidian
Rhossili
Worms Head
Port Eynon
Tywi
Cothi
M4
0 10 20 kilometres
0 10 miles
© Global Mapping / XYZ Maps

Glamorgan is a large county stretching from the Brecon Beacons in the north to the Bristol Channel in the south, and from the city of Cardiff in the east to the Gower Peninsula in the west. The area has a natural divide where the hills rise from the vale in a clear line of demarcation.

There are gardens opening for the NGS throughout the county, and in recent years the number of community openings has greatly increased and have been very successful.

A number of gardens open in villages or suburbs, often within walking distance of each other, providing a very pleasant afternoon for the visitors. Each garden has its own distinct character and the locality is full of hospitality and friendliness.

Gardens range from Mediterranean-style to gardens designed to encourage wildlife. Views from our coastal gardens are truly spectacular.

Our openings start around Easter with a woodland and spring bulbs garden and continue through to mid-September.

So just jump in the car – *Gardens to Visit* book in hand – and head west on the M4. The gardens in Wales are waiting for you!

Below: **17 Maes y Draneog**

Volunteers

County Organiser
Rosamund Davies
01656 880048
ros@sladewoodgarden.plus.com

County Treasurer
Trevor Humby
02920 512709
humbyt@cardiff.ac.uk

Publicity
Sara Bentley
02920 512709
sarajanebentley@googlemail.com

Rosamund Davies
(as above)

Booklet Co-ordinator
Lesley Sherwood
02920 890055
lesleysherwood@btinternet.com

Rosamund Davies
(as above)

Talks Co-ordinator
Frances Bowyer
02920 892264
frances5860@icloud.com

Health and Gardens Co-ordinator
Miranda Workman
02920 766225
miranda.parsons@talktalk.net

Assistant County Organisers
Sol Blytt Jordens
01792 391676
solinge22@yahoo.co.uk

Melanie Hurst
01446 773659
melanie@hurstcreative.co.uk

Ceri Macfarlane
01792 404906
ceri@mikegravenor.plus.com

Lesley Sherwood
(as above)

Miranda Workman (as above)

OPENING DATES

All entries subject to change. For latest information check **www.ngs.org.uk**

Map locator numbers are shown to the right of each garden name.

April

Saturday 21st
Slade 34

Sunday 22nd
Slade 34

Sunday 29th
Penllyn Court 26

May

Saturday 5th
NEW 38 South Rise 36

Sunday 6th
NEW 38 South Rise 36

Sunday 13th
19 Slade Gardens 35

Tuesday 15th
◆ Bordervale Plants 4

Saturday 19th
110 Heritage Park 16
Pontygwaith Farm 27

Sunday 20th
Pontygwaith Farm 27

Saturday 26th
NEW 17 Maes y Draneog 20

Sunday 27th
Llanmaes Gardens 18
Llantwit Garden 19
NEW 17 Maes y Draneog 20

June

Festival Weekend

Saturday 2nd
4 Clyngwyn Road 8
Rhos y Bedw 30

Sunday 3rd
4 Clyngwyn Road 8
Creigiau Village Gardens 11
Rhos y Bedw 30

Saturday 9th
NEW Cornerstone 9
The Old Post Office 22
NEW Pear Tree Cottage 24

Sunday 10th
◆ Bordervale Plants 4
NEW Cornerstone 9
The Old Post Office 22
NEW Pear Tree Cottage 24

Saturday 16th
NEW The Birches 3

Sunday 17th
Big House Farm 2
NEW The Birches 3
Cefn Cribwr Garden Club 6
NEW Pwll y Felin Isaf 28
The Retreat 29

Sunday 24th
Overton and Port Eynon Gardens 23

Saturday 30th
NEW Llandough Castle 17

July

Sunday 1st
NEW Llandough Castle 17
Ty Hosbis 37

Sunday 8th
◆ Bordervale Plants 4

Saturday 14th
Dinas Powys 13
NEW 38 South Rise 36

Sunday 15th
Creigiau Village Gardens 11
Dinas Powys 13
Maes-y-Wertha Farm 21
NEW 38 South Rise 36

Saturday 21st
Overton and Port Eynon Gardens 23
NEW Sea Breeze 33

Sunday 22nd
Bryn-y-Ddafad 5
Cyncoed and Penylan Gardens 12
50 Pen y Dre 25
Rose Cottage 31

Saturday 28th
47 Aneurin Road 1
77 Cefn Road 7
446 Gladstone Road 14
St Peter's Community Garden 32

Sunday 29th
47 Aneurin Road 1
77 Cefn Road 7
446 Gladstone Road 14
St Peter's Community Garden 32

August

Sunday 5th
Llantwit Garden 19

Monday 27th
◆ Bordervale Plants 4

September

Sunday 2nd
Penllyn Court 26

Sunday 9th
16 Hendy Close 15

By Arrangement

Big House Farm 2
Bryn-y-Ddafad 5
The Cottage 10
22 Dan y Coed Road, Cyncoed and Penylan Gardens 12
16 Hendy Close 15
Pontygwaith Farm 27
NEW Pwll y Felin Isaf 28
The Retreat 29

Penllyn Court

THE GARDENS

1 47 ANEURIN ROAD

Barry, CF63 4PP. Dave Bryant. *Barry Town. Head to Barry Police Station & YMCA Hub on Gladstone Rd then follow yellow NGS signs.* **Sat 28 July (11.30-6); Sun 29 July (12-6). Combined adm with 446 Gladstone Road by donation. Light refreshments.**

Small town front garden with an ever changing canvas reflecting the seasons and flowering cycle of a wide and varied arrangement of plants, grown in containers and hanging baskets. A vertical arranged garden with substantial collections of Clematis, Fuchsias Geraniums and Begonia's.

✻ ☕

2 BIG HOUSE FARM

Llanmadoc, Gower, Swansea, SA3 1DE. Mark & Sheryl Mead, 07831 725753, mark@bighousefarm.net. *15m W of Swansea. M4 J47, L A483 for Swansea, 2nd r'about R, A484 Llanelli 3rd r'about L, B4296 Gowerton T-lights, R B4295, pass Bury Green R to Llanmadoc.* **Sun 17 June (1-6). Combined adm with The Retreat £6, chd free. Home-made teas. Visits also by arrangement June to Aug for groups 10+.**

Multi awarded inspirational garden of around 1 acre at this lovely listed property combines colour form and texture, described by visitors as 'the best I've seen, a real gem. better than Chelsea & Gardeners World should visit'. Large variety of interesting plants and shrubs, with ambient cottage garden feel, Victorian glasshouse with rose garden pottager with beautiful views over sea country. Located on the Gower Peninsular, Britain's first designated Area of Outstanding Natural Beauty. Featured in TV and Garden News. Majority of garden accessible to wheelchairs.

♿ 🐕 ✻ 🚌 ☕

3 NEW THE BIRCHES

Dingle Close, Barry, CF62 6QR. Paul & Peta Goodwin. *W end of Barry. Along Porth y Castell, L onto Min y Mor, L onto Marine Drive. Park end Marine Drive, CF62 6QR. Walk down grassy slope to path through wildflower meadow. Entrance to garden through archway.* **Sat 16, Sun 17 June (2-6). Adm £4, chd free.**

Large coastal garden with terraces and different rooms combining hard and soft landscaping. Started 30 years ago by inexperienced owners on difficult steep plot which consisted mainly of rough grass. Now upper section has formal Mediterranean feel, lower part more relaxed, owners more experienced but still learning. Good design, beautiful plants and easy maintenance are equally important. Adjacent nature reserve with wood and wildflower meadow.

4 ◆ BORDERVALE PLANTS

Sandy Lane, Ystradowen, Cowbridge, CF71 7SX. Mrs Claire Jenkins, 01446 774036, bordervaleplants@gmail.com, www.bordervale.co.uk. *8m W of Cardiff. 10 mins from M4 or take A4222 from Cowbridge. Turn at Ystradowen postbox, then 3rd L & proceed ½m, follow brown signs. Garden on R. Parking in rd.* **For NGS: Tue 15 May, Sun 10 June, Sun 8 July, Mon 27 Aug (11-4). Adm £3, chd free. For other opening times and information, please phone, email or visit garden website.**

Within mature woodland valley (semi-tamed), with stream and bog garden, extensive mixed borders; mini wildflower meadow, providing diverse wildlife habitats. Children must be supervised. The Nursery specialises in unusual perennials and cottage garden plants. Nursery open: Fri - Sun (10-5), (and often open Mon - Thurs) mid Mar - mid Sept, when garden is also open mid May - mid Sept. Not for NGS. Awarded Silver Gilt Medal (for Unusual Welsh grown trees, shrubs & perennials) RHS Flower Show Cardiff. Wheelchair access to top third of garden as well as Nursery.

♿ ✻

5 BRYN-Y-DDAFAD

Welsh St Donats, Cowbridge, CF71 7ST. Glyn & June Jenkins, 01446 774451, junejenkins@bydd.co.uk, www.bydd.co.uk/garden. *10m W of Cardiff. 3m E of Cowbridge. From A48 follow signs to Welsh St Donats village (for SatNav use CF71 7SS). Follow brown tourist signs from Xrds, The entrance to the garden is a pick up and drop only, car parking on the verges.* **Sun 22 July (10.30-5). Adm £4.50, chd free. Home-made teas. Visits also by arrangement May to Sept groups 8+.**

A mature garden developed by the present owners from an overgrown state over a period of 40 yrs. Areas of unusual plantings give interest through the seasons. Terraced rear garden, mature trees, numerous flowering shrubs and roses. Lily pond, pergola of clematis and wisteria, leading to a bridge crossing the natural stream and bog garden. To the front of the house is a raised courtyard garden. Most of garden accessible by wheelchair.

♿ ✻ 🛏 ☕

GROUP OPENING

6 CEFN CRIBWR GARDEN CLUB

Cefn Cribwr, Bridgend, CF32 0AP. https://www.cefncribwrgardeningclub.com/. *5m W of Bridgend on B4281.* **Sun 17 June (11-5). Combined adm £4.50, chd free. Tea.**

6 BEDFORD ROAD
Carole & John Mason.

13 BEDFORD ROAD
Mr John Loveluck.

2 BRYN TERRACE
Alan & Tracy Birch.

CEFN CRIBWR GARDEN CLUB ALLOTMENTS
Cefn Cribwr Garden Club.

CEFN METHODIST CHURCH
Cefn Cribwr Methodist Church.

77 CEFN ROAD
Peter & Veronica Davies & Mr Fai Lee.
(See separate entry)

25 EAST AVENUE
Mr & Mrs D Colbridge.

15 GREEN MEADOW
Tom & Helen.

6 TAI THORN
Mr Kevin Burnell.

Cefn Cribwr is an old mining village atop a ridge with views to Swansea in the west, Somerset to the south and home to Bedford Park and the Cefn Cribwr Iron Works. The village hall is at the centre with teas, cakes and plants for sale. The allotments are to be found behind the hall. Children, art and relaxation are just some of the themes to be found in the gardens besides the flower beds and vegetables. There are also water features, fish ponds, wildlife ponds, summerhouses and hens adding to the diverse mix. Themed colour borders, roses, greenhouses, recycling, composting and much more. The chapel grounds are peaceful with a woodland trail meandering off. There will also be tea, coffee and cakes, craft stalls, games, raffles and a table top sale in the hall. For more information please see our website.

7 77 CEFN ROAD

CF32 0AW. Peter & Veronica Davies & Mr Fai Lee. **Sat 28, Sun 29 July (11-5). Adm £3, chd free. Home-made teas. Opening with Cefn Cribwr Garden Club on Sun 17 June.**

A large S-facing garden with flower borders, pots, vegetables, hens and several seating areas. There is a pond for wildlife next to a bog garden with large Gunnera and flanked by banana plants. The vegetable garden has 2 greenhouses, 4 no-dig beds, a composting system and a wood shed with a green roof. Views over the Vale and Bristol Channel.

8 4 CLYNGWYN ROAD

Ystalyfera, Swansea, SA9 2AE. Paul Steer, www.artinacorner.blogspot.com. *Follow NGS signs from Rhos y Bedw (combined opener).* **Sat 2, Sun 3 June (12-4.30). Combined adm with Rhos y Bedw £3.50, chd free. Light refreshments.**

The Coal Tip Cloister Garden is a small personal space created in order to help us unwind from our work as nurses. Its main character is enclosure and a sense of rest. It is not a flowery garden but is formed out of shrubs and trees - forming a tapestry of hedging with arches and niches being cut out in order to place seats and sculpture and to produce a visual rhythm. Publicised in South Wales Evening Post.

9 NEW CORNERSTONE

Charles Street, Cardiff, CF10 2GA. Mrs Lucy King. *The Cornerstone Sensory Garden is just off Queen St, behind Next and M&S and opp St David's Cathedral.* **Sat 9, Sun 10 June (10-4). Adm £5, chd free. Cream teas in cafe on site, next to garden.**

This is a brand new garden created from scratch in December 2016. It has been designed to facilitate disabled access and the needs of the Blind Gardening Club of Cardiff Institute for the Blind and has been planted with a mixture of plants to create highly visible contrasting colours and also scents. It is truly an inner city garden, being located in the centre of the city. The garden and adjoining buildings are fully accessible for wheelchair users and those with restricted mobility.

10 THE COTTAGE

Cwmpennar, Mountain Ash, CF45 4DB. Helen & Hugh Jones, 01443 472784, hhjones1966@yahoo.co.uk. *18m N of Cardiff. A470 from N or S. Then follow B4059 to Mountain Ash. Follow signs for Cefnpennar then turn R before bus shelter into village of Cwmpennar.* **Visits by arrangement May to July, groups 15 max. Adm £4, chd free. Home-made teas.**

4 acres and 40yrs of amateur muddling have produced what it is hoped is an interesting garden incl bluebell wood, rhododendron and camellia shrubbery, herbaceous borders, rose garden, small arboretum, many uncommon trees and shrubs. Garden slopes NE/SW.

GROUP OPENING

11 CREIGIAU VILLAGE GARDENS

Maes Y Nant, Creigiau, CF15 9EJ. *W of Cardiff (J34 M4). From M4 J34 follow A4119 to T-lights, turn R by Castell Mynach Pub, pass through Groes Faen & turn L to Creigiau. Follow NGS signs.* **Sun 3 June (1-5); Sun 15 July (12-5). Combined adm £5, chd free. Home-made teas at 28 Maes y Nant and Penybryn (June) 28 Maes y Nant and Waunwyllt (July).**

28 MAES Y NANT
Mike & Lesley Sherwood.
Open on all dates

31 MAES Y NANT
Frances Bowyer.
Open on Sun 15 July

PENYBRYN
Jen MacDonald.
Open on Sun 3 June

WAUNWYLLT
John Hughes & Richard Shaw.
Open on all dates

On the NW side of Cardiff and with easy access from the M4 J34, Creigiau Village Gardens incl four vibrant and innovative gardens. Each quite different, they combine some of the best characteristics of design and planting for modern town gardens with the naturalism of old fashioned cottage gardens. Each has its own forte; the garden at Waunwyllt has been achieved over 7yrs with coloured themed rooms. At 28 Maes y Nant, cottage garden planting reigns. This is in complete contrast to the strong architecture of 31 Maes y Nant, where the design coordinates water, the garden room and planting, incl a small scale prairie. Penybryn is a large garden with colourful planting and incl a kitchen vegetable plot. Anyone looking for ideas for a garden in an urban setting will not go away disappointed; enjoy a warm welcome, home-made teas and plant sales.

GROUP OPENING

12 CYNCOED AND PENYLAN GARDENS

Cyncoed, Cardiff, CF23 6SW. *From Hollybush Rd follow yellow NGS signs to Cyncoed Crescent & Danycoed Rd. 7 Cressy Rd is off Marlborough Rd, Penylan.* **Sun 22 July (2-6). Combined adm £4, chd free. Home-made teas.**

7 CRESSY ROAD
Victoria Thornton.

8 CYNCOED CRESCENT
Alistair & Teresa Pattillo.

22 DAN Y COED ROAD
Alan & Miranda Workman, 029 2076 6225, miranda.parsons@talktalk.net.
Visits also by arrangement Mar to Sept particularly in connection with 'Gardens and Health'.

KINSLEY, 3 LLYSWEN ROAD
Mrs Jill Davey-Karseras.

This is a group of four, 1930's suburban gardens. Each one has its own individual style. They have been designed by the owners and are continually evolving to create an eclectic collection of climber, perennials and shrubs that reflect the interests of these gardeners. Garden structures and summerhouses are used to add interest and to create different viewpoints over the gardens. All are within walking distance from each other except Penylan, which is a 5 mins drive away. Partial wheelchair access only.

GROUP OPENING

13 DINAS POWYS

Dinas Powys, CF64 4TL. *Approx 6m SW of Cardiff. Exit M4 at J33, follow A4232 to Leckwith, onto B4267 & follow to Merry Harrier T-lights. Turn R & enter Dinas Powys. Follow yellow NGS signs.* **Sat 14, Sun 15 July (11-5). Combined adm £5, chd free. Home-made teas at most gardens.** Donation to Dinas Powys Voluntary Concern.

BROOKLEIGH
Duncan & Melanie Syme.
Open on all dates

NEW **40 DENYS CLOSE**
Mr & Mrs Sue and Alan Rimmer.
Open on all dates

32 LONGMEADOW DRIVE
Julie & Nigel Barnes.
Open on Sat 14 July

NEW **5 THE MOUNT**
Mrs Maureen Bater.
Open on Sun 15 July

NIGHTINGALE COMMUNITY GARDENS
Keith Hatton.
Open on all dates

An inspiring and eclectic group of 5 gardens in this small friendly village, all with something different to offer. There are ponds of all sizes and styles, planting in shade and sun, boggy areas, pergolas, mature shrubs and trees, vegetables and fruit, challenging terraced designs and wild areas. Plus we have our community gardens opening with lovely displays of vegetable and fruit. Our village church, St Peters, is also opening with displays of flowers, classic cars and other attractions. Lovely home-made teas will be served, incl gluten free options; wine served at Brookleigh. There are many restful and beautiful areas to sit and relax. Plant sales are also an attraction. Good wheelchair access at the community gardens. Partial access elsewhere.

14 446 GLADSTONE ROAD

Barry, CF63 1QG. Kelly Bryant. *Head to Barry Police Station & YMCA Hub on Gladstone Rd then follow yellow NGS signs.* **Sat 28, Sun 29 July (12-6). Combined adm with 47 Aneurin Road by donation. Light refreshments.**

Small town house garden, currently in development that has to cater for a children's play area but still has a good arrangement of planting that could survive the occasional damage!

15 16 HENDY CLOSE

Derwen Fawr, Swansea, SA2 8BB. Peter & Wendy Robinson, 07773 711973, robinsonpete1@hotmail.co.uk. *Approx 3m W of Swansea. A4067 Mumbles Rd follow sign for Singleton Hospital. Then R onto Sketty Lane at mini r'about, turn L then 2nd R onto Saunders Way. Follow yellow NGS signs. Please park on Saunders Way if possible.* **Sun 9 Sept (1-5). Adm £6, chd free. Home-made teas. Refreshments are included in the entry price. Visits also by arrangement June to Sept, groups 10+.**
Originally the garden was covered with 40ft conifers. Cottage style, some unusual and mainly perennial plants which provide colour in spring, summer and autumn. Hopefully the garden is an example of how to plan for all seasons. Visitors say it is like a secret garden because there are a number of hidden places. Plants to encourage all types of wildlife in to the garden.

16 110 HERITAGE PARK

St Mellons, Cardiff, CF3 0DS. Sarah Boorman. *Leave A48 at St Mellons junction, take 2nd exit at r'about. Turn R to Willowdene Way & R to Willowbrook Drive. Heritage Park is 1st R. Park outside the cul-de-sac.* **Sat 19 May (1-5). Adm £3, chd free. Home-made teas. Gluten free available.**
An unexpected gem within a modern housing estate. Evergreen shrubs, herbaceous borders, box topiary and terracotta pots make for a mix between cottage garden and Italian style. With numerous seating areas and a few quirky surprises this small garden is described by neighbours as a calm oasis.

17 NEW LLANDOUGH CASTLE

Llandough, Cowbridge, CF71 7LR. Mrs Rhian Rees. *1½m outside Cowbridge. At the T-lights in Cowbridge turn onto the St Athan Rd. Continue then turn R to Llandough. Drive into the village and park in Castle Precinct. Walk up a short lane and into the gardens.* **Sat 30 June, Sun 1 July (10.30-4.30). Adm £5, chd free. Home-made teas.**

Set within castle grounds and with a backdrop of an ancient monument, the 3½ acres of garden incl a contemporary twist on a Victorian kitchen garden with a hint of the Mediterranean, formal lawns and herbaceous beds, a wildlife pond with waterfall and a woodland garden with stumpery and sculpture. Although some of the gardens are flat, areas like the woodland may be difficult for wheelchair access.

GROUP OPENING

18 LLANMAES GARDENS

Llanmaes, Llantwit Major, CF61 2XR. *5m S of Cowbridge. From Mehefin & West Winds travel to Church via Church House, continue down lane for 1km to Old Froglands.* **Sun 27 May (12-5). Combined adm £5, chd free. Light refreshments at Old Froglands & Mehefin.**

CHURCH COTTAGE
Annie Grujic.

MEHEFIN
Mrs Alison Morgan, 01446 793427, bb@mehefin.com, www.mehefin.com.

OLD FROGLANDS
Dorne & David Harris, 07702502950, dorneharris@hotmail.co.uk.

WESTWINDS
Ms Jackie Simpson.

Llanmaes, 1m from Llantwit Major, is a pretty village with attractive village green, stream running through and C13 church. Old Froglands is an historic farmhouse with streams and woodland areas linked by bridges. Ducks swim and chickens roam free. The vegetable plot is now productive. Plantings are varied with interesting foliage. Church Cottage has a pretty little garden to the rear newly acquired and the owner is still discovering its unknown delights. Mehefin is an enchanting garden with bursts of colour and Westwinds a surprise in store!

19 LLANTWIT GARDEN

21 Monmouth Way, Boverton, Llantwit Major, CF61 2GT. Don & Ann Knight. *At Llanmaes rd T-lights turn onto Eagleswell Rd, next L into Monmouth Way, garden ½way down on R.* **Sun 27 May, Sun 5 Aug (11-5). Adm £3.50, chd free. Home-made teas.**

This is a Japanese garden with a Zen gate, Torri gate and Japanese lanterns featuring a large collection of Japanese style trees, which incl an English elm, oak, larch etc., a pagoda and 3 water features which incl the great Amazon waterfall along with large Buddha's head and new pond. Has been shown on ITV Wales news as well as a garden programme on S4C. Wheelchair access via rear garden.

20 NEW 17 MAES Y DRANEOG

Maes Y Draenog, Tongwynlais, Cardiff, CF15 7JL. Mr Derek Price. *North of M4 Cardiff. From South: M4 , J32, take A4054 into village. R at Lewis Arms pub, up Mill Rd. 2nd L into Catherine Drive, park in signed area (no parking in Maesydraenog). Follow signs to 17 Maesydraenog.* **Sat 26, Sun 27 May (1-6). Adm £4, chd free. Light refreshments.**

Visitors be surprised - a hidden gem of a garden, in the shadow of Castell Coch, fed by a stoned mountain stream. Footbridge invites you to naturalised areas, set against a woodland backdrop. Developed over 10 yrs with a good variety of plants, filling two main borders of herbaceous plants for spring and summer. Garden structures, summer house, patios, greenhouse and small veg area. Mountain stream with wooden footbridge, Summer house, greenhouse and variety of plants in borders around house. Set against woodland. Not suitable for young children and partial access for wheelchair users.

21 MAES-Y-WERTHA FARM

Bryncethin, CF32 9YJ. Stella & Tony Leyshon. *3m N of Bridgend. Follow sign for Bryncethin, turn R at Masons Arms. Follow sign for Heol-y-Cyw garden about 1m outside Bryncethin on R.* **Sun 15 July (1-7). Adm £5, chd free. Tea.**

A 3 acre garden. Informal mixed beds with large selection of perennial plants, shrubs, conifers and trees. Water garden fed by natural spring. Large grass area under new planting. Mural in the summerhouse by Daniel Llewelyn Hall contemporary artist. His work is represented in the Royal Collection and House of Lords.

22 THE OLD POST OFFICE

Main Road, Gwaelod-Y-Garth, Cardiff, CF15 9HJ. Ms Christine Myant. *N of Cardiff nr Radyr & Pentyrch. Entry and exit to both gardens is via The Old PO which is on the same side as pub, 4 houses pass pub. Parking in school car park further down hill.* **Sat 9, Sun 10 June (11-5). Combined adm with Pear Tree Cottage £4, chd free. Home-made teas.**

Situated in the popular village of Gwaelod-y-Garth on the northern edge of Cardiff. This year The Old Post Office will be opening alongside its neighbouring garden attached to Pear Tree Cottage. Gwaelod Inn only a stone's throw away and serves great food and drink.

GROUP OPENING

23 OVERTON AND PORT EYNON GARDENS

Overton Lane, Port Eynon, Swansea, SA3 1NR. *16.8m W of Swansea on Gower Peninsula. From Swansea follow A4118 to Port Eynon. Parking in public car park in Port Eynon. Yellow NGS signs showing gardens. Maps of gardens locations available.* **Sun 24 June, Sat 21 July (2-5.30). Combined adm £4.50, chd free. Home-made teas.**

THE BAYS FARM
Sol Blytt Jordens.
Open on all dates

6 THE BOARLANDS
Robert & Annette Dyer.
Open on all dates

BOX BOAT COTTAGE
Ms Christine Williams.
Open on Sun 24 June

WESTCLIFFE HOUSE
David Carlsen-Browne.
Open on Sat 21 July

Overton offers breathtaking views of the Gower Peninsula. Port Eynon is the most southerly point on the Gower. Set in the heart of Port Eynon, Box Boat Cottage is a delight set with pretty borders and a riot of colour. 6 The Boarlands is a plantman's paradise! A gently sloping garden designed for yr-round interest lots of shrubs bulbs and perennials. Westcliffe House a garden of interest diversity and surprise. The Bays Farm an ever developing garden!

24 NEW PEAR TREE COTTAGE

Main Road, Gwaelod-Y-Garth, Cardiff, CF15 9HJ. Yvonne Reid. *Opening jointly with The Old Post Office and 3rd house on L after Gwaelod pub.* **Sat 9, Sun 10 June (11-5). Combined adm with The Old Post Office £4, chd free. Home-made teas.**
New to NGS and opening in conjunction with The Old Post Office next door Pear Tree Cottage offers a different take on gardening on a sloping site with hard won solutions to some tricky problems. The garden has wide beds packed with plants and shrubs and various seating areas from which to enjoy the views. Entry and exit via The Old Post Office.

25 50 PEN Y DRE

Rhiwbina, Cardiff, CF14 6EQ. Ann Franklin. *N Cardiff. M4 J32, A470 to Cardiff, 1st l to mini r'about, turn R. At T-lights in village, turn R to Pen-y-Dre.* **Sun 22 July (11-4.30). Adm £3, chd free. Homemade cakes.**
Mixed mature borders in cottage garden style with many old favourites incl vegetable plot.

26 PENLLYN COURT

Penllyn, Penllyn, Cowbridge, CF71 7RQ. Mr & Mrs John Homfray. *17m W of Cardiff. 1m from A48 in village of Penllyn from Pentre Meyrick Xrds, 3m from Cowbridge towards Bridgend, 5m from Bridgend heading Cardiff way, 5m from M4 exit 35.* **Sun 29 Apr, Sun 2 Sept (2-6). Adm £4, chd free. Home-made teas.**
Large family garden with semi-formal walled garden, orchard with fruit trees and bulbs, stumpery, mixed plantings of shrubs and herbaceous perennials for all the months of the year, roses. Vegetable garden and small amount of woodland plantings, secret garden, all set amongst the rolling hills of a beautiful estate. Only access not wheelchair friendly are the flower beds around the swimming pool area which is reached by steps.

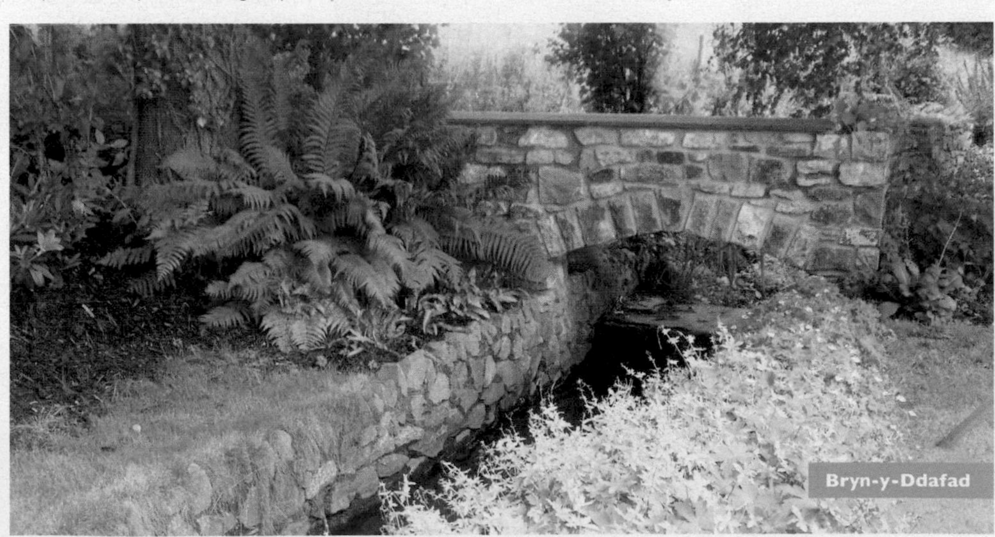
Bryn-y-Ddafad

27 PONTYGWAITH FARM

Edwardsville, nr Treharris, CF46 5PD. Mrs D Cann, 07511 744976. *2m NW of Treharris. N from Cardiff on A470. At r'about take A4054 N towards Aberfan. 1m after Edwardsville turn sharp L by black bus shelter. Garden at bottom of hill.* **Sat 19, Sun 20 May (10-5). Adm £4, chd free. Light refreshments. Visits also by arrangement May to Aug, groups 10 max.**

Situated in a picturesque wooded valley is a truly magical garden with a surprise around every corner - woodland walk, fish pond, perennial borders, vegetable patch, lakeside walk, rose garden, Japanese garden, Grade 2 listed humpback bridge, all surrounding C17 farmhouse adjacent to Trevithick's Tramway. Welcome to visitors on the Taff Trail (April - Sept, 10am - 5pm). Partial wheelchair access due to steep slope to river, gravel paths.

28 NEW PWLL Y FELIN ISAF

Glynogwr, Glynogwr, Blackmill, CF35 6EN. Ms Chrissy Langmaid & Mr Mark Farrant, 07738072007, mc1810@btinternet.com. *on A4093. 2m from Blackmill T-lights garden on L at bottom of hill, after bend. Parking in field opp drive. From Tonyrefail, enter Bridgend Borough, then parking on L, garden opp.* **Sun 17 June (10.30-6). Adm £4.50, chd free. Cream teas. Visits also by arrangement May to Aug open day and by pre arranged appointment. Groups of 10 maximum.**

8yrs of passion & hard work has resulted in the transformation of an acre of unloved land into lawns, shrubberies, a small orchard, pretty cottage garden and a peaceful pond area with bluebell wood. Hidden garden to the east of the property mixing flowering shrubs with fruit bushes, rambling strawberries, tomato greenhouse and polytunnel. Various seating areas for all gardens to be enjoyed. Most gardens accessible by wheelchair. Parking on drive for disabled visitors.

29 THE RETREAT

Llanmadoc, Swansea, SA3 1DE. Richard & Sue McCauley, 01792 386619, susanamccauley@googlemail.com. *15m W of Swansea. M4 J47, L A483 for Swansea, 2nd r'about R, A484 Llanelli 3 r'about L, B4296 Gowerton T-lights, R B4295, pass Burry Green R to Llanmadoc.* **Sun 17 June (1.30-5.30). Combined adm with Big House Farm £6, chd free. Visits also by arrangement June to Aug will open alongside Big House Farm. minimum 10 visitors.**

Our garden has evolved over many yrs. It now has several distinct areas, varied borders range from cottage style perennial planting, an area of large structured plants, a vegetable garden along with a small orchard in a wildlife friendly area. The garden is also one of a group which has won awards in the Swansea in Bloom competition. Some steps and uneven ground. Partial wheelchair access, gravel path around bungalow to rear terrace.

30 RHOS Y BEDW

4 Pen y Wern Rd, Ystalyfera, Swansea, SA9 2NH. Robert & Helen Davies. *13m N of Swansea. M4 J45 take A4067. Follow signs for Dan yr Ogof caves across 5 r'abouts. After T-lights follow yellow NGS signs. Parking above house on rd off to R.* **Sat 2, Sun 3 June (12-5). Combined adm with 4 Clyngwyn Road £3.50, chd free. Home-made teas. Gluten free options available.**

A haven of peace and tranquility with spectacular views, this glorious compact garden with its amazing array of planting areas is constantly evolving. Our diverse planting areas incl cottage, herb, and bog gardens also an array of roses and a knot garden are sure to provide inspiration. A garden with something different around every corner to be savored slowly, relax and enjoy. Home-made cakes available incl gluten free option.

31 ROSE COTTAGE

32 Blackmill Road, Bryncethin, Bridgend, CF32 9YN. Maria & Anne Lalic, www.marialalic.co.uk. *1m N of M4 J36 on A4061. Follow A4061 to Bryncethin. Straight on at mini r'about for approx 400 metres. Just past Used Car Garage, turn R onto side rd at grassed area.* **Sun 22 July (12-5). Adm £3.50, chd free. Home-made teas.**

If you want a proper garden with

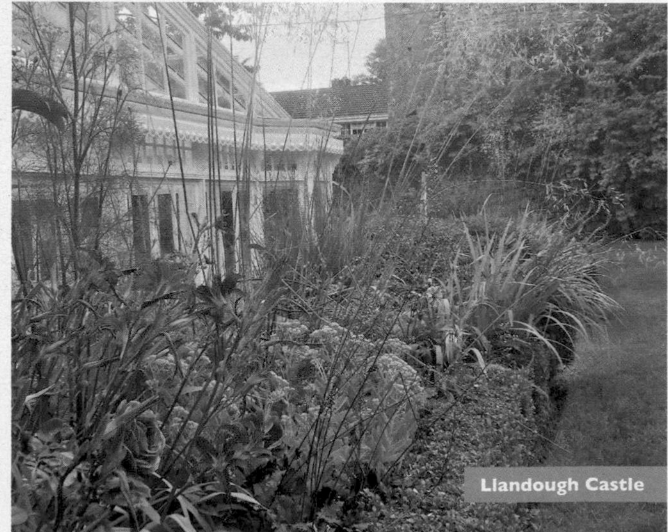

Llandough Castle

manicured borders & Latin plant names, Rose Cottage isn't the place for you. We have a traditional Welsh working cottage garden with jumbled flower beds, a herb yard, seasonal growing of fruit & vegetables, ideas borrowed from permaculture, no-dig and companion planting to help us with our simple, self-reliant way of life. A raised terrace area next to the conservatory allows viewing of the field where the goats, chickens and ducks graze. Our pop up tea room sells tea, coffee & home-made cakes served on vintage china and there'll be a selection of preserves & cordials to taste. Maria leads tours around the garden. Main path and gateways suitable for wheelchairs. Narrower, bark chip paths and grass paths are uneven and care should be taken.

32 ST PETER'S COMMUNITY GARDEN

St Fagans Road, Cardiff, CF5 3DW. Father Colin Sutton, www.stpeterschurchfairwater.org.uk. *Next Door to Church, set back from St Fagans Rd. A48 to Culverhousecross r'bout take A48 Cowbridge Rd West to Ely r'bout 1st L. At T-lights go L B4488 to Fairwater Green, follow yellow NGS signs.* **Sat 28, Sun 29 July (10-3.30). Adm £3, chd free. Home-made teas.**

Secret garden in city suburb. Unusual combination of flower beds, raised vegetable beds and nature reserve, all created by volunteers. Features incl a large natural pond surrounded by wild plants, Welsh heritage apple trees, long herb border and wild flower meadow., Latest editions Two bee hives and our completed Quiet Garden with water feature and planned planting. Fairtrade, Book and Craft Stalls. Disabled WC available.

33 NEW SEA BREEZE

Oyster Bend, Sully, CF64 5LW. Chris & Derek Richards. *5m W of Penarth. From A4232 take A4055 to Dinas Powys. L at B4267 after Merry Harrier Pub to Redlands Rd. Continue on for approx 4m. In Sully L onto Clevedon Ave then R Smithies Ave. 1st L into Oyster Bend.* **Sat 21 July (11-5.30). Adm £3.50, chd free. Home-made teas.**

A plantsperson's garden near the sea, exciting around every corner. Coastal haven overflowing with unusual tropical plants. Colourful decking surrounds pond and tree seat. Braheas, iochromas and hedychiums. Small Japanese garden holds 40 maples in slate borders complementing granite pathways and Japanese sculptures.

34 SLADE

Southerndown, CF32 0RP. Rosamund & Peter Davies, 01656 880048, ros@sladewoodgarden.plus.com, www.sladeholidaycottages.co.uk. *5m S of Bridgend. M4 J35 Follow A473 to Bridgend. Take B4265 to St. Brides Major. Turn R in St. Brides Major for Southerndown, then follow yellow NGS signs.* **Sat 21, Sun 22 Apr (2-5.30). Adm £4.50, chd free. Home-made teas.**

Hidden away Slade garden is an unexpected jewel to discover next to the sea with views overlooking the Bristol Channel. The garden tumbles down a valley protected by a belt of woodland. In front of the house are delightful formal areas a rose and clematis pergola and herbaceous borders. From terraced lawns great sweeps of grass stretch down the hill enlivened by spring bulbs and fritillaries. Heritage Coast wardens will give guided tours of adjacent Dunraven Gardens with slide shows every hour from 2pm. Partial wheelchair access.

35 19 SLADE GARDENS

West Cross, Swansea, SA3 5QP. Norma & Peter Stephen. *5m SW of Swansea. At mini r'about on Mumbles Rd A4067 take 2nd exit (Fairwood Rd), 1st L onto West Cross Lane & follow yellow NGS signs.* **Sun 13 May (2-5). Adm £3, chd free. Home-made teas.**

A very small enclosed front and rear garden, designed to lead you around its informal planting of over 200 species. A garden to sit in! Narrow paths and steps make access difficult for less mobile visitors.

36 NEW 38 SOUTH RISE

Lanishen, Cardiff, CF14 0RH. Dr Khalida Hasan. *N of Cardiff, from Llanishen Village Station Rd past Train Stn go R down The Rise or further onto S Rise directly. Following yellow signs.* **Sat 5, Sun 6 May, Sat 14, Sun 15 July (11.30-5.30). Adm £4, chd free. Home-made teas.**

A relatively new garden backing on to Llanishen Reservoir gradually establishing with something of interest and colour all yr round. Herbaceous borders, vegetables and fruit plants surround central lawn. Wild life friendly; variety of climbers and exotics. In front shrubs and herbaceous borders to a lawn. Stepping stones leading to childrens play area and vegetable plot. Wheelchair access to rear from the side of the house.

37 TY HOSBIS

Whitchurch Hospital Grounds, Park Road, Whitchurch, Cardiff, CF14 7BF. City Hospice Trust Ltd, www.cityhospice.org.uk. *Follow M4 to J32. Take A4054 signed Whitchurch. After 1m turn R through gates into Whitchurch Hospital, follow directions to Ty Hosbis and City Hospice.* **Sun 1 July (2.30-4.30). Adm £3.50, chd free. Cream teas.**

Hospice garden of 0.8 acres, designed for patient enjoyment and relaxation. Hosts established trees, shrubs, and planting providing yr-round colour. Wildlife pond stocked with fish and aquatic plants with a rock waterfall feature and a second pond with waterfall providing comforting sounds with natural woodland as a backcloth. Tended by volunteers, the paths and seating allow easy access for all.

GWENT

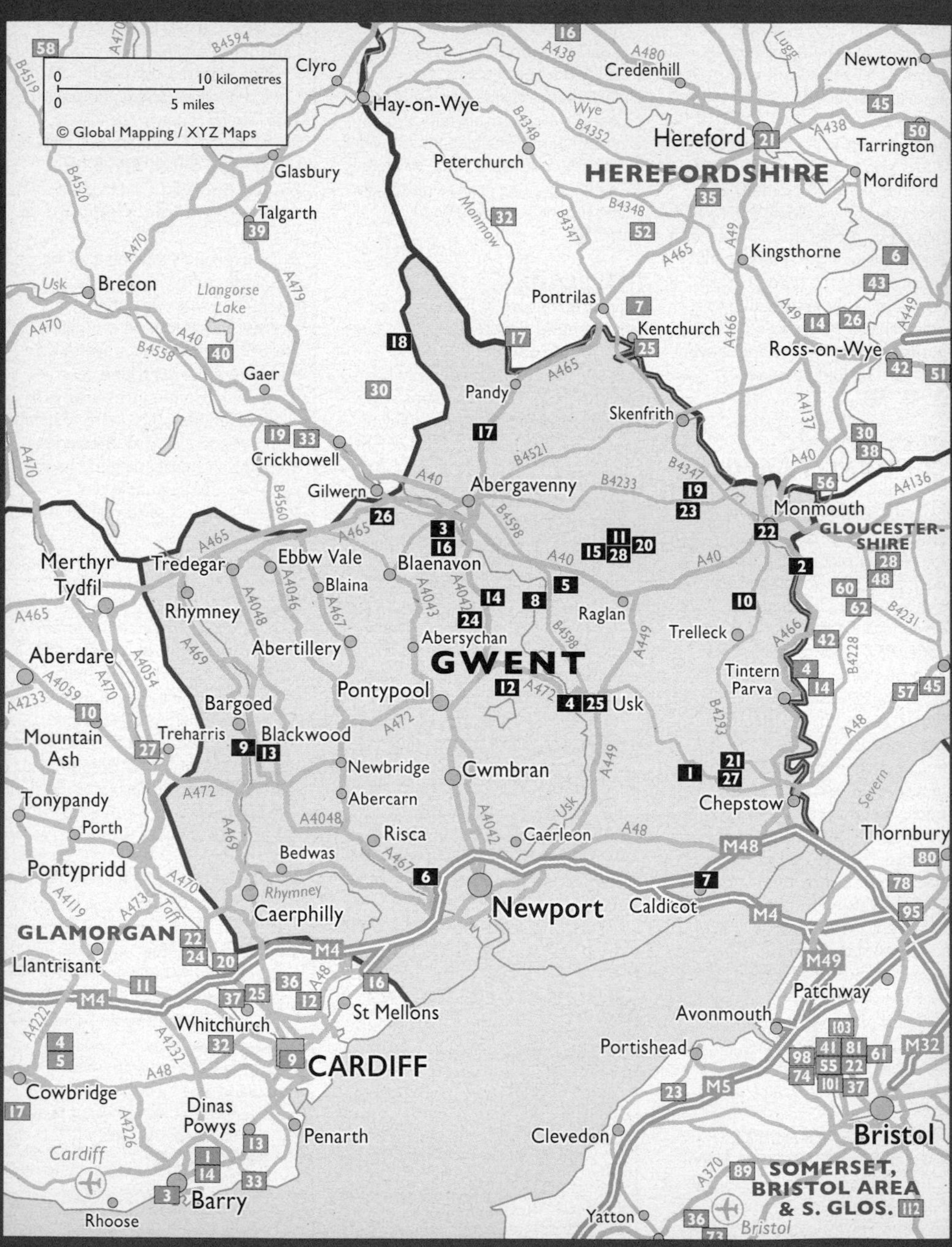

0
10 kilometres
0
5 miles
© Global Mapping / XYZ Maps
GWENT
HEREFORDSHIRE
GLOUCESTERSHIRE
GLAMORGAN
SOMERSET, BRISTOL AREA & S. GLOS.
Clyro
Hay-on-Wye
Glasbury
Talgarth
Brecon
Llangorse Lake
Gaer
Crickhowell
Gilwern
Merthyr Tydfil
Tredegar
Ebbw Vale
Blaina
Blaenavon
Rhymney
Abertillery
Abersychan
Aberdare
Mountain Ash
Bargoed
Treharris
Blackwood
Pontypool
Newbridge
Abercarn
Cwmbran
Tonypandy
Porth
Pontypridd
Risca
Bedwas
Caerleon
Caerphilly
Newport
Caldicot
Llantrisant
Whitchurch
St Mellons
CARDIFF
Cowbridge
Dinas Powys
Penarth
Barry
Rhoose
Cardiff
Credenhill
Hereford
Peterchurch
Pontrilas
Kentchurch
Pandy
Skenfrith
Abergavenny
Raglan
Usk
Trelleck
Tintern Parva
Chepstow
Monmouth
Newtown
Tarrington
Mordiford
Kingsthorne
Ross-on-Wye
Thornbury
Patchway
Avonmouth
Portishead
Clevedon
Bristol
Yatton
Wye
Lugg
Monnow
Usk
Severn
Taff
Rhymney
M4
M48
M49
M5
M32
A40
A48
A49
A438
A480
A465
A466
A470
A4059
A4233
A4054
A469
A472
A4048
A4046
A467
A4043
A4042
A449
A4137
A4136
A4119
A473
A4222
A4232
A4226
A370
B4594
B4519
B4520
B4558
B4560
B4348
B4352
B4347
B4521
B4233
B4598
B4293
B4228
B4231
A479

From the old coal mining villages in the west to the rolling pastures on the east side of the county, from the sea and estuaries in the south to the rugged mountains in the north, Gwent is Wales writ small.

These contrasts are reflected in our Open Gardens; from small town gardens to rambling estates, from sea level to over 1200 feet, from highly manicured to blending into the landscape, there'll be a garden that will suit all tastes.

Some of our gardens are clustered around the delightful market towns of Monmouth and Abergavenny, many with breathtaking views of the surrounding hills and valleys. The historic small town of Usk opens around 20 varied gardens over a June weekend.

Gwent is a most accessible county, easily reached from Cardiff or Bristol, from Hereford or the Midlands. Gwent gardeners are proud of their efforts, and really enjoy talking about what they have achieved and what they are planning for the future. Come and join in those conversations - and do your bit for the wonderful National Garden Scheme charities at the same time.

Volunteers

County Organiser
Cathy Davies
01291 672625 / 07976 633 743
cathy-davies@btconnect.com

County Treasurer
Ian Mabberley
01873 890219
ian.mabberley@ngs.org.uk

Publicity
Ian Mabberley
(as above)

Assistant County Organiser
Sue Torkington
01873 890045
sue@torkington.myzen.co.uk

Veronica Ruth
01873 859757
vruth@btinternet.com

Below: Croesllanfro Farm

OPENING DATES

All entries subject to change. For latest information check **www.ngs.org.uk**

Extended openings are shown at the beginning of the month.

Map locator numbers are shown to the right of each garden name.

March

Sunday 25th
Llanover 14

April

Every day from Monday 9th to Sunday 15th
Woodlands Farm 28

Friday 13th
Woodlands Farm 28

Saturday 21st
Glebe House 8

Sunday 22nd
Glebe House 8

Sunday 29th
High Glanau Manor 10

May

Sunday 6th
High House 11
The Old Vicarage 20

Saturday 12th
NEW Park House 21
NEW Woodhaven 27

Saturday 19th
The Alma 1
NEW Dan-y-Warren

Sunday 20th
NEW Dan-y-Warren

Saturday 26th
Hillcrest 13

Sunday 27th
Hillcrest 13
Wenallt Isaf 26

Monday 28th
Hillcrest 13

June

Every day from Saturday 23rd to Thursday 28th
Castle House 4

Festival Weekend

Sunday 3rd
Rockfield Park 22

Sunday 10th
Castell Cwrt 3
Middle Ninfa Farm & Bunkhouse 16

Saturday 16th
Ty Boda 24

Sunday 17th
Ty Boda 24

Saturday 23rd
Usk Open Gardens 25

Sunday 24th
Usk Open Gardens 25

Friday 29th
Mione 17

July

Sunday 1st
Hill House 12
Mione 17

Friday 6th
Mione 17

Saturday 7th
Longhouse Farm 15

Sunday 8th
Longhouse Farm 15
Mione 17

Saturday 14th
14 Gwerthonor Lane 9
◆ Nant y Bedd 18

Sunday 15th
14 Gwerthonor Lane 9
◆ Nant y Bedd 18

Sunday 22nd
Birch Tree Well 2
Clytha Park 5

Saturday 28th
Woodlands Farm 28

Sunday 29th
Woodlands Farm 28

August

Sunday 19th
Croesllanfro Farm 6

September

Sunday 16th
NEW Old Llangattock Farm 19

Sunday 23rd
Sunnyside 23

October

Sunday 14th
Castell Cwrt 3
◆ Dewstow Gardens & Grottoes 7

By Arrangement

Birch Tree Well 2
Castle House 4
Croesllanfro Farm 6
NEW Dan-y-Warren
Glebe House 8
Hillcrest 13
Llanover 14
Longhouse Farm 15
NEW Old Llangattock Farm 19
Rockfield Park 22
Sunnyside 23
NEW Woodhaven 27
Woodlands Farm 28

THE GARDENS

1 THE ALMA

Bully Hole Bottom, Usk Road, Shirenewton, NP16 6SA. Dr Pauline Ruth. *Southwest facing slope overlooking valley. B4235 Usk to Chepstow signposted Bully Hole Bottom. Down hill over bridge up to T junction. Drive straight ahead along track signposted The Alma. Parking in meadow on L.* **Sat 19 May (1-6). Adm £4, chd free. Home-made teas.**

Large and beautiful sheltered SW facing garden in development, planted with uncommon trees and acid loving shrubs. Long border, hot border, wildlife pond, sunset arbour and riverside path. Driveway packed with native daffodils, snowdrops and bluebells in the spring. Sunny terrace for teas. Wheelchair access to level terrace.

2 BIRCH TREE WELL

Upper Ferry Road, Penallt, Monmouth, NP25 4AN. Jill Bourchier, gillian.bourchier@btinternet.com. *4m SW of Monmouth. Approx 1m from Monmouth on B4293, turn L for Penallt & Trelleck. After 2m turn L to Penallt. On entering village turn L at Xrds & follow yellow signs.* **Sun 22 July (2-5.30). Adm £4, chd free. Cream teas. Visits also by arrangement May to Sept groups welcome but limited parking.**

Situated in the heart of the Lower Wye Valley, amongst the ancient habitat of woodland, rocks and streams. These 3 acres are shared with deer, badger and fox. A woodland setting with streams and boulders which can be viewed from a lookout tower and a butterfly garden planted with specialist hydrangeas incl many plants to also attract bees and insects. Live music will be played (harp and cello). Children are very welcome (under supervision) with plenty of activities in the form of treasure hunts. Not all areas of garden suitable for wheelchairs but refreshments certainly are!

3 CASTELL CWRT

Llanelen, Abergavenny, NP7 9LE. Lorna & John McGlynn. *1m S of Abergavenny. From Llanfoist B4629 signed Llanelen. ½m R up single track rd. Approx 500yds past canal, garden entrance 2nd on L. Disabled parking. On combined opening day (June) main parking at Castell Cwrt.* **Sun 10 June (2-6). Combined adm with Middle Ninfa Farm & Bunkhouse £5, chd free. Sun 14 Oct (2-5). Adm £3.50, chd free. Home-made teas.**

Large informal wildlife friendly, family garden on 10 acre small holding with fine views overlooking Abergavenny. Lawns with established trees, shrubs and perennial borders. Soft fruit and vegetable gardens. Woodland and hay meadow walks, chickens and geese, bees, livestock in fields and family pets. Children very welcome, animals to see and space to let off steam. Farm Shop with own produce. Hay meadow in bloom in June, autumn colour in October. Canal & Hill Walking on the doorstep! Some gravel paths.

4 CASTLE HOUSE

Castle Parade, Usk, NP15 1SD. Mr & Mrs J H L Humphreys, 01291 672563, info@uskcastle.com, www.uskcastle.com. *200yds NE from Usk centre. Footpath access signed to Usk Castle 300yds E from town square, opp Fire Station. Vehicles 400yds (next L) on Castle Parade in Usk.* **Daily Sat 23 June to Thur 28 June (10-5). Adm £5, chd free. (23rd & 24th June, adm incl in Usk Open Gardens). Light refreshments in Conservatory or Tithe Barn. Visits also by arrangement throughout the year. Refreshments for groups on request.**

Overlooked by the romantic ruins of Usk Castle which is also open, the gardens were established over 100 years ago, with yew hedges and topiary, long border planted as a pictorial meadow, croquet lawn and pond. The herb garden has plants that would have been used when the castle was last lived in c.1469. Most areas easily accessible to wheelchair users.

5 CLYTHA PARK

Abergavenny, NP7 9BW. Jack and Susannah Tenison. *Between Abergavenny (5m) & Raglan (3m). On old A40 signed Clytha at r'abouts either end.* **Sun 22 July (2-5). Adm £5, chd free. Home-made teas.**

Large C18/19 garden around lake with wide lawns and specimen trees, original layout by John Davenport, with C19 arboretum, and H. Avray Tipping influence. Visit the 1790 walled garden and the newly restored greenhouses. Some stalls. Gravel and grass paths.

6 CROESLLANFRO FARM

Groes Road, Rogerstone, Newport, NP10 9GP. Barry & Liz Davies, 01633 894057, lizplants@gmail.com. *3m W of Newport. From M4 J27 take B4591 towards Risca. Take 3rd R, Cefn Walk (also signed 14 Locks Canal Centre). Proceed over bridge, cont ½m to island in middle of rd.* **Sun 19 Aug (1.30-5). Adm £4.50, chd free. Home-made teas. Visits also by arrangement May to Sept for any size group.**

Two acres of informal, mass planted perennial borders. Spring and early summer is a tapestry of green concentrating on leaf form and texture. Late summer and early autumn brings the the garden to a finale with an explosion of colour. A barn stands in a large formal courtyard designed on 6 different levels. Children can explore the folly, grotto and try the treasure hunt! Folly, grotto and large barn open to the public. Owner co-author of Designing Gardens on Slopes and featured in Country Homes and Interiors. Some gravel paths and shallow steps to main area of garden.

Hill House

NEW DAN-Y-WARREN

Crickhowell Road, Gilwern, Abergavenny, NP7 0EH. Mrs Olive Scurr, 01873 830274. *From centre of Gilwern, turn R for Crickhowell & Brecon. Proceed about 1½ miles, entrance is on the R.* **Sat 19, Sun 20 May (2-6). Adm £4, chd £1. Home-made teas. Visits also by arrangement Jan to Sept.**

Dan-y-Warren was originally part of the Dan-y-Parc Estate. It borders the River Usk and has large old oaks, a circle of Redwoods and other interesting trees. The garden contains a variety of rhododendrons, azaleas, flower borders, an orchard, vegetable beds and a fruit cage. A woodland walk through a dell and newly planted valley goes down to the River Usk. No wheelchair access to woodland walk.

♿ ☕

7 ◆ DEWSTOW GARDENS & GROTTOES

Caerwent, Caldicot, NP26 5AH. John Harris, 01291 431020, info@dewstowgardens.co.uk, www.dewstowgardens.co.uk. *Dewstow House, 6m W of Chepstow. 8m E of Newport. A48 Newport to Chepstow rd, drive into village of Caerwent. Follow brown tourist daisy signs to Gardens. (1½m from Caerwent Village).* **For NGS: Sun 14 Oct (10-3.30). Adm £6, chd free. Light refreshments. For other opening times and information, please phone, email or visit garden website.**

5 acre Grade I listed unique garden which was buried and forgotten after World War II and rediscovered in 2000. Created around 1895 by James Pulham & Sons, the garden contains underground grottoes, tunnels and ferneries and above ground stunning water features. You will not be disappointed. Various events throughout the season. No wheelchair access to underground areas. Partial access elsewhere.

♿ ✿ 🚌 ☕

8 GLEBE HOUSE

Llanvair Kilgeddin, Abergavenny, NP7 9BE. Mr & Mrs Murray Kerr, 01873 840422, joanna@amknet.com. *Midway between Abergavenny (5m) & Usk (5m) on B4598.* **Sat 21, Sun 22 Apr (2-6). Adm £5, chd free. Home-made teas. Visits also by arrangement Apr to July.**

Orchard and borders bursting with spring bulbs and tulips. South facing terrace, decorative veg garden and wildflower meadow in development. Some topiary and formal hedging in 1½ acre garden set in AONB in Usk valley. Old rectory of St Mary's, Llanfair Kilgeddin which will also be open to view famous Victorian Scraffito Murals. Featured in Country Homes and Interiors. Some gravel and gently sloping lawns.

♿ ✿ ☕

9 14 GWERTHONOR LANE

Gilfach, Bargoed, CF81 8JT. Suzanne & Philip George. *8m N of Caerphilly. A469 to Bargoed, through the T-lights next to school then L filterlane at next T-lights onto Cardiff Rd. First L into Gwerthonor Road, 4th R int Gwerthonor Lane.* **Sat 14, Sun 15 July (11-6). Adm £3, chd free. Light refreshments.**

The garden has a beautiful panoramic view of the Rhymney Valley and is in a semi-rural setting. A real plantswoman's garden with over 600 varieties of perennials, annuals, bulbs, shrubs and trees. There are numerous rare and unusual plants combined with traditional and well loved favourites (many available for sale). A pond with a small waterfall adds to the tranquil feel of the garden.

♿ ✿ ☕

10 HIGH GLANAU MANOR

Lydart, Monmouth, NP25 4AD. Mr & Mrs Hilary Gerrish. *4m SW of Monmouth. Situated on B4293 between Monmouth & Chepstow. Turn R into Private Rd, ¼m after Craig-y-Dorth turn on B4293.* **Sun 29 Apr (2-6). Adm £6, chd free. Home-made teas.**

Listed Arts and Crafts garden laid out by H Avray Tipping in 1922. Original features incl impressive stone terraces with far reaching views over the Vale of Usk to Blorenge, Skirrid, Sugar Loaf and Brecon Beacons. Pergola, herbaceous borders, Edwardian glasshouse, rhododendrons, azaleas, tulips, orchard with wild flowers. Originally open for the NGS in 1927. Garden guide by owner, Helena Gerrish, available to purchase.

✿ 🚌 ☕

11 HIGH HOUSE

Penrhos, NP15 2DJ. Mr & Mrs R Cleeve. *4m N of Raglan. From r'about on A40 at Raglan take exit to Clytha. After 50yds turn R at Llantilio Crossenny. Follow NGS signs, 10mins through lanes.* **Sun 6 May (2-6). Combined adm with The Old Vicarage £6, chd free. Home-made teas.**

3 acres of spacious lawns and trees surrounding C16 house (not open) in a beautiful, hidden part of Monmouthshire. South facing terrace and extensive bed of old roses. Swathes of grass with tulips, camassias, wild flowers and far reaching views. Espaliered cherries, pears and scented evergreens in courtyard. Large extended pond, orchard with chickens and ducks, vegetable garden. Partial wheelchair access, some shallow steps, sloping lawn, gravel courtyard.

♿ ✿ ☕

12 HILL HOUSE

Church Lane, Glascoed, Pontypool, NP4 0UA. Susan & John Wright. *Between Usk & Pontypool. Approx 2m W of Usk via A472 turn L before Beaufort Arms into Glascoed Lane. Bear L up hill, Church Lane 1st turn on R. House at very end of narrow lane, do not turn off.* **Sun 1 July (1-6). Adm £5, chd free. Home-made teas.**

Developing garden on ex-wasteland around modest farmhouse. Exposed hilltop site, fine views. Small orchard, reflecting pond, herbaceous borders, grasses, farmyard garden with standard parrotia and massed crocosmia (under reconstruction), picket beds. Many seats. 30 mins walk through fields, steep return climb. Restricted parking, marshals in attendance. Some gravel paths. No disabled WC.

♿ ☕

13 HILLCREST

Waunborfa Road, Cefn Fforest, Blackwood, NP12 3LB. Mr M O'Leary & Mr B Price, 01443 837029, bev.price@mclweb.net. *3m W of Newbridge. Follow A4048 to Blackwood town centre or A469 to Pengam (Glan-y-Nant) T-lights, then NGS signs.* **Sat 26, Sun 27, Mon 28 May (11-6). Adm £4, chd free. Cream teas. Visits also by arrangement Apr to Oct guided tours need to be booked in advance. Refreshments on request when booking.**

A cascade of secluded gardens of distinct character, all within 1½ acres. Magnificent, unusual trees with interesting shrubs and perennials. With choices at every turn, visitors exploring the gardens are well rewarded as hidden delights and surprises are revealed. Well placed seats encourage a relaxed pace to fully appreciate the garden's treasures. Delicious cream teas to be enjoyed. Tulips in April and trees in their autumnal splendour in October. Featured in the Western Mail. Lowest parts of garden not accessible to wheelchairs.

14 LLANOVER

nr Abergavenny, NP7 9EF. Mr & Mrs M R Murray, 07753 423635, www.llanovergarden.co.uk. *4m S of Abergavenny, 15m N of Newport, 20m SW Hereford. On A4042 Abergavenny - Cwmbran Rd, in village of Llanover.* **Sun 25 Mar (2-5). Adm £5, chd free. Home-made teas. Visits also by arrangement Feb to Nov groups min 15 for tours.**

Stunning 15 acre garden laid out in C18. The Rhyd-y-Meirch stream flows through ponds and the round walled garden, over cascades and beneath flagstone bridges. Children can run on the lawns, play pooh-sticks along the streams or hide and seek amongst the trees. Home of Llanover Garden School where renowned gardeners & plantsmen share their knowledge with participants. The house (not open) is the birthplace of Augusta Waddington, Lady Llanover, C19 patriot and supporter of the Welsh Language Descendants. The flock of Welsh Black Mountain sheep which she introduced, can be seen grazing in the park. Historic listed garden laid with a ha-ha, circular garden and ponds. Gravel and grass paths and lawns. No disabled WC.

15 LONGHOUSE FARM

Penrhos, Raglan, NP15 2DE. Mr & Mrs M H C Anderson, 01600 780389, m.anderson666@btinternet.com. *Midway between Monmouth & Abergavenny. 4m from Raglan. Off Old Raglan/Abergavenny rd signed Clytha. At Bryngwyn/Great Oak Xrds turn towards Great Oak - follow yellow NGS signs from red phone box down narrow lane.* **Sat 7, Sun 8 July (2-6). Adm £5, chd free. Home-made teas. Visits also by arrangement June to Sept.**

Hidden 2 acre garden with S-facing terrace, collection of pelargoniums, millrace wall, pond and spacious lawns with extensive views. Colourful and unusual plants in the borders, a malus avenue and a recently revamped productive vegetable garden. A woodland walk is being created with a stream, hidden ponds and massed bluebells in spring.

16 MIDDLE NINFA FARM & BUNKHOUSE

Llanelen, Abergavenny, NP7 9LE. Richard Lewis, 01873 854662, bookings@middleninfa.co.uk, www.middleninfa.co.uk. *2½m SSW Abergavenny. At A465/ B4246 junction, S for Llanfoist, L at mini r'about, B4269 towards Llanelen, ½m R turn up steep lane, over canal. ¾m to Middle Ninfa on R. Main parking at Castel Cwrt.* **Sun 10 June (2-6). Combined adm with Castell Cwrt £5, chd free.**

Large terraced eco-garden on east slopes of the Blorenge mountain. Vegetable beds, polytunnel, 3 greenhouses, orchard, flower borders, wild flowers. Great views, woodland walks, cascading water and ponds. Paths steep in places, unsuitable for less able. Campsite and small bunkhouse on farm. 5 mins walk uphill to scenic Punchbowl Lake and walks on the Blorenge.

17 MIONE

Old Hereford Road, Llanvihangel Crucorney, Abergavenny, NP7 7LB. Yvonne & John O'Neil. *5m N of Abergavenny. From Abergavenny take A465 to Hereford. After 4.8m turn L - signed Pantygelli. Mione is ½m on L.* **Fri 29 June, Sun 1, Fri 6, Sun 8 July (10.30-6). Adm £3, chd free. Home-made teas.**

Beautiful garden with a wide variety of established plants, many rare and unusual. Pergola with climbing roses and clematis. Wildlife pond with many newts, insects and frogs. Numerous containers with diverse range of planting. Several seating areas, each with a different atmosphere. Lovely home-made cakes, biscuits and scones to be enjoyed sitting in the garden or pretty summerhouse.

18 ◆ NANT Y BEDD

Grwyne Fawr, Fforest Coal Pit, Abergavenny, NP7 7LY. Sue & Ian Mabberley, 01873 890219, garden@nantybedd.com, www.nantybedd.com. *In Grwyne Fawr valley. From A465 Llanv Crucorney, direction Llanthony, then L to Fforest Coal Pit. At grey telephone box cont for 4½m towards Grwyne Fawr Reservoir.* **For NGS: Sat 14, Sun 15 July (12-6). Adm £5, chd free. Home-made teas.** For other opening times and information, please phone, email or visit garden website.

Blending wild and tame, 6½ acre garden described as 'Absolutely enchanting, of the place, so imaginative'. Set high in the Black Mountains by the Grwyne Fawr river with lots of places to sit and enjoy the tranquility. An inspiring mix of vegetables and fruit, mature trees and shrubs and water. A garden for everyone, loved by photographers. Productive organic vegetable and fruit gardens, stream, forest and river walk, wildflowers, natural swimming pond, tree sculpture, shepherd's hut and eco-features. Ducks, chickens, sheep, pigs, cats. Plants and garden accessories for sale. See www.nantybedd.com for details. Featured in Country Homes & Interiors (Gwent's Most Magical Garden), House & Garden, The Organic Way.

19 NEW OLD LLANGATTOCK FARM

Llangattock Vibon-Avel, Monmouth, NP25 5NG. Dr Cherry Taylor, 01600 715404. *4 miles west of Monmouth. Follow B4233 Monmouth to Abergavenny rd, turning right after ~3 miles, signposted Llangattock. Follow road for 1 mile, turning left at the lodge onto dirt track leading to the garden.* **Sun 16 Sept (2-6). Adm £4, chd free. Home-made teas. Visits also by arrangement Feb to Nov for groups of 1-10 people.**

Organic, no-dig garden started in late 2015, with unusual plants in colour-rich beds, plus a large vegetable garden, orchard and field totalling 1¾ acres. No-dig methods have enabled rapid progress & the garden has been used by no-dig guru, Charles Dowding, in courses to demonstrate his methods. Far-reaching views of the Blorenge, Skirrid and Black Mountains. Gravel and woodchip paths. Featured on Charles Dowding's website as an example of a no-dig garden.

20 THE OLD VICARAGE

Penrhos, Raglan, Usk, NP15 2LE. Mrs Georgina Herrmann. *3m N of Raglan. From A449 take Raglan exit, join A40 & move immed into R lane & turn R across dual carriageway. Follow yellow NGS signs.* **Sun 6 May (2-6). Combined adm with High House £6, chd free.**

The Old Vicarage has a series of gardens surrounding a 151yr old (1867) Victorian Gothic house which invites you to explore as the eye is drawn from one garden into the next. With sweeping lawns and a variety of young and mature trees, a summer house and formal garden, two ponds and a kitchen garden enhanced by imaginatively placed pots, this gem is not one to be rushed and gets better each year. Plant stall.

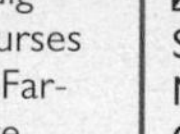

21 NEW PARK HOUSE

School Lane, Itton, Chepstow, NP16 6BZ. Professor Bruce & Dr Cynthia Matthews. *as above. From M48 take A466 Tintern. At 2nd roundabout turn L B4293 After blue sign Itton turn R Park House is at end of lane. Parking 200m before house. From Devauden B4293 1st L in Itton.* **Sat 12 May (10-5). Combined adm with Woodhaven £6, chd free. Home-made teas at Woodhaven.**

Approx one acre garden with large vegetable areas and many mature trees, rhododendrons, azaleas, camellias in a woodland setting. Bordering on Chepstow Park Wood. Magnificent views over open country. A few small steps. and irregular paths too narrow for wheelchairs. Disabled parking adjacent to house.

22 ROCKFIELD PARK

Rockfield, Monmouth, NP25 5QB. Mark & Melanie Molyneux, 07803 952027. *On arriving in Rockfield village from Monmouth, turn R by phone box. After approx 400yds, church on L. Entrance to Rockfield Park on R, opp church, via private bridge over river.* **Sun 3 June (11-5). Adm £5, chd free. Home-made teas. Visits also by arrangement June & July, group size 20 Max.**

Rockfield Park dates from C17 and is situated in the heart of the Monmouthshire countryside on the banks of the River Monnow. The extensive grounds comprise formal gardens, meadows and orchard, complemented by riverside and woodland walks. Possible to picnic on riverside walks. Main part of gardens can be accessed by wheelchair but not steep garden leading down to river.

23 SUNNYSIDE

The Hendre, Monmouth, NP25 5HQ. Helen & Ralph Fergusson-Kelly, 01600 714928, helen_fk@hotmail.com. *4m W of Monmouth. On B4233 Monmouth to Abergavenny rd.* **Sun 23 Sept (12-6). Adm £4.50, chd free.**

Rockfield Park

Home-made teas. Visits also by arrangement May to Nov for single visitors or groups 25 max (evenings and weekends).

A sloping ⅓ acre garden on the old Rolls estate. There is much to be enjoyed throughout the yr with formal plant and topiary structure. The garden builds to a profusion of colour towards the end of the summer from russet tones of grasses then bold injections of scarlet, cerise, violet and gold from bulbs, perennials and trees. Quiet seating areas to enjoy views of the Monmouthshire countryside. Some gravel paths.

24 TY BODA

Upper Llanover, Abergavenny, NP7 9EP. Mike & Mary Shooter. *Off A4042. Follow directions to Upper Llanover (coming from Abergavenny) or Pencroesoped (coming from Cwmbran), narrow lanes. Watch out for signs to Goose & Cuckoo Pub. If you get there, you've past us!* **Sat 16, Sun 17 June (11-5). Adm £5, chd free. Home-made teas.**

A 4 acre hillside garden with stunning views out over the Vale of Usk. Wildlife pond, stream and winding paths through a meadow newly planted with fifteen hundred native trees. Medieval style medicinal herb garden, potager, fernery, orchard, rope swing, stone circle and roses, roses everywhere. Steep slopes and slippery steps, so come prepared! Scrumptious home-made cakes and tea.

GROUP OPENING

25 USK OPEN GARDENS

Twyn Square, Usk, NP15 1BH. 07944 616448, UskOpenGardens@gmail.com, www.uskopengardens.com. *From M4 J24 take A449, proceed 8m N to Usk exit. Free parking in town. Blue badge car parking in main car parks & at Usk Castle. Map of gardens provided with ticket.* **Sat 23, Sun 24 June (10-5). Combined adm £7.50, chd free.**

Winner of Wales in Bloom for over 30yrs, Usk is full of hanging baskets and boxes and a wonderful backdrop to around 20 gardens from small cottages packed with colourful and unusual plants to large gardens with brimming herbaceous borders. Romantic garden around the ramparts of Usk Castle. Gardeners' Market with interesting plants. Great day out for all the family with lots of places to eat and drink incl places to picnic. Various cafes, PH and restaurants available for refreshments, plus several volunteer groups offering teas and cakes; one garden has a pop up Pimms, Prosecco and ice cream bar with a picnic and children's play area by their lake. Usk Castle and school fully accessible but not all gardens/ areas of gardens fully wheelchair accessible. Accessibility noted on ticket.

26 WENALLT ISAF

Twyn Wenallt, Gilwern, Abergavenny, NP7 0HP. Tim & Debbie Field. *3m W of Abergavenny. From Abergavenny follow A465 towards Merthyr. At Gilwern roundabout follow yellow NGS signs.* **Sun 27 May (2-6). Adm £4, chd free. Home-made teas.**

2½ acre garden 650ft up on a N-facing hillside with magnificent views of the Black Mountains. Mature trees, flowering shrubs, borders, productive vegetable garden, small polytunnel, orchard, pigs, chickens, 2 bee hives and plenty of space to run about.

27 NEW WOODHAVEN

Itton, Chepstow, NP16 6BX. Mr & Mrs Kelly, 01291 641219. *Take the B4293 at Chepstow Racecourse r'about at Itton Common triangle, turn L at red tel box, and then L along the the road to Shirenewton, Woodhaven is on the L.* **Sat 12 May (10-5). Combined adm with Park House £6, chd free. Home-made teas. Visits also by arrangement May to Oct groups of 10-25. Parking for a coach can be arranged after drop off.**

A modern house built on the site of a former sawmills for the Itton Court Estate. Garden of two-thirds of an acre developed over the last twenty years for all yr round colour and interest. Level front garden and gently sloping rear garden with extensive views over the valley. Lots of seating areas to enjoy the views. Meadow area with bulbs, fruit trees and wild flowers. Wheelchair access for the front garden and rear terrace with views only.

28 WOODLANDS FARM

Penrhos, NP15 2LE. Craig Loane & Charles Horsfield, 01600 780203, Woodlandsfarmwales@gmail.com, www.woodlandsfarmwales.com. *3m N of Raglan. From A449 take Raglan exit, join A40 & move immed into R lane & turn R across dual carriageway towards Tregare. Take first L down narrow lane. Follow yellow NGS signs.* **Daily Mon 9 Apr to Sun 15 Apr (2-6). Adm £5, chd free. Home-made teas in the Pavilion at Woodlands Farm Barns. Evening opening Fri 13 Apr (6-8). Adm £6. Wine in the Pavilion at Woodlands Farm Barns. Sat 28, Sun 29 July (2-6). Adm £5, chd free. Home-made teas in the Pavilion at Woodlands Farm Barns. Visits also by arrangement Apr to Oct.**

A design led garden that's built to entertain. Many rooms & hidden spaces draw you in. With ponds, viewing platform, hard landscaping, sculptures & more, there's something for all. In response to last year's success (700+ visitors) we're offering a week of events, incl guided walks, floristry & an evening with wine & music. See www.woodlandsfarmwales.com for details.

GWYNEDD & ANGLESEY

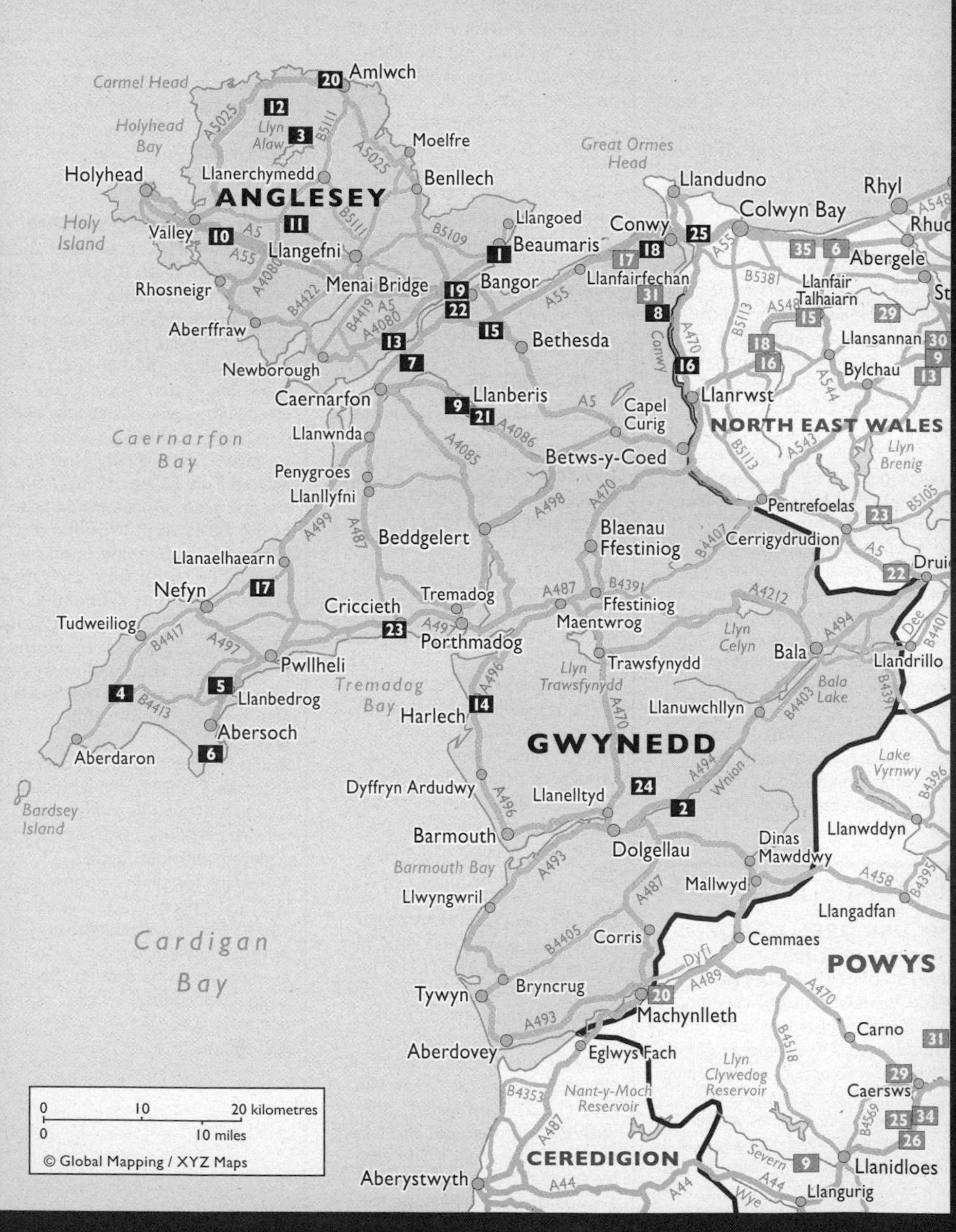

Gwynedd is a county rich in history and outstanding natural beauty. Bordered by the Irish Sea and home to Snowdonia National Park, Gwynedd can boast some of the most impressive landscapes in the UK.

The mountains in Gwynedd are world famous, and have attracted visitors for hundreds of years – the most famous perhaps, was Charles Darwin in 1831. As well as enjoying the tallest peaks in the UK, Gwynedd has fine woodland – from hanging oak forests in the mountains to lush, riverside woods.

Holiday-makers flock to Gwynedd and Anglesey to take advantage of the sandy beaches, and many can enjoy sightings of dolphins and porpoises off the coast.

The gardens of Gwynedd and Anglesey are just as appealing an attraction for visitors. A variety of gardens open for Gwynedd NGS, ranging from Crowrach Isaf a two-acre garden with views of Snowdonia and Cardigan Bay to Ty Capel Ffrwd, a true cottage garden in the Welsh mountains.

So why not escape from the hustle and bustle of everyday life and relax in a beautiful garden? You will be assured of a warm welcome at every garden gate.

Below: Treborth Botanic Garden, Bangor University

Volunteers

North Gwynedd & Anglesey
County Organiser
Hazel Bond
01407 831354
nigel@cae-newydd.co.uk

County Treasurer
Nigel Bond
01407 831354
nigel.bond@ngs.org.uk

Assistant County Organisers
Grace Meirion-Jones
01286 831195

Janet Jones
01758 740296
janetcoron@hotmail.co.uk

Delia Lanceley
01286 650517
delia@lanceley.com

South Gwynedd

County Organiser
Hilary Nurse
01341 450255
antique_pete@btinternet.com

County Treasurer
Michael Bishton
01654 710882
m.bishton@btopenworld.com

OPENING DATES

All entries subject to change. For latest information check **www.ngs.org.uk**

Extended openings are shown at the beginning of the month.

Map locator numbers are shown to the right of each garden name.

March

Friday 30th
Llyn Rhaeadr 14

Saturday 31st
Llyn Rhaeadr 14

April

Every day from Sunday 1st to Friday 6th
Llyn Rhaeadr 14

Wednesday 25th
Plas Cadnant Hidden Gardens 19

Saturday 28th
Llanidan Hall 13

Sunday 29th
Maenan Hall 16

May

Every day from Sunday 27th to Thursday 31st
Llyn Rhaeadr 14

Sunday 6th
Llyn Rhaeadr 14
Sunningdale 20

Monday 7th
Llyn Rhaeadr 14

Saturday 12th
Sunningdale 20

Saturday 19th
Coron 5
Ty Capel Ffrwd 24

Sunday 20th
Bryn Gwern 2
Coron 5
Llys-y-Gwynt 15
Ty Capel Ffrwd 24

Saturday 26th
Gwaelod Mawr 10

Sunday 27th
Gwaelod Mawr 10
NEW Mynydd Heulog 17

June

Festival Weekend

Friday 1st
Llyn Rhaeadr 14

Saturday 2nd
◆ Crûg Farm 7
Glan Llyn 9
Llyn Rhaeadr 14
Sunningdale 20

Sunday 3rd
Gilfach 8
Llyn Rhaeadr 14
NEW Mynydd Heulog 17
◆ Pensychnant 18
NEW Swn-Y-Gwynt 21

Saturday 9th
Cae Newydd 3

Sunday 10th
Cae Newydd 3

Saturday 16th
Crowrach Isaf 6

Sunday 17th
Crowrach Isaf 6

Sunday 24th
Sunningdale 20

Saturday 30th
Llanidan Hall 13

July

Sunday 1st
Gwyndy Bach 11
Llys-y-Gwynt 15

Saturday 7th
NEW Beaumaris Allotments 1

Sunday 8th
NEW Beaumaris Allotments 1

Saturday 14th
Llanidan Hall 13

Sunday 15th
41 Victoria Drive 25

Saturday 21st
NEW Trefaes 23

Sunday 22nd
◆ Pensychnant 18
NEW Trefaes 23

Sunday 29th
Bryn Gwern 2
NEW Llanfechell Allotments 12
Maenan Hall 16

August

Every day from Sunday 26th to Thursday 30th
Llyn Rhaeadr 14

September

Saturday 1st
Llyn Rhaeadr 14

Sunday 2nd
Llyn Rhaeadr 14

Saturday 22nd
NEW Treborth Botanic Garden, Bangor University 22

By Arrangement

Bryn Gwern 2
Coed Ty Mawr 4
Crowrach Isaf 6
Gilfach 8
Gwaelod Mawr 10
Gwyndy Bach 11
Llys-y-Gwynt 15
Maenan Hall 16
NEW Mynydd Heulog 17
Sunningdale 20

Swn-Y-Gwynt

THE GARDENS

1 NEW BEAUMARIS ALLOTMENTS

Beaumaris, LL58 8RA. Beaumaris Allotments Society, www.beaumaris/allotments.weebly.com. *Beaumaris Anglesey North Wales. Past Beaumaris Castle L into car park gate at top.* **Sat 7, Sun 8 July (10-5). Adm £3, chd free. Light refreshments at nearby Happy Valley Cafe.**

Est 1917 the allotments are set in an idyllic location overlooking Beaumaris castle, Menai Strait and Snowdonia mountains. 60+ plots growing veg, flowers and fruit. Site is a short walk from town centre. Produce for sale. Grass paths partially accessible by wheelchair when dry.

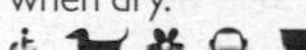

2 BRYN GWERN

Llanfachreth, Dolgellau, Gwynedd, LL40 2DH. H O & P D Nurse, 01341 450 255, antique_pete@btinternet.com. *5m NE of Dolgellau. Do not go to Llanfachreth, stay on Bala road, 5m from Dolgellau, 14m from Bala.* **Sun 20 May, Sun 29 July (10-5). Adm £3.50, chd free. Home-made teas. Visits also by arrangement May to Oct.**

Sloping 2 acre garden in the hills overlooking Dolgellau with views to Cader Idris, originally wooded but redesigned to enhance its natural features with streams, ponds and imaginative and extensive planting and vibrant colour. The garden is now a haven for wildlife with hedgehogs and 27 species of birds feeding last winter as well as being home to ducks, dogs and cats. Stone mason at work and items for sale or orders taken. Wheelchair access to main area of garden but only when dry.

3 CAE NEWYDD

Rhosgoch, Anglesey, LL66 0BG. Hazel & Nigel Bond. *3m SW of Amlwch. A5025 from Benllech to Amlwch, follow signs for leisure centre & Lastra Farm. Follow yellow NGS signs (approx 3m), car park on L.* **Sat 9, Sun 10 June (11-4). Adm £4, chd free. Light refreshments.**

Maturing country garden of 2½ acres which blends seamlessly into the open landscape with stunning views of Snowdonia and Llyn Alaw. Variety of shrubs, trees and herbaceous areas, large wildlife pond, polytunnel, greenhouses, raised vegetable beds. Collections of fuchsia, pelargonium, cacti & succulents. An emphasis on gardening for wildlife throughout the garden. Hay meadow. Lots of seating throughout the garden, visitors are welcome to bring a picnic. Garden area closest to house suitable for wheelchairs.

4 COED TY MAWR

Ty Mawr, Bryncroes, Pwllheli, LL53 8EH. Nonni & David Goadby, 01758 730359, nonni@goadby.net, www.coed-ty-mawr.co.uk. *12m W of Pwllheli. Take B4413 Llanbedrog to Aberdaron. 1¾m past Sarn Meyllteyrn. Turn R at Penygroeslon sign. From Nefyn take B4417, at Xrds with B4413 turn L.* **Visits by arrangement Mar to Sept no minimum, maximum 50. Adm £5, chd free. Home-made teas.**

Outstanding 5 acre woodland garden created from wilderness and situated among some of the most beautiful scenery of Wales. Over 3,000 trees and shrubs incl growing collections of magnolia, rhododendron, hydrangea and cornus. Also large pond, orchard, fernery, vegetable, and sea view gardens. Plenty of seating. Sit on the raised deck, take in the sea views and enjoy a home-made tea. Grass paths.

5 CORON

Llanbedrog, LL53 7NN. Mr & Mrs B M Jones. *3m SW of Pwllheli. Turn R off A499 opp Llanbedrog Village sign, before garage, up private drive.* **Sat 19, Sun 20 May (10.30-5). Adm £4, chd free. Cream teas.**

6 acre mature garden overlooking Cardigan Bay. Featuring a Davidia Involucrata, 3 superb, huge specimens of Tasmanian Blue Gum, Eucalyptus, pathways leading through extensively planted areas with rhododendrons, embothriums, azaleas, camellias, bluebell walks, wooded slopes and rock outcrops providing shelter for tender plants. Lakes and bog gardens; orchard, walled vegetable and formal garden. Featured on S4C Pobol A'i Gerddi (People and their Gardens). Some areas accessible for wheelchair users.

6 CROWRACH ISAF

Bwlchtocyn, LL53 7BY. Margaret & Graham Cook, 01758 712860, crowrach_isaf@hotmail.com. *1½m SW of Abersoch. Follow rd through Abersoch & Sarn Bach, L at sign for Bwlchtocyn for ½m until junction & no-through rd - TG Holiday Complex. Turn R, parking 50 metres on R.* **Sat 16, Sun 17 June (1-5). Adm £4, chd free. Cream teas. Visits also by arrangement June to Sept groups 20+.**

2 acre plot incl 1 acre fenced against rabbits, developed from 2000, incl island beds, windbreak hedges, vegetable garden, wild flower area and wide range of geraniums, shrubs and herbaceous perennials. Views over Cardigan Bay and Snowdonia. Grass and gravel paths, some gentle slopes.

7 ◆ CRÛG FARM

Griffiths Crossing, Caernarfon, LL55 1TU. Mr & Mrs B Wynn-Jones, 01248 670232, sue@crug-farm.co.uk, www.crug-farm.co.uk. *2m NE of Caernarfon. ¼m off main A487 Caernarfon to Bangor rd. Follow signs from r'about.* **For NGS: Sat 2 June (9.30-4.30). Adm £3, chd free. Home-made teas. For other opening times and information, please phone, email or visit garden website.**

3 acres; grounds to old country house (not open). Gardens filled with choice, unusual plants collected by the Wynn-Jones. Woodland garden with shade loving plants, many not seen in cultivation before. Walled garden with more wonderful collections growing. Chelsea Gold Medallists and winners of the President's Award among other many prestigious awards. Exhibiting at Chelsea 2018. Partial wheelchair access.

NPC

Beaumaris Allotments

Spanish style patio and laburnum arch lead to sunken garden and wooden bridge over lily pond with fountain and waterfall. Peaceful Chinese orientated garden offering contemplation. Separate Koi carp pond. Abundant seating throughout. Mainly flat, with gravel and stone paths, no wheelchair access to sunken lily pond area.

11 GWYNDY BACH

Tynlon, Llandrygarn, LL65 3AJ. Keith & Rosa Andrew, 01407 720651, keithandrew.art@gmail.com. *5m W of Llangefni. From Llangefni take B5109 towards Bodedern, cottage exactly 5m out on L. Postcode good for SatNav.* **Sun 1 July (11-4.30). Adm £3.50, chd free. Home-made teas. Visits also by arrangement May to July.**

¾ acre artist's garden, set amidst rugged Anglesey landscape. Romantically planted in informal intimate rooms with interesting rare plants and shrubs, box and yew topiary, old roses and Japanese garden with large Koi pond (deep water, children must be supervised). National Collection of Rhapis miniature Japanese palms. Gravel entrance to garden.

NPC

8 GILFACH

Rowen, Conwy, LL32 8TS. James & Isoline Greenhalgh, 01492 650216, isolinegreenhalgh@btinternet.com. *4m S of Conwy. At Xrds 100yds E of Rowen S towards Llanrwst, past Rowen School on L, turn up 2nd drive on L.* **Sun 3 June (2-5.30). Adm £3.50, chd free. Home-made teas. Visits also by arrangement Apr to Aug coffee/ biscuits (am), tea/cake (pm). Groups 45 max.**

1 acre country garden on S-facing slope with magnificent views of the River Conwy and mountains; set in 35 acres of farm and woodland. Collection of mature shrubs is added to yearly; woodland garden, herbaceous border and small pool. Spectacular panoramic view of the Conwy Valley and the mountain range of the Carneddau. Classic cars. Large coaches can park at bottom of steep drive, disabled visitors can be driven to garden by the owner.

9 GLAN LLYN

Llanberis, Caernarfon, LL55 4EL. Mr Bob Stevens. *On A4086, ½m from Llanberis village. next door to the Galty-Glyn Hotel (Pizza & Pint Restaurant) opp DMM factory.* **Sat 2 June (11-4). Adm £3.50, chd free. Tea.**

A 3 acre woodland edge garden incl 2 acres of woodland, wildlife ponds, stream, wildflower area, raised sphagnum bog garden, three green roofs, 3 glass houses for cacti and succulents, Australasian and South African beds, sand bed, many unusual trees, shrubs and herbaceous perennials. The garden is on fairly steep sloping ground, no wheelchair access to the woodland.

10 GWAELOD MAWR

Caergeiliog, Anglesey, LL65 3YL. John & Tricia Coates, 01407 740080, patriciacoates36@gmail.com. *6m E of Holyhead. ½m E of Caergeiliog. From A55 J4. r'about 2nd exit signed Caergeiliog. 300yds, Gwaelod Mawr is 1st house on L.* **Sat 26, Sun 27 May (11-5). Adm £4, chd free. Home-made teas. Visits also by arrangement May to Aug.**

2 acre garden created by owners over 20 yrs with lake, large rock outcrops and palm tree area.

12 NEW LLANFECHELL ALLOTMENTS

Brynddu Road, Llanfechell, Amlwch, LL68 0PU. Mike Harris, Secretary. *5 miles NW of Amlwch, 1 mile S of Cemaes on Anglesey. From Amlwch on A5025 take L just before Cemaes: from Holyhead on A5025 take R just before Cemaes: from Llangefni, take R at Sportsman's Lodge in Rhosgoch then follow NGS signs.* **Sun 29 July (10.30-5). Adm £3, chd free. Light refreshments in nearby community cafe.**

Established just a few years ago and building on initial success, we now have 18 plots, sheds and greenhouses, and grow a variety of vegetables, soft fruit and flowers. A short walk from car park along road leads to grass paths inside. Walled garden at Brynddu, C17 manor house home of Anglesey diarist

W Bulkeley also open. Visit Llanfechell church and/or take short local walk (maps available).

13 LLANIDAN HALL

Brynsiencyn, LL61 6HJ. Mr J W Beverley (Head Gardener). *5m E of Llanfair Pwll. From Llanfair PG follow A4080 towards Brynsiencyn for 4m. After Hooton's farm shop on R take next L, follow lane to gardens.* **Sat 28 Apr, Sat 30 June, Sat 14 July (10-4). Adm £3.50, chd free. Light refreshments.** Donation to CAFOD.

Walled garden of 1¾ acres. Physic and herb gardens, ornamental vegetable garden, herbaceous borders, water features and many varieties of old roses. Sheep, rabbits and hens to see. Children must be kept under supervision. Well behaved dogs on leads welcome. Llanidan Church will be open for viewing. The walled garden will be open early in the season for viewing of the spring bulbs. Hard gravel paths, gentle slopes.

14 LLYN RHAEADR

15 Parc Bron-y-Graig, Centre of Harlech, LL46 2SR. Mr D R Hewitt & Miss J Sharp. *From A496 take B4573 into Harlech, take turning to main car parks S of town, L past overspill car park, garden 75yds on R.* **Fri 30 Mar (2-5); Sat 31 Mar (2.30-5). Daily Sun 1 Apr to Fri 6 Apr (2-5). Sun 6, Mon 7 May (2-5). Daily Sun 27 May to Thur 31 May (2-5). Fri 1, Sat 2, Sun 3 June (2-5). Daily Sun 26 Aug to Thur 30 Aug (2-5). Sat 1, Sun 2 Sept (2-5). Adm £3.50, chd free.**

Landscaped hillside garden blending natural areas with garden plants, shrubs and trees with wildlife, small lake with many species of unusual ducks, fish and wildlife ponds, waterfalls, woodland, gazebos, rockeries, lawns, borders, snowdrops, daffodils, bluebells, ferns, heathers, camellias, azaleas, Rhododendrons, wild flowers. Good paths and seating views of Tremadog Bay, Lleyn Peninsula. Waterfowl collection.

15 LLYS-Y-GWYNT

Pentir Road, Llandygai, Bangor, LL57 4BG. Jennifer Rickards & John Evans, 01248 353863. *3m S of Bangor. 300yds from Llandygai r'about at J11, A5 & A55, just off A4244. Follow signs for services (Gwasanaethau). No through rd sign, 50yds beyond. Do not use SatNav.* **Sun 20 May, Sun 1 July (11-4). Adm £4, chd free. Cream teas. Visits also by arrangement, yr round interest.**

Interesting, harmonious and very varied 2 acre garden incl magnificent views of Snowdonia. An exposed site incl Bronze Age burial cairn. Winding paths and varied levels planted to create shelter, yr-round interest, microclimates and varied rooms. Ponds, waterfall, bridge and other features use local materials and craftspeople. Wildlife encouraged, well organised compost. Good family garden.

16 MAENAN HALL

Maenan, Llanrwst, LL26 0UL. The Hon Mr & Mrs Christopher Mclaren, 01492 640441, cmmclaren@gmail.com. *2m N of Llanrwst. On E side of A470, ¼m S of Maenan Abbey Hotel.* **Sun 29 Apr, Sun 29 July (10.30-5.30). Adm £4, chd free. Light refreshments. Visits also by arrangement Apr to Sept for groups 8+.** Donation to Wales Air Ambulance.

A superbly beautiful 4 hectares on the slopes of the Conwy Valley, with dramatic views of Snowdonia, set amongst mature hardwoods. Both the upper part, with sweeping lawns, ornamental ponds and retaining walls, and the bluebell carpeted woodland dell contain copious specimen shrubs and trees, many originating at Bodnant. Magnolias, rhododendrons, camellias, pieris, cherries and hydrangeas, amongst many others, make a breathtaking display. Treasure Hunt (£1) on both open days. Upper part of garden accessible but with fairly steep slopes.

17 NEW MYNYDD HEULOG

Llithfaen, Pwllheli, LL53 6PA. Mrs Christine Jackson, 01758 750400, christine.jackson007@btinternet.com. *Llithfaen. From A499 take B4417 road at r'about signed Nefyn, approx 3m enter Llithfaen, 1st R turn opp chapel. Follow NGS signs, garden last property on R, limited parking.* **Sun 27 May, Sun 3 June (11-5). Adm £3.50, chd free. Home-made teas. Visits also by arrangement May & June.**

Mynydd Heulog is an C18 stone cottage set in approx. 1 acre of sloping garden with amazing views over the Lleyn and Cardigan Bay. Gradually being developed over 25 years, the garden is now an eclectic mix of mature trees, shrubs, perennials and exotics. Features incl arches, statues, bridges, summer house and shepherds hut. Large terrace and verandah with views and secret seating areas.

18 ◆ PENSYCHNANT

Sychnant Pass, Conwy, LL32 8BJ. Pensychnant Foundation; Wardens Julian Thompson & Anne Mynott, 01492 592595, jpt.pensychnant@btinternet.com, www.pensychnant.co.uk. *2½m W of Conwy at top of Sychnant Pass. From Conwy: L into Upper Gate St; after 2½m Pensychnant's drive signed on R. From Penmaenmawr: fork R, up pass, after walls U turn L into drive.* **For NGS: Sun 3 June (10-5). Home-made teas. Sun 22 July (10-5). Cream teas. Adm £3.50, chd free. For other opening times and information, please phone, email or visit garden website.**

Wildlife Garden. Diverse herbaceous cottage garden borders surrounded by mature shrubs, banks of rhododendrons, ancient and Victorian woodlands. 12 acre woodland walks with views of Conwy Mountain and Sychnant. Woodland birds. Picnic tables, archaelogical trail on mountain. A peaceful little gem. Large Victorian Arts and Crafts house (open) with art exhibition. Partial wheelchair access, please phone for advice.

19 PLAS CADNANT HIDDEN GARDENS

Cadnant Road, Menai Bridge, LL59 5NH. Mr Anthony Tavernor, 01248 717174, plascadnantgardens@gmail.com, **www.plascadnantgardens.co.uk.** *½m E of Menai Bridge. Take A545 & leave Menai Bridge heading for Beaumaris, then follow brown tourist information signs.* **Wed 25 Apr (12-5). Adm £7, chd £2. Light refreshments in traditional Tea Room.** Donation to Wales Air Ambulance; Anglesey Red Squirrel Trust; Menai Bridge Community Heritage Trust.

Early C19 picturesque garden undergoing restoration since 1996. Valley gardens with waterfalls, large ornamental walled garden, woodland and early pit house. Recently created Alpheus water feature and Ceunant (Ravine) which gives visitors a more interesting walk featuring unusual moisture loving Alpines. Restored area following flood damage. New guidebook available. Visitor centre open. Partial wheelchair access to parts of gardens. Some steps, gravel paths, slopes. Access statement available. Accessible Tea Room and WC.

The National Garden Scheme is the largest single funder of the Queen's Nursing Institute

20 SUNNINGDALE

Bull Bay Road, Bull Bay, Amlwch, LL68 9SD. Mike & Gill Cross, 01407 830753, mikeatbb@aol.com. *1½m NW of Amlwch. On A5025 through Amlwch towards Cemaes. No parking at house but parking will be signed.* **Sun 6, Sat 12 May, Sat 2, Sun 24 June (1-5). Adm £3.50, chd free. Home-made teas. Soup available in May. Visits also by arrangement May & June for groups 8+.**

A seaside garden. Headland has cliffs, steps, wild flowers and seating, spectacular views and sheer drops! Front garden has raised pond and planting to cope with hostile weather. The relatively sheltered rear garden is cottage style with lots of different rooms, no large lawn here! There are different plants, paths, seats, pots and a raised bed vegetable area. Bluebells are spectacular on Headland in May/June. The 50 yr old Scottish laburnum creates a large canopy of yellow to enjoy from below. Wheelchair access to front garden only.

21 NEW SWN-Y-GWYNT

High Street, Llanberis, Caernarfon, LL55 4EN. Mr Keith Chadwick. *Llanberis the mountain village at the foot of Snowdon. Turn off the A4086, follow NGS sign onto Llanberis High St then a green sign for Swn-y-Gwynt with the driveway entrance and private car park.* **Sun 3 June (11-4). Adm £3.50, chd free. Light refreshments.**

A S-facing terraced garden with dramatic views of Snowdon and surrounding hills. Steep slate steps lead to the garden comprising of a variety of conifers, mature acers, azaleas, rose bed and herbaceous perennial border with a variety of spring bulbs complemented by hellebores and ferns. There is also a secluded small pond area leading onto slate steps towards a Scots pine terraced area. Children must be supervised at all times.

22 NEW TREBORTH BOTANIC GARDEN, BANGOR UNIVERSITY

Treborth, Bangor, LL57 2RQ. Natalie Chivers, treborth.bangor.ac.uk. *On the outskirts of Bangor towards Anglesey. Approach Menai Bridge either from Upper Bangor on A5 or leave A55 J9 and travel towards Bangor for 2m. At Antelope Inn r'bout turn L just before entering Menai Bridge.* **Sat 22 Sept (1-4). Adm £3, chd free. Home-made teas. Guided walks.**

Owned by Bangor University and used as a resource for teaching, research, public education and enjoyment. Treborth comprises planted borders, species rich natural grassland, ponds, arboretum, Chinese garden, ancient woodland, and a rocky shoreline habitat. Six glasshouses provide specialised environments for tropical, temperate, orchid and carnivorous plant collections. Wheelchair access to some glasshouses and part of the garden. Woodland path is surfaced but most of the borders only accessed over grass.

23 NEW TREFAES

Y Maes, Criccieth, LL52 0AE. Patricia Stephens. *Criccieth, Gwynedd. On entering Criccieth High St take the Caernarfon rd. The garden is on the R at the top of the hill looking down on the green with a front hedge. Roadside parking by house and public car park.* **Sat 21, Sun 22 July (2-5). Adm £3, chd free. Light refreshments.**

The garden is on three levels, the bottom level has a lawn with borders, an apple tree and a large display of container pots set on slate chippings and flagstones and a rockery. The centre has a pond, a raised vegetable bed and an island bed. The top has a lawn surrounded by herbaceous borders with trees and shrubs. Part of the garden trail in the annual Criccieth Festival.

24 TY CAPEL FFRWD

Llanfachreth, Dolgellau, LL40 2NR. Revs Mary & George Bolt. *4m NE of Dolgellau, 18m SW of Bala. From Dolgellau 4m up hill to Llanfachreth. Turn L at War Memorial. Follow lane ½m to chapel on R. Park & walk down lane past chapel to cottage.* **Sat 19, Sun 20 May (11-5). Adm £3.50, chd free. Cream teas.**
True cottage garden in Welsh mountains. Azaleas, rhododendrons, acers; large collection of aquilegia. Many different hostas give added strength to spring bulbs and corms. Stream flowing through the garden, 10ft waterfall and on through a small woodland bluebell carpet. For summer visitor's there is a continuous show of colour with herbaceous plants, roses, clematis and lilies, incl cardiocrinum giganteum. Harp will be played in the garden.

25 41 VICTORIA DRIVE

Llandudno Junction, LL31 9PF. Allan Evans. *Llandudno Junction. A55 J18. From Bangor 1st exit, from Colwyn Bay 2nd exit, A546 to Conwy. Next r'about 3rd exit then 1st L.* **Sun 15 July (2-4). Adm £3, chd free. Home-made teas.**
A very interesting small urban garden, offering so much in creative ideas incl growing exhibition sweet peas and dahlias and colourful bedding and other shrubs and herbaceous plants. Featured in Amateur Gardening and on S4C Gerddi Cymru.

Llyn Rhaeadr

NORTH EAST WALES

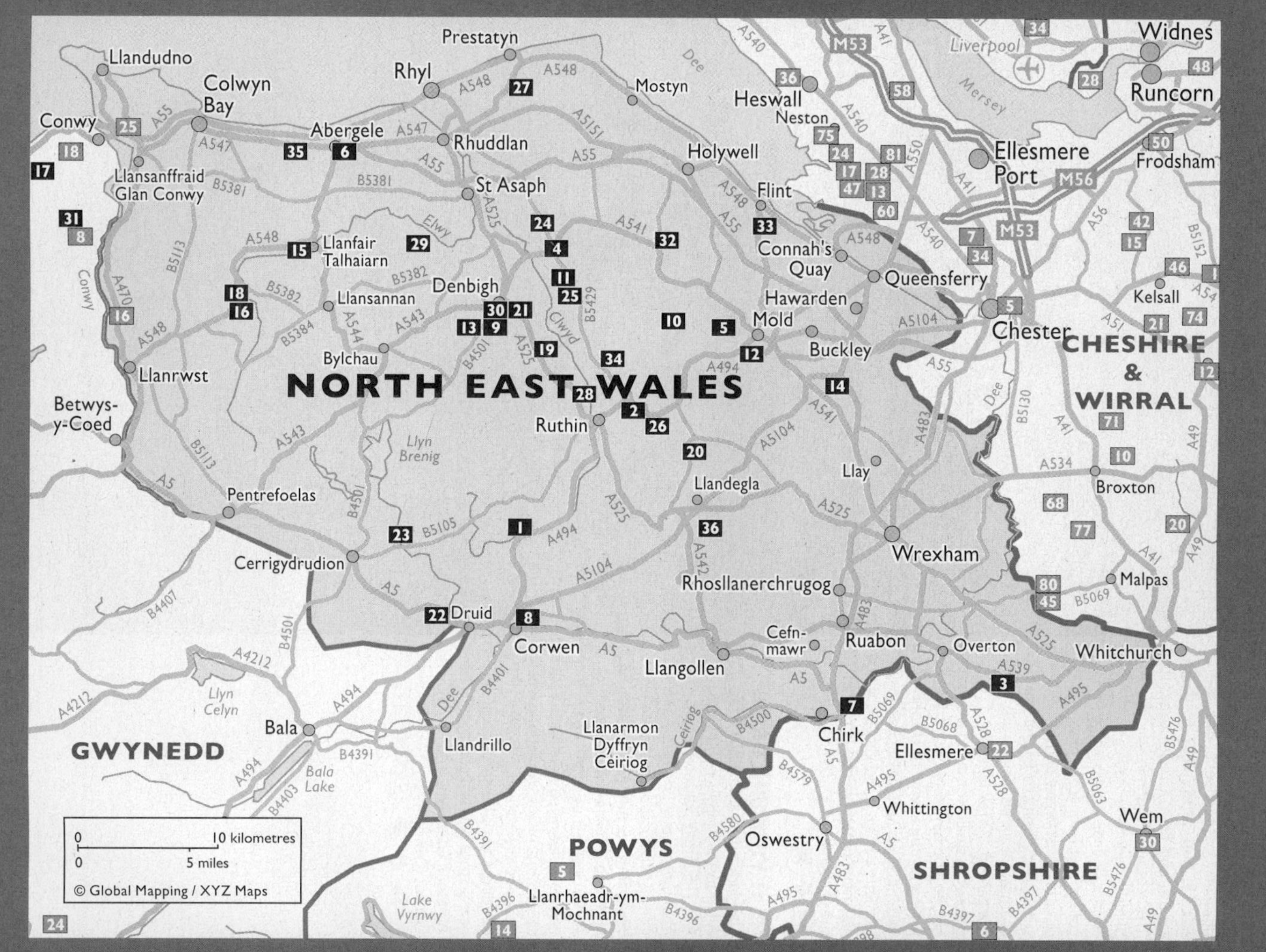

With its diversity of countryside from magnificent hills, seaside vistas and rolling farmland, North East Wales offers a wide range of gardening experiences.

Our gardens offer a wealth of designs and come in all shapes and sizes, ranging from abundant plantsmen's gardens to informal natural hillside planting. Visitors will have something to see from the frost-filled days of February through till the magnificent colourful days of autumn.

The majority of our gardens are within easy reach of North West England, and being a popular tourist destination make an excellent day out for all the family.

Come and enjoy the beauty and the variety of the gardens of North East Wales with the added bonus of a delicious cup of tea and a slice of cake. Our garden owners await your visit.

Volunteers

County Organiser
Jane Moore
07769 046317
jane.moore@ngs.org.uk

County Treasurer
Iris Dobbie
01745 886730
irisd@cactus5.freeserve.co.uk

Publicity
Trish Morris
01745 550121
trishmorris61@yahoo.co.uk

Booklet Co-ordinator
Roy Hambleton
01352 740206
royhambleton@btinternet.com

Assistant County Organisers
Fiona Bell
07813 087797
bell_fab@hotmail.com

Ann Knowlson
01745 832002
apk@slaters.com

Ann Rathbone
01244 532948
rathbone.ann@gmail.com

Carol Perkins
07808 988556
carolperkins24@yahoo.co.uk

Left: **6 Lon Cilan, Cilcain Village Gardens**

OPENING DATES

All entries subject to change. For latest information check **www.ngs.org.uk**

Map locator numbers are shown to the right of each garden name.

February

Snowdrop Festival

Wednesday 14th
Clwydfryn 11

March

Wednesday 14th
Clwydfryn 11

April

Wednesday 4th
Aberclwyd Manor 1

Wednesday 11th
Clwydfryn 11

Wednesday 18th
Aberclwyd Manor 1

May

Wednesday 2nd
Aberclwyd Manor 1

Wednesday 9th
Clwydfryn 11

Wednesday 16th
Aberclwyd Manor 1

Sunday 20th
Maesmor Hall 22

Saturday 26th
Hafodunos Hall 18

Sunday 27th
Caereuni 8
Hafodunos Hall 18

Monday 28th
Caereuni 8
Garthewin 15

Wednesday 30th
Aberclwyd Manor 1

June

Saturday 9th
The Laundry 19

Sunday 10th
NEW Castle Hill Gardens 9
The Laundry 19
Woodlands 33

Wednesday 13th
Aberclwyd Manor 1
Clwydfryn 11

Saturday 16th
NEW Rhewl Village Gardens 28

Sunday 17th
NEW Lower Denbigh Gardens 21

Saturday 23rd
Llanarmon-yn-Ial Village Gardens 20

Sunday 24th
The Beeches 3
Caereuni 8
Tal-y-Bryn Farm 29
Y Bwthyn 35

Wednesday 27th
Aberclwyd Manor 1

Saturday 30th
33 Bryn Twr and Lynton 6
Gwel Yr Ynys 17

July

Sunday 1st
33 Bryn Twr and Lynton 6
Gwel Yr Ynys 17

Thursday 5th
Brynkinalt Hall 7

Saturday 7th
NEW Cilcain Village Gardens 10

Sunday 8th
NEW Bella Vista 4
NEW White Croft 32

Wednesday 11th
Aberclwyd Manor 1
Clwydfryn 11

Sunday 15th
The Cottage Nursing Home 12
NEW Prestatyn Town Gardens 27

Wednesday 25th
Aberclwyd Manor 1

Sunday 29th
Caereuni 8
Plas Ashpool 25

August

Sunday 5th
Dove Cottage 14

Wednesday 8th
Aberclwyd Manor 1

Wednesday 22nd
Aberclwyd Manor 1

Sunday 26th
Caereuni 8

Monday 27th
Caereuni 8

September

Wednesday 5th
Aberclwyd Manor 1

Wednesday 19th
Aberclwyd Manor 1

Sunday 30th
Caereuni 8

February 2019

Thursday 14th
Glog Ddu 16

Sunday 17th
Glog Ddu 16
Hafodunos Hall 18

Thursday 21st
Glog Ddu 16

By Arrangement

Aberclwyd Manor 1
NEW Aynho 2
NEW Bella Vista 4
5 Birch Grove, Prestatyn Town Gardens 27
Bryn Bellan 5
33 Bryn Twr and Lynton 6
NEW 86 Crud y Castell, Lower Denbigh Gardens 21
Crud-y-Gwynt, Llanarmon-yn-Ial Village Gardens 20
Dolhyfryd 13
Dove Cottage 14
Garthewin 15
Gwel Yr Ynys 17
NEW Hillbre, Prestatyn Town Gardens 27
The Laundry 19
The Old Rectory 23
Peacock House, Castle Hill Gardens 9
Pen Y Graig Bach 24
NEW Plas Y Nant 26
NEW Ty Brombil 30
Ty Hwnt Yr Afon 31
Wylan 34
Y Graig 36

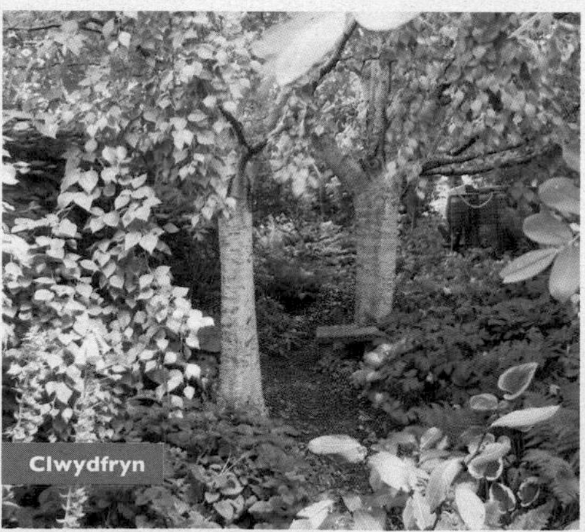
Clwydfryn

THE GARDENS

1 ABERCLWYD MANOR

Derwen, Corwen, LL21 9SF. Miss Irene Brown & Mr G Sparvoli, 01824 750431, irene662010@live.com. *7m from Ruthin. Travelling on A494 from Ruthin to Corwen. At Bryn S.M service station turn R, follow sign to Derwen. Aberclwyd gates on L before Derwen.* **Wed 4, Wed 18 Apr, Wed 2, Wed 16, Wed 30 May, Wed 13, Wed 27 June, Wed 11, Wed 25 July, Wed 8, Wed 22 Aug, Wed 5, Wed 19 Sept (11-4). Adm £3.50, chd free. Cream teas. Visits also by arrangement Feb to Oct for groups 10+, daytime or evenings.**

4 acre garden on a sloping hillside overlooking the Upper Clwyd Valley. The garden has many mature trees underplanted with snowdrops, fritillaries and cyclamen. An Italianate garden of box hedging lies below the house and shrubs, ponds, perennials, roses and an orchard are also to be enjoyed within this cleverly structured area. Mass of cyclamen in Sept. Abundance of Spring flowers. Mostly flat with some steps and slopes.

2 NEW AYNHO

4 Tan Y Bryn, Llanbedr Dyffryn Clwyd, Ruthin, LL15 1AQ. Mrs Rita Anderson, 01824 704121. *Take A494 from Ruthin past Llanbedr church & turn L into Lon Cae Glas. Follow road till R hand turn & bungalow is located third R.* **Visits by arrangement May to July maximum group of 12. Adm £3, chd free. Tea.**

Beautifully maintained village garden with stunning views over the Vale of Clwyd. A mature pink crab apple and fruit trees adorn the front lawned garden. The side garden opens onto mixed beds around a fish pond. There are seating areas, some under pergolas with flowering climbing plants. Many plants have been grown from cuttings or seeds.

3 THE BEECHES

Vicarage Lane, Penley, Wrexham, LL13 0NH. Stuart & Sue Hamon. *Western edge of village. From Overton turn 1st L after 30mph sign. From Whitchurch go along A539 through village & turn R just after church, signed to Adrefelyn. N.B. SatNavs may show Vicarage Lane as Hollybush Lane.* **Sun 24 June (1-5). Adm £3.50, chd free. Home-made teas.**

The garden surrounds an 1841 former vicarage and extends to 3½ acres. It has been redesigned to create an attractive open garden laid mainly to lawn with a mixture of mature and younger specimen trees and shrubs. There are shrub, rose and herbaceous beds together with a productive vegetable and fruit area. The walled courtyard has tender plants incl many varieties of agapanthus and hostas. We are delighted to announce that Bernard Porter, The Head Gardener at Bridgemere Nursery in south Cheshire, will be on hand to answer visitors gardening questions. Bernard has over 30yrs professional gardening experience incl running the 6 acre, award winning, garden at Bridgemere. A mostly flat garden with gravelled paths. Grass is usually firm allowing easy access. Courtyard access has three very shallow steps.

4 NEW BELLA VISTA

Tremeirchion Road, Bodfari, Denbigh, LL16 4EG. Mr & Mrs Alex & Dee Jones, 01745 710495, dee@valeside.co.uk. *3m NE Denbigh. J31 off A55 through Caerwys to Mold/Denbigh rd. Go R 3m to Bodfari. Turn R to Tremeirchion B5429, pass PH, parking 300yds on R.* **Sun 8 July (11-5). Adm £3.50, chd free. Home-made teas. Visits also by arrangement Apr to Sept.**

Situated on a hillside below an area of mixed woodland. A variety of vegetables, some in raised beds; shrubs and herbaceous borders, with areas under development. A wooden Summer House overlooks the patio where refreshments will be served and to enjoy spectacular views across the valley. Parking is available on an area of hard standing at the lower edge of the adjoining paddock.

5 BRYN BELLAN

Bryn Road, Gwernaffield, CH7 5DE. Gabrielle Armstrong & Trevor Ruddle, 01352 741806, gabriele@indigoawnings.co.uk. *2m W of Mold. Leave A541 at Mold on Gwernaffield Rd (Dreflan), ½m after Mold derestriction signs turn R to Rhydymwyn & Llynypandy. After 200yds park in field on R.* **Visits by arrangement May to Sept for groups 8+. Please discuss when making arrangements to visit..**

This tranquil, elegant garden is perfect for relaxing with friends for morning coffee, afternoon tea or evening glass of wine with nibbles. A partly walled upper garden has a circular sunken lawn featuring a Wellingtonia and mixed borders. The lower garden has an ornamental cutting garden, vegetable garden, orchard and bijou potting shed. Many spring bulbs, iris, peonies, hydrangeas and cyclamen. Some gravel paths.

The National Garden Scheme is committed to helping unpaid carers

6 33 BRYN TWR AND LYNTON

Lynton, Highfield Park, Abergele, LL22 7AU. Mr & Mrs Colin Knowlson and Bryn Roberts & Emma Knowlson-Roberts, 07712 623836, apk@slaters.com. *From A55 heading W take slip rd into Abergele town centre. Turn L at 2nd set of T-lights signed Llanfair TH, 3rd rd on L. For SatNav use LL22 8DD.* **Sat 30 June, Sun 1 July (1-5). Adm £4, chd free. Home-made teas, gluten free option available. Visits also by arrangement June & July for any size group. Home-made teas incl gluten free option.**

More changes have been made to the gardens for 2018, mixed herbaceous and shrub borders, some trees plus many unusual plants. Lawn at Lynton replaced with slate chips and more planting. Garage with interesting fire engine; cars and memorabilia; greenhouse over water capture system; surrounding planting coming along nicely, hens now kept at Bryn Twr. Featured in Garden Answers. Partial wheelchair access.

7 BRYNKINALT HALL

Brynkinalt, Chirk, Wrexham, LL14 5NS. Iain & Kate Hill-Trevor, www.brynkinalt.co.uk. *6m N of Oswestry, 10m S of Wrexham. Come off A5/A483 and take B5070 into Chirk village. Turn into Trevor Rd (beside St Mary's Church). Continue past houses on R. Turn R on bend into Estate Gates. N.B. Do not use postcode with SatNav.* **Thur 5 July (2-5). Adm £4, chd free. Home-made teas.**

5 acre ornamental woodland shrubbery, overgrown until recently, now cleared and replanted, rhododendron walk, historic ponds, well, grottos, ha-ha and battlements, new stumpery, ancient redwoods and yews. Also 2 acre garden beside Grade II* house (see website for opening), with modern rose and formal beds, deep herbaceous borders, pond with shrub/mixed beds, pleached limes and hedge patterns. Home of the first Duke of Wellington's grandmother. Article in Shropshire Magazine. Partial wheelchair access. Gravel paths in West Garden and grass paths and slopes in shrubbery.

8 CAEREUNI

Ffordd Ty Cerrig, Godre'r Gaer, Corwen, LL21 9YA. Mr S Williams. *1m N of Corwen. A5 Corwen to Bala rd, turn R at T-lights onto A494 to Chester. 1st R after lay by. House ¼m on L.* **Sun 27, Mon 28 May, Sun 24 June, Sun 29 July, Sun 26, Mon 27 Aug, Sun 30 Sept (2-5). Adm £3.50, chd free.**

A plantsman`s garden of rare trees, shrubs, topiary and containers of tender plants set in a quirky themed much loved ⅓ acre garden. To celebrate the 30th anniversary of this garden a Harry Potter inspired tower is being built, and an extra opening is added at the end of September so the exotic late flowering plants can be fully appreciated. No teas at Caeruni but Glyndwr Plant Centre and Coffee Shop LL12 9BU approx 1m from garden.

GROUP OPENING

9 NEW CASTLE HILL GARDENS

Denbigh, LL16 3NB. *Narrow rds and limited parking in the castle area. Use LL16 3RJ then follow our signs for easiest route up. Or park in town and walk up through Temple Bar Gardens signed from High St by Boots.* **Sun 10 June (1-5). Combined adm £5, chd free. Tea at Bryn Awelon.**

NEW BRON Y GAER
Mr & Mrs Tony & Lorna Scharer.

NEW BRYN AWELON
Dr & Mrs Martin Giles.

NEW 52 CASTLE HILL
Ms Rachel Smith.

NEW 2 LEICESTER TERRACE
Mrs Judith Huxley.

PEACOCK HOUSE
Mr & Mrs Peter Ellis, 01745 814068.

Visits also by arrangement June to Sept no more than 15 in a group refreshment details to be arranged when booking.

Overlooking the stunning Vale of Clwyd the historic market town of Denbigh has more listed buildings than any other town in Wales with a 13C castle at the top of the hill. All these gardens sit within the ancient town walls. Peacock House was much admired when it opened 2 yrs ago and has a listed gazebo, old box hedges, borders and many acers. A steep slope leads to the terrace and then steps to the main garden. Bron y Gaer is a small sunny garden on a steep restricted site created by retired nursery owners. Bryn Awelon used to be a pub centuries ago, its garden area is now going to be the place to enjoy tea and cake. It has old shrubs and roses and some new plantings enhance the area. 52 Castle Hill is the cleverly planted tiny front garden of a crenulated stone house, showing what can be achieved in the smallest of places. 2 Leicester Terrace is a backyard garden full of colourful potted plants, including many climbers to maximise the space and fill the walls with colour.

GROUP OPENING

10 NEW CILCAIN VILLAGE GARDENS

Cilcain, CH7 5PL. *Cilcain is signed from A541.* **Sat 7 July (11.30-5). Combined adm £5, chd free. Home-made teas at Village Hall.**

NEW DELFRYN
Mr & Mrs Phil & Angela Parsons.

NEW 6 LON CILAN
Mrs & Mr Val & Phil Higgins.

NEW NYTH Y WENNOL
Mr & Mrs Keith & Margaret Humphreys.

NEW TY MAWR
Mr & Mrs Peter & Susan Richards.

Cilcain is a very pretty and colourful village and as a community run their own Village Hall, Show and Plant Fair. They now invite you to come along and enjoy 4 of their gardens to raise funds for the NGS and their Village Hall garden conversion.

Some parking at the Village Hall and in the village, and at the bottom of Pentre Hill for Delfryn, or enjoy a circular walk of ⅔m to cover all gardens. Rest and admire the views at Nyth y Wennol with its borders and veg plot, then carry on to the bottom of the hill turn left and see Delfryn a large well planted cottage garden with pond, woodland, large veg plot, roses and seats. Only disabled parking on drive otherwise by grey shed. Then walk left and up hill to Ty Mawr with its flowery meadow and specimen trees and shrubs. A short walk back towards the A541 brings you to Lon Cilan where the immaculate No. 6 can be found on the right hand side. Tickets, maps and good cakes at the Village Hall. Wheelchair access not easy through all the gardens.

♿ 🐕 ✿ ☕

11 CLWYDFRYN

Bodfari, LL16 4HU. Keith & Susan Watson. *5m outside Denbigh. Halfway between Bodfari & Llandyrnog on B5429. Yellow signs at bottom of lane.* **Wed 14 Feb, Wed 14 Mar, Wed 11 Apr, Wed 9 May, Wed 13 June, Wed 11 July (11-4). Adm £4, chd free. Home-made teas.**

¾ acre plantswoman's garden, well worth a visit any time of the year. Collection of snowdrops, epimediums, hellebores and daffodils in spring. Many unusual bulbs, shade loving plants and perennial borders in summer. Alpine house with sand plunge beds new in 2016 to house alpine plants and bulbs. Orchard and colourful cottage garden potager. Garden access to a paved area at back of house for wheelchair users.

♿ ☕

12 THE COTTAGE NURSING HOME

54 Hendy Road, Mold, CH7 1QS. Mr. A.G. Lanini. *12m W of Chester. From Mold town centre take A494 towards Ruthin then follow yellow NGS signs.* **Sun 15 July (2-5). Adm £2, chd £0.50. Light refreshments.** Donation to British Heart Foundation.

Beautiful garden set in approx 1 acre. Well-established shrubs, herbaceous plants and abundance of colourful window boxes and tubs. Recently re-modelled garden we have now added a waterfall feature incl a fish pond and small area to grow vegetables. The central courtyard has two water features. At the bottom of the garden lies a wooden summer house and extended seating.

♿ 🐕 ✿ ☕

13 DOLHYFRYD

Lawnt, Denbigh, LL16 4SU. Captain & Mrs Michael Cunningham, 01745 814805, virginia@dolhyfryd.com. *1m SW of Denbigh. On B4501 to Nantglyn, from Denbigh - 1m from town centre.* **Visits by arrangement Mar to Sept families with children welcome to explore. Adm £5, chd free. Light refreshments.**

Established garden set in small valley of River Ystrad. Acres of crocuses in late Feb/early Mar. Paths through wildflower meadows and woodland of magnificent trees, shade loving plants and azaleas; mixed borders; walled kitchen garden. Many woodland and riverside birds, incl dippers, kingfishers, grey wagtails. Many species of butterfly encouraged by new planting. Much winter interest, exceptional display of crocuses. Gravel paths, some steep slopes.

♿ 🐕 ✿ ☕

14 DOVE COTTAGE

Rhos Road, Penyffordd, Chester, CH4 0JR. Chris & Denise Wallis, 01244 547539, dovecottage@supanet.com. *6m SW of Chester. Leave A55 at J35 take A550 to Wrexham. Drive 2m, turn R onto A5104. From A541 Wrexham/Mold Rd in Pontblyddyn take A5104 to Chester. Garden opp train stn.* **Sun 5 Aug (2-5). Adm £3.50, chd free. Home-made teas. Visits also by arrangement July & Aug for groups 10+ only.**

Approx 1½ acre garden, shrubs and herbaceous plants set informally around lawns. Established vegetable area, 2 ponds (1 wildlife), summerhouse and woodland planted area. Gravel paths.

♿ ✿ 🛏 ☕

Glog Ddu

16 GARTHEWIN

Llanfairtalhaiarn, LL22 8YR. Mr Michael Grime, 01745 720288, michaelgrime12@btinternet.com. *6m S of Abergele & A55. From Abergele take A548 to Llanfair TH & Llanrwst. Entrance to Garthewin 300yds W of Llanfair TH on A548 to Llanrwst. SatNav misleading.* **Mon 28 May (2-6). Adm £4.50, chd free. Home-made teas. Visits also by arrangement Apr to Oct, groups 50 max. Regret, no coaches.**

Valley garden with ponds and woodland areas. Much of the 8 acres have been reclaimed and redesigned providing a younger garden with a great variety of azaleas, rhododendrons and young trees, all within a framework of mature shrubs and trees. Teas in old theatre. Chapel open. Some stalls to promote local arts, crafts and foods.

17 GWEL YR YNYS

Parc Moel Lus, Penmaenmawr, LL34 6DN. Mr Dafydd Lloyd-Borland, 07968 243119, garden@gwelyrynys.com, www.gwelyrynys.com. *Take J16 from A55. At Mountain View PH take v.sharp L onto Conwy Old Rd. In ½m take sharp R into Graiglwyd Rd. Park at Ysgol Pen Cae, bus to garden. Disabled parking available at garden, please ring.* **Sat 30 June, Sun 1 July (11-3.30). Adm £3.50, chd free. Home-made teas. Visits also by arrangement Mar to Sept for groups min 10, max 20.**

A dynamic and exciting ¾ acre hillside garden 650ft above sea level. Imaginative landscaping has been undertaken to complement and blend with the countryside beyond. Natural planting incl a large range of herbaceous plants shrubs and trees. Garden structure benefits from streams, freshwater pond, woodland 'dell' area, bog garden, and many ferns and hostas. Excellent views out to sea. Chickens. Featured on BBC Gardeners World,. Most areas accessible for wheelchair users.

18 HAFODUNOS HALL

Llangernyw, Abergele, Conwy, LL22 8TY. Dr Richard Wood, www.hafodunoshall.co.uk. *1m W of Llangernyw. ½ way between Abergele & Llanrwst on A548. Signed from opp Old Stag PH. On combined snowdrop day park here and take the bus to within 250m of Glog Ddu. Followed by a steep walk down.* **Sat 26, Sun 27 May (11-5). Adm £5, chd free. Light refreshments. Cream teas, coffee and cakes in Victorian conservatory. Lunchtime barbecue weather permitting. 2019: Sun 17 Feb.**

Historic garden undergoing restoration after 30yrs of neglect surrounds a Sir G G Scott Grade I Hall derelict after an arson attack. ½ m treelined drive, formal terraces, woodland walks with ancient redwoods, laurels, yews, lake, streams, waterfalls and a gorge. Unique setting. Carpeted with snowdrops in spring. Some uneven paths and steep steps. Children must be supervised by an adult at all times. Most areas around the hall accessible to wheelchairs by gravel pathways. Some gardens are set on slopes.

19 THE LAUNDRY

Llanrhaeadr, Denbigh, LL16 4NL. Mr & Mrs T Williams, 01745 890515, tomjenny@btinternet.com, thelaundryrocks.wordpress.com. *3m SE of Denbigh. Entrance off A525 Denbigh to Ruthin Rd.* **Sat 9, Sun 10 June (2-6). Adm £5, chd free. Home-made teas. Visits also by arrangement May to Sept, groups strictly 10+.**

Terraced courtyard garden developed since 2009 surrounded by old stone walls enclosing cottage style planting and formal hedging. 5yrs ago work started on the old kitchen walled garden with a view to incorporating it within the whole garden plan. A chance to see a new garden evolving within an old setting. Woodland walk, roses, pleached limes, peonies and herbaceous planting. Some deep gravel areas, may prove difficult for wheelchair users.

GROUP OPENING

20 LLANARMON-YN-IAL VILLAGE GARDENS

Mold, CH7 4PZ. *6m S of Mold. From Mold to Ruthin Rd (A494) turn into B5430. After 2 miles turn R to B5431 into Llanarmon. Or 3m from A525 & A5104, join B5430 and turn L to Llanarmon.* **Sat 23 June (11-4). Combined adm £6, chd free. Home-made teas at The Old Schoolroom.**

ARDWYN
Gill & Pete Hodson.

BRONALLT
Brenda & Tony Rigby.

BRYDAL COTTAGE
Jill Finlow.

CRUD-Y-GWYNT
Elaine & Gareth Jones, 01824780798, Elaineandgareth@btinternet.com.
Visits also by arrangement in June.

7 MAES IAL
Viv & Don Bennion.

12A MAES IAL
Beryl Campbell.

RAVEN INN
Sue Willis.

Entering Llanarmon-yn-Ial from the B5430 drive over the ancient stone bridge, up the hill to The Old Schoolroom - Yr Hen Ysgoldy. Tickets & refreshments available here & limited disabled parking. Some parking in the village or follow signs for main car park 350 yards out of village on Llandegla Road. Maps of gardens incl with ticket. The gardens are all close to the heart of the village and tickets will also be available at some gardens and main car park. The people of Llanarmon-yn-Ial have been successfully running the Raven Inn and Village Shop as community ventures for many years now. Percentage of the proceeds to the Church of St Garmon in the village.

GROUP OPENING

21 NEW LOWER DENBIGH GARDENS

Denbigh, LL16 4PT. *signed from the r'about on Ruthin side of town.* **Sun 17 June (1-5). Combined adm £5, chd free. Home-made teas at Llys Allen.**

NEW 86 CRUD Y CASTELL
Mr & Mrs Mel & Bernie Royles, 01745 816660.
Visits also by arrangement Mar to Sept.

NEW LLYS ALLEN
Mrs Iona Thomas.

NEW TRYFAN
Mrs Alison Devine.

Here are three town gardens of different styles. Llys Allen is an ex farmhouse and its cottage garden, fruit trees, water feature and hidden areas gives it a lovely atmosphere. Next door the garden at Tryfan has been designed by a busy family to keep work to a minimum. It has lawns and borders and the family enjoy growing veg. Both these gardens are on Ruthin Rd near the r'about on the Ruthin side of town. There is some parking in front of these houses. The third garden is a 5-10min walk away (map at Llys Allen) or move your car to Ystrad Rd, park by the cemetery and follow the signs back to 86 Crud y Castell. An excellent plantsman`s garden full of rare and unusual plants and shrubs. It really needs to be seen to believe what can be achieved in a smallish garden with part of it on the steep bank of an old railway bridge. Partial wheelchair access.

22 MAESMOR HALL

Maerdy, Corwen, LL21 0NS. Dr & Mrs G M Jackson, 01490 460411, www.maesmor.com. *5m W of Corwen. Take A5 from Corwen, through 2 sets of T-lights. In Maerdy take 1st L after church & opp The Goat PH.* **Sun 20 May (12-5). Adm £4, chd free. Home-made teas.**

Garden with riverside and estate walks featuring a water and white plant garden. The rhododendrons are extensive and provide a fitting backdrop to the parkland. New and large azalea beds are a mixture of colour. Wooded walks around the hall go towards a new folly amongst the bluebells in the arboretum.
A 100yr old Fig and Vine House has been restored and incl exotic plants, flowers, pomegranates, lemons, oranges, and bananas. Also many patios and front of hall rose displays. A nut arch sits by a soft fruit wall and there is an enormous stone table which has been brought down from the surrounding mountain - it could have been King Arthur's. Gravel paths.

23 THE OLD RECTORY

Llanfihangel Glyn Myfyr, Corwen, LL21 9UN. Mr & Mrs E T Hughes, 01490 420568, elwynthomashughes@hotmail.com. *2½m NE of Cerrigydrudion. From Ruthin take B5105 SW for 12m. From Cerrigydrudion take B5105 for 3m.* **Visits by arrangement please discuss refreshments when booking. Adm £4, chd free.** Donation to Cancer Research U.K.

This one acre garden is in a beautiful setting along the Afon Alwen valley and has mixed borders; water, bog, and gravel gardens; walled garden with old roses, pergola, bower and garden of meditation. In early spring a number of different varieties of snowdrops may be seen together with hellebores, crocus and other spring flowers. Also hardy orchids, gentians, daffodils, rhododendrons and acers. Partial wheelchair access.

24 PEN Y GRAIG BACH

Tremeirchion, St Asaph, LL17 0UR. Roger & Christine Pawling, 07875 642270, christinehoyle@gmail.com. *4m SE of St Asaph. Off A55 take J28/29/30 to Tremeirchion, then B5429 to Bodfari, go 0.7m (wide verge), turn L up hill, L at fork, cont to rd end. From Bodfari take B5429 take 2nd R (after 1¼m).* **Visits by arrangement Apr to Sept tea, coffee or juice with biscuits. Cake and wine on request. Adm £4, chd free. Light refreshments.**

2 acre wildlife friendly rural cottage garden. Succession of colour throughout the year. Box hedges and fruit trees enclose 5 plots of herbaceous perennials, unusual climbers, flowering shrubs, soft fruit and vegetables. Over 200 native and ornamental trees. 4 ponds and 3 paddocks which are managed organically for wild flowers and hay. Beehives. At 560ft with stunning views from sea to mountains. Partial wheelchair access, gravel paths between box hedges and grass paths.

25 PLAS ASHPOOL

Llandyrnog, LL16 4HP. Fiona Bell. *5m outside Denbigh. ½ way between Bodfari & Llandyrnog on B5429.* **Sun 29 July (2-5.30). Adm £3.50, chd free. Home-made teas.**

This country house garden with views of the Clwydian hills and Vale of Clwyd was developed over 40yrs ago by present owner's family and is now undergoing restoration. The herbaceous and shrub borders, orchard, vegetable garden and sunken rose garden are surrounded by historic farm buildings, now being rescued from disrepair. Wild flowers, hens, bees complete this rural picture. Partial wheelchair access.

26 NEW PLAS Y NANT

Llanbedr Dyffryn Clwyd, Ruthin, LL15 1YF. Lesley, Ian, Dan, Sam & Jamie Callister, 01824 705444, lesleycallister@icloud.com. *From A494 turn onto B5429 Graigfechan,approx 1m,4th turning L private rd. If using Satnav follow postcode LL15 2YA. Proceed through farmyard continue and keep L, uphill to cottage on R, go straight onto forest track. Travel 0.8 m on track, drive on R.* **Visits by arrangement Apr to Aug groups welcome daytime or evening. Wine available. Adm £4, chd**

free. Light refreshments can be discussed when booking.
Listed Gothic Villa in a serene upland valley (AONB) amid seven acres of gardens, bluebell woods and stream. Rhododendrons,magnolia and specimen trees abound, formal parterre of clipped box and yew. Embryonic dragons head rose garden and trelliage. Procession of seasonal colour led by snowdrops, primroses and daffodils. Other aspects incl water features, loggia, summer and greenhouses, beehives.

GROUP OPENING

27 NEW PRESTATYN TOWN GARDENS

5 Birch Grove, Woodland Park, Prestatyn, LL19 9RH. Mrs Iris Dobbie. *Off A547 Prestatyn to Rhuddlan rd. Turn up The Avenue, Woodland Park. Take care if coming from Rhuddlan, it's just after the bridge. 1st R into Calthorpe Dr, 1st L Birch Gr. Or 10min walk from town centre - at top of High st, turn R.* **Sun 15 July (1-5). Combined adm £5, chd free. Home-made teas at 3 Oak Hill Drive Prestatyn LL19 9PY.**

5 BIRCH GROVE
Mrs Iris Dobbie, 01745 886730, irisd.cactus5@gmail.com. **Visits also by arrangement May to Sept for groups up to 20.**

NEW HILLBRE
Robert & Margaret Smith, 01745853628, margaret.smith810@btinternet.com. **Visits also by arrangement Apr to Aug.**

NEW 3 OAK HILL DRIVE
Tim and Ann Walkden-Williams.

Prestatyn nestles between sandy beaches and the spectacular slopes of the Clwydian Range. Its history goes back to Roman times and it's the start/finish of Offa's Dyke Path National Trail. The town boasts a shopping park and a wealth of independent traders. This is the first time the Prestatyn Town Gardens has opened for the NGS. 5 Birch Grove is a well-established town garden with a variety of borders incl. woodland, grass, herbaceous, shrub, alpine, drought, tropical and bog planting. Hillbre is surrounded by a cottage garden with a fish pond, soft fruit, top fruit and herbaceous planting. It is steeply terraced with many steps (care required) and beautiful views. 3 Oak Hill Drive is a secluded garden with shrubs and tree borders and colourful herbaceous planters with a small pond. Tickets and maps at 5 Birch Grove. Homemade teas served at 3 Oak Hill Drive. Birch Grove garden received first prize in both front and back garden competitions at the Prestatyn Flower Show for the last two years. Partial wheelchair access.

GROUP OPENING

28 NEW RHEWL VILLAGE GARDENS

Rhewl, Ruthin, LL15 2UD. Mrs Jean Wallis. *On A525 between Ruthin & Denbigh. Park at The Drovers Arms. The Drovers Cottage is next door.* **Sat 16 June (11-4). Combined adm £3.50, chd free. Home-made teas at Drovers Cottage.**

NEW THE DROVERS ARMS
Mrs Michelle Strang.

NEW DROVERS COTTAGE
Mrs Jean Wallis, 01824 703954, jean.droverscottage@gmail.com.

The Drovers Arms is where the Welsh Drovers would stop for ale on the way to London, and the Drovers Cottage is the converted Cattle Barn next door. Both gardeners are members of the Rhewl Gardening Club and have enjoyed creating their gardens over many years. The pub has a rear garden which can be accessed through the pub or through the side gate and can be seen and enjoyed by diners in the rear conservatory. A small garden packed full of enthusiasm, with a quirky touch and overseen by artistic eye. This country cottage style garden has taken it's own path over ten years and with some gentle nurturing has created some interesting spaces around the garden for wild life. The Drovers Cottage has a courtyard front garden with raised bed of shrubs & perennials and wisteria climbing over the house. The rear garden has acers, shrubs, a pond (loved by birds) and quirky entertaining ornaments. Partial wheelchair access.

29 TAL-Y-BRYN FARM

Llannefydd, Denbigh, LL16 5DR. Mr & Mrs Gareth Roberts, 01745 540256, falmai@villagedairy.co.uk, www.villagedairy.co.uk. *3m W of Henllan. From Henllan take rd signed Llannefydd. After 2½m turn R signed Bont Newydd. Garden ½m on L.* **Sun 24 June (2-5.30). Adm £4, chd free. Tea. Adm includes a cup of tea and slice of barabrith.** Donation to Elderly Committee of Llannefydd.
Medium sized working farmhouse cottage garden. Ancient farm machinery. Incorporating ancient privy festooned with honeysuckle, clematis and roses. Terraced arches, sunken garden pool and bog garden, fountains and old water pumps. Herb wheels, shrubs and other interesting features. Lovely views of the Clwydian range. Water feature, new rose tunnel, vegetable tunnel and small garden summer house.

30 NEW TY BROMBIL

Broomhill Lane, Denbigh, LL16 3NH. Mr & Mrs Christopher Sanders, 01745 813852, c-sanders@btconnect.com. *Denbigh Town Centre. Closest council car park LL16 3TS. Walk up alley to High St. Garden Gate is next door to Halifax BS. Entry phone button for House.* **Visits by arrangement May to Sept for groups of 5 -**

20. Adm £4, chd free.
Open the gate to a unique hidden garden below a striking contemporary home. The house and garden are located on a very steep and rocky site. The garden consists of several outdoor 'rooms' at various levels linked by short flights of steps between the buildings. Stone walls, architectural planting, fruit trees, vines and pots make for a rare and very interesting, private urban garden. Steep steps could make access difficult for less mobile visitors.

31 TY HWNT YR AFON
Rowen, Conwy, LL32 8YT. Ian & Margaret Trevette, 01492 650871, ian.trevette@btopenworld.com. *Take B5106 from Conwy, R at Groes Inn. Follow signs. Park on rd below Ty Gwyn Hotel, garden 500yds thru village on L fork in rd. Disabled parking on drive.* **Visits by arrangement May to July for groups up to 25. Adm £3.50, chd free. Light refreshments.**
¾ acre garden re-landscaped by owners over last 7yrs. With the backdrop of River Ro and preserved woodland beyond have used the gardens natural features of glacial stone, stream and springs to create an amphitheatre of garden shrubs and plants incl spring bulbs, acers, azaleas, camellias, rhododendrons and a multitude of other favourite perennials. Wheelchair access to view most of garden and for home-made teas on the sun terrace provided by Friends of ChildLine North Wales. Some steps.

32 NEW WHITE CROFT
19 Ffordd Walwen, Lixwm, Holywell, CH8 8LW. Mr & Mrs John & Mary Jones. *From A541 turn onto the B5121 for Lixwm, From A55 come off at J32 or J32A. Drive South follow Lixwm signs.* **Sun 8 July (1-5). Adm £4, chd free. Home-made teas.**
Wrap around garden incl Cottage style planting, Dahlia bed, Rock garden, Vegetable plot, Fruit trees. Greenhouse, Stream and Fish pond, Pagola, Balcony views over Clwydian Range and Japanese style garden. The garden has been established over the last 6 yrs. It was originally just lawn and conifer trees. A double garage containing a Westfield Kit Car and a sports car. Car park available.

33 WOODLANDS
31 Halkyn Road, Flint, CH6 5QX. Alun & Lorraine Jones. *¾m from Flint town centre. A548 - up Church St through T-lights bear R at the fork - continue R to the top of rd and follow signs from A55 - continue on the A5119 entering Flint take a sharp turning L.* **Sun 10 June (11-5). Adm £3.50, chd free. Light refreshments.** Donation to St Kentigerns St Asaph Hospice.
Medium sized terraced garden informally planted with herbaceous plants and shrubs, leading past old mill race and wooded area to Swinchard river. Partial wheelchair access.

34 WYLAN
Llangynhafal, Ruthin, LL15 1RU. John & Carol Perkins, 07808 988556, carolperkins24@yahoo.co.uk. *3m N of Ruthin. Take A494 from Ruthin to Llanbedr then B5429. After ½m turn R signed Llangynhafal 1½m. Entrance on R by large clump of trees.* **Visits by arrangement May to July no minimum and up to 25 maximum. Adm £3.50, chd free. Light refreshments.**
One acre garden designed by owners for all parts to be easily accessible. Magnificent panoramic views. Mature shrubs, mixed borders and water features. Pergola leading into sunken patio with colourful summer planted containers. Winner of Best Kept Country Garden in Ruthin Flower Show 7 times. Gradual grass slope at end of front garden to access back garden.

35 Y BWTHYN
New Road, Llanddulas, Abergele, LL22 8EL. Mr David Roberts & Mr Mark Cooke. *J23 on A55. Through village pass Valentine Inn (R) then take 1st R (Beaula Av), 2nd L (New Rd). Y Bwthyn, last bungalow on L at top of hill.* **Sun 24 June (1-5). Adm £4, chd free. Home-made teas. share to St Kentigern Hospice.**
A garden with meandering paths that leads the eye to explore the varied themes created within the different 'rooms'. From a cottage garden (busy and lush) to a lawned area of tranquility and space. From a shady grove to a watery nook, all within the back drop of the beautiful Llanddulas mountain. An artist's garden with roses, clematis, hostas and ferns featured as some of the favourites. Featured in the Garden Weekly Magazine.

36 Y GRAIG
Llandegla, Wrexham, LL11 3BG. Janet Strivens & Phillip Tidey, 01978 790657, janet@ygraig.org.uk. *8m SE of Ruthin. From Wrexham take A525 towards Ruthin. After approx 7m enter a 40 mph zone. ½ mile further turn L at a red postbox on L. immed before a car parking area, garden is 1m up narrow winding rd.* **Visits by arrangement Apr to Sept. Adm £4, chd free. Home-made teas.**
½ acre of enchanting informal hillside garden at around 1000 ft beneath a limestone outcrop. which gives protection to the old Welsh longhouse from prevailing winds. Herbaceous beds full of colour, rockeries, many clematis and old roses, small ponds and water lilies. 3 acres of field with recently established woodland incl specimen trees. with wonderful views over the Clwydians. Partial wheelchair access due to gravel areas, some steps and steep slopes especially in woodland walk.

POWYS

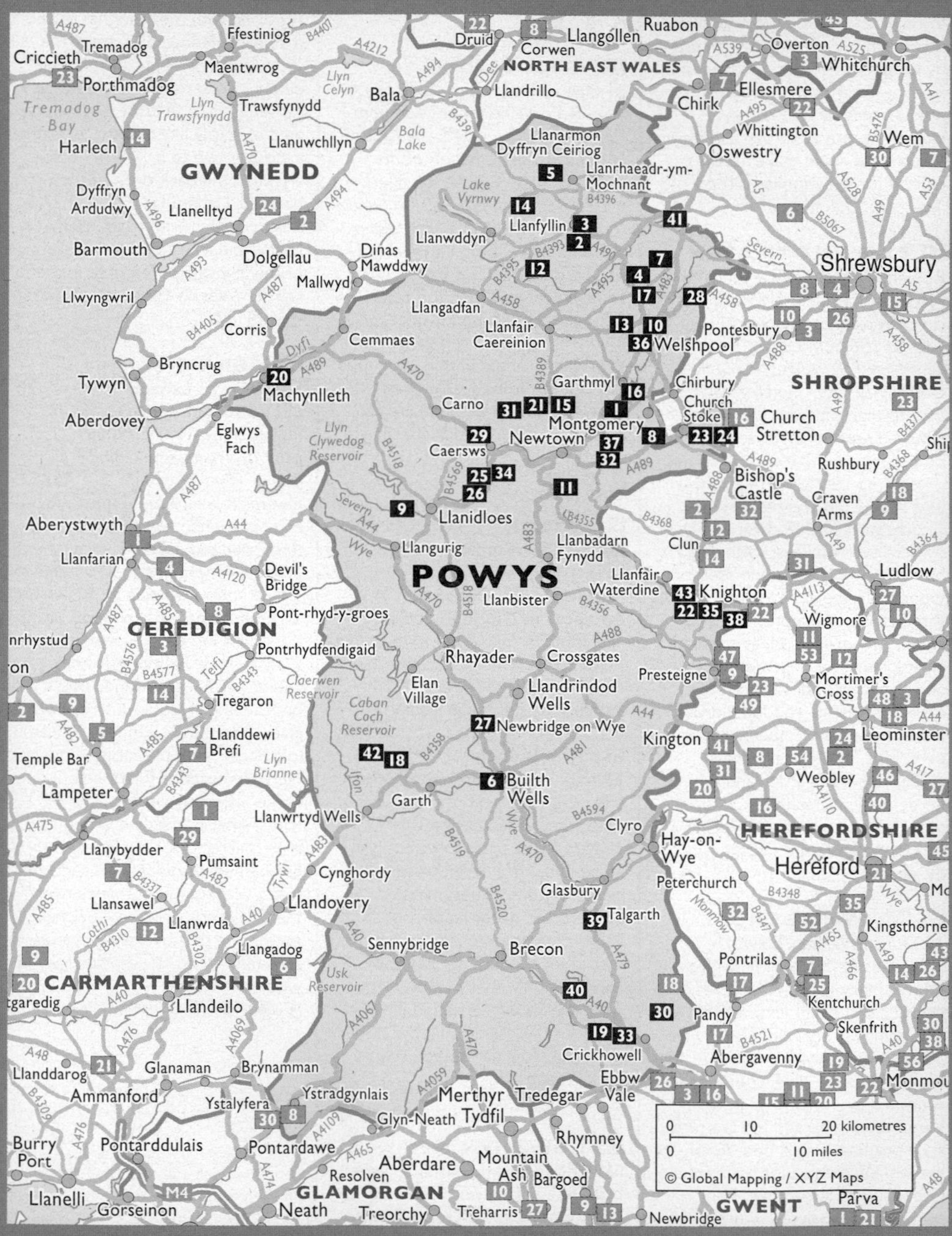
POWYS
GWYNEDD
NORTH EAST WALES
SHROPSHIRE
CEREDIGION
HEREFORDSHIRE
CARMARTHENSHIRE
GLAMORGAN
GWENT
Shrewsbury
Welshpool
Newtown
Montgomery
Llanidloes
Rhayader
Llandrindod Wells
Builth Wells
Brecon
Crickhowell
Hay-on-Wye
Knighton
Presteigne
Machynlleth
Aberystwyth
Hereford
Abergavenny
0 10 20 kilometres
0 10 miles
© Global Mapping / XYZ Maps

A three hour drive through Powys takes you through the spectacular and unspoilt landscape of Mid Wales, from the Berwyn Hills in the north to south of the Brecon Beacons.

Through the valleys and over the hills, beside rippling rivers and wooded ravines, you will see a lot of sheep, pretty market towns, half timbered buildings and houses of stone hewn from the land.

The stunning landscape is home to many of the beautiful NGS gardens of Powys. Some are clustered around the eastern side of the county, where Wales meets the Marches. There are a few in town centres, and the rest, both large and small, are scattered throughout this agricultural paradise.

Powis Castle, whose 18th century Italian terraces set the gold standard for the other gardens, owes much of its wealth to the farming and mining in the area. The Dingle is world-renowned for the dark, still lake at the centre of fantastic planting.

Here in Powys is the spectacular, the unusual, the peaceful and the enchanting, all opened by generous and welcoming garden owners.

Below: **Gilwern**

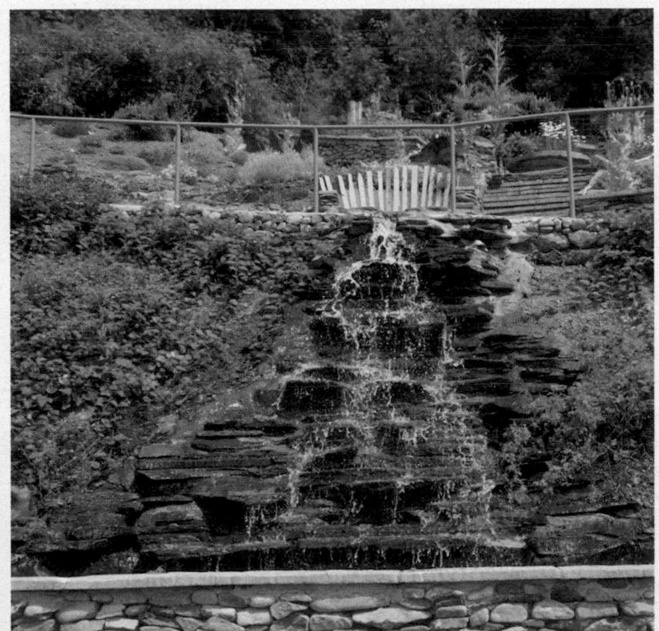

Volunteers

North Powys County Organiser
Susan Paynton
01686 650531
susan.paynton@ngs.org.uk

County Treasurer
Gwyneth Jackson-Jones
01691 648578
gjacksonjones@icloud.com

Publicity
Helen Anthony
01686 941795
powys.ngs.publicity@gmail.com

Social Media
Jude Boutle & Sue Cox
powys.socialmedia@ngs.org.uk

Booklet Co-ordinator
Carole Jones
01650 511176
carole.jones@ngs.org.uk

Assistant County Organisers
Penny Davies
01691 828373
digbydavies@aol.com

South Powys County Organiser
Katharine Smith
01982 551308
katharinejsmith@hotmail.co.uk

County Treasurer
Steve Carrow
01591 620461
stevetynycwm@hotmail.co.uk

Assistant County Organisers
Christine Carrow
01591 620461
stevetynycwm@hotmail.co.uk

OPENING DATES

All entries subject to change. For latest information check www.ngs.org.uk

Map locator numbers are shown to the right of each garden name.

April

Sunday 8th
Maesfron Hall and Gardens 28

Sunday 15th
Cartref 7

May

Saturday 12th
1 Church Bank 10
◆ Dingle Nurseries & Garden 13

Sunday 13th
1 Church Bank 10
◆ Dingle Nurseries & Garden 13

Thursday 17th
NEW Gilwern 18

Saturday 19th
Cyfie Farm 12
Rock Mill 37

Sunday 20th
Cyfie Farm 12
Fraithwen 15
Gliffaes Country House Hotel 19
Penmyarth House 33
Rock Mill 37

Thursday 24th
NEW Gilwern 18

Saturday 26th
NEW Hyssington Gardens 24

Sunday 27th
NEW Hyssington Gardens 24
Llandinam, Little House 25

Monday 28th
NEW Bodfach Hall 3
Llysdinam 27

Wednesday 30th
◆ Grandma's Garden 20

Thursday 31st
NEW Gilwern 18

June

Festival Weekend

Sunday 3rd
The Neuadd 30

Thursday 7th
NEW Gilwern 18

Saturday 9th
Hurdley Hall 23

Sunday 10th
NEW Ger-y-Nant 17
Hurdley Hall 23

Thursday 14th
NEW Gilwern 18

Saturday 16th
NEW Hyssington Gardens 24
1 Ystrad House 43

Sunday 17th
◆ Gregynog Hall & Garden 21
NEW Hyssington Gardens 24
NEW Observatory 31
Tyn y Cwm 42
1 Ystrad House 43

Thursday 21st
NEW Gilwern 18
◆ Powis Castle Garden 36

Saturday 23rd
NEW The Old Court 32
NEW Rose Cottage 38
Tremynfa 41

Sunday 24th
Garthmyl Hall 16
NEW The Old Court 32
NEW Rose Cottage 38
Tremynfa 41

Monday 25th
Garthmyl Hall 16

Wednesday 27th
Foel Ortho 14

Thursday 28th
NEW Gilwern 18

Saturday 30th
1 Church Bank 10
Llandinam, Little House 25
Llandinam, Neuaddllwyd 26
Talgarth Mill 39

July

Sunday 1st
1 Church Bank 10
Cwm-Weeg 11
Llandinam, Little House 25
Llandinam, Neuaddllwyd 26
Talgarth Mill 39

Thursday 5th
NEW Gilwern 18

Saturday 7th
NEW Ceunant 9
Hurdley Hall 23

Sunday 8th
NEW Ceunant 9
Hurdley Hall 23
The Mill 29

Thursday 12th
NEW Gilwern 18

Sunday 15th
Broniarth Hall 4

Saturday 21st
Bachie Uchaf 2

Sunday 22nd
Bachie Uchaf 2
Broniarth Hall 4
Fraithwen 15

Thursday 26th
NEW Gilwern 18

Sunday 29th
Treberfydd House 40

August

Thursday 2nd
NEW Gilwern 18

Sunday 5th
Tyn y Cwm 42

Thursday 9th
NEW Gilwern 18

Saturday 11th
NEW Hebron 22

Sunday 12th
NEW Hebron 22

Thursday 16th
NEW Gilwern 18

Saturday 18th
NEW Ceunant 9

Sunday 19th
NEW Ceunant 9

Thursday 23rd
NEW Gilwern 18

Thursday 30th
NEW Gilwern 18

September

Thursday 6th
NEW Gilwern 18

Thursday 13th
NEW Gilwern 18

Thursday 20th
NEW Gilwern 18

Thursday 27th
NEW Gilwern 18

October

Thursday 4th
NEW Gilwern 18

Thursday 11th
NEW Gilwern 18

Saturday 13th
◆ Dingle Nurseries & Garden 13

Sunday 14th
◆ Dingle Nurseries & Garden 13
◆ Gregynog Hall & Garden 21

By Arrangement

Abernant 1
Broniarth Hall 4
Bryn y Llidiart 5
Caer Beris Manor Hotel 6
Cartref 7
Castell y Gwynt 8
NEW Ceunant 9
1 Church Bank 10
Fraithwen 15
NEW Gilwern 18
Gorsty House, Hyssington Gardens 24
NEW Hebron 22
Hurdley Hall 23
Llysdinam 27
The Neuadd 30
Plas Dinam 34
Pont Faen House 35
Tyn y Cwm 42

Ceunant

THE GARDENS

1 ABERNANT

Garthmyl, SY15 6RZ. Mrs B M Gleave, 01686 640494, john.gleave@mac.com. *1½m S of Garthmyl. On A483 midway between Welshpool & Newtown (both 8m). Approached over steep humpback bridge with wooden statue of a workman to one side, then straight ahead to the house and parking.* **Visits by arrangement Mar to Aug groups 5+ Evening openings in June and July for groups 10+. Adm £4, chd free. Home-made teas.**

Approx 3 acres incl orchard with 90 cherry trees, knot garden, box hedging, roses, rockery, pond, shrubs, ornamental trees, raised specimen fern beds in natural setting. Examples of archaic sundials, fossilized wood and stone heads. Additional woodland of 9 acres, pond and stream with borrowed views of the Severn Valley. Late April: 90 cherry trees in blossom. Late June: roses. Picnics welcome from 12pm.

2 BACHIE UCHAF

Bachie Road, Llanfyllin, SY22 5NF. Glyn & Glenys Lloyd. *S of Llanfyllin. Going towards Welshpool on A490 turn R onto Bachie Rd after Llanfyllin primary school. Keep straight for 0.8m. Take drive R uphill at cottage on L.* **Sat 21, Sun 22 July (1.30-5). Adm £4.50, chd free. Home-made teas.**

Inspiring, colourful hillside country garden. Gravel paths meander around extensive planting and over streams cascading down into ponds. Specimen trees, shrubs and vegetable garden. Enjoy the wonderful views from one of the many seats; your senses will be rewarded.

3 NEW BODFACH HALL

Llanfyllin, SY22 5HS. Simon & Maggie Baynes, www.bodfachtrust.org.uk. *½ mile NW of Llanfyllin. On A490 drive west through Llanfyllin. Just outside town turn R into parkland at lodge, over small bridge, take L fork. Park near white gates to the gardens.* **Mon 28 May (2-5.30). Adm £3.50, chd free. Home-made teas.**

Gardens of 10 acres surrounded by parkland dating back to C18th. Owners are restoring the gardens with recent discovery of a secret well. Stunning display of mature rhododendrons and azaleas from mid-May. Formal, courtyard and cottage gardens complement Georgian and Victorian architecture. Topiary, specimen trees and spring walk. Small lake, iris beds in statue garden and Victorian dog kennels. Music by Montgomeryshire Musicians. Charity stalls and raffle. Art exhibition. Children's play area. Featured in local newspapers and magazines.

4 BRONIARTH HALL

Pentrebeirdd, Guilsfield, Welshpool, SY21 9DW. Mrs Janet Powell, 01938 500639, janet09br@hotmail.co.uk. *From Londis petrol station, Guilsfield, take A490 towards Llanfyllin for approx 2m. Turn R towards Sarnau. After 1m turn R for Broniarth Hall.* **Sun 15, Sun 22 July (2-5.30). Adm £3.50, chd free. Cream teas and home-made cakes. Visits also by arrangement in July groups of 10-20.**

Broniarth Hall is a C17 farm house (not open) with bijou SE facing cottage garden with 2 small ponds, Summerhouse, perennial filled beds and aviary. Unique and quirky features and containers incl a collection of approx 70 heucheras. Stunning views from patio areas with summer bedding and foliage plants.

5 BRYN Y LLIDIART

Cefn Coch, Llanrhaeadr ym Mochnant, Oswestry, SY10 0BP. Dr John & Mrs Christine Scott, 01691 780080, christine.scott@ngs.org.uk. *2m W of Llanrhaeadr ym Mochnant. On rd between Llanrhaeadr village & Penybontfawr. Follow yellow NGS signs R up hill on single track rd for 1m.* **Visits by arrangement May to Sept, individuals/groups max 30 visitors. Adm £5, chd free. Home-made teas. Wine and nibbles as an alternative by prior arrangement.**

Up the airy mountain you are in for a big surprise at 1100ft! Lush planting around the house melts into the spectacular landscape of the Berwyns. Wander mown paths through wildflower meadows, pass huge erratic boulders to discover a 'sitouterie' in the Welsh Orchard, veggie garden, and a wildlife pool. Then follow the tumbling stream to the bog garden, exotic 'Twitter' garden and a green roof. Good footwear required. Childrens' Quiz. Featured in County Times, and on Gardeners World. Partial wheelchair access, shale and rough grass paths, some steps. Small coaches only up to 10 metres.

6 CAER BERIS MANOR HOTEL

Builth Wells, LD2 3NP. Mrs Nika Yusifova, 01982 552601, caerberis@btconnect.com, www.caerberis.com. *W edge Builth Wells. From Builth Wells town centre take A483 signed Llandovery. Caer Beris Manor is on L as you leave Builth.* **Visits by arrangement May to Oct. Home-made teas.**

An original 1927 NGS pioneer garden. 27 acres of mature parklands, with the River Irfon bordering the property. The grounds were planted early C20 by the Vivien family who were plant hunters. Many varied specimen trees form an Arboretum. Large displays of rhododendrons. An Edwardian Rose archway has been recently replanted with David Austin roses. Sunday lunches and afternoon teas available. Lower parkland can be accessed by car or wheelchair.

7 CARTREF

Sarnau, Arddleen, Llanymynech, SY22 6QL. Neil & Stella Townsend, 01938 590485, mail@stellatown.plus.com. *8m N of Welshpool. Take A483 from Welshpool towards Oswestry. Turn L after 6m at Arddleen, bear R then turn R towards Sarnau. Turn R after 1m. Cont for approx ½m. Cartref is on L.* **Sun 15 Apr (1-5). Adm £3.50, chd free. Home-made teas. Visits also by arrangement Mar to May individuals/groups max 30.**

1 acre modern cottage garden in open countryside with an emphasis on attracting wildlife. Spring bulbs make the garden particularly pretty in spring. Woodland, ponds, perennial borders and a kitchen garden give yr-round interest. Meandering paths join areas and give unexpected views within the garden. Tulips in the spring. The garden as a whole is not wheelchair accessible but the patio area directly outside the house is and gives good views of the garden.

8 CASTELL Y GWYNT

Llandyssil, Montgomery, SY15 6HR. John & Jacqui Wynn-Jones, 01686 668569, jacquiwj@btinternet.com. *2m out of Montgomery on the Sarn Rd, 1st R, 1st R.* **Visits by arrangement May to July single visitors/small groups 30 max. Prior booking necessary as parking limited. Adm £5, chd free. Home-made teas.**

1½ acre garden at 900ft, set within 6 acres of land managed for wildlife. Native woodland corridors with mown rides surround hayfield/ wildflower meadow and pool with turf roofed summerhouse. Enclosed kitchen garden with boxed beds of vegetables, fruit and cutting flowers, greenhouse and orchard. Shrubberies, deep mixed borders and more formal areas close to house. Outstanding views of Welsh mountains. Circular path around the whole property which gives unique views of the house, garden and surrounding countryside. Bring good footwear and enjoy the walk.

9 NEW CEUNANT

Old Hall, Llanidloes, SY18 6PW. Sharon McCready, 01686 412345, sharon.mccready@yahoo.co.uk, www.gardenthesevernway.com. *2m W of Llanidloes. Leave Llanidloes over Shortbridge St, turn L along Pen y Green Rd, approx ½m turn L signposted Llangurig, Glyn Brochan. Follow signs property is on R.* **Sat 7, Sun 8 July, Sat 18, Sun 19 Aug (1-5). Adm £4, chd free. Home-made teas. Visits also by arrangement May to Sept individuals/groups max 30 Home made pizzas available from our own clay oven for group bookings.**

4 acre riverside garden started in 2013 in a beautiful setting on River Severn just 7m from the source. Wooded wildlife area and wildlife pond, orchard, ornamental garden, herbaceous borders, scented seating areas. Riverside path, meadow and veg plot. A developing garden full of unusual features, new areas being added all of the time. Planting is aimed at pollinators and to encourage wildlife. Sleeping mud maid, clay oven and brook home to Indian Runner ducks. Accommodation available in shepherd's hut.

10 1 CHURCH BANK

Welshpool, SY21 7DR. Mel & Heather Parkes, 01938 559112, melandheather@live.co.uk. *Centre of Welshpool. Church Bank leads onto Salop Rd from Church St. Follow one way system, use main car park then short walk. Follow yellow NGS signs.* **Sat 12, Sun 13 May, Sat 30 June, Sun 1 July (12-5). Adm £3.50, chd free. Home-made teas. Visits also by arrangement May to Sept for groups min 6, max 20.**

A jewel in the town. Explore the ground floor of this C17 barrel maker's cottage and walk into a large garden room which also houses a museum of tools from different trades. Mystic pool of smoke and sounds. Outside a Gothic arch and zig zag path lead to a shell grotto and bonsai garden, fernery and many unusual features. Sounds of water fill the air and interesting plants fill the intimate space. Children's garden quiz. Museum of country life.

11 CWM-WEEG

Dolfor, Newtown, SY16 4AT. Dr W Schaefer & Mr K D George, 01686 628992, wolfgang@cwmweeg.co.uk, www.cwmweeg.co.uk. *4½m SE of Newtown. Take A489 E from Newtown for 1½m, turn R towards Dolfor. After 2m turn L down asphalted farm track, signed at entrance. Do not rely on SatNav. Also signed from Dolfor village.* **Sun 1 July (2-5). Adm £5, chd free. Home-made teas.**

2½ acre garden set within 24 acres of wildflower meadows and bluebell woodland with stream centred around C15 farmhouse (open by prior arrangement). Formal garden in English landscape tradition with vistas, grottos, sculptures, stumpery, lawns and extensive borders terraced with stone walls. Translates older garden vocabulary into an innovative C21 concept. Under cover area for refreshments if wet. Partial wheelchair access. For non NGS openings please see garden website.

12 CYFIE FARM

Llanfihangel, Llanfyllin, SY22 5JE. Matthew and Teresa Palmer, 01691 648451, enquiries@cyfiefarm.co.uk, www.cyfiefarm.co.uk. *6m SE of Lake Vyrnwy. ½m N Llanfyllin on A490 turn L B4393 towards L Vrynwy. 4m turn L B4382 signed Llanfihangel go straight through, 1½m, 1st L, 3rd on L.* **Sat 19, Sun 20 May (10.30-4). Adm £4, chd free. Home-made teas.**

Enjoy the spectacular views across Vyrnwy valley and the Welsh hills from our beautiful 1 acre hillside garden. Wander around our lower garden and then through the secret doorway to our woodland garden with many rhododendrons, camellias and azaleas along our bluebell banks. Since arriving in 2017 we have been introducing more areas of interest with new planting and seating. Spectacular views, peaceful setting. Partial wheelchair access to the front of the farmhouse with views over the lower garden.

13 ◆ DINGLE NURSERIES & GARDEN

Welshpool, SY21 9JD. Mr & Mrs D Hamer, 01938 555145, www.dinglenurseries.co.uk. *2m NW of Welshpool. Take A490 towards Llanfyllin & Guilsfield. After 1m turn L at sign for Dingle Nurseries & Garden.* **For NGS: Sat 12, Sun 13 May, Sat 13, Sun 14 Oct (9-5). Adm £3.50, chd free. Tea and coffee available. For other opening times and information, please phone or visit garden website.**

RHS recommended 4½ acre garden on S-facing site, sloping down to lakes surrounded by yr-round interest. Beds mostly colour themed with a huge variety of rare and unusual trees, ornamental shrubs and herbaceous plants. Set in hills of mid Wales this beautiful and well known garden attracts visitors from Britain and abroad. Open all yr except 24 Dec - 2 Jan.

14 FOEL ORTHO

Penybontfawr, SY10 0HU. Eddie Matthews & Jenny Miller, 01691 870626, www.farmhouseinwales.com. *16m W of Oswestry. 2m SW of Penybontfawr. From Penybontfawr take rd towards Lake Vyrnwy. After ¼m bear L up steep hill then along side of valley for 1m. Sign 'Foel Ortho' and 'Bunkhouse' and yellow sign on LHS. Turn sharp L down track.* **Wed 27 June (11.30-7). Adm £3.50, chd free. Home-made teas.**

Exciting, eccentric, steeply terraced hillside garden. Paths through lovely planting wind upwards past water, through turrets, boules arena to 'pueblo' and amphitheatre, with outsize chess court all set in remote idyllic landscape. Live, easy-listening jazz played by Eddie & Jenny. Due to steep steps children must be supervised by an adult at all times.

15 FRAITHWEN

Tregynon, SY16 3EW. Sydney Thomas, 01686 650307. *6m N of Newtown. On B4389 midway between villages of Bettws Cedewain & Tregynon.* **Sun 20 May, Sun 22 July (2-5). Adm £3.50, chd free. Home-made teas. Visits also by arrangement Feb to Oct individuals/groups max 30.**

1½ acre plantswoman's garden with herbaceous borders, rockeries and ponds. Planted with rare plants for yr-round interest and for pollinators. Plants in flower every day of the year: spring bulbs, alpines, alstroemeria collection, lilies, vegetable plot and pool. Collector of unusual snowdrops. Snowdrops and hellebores in flower February and carpets of cyclamen in September. Partial wheelchair access. Some steps, gravel and slopes.

16 GARTHMYL HALL

Garthmyl, Montgomery, SY15 6RS. Julia Pugh, www.garthmylhall.co.uk. *On A483 midway between Welshpool & Newtown (both 8m). Turn R 200yds S of Nag's Head Pub.* **Sun 24, Mon 25 June (1-4.30). Adm £3.50, chd free. Home-made teas served in summerhouse.**

Grade II listed Georgian manor house (not open) surrounded by 5 acres of grounds currently under restoration. Over 100 metres herbaceous borders, newly restored 1 acre walled garden with gazebo, circular flowerbeds, lavender beds, two fire pits and gravel paths. Fountain, 3 magnificent Cedar of Lebanon and giant redwood. Partial wheelchair access. Accessible WC.

17 NEW GER-Y-NANT

Glyndwr Crescent, Guilsfield, Welshpool, SY21 9QA. Jennie Lock & Hugh Williams. *2m north of Welshpool on A490 turn r signposted Guilsfield. Follow NGS signs into centre of village. Garden on L opp Costcutter shop.* **Sun 10 June (2-5). Adm £3, chd free. Home-made teas.**

Small garden developed over past 6 yrs. Herbaceous borders, climbing roses and shrubs, kitchen garden raised veg beds, apple trees, greenhouse and polytunnel with peach tree, grape vine and strawberries. Tiny wildlife pond with waterlilies, bird boxes and 'bug house'. Gravel paths and some steps. On-road parking please respect neighbours' access.

18 NEW GILWERN

Beulah, LD5 4YG. Mrs Penelope Bourdillon, 01591 620203, pbourdillon@gmail.com, www.gilwerngarden.co.uk. *2m N of Beulah. Turn L exactly ¾m from Beulah on B4358. Follow rd for over 1m. Past Cefnhafdref Farm. L at T junction. In 600 yds fork L through stone gateposts.* **Open every Thurs from 17th May to 11th Oct (except 19th July). (10-5). Adm £4, chd free. Home-made teas. Visits also by arrangement May to Oct.**

Terraced garden in the making, on very challenging site situated on steep rocky hillside in the beautiful and secluded Cammarch Valley. Roses, herbaceous and shrub borders. Fine walling and gate posts making use of stone found in the garden. Man-made waterfall. The situation, on a rocky slope, is fairly dramatic and makes it interesting. Also perhaps the fact that work is still in progress. The waterfall is quite a feature. The roses are late: mid July to mid August. Hopefully the peonies will be worth seeing. Much of the garden can be seen from a wheelchair. Good access for tea and toilet.

19 GLIFFAES COUNTRY HOUSE HOTEL

Gliffaes Rd, Crickhowell, NP8 1RH. Mrs N Brabner & Mr & Mrs J C Suter, 01874 730371, calls@gliffaeshotel.com, www.gliffaes.com. *3½m W of Crickhowell. 1m off A40, 2½ m W of Crickhowell.* **Sun 20 May (2-5). Adm £5, chd free. Cream teas.**

The Gliffaes gardens lie in a dream position on a plateau 120ft above the spectacular fast flowing River Usk. As well as breathtaking views of the Brecon Beacons and 33 acres of parkland and lawns, there are ancient and ornamental trees, fine maples, new tree plantings, spring bulbs, rhododendrons, azaleas, many shrubs and an ornamental pond. Gliffaes is a country house hotel and is open for lunch, bar snacks, afternoon tea and dinner to non residents and garden visitors. Wheelchair ramp to the west side of the hotel. In dry weather main lawns accessible, but more difficult if wet.

20 ◆ GRANDMA'S GARDEN

Dolguog Estates, Felingerrig, Machynlleth, SY20 8UJ. Richard Rhodes, 01654 702244, info@plasdolguog.co.uk, www.plasdolguog.co.uk/grandmasgarden. *1½m E of Machynlleth. Turn L off A489 Machynlleth to Newtown rd. Follow brown tourist signs to Plas Dolguog Hotel.* **For NGS: Wed 30 May (10.30-4.30). Adm £4, chd £1.50. Light refreshments. For other opening times and information, please phone, email or visit garden website.**

Inspiration for the senses, unique, fascinating, educational and fun. Strategic seating, continuous new attractions, wildlife abundant, 9 acres of peace. Sculptures, poetry arboretum. Seven sensory gardens, wildlife pond, riverside boardwalk, stone circle, labyrinth. Azaleas and bluebells in May. Children welcome. Plas Dolguog Hotel open their café in the conservatory - the hotel is the admission point - serving inside and out on patio overlooking gardens.

21 ◆ GREGYNOG HALL & GARDEN

Tregynon, Newtown, SY16 3PW. Gregynog, 01686 650224, enquiries@gregynog.org, www.gregynog.org. *5m N of Newtown. From main A483, take turning for Berriew. In Berriew follow sign for Bettws then for Tregynon (£2.50 car parking charge applies).* **For NGS: Sun 17 June, Sun 14 Oct (11-4). Adm £3, chd £1. Home-made teas at Courtyard Cafe. For other opening times and information, please phone, email or visit garden website.**

Grade I listed garden set within 750 acres of Gregynog Estate which was designated a National Nature Reserve in 2013. Fountains, lily lake and water garden. A mass display of rhododendrons and yew hedge create a spectacular backdrop to the sunken lawns. Azaleas and unusual trees. Fantastic autumn colour. Courtyard cafe serving morning coffee, light lunches and Welsh afternoon teas. Some gravel paths.

22 NEW HEBRON

Ludlow Road, Knighton, LD7 1HP. Kevin Collins & Anita Lewis, 01547 529576, kd.collins@hotmail.co.uk. *From Knighton, take A4113 towards Ludlow, house on R opposite playing fields where parking is available.* **Sat 11, Sun 12 Aug (12-6). Adm £3.50, chd free. Home-made teas. Visits also by arrangement May to Sept individuals/groups max 20.**

½ acre Victorian town garden. Surprises await the visitor: garden is divided into distinct rooms by yew & beech hedges. Variety of trees incl large silver birches, magnolia, weeping willow and cherry. Many shrubs provide colour throughout the season. Heathers, herbs, vegetables and flower beds. Plenty of seating. Beehives and garden art add an interest. Slate/stone letter cutter/carver will be present. Music.

23 HURDLEY HALL

Hurdley, Churchstoke, SY15 6DY. Simon Cain & Simon Quin, simon.cain@westbourneconsulting.com. *2m from Churchstoke. Take turning for Hurdley off A489, 1m E of Churchstoke. Garden is approx 1 m from here.* **Sat 9 June (1-5); Sun 10 June (11-5); Sat 7 July (1-5); Sun 8 July (11-5). Adm £4.50, chd free. Home-made teas.**
Visits also by arrangement June to Aug for groups 10+.
2 acre garden set around C17 house with additional 18 acres adjoining Roundton Hill National Nature Reserve. Herbaceous and mixed borders, orchard, ponds, topiary and kitchen garden. Mown paths lead to a 5 acre Coronation Meadow, large newly planted orchard, pastures and new and ancient woodland with brook. Uneven ground and steep slopes give wide ranging views but may restrict access. Live music by Bishops Castle Swing Band on Sun 8 July from 2pm.

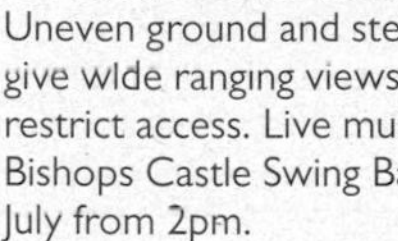

GROUP OPENING

24 NEW HYSSINGTON GARDENS

Hyssington, Montgomery, SY15 6AT. *A488 from Bishop's Castle. Approx 3½m, turn L (signed Hyssington), then follow yellow NGS signs. Also signed A489 E from Churchstoke. Park at Village Hall for Gorsty House and Old Barn, parking for Llanerch Lodge next to house.* **Sat 26, Sun 27 May, Sat 16, Sun 17 June (1-5.30). Combined adm £5, chd free. Home-made teas.**

GORSTY HOUSE
Gary & Annie Frost, 01588 620953, frostiesuk@msn.com.
Visits also by arrangement Apr to Sept. Please ring to discuss visits. Groups 10+.

NEW LLANERCH LODGE
Martin Bonathan & Sara Metcalf.

THE OLD BARN
Avril & Stuart Dickinson.

Three very different gardens in and around Hyssington. Gorsty House is an ongoing renovation of a neglected garden with 2+ acres planted to attract wildlife, incl an acre of wildflower meadow, abundant cottage garden planting, new orchard, and pond. Beautiful views to Long Mynd. The Old Barn is a peaceful ½ acre hideaway with colourful mixed borders, evergreens and mature trees, incl a handkerchief tree. There is a wildlife pond, vegetable and soft fruit areas, against a woodland backdrop. Llanerch Lodge is a smallholding in the lee of Roundton Hill, which offers a productive vegetable plot with raised beds, a lovely cottage garden, wildflower meadow, pond, cutting garden and newly planted nuttery and fruit trees, as well as sheep and poultry. Something to interest everyone.

25 LLANDINAM, LITTLE HOUSE

Llandinam, SY17 5BH. Peter & Pat Ashcroft, www.littlehouse1692.uk/. *1m from Llandinam Lion Hotel. Cross river at statue of David Davies on A470 in Llandinam. Follow rd for just under 1m, Little House is black & white cottage on roadside. Limited parking.* **Sun 27 May (1-5). Adm £3.50, chd free. Sat 30 June, Sun 1 July (1-5). Combined adm with Llandinam, Neuaddllwyd £5, chd free.**
Little House is on a quiet lane surrounded by fields and woodland, bordered by a stream. Slate and bark paths give access to the many features in the ⅓ acre garden incl fish and wildlife ponds, woodland, conifer, azalea, grass and mixed beds, vegetable garden, mini meadow, sensory garden, grotto water feature and alpine/cactus house. Every step, something different to see. Refreshments at Neuaddllwyd June and July only.

Bodfach Hall

26 LLANDINAM, NEUADDLLWYD

Llandinam, SY17 5AU. Roger & Pat Scull. *Take A470 to Llandinam, turn off main rd over bridge by statue. Take 1st lane on L, follow track for ¾m. Garden on L. Do not use SatNav.* **Sat 30 June, Sun 1 July (1-5). Combined adm with Llandinam, Little House £5, chd free. Home-made teas.**

1 acre garden set within 4 acres of wildlife meadows around C19 Grade II listed farmhouse (not open). Shrub and herbaceous borders, lawn with magnificent Monkey Puzzle tree leading down to R Severn with glorious views to hills beyond. Cottage garden area with roses, old orchard, pond, water feature, wooded area and a small allotment used by Llandinam Village. Species Habitat Group will be in attendance to explain their work. Partial wheelchair access.

Funds from National Garden Scheme gardens help Macmillan support thousands of people every year

27 LLYSDINAM

Newbridge-on-Wye, LD1 6NB. Sir John & Lady Venables-Llewelyn & Llysdinam Charitable Trust, 01597 860190, llethr@outlook.com, llysdinamgardens.co.uk. *5m SW of Llandrindod Wells. Turn W off A470 at Newbridge-on-Wye; turn R immed after crossing R Wye; entrance up hill.* **Mon 28 May (2-5). Adm £4, chd free. Home-made teas.**
Visits also by arrangement conducted tours/refreshments for groups 15+.

Llysdinam Gardens are among the loveliest in mid Wales, especially noted for a magnificent display of rhododendrons and azaleas in May. Covering some 6 acres in all, they command sweeping views down the Wye Valley. Successive family members have developed the gardens over the last 150yrs to incl woodland with specimen trees, large herbaceous and shrub borders and a water garden, all of which provide varied and colourful planting throughout the yr. The Victorian walled kitchen garden and extensive greenhouses grow a wide variety of vegetables, hothouse fruit, and exotic plants. Gravel paths.

28 MAESFRON HALL AND GARDENS

Trewern, Welshpool, SY21 8EA. Dr & Mrs TD Owen, www.maesfron.co.uk. *4m E of Welshpool. On N side of A458 Welshpool to Shrewsbury Rd.* **Sun 8 Apr (2-5). Adm £5, chd free. Cream teas and speciality sandwiches.**

Georgian house (partly open) built in Italian villa style set in 4 acres of South-facing gardens on lower slopes of Moel-y-Golfa with panoramic views of The Long Mountain. Terraces, walled kitchen garden, tropical garden, restored Victorian conservatories, tower, shell grotto and hanging gardens below tower. Hundreds of daffodils in spring. Explore the ground floor and outbuildings. Parkland walks with a wide variety of trees. Adjacent 3 acre Equestrian Centre. Teas served in the dining room or on the terrace. Some gravel, steps and slopes.

29 THE MILL

Pontdolgoch, Caersws, SY17 5JE. Les & Kris George. *A470 2m from Caersws towards Carno.* **Sun 8 July (11-5). Adm £4, chd free. Home-made cakes and scones.**

S-facing ½ acre garden with beautiful herbaceous borders, roses, shrubs and trees creating a haven of peace and tranquillity. Sit and relax by Cornus controversa 'Variegata' (wedding cake tree) surrounded by roses with the sound of the river nearby. Raised beds, fruit trees and vegetable garden. Stunning mill pond with walk onto balcony over the old mill wheel. Pontdolgoch Water Mill was the last working watermill in Montgomeryshire. Inside view some of the workings and history of the Mill. Mostly wheelchair accessible apart from shady garden which has steps.

30 THE NEUADD

Llanbedr, Crickhowell, NP8 1SP. Robin & Philippa Herbert, 01873 812164, philippahherbert@gmail.com. *1m NE of Crickhowell. Leave Crickhowell by Llanbedr Rd. At junction with Great Oak Rd bear L, cont up hill for approx 1m, garden on L. Ample parking.* **Sun 3 June (2-6). Adm £5, chd free. Home-made teas.**
Visits also by arrangement May to Sept, adequate parking spaces for cars/mini buses.

Robin and Philippa Herbert have worked on the restoration of the garden at The Neuadd since 1999 and have planted many unusual trees and shrubs in the dramatic setting of the Brecon Beacons National Park. One of the major features is the walled garden, which has both traditional and decorative planting of fruit, vegetables and flowers. There is also a woodland walk with ponds and streams and a formal garden with flowering terraces. Water and spectacular views. Featured in Daily Telegraph, 3 June 2017 and local papers. The owner uses a wheelchair and most of the garden is accessible, but some steep paths.

31 NEW OBSERVATORY

Bwlch-y-Ffridd, Newtown, SY16 3JB. Mr & Mrs Jim and Anne Wren. *Approximately 2m NW of Bwlch-y-ffridd nr Newtown. From Newtown through Aberhafesp, from Caersws leave village with Red Lion on L, from Tregynon/Adfa head towards Bwlch-y-Ffridd and follow yellow arrows.* **Sun 17 June (2-5). Adm £3.50, chd free. Home-made teas. Gluten free alternative.**
Located in the hills at 1100 feet but very sheltered on all sides. Observatory offers superb views of the Severn Valley and beyond. Developed with the aim of encouraging wildlife, our garden is home to a large number of birds, bees, butterflies and other pollinating insects. Wildlife pond, meadow, pretty cottage garden with colourful borders of perennials, shrubs and roses. Fruit garden, polytunnel, beehives and pet hens. The house is accessed via a track. The areas around the house are level with gravel paths and parts of the garden are on a slope.

32 NEW THE OLD COURT

Kerry, Newtown, SY16 4LU. Paul & Debbie Gurden. *4½m East of Newtown. Situated off the B4386 Kerry to Abermule rd nr Hodley.* **Sat 23, Sun 24 June (2-5). Adm £4, chd free. Home-made teas.**
Acre garden plus fields & orchard. Originally part of 22 acre smallholding, The Old Court 1575, and its gardens have been restored after many years of neglect. Victorian style walled vegetable garden, rose and herbaceous borders, pond, ancient yew & mature trees create a relaxing environment. The orchard, replanted in 2010 homes our beehives. Alpacas & chickens complete the scene! Wheelchair access to most grassed areas (some slopes).

33 PENMYARTH HOUSE

The Glanusk Estate, Crickhowell, NP8 1LP. Mrs Harry Legge-Bourke, 01873 810414, info@glanuskestate.com, www.glanuskestate.com. *2m NW of Crickhowell. Please access open garden via main estate entrance off A40 & follow signs to car park.* **Sun 20 May (11-4). Adm £6.50, chd free. Light refreshments.**
The garden is adorned with many established plant species such as rhododendrons, azaleas, acers, camelia, magnolia, prunus and dogwood giving a vast array of colour in the spring and summer months. Alongside the Open Garden, we will be holding the annual Estate Fayre, showcasing over 30 artisans with exhibits of works for sale. Penmyarth Church, a short distance from the gardens, will be open. Updates about the Glanusk Estate Fayre and NGS Open Gardens can be found at www.glanuskestate.com, the Glanusk Facebook page and the Glanusk Twitter and Instagram feeds. Home-made cakes, coffee, tea and gourmet catering, licensed bar. 30 artisan stalls. Talks and garden tours.

34 PLAS DINAM

Llandinam, SY17 5DQ. Eldrydd Lamp, 07415 503554, eldrydd@plasdinam.co.uk, www.plasdinamcountryhouse.co.uk. *7½m SW Newtown. on A470.* **Visits by arrangement Mar to Nov for groups 10+ (weekdays only, excl school holidays). Home-made teas.**
12 acres of parkland, gardens, lawns and woodland set at the foot of glorious rolling hills with spectacular views across the Severn Valley. A host of daffodils followed by one of the best wildflower meadows in Montgomeryshire with 36 species of flowers and grasses incl hundreds of wild orchids; Glorious autumn colour with parrotias, liriodendrons, cotinus etc. Millennium wood. From 1884 until recently the home of Lord Davies and his family (house not open).

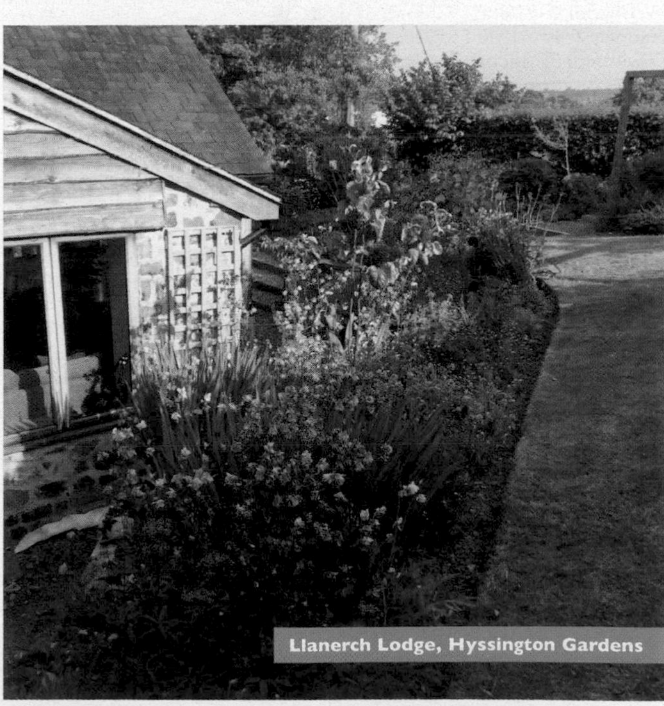

Llanerch Lodge, Hyssington Gardens

35 PONT FAEN HOUSE

Farrington Lane, Knighton, LD7 1LA. Mr John & Mrs Brenda Morgan, 01547 520847. *S of Knighton off Ludlow Rd. W from Ludlow on A4113 into Knighton. 1st L after 20mph sign before school.* **Visits by arrangement Mar to Sept individuals/large groups. Adm £4, chd free. Home-made teas.**

Colourful ½ acre garden, full of flowers surrounds house on edge of town. Paths through floriferous arches and gazebos lead from shady, ferny corners to deep borders filled with a large range of colourful perennials, annuals, rhododendrons, azaleas, alstromerias, hydrangeas and 40 varieties of roses. Water features, fish pond. Enjoy the views of the hills from many seats in this flat garden. Yr round colour: daffodils, tulips, clematis, ten varieties alstroemerias, rudbeckias, inulas. Disabled parking in garden.

36 ◆ POWIS CASTLE GARDEN

Welshpool, SY21 8RF. National Trust, 01938 551920, powiscastle@nationaltrust.org.uk, www.nationaltrust.org.uk. *1m S of Welshpool. From Welshpool take A490 S towards Newtown. After ¾m turn R into Red Lane. Cont up lane for ¼m & turn R into property.* **For NGS: Thur 21 June (10-5.30). Adm £13, chd £6.50.** For other opening times and information, please phone, email or visit garden website.

Laid out in early C18 the garden features the finest remaining examples of Italian terraces in Britain. Richly planted herbaceous borders; enormous yew hedges; lead statuary, orangery and large wild flower areas. One of the NT's finest gardens. National Collection of *Laburnum*. Short introductory talks about the castle and garden run throughout the day. Refreshments served in the Courtyard Restaurant and Garden Coffee Shop. To be featured on Channel 5 - Secrets of the National Trust. Step free route around the garden, gravel paths, due to steep slopes only 4 wheeled PMV's permitted.

NPC

37 ROCK MILL

Abermule, Montgomery, SY15 6NN. Rufus & Cherry Fairweather. *1m S of Abermule on B4368 towards Kerry. Best approached from Abermule village as angled entrance into field for parking.* **Sat 19, Sun 20 May (2-5). Adm £4, chd free. Home-made teas.**

2 acre riverside garden on different levels in a wooded valley. Colourful borders and shrubberies, specimen trees, terraces, woodland walks, bridges, extensive lawns, fishponds, orchard, herb and vegetable gardens. Features incl beehives, dovecote, heather thatched roundhouse and remnants of industrial past (corn mill and railway line). Child friendly activities (supervision required) incl sunken trampoline, croquet and badminton, animal treasure hunt, interactive quiz, wilderness trails. Sensible shoes and a sense of fun/ adventure recommended.

38 NEW ROSE COTTAGE

Reeves Lane, Knighton, LD7 1NA. Jane Willis & Phil Pallett. *4m east of Knighton. on A4113 to Leintwardine. The lane is next on R after the 'Welcome to England' sign. The cottage is the first house on L, ½m along the narrow road which has passing places.* **Sat 23, Sun 24 June (11-4). Adm £3, chd free. Home-made teas.**

¾ acre wildlife rich garden in process of development. Informal, sloping garden with roses, flower and shrub borders, wild areas, vegetable plot, greenhouse, polytunnel and apiary. Pond planted with a variety of water plants which provide habitat for a wide range of creatures. A peaceful atmosphere and glorious views are part of the garden's charm.

39 TALGARTH MILL

The Square, Talgarth, Brecon, LD3 0BW. Talgarth Mill, www.talgarthmill.com. *In centre of Talgarth. Park in free car park opp rugby club, turn L out of car park entrance, follow High St to end, cross bridge, the Mill is on your R.* **Sat 30 June, Sun 1 July (10-4). Adm by donation. Light refreshments. Refreshments available from The Bakers' Table.**

A pretty riverside garden, maintained by volunteers. Along the riverside there is mixed herbaceous planting, a shady area, and steps up to a productive garden with espalier fruit trees, vegetables, soft fruits and a wildlife area. Places to sit and watch the river and its bird life (dippers, wagtails, kingfishers, herons) and the mill wheel turning. Garden is part of a working water mill that produces high quality flour (Great Taste 1 and 2 star), with our staple bread wheat grown just 7 miles away. Award winning cafe and bakery which champions local, seasonal produce, gourmet coffee and tea. Open 10-4pm. Garden can be accessed by lift. Wide, flat paths for wheelchair access.

40 TREBERFYDD HOUSE

Llangasty, Bwlch, Brecon, LD3 7PX. David Raikes & Carla Rapoport, www.treberfydd.com. *6m E of Brecon. From Abergavenny on A40, turn R in Bwlch on B5460. Take 1st turning L towards Pennorth & cont 2m along lane. From Brecon, turn L off A40 towards Pennorth in Llanhamlach.* **Sun 29 July (1-5.30). Adm £4, chd free. Home-made teas.**

Grade I listed Victorian Gothic house with 10 acres of grounds designed by W A Nesfield. Magnificent Cedar of Lebanon, avenue of mature Beech, towering Atlantic Cedars, Victorian rockery, herbaceous border and manicured lawns ideal for a picnic. Wonderful views of the Black Mountains. Plants available from Commercial Nursery in grounds - Walled Garden Treberfydd. House tours every half hour (additional £2), last tour 4pm. Easy wheelchair access to areas around the house, but herbaceous border only accessible via steps.

41 TREMYNFA

Carreghofa Lane, Llanymynech, SY22 6LA. Jon & Gillian Fynes. *Edge of Llanymynech village. From N leave Oswestry on A483 to Welshpool. In Llanymynech turn R at Xrds (car wash on corner). Take 2nd R then follow yellow NGS signs. 300 yds park signed field, limited disabled parking nr garden.* **Sat 23, Sun 24 June (1-5). Adm £4, chd free. Home-made teas.**

S-facing 1 acre garden developed over 10yrs. Old railway cottage set in herbaceous and raised borders, patio with many pots of colourful and unusual plants. Garden slopes to productive fruit and vegetable area, ponds, spinney, wild areas and peat bog. Patio and seats to enjoy extensive views incl Llanymynech Rocks. Pet ducks on site, Montgomery canal close by. 100s of home grown plants for sale. Featured in Amateur Gardening magazine.

42 TYN Y CWM

Beulah, Llanwrtyd Wells, LD5 4TS. Steve & Christine Carrow, 01591 620461, stevetynycwm@hotmail.co.uk. *10m W of Builth Wells. On A483 at Beulah take rd towards Abergwesyn for 2m. Drive drops down to L.* **Sun 17 June, Sun 5 Aug (2-5.30). Adm £4, chd free. Home-made teas. Visits also by arrangement Apr to Aug.**

Garden mainly started 16yrs ago, lower garden has spring/woodland area, raised beds mixed with vegetables, fruit trees, fruit and flowers. Perennial borders, summer house gravel paths through rose and clematis pergola. Upper garden, partly sloped, incl bog, winter, water gardens and perennial beds with unusual slate steps. Beautiful views. Property bounded by small river.

43 1 YSTRAD HOUSE

1 Church Road, Knighton, LD7 1EB. John & Margaret Davis. *At junction of Church Rd & Station Rd. 225yds along Station Rd (A488 Clun) opp Knighton Hotel. Yellow House at junction with Church Rd.* **Sat 16, Sun 17 June (2-5). Adm £4, chd free. Home-made teas.**

An unsuspected town garden hidden behind Ystrad House, a Regency villa of earlier origins. Developed over the last 10yrs with an emphasis on tranquillity and timelessness: having broad lawns and wide borders, mature trees and more intimate features adding interest and surprise. The formal areas merge with wooded glades leading to a riverside walk alongside the River Teme. Cellists will be playing on the Sunday. Lawns and gravelled paths mostly flat except access to riverside walk..

Foel Ortho

Early Openings 2019

Plan your garden visiting well ahead – put these dates in your diary!

Gardens across the country open early – before the next year's guide is published – with glorious displays of colour including hellebores, aconites, snowdrops and carpets of spring bulbs.

Bedfordshire

Sun 24 February (2-4.30)
King's Arms Garden

Cheshire & Wirral

Sun 24 February (1-3)
Bucklow Farm

By arrangement in February
The Well House

Devon

Fri 8, Fri 15, Sat 23 February (2-5)
Higher Cherubeer

Gloucestershire

Sun 27 January, Sun 10 February (11-3)
Home Farm

Hampshire

Sun 17, Mon 18, Sun 24, Mon 25 February (2-4.30)
Little Court

Herefordshire

Thurs 7, 14, 21, 28 February (9-4)
Ivy Croft

Fri 22 February (11-5)
The Picton Garden

Kent

Sun 10, Sun 17 February (12-4)
Copton Ash

Sat 16, Sun 17, Mon 18 February (11-3)
Knowle Hill Farm

Sun 17, Sun 24 February (2-5)
Mere House

By arrangement in February
The Old Rectory
Spring Platt

Lincolnshire

Sat 23, Sun 24 February (11-4)
21 Chapel Street

North East Wales

Thur 14, Sun 17, Thur 21 February (12-4)
Glog Ddu

Sun 17 February (12-4)
Hafodunos Hall

Oxfordshire

Sun 17 February (1.30-5)
Hollyhocks

Somerset, Bristol & South Gloucestershire

Sun 3, Sun 10 February (11-4)
Rock House

Sun 10, Mon 11 February (11-4)
Sherborne Garden

Sun 17 February (10-5)
East Lambrook Manor Gardens

Sussex

By arrangement in February
Pembury House

Wiltshire

Sat 23 February (10.30-5.30)
Lacock Abbey Gardens

Yorkshire

Sun 17 February (1.30-5.30)
Fawley House

Plant Heritage

National Council for the Conservation of Plants and Gardens

Nearly 70 gardens that open for the National Garden Scheme are guardians of a Plant Heritage National Plant Collection although this may not always be noted in the garden description. These gardens carry the NPC symbol.

Plant Heritage, 12 Home Farm, Loseley Park, Guildford, Surrey GU3 1HS. 01483 447540 www.plantheritage.com

ABIES SPP.
The Yorkshire Arboretum, Yorkshire

ACER (EXCL. PALMATUM CVS.)
Blagdon, North East

AGAPANTHUS – FAIRWEATHER NURSERY TRIALS COLLECTION (HORTICULTURAL)
Fairweather's Nursery, Hampshire

AGAPANTHUS (PINE COTTAGE CVS.)
Bowdens, Devon

AKEBIA
190 Barnet Road, London

ALNUS
Blagdon, North East

ANEMONE NEMOROSA
Avondale Nursery, Warwickshire

Kingston Lacy, Dorset

ARALIACEAE
Meon Orchard, Hampshire

ARUNCUS
Windy Hall, Cumbria

ASTER & RELATED GENERA (AUTUMN FLOWERING)
The Picton Garden, Herefordshire

ASTER NOVAE-ANGLIAE
Avondale Nursery, Warwickshire

Brockamin, Worcestershire

ASTILBE
Holehird Gardens, Cumbria

ASTRANTIA
Norwell Nurseries, Norwell Gardens, Nottinghamshire

BRUNNERA
Hearns House, Oxfordshire

BUDDLEJA DAVIDII CVS. & HYBRIDS
Shapcott Barton Knowstone Estate, Devon

CAMELLIAS & RHODODENDRONS INTRODUCED TO HELIGAN PRE-1920
The Lost Gardens of Heligan, Cornwall

CARPINUS
Sir Harold Hillier Gardens, Hampshire

CARPINUS BETULUS CVS.
West Lodge Park, London

CEANOTHUS
Eccleston Square, London

CERCIDIPHYLLUM
Hodnet Hall Gardens, Shropshire

Sir Harold Hillier Gardens, Hampshire

CHRYSANTHEMUM (KOREAN, RUBELLUM & HARDY SPRAY)
Hill Close Gardens, Warwickshire

CLEMATIS VITICELLA
Longstock Park, Hampshire

CLEMATIS VITICELLA CVS.
Roseland House, Cornwall

CODONOPSIS
Woodlands, Fotherby Gardens, Lincolnshire

CONVALLARIA
Kingston Lacy, Dorset

CORIARIA
Crûg Farm, Gwynedd & Anglesey

CORNUS
Sir Harold Hillier Gardens, Hampshire

CORNUS (EXCL. C. FLORIDA CVS.)
Newby Hall & Gardens, Yorkshire

CORYLUS
Sir Harold Hillier Gardens, Hampshire

COTONEASTER
Sir Harold Hillier Gardens, Hampshire

CYCLAMEN (EXCL. PERSICUM CVS.)
Higher Cherubeer, Devon

CYDONIA OBLONGA
Norton Priory Museum & Gardens, Cheshire & Wirral

DABOECIA
Holehird Gardens, Cumbria

DAHLIA
Varfell Farm, Cornwall

DESCHAMPSIA
The Walled Gardens of Cannington, Somerset, & South Gloucestershire

DIERAMA SPP.
Yew Tree Cottage, Staffordshire

ERICA & CALLUNA - SUSSEX HEATHER CVS
Nymans, Sussex

EUCALYPTUS
Meon Orchard, Hampshire

EUCALYPTUS SPP.
The World Garden at Lullingstone Castle, Kent

EUCRYPHIA
Whitstone Farm, Devon

EUONYMUS (DECIDUOUS)
The Place for Plants, East Bergholt Place Garden, Suffolk

EUPHORBIA (HARDY)
Firvale Allotment Garden, Yorkshire

GERANIUM SANGUINEUM, MACRORRHIZUM & X CANTABRIGIENSE
Brockamin, Worcestershire

GERANIUM SYLVATICUM & RENARDII - FORMS, CVS. & HYBRIDS
Wren's Nest, Cheshire & Wirral

GEUM
1 Brickwall Cottages, Kent

HAKONECHLOA
12 Woods Ley, Kent

HAMAMELIS
Sir Harold Hillier Gardens, Hampshire

HARDY CHRYSANTHEMUM
Norwell Nurseries, Norwell Gardens, Nottinghamshire

HEDERA
Ivybank, Pebworth Gardens, Warwickshire

HILLIERS (PLANTS RAISED BY)
Sir Harold Hillier Gardens, Hampshire

HOHERIA
Abbotsbury Gardens, Dorset

HOSTA (EUROPEAN AND ASIATIC)
Hanging Hosta Garden, Hampshire

HOSTA (HALCYON & SPORTS)
Bowdens, Devon

HYPERICUM
Sir Harold Hillier Gardens, Hampshire

JUGLANS
Upton Wold, Gloucestershire

LABURNUM
Powis Castle Garden, Powys

LEUCANTHEMUM X SUPERBUM (CHRYSANTHEMUM MAXIMUM)
Shapcott Barton Knowstone Estate, Devon

LEWISIA
'John's Garden' at Ashwood Nurseries, Staffordshire

LIGUSTRUM
Sir Harold Hillier Gardens, Hampshire

LITHOCARPUS
Sir Harold Hillier Gardens, Hampshire

MALUS (CVS. FROM NOTTS & DERBY, LINCS, LEICS & YORKS)
Clumber Park Walled Kitchen Garden, Nottinghamshire

MALUS (ORNAMENTAL)
Barnards Farm, Essex

MECONOPSIS (LARGE PERENNIAL SPP. & HYBRIDS)
Holehird Gardens, Cumbria

METASEQUOIA
Sir Harold Hillier Gardens, Hampshire

MONARDA
Hole's Meadow, Devon

MUSCARI
16 Witton Lane, Norfolk

NEPETA
Hole's Meadow, Devon

NERINE SARNIENSIS CVS
Bickham Cottage, Devon

OMPHALODES
Hearns House Oxfordshire

PARIS
Crûg Farm, Gwynedd & Anglesey

PELARGONIUM
Ivybank, Pebworth Gardens, Warwickshire

PENNISETUM
Knoll Gardens, Dorset

PENSTEMON
Froggery Cottage, Northamptonshire

PHLOMIS
Foamlea, Devon

PHOTINIA
Sir Harold Hillier Gardens, Hampshire

PICEA
The Yorkshire Arboretum, Yorkshire

PINUS (EXCL DWARF CVS.)
Sir Harold Hillier Gardens, Hampshire

PINUS SPP.
The Lovell Quinta Arboretum, Cheshire & Wirral

PODOCARPUS & RELATED PODOCARPACEAE
Meon Orchard, Hampshire

POLYGONATUM
Crûg Farm, Gwynedd & Anglesey

POLYSTICHUM
Holehird Gardens, Cumbria

PTEROCARYA
Upton Wold, Gloucestershire

QUERCUS
Chevithrone Barton, Devon

Sir Harold Hillier Gardens, Hampshire

RHAPIS SPP. & CVS.
Gwyndy Bach, Gwynedd & Anglesey

RHEUM (CULINARY CVS.)
Clumber Park Walled Kitchen Garden, Nottinghamshire

RHODODENDRON (GHENT AZALEAS)
Sheffield Park and Garden, Sussex

RHODODENDRON KURUME AZALEA WILSON 50
Trewidden Garden, Cornwall

RODGERSIA
The Gate House, Devon

ROSA - HYBRID MUSK INTRO BY PEMBERTON & BENTALL 1912-1939
Dutton Hall, Lancashire

ROSA (RAMBLING)
Moor Wood, Gloucestershire

SANGUISORBA
Avondale Nursery, Warwickshire

SANTOLINA
The Walled Gardens of Cannington, Somerset, Bristol & South Gloucestershire

SAXIFRAGA (LIGULATAE GROUP)
Waterperry Gardens, Oxfordshire

SAXIFRAGA SUB SECTION POROPYLLUM, CULTIVARS & SPECIES
Waterperry Gardens, Oxfordshire

SIBERIAN IRIS CVS: BRITISH, AWARD WINNERS & HISTORICALLY SIGNIFICANT
Aulden Farm, Herefordshire

SOLENOSTEMON
Croxteth Park Walled Garden, Lancashire

SORBUS
Blagdon, North East

Ness Botanic Gardens, Cheshire & Wirral

STEWARTIA - ASIAN SPP.
High Beeches Woodland and Water Garden, Sussex

STYRACACEAE (INCL HALESIA, PTEROSTYRAX, STYRAX, SINOJACKIA)
Holker Hall Gardens, Cumbria

TAXODIUM SPP. & CVS.
West Lodge Park, London

TULBAGHIA
Marwood Hill Garden, Devon

YUCCA
Renishaw Hall & Gardens, Derbyshire

Society of Garden Designers

The [D] symbol at the end of a garden description indicates that the garden has been designed by a Fellow, Member or Pre-Registered Member of the Society of Garden Designers.

Fellow of the Society of Garden Designers (FSGD) is awarded to Members for exceptional contributions to the Society or to the profession

Rosemary Alexander FSGD
Roderick Griffin FSGD
Ian Kitson FSGD
Sarah Massey FSGD
David Stevens FSGD
Robin Templar-Williams FSGD
Julie Toll FSGD

Member of the Society of Garden Designers (MSGD) is awarded after passing adjudication

Sue Adcock MSGD
Jill Fenwick MSGD
Joanna Herald MSGD
Thomas Hoblyn MSGD
Barbara Hunt MSGD (retired)
Arabella Lennox-Boyd MSGD
Chris Parsons MSGD
Dan Pearson MSGD
Emma Plunket MSGD
Jilayne Rickards MSGD
Debbie Roberts MSGD
Charles Rutherfoord MSGD
Ian Smith MSGD
Tom Stuart-Smith MSGD
Sue Townsend MSGD
Cleve West MSGD
Rebecca Winship MSGD

Pre-Registered Member is a member working towards gaining Registered Membership

Tamara Bridge
Fiona Cadwallader
Wendy Cartwright
Kristina Clode
Linsey Evans
Anoushka Feiler
Louise Hardwick
Sarah Murch
Sarah Oxby
Anne-Marie Powell
Faith Ramsay
Daniel Shea
Amanda Shipman
Julia Whiteaway

Acknowledgements

Each year the National Garden Scheme receives fantastic support from the community of garden photographers who donate and make available images of gardens. We would like to thank them for their generous donations. Our thanks also to our wonderful garden owners who kindly submitted images of their gardens.

Unless otherwise stated, photographs are kindly supplied by permission of the garden owner.

The 2018 Production Team: Elna Broe, Jack Claramunt, Linda Ellis, Louise Grainger, Kali Masure, Tina Napier, Araminta Pender, George Plumptre, Helena Pretorius, Jane Sennett, Catherine Swan, Sarah Turner, Georgina Waters, Anna Wili. With heartfelt thanks to our dedicated County Team Volunteers.

CONSTABLE
First published in Great Britain in 2018 by Constable

A CIP catalogue record for this book is available from the British Library.

ISBN: 978-1-4721-2911-6

Designed by Level Partnership
Maps by Mary Spence © Global Mapping and XYZ Maps
Typeset in Gill Sans
Printed and bound in Italy by Rotolito S.p.A.

Constable
An imprint of Little, Brown Book Group
Carmelite House, 50 Victoria Embankment,
London EC4Y 0DZ

An Hachette UK Company
www.hachette.co.uk www.littlebrown.co.uk

If you require this information in alternative formats, please telephone 01483 211535 or email hello@ngs.org.uk